אגרת הקודש
קונטרס אחרון

THE STEINSALTZ TANYA

Iggeret HaKodesh

Kuntres Aḥaron

VOLUME VI

Steinsaltz
Center

MAGGID

THE MAGERMAN EDITION

THE STEINSALTZ
TANYA

IGGERET HAKODESH 27–32
KUNTRES AHARON

COMMENTARY & TRANSLATION BY
RABBI ADIN EVEN-ISRAEL STEINSALTZ

Steinsaltz Center
Maggid Books

The Steinsaltz Tanya:
Iggeret HaKodesh 27–32 and Kuntres Aharon, Volume 6
First edition, 2024

Maggid Books
An imprint of Koren Publishers Jerusalem Ltd.

POB 8531, New Milford, CT 06776-8531, USA
& POB 4044, Jerusalem 9104001, Israel
www.maggidbooks.com

This book was published in cooperation with
the Israeli Institute for Talmudic Publications.
All rights reserved to the Steinsaltz Center Ltd.

We acknowledge with gratitude the generous support of
Terri and Stephen Geifman, *who made possible an earlier edition of this*
commentary.

The right of Adin Steinsaltz to be identified as the author
of this work has been asserted by him in accordance
with the Copyright, Designs & Patents Act 1988.
Steinsaltz Center is the parent organization of institutions
established by Rabbi Adin Even-Israel Steinsaltz
POB 45187, Jerusalem 91450 ISRAEL
Telephone: +972 2 646 0900, Fax +972 2 624 9454
www.steinsaltz-center.org

Cover design by Tani Bayer

ISBN 978-1-59264-589-3 hardcover

Printed and bound in the United States

Dedicated to

my wife, **Debra**,

and my children,
Elijah, **Zachary**, **Sydney**, and **Lexie**.

May this new translation of the Tanya,
along with the commentary from Rabbi Steinsaltz (*z"l*),
bring us closer to hasidic teaching and
help us connect with the mystical meaning
behind the Torah.

*May all the children of Israel use
the Tanya's knowledge and wisdom
to work together to hasten the coming of Mashiaḥ.*

DAVID M. MAGERMAN

ספר התניא מלמד אותנו שהנפש האלוקית מסורה כל כולה
לקב"ה והיא מבחינה זו חסרת אנוכיות או תחושת ישות. הנפש
הבהמית לעומת זאת מרוכזת בעצמה ומסורה לקיומה הנפרד.

לפיכך לימד אותנו האדמו"ר האמצעי שכאשר שני יהודים
לומדים או משוחחים בעניני עבודת ה' הרי אלו שתי נשמות
אלוקיות כנגד נפש בהמית אחת. הנפש הבהמית לא מצטרפת
עם חבירתה משום שכאמור היא מסורה לעצמה אבל הנפשות
האלוקיות מצטרפות יחד בלי כל חציצה או הבדל.

(מתוך: "היום יום" כ' לטבת)

לזכות
משה ליב בן זיסל שיחי' לאיוש"ט
שולמית בת זהרה שתחי' לאיוש"ט

The *Tanya* teaches us that the divine soul is fully devoted to
G-d, and therefore it is selfless. By contrast, the animal soul
is selfish, devoted only to maintaining its own existence.

The Mitteler Rebbe, Rabbi Dovber of Lubavitch, taught
that when two Jews learn or discuss matters pertaining
to service of God, there are two divine souls against one
animal soul. The animal soul thinks only of itself and will
not attach itself to the animal soul of the other. But the two
divine souls are joined together with no division or barrier.

(Cited from *HaYom Yom*, 20 Tevet)

In the merit of
MOSHE LEIB BEN ZISEL
SHULAMIT BAT ZOHARA

A blessing from the Lubavitcher Rebbe, Rabbi Menaḥem Mendel Schneerson, dated 21 Av 5721 (August 3, 1961), viewing with favor Rabbi Steinsaltz's project of writing a short commentary, with longer explanations, on the *Tanya* in a style accessible to the contemporary reader:

(ושאלות ותשובות – כהמצורף למכתבו) בעניינײ המובאים בתניא, כן ביאור קצר או גם ארוך, ובסגנונו, ערוכים בלשון בני דורנו...

בברכה לבשו"ט

In December 2012, the final volume of the Hebrew edition of *The Steinsaltz Tanya* was published. That year, at a hasidic gathering, Rabbi Adin Steinsaltz shared why he wrote the book. He explained that Rabbi Shneur Zalman of Liadi, the author of the *Tanya*, had poured his entire soul, his love and awe, his soul-wrenching oneness with God into that concise book, into pages that obscured his immense spirit so well. Through his commentary, Rabbi Steinsaltz strove to reveal to us this spirit, that powerful fire just barely contained by the words of the *Tanya*.

And he certainly succeeded. Yet he failed to mask his own burning spirit, his own love, awe, and closeness to God, as he had attempted to do his entire life.

The publication of this English edition of *The Steinsaltz Tanya* is the fulfillment of Rabbi Steinsaltz's vision to make the teachings of the *Tanya* accessible to every single individual. At the height of the preparations for this edition, our teacher Rabbi Adin Even-Israel passed away.

In this book, one learns how the life of the tzaddik lives on in this world, in those who learn his works. It is through those students who are open to receiving his teachings and are inspired to build upon his words that his light remains with us. We pray that this commentary of Rabbi Steinsaltz will introduce many generations of Jews to the world of the *Tanya* and to the path of authentic devotion to God.

May it serve to elevate his soul.

Contents

For the Hebrew Tanya Vilna edition, open from the Hebrew side of the book.

אִגֶּרֶת הַקֹּדֶשׁ

Iggeret HaKodesh

The Holy Epistle

Epistle 27

EPISTLE 27, ONE OF THE MOST WELL-KNOWN OF THE *Iggerot HaKodesh*, is a condolence letter to the hasidim of the tzaddik Rabbi Menaḥem Mendel of Vitebsk (or, as Chabad hasidim call him, Rabbi Menaḥem Mendel of Horodok) following his passing away in the Land of Israel in 5548 (1788).

This letter is very personal, particularly its first part. One can feel the pain and personal connection of the author of the *Tanya,* who viewed Rabbi Menaḥem Mendel as his rebbe. But the significance of this letter transcends that specific event. This letter[1] presents a seminal perspective on the meaning of a tzaddik's *histalkut* (literally, "elevation," referring to a tzaddik's death) and on how to relate to him after his death. This topic is especially important in the hasidic movement, in which the influence and inspiration of the tzaddik – not only through his writings and his students but through his person – transcends his place and time. This letter establishes the fundamental principles of how to understand these profound matters (which have been discussed by subsequent Chabad Rebbes as well[2]).

More than any other epistle of the author of the *Tanya,* this letter is written in a classical literary style weaving together verses and rabbinical statements. This is possibly an outcome of the nature of this letter: because, in words

---

1. As well as the following letter, epistle 28. And in greater detail in the discourses of the author of the *Tanya* 5566, Part 1, p. 147.
2. The letter is printed in full with a commentary in *Kuntres Inyan HaHishtatḥut* by the second Lubavitcher Rebbe, Rabbi Dovber Schneuri, and parts of it have been inserted in other essays and talks over the course of generations.

of consolation, there is no place for the presence of the consoler, the author of the *Tanya* conceals himself almost entirely in these phrases. Nevertheless, like everything else that he wrote, this letter is something that every person can study and apply throughout his entire life. Thus, this letter has two aspects. One, it is a short letter of condolence, speaking to the hearts of the mourners. And two, it transmits a profound perspective on the tzaddik following his *histalkut*: where he is now, how he continues to exercise an influence on his followers, and how they should conduct themselves. This spoke to the hearts of Rabbi Menaḥem Mendel's hasidim, who had loved him and had been connected to him, and who were now grieving. But for other hasidim who were not of this group, this letter remained almost completely sealed. And therefore, in an uncharacteristic maneuver, the author of the *Tanya* appended an "explanation" to this letter.

The letters in *Iggeret HaKodesh* are arranged thematically. Therefore, although this is one of the earliest letters, it is placed toward the end. Seemingly, however, it is completely different from the previous letter, which has no connection to any specific event but deals entirely with an abstract topic, in contrast to the present letter, which is of a personal nature – more so, perhaps, than any other in *Iggeret HaKodesh* – discussing a particular event. However, a connection between these two letters does exist. The previous letter discussed the revealed and hidden Torah. The revealed Torah is clothed in this world's concepts and physicality, and the hidden Torah is the Torah's inner aspect that is not clothed in this world, nor in any other world, but transcends this world's existence. That idea is connected to this letter, which discusses the tzaddik's influence: an influence that is both clothed in this world (in his body and in the matters of this world with which he is involved) and beyond this world, after he has passed away. The latter influence parallels the hidden Torah, which is not clothed in this world and so continues in the World to Come. The tzaddik's life, which is entirely spiritual and dedicated to serving God – since all of his days are holy and separate from the things of this world in and of themselves – continues after his *histalkut*. This consists of a continuation for his hasidim in this world, because he remains with them even after he leaves his body, and it is a continuation as well for the tzaddik, even as his soul rises ever higher.

The editors added an introduction to this letter, as they did in the case of a few other epistles as well,[3] as follows.

(מַה שֶּׁכָּתַב לְיוֹשְׁבֵי אַרְצֵנוּ הַקְּדוֹשָׁה (This is a letter **that** the author of
תִּבָּנֶה וְתִכּוֹנֵן בִּמְהֵרָה בְיָמֵינוּ אָמֵן the *Tanya* **wrote to those who dwell in our Holy Land – may it be built and established quickly, in our days, amen.**

To whom was this letter written? In Lubavitcher Rebbe, Rabbi Menaḥem Mendel Schneerson's list of errata, he notes that the words "to those who dwell in our Holy Land…" are an error, because the letter was written to Chabad hasidim outside the Holy Land. *Beit Rebbe,* too, states that this phrase is clearly a mistake, as may be seen from the body of the letter – and in particular from its second half (which was not published in *Iggeret HaKodesh*) in which the author of the *Tanya* explicitly addresses the hasidim outside the Holy Land, telling them to continue sending money to the Holy Land. However, the Lubavitcher Rebbe states further on that erasing this phrase would be wrong, because it was allowed to remain by the rebbes of Chabad throughout the generations, beginning with the author's sons (who edited and approved the text of *Iggeret HaKodesh* as published in the introductions to the *Tanya*) and the Tzemaḥ Tzedek, and this is how it appears in the first edition of *Kuntres Inyan HaHishtatḥut*. Therefore, this phrase possesses a certain level of authority. The Lubavitcher Rebbe proposes that both versions of the text be preserved, with the presumption that one version of the letter (which was preserved only

---

3. Epistles 2, 16, 28.

in part) was sent to the hasidim in the Land of Israel, and another version – the version that we possess in full – was sent to the hasidim outside the Holy Land.

לְנַחֲמָם בְּכִפְלַיִם לְתוּשִׁיָּה   **To console them with double alleviation** (Job 11:6),

The author of the *Tanya* characterizes his words of consolation as possessing "double alleviation." This alludes to the character of the entire letter, and may even be considered its motto. Words of consolation, in particular those of a rebbe, not only express the consoler's participation in the mourner's suffering, which is itself deeply comforting, but are an attempt to transform the situation. The suffering and loss are a reality that cannot be changed, but other aspects can help a person elevate himself. In the midst of their suffering, mourners cannot as a general rule see these other aspects, and so other people's words of consolation are required. Therefore, in this letter, the author of the *Tanya* explains that the tzaddik's passing away brings about rectification and elevation on the level of "double alleviation": referring to the reality after he has passed away and even retrospectively to the situation prior to his having passed away. ☞

עַל פְּטִירַת הָרַב הַגָּאוֹן הַמְפוּרְסָם,   **on the passing away of the famous,**
אִישׁ אֱלֹקִים קָדוֹשׁ, נֵר יִשְׂרָאֵל,   **brilliant rabbi, the holy man of**
עַמּוּד הַיְמִינִי, פַּטִּישׁ הֶחָזָק   **God, the lamp of Israel, the pillar on the right side, the powerful hammer,**

This is a description of Rabbi Menaḥem Mendel's greatness in Torah.[4]
    The tzaddik is like a lamp, and he is the soul of the entirety of the people of Israel.[5]

---

4. See Kings II 4:9. This in keeping with the term, "Moses, the man of God" (Deut. 33:1, and elsewhere).
5. See II Sam. 21:17. See the commentators who state that this is comparable to the life and soul of all Israel; and that if it were extinguished, heaven forbid, the lamp of all Israel would be extinguished.

He is the principal pillar upon which the house stands.[6]

This relates to his greatness in Torah, in keeping with our Sages' interpretation of the verse, "like a hammer that shatters the rock" (Jer. 23:29).

All of these descriptions are how Rabban Yoḥanan ben Zakkai was eulogized by his students (*Berakhot* 28b). In using them here, the author of the *Tanya's* sons hint that Rabbi Menaḥem Mendel was a leader of Israel on a rarely equaled scale.

מוֹרֵנוּ הָרַב וְרַבֵּנוּ רַבִּי מְנַחֵם   our master, the rabbi, and our rabbi,
מֶענְדְל נִשְׁמָתוֹ עֵדֶן)   Rebbe Menaḥem Mendel, his soul is in Eden).

Rabbi Menaḥem Mendel of Vitebsk was among the greatest students of the Maggid of Mezeritch. After the Maggid passed away, Rabbi Menaḥem Mendel was recognized as his successor. In fact, he was the last hasidic leader to be unilaterally accepted by all of the other hasidic leaders. The author of the *Tanya,* who was among the youngest students

DOUBLE ALLEVIATION

☞ This expression appears as well in *Likkutei Amarim* (chap. 35, and elsewhere). There, it describes the consolation given to a soul upon its descent into a body in this world. That descent parallels the descent from the level of a tzaddik to the level of a *beinoni.* All of a person's service of God in this world cannot restore to his soul the love and fear that it had possessed before its descent. (See *Likkutei Amarim,* chap. 12 and onward.) Nevertheless, despite all of the hardship and even suffering caused by this descent, the soul can now attain a level even than it could have attained previously. Therefore, this apparent descent contains the potential for ascent immeasurably greater than had existed previously. That reflects the entire aim of the hasidic approach and of a person's service of God: to transform the mundane into holiness, darkness into light, and descent into ascent. This message is consolation with "double alleviation."

In using this expression here, the author of the *Tanya* expresses the same idea: that with the passing away of Rabbi Menaḥem Mendel, his students and hasidim have experienced a descent. But now they can ascend even higher than they could have before.

---

6. See I Kings 7:21.

of the Maggid, related to him as his own rebbe, although even in Rabbi Menaḥem Mendel's lifetime, The author of the *Tanya* had already set forth his own path of Chabad Hasidism. ☞

This concludes the introduction to the letter. Now the letter itself begins.

<table>
<tr><td>12 Ḥeshvan
11 Ḥeshvan
(leap year)</td><td>אֲהוּבַיּ אַחַיּ וְרֵעַיּ אֲשֶׁר כְּנַפְשִׁי
כו׳</td><td>**My beloved ones, my brothers and friends who are** as close to me **as my soul…**,</td></tr>
</table>

The salutation has always been meaningful in letters written by hasidic tzaddikim. This greeting, "My beloved, my brothers and friends who are [as close to me] as my soul…," which is found in a number of the letters (9, 16, 22, addenda to 22 and 23), expresses exceptional closeness and affection. This greeting relates to what the author of the *Tanya* will say later on. He is addressing those who are especially

RABBI MENAḤEM MENDEL AND THE AUTHOR OF THE *TANYA*

☞ In the year 5537 (1776-77), Rabbi Menaḥem Mendel led a large group of hasidim to the Land of Israel. He went for a number of reasons, among which were the personal attacks directed against him by the opponents of Hasidism. Initially, the author of the *Tanya* wished to join this group, but he did not do so, principally because Rabbi Menaḥem Mendel requested that he remain in his place. Later on, Rabbi Menaḥem Mendel appointed the author of the *Tanya* his successor in Lithuania and White Russia (see *Sefer HaToledot* 18, and also *Iggeret HaKodesh*, epistle 122, from the Kherson archive). Even after Rabbi Menaḥem Mendel's ascent to the Land of Israel, the two maintained a close connection. Rabbi Menaḥem Mendel sent many letters to the author of the *Tanya*, and put him in charge of collecting money for his hasidim's support. Rabbi Menaḥem Men-

del's passing away was a hard blow for hasidim everywhere, and raised the question of who would lead the movement, both in and outside the Land of Israel. Outside the Land of Israel, in those areas that had been under the influence of Rabbi Menaḥem Mendel, the author of the *Tanya* was recognized as his successor and as a significant figure in his own right. The author of the *Tanya*'s unique approach of Chabad Hasidism was already an independent movement that had grown significantly beyond the dimensions of the other students of the Maggid and Rabbi Menaḥem Mendel. The author of the *Tanya* also saw himself as responsible to an extent for the hasidim in the Land of Israel. That is the background against which he wrote his letter of condolence to the hasidim, both in and outside the Land of Israel.

close to him and he will implicitly demand a great deal from them: not only to overcome their loss emotionally but to elevate the situation so that each person will receive something from the tzaddik and, with the attendant strength and responsibility, will himself be like the tzaddik. ☞

ה' עֲלֵיהֶם יִחְיוּ "חַיִּים עַד הָעוֹלָם" (תהלים קלג,ג), וְצֶאֱצָאֵיהֶם אִתָּם, זֶרַע אֱמֶת (ירמיה ב,כא) בְּרוּכֵי ה' הֵמָּה, "מֵעַתָּה וְעַד עוֹלָם"

may God be over them, that they should live "life for eternity" (Ps. 133:3), and their offspring with them, who will be a seed of truth (Jer. 2:21) they are blessed by God, from now and forever.

The author of the *Tanya* blesses the hasidim for the future. The blessing that these mourners need after the passing away of the tzaddik is life (see Isa. 38:16). As the verse states, "The Lord commanded the blessing of life for eternity" (Ps. 133:3). Not only do they need a replacement of the life they lost, whose stay on earth was temporary, but they need life that will last forever.

This blessing continues beyond their days, to their offspring after

MY BELOVED ONES

☞ *Likkutei Hagahot LaTanya* (p. 81) comments on these phrases in keeping with hasidic explanations (see e.g., *Torah Or* 36d; *Likkutei Torah*, Lev. 35a, 74b) that are based on the following midrash: "A king had an only daughter..., whom he called 'my daughter.' He came to love her so much that he called her 'my sister.' At last, he called her 'my mother'..." (*Shemot Rabba* 52:5). *Likkutei Hagahot LaTanya* draws a correlation between the phrases of the author of the *Tanya*'s salutation and the king's locutions.

"My beloved" corresponds to "my daughter."

"My brothers" corresponds to "my sister."

"Friends" corresponds to "my mother."

"Who are [as close to me] as my soul" corresponds to the level of calling them "by my very name," to the essence of the soul."

The ellipsis corresponds to *yehida*.

"May God give them life." Previously the author of the *Tanya* spoke about the level of the "inner essence" and now he speaks about the level of "encompassing."

"Life forever." This implies the binding between the encompassing with the inner essence.

them, so that the latter will be "a seed of truth blessed by God,[7] from now and forever,[8]" that is to say, blessed with true, eternal life. ☞

These words of opening and blessing are not simply expressive, but rather, they are intended to foreshadow the content of the epistle, which will show how these words of blessing actually happen, and how they can and should be received.

אַחֲרֵי דְּרִישַׁת שְׁלוֹמָם כַּמִּשְׁפָּט לְאוֹהֲבֵי שְׁמוֹ **After inquiring after their well-being, as is proper for those who love His Name,**

"Those who love His Name"[9] refers to every Jew. As *Likkutei Amarim* explains (chaps. 14 –15) every Jew's divine soul possesses a hidden love for God. This love is so great that when it is revealed it vanquishes a person's entire being, to the extent that he will be prepared to literally sacrifice himself. This is so characteristic of a Jew, that Jews are called "those who love His Name."

בָּאתִי לְדַבֵּר עַל לֵב נִדְכָּאִים הַנֶּאֱנָחִים וְהַנֶּאֱנָקִים **I have come to speak to the heart of those who are downcast, the sighing and the mournful,**

Those who are "downcast, sighing and mournful" are the hasidim mourning the loss of their rebbe. The halakha states that a student must mourn for his principal rabbi even to the extent of tearing his

A SEED OF TRUTH

☞ The expression, "a seed of truth," has an additional meaning. In exile, as the Divine is concealed (in particular, when a tzaddik passes away) the people of Israel are like a seed planted in the ground that disintegrates yet which afterward grows far beyond what it had been. Thus, during this period of suffering, when the hasidim are depressed and desolate, the author of the *Tanya* blesses them that they will be like a seed that flourishes multiple times beyond its crushed state.

7. This expression is based on Isa. 65:23: "For they are the descendants of the blessed of the Lord, and their offspring with them."
8. In a number of places in Prophets and the Writings; for instance, Isa. 9:6, ibid. 59:21, Ps. 113:2, 115:18, and elsewhere.
9. See Ps. 119:132 (and see also ibid. 69:36).

clothes – and how much more must hasidim mourn their rebbe. For the hasidim, the rebbe to whom they are attached is more than a rabbi who has taught them wisdom; he is also their father and king. His loss affects almost every area of their lives: Torah, prayer and the commandments (which, overall, comprise the entire life of this world). And this loss affects the life of their spirit as well: the *sefira* of Ḥesed, associated with love, corresponds to the father; the *sefira* of *Gevura*, associated with fear, corresponds to the king; and the *sefira* of *Tiferet* corresponds to the rabbi. A person who loses all of these has nowhere to escape from his sorrow. ☞

וּלְנַחֲמָם בְּכִפְלַיִים לְתוּשִׁיָּה, אֲשֶׁר שָׁמְעָה אָזְנִי וַתָּבֶן לָהּ (איוב יג, א) עַל מַאֲמַר רַבּוֹתֵינוּ ז"ל 'דְּשָׁבַק חַיִּים לְכָל חַי'

and to console them with double alleviation that my ear has heard and understood regarding the description of our Rabbis of blessed memory that a person who has died is someone **"who has left life for all the living."**

"My ear has heard and understood" (Job 13:1): "My ear has heard" from others, "and [I] understood" myself (*Likkutei Hagahot LaTanya*).

"Who has left life for all the living":[10] This expression has a secondary

DOWNCAST, THE SIGHING AND THE MOURNFUL

☞ This terminology may support the proposal of the Lubavitcher Rebbe, Rabbi Menaḥem Mendel Schneerson, that at least a partial version of the letter was written to the hasidim of the Land of Israel. That is because for the hasidim outside the land, the image of Rabbi Menaḥem Mendel was no longer vivid. More than ten years had passed since he had made aliya, and although there were still those who remembered him or who had heard stories about him, his presence was no longer so powerful that his death would cause them to be "downcast, sighing and mournful."

---

10. A similar phrase appears in the words of our Sages: "The Master has not left life to any person" (*Berakhot* 61b, quoted as well in *Likkutei Amarim*, chap. 1. And see a variant in *Bava Kama* 91b, and elsewhere). However, that phrase is speaking of this as something negative, not as the description of a person passing away from the world. In terms of the meaning used by the author of the *Tanya* here as referring to someone passing away, this expression appears in the words of the

meaning that offers consolation: the tzaddik has left his life here, giving it to those who live in this world.

Now, the author of the *Tanya* explains the meaning of the tzaddik's life while he was alive and the power of the life he leaves behind.

כִּי "צַדִּיק בֶּאֱמוּנָתוֹ יִחְיֶה" (חבקוק ב,ד), וּבְ"יִרְאַת ה' לְחַיִּים" (משלי יט,כג), וּבְרִשְׁפֵּי אֵשׁ שַׁלְהֶבֶת אַהֲבָתוֹ	This is **because "the tzaddik lives by his faith"** (Hab. 2:4), **by "the fear of the Lord, which leads to life"** (Prov. 19:23), **and by the flames of fire, a burning flame of his love** for God.

Clearly, the tzaddik's life – that which engages him, moves him and fills his soul all the days of his life – is not like that of other people. Most people are involved first and foremost with the life of this world, with its benefits, victories, fears, and so forth – in short, with themselves and their survival, and everything connected to that. Their life of this world is ongoing, whereas their thoughts of God are sporadic. However, for some people, God is everything, and it is with this that they live (and as for the life of this world, they think of it only in connection with the Divine). These people are the tzaddikim. A tzaddik's life therefore consists of his relationship with God, which includes faith, fear and love. He lives with faith because for him faith is not a cloudy concept but an existential reality. He lives with the fear of God because it is what he experiences. When a person is frightened of something in this world, he has no rest and no life, because everything is colored by that fright. But the tzaddik fears God. That is his life. And he lives with the love of God. Sometimes a person experiences a fiery love that fills his entire life until nothing else interests him, and he cannot deal with anything but the object of his love. In the same way, the tzaddik's love of God constitutes his life.

Rishonim in a somewhat different form in the text of the *ḥalitza* document (see, for instance, Rambam, *Hilkhot Yibum VeHalitza* 4:30: "and when he dies and leaves life to the rabbis and to all Israel"). Only later on (perhaps at the end of the period of the *Rishonim*) is the expression used with the meaning familiar to us: of someone passing away (as in *Responsa Maharam Padua* 73, *Responsa Rabbi Moshe Alsheikh* in a number of places, and elsewhere).

מְחַיִּים לְכָל בָּהֶן, חַיֵּי רוּחוֹ These traits are even greater **than life** for
[נוּסָח אַחֵר: וְנִשְׁמָתוֹ] כָּל the tzaddik, so that **he incorporates into**
יְמֵי חֶלְדּוֹ **them the life of his** *ruaḥ* [a different version: and of his *neshama*] all the days of
his earthly life.

The tzaddik's faith, fear and love are even more real and critical for him
than life[11] itself, more than what others see as life, more than everything
that connects him to the life of this world.[12] Throughout all the days
of his life in this world, the sole involvement of his *ruaḥ*[13] (and his
neshama[14]) is the fear and love of God. In matters of this world, only
his body and his vital *nefesh* are engaged and only regarding his most
basic survival needs, whereas the entire inner being of his *nefesh*, *ruaḥ*
and *neshama* are involved in the Divine.[15]

"וַיְהִי בְּהַעֲלוֹת ה'" (מלכים "And when the Lord raises" (II Kings 2:1)
ב ב,א), "רוּחוֹ וְנִשְׁמָתוֹ אֵלָיו "and gathers his *ruaḥ* and his *neshama*
יֶאֱסוֹף" (איוב לד,יד) וְיַעֲלֶה **to Himself**" (Job 34:14), **and he rises,**
בְּעִילּוּי אַחַר עִילּוּי עַד רוּם **elevation after elevation, to the exalted**
הַמַּעֲלוֹת **heights,**

---

11. See Ps. 63:4: "For Your kindness is better than life."

12. Regarding the wording of, "the days of his earthly life," see *Likkutei Amarim*,
end of chap. 31.

13. See Isa. 38:16.

14. The difference between the texts is a disagreement as to whether the tzaddik's
influence on the hasidim is only on the level of the *ruaḥ* or also on the level of the
neshama. *Likkutei Hagahot LaTanya* notes that apparently the tzaddik's influence
on his students reaches only as far as the level of the *ruaḥ*. If so, the variant reading
is to be rejected. And *Likkutei Hagahot LaTanya* adds that possibly the variant text
relates to the tzaddik's influence on his son. And see *HaLekaḥ VeHaLibuv*, which
states that "his *ruaḥ*" includes the "faith, fear and love" mentioned earlier, whereas
the additional variant text, "and his *neshama*" relates to the statement at the end
of the commentary on this letter that there is yet another level of illumination
for the tzaddik's students, which comes from the elevation of his *ruaḥ* and his
neshama to the Source from which he was hewn.

15. This is in keeping with the author of the *Tanya's* teaching in a number of
places on the verse "The toil of your hands…," that in regard to matters of this
world, one needs toil of the hands only and not the intellect and the inner being
of the *nefesh*. See *Likkutei Torah, Derushim LeRosh HaShana* 63b, and elsewhere.

When a tzaddik passes away, his *ruah* and *neshama*[16] that were connected to his body and to his life in this world are freed and rise, and God gathers them to Himself.

In addition, when the souls of different people are elevated, they are gathered together. In this world, the people's souls were separated from each other, each one experiencing itself as a separate entity. But when they rise from this world of separation, they gather together to be with the one God.

The tzaddik rises, ascent after ascent. Usually, when a person dies, as his *ruah* and *neshama* rise, they are disconnected from his body and from this world.

On the other hand, if a person was so deeply connected to his body that his life consisted solely of what occurs in this world, something of that connection remains like a pleasant memory even after he passes away, and that prevents his spirit from freeing itself entirely to be able to rise.

But the tzaddik is not like either of these two types of people. During his lifetime in this world, his soul was connected to the upper worlds. His entire connection to his body and this world was imposed upon him from without, and he only awaited his moment of release. Therefore, his passing away is a mighty, unlimited liberation. All of the parts of his divine *nefesh*, *ruah* and *neshama* unite and rise toward their supernal root, that being "a portion of the Divine above." He had been connected, to some extent, to the forms of this world: to people, to practical commandments. However, these connections do not hinder him after his passing. Instead, he considers them, takes them into account, and then rises further, elevation after elevation. Since his life below had been meaningful, there is meaning as well to every level that he passes through until he reaches the highest heights. ☞

שָׁבַק חַיֵּי רוּחוֹ, פְּעוּלָתוֹ אֲשֶׁר
עָבַד בָּהּ לְפָנִים בְּיִשְׂרָאֵל

he then **leaves behind the life of his** *ruah*, and **his activity that he had formerly engaged in among** the people of **Israel.**

---

16. His *ruah* and his *neshama*, but not his *nefesh*. That is because the level of the *nefesh*, which is connected to the body, retains that connection and does not rise, elevation after elevation.

Although the tzaddik rises, he does not entirely take leave of the lower realm. What remains of a person after he dies? If he had lived only in the physical realm, it is possible that after his death nothing remains. But regarding the tzaddik, whose life had been spiritual, the death of his body is not the death of his spirit. That continues to exist, even if not via the body, but through the "activity that he had formerly engaged in." The tzaddik acted in this world and worked in it, he influenced it and improved it. And this activity remains in the world even after his *histalkut* as a vessel for his spirit. The Hebrew for "formerly" can also be translated as "inner being." The tzaddik's activity and work affect the inner dimension of the world. Work that affect the world's external realm, which is no more than preparation for something else, may not last, because its scope is temporal and local. But an activity aimed at inner essence lasts forever. And all of these things are recognized and impressed in this world in a Jew's soul and life.

Below, the author of the *Tanya* specifies who receives the life that the tzaddik leaves behind.

"פְּעֻלַּת צַדִּיק לְחַיִּים" (משלי "The tzaddik's activity is for the living" י,טז), לְכָל חַי, הִיא נֶפֶשׁ כָּל (Prov. 10:16): **for every living being,** חַי הַקְשׁוּרָה בְּנַפְשׁוֹ בַּחֲבָלֵי which **is the soul of every living being** עֲבוֹתוֹת 'אַהֲבָה רַבָּה' וְ'אַהֲבַת who **is connected to his soul with the** עוֹלָם' בַּל תִּמּוֹט לָנֶצַח **thick cords of a tremendous love and a worldly love that will not be moved for all eternity.**

The tzaddik's activity that remains in the world after his *histalkut* is life for the living; for those who are alive. In a simple sense, this refers to those who are alive in this world. More deeply, it refers to those who not

---

HISTALKUT

☞ The tzaddik's passing away is called *histalkut*, "elevation." "Death" is a descent, which is something that has absolutely no connection to the tzaddik. "Passing away" relates to those who remain, those whom the dead person has left behind. That too does not pertain to the tzaddik (as this letter will explain). But *histalkut* is elevation: the tzaddik is liberated and rises upward, yet without being disconnected from what remains below.

only exist in the world but who may be as though spiritually dead, but those who are truly alive because they serve God and apply themselves to the Torah and its commandments. Not everyone can receive life from the tzaddik, and certainly not what the tzaddik leaves after his *histalkut*. The only people who can do that are those who are "alive," those who possess the "vessels" of Torah and the commandments - to receive an enhanced life from the tzaddik.

Another parameter of whether a person will be able to receive from the tzaddik is whether he was connected to the tzaddik while the tzaddik was in this world and is connected to the tzaddik now. In order that the inner stream of abundance may flow, two parties are required: giver and recipient. The recipient must want and need to have the vessels with which to receive. A person who was connected to the tzaddik, who knew him, his ways and his teachings, who received from him in the past and wants to receive from him now as well, can continue to do so. Moreover, a person who is connected with the tzaddik's soul is more than just a student; he is what hasidim call "a hasid connected to the rebbe." That connection impels the tzaddik's life force to come him.

Two ropes bind the hasid to the tzaddik: "tremendous love" and "worldly love." In general, the hasid's connection to the rebbe is based on love. (The hasid also experiences a fearful respect of the rebbe, and even a lower fear of punishment. But the connection is based on love.) The entire hasidic movement, as its name suggests, is built on *ḥesed*, "kindness." It is a movement that comes from the faculties of love, associated with "running forth" to escape vessels and parameters. It is based on activity involving a connection to that which is beyond the requisite[17] and beyond present existence. And certainly, this is true of the core of the hasid's heart in his connection to the rebbe, which is principally a connection of love. ☞

אֲשֶׁר "מִי הָאִישׁ הֶחָפֵץ חַיִּים" (תהלים That **"person who desires life"**
לְהָיָג), לְדָבְקָה בה׳ חַיִּים בַּעֲבוֹדָתוֹ (Ps.34:13) – who desires **to cling**
תִּדְבַּק נַפְשׁוֹ **to the living God – his soul will cling through his service**

---

17. See *Kuntres Inyana shel Torat HaḤasidut* (by the Lubavitcher Rebbe), section 1.

The author of the *Tanya* describes who receives the life of the tzaddik: it is the person who desires the supernal life that the tzaddik brings down, a life that consists of clinging to God with faith, love, and fear.

In this sentence, the word "life" refers to the hasid, to his desire for life and his clinging to the ways of the tzaddik, and the word "living" refers to his receiving the life of the tzaddik, which becomes his own life.

A TREMENDOUS LOVE AND A WORLDLY LOVE

☞   These two terms refer to fundamental Chabad concepts (see, e.g., *Likkutei Amarim*, chap. 43; *Torah Or* 47b). One may assume that the hasidic meaning of these terms – terms that are found in the literature of our Sages and in the prayer book – was already complete in the author of the *Tanya's* thought, although this letter dates much earlier (written about ten years before the publication of the *Tanya*).

The use of these terms here is unusual, because in general they apply to love of God, and not – as they are used here – to the hasid's connection with his rebbe. But the basis of the hasid's relationship with his rebbe is the hasid's relationship with God. His relationship with his rebbe only provides a model for his relationship with God. His love for his rebbe is nothing in and of itself. It is on the level of "He and His essence are one" (meaning, "He and His vessels, His traits, are one"). The use of these terms here may be explained in light of that. Generally, the term "tremendous love" refers to a person's supernal love for God Himself, beyond all of His revelations. Such a love is infinite and not conditioned on any external factor. In contrast, "worldly love" is connected to the world, in two ways. First, it relates to God as He is revealed as Creator and Guide. And second, the way a person attains this love, feels it and is influenced via this world, that is, via contemplating the world and having a feeling about the world. In this sense, the hasid's connection to the rebbe with ropes of tremendous love is, in essence, his inner connection to God, who is to be found in all of the rebbe's affairs, intentions and personality. As for "worldly love," it too, is love for God, but it proceeds via the hasid's relationship with the rebbe: his personality, manner and form, and the beauty with which he imbues things. This love is apparently limited to the time and state during which the hasid is with the rebbe in this world. Nevertheless, the author of the *Tanya* says that this love "will not be moved for eternity." This "eternity" is neither finite nor infinite. The concept of "forever" relates to an existence and form within time, into which the infinite that transcends time shines its light (see *Likkutei Torah*, Deut. 67c, where it is similarly explained that it is a concept that relates to the trait of *Malkhut*). It is precisely this, that the author of the *Tanya* is discussing here: the being of the tzaddik, which is within time, within a certain person living in this world as a soul in a body and so forth, yet which also exists beyond that, insofar as the tzaddik possesses faith and the fear and love of God.

The soul of the person who desires life will cling to the way of service that the tzaddik taught the hasidim in general and him in particular.

וְהָיְתָה צְרוּרָה בִּצְרוֹר הַחַיִּים אֶת ה' בְּחַיֵּי "רוּחַ אַפֵּינוּ" (איכה ד,כ), "אֲשֶׁר אָמַרְנוּ בְּצִלּוֹ נִחְיֶה בַגּוֹיִם" (איכה שם)

and his soul **will be bound in the bond of life with God**, and it will be bound **with the life of** the tzaddik, the one who is **"the spirit of our nostrils"** (Lam. 4:20) **"of whom we have said, 'In his** protective **shadow, we will live among the nations'"** (ibid.).

As explained elsewhere,[18] "the bond of life" (see I Sam. I 25:29) may be thought of as a garment for the soul. A person, who is a created and limited being, can only receive God's pure and infinite light via a garment that is as pure as that light. This garment is made from the Torah and the mitzvot that this person engaged in during his lifetime.

A person creates another garment through his choice of neighborhood and his neighbors, the people around him, what he speaks about, how he speaks, how he interacts with others, and so forth. And he creates yet another type of garment if his thoughts and words in this world are materialistic. After he dies, these become the garments of his soul in the World to Come, with all of the grotesqueness and pointlessness of physicality within that world.

But if a person's deeds and thoughts are in Torah and good deeds, in faith, in love and in the fear of God, after he passes away that will be his bond, his garment of life. He will be together with God.

The tzaddik leaves behind his thoughts, words, teachings and prayers to everyone in this world. They give life to those who desire life, who desire the inner essence life as much they desire to breathe air. The tzaddik's influence is all-encompassing. The two terms, "the spirit of our nostrils" and "in his [protective] shadow, we will live," refer to the totality of the tzaddik's spiritual influence upon the hasid and to the connection of the hasid with the tzaddik. ☞

---

18. See *Likkutei Amarim*, chap. 4; epistle 29; *Torat Ḥayyim, Parashat Mishpatim* 285c.

אֲשֶׁר שָׁבַק לָנוּ בְּכָל אֶחָד וְאֶחָד
כְּפִי בְּחִינַת הִתְקַשְּׁרוּתוֹ בֶּאֱמֶת
וְאַהֲבָתוֹ אַהֲבַת אֱמֶת הַטְּהוֹרָה
מִקֶּרֶב אִישׁ וְלֵב עָמוֹק כִּי "כַּמַּיִם
הַפָּנִים וכו'" (משלי כז,יט) וְרוּחַ
אַיְיתֵי רוּחַ וְאַמְשִׁיךְ רוּחַ

All this the tzaddik **has left** for **us, each person corresponding to the level of his genuine connection and his pure love** – his **true love** – with the tzaddik, **from within himself** and from **the depth of** his **heart** (see Psalms 64:7). That is **because "As water reflects** a face to the face, so does the heart of a person to a person" (Prov. 27:19), **and "spirit brings spirit and draws forth spirit"** (*Zohar* 2:166b and elsewhere).

Now, after the tzaddik's *histalkut*, we do not seek his influence externally but we seek it by looking within ourselves. Each person may find the tzaddik in his soul.

The text uses the adjectives "genuine" and "pure," indicating something true, because, as the author of the *Tanya* states in a number of places, truth is something that does not change. The truth is an entity's central, inner and essential core, unaffected by any external alterations. Thus, the hasid's genuine connection to and pure love for his rebbe does not change just because the rebbe is no longer in his body. The only difference is that the "garments" have changed.

THE SPIRIT OF OUR NOSTRILS

☞ This metaphor is more extreme than the more common metaphor of food. A person's dependence on food is not as acute as his dependence on air. Without the life that a person receives from the tzaddik, he has no life at all – not even a momentary illusion of some other, worldly life.

"The spirit of our nostrils" and "in his protective shadow, we will live."

This is speaking overall of two levels of spiritual influence: inner and encompassing. Food and air are metaphors for inner influence. There is a difference between an inner influence and its recipient. The recipient has his own existence, and the influence is a life force that he receives. Conversely, an encompassing influence not only gives life to its recipient, but it constitutes the essence of his existence. He exists only within that encompassing influence. That is the meaning of "in his [protective] shadow, we will live." The shadow is encompassing, and the hasid is within it. The hasid receives the encompassing illumination of the tzaddik in such a way that there is no difference between the influence and the recipient. The hasid has no inherent existence.

To the degree that the hasid's connection to and love of his rebbe in his lifetime was pure – without any admixture, without any superficial motivations – it will grow even stronger after the tzaddik's *histalkut*.

The hasid's connection to the tzaddik must emerge from the depth of his heart: from the core of his heart and the essence of his soul. The more the hasid's connection is genuine and pure, the more it will bring the tzaddik's influence down to him from the tzaddik's inner point of truth and the depth of the tzaddik's heart. Then it will enter and influence the hasid's inner being and depth of his heart.

This metaphor describes the arousal from below: the face that one presents to water is the face that is reflected in them. When a person smiles, the water smiles back. Similarly, that which a person feels in his heart toward another person, that person returns to him.[19] In this context, that which the hasid feels and seeks, he receives from the rebbe.

This phrase expresses the same concept in the language of the *Zohar*, and is discussed at length in hasidic teachings in this context of an arousal from below. The hasid's spirit of connection with his rebbe and love for him draws a spirit of love and connection from the rebbe to him. ☞

וְרוּחוֹ עוֹמֶדֶת בְּקִרְבֵּינוּ מַמָּשׁ, כִּי בִּרְאוֹתוֹ יְלָדָיו, מַעֲשֵׂה יָדָיו בְּקִרְבּוֹ יַקְדִּישׁוּ שְׁמוֹ יִתְבָּרֵךְ אֲשֶׁר יִתְגַּדֵּל וְיִתְקַדֵּשׁ

The tzaddik's **spirit truly remains in our midst when he sees his children, the work of his hands in his midst, sanctifying** God's **name, may He be blessed, which is magnified and sanctified,**

Even now. This is literally the tzaddik's spirit: not only memories of experiences that we had, but the tzaddik's living spirit within our own spirit.

"His children" refers to the tzaddik's students,[20] his hasidim. When the tzaddik's spirit sees that his students are connected to him as

---

19. Regarding the way of service of "like water, face answers to face…," see at length *Likkutei Amarim*, chaps. 46 and 49.

20. Students are called children, as in Scripture and in the words of our Sages. "Children of the prophets" are the students of the prophets. Elisha calls Elijah "my father." And this is expressed in various statements of the Sages, such as, "Whoever teaches his comrade's child Torah is considered by Scripture as though he fathered him" (*Sanhedrin* 19b).

children are connected to their father and, moreover, that they are like "the work of his hands," in that they embody and express his fear and love of God, God's name is truly "magnified and sanctified,"[21] just as it is by the tzaddik. "Magnified" means that it is made greater, spreading and permeating all existence. And "sanctified" means that God's holiness is revealed; the fact that He is separate from and higher than all existence. As explained in hasidic teachings, these are the two levels of the revelation of the divine light: inner and encompassing, also referred to as "filling all worlds" and "encompassing all worlds." ☞

"AS WATER REFLECTS A FACE TO THE FACE"

☞   Physical water reflecting one's face" is a tangible metaphor from the nature of the world, whereas "spirit brings spirit" emphasizes that the same principle applies in the spiritual realm.

Furthermore, an additional aspect exists in the spiritual dimension: not only does spirit bring spirit but it draws forth more spirit. As stated elsewhere (see Ha-Yom Yom, 20 Adar Sheni), "spirit from below brings spirit from above, and draws spirit from above and higher." In terms of the physical metaphor, what we show to water reflects back to us, no more and no less. But in terms of the spiritual metaphor, the spirit that rises from below draws spirit from the highest heights, which is much more than the spirit from below. It is important to emphasize this here, because otherwise a person might have thought that the hasid's connection to the tzaddik after the latter's *histalkut* is only a type of memory, that he merely recaptures what had once been. Therefore, the author of the Tanya stresses that a new spirit comes from the tzaddik, which in scope and tangibility, is far greater than what the hasid had received from the tzaddik in the latter's lifetime.

WHICH IS MAGNIFIED AND SANCTIFIED

☞   These are the words with which the kaddish begins, the prayer recited in a quorum to magnify and sanctify God's name as well as to elevate the soul of a person who has passed away – in particular, when he was connected to the person reciting the kaddish. As used here, this term teaches that the hasid's connection to the tzaddik's life after the latter's *histalkut* and the hasid's walking in the tzaddik's ways, magnify and sanctify God's name. This connection elevates the soul of that tzaddik as well, since the hasid's service of God is powered by him. Then, as this letter will go on to explain, the more the tzaddik's spirit rises, the more abundance it causes to flow down onto the hasid, even more than he had received in the tzaddik's lifetime, both in the inner being of the hasid's soul and in the encompassing illumination from above.

---

21. See Isa. 29:23.

כַּאֲשֶׁר נֵלֵךְ בְּדֶרֶךְ יְשָׁרָה אֲשֶׁר **when we will go on the straight road**
הוֹרָנוּ מִדְּרָכָיו, וְנֵלְכָה בְּאוֹרְחוֹתָיו **that he taught us of his ways, and we will go on his paths,**

All of this is the case when the hasidim continue to walk on the path that the tzaddik taught them in his lifetime. Through this, they will continue to go in his ways and they will be connected to him forever, so that no circumstances – in life nor in death, in body nor in soul – will interfere with this living connection.[22] ☞

נֶצַח סֶלָה וָעֶד **eternally, always, forever.**

As explained elsewhere,[23] in keeping with what is explained in the words of the Sages (see *Eiruvin* 54a), whenever Scripture uses any of

HIS ROADS AND HIS PATHS

☞ The *Zohar* explains, as does somewhat differently the Ba'al Shem Tov, that there is a difference between a "road" and a "path." It may be noted that The Lubavitcher Rebbe, Rabbi Menaḥem Mendel Schneerson, also references the *Zohar* 2:215a and *Likkutei Torah*, Song. 12a, which discusses the connection between *oreaḥ*, "guest," and *oraḥ*, "path." See *Ba'al Shem Tov al HaTorah, Parashat Yitro* 4, *Tzava'at HaRibash, Keter Shem Tov* and *Likkutim Yekarim*. In brief, a "road" is paved, as when a person separates himself from this-worldly matters and engages solely in Torah, day and night, and "path" is the way in which a person speaks with people and about this-worldly matters, but does all of that for the sake of heaven. Thus, a "road" is paved, a way on which many have gone and still go. What the tzaddik teaches others is a straight way on which the tzaddik and others have walked. A "path," on the other hand, is unpaved and, moreover, has dangers and surprises. It is every individual's personal path. A person cannot only walk upon the straight road that his rabbis taught him. As he lives in the world, he faces opportunities and tests to which he must respond in his own unique way. Although these are the person's own paths, the author of the *Tanya* calls them the tzaddik's paths, because the tzaddik teaches the hasid how to walk upon the unpaved path, the path that his particular soul descended to the world to walk upon, a path that is not outlined in the *Shulḥan Arukh*. The "path" comes from the tzaddik – especially after his *histalkut*. Nevertheless, he leaves something for the hasid beyond making a simple choice between good and evil. Therefore, "we" – his hasidim – "will go on his paths."

---

22. See Ps. 107:7 and Isa. 2:3 (also Mic. 4:2).

23. See *Likkutei Torah, Pekudei* 5a, which cites the *Zohar* 3:20a and refers as well to *Mikdash Melekh*, ibid.

these three synonyms it means something that will never cease. By using all three terms, the author of the *Tanya* emphasizes that the tzaddik's life and his guidance of his hasidim never cease.

וְזֶה שֶׁכָּתוּב בַּזוֹהַר הַקָדוֹשׁ (חלק ג עא,ב): דְצַדִיקָא דְאִתְפַּטַר אִשְׁתַּכַּח בְּכֻלְהוּ עָלְמִין יַתִיר מִבְּחַיוֹהִי דְהַיְינוּ שֶׁגַם בְּזֶה הָעוֹלָם הַמַעֲשֶׂה, "הַיוֹם לַעֲשׂוֹתָם" (דברים ז,יא)

And so is it written in the holy *Zohar* (3:71b), "**a tzaddik who passes away is found in all worlds more than** [he was] **in his lifetime**" that is, **even in this world of action,** of which it is written, "**today to do them**" (Deut. 7:11).

13 Heshvan
12 Heshvan
(leap year)

The fact that after the tzaddik has left his physical body he exists in the upper world is easy to understand. But the fact that his soul still exists, even more than when he was alive, in the physical world is hard to comprehend, because the tzaddik now has no physical body with which to act, with which to speak, and with which to be in the world of action. However, even though the tzaddik's life is not in his body, it exists in the bodies of the hasidim connected to him, and so through them he continues to fulfill the purpose of the world of action: "today to do them" (Deut. 7:11).

אִשְׁתַּכַּח יַתִיר כִּי הַמַעֲשֶׂה (גָדוֹל) [גָדֵל] וְהוֹלֵךְ, גִידוּלֵי גִידוּלִין מִן אוֹר זָרוּעַ לַצַדִיק בַּשָׂדֶה אֲשֶׁר בֵּרְכוֹ ה'

The tzaddik **is present more** than when he was alive. That is **because the action** of his disciples **continuously grows,** producing **successive** generations of **offshoots, from "the light planted for the righteous"** (Ps. 97:11) **in "the field that the Lord has blessed"** (Gen. 27:27).

This is in keeping with our Sages' statement (*Eiruvin* 22a) that "today" refers to the world of action, the arena designated for the commandments that can be performed only in a physical body. Therefore, the physicality of the world of action and the fact that it conceals the Divine and expresses God's inner intent is an end in itself and not just a means toward some other goal. One cannot say that physicality is secondary to spirituality – that the tzaddik had been in the world of action and now, at a more advanced stage, he is no longer there. That is not so. Even after his *histalkut*, the tzaddik is more present in the world of deed.

That is because the deeds that the hasidim perform in this world continuously grow,[24] beyond that which the tzaddik did and was able to do while in his body. That indicates not only the growths that the tzaddik grew in his lifetime – his own students – but their successive generations of offshoots as well: their own students and children.

The tzaddik's influence is comparable to a seed planted in the earth. After it disintegrates, it grows into a plant that is much greater than what had been manifest in the seed. And that plant itself goes on to produce its own offshoots. ☞

הַמֵּאִיר לָאָרֶץ וְחוּצוֹת   Shining on the Land and on the outside places.

The light shines down to the land below, that being the Land of Israel, and to the "outside places," those being the areas outside the Land of Israel.[25]

Most of Rabbi Menaḥem Mendel of Vitebsk's hasidim lived in the Land of Israel, where he had lived and had been active for the last ten years of his life. But even outside the Land, many hasidim had remained connected to him and stayed in touch with him via messengers and

---

"IN THE FIELD THAT THE LORD HAS BLESSED"

☞ What is the meaning of this expression, which was spoken by Isaac to Jacob? Is the "field" the Garden of Eden (as implied by Rashi there, based on *Tanḥuma*), the Temple, or, in the language of the kabbalists, the *sefira* of *Malkhut*? Whatever it is, the author of the Tanya is apparently alluding to the inclusive "supernal earth": a spiritual "earth" where the tzaddik exists after his *histalkut*. This spiritual existence is the supernal, rectified and holy aspect of our world. Since the tzaddik is in that spiritual world, it relates to our own world. Since, in his lifetime, the tzaddik lived in "the field that the Lord has blessed," his link with this earth remains even after his *histalkut*.

---

24. This phrase is possibly based on I Sam. 2:26: "The lad Samuel was steadily growing."

25. See the blessing of *Yotzer Or*, and also Prov. 8:26. Rashi interprets "land and the outer places" as referring to "the Land of Israel and the other lands."

letters. And in a more extended circle, hasidim had a connection to him via the author of the *Tanya* and via giving charity to the author of the *Tanya*, which he sent to the Land of Israel to support the hasidic community there.

וְגַם אֲנַחְנוּ אֵלֶּה פֹּה הַיּוֹם כּוּלָנוּ חַיִּים בִּדְרָכָיו, דֶּרֶךְ הַקֹּדֶשׁ יִקָּרֵא לָה

We as well who are here today, all of us who live in his ways, "which is called the way of holiness" (Isa. 25:8).

"We as well…all of us who live" is a reference to Deuteronomy 4:4. "Here" means outside the Land, while "today," indicates that after the tzaddik's *histalkut*, every person can receive the tzaddik's illumination.

The author of the *Tanya* calls the tzaddik's way "the way of holiness" because the tzaddik's life in this world has no connection to the things of this world, but it is dedicated entirely to God. "The way of holiness" also alludes to the person who goes on this way. Although he is not literally like the tzaddik, who is intrinsically separate from the things of this world, and although he does not feel the presence of the tzaddik as it was in this world, he nevertheless goes on the tzaddik's way, a way that is not dependent on and not influenced by the environment that surrounds him.

זֹאת בַּעֲבוֹדַת ה' בְּמִילֵי דִשְׁמַיָּא. וּבְמִילֵי דְעָלְמָא בְּפֵירוּשׁ אִתְּמַר בַּזּוֹהַר הַקָּדוֹשׁ (חלק ג עא,ב) דְּצַדִּיקַיָּא מְגִינִין עַל עָלְמָא, וּבְמִיתָתְהוֹן יַתִּיר מִבְּחַיֵּיהוֹן, וְאִלְמָלֵא צְלוֹתָא דְצַדִּיקַיָּא בְּהַהוּא עָלְמָא לָא אִתְקַיֵּים עָלְמָא רִגְעָא חֲדָא

This relates to the service of God in matters of heaven. And in matters of the world, the holy *Zohar* explicitly states (3:71b) that the righteous people protect the world – in their death even more than in their lifetime. And if not for the prayer of the righteous in that world, this world would not last a moment.

The spiritual work of ascending to the upper worlds and to their abundance. This spiritual work does not relate to any revelation of

Godliness, but to God Himself, beyond the existence of all worlds, even the spiritual worlds.

Matters of the world refers to the spiritual work that relates to the worlds overall and to this world in particular, in order to make it a dwelling place for holiness.

The tzaddikim have the power to pray for the world and to guard it from all evil. The *Zohar* here adds that after a tzaddik's *histalkut*, he possesses even more power to protect the world by means of his prayer than he had possessed during his lifetime. ☞

וְכֹל הַקָּרוֹב קָרוֹב אֶל מִשְׁכַּן ה' **And whoever was closer to** the tzad-
בְּחַיָּיו - קוֹדֶם לַבְּרָכָה dik, who is **the tabernacle of the Lord during his lifetime, has precedence to** receive **the blessing.**

The tzaddik is called "the tabernacle of the Lord" because he is like a tabernacle, a place where the Divine Presence dwells: "and I will dwell in their midst.... " The closer something was to the Tabernacle, the more sanctified it was (the camp of the Divine Presence was more sanctified than the Levite camp, which was in turn more sanctified than the Israelite camp.) So too, a person who is close to the tzaddik receives directly and deeply, whereas a person further away receives indirectly and superficially. In accordance with a person's closeness to the tzaddik in the latter's lifetime, so will he receive from the tzaddik's blessing after his *histalkut*. [26] ☞

THE RIGHTEOUS PEOPLE PROTECT THE WORLD

☞   Even when the tzaddik lives in this world, he is not truly a part of it. He is always a little above it. It may be said that he is a stage higher in the chain of cause and effect, that he exists a moment before the trait of judgment determines how the world will be. (In kabbalistic terminology, he is comparable to *Yesod* that influ- ences *Malkhut*, which corresponds to the world.) From there, he can nullify decrees and change events – to which many de- scriptions of the tzaddikim throughout the generations attest. This connection of the tzaddik with the world and its people ex- ists even after his *histalkut*. This is the top- ic discussed in this letter.

26. "Whoever is closer.... " See Num. 17:28. Regarding "has precedence to [receive] the blessing," see *Berakhot* 41a on the laws of blessings on items from

The following is the continuation of the letter:

And that is particularly so when my speech – my prayer and my request – is expansive on behalf of Rabbi Menaḥem Mendel's **lovely and pleasant son, who is wondrous and outstanding, a stream of God, filled with knowledge and the fear of God: his holy honor, our teacher Rabbi Moshe, may his light shine. That is in keeping with the statement of our Rabbis of blessed memory that a** father's **disposition is inclined to** that of **his son** (*Bava Batra* 142b).

Therefore, I pour forth my prayerful **speech that those close** to Rabbi Menaḥem Mendel **should not distance** themselves, **heaven forbid. I have heard the speech of the** morally **impoverished of the flock who speak without knowledge, judging that the son should** now **receive less money, heaven forbid, from all the sanctified money that** people **dedicate to God** as charity **every year regularly, from**

AND WHOEVER IS CLOSER...HAS PRECEDENCE
TO RECEIVE THE BLESSING

☞ This sentence emphasizes something that could have been understood as well from what was stated earlier regarding the connection between the tzaddik's influence prior to and following his *histalkut*. Certainly, this has a spiritual meaning, but more simply it may be understood in the context of the next part of this letter, which was not published in *Iggeret HaKodesh*. That continuation of the letter deals principally with the practical and material ramifications of Rabbi Menaḥem Mendel's *histalkut* (for which reason it was not published in *Iggeret HaKodesh*), in requesting that the hasidim outside the Land continue their support of the hasidim dwelling in the Holy Land. The hasidim outside the Land were not wealthy, and what they gave was not from discretionary funds. Therefore (as may be seen in many of the other holy epistles), the author of the *Tanya* had to provide them with a good reason for why they must give. Rabbi Menaḥem Mendel had been the head of the hasidim (including those outside the Land). Thus, the hasidim had felt that sending charity to him was of benefit to themselves as well. But after his *histalkut*, it was necessary to emphasize that even now they could be connected to the tzaddik, to some extent, via those close to him: His son, the hasidim in the Land of Israel, his successor. That being the case, they must continue to maintain and strengthen this connection, both materially and spiritually.

---

which one derives benefit. Regarding the seven varieties of praiseworthy produce of the Land of Israel, whatever is mentioned first and is closer to the word "Land" in the verse takes precedence in the order of reciting a blessing.

each person whose heart inspires him, on behalf of our rabbis in the Land of Israel, may it be built and established quickly in our days, amen, who have until now divided their money into equal parts.

"Behold, how good and how pleasant it is for brothers to sit together" (Ps. 133:1). Now as well, so should matters be performed in keeping with their words of the past, their words that are alive and established. Heaven forbid, that we act in a way that will leave "the righteous man abandoned, and his offspring ...," heaven forbid.

This beloved and pleasant son was supported at the table of his father, may his memory be for the life of the World to Come. And almost half of Rabbi Menaḥem Mendel's expenses went to him and to his family: the minors dependent on him and his wife, "the wife of a colleague, who is like the colleague," and his grandchildren and grandchildren, these last being the daughters of his daughter, who also require a great deal of money to take care of all their needs, to "raise them to the wedding canopy and engaging in good deeds." And that which remains will go to repay the debts that are well-known to all, the collateral for which consists of his house and his inheritance, the inheritance of God, which should go to the children and not to strangers, heaven forbid.

Therefore, my request is repeated to all of my beloved and friends: not to diminish, heaven forbid, even by one small coin, heaven forfend, not to give any less to the holy charity, heaven forbid. The amount of money should be complete, all of it, so that it is favorable to God.

Furthermore, I ask and request that you should be swift in performing a mitzva this year: that all the money going up to the Land of Israel from our country should be counted and received by the hand of a faithful agent, may he live, before this Passover coming upon us for the good, to be sent immediately after Passover to the holy community of Brod and from there to Triest, so that it will rise and come and arrive in our Holy Land in the autumn. Because: know clearly that the extra profit of the money that arrives in autumn constitutes almost half of the entire amount that is sent from our country - as the person who transmits this letter, may he live, will explain my speech.

And so, my beloved, my brothers and my friends, do you not

know, have you not heard about the precious beauty of the greatness of the commandment of strengthening the settlement of the Land? This commandment is great. Even for the sake of acquiring of just one house in the Holy Land, the Sages set aside the severe commandment of the Sabbath in terms of a rabbinic decree. And certainly we should be equally dedicated, in order to give life to quite a number of clean souls who serve God with holiness and purity, who sanctify themselves and purify themselves, drawing from the sanctity and holy purity of the holy rabbi, our master, teacher and rabbi, the master, Avraham HaKohen, the greatest among his brothers, may he live, who has succeeded our holy rabbi, Rabbi Menaḥem Mendel, may his memory be for a blessing of the life of the World to Come, with wisdom and fear.

And when a person considers in his heart with his knowledge and understanding, saying, "How fortunate we are, how good is our portion, and how pleasant our fate," his heart will rejoice in God and he will be glad with gladness and song. And the donors will rejoice in God as they remit the debts of the hasidim, in keeping with the saying of our Rabbis of blessed memory, "My sons have borrowed on My behalf, and I will repay." If you do so, as we are commanded, God will give you goodness in all matters that benefit soul and flesh. "Be good, Lord, to the good, and to the upright in their hearts."

In resonance with their soul and every soul that seeks their wellbeing, loving their soul from my heart and my willing soul.

Shneur Zalman, son of my master and my rabbi,
Rabbi Barukh, may his light shine.

This marks the end of the author of the *Tanya*'s condolence letter to Rabbi Menaḥem Mendel's bereaved hasidim. This short letter touches on fundamental concepts of Kabbala and emergent Hasidism regarding the connection that transcends time and space between the rebbe and his hasidim. Since the letter was written at a time of emotional distress, its principal purpose was to console the hasidim. Therefore, the author of the *Tanya* wrote succinctly, without employing kabbalistic and hasidic terminology, since such terminology is not universally understood and also, because it would have been out of place. However, at a later stage and for a broader audience of hasidim, it was necessary to discuss this topic more extensively, and in the author of the *Tanya*'s later hasidic language. And so, he penned an "explanation," of this letter, which was published in *Iggeret HaKodesh* directly following this letter.

A commentary by the author of the *Tanya* on his own hasidic teaching is unusual in the *Tanya* and in *Iggeret HaKodesh*, although it is often found in other works. One might have expected that such a commentary would be a restatement of the original in easier and less specialized language. But on the contrary, these commentaries, which focus on certain points in greater depth than the original teaching, are written using more kabbalistic language. The commentary here is not typical, because it does not come to analyze a characteristic hasidic teaching but rather to explain a hasidic teaching that was written succinctly and poetically (without using hasidic terminology) presenting it in the common language of later hasidic teachings. ☞

<table>
<tr>
<td>

14 Heshvan

13 Heshvan
(leap year)

</td>
<td>

אִיתָא בַּזוֹהַר הַקָּדוֹשׁ דְּצַדִּיקָא
דְּאִתְפְּטַר אִשְׁתַּכַּח בְּכֻלְהוּ עָלְמִין
יַתִּיר מִבְּחַיּוֹהִי כו'

</td>
<td>

So **is it written in the holy** *Zohar* (3:71b), **"a tzaddik who passes away is found in all worlds more than** he was **in his lifetime…"**

</td>
</tr>
</table>

These words appeared in the letter, and constitute its essence. Therefore, the author of the *Tanya* will explain them here at length. ☞

EXPLANATION

☞   In order to understand why this article is called an "explanation," one must bear in mind the background of the hasidim whom the author of the *Tanya* was addressing. This was the period of the inception of Hasidism in general and Chabad Hasidism in particular. The hasidim had no tradition of hasidic life and doctrines. Every hasidic topic (and in particular the doctrine of Chabad) was new: the concepts, the direction of thought, and so forth. On the oth-er hand, the members of the author of the *Tanya*'s close circle had already learned a great deal of both the revealed Torah and Kabbala. When such a person heard hasidic teachings for the first time, it was hard for him to understand them and how they fit into what he already knew. Therefore, the author of the *Tanya* provided an explanation of how the elements of a hasidic teaching were derived from kabbalistic doctrines or sayings of the Sages.

וְצָרִיךְ לְהָבִין, תִּינַח בְּעוֹלָמוֹת
עֶלְיוֹנִים אִשְׁתַּכַּח יַתִּיר בַּעֲלוֹתוֹ שָׁמָּה,
אֲבָל בָּעוֹלָם הַזֶּה אֵיךְ אִשְׁתַּכַּח יַתִּיר

We must understand this. Granted that he is now **found more in the upper worlds, since he has risen there. But how is he** now **found more in this world?**

וְיֵשׁ לְפָרֵשׁ עַל דֶּרֶךְ מַה שֶּׁקִּבַּלְתִּי עַל
מַאֲמַר חֲזַ״ל: דִּשָׁבַק חַיִּים לְכָל חַי

One may interpret this in the way that I received regarding the statement of our Sages, of blessed memory, "He has left life for all the living."

The author of the *Tanya* presumably received this from his teacher, the Maggid of Mezeritch.[27] As was explained earlier, "he has left life for all the living" cannot mean that the tzaddik left his followers behind as he rose upward. Rather, it means that he left his life here for all of those who remain alive. What is the meaning of that life that he left to us?

כַּנּוֹדַע, שֶׁחַיֵּי הַצַּדִּיק אֵינָם חַיִּים
בְּשָׂרִים כִּי אִם חַיִּים רוּחָנִיִּים

As is known, the tzaddik's life is not a life of flesh but a life of the spirit,

IN THE UPPER WORLDS

☞ This is also difficult to understand. How can the tzaddik have risen to the upper worlds, since even when he had lived in this world, he had been stripped of physicality? The apparent answer is that when the tzaddik is in his body, he is to some degree involved in this world. Even if he does not feel its limitation, he feels his responsibility to it. Moreover, since the connection is bidirectional, it is particularly intense. People project their needs onto him in an especially immediate and demanding fashion. Therefore, his soul is in this world as well. But after his *histalkut*, his connection to this world is not direct. And whatever connection does exist travels through the intermediary of the upper worlds. He sees and feels the things of this world as they are seen and felt there. In that sense, he is essentially there and not here in this world.

---

27. *HaLekaḥ VeHaLibuv* infers that since the author of the *Tanya* wrote "I received" in the singular, he alone received this. As known, the author of the *Tanya* had a regular private learning schedule with the Maggid.

The author of the *Tanya* briefly alluded to this idea earlier. Here he states it explicitly.

Every person has something that enlivens him: that excites him, that he yearns for, that he fears. It is in relation to that entity that he thinks, speaks and acts – that he lives. There are people for whom the things of this world, material and non-material, provide life. Even if such a person thinks about and does other things, he does so superficially, only because he thinks that he needs to. But he receives his sense of life from whatever excites him: the food that he eats, a compliment that he receives, his family whom he loves, and so forth. The tzaddik is different from everyone else because his life force does not come from this world. He too, may have worldly things, but his essence exists elsewhere. And so, not only do worldly things fail to enliven him, but they may even detract from his life. Any love, or expression of love, for something worldly, hides and weakens his love for the Divine. ☞

שֶׁהֵם אֱמוּנָה וְיִרְאָה וְאַהֲבָה   which consists of **faith, fear and love.**

A person's spiritual life may be divided into three elements: faith, fear, and love.

The spiritual life that the author of the *Tanya* speaks about is a life of holiness. A person might think that music, poetry or abstract thought are spiritual. But that is not what the author of the *Tanya* is talking about. Rather, he is talking about a life whose focus is faith, and the fear and love of God. ☞

THE TZADDIK AND THIS WORLD

☞ The fact that the tzaddik's life is spiritual does not mean that he does not live in this world. Rather, it means that he sees, feels, and thinks about this world as it appears from above, in its spiritual roots. And so, the tzaddik can see what other people do not see: what a person's soul needs and what its purpose is, and the spiritual stages that precede the appearance of occurrences in this world. He is even capable of transforming occurrences before they manifest themselves in this world.

FAITH, FEAR AND LOVE

☞ Why these three? Life, in the sense of that which gives a sense of life, is embedded in a person's character. When one's attributes become excited, they cause him to think, speak, act and move – in one word, to live. Love and fear are the essence and archetypes of a human being's traits from which all the rest develop (perhaps one

The author of the *Tanya* derives from verses how each of these three is called "life":

כִּי בֶּאֱמוּנָה כְּתִיב: "וְצַדִּיק בֶּאֱמוּנָתוֹ יִחְיֶה" (חבקוק ב,ד), וּבְיִרְאָה כְּתִיב: "וְיִרְאַת ה' לְחַיִּים" (משלי יט,כג), וּבְאַהֲבָה כְּתִיב: "רוֹדֵף צְדָקָה וָחָסֶד יִמְצָא חַיִּים" (משלי כא,כא), וְחָסֶד הוּא אַהֲבָה

That is **because, regarding faith, it is written, "But the righteous will live by his faith"** (Hab. 2:4). **And regarding fear, it is written, "The fear of the Lord leads to life"** (Prov. 19:23). **And regarding love, it is written, "He who pursues righteousness and kindness will find life"** (Prov. 21:21). **And "kindness" is "love."**

The inner essence of kindness is love.[28] ☞

---

may add as well, the third fundamental trait: compassion (*Tiferet*, truth), which is connected to faith). A tzaddik is fully alive when his love and fear are directed totally toward God. (Such an illuminated life force can occasionally be experienced by an ordinary individual when he is praying, and the like; at that moment, he is similar to the tzaddik.)

However, there are corners of one's life that love and fear do not fill. When the soul does not clothe itself in love and fear,

faith is the power of life that fills everything. Faith is a power of the soul that is not part of the intellect nor any particular attribute of the soul. It is an expression of the essence of the Jewish soul, which fills all of the space between definable reality.

Faith, fear and love of God therefore describe the totality of life. A person who enters into that totality receives his life solely from the Divine, which is entirely disconnected from the life force of this world. And that person is the tzaddik.

"IT IS WRITTEN"

☞ This string of verses is not placed here solely for rhetorical effect. When a person is shown a verse in Scripture as the source of an idea, he is inspired beyond logic and human experience (see also *Siddur Im Divrei Elokim Ḥayyim*, p. 238b, on the verses of sovereignty, remembrances and shofar in the Rosh HaShana prayers). The truth of the Torah is absolute. It is anchored in an infinite expanse beyond all worlds, beyond all that was and will be. A person needs such

inspiration because the tzaddik's life about which the author of the *Tanya* speaks, is not a life that we truly know. Even if we can sense it, we do not really know the extent to which it reaches. Therefore, the author of the *Tanya* cites Scriptural sources in which this idea is embedded in a realm beyond our comprehension: that faith, fear and love are essentially the true life beyond the life of this world. And they constitute the life of the tzaddik.

---

28. See above, epistle 15.

וּשְׁלֹשָׁה מִדּוֹת אֵלּוּ הֵם בְּכָל עוֹלָם וְעוֹלָם עַד רוּם הַמַּעֲלוֹת הַכֹּל לְפִי עֶרֶךְ בְּחִינַת מַעֲלוֹת הָעוֹלָמוֹת זֶה עַל זֶה, בְּדֶרֶךְ עִילָה וְעָלוּל כַּנּוֹדָע

And these three attributes exist in every world up to the highest levels, everything in keeping with the level of the category of the position of the worlds, one higher than the next, by way of cause and effect, as is known.

Some matters exist only in one specific world. Even the life force connected to that matter exists nowhere else. For instance, a person who loves steak will not find it in the world of music. A person whose life is conditioned on some sort of material existence will not find life in the spiritual worlds. In contrast, these three attributes of the tzaddik's life exist in all worlds, up to the highest levels, because they are the attributes that relate to the Divine, which is found within each person and which is higher than all of the worlds.

Of course, these traits do not exist in each world to an equal extent. They change in each world in keeping with its level.

The descent of worlds occurs in a process of cause and effect. A lower world is in a sense an outcome, the externalization of an idea in the world above it. In this way, lower worlds emerge from higher, almost-entirely abstract worlds that have no boundary, descending in a process of cause and effect to worlds bound by boundaries and parameters, down to this world in which the life force within the garment is no longer visible, but in which only the garments of nature and materiality are visible.

15 Ḥeshvan

14 Ḥeshvan (leap year)

וְהִנֵּה בִּהְיוֹת הַצַּדִּיק חַי עַל פְּנֵי הָאֲדָמָה, הָיוּ שְׁלֹשָׁה מִדּוֹת אֵלּוּ בְּתוֹךְ כְּלִי וּלְבוּשׁ שֶׁלָּהֶם, בִּבְחִינַת מָקוֹם גַּשְׁמִי שֶׁהִיא בְּחִינַת נֶפֶשׁ הַקְּשׁוּרָה בְּגוּפוֹ

And when the tzaddik lived upon the face of the earth, these three traits were in their vessel and garment, on the level of a physical place, which is the category of the soul connected to his body.

When the tzaddik was alive, his faith and his fear and love of God were clothed in the parameters of this material world. ☞

וְכָל תַּלְמִידָיו אֵינָם מְקַבְּלִים רַק הֶאָרַת מִדּוֹת אֵלּוּ וְזִיוָן, הַמֵּאִיר חוּץ לִכְלִי זֶה עַל יְדֵי דִּבּוּרָיו וּמַחְשְׁבוֹתָיו הַקְּדוֹשִׁים

And all of his students receive only an illumination of these traits and their radiance, an illumination **that shines out of this vessel** of his physicality **via his holy words and thoughts.**

That which travels through the physical realm is only physical. Thus, what reaches other people is not the tzaddik's traits but only their illumination. That is comparable to a person's written message that transmits only a part of his oral speech. ☞ ☞

THE SOUL CONNECTED TO THE BODY

☞ The love and fear of God and faith are bound to the physical body via the lowest level of the soul, which is connected to the body and gives it life. This level of the soul creates a bridge. It translates the soul into the vessel of the body. Nevertheless, the essence of the soul is not present. That essence is absolutely meaningless in the material world. In order for the soul to exist here, in order that it may feel and be felt, it needs a garment that will translate it into the language of this world. And that is the level of the part of the soul that is connected to the body. A person's body – even his brain, with all of its complexity and incomprehensible perfection – is ma-terial. And when the soul travels through its nerve cells, when the soul travels through the blood vessels and movements of the body, it constricts itself into these boundaries, into the forces that the materiality of the body contains. Through this physicality, the soul speaks to the person. That communication is of course very limited compared to what the soul itself can experience. The limitation of this communication creates difficulties and limitations first and foremost for the person himself, for his ability to nullify himself to the awe of God's exaltedness or to exude an infinite love of God. But most of all, this limits his ability to connect with and influence other people.

AN ILLUMINATION OF THESE TRAITS

☞ The body does not only constrict the soul's life force. It conceals it entirely. Only a glimmer of that life force extends beyond the body. Thus, the tzaddik's divine life – his faith, and his love and fear of God – are almost entirely hidden by his body and the physical world. What reaches the world is merely a glimmer. This glimmer cannot even be called the externality of the soul's life force, because the illumination is, in a sense, entirely separated from its source. When a source radiates light, its own brightness is not dimmed, and the radiated light does not return to it. Whether or not people receive that radiance, and if they do, how and how much, is not relevant to the source of the light.

VIA HIS HOLY WORDS AND THOUGHTS

☞ How is it possible for anyone to receive the tzaddik's thoughts? *Likkutei Levi* *Yitzḥak al HaTanya*, p. 50, offers an explanation in keeping with the verse: "The

וְלָכֵן אָמְרוּ רַבּוֹתֵינוּ ז"ל שֶׁאֵין אָדָם עוֹמֵד
עַל דַּעַת רַבּוֹ וכו' (עבודה זרה ה,ב)

And therefore, our Sages of blessed memory said that a person does not understand his rabbi's mind… (*Avoda Zara* 5b).

A person does not understand his rabbi's mind until forty years have passed. If a student could receive the entirety of his teacher's good traits, fear and love, or his intellect, he would learn immediately, and he would become like him. But since the teacher can only transmit an illumination, the teaching process takes time. Also, the student does not receive what the teacher has to teach as a whole, but only as separate points, which he must take time to assimilate and integrate. And for this to happen, both the teacher and his student must be capable.[29]

אֲבָל לְאַחַר פְּטִירָתוֹ, לְפִי שֶׁמִּתְפָּרְדִים
בְּחִינַת הַנֶּפֶשׁ, שֶׁנִּשְׁאֲרָה בַּקֶּבֶר, מִבְּחִינַת
הָרוּחַ שֶׁבְּגַן עֵדֶן שֶׁהֵן שָׁלֹשׁ מִדּוֹת הַלָּלוּ

However, after the tzaddik passes away, because the level of his *nefesh*, which remains in the grave, separates itself from the level of his *ruaḥ* in the Garden of Eden, which consists of these three traits,

wisdom of a man illuminates his face" (Eccles. 8:1): A person's thoughts have an influence on those around him. Another answer is that when a person – in particular, a tzaddik – thinks about others, he impacts them. This occurs when he judges someone positively, when he feels love for someone, or even when he thinks of how to help someone. This happens also when he speaks, since his words are united with his thoughts. Conversely, a person's words that are not connected to his thoughts do not exercise any influence. This is in keeping with the statements, "When a person has the fear of heaven, his words are heard" (*Berakhot* 6b) and "Words that come from the heart enter the heart" (Rabbeinu Tam's *Sefer HaYashar*, gate 13, quoted in the *Shelah*, *Sha'ar HaOtyiot* 30).

---

29. According to the Talmud ibid. (as explained by Rashi) the teacher represents God and the student represents Moses. Accordingly, the limitation is due neither to the teacher nor the student, but is ontologically intrinsic.

After a person passes away, his soul is separated from his body. The soul is composed of several levels: *nefesh, ruaḥ, neshama, ḥaya,* and *yeḥida.* In this world, the soul is centered in the body. Only through the body does it feel, think, and act. But with a person's death, only the lowest part of the soul, the *nefesh,* remains connected to the body, whereas the other parts remove themselves and go to where they belong. In particular, the *ruaḥ,* is the level of the revelation of the divine traits in the soul, while the neshama sits in the brain, the *ḥaya* and *yeḥida* are manifest on the levels of the encompassing *Keter.* Faith, which is the inner source of these traits, and fear and love, which are the main traits – rises to the level of the Garden of Eden, where these traits are revealed. ☞

This is particularly true regarding the life of the tzaddik. Even when he had been in this world, the entirety of his life had consisted of faith, and the fear and love of God, so that even when he was alive, these attributes did not have any trace of this world. Therefore, after he passes away, they completely separate from this world; with absolutely nothing limiting them.

לְפִיכָךְ יָכוֹל כָּל הַקָּרוֹב אֵלָיו לְקַבֵּל חֵלֶק מִבְּחִינַת רוּחוֹ שֶׁבְּגַן עֵדֶן, הוֹאִיל וְאֵינָהּ בְּתוֹךְ כְּלִי וְלֹא בִּבְחִינַת מָקוֹם גַּשְׁמִי

therefore, **whoever is close to** the tzaddik **can receive a part of the level of his** *ruaḥ* **that is in the Garden of Eden, since** that *ruaḥ* is now **not within a vessel, and not on the level of physical space.**

THE *RUAḤ* IN THE GARDEN OF EDEN

☞ As explained in many other sources, the Garden of Eden is not one single realm or level, but rather many different levels, one progressively higher than the next. In general, the Garden of Eden is that which is revealed to a soul on every level. When a person affects this world for the good, he also affects all worlds, just as he affects all levels of his soul, although this impact is unbeknownst to him. After he passes away, when his soul rises from this previously closed world, it discovers in every single world what was hidden to him in the physical world when he was performing the holy act. This revelation of the power and brilliance of what he had accomplished, is his very reward, his personal Garden of Eden.

Whoever was close to the tzaddik in his lifetime and remains close to him now as well, drawing closer to his ways and teachings, can receive a part of the level of his *ruaḥ* that is in the Garden of Eden. When the *ruaḥ* is in the body, it is necessarily limited to the body and its physical locus. But in the Garden of Eden, when the *ruaḥ* is not constrained by a physical vessel and location, it can spread without l imit.

It is true that vessels exist on every level of the Garden of Eden, because there can be no revelation without a vessel. But these are spiritual vessels, which do not possess the limitations of a physical body. Thus, the three traits of the tzaddik's life are no longer limited by his body and place. They exist in *ruaḥ* beyond spatiality. Each person everywhere can receive them as they are and not only as an illumination via the tzaddik's body, words and books, or via other people.

כַּנּוֹדַע מַאֲמַר רַבּוֹתֵינוּ ז"ל עַל יַעֲקֹב אָבִינוּ עָלָיו הַשָּׁלוֹם שֶׁנִּכְנַס עִמּוֹ גַּן עֵדֶן

This is in keeping with the well-known statement of our Rabbis of blessed memory that when Jacob came before Isaac, **the Garden of Eden entered with Jacob our Patriarch, may he rest in peace.**

When Jacob approached Isaac to receive his blessing, Isaac "smelled the scent of his garments, and he said, 'See, the scent of my son is like a field that the Lord has blessed'" (Gen. 27:27). The midrash states: "This teaches that the Garden of Eden entered with [Jacob]". And later on, the midrash states that when Esau entered, Gehenna entered with him.[30] These sources thus point to the fact that the Garden of Eden and Gehenna are not geographic locations that souls enter, but rather are spiritual realities that reflect the state of a person's soul, deeds and thoughts as they appear from the perspective of a higher and more revealed level of existence. Isaac sensed the atmosphere of the Garden of Eden that accompanied Jacob in its entire scope and significance.

---

30. *Bereshit Rabba* 65:22; *Tanḥuma, Toledot* 11; *Zohar* 3:84a; and cited by Rashi on Gen. 27:27.

וְכֵן כָּתַב בְּסֵפֶר 'עֲשָׂרָה מַאֲמָרוֹת' And it is likewise written in the
שֶׁאֲוִיר גַּן עֵדֶן מִתְפַּשֵּׁט סְבִיב book *Asara Ma'amarot* that the
כָּל אָדָם, וְנִרְשָׁמִים בַּאֲוִיר זֶה כָּל atmosphere of the Garden of Eden
מַחְשְׁבוֹתָיו וְדִבּוּרָיו הַטּוֹבִים בַּתּוֹרָה surrounds every person, and all of
וַעֲבוֹדַת ה' his good thoughts and his words
of Torah and service of God are
impressed in this atmosphere.

The atmosphere of a person's Garden of Eden surrounds him even in this world.[31] The air of the Garden of Eden is like the primordial Edenic matter that reflects one's good thoughts and words, that he spoke his whole life. This air is a good fabric comprised of light and Divine delight, that hints at more divine delight to come. It receives its structure and form from the person's deeds and thoughts. Little by little, it crystallizes and develops until, by the end of a person's days in this world, it reflects his entire life and reveals everything that his life had not revealed to him: its meaning and connections, and the infinite delight that exists within them.

(וְכֵן לְהֵיפֶךְ, חַס וְשָׁלוֹם, נִרְשָׁמִים (And so too the converse, God
בַּאֲוִיר הַמִּתְפַּשֵּׁט מִגֵּיהִנָּם סְבִיב forbid, are impressed in the atmo-
כָּל אָדָם) sphere that spreads from Gehenna
around each person.)

Just as the atmosphere of the Garden of Eden is the material in which a person's good thoughts, words of Torah, the commandments, and so forth are impressed, so too, the atmosphere of Gehenna is the material in which his bad thoughts and words are impressed.

Nothing is erased. All of a person's life, for good or for evil, in general and in detail, leaves an impression in the air around him, in all of the levels of existence that surround this world. And when his soul is freed from its connections to his body and this world, it begins to see those impressions. Moreover, since overall, it no longer has a tangible continuation to this-worldly life, it connects to and exists only on the level of those impressions. And then it is said to be in the Garden of Eden or, heaven forbid, in Gehenna.

---

31. By Rabbi Menaḥem Azaria of Fano, *Ma'amar Ḥakor Din*, part 2, chap. 12.

הִלְכָּךְ נָקֵל מְאֹד לְתַלְמִידָיו
לְקַבֵּל חֶלְקָם מִבְּחִינַת רוּחַ
רַבָּם הָעַצְמִיִּת, שֶׁהֵם אֱמוּנָתוֹ
וְיִרְאָתוֹ וְאַהֲבָתוֹ אֲשֶׁר עָבַד
בָּהֶם אֶת ה', וְלֹא זִיוָם בִּלְבָד
הַמֵּאִיר חוּץ לַכְּלִי

Therefore, it is very easy for the tzaddik's students to receive their portion from the level of the independent, unembodied *ruaḥ* of their rabbi – that being his faith, fear and love with which he served God, and not only their radiance that shines beyond the vessel.

Now, after the tzaddik's *histalkut*, his spirit – and not just a glimmer of his radiance – is revealed. This allows those people who are still enclosed in a body to receive from it. The radiance of the spirit must be received little by little and then rebuilt in the recipient's soul, all of which requires time and effort. And after all that, what the person receives is only similar to the tzaddik's *ruaḥ*. On the other hand, when a person receives directly from the tzaddik's spirit – from his faith, fear and love – an actual portion of the tzaddik's fear of God becomes his fear, a portion of the tzaddik's love of God becomes his love, and so forth.

But how is it possible for the tzaddik's unembodied spirit to join with the student's embodied spirit? In addition, after the tzaddik's *histalkut*, his spirit – consisting of his faith, fear and love – rises ceaselessly. Even in this world, one cannot receive from another person when he is involved in his own learning, in his own elevation, in his own feelings. So how can the student bind his spirit to that of the tzaddik?

The author of the *Tanya* now addresses these questions.

לְפִי שֶׁבְּחִינַת רוּחוֹ הָעַצְמִית
מִתְעַלָּה בְּעִילּוּי אַחַר עִילּוּי,
לְהִכָּלֵל בִּבְחִינַת נִשְׁמָתוֹ
שֶׁבְּגַן עֵדֶן הָעֶלְיוֹן שֶׁבָּעוֹלָמוֹת
הָעֶלְיוֹנִים

That is because the level of the tzaddik's independent, unembodied *ruaḥ* rises, elevation after elevation, to be incorporated into the level of his *neshama* in the supernal Garden of Eden in the supernal worlds.

The supernal Garden of Eden (which corresponds to the world of *Beria*) is not contiguous to this world and does not relate directly to it. That is in contrast to the lower Garden of Eden (which corresponds to the world of *Yetzira*).

The difference between the supernal and lower Gardens of Eden parallels the difference between the revelation of the *neshama*, which is overall the revelation in the *moḥin* (the intellect), and the revelation of the *ruaḥ*, which is the revelation in the *middot* (the traits).

The tzaddik's unembodied spirit – his faith, fear and love – which is related to his personal experience, to his bond with God, is not confined to the lower Garden of Eden but rises ever higher. Contrary to what one may think, after a person passes away, his soul does not rest as in sleep (the life that it had had in this world does come to a rest, but the soul continues having more experiences). The *neshama* must work through what it underwent in this world, removing blockages, purifying experiences and rising ever higher. As time passes, the *neshama* grows increasingly distanced from this world. Even those elements from this world that it takes – its good deeds, Torah study and the commandments – lose the form that they previously had. In particular, the tzaddik – who even while he was alive was not pulled down by his speech or thought, since his life consisted entirely of faith and the fear and love of God – now rises, step by step, ceaselessly and unhindered. He only pauses at various levels of the Garden of Eden to extract the meaning of his life that relates to these levels. Once his soul has extracted the infinite delight in his love and fear of God in the lower Garden of Eden, it rises to the supernal Garden of Eden, and onward to its root and essence.

We cannot receive from the tzaddik's personal *ruaḥ* and experience, because that rises ceaselessly. But on the other hand, as the author of the *Tanya* will now explain, this swift ascent makes the apparently impossible possible: we are able to receive something from the essence of his spirit that remains in the lower Garden of Eden and that relates to our world.

וְנוֹדַע שֶׁכָּל דָּבָר שֶׁבִּקְדוּשָׁה אֵינוֹ נֶעֱקָר לְגַמְרֵי מִכֹּל וָכֹל מִמְּקוֹמוֹ וּמַדְרֵגָתוֹ הָרִאשׁוֹנָה, גַּם לְאַחַר שֶׁנִּתְעַלָּה לְמַעְלָה לְמַעְלָה

It is known that no holy entity is ever entirely, completely uprooted from its place and from its original level, even after it has risen higher and higher.

When something has the status of a holy article, this means that it is a vessel for holiness, absolutely nullified to God, without any will of its own, without any intrinsic existence. Such an entity grows and rises continuously. Actually, it does not rise, because it is already at the highest heights. Rather, existence around it collapses, exposing its essence stage by stage. Yet on the other hand, it is never entirely uprooted from its previous place below. That is because even when it was below, it was essentially above. Even when it is above, it is still below.[32] And so is it always: the revelation of the tzaddik's essence rises constantly so that we never grasp him at any time and place, since he has already ascended. Nevertheless, his presence that had been there is not uprooted from its place. ☞

וּבְחִינָה זוֹ הָרִאשׁוֹנָה, שֶׁנִּשְׁאֲרָה לְמַטָּה בְּגַן עֵדֶן הַתַּחְתּוֹן, בִּמְקוֹמוֹ וּמַדְרֵגָתוֹ הָרִאשׁוֹנָה הִיא הַמִּתְפַּשֶּׁטֶת בְּתַלְמִידָיו

This first level that remains below in the lower Garden of Eden spreads among the tzaddik's **students in its original place and level.**

The lower Garden of Eden is the reflection and revelation of the tzaddik's life in this world. It is the significance and supernal delight that his deeds and thoughts in this world still retain. This is the tzaddik's

---

NOTHING HOLY IS UPROOTED FROM ITS PLACE

☞ That is not the case with something that is not holy. It exists due to the power of the holy spark in it, but the spark's existence is one of exile within the unholy "husk." And so, from the moment that the spark is liberated, it rises and does not remain below where it had been. Something holy, on the other hand, is not hidden by a garment and the lower vessel. Instead, the garment and vessel are themselves transformed into holiness. Therefore, even when the core of something holy rises, that core is everywhere and accessible to everyone.

For example, when a holy person lives in this world, everything he does – how he dresses, how he eats, how he wishes people a good morning – becomes not only a vessel and locus for holiness but in a sense, actual holiness. When this holy person rises from that place, the holiness is not uprooted. It remains in the "garments" of how he ate and how he walked. From now on, whoever acts in that way will undoubtedly receive something of that holiness. And if that is the case in the physical realm, how much more in the spiritual realm of the lower Garden of Eden (as will be explained).

---

32. In Kabbalistic books, such as *Pardes Rimmonim*, gate 14, chap. 1; *Etz Ḥayyim*, gate 34, chap. 3; the Arizal's *Likkutei Torah, Parashat Vayera*; *Emek HaMelekh*, gate 14, chap. 85, and elsewhere.

ruaḥ as it remains in the lower Garden of Eden even after his *neshama* has risen.

Although the tzaddik's *neshama* has risen and will rise yet more and no one can keep up with it, his students can still receive from his *ruaḥ*, because his *ruaḥ* has not moved from its place. The lower Garden of Eden reveals the supernal, holy aspect of this world in which the tzaddik and the hasidim had been together. Therefore, the revelation there relates to both the tzaddik and his hasidim. From there, the hasid can receive the aspects of the tzaddik's spirit that relate to him even after the tzaddik's *histalkut*. ☞

However, the question still remains: how can the hasidim, who are in their bodies in this world, receive from this *ruaḥ*? We receive from other people by hearing their words and seeing their deeds. But how is it possible to receive – not via the physical senses – from a purely spiritual entity? The author of the *Tanya* now addresses this question.

כָּל אֶחָד כְּפִי בְּחִינַת הִתְקַשְּׁרוּתוֹ וְקִרְבָתוֹ אֵלָיו בְּחַיָּיו וּבְמוֹתוֹ

It spreads to **every person in keeping with the level of his connection and closeness to** the tzaddik, **in** the tzaddik's **lifetime and after his death.**

This is not a miraculous, "supernatural" connection, but a continuation of what had existed when the tzaddik had been alive. This continuation proceeds further than might have first been imagined. The key is a

THE TZADDIK'S *RUAḤ* SPREADS AMONG HIS STUDENTS

☞ This aspect of the tzaddik that spreads among his students is his essential *ruaḥ* – his faith, his fear and his love of God – and not merely an illumination (such as that which had been revealed via his speech and so forth when he had been alive). In fact, this *ruaḥ* might be an even more essential part of the tzaddik than his ruaḥ in the Garden of Eden. It is axiomatic that every influence of holiness in this world contains more of the essence of holiness than an influence of holiness in the spiritual, supernal world. God's in-fluence upon and connection to matters of this world is more intrinsic than His illumination alone in the Garden of Eden. And the same applies to the tzaddikim, who are "similar to their Creator." At this point, when the tzaddik's personal *ruaḥ* has risen so high, his students can connect with and receive an intrinsic part of that *ruaḥ*, which exists in and relates to this world. Thus, his faith becomes their faith, his fear of God becomes their fear of God, and his love of God becomes their love of God.

person's connection to the tzaddik: both in the tzaddik's lifetime (in seeing him, in hearing his words, and in being in his presence) and after his *histalkut* (in one's memories, in learning his teachings, in emulating his ways and keeping his directives). That is the way to receive the tzaddik's spirit. As long as that connection continues, the tzaddik's influence and the student's receiving continue. And as the connection grows stronger, it dissociates more fully from the recipient's physical vessels and concepts. Then, its influence and the way it is received become more independent and more powerful.

בְּאַהֲבָה רַבָּה, כִּי הַמְשָׁכַת כָּל רוּחָנִיּוּת אֵינָהּ אֶלָּא עַל יְדֵי אַהֲבָה רַבָּה

It spreads **with tremendous love.** That is **because the drawing forth of all spirituality** comes about **solely by means of great love.**

The student's connection to the tzaddik, which draws forth the tzaddik's spirit, comes about solely by means of the student's great love for God. After the student cultivates his "physical" connection to the tzaddik by learning his teachings and acting in keeping with his directives, he draws forth the tzaddik's spirit. He can do so only by having a "great love" for God.

In general, a person draws forth and expands spiritual influence by means of love and kindness. Unlike fear of God, which is characterized by gathering in, love of God is characterized by spreading out: expanding and broadening holiness. With "great love" in particular, a person rises above his ego.

"Great love" is so-called in contrast to "small love," which refers to a person's love for the things in his world that he knows are worth loving. In general, that is the "worldly love" mentioned many times by the author of the *Tanya*, which a person experiences when he contemplates the world and realizes how fitting it is to love the One Who created it and Who guides it and himself in particular. "Great love," however, relates to God Himself beyond the fact of His being the Creator and Guide of the world, beyond all comprehension. Small love is part of a person. It is the emotional distillation of what he comprehends and knows. It magnifies his holy traits, and cleans and improves them – but it remains his own "small love." Therefore, a person also needs "great love" that transcends his being in order to connect himself to the tzaddik and draw forth the tzaddik's spirit.

כְּמוֹ שֶׁכָּתוּב בַּזוֹהַר הַקָדוֹשׁ דְּרוּחַ דִּרְעוּתָא דְּלִבָּא אַמְשִׁיךְ רוּחַ מִלְעֵילָא   As written in the holy *Zohar* (2:162b, and elsewhere), **"the spirit of the will of the heart draws forth the spirit from above"**

"The will of the heart" refers to a person's great love for God: a love beyond the powers of his soul. It is like the power of the *Ratzon* (will) in his soul, which transcends all the powers of his soul, including his intellect and his entire consciousness. This vast, inner love is the love of the essence of the soul, not what it comprehends with the intellect but what it connects to from its core. This love relates to God Himself, beyond all of His revelations and activities, beyond what may be comprehended in any way.[33]

When the tzaddik was in this world, the student had no need to experience this vast love in order to receive the illumination of the tzaddik's spirit. But after the tzaddik's *histalkut*, in order for the student to draw forth the tzaddik's traits and transform them into his own so that he himself is transformed he requires this vast love, a love that transcends his intellect and character traits.

רַק אִם יָכוֹן לִקְרַאת אֱלֹהָיו בַּהֲכָנָה רַבָּה וִיגִיעָה עֲצוּמָה, לְקַבֵּל שָׁלֹשׁ מִדוֹת הַלָלוּ כְּדֶרֶךְ שֶׁהוֹרָהוּ רַבּוֹ   **only when** a person **prepares to meet his God with great preparation and mighty effort in order to receive these three traits in the way that his rabbi taught him.**

The author of the *Tanya* adds here, that even the hasid's connection to the tzaddik and great love for God do not suffice, because this hasid is still in his body and his animal *nefesh*. The tzaddik's spirit is in the Garden of Eden, liberated from the bonds of the body, but the hasid is not on that level. In order for him to receive from the tzaddik's spirit, he must break through and beyond the boundaries of his connections

---

33. See *Likkutei Torah, Bemidbar* 81d and also *Torah Or* 27a, stating that no thought grasps God, but that He may be grasped by the will of the heart.

to his body. For this there are no shortcuts. He must work hard, "with a tremendous preparation and mighty effort." ☞

HE MUST PREPARE TO MEET HIS GOD

☞ The author of the *Tanya* states (as does the approach of Chabad in general) that it is not enough for the hasid to have a connection with the tzaddik. Even when the tzaddik can apparently do everything for the hasid, physically and spiritually, the hasid must do the work himself. He himself must toil.

The directive, "Prepare to meet your God, O Israel" (Amos 4:12) means that before a person serves God he must cleanse and prepare his mind and body (see e.g., *Berakhot* 23a, *Shabbat* 10a; *Shulḥan Arukh HaRav, Oraḥ Ḥayyim* 1:1; *Shulḥan Arukh, Oraḥ Ḥayyim* 92:1 and *Mishna Berura* there). In the present context, this means that the student must stand before God as he himself attains the fear and love possessed by the tzaddik, without the interposition of the limitations of his own soul (of his own love and fear of God, which are aligned with his character traits). He himself stands before God, as the tzaddik only guides him.

The author of the *Tanya* explains similarly in *Likkutei Amarim* (chap. 42; see also a comment in this vein in *Likkutei Hagahot LaTanya*), that in order for a person to make such a connection he needs to engage in "effort of the soul and effort of the flesh" to deal with the fact that his soul is tied to his body. The "great preparation" mentioned here corresponds to the "effort of the soul" mentioned in *Tanya*. This person must engage in profound and prolonged contemplation until something changes in his perception of these matters. The "mighty effort" mentioned here corresponds to the "effort of the flesh" mentioned in *Likkutei Amarim*, as a per-son "batters" and subjugates his body so that it will not darken the light of his soul. How does he batter his body? By engaging in thoughts of repentance in the depths of his heart, which shatter the concealment caused by his body. A person must cease to pursue his body's lusts and desires, shattering its monopoly on his feelings, until his body no longer conceals the light of his soul hidden within it.

Regarding the words, "if [a person] prepares to meet his God with a tremendous preparation and mighty effort," the sixth Lubavitcher Rebbe, Rabbi Yosef Yitzḥak Schneerson, teaches (see *Sefer HaMa'amarim* 5692 p. 276) that the student must – with faith and with fear and love – bring these traits of the tzaddik "into fleshly life...by learning the Torah and keeping the commandments in actuality, literally." In order to receive these traits, having the appropriate feelings does not suffice. A person must engage in the requisite actions, in keeping with the tzaddik's directions.

This may be understood in a number of ways. For instance, a person's preparation to receive the tzaddik's traits must involve his serving God with his body in this world of action. The tzaddik's spirit is found precisely in the context of the world of action, clothed in the fleshly life, in practical Torah and the practical commandments. The tzaddik's intellect and feelings rise ever higher. Yet his inner essence, will, and delight continue to be connected to this world below. So too, the hasidim's drawing forth of the tzaddik's spirit is expressed in that spirit's worldly, practical applications of faith, fear and love. The fact that these actions occur in

וּכְמַאֲמַר רַבּוֹתֵינוּ ז"ל: יָגַעְתָּ
וּמָצָאתָ תַּאֲמִין (מגילה ו,ב)

And that is in keeping with the statement of our Rabbis of blessed memory, "If someone tells you that he **toils and finds** success, **believe** him" (*Megilla* 6b).

That applies here as well. A person must believe that if he toils to draw forth the tzaddik's spirit after the latter's *histalkut* – an achievement that may appear to be wondrous, bordering on the miraculous - he will "find." ☞

From this point onward to the end of the letter, the author of the *Tanya* shifts from addressing Rabbi Menaḥem Mendel's hasidim after his *histalkut* to discussing other aspects of a tzaddik's influence following his *histalkut*: spiritual heights that are not directly connected to our world, and future generations that are not directly connected to the tzaddik.

וְהִנֵּה יֵשׁ עוֹד בְּחִינַת הָאָרָה
לְתַלְמִידָיו רַק שֶׁאֵינָהּ מִתְלַבֶּשֶׁת
בְּתוֹךְ מוֹחָם מַמָּשׁ כְּרִאשׁוֹנָה, רַק
מְאִירָה עֲלֵיהֶם מִלְמַעְלָה

There is another level of how the tzaddik **illuminates his students** after his *histalkut*. **But that** level **does not,** as did the first, truly clothe itself in their mind. Instead, it shines upon them from above.

16 Ḥeshvan

15 Ḥeshvan (leap year)

Here the author of the *Tanya* is referring not only to the tzaddik's immediate students, but to all those who will learn his teachings in the future.

this physical world does not diminish their value, because they are imbued with an inner life force that makes them meaningful in all worlds and that transforms the lower realm into a dwelling place for the light of the *Ein Sof.*

BELIEVE HIM

☞ This "toiling" refers to a person's work in this world to overcome materiality and the harsh "husks." Added to this difficulty is the fact that a person does not see results immediately. The verb "found" indicates that the result is even greater than the toil. (That is in contrast to the term "reward." A reward is simply commensurate with the extent of a person's work.) "Believe him" A person who is toiling must continue his efforts even if he does not see progress. Even if the toil does not seem to result in "finding," he must continue to believe.

Illumination that clothes itself in the students' mind does so directly and deeply. This is comparable to a person explaining a concept to someone else, which the latter understands and internalizes. Until now this epistle has been discussing that sort of illumination and influence. This illumination also has a hidden aspect: how the students receive from the spirit of the tzaddik after his *histalkut*. In general, this sort of influence speaks of students who had been connected to the tzaddik during his lifetime, who had learned from him and who now continue that connection. In general, this is called an "inner illumination" because it penetrates the student's inner world and aligns itself with the vessels of his soul. But from this point onward, the author of the *Tanya* will discuss an "encompassing illumination," which is not clothed in the mind and faculties of the student's soul, but rests upon them from above. It may be said to clothe and encompass them – or, alternatively, it may be described as the context in which they exist. ☞

וְהִיא מֵעֲלִיַּית רוּחוֹ וְנִשְׁמָתוֹ לִמְקוֹר חוּצְבוֹ   **It comes from the ascent of** the tzaddik's *ruaḥ* **and** *neshama* **to the source from which it is hewn –**

This influence comes not only from the impression made by the tzaddik's *ruaḥ* that remains in the lower Garden of Eden. The tzaddik's *ruaḥ* rises after his *histalkut* from level to level, from the lower Garden of Eden to the supernal Garden of Eden and higher, until it reaches the source from which it was hewn: the source from which his *neshama* was hewn, a particular *neshama* from the source of all souls, like a stone hewn from a quarry. The light of the *neshama* on this supernal

SHINES UPON THEM FROM ABOVE

☞ As explained in *Likkutei Amarim* (chap. 48) the spiritual concepts of "encompassing" and "from above" describe a state in which something is not grasped by the "vessels" of a person's soul: by his intellect and traits. It is hidden from everything and illuminates everything equally. It is not intellect or feeling. It is nothing that can be defined within our "vessels" and concepts.

For instance, we see with our eyes and hear with our ears, but there is also an intangible atmosphere, to which some people are particularly sensitive. That is similar to an illumination from above. Although a person does not see, hear or understand anything new, he can tell that something new is in the air.

level relates to the tzaddik alone. It does not shine on his students and other people with an inner illumination, but it encompasses them from above.

דְּהַיְינוּ לַחֲקַל תַּפּוּחִין קַדִּישִׁין   **that is, to the field of sacred apples.**

The ascent of the tzaddik's soul to the source from which it is hewn is called an ascent to the field of sacred apples, because the *Zohar* calls the source of the souls of Israel "the field of sacred apples." The Kabbalistic literature explains that this is the level of *Malkhut* of *Atzilut*, which is the level of the Congregation of Israel. All of the souls of Israel are gathered in it together. It is called a field because in it are planted, as in a field, all of the holy sparks that the people of Israel raise from this world in their service of God.[34] The sparks are parts of the holiness found in everything, sparks of the Divine Presence that souls have descended into the world to raise. In a sense, these sparks are parts of the souls themselves (because they are the parts of the world related to the souls) which rise to the source from which they were hewn. Throughout a soul's lifetime, it descends and clings to the parts of holiness that it finds, and raises them. When a person dies and his soul has no more connections and obligations to the body and the world, it disconnects itself from them and ascends limitlessly to this field in *Atzilut*, which is higher than all the worlds.

וְעַל יְדֵי זֶה נַעֲשֶׂה שָׁם יִחוּד עַל יְדֵי הַעֲלָאַת מַיִין נוּקְבִין מִכָּל מַעֲשָׂיו וְתוֹרָתוֹ וַעֲבוֹדָתוֹ אֲשֶׁר עָבַד כָּל יְמֵי חַיָּיו   **As a result of this, a unification is affected there. It** comes **as a result of the elevation of the feminine waters from all of** the tzaddik's **actions, Torah** learning, **and service that he engaged in all the days of his life.**

All of the parts of the Divine Presence that were connected to the tzaddik in this world ascend and are united in their root: in *Malkhut* of *Atzilut*. That brings about an inclusive and meaningful unity of God and the Divine Presence. Every unification, on every level, is a part of the prin-

---

34. See *Torah Or* 28a, *Likkutei Torah*, *Devarim* 36d, and elsewhere, which explains why it is called "a field of apples."

cipal unification: that of the Holy One, blessed be He, with His Divine
Presence, of the transcendent, essential Divine light with the immanent
Divine light, a light that brings all elements into being and vitalizes them.
The unification mentioned here, as the tzaddik ascends to the field of
holy apples, is encompassing and meaningful for many people: those
in his generation and those subsequent to his generation.

This unification is meaningful not only because the tzaddik's soul
now rises. The particular significance of an ascent after a descent is that
something new exists that did not exist prior to the descent. That is the
meaning of the elevation of the feminine waters, which are the "lower
waters," the lower divine light that was hidden within things, within the
lower worlds and the "husks." The "lower waters" are a term referring
to holiness (the Divine Presence) that is hidden in everything, that is
not revealed and cannot by itself rise and bind itself to the source of
holiness (the Holy One, blessed be He) up above. It is called "feminine
waters" because it cannot rise by itself, but waits for someone or
something to raise it. And that which raises it is a person's soul – and in
particular, the soul of a tzaddik – that descends and, with its work in Torah and the commandments, arouses, reveals and raises those feminine
waters.

וְנִזְרְעוּ בַּחֲקַל תַּפּוּחִין קַדִּישִׁין אוֹרוֹת
עֶלְיוֹנִים מְאֹד לְעוּמַת תַּחְתּוֹנִים אֲשֶׁר
הֵם תּוֹרָתוֹ וַעֲבוֹדָתוֹ

**Very supernal lights are planted
in the field of holy apples.** They
correspond to and result from
the illuminations in the **lower
realms, which are** the tzaddik's
Torah and service.

This supernal holy field blossoms due to that which rose from the lower
realms and was planted in it: the tzaddik's Torah and service. And now
this field brings forth supernal and multitudinous lights. This process
is comparable to an apple seed planted in the soil that produces a great
apple tree with sweet fruits.

וְהֶאָרַת אוֹרוֹת עֶלְיוֹנִים אֵלּוּ מְאִירָה
עַל כָּל תַּלְמִידָיו שֶׁנַּעֲשׂוּ עוֹבְדֵי ה' עַל
יְדֵי תּוֹרָתוֹ וַעֲבוֹדָתוֹ

**The illumination of these super-
nal lights shines on all of the**
tzaddik's **students who became
servants of God due to** the influence **of his Torah and his service.**

The supernal lights that were aroused by the tzaddik and that now shine in all the worlds shine in particular on his students – not only those who were his students in his lifetime, but every individual who became a servant of God because of his teachings and his service, every individual who relates to and is connected to the conduits of holiness that the tzaddik opened. The expression, "who became servants of God due to [the influence of] his Torah," emphasizes that the connection must be deep. It does not apply to every person who only bought or even read his book, but only to an individual who was changed in some way by his teachings. The tzaddik's power and path rectified and prepared this individual to receive the supernal lights.

וְהֶאָרָה זוֹ שֶׁעֲלֵיהֶם מִלְמַעְלָה מַכְנֶסֶת בְּלִבָּם הִרְהוּרֵי תְּשׁוּבָה וּמַעֲשִׂים טוֹבִים

This illumination that comes **upon the** students **from above brings thoughts of repentance and good deeds into their heart.**

This is an encompassing illumination from above. A person who connects himself to the tzaddik and prepares himself to be in touch with holiness receives this encompassing love and fear only if he brings thoughts of repentance and good deeds into his heart. Such reflections do not constitute actual repentance and good deeds. They do not even constitute a person's intellectual and emotional intent to repent and perform good deeds. These reflections, rather, are precursors to thoughts. They are an atmosphere of thought, a state of wanting to repent and engage in good deeds. That is something great that should not be denigrated – nevertheless, it is not yet something that the soul has attained. A person does not receive reward for these reflections. They do not raise the female waters and do not cause any arousal above. Nevertheless, these reflections can turn into actual thoughts and deeds. Thus, they place a person at the starting point, from which he can and must begin to walk upon the path of repentance and good deeds in his service of God. Corresponding to these, the illumination of the tzaddik comes from above, preceding the arousal of this person from below. ☞

AN ILLUMINATION FROM ABOVE

☞ In general, an arousal from below precedes and sparks an arousal from above.

However, elsewhere it is explained that the illumination from above mentioned here,

וְכָל הַמַּעֲשִׂים טוֹבִים הַנּוֹלָדִים מֵהָאָרָה זוֹ, שֶׁמְּאִירָה מְאוֹרוֹת הַזְּרוּעִים בַּשָּׂדֶה הַנִּזְכָּר לְעֵיל, נִקְרָא גִּידוּלֵי גִּידוּלִין

All of the good deeds engendered by this illumination, which shines from the lights planted in the field mentioned above, are called secondary growths.

The tzaddik's ascent and service of God constitute planting in the field of apples. That arouses an illumination descending from above, which constitutes the growths that the field produces. These growths are immeasurably more numerous and brighter than what was planted. And if people on earth do something good as a result, those are "secondary growths."

וְהָאָרָה זוֹ הִיא בְּהֶעְלֵם וְהֶסְתֵּר גָּדוֹל כְּמוֹ שֶׁמֶשׁ הַמֵּאִיר לַכּוֹכָבִים מִתַּחַת לָאָרֶץ

This illumination is very greatly hidden and concealed. It is compared to the sun that shines from below the earth onto the stars.

This is an encompassing illumination. Unlike an inner light, it does not appear in a person's intellect and emotions.

We understand and feel the significance and power of an inner illumination. It therefore impels us to think and act in accordance with it. In contrast, an encompassing illumination does not impel its recipients to absorb it or to act in accordance with it. Therefore, the actions that it does engender are called "secondary growths." They are an indirect outcome, which is dependent on a person's free will and effort. And precisely because of that, precisely because they are secondary growths, they grow even more than do the direct growths.

This is comparable to the sun that shines from below the earth onto the stars. They have no light of their own. The light that we see is the light of the sun that they reflect, whereas we do not see the sun itself.

precedes the arousal from below. In certain circumstances, a new arousal is generated from above, so supernal that it is not measured at all in terms of the values of the actions, thoughts and prayers of people on earth. That is an illumination from God Himself, as it were, not in response to, nor in connection with what we think, want, and need. Nevertheless, it is not given to everyone, but only to those individuals to whom the Giver wishes to grant it.

כִּדְאִיתָא בַּתִּיקוּנִים, עַל מֹשֶׁה
רַבֵּינוּ עָלָיו הַשָּׁלוֹם שֶׁאַחַר
פְּטִירָתוֹ מִתְפַּשֶּׁטֶת הָאָרָתוֹ
בְּכָל דָּרָא וְדָרָא לְשִׁשִּׁים רִבּוֹא
נְשָׁמוֹת

As the *Tikkunim* state, after Moses our
teacher, peace be upon him, passed
away, his illumination spread throughout every generation to the 600,000
souls of Israel.

Moses is the archetype of the tzaddik, because through him we received
the Torah in its totality, and because he was the leader and shepherd
of Israel who spread faith and the knowledge of God throughout his
generation and all subsequent generations.[35]

The 600,000 souls of Israel constitute the totality of the people of
Israel, composed of 600,000 root souls. Those are the 600,000 men
whom Moses brought out of Egypt, from whom come branches and
sparks of souls in every generation. The author of the *Tanya* thus speaks
about Moses' influence not only on those of his generation, but on
every Jew, who ever lived and will live.[36]

And how do we receive that illumination? We do not receive it
directly, because we do not see it physically, but we receive it in a
concealed way, comparable to the way in which the presence of the
sun shining from below the earth is perceived indirectly. We do not
always understand and feel that God is true and His Torah is true
(and certainly not as Moses did). But every Jew in every generation
possesses that as a basic assumption. In how many ways does a person
apply this assumption? How much do the details of a person's life – his
thoughts and actions *Hemshekh* express and reveal everything that
this assumption contains? That depends on the individual, on the
generation, and on its leader, the Moses of his generation.

---

35. And see also *Likkutei Amarim*, chap. 42, which states that a spark of Moses
exists in every soul of Israel. And he is clothed in a revealed way in the leaders of
each generation to guide Israel with faith in God, as did Moses in his generation.
36. The Lubavitcher Rebbe, Rabbi Menaḥem Mendel Schneerson, notes (based
on Lessons in *Tanya*): "At present, I found the entire topic [discussed] in *Zohar*
3:273b. But in the *Tikkunim* (*Tikkun* 69, 112a, 103a, *Tikkun* 70, 138a), I found only
a part of this explanation. And perhaps [this citation] in *Iggeret HaKodesh* is a
copyist's error, influenced by the citation 'in the *Tikkunim*' in *Tanya*, 44."

כְּמוֹ שֶׁמֶשׁ הַמֵּאִיר מִתַּחַת It is **comparable to the sun that shines**
לָאָרֶץ לְשִׁשִׁים רִבּוֹא כּוֹכָבִים **from under the earth to the 600,000
stars.**

This assumption that shines within each Jew is like the radiance of the
sun shining from under the earth. We do not see the sun itself, and we
do not know with certainty that the sun is the source of the radiance.
However, we receive something from the sun – and that constitutes
everything that we possess. All of the forms and colors that reveal and
communicate all sorts of things ultimately reveal only one thing: the
light of the sun from under the earth. This "sunlight" is a metaphor for
the Divine Presence that brings everything into being out of absolute
nothingness and vitalizes it.

There is always a basic illumination from under the earth. That is a
Jew's basic faith, his fundamental assumption. That is the equivalent of
the encompassing illumination from above that the author of the *Tanya*
described at the end of the letter. There is also an inner illumination
that the author of the *Tanya* initially described, which is transmitted
from the tzaddik to a person's soul and life.

The author of the *Tanya* mentions Moses' soul illuminating all
souls of Israel as an example of the illumination of the tzaddik's soul.
The illumination of a tzaddik's soul in a particular generation is not
an overall illumination such as was that of Moses, but an illumination
that focuses on the generation in which he lives, as well as on future
generations.

This is a letter of condolence filled with timeless truths that give the
mourners a tangible replacement for what they have lost. It does not
give them something new, but a different aspect of what they had:
something that, because they are in mourning, they cannot presently
see. Having lost their rabbi, they yearn for him in the form he had been
when he had been alive, but of course they will not find him. Therefore,
the author of the *Tanya* guides the hasidim to seek his soul and not
his body, to seek his faith, fear and love, and not his material life. This
provides more than just a substitute. It becomes "a double alleviation,"
because now they can cling to the tzaddik and receive from him even
more than they did when he was alive.

It is true that there is now a lack that cannot be filled: a lack of a personal connection to a fatherly figure. As much as one may explain to the hasid the superiority of a rebbe who exists in an abstract, non-physical form, the hasid had previously had a rabbi, father and king who had been everything for him, and who is now no more. Beyond the body, the tzaddik's wisdom, Torah, love and fear can still exist, but he is no longer the person, rabbi and father he had been. The author of the *Tanya* knows this from personal experience, because Rabbi Menaḥem Mendel of Vitebsk had been his own rabbi and colleague. Nevertheless, he calls this consolation a "double alleviation." Now there is sadness and a feeling of loss, which are legitimate stages in a person's life. But, as the author of the *Tanya* explains in *Likkutei Amarim* (chap. 26) on the verse, "In all toil there will be gain" (Prov. 14:23) the next stage will be more than what had existed before the sadness. The more a person was connected to his rabbi and the more pain and loss he now suffers, the more significant and closer will be the connection he will be able to forge with the tzaddik after the latter's *histalkut*. The hasid who was connected with all his soul and might to the tzaddik will now find that his rabbi's faith is his own. And a hasid cannot cling more closely to his rebbe than that.

The pain and loss will never disappear, but a person must go forward. It is somewhat sad when a seed that is planted in the ground disintegrates until it no longer exists. But it is necessary so that something else will blossom: a great tree bearing sweet fruits.

The "explanation" of this letter, which was apparently written at a later date and is not directly connected to the tzaddik's *histalkut*, has timeless significance for all Jews wherever they may be. It describes an encompassing illumination that is not limited by the physicality of a tzaddik nor by the hasidim's memory of him and personal relationship with him, an illumination that loses the characteristics and parameters it had possessed during the tzaddik's lifetime and blossoms anew for everyone who has resolved to follow in his footsteps.

In its personal sense as well, as a letter of condolence, this letter accompanies every hasid in every generation who has lost his rebbe. Whoever has experienced the blow of a tzaddik's *histalkut* has no consolation besides this letter, which during difficult hours displays a consoling aspect with "double alleviation."

Epistle 28

LIKE THE PREVIOUS LETTER, THIS IS A LETTER OF CON-
solation. However, it is different in a number of ways. First,
it was written at a different time. The previous letter was
written at the beginning of the author of the *Tanya*'s time
as rebbe (5537), whereas this letter is one of the last that he
wrote (5566).[1] Moreover, these letters differ in character
and content. The previous letter was written to the hasidim
of Rabbi Menaḥem Mendel of Vitebsk on the occasion of
his *histalkut*. It was addressed to them by Rabbi Menaḥem
Mendel's successor, as a rebbe writing to his hasidim. On the
other hand, the author of the *Tanya* wrote the present letter
to his colleague and in-law, Rabbi Levi Yitzḥak of Berditchev,
on the occasion of the passing away of the latter's son. And
of course, it was not written as a rebbe writing to his hasidim
but as a person writing to his equal – more specifically, as
one rebbe writing to another.

We are familiar with what a rebbe writes to his hasidim,
as well as with what a hasid writes to his rebbe. But what
does one rebbe write to another? A glimpse of that may be
seen in this letter.

As was stated in the commentary on the previous letter,
a rebbe's words of consolation are more than his empathic
participation with the sufferer's pain: They explain that the
misfortune itself contains goodness, something superior to
the earlier situation. The previous letter had a single nexus:
the tzaddik who is gone. The present letter has two nexuses:

---

1. As noted by the Lubavitcher Rebbe in *Shiurim BeSefer HaTanya*.

the tzaddik who is gone and the tzaddik whom the author of the *Tanya* is addressing. The previous letter stressed that there is an ongoing connection with departed tzaddikim. That emphasis is not needed in this letter because Rabbi Levi Yitzḥak of Berditchev, as a tzaddik himself, was not truly living in this world. The only question that remains is whether the *histalkut* itself has meaning. That question is addressed in this letter.

Around this time, the author of the *Tanya* delivered a talk to his hasidim that constitutes a sort of commentary on this letter (*Ma'amarei Admor HaZaken 5566*, Part 1), which will serve as a source for understanding this letter.

Because this is a private letter, when it was edited to be published in *Iggeret HaKodesh,* all of its personal sections were removed. In their place, the editors supplied a brief introduction:

(מַה שֶׁכָּתַב לִמְחוּתָנוֹ, הָרַב הַגָּאוֹן הַמְפוּרְסָם אִישׁ אֱלֹקִים קָדוֹשׁ ה׳, נֵר יִשְׂרָאֵל, עַמּוּד הַיְמָנִי, פַּטִּישׁ הֶחָזָק, מוֹרֵנוּ וְרַבֵּנוּ הָרַב לֵוִי יִצְחָק נִשְׁמָתוֹ עֵדֶן, אַב בֵּית דִּין דִּקְהִילַת קֹדֶשׁ בְּאַרְדִּיטְשׁוֹב לְנַחֲמוֹ עַל פְּטִירַת בְּנוֹ הָרַב הֶחָסִיד מוֹרֵנוּ וְרַבֵּנוּ הָרַב מֵאִיר נִשְׁמָתוֹ עֵדֶן)

(**This is** a letter **that** the author of the *Tanya* **wrote to his relative by marriage, the rabbi, the brilliant Torah scholar, the well-known man of God, a holy man of God, the lamp of Israel, the right pillar, the strong hammer, our teacher and our rabbi, Rabbi Levi Yitzḥak, his soul is in Eden,** who was **head of the rabbinical court of the holy community of Berditchev, to console him on the passing of his son, the pious rabbi, our teacher and our rabbi, Rabbi Meir, his soul is in heaven.**)

These honorifics[2] are copied from our Sages' eulogy for Rabban Yoḥanan ben Zakkai (*Berakhot* 28b), which became the prototype for the encomiums of great sages throughout the ages.

---

2. "A holy man of God" (see II Kings 4:9), "the lamp of Israel" (see II Sam. 21:17), "the right pillar" (see I Kings 7:21), "the strong hammer" (a term indicating his greatness in Torah; see Jer. 23:29). Rebbetzin Beila (the daughter of the second

Rabbi Levi Yitzḥak had been a close colleague of the author of the *Tanya* from the time when they were both students of the Maggid of Mezeritch, and they loved, appreciated, and respected each other. When the author of the *Tanya* was arrested for the first time (in 5559) and before he was taken to prison, he sent a *pidyon nefesh* (a petitionary note for heavenly assistance with an attached charitable donation) to Rabbi Levi Yitzḥak.[3]

Rabbi Levi Yitzḥak had three sons, the oldest of whom was Rabbi Meir. This son, to whom the author of the *Tanya* refers as "tzaddik," was spiritually accomplished and also apparently a considerable Torah scholar. He authored a book called *Keter Torah*, some of whose teachings Rabbi Levi Yitzḥak quotes in his *Kedushat Levi*. His premature death was a source of profound grief for Rabbi Levi Yitzḥak, who loved and valued him.

This letter constitutes a kabbalistic and hasidic explanation of a statement of the Sages. It begins by quoting that statement:

לָמָּה נִסְמְכָה פָּרָשַׁת מִרְיָם לְפָרָשַׁת פָּרָה לוֹמַר לְךָ מַה פָּרָה מְכַפֶּרֶת וכו'

Our Sages ask: "**Why is the passage about** the passing away of **Miriam placed adjacent to the passage about** the red **heifer?** The answer is **to tell you that just as the** red **heifer grants atonement,** so does the passing away of the righteous" (*Moed Katan* 28b; quoted by Rashi on Num. 20:1).

17 Ḥeshvan

16 Ḥeshvan (leap year)

The passage in the Torah about Miriam's death (Num. 20:1) immediately follows the passage about the red heifer (Num. 20:19). The talmudic Sages state that these two passages appear together because

Lubavitcher Rebbe and granddaughter of the author of the *Tanya*) was married to Rabbi Levi Yitzḥak's grandson, Rabbi Yekutiel Zalman. The wedding, known as "the great wedding" and about which many stories are told, took place in Sivan 5567 (1807). The author of the *Tanya* delivered hasidic talks there that have been preserved. It would appear that at the time when this letter was written, they were not yet in-laws, and so the phrase "to his relative by marriage" was added later by the editors.

3. See *Beit Rebbe*, chap. 20, and *Sefer HaToledot: Admor HaZaken*, 3:672.

they share the theme of atonement: Just as the red heifer grants atonement, so too does the passing away of a righteous person.

This statement raises a question:

וְצָרִיךְ לְהָבִין לָמָּה נִסְמְכָה
דַּוְקָא לְפָרָה אֲדוּמָה הַנַּעֲשָׂה
חוּץ לְשָׁלֹשׁ מַחֲנוֹת

But the following **must be understood: Why was** the passage about the passing away of Miriam **placed adjacent to, in particular,** the passage about **the red heifer, which is prepared outside the three camps** of the people of Israel?

All of the sacrificial offerings grant atonement when they are placed on the altar. The red heifer is not this type of offering, since it is not placed on the altar. In fact, its ceremony is not even performed in the Temple but outside the "three camps,"[4] completely removed from holiness and the Sanctuary, a place that is entirely mundane. If the Torah intended to teach that the tzaddik's passing away grants atonement, why was the passage about Miriam's death placed next to the passage about the red heifer? ☞

אֶלָּא דְּחַטָּאת קַרְיֵיהּ רַחֲמָנָא
[בִּכְתַב יַד הַנּוּסְחָא: הַנַּעֲשָׂה
בַּחוּץ. וּמִן תֵּיבַת 'לְשָׁלֹשׁ' עַד

Although the Compassionate One calls it a "sin offering" [a manuscript version reads, **"which is prepared out side,"**

THE THREE CAMPS

☞ In the desert (see end of Tractate *Zevahim*, *Tosefta Keilim* 1:11, and elsewhere), the children of Israel camped in three concentric circles: a) at the center, the camp of the Divine Presence, that being the *Mishkan*; b) around that, the Levite camp; c) around that, the camp of Israel. All of these were in the realm of holiness. These three circles had their parallels in the later Temple: a) corresponding to the camp of the Divine Presence was the *azara* (the central courtyard); b) corresponding to the Levite camp was the Temple Mount; and c) corresponding to the Israelite camp was Jerusalem. The expression "outside the camp" relates to the mundane area outside the three camps in the desert or, correspondingly, outside Jerusalem. That is where the red heifer was slaughtered and burned – not like an offering brought in the Sanctuary!

---

4. See Rashi on Num. 19:3.

תֵּיבַת 'דְּרַחֲמָנָא' לֵיתָא בִּכְתַב
[דְ

omitting the section **from the phrase "the three" until "the Compassionate One"**]

In a few places, the Torah refers to the red heifer as a "sin offering,"[5] from which our Sages derive[6] that it is like a sin offering in a number of respects, although otherwise it is only considered to be "sacred material for the upkeep of the Sanctuary" and not "sacred material that goes upon the altar."[7]

"A manuscript version reads, 'which is prepared outside,' omitting 'although the Compassionate One calls it a sin offering'":[8] It is possible that these two versions are expressing a difference in emphasis. The statement that the red heifer is burned "outside the three camps" underscores the difference between it and the sin offering. The manuscript version, "which is prepared outside," refers to the sanctification of the waters associated with the red heifer – that is, the addition of the red heifer's ashes to a container of water (which the letter will discuss further on). That does not occur outside the three camps. Still, that may be done outside the Sanctuary, unlike the sin offering.

וְלֹא נִסְמְכָה לְפָרָשַׁת חַטָּאת הַנַּעֲשָׂה
בִּפְנִים עַל גַּבֵּי הַמִּזְבֵּחַ כַּפָּרָה מַמָּשׁ?

Why is the passage about Miriam's passing away **not placed,** rather, **adjacent to the passage about the sin offering, which is prepared within** the Sanctuary **on the altar** – the act that brings about **actual atonement?**

---

5. For instance, Num. 19:9: "It is a sin offering."

6. See *Avoda Zara* 23b, and Ritva and Meiri there.

7. There are two categories of items dedicated to the Sanctuary: 1) offerings brought upon the altar, and 2) everything else brought for the Sanctuary, such as materials for maintenance and improvement, wages, and so forth. Although the red heifer is not brought as an offering on the altar, it is slaughtered and burned as an offering is, and its sanctity is even greater than that of offerings brought on the altar.

8. The Lubavitcher Rebbe notes in *He'arot VeTikkunim BeDerekh Efshar* that the words from "is prepared" to "Compassionate One" should be placed in parentheses.

In order to teach that the death of the righteous grants atonement, the Torah should apparently have placed the passage of Miriam's death next to the passage of the sin offering, because what grants atonement is the act of placing the offering upon the altar. It is true that Scripture calls the red heifer a "sin offering" – but it is not truly so.

This letter will provide a kabbalistic answer to this question. That is not to imply that there is no straightforward answer. Rather, the author of the *Tanya* intends to teach something deeper and more particular, which only utilizes this question as its vehicle.

The author of the *Tanya* will begin by presenting a kabbalistic explanation of the offerings overall, and he will then explain the red heifer's superiority to them.

אָמְנָם נוֹדַע מִזוֹהַר הַקָּדוֹשׁ (חלק א סד,ב) וְהָאֲרִ"י ז"ל סוֹד הַקָּרְבָּנוֹת שֶׁעַל גַּבֵּי הַמִּזְבֵּחַ הֵן בְּחִינַת הַעֲלָאַת 'מַיִין נוּקְבִין'

The answer is as follows. **The secret** meaning **of the offerings upon the altar is known from the holy *Zohar* (1:64b) and the Arizal,** which is that these offerings bring about **the ascension of the feminine waters**

"The secret [meaning] of the offerings" refers to their inner effect, that which is hidden from the physical eye.

A "secret" is something that is not revealed in the exterior aspect of life and in social relationships. A person's usual way of seeing and thinking cannot show him such a secret. In order for him to see it, someone must explain it to him (reveal it and transmit it). And then, after extended review and contemplation, he too can see it with his own eyes.

The secret of the offerings is the raising of the feminine waters.[9] With our eyes of flesh, we see sheep and rams being brought up to the altar. But on the inner, secret level, what is occurring is the raising of the feminine waters.

The divine influence in the worlds is compared to water: lower waters and upper waters. The lower waters provide divine influence within entities, maintaining them in a hidden way. Conversely, the

9. The source from the Arizal is *Likkutei Torah, Parashat Vayikra. Likkutei Hagahot LeTanya* references *Etz Ḥayyim*, Gate 50 (*Sha'ar Kitzur Abiya*), end of chap. 2.

upper waters provide abundance and divine kindness from above whenever the Creator reveals Himself and embraces the lower spheres. The lower waters are called "feminine waters," whereas the upper waters are called "masculine waters." The lower waters are comparable to a female, who does not bestow new things but distils and reveals what is in her, what she is. The raising of the feminine waters is not an influence upon that which is above (which would be an analogue to the downward flow of masculine waters). Rather, it is like a person with a request who opens his hand, like someone who wants to know more and opens his mind. This is the opening up of the "husk" of an entity, the "husk" that ordinarily hides the divine flow from that entity. This opening, which shatters and nullifies the concept of lower existence, constitutes the raising of the lower waters. From the moment the cover is removed, the lower waters bond with their supernal root and source. Therefore, "the raising of feminine waters" is the secret aspect of the sacrificial offerings. The offerings represent the elevation of the animal kingdom, the plant kingdom, and all of the elements of this world.[10]

מִנֶּפֶשׁ הַבַּהֲמִית שֶׁבְּנוֹגַה   **from** a person's **animal soul, which is in *noga*,**

The sacrificial offerings come from kosher animals: oxen, sheep, and so forth. These represent the husk of *noga*, a husk that contains light that can be elevated. The soul of these animals is their life and spirit, their "lower waters" that rise upward, whereas their body is a covering of physicality and materiality that keeps this life below, separate from the upper waters. The animal's body is slaughtered, burned, and eaten. It is destroyed as an entity in itself. With that, its soul rises.

And then the animal soul of the person bringing the offering is offered up and elevated. That also occurs when a person recites the *Shema* and prays, and more generally whenever he overcomes impediments caused by his animal soul and raises it to its root so that it is absorbed and nullified into his divine soul and into divinity. At that time, everything that relates to the person's animal soul – his body,

---

10. See the Arizal's *Likkutei Torah* there, which explains how the different elements of the offerings – the salt, the wine and oil, the animals, the birds, and so forth – represent all of the components of the world.

his food, his clothing and everything he uses, as well as the material aspect of a commandment that he performs, the preparatory materials connected with that commandment, and so forth. ☞

אֶל שָׁרְשָׁן וּמְקוֹרָן הֵן בְּחִינַת ד' חַיּוֹת שֶׁבַּמֶּרְכָּבָה הַנּוֹשְׂאוֹת אֶת הַכִּסֵּא - פְּנֵי שׁוֹר וּפְנֵי נֶשֶׁר וכו' — to their root and their source – that being the four ḥayot on the heavenly chariot that carry the throne: the face of the ox, the face of the eagle...

The life-providing root of animals is the ḥayot – the "animals" – on the heavenly chariot described in the book of Ezekiel (1:10). The chariot (the throne, the ḥayot that carry it, and so forth) is a visual representation of the supernal structure upon which God, who creates and guides the created worlds, "rides," as it were. It is an instrument and model for the creation of His world. Every detail in the created world receives its form and characteristics from the form and characteristics of the tool by which it was made. This chariot does not belong to the world of *Atzilut* but to the world below it, that of *Beria*, the level of the supernal pattern by which creation was given shape. Everything that exists in our world has its supernal, spiritual root and source in the chariot. The ḥayot described there are supernal angels that are the root and source of every animal and human being in this world. The

THE ANIMAL *NEFESH* IN *NOGA*

☞ The husk, including the husk of *noga*, keeps a person's animal soul separate from the Divine. There are two sorts of husks: a) three impure husks and b) one husk of *noga* (see *Likkutei Amarim*, chap. 6, and elsewhere). The impure husks hide the Divine absolutely. They are the place of darkness, death, and the depth of evil. (They will be discussed further on.) And the husk of *noga* is, as the term indicates, a husk that glows. That is to say, although it conceals the Divine and so it is a husk, this concealment is not absolute darkness in which nothing can be seen, but an obfuscation in which a little may be seen – unclearly, but sufficiently so that it may be under-

stood as well as the generality constructed from it. In other contexts, this husk is referred to as the realm of the mundane – that is to say, the totality of the existence of this world. Although it is coarse, animalistic, and not nullified to the Divine, it is not inherently forbidden and evil. It is overall the realm in which we serve God, the realm of what is permitted: the realm that we raise and join to holiness when we act for the sake of Heaven. Therefore, the offerings that are brought on the altar, like all of the parts of the world that we use in performing the commandments, relate to the husk of *noga*.

ox is the source of domesticated animals, the lion is the source of wild animals, the eagle is the source of birds, and so forth.

A sacrificial offering raises an animal to its root in the angel of the chariot. In contrast to the earthly animal, the "animal" angel of the chariot feels itself subsumed in the divinity that acts upon it. It is like a chariot in relation to its rider – comparable to a person's limb, which does not have its own existence, will, and intelligence, but which is like a tool for him to utilize.

The elevation of a person's animalistic aspect in his service of God, whether he is bringing an offering upon the altar or is engaged in something spiritual in his personal service, involves the elevation of these lowly, particularized forms and their bonding to the transcendent structure of the chariot's ḥayot. The goal of this service is to nullify, in one way or another – by slaughtering and burning the offering or by subjugating and nullifying oneself – one's animalistic being, and in that way to see and recognize that one's animal nature is only a particular projection of the nature of the supernal chariot. ☞

וְעַל יְדֵי זֶה זֶה נִמְשָׁכִים וְיוֹרְדִים מַיִין דְּכוּרִין מִבְּחִינַת אָדָם שֶׁעַל הַכִּסֵּא, הַנִּקְרָא בְּשֵׁם מַלְכָּא וז"א

As a result of this raising of the feminine waters, **the masculine waters are drawn forth and descend from the level of the "person upon the throne"** (see Ezek. 1:26), **which is** also **called the King and *Zeir Anpin*.**

THE LOWER WATERS WEEP

☞   As stated earlier, the lower waters are the divine vitality that exists below: that which vitalizes every entity from within itself. The divine vitality is apparently not bound to the divine being itself beyond these entities. This situation is required so that existence will exist as it is. But in essence the lower waters also belong above, and so they weep, because they do not want to be separated and distant from God. They too want to be united above (see *Tikkunei Zohar, Tikkun* 5 19b: "The lower waters weep [and say], 'We too want to be before the King'"). A person's role in his life and in his service of God is to bring about this wondrous matter: to raise the lower waters and unite them with the supernal Divine, even as the lower waters continue to maintain the existence of lower reality (for which reason this can only be accomplished by human beings here below). This unification, which every individual attains little by little, detail by detail, is called overall "the unification of the Holy One, blessed be He, and His Divine Presence." That is the purpose of all existence and of man's service of God.

The elevation of the lower waters from the worlds causes – like water that reflects a person's face (see Prov. 27:19) – a descent of the upper waters from above, from the level of *Zeir Anpin* in *Atzilut* (which is called the King), down to *Malkhut*, and to the worlds.

There are *ḥayot* that carry the throne, there is the throne, and upon the throne is "an image like the visage of a man" (Ezek. 1:26). The *ḥayot* of the chariot are, as stated earlier, the roots above of domestic animals, wild animals, and earthly existence. The "person upon the throne" is the image of the supernal, divine "man": that is to say, the structure of the *sefirot* of the world of *Atzilut* (that is, *Zeir Anpin* within *Atzilut*).[11] The throne exists between the *ḥayot* and the supernal man upon it. It both separates them and connects them. That is to say, it is between *Beria* and the infinite divine (and it is thus also called the world of *Beria*).[12] It separates them to keep everything from becoming infinity, and it connects them by transmitting the divine life force downward to the worlds, which those worlds need, and transmitting to the Divine the awareness and yearning of the creatures below. ☞

THE THRONE

☞ The throne is, by way of analogy, like a physical chair that a person sits on. When a person sits on a chair, he lowers himself onto it while he is still standing. In spirituality, he descends in order to relate to a lower state of being, one that does not exist on his essential level. The seat of a chair separates a person's feet from his torso. His torso and head are above the seat, and his feet are below it. Analogously, now it is possible to receive from the "feet" of the "person" alone (see *Torah Or* 77a, 83a), and not from his torso and head. Switching the metaphor, the worlds of *Beria, Yetzira,* and *Asiya* and everything in them receive only from externality and the back side. They do not receive from the interiority of *Atzilut*, where God, His light, and His influence are all one. If they did receive from the interiority of *Atzilut*, it would be impossible for them not to be aware of the divine essence that is present and making everything exist.

The Hebrew word for "throne," *kisei*, is spelled *kof samekh alef*. The letters *kof samekh* form the word *kas*, which means "covering." This covering conceals the *alef*, which is the essence of the divine light, the *Aluf*, the "Master," of the world. This covering does not transmit the character of the *alef* (because if it did, everything would be that *alef*). Rather, it transmits the knowl-

---

11. Specifically, the "person upon the throne" is the *partzuf* of *Zeir Anpin* in *Atzilut*, and at times the *partzuf* of *Arikh Anpin*.

12. *Likkutei Amarim*, chap. 39

The elevation of the feminine waters annuls the separation that had existed previously. From now on, not only do the lower waters rise and nullify the separateness of their existence, but the upper waters pour down. The ascent is like removing a screen so that one sees that there is something above: that there are upper waters, the light of *Ein Sof*. And the masculine waters descend of their own accord to be down here, no longer above but below, in a unity.

In the context of the sacrificial offerings, this unification occurs when the offering is brought onto the altar, and fire descends from above and consumes it. In prayer, the altar is the heart. With a person's contemplation of God and service of Him, he raises his animal aspect and earthly nature to the love of God that he arouses in his heart. And then God's great love (His vast love) descends, completely eradicating the animal nature that the person had elevated. ☞

The author of the *Tanya* has explained the concept of the offerings brought on the altar so that he may now proceed to discuss that which is on a higher level: the red heifer, which has a connection with the death of tzaddikim.

edge that it is covering the *alef*, that an *alef* exists. And that is the world of *Beria*. It is stated in various contexts that in the realm of the "husk," the *kas* is separate from the *alef* and remains only a concealing cover, as the *alef* is hidden below. And thus the verse states of Amalek: "Because there is a hand upon the *kas* [Rashi: 'incomplete throne']..." (Ex. 17:16).

THE KING AND *ZEIR ANPIN*

☞ The divine flow that is drawn down as a result of this service of God comes from the level of *Atzilut* that relates to *Malkhut* of *Atzilut* and to the worlds of *Beria, Yetzira,* and *Asiya*. That level is called the King or *Zeir Anpin*. *Zeir Anpin* means "small countenance." That is in contrast to the "large countenance," which refers to *Arikh Anpin*. By way of analogy, when relating to a small child, a person puts on a "small face," by using a small intellect, concepts that are appropriate for young people, with a smile that is suited for children, and so forth. He keeps the large countenance for himself or for someone on his level. So too God relates to the created worlds with a small countenance, *Zeir Anpin*. That is analogous to the masculine waters, which the feminine waters draw down when an offering is raised onto the altar. The offerings that we raise upon the altar, like our service of prayer, are in keeping with the mitzvot: they accord with the proper structure of the world (as it is structured by the Torah) on its supernal level, even as it remains a world.

אָכֵן בִּשְׂרֵיפַת הַפָּרָה אֲדוּמָה, **Indeed, with the burning of the red**
הִנֵּה עַל יְדֵי הַשְׁלָכַת עֵץ אֶרֶז **heifer** – in particular, **as a result of the**
וְאֵזוֹב וכו' וּנְתִינַת מַיִם חַיִּים אֶל **casting of the cedar wood and hyssop**
הָאֵפֶר נִקְרָא בְּשֵׁם 'קִידּוּשׁ מֵי **living,** running **water into the ashes**
חַטָּאת' בַּמִּשְׁנָה וְהִיא בְּחִינַת (see Num. 19:27) – a process that **the**
קֹדֶשׁ הָעֶלְיוֹן הַנִּקְרָא בְּשֵׁם **Mishna calls "sanctification of the**
'טַלָּא דִּבְדוֹלְחָא' **purifying waters," which is the** level
of the **supernal sanctity called "dew
of crystal,"**

The entire purpose of the ceremony of the red heifer is to attain the purifying waters that are sprinkled on people rendered impure by contact with the dead. There were two stages in the preparation of the purifying waters. The first stage was the burning of the red heifer, which took place on the Mount of Olives outside Jerusalem. Cedar wood and hyssop were then thrown onto the burning carcass, and afterward the ashes were kept.

In the second stage, water was drawn from a wellspring into a vessel, and these ashes were mixed into it.[13] This stage was called the "sanctification of the purifying waters,"[14] for which the author of the *Tanya* offers a kabbalistic explanation.

The spiritual root of the waters into which the ashes of the heifer were placed was on a level of supernal holiness transcending and separate from the world and the speaking soul. The *Zohar* calls this level "dew of the crystal."[15] Dew indicates a very high level of spiritual influence, higher than rain. Rain expresses an influence from above that comes in response to an awakening from below, connecting to and relating to that awakening.[16] It is comparable to giving a person some-

---

13. Actually, the ashes were placed into the water. The phrase indicating that the water was placed onto the ashes means that the water was mixed with the ashes (Rambam, *Mishneh Torah, Sefer Tahara, Para Aduma* 9:1).

14. Numerous times; in particular, *Para* 5 and onward.

15. *Zohar* 3:49a. This corresponds to the white, supernal dew. The *Zohar's* implication is that this has the same quality as the purifying waters.

16. Similarly, our Sages state that a raindrop does not descend from above without two corresponding drops rising from below. See *Zohar* 3 (*Raya Meheimna*) 247b,

thing after he has requested it, which is within the parameters of what he requested. Dew, on the other hand, is a flow and giving that is not a response to an awakening or request from below. It is not dependent on such a request and preparation, neither in its essence (therefore, it is constant, unlike rain), nor in its quality. It can therefore possess an abundance and quality beyond the limited concepts of the recipients. And the highest level of dew is the "dew of crystal." This crystal stone is of a supernal color that transcends all colors and includes them all. This was also the level of the manna:[17] "Its appearance is like the appearance of crystal" (Num. 11:7). That was the bread that was given to Israel from heaven, unlike bread from the earth, which must be plowed, planted, reaped, and so forth.

Indeed, this influence of the dew of crystal has meaning below as well, in a more occluded way, in the manner of a ruling and decree from above, but in an entirely clear way, which is impossible without existence below. When the purifying waters are sanctified, the ashes and water meet. The ashes represent the very lowest and the water represents the very highest.

It is precisely in this way that the supernal flow is drawn through all existence. Only the very highest can descend to the very lowest, to absolute darkness, to death, in order to purify it from the impurity of the dead – and, in the future, to revive the dead.[18]

כְּמוֹ שֶׁכָּתוּב בַּזּוֹהַר הַקָּדוֹשׁ (חלק ג מט,א), שֶׁהִיא בְּחִינַת חָכְמָה עִילָאָה וּמוֹחָא סְתִימָאָה דְּאֲרִיךְ אַנְפִּין	which the holy *Zohar* (3:49a) states is the supernal wisdom and "sealed brain" of *Arikh Anpin*,

The "sealed brain" of *Arikh Anpin* is in *Keter*. Sanctity is the level of *Ḥokhma*,[19] the beginning of the soul and of the influence of Godliness

---

Ta'anit 25b, and elsewhere. And see *Likkutei Torah, Bemidbar* 42:2, and *Tziyunim Umar'ei Mekomot*, there.

17. See *Torah Or* 65c and 89a, *Likkutei Torah, Devarim* 14b, and elsewhere.

18. Those are the 288 sparks that fell with the shattering of the vessels. The vessels are referred to as being "dead."

19. See *Likkutei Amarim,* chap. 19, and many other places, which state that *Ḥokhma* is called "holy," etc.

upon the world. The transcendent light of *Ein Sof* is clothed in it.[20] Therefore, *Ḥokhma* reveals and presents the separate and holy *Ein Sof* to the other *sefirot* below *Ḥokhma*, to the entire world. And "supernal sanctity" is the level of *Ḥokhma* that is higher than *Ḥokhma*. It is the *Ḥokhma* in *Keter* (*Arikh Anpin*), which is called the "sealed brain." It is the hidden *Ḥokhma* that cannot be related to from below. It is only a hidden source, not dependent on and not limited to *Ḥokhma* in *Atzilut*. ☞

וַעֲלָהּ אִיתְּמַר בְּדוּכְתֵּי טוּבָא בַּזוֹהַר הַקָדוֹשׁ 'בְּחָכְמָה אִתְבְּרִירוּ'   and **regarding which the holy** ***Zohar* states in many places that "with wisdom – *Ḥokhma* – they are refined** (*birurim*)" –

The work of refining is achieved essentially by means of wisdom, *Ḥokhma*. Here the author of the *Tanya* is saying that the statement of the Zohar, "with wisdom – *Ḥokhma* – they are refined," refers essentially to the hidden *Ḥokhma* (the "sealed brain") in *Keter*. It is true that revealed wisdom, that being the *Ḥokhma* in *Atzilut*, also refines. But as will soon be explained, refining the darkness that has no light (the impure "husk") and no wisdom (life force) requires the hidden *Ḥokhma* in supernal *Keter*, the dew of crystal, which descends to the depths even when there is no awakening from below.[21] ☞

וְאִתְהַפְּכָא חֲשׁוֹכָא לִנְהוֹרָא   "**darkness is transformed into light**" –

CONCEALED ḤOKHMA

☞ That higher, inner, concealed *Ḥokhma* is within the *partzuf* of Arikh Anpin, which is within *Keter* (above the world of *Atzilut*). That is the countenance, as it were, of the Holy One, blessed be He. It is within God's independent will that includes all of the worlds that will be, insofar as for Him everything already is. This *Ḥokhma* does not relate to the existence of the worlds but only to the essential will that a world will exist. And since the will at this stage is unlimited, the wisdom – *Ḥokhma* – that relates to it is concealed and unlimited.

---

20. See *Likkutei Amarim*, chap. 18, and the sidenote in chap. 35.
21. See more on how refining occurs by means of the "hidden wisdom" within

This refining transforms darkness into light. There is nothing that
is literally darkness: there is only light that is not seen. The refining
arranges things into an order: it matches up a person who sees with
what he sees, so that his eyes are not closed and nor is the object hidden.
Existence is filled with entities (comparable to letters of the alphabet);
as long as we do not see the connection between them – the structure,
the intelligence within everything – then what we see only conceals
and confuses. But when we see the structure and meaning (and that
in particular is the power of the illumination of Hokhma), everything
that had been hidden communicates, reveals, shines more and more
light. And that is the refining that transforms the darkness to light.

Regarding the expression "darkness is transformed into light," it

WITH WISDOM – HOKHMA – THEY ARE REFINED

☞ A number of reasons have been proposed for why it is precisely wisdom –
Hokhma – that refines. One reason is that
refining is a type of rectification. Only an
entity that is itself rectified can rectify (see
Likkutei Torah, Bemidbar 69b–c. And that
states that there is refining in Hokhma and
a deeper refining that comes from the level
of Keter). In the case of human beings, only
a person who can hear the essence within existence can refine and arrange its external confusion. And in the context of the
sefirot, only Hokhma is intrinsically rectified. That is because its existence is nullified before the light of Ein Sof that shines
within it. It is to the other sefirot what Atzilut is to the created worlds of Beria, Yetzira, and Asiya (Atzilut is in a rectified state
in comparison to them).

Wisdom is, in a sense, both vessel and
light. The light is, in the broadest and most
abstract sense, the light of Ein Sof, which
nothing can limit and hide. This light is

what refines. However, since Hokhma is itself ayin, "nothingness," the level of absolute nullification in the soul, only Hokhma
can receive this unlimited light to be a vessel for infinite light. That being the case,
the refining power of Hokhma comes
not only from its aspect as light but also
from its aspect as vessel, which means
Hokhma's absolute nullification. As for why
the world is not refined, that is because it
contains entities that are not nullified to
the divine light: cells of darkness and death
that do not shine with divine light and life
force, that create concealment and confusion in the entirety of existence. Refining –
in general and in particular – is due to the
fact that there is a refining entity that is in
itself a point of nullification within existence and that is a vessel for the refining
light of Ein Sof, even as it is also a vessel
that can perceive this, that can receive this
nullification, and in that way draw it into
entities, overall and in particular.

Keter in Likkutei Torah, Bemidbar 59d, and onward. And see a different approach
in the addendum to Torah Or 107c and onward.

has been noted[22] that the author of the *Tanya* is being precise in his language: not only is the darkness "subdued," but it is "transformed." "Subduing" and "transforming" are key terms in Hasidism. In general, they relate to a person's service of God – whether he only subdues his evil traits but does not transform them to good or whether he transforms those traits. Presumably, by using the term "transformed," the author of the *Tanya* means that the darkness is not only subdued. That is because when the refining *Ḥokhma* is on a level that is related to the world and soul that it is refining, the refining is not absolute, because the overall situation cannot change. A person may know that a situation is dark and should not exist, but the darkness is not transformed to light. Having this knowledge, the person can either act in accordance with his natural inclination or in opposition to it – the latter would be a "subduing" of his inclination. Only when the power of the refining comes from above – that is, from the hidden *Ḥokhma* in *Keter* – can darkness be transformed into light.

דְּהַיְינוּ עוֹלָם הַתִּיקוּן, שֶׁנִּתְבָּרֵר וְנִתְתַּקֵּן עַל יְדֵי מוֹחָא סְתִימָאָה דא"א מֵעוֹלָם הַתֹּהוּ וּשְׁבִירַת הַכֵּלִים שֶׁנָּפְלוּ בבי"ע וכו' כַּנּוֹדָע

that is to say, it is transformed into **the world of rectification, which is refined and rectified by the "sealed brain" of** *Arikh Anpin* **out of the world of chaos –** *tohu* **– and the shattering of the vessels, which had fallen into** the worlds of ***Beria, Yetzira, Asiya*...**, as is known.**

The existence of the broken world of *tohu* and its fragments that fell to the created worlds is rectified by hidden *Ḥokhma* in *Keter*. The rectified existence is called the "world of rectification."

The rectification of the world of *tohu* and of the shattering of the vessels are among the most central and most discussed topics in the Kabbala of the Arizal, as well as in Hasidism. Therefore, the author of the *Tanya* here notes, "As is known." ☞

---

22. Thus notes the Tzemaḥ Tzedek in this context. See his *Or HaTorah, Bemidbar* 3:803.

וְלָזֹאת מְטַהֶרֶת טוּמְאַת
הַמֵּת, אַף שֶׁהוּא אֲבִי אֲבוֹת
וכו' וּלְמַטָּה מַטָּה מִנּוֹגַהּ

That is what the red heifer does. It **purifies** a person from **the impurity of** contact with **the dead, even though** a corpse **is the ultimate** impurity, **and much, much lower than** *noga*.

The red heifer brings about refining and rectification, continuing from the hidden *Hokhma* in *Keter*. It can thus even purify a person from the impurity of contact with the dead, which is the most severe level of impurity. All impurity is connected in some way to death, the absence of life. Therefore, a corpse itself is the primal source, the root, of all impure existence.

The husk is the source of impurity. And just as there are two levels of the husk – the husk of *noga* and below it the impure husks[23] – so too there are two levels of impurity: regular impurity and the severe, ultimate impurity of a corpse. The husk of *noga*, as its name indicates, is a husk that possesses light (*noga*); thus, the impurity related to it is

THE WORLD OF RECTIFICATION

☞ Our world has an old "story": something occurred in the distant past, to which everything that exists and occurs in our world is linked. One may say that in our world there is nothing else than the materials that remain from that story in a scattered and confused state, as though something fell and was shattered. In the language of the Kabbala, it is the story of the world of chaos – *tohu* – which existed and was broken, and of the fragments that lost their meaning, their life force, falling like corpses to the worlds of *Beria, Yetzira*, and *Asiya*. In contrast to the world of *Atzilut*, where the divine vitality is completely revealed, in the created worlds it is covered by husks. The vitality is not clear and obvious but is fallen on a variety of levels,

until in this physical world it is entirely hidden, as though resting in lifeless bodies. In the supernal worlds the concealment is not absolute. A measure of divine life force always exists, rises, and is revealed. But in our world, the concealment has reached its ultimate extent: We do not see at all. All we see are silent objects and broken vessels scattered in inanimate matter, plant life, animal life, and man. On the other hand, a human being has the ability to change direction: not just descending and shattering, but he can ascend and rectify. When he does so, this world grows more refined and more rectified, little by little, person by person, and generation by generation, and it is accordingly called "the world of rectification."

23. *Likkutei Amarim*, chap. 6.

a scarcity, not an absolute absence, of life force. That is not the case regarding the impure husks and the corresponding impurity of a corpse, where there is not only a diminution of light but its absolute concealment. It is a husk that has no light; it is impurity that has absolutely no life force. Here the author of the *Tanya* states that only hidden *Ḥokhma* in *Keter* can rectify this level of impurity and husk. ☞

Until now, this letter has been discussing the atonement effected by the red heifer in contrast to the atonement effected by the offerings placed on the altar. Further on, the author of the *Tanya* will explain how this is connected to the death of the tzaddikim. The Midrash infers this connection from the fact that the biblical passages about Miriam and the red heifer are adjacent to each other. But the inner aspect of the Torah does not stop there. The Kabbala, and in particular Hasidism, seeks those inner connections and reasons, that inner aspect of the Torah.

<table>
<tr><td>18 Ḥeshvan</td><td>וְהִנֵּה מוּדַעַת זֹאת דְּאַבָּא יוֹנֵק</td><td>It is known that Abba draws its suste-</td></tr>
<tr><td>17 Ḥeshvan
(leap year)</td><td>מִמַּזָּל הַשְּׁמִינִי</td><td>nance from the "eighth mazal."</td></tr>
</table>

AND MUCH, MUCH LOWER THAN NOGA

☞ Regarding God's descent to Egypt to liberate the children of Israel there, the Haggada states, "I and not an angel.... " Only God Himself could distinguish between the Egyptians and the children of Israel. Similarly, the Midrash states that when God split the Red Sea, the ministering angels protested: "Both [the Egyptians and the children of Israel] are idolaters," since an angel cannot distinguish between the two. An angel can differentiate between righteousness and evil, but not between a wicked person who has a holy soul and a wicked person who does not have a holy soul. It can differentiate revealed entities and the factors that define them. It can create categories in a normative world that adheres to known laws of action. But it cannot perceive if there is something in the dark. It cannot imagine what would happen if the entire existence of this dark

would be overturned, what would happen if all of these factors existed within other dimensions. That is something, in the language of the Midrash, that only God can do: the divine power itself, separated from all of the powers that maintain and manage the world. In the words of the author of the *Tanya*, this is the transcendent point of wisdom, the hidden wisdom in *Keter*.

The realm of the husk of *noga*, which is the arena of our lives and our Jewish service of God, is the arena within the three camps, the arena of the offerings upon the altar. But the realm below the husk of *noga*, which just glances at us from the impure husks, from the forbidden things, is refined by the ashes of the red heifer that comes from there, from outside the three camps, and with the sanctification of the purifying waters draws forth holiness from above the camps of holiness.

"*Abba*" is the term for *Ḥokhma* in *Atzilut*. This supernal *Ḥokhma* in *Atzilut* (which is the initial stage of the world of *Atzilut*, which receives its vitality from that which is above *Atzilut*) draws its vitality, its content, from the "eighth *mazal*."[24] But that *mazal* is not the source of this influence: it only acts to transmit it from hidden *Ḥokhma* in *Keter* to *Ḥokhma* in *Atzilut*. That (as was explained earlier) is drawn down by the purifying water of the red heifer. And (as will be explained below) that is also what occurs upon a tzaddik's *histalkut*. ☞ ☞

THE MAZALOT

☞ The *mazalot* (pl. of *mazal*) are the influences that drip down (*nozlot*) to the worlds from a realm that transcends the worlds – generally speaking, from *Keter* to *Ḥokhma* of *Atzilut* and to the world of *Atzilut* as a whole, and from there to the subsequent worlds (*Beria, Yetzira,* and *Asiya*). The *mazalot* are also referred to as the thirteen traits of compassion that God revealed to Moses (Ex. 34:6–7) and as the "rectifications of the beard" (that is, thirteen areas of the beard). They are the totality of the archetypal ways in which the transcendental powers that surround the worlds penetrate to the inner forces within the worlds and within the soul. Transcendental powers are not limited by the rules and parameters of the worlds. Therefore, they are traits of "compassion," which override the determinations of reason and judgment. They are also called "hairs," because the hairs of the beard (as explained in a number of places) represent the way in which that which is transcendent and encompassing penetrates to the lower being, like

a hair that does not directly transmit life force (in contrast to a bodily limb). When we cut a hair, we do not feel anything; nevertheless, something of the inner life force – something constricted, something that is impossible to explain and define – passes outward via the skin. In spirituality, this is said to be a transmission downward from a transcendent, encompassing state. And that is *mazal*: an influence that "drips down" from an essence that is not yet defined and "clothed." The verse states, "I, Daniel, alone, saw the vision, and the men who were with me did not see the vision; however, a great trembling overcame them" (Dan. 10:7). The Sages question this: "If they did not see, why did trembling overcome them?" And they answer, "Although a person does not see, his *mazal* sees" (*Megilla* 3a). Hasidism explains that the *mazal* is an illumination that comes from the soul's deepest levels. It is not clothed in the body and its abilities, but it expresses itself in an inner sense that is aware of even a reality that the mind's eye does not see.

THE EIGHTH MAZAL

☞ As explained in kabbalistic writings (see *Etz Ḥayyim*, Gate 13 – *Sha'ar Arikh* *Anpin* – chap. 9, and elsewhere), there are thirteen *mazalot*, corresponding to the

24. See *Zohar* 3:289; *Etz Ḥayyim, Sha'ar HaKelalim,* chap. 5, and Gate 13 (*Sha'ar Arikh Anpin*), chap. 9, *Biur Kol HaYod Gimmel Tikkunim*; see also *Sha'ar 14* (*Heikhal Abba VeIma*), chap. 3 and chap. 8, and elsewhere.

הוּא תִּיקוּן "נוֹצֵר חֶסֶד", "נוֹצֵר" אוֹתִיּוֹת רָצוֹן That eighth *mazal* **is the rectifying factor** called *notzer ḥesed,* **"and preserves** kindness." The word *notzer* is composed of **the letters of *ratzon,*** "will, favor."

In keeping with the names of the traits of compassion mentioned in Scripture (Ex. 34:6–7), the eighth rectifying factor is called *notzer ḥesed,* "preserves kindness."

The letters of the word *notzer,* "preserves," may be rearranged to spell *ratzon,* which means "will" or "favor." The names of the divine attributes in Scripture have, in addition to their straightforward meaning, a kabbalistic meaning. That is because they come from a supernal and hidden place (namely hidden *Ḥokhma*). One way of revealing such a hidden meaning is to rearrange the letters. *Ratzon* is the supernal power of the soul, higher than all its other powers. In terms of the *sefirot,* it is *Keter,* which transcends all the other *sefirot.* Thus, the rectifying factor *notzer* has the letters of *ratzon,* because it draws down hidden *Ḥokhma* in *Keter* to the worlds. ☞

thirteen rectifying factors (*tikkunim*) of the beard, thirteen locations in the beard, thirteen aspects and ways of drawing forth this illumination of hairs. The first through seventh rectifying factors are parts of the beard on the upper part of the face, whereas the eighth rectifying factor corresponds to the part of the beard below the mouth, descending from the face. It expresses the flow downward, in that it brings together the flow of all of the *mazalot* above it and transmits it downward. The Kabbala explains that this is the role of the eighth through the thirteenth *mazalot* (including the parts of the beard near the neck in the thick section of the beard). In the flow of the beard from the eighth to the thirteenth *mazalot,* there is an upper part and a lower part. The upper part is the eighth *mazal,* which draws light down to *Ḥokhma* (as stated here), and the lower part is the thirteenth *mazal,* which draws down to *Bina.*

The phrase "draws its sustenance" (from the eighth *mazal*) literally means "suckles." The imagery is that of a nursing baby. That is to say, this flow is very constricted, like that which a mother transmits to her infant in a way that it can receive. This means that, even after the nursing, *Ḥokhma* in *Atzilut* will not be like hidden *Ḥokhma* in *Keter.* Therefore, in those special situations in which there is a direct drawing forth from hidden *Ḥokhma* in *Keter* to the worlds, it refines and purifies matters in the lower realms more than *Ḥokhma* in *Atzilut* does: it brings about the purification from contact with a corpse and the atonement of sins, and it even rectifies the impure husks below the husk of *noga.*

וְהִיא 'עֵת רָצוֹן' הַמִּתְגַּלֶּה וּמֵאִיר
בִּבְחִינַת גִּילּוּי מִלְמַעְלָה לְמַטָּה
בְּעֵת פְּטִירַת צַדִּיקֵי עֶלְיוֹן

That refers to "a time of favor," which is revealed and shines – as a revelation from above to below – at the time of the passing away of supernal tzaddikim,

That drawing forth of this *ratzon* from sealed Ḥokhma is "a time of favor." This is a time when the supernal *ratzon* is revealed. That is not only a time on the calendar, but a state of being that is created from the blending of particular factors, such as prayer with clinging to God and dedication, which is called "a time of favor"[25] and which creates a reality – in the dimension of time, at any rate – of the revelation of the supernal will (as was explained earlier). And this applies especially at the time that a tzaddik passes away.

One may easily understand that focused prayer or a good deed – in

NOTZER AND RATZON

☞ The link between *notzer* and *ratzon* is the link between exteriority and interiority (as described in *Ma'amarei Admor HaZaken* 5566, p. 146). *Notzer* emphasizes the ability to transmit that hidden will downward, to maintain it as it is in its supernal realm, which is higher than Ḥokhma in *Atzilut*, as it descends to that Ḥokhma and to the worlds in general. And *ratzon* emphasizes the character of the will itself as it is above. This may be compared to a person's will to perform a kind deed. The will does not come from his recognition that performing that kind deed is a good thing to do. It is not any particular attribute of his soul, but the inclination of his soul itself. Such a supernal will transcends recognition and wisdom. It is not limited even by the limitations of the attributes of the world of *Atzilut*. The attributes of *Atzilut* are the attributes of God. These attributes do not have an intrinsic limitation, but they have limitation from the aspect of the other attributes, from the aspect of their being part of the complex picture of the world of *Atzilut*. Conversely, the attribute in *Keter*, that being the attribute in *ratzon*, is not a particular attribute – ḥesed, gevura, and so forth. Rather, it is the essence of the soul as it inclines toward kindness and the like. In *Keter*, there is no limitation and separation, because *Keter* is the essential point of the soul, which is not divided. The essence is in a general way like inanimate matter, but if and when it is drawn through the *ratzon* into the soul and into our world, that is literally like granting new life to the soul or the world.

25. As in the verse "But as for me, let my prayer come to You, Lord, at a time of favor" (Ps. 69:14).

particular, if it is performed with total dedication – creates a time of favor. But why should the death of a tzaddik do so?

In order to understand the meaning of a tzaddik's death, one must understand the meaning of his life. There is no part of a tzaddik's life that does not participate in completing the expression of his divine soul. His passing away is the refining of his life, the moment at which his entire life joins with a single summarizing line of holiness, a line that illuminates the worlds even more than it did when he was alive.

עוֹבְדֵי ה' בְּאַהֲבָה בִּמְסִירַת נַפְשָׁם לה' בְּחַיֵּיהֶם עַרְבִית וְשַׁחֲרִית בִּקְרִיאַת שְׁמַע

those who serve God with love, with the self-sacrifice of their soul to God in their lifetime, evening and morning, with the recitation of the *Shema*,

The tzaddik's life is one of uninterrupted service of God with love and dedication. That dedication exists in all parts of his life, but it is refined in an eruption of revelation when he recites the *Shema*, morning and evening.

Regarding one's dedication in reciting the *Shema*, there are two principal levels in serving God and relating to Him, both of them referred to in the *Shema*. Sometimes a person attains only one of them, and sometimes both. One is referred to in the first verse of the *Shema*, in the word "one," as a person contemplates and feels as deeply as possible that God is one and there is no other, that everything – including himself – is absolutely nullified within the divine oneness. This level is called "supernal unification." And the other is referred to by the phrase "with all your soul" – meaning, even if He takes your soul.[26] That is in general a dedication that emerges out of a person's awareness of living and existing in the world. This level is called "lower unification" or "nullification of being." ☞ ☞

שֶׁעַל יְדֵי זֶה הָיוּ מַעֲלִים מַיִּין נוּקְבִין לאו"א בִּקְרִיאַת שְׁמַע כַּיָדוּעַ

by means of which they would raise the feminine waters to *Abba* and *Imma* with their recitation of the *Shema*, as is known.

---

26. And in a variant of that level, "with all your might." See *Likkutei Torah, Devarim* 44:4.

The tzaddikim would raise the feminine waters to *Abba* and *Ima* by dedicating their soul to God as they recited the *Shema*. The elevation of feminine waters is essentially the elevation of the divine life force within the lower entities – the holy sparks held captive in those entities – to be absorbed into and united with the divine holiness that transcends them. An individual experiences that as the utter dedication of his soul. That is to say, when he nullifies his sense of separateness from the Divine, which is felt whenever he relates to every element in

DEDICATION IN SERVICE OF GOD

☞ A person's will in his service of God is an expression of the essential core of his soul, a core that is united with the Divine and that reveals itself at the time of his dedication to God. What is dedication? It is not necessarily a good deed, a mitzva, or even love of God. A person may perform a mitzva because he thinks that it is the right thing to do or because he loves God in his heart or mind – in other words, because of a certain attribute. But when a person dedicates his soul to God (in deed, in speech, or simply with a feeling), that is not an expression of a specific attribute in his soul, because no particular attribute in a person's soul is capable of leading him to dedicate his soul. Rather, that dedication is an expression of the essence of his soul, of his inner, essential will, in which his soul itself shines.

DEDICATION OF THEIR SOUL TO GOD
WITH THE RECITATION OF THE *SHEMA*

☞ The tzaddik lives every day with a total, self-effacing dedication of the soul. However, that dedication is not explicit and revealed, because he is living and acting in this world. Even when he clings to God and he is on the level of the chariot – that is, when his thoughts, words, and deeds are on a supernal level – he is still living and acting in this world, and so his soul's dedication is hidden. Possibly it is hidden in an even higher dedication of the soul, of "against your will you live," meaning that he has accepted God's decree that he be immersed in this-worldly reality for the sake of serving God. Nevertheless, it is hidden.

Any revelation of the self-sacrifice of a person's soul necessarily interrupts his life and activities. That is so not only when that self-sacrifice of the soul is actualized. Even the very thought of such dedication of the soul constitutes such a dedication and interruption. And a person's life and his activity in the service of God seemingly require a periodic readjustment, a point at which his dedication of the soul is revealed so that he can think about it and feel it (see *Likkutei Amarim,* chap. 25, which states that a person's keeping the Torah and the commandments is dependent on remembering how, when he recited the *Shema,* he was ready to sacrifice his life for the sake of the oneness of God). That point is reached during the twice-daily recitation of the *Shema,* morning and evening (see *Zohar* 1:124b; *Pri Etz Ḥayyim, Sha'ar Keriat Shema,* chap. 12; *Baḥ* on *Tur Oraḥ Ḥayyim,* beginning of 61, and elsewhere).

his life, and he commits to God the life force that he receives from that element, he is dedicating his soul to God; he is integrating himself and uniting himself with the Divine.

The tzaddikim elevate the feminine waters to the level of *Abba* and *Ima* (which are Ḥokhma and *Bina*). In general, when an ordinary person raises the feminine waters, where do they rise to? They rise to where his thought and intent are found. When a person performs a mitzva and a good deed, he relates to some parameter of existence that he is rectifying or wants to rectify: an existence of light contained in vessels. That is the case even when he does so with the dedication of his soul. In the terminology of the Kabbala, he raises the feminine waters to *Zeir* and *Nukva*, which are the "attributes." These are the levels in the world of *Atzilut* that are the "body" of *Atzilut* and that relate to the created worlds. That is in contrast to *Abba* and *Ima*, which are the head of *Atzilut*, and which relate to that which is above them. Therefore, when a person performs a mitzva while thinking about and relating to something this-worldly, he raises the feminine waters to *Zeir* and *Nukva*. But when a person recites the *Shema* and dedicates his soul with a movement of nullification of his own parameters, his thought and his intent relate literally to *Ein Sof*, who transcends the parameters of the worlds. In the language of the Kabbala, he raises the feminine waters to *Abba* and *Ima*. And the light that is consequently drawn down to Ḥokhma of *Atzilut* (for the sake of the unification of Ḥokhma and *Bina*) is a new light that is drawn to the worlds from *Ein Sof*, who transcends the worlds.[27]

(וְכֵן בְּתַלְמוּד תּוֹרָה, דְּמֵחָכְמָה נָפְקָא) **(And the same applies to their Torah study, which emerges from Ḥokhma.)**

Here the author of the *Tanya* adds that the feminine waters are raised to *Abba* and *Ima* (that is, to Ḥokhma and *Bina* in *Atzilut*) not only when a person recites the *Shema* but also when he studies Torah. The Torah "emerges from Ḥokhma":[28] that is to say, it emerges from its root above the worlds to enter the worlds on the level of Ḥokhma of *Atzilut*.

27. See *Likkutei Torah, Vayikra* 33:2, and onward.
28. See *Zohar* 2:121a, 85a, and elsewhere.

Therefore, when a person in this world studies Torah, he is connecting, via a level of wisdom within himself, to the supernal *Ḥokhma*, which itself receives from above itself: from the hidden *Ḥokhma*. In this way, he raises the feminine waters to *Ḥokhma* from every part of his soul and body and from every part of the world that he brings into partnership with this study. ☞

וְעַל יְדֵי זֶה הָיוּ נִמְשָׁכִים וְיוֹרְדִים בְּחִינַת 'מַיִּין דְּכוּרִין' מִתִּיקּוּן 'וְנוֹצֵר חֶסֶד'

As a result of this, the masculine waters were drawn forth and descended from the rectifying factor of "and preserves kindness."

"As a result of" the dedication of the soul of the tzaddikim, "the male waters were drawn forth and descended from the rectifying factor of 'and preserves kindness.'" The rising feminine waters prompt the masculine waters to descend. When the feminine waters rise to *Abba*

AND THE SAME APPLIES TO THEIR TORAH STUDY

☞ Indeed (and perhaps that is why this sentence is in parentheses), unlike the dedication of a person's soul when he recites the *Shema* – when he is aware of and senses the level of *Ein Sof*, to whom he is giving his soul – when he is learning Torah, that awareness exists only in the background. Even if he knows that the Torah emerged from *Ḥokhma*, while he is learning he is apparently dealing with this-worldly topics – with an ox and donkey, with woolen *tzitzit*, with an *etrog*, and so forth – and he does not feel that he is engaging in God's wisdom. That being the case, one might say that he is not raising the feminine waters to *Abba* and *Ima*. But that is not so. First of all, even when a person is studying the revealed aspect of the Torah, he must have in mind that he is engaged in God's wisdom, and not just in a general way: he must try to draw that wisdom into what he is studying and into his feelings at every moment and in every detail (see *Likkutei Amarim*, chap. 41). Second, even if a person does not have that in mind and he does not sense that, he is still engaging in God's wisdom. In the Torah (unlike the worlds or the levels of the soul), *Ḥokhma* is not found only at the beginning but at every level to which it descends. Even when *halakha* is clothed in physical matters, it is God's wisdom. *Halakha* is not only an expression and outcome that devolves from God's *Ḥokhma*, but it is the essence of the *Ḥokhma* itself. Ultimately, then, even if a person does not sense that he is thinking about divine wisdom, that is what he is doing (unless there is an interference through a contrary intent and thought). Therefore, the feminine waters rise to *Ḥokhma* and *Bina*.

and *Ima*, they cause the masculine waters above them to descend to them. In particular, *Abba* draws down sustenance from the eighth *mazal*, which is the rectifying factor of "and preserves kindness."

The feminine waters do more than initiate the descent of something that had previously existed. They generate something new. This may be compared to a student who asks his teacher a challenging question. He inspires the teacher to produce an answer that is not only beyond the mind of the student but that was also beyond the mind of the teacher, something new that had transcended both of them. Similarly, a woman who arouses a man arouses something new in him that was not revealed to him, something that now includes and unites them both.[29]

וְהֵם הֵם הַמְּאִירִים בִּבְחִינַת גִּילּוּי בִּפְטִירָתָם כַּנּוֹדָע שֶׁכָּל עֲמַל הָאָדָם שֶׁעֲמָלָה נַפְשׁוֹ בְּחַיָּיו לְמַעְלָה, בִּבְחִינַת הֶעְלֵם וְהֶסְתֵּר, מִתְגַּלֶּה וּמֵאִיר בִּבְחִינַת גִּילּוּי מִלְמַעְלָה לְמַטָּה בְּעֵת פְּטִירָתוֹ

These masculine waters from the rectifying factor of "and preserves kindness" **shine in a revealed way when** the tzaddikim **pass away. As is known, the entire toil of a person, the toil of his soul when he is alive** that exists **above in a hidden and concealed way, is revealed and shines in a revealed way from above to below when he passes away.**

When the tzaddik passes away and the limitations of his body and this-worldly life are removed, all of the spiritual abundance that had gathered above because of him and had been concealed is now revealed.

The elicitation of the masculine waters transcends that which a person unveils with the elevation of the feminine waters. That is to say, the spiritual abundance descends from a level that transcends everything that he himself could have uncovered in himself and shared with others in his lifetime. Therefore, it cannot be revealed while he is alive in this world and in his body. It is stored on a hidden, supernal plane, where it increases from day to day as he dedicates his soul to the service of God. At that time, only a minor illumination is revealed. But his passing away results in its complete revelation. ☞

---

29. And thus the phrase "to arouse the unification of *Abba* and *Ima*..." appears occasionally.

A question remains. In order for that illumination to be revealed in this world, it requires a vessel that can contain it. If even the tzaddik had been unable to function as a vessel for this in his lifetime, how will other people be able to do so after he has passed away? To answer this, the author of the *Tanya* adds:

וְהִנֵּה עַל יְדֵי גִילוּי הֶאָרַת תִּיקוּן 'וְנוֹצֵר חֶסֶד' בִּפְטִירָתָן מֵאִיר חֶסֶד ה' מֵעוֹלָם עַד עוֹלָם עַל יְרֵאָיו

In consequence of the revelation of the illumination of the rectifying factor of "and preserves kindness" when tzaddikim **pass away, God's kindness shines from world to world upon those who fear Him,**

Because this illumination is so elevated, coming from the rectifying factor of "and preserves kindness," the place of supernal will that transcends supernal *Ḥokhma* of *Atzilut* and all parameters of the worlds, it shines from the highest world to the lowest. ☞

THE REVELATION FROM THE TZADDIK WHEN HE PASSES AWAY RELATES TO EVERY JEW

☞ The special quality of the masculine waters that the tzaddik draws down is not only their elevated level (the fact that they come from the *mazal* of "preserves kindness") but the fact that they relate to every Jew. If a person is not a tzaddik, then even if he has involved himself with the holiness of the Torah and the commandments throughout his entire life, the focus of his life has been his struggle for personal survival and elevation. Even that which he draws down from above relates to his personal realm (something that is not inconsequential for him). But the tzaddik is different. He has a universal soul. Even if he is not a leader of the generation or of a community, his life in this world always relates to the supernal character of the totality of the people of Israel, to the Divine Presence. He knows that his soul descended to this world to help the entire people of Israel. That is what interests and engages it. Moreover, the tzaddik's existence as a particular individual is not only uninteresting to him but it is even like a "sin," like a deterioration of, a separation from, his state of unity with God and his clinging to God. That being the case, just as the life of the tzaddik is the life of the Divine Presence, the life of every individual of Israel, so too the revelation that ensues when he passes away relates to every Jew.

ON THOSE WHO FEAR HIM

☞ When the light is higher than a particular vessel, there is no way for that vessel to receive it. However, when it is beyond the parameters of all vessels, when it is not in

וּפוֹעֵל יְשׁוּעוֹת בְּקֶרֶב הָאָרֶץ   and brings about "deliverance in the
לְכַפֵּר עַל עֲוֹן הַדּוֹר   midst of the land" to grant atonement
for the sin of the generation,

This tremendous illumination brings about "deliverance in the midst of
the land" – in our world – that is not commensurate with the level and
capability of this world itself. That is to say, it saves a person, wherever
he may be, from his deeds and thoughts, from what he deserves or does
not deserve, as these are determined by the order of the world and even
by the judgment of the Torah. This illumination, which comes from the
supernal *mazalot*, from the thirteen traits of compassion, transcends
Ḥokhma and the intellect that determine all of the structures of the
world. Therefore, it can grant atonement for the generation's sin that
has violated the structures of the world.[30] ☞

the parameter of a vessel at all, there is another way that each one can receive it. It is
only necessary to open an ear of a different sort. And thus the text speaks of "those
who fear Him." That is to say, not an ear of
understanding and knowledge with which
Ḥokhma listens, but an ear of the fear of
God, with which Ḥokhma also listens. As is
known, the supernal kindness and all of the
attributes within *Keter* are first revealed in
the soul and in the world in the attributes,
which are specifically the vessels to receive the supernal attributes (higher than
Ḥokhma and Bina).).

FOR THE SIN OF THE GENERATION

☞ This recalls the Sages' use of this expression (such as in Tractate *Kalla*, chap.
6). The tzaddik commits himself to repair,
or he is at least responsible for, the sins
of the generation. He has a connection
with and responsibility toward his entire
generation – not only those people who
were connected to him as his students
and Hasidim. This is a concept of a connection that exists at the substructure of
being, even deeper than Ḥokhma and intellect. Therefore, the second aspect of
this commitment is the tzaddik's ability to
gain atonement for the sin of the generation even when doing so is not his direct
responsibility and even when he is apparently unaware of this.

The Ba'al Shem Tov (See *Ba'al Shem Tov
al HaTorah, Parashat Ki Tisa,* 9–11, quoted
there in the name of Rabbi Levi Yitzḥak of
Berditchev) develops the concept of this
connection further. There are two ways
to view the sin of the generation. The first
is that the tzaddik is weak and has some
wrongful thought, and that expresses itself among the masses as actual sin. And
the second is that the people's sinning results in the tzaddik's having some wrongful

---

30. See Ps. 74:2. "For God is my King from the times of old, working deliverance…." The Hebrew word for "times of old," *kedem*, refers to something

אַף גַּם עַל הַזְּדוֹנוֹת שֶׁהֵן מִג׳ קְלִיפּוֹת הַטְּמֵאוֹת שֶׁלְּמַטָּה מִנּוֹגַהּ

even for intentional sins that are of the three impure husks below *noga*.

The "sin of the generation" for which the tzaddik's passing away provides atonement includes not only the subtle sins of great, pious men and the errors of a simple Jew, but even actual sins that people have performed intentionally against God's express will. ☞

לְפִי שֶׁמַּזָּל דְּ׳נוֹצֵר׳ מְמוֹחָא סְתִימָאָה דָּא״א מְקוֹר הַבֵּירוּרִים

That is because the *mazal* of "preserves kindness" is drawn from the "sealed brain" of *Arikh Anpin*, which is the source of the refinings,

The "sealed brain" is *Ḥokhma* in *Arikh Anpin*, which is *Keter*. That "sealed brain" is the source of revealed *Ḥokhma* that exists in *Atzilut*.

thought and an extremely subtle ulterior motive. The Ba'al Shem Tov says – and this is a fundamental idea in Hasidism in general – that the tzaddik must always adopt the first view: that whatever happens to every Jew in his generation depends on him. It emerged from him, and the responsibility is his. That concept doubtless underlies this letter: that the tzaddik gains atonement for the sin of the generation. In order to do so, he must accept responsibility for the generation and be prepared to be ensnared in its sin.

INTENTIONAL SINS FROM THE IMPURE HUSKS

☞ Intentional sins come from the three impure husks, whereas errors come from the husk of *noga*. The concept relevant to error and intentional sin is that of intent, whereas the concept relevant to the husk of *noga* and the impure husks is that of deed. The connection between these two concepts is as follows. When a person acts unwittingly, there is nothing illicit in his intent; he is only guilty of inattention. Therefore, he is comparable to the husk of *noga*, which is not something forbidden and which can be elevated. But when one sins intentionally, he is committing a forbidden act. That is comparable to the impure husks, which cannot be elevated.

that precedes the beginning, which is *Ḥokhma* (see *Torah Or* 87s). That idea corresponds to what is stated here: that "working deliverance" relates to the revelation of the illumination of the *mazal*, "preserves kindness," which precedes and is the source of *Ḥokhma*.

Unlike revealed *Hokhma* in *Atzilut*, which is *Hokhma* within its own vessel, illuminating and revealed, it is a higher, hidden level, and it constitutes the roots of the revealed *Hokhma*. Like the will, it is a sort of inclination of the soul itself toward the direction of *Hokhma*, etc. (as explained above). This supernal will, which together with the hidden *Hokhma* penetrates into our world, can grant atonement even for intentional sins and can reach lower than the husk of *noga*.

Just as hidden *Hokhma* is the source of revealed *Hokhma*, so is it the source of the refinings that revealed *Hokhma* brings about ("with wisdom – *Hokhma* – they are refined").

Here the author of the *Tanya* is speaking about the source of the refinings. Thus, the text here is not only speaking about refinings that affect the husk of *noga* and human errors, and which are generated by revealed *Hokhma*. When revealed *Hokhma* sees matters as they need to be – meaning, as they truly are – then good is refined from evil and the sparks of holiness from among the husks. But the letter here is speaking of a refining that reaches down to a level lower than *noga*, to intentional sins that exist in the realm of the three impure husks. That requires the power of the source of refinings, which is in hidden *Hokhma*. The power to refine in the source of revealed *Hokhma* is the light of *Ein Sof* in *Hokhma*, to which holiness clings and from which the husk flees. This is not only an intellectual refining, which distinguishes between good and evil, but an intrinsic refining. The essence of the soul is revealed, and as a result of the uncovering of the light of *Ein Sof* in the soul, matters are refined automatically. It is the source of the revealed intellect's ability to refine. The intellect, which distinguishes, sees, compares, weighs, and knows, receives its power to make determinations – between pure and impure, between husk and holiness, and so forth – from the transcendent source, from the source of the refinings, which exists in hidden *Hokhma*.

וְאִתְהַפְּכָא חֲשׁוֹכָא דִּשְׁבִירַת הַכֵּלִים לִנְהוֹרָא דְּעוֹלָם הַתִּיקוּן
and the darkness of the shattering of the vessels is transformed into the light of the world of rectification.

That is the purpose of the refining.

This deep refining is brought about through the purifying waters of the red heifer and the passing away of the tzaddikim. It is the fundamental refining of the roots of evil and concealment, which are embedded in the shattering of the vessels. That shattering occurred, in a sense, even before the world was created, before man was created in it, and before he sinned. That shattering of the vessels cannot be explained in terms of the logic of the world and its wisdom, but only in terms of the roots prior to its existence. The rectification that now occurs not only affects the darkness of the shattered vessels, by diminishing or illuminating it. Rather, it transforms the darkness itself into light. Light now comes from where darkness had come,

This light that comes from the dark is the light of the world of rectification. The shattering of the vessels brought darkness into this world. Our work only removes the dark, so that the world can at best return in specific ways to the reality prior to the shattering of the vessels. But the transformation of the dark to light is the refining of the purpose of everything. Certainly, the entire descent wasn't only for the sake of returning to the starting point. Rather, it was in order to reveal the ascent within the descent itself: to reveal the light in the dark and the rectification in the *tohu*, the chaos. Only when that which was dark is transformed to light and that which was hidden is revealed is the full meaning of the rectification, which is higher than the dark and the light, revealed.

Until this point, the author of the *Tanya* has discussed the depth of the rectification and atonement that are brought about either via the red heifer or, in a more abstract and encompassing way, by the *histalkut* of the tzaddikim.

מַה שֶּׁאֵין כֵּן בַּקָּרְבָּנוֹת שֶׁעַל גַּבֵּי הַמִּזְבֵּחַ שֶׁאֵינָן מְכַפְּרִים אֶלָּא עַל הַשְּׁגָגוֹת, שֶׁהֵן מֵהִתְגַּבְּרוּת נֶפֶשׁ הַבַּהֲמִית שֶׁמְּנוֹגַהּ, כְּמוֹ שֶׁכָּתוּב בְּלִקּוּטֵי תּוֹרָה פָּרָשַׁת וַיִּקְרָא

That is not the case with the offerings brought **upon the altar. They atone only for** people's **unwitting sins, which** result **from the strengthening of the animal soul,** which comes from *noga*, **as is written in** the Arizal's *Likkutei Torah, Parashat Vayikra.*

For instance, the sin offering only atones for unwitting transgressions. These sins result from the strengthening of the animal soul, which comes from the husk of *noga* and not from the impure husks, which are below *noga*.

A person sins unwittingly not because he intended to do so, but because he was forgetful, he was not paying attention. At that time, his animal soul gained ascendancy over his divine soul. As explained in *Likkutei Amarim* (chap. 9 and elsewhere),[31] these two souls battle constantly within a person for control of the "small city" – the person's body, senses, thoughts, and so forth. When the divine soul gains strength, when it is the one that thinks, feels, recognizes, and so forth, the person is not forgetful and his mind is not distracted. But when the animal soul gains strength and the person is living on the plane of the life and activity of this world, he is liable to cease paying attention.

An unwitting transgression may be rectified by the offerings on the altar. That is to say, there is a way of rectifying such a sin in accordance with the Torah. There is no need to go outside the Torah, to arouse that which is beyond the laws of the Torah, as it were, because the Torah itself, which delineates the sin, provides the way to rectify it. The unwitting sin is the husk of *noga*, the husk that possesses light, which makes it possible for the Torah to grant atonement for it. In contrast, the law of the Torah does not provide a way to rectify intentional sins, forbidden acts.

It is true that there is repentance, which penetrates beyond everything that is written in the Torah, beyond both unwitting and intentional acts, and that nothing supersedes repentance. But a person must engage in repentance from below to above. Here, however, the text is speaking about another facet, one that is not personal: of rectification and atonement for the "sin of the generation" – something that the tzaddik performs on behalf of the people of his generation, similar to an illumination that comes from above and similar to the red heifer, which after all is also a commandment written in the Torah.

---

31. This is apparently referring to *Ta'amei HaMitzvot* there., s.v. *mitzvot al kol korbanekha takriv melaḥ*. And it is said there that the turbidity of man's animal soul causes him to sin (unwittingly). Therefore, when a person sins, he offers the soul of the animal, because the animal soul is what caused him to sin. And a fire descends from above and burns his sins.

וְלָכֵן נִסְמְכָה לְפָרָשַׁת פָּרָה דַּוְקָא
מַה פָּרָה וכו' וּבַיַּלְקוּט פָּרָשַׁת
שְׁמִינִי הֵגִיהַּ 'מֵי חַטָּאת וכו'"

Therefore, the passage about Miriam's death **is placed adjacent to the passage of the heifer specifically.** As the Midrash says, "**Just as the heifer** grants atonement…" **And** *Yalkut, Parashat Shemini,* **revises** the text from "the heifer grants atonement" to "**the waters of purification** grant atonement…"

The passage in the Torah about the death of Miriam, which indicates that the death of a tzaddik grants atonement for an intentional sin and a forbidden act, which derives from the three impure husks, is placed adjacent to the passage of the red heifer, which purifies a person from the impurity that comes from contact with a corpse, which too comes from the three impure husks. In the language of the Talmud: "Just as the heifer grants atonement, so too the death of the tzaddikim grants atonement…."

"*Yalkut, Parashat Shemini,* revises" the text from "the heifer grants atonement" to "the waters of purification" grant atonement.[32] Why does the author of the *Tanya* cite this textual variant? One may say that his intent is to transfer the emphasis from the heifer and its ashes to the water – which is to say, from the elevation to the drawing down.[33] As explained earlier, the aspect of the red heifer ceremony that is similar to the passing away of the tzaddik is not the elevation from below but the drawing down from above – not the heifer that is burned to ash but the waters that grant purification to those made impure by contact with the dead. The function of the waters is similar to the drawing down of masculine waters from the *mazal*, the rectifying factor, of "and

32. This variant does not appear in our texts. In the *Yalkut* as we have it, the text states, "Just as the ash of the heifer grants atonement…" (*Parashat Shemini, remez* 525). And that is what appears in *Midrash Rabba* and *Tanḥuma*. And this requires further study.
33. As explained at length in *Likkutei Torah, Parashat Ḥukat* (56a and onward), the concept related to the commandment of the red heifer is that of "running and returning," of raising and drawing down.

preserves kindness," which is drawn down when the tzaddik passes away to grant atonement for the sin of the generation.[34]

This second letter of consolation is very different from the first. It lacks the personal, emotional connection, with its sense of loss and search for a continued connection, which were principal elements of the previous letter. The consolation that the present letter provides is not based on the idea that the connection with the departed tzaddik still exists and that essentially, he is still with us. Nevertheless, there is a common denominator binding the two letters: the idea that the tzaddik's *histalkut* is not a fall; it is not death and separation. On the contrary, it is an ascent and unification, and even a way of sharing with others the illumination of eternal life. The previous letter told the Hasidim that their connection with the tzaddik still continued and that it could – although in a different way – be closer, deeper, and more attached than it had been when he was alive. In this letter, the relationship to the tzaddik who has passed away is experienced in a less personal and experiential way. Precisely for this reason, it can address the non-personal aspect of the tzaddik's *histalkut*. This non-personal aspect extends to the widest possible degree. The tzaddik's *histalkut* has meaning beyond what his Hasidim need or are able to undertake. It relates to the needs of the entirety of Israel, including even those who are unaware, those who are in absolute darkness, in a place that receives no light from the Torah and the living tzaddikim. That which the author of the *Tanya* refers to in this letter as "the sin of the generation," ranging from the slightest of misdeeds to the depths of the impure husks, is atoned for with the *histalkut* of the tzaddik.

In contrast to the previous letter, which discussed the situation following the tzaddik's *histalkut*, this letter deals with the *histalkut* itself. At that juncture, the tzaddik's entire life is refined: his thoughts, his deeds, and in particular his soul's dedication, which in his lifetime had no limit and no vessel and which is now liberated with an eruption that shakes all the worlds. This elevation of the personal infinite fractures the barriers of the worlds and then proceeds all the way downward from the transcendent *Ein Sof* to every world, and to each world's spirit

---

34. See also *Shiurim BeSefer HaTanya*.

and intellect. It floods over the barriers of the dark husk, within which the world does not shine, and provides an opportunity for the person who has already lost all his opportunities.

Does this provide consolation? Perhaps not for the Hasidim; therefore, in the previous letter addressed to them, the author of the *Tanya* discussed other things. But for Rabbi Levi Yitzḥak of Berditchev, this letter from the author of the *Tanya*, speaking as colleague to colleague and rebbe to rebbe, does offer consolation.

Although the author of the *Tanya* does not console Rabbi Levi Yitzḥak of Berditchev by referring to an ongoing connection with the departed, with the idea that in a sense the evil fact of the death of Rabbi Levi Yitzḥak's son did not occur, he addresses a topic that offers Rabbi Levi Yitzḥak a greater measure of consolation: the granting of atonement for the sin of the generation. The life of the tzaddik, Rabbi Levi Yitzḥak of Berditchev, is not only a spiritual life of faith, love, and fear, but a life of absolute self-negation. In this self-negation, there is no individual, no one who loves and who is connected to God. There is only one factor: the unification of God with the congregation of Israel. And that which grants atonement for the sin of the generation (a sin that separates the generation from God, as the verse states, "Your iniquities have been separating between you and your God" [Isa. 59:2]; see *Iggeret HaTeshuva*, chap. 5) is a consolation beyond time and beyond the individual – and it consoles the tzaddik.

And this also provides a measure of personal consolation, because these exceedingly comprehensive and abstract matters are transmitted via a particular personal path. The purpose of this letter is to bring matters down to the individual: a person who has done such-and-such, who feels this and that. The narrow path leading there is necessarily delineated within a particular time, within a particular way, and for a particular individual. Thus, precisely because the author of the *Tanya* knows the soul of his colleague, Rabbi Levi Yitzḥak of Berditchev, he touches on the general point. But he also describes the path of that general point, because that is what will provide personal consolation to Rabbi Levi Yitzḥak.

And the core of the message of consolation of the author of the *Tanya* is that nothing is lost. Even if the body is lost, its meaning and significance are not. The departed tzaddik, Rabbi Levi Yitzḥak's son, still lives on in everything relating to him: his deeds, his character, and his path, the essential point to which he dedicated himself his entire life, the path and the means by which atonement is now granted for the sin of the generation.

Epistle 29

THIS EPISTLE IS ONE OF SEVERAL THAT WERE APPAR-
ently initially penned as explanations of and discourses on
Hasidism. It discusses a topic that is addressed by several of
the other epistles as well: Studying the *halakhot* of the Oral
Torah. This epistle is not addressing the practical necessity of
knowing how to act (as is the case for Epistle 23, for example),
or the spiritual function of studying *halakha* – that is, the
work of "refinement," *birurim* (as explained in Epistle 26).
Its purpose is to teach one how to act in preparation for the
life and experiences of the Garden of Eden. As explained
in previous epistles, this is related to life in this world: First,
because the Garden of Eden exists here as well, and second,
because the soul prepares itself in this world to attain the
garment in which it must clothe itself in order to attain the
divine delight of the Garden of Eden.

Since studying and clarifying *halakha* is the essence of
the Oral Torah, this epistle addresses another topic as well
(one that the author of the *Tanya* has already discussed at
great length in *Iggeret HaKodesh*): the relationship between
the Written Torah and the Oral Torah, and in particular
the supreme importance of the Oral Torah, which reveals
everything that cannot be disclosed in the Written Torah.

As is common in many hasidic teachings, the epistle
quotes relevant sources from Scripture and the Talmud,
before raising a difficulty with regard to their meaning,
which leads to a discussion that forms the basis for the
epistle's message.

19 Ḥeshvan

18 Ḥeshvan
(leap year)

"אֵשֶׁת חַיִל עֲטֶרֶת בַּעְלָהּ כו'"   "A woman of valor is the crown of her

(משלי יב,ד)   husband …" (Prov. 12:4).

The author quotes a verse that will serve as a motto for the entire teaching.

According to kabbalistic writings, this verse is describing the relationship between *Malkhut* and the *sefirot* above it. The "woman of valor" is the receptive *Malkhut*, while "her husband" refers to the *sefirot* that pour abundance down to her. The verse teaches that *Malkhut* may also be viewed as above the other *sefirot*. In that configuration, *Malkhut* is the coronet, the crown, which bestows upon the other *sefirot*. Although this configuration is hidden at present, it exists in certain aspects of reality, and in the messianic future it will be the revealed reality in which we will live.

There are many facets to the relationship between *Malkhut* (the "woman of valor") and the other *sefirot*. In this epistle, *Malkhut* corresponds to the Oral Torah, in which the *halakhot* are clarified and studied, whereas the other *sefirot* ("her husband") correspond to the Written Torah. As will be explained, when we study the *halakhot* of the Oral Torah, the messianic configuration of the *sefirot*, in which the "woman of valor is the crown of her husband," already exists.

אִיתָא בַּגְּמָרָא פֶּרֶק ד' דִּמְגִילָה   It says in the Talmud, chapter 4 of

(כח,ב): וּדְאִשְׁתַּמֵּשׁ בְּתַגָּא חֲלָף   *Megilla* (28b): The teaching in *Avot*

כו' זֶה הַמִּשְׁתַּמֵּשׁ בְּמִי שֶׁשּׁוֹנֶה   5 that "a person who makes use of

הֲלָכוֹת, כִּתְרָהּ שֶׁל תּוֹרָה כו'   the diadem will pass away…" applies to "a person who allows himself to be served by someone who studies *halakhot*, which are the crown of the Torah…."

The talmudic passage reads, more fully:

We learned in a mishna (*Avot* 1:13): "A person who makes use of the diadem will pass away." Reish Lakish explains: This is a person who [allows himself to be] served by someone who studies *halakhot*, which are the crown of the Torah.[1]

---

1. The phrase "the crown of the Torah" does not appear in the glosses of the *Baḥ*

We see from this that the *halakhot* are called "a diadem" and "the crown of the Torah."[2]

תָּנָא דְּבֵי אֵלִיָּהוּ כָּל הַשּׁוֹנֶה הֲלָכוֹת מוּבְטָח לוֹ כו׳

This talmudic passage continues, "**The Academy of Elijah taught: Whoever studies *halakhot* is assured** of a share in the World to Come…"

The emphasis in this source[3] is on studying *halakhot*, rather than other topics of the Torah.

וְצָרִיךְ לְהָבִין, לָמָּה נִקְרְאוּ הַהֲלָכוֹת בְּשֵׁם תָּגָא וְכִתְרָה שֶׁל תּוֹרָה?

Now, one must understand: Why are the *halakhot* referred to as a "diadem" and "the crown of the Torah"?

In other words, why does their name imply that they are loftier than every other part of the Torah, like a crown upon the head, when they apparently deal with the lowest matters in the material world of action?

וְגַם לָמָּה הַשּׁוֹנֶה הֲלָכוֹת דַּוְקָא מוּבְטָח לוֹ כו׳, וְלֹא שְׁאָר דִּבְרֵי תּוֹרָה?

Also, why is it particularly a person who studies *halakhot* who is "assured…," and not someone who studies other areas of Torah?

(see *HaLekaḥ VeHalibbuv; Lessons in Tanya*). Nevertheless, the author of the *Tanya* includes them, as in our printed editions of the Talmud.

2. The Talmud goes on to relate that Reish Lakish asked the man if he had read the Written Torah. The man replied affirmatively, and Reish Lakish continued accepting his service. Reish Lakish then asked him if he had studied Mishna, which constitutes the laws of the Oral Torah. When the man again answered in the affirmative, Reish Lakish no longer wished to be served by him.

3. *Tanna deVei Eliyahu Zuta*, 2; see also *Nidda* 73a, Jerusalem Talmud, *Megilla* 1:5. This passage is included in the daily prayer service (in the passage beginning *Ein Kelokeinu*). For a commentary on it, see *Likkutei Torah*, Song 29d.

There is no difference in the absolute value of the different parts of the Torah: they are all God's wisdom, which is enclothed in different topics and areas. Thus, there is no difference between one verse and another, between "Timna was a concubine" (Gen. 36:12) and "Hear O Israel etc." (Deut. 6:4), because "everything was given from the mouth of the Almighty."[4]

וְכֵן לְהָבִין מַאֲמַר רַבּוֹתֵינוּ ז"ל בְּפֶרֶק י"א דִּמְנָחוֹת (צט,ב): אֲפִילוּ לֹא שָׁנָה אָדָם אֶלָּא פֶּרֶק אֶחָד שַׁחֲרִית כו', יָצָא יְדֵי חוֹבָה

Furthermore, one must **understand the statement of our Rabbis** in chapter 11 of *Menaḥot* (99b) that **"even if a person only studied one chapter in the morning** and one chapter in the evening…, **he has fulfilled his obligation** to learn Torah."

As the Talmud explains, this statement refers to studying a chapter of Mishna, which is essentially a summary of the halakhic decisions of the Oral Torah. Thus, although the commandment to learn Torah applies all day and all night – as the verse states: "This book of the Torah shall not depart from your mouth, and you shall ponder it day and night" (Josh. 1:8) – if a person cannot do that, it is enough if he studies one chapter of Mishna in the day and one at night. The difficulty with this source is as follows:

וְלָמָּה אֵינוֹ יוֹצֵא יְדֵי חוֹבָה בִּשְׁאָר דִּבְרֵי תּוֹרָה?

Why doesn't a person **fulfill** his obligation by studying **other parts of the Torah** as well?

Not only is *halakha* accorded a status superior to that of other areas of the Torah, and not only is one who studies it granted a greater reward, but it is only when a person studies *halakha* that he fulfills his obligation to study Torah. This despite the fact that every other area of the Torah is also genuinely Torah.

---

4. Rambam's *Commentary on the Mishna, Perek Ḥelek* (*Sanhedrin*, chap. 10) in the eighth of the Thirteen Principles of Faith, quoted in *Likkutei Torah*, Lev. 5b, and several hasidic sources. See also *Sanhedrin* 99b and Rashi there, and Rashi on Deut. 32:47, and elsewhere.

A simple explanation is that *halakha*, which summarizes how a person must act, is the distillation of the identity of the Torah. It is inclusive in a way that other parts of the Torah are not, because it transmits the central import of the Torah. In the ensuing discussion, this epistle will explain more fully why *halakha* is called the crown of the Torah, why it is so meaningful for the World to Come, and why it is revealed specifically through the Oral Torah.

אַךְ מוּדַעַת זֹאת מַה שֶּׁכָּתַב
הָאֲרִ"י ז"ל, שֶׁכָּל אָדָם מִיִּשְׂרָאֵל
צָרִיךְ לָבֹא בְּגִלְגּוּלִים רַבִּים עַד
שֶׁיְּקַיֵּים כָּל תַּרְיַ"ג מִצְוֹת הַתּוֹרָה
בְּמַחֲשָׁבָה דִּיבּוּר וּמַעֲשֶׂה

But it is well known that the Arizal said that every Jew must undergo many incarnations until he will keep all 613 commandments of the Torah in thought, speech, and deed:

An "incarnation" means that the soul returns to this world in another body and lives a different life. The reason for this is as stated here, in order that "he will keep all 613 commandments of the Torah."[5] ☞

MANY INCARNATIONS

☞ Every person must attain perfection, which means that he must keep all of the Torah's 613 commandments, corresponding to the 613 parts of a person's body and soul (365 sinews and 248 organs). No limb of a person's body and soul was created without a purpose, and similarly there is no day in his life that was given to him without a goal. Every limb and every minute in a person's life is designed so that he will observe or participate in the fulfillment of a particular mitzva, until he has kept all 613.

If he lacks a mitzva, he lacks completion. A person who fails to keep a mitzva – whether because he was unwilling or unable to do so – will return for at least one more incarnation, with another consciousness and different abilities, until he ultimately fulfills this requirement.

A person's will and knowledge are not transmitted from one incarnation to the next. Furthermore, one's identity encompasses more than is manifest in a single incarnation. This is similar to the identity of a

---

5. Note of the Lubavitcher Rebbe (printed in *Lessons in Tanya*): "*Sefer HaGilgulim*, chap. 4; *Sha'ar HaGilgulim*, Introduction 11:16. In the Introduction to *Sha'ar HaMitzvot* (and in *Etz Ḥayyim, Sha'ar* 49, chap. 5) he was concise, and therefore one cannot raise a question [regarding any apparent contradiction] from there. See also *Shenei Luḥot HaBerit*, the beginning of *Torah Shebikhtav* (264b and onward)." This idea is mentioned in many other hasidic teachings as well; see e.g., *Torah Or* 16d and 32d; *Likkutei Torah*, Num. 38:4; *Or HaTorah*, Num. section 4, p. 1490.

The reference to "thought, speech, and deed" means that a person utilizes these three garments in which his soul is enclothed, in order to uphold the practical commandments.[6] The soul cannot act in this world without a garment, because it belongs to a higher and more abstract reality. Only when it is clothed in a body and acts upon the body with thought, speech, and deed can it sense this world and act in it. These three garments are not only aspects of the body; they are aspects of the soul itself. The higher, more interior parts of the soul are enclothed in thought, those that turn outward are enclothed in speech, and those that are related to action are enclothed and revealed through deeds. ☞

Some commandments are kept principally through one's thought and intent (such as reciting *Shema* and praying, which one must recite with intent in order to fulfill his obligation). He keeps some commandments through speech (such as studying Torah), while others he observes through action.[7] Alternatively, it can be said that each commandment involves these three garments: The "thought" is a person's intent while performing the commandment; the "speech" is his study of the commandment; and the "deed" is his actual observance of the commandment.

At any rate, since the soul can keep the commandments only by being enclothed in these three garments, and since no single incarnation

nation, which binds together many people into a single unity. Likewise, an individual's incarnations bind together several lives and bodies that are a single being, until that being completes its existential purpose.

THE THOUGHT, SPEECH, AND DEED OF THE DIVINE SOUL

☞ A distinction may be made between the garments of the animal soul and the garments of the divine soul (see *Likkutei Amarim*, chap. 4). This distinction relates to what a person thinks, says, and does. The animal soul is enclothed in matters of this world, whereas the divine soul is enclothed in matters pertaining to God and His service Him by means of the Torah and the commandments. According-ly, it can be said that the part of a person that is reincarnated in order to complete the observance of the 613 commandments is his divine soul, whereas his animal soul breaks apart with the death of an incarnation, and remains (in a sense like the dead body) only in the memories of the divine soul regarding the ways in which it affected the life and body of that incarnation.

6. See *Likkutei Amarim*, 4.
7. See *Likkutei Torah, Bemidbar* 38d.

can observe them all (because some commandments relate only to women, others to men alone, yet others solely to priests, and so forth, and also because conditions change, and sometimes the soul fails to do what it was supposed to do), the soul must return to another life in a different body.[8]

לְהַשְׁלִים לְבוּשֵׁי נַפְשׁוֹ, וּלְתַקְּנָם "To complete the garments of his
שֶׁלֹּא יְהֵא לְבוּשָׁא דְחָסְרָא כו' soul and to rectify them so that no garment will be missing with respect to any of his limbs.

Before a person has kept all 613 commandments, some garments of his soul are unrectified, with others are missing. If the "garments" of a person's thoughts, speech, and actions are not garments of mitzvot, or if those garments of mitzvot are flawed, he must attend to them. If he fails to so in one incarnation, he will have to complete the mission in another.

When a garment is missing, it is as though the person is blemished. Without that garment, the spiritual limb[9] with which that garment is associated has no meaning. The soul thinks, feels, and acts only through the garment. If the garment is not there, the soul is incomplete; it lacks a spiritual hand or foot, the ability to love or understand, and so forth.

לְבַד מִצְוֹת הַתְּלוּיוֹת בַּמֶּלֶךְ שֶׁהוּא "This is with the exception of the
מוֹצִיא כָּל יִשְׂרָאֵל כִּי הוּא כְּלָלוּת commandments unique to and
כּוּלָם כו' incumbent upon the king, who fulfills the obligation of all Israel in performing those mitzvot, because he is the totality of them all …

---

8. A person might keep a mitzva with his *nefesh* but not with his body, with his *ruah* rather than with his *neshama*, with speech and not with deed, and so forth. Furthermore, a person can sometimes keep a mitzva by substituting one activity for another. Thus, the Sages state that a person who studies the laws of the burnt offering is considered as though he has actually brought a burnt offering (end of *Menahot*). See also *Shulhan Arukh HaRav, Orah Hayyim* 1:13 and onward (in the first edition; 1:9, and in the later edition, ibid. 9); *Likkutei Torah*, Num. 57a, 68a; see also *Likkutei Sihot*, vol. 18, p. 413).

9. See *Zohar* 1:224a.

An exception to this rule is the unique set of commandments that are incumbent upon a king. This is not only because it is impossible for everyone to be king (for the same applies to those commandments specific to the priests, and the High Priest in particular), but also because the king, as the head of the people, embodies the entire nation of Israel.[10] Accordingly, when he keeps these commandments, it is as though everyone is doing so.

וְהַטַּעַם הוּא, כְּדֵי לְהַלְבִּישׁ כָּל תַּרְיַ"ג בְּחִינוֹת וְכֹחוֹת שֶׁבְּנַפְשׁוֹ אַחַת מֵהֵנָּה לֹא נֶעְדָּרָה כו'

"**The reason** that a person must have the garments of all 613 commandments **is so that** he will **clothe all 613 aspects and faculties of his soul, and then not a single one of them will be missing…**"

If even a single faculty or aspect in a person's soul is unclothed, that constitutes a blemish. A person's limbs and faculties are not a collection of discrete entities but an organic, integrated structure. A blemish in any one of them is a blemish in the whole and in all the other ones.

וּבֵיאוּר עִנְיַן הַכְרֵחַ וְצֹרֶךְ לְבוּשִׁים אֵלּוּ מְבוֹאָר בַּזֹּהַר וּמוּבָן לְכָל מַשְׂכִּיל

An explanation of the necessity for and indispensability of these garments is given in the *Zohar*, and can be understood by every intelligent person.

The author of the *Tanya* returns to the question of why the soul needs these garments.

Although the ideas he presents are based on kabbalistic teachings from the *Zohar*,[11] in essence they are rational, and every intelligent person who understands something about the nature of man and the world of God can comprehend them.

כִּי לִהְיוֹת שֶׁנֶּפֶשׁ רוּחַ וּנְשָׁמָה שֶׁבָּאָדָם הֵן בְּחִינוֹת נִבְרָאִים

It is **because the *nefesh*, *ruaḥ*, and *neshama* in man are created entities,**

10. See the Lubavitcher Rebbe's notes here, in *Lessons in Tanya*.
11. *Zohar* 2:210b and 229b.

Not only is a person's body a created entity, but his soul is as well. This is true not only of the lowly part of his soul – the *nefesh*, which is enclothed in the body and belongs to the physical world – but even of the higher parts of his soul, the *ruaḥ* and *neshama*, which relate to the abstract, spiritual worlds. ☞

THE *NEFESH*, *RUAḤ*, AND *NESHAMA* ARE CREATED ENTITIES

☞ To be created means to be an "entity" [*yesh*] and not a "nothingness" [*ayin*], a being with its own parameters, apparently separate from the indefinable and incomprehensible "nothing." Our most basic concept of reality is bipolar: The created and the Creator; the world and the Divine. The Creator is not only the incomprehensible "nothing." He is also all of His powers through which He acts and affects creation: *Ḥokhma, Bina, Ḥesed, Gevura*, and all of the other *sefirot* of the world of *Atzilut*. As for created existence, it is not merely physical reality; it is the entire breadth of existence up to the higher level that receives from the Divine and that defines itself as a receiving entity. Therefore, the basis of a created being's awareness is that it is an independent entity, although it can also be aware that it receives everything from the Divine, and that its very separateness from God comes from God Himself.

However, the statement here that the human soul is created is puzzling, because it is often stated that the soul is "a divine portion from above" (*Likkutei Amarim*, 2). Not only at its root but on every level, it is truly a portion of divinity, with a divine identity. Yet, as stated here, and in keeping with every person's sense of himself, it a defined and limited entity, a part of the overall creation. Accordingly, it can be said that there is a complex parameter here that goes beyond the simplistic dichotomy of Creator and created being. Although

the soul is created, it is not like other created beings. It is also an aspect of divinity. In the language of the hasidic texts (see *Hemshekh Samekh Vav*, 5666, pp. 459, 470), it is as though divinity has been made into a created being. The soul is not only the power and vitality of divinity in a created being, but it is like a created being in the divine itself. This is because the soul is actually a portion of divinity that can also relate to the created world. In other words, the soul is the divine enclothed. It is not only a divine influence, action, and even power, but the divine essence enclothed in created reality. Therefore, in many ways a person thinks and feels like his soul. However, he can also transcend that, and unite with the Divine.

Every person may on occasion sense this, that his soul runs deeper than the reality in which he lives. He is aware that everything around him serves only as an instrument and tool for his soul. This awareness is an expression of the divine nature within him, which is always deeper than anything else.

In conclusion, the soul is more internal than everything else because it contains the divine intent. The soul is the purpose of all creation. It is the divine will and delight that are more internal than everything, and the rest of creation is merely a vehicle for the soul. Nevertheless, it is precisely for this reason that the soul is enclothed in creation (so much so that it engages in physical activity), because it is only by feel-

וְאִי אֶפְשָׁר לְשׁוּם נִבְרָא לְהַשִּׂיג
שׁוּם הַשָּׂגָה בַּבּוֹרֵא וְיוֹצֵר הַכֹּל
אֵין סוֹף בָּרוּךְ הוּא

and it is impossible for any created entity to attain any comprehension of the Creator and Maker of all, *Ein Sof*, blessed be He.

The definition of creation is existence out of nothingness. A created being is a tangible entity limited by its conception of itself and its environment, whereas the Creator, who stands beyond creation, is "nothingness," and He does not exist within created reality. Therefore, by definition a created being cannot comprehend the Creator.

The Creator is the Maker of everything. There is a difference between "Maker" and "Creator." A maker (including a person who makes things in his world) is a being who combines entities – stones, materials, letters – in new permutations. He does not fashion existence out of nothingness, because he uses the materials at his disposal. Nor does he make everything, because there is always something in existence that he did not make. There is only One who is "the Maker of everything," of all that exists: The Creator Himself.

Kabbalistic literature calls God Himself "*Ein Sof* [the Infinite One], blessed be He." The Creator, who is one, created from nothing [*ayin*] not only the entire limited creation, but finiteness itself; not only that which exists in time and space, and so forth, but time and space themselves. Accordingly, from the perspective of the worlds, the most far-reaching appellation for God as a Being entirely separate from creation, a designation that negates any limitation at all, any dependence of the Creator on the created, is *Ein Sof*. ☞

ing itself a created entity and through its work in a created reality, created by God, that it can serve as the self-expression of the Divine. It could not do so in its state preceding the creation of the world, before its descent to become a created entity.

Nevertheless, at the time when the soul is living in the body and operating in this world, it senses itself as a created being.

THE *EIN SOF* IN RELATION TO CREATION

☞ The important point is that there can be no connection between the finite and infinite. As much as the finite grows, it will never be infinite. Similarly, no matter how much as the infinite contracts, it will never be finite. For instance, take the infinite sequence of natural numbers. If only the even numbers are chosen or only one from each thousand, the total will still remain infinite.

וְגַם אַחֲרֵי אֲשֶׁר הֵאִיר ה' מֵאוֹרוֹ יִתְבָּרֵךְ, וְהֶאֱצִיל בִּבְחִינַת הִשְׁתַּלְשְׁלוּת מַדְרֵגוֹת רַבּוֹת, מַדְרֵגָה אַחַר מַדְרֵגָה

And even after God, may He be blessed, has illuminated from His light and emanated an unfolding of numerous descending levels, level after level,

There can be no conception of the *Ein Sof* Himself. Moreover, even an illumination from *Ein Sof* is beyond conception. The fact that, as stated here, this illumination comes "after" means that it has some relationship to the existence of time, which is an integral part of the creation of the world. Consequently, it is no longer *Ein Sof* Himself, who is entirely separate from creation, but an illumination of *Ein Sof* upon the created worlds, which relates to them.

Yet that illumination is not a creation but an emanation, which is a type of transmission. Although it is immeasurably distant and separate from the Emanator, the illumination is still with Him, in His realm. In relation to *Ein Sof*, this "world of emanation" is not created, not the creation of existence out of nothingness. Rather, it still partakes of the nature of the Emanator, and is as infinite as He is.

Yet this emanation from *Ein Sof*, from His perspective, is an unmeasurable descent and contraction: A descent to the lowest end imaginable, and again another descent, and yet another and another. ☞

NUMEROUS LEVELS, LEVEL AFTER LEVEL

☞ This can be compared to someone attempting to see infinitely far away, trying as much as possible to imagine the immeasurable. Then, having reached that furthest extent, he tries again to think beyond the infinity he had just imagined. And he does this repeatedly. The conception presented here of a great distance divided into discrete stations is not only a way to present something that will enable us to appreciate distances that are far beyond our comprehension. It is in fact a true description of those distances. A spiritual distance is not like a physical distance of meters or light years, but a distance that is measured by the breadth of one's comprehension and awareness. How large is the spiritual realm? It is as large as the area encompassed by a person's awareness. There is a realm of matters grasped by a child's thought and awareness; there is a larger realm that is incorporated into the awareness of an adult; and there are matters that human thought as a whole can comprehend and contemplate, which is an even greater spiritual expanse.

The concept of many levels makes it possible for a finite being to imagine the infinite. This conception begins with the ultimate extent of what a person can com-

בִּבְחִינוֹת צִמְצוּמִים עֲצוּמִים וּלְבוּשִׁים
רַבִּים וַעֲצוּמִים הַיְדוּעִים לְיוֹדְעֵי חֵן

on the level of immense contractions and numerous, immense garments that are known to those initiated in the esoteric wisdom of Kabbala,

This contraction is a type of garment, not a physical garment, which is like a different body in relation to the enclothed light, but a garment that is like a dimmer, more external light. A contraction is a part, and as a part it is surrounded by something that it is not, something whose existence is recognized but whose nature is not known. This is comparable to the exteriority of light that clothes the interior.

These supernal levels of the intrinsic contraction of the divine light even before creation, and in a sense even before emanation, are described only in kabbalistic writings, and not even in all of them.[12] ☞

וְנִקְרָאִים בָּאִדְרָא רַבָּה בְּשֵׁם 'שְׂעָרוֹת'
וּכְדִכְתִיב בְּדָנִיֵּאל (ז, ט): "וּשְׂעַר רֵישֵׁיהּ
כַּעֲמַר נְקֵא כו'"

and they are called in the *Idra Rabba* "hairs," as written in Daniel (7:9), "And the hair of His head like pure wool …"

prehend, and then doubles it, again and again. It is possible to speak of the expanse of the concept of the divine, the One that contains everything. However, that description lacks meaning for created beings. It belongs to the unknown, the transcen-

dent reality, in contrast to this pictorial presentation of consecutive stations. Even if these stations are infinitely numerous, they make the descent of the light to the finite realm possible, so that it ultimately becomes comprehensible, even to mortals.

THOSE INITIATED IN THE ESOTERIC WISDOM

☞ The definition of a person who knows the esoteric wisdom is not one who studies kabbalistic writings, but someone who has an intrinsic understanding of these ideas (see *Ḥagiga* 11b). Studying esoteric wisdom in general, and certainly these difficult topics, requires more than intellectual understanding. One's soul must be refined

and able to separate itself from this world and relate to a reality beyond this world – to that reality's experience and concepts. We can only try to express aspects of that reality by using ideas and words borrowed from our world. Only someone who has an inner image of what these words are referring to can understand them properly.

---

12. For example, in the entire *Tanya* these concepts are mentioned only by way of allusion, as is the case here, or in a gloss, such as in *Sha'ar HaYiḥud VeHa'emuna*, 9.

The *Idra Rabba* is part of the *Zohar* (which appears in our editions in *Parashat Naso*). "*Idra*" means "gathering," and it alludes to an occasion when Rabbi Shimon bar Yoḥai gathered his select students and revealed exceptionally lofty secrets to them.[13] In the *Idra Rabba*,[14] the elevated levels and contractions discussed here are referred to as "hairs."

The verse from Daniel refers to a particularly high level of the revelation of the divine (*Atik Yomin*). Of course, this "hair" is not something physical but rather a spiritual reality. ☞

אַף עַל פִּי כֵן, לֹא יָכְלָה הַנֶּפֶשׁ אוֹ   **nevertheless, neither** *nefesh* **nor** *ruaḥ*
הָרוּחַ וּנְשָׁמָה, לְמִסְבַּל הָאוֹר כִּי   **and** *neshama* **could endure the light.**

THE HAIR OF THE HEAD

☞ Elsewhere (e.g., *Torah Or* 82b, *Likkutei Torah*, Num. 33a and 31a), the author of the *Tanya* discusses the metaphor of hairs at length. In brief (and in relation to the topic discussed here), "hairs" is a way of speaking about contraction and transmission from the divine essence in itself (which lies beyond the comprehension of created beings), so that created beings will be able to relate to the divine. The physical hair emerges from and derives its vitality from the brain in the head. Nevertheless, it is not a part of the brain, not even an offshoot of it, but merely an emanation. At the same time, it is more than a hat on one's head, since it comes from the person himself. This "hair" refers to an illumination. Even if it is an extremely contracted illumination, it is an illumination that is itself divine, not a created entity.

On a more abstract level, the author of the *Tanya* explains elsewhere (see *Likkutei Torah*, Num. 33a and onward) that the content transmitted via the hairs is like meaning conveyed by means of a metaphor. A metaphor is not a direct extension of the original idea, but like an understanding added to the original idea. The original idea and the metaphor are separated by an intellectual-conceptual leap, which is like crossing between two worlds. Nevertheless, a metaphor is not entirely separate from the original meaning. It is an image that places the original meaning in another reality and on a different level. Therefore, one can use another metaphor to explain the original metaphor, and so forth (see e.g., *Torah Or* 11c), because on every level the inner light – the original meaning – that is drawn through the hair expresses itself through another metaphor. At any rate, a metaphor, like hair, is more than a means of transmission from one level to the next: it is a shift from one reality to another, so that it is no longer above a given reality but within it.

---

13. Just as there is an *Idra Rabba*, so is there an *Idra Zuta* ("Small Gathering"), at the end of *Parashat Haʾazinu*, which records Rabbi Shimon bar Yoḥai's final words to his students before he passed away.

14. *Zohar* 3:128b and onward.

טוֹב וּמָתוֹק הָאוֹר וכו' That is because **"the light is good and sweet…"** (cf. Eccles. 11:7).

Despite all the constrictions, this light is truly divine. Accordingly, the levels of the human soul, which are created entities, could not endure it without breaking apart. They could not remain as they were. They are able to endure this light because what they receive is tailored to their level and they possess something of its nature. Otherwise, if the soul reached a state of awareness of delight and wisdom beyond anything that it itself possesses, it would no longer be able to maintain its awareness and feeling, and it would be extinguished – that is, it would leave its state and be unable to return.

This light that the soul cannot endure, in which the soul expires, is the goodness and sweetness of *Ein Sof*. When all the goodness that a person has recognized and all the sweetness that he has felt are nullified because he has attained even the slightest taste of divine existence, this is termed an extinction of the soul.

כְּמוֹ שֶׁכָּתוּב (תהלים כז,ד): "לַחֲזוֹת בְּנֹעַם ה'" לְשׁוֹן נְעִימוּת וַעֲרִיבוּת וּמְתִיקוּת וְתַעֲנוּג עָצוּם לְאֵין קֵץ As the verse states (Ps. 27:4): **"To behold the goodness of the Lord,"** a term signifying **pleasantness, agreeableness, and sweetness, and intense delight without end.**

The "goodness of the Lord" is, as will be explained below, the light that was hidden away for the righteous in the messianic future, a light that is so intensely pleasant, agreeable, and sweet that it cannot be endured in this world.

כְּמוֹ שֶׁכָּתוּב (ישעיה נח,יד): "אָז תִּתְעַנַּג עַל ה'" "וְהִשְׁבִּיעַ בְּצַחְצָחוֹת כו'" (שם פסוק יא), לְשׁוֹן "צִחֵה צָמָא" (שם ה,יג) כְּמוֹ שֶׁכָּתוּב בַּזֹּהַר (חלק ב רי,ב) As Scripture states (Isa. 58:14): **"Then you will delight in the Lord"** and **"He will satisfy** your soul **in drought** [*tzaḥtzaḥot*]…" (Isa. 11), related to **"parched** [*tziḥa*] **with thirst"** (Isa. 5:13), **as written in the** *Zohar* (2:210b).

"Then," in the messianic future, when all present-day reality will change, when the relationship between God and the world will be different and the existence of the world will no longer consist of divine concealment but of divine revelation, "you will delight in the Lord." This phrase can be read as "you will delight *upon* the Lord": A delight that is higher than the name of God. The source of every delight that we are familiar with comes from the name of God, with which He brings our world into being and relates to it. In the messianic future, by contrast, the source of delight will come from God Himself, higher than His Name, in the light of *Ein Sof* that transcends His relationship to the existence of the worlds – from God's own delight, as it were.

"He will satisfy [your soul] in drought."[15] Simply understood, this verse is stating that God will satisfy a person when there will be physical thirst in the land. However, the *Zohar* applies this verse to the revelation of the divine light to the soul, reading *tzaḥ* as "pure." In other words, the soul in this world, which lacks a revelation of the divine, is thirsty for the revelation of purity, the pure divine light that transcends the limitations of the body and this world, the divine light as in the Garden of Eden, the light of the goodness of the Lord and endless agreeableness and sweetness. This is a thirst for an agreeableness and sweetness that have no end, which will always leave the soul thirsty for even more pleasantness and sweetness. ☞

THE GOODNESS OF THE LORD AND *TZAḤTZAḤOT*

☞ In his notes, the Lubavitcher Rebbe cites explanations from hasidic teachings (*Torah Or*, Est. 98b; *Or HaTorah, Shemot*, part 4, p. 1606; see also *Pardes Rimmonim, Sha'ar HaTzaḥtzaḥot*) that the goodness of the Lord and *tzaḥtzaḥot* are an illumination that comes from *Atik Yomin*, which is the interior aspect of *Keter*. The parallel to this level in the soul is its delight, which is its highest and most intrinsic level. It is the root of all of one's faculties and activities. The soul's delight exists beyond functionality, emotion, and intellect, and even beyond the simple will. This delight is not only enjoyment and good feelings, but an

expression of wholeness, of the integration of all parts of one's essence. In the realm of the divine, it is the level that transcends all His manifestations in the worlds and in their relationship to the worlds. The entire realm of *Atzilut*, from *Malkhut* up to *Ḥokhma*, is the revelation of God in relation to the worlds. Yet above that, *Keter* is the divine reality beyond the worlds. Furthermore, there is interiority and exteriority in *Keter* itself. The exteriority, which is *Arikh Anpin*, is the root of emanated existence: It is the supernal will for the creation of beings (in relation to the worlds, which is said to "encompass all worlds"). The interi-

---

15. This translation follows the commentary of the Radak.

וְאֵין בְּכֹחָהּ לְקַבֵּל הַנְּעִימוּת וַעֲרִיבוּת
הַצַּחְצָחוֹת, שֶׁלֹּא תֵּצֵא מִנַּרְתְּקָהּ
וְתִתְבַּטֵּל מִמְּצִיאוּתָהּ כְּנֵר בָּאֲבוּקָה

The soul **does not have the strength to endure the pleasantness and agreeableness of the** *tzaḥtzaḥot* **without exiting its sheath and being nullified out of existence, like a flame** nullified **in a torch,**

The human soul, which is created and limited, lacks the ability to receive the endless pleasantness and agreeableness of the *tzaḥtzaḥot*. The soul's "sheath" is the medium through which it experiences, feels, and acts. It is not only the body and life in this world, but the entire manner in which the soul thinks and feels. If the soul were to experience this light that transcends its sheath, it would leave it and cease to exist.

When a flame is brought close to a torch, the flame is extinguished. This is an ancient metaphor for the nullification of an entity within a totality that transcends it. Just as the small flame is nullified within the larger flame when the boundaries between them are broken, so too the soul is nullified when it undergoes an experience that breaches its boundaries, when it encounters the realm of the awareness and experience that transcends it, like a drop that encounters the sea and like "a flame nullified in a torch."

That is the meaning of the phrase "[the soul] does not have the strength": It does not have the power to maintain its existence, the flow of its consciousness in its reality.

אִם לֹא שֶׁמִּבְּחִינַת אוֹר זֶה עַצְמוֹ
תִּשְׁתַּלְשֵׁל וְתִמָּשֵׁךְ מִמֶּנּוּ אֵיזוֹ הֶאָרָה
מוּעֶטֶת בְּדֶרֶךְ הִשְׁתַּלְשְׁלוּת, מַדְרֵיגָה
אַחַר מַדְרֵגָה בְּצִמְצוּמִים רַבִּים, עַד

were it not for the fact **that from this very light some slight illumination will unfold and be drawn forth by way of unfolding, level after level with numerous**

ority, which relates to the Emanator, is *Atik Yomin* in *Keter*, which is separated [*ne'eteket*] from the existence of the worlds, and resembles God's intrinsic delight in matters such as our mitzvot. This is because a person's will relates to what he desires, whereas the delight relates to the one who experiences the delight. With regard to a person's divine soul, when it is exposed to this supernal level it intrinsically experiences "the goodness of the Lord" with an unlimited delight and sweetness.

שֶׁיִּבָּרֵא מִמֶּנָּה לְבוּשׁ אֶחָד נִבְרָא
מֵעֵין מַהוּת אוֹר זֶה לְהַלְבִּישׁ
הַנֶּפֶשׁ רוּחַ וּנְשָׁמָה. וְדֶרֶךְ לְבוּשׁ
זֶה, שֶׁהוּא מֵעֵין אוֹר זֶה, תּוּכַל
לֵיהָנוֹת מִזִּיו אוֹר זֶה וּלְהַשִּׂיגוֹ,
וְלֹא תִתְבַּטֵּל מִמְּצִיאוּתָהּ

contractions, until a single garment will be created from this contracted light, a created entity with something of the nature of this light's essence, with which to clothe the *nefesh, ruaḥ,* and *neshama.* And through this garment, which has something of the nature of this light, it will be able to delight in and comprehend the radiance of this light, and will not be nullified out of its existence.

The human soul is created and finite, whereas the divine light is infinite, and therefore there is no evident way to join the two. As soon as contact is made between them, either they will not combine or they will do so and the soul will cease to exist. The entire process of reality, as we understand it, is that there will indeed be a connection: People in this world will attain a comprehension of the divine light and delight in it. The author of the *Tanya* therefore refers solely to this second option: How to safeguard the soul so that with its apprehension and experience of the divine it will remain the same – not precisely the same, since it is now comprehending and experiencing new things, but it will at least remain a created soul that is receiving the divine light, while the divine light will remain divine light.

However, these two – the soul and the divine, the created and the infinite – cannot meet either in this world (in which the divine is not revealed) or in the divine existence (which does not have the character of created reality). Therefore, a meeting place is required, a special environment like a garment that is able to contain and express the infinite, divine light on the one hand and the soul on the other. This place, this garment, must partake of the divine, infinite light, because only the infinite can contain infinity, and it must also be a created entity, because it is only in a created place that the soul will not be nullified.

To that end, "some slight illumination" is drawn from the divine light, which descends through many contractions until from it, from numberless possibilities, a single possibility is created, a single garment, which still has something of the nature of that divine light's essence. In other words, the divine light itself, not a vessel that receives the light, devolves and descends repeatedly without any admixture and distortion, until finally the created being attains a deep, direct connection with the divine entity, although that created being still belongs to the created world with its parameters and boundaries.

By way of analogy, if one wishes to convey to a child information that is beyond his intellect and comprehension, he must carve out a kind of "place" or "garment" where the child and the information can coexist. One must tell a story or describe a situation with which the child can identify. For example, if we wish a child to know that wealthy countries exploit weak countries, we can tell him about a boy who has many toys and another boy who has only one old toy. The metaphor is not a different story, but a superficial rendering of the original content. The metaphor must maintain at least some of the original, higher message without inverting or distorting its meaning. Similarly, in order for a human being, who lives in a created and finite world, to receive an illumination, idea, or feeling from *Ein Sof*, he must heed the metaphor and story that He is telling him, by entering into it. This takes work, indeed the labor a lifetime, to align all of one's limbs and faculties to those transcendent dynamics. This is a person's performance of the 613 commandments in this world, which reflect their existence above, and that constitutes a "garment."

וְכִמְשַׁל הָרוֹאֶה בַּשֶּׁמֶשׁ דֶּרֶךְ עֲשָׁשִׁית זַכָּה וּמְאִירָה וכו׳   This is analogous to a person who looks at the sun through a relatively clear and bright lantern glass…,

Here the author of the *Tanya* speaks in terms of a garment that has something of the nature of the light, by using a physical analogy. Our eyes cannot look at the sun, because if they were to see the sun one would go blind. However, one can place a barrier between the eye and sun; neither an entirely opaque barrier, because then what he would see would no longer be the light of the sun, nor an absolutely transparent one, because then the eye would not be able to see. Rather, it must be as though he is looking through a transparent glass (which is in some ways like the light), but which is tinted, so that a portion of the light itself will pass through.

וּכְמוֹ שֶׁכָּתוּב: "וַיָּבֹא מֹשֶׁה בְּתוֹךְ הֶעָנָן and as the verse states, "Moses
וַיַּעַל כו'" (שמות כד,יח) שֶׁנִּתְלַבֵּשׁ בֶּעָנָן, entered into the midst of the
וְעָלָה וְרָאָה דֶּרֶךְ הֶעָנָן וכו', כְּמוֹ שֶׁכָּתַב cloud and went up to the moun-
בַּזֹּהַר חֵלֶק ב' דַּף ר"י וְרכ"ט taintop" (Ex. 24:18). That is, he
was clothed in the cloud, and he
ascended and saw by way of the
cloud ..., as written in the *Zohar*,
2:210 and 229.

The "cloud" that Moses entered in order to ascend to God is the
"garment" referred to here, through which the soul can attain the
light of God.[16] Moses was enclothed in the cloud, and he rose in this
garment up to Mount Sinai, and via the cloud he attained the divine
revelations.

Even Moses, who surpassed every other human being, whose body
was purified to the ultimate degree, could not receive those revelations
without a garment. The function of this garment is not only to help
the weak and limited. Its function is essential for each created being,
at all times and on every level. No matter how high one may be, he
necessarily remains a created being that receives infinite, divine light –
and for that purpose he needs a garment.

וְהִנֵּה אוֹר זֶה, הַגָּנוּז לַצַּדִּיקִים לֶעָתִיד Now this light, which is hidden
לָבוֹא, הַנִּקְרָא בְּשֵׁם: 'נֹעַם ה'' for the righteous in the future
וְ'צַחְצָחוֹת' לְהִתְעַנֵּג עַל ה' time, is called "the pleasantness
of God" and the "*tzahtzahot*" to
delight in God.

The light that the soul attains within this garment is set aside for the
righteous in the messianic future, the time of the resurrection of the
dead. It is called "the pleasantness of God" and *tzahtzahot*, for its

---

16. As explained in the *Zohar* (see below). See also *Torah Or* 16a: In order for
Moses to feed his physical body with spiritual food (like the angels) during the
forty days that he was on Mount Sinai, he had to clothe himself in the cloud.
The "garment" serves to bind two opposites, as clarified here, in order to serve as
an intermediary between them, without either of them losing their parameters.

pleasantness and delight are infinite. Therefore, it is never sated, and the soul constantly thirsts for more. ☞

As stated, the phrase "to delight in God" literally means "to delight *upon* God": To connect oneself to the supernal delight, the interiority of *Keter* that is above the Name of God, and to receive from that level. ☞

וְד' מֵאוֹת עָלְמִין דְּכִסּוּפִין
דְּמִתְעַנְגֵּי בְּהוֹן צַדִּיקַיָּיא כו'
כְּמוֹ שֶׁכָּתוּב: "אַרְבַּע מֵאוֹת
שֶׁקֶל כֶּסֶף כו'" (בראשית
כג,טז)

And it is called **"the four hundred worlds of yearning [*kissufin*]" in which the righteous delight... As the verse states: "Four hundred shekels of silver [*kesef*]"** (Gen. 23:16).

THE FUTURE TIME

☞   The concept of "the future time" relates to the reality that follows this world – either overall, after the cessation of this world at the time of the resurrection, or for the individual soul after its life in this world. This light is revealed only after life in this world, not beforehand. Prior to the existence of the world and the soul's descent into it, the soul – pure though it be – cannot receive from the light of *Ein Sof* Himself, the light of the pleasantness of God and the *tzaḥtzaḥot*, in order to take delight in God. Until its descent into this world, it is merely a soul. True, it is on a very high level, but still it is a created being. Only after it has taken on the garb of a body and the life of this world can it receive the garment with which it rises beyond its initial place and connects to and receives from the light of *Ein Sof* Himself, uniting with the Divine on the level of intrinsic delight. Before the soul's descent to the world, even if it studies the entire Torah (as our Sages state in *Nidda* 30b, with respect to a fetus in its mother's womb), it is not truly enclothed in these ideas; it only thinks about them and understands that they exist. Only in this world does the soul clothe itself in matters of Torah: What it means to be enslaved in and then leave Egypt; what it means to observe negative commandments by overcoming the evil inclination; what it means to give charity with money that one toiled to earn; what it means to exert oneself in Torah study, and how to understand the Torah. The garment for the soul is forged from all of this, the garment that binds the soul to *Ein Sof*.

UPON GOD

☞   The name here is the name *Havaya* (the Tetragrammaton). It represents the world of *Atzilut* and the overall way that the Divine relates to the worlds. To delight *upon* the name is higher than all of that; higher than this logic, and even higher than the will that desires it. It relates solely to the intrinsic divine delight, to God's delight within Himself, as it were. As explained earlier, this delight is even deeper than will, because in a sense it is the delight that fulfills the will. Thus, delight always occurs in the innermost realm, to a greater depth than any other relationship and feeling. Accordingly, as it were, above the name.

These four hundred worlds of yearning are four hundred[17] forms of delight in and yearning for the light of *Ein Sof*, which the tzaddikim will attain in the messianic future (*Zohar* 1:123b; *Idra Zuta* 288a and elsewhere; see also *Torah Or* 16a and elsewhere), each one in keeping with his measure and service. These constantly yearn and rise.

The Hebrew word for "silver," *kesef*, is related to the word for "yearning," *kissufin*.[18] The four hundred silver shekels that Abraham (who exemplifies the trait of kindness and abundant generosity) paid to Ephron for the Cave of Makhpela are the supernal illumination of these four hundred worlds of yearning. The source of this illumination is in *Atika Kaddisha*, the interiority of *Keter*, the intrinsic divine delight that draws forth to the essence of a person's soul, which will be revealed in the righteous in the messianic future. These shekels are said to be "ready currency" (Gen. 23:16) because they pass directly from the divine essence above the worlds and the created beings, from the level that encompasses all worlds. For now, they are drawn down to Ephron in order to effect spiritual refinements so that they may later be brought out from him with an added blessing. At present, they are not in the world as "worlds of yearning" but as silver shekels. When they will be refined and elevated, they will be turned into a "garment" that can receive the four hundred worlds of yearning. In the meantime however, they have descended even further, into the husks, becoming the four hundred men of Esau (Gen. 32:7). In the future, when all the refinements will have been completed and the universal reward will be revealed, the four hundred levels will be revealed as supernal worlds of yearning, as the four hundred types of yearning in which the righteous will take delight. ☞

FOUR HUNDRED SHEKELS OF SILVER

☞ These four hundred worlds of yearning exist not only in the messianic future but even here and now. What will occur in the messianic future will be the revelation of the pleasantness of God as the worlds of yearning. At present, this pleasantness of God exists in our world as "four hundred shekels of silver" and even as the "four

---

17. Various explanations are given for why there are four hundred. See *Zohar* 1:123b and *Peri Tzaddik* on *Parashat Shekalim* (there are four worlds, in each of which are ten *sefirot*, and each *sefira* is in turn comprised of ten *sefirot*).

18. See *Zohar* 3:128a and 288a. See also *Torah Or* 24a.

הִנֵּה יֵשׁ בּוֹ מַעֲלוֹת וּמַדְרֵגוֹת This light **has a very great many quali-**
רַבּוֹת מְאֹד, גָּבוֹהַ מֵעַל גָּבוֹהַ **ties and levels, rising ever higher.**

This light is much higher than our words and concepts, not just by
one level but by a great many levels. "High" is what we comprehend as
high; "ever higher" surpasses by many levels even the highest that we
can comprehend. Nevertheless, when we say that this light has many
qualities and levels, we mean that there is a bond between the higher
and lower; the two are not separate. The existence of all these levels
testifies to the fact that they are a single continuum.

אַךְ הֶאָרָה מוּעֶטֶת הַיּוֹרֶדֶת **But the minute illumination that**
מַדְרֵגָה אַחַר מַדְרֵגָה לִבְרוֹא **descends level after level to create this**
לְבוּשׁ זֶה הִיא מִבְּחִינַת מַדְרֵגָה **garment belongs to the lowest level of**
הָאַחֲרוֹנָה שֶׁבְּאוֹר זֶה **this light.**

Just as there are levels that rise ever higher, so are there are levels that
descend ever lower. The exalted light descends, level after level, until
it creates the garment that can receive and contain the light even at its
highest level.

What is this garment that is so high and yet also a created entity,
both light and a garment (a vessel)? This question is central to the epistle. The answer is that the garment that can contain this supernal light
cannot be something different from the light. It must be comprised
of the light itself. Therefore, the descent of this light is not a descent
of lights into vessels, with the light being revealed below by means of
something else, but a descent of the light itself. ☞

hundred men with Esau," which we must
process and refine. It is true that ours is a
time of service, whereas the future will be a
time of reward, and each of these comprises a separate chapter. Nevertheless, when

the soul has the fitting garment, it can see
even now – within the silver shekels and
men of Esau – the four hundred worlds of
yearnings, the pleasantness of God and
the *tzaḥtzaḥot*.

TWO WAYS THAT THE LIGHT CAN DESCEND

☞   In contrast to the descent of the light
described here, it can also descend via a
vessel that is not the light itself. In that case,

the light passes from one realm to another, one that has its own rules and intercon-
nections that are not directly connected to

וְנִקְרֵאת בְּשֵׁם מַדְרֵגָה הַחִיצוֹנָה וַאֲחוֹרַיִים דֶּרֶךְ מָשָׁל **Metaphorically speaking, it is called the external level and that which is the back side [aḥorayim],**

The descent of the light is the transition of interiority to exteriority and to the back side. Regarding the light itself, if there is no reference to where it is shining, one cannot speak of high and low. However, it is possible, with care, to speak about the inner and outer. High and low relate to location: a world, a "vessel," whereas inner and outer relate to the light itself: When it relates to its source, it is inner, whereas in reference to the vessel, to the place which it is illuminating, it is exterior. ☞

the quality and level of the supernal light. By way of analogy, imagine that someone expresses his love for someone else by giving him a monetary gift. This money is like a vehicle for the love. It transmits the feeling of love to something other than the realm of emotions. In certain situations and with the proper understanding, this money will indeed express love and show that the giver desires to provide benefit to the recipient and draw closer to him. Yet since it is money first of all, the gift could also signify the opposite message.

METAPHORICALLY SPEAKING

☞ The expression "metaphorically speaking" has an additional meaning. The garment under discussion here, which was created from the light and which descended from the internal to the external, is itself a kind of metaphor (see *Torah Or* 16a, s.v. "*vaAvraham zaken*," and 32d, s.v. "*tannu rabbanan, ner Ḥanukka Beit Shammai omrim*"). When we want to explain a profound concept to someone who does not have access to our conceptual and experiential world, we use a metaphor – we tell a story or describe a situation, using the reality and concepts with which he is familiar. Now, when he comprehends this situation with its relationships, he can in some way also comprehend the inner concept and light. The metaphor is not something separate from the light. It does not hide the light entirely and transmit something else in its place. It is simply a garment for the light.

In this sense, when the garment is "higher," more "abstract" and more transparent to its source, the light is more "interior," whereas when the garment relates to lowly worlds and less abstract and more impermeable levels, the light is more "exterior" and the "back side." A metaphor (which is like a vessel) is never autonomous. The moment it becomes autonomous, it is ruined, for it is ceases to be a metaphor. A metaphor is designed only to restore the light, to transform it from an "interior" to an "exterior" state. It projects the light, revealing the light shining within itself. The difference between a metaphor and what it is describing is like the difference between "outer" and "inner." The "inner" is understood only by the person providing the metaphor. The "external," by contrast, is in keeping with what the recipient, who is on a lower level, can grasp. The meta-

כְּמוֹ שֶׁכָּתוּב בַּזֹּהַר דַּף ר"ח עַמּוּד
ב (עַיֵּין בְּסֵפֶר מִקְדָּשׁ מֶלֶךְ) וְר"י
עַמּוּד ב: וּמַה דְּאִשְׁתָּאַר כו'

as stated in the *Zohar* 208b (see *Sefer Mikdash Melekh*) and 210b: "And that which remains…"

The *Zohar* refers to garments of the soul in the upper and lower Gardens of Eden.[19] A person's performance of the mitzvot creates garments of the lower Garden of Eden, and his intent in performing the mitzvot, as well as his Torah study and prayer, creates garments of the upper Garden of Eden. The *Zohar* explains (this is stated more explicitly in *Mikdash Melekh*[20]) that the essence of a unification that a person forms here below, by performing the mitzvot with the intent of the heart, occurs in the supernal reality of the world of *Atzilut*. Nevertheless, something of this unification affects the person here below as well. That is to say, when a person performs a mitzva – particularly, when the faculties of his soul and thought and the intent of his heart are involved – he performs a "supernal unification," a kind of line of unification that runs from his deed and thought to the highest heights, higher than all worlds, to the realm of God Himself. The unification that occurs above (in relation to which everything else is nullified and insignificant) is meaningful for all worlds. Yet some aspect of this remains with this individual in his state below. It becomes his garment and the path along which he can rise in order to be influenced by that supernal unification and light. ☞

phor is in essence the recipient: It is his understanding and concepts, the structure of his soul, the way he receives and relates to that inner light. The wisdom of the metaphor is thus even deeper than the interiority of the light, because the metaphor can convey the light from the inside to the outside, from one world to another, without extinguishing it.

---

19. The language in the *Zohar* is: "A portion remains for that person from which are made garments of light that the *neshama* wears in order to rise upward."
20. A basic commentary on the *Zohar*, in keeping with the Kabbala of the Arizal, by Rabbi Shalom Buzaglo, mentioned often in the writings of the author of the *Tanya*. The comment in question is on the *Zohar* 2:210b. It states, "And of that which remains, garments are made…. ' Every act of a person, who is basically dust, effects a unification above. And from that unification itself illumination is drawn to him from it." See also *Or HaTorah, Shemot*, part 8, p. 3072.

וְהִנֵּה כְּמוֹ שֶׁבְּנִשְׁמַת הָאָדָם יֵשׁ בָּהּ
כֹּחַ הַתַּעֲנוּג, שֶׁמִּתְעַנֶּגֶת מִמַּה שֶּׁיֵּשׁ
לָהּ עֹנֶג מִמֶּנּוּ

And this is in keeping with **the soul of man possessing the faculty of delight, delighting in what it finds delightful,**

This is referring to the divine light. The way for a person to understand something of the divine light is first of all to contemplate these concepts as they apply to his soul.

This faculty of delight is the innermost expression of the soul. This is signified by the way the soul receives delight from the attributes associated with all of the *sefirot*: from kindness and love (*ḥesed*); from strengthening and restraint (*gevura*); from vanquishing (*netzaḥ*); from splendor (*hod*); and from communication (*yesod*). The delight is not limited to any one faculty or attribute, but rather it is found in them all. This delight is thus the interiority of the entirety of the soul. It is revealed in every aspect and faculty manifested by the soul, and accordingly it expresses the essence of the soul. ☞

כְּמוֹ מֵהַשְׂכָּלַת שֵׂכֶל חָדָשׁ וּכְהַאי
גַּוְונָא

as when it experiences **a new intellectual insight, and the like,**

With regard to all of the *sefirot* and their associated faculties as experienced in the soul, when an attribute is revealed, the soul experiences delight. The author of the *Tanya* provides the example of the delight

AND THAT WHICH REMAINS

☞ That which remains is something that is on the highest level of exteriority. It remains even where interiority has departed and disappeared. It is like a tzaddik's *shirayim*, the food that he leaves behind at a ceremonial *tisch* ("table"). This food has no apparent connection to his soul's inner being, and yet it contains something of that inner being in a form that even simple people can absorb.

THE DELIGHT OF THE ESSENCE OF LIFE

☞ This delight in and of itself, not as a result of anything else, nor as an element revealed in something else, is not manifested in the exteriority of our lives. It is comparable to an awareness that a person sometimes has of the essence of life and even of the essence of existence. This awareness generally finds expression in relation to the essential needs of life: Food, warmth, love, intellect, and so forth. However, on occasion, in extreme situations, when a person is saved from a great danger, he experiences a delight that most closely resembles the soul's inner, intrinsic delight.

that a person feels when he attains a new understanding, a new intellectual insight. Each person speaks from experience, and the author
certainly had experiences of this kind. There may, however, be several
more specific reasons for his use of this particular example. First, the
intellect is the initial faculty of the soul, in contrast to the attributes,
which receive from the intellect before they manifest as attributes.
Therefore, the delight that accompanies an intellectual insight is delight
in its initial and abstract form, like one that is drawn directly from its
supernal locus, transcending all the faculties of the soul. Furthermore,
in the attributes the delight is so completely enclothed in the nature of
each attribute that it is impossible to distinguish it from the attribute,
whereas the delight that accompanies the intellect appears as a distinct,
"emotional" experience separate from the intellect. The intellect has its
own identity, and the delight likewise has its own identity. Here the
author of the *Tanya* wishes to speak about the delight in and of itself,
as the inner expression of the soul, which is on a higher level than all
the soul's sensing of itself through its attributes and its actions.

וּבְחִינַת חִיצוֹנִיּוּת וַאֲחוֹרַיִים שֶׁל **and the exterior and the back side**
כֹּחַ וּבְחִינַת הַתַּעֲנוּג שֶׁבָּהּ, הִיא **aspect of the** soul's **power and delight**
בְּחִינַת כֹּחַ הָרָצוֹן שֶׁבָּהּ **is its power of will.**

Like delight, the faculty of will is a single, encompassing faculty that
expresses the essence of the soul. However, unlike delight, which
expresses the essence of the soul in and of itself, the will expresses
the relationship of the essence of the soul toward the outside, to that
which it desires. ☞

THE UPPER WILL AND THE LOWER WILL

☞ This is not referring to a person's will
in terms of desiring something which he
understands to be good for him. That sort
of will is called the "lower will," because it
is lower than the intellect. What is being
discussed here is the "upper will," which is
higher than all the faculties of the soul, even
intellect and awareness. As the author of
the *Tanya* will state, the person wants what
he wants. That is to say, he does not want

something external to what the soul wants
(something that he thinks is good, something that he loves, and so forth), but rather
he wants what the soul wants in and of itself.
Such a will is not engendered by the intellect. Moreover, it itself engenders and directs the intellect in accordance with what
it wants, so that the intellect will understand
what it wants, why it wants it, and how to
act in order to attain it.

שֶׁהוּא רוֹצֶה מַה שֶׁהוּא רוֹצֶה, דְּהַיְינוּ דָּבָר שֶׁאֵינוֹ צַעַר, שֶׁהַצַּעַר הֵיפֶךְ הַתַּעֲנוּג

That means that the will **wants what it wants; that is, something that is not painful, because pain is the opposite of delight,**

A person's will does not necessarily want everything that provides delight, because "delight" is only an expression of the soul, and the will, like the delight, is also an expression of the essence of the soul (not an expression of an expression). For this reason, the author of the *Tanya* does not state that the will wants delight. Instead, he uses an expression of negation: The will wants something that is not painful (because pain is the opposite of delight).[21] ☞

וְכָכָה עַל דֶּרֶךְ מָשָׁל בְּאוֹר אֵין סוֹף בָּרוּךְ הוּא גַם כֵּן כִּבְיָכוֹל הָרָצוֹן הָעֶלְיוֹן בָּרוּךְ הוּא הִיא בְּחִינַת חִיצוֹנִיּוֹת וַאֲחוֹרַיִים לִבְחִינַת 'עֹנֶג הָעֶלְיוֹן' וְ'נוֹעַם ה'' וְ'צַחְצָחוֹת' וְ'עָלְמִין דִּכְסוּפִין' הַנִּזְכָּר לְעֵיל

and the same, metaphorically speaking, **applies, as it were, to the light of *Ein Sof*, blessed be He, as well. The blessed supernal will is the external and the back side aspect of the aforementioned aspect of supernal delight, the "pleasantness of God," "*tzaḥtzaḥot*," and "the worlds of yearning."**

The will is something "external" in that it is a faculty that leads from the potential to the actual, which actualizes, completes, and moves outward. This is necessarily a faculty that responds to, relates to, and is built on another faculty, one that is more inward, which does not move in an outward direction. This inner faculty that does not move outward is called, in relation to the will, *ta'am* (reason, or cause, source). Every will has a *ta'am*, whether an essentially intellectual cause, as in the lower will, or whether it is a *ta'am* in the sense of delight, as in the supernal will.

A PERSON'S WILL WANTS SOMETHING THAT IS NOT PAINFUL, BECAUSE PAIN IS THE OPPOSITE OF DELIGHT

☞ This unusual formulation – that a person's will wants something that is not painful (rather than that it "wants something that is delightful") – possibly relates to a fundamental question, the answer to which is not clearly established in the kabbalistic and hasidic literature: Which is the primary faculty, delight or will? Although the view expressed here, as in hasidic teachings overall, is that delight is *interior*

---

21. As in the well-known formulation that we cannot say, for instance, that God is wise, but only that He is not unwise.

This "supernal will" is not only supernal with respect to man. It is the will of God Himself. In other words, it is not the will that is revealed in the worlds God created, in the framework, manner, and intellect in which they act and develop. Rather, it goes beyond all that. It is, as it were, God's intrinsic will, that which He Himself wants. This is what the author of the *Tanya* is referring to here, a will that is "external" only in relation to the supernal delight, which he has already discussed in this epistle.

Yet as always, there is a difference between the metaphor and its reference. Not everything that the metaphor is applied to finds expression in the metaphor itself, and not every detail in the metaphor aligns with that which it comes to clarify. (This is particularly true of metaphors that relate to *Ein Sof*, because a perfect metaphor for the Infinite One cannot be found within the finite worlds.) The author of the *Tanya* proceeds to discuss these differences:

הֲגַם שֶׁהֵם מְיוּחָדִים בְּתַכְלִית הַיִּחוּד, שֶׁהוּא יִתְבָּרֵךְ וּרְצוֹנוֹ אֶחָד, וְלֹא כִּרְצוֹן הָאָדָם חַס וְשָׁלוֹם, לָא מִינֵּיהּ וְלֹא מִקְצָתֵיהּ וְאֵין דִּמְיוֹן בֵּינֵיהֶם כְּלָל

Although the supernal delight and supernal will **are united in an absolute unity, since He, may He be blessed, and His will are one, which is not in the least like the will of a human being, Heaven forbid, and there is no comparison between them at all,**

The supernal will and the supernal delight are entirely united in God, because God and His will are one. That is not in the least like the

to the will, that is not exactly the same thing. From the aspect of the relationships between them and from the aspect of functionality, delight is indeed interior. However, the abstract question of which is the primary faculty has no clear resolution. It can be understood from here that the will at its core is a fundamental force that in a sense has even greater primacy than the delight. In terms of the soul, the "supernal will" is the will to maintain the soul's existence in the most basic form, to be what it is, only more tangible and more actualized. The idea expressed here can

also be explained in the following terms: This will, which wishes to advance more and more, covers and limits the delight. The limitation is where there is no delight, where there is pain, which is the opposite of delight: There, the will is not revealed. In this sense, the will does not particularly want delight. The will is broader and more fundamental, and it is impossible to define it at all – not even in terms of delight. The only way in which it may be defined or revealed is through its negation of delight, when there is pain. Therefore, wherever there is no pain, the will is revealed.

will of a human being. A person's will is not absolutely united with him in the manner that the supernal will is united with God. There is no similarity at all between the metaphor and that which it refers to, between the human will and the divine will. First, there is a difference in the order of magnitude. God's traits are immeasurably greater in scope and depth. Moreover, there is an intrinsic difference, which is[22] that God's attributes – and these certainly include His supernal will and delight – are united in Him, and accordingly they are united in each other. Conversely, a person's will relates to something outside of himself. A person wants something that he lacks or at the very least is not manifest in him. This is almost the definition of a person's will, because if he had that object, he would not want it. In contrast, in regard to God it is impossible to speak of anything outside Him, of anything that is not in Him (and "there is no other than God"). As stated[23] with regard to knowledge, He, His knowledge, and what He knows are all one. The same applies to will and delight: He, His will, and what He wants are all absolutely one. There is no difference between Him and His will, and there is no difference between the will and the delight, between the inner and the outer. Any difference exists only from our perspective, in the way that we can comprehend these matters. ☞

The oneness that exists above, between the divine will and the

AND NOT LIKE THE WILL OF A HUMAN BEING

☞ Nevertheless, there is something within human beings that resembles that oneness. As mentioned earlier, the supernal delight in the soul is somewhat similar to the delight that a person can occasionally experience in living and existing. The same applies to the will. The will that is the essence of human existence – to be, to act, to love, and so forth – does not exist outside of the person. It does not desire anything that does not yet exist. Rather, it exists in everything that has been and that will be. If one were to isolate it, it is an *a*

priori fundamental stage that is found in every will and that can, like delight, manifest itself in unusual situations. The hidden will and delight are not separate from the essence of the soul, and it is impossible to make a clear demarcation: "Here is the soul and there is its will." In a sense, it is even impossible to say, "here is the will and there is delight." Accordingly, it is possible to gain some slight conception of a person's intrinsic will and delight, and even of the divine will and delight that the author of the *Tanya* is discussing here.

---

22. As explained at length in other places as well. See e.g., *Sha'ar HaYiḥud VeHa'emuna* 8.

23. See *Sha'ar HaYiḥud VeHa'emuna* 7 and 8, in the name of the Rambam.

delight, is accorded a special meaning in this epistle. The epistle discusses the garment that can receive the light of the divine delight, the pleasantness of God, and *tzaḥtzaḥot*, and so forth. That garment must share the nature of this light. In other words, the garment must be an extension of the inner delight; not an enclothing of the delight in something else, but its enclothing in another aspect of the delight. This can happen only through the unification of the attributes of will and delight, as is the case in the divine. In the human soul, while there is a closeness, there is no actual unity. In the human soul, the will is the back side of delight, but the will is also an autonomous entity. Therefore, it does not enclothe and receive the delight in itself, as it is, but only in something else. That is not true of the divine will in the Torah and the commandments. Therefore, the author of the *Tanya* emphasizes here that there is nothing but the divine will, which is the back side of the divine delight.

אַף עַל פִּי כֵן, דִּבְּרָה תּוֹרָה כִּלְשׁוֹן בְּנֵי אָדָם, לְשַׁבֵּךְ הָאֹזֶן מַה שֶּׁיְּכוֹלָה לִשְׁמוֹעַ **the Torah nevertheless speaks in the language of men to attune the ear to what it is able to hear**

Despite the intrinsic difference between human will and delight and divine will and delight, the Torah uses language appropriate to human beings,[24] utilizing concepts of will and delight as they exist among human beings so that we can relate to them. All of the words are those utilized in the language of human experience; we have no others. We cannot hear and absorb speech that cannot be verbalized. Yet this is still communication, because one's comprehension is not limited to words alone. Furthermore, even within the human realm, words have different levels of meaning. Someone who understands words on one level might not grasp them on a more abstract level. In that sense, the words and language that we use and understand here on earth are not necessarily different from those used to describe heavenly matters. Consequently, it can be said that these words are not only "human language" but "divine language" as well. The difficulty therefore es-

---

24. See Rambam, *Sefer HaMadda, Hilkhot Yesodei HaTorah* 1:9.

sentially lies in attaining a higher understanding of the words that are
being used.[25]

בְּמָשָׁל וּמְלִיצָה מִנִּשְׁמַת הָאָדָם with **metaphor and oratory** relating to
הַכְּלוּלָה מִכֹּחַ הַתַּעֲנוּג וְהָרָצוֹן **the soul of the human being, which**
וְהַחָכְמָה וְהַבִּינָה וכו' **is comprised of the faculty of delight,**
will, wisdom, and understanding...

The meaning as grasped in our soul is a metaphor for that how they
are to be understood with respect to the divine. Like the divine nature
and light, the human soul is comprised of delight, will, wisdom, and
so forth. We comprehend the divine faculties with them and by means
of them. ☞

וְכַנִּרְאָה בְּחוּשׁ שֶׁכְּשֶׁאָדָם And **as seen in actuality, when a per-**
מַשְׂכִּיל אֵיזֶה שֵׂכֶל חָדָשׁ נִפְלָא **son comprehends some wonderful**
אֲזַי בְּאוֹתָהּ רֶגַע עַל כָּל פָּנִים **new intellectual insight, a wonderful**
נוֹלָד לוֹ תַּעֲנוּג נִפְלָא בְּשִׂכְלוֹ **delight is born in his intellect at that**
moment, at any rate.

We feel what occurs in our soul without having to learn about it from a
book or from another person. However, at times it is necessary for ideas
to be explained for us, and that is what the author of the *Tanya* does
here. When one attains a new insight, it is akin to a bolt of lightning,
separate from the awareness that he had earlier possessed.

THE HUMAN SOUL AS METAPHOR

☞ The ten supernal *sefirot* in *Atzilut* are
mirrored, in a narrow and constricted way,
in the human soul. This comparison, despite its problematical and dangerous nature, is the only way that we can think and
speak about these matters – not only because we have no other choice, but because this is how God created us, and it is
His will that we should contemplate and
ascend to Him in this manner. Therefore,
what I see and I understand are true. Admittedly, this is not the ultimate, singular
and objective truth. Yet we cannot speak in
such absolute concepts with respect to the
elevated and divine realms, but only with
the truth of one who is observing, understanding, and relating to them under the
present conditions.

---

25. See *Torah Or* 75a, and in several other places.

Together with the new insight, a delight is born as well. At this initial stage, when a new understanding has arrived only as far as the intellect and not reached the attributes of the soul, the delight is also yet to be felt by the attributes of the soul, but rather it stands alone. It does not yet possess its own presence in the soul's faculties and structure. It is not in a relational state with the person, but it accompanies him. It is like a silhouette and background that appears with his new insight. In a sense, the insight itself reveals the delight. Since a constant delight is not a delight,[26] the revelation of the delight at this stage is only momentary.

מִכְּלָל שֶׁהַתַּעֲנוּג הוּא לְמַעְלָה **This delight is much higher than**
מַעְלָה מִבְּחִינַת הַשֵּׂכֶל וְהַחָכְמָה, **the level of intellect and Ḥokhma.**
רַק שֶׁמְּלוּבָּשׁ בִּבְחִינַת שֵׂכֶל וְחָכְמָה **However, it is clothed in the level of intellect and Ḥokhma.**

The delight is revealed together with Ḥokhma [wisdom], which is the initial level of the soul. This indicates that the source of the delight is higher than Ḥokhma, and indeed higher than all of the soul's faculties. Since, as explained, this delight relates to a reality that transcends all of the soul's faculties, to the essence of the soul, higher than all of the soul's parameters and illuminations, the delight possesses no vessel of its own in the soul. Thus, the delight is revealed together with and in the garment of Ḥokhma, and subsequently in all the faculties of the soul.

וּכְשֶׁהָאָדָם מַרְגִּישׁ הַשֵּׂכֶל וְחָכְמָה, **And so, when a person feels that**
דְּהַיְינוּ שֶׁמַּשִּׂיגָה וּמְבִינָה הֵיטֵב, **intellect and Ḥokhma – that is, when**
אֲזַי מַרְגִּישׁ גַּם כֵּן בְּחִינַת הַתַּעֲנוּג **he comprehends it and understands**
הַמְלוּבָּשׁ בַּחָכְמָה **it well – then he also senses the aspect of delight clothed in Ḥokhma.**

Intellect descends from Ḥokhma to Bina and from there to all of the other faculties of the soul,[27] at which point a person feels the delight that is clothed in Ḥokhma. The delight is born when Ḥokhma becomes

26. See *Keter Shem Tov*, 121. See the references in the Kehot edition to similar ideas expressed by the rabbinic Sages, the *Rishonim*, and in numerous hasidic teachings.
27. *Likkutei Amarim*, chap. 3.

manifest. However, like *Ḥokhma* itself, the delight is still not felt by the soul. It is only when a person understands and knows the *Ḥokhma* that the delight grows, expands, and settles in the soul and its senses. Just as *Bina* alone is the mother that brings forth the attributes and emotions in the soul, so too the delight is truly felt only in *Bina*.

וְלָכֵן נִקְרֵאת בְּחִינַת בִּינָה בְּשֵׁם עוֹלָם הַבָּא בַּזוֹהַר הַקָּדוֹשׁ שֶׁהִיא בְּחִינַת הִתְגַּלּוּת הַחָכְמָה עִם הַתַּעֲנוּג הַמְלוּבָּשׁ בָּהּ שֶׁמַּשִּׂיגִים הַצַּדִּיקִים בְּגַן עֵדֶן וּמַשְׂכִּילִים בִּפְנִימִיּוּת הַתּוֹרָה

Therefore, the aspect of *Bina* is called "the World to Come" by the holy *Zohar* because it is the aspect of the manifestation of *Ḥokhma* together with the delight clothed in it, which the righteous in the Garden of Eden comprehend and apprehend in the inner aspect of the Torah.

The "World to Come" is a broad term that includes the reality that will exist after our present reality (the world of the resurrection and so forth). Here the term is used in a more restricted sense: The manifest state of *Ḥokhma* together with the delight enclothed in it that the righteous attain in the Garden of Eden. *Ḥokhma* in itself is not a world; it is a point without length and breadth. The world and "palace" in which *Ḥokhma* is revealed and settled is *Bina*. Therefore, *Bina* is the "World to Come" (*Zohar* 3:82b (*Likkutei Hagahot LeTanya*) and 158b), the place where *Ḥokhma*, together with its accompanying delight, is revealed. ☞

THE MANIFESTATION OF DELIGHT IN THE WORLD TO COME

☞ In contrast to this world, which is the world for performing the mitzvot, in the World to Come we receive their reward. "I command you today to do them" (Deut. 7:11): 'Today' to do them, tomorrow to receive reward for [having done them]" (*Eiruvin* 22a). The reward is, in essence, the delight. The direction of the performance of the mitzvot is from within to without: From a person's *Ḥokhma* to his attributes and thought, and from there to his speech and deeds. The inner point is brought out to the consciousness of the soul, and then further out to other souls, and subsequently entirely outward to actions that affect physical reality. In contrast,

What do the righteous do in the Garden of Eden? They gain insights into the interiority of the Torah. The body and this world do not exist there. Therefore, there is nothing to do there. All they can do is think about what they did in this world. The contemplation of supernal matters is in essence thinking about them as they are in the Torah; in other words, to engage with the supernal Torah, the inner being of the Torah, which is the Torah that is enclothed not in this world but in the upper worlds, for each person in keeping with the level of the Garden of Eden where his soul is situated.

דְּאוֹרַיְיתָא מֵחָכְמָה נָפְקָא וְאוֹרַיְיתָא וקב״ה כּוּלָּא חַד	That is **because Torah emerges from Ḥokhma, and Torah and the Holy One, blessed be He, are entirely one.**

The statement that the Torah emerges from Ḥokhma means that the Torah is higher than Ḥokhma, and it merely emerges to be revealed to the worlds via the vessel and expression of Ḥokhma. This explains the earlier statement about how the metaphor of the human soul is applied to God. The Torah itself, which is higher than Ḥokhma and any relationship to the worlds, is on the level of God's intrinsic delight,

receiving the reward returns from without to within: From the extreme outer boundary, the outcomes of a person's good deeds, back to the person, to the essence of his soul, which is the manifestation of delight. A person's good deeds are a manifestation of the essence of his soul on the extreme outer boundary, whereas receiving the reward is solely a manifestation of the matter above, in the essence of the soul; that is, an infinite delight.

Although the revelation of the delight exists in all of the soul's faculties, the revelation of the delight in the Garden of Eden refers primarily to the revelation of the delight in the soul's intellectual comprehension. As explained earlier, the revelation of the delight in the intellect is the soul's in-

trinsic delight. The delight enclothed in a person's lower attributes is connected in one way or another to his life in a body and in this world. The delight of the soul itself, after it has been disconnected from this world, is the delight in the World to Come. Therefore, the soul can experience delight only through intellectual comprehension. It is true that there are lower levels of the Garden of Eden (the lower Garden of Eden and the world of *Yetzira*), in which even intellectual attainment relates to the realm of the lower attributes, such the awareness that relates to the attribute of love, and so forth. However, this is still comprehension with wisdom (Ḥokhma) and understanding (Bina), even when the topic is love and the like.

as it were,[28] united with God at the most essential point that one can contemplate. The special quality of the Torah, above and beyond all created beings, is that it does not have a "back side" aspect, but it is completely interiority, in every form and aspect by which it manifests. We who receive the Torah relate to matters as having "front and back." However, the Torah itself, from the level of will and wisdom down to actual deed, is interiority. That is the meaning of the saying that the Torah and God are entirely one: It means that the light of the Torah even on its external level is the light of intrinsic divine delight.

Later, the author of the *Tanya* will explain the nature of the external illumination that reaches us, and how it becomes a garment for the soul to receive the interiority.

וְהִנֵּה רָצוֹן הָעֶלְיוֹן בָּרוּךְ הוּא מְכוּנֶּה וְנִקְרָא בְּפִי חַכְמֵי הָאֱמֶת בְּשֵׁם 'כֶּתֶר עֶלְיוֹן' וּבוֹ תר"ך עַמּוּדֵי אוֹר וכו'	**And the blessed supernal will is termed and referred to by the sages of the Kabbala as "supernal crown" [*Keter Elyon*]. In it are 620 pillars of light...**	21 Ḥeshvan 20 Ḥeshvan (leap year)

The human will is a supernal faculty, higher than all of the other faculties and incorporating all of them. In the realm of divinity, the will is *Keter*, which transcends all of the other *sefirot*, encompassing and incorporating them all.

In Hebrew numeration, the number 620 consists of the letters that spell the word *Keter*. The will is related to the nature of *Keter*. In addition, there are 620 commandments (613 Torah commandments and seven rabbinic commandments), and thus the nature of *Keter* is connected to the practical commandments, which are like "pillars of light" (see *Pardes Rimmonim, Sha'ar* 8, chap. 3).

What is the meaning of the idea that the commandments are like pillars of light?

---

28. See *Likkutei Torah*, Num. 17d, s.v. *"ve'ehyeh etzlo amon,"* and in particular the explanation there 19b–19c.

פֵּירוּשׁ, דֶּרֶךְ מָשָׁל, כְּמוֹ שֶׁיֵּשׁ
עַמּוּדִים בְּבֵית חוֹמָה גָדוֹל נִצָּבִים
בָּאָרֶץ וְרֹאשָׁם מְחוּבָּר בַּתִּקְרָה,
כָּכָה מַמָּשׁ עַל דֶּרֶךְ מָשָׁל, כֶּתֶר
עֶלְיוֹן בָּרוּךְ הוּא

That means, by analogy, that just as there are pillars in a large building standing on the ground, with each pillar's head connected to the ceiling, the blessed supernal crown is exactly the same, metaphorically speaking.

Supernal *Keter* is like those pillars that connect the ceiling to the floor.

These pillars are the commandments, which are the supernal will that transcends all the *sefirot*, all faculties, existences, and parameters, like a ceiling above a house. They descend to the floor, because they are the practical commandments that express the supernal will in the material world of deed, which is lower than all of the other worlds, like a floor. ☞

הוּא לְמַעְלָה מִבְּחִינַת מַדְרֵגַת
הַחָכְמָה, וְהוּא מִלְשׁוֹן כּוֹתֶרֶת,
שֶׁהוּא מַכְתִּיר וּמַקִּיף עַל הַמּוֹחִין
שֶׁבָּרֹאשׁ, שֶׁהֵם בְּחִינַת חב"ד

Keter transcends the level of wisdom. The word *Keter* is related to *koteret*, a coronal "capital," because *Keter* crowns and encompasses the intellect in the head, which are the faculties of Ḥokhma, Bina, and Daʾat.

Keter is higher than Ḥokhma and all of the other *sefirot*. Its superiority to Ḥokhma is not like Ḥokhma's superiority to Bina, and so forth. Rather, it can be described as a capital that crowns, surrounds, and encompasses the entirety of Ḥokhma and all the other *sefirot*. In this sense, *Keter* is not only above all the *sefirot* but it is below them as well, like a pillar that stands on the floor and rises up to support the ceiling.

IS EXACTLY THE SAME, METAPHORICALLY SPEAKING

☞ There is clearly a difference between a metaphor and what it denotes. However, in this case the metaphor actually resembles its references. This metaphor has more than just one external point of connection with its application; they have a multilayered connection with each other, with more than one dimension and more than one layer of meaning in common. These must be "unpacked" (as will be seen below).

In this sense, *Keter* does not have its own content, unlike Ḥokhma and *Bina*. Its content, as far as it is possible to speak of such a thing, is like that of the will (and delight), which, as explained above at length, does not relate intrinsically to any content, faculty, and direction in the soul (something that is fully exhausted by the ten *sefirot*; *Keter* does not count as one of the *sefirot*), but which can enclothe itself in and accompany each of them.

וְרָצוֹן זֶה נִתְלַבֵּשׁ בְּתַרְיַ״ג מִצְוֹת הַתּוֹרָה וּז׳ מִצְוֹת דְּרַבָּנָן, שֶׁרוּבָּם כְּכוּלָם הֵן מִצְוֹת מַעֲשִׂיּוֹת

And this supernal **will is clothed in the 613 commandments of the Torah and the seven rabbinical commandments, almost all of which are practical commandments,**

In itself, this supernal will merely passes through the upper worlds, but it does not remain there and it is not enclothed there. As it passes through them, it receives form, direction, and parameters, its "how" and "what," but it remains the same will, the same supernal light, descending lower and lower. Only at the lowest point of all the levels, in this material world of action, is it enclothed, halted, and fulfills the purpose of its descent through all of the worlds. That is related to the expression:[29] "The final action was first in thought." On the level of action, which is the lowest of all levels, is embedded the beginning of thought, that is, the supernal will, which precedes thought. These are the commandments, which are the 613 commandments of the Torah plus the seven rabbinical commandments. Together they equal 620, the numerical value of the word *Keter*, which expresses the connection between the highest and the lowest.

Here delight, will, and the *halakhot* are connected. The will, which is the exteriority of the delight, is revealed through the *halakhot* of the Torah in this world, and the interiority of this comprehension is the interiority of the Torah that reveals the intrinsic supernal delight, the pleasantness of God, and so forth, in the Garden of Eden. Together, they are the *sefira* of *Keter* that surrounds and connects all of the extremities of reality, from the supernal Ḥokhma down to the world of action.

---

29. From the liturgical song *Lekha Dodi*, by Rabbi Shlomo Alkabetz.

וְגַם הַתְּלוּיוֹת בְּדִבּוּר, הָא קַיְימָא and even those dependent on speech,
לָן דַּעֲקִימַת שְׂפָתָיו הָוֵי מַעֲשֶׂה because we have a principle that the
movement of the lips is a deed (San-
hedrin 65a),

This also applies to the commandments that are dependent on speech,
such as reciting blessings and studying Torah, which are not practical
commandments in the usual sense, because we implement them
through speech alone. However, due to the movement of the lips and
the five articulations of the mouth to produce the consonants, even
speech is considered a deed. ☞

וְגַם הַתְּלוּיוֹת בְּמַחֲשָׁבָה אוֹ and even those that are dependent on
בַּלֵּב, הֲרֵי הַמִּצְוָה נִיתְּנָה לָאָדָם thought or those that are performed in
הַגַּשְׁמִי שֶׁבָּעוֹלָם הַזֶּה דַּוְקָא the heart. That is because each commandment is given to the physical
human being precisely in this world,

The more spiritual commandments – those that we perform even
without speech, commandments that are dependent on thought or the
feeling of the heart, such as the commandment to believe in God, to
love God, and to fear God – are also considered "practical commandments," because it is given to a physical person in this physical world.

THE MOVEMENT OF THE LIPS IS A DEED

☞ Why must it be said that "the movement of the lips is a deed" and "we have a
principle..."? Isn't it clear, by virtue of the
fact that we hear speech, that speech is a
physical act? It can be suggested that the
issue is that unlike deeds, speech does
not act directly upon the material world.
It transmits something via a material medium, but that which is transmitted is information and not literally material. In that
sense, speech is a deed but not a literal
deed. It is a deed as it relates to the speaker,
but is not a deed with respect to its product. Therefore, it is necessary to stress that

"the movement of the lips is a deed" – that
the deed performed through the articula-
tion of the letters is literally a deed. It is also
possible to say, in keeping with a conception that is emphasized in hasidic teachings, that human speech in a sense is like
divine speech, for it "creates" that which
it speaks about. Accordingly, the author
states that "we have a principle," because
although we cannot perceive it, we accept
and believe that speaking – in particular,
words of Torah and prayer – affects the
world like actual deeds.

We give charity with the hand, we speak words with our mouth, we think with the physical brain, and we feel with the heart. The soul acts, thinks, and feels through the body. It has no other way to express and reveal itself. Even an act that has no apparent connection whatsoever to the world and the physical body, such as love and abstract thought, cannot avoid relating to the world and the physical body. At the very least, the physical realm must be prevented from disturbing or distorting that thought, until the abstract thinking is utilizing the relationship to the body and world to the point that the body and world are nullified by the thought.

שֶׁהוּא בַּעַל בְּחִירָה לְהַטּוֹת לְבָבוֹ לְטוֹב וְכוּ'. מַה שֶׁאֵין כֵּן הַנְּשָׁמָה בְּלֹא גוּף אֵין צָרִיךְ לְצַוּוֹתָהּ עַל זֶה

because he has the free will to turn his heart to good..., which is not the case with the soul without a body. There is no need to command it regarding this.

The pure soul, before its descent to the body, does not have free will. Certainly, it does not have free will with regard to an act, because it has no body with which to act. Yet even in the spiritual realm, it has no free will – that is, as to whether or not to love God and fear Him, and so forth. One's free will depends on the fact that he has options, whereas the pure soul does not have the option not to love and fear God. If there is no free will, no commandments apply either. The supernal will in the commandment is not only the will that the commandment be performed. It is that the person will perform it not only because he desires the outcome or because he does not desire another outcome, but because God commanded it. Only then does the commandment serve as a bond between the highest and the lowest, between God and man below, and all parts of reality from top to bottom.

וְנִמְצָא שֶׁהַמִּצְוֹת הֵן עַל דֶּרֶךְ מָשָׁל כְּמוֹ הָעַמּוּדִים, נִצָּבִים מֵרוּם הַמַּעֲלוֹת, הוּא רָצוֹן הָעֶלְיוֹן בָּרוּךְ הוּא, עַד הָאָרֶץ הַלֵּזוּ הַחוֹמְרִית

Thus, the commandments are, metaphorically speaking, like pillars that stand from the highest height – which is the blessed supernal will – and reach to this material world.

Every commandment is like a pillar that connects the highest to the lowest, the supernal will that gives the commandment to the earth below, where the commandment is performed. The comparison of a commandment to a pillar indicates that there is something that connects each end of an unending number of levels separating the two extremities of reality to the other. It is not a passage from one level to another, and from there to yet another, of devolution from one world to another. Rather, there is one entity that is the same below as above. This entity is the commandment.

וְהֵן עַל דֶּרֶךְ מָשָׁל כְּמוֹ הָעַמּוּדִים **Metaphorically speaking,** the com-
חֲלוּלִין שֶׁמַּקִּיפִין וּמַלְבִּישִׁין mandments **are like hollow pillars that**
נִשְׁמַת הָאָדָם אוֹ רוּחוֹ אוֹ נַפְשׁוֹ **encompass and clothe the** neshama **of**
כְּשֶׁמְּקַיֵּים הַמִּצְוֹת **the person or his** ruaḥ **or his** nefesh
when he keeps the commandments.

Here other facets of this metaphor are revealed. Besides the fact that the pillars form a connection, they are also hollow. That means that they encompass an expanse that can contain a person's neshama, ruaḥ, or nefesh. This encompassing does not link the parts in a manner involving comprehension or through any other causal connection. Rather, it is like a space, palace, or garment in which all of the parts and levels are found together.

The mention of the levels of the soul – "neshama of the person or his ruaḥ or his nefesh" – serves to emphasize each one separately. This means that the enclothing is not only general, but it relates to one's actions when performing a mitzva. For example, when he acts through his intellect to study a halakha, he enclothes the level of neshama; when he acts through the power of the attributes to inspire himself to act with love and fear, he enclothes the level of ruaḥ; and when he acts with the powers of the nefesh that are directed to an act – meaning, the way in which he will act and the performance of that act – he enclothes the level of nefesh.

וְדֶרֶךְ עַמּוּדִים אֵלּוּ עוֹלִין הנר"ן **Through these pillars, his** nefesh, ruaḥ,
שֶׁלּוּ עַד רוּם הַמַּעֲלוֹת לִצְרוֹר **and** neshama **rise to the highest height,**
בִּצְרוֹר הַחַיִּים אֶת ה' **to be bound "in the bond of life with**
the Lord" (I Sam. 25:29).

The pillars are the commandments that enclothe the *nefesh, ruah,* or *neshama* of the person performing them. The commandments bring the *nefesh, ruah,* or *neshama* to this level that encompasses them. This is the level of the will in the soul, which is now united with the supernal, divine will. This level, in which the essence of the soul is united with the essence of the divine, is called "the bond of life"[30] because all the souls that have ever existed and that will ever exist are joined together there. This is truly "with the Lord" Himself.

פֵּירוּשׁ, לִהְיוֹת צְרוּרוֹת וּמְלוּבָּשׁוֹת בְּאוֹר הַכֶּתֶר, הוּא רָצוֹן הָעֶלְיוֹן בָּרוּךְ הוּא

That means that the souls **are bound and clothed in the light of** *Keter*, **which is the blessed supernal will,**

"The bond of life" is not another location to where the soul moves, as it were, so that it is no longer in its original place. Rather, it is in a way the essential root of the soul with which the soul rises and unites. Therefore, when the soul performs the commandment, it remains where it is, and at the same time it is incorporated into its own supernal will, which is in turn incorporated into the light of *Keter*, the supernal divine will. This is the commandment that the person performs.

וְעַל יְדֵי לְבוּשׁ זֶה יוּכְלוּ לַחֲזוֹת בְּנוֹעַם ה'' וְ'צַחְצָחוֹת', שֶׁלְּמַעְלָה מִמַּעֲלַת הַכֶּתֶר, וְהֵן פְּנִימִיּוּתוֹ עַל דֶּרֶךְ מָשָׁל

and by means of this garment, they can gaze upon "the pleasantness of God" and the *tzahtzahot*, **which are higher than the level of** *Keter*, **and which are** Keter's **inner being, metaphorically speaking.**

By means of this garment, comprised of the mitzva and the supernal will, souls can gaze upon the "pleasantness of God" and *tzahtzahot*, which are the light of the divine delight, and which is higher than *Keter*. This garment is the will and exteriority of *Keter*, whereas the pleasantness of God etc., are the interiority of *Keter*. As in the earlier

---

30. Cf. I Sam. 25:29: "And the soul of my lord will be bound in the bond of life with the Lord your God...." See *Torat Ḥayyim, Parashat Mishpatim*, p. 285b and onward, where it is explained that the bond of life is the garment of the divine soul in the Garden of Eden, which is comprised of the commandments, as mentioned here.

metaphor, the soul's inner light is the essential delight, while the supernal will is external to it.

That is the answer to the question posed at the beginning of the epistle: Why does the soul need the garments of the commandments? Why is it that by means of the garment of the commandments in particular the soul can gaze upon the pleasantness of God and the supernal delight? The answer of the author of the *Tanya* here is that the garment comprised of the commandments is the garment composed of the supernal will, which is the exteriority of delight, while the exteriority is the vessel through which the interiority is transmitted. It is impossible to transmit the interior itself. A person cannot communicate his personal inner feeling to someone else. However, if there is an exterior garment that matches that interiority, it can be transferred. This is the nature of the garment of the commandments. God transfers a commandment to us and in it is enclothed the supernal delight, "the pleasantness of God," and the *tzaḥtzaḥot*, which in this manner are transmitted to our soul.

The author of the *Tanya* now comments parenthetically on the statement that the commandments are a garment for the supernal delight.

(וְהַגַּם שֶׁנִּתְבָּאֵר בְּמָקוֹם אַחֵר שֶׁהַמִּצְוֹת הֵן פְּנִימִיּוּת רָצוֹן הָעֶלְיוֹן בָּרוּךְ הוּא, הִנֵּה מוּדַעַת זֹאת לְיוֹדְעֵי חֵן רִיבּוּי בְּחִינוֹת וּמַדְרֵגוֹת שֶׁיֵּשׁ בְּכָל בְּחִינָה וּמַדְרֵגָה מִמַּדְרֵגוֹת הַקְּדוּשָׁה. כַּמָּה בְּחִינוֹת פָּנִים לְפָנִים וְכַמָּה בְּחִינוֹת אֲחוֹרַיִים לַאֲחוֹרַיִים לְאֵין קֵץ וְכוּ')

(Although it is explained elsewhere that the commandments are the inner being of the blessed supernal will, those initiated in the esoteric wisdom of Kabbala know the multiplicity of aspects and levels present in every aspect and level of the levels of holiness. There are many aspects of "face to face" and many aspects of "back side to back side" without end ...)

It is stated elsewhere[31] that the commandments are the interiority of the supernal will. This apparently contradicts the statement here that

31. See *Likkutei Amarim*, chap. 23; *Likkutei Torah, Derushim LiShemini Atzeret* 83c; *Sefer HaMa'amarim* 568, p. 334.

they are the externality of *Keter*. However, it is not a real contradiction, because there are many aspects and levels within the realm of holiness. Each aspect and level is comprised of other levels. For instance, every level has a front and back, and the front itself has a front and back, and so on and so forth. Thus, in this epistle, the author of the *Tanya* is describing an aspect in which the commandments are the external expression of the inner light, and therefore they constitute the garment through which the soul can receive that inner light. The other sources, by contrast, are coming from a different perspective, one in which the commandments reveal the interiority of the divine will, in contrast to the exteriority of the will that creates and sustains the worlds, the exterior framework that enables the realization of the inner will through the performance of the commandments. ☞

וְהִנֵּה ז' מִצְוֹת דְּרַבָּנָן אֵינָן   **And the seven rabbinical command-**
נֶחְשָׁבוֹת מִצְוֹת בִּפְנֵי עַצְמָן   **ments are not considered commandments in themselves,**

Initially, the author of the *Tanya* spoke of a garment made of the 613 commandments that enclothes the 613 aspects and faculties of the human soul. Subsequently however, in reference to *Keter*, he spoke about 620 commandments (the numerical value of the word *Keter*). If so, which of these figures is the correct one for the present discussion? Moreover, how is it possible for rabbinical commandments to be counted together with the Torah commandments?

THE MULTIPLICITY OF ASPECTS AND LEVELS IN EVERY ASPECT

☞ This explanation accords with the principle discussed widely in kabbalistic literature that the meaning of every statement depends on its context. No statement is correct in every aspect and on every level, because a crucial part of understanding something is knowing its context. A major problem in studying Kabbala is that we lack the concepts and words to express otherworldly realities, and therefore we have to use words and models from essentially physical realms. Further-more, in the spiritual worlds, matters are often more subtle and complex than in their physical counterparts. Therefore, the number of words (and frameworks of thought) that we have is limited, and we necessarily use the same words in order to express different concepts, sometimes even when they are opposite in nature. When questions and contradictions subsequently arise, the solution is to clarify the precise context.

שֶׁהֲרֵי כְּבָר נֶאֱמַר: "לֹא תוֹסֵף"
(דברים יג,א) אֶלָּא הֵן יוֹצְאוֹת
וְנִמְשָׁכוֹת מִמִּצְוֹת הַתּוֹרָה
וּכְלוּלוֹת בָּהֶן בְּמִסְפַּר תַּרְיַ"ג
לְהַלְבִּישׁ תַּרְיַ"ג בְּחִינוֹת וְכֹחוֹת
שֶׁבְּנֶפֶשׁ רוּחַ נְשָׁמָה הָאָדָם

because it has already been said, "You shall not add" (Deut. 13:1). But the explanation is that the rabbinical commandments are derived from and issue from the commandments of the Torah and are included in them, in the sum of 613, to enclothe the 613 aspects and powers in a person's *nefesh, ruaḥ,* and *neshama,*

The Torah states: "All this matter that I command you…you shall not add to it and you shall not subtract from it" (Deut. 13:1). This verse prohibits making additions to the words of the Torah.[32] However, the seven rabbinical commandments are not considered additions to the commandments of the Torah, because they are extensions of them, for they elaborate on and develop them. Therefore, they are included in the sum total of the 613 commandments, which means that there are in fact no more than the 613 commandments of the Torah. Even those rabbinical commandments that appear to be separate commandments are actually drawn from the Torah's command to heed the words of the prophets and sages in each generation:[33] "Him you shall heed" (Deut. 18:15).

The number 613 is important because it expresses the unique connection between the Torah and the soul. Just as the soul's 613 aspects and faculties relate to the corresponding 613 limbs of the body, so too the Torah relates to the soul. Thus, there is an intrinsic connection that joins together the Torah, soul, and body at their roots. If the number was not identical, the connection (even if it was temporarily intense) would be merely partial, existing only in a particular aspect and for a certain purpose. But when the entire framework is identical, the connection is whole, and the interiors of Torah, soul, and body are totally identical, albeit revealed in a different form and on a different level.[34]

---

32. *Sefer HaMitzvot,* prohibition 313.
33. Rambam, *Sefer HaMadda, Hilkhot Yesodei HaTorah* 9:3.
34. See the oft-cited expression: "Israel, Torah, and the Holy One, blessed be

וְזֶה שֶׁכָּתוּב בַּזוֹהַר הַקָדוֹשׁ פָּרָשַׁת
פְּקוּדֵי (דַף רכ״ט עַמוּד ב), דְּאִינוּן
עוּבְדִין טָבִין דְּעָבֵיד בַּר נַשׁ מָשְׁכֵי
מִנְּהוֹרָא דְזִיווָא עִילָּאָה לְבוּשָׁא כו׳
וְחָמֵי כו׳ בְּנוֹעַם ה׳ וכו׳

and this is the meaning of the statement in the holy *Zohar, Parashat Pekudei* (229b), that "the good deeds that a person performs elicit a garment from the light of supernal radiance… and he beholds… the pleasantness of God…"

This statement, which discusses the garment that allows the soul to gaze upon the pleasantness of God, was mentioned at the beginning of this epistle. Here the author of the *Tanya* quotes its continuation, which clarifies the nature of the garment: It consists of the "good deeds," the commandments that a person performs. These, as explained, are extensions of the light of the supernal will that enclothe him in a garment that will enable him to see and experience the inner being of the supernal light, which is the pleasantness of God etc.

Later, the author will clarify whether those are merely garments of deeds, such as the deed of a commandment, or garments on a spiritual level as well. Just as in a person's life in this world there are additional, spiritual levels of thought and feeling that are on a higher plane than the materiality of this world, so too, in the World to Come (the Garden of Eden) there are relatively high levels that function as garments to which the soul can rise and at which it can receive the significance and delight that are revealed on those levels.

וְהַגַם דְּהָתָם מַיְיֵרי בְּגַן עֵדֶן
הַתַּחְתּוֹן, שֶׁהַלְבוּשִׁים שָׁם הֵם
מִמִּצְוֹת מַעֲשִׂיוֹת מַמָּשׁ

Although there the *Zohar* is speaking **about the lower Garden of Eden, where the garments derive from the actual practical mitzvot,**

The garments that are made from the deeds of the commandments belong to the level of the lower Garden of Eden. The lower Garden of Eden parallels the world of *Yetzira*, which relates directly to the world of *Asiya* below it, including our physical world. Accordingly, the

---

He, are one" (attributed in many places in the hasidic texts to the *Zohar*; a similar formula does appear in the *Zohar*, 3:73a).

garments for the *neshama* that relate to the lower Garden of Eden are the garments made from the performance of the mitzvot. ☞

אֲבָל בְּגַן עֵדֶן הָעֶלְיוֹן הַלְבוּשִׁים הֵם מֵרְעוּתָא וְכַוְּונָה דְּלִבָּא בְּאוֹרַיְיתָא וּצְלוֹתָא כְּמוֹ שֶׁכָּתוּב בַּזֹּהַר שָׁם (דַּף ר"י)

but in the upper Garden of Eden the garments are derived from the will and intent of the heart in Torah and prayer, as written in the *Zohar* there (210).

The upper Garden of Eden relates to the higher levels of the worlds and souls, that is, to *Beria*, which has no direct connection to the world of action. There, the garments come from the will and intent of a person's heart in Torah and prayer. The soul's garments that relate to the upper Garden of Eden are fashioned not from one's deeds but from his feelings and understanding. That is to say, the garments are made from the supernal will itself, not as that will manifests itself in one's deed but as it manifests itself in the intent behind his deed and the intent itself within the person's mind and heart. ☞

THE REASON AND SIGNIFICANCE OF THE WORLD THAT IS REVEALED IN THE GARDEN OF EDEN

☞ In general, the Garden of Eden is the "place" where the meaning of the life of this world is revealed: Not only the significance that things have in this world, but also the true meaning that goes beyond this world. This is the meaning that inheres in repentance, good deeds, Torah, and mitzvot; everything in one's life that relates to God. God alone exists beyond the worlds, and therefore there is meaning and purpose in everything that occurs in them only in their relationship to Him. The reason for this meaning is the infinite delight whose root is the intrinsic divine delight (as explained in this epistle). The infinite levels of the Garden of Eden correspond to the infinite levels of the worlds. Nevertheless, we generally speak of two overall levels of the Garden of Eden, the lower and the upper.

THE WILL OF THE HEART

☞ The will of the heart is the supernal will as it is expressed in the feeling in the heart. In other words, the garment for this will, the completion of its expression, is the feeling in the heart. There is a feeling in the heart, such as love or fear, which relates to a certain awareness. We understand things and recognize their existence, and in relation to them we develop feelings: Attraction, repulsion, love, fear, and so forth. Yet there is another will in the heart which is intrinsic, what a person wants and feels – not what he understands, not what his neighbors or society deems proper, but

The difficulty here is that the *Zohar* is now apparently speaking of a previously unmentioned level of garments, one that is not connected to the level of deed. This is in contrast to the *Zohar*'s earlier statement that the garments are made from the level of deeds, like a garment for the spiritual faculties of the soul. In other words, the garment and the vessels for the divine and infinite will, which transcend human feelings and understanding, are made precisely from what we do not understand and feel. If so, how is one to understand the statement here that the garments of the soul in the upper Garden of Eden are made from the will and intent of the heart?

הֲרֵי הַכַּוָּונָה הִיא כַּוָּונַת עָסְקוֹ
בַּתּוֹרָה לִשְׁמָהּ מֵאַהֲבַת ה',
וּמִצְוַת תַּלְמוּד תּוֹרָה הִיא גַם כֵּן
מִכְּלַל מִצְוֹת מַעֲשִׂיּוֹת, דַּעֲקִימַת
שְׂפָתָיו הָוֵי מַעֲשֶׂה, וְהִרְהוּר לָאו
כְּדִיבּוּר דָּמֵי, וְאֵינוֹ יוֹצֵא יְדֵי חוֹבָה
בְּהִרְהוּר לְבַדּוֹ, וְכֵן בִּתְפִלָּה

This intent is a person's **intent** as he **engages** in learning **the Torah for its own sake out of love for God. And the commandment of Torah study is also one of the practical commandments, because** "the movement of the lips is a deed." **But thought is not similar to speech, and** a person **does not fulfill his obligation** to learn Torah **with thought only. And the same applies to prayer,**

what his heart wants. As stated earlier, the faculty of will in general is nothing other than the inclination of the essence of the soul in a certain direction. Likewise, the will of the heart is the inclination of the essence of the soul, but in the realm of the heart: How the soul itself is drawn to love, what sort of love, what it loves – here, the essence of the soul is revealed. The author of the *Tanya* offers the following metaphor: When a person feels that his entire life depends on this love, that he cannot exchange it for anything else, this means that the essence of his soul is clothed in the love, and this is the "will of the heart."

The will of the heart of the Jewish soul is revealed through garments comprised of Torah and prayer. On the highest and most intrinsic level, the soul is one with the divine, and as such it can manifest itself only in divine garments. It is manifested in one manner through the Torah, which reveals the divine will and wisdom, and in another way in prayer, which expresses the human will when one pours out his soul to the Divine. This is not referring to the act of the commandments, because the "will of the heart" does not reach down to the level of deed. Rather, it is fully expressed in the levels of a person's soul, and revealed in his spiritual undertakings: In his Torah study and prayer.

The garments are made from more than just a person's intent and feeling in Torah and prayer. Although the will of the heart is revealed in his feeling – in love and in fear – this feeling cannot remain abstract. It must be related to something that a person thinks about and expresses in speech. If he does not articulate the words of Torah or prayer, he does not fulfill his obligation (for it is only by connecting the speech to deed that he maintains the connection between above and below; otherwise, he does not create the "garment"). Therefore, the garments created by the heart's will and intent do not negate the aspect of deed; rather they add to it a revelation on the levels of the soul. ☞

וּמַה גַם כִּי מַעֲלַת הַכַּוָּונָה עַל הַדִּבּוּר
וּמַעֲשֶׂה אֵינָה מִצַּד עַצְמָה כוּ', אֶלָּא
מִצַּד הָאָרַת רָצוֹן הָעֶלְיוֹן כוּ', כְּמוֹ
שֶׁנִּתְבָּאֵר בְּלִקּוּטֵי אֲמָרִים חֵלֶק א'
פֶּרֶק ל"ח בַּאֲרִיכוּת, עַיֵּין שָׁם

and also because the superiority of intent over speech and deed is not due to intent's intrinsic merits, and so on, but because it comes from the illumination of the supernal will, and so on, as explained in *Likkutei Amarim* volume 1, chapter 38, at length; see there.

THE LOWER AND THE UPPER GARDENS OF EDEN

☞   The garments of the lower Garden of Eden enclothe only the limbs of deeds in the soul, and therefore what they reveal relates to the realm of action alone. Although they reveal the infinite divine (as explained at the beginning of the epistle), this is only in the intellect as it relates to deeds, in feeling as it relates to deed, and in the implementation of the deed. By contrast, in the upper Garden of Eden the garments of the soul – which are fashioned from the will of the heart – not only enclothe the light of *Ein Sof* through their aspect of action but they also enclothe the realm of the person's abstract feeling and thought. Accordingly, in the upper Garden of Eden they reveal a more wondrous divine delight, which is more disconnected from this physical world and more connected and open to the divine being and

delight itself. By way of analogy, consider a mundane printer. One might be impressed by the way it prints text on paper, by its fine quality, by its speed of operation, by the ingenuity of its construction, by the harmonious operation of its parts, and so forth. On a higher plane, one might be impressed by the technological and scientific principles underlying the device's construction. On a much higher level, he may be impressed by the content of the written material, and even by the intent of the person who wrote it, such as the love that it expresses. All of these aspects cannot be separated from the final product; they have no meaning without that last stage when the machine prints words on the page. If this does not occur, none of those abstract ideas can be conveyed.

From the aspect of the infinite divine, the spiritual is not superior to the physical, nor is intent superior to speech. Their superiority derives from the supernal will's illumination. This observation applies not only here but also more generally to the relationship between deed and intent. After explaining the central and vital place of deeds in the service of God, including the words of Torah and prayer, as well as the importance of intent, the author of the *Tanya* provides a metaphor that is key to understanding the relationship between deed and intent: Prayer without intent is like a body without a soul. The "body" of prayer, like the physical body, is the essence of its existence, while the "soul" is the vitality that is enclothed and revealed in it. Speech and deed are the "body"; the intent of the heart is the soul. Thus, the intent of the heart has no meaning without the "body" of the deed, through which the intent is revealed. "Body" and "soul" have no actuality apart from each other. The difference between them is only with respect to the revelation and illumination of the supernal will (in the terms of the *Tanya* in in *Likkutei Amarim* 1:38, the contraction and expansion of the illumination). The supernal will is implemented through a person's deed, and the more intent he has, the more the intent shines and is revealed. The loftier a person's intent – the more refined his feeling and awareness – the higher and clearer the revelation of the supernal will, and the more separated from matters of this world.

Now the author of the *Tanya* will proceed to speak about the part of the Torah that relates to deed: Studying the *halakhot* of the Oral Torah, which is called "the crown of Torah," the topic with which he began this epistle. He will thereby explain the overall value of the Oral Torah, and the relationship between it and the Written Torah.

וְהִנֵּה מוּדַעַת זֹאת, כִּי הִנֵּה רָצוֹן הָעֶלְיוֹן בָּרוּךְ הוּא הַמְלוּבָּשׁ בְּתַרְיַ״ג מִצְוֹת שֶׁבַּתּוֹרָה שֶׁבִּכְתָב, הוּא מוּפְלָא וּמְכוּסֶּה טָמִיר וְנֶעְלָם.	And it is known that the blessed supernal will, which is clothed in the 613 commandments in the Written Torah, is hidden and covered, cloaked and obscured.	23 Heshvan ___ 22 Heshvan (leap year)

The Written Torah does not reveal the supernal will. It only reveals the fact that there are practical commandments through which God reveals His will to us. However, their precise nature and how we perform them in all their details and in various circumstances remain concealed. To put it another way, the Written Torah reveals the spoken word of God speaks, while what that communicates to us on all levels and in all senses is contained in the Oral Torah. ☞

וְאֵינוֹ מִתְגַּלֶּה אֶלָּא בַּתּוֹרָה   And it is revealed only in the Oral Torah,
שֶׁבְּעַל פֶּה

That which is hidden in the Written Torah is revealed in the Oral Torah. The Oral Torah is a tradition that passes from generation to generation, from one person to another, from mouth to mouth. It consists of things that cannot be written or even formulated: How we are to understand matters, how we are to think about them, how we are to relate to them. Only living people who see each other, who recognize each other, who think together, can communicate to each other such matters that lie beyond words. This is the Oral Torah.

It is not only that the Written Torah often does not provide sufficient information, or that one cannot understand something, or that a specific circumstance is left undescribed. Rather, the Written Torah in general is not designed to teach practical *halakha*. The parameters of the *halakhot* – how we perform them, all of the minutest details –

HIDDEN AND COVERED, CLOAKED AND OBSCURED

☞ The author of the *Tanya* describes that which is hidden in the Written Torah with four terms: "Hidden and covered, cloaked and obscured." Perhaps this is to be understood in the context of his aforementioned statement in chapter 38 of *Likkutei Amarim* that the divine will is revealed on two general levels that can be divided into four. The two general levels are deed and intent. Deed can be divided into action and speech (which includes thought), while intent can be divided into intent that relates to the human aspect and intent relating to one's animal aspect. It can be said that the four levels of the revealed Oral Torah mentioned there correspond to the four levels of concealment in the Written Torah stated here. (In general, these four levels of revelation appear in various formulations, and their archetype are the four letters of the name of *Havaya*. See *Likkutei Levi Yitzḥak al HaTanya* here at length, where these four are also divided into two: "Hidden and covered" corresponds to the letters *yod heh* of the name of *Havaya*, while "cloaked and obscured" corresponds to the *vav heh* of the name of *Havaya*. He adds that all of this is revealed in the Oral Torah, which corresponds to the name of *Adnut*).

remain obscure, unexplained, and unknowable. The Written Torah merely alludes to these matters, which must be elucidated by the Oral Torah. The Written Torah be understood only in light of the Oral Torah. ☞

Therefore, as the author of the *Tanya* says in this epistle, it is precisely the Oral Torah that transmits the level of *Keter*, that which is hidden, which cannot be expressed in the supernal, eternal words of the Written Torah. For that which cannot be taught from above to below can be taught from below to above. Only we here, who continue to study the Oral Torah, can successfully transmit onward, from mouth to mouth, that which all of the supernal worlds do not know.

The author of the *Tanya* proceeds to present an example of this:

IT IS REVEALED ONLY IN THE ORAL TORAH

☞ This is somewhat true of every word that one says to someone else. What the speaker says are only words; in order to understand their import, the listener must have the inherent ability to understand the topic, their reference. Otherwise, he will be unable to comprehend anything. This is especially the case when there is a conceptual distance between speaker and listener. When people have a shared understanding, each can easily grasp the other's meaning. Yet the further they are from each other in perspective, the greater the distance between their understanding of the words, until communication grows impossible. Accordingly, the revelation of God's supernal will to the people would have been absolutely impossible were it not for the Oral Torah.

It is a principle of Jewish faith that the Oral Torah was given to Moses. The level of Moses's prophecy (and in a sense the prophetic level of all the people at the Giving of the Torah) was so high that his mind – his understanding and feeling – was close, as it were, to the place from where God was speaking. When God issued forth a statement, Moses understood what was being said. He saw the picture, as it were, of what God is thinking and wanting. At that time, all the souls of Israel ascended and were singed by that fire that is beyond words. However, they were unable to transmit their insights back to their daily lives. For that, they needed Moses to explain in detail how all these matters fit into the life of this world; that is, they needed him to teach them the Oral Torah. What Moses taught the people was not only what he understood of the Written Torah, but more essentially how to transmit the spirit and meaning that have no words via those words, a meaning that requires an appropriate form for every generation and individual.

כְּמוֹ מִצְוַת תְּפִילִין עַל דֶּרֶךְ מָשָׁל, שֶׁנֶּאֱמַר בַּתּוֹרָה שֶׁבִּכְתָב: "וּקְשַׁרְתָּם לְאוֹת עַל יָדֶךָ וְהָיוּ לְטוֹטָפֹת בֵּין עֵינֶיךָ" (דברים ו,ח). וְהוּא מַאֲמָר סָתוּם וְנֶעֱלָם, שֶׁלֹּא פֵּרֵשׁ הַכָּתוּב אֵיךְ וּמַה לִקְשׁוֹר וּמַהוּ "טוֹטָפוֹת" וְהֵיכָן הוּא "בֵּין עֵינֶיךָ" וְ"עַל יָדֶךָ" עַד שֶׁפֵּירְשָׁה תוֹרָה שֶׁבְּעַל פֶּה: שֶׁצָּרִיךְ לִקְשׁוֹר בַּיִת אֶחָד עַל הַיָד וד' בָּתִּים עַל הָרֹאשׁ וּבְתוֹכָם ד' פָּרְשִׁיּוֹת וְהַבָּתִּים יִהְיוּ מֵעוֹר מְעוּבָּד וּמְרוּבָּעִים דַּוְקָא וּמְקוּשָּׁרִים בִּרְצוּעוֹת שֶׁל עוֹר שְׁחוֹרוֹת דַּוְקָא וְכָל שְׁאָר פְּרָטֵי הִלְכוֹת עֲשִׂיַּית הַתְּפִילִין שֶׁנֶּאֶמְרוּ בְּעַל פֶּה

like the commandment of *tefillin*, for instance, as it says in the Written Torah, "You shall bind them as a sign on your arm, and they shall be for ornaments between your eyes" (Deut. 6:8). That is a hidden and concealed statement, because Scripture did not explain how and what to bind, nor what "ornaments" are, nor the locations indicated by "between your eyes" and "on your arm," until the Oral Torah explained that one must bind one box on the arm and four boxes on the head, containing four passages, and the boxes are to be of processed leather, and specifically square, and tied with straps of leather, which must be black, and all of the other details of the *halakhot* of making *tefillin*, which were communicated orally.

The Oral Torah exposes what has been hidden. It expands upon that which was contained in a few words in the Written Torah. This example illustrates how the Oral Torah not only explains each word but how it provides a plethora of information for which there is no obvious allusion in the Written Torah. Only by knowing all the information contained by the Oral Torah can we unwrap the meaning of the words in the Written Torah.

וְ"עַל יָדֶךָ" הִיא הַזְּרוֹעַ דַּוְקָא וְלֹא כַּף הַיָד, וּ"בֵין עֵינֶיךָ" זֶה קָדְקוֹד וְלֹא הַמֵּצַח

And "on your arm" is specifically the upper arm and not the palm of the hand, and "between your eyes" is the mid-frontal skull and not the forehead.

Although elsewhere the phrases "on your arm" and "between your eyes" are read literally, the Oral Torah reveals that this is not the case here.[35] Thus, the Oral Torah reveals not only the logic and cohesiveness of the words, but also the absence of logic in certain cases, which could not have been understood in the correct manner if their meaning had not been revealed by the Oral Torah.

וְכֵן כָּל מִצְוֹת שֶׁבַּתּוֹרָה, בֵּין מִצְוֹת עֲשֵׂה בֵּין מִצְוֹת לֹא תַעֲשֶׂה, אֵינָן גְּלוּיוֹת וִידוּעוֹת וּמְפוֹרָשׁוֹת אֶלָּא עַל יְדֵי תּוֹרָה שֶׁבְּעַל פֶּה כְּמִצְוַת לֹא תַעֲשֶׂה שֶׁנֶּאֱמַר בְּשַׁבָּת: "לֹא תַעֲשֶׂה מְלָאכָה" (דברים ה,יג. שמות כ,י), וְלֹא פֵּירֵשׁ מַה הִיא מְלָאכָה, וּבַתּוֹרָה שֶׁבְּעַל פֶּה נִתְפָּרֵשׁ שֶׁהֵן ל"ט מְלָאכוֹת הַיְדוּעוֹת, וְלֹא טִלְטוּל אֲבָנִים וְקוֹרוֹת כְּבֵידוֹת

And likewise all of the commandments in the Torah, whether the positive commandments or the negative commandments, are only revealed, known, and explained through the Oral Torah. For instance, the negative commandment is stated regarding Shabbat, "You shall not perform any labor" (Deut. 5:14; Ex. 20:10). Here, the verse **did not explain what constitutes labor. The Oral Torah explains that this** refers to **the thirty-nine known** types of **labor, not to moving stones and heavy beams.**

After presenting an example of a positive commandment – *tefillin* – the author of the *Tanya* now provides an example of a negative commandment – work on the Sabbath. An understanding derived from the Written Torah alone – "so that you may rest…" – might be that this refers to moving stones and heavy beams, and the like. However, the teachings of the Oral Torah are not always in keeping with our intellect and understanding. If that were the case, perhaps we would not need the Oral Torah. We would simply read the Written Torah and be able to infer the rest. Yet in actual fact, not only does the Written Torah lack sufficient information, even what it does convey is not always aligned with what we learn is the *halakha* from the Oral Torah.

---

35. This follows a comment of the Lubavitcher Rebbe (see *Lessons in Tanya*).

וְכַיוֹצֵא בָּהֶן הֵן כָּל הַמִּצְוֹת, בֵּין מִצְוֹת
עֲשֵׂה בֵּין מִצְוֹת לֹא תַעֲשֶׂה, הֵן סְתוּמוֹת
וְלֹא מְפוֹרָשׁוֹת וּגְלוּיוֹת וִידוּעוֹת אֶלָּא
עַל יְדֵי תּוֹרָה שֶׁבְּעַל פֶּה

And similar to these, all of the commandments, whether positive commandments or negative commandments, are hidden and are only explained, revealed, and known by means of the Oral Torah.

The author of the *Tanya* points out that this pertains to both the positive and the negative commandments. There is an intrinsic difference between the revelation of the supernal will through the positive commandments and that revelation through the negative commandments.[36] In the positive commandments the supernal will is revealed in the form of specific thing that expresses the supernal will below: A person should do such-and-such in such-and-such a manner. In the negative commandments, it seems that there is no specific revelation of what the supernal will is, but at most what it is not. Yet the Oral Torah reveals this as well: A garment that is not of deed but of non-deed, which can reveal to the soul even that which lies beyond all levels and parameters. This can also serve as a garment of light for the entirely concealed delight.

וּמִשּׁוּם הָכֵי כְּתִיב עַל תּוֹרָה שֶׁבְּעַל
פֶּה: "אַל תִּטּוֹשׁ תּוֹרַת אִמֶּךָ" (משלי
א,ח), כְּמוֹ שֶׁכָּתוּב בַּזֹּהַר

And therefore the verse states concerning the Oral Torah, "Do not forsake the teaching of your mother" (Prov. 1:8), as is written in the *Zohar*.

"Hear, my son, the admonition of your father, and do not forsake the teaching of your mother." The *Zohar*[37] states that the written Torah is "the admonition of your father," while the Oral Torah is "the teaching

---

36. See *Likkutei Torah, Parashat Pekudei, Ma'amar* s.v. "*eileh pekudei hamishkan,*" where it is said that the positive commandments correspond to the letters *vav heh* in the name of *Havaya* and the negative commandments to *yod heh*. As mentioned above, this is similar to the division of the four levels into two sets of two.

37. *Zohar* 2:276b. See also *Kanfei Yona*, part 1, chap. 4; *Mateh Moshe, Sha'ar* 3, in the name of the Sages (*Likkutei Hagahot LeTanya*). See also *Or HaTorah*, Prayer Book, p. 98; *Yahel Or*, p. 641, which references the *Zohar* 2:85a (*Tanya BeTzeruf Likkutei Peirushim*).

of your mother." The relationship between them is analogous to that of a father and mother.

מִשּׁוּם שֶׁעַל דֶּרֶךְ מָשָׁל, כְּמוֹ שֶׁכָּל אֶבְרֵי הַוָּלָד כְּלוּלִים בְּטִיפַּת הָאָב בְּהֶעְלֵם גָּדוֹל, וְהָאֵם מוֹצִיאַתּוּ לִידֵי גִּילּוּי בְּלֵידָתָהּ וָלָד שָׁלֵם בִּרְמַ״ח אֵבָרִים וּשְׁסָ״ה גִידִים, כָּכָה מַמָּשׁ כָּל רְמָ״ח מִצְוֹת עֲשֵׂה וּשְׁסָ״ה מִצְוֹת לֹא תַעֲשֶׂה בָּאִים מֵהֶעְלֵם אֶל הַגִּילּוּי בַּתּוֹרָה שֶׁבְּעַל פֶּה

That is **because, metaphorically speaking, just as all of the child's organs are incorporated in the father's** drop of **semen in** a state of **extreme concealment, and the mother causes it to emerge to** a state of **manifestation when she gives birth to an infant** who is **complete with 248 limbs and 365 sinews, so too exactly, all of the 248 positive commandments and 365 negative commandments pass from concealment to manifestation in the Oral Torah,**

The father provides a drop, a single seed that contains the root and hint of everything that the child will become. The drop does not look like the child, it does not have the distribution of limbs like a child; it is merely a drop. Accordingly, it is analogous to the Written Torah and the commandments as they are written in it. The mother receives the drop from the father, which she develops and grows immeasurably, such that when it is born it has the form of an entire human being with all its limbs. Similarly, in the Oral Torah each commandment is constructed and attains completion in all of its details. In every "birth" – in each halakhic ruling in the summation of the Oral Torah – a complete form is achieved, with all the details and particulars of the "drop" of the commandment that is transmitted in the Written Torah.

וְרֵישֵׁיהּ דִּקְרָא ״שְׁמַע בְּנִי מוּסַר אָבִיךָ״, קָאֵי אַתּוֹרָה שֶׁבִּכְתָב דְּנָפְקָא מֵחָכְמָה עִילָּאָה, הַנִּקְרֵאת בְּשֵׁם אָב׳

whereas **the beginning of the** verse: **"Hear, my son, the admonition of your father," refers to the Written Torah, which emerges from supernal wisdom, which is called "father."**

The Written Torah is called "father" not only in relation to the Oral Torah, which is called "mother," but also because it emerges from Ḥokhma, which is itself called "father." Just as Ḥokhma is the initial level, the highest of the sefirot, so too the Written Torah is the initial level, prior to all other levels of the revelation of the Torah, as it brings the initial kernel of the divine revelation into everything that will subsequently develop into our world. Furthermore, just as Keter, which is not counted as one of the sefirot but encompasses them, is above Ḥokhma, so too that which can be called the "spirit of the Torah," the presence of the Torah as it is beyond the revelation in the letters of the worlds, exists above the Written Torah. This "spirit of the Torah" is revealed in the Oral Torah and the halakhot.

וְזֶה שֶׁכָּתוּב: "אֵשֶׁת חַיִל עֲטֶרֶת בַּעְלָהּ" (משלי יב, יד) כִּי הַתּוֹרָה שֶׁבְּעַל פֶּה הַנִּקְרֵאת 'אֵשֶׁת חַיִל', הַמּוֹלִידָה וּמַעֲמֶדֶת חֲיָלוֹת הַרְבֵּה

And thus the verse states, "A woman of valor is the crown of her husband" (Prov. 12:14), because the Oral Torah is called "a woman of valor," who gives birth to and establishes many legions.

Here the author of the Tanya repeats the verse quoted at the beginning of the epistle. Now we can understand who the woman of valor is and why she is called a crown. The woman of valor is the Oral Torah, which reveals to us down below the supernal will, which is Keter, higher than the Written Torah (the "husband" of the Oral Torah).

The Hebrew word for "valor," ḥayil, is related to ḥayal, "soldier." The Oral Torah is called a woman of valor because it engenders and raises many legions of soldiers who, directed from above, descend to battlefields in remote locations, where the divine source cannot be seen, to take arms against numerous "troops" that are cut off from holiness and the divine revelation and will. These legions are a person's performance of the practical commandments in the physical world.

כְּמוֹ שֶׁכָּתוּב: "וַעֲלָמוֹת אֵין מִסְפָּר" (שיר השירים ו, ב), אַל תִּקְרֵי עֲלָמוֹת אֶלָּא עוֹלָמוֹת,

As the verse states, "And young women without number" (Song 6:8). Do not read alamot, "young women,"

אֵלוּ הֲלָכוֹת דְּלֵית לוֹן חוּשְׁבָּנָא, כְּמוֹ שֶׁכָּתוּב בַּתִּיקוּנִים (הקדמת תיקוני זהר [יד,ב])

but *olamot*, "worlds" (see *Shir HaShirim Rabba* 10:12; *Avoda Zara* 35b). These worlds **are the *halakhot* that are without number, as written in the *Tikkunim*** (Introduction to *Tikkunei Zohar* 14b).

Every *halakha* is like a world in and of itself. Just as there is no end to the worlds, so too there is no end to all of the details of halakhic decisions. Although there are a finite number of commandments in the Torah, the *halakhot* in the Oral Torah are infinite. Each application of a commandment in the world of action, in a certain situation and at a particular time, is a distinct *halakha*, and these are innumerable.

וְכוּלָן הֵן בְּחִינַת גִּילּוּי רָצוֹן הָעֶלְיוֹן בָּרוּךְ הוּא, הַנֶּעֱלָם בַּתּוֹרָה שֶׁבִּכְתָב

And these *halakhot* are all an aspect of a revelation of the blessed supernal will, which is concealed in the Written Torah.

Each halakhic decision, in every detail of a commandment and in each of its encounters with reality and other commandments, is a unique revelation of the supernal will, which was concealed in the Written Torah.

וְרָצוֹן הָעֶלְיוֹן בָּרוּךְ הוּא - הוּא לְמַעְלָה מַעְלָה מִמַּעֲלַת חָכְמָה עִילָּאָה, וּכְמוֹ כֶּתֶר וַעֲטָרָה שֶׁעַל הַמּוֹחִין שֶׁבָּרֹאשׁ, לָכֵן נִקְרְאוּ הַהֲלָכוֹת בְּשֵׁם 'תָּגָא' וְ'כִתְרָה שֶׁל תּוֹרָה'

And the blessed supernal will is much higher than the level of supernal wisdom, and it is like a crown and coronet over the intellect in the head. Therefore, the *halakhot* are called a "diadem" and "the crown of the Torah,"

The supernal will, which the *halakhot* express, is higher than the supernal wisdom, which is the Written Torah. The supernal will is like a crown upon the supernal wisdom.

Thus, at the end of the epistle the question that was posed at its beginning receives its answer. Why are the *halakhot* called "the crown of the Torah"? If you say it is because the *halakhot* are an expression of the supernal will, apparently everything in the world is an expression of the supernal will. The answer is that since the revelation of the supernal will in the *halakhot* does not pass through Ḥokhma (and all the levels of descent), the *halakhot* themselves, as they are here below, can be described as a revelation of the supernal will and of the crown, *Keter*, themselves. For beyond all of the noble justifications, material and spiritual, for performing the commandments, there is in fact one reason alone: Because God commands us to do so.

וְהַשּׁוֹנֶה הֲלָכוֹת מוּבְטָח לוֹ שֶׁהוּא בֶּן עוֹלָם הַבָּא (מגילה כח,ב) עַל יְדֵי הִתְלַבְּשׁוּת נֶפֶשׁ רוּחַ נְשָׁמָה שֶׁלּוֹ בָּרָצוֹן הָעֶלְיוֹן בָּרוּךְ הוּא, כַּנִּזְכָּר לְעֵיל:

and "whoever studies *halakhot* is assured of a share in the World to Come" (*Megilla* 28b), **as a result of enclothing his** *nefesh, ruaḥ,* **and** *neshama* **in the blessed supernal will, as mentioned above.**

This addresses the second question posed at the beginning of the epistle: Why is one who studies *halakhot* assured of a share in the World to Come, rather than other areas of Torah? The answer is that this is because his *nefesh, ruaḥ,* and *neshama* are enclothed in the supernal will within the *halakhot*. The Hebrew for "is assured of a share in the World to Come" can be read as "is in the World to Come": He is already there and experiencing it. As stated earlier, our created soul cannot endure the World to Come. In order to be in the World to Come, to experience it and attain the revelation of the divine light and the infinite delight there, the soul must be enclothed in a garment that resembles that light, which is the garment of the commandments. Therefore, a person who attains these garments while alive in this world, one who engages in this aspect of the Torah that reveals the supernal will – the *halakhot* – is "in the World to Come." ☞

The central topic of Epistle 29 was the study of the *halakhot* of the Oral Torah. It was explained that the *halakhot* are "the crown of the Torah," since they draw forth *Keter*, which is the supernal, divine will, to the land below, like pillars that connect the earth to a supernal, encompassing ceiling. Like hollow pillars, the *halakhot* enclothe the person who engages in them in a garment of divine will through which the soul can attain in the Garden of Eden the interiority of the will, the intrinsic divine delight that is revealed through the performance of the commandments.

Since the *halakhot* are studied as part of the Oral Torah, at its end the epistle describes the excellent nature of that Torah in words that echo its introductory comments, that the Oral Torah is "a woman of valor, the crown of her husband." This is because studying the *halakhot* – how exactly here below we can implement the highest will – is found

THE ENCLOTHING OF THE *NEFESH, RUAḤ,* AND *NESHAMA*

☞ The author of the *Tanya* mentions the three levels of the soul – *nefesh, ruaḥ,* and *neshama* – because each one is enclothed in a different manner and on a different level when it wears the garment of the supernal will that expresses itself in the *halakhot.* The levels of the soul are like stages on the way to a goal, stages of development and ascent, through which a person rises from this world to the divine. As the *Zohar* states (2:94b): "When a person is born, he is given a *nefesh.* If he merits more, he is given a *ruaḥ.* If he merits more, he is given a *neshama.*" In other words, as soon as a person is born, the aspect of *nefesh* is drawn down to him. Afterward, by means of his service, he rises to the aspect of *ruaḥ,* until he reaches the level of *neshama* (see the beginning of *Kuntres HaAvoda* by the fifth Lubavitcher Rebbe, Rabbi Sholom Dovber Schneerson). Moreover, each level has its own root and purpose. A commandment that is performed on the level of the *neshama* cannot substitute for one performed on the levels of the *ruaḥ* and *nefesh,* and so forth. There is intrinsic meaning and significance to keeping the commandments and studying *halakha* on each level of the soul.

On the level of *nefesh,* what is important is the performance of the deed and one's awareness of its performance. On the level of *ruaḥ,* the important thing is one's at-titude itself, such as his love, which leads him to keep the positive commandments, and his fear, which leads him to observe the negative commandment. On the level of *neshama,* what is important is an entirely abstract relationship to commandments, without a person's reference to himself, his sense of self, his sense of his own existence. Here there is no "I" who loves or who acts. Corresponding to these three levels of soul that are enclothed within the *halakhot,* there are three levels in the Garden of Eden, in each of which the supernal, divine delight is enclothed (although in general we speak of two levels, the upper and lower Garden of Edens, that is only a general picture; on closer inspection there are many levels, all in accordance with the individual and his soul). On the level of the *nefesh,* the Garden of Eden is connected to and revealed through the garments of all of the details of this physical world. On the level of the *ruaḥ,* the Garden of Eden is in the world of feeling, albeit connected to this world, but as the divine existence feels the world, with its love, might, and compassion, as a person's *ruaḥ* now feels them and in which it participates. Finally, on the level of the *neshama* the Garden of Eden is itself, with a divine awareness, as it were, that a person's *neshama* also takes delight in attaining.

not in the Written Torah but only in the Oral Torah, in the infinite renewal that is required in response to the infinite renewal and change of our lower existence. Accordingly, it is precisely when we study the *halakha* in the Oral Torah that we attain the crown of the Torah, which is loftier than that which can understood and comprehended by human wisdom.

Each individual can take from these ideas, with respect to the service of the soul, another perspective on studying *halakha*. Although the *halakha* is so focused on worldly matters that one who engages in it might imagine that he is immersed in this world, its study also pertains to the highest pinnacle of all learning. It is not a method of study through which we cogitate and experience divine wisdom and delight. Rather, it is the analysis of details and connections. For the very reason that we do not relate to their inner meaning, they weave a garment for the soul: One detail after another, a garment for each limb and ability in *nefesh*, *ruah*, and *neshama*, so that when the soul is enclothed in it, it can experience that which it is impossible for a created soul to attain. In sum, by studying the *halakha*, the soul fulfills the obligation of its descent to this world, both in deed and in the spiritual attainment mentioned above: To draw forth the divine delight by making an abode here for God.[38]

---

38. See *Tanya*, 36, and many other places. God's abode in the lower worlds is the revelation of the intrinsic divine delight on all levels of existence.

Epistle 30

THIS SHORT EPISTLE IS ONE OF A NUMBER THAT THE author of the *Tanya* wrote to his hasidim in the context of raising funds for those hasidim living in the land of Israel. The text indicates that it is addressed to a particular community whose members had recently given less charity than they were accustomed to giving and that they should have been giving. The author of the *Tanya* reproves them for that, and he encourages them to make up the deficit. But in addition, since this is a letter of a rebbe to his hasidim, he discusses the spiritual meaning of this topic: what is the meaning of a mitzva, charity in particular, which should have been performed but was not – and on the essence of a spiritual reality that has not been completed in actuality and is now incomplete.

Out of this context, the epistle discusses the value of a plenitude of charity: a plenitude of instances of giving charity and a plenitude of coins (the sum). What is the spiritual meaning of a plenitude of charity, since by its nature giving charity is an immeasurable act? What place do sums and amounts have in the spiritual world and in divine influence overall? When a person gives charity, that draws the divine blessing of peace into the world. And how specifically through calculated large sums of that which seemingly has no measurement do we draw peace into the world?

Other epistles have related primarily to the personal meaning of an awakening from above – particularly, in regard to what an individual who has given charity receives. This epistle, on the other hand, discusses the overall meaning of giving charity here below, the influence of the supernal will upon the source of life of all worlds and created beings. This overall influence must exist unceasingly, which is to say that there must be a constant giving at all periods of time without interruption. Therefore, the awakening from below discussed by the author of the *Tanya* in this epistle is an ongoing giving of charity that a person is accustomed to engaging in – despite the hindrances and difficulties that arise daily.

24 Ḥeshvan

23 Ḥeshvan
(leap year)

מוּדַעַת זֹאת מַה שֶּׁאָמְרוּ רז״ל: כָּל הָרָגִיל לָבֹא לְבֵית הַכְּנֶסֶת וְיוֹם אֶחָד לֹא בָּא, הקב״ה שׁוֹאֵל עָלָיו

The Sages' statement is well known: Whoever is accustomed to coming to the synagogue, and one day he does not come, the Holy One, blessed be He, asks about him,

When a person regularly attends synagogue daily, and one day he does not attend, God senses this person's absence.[1] The implication is that when a person does come to the synagogue every day, God senses his coming. Although habituation may dull a person's feeling of the holiness of the synagogue, and the supernal significance of his going there, God does sense it. The world grows habituated, the angel grows habituated, but God never grows habituated and never grows weary. Similarly, should a person fail to perform a mitzva, even without caring about it anymore, God is aware, and He Himself inquires after that person.

שֶׁנֶּאֱמַר: ״מִי בָכֶם יְרֵא ה' וכו'״ (ישעיה נ,י) וְכֵן בְּכָל הַמִּצְוֹת וּבִפְרָט מִצְוַת הַצְּדָקָה שֶׁשְּׁקוּלָה כְּנֶגֶד כָּל הַמִּצְוֹת הֲגַם שֶׁהִיא בְּלִי נֶדֶר חַס וְשָׁלוֹם

as it is stated: "Who among you fears the Lord…" (Isa. 50:10). The same applies to all the mitzvot, especially the mitzva of charity, which is equivalent to all the other mitzvot, although it should be performed **without a vow, God forbid.**

---

1. See *Berakhot* 7b and *Yalkut Shimoni, Yeshaya* 473. Rabbi Menaḥem Mendel Schneerson, the Lubavitcher Rebbe, notes here that the text in our Talmud differs: "And if one day he does not come, the Holy One, blessed be He, asks after him." But in *Yalkut Shimoni*, above, the text is as it is here: "And he did not come one day…."

The verse states, "Who among you fears the Lord, hears the voice of His servant, who walked in darkness and there was no light for him..." (Isa. 50:10). Our Sages interpret this to mean that a person who fails to attend the synagogue one day, walks in darkness. He did not come to the synagogue, he did not join this mitzva act, because he was in a state of "darkness," meaning, distress, confusion, and anguish. Had he overcome his obstacles and went to the synagogue, despite his feeling no need and desire to do so but only because he is accustomed to doing so every day, he would have seen light there (*Berakhot* 6b; see the commentators).

Every mitzva is comparable to coming to the synagogue, to a holy place. Every mitzva is an encounter. It is where a person is together with God. Therefore, when a person does not perform a mitzva that he has been accustomed to performing, it is as though he has not come to the meeting, and God inquires after him.

All of the mitzvot are like charity that God gives to us and the world. Every mitzva stems from God's infinite divine being, that lacks nothing. His giving of the mitzvot to imperfect man and the world to connect with us, can be defined as charity and an outright gift. *Likkutei Amarim* (chap. 37) points out that the Jerusalem Talmud simply calls charity "the mitzva." There he emphasizes in the name of the Sages (*Bava Batra* 9a), that the purpose of the mitzvot is to refine the world and elevate the holy parts of it. In this, the mitzva of charity has no equal. When a person gives charity, he raises sparks more than he does by performing any other mitzva. When he gives away money that he would otherwise have spent on his material needs, it is as though he is giving away his animal soul. In addition, the mitzva of charity is not limited to any specific object with which one performs the charity. Everything that one gives to charity is elevated. Moreover, everything connected to what a person gives—directly or indirectly, from all parts of the world and parts of the soul and life that he invested to acquire that contribution— is elevated. All of that rises when he gives charity. ☞

THE MITZVA OF CHARITY AND HASIDISM

☞ The idea that charity is equivalent to all the other mitzvot was expressed by the Sages in several places (see *Bava Batra* 9a, and Jerusalem Talmud, *Pe'a* 1:1), and the author of the *Tanya* emphasizes this often in his teachings and letters. The topic

The halakha states that when a person performs a good deed a number of times, it is as though he has vowed to continue doing so.[2] Therefore, it is recommended that, to obviate such an obligation, he must state explicitly in advance that he will engage in that act "without a vow." That is what the author of the *Tanya* is referring to here. When this person who intends to gives charity consistently at set times states explicitly that he will do so "without a vow," he has no formal obligation to continue doing so. (He makes that stipulation so that, should he need to cease that activity, he will not be guilty of violating a vow.)

אַף עַל פִּי כֵן, כָּל הַחַיִל אֲשֶׁר נָגַע
יִרְאַת ה' בְּלִבָּם לֹא יָאֶתָה לְנַפְשָׁם
הָאֱלוֹקִית לָתֵת מִגְרָעוֹת בַּקֹּדֶשׁ

Nevertheless, it is unbecoming for the divine soul of any of the host whose heart has been touched by the fear of God to give a reduced amount of the holy,

The author of the *Tanya* turns here to his hasidim, "the host whose heart has been touched by the fear of God," of whom more is expected than of

of charity seems to have been especially meaningful to him. Beyond the hasidic community's existential need for charity in the most practical sense, it is a "hasidic" mitzva because, perhaps more than any other, it expresses the character of the hasidic movement. Simply put, although there is a general obligation for everyone to give charity, that obligation does not specify details: how much, when and in what manner. Therefore, every time a person gives charity there is an aspect of generosity, of going beyond the letter of the law. This points to the essence of Hasidism (see *Nidda* 17a and *Tosafot* there. And the sixth Lubavitcher Rebbe, Rabbi Yosef Yitzḥak Schneerson in *Likkutei Dibburim, Shemini Atzeret VeSimḥat Torah* 5694 (3), section 12 on the term "hasid.").

Another aspect is that, like every other mitzva, charity is above as it is below. Just as below it entails giving to a person who is lacking, including to a person who cannot pay, neither in a physical nor in a spiritual manner, so too above it entails the giving of an outright gift to a person who is lacking. That is to say, it is the highest, most essential giving, with no parallel. (Therefore, it entails giving to someone who is lacking, because the recipient has nothing of commensurate value to repay it). The mitzva of charity is therefore the mitzva with which a person connects to the highest place and draws it into the lowest place. He connects and unites everything that is, in the most tangible way. This is the whole thrust of the hasidic movement.

2. See *Shulḥan Arukh, Yoreh De'a,* 214.

anyone else. That is not to say that hasidim are special people, but that
the hasidic movement in general sets the bar at a higher level than the
basic requirements of the Torah. The very minimum that is expected
of every hasid is to be "the host whose heart has been touched by the
fear of God." They are the men conscripted to a purpose beyond their
personal lives, who are even obligated, if necessary, to give their lives
for that purpose. The hasid is obligated to act not on behalf of himself
and his family but on behalf of the entire people of Israel, and not only
due to a formal obligation to follow the *Shulḥan Arukh* but to abide
by the entire breadth of the Torah beyond fixed obligations. As the
epistle states, the fear of God has touched their heart. When the fear
of God touches a hasid's heart, when it becomes a part of who he is, he
begins his journey. It is from this point that the Rebbe tells him – in
this epistle and in general – to go forward.

It is not fitting for a person's divine soul, which this epistle is
addressing, to give less charity than he has been used to doing, to
diminish and damage the holy building that already exists.

What the author of the *Tanya* expects of the hasid is not that he
wage a new battle, that he scale a new mountain, but rather, only that
he guard the already existing portion of holiness from being damaged.
He should do so not in a strident, confrontational way, but in a way that
is comparable to surfing a wave. As the surfer rides a wave of holiness
down from the crest, he draws holiness downward. Nothing less than
that is expected of him.

When a person gives charity, he draws forth holiness, the light of the
infinite one, to *Malkhut*, which "has nothing of its own."[3] Therefore,
when a person gives charity repeatedly, that is not merely a pulse of
holiness. It is a stream of holiness, a reality and structure of holiness.
And if he does not give charity one time, he damages and diminishes
that holy reality.

מֵאֲשֶׁר כְּבָר הוּרְגְּלוּ מִדֵּי שָׁנָה	**than that which they have become**
לְהַפְרִישׁ מִמְּאוֹדָם	**accustomed to set aside on a yearly basis from their capital** (*me'odam*).

---

3. *Zohar*, see 1:181a, *Zohar*, 249b, and *Zohar* 2:218b. And see also *Etz Ḥayyim*,
Shaʿar 6 (*Shaʿar HaʾAkudim*), chap. 5.

The Hebrew word *me'odam* simply means "their capital." As the verse states, "You shall love the Lord your God with all your capital (*me'odekha*)." The Mishna explains that *me'odekha* means "with all your money" (*Berakhot* 9:5). But a number of hasidic texts[4] understand *me'odekha* as without boundary, something that goes beyond the maximum. Although these two explanations appear to contradict each other, both are true. When a person donates money that is not from his surplus of financial cushion, but rather from what he would otherwise have used for his basic needs, he is giving all his money, and he is going beyond the maximum. This can be seen as even greater than giving up one's life, because the latter is a one-time act and furthermore, at the moment of self-sacrifice, a person can feel the meaning in it. In contrast, when a person gives charity on the level of "with all your money" consistently every day, irrespective of his mood, that is with all of his unbounded *me'od*. ☞

לְהַחֲיוֹת רוּחַ שְׁפָלִים וְנִדְכָּאִים, דְּלֵית לְהוֹן מִגַּרְמֵיהוֹן הִיא בְּחִינַת "סוּכַּת דָּוִד הַנּוֹפֶלֶת וכו'" לְקוֹמֵם וּלְרוֹמֵם וכו', לְמֶהֱוֵי אֶחָד בְּאֶחָד וכו'

The purpose of charity is **to revive the spirit of the humble and the downtrodden, who have nothing of their own.** The *Malkhut* corresponds to **"the fallen booth of David...," to raise and uplift..., to be united in one...,**

A person is poor in the sense that he is incapable of paying for what he receives, whether that is physical or spiritual. Charity to such a person is therefore the deepest sort of free gift. In that sense, a person who gives charity is similar to God Himself, whose whole influence

---

FROM THEIR CAPITAL

☞ The author of the *Tanya* writes elsewhere (see *Torah Or* 69d and *Likkutei Torah*, Num. 28b) that the infinitude indicated by the word *me'odekha* is always connected to what a person does here on earth. Here on earth, material possessions are merely physical: financially speaking, it is just money or even worse, *kelippot*. However, when these are transformed into holiness, they reach a state of infinitude that is beyond anything that descends from above. And so, the phrase, "with all your capital," which translates literally as, "with all of your might," refers not to the money itself, but to what exists when the money (or the like) is transformed to holiness.

---

4. *Likkutei Torah*, Num. 42, *Torah Or* 53, and elsewhere.

upon existence is ultimately an undeserved gift to *Malkhut*, which "has nothing of own," and to the "children of *Malkhut*," the poor.

During the time of exile, *Malkhut* corresponds to the fallen booth of David (Amos 9:11.) The booth of David is the *Malkhut*, the sovereignty, of David[5] as it was in its time and, even more so, as it will be in the future redemption. It is synonymous with the revelation of the sovereignty of God in all worlds. The "booth" signifies that at that time, it will be like a crown that surrounds all existence. During the time of exile, however, it is "the fallen booth of David." The crown and glory of that sovereignty have fallen to the *kelippa* and to exile. That is exile in the broadest sense: the fall of the holy sparks, darkness and ruin, concealment of the Divine that provides life to an existence that does not recognize it. At this time of exile, the principal way of serving God is by giving charity, which shines light into the darkness and into the *kelippot* even when we do not see the fallen holiness, even when we do not receive even the slightest reflection of light. That is the essence of the service of charity: giving to a person who has nothing, and who seemingly, gives nothing back.

The author of the *Tanya* relates the words "to raise and uplift" to the verse that states, "On that day, I will raise the fallen booth of David." The ultimate level of the service of charity is to elevate the fallen holiness.[6]

At that time there will be a revelation of oneness between every Jew. That oneness will then unite with the oneness above, and all will be enveloped in a single holiness: "united in one."[7] ☞

TO BE UNITED IN ONE

☞ The purpose of all service of God is the achievement of the state of "the unity of the Holy One, blessed be He, with His Divine Presence." At the present time of

---

5. And so, *Targum Yonaton* translates "the booth of David" as "the sovereignty of the house of David."

6. See *Likkutei Amarim*, chap. 37.

7. From the well-known passage in the *Zohar* (2:135a) called *Kegavna*. It is recited (according to the hasidic custom) before evening prayers on Shabbat eve, because at that time – which is a foretaste of the World to Come and the redemption – the disjointed created world, rises to the world of unity (the world of *Atzilut*), to be "united in one."

וְהַכֹּל לְפִי רוֹב הַמַּעֲשֶׂה וכו' וּלְפִי   and everything is in accordance with
הַחֶשְׁבּוֹן   the abundance of actions..., and in
accordance with the sum.

As the author of the *Tanya* explained in epistle 21, the service of charity is measured not only by the amount that a person gives (providing practical benefit to the recipient) but also by the number of times that he gives (the spiritual benefit created by the act of giving). ☞

This applies not only to the giver but to the recipient as well because, beyond the physicality that he receives, he becomes a part of the mitzva of charity. It is impossible for the giver to give if there is no one to receive. In all giving, there is receiving, which, on a deeper level, is also giving, because only with a recipient can the giver give. That is certainly the case if the recipient shares the intent of the mitzva

exile, we do not see the oneness of God who is one with the Divine Presence. That is because the holiness and oneness of the Divine Presence are hidden and scattered among the *kelippot*. However, when a person gives charity repeatedly, the sparks rise from the *kelippot* and unite into a single oneness. And whenever they are one here below, they unite with the one above, "to be united in one."

Being "united in one" means that the worlds and souls here below unite with each other, after which they can rise to oneness above. The opposite of oneness, separation, means being enclosed within the husk of the *kelippa*. Just as the *kelippa* separates created existence from the *Ein Sof*, so does it separate the created entities

from each other. Therefore, the first stage is to break the *kelippa* that separates one being from another here below, one spark from another, one soul from another. This leads to oneness, which can then be drawn to the supernal oneness.

All of that begins when a person gives charity in a basic sense. When two Jews are separated by the fact that one has and the second lacks, whether in physicality or spirituality, the separation between them evolves into competitiveness and hatred. But when people give charity, they stop and reverse the process of separation, and they begin a process of bonding and unification, until the state of being "united in one" is reached.

THE ABUNDANCE OF ACTIONS

☞ Simply put, epistle 21 explains (in keeping with the Rambam's commentary on the *Mishna*) that a person's performance of multiple good deeds purifies his soul. On a deeper level, it explains that the main purpose of every mitzva is not what the

mitzva accomplishes, but rather, that the person should perform the mitzva action. God commands and a person acts: that is the value of the mitzvot. The principal element, therefore, is the person's action, as he overcomes physical and spiritual obsta-

of charity: when he does not think that the charity is his by right, but rather, recognizes that he is receiving an outright gift from God's supernal lovingkindness, and that the giver is the instrument used to transfer that to him. A recipient with that awareness is a full partner in the reward of the mitzva and in "the abundance of actions."

There is "the abundance of actions," and then there is the sum – that is, the outcome of all of the actions, which is important as well.

כְּמַאֲמַר רַבּוֹתֵינוּ ז"ל: כָּל פְּרוּטָה וּפְרוּטָה מִצְטָרֶפֶת לְחֶשְׁבּוֹן גָּדוֹל וכו' (בבא בתרא ט,ב) עַל דֶּרֶךְ מַאֲמַר רַבּוֹתֵינוּ ז"ל: אֵימָתַי גָּדוֹל הֲוָיָ"ה? כְּשֶׁהוּא בְּעִיר אֱלֹהֵינוּ וכו'

As the Rabbis stated: Each and every *peruta* that one gives combines to form a great sum – (*Bava Batra* 9b), in the manner of the Rabbis' statement: When is *Havaya* great? When He is in the city of our God...

Every act of giving charity (and giving even a single *peruta* – a coin of trifling value) is important in itself. Yet there is also meaning in the accumulation of all one's acts of giving; they combine into a great sum.

But why should that be important? This is a mitzva, drawn down literally from the *Ein Sof*, and in that context, what difference does it make whether a person has donated two *perutot* or three, a small sum or a large sum? But it certainly does make a difference for the poor person, and therefore it makes a difference from the perspective of the giver and from the aspect of the absolute value and meaning of the mitzva. The mitzva of giving charity is not an act that is performed abstractly

cles with alacrity, love and fear that lead to deed. That is the most meaningful outcome - not only for the person's soul but for all worlds, because through his performing the mitzvot they reveal their inner meaning.

Our Sages teach that "the principal element is the deed" (see *Avot* 1:17; see also the Rambam's commentary on the *Mishna*, there). According to this statement, the principal element is not the outcome of his action, but rather, his deed, which is the culmination and test of the authen-

ticity and effect of all his inner work up to that point. When it comes particularly to the mitzva of charity, the practical outcome of which is clearly measurable by the effect on the recipient's physical well-being, the number of times that the giver performs the deed, "the abundance of actions," seems irrelevant. Therefore, the author of the *Tanya* emphasizes that even in the case of giving charity "everything is in accordance with the abundance of actions."

between a person's soul and God. It is performed in this world, and this world has something to say about its value.

There is an even more profound explanation of the Sages' statement, "When is *Havaya* great? When He is in the city of our God...."[8] When discussing the Divine, the *Ein Sof*, how is it possible to speak of a sum? A sum involves numbers, and what meaning does any number, whether large or small, have in relation to the infinite? To explain this, the epistle quotes the *Zohar's* statement, "When is *Havaya* great?" When is there meaning to great and small? "When He is in the city of our God." The "city of our God" alludes to *Malkhut* as the divine speech. *Sefer Yetzira* states that the letters are called "stones" and words are called "houses." By extension, statements are called a "city." Therefore, God's greatness is revealed "in the city of our God," in His Divine speech. That is where the great divine meaning is revealed. Within His letters and words, the multitude of vessels and levels, there is meaning to the statement that God is great. This does not refer to God's essential greatness, but rather, to the "city," to the revelation of His greatness to those within it. ☞

A GREAT SUM

☞ That which is beyond sum, beyond the concepts of great and small, does not essentially exist in our world. It follows that the divine revelation and presence in this world must always be within a certain measure or amount, which is called the sum. Therefore, a sum in its simple sense – the monetary value of the charity – is important not only to the poor person, but because it expresses a certain amount of divine revelation. The number of *perutot* is not, of course, the parameter and measure of God, but it provides some measure that we can relate to. As one *peruta* joins another, divine revelation in one point joins another, and when added up amounts to a "great sum." Although it is fi-

nite, it is "great," meaning that it points toward greatness, even to greatness beyond a sum. Out of this great amount, which grows beyond a person's ability to count, we can see a divine accounting, divine reality within this world. Moreover, it is precisely from the amount that we are able to perceive its greatness that is beyond this world. That is because the "great sum" points from our world to that which is beyond the world and beyond a sum (see *Likkutei Torah*, Num. 70a, which states that "a great sum" is defined as a number and amount "that cannot be counted," comparable to grains of sand, which have a number but are so many that they cannot be counted. Therefore, this "great sum" in-

---

8. See *Zohar* 2:35a, 3:5a, and elsewhere. Based on Ps. 48:2.

הִיא בְּחִינַת וּמְקוֹם הַחֶשְׁבּוֹן כְּמוֹ
שֶׁכָּתוּב: "עֵינַיִךְ בְּרֵכוֹת בְּחֶשְׁבּוֹן"
(שיר השירים ז,ה)

The city of our God **is the aspect and place of the sum** [heshbon], **as it is written: "Your eyes are pools in Ḥeshbon"** (Song 7:5).

The "city of our God" refers to *Malkhut* of *Atzilut*. *Malkhut* and everything that is drawn down from it – the letters, the worlds that are created on all their levels and with all their details – constitutes a place where the divine life force in it is within vessels that are so detached and finite that we do not see infinitude and Divinity but only disconnected, ambiguous sparks. In such a place, only via a sum, only when we calculate, combine and arrange all of these factors, do we see Godliness. Therefore, this place is called "the place of the sum."

The verse states, "Your eyes are pools in Ḥeshbon." The eyes are *Ḥokhma*,[9] and the light of the *Ein Sof* that is revealed in *Ḥokhma* descends and gathers in the pool, which is the "place of the sum," that being *Malkhut*. That is to say, the light of the *Ein Sof* that descends and is drawn down comes to the place of the sum. There it does not descend any further but is gathered together and consolidated. And that is "the sum of the world," from which point it then ascends.

Perhaps this verse hints as well to what occurs next: the eyes, which are *Ḥokhma*, look at the sum, which is *Malkhut*, like water in a

dicates the drawing forth from *Keter* to *Malkhut*, from that which "surrounds all worlds" to that which "fills all worlds").

Elsewhere, (see *Likkutei Torah*, Num. 66d) the difference between "sum" and "great sum" is explained. "Sum" is the spreading forth of the life force of the light that fills all worlds, *Malkhut* of *Atzilut*, the divine speech in the letters that created the universe. And "great sum" is the light that "encompasses all worlds." It is a

"sum" because it relates to the world that it surrounds. Yet, it is "great" because it is greater than the world and the light that fills it, which reveals God in terms of how He acts and creates. A "great sum" therefore characterizes the revelation of the essential divine in the world, which is drawn forth and revealed in it as a result of a person performing the mitzvot in general and in particular the mitzva of giving charity.

---

9. The phrase, "the eyes of the congregation" (Num. 15:24), refers to the sages of the congregation. In general, eyes and seeing allude to *Ḥokhma* (see epistle 14 and *Torah Or* 40a, and elsewhere).

pool that reflects everything. The eyes are then aroused from above, "as water reflects a face to the face, so does the heart of a person to a person" (Prov. 27:19).

וְהַמְכַוִּן כַּנּוֹדַע כִּי בְּאִתְעָרוּתָא   **The intention** of these assertions **as is**
דִּלְתַתָּא   **known, is that by an awakening from below,**

The author of the *Tanya* expands upon the intention of that which has been said about the mitzva of charity, of kindness in its unbounded essence, that a person performs here below in a world of calculated amounts.

According to that which is known generally and explained in other epistles that discuss charity.

The charity that a person does below engenders an arousal from below that impacts the heavenly spheres. Like a mirror in which someone above sees himself, and is aroused, as it were, to feel and act the same way towards those below: to the worlds in general, and in particular, to the person who awakened him above from below. ☞

WITH AN AWAKENING FROM BELOW

☞ Between the upper and lower realms, there is a back-and-forth movement of life force. Life force is not static. It is that which flows, acts and happens within existence. Therefore, it appears in the form of pulses: something occurs and then ceases, something rises and then descends (thus, in the realm of time ("year"), the soul manifests itself in the world in a movement of racing forth and returning. (See *Likkutei Torah*, Num. 64d, and onward). It is a sort of an intertwined arrangement of life force that passes from one periphery to the other, of a pulse of life on one side arousing and initiating a pulse of life on the other side. Of course, the drawing forth of life force from above and the drawing forth of life force from below are not equal. That is because the sole source of life is God Himself

above. Therefore, we do not speak about a flow of life force coming from below but about an arousal by man from below and an arousal by God from above (this is the source of the concept that subsequent to the creation of man, every flow of abundance from above depends on the arousal of man from below.)

Seemingly, in a perfect and pure reality, the arousal from below would have to act exactly as that from above, so that whatever a person said and did below would simply be performed above. For instance, when a person would recite the words in prayer, "He brings down the rain," rain would fall. As the Talmud relates: "Rabbi Yehuda HaNasi decreed a fast, and the Sages brought Rabbi Ḥiyya and his sons down to the pulpit to pray on behalf of

הַמְשָׁכַת חַיִּים חֵן וָחֶסֶד בְּמַעֲשֵׂה which is **the drawing down of life,**
הַצְּדָקָה בִּרְצוֹן הַטּוֹב וְסֵבֶר פָּנִים **grace, and kindness through an act**
יָפוֹת **of charity** performed **with good will**
and a pleasant countenance,

When a person gives charity, he draws forth life and undeserved, unlimited kindness to a needy person.

That is particularly so when he gives charity with a good will and a pleasant countenance. Giving charity in this way is not only preferable and recommended, but an integral part of the mitzva, and indeed halakhically mandated.[10] A pleasant countenance is more than the person's thoughts and feelings as he performs this mitzva. It is itself a spiritual gift, whose importance is no less than that of the physical gift. In particular, in regard to charity as an arousal from below to above, the intention and the spiritual giving are especially important, because those are what rise up through the worlds.

אִתְעָרוּתָא דִלְעֵילָא: "יָאֵר הֲוָי"ה one engenders **an awakening from**
פָּנָיו" (במדבר ו,כה) **above: "The Lord shall shine His countenance"** (Num. 6:25).

the congregation. Rabbi Ḥiyya recited the phrase in the Amida prayer: Who makes the wind blow, and the wind blew. Rabbi Ḥiyya recited the next phrase: Who makes the rain fall, and rain fell." (*Bava Metzia* 85b).

When a person recites the prayer for healing, the words themselves should heal. Indeed, for men of stature – the perfect tzaddikim who are constantly clinging to God and absolutely nullified to the supreme will, without a trace of personal motive – there can exist something like "the tzaddik decrees and God fulfills" (see *Ta'anit* 23a; *Shabbat* 59b; *Zohar* 2:15a). But even in more common and complex situations, this dynamic of life stands at the foundation of the existence of the world: arousal from below and arousal from above. That which a person does below arouses an action from above. But how much, to what extent, in which world and on which level all depends on various factors.

10. See *Shulḥan Arukh, Yore De'a* 249:3, which states that a person who gives charity with a miserly will and an unpleasant expression loses the merit of the mitzva and, furthermore, transgresses the negative commandment of "Your heart shall not be grieved when you give" (*Deut.* 15:10).

The arousal from below of giving charity with a pleasant countenance elicits from above the illumination of the countenance of God to us. This benediction is the second of the three priestly blessings of the *kohanim*. The overall power of these blessings is the illumination of the divine countenance and special Godly outpouring of goodness to us with a good will and a pleasant countenance. A number of Hasidic teachings[11] explain that this is precisely what the priestly blessings do: they shine the light of God's inner essence upon us. This illumination does not go through all of the stages of the order of progression, which have a "face" and a "backside," and therefore does not incur externality and concealment of its inner dimension. Rather, it remains an illumination of the divine countenance that shines its inner essence directly from the highest place to the lowest place. It is an illumination that does take into account whether or not we deserve its divine light. It is an unconditional illumination that does not depend on anything in return, just like the giving of charity here below.

הוּא הָאָרַת וְהַמְשָׁכַת חֵן וְחֶסֶד
וְרָצוֹן עֶלְיוֹן מֵחַיֵּי הַחַיִּים אֵין סוֹף
בָּרוּךְ הוּא, אֲשֶׁר לִגְדוּלָתוֹ אֵין
חֵקֶר וְהַשָּׂגָה כְּלָל

This is the illumination and drawing down of grace, kindness, and supernal will from the infinite source of life, *Ein Sof*, blessed be He, whose greatness cannot be fathomed or comprehended at all,

This flow comes from so high that it cannot by any means be appraised and measured in relation to anything that occurs below. Therefore, it cannot be considered as payment and reward for anything that is done below, but is to be considered an illumination of outright kindness. The level from which this influence comes is called "the supernal will," which is the intrinsic will that expresses the divine essence that transcends all divine manifestations. This is not as we understand the will as it relates to lower existence and is revealed in it, but as it is in itself. This supernal will is the life of life: the life force that exists in all worlds, life that has no end and intrinsically cannot be comprehended.

---

11. *Likkutei Torah* 55c; *Derekh Mitzvotekha, Birkat Cohanim* 112a.

This powerful and inner illumination is aroused above by means of the act of charity that is performed below.

אֶל בְּחִינַת "מַלְכוּתְךָ מַלְכוּת כָּל עוֹלָמִים"   **to the aspect of "Your king-**
(תהלים קמה,יג)   **ship is the kingship of all the**
    worlds" (Ps. 145:13),

This giving reaches the lowest place, which is *Malkhut*, which flows down and maintains all of the worlds.

The phrase "Your kingship is the kingship of all worlds" describes the divine life force that descends to the lowest level at the greatest distance from holiness.[12] The level of *Malkhut* is the culmination of the divine revelation. After the descent of the supernal will to the intellect and the supernal attributes – through which His will can be understood and conceptualized – an actually existent entity emerges: that is to say, *Malkhut*. This is not God's intellect nor His love, but their outcome that is projected from them upon the opaque screen that separates *Atzilut* from the world. (That is to say, *Malkhut* of *Atzilut* receives all of the supernal lights that contain the supernal will, but it does not transfer them onwards as they are intrinsically.) Furthermore, the light of "Your kingship" (*Malkhut* of *Atzilut*) is repeatedly cast further onward in a constricted form onto "the kingship of all worlds" – meaning, onto *Malkhut* of every world, until it constitutes the reality of every person's daily life, in all of its details.

עָלְמָא דְּאִתְגַּלְיָא, הַמְחַיֶּה כָּל הַבְּרוּאִים   **the revealed world, which**
שֶׁבְּכָל הַהֵיכָלוֹת עֶלְיוֹנִים וְתַחְתּוֹנִים   **sustains all created beings**
    that are in all the sanctums,
    both higher and lower,

This level of "Your kingship is the kingship of all worlds" is the divine illumination and life force that is called the "revealed world" and the light that "fills all worlds." It is the divine light not as it is in essence, but

---

12. A similar hasidic teaching is applied to the Sages' designation of God as the exalted "King, King of kings, the Holy One, blessed be He" (as in the Passover Haggadah; see the explanation in the Haggadah of the author of the *Tanya*; *Likkutei Torah, Vayikra* 12b; *Ma'amarei Admor HaZaken* 5569, p. 71).

as it is constricted and becomes compatible with the parameters and concepts of every world, high and low, to give it life according to those parameters. Therefore, it is also the divine illumination that is revealed to lower beings (the "revealed world"): that which every creature and every world can comprehend and relate to as it enters the boundaries and concepts relevant to them. Beyond it, is what is concealed, that which "surrounds all worlds."

שֶׁהֵן בִּבְחִינַת מִסְפָּר וְחֶשְׁבּוֹן כְּמוֹ שֶׁכָּתוּב: "אֶלֶף אַלְפִים יְשַׁמְּשׁוּנֵיהּ" (דניאל ז,י)

which are on the level of numbers and sum, as it is written: "Thousands upon thousands serve Him" (Dan. 7:10),

The revealed worlds and what they contain are within the dimension of numbers and amount. Higher than that, in the hidden worlds, number and amount do not exist. Therefore, even if we speak of that higher realm as a "world," it is a world without measurements, a world that cannot be comprehended or even thought about. In contrast, the revealed worlds, which are essentially the worlds within *Malkhut* on all levels, necessarily have number and amount that distinguish them from the *Ein Sof*. This can be compared to the difference between a person's speech on the one hand and his feelings or understanding on the other. The powers of a person's soul – his intellect and emotional attributes - are hidden: not only from others but even from himself, because fundamentally a person is only aware of what is clothed in the letters of his thought, of that which is quantifiable by number and amount, since only that can be revealed.

The "thousands upon thousands" of angels in the supernal worlds have a number: thousands upon thousands. And if there is number in the upper worlds, which are the root and source of everything that occurs in the lower worlds, how much more so is there number in the lower worlds. ☞

וְזֶהוּ 'חֶשְׁבּוֹן גָּדוֹל'   and this is "a great sum."

Here the author of the *Tanya* returns to the topic of charity, as was explained earlier. "Great sum" alludes to the light that "surrounds all worlds." Although this infinite divine light, in and of itself, is beyond the parameters of all worlds, it relates to the worlds. "Great" alludes to God. When is He considered "great"? When He is "in the city of our God": that is, in the sum of the letters, of the structures, of this world. That is to say, when a person gives charity, God Himself, the infinite one, is revealed. through finite amounts. But how is it possible for there to be a "great sum," a revelation of everything infinite, within the finite? Not even all the angels at the heights of the upper world could accomplish that! The answer is as follows.

| שֶׁעַל יְדֵי רוֹב מַעֲשֵׂה הַצְּדָקָה שָׁלוֹם כִּי פֵּירוּשׁ שָׁלוֹם הוּא דָּבָר הַמְחַבֵּר וּמְתַוֵּוךְ ב׳ קְצָווֹת הַפְּכִיִּים | For by means of the abundance of the act of charity there is peace, because "peace" means something that connects and mediates between two opposite extremes. |

As a result of a person's many uninterrupted acts of charity, the *perutot* combine into a "great sum." In a sense, when a person gives charity, he becomes like God Himself, higher than all of the revealed worlds. Everything that he gives to the needy person is in the category of outright kindness to a person who is lacking. However, this is the main emphasis of this epistle, giving once or even a few times does not suffice if there is a subsequent interruption. That interruption creates a wall, at which point the giving is no longer infinite, because there is a boundary to the sum and it is no longer "great." Only by means of "the abundance of the act" does the amount become "a great sum." This great amount is not the total number of *perutot* but their combining with each other in a vastness beyond number. And that can occur only when there is no interruption between one *peruta* and the next, between one act of giving and the next. Only then is the giving not grasped by finitude, but

THOUSANDS UPON THOUSANDS

☞ The supernal angels represent the largest number that it is possible to think about. Thus, this term represents the largest number that can be expressed. From this abundant quantity, the angels praise God as much as they can, but not beyond that. Meaning, the whole plurality of this light is comprised only of that number and amount that is in it; it does not draw down from the *Ein Sof* beyond that which is revealed to it, and does not have access to the hidden that is not yet revealed.

rather, summons the *Ein Sof* beyond worlds to make "peace" between the finite entities in the worlds.

The concept of "peace," on all levels and in all senses, is a bonding of factors that are distant and opposite from each other, like adversaries that could not otherwise be together in the same place, since they act in opposition to one another. Peace is the arena that puts them together, and makes it so that they are no longer opposites.

שֶׁהֵן קְצֵה הַשָּׁמַיִם לְעֵילָא, בְּחִינַת "וְלִגְדוּלָּתוֹ אֵין חֵקֶר" (תהלים קמה,ג) וּקְצֵה הַשָּׁמַיִם לְתַתָּא, הַמִּתְלַבֵּשׁ בִּבְרִיאָה יְצִירָה עֲשִׂיָּיה, בְּחִינַת גְּבוּל וּמִסְפָּר, וְדַי לַמֵּבִין

One of these opposites **is the edge of the heavens above, as in "His greatness is unfathomable"** (Ps. 145:3), **and** the other opposite is **the edge of the heavens below, which is enclothed in the worlds of *Beria*, *Yetzira*, and *Asiya*, in the form of a limit and number, and this is sufficient explanation for one who understands.**

The epistle refers to two opposite extremities. At the upper perimeter of heaven, "His greatness is unfathomable" (Ps. 145:3) because He is infinite, and the infinite lies beyond inquiry and comprehension. And the lower perimeter of heaven is clothed in the worlds of *Beria*, *Yetzira* and *Asiya*, which are characterized by boundary and number. The peace that the epistle discusses is the most comprehensive peace between the two farthest extremities: the infinite above and the finite below. Although below, within boundaries, there are endless levels and variations, essentially, all of that has no meaning compared to the infinite. Between the finite and the infinite there is an inherent contradiction that encompasses every actual and possible dichotomy of reality. ☞

THE EDGE OF THE HEAVENS ABOVE AND BELOW

☞ The author of the *Tanya* speaks here of two extremities of heaven, not the extremities of heaven and earth. That is because, once some degree of limitation exists in heaven, in divine existence itself (in the world of *Atzilut*), then the meaning and possibility of finitude throughout the entire descent of created worlds through *Beria*, *Yetzira* and *Asiya* is merely an extension that develops from that initial

The epistle concludes by speaking about peace, which the culmination of all of the contents discussed therein. Only that which transcends the two opposite extremities can make peace between them (see epistle 12 and many teachings of the author of the *Tanya*). Therefore, only God Himself "makes peace in His heights" (Job 25:2): between Michael (angel of water) and Gabriel (angel of fire), between fire and water, between Ḥesed and Gevura, between the power of spreading out and the power of reining in. Only in the context of God's supernal will and wisdom, that transcend Ḥesed and Gevura and that encompass both of them in a single perspective of the world, do we see that Ḥesed and Gevura are not opposed to each other but that essentially their contending actions generate the existence of the world and everything in it.

The same applies to the parameters of the more abstract extremities of finitude and infinitude. Only God Himself, who is beyond finite and beyond infinite, makes peace. There is a reality that transcends the infinite. That is because the infinite is limited insofar as it relates to the finite. Its very infinitude exists because it is in relation to the finite. It is infinitude that has, as it were, finitude, in that it is defined as being infinite. This is explained in hasidic teachings based on *Avodat HaKodesh* 1, beginning of chapter 8.

This epistle has explained that the aspect of the divine essence, which is higher than finitude and infinitude both, draws God's "charity" into the worlds. Only charity, which is an undeserved gift for a needy recipient, can bridge the infinite gap – something that appears to be absolutely impassible – so that God Himself descends and enters into

differentiation. In the three lower worlds, there is no new fundamental, intrinsic differentiation, but only a partial reiteration at low intensities of that primary differentiation. This may be compared to secondary earthquakes that only express reverberations of the original great earthquake.

Perhaps that is why the epistle concludes with the words, "This is sufficient explanation for one who understands." This suffices for a person who understands that the extremities of heaven above and heaven below express the two types of divine light that the Kabbala and Hasidism call "light that surrounds all worlds" and "light that fills all worlds." In hasidic thought, these two express the root of the most primordial differentiation that constitutes the foundation of the existence of the worlds and the Divine. The making of "peace" between the two – unifying the Holy One, blessed be He, and His Divine Presence – is the purpose of all service of God.

this world. When a human being performs the mitzva of giving charity to another person, he becomes a partner with God Himself Who gives the mitzvot. This person arouses from below the divine act of charity and its entrance into our world.

This epistle emphasizes that a person should give charity generously and frequently, because that arouses the *Ein Sof* to give from above. Charity, on a deeper level, is an outright gift whose character is infinite. For its exterior action to be infinite as well, it must be frequent and ongoing, repeatedly in every period of time, without any interruption. That prevents any interruption between charity below and charity above, because the deed below truly affects the infinite above, with an ever-increasing resonance. Should there be an interruption, heaven forbid, should a person does not come one day, then God inquires after him. That inquiry is itself an interruption of the flow from above, an interruption in the state of peace that had existed between the extremity above and the extremity below. By way of illustration, imagine a group of people who work well together, who get along, who inspire each other, who together create an atmosphere of increasing kindness, holiness and creativity (or imagine an individual who experiences such a state of compatibility among the parts of his soul). Should someone or something suddenly be out of place, and the question is asked: "What is going on? Why is everything stuck?" At that moment, the members of the group find themselves outside. Suddenly they begin to reflect from the outside: "What a beautiful thing we had here!" because it no longer exists. The one-time peace is broken, and disjunction, in which various factors pull in opposite directions, returns.

Giving frequently and without interruption is not only a particular way of giving charity. It is essential to the act of giving charity, which must be precisely in that way. All charity is inherently not limited by the character of the recipient, by how much he deserves, and so forth. When the giving is uninterrupted and it continues on and on without interruption in the life of the giver, it is also infinite in actuality. It then arouses a flow of infinite kindness and favor from the very highest level to all of the worlds.

Epistle 31

THIS SMALL AND CONCENTRATED EPISTLE IS APPAR-
ently part of a letter that was intended to effect a reconciliation among hasidim, perhaps following some specific
occurrence. In it, the author of the *Tanya* explains the importance of closeness and concord among people, and the
dangers to which the lack of these may lead.

נוֹדָע בַּשְּׁעָרִים   It is **"known in the gates"**   25 Ḥeshvan

24 Ḥeshvan
(leap year)

In this epistle, the author of the *Tanya* will write on a topic that pre-
sumes a certain degree of prior knowledge on the part of his readers.
With this assumption, he briefly summarizes an explanation of the
background, and then immediately delves into the main topic of the
letter. ☞

"KNOWN IN THE GATES"

☞ It is unusual for the author of the *Tan-ya* to employ this expression instead of the more typical "it is well known" which appears often in the *Tanya*, and alludes to matters that people know or may be presumed to know, which includes Kabbalistic concepts (see epistles 28, 29). Here, on the other hand, the author of the *Tanya* will discuss a topic that is not universally known. Furthermore, he will not explain it, but only derive applicable conclusions from it that relate to serving God. Therefore, he employs the phrase, "known in the gates [*she'arim*]," according to its hasidic interpretation that a matter is known

to an individual through the way that he conceives of it (*mesha'er*) in his heart. This is in keeping with the *Zohar's* statement (1:103b) that the Holy One, blessed be He (the "Husband" of the Congregation of Israel) is known to each individual through the particular way that he imagines in his heart. This is cited in many hasidic sources, such as the introduction to the *Tan-ya* and chapter 44 (and see *Likkutei Torah, Bemidbar* 85b, and *Torat Menaḥem*, vol. 17, p. 179.) That is to say, according to a person's measure (*shiur*), his character, he connects himself to a topic via the understanding and feelings of his heart. This

מַה שֶּׁכָּתוּב בַּתִּיקוּנִים דִּשְׁכִינְתָּא   that which is written in *Tikkunei*
אִיהִי מַרְעָא בְּגָלוּתָא כִּבְיָכוֹל   *Zohar:* that "the Divine Presence
is sick in exile," as it were.

This statement presents a fundamental description of the exile of the Divine Presence: it is as though the Divine Presence is ill. In other words, exile is an unhealthy, unnatural, and dysfunctional state. A person may conceptualize and experience exile as a stage of development and learning that is a part of an operative process; that in order to reach the redemption, which is a more mature and improved state of existence, we must endure stages of exile. In contrast to that understanding, the *Zohar*[1] states that exile, at least in human eyes, is to be conceived of as a state of illness, of impairment, which lacks even temporary legitimacy. Accordingly, we must relate to exile not as to something vital (although difficult) that one must undergo, but as a state of being whose cessation one must bring about by all possible means.

פֵּירוּשׁ, עַל דֶּרֶךְ מָשָׁל כְּמוֹ חוֹלִי   This means, figuratively speaking,
הַגּוּף הַמַּבְדִּיל בֵּין קֹדֶשׁ וכו'   that exile is **like a sickness of the
body** – while being careful to **"dis-
tinguish between the holy** and the
mundane."

knowledge is not structured in a way that allows a person to easily transmit it to another; the person himself might not necessarily have a clear knowledge of the matter. Nevertheless, what the author of the *Tanya* will write here is enough to connect the reader to the content of the ideas and to its subsequent conclusions.

The phrase is derived from Prov. 31:23: "Her husband is known in the gates when he sits with the elders of the land." Rab-

bi Menaḥem Mendel Schneerson, the Lubavitcher Rebbe (see *Lessons in Tanya*), quotes the *Metzudat David*'s comment that the husband is known because of his fine garments (which his wife has made for him). This may be understood as referring to the knowledge that a person attains congruent with the garments of his soul, the garments that he himself has prepared as well as those which his forefathers prepared for him.

---

1. *Tikkunei Zohar*, Tikkun 25 (70b); in *Lessons in Tanya*, the Rabbi Menaḥem Mendel Schneerson, the Lubavitcher Rebbe notes: "See this *Tikkun* at length".

The Divine Presence and its exile are abstractions that we have no direct way of understanding. Therefore, the author of the *Tanya* utilizes a physical analogy taken from the human body.

We can understand the use of this quotation here as a warning (appropriate for every analogy) that just as there is a difference between the holy and the mundane, so there is a difference between the analogy and what it alludes to. The analogy only helps us understand an aspect of the object of the analogy. It alludes to, but is not in absolute correspondence with, its object. Therefore, one must be careful not to make inferences that go beyond a limited equivalency. That is particularly the case here (and essentially in all of the physical analogies in the Torah), where the difference is not only one of magnitude but one of distinguishing between the holy and the mundane. Any inferences that go too far can be a literal desecration of the holy. ☞

שֶׁסִּיבַת הַחוֹלִי וְהַבְּרִיאוּת הִיא הִתְפַּשְׁטוּת וְהִילוּךְ הַחַיּוּת מֵהַלֵּב אֶל כָּל הָאֵבָרִים הַמְלוּבֶּשֶׁת בְּדַם הַנֶּפֶשׁ הַיּוֹצֵא מֵהַלֵּב אֶל כָּל הָאֵבָרִים	That is **because the cause of sickness or health is the spread and procession from the heart to all the organs of the vitality that is enclothed in the blood of the soul, emerging from the heart to all the organs,**

BETWEEN THE HOLY AND THE MUNDANE

☞ The use of this terminology appears to allude to a more extensive meaning. A number of hasidic texts explain that the Hebrew word for "illness," *maḥalah*, is related to the word *ḥullin*, "mundane" (see *Or HaTorah, Shemot* 4, p. 1228; and *Hemshekh Ayin Bet, 5672,* 2:1202). This indicates that, compared to the holy, the mundane is like an illness, something that prevents and interferes with the existence of the holy. The holy is life, whereas the mundane and illness, even if not themselves impure, can bring about impurity and death.

The mundane is the existence of a world of natural powers and laws, a world that has no place for the Divine and the holy. Although this world is apparently neither evil nor holy, it is in a state of illness, and a person must battle against it without slackening, because it is the manifestation of the exile of the Divine Presence. The exile of the Divine Presence exists not only in death and horror. Its exile is in essence the mundane, the reality of living each day without sensing holiness. It is not necessarily the state of the impure *kelippa,* but rather, it makes such a "distinction between holy and mundane" until we totally lose sight of the holy. Our struggle is not to demolish the mundane but to trans-

The author of the *Tanya* draws an analogy to sickness of the body. Physical health depends on a properly functioning stream of vitality from the heart to the organs. A person's vitality, the vitality of his soul that enlivens his body, is clothed in his blood that flows from his heart to all of his organs. The blood emerging from the heart carries the soul's life force. In the blood, the body and soul meet. The blood is where one's spiritual vitality and his body and its physicality, connect. Therefore, it is called "the blood of the soul."

וְסוֹבֵב סוֹבֵב הוֹלֵךְ הָרוּחַ חַיִּים וְהַדָּם תּוֹךְ תּוֹךְ כָּל הָאֵבָרִים וְהַגִּידִים הַמֻּבְלָעִים בָּהֶם וְחוֹזֵר אֶל הַלֵּב

and the spirit of life with **the blood circulates and circulates, deep, deep within all the organs and the sinews that are embedded in** the organs, **and returns to the heart.**

The blood, and the spirit of life within it, circulate from the heart to all the organs (see Eccl. 1:6), entering into each organ and cell in the body,[2] and then return to the heart. This movement of the blood with every heartbeat is our pulse of life.

וְאִם סִיבוּב וְהִילוּךְ הָרוּחַ חַיִּים הַלָּז הוּא כְּהִלְכָתוֹ, תָּמִידִי כְּסִדְרוֹ הַמְסוּדָּר לוֹ מֵחַיֵּי הַחַיִּים בָּרוּךְ הוּא, אֲזַי הָאָדָם בָּרִיא בְּתַכְלִית

And if the circulation and procession of this spirit of life functions properly and **continuously, in accordance with its order, as was arranged for it by the ultimate source of life, blessed be He, then the person is completely healthy.**

Health depends on the free passage, without any blockages, of the flow of blood and vitality, as well as on the proper modulation of how much life, how and when, each organ should receive.

form it into holiness. This epistle will go on to discuss the fact that we are called upon, in our own inner work and with others, to open obstructions and make the proper connections until all souls and issues will not conceal the Divine (as mundane reality and illness do), but will reveal the hidden divine light within. This constitutes the redemption of the Divine Presence.

2. In *Ha'arot VeTikkunim Bederekh Efshar*: "by means of the sinews."

כִּי כָּל הָאֵבָרִים מְקֻשָּׁרִים יַחַד
וּמְקַבְּלִים חַיּוּתָם הָרָאוּי לָהֶם
מֵהַלֵּב, עַל יְדֵי סִיבוּב הַלָּז

That is **because all the organs are connected together and receive their appropriate vitality from the heart by means of this circulation.**

This is not merely a simplistic system of heart and body, but a system composed of many various organs – large and small, cold and hot…. – all of which are connected to and dependent on each other. In order for each to receive the vitality it needs, without the interference of any other organ, and, moreover, for all the organs to work harmoniously together, with each receiving what it needs individually and collectively, they require an organized system from the source of life.

The ultimate source of life is the final, hidden life-of-all-life beyond the individual life vitality within each organ. This is the source, in light of which, the separate identities of all the organs dissolve, and are subsumed into their all-encompassing essence. Ultimately, the foot cannot ignore the existence of the hand, because on a deeper level that underlies all the details of each limb, the hand is a part of the foot and the foot is a part of the hand, and of every other organ.

אַךְ אִם יֵשׁ אֵיזֶה קִלְקוּל בְּאֵיזֶהוּ
מְקוֹמָן, הַמּוֹנֵעַ וּמְעַכֵּב אוֹ מְמַעֵט
סִיבוּב וְהִילוּךְ הַדָּם עִם הָרוּחַ חַיִּים
הַמְלוּבָּשׁ בּוֹ, אֲזַי נִפְסַק אוֹ מִתְמַעֵט
הַקֶּשֶׁר הַלָּז הַמְקַשֵּׁר כָּל הָאֵבָרִים
אֶל הַלֵּב עַל יְדֵי סִיבוּב הַלָּז, וַאֲזַי
נוֹפֵל הָאָדָם לְמִשְׁכָּב וְחוֹלִי, ה׳
יִשְׁמְרֵנוּ

However, if there is some malfunction anywhere that prevents and blocks or decreases the circulation and procession of the blood with its enclothed spirit of life, then this connection, which connects all the organs to the heart by means of this circulation, is interrupted or diminished, and then the person will fall onto his sickbed, may the Lord preserve him.

If any organ is not working properly, no matter which one or where it is located, the entire body is affected.[3] There is a single flow from the heart to all of the organs, and wherever it is blocked, the overall flow that connects all the organs is damaged. This becomes no longer

---

3. The phrase "anywhere" is from *Zevaḥim* 5:1.

just a problem of one particular organ, but of the entire person – and
he falls sick.

This analogy clearly expresses the close and vital connection among
the organs of the body. However, in the object of the analogy, in the
societal and spiritual systems, the critical nature of such connections is
not as clear. Therefore, this analogy is so important, because it clarifies
and emphasizes that connection.

וְכָכָה מַמָּשׁ עַל דֶּרֶךְ מָשָׁל הִנֵּה כָּל **In literally the same way, figura-**
נִשְׁמוֹת יִשְׂרָאֵל נִקְרָאִים בְּחִינַת 'אֲבְרֵי **tively speaking, all the souls of**
דִּשְׁכִינְתָּא' הַנִּקְרֵאת בְּשֵׁם לֵב **Israel are called "the organs of**
the Divine Presence," which is
called the heart.

Now the author of the *Tanya* discusses the object of the analogy: the
exile of the Divine Presence. Exile can be compared to the illness of
the Divine Presence.

First, the author of the *Tanya* shows how the particulars of the
analogy apply to the object of the analogy. The organs of the body
correspond to the souls of Israel.[4]

The Divine Presence is the totality of all of these souls together,[5]
also called "the Congregation of Israel." That is to say, the unified
essence of the totality of the souls of Israel expresses the divine light
that is called the Divine Presence. The totality of souls is like the totality
of the organs of a body. Just as all of the organs of the body are a single
entirety whose components cannot be separated, so too all the souls
of Israel are a single entirety that reveals in its totality, and only in its
totality, the Divine Presence.

The analogy discusses the heart and the organs; if the limbs are the
souls of Israel, then the heart is the Divine Presence.

כְּמוֹ שֶׁכָּתוּב: וְ"צוּר לְבָבִי" (תהלים **As it is written: "God is the**
עג,כו) וּכְמוֹ שֶׁכָּתוּב: "וְשָׁכַנְתִּי **strength of my heart"** (Ps. 73:26),
and as it is written: "I will dwell

---

4. On the expression "limbs of the Divine Presence," see this commentary on
Likkutei Amarim, chaps. 21 and 37, and on epistle 5, above.
5. *Zohar* 3:17a.

בְּתוֹכָם" (שמות כה,ח)   [veshakhanti] **among them**" (Ex. 25:8).

The verse states, "God is the strength of my heart and my portion forever" (Ps. 73:26). This verse is explained elsewhere[6] to indicate that the heart represents the Divine – that is, the Divine Presence – that vivifies the world. Just as the heart imparts life to all of the organs, so too the Divine Presence imparts life to the entire world.

The Torah states that through the service performed in the Tabernacle, God will dwell in the midst of the children of Israel. This is because the Tabernacle is like a house and vessel in this world in which the Divine Presence resides and is made manifest.[7]

פֵּירוּשׁ, כִּי לְשׁוֹן 'שְׁכִינָה' הוּא שְׁאוֹר הֲוָי"ה שׁוֹכֵן בְּעוֹלָמוֹת בְּרִיאָה יְצִירָה עֲשִׂיָּה לְהַחֲיוֹתָם   **The meaning is that the term Divine Presence** [*Shekhina*] **denotes that the light of** *Havaya* **resides** [*shokhen*] **in the worlds of** *Beria, Yetzira,* **and** *Asiya,* **in order to vivify them.**

The "light of *Havaya*" is the illumination of the name *Havaya*. That is the great divine name that represents God Himself (the name of His essence), and its illumination is the greatest revelation possible of God in the totality of His powers. As explained in the Kabbalistic literature, this illumination manifests itself in two ways: "light that surrounds all worlds" and "light that fills all worlds."[8] The light that fills all worlds, the light and vitality that fill every entity and give it life as it is, is that which is called here the Divine Presence. The concept of the Divine Presence is very broad and encompassing.[9] However, as it is discussed here, it relates to the light that dwells in, fills and vivifies the created worlds – *Beria, Yetzira,* and *Asiya* – but not *Atzilut*, because in relation to the worlds of *Beria, Yetzira,* and *Asiya,* the world of *Atzilut* is Divinity,

---

6. See *Torah Or* 29d; *Likkutei Torah, Derushim LeRosh HaShana* 59d; and *Likkutei Torah, Derushim LeSukkot* 82c.

7. See *Likkutei Amarim,* chap. 52, which states that this verse is the source of the concept of the Divine Presence.

8. See essay of the Rabbi Menaḥem Mendel Schneerson, the Lubavitcher Rebbe, 2 Tammuz 5717 (published in *Sefer HaMa'amarim Melukat* part 2, p. 61).

9. See the beginning of *Hemshekh, Bati LeGani* on the concept of the essence of the Divine Presence.

beyond the worlds. Only the trait of *Malkhut* of *Atzilut* is clothed in the created worlds as the Divine Presence that gives them life. This may be compared to speech. Of all the powers of a person's soul, only speech is clothed in another person, giving life and existence to the idea that has been transmitted to the latter.

וְהַמְשָׁכַת חַיּוּת זוֹ הִיא עַל יְדֵי הִתְלַבְּשׁוּת תְּחִלָּה בְּנִשְׁמוֹת יִשְׂרָאֵל **The drawing forth of this vitality** to the worlds **is achieved by a prior enclothing** of the vitality **in the souls of Israel.**

The drawing forth of vitality from the Divine to the worlds so that the Divine will dwell in their midst and give them life is indirect. There is no unmediated, deliberate relationship of the Divine to the worlds. The Divine relates to the world only via the souls of Israel. In other words, none of the worlds are important to God in and of themselves. Only because the Jewish people lives in the worlds, does He value them and give them life.

לְפִי שֶׁכָּל הַנִּבְרָאִים אֵין עֲרוֹךְ לָהֶם אֶל הַבּוֹרֵא יִתְבָּרֵךְ, דְּכוּלָּא קַמֵּיה כְּלָא מַמָּשׁ חֲשִׁיבִין, וְאִי אֶפְשָׁר לָהֶם לְקַבֵּל חַיּוּת מֵאוֹרוֹ וְשִׁפְעוֹ יִתְבָּרֵךְ לִהְיוֹת נִבְרָאִים מֵאַיִן לְיֵשׁ וְחַיִּים וְקַיָּמִים **That is because no created beings have any value in relation to the Creator, may He be blessed, since everything before Him is considered truly nothing, and they cannot receive vitality from His light and sustenance, may He be blessed, to be created from nothingness and to live and exist**

Since the worlds are unimportant in His eyes, being inherently nothing before Him, they cannot receive from Him. He has no desire nor interest in giving them life and existence for their own sake, as it were. So how, despite all that, do they receive vitality and existence? The answer is because the vitality is initially clothed in the souls of Israel. Since God desires the souls of Israel (whom He chose, and who perform His commandments and learn His Torah), and He sends them life and favor, that life and favor travel through them to all of the worlds. By way of analogy, a father prepares a special room for his child in which he places the child's toys, clothes, and so forth. All of these are unimportant and meaningless to the father. He does not need them. They are "considered as nothing." But since his child is important to him, he involves himself in and maintains these items that the child needs.

כִּי אִם עַל יְדֵי הַנְּשָׁמוֹת שֶׁעָלוּ בַּמַּחֲשָׁבָה וְקָדְמוּ לִבְרִיאַת עוֹלָמוֹת שֶׁעַל יְדֵי בְּחִינַת הַדִּבּוּר

except by means of the souls of Israel **that arose in** God's **thought and preceded the creation of worlds** that came about **through the aspect of speech.**

All of the worlds were created by God's speech:[10] that is, by His ten utterances recorded in the opening chapters of Genesis that describe the Creation. This is in contrast to the way God created the souls of Israel, which "arose in God's thought." This offers a glimpse into the relationship between the souls of Israel and all the worlds: Israel is the thought, the inner impulse that precedes divine speech. When it comes to a person, speech is that which emerges outward and is but a small, negligible expression of his inner world. Therefore, if we relate to his speech as to something in and of itself – the way that a second party would treat it as purely external, with no connection to the thought or soul behind it, it becomes meaningless. It is like superficial noise, a *kelippa* devoid of its inner dimension. When is it significant? When it is connected to thought, not merely speech, but rather, speech that expresses thought, which in turn, manifests the soul itself. At that moment, it is not only speech, but the tip of an inner process that comes from the essence of the soul. Then, and only then, all speech, every word and sentence, every detail of Creation, express and reveal God's thought and intent, as well as He Himself. That is what is stated here: that all of the worlds receive vitality only after they have first been clothed in the souls of Israel. Then speech receives its life and its meaning from the thought that preceded it.

כְּמַאֲמַר רַבּוֹתֵינוּ ז"ל: בְּמִי נִמְלַךְ הקב"ה וכו', כַּנּוֹדָע בְּמָקוֹם אַחֵר

As our Rabbis stated: "With whom did the Holy One, blessed be He, take counsel....?" which is explained elsewhere.

---

10. See the Sages' statement, "Israel arose in His thought." See *Bereshit Rabba* 1:4. And see *Likkutei Torah, Shir HaShirim* 17d.

With whom did God take counsel when He came to create the world? With the souls of the righteous.[11] Simply understood, this is an imagistic way of expressing the earlier statement that Israel arose in God's thought. It is as though God took counsel with the souls of Israel: if righteous people will exist in the world, God will delight in them and in the world, and it will be worthwhile creating[12] — and if not, then not. In that sense, the souls of Israel provided the rationale and cause for the creation of the world.

This statement of the Sages has a deeper meaning as well: not only did the souls of the righteous exist even before the world was created, comparable to thought that preceded speech, but God took counsel with them. That is to say: unlike thought and speech, both of which are part of a continuous stream of influence from within outward, He took counsel with the souls of Israel. He took counsel with the essence of that which is drawn forth as to whether or not to draw it forth. He took counsel regarding the essence of the initial will to enter into this entire matter. When God took counsel with the souls of Israel regarding whether to create the world, this refers to God Himself as He was before the beginning of Creation, much higher than speech and even thought. ☞

In the analogy of the organs and the heart, there is a movement of life from the heart to the organs, as well as an opposite movement from the organs to the heart. The author of the *Tanya* will now discuss both of these movements as they apply to the object of the analogy.

THE SOULS OF THE RIGHTEOUS

☞ This actually refers not only to the righteous, but to all souls of Israel because, before being clothed in a body, all souls are characterized as righteous. And even after a soul descends into the body, that soul in itself always possesses the charac-ter of the righteous. Despite what it may undergo in its life, it does not change. As the verse states; "And your people, they are all righteous," as quoted in that context in the hasidic literature (Is. 60:21; and see *Sanhedrin* 10:1).

---

11. *Rut Rabba* 2:3; *Bereshit Rabba* 8:7.

12. See as well *Besht Al HaTorah, Bereshit* 6; *Or Torah* by the Maggid of Mezeritch, 237.

וְנוֹדָע בַּשְּׁעָרִים כִּי כָּל הַמְשָׁכַת
הַחַיּוּת וְהַהַשְׁפָּעָה מֵעֶלְיוֹנִים
לַתַּחְתּוֹנִים מֵהֶם הֵן כְּמוֹ שֶׁכָּתוּב
בְּסֵפֶר יְצִירָה 'נָעוּץ תְּחִלָּתָן בְּסוֹפָן
וְסוֹפָן בִּתְחִלָּתָן'

It is "**known in the gates**" that the whole drawing forth of vitality and sustenance from the higher to the lower realms is in keeping with what is written in *Sefer Yetzira*: "**Their beginning is wedged in their end, and their end in their beginning.**"

The expression "it is known in the gates," which appeared at the beginning of the epistle, appears here again, yet this time, in relation to that particular information that "cannot be thoroughly clarified in a letter" (a phrase that will appear in this epistle further on), information that can only truly be "known" according to an individual's subjective internal experience.

There is a connection between the beginning and end of the vitality and sustenance, a direct connection between the first point and the last that passes through all of the intermediary layers: between the first thought, which appears as a sort of initial idea and will, to the final point of existence that comes about after all the spiritual and physical processes. This connection has two aspects: from above downward ("their beginning is embedded in their end") and from below upward ("and their end in their beginning.") ☞

THEIR BEGINNING IN THEIR END AND THEIR END IN THEIR BEGINNING

☞ The epistle began by discussing the perspective of "their beginning in their end": the drawing down of divine vitality from God to all the worlds through the souls of Israel, and because of the souls of Israel. That initial connection, of supernal, initial divine thought, bound to the root of the souls of Israel, is connected to the end of all worlds, meaning, the physical reality in which these souls live and function in a body. Everything in the middle – the spiritual worlds, the angels and the seraphim, to the highest heights – receive only from a transfer of vitality from God through them, a vitality that strives towards the absolute

lowest point where the souls of Israel are clothed in a physical body.

While the second connection corresponds to the perspective of "their end in their beginning." The entire intermediary expanse is like a giant mechanism that is built around the single point of a soul in a body, which is the only point that is not an automatic mechanism. It is for that soul's sake that everything in the universe works and flows. The whole point of creation, is that from this point, that is not a programmed cog in the mechanism of creation, and is not merely a transparent channel of that flow from above, some-

וּבְכִתְבֵי הָאֲרִ״י ז״ל מְכוּנָּה בְּשֵׁם   In the writings of the Arizal this
'אוֹר יָשָׁר' וְ'אוֹר חוֹזֵר'   is called the "direct light" and the
"returning light,"

The drawing down from above and the drawing up from below are called, respectively, the "direct light" and the "returning light." The direct light is the light that God sends to maintain and vivify all of the worlds, and the returning light is the light that returns from them. The direct light is called direct because it comes directly from God, the source of life and light. While, the returning light is the light that returns from the opposite axis, the lowest level that light reaches.

The author of the *Tanya* emphasizes here that the light that comes from below is not a different light, but the very light and vitality that descended from above. This cyclic dynamic is not comprised of different elements, but between various aspects and perspectives of the same thing. There is a single unity. The more its oneness is revealed, the more the flow improves, without barriers. This "other" formation, as it were, of the latter side, creates a tension, an energy, that impels the entire universe. However, it is important to remember that this tension is not intended to reveal, by way of analogy, an "other" that is outside but rather, the "other" that is within: an additional layer of the depth of essence that is even more authentic. ☞

thing will occur that is not entirely foreseeable. That is a signal of an answer from below: "Received!" This small signal that rises from below, pierces the intermediate worlds, directly reaches the supernal heights that transcend the entire order of worlds, and reaches God's essence. This is all God was waiting for, as it were. This signal, even if at its origin sounds weak and small, gains strength as it rises. It becomes more meaningful than anything else that exists. That is the meaning of "their end in their beginning."

THE DIRECT LIGHT AND THE RETURNING LIGHT

☞ In contrast to what might have been expected, it is explained that it is precisely the returning light that is a "new light," because only in it is there something new, in relation to the direct light (see *Torah Or* 8b). That "new" factor is not a new source of light and vitality that did not previously exist, but a new revelation, a new illumination, of that one source itself. An illumination is like a revelation, and every illumination is essentially a revelation of the light source, of the essence. In that sense, a new light is a new revelation, more internal and essential than that which was

וּכְמוֹ שֶׁכָּתוּב: "וְהַחַיּוֹת רָצוֹא **As it is written: "The creatures were**
וָשׁוֹב" (יחזקאל א,יד) **racing forward and returning"** (Ezek.
1:14).

The word "creatures," ḥayot, can also be vowelized as ḥiyyut, "vitality."
This means that life and vitality in general are not something that
merely exists, but something that goes out and comes back with a
movement of "racing forward" and "returning." Racing forward is the
emergence of the vitality from the vessel, that is, of the soul from the
body. It races with yearning to bond with and be nullified in the source
of the divine light. While "returning" is the opposite movement, the
return of the vitality to the body and the world. "Racing forward" is
the soul's response to its contemplating its position below, entrenched
in darkness and concealment. It is an expression of its yearning for the
infinite divine, and to break free of its limited faculties to connect with
God. While "return" is the soul's response to its contemplation from
above, when divine reality is no longer a distant goal it yearns for, but
rather, the reality in which that soul exists. At that moment, besides the
awe that the soul experiences, it sees that there is no difference between
above and below, but that the Divine exists in everything, even where
the body is below. Then, the movement of the soul is a return to the
body in which it exists, to worldly life and to that which the soul must
accomplish here. ☞

revealed in the previous illumination. This
is the systematic meaning of this returning,
new light, which moves the system from
stasis to a living, breathing state, a system that changes and develops with every
added pulse of returning light. Therefore,
those that cause the light to return – the
souls in the body – are called "those who
walk," in contrast to the angels and all of
Creation, which are called are called "those
who stand" (see Zech. 3:7: "and I allowed
you to be those who walk among those
who stand"; see *Likkutei Torah, Vayikra* 45c,
Likkutei Torah, Bemidbar 71c).

THE "DIRECT LIGHT" AND THE "RETURNING LIGHT" CORRESPOND TO "RACING FORWARD" AND "RETURNING"

☞   The difference between these sets
of concepts is the direction from which
one is looking. With "racing forward and
returning," one is looking up from below.
Therefore, the "racing forward" goes upward, and then comes back down with the
"returning." In contrast, "direct light" and
"returning light" express one's perspective
from above. The direct light comes down,
and the returning light goes back up.

אֲשֶׁר עַל כֵּן, עַל פִּי הַדְּבָרִים
וְהָאֱמֶת הָאֵלֶּה, אֲשֶׁר אִי אֶפְשָׁר
לְבָאֵר הֵיטֵב בְּמִכְתָּב, נִקְרֵאת
הַשְּׁכִינָה בְּשֵׁם לֵב וְהַנְּשָׁמוֹת
בְּשֵׁם אֵבָרִים

For this reason, in accordance with these words and truth, which cannot be thoroughly clarified in a letter, the Divine Presence is called "heart" and the souls are called "organs,"

The author of the *Tanya* presented here the background to help explain the object of the analogy, even though ultimately such an explanation cannot be adequately conveyed in a letter. His explanation here of the object of the analogy is too abstract and too distant from the reality of one's daily life, and so the topic can be best explained only by presenting an analogy. Therefore, particularly in this case, when the distance between the physical analogy and its divine object is so great, there is no unequivocal wording that will directly connect the two that can be written down for all people in all places and at all times. Rather, these are matters that, as was noted initially, "are known in the gates [*she'arim*]." That is to say, the knowledge of them depends on the measure (*shiur*) of each individual at the time that he hears it. They can be transmitted only in person orally, if at all. All this being said, according to these introductory words, each person can, according his measure, understand the object of the analogy: the heart and organs allude to the Divine Presence and to souls. ☞

Even if the topic cannot be explained objectively or intellectually, a person can, precisely because of that, get a sense of the infinite gap between the analogy and the object of the analogy, and grasp some true feeling regarding the object of the analogy. Most importantly, and it is with this that the epistle continues, a person can arrive at concrete

THE ANALOGY VERSUS ITS OBJECT

☞ The truth is that every analogy has a hidden point of transition from the analogy to its object, which is difficult to convey in writing. Therefore, often, a person does not even try to do so, and the analogy remains a tool that the listener receives and uses – each person according to his measure. Indeed here, as in a number of plac-es where the object of an analogy refers to the Divine, there is an especial need to relate to and focus on the object of the analogy due to its great distance from the analogy and due to the fact that the object of the analogy has an added, infinite dimension that has no parallel in the analogy and in this world.

conclusions from these concepts: How he can apply this understanding
in his down-to-earth life, how he can truly serve God here with what he
has. The author of the *Tanya* will discuss these practical ramifications
that can be drawn from the analogy – the heart, the organs and the
health of the body – and with that, he will conclude this epistle.

לְהוֹרוֹת לָנוּ כִּי כַּאֲשֶׁר כָּל
הַנְּשָׁמוֹת דְּבוּקוֹת וּמְקוּשָׁרוֹת
יַחַד אֲזַי סִיבּוּב וְהִילוּךְ הַחַיּוּת
וְהַהַשְׁפָּעָה סוֹבֵב סוֹבֵב, וְנָעוּץ
סוֹפָן בִּתְחִלָּתָן

**to teach us that when all souls cleave
and connect together, then the circulation and the procession of vitality
and sustenance circulates and circulates, and their end is wedged in their
beginning,**

The existence of vitality (as well as the illumination of the essence of
existence itself) is its flow: from beginning to end and from end to
beginning, as explained earlier. If there is no movement, if there is no
stream that races forward and returns, there is no life. As in the breath
or the heartbeat, a person cannot live with only inhalation or exhalation,
but rather, with rhythmic recurrence. Therefore, so that the vitality will
stream from one part to another, from one soul to another, these parts
must cling to each other, without any interruption and interposition
that would interfere in the slightest way with the movement of life.

The emphasis is specifically on the connection between the souls
of Israel, because all the worlds receive their life vitality from these
souls. The souls of Israel are the inner dimension of all existence,
giving its every element life. They justify and give meaning to the
external, visible layer of life. The vitality of each soul lends vitality to
the part of the world that relates to it. Therefore, if the vitality is not
clothed completely in that soul, there is a blemish in that part of the
world. All of these souls are connected to each other, like the organs
of a body, in a single entirety that is called the Congregation of Israel,
which is the Divine Presence – which is, by way of analogy, the heart
of the entire world. ☞

THEIR END IS IN THEIR BEGINNING

☞ This statement highlights an additional aspect as well: that this movement must

encompass everything, from beginning to
end via everything in-between. Further-

The analogy communicates yet more: this heart from which vitality spreads to all of the organs is not something that exists apart from the person. So too, the Divine Presence, the source of the divine vitality in all souls and worlds, is not something separate from them. The worlds, the souls of Israel and the Divine Presence are one. Therefore, just as the oneness of a person's body is revealed only when he is alive (whereas when he is not alive, every organ is separate), so too the Congregation of Israel, which is the Divine Presence, a single divine life force in all parts of the worlds, is revealed only when the stream of life among souls flows freely.

לְקַשֵּׁר וּלְחַבֵּר כּוּלָן לַהֲוָיַ"ה
אֶחָד וּלְדָבְקָה בּוֹ יִתְבָּרֵךְ

to connect and join them all into the one essence [Havaya] and to cleave to Him, may He be blessed.

The bonding of souls together leads to their bonding with and clinging to the one God. That is because the revelation of the Divine Presence has infinite significance. The revelation of the Divine Presence means that everything is divine vitality. Divine vitality means that the Divine is present right here. It is the presence of the infinite one who fills everything and encompasses everything, who is actually the only existence. In the language of the Kabbalists, the revelation of the Divine Presence means "the unification of the Holy One, blessed be He and His Divine Presence." That is to say, everything that the analogy states regarding the vitality and health of the body applies to the object of the

more, the statement, "their end is embedded in their beginning" does not mean, as one might have thought, that the beginning and end points are of primary significance, while everything in-between is of secondary significance. Rather, this is comparable to the organs in the body, and to the entirety of the souls of Israel, each unit of which is both an end point and a beginning. Each one is an end in and of itself because it is the purpose of the creation of all the worlds. It is also a starting point because through it, the rest of the universe

receives its vitality. Therefore, the author of the Tanya speaks about the circulation of the vitality, about circular movement between points that are neither higher nor lower than any other. There is no particular end. Rather, each point is an axis to which vitality streams and from which it flows.

(It is true that there are souls that correspond to the head and souls that correspond to the foot, and so forth. However, that is only a functional measure of importance in relation to other souls, and not a statement of intrinsic value.)

analogy, to the unification with and clinging to that which is beyond the body and the vitality within it. ☞

וּכְמוֹ שֶׁכָּתוּב: "אַתֶּם נִצָּבִים הַיּוֹם כֻּלְּכֶם לִפְנֵי הֲוָיָ"ה אֱלֹקֵיכֶם" (דברים כט,ט) "כֻּלְּכֶם" דַּיְקָא וְ"לִפְנֵי" דַּיְקָא, "רָאשֵׁיכֶם כוּ' מֵחוֹטֵב עֵצֶיךָ כוּ'"

As it is written: "You are standing today, all of you, before *Havaya* your God" (Deut. 29:9) – the verse specifically states "all of you," and specifically states "before," "your heads…," "from the hewer of your wood.…"

All of the souls of Israel must without exception stand in a state of love and oneness, and "before Me." Only when they are all one, do they rise to the countenance of God Himself. God too has a front and back, as it were. The back relates to the externality of existence and to the multitude of revelations in it: the multitude of worlds and created beings. While the "countenance" (*panim*), the inner essence (*penimi*), relates to the oneness within the entire multiplicity. Each entity has many external revelations and a single essence that lies underneath all the revelations.

Hasidic teachings explain that "before *Havaya*" means that He Himself is before and above existence that is enclothed in the name *Havaya*, the name that creates everything. "Before *Havaya* your God" refers to God prior to His being the power and life force of the souls of Israel. That being the case, when all of you stand together, connected and bonded to each other, it is precisely then that you stand "before *Havaya* your God."

The verse goes on to detail what constitutes "all of you": "your heads, your tribes, your elders, and your police, each man of Israel, your infants, your wives, and your convert in the midst of your camp, from your

HAVAYA IS ONE

☞ God's name *Havaya*, whose four letters symbolize the ten *sefirot* and the four worlds, symbolizes the encompassing oneness of existence in divine revela-tions (the *sefirot*) and in the worlds. (See *Iggeret HaTeshuva*, chap. 4, and many hasidic teachings.)

woodcutter to your water drawer." It is explained[13] that this itemization alludes to the ten levels of souls of Israel,[14] from "your heads" to "your water drawer." Additionally, the number ten, like the ten *sefirot* and the ten powers of the soul, indicates an overall wholeness.

וּבָזֶה יוּבָן מַאֲמַר רַבּוֹתֵינוּ ז״ל כִּי חוּרְבָּן בַּיִת שֵׁנִי וּנְפִילַת יִשְׂרָאֵל בַּגָּלוּת, וְהִסְתַּלְקוּת הַשְּׁכִינָה, וִירִידָתָהּ לֶאֱדוֹם בִּבְחִינַת גָּלוּת כִּבְיָכוֹל

Based on this, the following **statement of our Rabbis may be understood: that the destruction of the Second Temple, and Israel's fall into exile and the departure of the Divine Presence and its descent to Edom in the form of exile, as it were,**

The destruction of the second Temple represented a new descent into exile, more encompassing and deeper than what we had known until then.[15] The Temple is the place where the Divine Presence resides and is revealed.[16] The destruction of the Temple entails the departure of the Divine Presence, in the sense of its concealment, so that it is no longer revealed in the world as it had been before.

The departure of the Divine Presence is also its descent into exile, because "departure" means that only in the heights is it revealed, but below it becomes more concealed. In spiritual terms, concealment is descent: the deeper the concealment, the deeper and more intense is the descent.

The Sages call this exile since the destruction of the second Temple to our day "the exile of Edom." Simply understood, "Edom" refers to the Roman Empire, which destroyed the Temple and brought about this present exile that scattered Israel across the Roman empire and introduced the culture of Rome and that of Rome's heirs, the Christians, to this day, to the Jewish people. In a deeper sense, Edom

---

13. See *Likkutei Torah, Devarim* 44a, based on the *Zohar* 2:82a.

14. See as well *Kiddushin*, beginning of chapter 4, "ten categories of lineage...."

15. *Yoma* 9b.

16. And *Likkutei Amarim*, chap. 53, utilizing Kabbalistic language, describes in detail the level of the revealed state of the Divine Presence in the first and second Temples.

is Esau (Gen. 36:43), that being the *kelippa* of severe *Gevura* (Esau was the corrupt son of Isaac, the latter being the trait of holy *Gevura*). Therefore, since Esau is close to holiness ("Is Esau not a brother to Jacob?" Mal. 1:2), he is especially deep and problematical. Despite that and because of that, the rectification of this *kelippa* will entail the complete rectification of the character of Israel and of the exile of the Divine Presence overall.

However, this descent to exile is not a real descent. Although it appears as such, in truth there is no true concealment of the Divine Presence, of Godly presence, within existence, but only the appearance of such. Therefore, in the most general way one may say that from the moment that we conduct ourselves as though there is no concealment, as though God exists and is revealed here, in our mind, in our thoughts and in our keeping all of His mitzvot, that is already the revealing of the Divine Presence and the redemption from our personal exile.

הַכֹּל הָיָה בַּעֲוֹן שִׂנְאַת חִנָּם וּפֵירוּד לְבָבוֹת רַחֲמָנָא לִיצְּלַן וְלָכֵן נִקְרֵאת 'חוֹלָה', עַל דֶּרֶךְ מָשָׁל

were all due to the sin of baseless hatred and the separation between hearts, may the Merciful One save us. And therefore, the exiled Divine Presence is called "sick," figuratively speaking.

The exile of the Divine Presence in Edom is the most severe and profound exile of all. The Divine Presence is now said to be sick. The epistle opened with the analogy of the body growing ill because the flow of blood from the heart to the organs has been impeded. The object of this analogy is the exile of the Divine Presence. The illness is the impeding of the flow of the vitality from the Divine Presence to the souls of Israel and to all existence.

Baseless hatred occurs when people hate each other without cause. They hate each other because there is no true connection among them. To hate a Jew is never good. It is a sin forbidden by the Torah.[17] But at least when there is a reason to hate someone, there is a connection with him. A person is enraged because he cares. However, baseless hatred

17. Lev. 19:17: "You shall not hate your brother in your heart."

means that there is no connection, and that is a problem of a different scope: not only a functional difficulty, but an illness. ☞

כְּמוֹ שֶׁאוֹמְרִים "סוֹמֵךְ נוֹפְלִים
וְרוֹפֵא חוֹלִים", לְשׁוֹן רַבִּים, הֵם
כָּל הָאֵבָרִים וכו'

As we say "Who supports those who are fallen and heals those who are sick" in the plural form, because **that** refers to **all the organs....**

Why is this phrase in the *Shemoneh Esrei* prayer stated in the plural? The author of the *Tanya* explains that, in essence, it is referring to the healing and redemption of the Divine Presence. The plural is used because it is referring to all the souls of Israel, which are like organs of the Divine Presence. They are ill in that they are not united, and they heal when they attain oneness and harmony among themselves.

It is true that all of the blessings in the *Shemoneh Esrei* prayer are stated in the plural. However, this instance has a special meaning that sheds light on the entire *Shemoneh Esrei*. This part of the *Shemoneh Esrei* prayer is a request for the healing of a multiplicity. The very fact that there is a multiplicity indicates illness and lack. As in the analogy, if a person does not feel the unity of his organs and they express themselves, as it were, in the plural, something is not healthy. Therefore, we ask God to restore wholeness to their lack so that they will be one in His oneness and not multiple, not separated from Him. ☞

THE EXILE OF THE DIVINE PRESENCE IS AN ILLNESS

☞ The exile of the Divine Presence occurs when, instead of revealing and expressing itself – the Divine within everything – it is forced to give the power of its vitality to that which conceals the holiness and is separate from the Divine Presence. That is the internal illness that the author of the *Tanya* is speaking about: not only is the Divine Presence concealed, but it gives its power and vitality to that which conceals it, as in certain bodily illnesses in which the power of the vitality of the body itself enlivens and increases that which is killing it. At that time, the regimen for that illness can no longer be local and external, but it must treat the deepest roots of the problem.

The author of the *Tanya* defines the illness as "baseless hatred and separation of hearts." Earlier, the epistle spoke of the separation of organs from the heart. While they do not receive the vitality that they need, they still feel like organs, like parts that ultimately need to receive from the center. However, when there is a "separation of hearts," when each feels that it itself is the heart and center of life, the illness is deeper and more severe.

This epistle discussed the exile of the Divine Presence, which is separation between souls. The uniqueness of this letter lies in its view of exile and alienation as illness. Although the exile is not a good state, a person might nevertheless get used to it and feel that this is just how things are. However, if he sees exile as an illness, then he finds it unbearable. He cannot accept it, and will not accustom himself to it. However, the epistle does not stop there. It goes on to explain what sort of illness this is. There are local illnesses, which are essentially the body's response to something that attacks it from without. That too, is a sort of exile of the Divine Presence. Yet here, the author of the *Tanya* speaks of the exile of the Divine Presence as the exile imposed by Edom, which is deeper than all other exiles, and is a more internal and profound illness. As explained earlier and in *Likkutei Torah, Bemidbar* 85d, *heiḥaltzu*, this exile is the exile of Edom that has had power since the destruction of the second Temple, due to the sin of causeless hatred, in contrast to the other exiles. The illness that is the root and cause of all illnesses occurs when the movement of life among the organs and between the heart and organs is disordered, when a blockage prevents the stream of life from reaching every place at the necessary time and in the right way. The problem then, is not the particular organ that has been harmed – it would be a mistake to think so – but harm to the inner stratum of the life of all the organs, when that which unites them is not functioning

THE ANALOGY OF EXILE AS A BODILY ILLNESS

☞   This is more than just an analogy. Illness is a particular occurrence that serves as a tangible model of all existence. A person's health is the health of the Divine Presence, and his illness is its exile. They are connected. As the Mishnah states: "At the time that a person suffers, the Divine Presence, what does it say, as it were? My head is heavy, my arms are heavy" (*Sanhedrin* 6:5). The analogy and its object, the individual and the whole, move from one to the other and back again. A person feels the "analogy" of illness in his body in a sensory and immediate way: something is wrong, an organ of his body or his soul is ill and does not sense the other organs. The stream of his vitality is not functioning properly. He must apply this to the object of the analogy: to the exile of the Divine Presence, which similarly is not drawn into the totality of the worlds. On the other hand, he must apply the alienation that he feels regarding another person and regarding the concept of the Divine Presence overall, to his body, to feel in relation to the Divine Presence as he feels in relation to one of his organs that does not receive vitality, just as his hand, his head and his heart suffer when another organ is not connected to them.

properly. In the object of the analogy, the organs allude to the souls of Israel. Every soul, every person, is an organ of the Divine Presence. Therefore, when a problem arises in the connection between souls, when they view themselves as separate from each other, the Divine Presence, which is their totality – the congregation of Israel – cannot be revealed. It does not shine forth and reveal what it is: divinity within Creation. That is the exile of the Divine Presence: instead of revealing the Divine, in all of its colorful beauty, it invests its power in concealing divinity and life, and exhibits symptoms of illness.

Describing exile as an illness brings about the healing. If the illness lies in the separation of souls, the healing lies in their unification. When the souls bond to each other and are connected, then the Divine Presence, which is the divine vitality, pulses in them through and through via all the intermediary details, and reveals its oneness and essence; a single unity with the one God. That constitutes the redemption of the Divine Presence from exile, with all of the particulars that it gathers from the exile, one by one.

Epistle 32

THIS IS THE FINAL EPISTLE IN *IGGERET HAKODESH*, AND it appears that the editors of this collection[1] deliberately chose it as such. Since it resembles the first epistle in several ways, it can be said that the end of *Iggeret HaKodesh* is embedded in its beginning. Like the first epistle, this one opens with a blessing for the hasidim in response to a good report about them that the author had received. In the first epistle, that good report was related to the Torah – that they had collectively learned the entire Talmud – whereas here it refers to a great act of charity. The two epistles also share a common underlying factor in that they both offer gratitude and make no explicit requests of the hasidim. However, the Rebbe's statement of thanks is not merely an expression of appreciation. He also analyses the deeper meaning of the topic at hand, implicitly challenging the hasidim to integrate their understanding into their inner service: The service of the heart, which is prayer. Thus, this epistle, like the first one, concludes by connecting the topic at hand to prayer.[2]

בָּרֵךְ ה' חֵילָם וּפוֹעַל יָדָם יִרְצֶה **Bless, O Lord, their might, and accept the work of their hands** (see Deut. 33:11)

26 Ḥeshvan

25 Ḥeshvan (leap year)

---

1. By the sons of the author of the *Tanya* (as mentioned in *Haskamat HaRabbanim SheYiḥyu, Benei HaGaon HaMeḥaber Zal, Nishmato Eden*, which is printed at the beginning of the *Tanya*).
2. The Lubavitcher Rebbe, Rabbi Menaḥem Mendel Schneerson, notes an additional connection between the two epistles, that they are both related to the service of prayer (*Iggerot Kodesh*, vol. 23, letter 8987; *Lessons in Tanya*).

The author of the *Tanya* will typically begin an epistle with a rhetorical flourish derived from Scripture. These paraphrases of verses and their interrelations contain allusions to the topic he will proceed to discuss. The opening words here are taken from Moses's blessing of the tribe of Levi (with a change from the singular to the plural). The might and work of the hands of the Levites – to be more precise, of the priests – are expressed in their service in the Temple.[3] Thus, the author of the *Tanya* is comparing the service of charity performed by the people to the holy service in the Temple.[4] This is because charity in general, and more specifically charity for the community, like the service of the offerings, is a general mitzva of the public realm, in which one gives and draws something from this world to God. In the case of sacrificial services, we give of ourselves and our essence to God without making any worldly calculations. Similarly, the ethic of giving charity is ultimately not a heavenly calculation rather than a worldly one. A poor person is not expected to pay back what he receives. Rather, God Himself becomes the donor's debtor, as it were. ☞

BLESS, O LORD, THEIR MIGHT

☞   The author of the *Tanya* had been apprised of a charitable deed that was apparently performed not by a few individuals but as an organized activity of the entire community. Accordingly, he begins the epistle by bestowing a special blessing upon them. As in the first epistle, an organized activity of a community of hasidim – in that case studying the entire Talmud, here a charitable donation – indicates an enhanced closeness of the hasidim to the Rebbe. There are two reasons why these activities are more pleasing than those the hasidim perform as individuals. First, the service of a community is particularly expressive of the connection between the Rebbe and the hasidim. Second, it reflects the community's attitude toward God, for a service performed by the people as a whole, like the prayer of the people collectively, is qualitatively different than that of an individual. It is in this context that these words of blessing, connecting the service of charity to the holy service in the Temple, are to be understood.

---

3. As taught by the Sages in a number of places. See e.g., *Pesaḥim* 22b and 72b.
4. See the statement in *Bava Batra* 9a that when the Temple is not standing the mitzva of giving charity provides atonement and it corresponds to the sacrificial services (in *Lessons in Tanya* a relevant statement is cited from *Avot deRabbi Natan*, first version, 4:5).

לְרָצוֹן לָהֶם לִפְנֵי ה׳ תָּמִיד   **so that they may gain favor before the Lord always** (see Ex. 28:38).

Their activity should always be pleasing to God. That is to say, it should be directed to the interiority of His supernal will and placed "before the Lord." "The Lord" refers to the name of *Havaya*, whose letters allude to all ten *sefirot*, through which God reveals Himself and bestows upon His creatures. Thus, "*before* the Lord" means that the hasidim should be on a level before – in the sense of prior to – His entire relationship to the fluctuating world, on a level that is eternal and always pleasing.

As we will see below, this is referring to a person who influences others to give. The activity of such an individual is more profound than the act of charity itself, than the entire world of action. It is comparable to the inner divine will that precedes actual creation, which precedes the name of *Havaya*, the name applied to God when He brings the world into existence and acts upon it. In this and in other senses, the action of such a person relates to the inner divine will that is "before the Lord always." ☞

כֹּה יִתֵּן וְכֹה יוֹסִיף ה׳, לְאַמֵּץ   **So may God grant and so may He con-**
לָבָם בַּגִּבּוֹרִים   **tinue to fortify their hearts among the mighty.**

May God give them and continue to give to them in keeping with their donation and even beyond that measure. May He fortify their hearts among the mighty so that they will be the mightiest of all.[5] Although giving charity is an expression of kindness to another, it also requires

SO THAT THEY MAY GAIN FAVOR BEFORE THE LORD

☞   The verse from which this phrase is taken is dealing with the golden headband, the *tzitz*, worn by the High Priest, which granted atonement for any service of the priests that had been performed improperly (that is, in a state of ritual impurity). Here too, the author's intent is to bless his hasidim with the wish that the service of giving charity that they performed will always please God, even if here and there the sanctity of their act and intent might have been imperfect.

---

5. "So shall God do to me and so shall He continue" (see II Sam. 19:14 and elsewhere) "[to fortify] the courageous of heart among the valiant" (see Amos

a person to act with fortitude toward himself, because he is taking something away from himself in order to give to the other. Thus, the author of the *Tanya* blesses his hasidim with the wish that their courage and might should increase.

וְנָדִיב עַל נְדִיבוֹת יָקוּם לִהְיוֹת
גְּדוֹל הַמַּעֲשֶׂה בְּכָל עִיר וּמְנָיָן,
וְתֵחָשֵׁב לוֹ לִצְדָקָה

And may each generous person be established through his **generous** deeds **to be great because he causes others to act** charitably **in every city and congregation. And may** their charity **be considered his own charity.**

One might be worried that his charitable generosity could undermine his financial security. Therefore, the author of the *Tanya* blesses his hasidim that, on the contrary, they will be well established on account of their generosity.

Furthermore, a person who causes others to give, who inspires the community to be generous, attains even greater merit, reward, and stature than those who themselves give.[6] That is because a person who causes others to give is greater than one who performs the deed of giving itself. ☞

The greatness and value of a deed depend on many factors: Its difficulty, the psychological and financial situation of the parties involved, and so forth. No two cases are exactly alike. Therefore, the

---

A PERSON WHO CAUSES OTHERS TO ACT IS GREATER

☞ The basis of this idea, discussed in various hasidic texts, is that something which causes an action to occur is necessarily greater than that action itself. Therefore, a person's service of repenting and performing good deeds, which leads to the reward of the World to Come, is greater than the World to Come itself. In this case too, one who influences others to give is greater than those who simply give.

2:16), "[and may] the generous [be established as he] counsels generously" (see Isa. 32:8) "to be great because he causes others to act [charitably]" (*Bava Batra* 9a), "[and may they be] accorded merit" (Ps. 106:31; see also Gen. 15:6).

6. *Hemshekh Ve'kakha* 5637 by the fourth Lubavitcher Rebbe, Rabbi Shmuel Schneerson, also known as the Rebbe Maharash, chap. 21, and see chap. 15. See also *Sefer HaMa'amarim* 5732, p. 178, and *Sefer HaMa'amarim* 5742, p. 26, and elsewhere.

author of the *Tanya* adds the phrase "in every city and congregation," to indicate that the greatness of a person who influences others is measured in relation to the specific population in question. It is as if he himself gave that charity.

Up to this point, the author of the *Tanya* has spoken of a person who moves others: One who organizes, persuades, and leads the community to give charity. He will return to this individual later on, but for now he turns his attention to one who himself acts.

וְעַל הָעוֹשֶׂה נֶאֱמַר: "צִדְקָתוֹ
עוֹמֶדֶת לָעַד" (תהלים קיב,ט)
"עוֹמֶדֶת" לְשׁוֹן נְקֵבָה, שֶׁמְּקַבֵּל
הִתְעוֹרְרוּת לִבּוֹ הַטָּהוֹר מִ׳גָדוֹל
הַמְעַשֶׂה,

With regard to one who acts, it is stated, "His charity stands forever" (Ps. 112:9). "Stands" is in the feminine form, because the person who acts receives the awakening of his pure heart from the greater person [*gadol*, in the masculine], the one who causes others to act.

With regard to one who gives charity, the verse states, "His charity stands forever" (Ps. 112:9). The word "stands" is in the feminine since he did not act of his own volition but because he was inspired by another. In spiritual matters, the "feminine" corresponds to the level of the recipient and the "masculine" to the level of the giver. Here the feminine form is applied to the act of giving charity because the giver is not acting on his own initiative but because he was inspired and influenced by another. Nevertheless, he did not reject this influence but accepted it and complied with it. That itself is a virtue, and therefore the charity is attributed to him and is called "*his* charity."

אַף עַל פִּי כֵן "עוֹמֶדֶת לָעַד".
פֵּירוּשׁ, שֶׁכָּל הַצְּדָקָה וְהַחֶסֶד
שֶׁיִּשְׂרָאֵל עוֹשִׂין בָּעוֹלָם הַזֶּה,
מִנִּדְבַת לִבָּם הַטָּהוֹר, הֵן הֵנָּה
חַיּוֹת וְקַיָּימוֹת בָּעוֹלָם הַזֶּה
הַגַּשְׁמִי עַד זְמַן הַתְּחִיָּיה

Nevertheless, his charity "stands forever." This means that all the charity and kindness that the people of Israel perform in this world out of the generosity of their pure hearts remain alive and in existence in this material world until the time of the resurrection,

The word "always" is attributed to one who inspires others to act. Here the author of the *Tanya* adds that the person who acts, and his action, also exist eternally.

This is one of the differences between masculine and feminine, between giver and receiver. The giver comes from above, from outside the system upon which he exerts his influence. Therefore, he and his influence transcend the internal changes within the system. He is in the realm of the "always" and the unchanging. In contrast, the receiver, the feminine, are dependent on what they receive, and are therefore not described as "always."[7] Nevertheless, since the giver has his own personality and free will to decide whether or not to accept the influence – and, if he does, in what manner – his acceptance essentially includes an aspect that is not only an act of receiving. Moreover, his receiving itself contains an aspect of giving, as has been explained[8] in reference to the Sages' statement that "more than the calf wants to suck, the cow wants to suckle" (*Pesaḥim* 112a). Through his very agreement to receive, it is as though he is providing the one who bestows with the will to bestow. Here too, the one who receives the influence and performs the act of charity is thereby elevated above the natural physical reality of his world, and thus through act of his he stands "forever."

However, the epistle's primary concern here is not the person giving the charity but the act of charity itself: What causes charity – in contrast to every other action in the world, which deteriorate, disintegrate, and erode – to "stand forever"?

The act of charity is exceptional because in a sense it is not entirely an act of this world. An act that is entirely charitable and kind, which is not dependent on receiving any recompense in this world and in general is unallied to any personal motive and anything in this world, although it is an action performed in this world, is not in fact part of this world. Rather, it is like a penetration of the infinite into this world. Therefore, even though it is enclothed in the world, it stands forever. ☞

---

7. The statement that "women are easily impressionable" (*Shabbat* 33b) applies to this context: A woman's mind is not set permanently but changes from time to time and from one issue to the next.

8. See e.g., *Sefer HaMa'amarim Melukat*, part 4, p. 163.

What is the nature of the life force that "stands forever" within the acts of charity, and in a sense within all of the commandments, which the people of Israel perform? Apparently, this world that God created should have been perfect and eternal, just as He is. However (as explained at length in the kabbalistic literature) in the past it was impaired, and therefore it is now not as straight as it had been when it was created, but distorted. As a result, it does not simply reflect the divinity that creates it and gives it life. Instead, it tells a different story, a false tale. When people hear this falsehood, believe it, are enticed by it, and live in accordance with it, they amplify it. This falsehood[9] is the source of the world's temporal nature. By contrast, when people perform commandments, and particularly when they perform acts of charity and kindness, this generates rectifications. As people perform acts of truth, things move to their proper places and connect with the truth. In this manner, the commandments slowly change the story of

THE CHARITY AND KINDNESS OF THE PEOPLE OF ISRAEL

☞ In order for an act of charity and kindness to exist in this manner, it must be performed by a person of "Israel," by someone who shares a portion of the divine, who is intrinsically not a part of this world but only enclothed in it. This is alluded to in the statement that "Israel arose in His thought" (see *Bereshit Rabba* 1:4), which Hasidism regards as referring to the thought that transcends the world which was created with speech. It is likewise explained in *Likkutei Amarim* that the souls of Israel are "a portion of the divine above, literally." Only such a person can cause this deed to penetrate into the world. However, since the people of Israel are enclothed in this world, in a body and an animal soul, by means of which they think and feel, the deed must come "out of the generosity of their pure hearts": Not from the aspect of their hearts that is enclothed and enwrapped in matters of this world, but from the aspect of their pure hearts that transcends such concerns, which exists just as their pure soul existed before it was enclothed in a body and animal soul. As we say in our prayers, "the soul that You placed within me is pure." This is referring to the holy soul before it was enclothed in the body (see e.g., *Likkutei Torah, Derushim LeYom HaKippurim* 69a and onward; it is also the aspect of the right chamber of the heart, as explained in *Likkutei Amarim*, chap. 9).

---

9. As explained in many places, the definition of falsehood is that, unlike truth, it changes and does not stand forever. "The language of truth will be established forever" (Prov. 12:19), whereas falsehood is like a desert stream that one day has water and the next day is dry.

the world, the order and meaning of matters in the world, until – when everything will come together and the entire world will speak the truth – the world will exist forever, unchanging.

The statement that charity and kind deeds are "alive and in existence in this material world until the time of the resurrection"[10] means precisely that they act to rectify and properly align this world. This is occurring even if we cannot observe it. By the nature of things, such an effect cannot be sensed until it is complete. The same applies to mundane cases: For example, a group of workers, each of whom is laboring within a large system, will be able to see the totality of their work only when everything is finished and the system begins to work. Therefore, at present, since the rectification is incomplete, because we only see, think, and feel in terms of this world in its current configuration, the infinite, eternal meaning of charity is hidden from us. However, all this applies only "until the time of the resurrection."

which is the time of the revelation in this world of the Divine and of the light of *Ein Sof*, blessed be He, which encompasses all worlds, שֶׁאָז הוּא זְמַן גִּילּוּי אֱלֹקוּת וְאוֹר אֵין סוֹף בָּרוּךְ הוּא מִבְּחִינַת סוֹבֵב כָּל עָלְמִין בָּעוֹלָם הַזֶּה

The "time of the resurrection" will be the era of the revelation of divinity and the infinite light surrounding all worlds, a light that expresses the divine itself. Not only does that light not exist within the world, but the world actually exists within it. That light surrounds and contains the dimensions of the world, namely time and space. It cannot be revealed in the world as it is now, but only at the time of the resurrection. Then the mitzva of charity that one performed in this world, which has been alive and in existence since then in a state of concealment, will be revealed. ☞ ☞

as was explained at length in my epistle of last year. וּכְמוֹ שֶׁנִּתְבָּאֵר בַּאֲרִיכוּת בְּמִכְתָּב דְּאֶשְׁתָּקַד

This is apparently a reference to epistle 17, which discusses in great detail the reward for performing the commandments that will be given

---

10. For a different explanation of these ideas, see the teaching of the Lubavitcher Rebbe that is published as an addendum to this epistle in *Lessons in Tanya*.

in the Garden of Eden and at the time of the resurrection of the dead, when the light that surrounds all worlds will be revealed. The author

THE TIME OF THE RESURRECTION

☞ The author of the *Tanya* speaks specifically about the time of the resurrection rather than an individual's attainment of the Garden of Eden or something similar. This is because in the Garden of Eden and wherever else the soul gains recompense and experience, the soul's delight is in the revelation of the divine light that fills all worlds, not the light that surrounds them. This is the nature of the World to Come, of the Garden of Eden. It is an experience of the revelation of everything that can be revealed, of the divine light within all things and their parameters, in essence of everything that we can apprehend in this world, but in interior aspect, illuminated by divine light and meaning. In contrast, at the time of the resurrection there will be a divine revelation on the level of the light that surrounds all worlds.

THE WORLD OF THE RESURRECTION AND THE SURROUNDING LIGHT

☞ Why will the light that surrounds all worlds be revealed specifically at the time of the resurrection? It is explained in several places that although the divine life force within things is not revealed in this material world, the world does contain the existence and the effect of transcendent divinity itself, of the light that surrounds all worlds. This makes it possible for intrinsic changes to occur in this world: From being to nothingness, from good to evil, from evil to good, and so forth. These cannot exist in the reality of a supernal world (the Garden of Eden, and the like), which simply has a revelation and then another revelation of the same thing – and those too in a structured and set manner that does not allow for fundamental changes. Therefore, in this world a person can change his own essence by repenting and performing good deeds (the commandments, which are a new light that did not previously exist in the world). The Sages accordingly state: "Better is one hour in repentance and good deeds in this world than the entire life of the World to Come" (*Avot* 4:17). Thus, the revelation in the World to Come is hidden in this world, and what exists in this world is hidden in the World to Come. At the time of the resurrection, when the soul will return to the body, when the World to Come will bond, in a sense, with this world, there will be – in addition to a revelation of the light that fills all worlds – a revelation of the light that surrounds all worlds.

The world following the resurrection of the dead will not return to its current state. It will be a world in which the bond between extremes will be different. Instead of a reality where physicality conceals the divine light (and therefore it can contain the light of *Ein Sof* that surrounds all worlds), there will be a reality in which physicality reveals the light that surrounds all worlds (and therefore it can reveal within itself the light that fills all worlds). In that world, the physical will fully reflect the divine that gives it life, as it comprehends, desires, and delights in the divine light. Physicality will not possess any evil, any concealment or restraint of the streaming of divine light between the spiritual and the physical, between high and low. Although we do not understand how, that reality will reveal the light that surrounds it, the inner will and inner delight of the One who created it.

of the *Tanya* refers to that epistle because his statement above about "the revelation in this world of the divine and of the light of *Ein Sof*, blessed be He, which encompasses all worlds" contains an internal contradiction. He cannot address that problem in his brief remarks here, but since it cannot simply be ignored, he refers to epistle 17, which discusses that topic at length.

וְצָרִיךְ לִהְיוֹת כְּלִי וּמָכוֹן לְהִתְלַבֵּשׁ בּוֹ אוֹר אֵין סוֹף בָּרוּךְ הוּא כְּמוֹ הַגּוּף לַנְּשָׁמָה עַל דֶּרֶךְ מָשָׁל

And there must be a vessel and abode in which the light of *Ein Sof*, blessed be He, can be enclothed – like the body for the soul, figuratively speaking.

Light without a vessel is a meaningless abstraction. It cannot be revealed and it cannot exert any influence. In order for the light to be revealed, for it to be meaningful in a particular place, it must be enclothed in a vessel. The analogy for this idea is the soul, which can be revealed and act within this world only when it is enclothed in a body.

כְּמוֹ שֶׁכָּתוּב: "הֲלֹא כֹה דְבָרִי כָּאֵשׁ" (ירמיה כג,כט), מָה אֵשׁ אֵינָה מְאִירָה בָּעוֹלָם הַזֶּה אֶלָּא כְּשֶׁנֶּאֱחֶזֶת וּמִתְלַבֶּשֶׁת בַּפְּתִילָה כוּ', כְּמוֹ שֶׁנִּתְבָּאֵר בְּמָקוֹם אַחֵר

As the verse states, "Truly, so is My word, like fire?" (Jer. 23:29) – just as fire shines in this world only when it is grasped by and enclothed in a wick..., as explained elsewhere.

Just as fire in an oil lamp has to grasp the wick and oil, so too the light of the divine soul shines in a person only when it has something to which it can grasp.[11] The animal soul is analogous to the wick, which burns as it is transformed into holiness (whether it is subdued or transformed into holiness), and the oil that maintains the fire represents one's good deeds, the mitzvot that he performs.

The object of this analogy is the illumination of the divine light that fills all worlds, and which shines and fills a person's soul and his life in

---

11. See e.g., *Likkutei Amarim*, end of 53; *Torah Or* 40b and onward; *Likkutei Torah*, Lev. 25c. Those sources refer to a different verse: "The Lord your God is a consuming fire" (Deut. 4:24; *Likkutei Torah* quotes both verses). Further study is required to resolve this discrepancy.

this world. However, one's service of performing the commandments in this world with his body and animal soul is not enough to bring forth the light of *Ein Sof* that surrounds all worlds. Something beyond that is necessary, something that is apparently impossible: A vessel that can contain that unlimited light that surrounds all worlds.

וְהַגּוּף וְהַכְּלִי לְאוֹרוֹ יִתְבָּרֵךְ הִיא
מִדַּת הַחֶסֶד וּנְדִיבַת הַלֵּב, לִיתֵּן
וּלְהַשְׁפִּיעַ חַיּוּת לְמַאן דְּלֵית לֵיה
כו׳

And the body and vessel for His light **is** a person's **attribute of kindness and generosity of heart,** as expressed in his **giving and bestowing vitality upon one who is lacking...,**

In order to contain infinitude, a vessel must itself be infinite, which is apparently impossible. Nevertheless, something of that sort does exist within a human being: Not an absolute infinitude, but a relative infinitude, a certain breaking forth out of the finite realm, which can serve as a vessel for the light that is literally infinite. All creatures apart from man exist and live within the parameters and boundaries of their nature, which they cannot break through, because these constitute their limits and essence. A human being, by contrast, can by virtue of his essential being freely choose to act against his nature and the nature and logic of the world. He can give charitably to someone who is undeserving or to one who has nothing and cannot give anything in return. This is not madness; it is an expression of the power of *Ein Sof* that is imprinted in this person. Here, in this body and in this world, he can perform an act of undeserved kindness that goes beyond finitude. He does not do so out of necessity; rather, he makes the decision on the basis of the power of the image of God within him, which only God can do, other than him. His decision to act in this manner forges a vessel down here below in which God Himself dwells and is revealed. ☞

THE VESSEL FOR HIS LIGHT

☞ How can a vessel for the infinite exist? A vessel is a limited, and is thus not infinite. Likewise, how can there be a vessel for God? Anything that enters a vessel – into any parameters, concepts, states of relationship – is by definition not God. Yet it can be said that the world was created precisely to resolve this problem: To be a dwelling place for God below (see *Likkutei Amarim,* 36–37 and elsewhere; see also the

כְּמוֹ שֶׁכָּתוּב בַּתִּיקוּנִים (הקדמת תיקוני as written in the *Tikkunim* (Intro-
זהר [יז,א]): וְכַמָּה גוּפִין תְּקִינַת לוֹן duction to *Tikkunei Zohar* 17a):
וְאִתְקְרִיאוּ בְּתִיקוּנָא דָא חֶסֶד דִּרוֹעָא "And You prepared a number of
יְמִינָא וְכָל הַגוּף נִכְלָל בִּימִין. bodies for them, which are called,
in this rectification, *Ḥesed*, which
is the right arm." The entire body
is incorporated into the right.

Even God's attributes have vessels for the light of *Ein Sof*, which are the
sefirot. The first vessel is the attribute of *Ḥesed*. The character of divine
Ḥesed is to give to one who, in comparison to the divine, has nothing.
Although the *Tikkunei Zohar* goes on to speak of the other *sefirot* as
well – "*Gevura* is the left arm, *Tiferet* is the body," and so forth, the
author of the *Tanya* here emphasizes that they are all included in *Ḥesed*.
Ḥesed is the first *sefira* in the order of the devolution of the attributes,
and in a sense, it incorporates them all. All of the other *sefirot* are ways
of defining, directing, and bestowing this *Ḥesed*. From the aspect of
the recipient, *Gevura* is *Gevura* of *Ḥesed*, the necessary constriction
of infinite *Ḥesed* so that the recipient may receive it. *Netzaḥ* and *Hod*
are the manner that *Ḥesed* relates to the recipient, how he may receive,
and so forth. All of the divine attributes, the vessels for the infinite
light, are essentially expressions of *Ḥesed*, of granting abundance to
one who is lacking. ☞

beginning of *Hemshekh Samekh Vav*, 5666), my cow." Actually, this is not merely a joke:
not to limit the infinite but to extend it, in Rothschild's wealth is, by the standards of
order that it will exist not only in infinitude the milkman, infinite, for he can acquire
but also in finitude; so that it will fill, as it whatever he wants. However, he cannot
were, this other part of existence that is buy the milkman's only cow, which is all the
finite and dark, which does not see divin- milkman has. He cannot understand and
ity. A very Jewish joke relates that a milk- feel what this cow that supports the milkman said, "If I were Rothschild, I would be man gives him: The problems, satisfac-
richer than Rothschild, because I would tions, and the texture of life that people in
have everything that Rothschild has, plus constrained circumstances experience.

THE ENTIRE BODY IS INCORPORATED INTO THE RIGHT

☞   The phrase used by the author of the sion of all of the *sefirot* in *Ḥesed*. This in-
Tanya here, "is incorporated into the right," clusion exists not only when *Ḥesed* is the
relates to an additional level of the inclu- first and highest in the order of the *sefirot*,

וְכָךְ אָמַר הַפַּיְּט: "לְבוּשׁוֹ צְדָקָה"   **And so did the liturgical poet say: "His garment is charity."**

God's garment, the vessel in which He is revealed, is charity.[12] That applies both above, in the supernal realm, insofar as everything that God does in relation to the worlds is charity, and also below, in that God's revelation in the worlds is manifested through the charity that the people of Israel perform.

וְזֶהוּ שֶׁאָמְרוּ רַבּוֹתֵינוּ ז"ל (סוכה מט,ב): אֵין הַצְּדָקָה מִשְׁתַּלֶּמֶת אֶלָּא לְפִי חֶסֶד שֶׁבָּהּ, שֶׁנֶּאֱמַר: "זְרְעוּ לָכֶם לִצְדָקָה קִצְרוּ לְפִי חֶסֶד" (הושע י,יב)   **And that is the meaning of the Rabbis' statement (*Sukka* 49b): "A person's charity is recompensed from Heaven only in accordance with the kindness in it, as the verse states, 'Sow charity for yourselves; reap according to kindness'"** (Hos. 10:12).

This statement of the Rabbis distinguishes between charity and kindness. Charity is the giving of money to a needy person. Kindness is the interiority of the deed: How the money is given, with what intent, whether it is done with a pleasant demeanor, how much effort is involved, and so forth. The comparison of charity to sowing seeds

when they are positioned in a single vertical line, but also when the *sefirot* are arranged in the more complex pattern of three parallel vertical lines: A line headed by Ḥesed on the right, a line headed by Gevura on the left, and a line headed by Tiferet in the middle. These powers, which are always found together within a single structure, are necessarily included within and combined with each other. But even so, the interrelationship possesses a preference to the right, which is the force that bonds and spreads out, in contrast to the constricting and separating force of the left line. This means that when the interrelationship is from the side of the right, it will be characterized by kindness and unity, whereas when it is from the side of the left, it will eventually lead to separation. Therefore, the statement that the entire body is incorporated into the right is not only an observation of existential reality; it mainly signifies a desirable reality, the definition of the purpose of our service in the world: To incorporate the left into the right, in the wording of the Zohar (3:178a; see also Torah Or 66b, Likkutei Torah, Num. 25b, and onward, and in many other places).

12. From the *piyyut*, *Ata Hu Elokeinu*, recited on the Days of Awe.

means that one who gives charity will receive a reward – comparable to the harvest that follows the sowing – commensurate with the measure of his kindness, rather than with the amount given.

The author of the *Tanya* now proceeds to reveal a deeper and more comprehensive meaning of this rabbinic statement.

שֶׁהַקָּצִיר הוּא גִּילּוּי הַזְּרִיעָה הַטְּמוּנָה בָּאָרֶץ, וְכָךְ הוּא הַצְּדָקָה וְהַחֶסֶד שֶׁיִּשְׂרָאֵל עוֹשִׂין בִּזְמַן הַגָּלוּת, הִיא טְמוּנָה וְנִסְתֶּרֶת עַד זְמַן הַתְּחִיָּה	That is **because the harvest is the revelation of the seed that was buried in the ground. And the same applies to the charity and kindness that** the people of **Israel perform during the time of exile: It is buried and concealed until the time of the resurrection,**

Giving charity is comparable to sowing. There is apparently no logic to sowing. We take a good seed, bury it, and it disintegrates in the ground. The same is true of charity: One gives a gift to someone who has nothing and from whom the giver will receive nothing in return. Yet just as one who sows does not see the reward of sowing seeds at the time, but only at the harvest, so too we do not see the reward of giving charity during the entire exile, but we will see it at the time of the redemption, at the resurrection of the dead. ☞

שֶׁיִּתְלַבֵּשׁ וְיָאִיר אוֹר אֵין סוֹף בָּרוּךְ הוּא בָּעוֹלָם הַזֶּה הַגַּשְׁמִי	**when the light of *Ein Sof*, blessed be He, will be enclothed and radiate in this material world.**

BURIED AND CONCEALED UNTIL THE TIME OF THE RESURRECTION

☞ It is true that – as explained in many places in the teachings of our Sages and in these holy epistles as well – we also receive a reward for charity during the exile. However, in this world too, the reward for giving charity is not revealed immediately, at the moment when one gives the charity, but only after a period of time, whethere in this world or in the Garden of Eden. Moreover, all of the reward constitutes only the "fruits" (as explained in epistle 17), whereas the essence of the reward, its principal – which is reward of an entirely different magnitude, coming as it does from the aspect of the light that surrounds all worlds – is concealed and hidden throughout the time of the exile. It will be revealed only in the future, at the time of the resurrection of the dead.

At the time of the resurrection, there will be a revelation of the bond between the light of *Ein Sof* that surrounds all worlds and the worlds themselves, which at present appears impossible. It will be revealed in this physical world, where the dead will be resurrected. The vessel and garment in which the light of *Ein Sof* will be revealed will be the charity sown in the earth, the charity that the people of Israel gave during the period of the exile.

That is the meaning of "reap according to kindness." The revelation at the time of the resurrection is not to any extent commensurate with the value of the material charity that was given, but it is commensurate with the kindness that inhered in those acts of charity, with the movement of the soul of the kindness: A flow that was not restricted by whether the giver will receive anything in return and what that might be. Just as the sowing of kindness involves a movement of the infinite beyond the reckonings of income and expenditure, the same will occur in the future harvest as well: The light of *Ein Sof* will shine regardless of what was sown.

How will the light of *Ein Sof* that surrounds all worlds be enclothed in the physical world? Nothing like this exists in our world. Nevertheless, there is a description closely resembling it (which exists in holy texts, at any rate) of the lights enclothed in the vessels of the world of *Atzilut*.[13]

The author of the *Tanya* now proceeds to explain something about how the light of *Ein Sof* that surrounds all worlds will be enclothed and revealed at the time of the resurrection.

וְאִיהוּ וְגַרְמוֹהִי חַד הֵם בְּחִינַת הַכֵּלִים דְּעֶשֶׂר סְפִירוֹת דַּאֲצִילוּת, And "He and His attributes are one" with the vessels of the ten *sefirot* of *Atzilut*,

With regard to the relationship between the light and vessels in the world of *Atzilut*, the *Zohar* says that they are one: There is a unity of revelation of light and vessel without any division between them.[14]

---

13. It is taught that the world of *Atzilut* is the rectified world that cannot be shattered and which does not experience exile. This will be the state of all reality at the time of the resurrection, with even greater intensity.
14. From the Introduction to *Tikkunei Zohar* (3b). See also epistle 20, above.

This idea can be explained as follows: In our world, while the vessel does effect revelation, it always conceals as well. The lower a world is, the greater the amount of concealment of a vessel in relation to the revelation (until in our world there might be no revelation of divinity at all). The higher and purer the world, the greater the revelation and the less the concealment, until the vessel does not conceal anything at all in the rectified and purified world of *Atzilut*. The vessel remains a vessel, but it is entirely united with the light in it in terms of purpose, means and even essence. They display a single essence that is fully revealed. ☞

וְכָל שֶׁכֵּן וְקַל וָחוֹמֶר אוֹר אֵין סוֹף בָּרוּךְ הוּא, הַסּוֹבֵב כָּל עָלְמִין מִלְמַעְלָה מַעְלָה מִבְּחִינַת אֲצִילוּת

all the more so is He one with **the light of *Ein Sof*, blessed be He, which encompasses all worlds above and beyond the aspect of *Atzilut*.**

The light in the world of *Atzilut* is the ultimate concept of light that we can imagine, the absolute revelation of everything that can be revealed. Yet this all applies only to the light that fills all worlds, the light that relates to the vessels. It is in contrast to the light that surrounds all worlds,

THE VESSELS IN *ATZILUT*

☞ The unique quality of the vessels in the world of *Atzilut* is that they are entirely subsumed within the light of *Atzilut*. They have no presence, no influence, of their own. They serve only as the complete and absolute expression of the light within themselves. This is in contrast to the lower worlds, and certainly the physical world of *Asiya*. There, the vessel is not a complete and absolute expression of the light currently enclothed within it. Rather, it always comprises other matters as well. For example, the garment for the power of a person's deed is an entity in itself. It possesses existence and presence apart from that person. This existence and presence affect his deed, and limit and conceal him: They conceal what he thought, felt, and intended when he performed the deed. On a higher plane, the garment of speech that enclothes his thought is yet closer and more connected to his thought, and conceals the speaking person less. As for his awareness and feelings (if it is possible to relate to them other than by way of his thought and speech, and the like), we cannot distinguish between them and the person himself. A person's understanding or love for God is a complete expression of himself, not of anything else. That is the closest we can get to grasping the vessels of the *sefirot* in *Atzilut*.

which is – as the phrase suggests – that which encompasses, which lies beyond all worlds, beyond relationship to any vessel, large or small, physical or entirely abstract. Therefore, just as in *Atzilut*, a light that is enclothed in a vessel is united with the vessel, with no interposition or distinction between them, that will certainly be the case when the light of *Ein Sof* that surrounds all worlds will be enclothed in this physical world. The vessel in which this light will be enclothed will be united with that light and absolutely nullified within it.

וּלְפִיכָךְ נִקְרֵאת ׳צְדָקָה׳, לְשׁוֹן נְקֵבָה ״צִדְקָתוֹ עוֹמֶדֶת לָעַד״ (תהלים קיב,ט), שֶׁמְּקַבֶּלֶת הֶאָרָה מֵאוֹר אֵין סוֹף הַסּוֹבֵב כָּל עָלְמִין הַמִּתְלַבֵּשׁ בְּתוֹכָהּ בָּעוֹלָם הַזֶּה הַגַּשְׁמִי בִּזְמַן הַתְּחִיָּה

Therefore, charity is called *tzedaka*, in the feminine form – "His *tzedaka* stands forever" (Ps. 112:9) – because it receives illumination from the light of *Ein Sof*, which encompasses all worlds and which will be enclothed in charity in this material world at the time of the resurrection.

The feminine is associated with the vessel. The feminine receives the influence of the masculine just as a vessel receives light. Since charity is a vessel in the broadest meaning of the term, a vessel to receive the surrounding light of *Ein Sof*, it is thus the concept of the feminine in the most complete sense.

Charity "stands forever." It does not go anywhere. It does not change and nor does it change anything else. Rather, it stands in its place and waits. In general, standing is self-nullification. Thus, "the standing prayer" [*Amida*] is the level of absolute self-nullification. Likewise, the angels are described as "standing" (see e.g., Isaiah 6:2) because they are nullified in relation to the divine light that shines in them. The same is true of the charity that we give in this world during the entire period of the exile. It stands, but its effects are not recognized. We give more and more – each person in accordance as he can afford – in every generation, and yet we do not receive anything in return. The world does not change and does not shine upon us in response. This is the nature of charity, which "stands forever," in a state of self-nullification, of absolute reception of the light, without any limit to its reception. Therefore, charity is that vessel which will, at the time

of the resurrection, forever receive the absolute influence of the light
of *Ein Sof* that surrounds all worlds.

Until now, the author of the *Tanya* has discussed the act of charity.
Now he will address the kindness in charity, which is the inner aspect
of its intent. What leads a person to give? What is this power within the
soul and what is the supernal meaning of this power that is awakened
and which motivates a person to give charity?

אֲבָל "צֶדֶק לְפָנָיו יְהַלֵּךְ" (תהלים
פה,יד), הוּא לְשׁוֹן זָכָר הִיא מִדַּת
הַחֶסֶד הַמִּתְעוֹרֶרֶת בְּלֵב הָאָדָם
מֵעַצְמוֹ

However, "Justice [*tzedek*] will go
before Him" (Ps. 85:14). *Tzedek* is
in the masculine form. That is the
attribute of Ḥesed [kindness] that is
awakened in a person's heart of his
own accord

In contrast to the feminine that "stands," the masculine "goes": It changes
itself, and it also changes and influences others. Not only does the masculine give charity, it rouses itself to do so and it awakens others as well.
Kindness is aroused in a person's heart of his own initiative. It is not the
case that another arouses and affects him. Therefore, this is referred to as
the masculine, and it possesses its characteristics, in that it does not stand
and receive but gives and goes forward. This distinction between *tzedek*
and *tzedaka*, between the act of charity and the attribute of kindness in
the soul, is the distinction to which the author of the *Tanya* referred at
the beginning of this epistle: Between the community that gives charity
and the individuals who inspire the community to give. Here, however,
the author applies this dynamic to the intrapersonal realm, to the element
in one's psyche that causes the other elements within him to act.

In the movement from the exterior to the interior, from the deed
to the heart, the author of the *Tanya* arrives at the inner plane of
serving God: The service of prayer (which includes the recitation of
the *Shema*).

עַל יְדֵי הִתְעוֹרְרוּת אַהֲבַת ה'
בִּקְרִיאַת שְׁמַע, וּלְדָבְקָה בּוֹ,
וְלִמְסוֹר נַפְשׁוֹ בְּ"אֶחָד"

by means of the awakening of a person's love for God when he recites the
Shema, and of the person's cleaving to
Him and giving over his soul when he
says the word "one"

The awakening of love for God is the interiority of the attribute of kindness.[15] Kindness and giving are an expression of love. The arousal of the attribute of love for God in a person's soul results from his inner service of reciting the *Shema* as he thinks about what he is saying and ponders seriously and deeply the idea that he should cleave to God and give over his soul at the recitation of the word "one." If one recites "Hear O Israel, the Lord our God, the Lord is one," while somberly bears in mind that God is one, including all reality, and that there is nothing other than God, not even the person himself, he thereby gives over his soul because he no longer regards himself as a separate being. As a result, he comes to love God. As the text of the *Shema* goes on to state: "And you shall love the Lord your God .... " (Deut. 6:5). ☞

ו"בְּכָל מְאֹדֶךָ" כִּפְשׁוּטוֹ וכו'   and when he says, "**With all your might**,"
וּבְאִתְעָרוּתָא דִּלְתַתָּא   in accordance with its plain meaning...,
and with his **awakening from below.**

THE AWAKENING OF LOVE FOR GOD THROUGH
THE RECITATION OF THE *SHEMA*

☞ The connection between a person's giving over his soul to God as he says "one" to him loving God is not immediately obvious. This problem is discussed in many hasidic writings. In brief, although a direct channel from the unity of "one" to loving God is possible, it requires a high degree of unity and love – that is to say, of "supernal unification" and "great love," of recognizing His oneness and of feeling love for God Himself beyond all His revelations through the creation of the world and in the person's soul. These require an absolute departure from this world, from its feelings and concepts. This is something that not every mind and heart can endure, certainly not twice every day. Therefore, the Sages instituted that the two verses, "...one" and "and you shall love...," should be separated by the statement: "Blessed be the name of His glorious kingdom for ever and ever." This statement refers to the divine sovereignty, to God as King of the world and the world as the domain of the King. It reflects the fact that we relate to God through our concepts and feelings about the world, each person on his own level and in his own way. This is because, if God is the King of the world, the world exists for every individual on his level (since "there is no king without a nation"; see *Sha'ar HaYihud VeHa'emuna* 7, and in many other places). It is true that in this respect as well, one must nullify his primary sense of his existence. However, this is not absolute self-nullification, but the nullification of his will and thought as he accepts the yoke of the kingdom of Heaven, each on his own level. From this unity (which is the lower unification), one becomes increasingly able to love God: To love the One who fashions and energizes this world that we feel, who gives us life and provides us with all of our familiar needs.

---

15. See epistle 15, above.

As stated in the *Shema*, one must love God "with all your heart and with all your soul and with all your might." Since the topic of this brief epistle is charity rather than the recitation of the *Shema*, the author does not enter into an explanation of the levels of service alluded to in the expression "with all your heart and with all your soul." Instead, he goes directly to the phrase "with all your might." The Mishna's[16] straightforward explanation of this phrase is that it means "with all your money." While there are many profound hermeneutical and kabbalistic interpretations of this, the simple meaning is that one should give his money to charity.

There are two stages in the service of prayer: The state of ascent and raising upwards, and the stage of descent and drawing down. The stage of ascent comes first: A person approaches prayer from the reality that he is living in, from feelings and an awareness that relate to his present life and current feelings. The first stage is to move from all of these to their root, to the root of love, of fear, and so forth: What he loves, and why he loves, and what love is, proceeding ever deeper until he reaches the depth of his heart that expresses the essence of his soul. From there, from the light of the essence of his soul, which is infinite in relation to the powers of his soul, he brings that light down and draws it into the vessels of love, which are transformed into love for God and into the power of kindness, of giving charity to a person in need.

One of the fundamental axioms in Judaism is that an awakening from below, from the person, leads to an awakening from above, from God. The deeds of a person in this world below are not disconnected from what occurs above and elsewhere. That which is above and that which lies below are connected to each other in every respect. Everything we do here, every person and every small movement, has meaning. We are not free to do whatever we desire, and God does not act in an arbitrary fashion, without taking us into account. There is more than a response to our deeds and their consequences: It is the same act of ours that returns to us from above, only on a grander scale, measured by God.

Prayer is our awakening from below. One awakens himself when he thinks about certain matters and does not think about other matters,

---

16. *Berakhot* 9:5.

and slowly he directs and raises his entire soul through understanding, knowledge, and feelings. The awakening is from below, from the point where he exists at that moment in his thought and feelings. When he thinks about the divinity in everything, he ascends and raises more and more, through his love for God and his relationship with Him.

וְ"כַּמַּיִם הַפָּנִים לַפָּנִים" (משלי
כז,יט) כֵּן לֵב אָדָם הָעֶלְיוֹן כו',
אִתְעָרוּתָא דִּלְעֵילָּא

And "as water reflects a face to the face" (Prov. 27:19), **so too** regarding **the heart of the Supreme "Person"...,** there is a reciprocal **awakening from above.**

"As water reflects a face to the face, so does the heart of a person to a person." This verse describes the process of an awakening from below that leads to an awakening from above. When a person looks into water, his reflection appears to him, and similarly, when he reveals his heart to someone else, he feels the heart of that other person turn to him. The author of the *Tanya* adds here (and this is a broad hasidic teaching) that this applies as well to the heart of the Supreme Person. God is called "the Supreme Person" because in His entire relationship to us and the world, He is enclothed in the form of a person, which consists of the ten *sefirot*, for they are in the form of the human soul (and body). Therefore, "as water reflects a face to the face, so does the heart of a Person to a person." As a person acts below, God is awakened from above.

הוּא הַמְשָׁכַת אוֹר אֵין סוֹף
בָּרוּךְ הוּא הַסּוֹבֵב כָּל עָלְמִין
לְמַטָּה מַטָּה בָּעוֹלָם הַזֶּה
הַגַּשְׁמִי בִּבְחִינַת גִּילּוּי בִּזְמַן
הַתְּחִיָּה כַּמְבוֹאָר בַּמִּכְתָּב
דְּאֶשְׁתָּקַד בַּאֲרִיכוּת

That awakening **is the drawing down of the light of** *Ein Sof,* **blessed be He, which encompasses all worlds, to the lowest depths in this material world on the level of the revelation at the time of the resurrection, as was explained at length in the epistle from last year.**

The awakening from below refers to the awakening of a person's heart, during the course of his prayers, to love God with all his might. In other words, it is an awakening of love for God from the essence of a person's heart, which is drawn down into the world of action and is expressed in his conduct as he gives his money to charity, to someone who has nothing of his own. Correspondingly, the awakening from above is the light that surrounds all worlds – the light of the essence of God in relation to the worlds – which is drawn forth like an act of charity to the lowest depths without any limitation and without any conditions, until the ultimate purpose of the descent, which is this physical world. At present, the world cannot receive such an abundance in an overt manner. It will be able to do so only when it changes at the time of the resurrection. ☞

As noted earlier, the earlier epistle referred to here is apparently epistle 17.

וְזֶהוּ "לְפָנָיו יְהַלֵּךְ", שֶׁמּוֹלִיךְ וּמַמְשִׁיךְ פָּנִים הָעֶלְיוֹנִים מִלְמַעְלָה מֵהָאֲצִילוּת עַד עוֹלָם הָעֲשִׂיָּה	And this is the meaning of "will go before Him": that *tzedek* guides and draws down the supernal countenance from above *Atzilut* to the world of *Asiya*.

Whereas *tzedaka* "stands forever," *tzedek* "will go before Him." *Tzedaka* is the act of charity itself, which is like a passive recipient, something that is done. By contrast, *tzedek* is the will, awareness, and love of the soul. "Will go before Him": It proceeds, engenders, and actualizes the performance of the deed.

The supernal countenance is the interior aspect of God's creation of the world. The exterior aspect is the act, whereas the interior is its thought and intent. There is an intent that runs even deeper than this

REVELATION AT THE TIME OF THE RESURRECTION

☞ Even at present, the light that surrounds all worlds is drawn into this physical world, albeit not as the recognizable revelation that it will be at that time. As stated earlier, the act of charity that "stands forever" is alive and exists in this physical world. The same can be said of the awakening of a person's kindness and justice that impels him and others to give charity. It finds fulfillment through the act of charity itself, when one is roused by this power, the power of *Ein Sof* that breaks through the boundaries of the world, to give charity to an indigent person. That is to say, the awakening from below and the awakening from above are not two different matters but two aspects, two perspectives, of a single reality. Sometimes, we see only one and cannot see the other. Yet the very fact that we see one means that the other exists as well, meaning that the light surrounding all worlds is drawn forth in this physical world even at the present time as well.

intent. The innermost intent is identified with the countenance that is above and beyond even the thought of creating the world, high and more inward than any relationship of the divine with any particular entity in the worlds, than any connection to the very idea of the existence of a world. This is the level of the light that surrounds all worlds, which is even higher than *Atzilut*. This drawing forth of the supernal countenance that is even higher than *Atzilut*, all the way to the world of *Asiya*, is awakened above in response to the awakening of a human being here below. This occurs when he recites the *Shema* with the dedication of his soul that is drawn to loving God on the level of "with all your might," with all of his money that he gives to charity.

וְכָעֵת עֵת לְקַצֵּר, וְכָל טוּב מֵהֶם לֹא יִבָּצֵר הֵטִיבָה ה׳ לַטּוֹבִים וְלִישָׁרִים בְּלִבּוֹתָם (תהלים קכה,ד), כְּנֶפֶשׁ תִּדְרְשֵׁנוּ.

But now is the time to be brief. And may no goodness be withheld from them. "Be good, Lord, to those who are good and to the upright of heart" (Ps. 125:4), **as is the wish of** myself, one **who seeks** that good for them (see Lam. 3:25).

This epistle focuses on a particular deed performed by a specific community that the author of the *Tanya* wishes to encourage and bless. Accordingly, since it is not the place for an extensive analysis, the issues under discussion are mentioned only briefly.

The author of the *Tanya* concludes with words of blessing: "May no goodness be withheld from them" (see Gen. 11:6). In Scripture, these words apply to the generation of the Tower of Babel, and they have a negative connotation: Had that generation been united, their evil schemes would not have been frustrated. However, the author of the *Tanya* transforms the meaning into the good: In light of the unity that this community has revealed – both in the performance of the mitzva of charity (a mitzva that unites everyone, rich and poor) and the fact that they performed it collectively as a communal mitzva – no goodness should be withheld from them.

The generation of the Tower of Babel had an evil intent: They wished to separate themselves from God. In contrast, the intent of the hasidim is for the good. Their heart is aligned with their deeds, and all of their deeds are for the sake of Heaven. They are seeking God and they wish to align themselves with His will and to draw close to Him.

This epistle, the last in *Iggeret HaKodesh*, is similar to many others in this collection in that it discusses charity. It begins by thanking and blessing the hasidim who have kept this mitzva. It goes on to present a profound explanation of this mitzva's essential nature, which is revealed in its reward. Finally, it concludes by discussing the stage that precedes and leads to the performance of the mitzva: One's awakening through his prayers to love God.

The author of the *Tanya* begins by discussing those who influence others to perform the mitzva of charity, in light of the Sages' statement that a person who inspires others to act is greater than those who perform the act. At the conclusion, the author of the *Tanya* applies these words to the realm of the soul, to the powers within a person's soul that lead him to perform a mitzva: Contemplation and arousing love, and that deepest, most essential power of the soul that leads one to bestow and give, without any calculation on the lowest level of existence, to someone who has nothing and who gives nothing in return. With these concluding words, the epistle goes beyond expressing thanks and issues a request to the hasidim: Not to wait for anyone or anything to inspire them to act but to be inspired by themselves with love for God, to dedicate their souls, when they say the word "one" in the *Shema*, with a love that is characterized by "'with all your might': with all your money."

Revelations will occur in the future, at the time of the resurrection. Yet even at present we draw the supernal countenance from above, from *Atzilut*, down to this world of *Asiya*, when we cause others to give charity and when we ourselves donate. The author of the *Tanya* is not waiting for the Garden of Eden or for the World to Come. This is reminiscent of the author's well-known statement: "I do not want your Garden of Eden, I do not want Your World to Come…. I only want You Yourself" (cited in the Tzemaḥ Tzedek's *Derekh Mitzvotekha*, *Shoresh Mitzvat HaTefilla*, chap. 40 [138a], and in *HaYom Yom*, 18 Kislev). Even if at present we do not appear to see or receive any of the divine influence, that itself constitutes our soul's dedication as we give charity:

We give without limit, and this breaks through all the limitations to God Himself.

The closing words of epistle 32 relate in a sense to all of the epistles and to the entirety of this collection. If *Iggeret HaKodesh* had a subtitle, it would be "Charity": Charity with all of its ramifications, social and personal; charity below from one person to another, and charity above from a person to God and from God to a person. This short epistle at the conclusion of *Iggeret HaKodesh* constitutes a summary of sorts to the topic of charity in its broadest sense: From the charity that a person gives here below, which becomes a vessel to receive the abundance from above, to the charity that God gives from above, which opens up the vessels to receive the divine light that is beyond them.

קוּנְטְרֵס אַחֲרוֹן

Kuntres Aḥaron

Last Tract

Preface to
Kuntres Aḥaron

Kuntres Aḥaron is the fifth and final [*aḥaron*] section of the *Tanya* in its current format, which has been in print since the year 1900. It contains notes and addenda written by the author of the *Tanya* concerning various chapters of his work. These were compiled in a separate volume at the end of the *Tanya* to avoid disrupting the continuity and coherence of the other volumes. Likewise, appended to *Shulḥan Arukh HaRav*, another work written by the author of the *Tanya*, is a volume called "*Kuntres Aḥaron*," comprising broader and more detailed analyses and discussions that complement the halakhic rulings in the book itself.

However, this description of *Kuntres Aḥaron* applies primarily to its first six essays. The remaining essays are epistles, like those found in *Iggeret HaKodesh*.[1] In many ways, *Kuntres Aḥaron* is regarded as part of *Iggeret HaKodesh*, which is how it appears on the title page and in the approbations at the beginning of the *Tanya*.[2] Nonetheless, it is also counted as a separate volume. It provides an additional layer of

---

1. In certain editions of the *Tanya*, two of these essays were included in *Iggeret HaKodesh*, and in other editions they were omitted altogether (Rabbi Yehoshua Mondshein, *Sefer HaTanya: Mahadurotav, Targumav, VeBiurav*).

2. In the Lemberg edition of the *Tanya* (5616) and other editions that followed it, the chapters of *Iggeret HaKodesh* and *Kuntres Aḥaron* are numbered sequentially as chapters 1–39. This numbering is also found in several discourses of the third Lubavitcher Rebbe, Rabbi Menaḥem Mendel Schneerson, and the fifth Lubavitcher Rebbe, Rabbi Sholom Dovber Schneerson. For example, in *Hagahot LeDibbur HaMathil Pataḥ Eliyahu 5658* (p. 6), the fifth Lubavitcher Rebbe refers to *Kuntres Aḥaron* 4 as chapter 36 (Rabbi Yehoshua Mondshein, *Sefer HaTanya: Mahadurotav, Targumav, VeBiurav*).

meaning to certain chapters of the *Tanya*, although it is not explicitly described as a commentary on those chapters.

The essence of *Kuntres Aharon* is described in the approbation by the sons of the author of the *Tanya*:[3]

Moreover, [these writings] contain new material, a last treatise [known as *Kuntres Aharon* (Last Treatise)] on certain chapters, which he penned while writing the book *Likkutei Amarim*. [This last treatise represents] a profound analysis and inquiry pertaining to passages in the *Zohar*, *Etz Ḥayyim*, and *Pri Etz Ḥayyim* that seem contradictory. With his understanding spirit, [our father] reconciles each statement in its context, based on what he wrote in *Likkutei Amarim*.

It is clear from this that the author of the *Tanya* did not write *Kuntres Aharon* after he had finished writing the *Tanya*, but that they were both written at the same time. Accordingly, it is not merely an addendum or an afterthought, but an organic part of the conception and formation of the *Tanya*. It may be said that the *Tanya* contains the condensed summary of an inner spiritual process, which the author of the *Tanya* presents to his followers. By contrast, *Kuntres Aharon*, which was appended to the *Tanya* by the author's sons, contains an actual part of the monumental spiritual process that produced the *Tanya*. Evidently, the author of the *Tanya* was right not to convey every aspect of this matter to the hasidim, instead simplifying his words. Nonetheless, his sons were also right to reveal some of the inner meaning. In addition to the intrinsic value of the words of *Kuntres Aharon*, they teach us about the *Tanya* as a whole. They attest to the fact that each idea in the *Tanya*, so simply and clearly stated, was formed through a lengthy process: It passed through each of the Torah's "chambers" and was formulated in accordance with a deep understanding of the complexity of the human soul and the physical world.

---

3. This is printed at the beginning of the *Tanya*.

Essay 1
One Who Reads All
the Narrative Stories

THE FIRST THREE ESSAYS IN *KUNTRES AḤARON* ADDRESS different aspects of the relationship between action and speech on the one hand, and intention on the other.[1]

The first essay is not comprised of notes or a commentary on the *Tanya* text. However, neither is it an entirely independent discourse. Its nature is described in the approbation of the sons of the author of the *Tanya*, as explained in the preface to *Kuntres Aḥaron*. This essay reveals a deeper layer of meaning to a matter discussed in several chapters of the *Tanya*, and provides additional kabbalistic sources that pertain to this topic.

The matter in question is discussed at length in *Likkutei Amarim*, chapters 38–40. Accordingly, this essay begins with a reference to *Likkutei Amarim*, which serves as a kind of heading.[2]

עַיֵּין בְּלִקּוּטֵי אֲמָרִים חֵלֶק א פֶּרֶק מ See *Likkutei Amarim*, volume 1, chapter 40,

---

1. In earlier editions, the first two essays of *Kuntres Aḥaron* appeared as one. Here and elsewhere, however, they are considered separate; see the introduction to *Kuntres Aḥaron* 2.
2. Evidently, the reference at the beginning of *Kuntres Aḥaron* does not pertain only to the first essay. It certainly relates to the following two essays just as much as to this one, and it applies more generally to a number of the other essays as well.

The opening sentence, which served as a kind of title for the essay, cites the chapter of *Tanya* that it relates to.

Although the same ideas were also discussed in the previous chapters, they are brought to a conclusion in chapter 40. It is important to note this because the *Tanya* is not merely a collection of concepts. Rather, the *Tanya* has a complex, organized structure. Chapter 40 is based on ideas found in the previous chapters (38–39) regarding the importance of intention. Those chapters, in turn, are based on ideas found in the preceding chapters (35–37) concerning the need for action, and so on. Thus, *Kuntres Aharon* must be understood in the context of that entire section of the *Tanya*. ☞

CHAPTER 40

☞   Chapter 40 of *Likkutei Amarim* deals with a topic that is addressed frequently by the author of the *Tanya*: the connection between intention on the one hand, and speech and action on the other. Speech has always been a theme in hasidic thought: its essence and power, as well as how we use it to serve God, study Torah, and pray. On the other hand, the importance of intention, understanding matters both as abstractly and as concretely as possible, is a theme that the author of the *Tanya* develops and emphasizes in the teachings of Chabad Hasidism. Consequently, the connection between these two elements and how they sustain, elevate, and give meaning to one another is a very important topic in the teachings of Chabad. Chapter 40 of *Likkutei Amarim* summarizes the view of the author of the *Tanya*: The two elements are essential to one another, like two parts of one body. Although action is of primary importance (see Mishna *Avot* 1:17), it is unable to ascend beyond the realm of action and to illuminate and confer meaningfulness in other realms unless it is accompanied by mental intentions of love and fear. In

chapter 40, the author of the *Tanya* compares action and speech to the body of a bird, and love and fear to its wings (in *Tikkunei Zohar* 25b, too, love and fear are referred to as "wings"). The wings are not essential to the bird's existence. However, it cannot fly without them. While the summary given in chapter 40 is fundamental, the relationship between action and intention is not fully explained there. We are not told what happens to each element when it is accompanied by the other and when it is not. In this essay in *Kuntres Aharon*, the author of the *Tanya* fills in some of these missing details, explaining the status of intention, or thought, that is not accompanied by action or speech. He asks whether there is any kind of ascent that takes place in this case, since there is nothing that rises. Moreover, if an ascent does take place, then what additional role does action play? Finally, he asks regarding words of Torah and acts of holiness: If love and fear are not present, do these words and acts still ascend to any degree from the physicality in which they were performed, and if so, to where?

לְהָבִין אֵיךְ הַקּוֹרֵא בְּסִיפּוּרֵי מַעֲשִׂיּוֹת **to understand how one who**
שֶׁבַּתּוֹרָה הוּא מְקוּשָׁר בְּחָכְמָה עִילָאָה **reads all the narrative stories**
in the Torah is connected to
the supernal wisdom,

"Narrative stories" may refer to anything in the Torah that is not a practical halakhic teaching. In its narrower definition it means, for example, the stories of the forefathers in the book of Genesis. However, more broadly, even the *halakhot* in the Written Torah are presented in the form of a narrative: God speaks to Moses, and so on.[3] Nevertheless, the author of the *Tanya* is referring here to the part of the Torah that we are unable to truly comprehend. It may be said that we are able to understand the halakhic sections: We know what we are required to do, and with regard to *halakha*, this is tantamount to a complete understanding. As a result, we are able to truly connect with supernal wisdom, *Ḥokhma* of the world of *Atzilut*, because we understand it with our human intellect, in our physical world. However, this kind of understanding is possible only with regard to the study of *halakha*, because *halakha* is expressed in the world of action, and we are able to truly comprehend this manifestation with our intellect. On the other hand, the narrative accounts in the Torah do not have the same association with our present-day reality. Even when we are able to understand their superficial structure in some form, our inner wisdom connects only to the level of wisdom that we are able to attain from this understanding, rather than to supernal wisdom. Thus, one may ask how a person who studies the narrative accounts in the Torah connects to supernal wisdom. ☞

NARRATIVE STORIES

☞ The distinction between narrative texts and halakhic texts is another topic that the author of the *Tanya* does not address in *Likkutei Amarim* but touches on in *Kuntres Aḥaron*. Although it is not the subject of this essay, it is significant here. This essay deals with intentions and thoughts that are not accompanied by spoken words, and this matter is emphasized more strongly when the thought pertains to the narrative sections of the Torah. As mentioned, regarding *halakha*, thought

---

3. See *Torah Or* 57d.

עַל פִּי מַה שֶׁכָּתוּב בַּ'כַּוָונוֹת' דַּף   in accordance with what is written in
ט"ז עַמּוּד ב'   *Kavanot*, page 16b:

Sefer HaKavanot is not merely the source of a single explanation of
this question.[4] Rather, the overall concept of *Sefer HaKavanot* itself
provides an explanation. This work deals with the higher spiritual
meaning of our actions when we observe mitzvot and customs, and
of our words when we recite blessings and prayers. It reveals a higher
level within the soul and within the words of the Torah, and this level
is the basis for the explanation given here by the author of the *Tanya*.

כְּמוֹ שֶׁהָאָדָם עוֹסֵק לְמַטָּה כָּךְ   Just as a person is engaged below, so
דִּיוֹקַן הָאָדָם הָעֶלְיוֹן לְמַעְלָה כו'   too the image of the supernal man
above...

When a person engages in matters of Torah in the lower realm, his "image," the root of his soul in the higher realm, does so in exactly the same
manner. This "image" is the supernal form of the human soul, which is
rooted in, and corresponds to, the image of the "supernal man," another
term for the structure of the ten *sefirot* of *Atzilut*.[5] This supernal image
of the human being's essence is bound to the individual in the lower

alone is also grounded in reality, by grasping its letters and substance. Although
this thought does not act or speak, it reflects upon both action and speech. On
the other hand, with regard to the narrative texts, supernal wisdom does not descend into the letters of speech or action.
Accordingly, the question regarding spiritual intentions that are not accompanied
by speech or action is even more pertinent
to thoughts about the narrative accounts
in the Torah.

---

4. The reference here is apparently to one of the anthologies of the Arizal's
Kavanot that were available at that time, and not to his prominent works *Pri Etz
Hayyim* and *Sha'ar HaKavanot*. These anthologies were compiled and edited by
the Arizal's students. This particular source is also cited elsewhere in the works of
the author of the *Tanya*, for example, "*Ethalekh Lozniya*," p. 160; *Ma'amarei Admor
HaZaken 5572*, p. 139. In Chabad literature, the source given is *Sefer HaKavanot*
(Venice, 5380). However, in that edition, the relevant words appear on page 12a.
5. This refers to the depiction of the structure of God's revelation and flow within
the worlds through the ten *sefirot*.

world, and operates together with him, especially when he is engaged in Torah, whose holiness is alike in the higher and lower realms. ☞

וְכֵן יֵשׁ לוֹמַר בְּהַרְהוּר בָּאוֹתִיּוֹת הַכְּתוּבוֹת   **And it should be said likewise with regard to contemplating written letters.**

SO TOO THE IMAGE OF THE SUPERNAL MAN ABOVE

☞ This does not pertain only to the soul that we human beings are aware of, each one of us on our own level. Rather, it refers to the full extent of human spiritual stature, which takes the form of the "supernal man." The Sages teach that before the sin, the height of Adam, the first man, extended from the ground to the skies (*Hagiga* 12a; see also Rashi, Deut. 4:32).[6] In any case, the Sages' statement is true in a certain sense even today, with regard to every human being: A person lives on this earth in a physical body, yet his soul rises to the highest realms. It acts and is acted upon in the highest levels of the world of *Beria*, and even on the divine levels of *Atzilut* and beyond. This is not only because his actions have meaning in those realms, but because the highest levels of his soul actually reach them. Of course, the soul in the lower world is unable to connect to these higher levels. As explained elsewhere (*Likkutei Torah*, Deut. 36d), the higher levels of the soul, *haya* and *yehida*, are not enclothed in the body or the faculties of the soul. Rather, they are on a level that surrounds us, a level that is beyond our perception. Nonetheless, they too are part of the soul's essence.

It is explained in Kabbala that the soul has five levels: *nefesh, ruah, neshama, haya,* and *yehida*. *Nefesh* is rooted in the world of *Asiya*, *ruah* in the world of *Yetzira*, *neshama* in the world of *Beria*, and *haya* and *yehida* in the world of *Atzilut* and that which is above *Atzilut* (see *Ma'amarei Admor HaZaken* 5572, p. 139). *Haya* and *yehida* are the levels that are "surrounding" in their essence, and thus connect to God Himself rather than merely to the divine light that gives life to the worlds. Thus, the human soul reaches all the way from *Asiya* to supernal wisdom, which is in *Atzilut*. Consequently, when a person reflects on the narrative accounts in the Torah, which are arranged in accordance with supernal wisdom, he is connected to them even if he does not comprehend them, because his soul is connected to supernal wisdom. As long as he engages with these stories in the lower world, every level of his soul connects to them, all the way up to the level of supernal wisdom.

Supernal wisdom descends from level to level within the words of the Torah. Ultimately, it reaches the world of *Asiya*, where it is revealed only in its external form, namely in the letters of the Hebrew alphabet. In much the same way, the human soul, too, descends from the highest

---

6. It is explained that since man was created "in the image of God" (Gen. 1:27), his height corresponded to that of the Creator of the world, the "Man" of *Atzilut*, or *Adam Kadmon* (see *Imrei Bina* 74b).

This explanation of the connection between supernal wisdom and the individual who reads the Torah's narrative accounts pertains to one who contemplates the written letters, without expressing them verbally. When a person speaks, his words and what they create move upward. In contrast, when he just thinks about the words, he is connected to supernal wisdom: Through his thinking, the lower part of his soul is joined with the higher part, which is connected to supernal wisdom. Hitherto, each level of the soul may have been concerned with a different matter, but now, the entire soul, up to the level of supernal wisdom, is united in one thought. ☞

אֲבָל הַדִּבּוּר, יֵשׁ לוֹמַר דְּבוֹקֵעַ
וְסָלֵיק לַאֲצִילוּת מַמָּשׁ

Speech, however, can be said to break through and ascend to actual *Atzilut*,

A person's contemplation of the narrative accounts in the Torah remains firmly entrenched in the "inner" soul, even though the soul itself extends all the way to the "image of supernal man." The abovementioned realm to the world of *Asiya*. Consequently, when the soul engages with the Torah's narrative accounts in the lowest realm, it has a pathway to the highest realm, which awakens and reveals the levels of the soul found along its length and attaches them to the levels of the Divine that are present to varying degrees in each and every level and world, all the way up to supernal wisdom.

Of course, these levels are always present in the soul, even when the person is not studying Torah. However, they are usually shadowy, imperceptible, and insignificant. On the other hand, when one engages with the Torah's stories in the lower world, he illuminates every level of his soul. He may not fully comprehend the essence of supernal wisdom as he does when he studies the halakhic sections of the Torah. Nonetheless, his understanding in the lower world is not completely detached from supernal wisdom either. It is the "foot," the activity ["*Asiya*"] of supernal wisdom, which is connected to its "head," just as the limbs of the human body are connected.

Thus, the more a person understands, on both the physical and spiritual plane, the narrative accounts in the Torah and the significance of the actions and relationships within them, the higher he will ascend and illuminate a loftier, more inner level. Of course, in his lower reality, where he is capable of understanding, certain matters will always be beyond his comprehension. Only the level of *ḥaya*, which is not enclothed in the created intellect, is able to grasp the essence of supernal wisdom. Nonetheless, the individual causes the higher part of his soul, the "image," to engage with this section of the Torah and illuminate it.

connection to supernal wisdom is not manifest in the lower soul, which is found in the human body, in the world of *Asiya*. Instead, it is manifest in the upper part of soul, in the "supernal image," which is intrinsically connected to supernal wisdom.

In contrast, when a person articulates his thoughts verbally, his speech breaks through the barriers of the soul and the physical world,

CONTEMPLATING WRITTEN LETTERS

☞ The term used here is *hirhur*, "contemplation," rather than *maḥshava*, "thought." On the simplest level, this is a reference to the talmudic statement "Contemplation is not tantamount to speech" (*Berakhot* 20b; *Shabbat* 150a). However, it may also indicate that there is a difference between contemplation and thought. The author of the *Tanya* writes in a number of places that contemplation is a more "internal," abstract kind of thought, which has not yet been formed, even mentally, into letters. In chapter 12 of *Likkutei Amarim*, for example, the author of the *Tanya* states that a *beinoni* may refrain from "thinking" evil thoughts, yet he has no control over whether or not he "contemplates" evil.[7]

---

7. Elsewhere, however, citing biblical verses to support his stance (see *Biurei HaZohar* by the Tzemaḥ Tzedek, p. 589), he expresses the opposite view, namely that contemplation is more "external" than thought, and is in fact closer to speech. This explains why the Talmud clarifies that "contemplation is not tantamount to speech." Since thought is further removed from speech, it is self-evident that it is not tantamount to speech either.

In *Iggerot Kodesh* (vol. 4, epistle 2054), the Lubavitcher Rebbe, Rabbi Menaḥem Mendel Schneerson, cites additional sources regarding the differences between thought and contemplation, and he resolves the discrepancy by explaining that there are two different types of contemplation: one that is on a higher level than thought, and one that is on a lower level. Furthermore, he makes a comment, printed in *Lessons in Tanya*: In the section beginning "To understand how one who reads" [this essay in *Kuntres Aḥaron*], and in volume 1 [*Likkutei Amarim*], chapter 38, [the author of the *Tanya*] sometimes uses the term "thought" and sometimes "contemplation," and this is the explanation: The term "thought" encompasses all levels of thought [see the end of *Iggeret HaKodesh*, epistle 19], and particularly [in relation to contemplation] "thought of thought." Contemplation, on the other hand, is the consideration of 1) how to speak, and 2) the written or spoken letters. See the beginning of *Biurei HaZohar*, at the end of s.v. *lehavin … pataḥ Rabbi Ḥizkiya*.

and ascends to the Divine. This refers to the world of *Atzilut* itself, and not just to the aspect of the Divine that is present on every level. ☞

As explained in *Likkutei Amarim* (chap. 40), the level to which speech ascends is determined by the person's intention. Love and fear are comparable to wings that carry speech and action to their intended destinations. A person's spiritual intention refers to his thoughts and emotions, his love and fear. When one's intention is on the level of "*atzilut*" in the soul, it elevates his speech and binds it to *Atzilut* itself. As explained below (and in *Likkutei Amarim*, chaps. 39–40), when a person's love and fear are intellectual, they elevate his speech to the world of *Beria*, and when his love and fear are natural and innate, they elevate his speech to the world of *Yetzira*. Lastly, when one's intention is purely to engage in the act of speech, which is the essential requirement for studying the Written Torah, his speech ascends to the holy realm of *Asiya*. ☞

אוֹ לִבְרִיאָה, בִּדְחִילוּ וּרְחִימוּ שִׂכְלִיִּים אוֹ
לִיצִירָה בִּדְחִילוּ וּרְחִימוּ טִבְעִיִּים

or to *Beria*, through intellectual fear and love, or to *Yetzira*, through natural fear and love.

SPEECH BREAKS THROUGH AND ASCENDS

☞   All speech, from human speech to *Malkhut*, divine Kingship, embodies the capacity to move away from the self and toward the other. Only speech is able to reveal the inner dimensions of a person's soul to others: his intellect, his emotions, and even his thoughts. Likewise, regarding one's Torah study and mitzvot, the words are able to ascend only when they are verbalized. They ascend in accordance with the level of his intention (as explained in *Likkutei Amarim*, chap. 40, and below), and can rise to the highest point of the world of *Atzilut*.

LITERAL ASCENT TO *ATZILUT*

☞   The love and fear that pertain to the world of *Atzilut* are on the level of supernal wisdom. On this level, there is complete nullification, not only of the person's physical being, but also of his love and fear, his emotions and intellect. Although he may experience love and fear, they are not truly "his." Instead, he experiences God's own love, thinks God's thoughts, knows with God's knowledge, and so on. Else-where, such an individual is referred to as the "chariot" of the Divine. Of course, not everyone is able to reach this level. Nonetheless, according to the definition of divine service provided by the author of the *Tanya*, every individual, on his own level, is capable of experiencing something similar, although perhaps not all the time and not in the world of *Atzilut* itself. This is because all souls are part of the Divine and are root-

At any given moment, the essence of an individual's intention is expressed through the fear and love that he is experiencing. His fear and love elevate his earthly speech and actions to the realm with which they are associated. When one's feelings of fear and love derive solely from his intellectual understanding, they convey his words to the world of *Beria*, the realm of the intellect. ☞ ☞

Natural love and fear elevate a person's spoken words to the world of *Yetzira*.

ed in the supernal image in the world of *Atzilut*. Furthermore, just as this quality of *Atzilut* is present in the large all-encompassing domain, (of the existence of the soul and all souls), it is likewise found within each level of the soul. Thus a person is not required to rise above his current situation, nor is he capable of doing so. Instead, he must identify the *Atzilut*, *Beria*, and *Yetzira* within himself and focus his intentions on them.

OR TO *BERIA*

☞   *Beria*, the realm of the intellect, is immediately below *Atzilut*. *Atzilut* is characterized by the complete nullification that precedes creation. It is pure, unadulterated divine revelation. *Beria*, on the other hand, is the realm in which the essence of the creation is established. The creations in *Beria* are not nullified: They perceive their own existence. However, their entire essence is their relationship to the Creator. The notion of creation is so important that they are wholly preoccupied by it. The connection between Creator and creation is extremely close: The creation is like a newborn infant, who does not yet relate to himself as a separate being, but rather is totally fixated on his Creator. He perceives the fact that he exists, but he also recognizes that he is "existence from nothingness." He regards the "nothingness" and is subsumed within it. The world of *Beria* is referred to as an "intellectual" process, like how we look at the "big picture" before considering the details. This is the nature of the world of *Beria*, the realm of pure intellect. Intellect alone determines the mental, emotional response, resulting in "intellectual" love and fear.

THROUGH INTELLECTUAL FEAR AND LOVE

☞   This does not refer to the intellect itself. The letters of speech, and the human soul, are elevated by the emotions of love and fear, which the *Zohar* refers to as "wings." The intellect is merely an onlooker: One's personal feelings and concerns are not integral parts of intellectual understanding, and therefore, intellectual understanding by itself does not lead a person to his intended destination. Instead, one's feelings regarding his intellectual understanding, namely love and fear, are what elevate him to be incorporated within the intellectual understanding. His true "self" is found in these emotions. When they ascend, they elevate him with them, as well as elevating the part of the world that he is engaging with through action or speech.

The world of *Yetzira* is the realm of the emotions, or the emotive attributes, which determine how we relate to the creations that were defined and given existence by the intellect. As mentioned, intellectual love and fear are elements of the intellectual realm. Here, on the other hand, the reference is to the love and fear themselves, as a world of their own, the realm of emotion. As mentioned, the emotive attributes of *Beria* comprise the emotions of the intellectual realm, namely intellectual love and fear. In the same way, the cognitive attributes of *Yetzira* form the intellectual aspect of the emotional realm.

This is why the author of the *Tanya* refers to "natural fear and love" in relation to the world of *Yetzira*. These emotions do not originate in the intellect. Instead, they are generated by their own, internal source within the essence of the world of *Yetzira*, which is the realm of emotion. The cognitive attributes of *Yetzira* awaken these emotions and help to develop and actualize them, but unlike in the world of *Beria*, they do not form them from nothingness. ☞

וּבְמִקְרָא סָלֵיק מֵעוֹלָם הַזֶּה לְעֶשֶׂר סְפִירוֹת דַּעֲשִׂיָּה מִשּׁוּם דְּבָקַע אֲוִירִין וכו׳

And in the case of the Written **Torah, it ascends from this world to the ten** *sefirot* **of Asiya, because it breaks through air spaces…**

NATURAL, CONCEALED LOVE AND FEAR

☞ The essence of natural love and fear is described at length in *Likkutei Amarim* (chaps. 16, 18 and onward), where they are referred to as "concealed" love and fear. Natural love is so called because it is inherent in the soul of every Jew, a legacy from our forefathers. Because this love is intrinsic to the soul and is not contingent on one's intellectual understanding, its capacity to move the soul is even greater than that of intellectual love and fear. It is capable of bringing a soul to the point of self-sacrifice for the sake of God, an act that the intellect could never endorse. The problem with natural love and fear in the world of *Asiya* is that they are concealed, obscured by the various "loves" and "fears" that are intrinsic to the animal soul. Nonetheless, since natural love and fear are innate, one does not need to be in the world of *Yetzira* in order for them to be manifest: They are part of the soul even in the world of *Asiya*. One needs only to be cognizant of this fact, and natural love and fear can be revealed in his actions and speech. They may not be manifest in his emotions in the realm of *Asiya*, yet they can be revealed as the spiritual force that impels him to act and speak. Then, as stated, when a person's words ascend to the world of *Yetzira* and elevate him with them, natural fear and love are revealed as emotions within his soul.

When a person enunciates the letters of the Written Torah, they ascend from this world of *Asiya*, where they are written and spoken, to the ten *sefirot* of the world of *Asiya*.

The unique element in the study of the Written Torah, in contrast to the various levels of the Oral Torah, is the enunciation of the written letters.[8] One's intention, the love and fear that he experiences at that moment, is insignificant with respect to the study of the Written Torah itself. Ostensibly, then, there are no "wings" that elevate this type of Torah study beyond *Asiya*. Instead, it rises from the level of *Asiya* itself, in the physical world, to the ten holy *sefirot* of *Asiya*.

Regarding every world, we can distinguish between the world itself and its ten *sefirot*. The world itself is the dimension of "reality," which includes time, space, and the creations that are found in that realm. The ten *sefirot*, on the other hand, comprise the divine element of that world, which forms it, sustains it, and embodies its conception of the Divine. Consequently, advancing from a particular world to the ten *sefirot* of the same world constitutes the most momentous transition. It involves progressing from the worldly realm to the divine realm, and this is certainly more significant than ascending from one world to another.

Unlike his thoughts, a person's speech always ascends, no matter what part of the Torah it is drawn from, and no matter what his level of intention is.

The words that we utter pierce the air around us and the firmament that separates us from all that is beyond us.[9] Even in the physical realm,

---

8. This is explained in numerous hasidic sources, e.g., *Likkutei Torah*, Lev. 5b.
9. The Lubavitcher Rebbe, Rabbi Menaḥem Mendel Schneerson, comments: This expression ["breaks through air spaces"] is also found in [*Sefer HaMa'am-arim*] "*Ethalekh Lozniya*," [which is a book of discourses that includes these essays from *Kuntres Aḥaron*]. [However,] this warrants a critical comparison of early editions and manuscripts, for in many places (*Likkutei Amarim*, chap. 40; *Zohar*, vol. 3, cited there), [the expression used is "breaks through] firmaments." (Printed in *Lessons in Tanya*)
   However, in my humble opinion, this variation is of no great significance, since there are sources in which both terms appear. These sources describe the voice that breaks through "atmospheres and firmaments" (see *Ma'amar HaZohar LeTikkun Ḥatzot*, printed in *Siddur im Divrei Elokim Ḥayyim* [5763], p. 428). Furthermore, it is explained that "atmospheres" refers to the air between the firmaments. Therefore, in this context, they have the same meaning.

speech emerges from one's personal space and enters the space of the other. The same thing happens in our relationship with God: Through the very act of verbalizing them, a person's words of Torah and prayer emerge from the human domain and ascend to the divine realm of the same world. This is true even if he does not experience intellectual or natural love and fear, although of course, he must not have any kind of intention that diminishes or suppresses his words.

These are the Torah's words, which are essentially the words of God Himself. When a person says these words and letters aloud, both the letters and the speaker are connected to the letters spoken by God. Regarding ordinary speech, a person's words emerge from his private domain, but they do not always reach their destination. However, when one restates another person's exact words, his words connect to the other person's intention and inevitably to the other person himself, as long as the speaker does not obstruct this connection with a different intention or thought. Thus, provided that one's intention is directed toward the essential holiness of his action or speech, he elevates the letters by verbalizing them. Even when his intention remains in the world of *Asiya*, the letters are raised up from the world itself, the physical domain, to the realm of holiness, which is where God's will, wisdom, and kindness give off their light.

מַה שֶּׁאֵין כֵּן בְּהִרְהוּר אֶלָּא הַדִּיּוֹקָן שֶׁהוּא שֹׁרֶשׁ נִשְׁמָתוֹ וְכוּ׳ **This is not the case for contemplation; rather, the image, which is the root of his soul…**

When a person does not say the words but only thinks them, they do not emerge, ascend, and unite with the divine being. However, as explained above, one's thoughts about the Torah's words do not remain in the lower realm, separate from supernal wisdom, either. Instead, they ascend within the person's soul to the image of supernal man, which is the soul's root in supernal wisdom. In this regard, a person's thoughts do not need to emerge or break through firmaments in order to enter a different realm, because they are able to reach the level of supernal wisdom within the soul. When one contemplates the Torah's words in the lower realm, his soul, situated in the upper realm, contemplates them as well.

Thus, when there is only contemplation, nothing truly shifts or breaks through firmaments. Only the soul's wondrous connection to supernal wisdom receives a new "melody," a new expression. It receives this new expression on account of the Torah's words, the words of God Himself, which pass through the person. It is as though it awakens from a slumber of inactivity and meaninglessness, and reveals an entirely new countenance.

וּמַה שֶּׁכָּתוּב בַּזֹּהַר חֵלֶק ג׳ דַּף קה״ה דְּהִרְהוּר לָא עָבֵיד מִידֵי כוּ׳, וְהַיְינוּ אֲפִילוּ לְטַב, עַיֵּין שָׁם	**As for what is written in the *Zohar* (3:105) that contemplation does not achieve anything…, and this means even for the good, see there**

This passage in the *Zohar* is concerned with the Sabbath.[10] The verse states, "You call the Sabbath a delight … you honor it by refraining from doing your business, from seeking your needs, and from speaking of matters" (Isa. 58:13). This teaches that in addition to refraining from desecrating the Sabbath through action, one must also refrain from doing so through mundane speech. The *Zohar* explains that unlike action, speech does not necessarily violate the holiness of the Sabbath in the lower world. However, when speech ascends to a higher level of existence, to the realm of speech, it becomes a solid reality, just like an action in the world of action. In that higher realm, speech does violate the holiness of the Sabbath. The *Zohar* goes on to say that this pertains specifically to speech. On the other hand, thought is not active in the higher realms. Consequently, the contemplation of mundane matters is permitted on the Sabbath. Thus, we learn that mere thoughts that are not "good" do not ascend to the higher realms, nor do they do any damage to those realms. Moreover, after quoting the *Zohar*, the author of the *Tanya* adds the phrase "even for the good." Evidently, even "good" thoughts, such as reflections on the Torah's words, do not ascend by contemplation alone, if unaccompanied by action or speech.[11]

---

10. It is cited as *Zohar* 3:105a in the gloss to *Likkutei Amarim*, chap. 40.

11. The Lubavitcher Rebbe, Rabbi Menaḥem Mendel Schneerson, makes mention of the fact, also noted in *Lessons in Tanya*, that in the section of *Sefer HaMa'amarim*, "*Ethalekh Lozniya*," that corresponds to this essay in *Kuntres Aḥaron*, the first word of this sentence is *ma*, and not *uma*, as written here. In other words, it is

וּבְדַף ל"א עַמּוּד ב' יֵשׁ לוֹמַר דְּהַיְינוּ
לְאִתְעָרָא לְעֵילָא שֶׁיּוּמְשַׁךְ מִשָּׁם
לְתַתָּא רַק מַחֲשַׁבְתּוֹ נִשְׁאֲרָה שָׁם
וּמוֹסִיפָה שָׁם אוֹר גָּדוֹל בְּתוֹסֶפֶת
וְרִיבּוּי הָאוֹר בַּאֲצִילוּת

and on page 31b, that is referring to
an awakening above which will be
drawn down from there to below.
Only his thought remains there,
adding a great light there, through
the addition and increase of the
light in *Atzilut*

The second source cited from the *Zohar* likewise speaks of a word that
is uttered in the lower world, and that ascends and breaks through
firmaments to evoke either good or evil, depending on its nature.

The words of the *Zohar* indicate that speech alone ascends and acts
in the upper realm. This seems to contradict what is said here, namely
that our thoughts also ascend and become connected to the supernal
image, which is in supernal wisdom, in the world of *Atzilut*.

However, when the *Zohar* states that thoughts do not "act" in the
upper realm, it does not mean that they do not ascend to the upper
realm, nor that they are insignificant in the upper realm. Rather, it
means that thoughts do not evoke a downward flow from the upper
realm.

Our holy thoughts certainly ascend to the upper realm, for that
is where they belong. When there is nothing physical binding a holy
thought to the lower world, it ascends and connects to its highest abode
within the soul, ultimately reaching its source in the world of *Atzilut*.
When it arrives at that point, it is not merely subsumed like a drop in
the sea. Rather, it adds something new that greatly increases the light
that was already present in the world of *Atzilut*. ☞

Now, the author of the *Tanya* relates to what was stated a few
paragraphs ago regarding the verbal expression of the Torah's words

---

written without the letter *vav*, a grammatical conjunction meaning "and." This is
a very significant change, because without the letter *vav*, this sentence no longer
comprises a question about what was stated previously, but instead marks the
beginning of a new topic. Here, this passage has been interpreted in accordance
with the version printed in the *Tanya*. However, it is worth noting that it is also
possible to interpret it differently.

and letters.[12] This speech ascends together with the thoughts and intentions the person had while speaking.

עַל יְדֵי מִקְרָא וּמִצְוֹת מַעֲשִׂיּוֹת שֶׁבַּעֲשִׂיָּה **by means of the** Written **Torah and mitzvot performed with a physical action in** *Asiya.*

Thought's capacity to ascend to supernal *Ḥokhma* of *Atzilut* is not comprised of only thought itself. When a thought ascends, it brings with it all that was tied to it the lower realms: If one articulated or acted on a thought, his speech or action ascends together with the thought, and furthermore, it rises to the very same height as the thought. When

---

ADDING LIGHT TO *ATZILUT*

☞ Ostensibly, the lights in *Atzilut* are already perfect, because *Atzilut* is the "rectified" world, which comprises the ideal connection between lights and vessels. The lights in *Atzilut* are not concealed by the vessels, but are revealed through them. By analogy, a well-crafted poem does not conceal the speaker's meaning, but reveals it on many levels. Of course, the lights in *Atzilut* are restricted by the vessels, but this does not cause any contradiction or conflict between them. Rather, it generates understanding and support, and ultimately, they are incorporated into one cause and action. It is not clear what human contemplation in the lower realm could possibly add to this, even if it does ascend to the upper realm. The answer is that it adds that which derives from imperfection, darkness, and all that is not found in *Atzilut*. *Atzilut* is intrinsically perfect, and

as such, it is unable to receive or to grow. Certain thoughts from the lower realm, from the imperfect reality of conflict, concealment, *kelippa* (husk), and evil, are capable of ascending. These are "rectified," holy thoughts. When they ascend, they emit a light into the world of *Atzilut* that was not found there previously: the light that emerges from the darkness. This light is beyond perfection. It is beyond *Atzilut* itself. The world of *Atzilut* can be compared to a righteous person, whose actions and thoughts are perfect. On the other hand, the thought that ascends from the world of *Asiya* can be compared to a penitent. The penitent attains the level of the righteous person starting from a place where the righteous person has never been. Consequently, the penitent adds strength and power to the existence of the righteous.

---

12. In the above section, the author of the *Tanya* posed a question about the words of the *Zohar* (3:105a) regarding thought alone and provided the answer. Here, there is a shift in focus. It is possible that there is a linking word missing from the text.

this happens, the increase in light in *Atzilut* is even more significant. Moreover, as mentioned, the additional light causes the light in the upper realm to flow down into the realm of *Asiya*, where the speech was uttered or the action performed. This will be explained below. ☞

שֶׁעִיקַר הַיִּחוּד הוּא לְמַעְלָה רַק הַפֵּירוֹת בָּעוֹלָם הַזֶּה עַל יְדֵי הַמְשָׁכַת אוֹר מְעַט מִזְעֵיר לְמַטָּה עַל יְדֵי הַדִּבּוּר וּמַעֲשֶׂה

For the primary union is above; only the fruits are in this world, by means of the drawing forth of a miniscule amount of light below, through speech and action.

The ascent from the lower realm creates a union, or merger, between the higher and lower realms. In the spiritual reality, entities are separate from one another as a result of their distinct spiritual levels. The world of *Yetzira* is separate from the world of *Beria*, not in the sense that one is in the east and the other is in the west, but rather, they constitute different spiritual levels. The two extremities of one level may be vastly different, yet they are still part of one system, one world. On the other hand, the differences between two distinct levels are fundamental, for they are like two separate worlds. Therefore, when that which is in the lower realm ascends, the primary union is formed and revealed in the upper realm. The highest realm is *Atzilut*, the world of unity. There, polar opposites are revealed in a state of unity: right and left, upper and lower, lights and vessels, one and many, and world and Divine.

VERBALIZING THE WORDS OF THE WRITTEN TORAH AND PERFORMING THE PRACTICAL MITZVOT IN *ASIYA*

☞ The author of the *Tanya* refers to the verbalization of the words of the Written Torah and the performance of the practical mitzvot, because like our thoughts, our speech and actions that ascend must have relevance and meaning in the upper realm. As mentioned, the principal way to engage with the Torah is through saying the words aloud, not through thinking about them or understanding their meaning. Consequently, the author of the *Tanya* emphasizes that although we enunciate the Torah's letters and words in physical *Asiya*, the lowest realm, these utterances are meaningful at every level, all the way up to the highest realm. Likewise, the act of performing a mitzva is significant at every level of the unfolding succession. Although this may not be evident in the lower realm, it becomes more and more obvious at the higher levels.

The "primary union," which is found in the upper realm, may be referred to as the "principal." On the other hand, the "fruits," which emerge from the upper realm and enter the physical world, correspond to the "proceeds," which do not reduce the principal. In the spiritual realm, this term refers to the emitted light, or flow, which has no value in relation to the supernal union. However, it has value and significance in the distant places which the light reaches, that is, the significance that the supernal union has in the vessels and concepts of the physical word. These vessels include the love between human beings, and any flow from above that translates into a physical blessing, such as livelihood, health, or children. All of these blessings embody a kind of union between the person in need and that which he lacks.

The downward flow of the "fruits" is an extremely small life force derived from the light of the supernal union. This miniscule amount of light is what the limited vessels of the lower world are able to receive, and accordingly, it has meaning for our lives in the physical world.

When the *Zohar* states that things are accomplished by means of speech and action, it is referring to the flow that is awakened and drawn down from *Atzilut* into the realm of action. ☞

מַה שֶּׁאֵין כֵּן בְּהִרְהוּר, לֹא נִמְשָׁךְ
כְּלוּם

This is not the case for contemplation, where nothing is drawn forth.

THROUGH SPEECH AND ACTION

☞   The light descends through speech and action because, simply put, speech and action themselves comprise a downward flow: They draw the soul, the light, and supernal meaning into physical matter. The soul that speaks shapes its self, its own supernal, holy form, in these physical shapes, and that descent draws down the supernal bounty, which are the "fruits" in this world. On a deeper level, it is possible to see this as an "awakening from below," or an "elevation of the feminine waters." This kind of elevation must take place in order for there to be an "awakening from above," which causes light to be transmitted to the lower realm. Supernal light, like the *neshama*, does not inherently desire to descend. Rather, it yearns to ascend and become subsumed in its source. Therefore, an awakening from below is necessary: Something must ascend from the lower realm to arouse the supernal light and induce it to emit a downward flow. The awakening from below does not simply provoke the supernal light or draw its attention. As explained at length elsewhere,

In the case of thought alone, without action or speech, all movement is in an upward direction.

Since nothing actually ascends from below, but instead, the soul that thinks in the lower realm thinks in the upper realm as well, nothing is drawn down either. In kabbalistic terms, if the feminine waters are not elevated, the masculine waters do not flow downward. By analogy, a scholar may reflect on some worldly concept without ever actually considering any of its physical elements, because he is thinking on higher, more abstract levels. The understanding that this scholar reaches does not give any meaning to the physical "metaphor," which is the worldly matter that he contemplates. The physical matter is of no interest to him: He is focused on its higher, abstract meaning, and on the possibility of attaining even higher levels of understanding.

וְלָכֵן לֹא יָצָא יְדֵי חוֹבָתוֹ מַה
שֶׁיָּרְדָה נִשְׁמָתוֹ לָעוֹלָם הַזֶּה
רַק לְהַמְשִׁיךְ אוֹרוֹת עֶלְיוֹנִים
לְמַטָּה, כְּמוֹ שֶׁכָּתוּב בְּעֵץ חַיִּים
שַׁעַר כ"ו 'לְהַמְשִׁיךְ אוֹר'

Therefore, he has not fulfilled his duty, as his soul descended to this world only to draw down supernal lights to below, as is written in *Etz Ḥayyim*, 26: "To draw forth light."

Thus, a person's duty is not fulfilled through thought alone. The soul's objective, rather than to ascend, is to draw down light into the lower world, where it is situated in the body.

It states in Etz Ḥayyim that the reason why the soul is required to become enclothed in physical matter, namely the body and the physical world, and in the spiritual garment [*tzelem*] that enables it to become enclothed in the body, is only in order to draw light into them and

---

it reaches a level that is even higher than the higher realm. As a result, it evokes an urge to connect to the lower realm, even if this is not a conscious thought or even an unconscious desire. It may simply be an incomprehensible feeling of obligation arising from the soul and from the essential, inexplicable truth of this matter that lies beyond words. It is our real, physical, worldly actions, and the letters of our spoken words, that ascend from the lower realm and give rise to all this. As explained at length in *Likkutei Amarim*, they ascend together with the person's intention, in accordance with the level of his love and fear.

rectify them.[13] The whole purpose of the soul's descent is to rectify the lower reality. It further states that the soul's descent into the body is akin to the exile of the Divine Presence, as well as the exile of the Jewish people among the nations, for it is a descent with a purpose that does not relate only to the soul itself. Simply put, the soul does not descend only in order to ascend, and likewise, the Jewish people were not exiled only in order to return. Rather, in each of these cases, there is a purpose that must be achieved in the lower realm, in the course of the descent or exile.[14] ☞

So too, a person's task in this world is to descend and draw down the supernal light. The problem with the lower realm is not its lowly position, but the fact that it perceives itself as separate from the Divine. Consequently, the way to rectify the lower realm is not by raising it up so that it is no longer "lower," but by drawing light into it from above. When this happens, it is still the lower realm, but it is no longer separate. In fact, it manifests the highest level of holiness. As explained

THE SOUL'S DUTY

☞ The soul's descent requires effort and it is an obligation. That obligation goes against nature and the soul's will because descending into the lower realm runs counter to the inclination of the soul (*Likkutei Amarim*, chap. 15). The soul's abode is in the upper realm. That is where it feels at ease, and where it reveals its true nature and inner delight. On the other hand, when it descends, concealed in the body and in the material world, it must work hard to fulfill its assigned task. Nonetheless, this exertion, which goes against its nature, is in fact the purpose of the soul's creation, and indeed, the purpose of all of creation. The natural order, though more familiar and more pleasant, is merely an extension of the act of creation, of the "direct light." However, unlike trees, rocks, and so on, which act in accordance with nature, the soul has an additional purpose: to perfect creation. It is able to achieve this only when it goes against nature and does that which the direct light does not do, namely reflect the light back to the upper realm.

---

13. *Etz Ḥayyim* 26 (*Sha'ar HaTzelem*), end of chap. 1.

14. The Sages say that the Jewish people were exiled among the nations only so that converts might be added to their ranks (*Pesaḥim* 87b). It is explained in kabbalistic and in hasidic writings that these converts are sparks of holiness that the Jewish people extricate from the exile and separate from the *kelippot*.

elsewhere, the purpose of creation is for God to desire a dwelling place in the lower world.[15]

אֲבָל לְהַעֲלוֹת מִמַּטָּה לְמַעְלָה הוּא
דַּוְקָא עַל יְדֵי 'מַחֲשָׁבָה טוֹבָה'

However, elevating from below to above is achieved specifically by means of "a good thought,"

Action and speech constitute the drawing down of the soul into vessels of the letters and physical matter. In contrast, a good, holy thought constitutes the elevation of the soul to its supernal image, its highest source. When the soul is elevated in this way, the letters of its speech ascend with it, as do the actions it performs. ☞ ☞

דְּבְלָא דְּחִילוּ וּרְחִימוּ לָא פָּרְחָא לְעֵילָא
וּכְמוֹ שֶׁכָּתוּב בְּשַׁעַר הַנְּבוּאָה פֶּרֶק ב',
וְהַמַּחֲשָׁבָה טוֹבָה כו'

for without fear and love it will not ascend upward, as is written in *Sha'ar HaNevua*, chapter 2: "And the good thought…"

ELEVATION BY MEANS OF A GOOD THOUGHT

☞ As mentioned, the soul's descent is a duty that goes against its nature. Conversely, the soul's nature and innermost desire is to ascend: to move toward its supernal source, which so high that it is always above the soul, regardless of the soul's current state. Thus, the soul does not need to speak or act in order to ascend. It continues to rise higher and higher simply through thought, which expresses its own essence.

A GOOD THOUGHT

☞ The author of the *Tanya* defines this term (based on *Kiddushin* 40a) in *Likkutei Amarim* (chaps. 16, 44). It relates to the intention behind a person's actions and words: the love and fear of God that lead him to do a certain mitzva, pray, study Torah, and so forth. An individual may not be able to evoke within himself the emotions of love and fear, but only the thought that these are the proper emotions to have. When such a person proceeds to act and speak as though he feels these emotions and is led by them, this thought is referred to as a "good thought." God attaches the good thought to the person's action, elevating the action as though there were actual love and fear in the person's heart.

---

15. See *Tanḥuma, Beḥukotai* 3, *Naso* 16; *Bereshit Rabba* 3:9; *Bemidbar Rabba* 13:6; see also *Likkutei Amarim*, chaps. 36–37. This matter is discussed in numerous discourses by the author of the *Tanya*. It is also explained at length at the beginning of *Hemshekh Samekh Vav*.

Actions and words do not ascend by themselves, even if they are "good" actions and words, namely mitzvot and words of Torah. They ascend only by means of the fear and love that the individual feels when he does or says them, or by means of a "good thought," as explained above.

It states in *Sha'ar HaNevua* that no words of Torah or prayer are spoken in vain: They all ascend and break through firmaments.[16] However, the magnitude of the ascent, and the nature of the angels that are created and borne by the words, are determined by the thoughts and intentions the person has while he is speaking. When one's intentions are lofty and free of worldly distractions, his words ascend to a higher level, and the angels that are created are loftier and purer, both in form and expression. It is further explained that a person's words are reflected back to him in the mouths of these angels. If his thoughts were good, the angels reveal supernal words of truth, but if his thoughts were worldly, they reflect words of falsehood.

To conclude this essay, the author of the *Tanya* elucidates another aspect of the complex relationship between intention and action. Having begun with the question of what happens to intentions that are not accompanied by speech, he ends by asking what happens to speech that is completely devoid of intention. Above, it was stated that without love and fear, our spoken words do not ascend. The author of the *Tanya* questions this based on the passage of the *Zohar* quoted above.

וּמַה שֶּׁכָּתַב דְּבָקַע רְקִיעִין וְכוּ׳, וְהַיְינוּ אֲפִילוּ בְּלֹא דְּחִילוּ וּרְחִימוּ, בְּ׳מְכָּל שֶׁכֵּן מִדְּבָרִים בְּטֵלִים	And regarding that which he wrote, that "it broke through firmaments…" – and that means even without fear and love, and all the more so from idle conversation

The *Zohar*, cited above, states that spoken words of Torah break through the firmaments and ascend beyond this world.[17] The author of the

---

16. The reference is probably to *Sha'ar HaYiḥudim*, also known as *Sha'ar HaYiḥudim VeNevua VeRuaḥ HaKodesh*. This is the fourth section of *Pri Etz Ḥayyim*, which was compiled and edited by Rabbi Meir Popperos from the writings of Rabbi Ḥayyim Vital (see Rabbi Yosef Avivi, *Kabbalat HaAri*, p. 651).

17. *Zohar* 3:105a.

Tanya explains that this applies even if the words are uttered without any holy intentions of love and fear for the sake of Heaven. Although this is not explicitly stated in the *Zohar*, the author of the *Tanya* argues that it may be inferred from the reference to idle, mundane talk. The *Zohar* teaches that if a person speaks of mundane matters on the Sabbath, his words ascend to the higher realm and detract from the sanctity of the Sabbath. Such a person is certainly not speaking with holy intentions, but just the opposite. Thus, if these mundane words ascend, then words of holiness, even if they are not stated with intention, certainly ascend as well.

[זֶה אֵינוֹ, דְּגַם שָׁם יֵשׁ אֵיזוֹ תַּאֲוָה   [this is not so, as there too there is
(בְּנוּסְחָא אַחֵר לֵיתָא תֵּיבוֹת אֵלּוֹ)]   some sort of lust (these words do not
appear in an alternative version)]

Ostensibly, this parenthetical statement negates the idea that our words ascend even when they are devoid of fear and love.[18] However, it can also be interpreted as further corroboration of this idea. It asserts that the assumption that idle talk is devoid of intention is incorrect. When a person engages in idle talk, he does so because he has some degree of spiritual lust for his subject, or for the act of speaking itself. This lust is a spiritual force, and although it may not be "holy," it elevates earthly speech to its own level of spirituality. Indeed, "spiritual" does not necessarily mean "holy." Just like the physical world, the spiritual worlds contain elements that are "good" and "holy," and elements that are not holy. There is "holy" love, and love that is not holy, yet both of them belong to the spiritual realm of love. Thus, the lust involved in idle talk elevates the words to its own level of spirituality, despite the fact that its spirituality is flawed. It is important to note, however, that on the higher, more spiritual levels of reality, that which is "not good" is flimsier. At each level, it gets closer to the good and the holy, until it is like the precursor to evil, or simply the possibility that evil might exist.

In any case, we can still infer from the *Zohar* that holy speech ascends, because holy speech cannot be completely bereft of intention and spirituality either. As explained at length in *Likkutei Amarim*, even when

---

18. The parenthetical statement does not appear in *Sefer HaMa'amarim*, "*Ethalekh Lozniya*," nor in manuscripts.

a person does not feel the emotions of love and fear, there are other spiritual forces that galvanize him to act and speak, despite the fact that he ostensibly lacks "intention." These are forces of direct and indirect conclusions, which are expressed through the person's acceptance of the yoke of Heaven, and even his habits of behavior. Thus, even if the love and fear of God that underlie a person's words and actions are "concealed," they are nonetheless capable of elevating those words and actions. For if worldly passion is capable of elevating frivolous talk, concealed love and fear must certainly be capable of elevating words of Torah.

דְּמִדָּה טוֹבָה מְרוּבָּה   **as the measure of good is greater –**

Whether or not the parenthetical statement above is included, there is a basic assumption here that "the measure of good is greater." The term "the measure of good" is used by the Sages to refer to the way in which God bestows His goodness upon the world and rewards us.[19] The simple explanation for the fact that it is "greater" is that the measure of good moves in the same direction as the flow, abundance, and kindness that embody creation itself. Thus it unites with and enhances the forces of creation, or in other words, the forces of giving, which form and sustain life. On the other hand, God's "measure of punishment" restricts, negates, and conceals. Since this attribute goes against the forces of creation, it only restricts and diminishes them.

It is the same with regard to human speech. Idle speech ascends even though it does not belong in the upper realm, and actually longs to descend. Consequently, it goes without saying that holy speech and holy intentions, which do belong in the upper realm, and in whose nature it is to ascend, ascend as well, and reach even higher.

In any case, the assertion of the *Zohar*, namely that our words ascend even without love and fear, seems to directly contradict what the author of the *Tanya* wrote above.

הַיְינוּ רְקִיעִין דַּוְקָא, שֶׁהֵן הַהֵיכְלוֹת וְהַבָּתִּים, וְלֹא בְּגוּף הָאָדָם הָעֶלְיוֹן   **that is** referring **specifically to firmaments, which are the chambers and the houses, not the body of the supernal man.**

---

19. See *Sota* 11a; *Sanhedrin* 100a; *Yoma* 76a.

The contradiction is resolved in the following way: The *Zohar* describes the ascent of words that, even if they are devoid of love and fear, break through firmaments. Yet the term "firmaments" refers to the external worlds only. On the other hand, regarding the ten *sefirot* of each world, our words cannot reach them without love and fear. ☞

וְכָל שֶׁכֵּן בְּנֶפֶשׁ רוּחַ נְשָׁמָה **And all the more so the** *nefesh, ruaḥ, neshama,*

THE CHAMBERS, NOT THE BODY OF THE SUPERNAL MAN

☞ Regarding each of the four worlds, *Atzilut, Beria, Yetzira,* and *Asiya,* it is necessary to distinguish between the world itself and the ten *sefirot* through which God acts and reveals Himself. The world itself is described here as "the chambers and the houses." It comprises the whole space of *Beria, Yetzira,* or *Asiya,* and everything that happens there. On the other hand, the ten *sefirot,* through which God rules the world in question and manifests Himself, are referred to as "the body of the supernal man." Throughout Kabbala, the human form is equated with the structure of the ten *sefirot* (as explained in detail in *Pataḥ Eliyahu*), and the structure of holiness in general. This is based on the verse in Ezekiel's vision of the divine chariot: "Upon the likeness of the throne was a likeness, like the appearance of a person upon it, from above" (Ezek. 1:26). Thus, the author of the *Tanya* explains that a person's words and actions that are devoid of love and fear, that lack spiritual intention, do indeed ascend from the purely physical plane, the plane of breath and sound, to a spiritual level in one of the four worlds. The letters of a person's speech are no longer simply letters or worldly objects. Instead, they have been verbalized by a human being, and as a result, they emerge from the realm of inaction, breaking through "firmaments," to enter a space of meaning, a space that relates to the connection between different objects and levels, just like the person himself does. However, these words do not ascend beyond that world to the "body of the supernal man," the ten *sefirot,* where God Himself is revealed.

By analogy, the events in a story do not affect the storyteller in any way, even though his thoughts and speech are what create them. A minor character may become the story's hero, yet the storyteller remains unmoved. A person who creates something, such as a story or a drawing, is affected by his creation only when an element of it relates to him personally. As he shapes the creation, some detail might emerge unexpectedly and evoke a personal association for him. This is the element of the work that touches him, that moves him to do more, beyond that drawing or story he created.

Similarly, when a person speaks without fear and love, his words ascend only in the sense that they move beyond their inanimate state. However, they are still part of the world and its "narrative." On the other hand, when one utters the Torah's words with love and fear of God, the words ascend and "touch" God Himself. This causes God to respond in kind, with His own love and fear, through the ten *sefirot* of the same world.

The "body of the supernal man" pertains to the "vessels" of the ten *sefirot*, while *nefesh, ruah*, and *neshama* are the "lights" within these vessels. The light within a vessel is analogous to the soul enclothed in the human body. Just as the soul contains the levels of *nefesh, ruah*, and *neshama*,[20] the lights within the vessels of the ten *sefirot* contain these levels as well. Consequently, if speech and actions that are unaccompanied by fear and love do not ascend to the body of the supernal man, they certainly do not ascend to *nefesh, ruah*, and *neshama* either. ☞

אֲפִילוּ בְּאָדָם דַּעֲשִׂיָּה' שֶׁהֵן   **even with regard to the "man of *Asiya*,"**
עֶשֶׂר סְפִירוֹת אוֹרוֹת וְכֵלִים   **which are the ten *sefirot*, lights, and vessels.**

Without the intention to do God's will, or in other words, without love and fear of God, our words and actions do not ascend even to the lowest order of the ten *sefirot*, namely the ten *sefirot* of *Asiya*. This is because, as explained above (and at length in *Iggeret HaKodesh*, epistle 20), the most substantial border in existence is the one that lies between a world and its *sefirot*. This assertion is true with regard to all worlds, even *Asiya*. It refers to the border between the worldly

---

NEFESH, RUAH, AND NESHAMA OF THE SUPERNAL MAN, OR SEFIROT

☞ When the soul ascends to the divine light, it connects to each of these levels. The differences between the levels of *nefesh, ruah*, and *neshama* in the divine light correspond to the differences between *nefesh, ruah*, and *neshama* in the soul. The first level, *nefesh*, is the inception of the connection that ascends in the divine realm of the *sefirot*. In the soul, this is a connection that touches the person himself, but specifically his external aspect, which connects to the outside world. Above *nefesh* is *ruah*, where the connection goes deeper. In the soul, it relates to the person's feelings toward this. Natural love and fear, which were discussed at the beginning of this essay, and which elevate speech to the world of *Yetzira*, belong on this level. Finally, the level of *neshama* has an even deeper connection. In the soul, it relates to the person's understanding of reality, which is even more in line with his essence, and which elevates the soul and its words to the level of *neshama* in the Divine. Intellectual love and fear, mentioned above, behave in this way, elevating speech to the world of *Beria*.

---

20. Since *haya and yehida* are levels that surround us rather than being enclothed in the body, they are not mentioned here.

and the Divine: Neither words nor souls can cross this border without
the presence of love and fear.

וְזֶה שֶׁכָּתוּב בַּתִּקּוּנִים דְּבִלָא   This is the meaning of **that which is**
דְּחִילוּ וּרְחִימוּ לָא יָכְלָא לְסַלְקָא   **written in the** *Tikkunim,* **that with-**
וּלְמֵיקָם קֳדָם ה' דַּוְקָא   **out fear and love it cannot ascend
                                              and stand before God** – specifically
                                              "before God."

The move from the external world to the ten *sefirot,* even of *Asiya,*
constitutes a shift from the external realm to the inner realm, or in other
words, from the act of focusing on that which God does and creates
to focusing on God Himself. The inner realm can be penetrated only
by means of love and fear of God.[21]

Love and fear are what enable us to connect to the souls of others.
We are certainly able to act and speak without forming any kind of
personal connection to others. One might do so out of habit, desire,
or a belief that it is necessary. However, a deep personal connection
develops, both for the individual who does the act and for the other
person, only when the act is performed out of love or fear. Likewise,
when one simply performs a mitzva or utters words of Torah or prayer
without love and fear, his words and actions remain in the world. However, when he does these things out of love and fear of God, because
they connect to his soul, his speech and actions ascend and penetrate
God's own love and fear, which are the ten *sefirot* of the particular world
in which he is speaking and acting.

As indicated by its first few words, this short essay provides an additional elucidation of certain chapters of *Likkutei Amarim.* It begins with
a question about a person who contemplates the narrative accounts in
the Torah, as opposed to the practical *halakhot.* This question raises
a fundamental issue that was barely addressed in *Likkutei Amarim:*
whether thoughts and intentions that are unaccompanied by speech
ascend and have meaning in other realms. The answer given is that
although they do not actually ascend to the higher worlds, they do

---

21. *Tikkunei Zohar* 25b.

ascend within the soul. Moreover, the human soul is the divine image, which extends to the level of supernal *Ḥokhma* of *Atzilut*. Accordingly, thoughts and intentions that are present in the soul in the lower realm ascend, within the soul itself, to the highest realm, and shine a great light into the world of *Atzilut*. Nonetheless, the author of the *Tanya* emphasizes the fact that intentions are most impactful when they are accompanied by speech. This is because the intentions elevate the letters of speech, and the reality that they convey, to the intentions' own level. Thus, the letters ascend from the "other side" of reality, and therefore, they are able to impel the divine essence, which is beyond the entire unfolding succession, to emit a new, divine light into the lower realm. As mentioned, this flow of light is the main purpose of the creation of humanity and the world. Thus it is the obligation of each human being, whose soul descended into the physical world, to speak and act there, in order to draw the supernal light down into the lower realm.

To complete the picture, the author of the *Tanya* addresses the opposite situation: What happens to holy speech that is unaccompanied by intentions of love and fear. He concludes that since it is holy, this speech does ascend, but only within the world in which it was spoken. However, it does not reach the realm of the Divine, namely the ten *sefirot*.

This addendum of sorts to *Likkutei Amarim* reveals the essence of the relationship between action and intention. The intentions of love and fear of God constitute the "force of elevation." Intentions ascend by themselves in any case, and when they are accompanied by the letters of speech or action, they elevate them as well, together with whatever worlds they are attached to. Speech and action, on the other hand, constitute the "downward force," which awakens, in the upper realm, the desire to flow downward. Speech cannot truly ascend without thought, and thought cannot draw anything down without speech. Accordingly, each world exists and fulfills its purpose only through the combination of intention and action, or in other words, through elevation and the ensuing downward flow.

Essay 2
See *Etz Ḥayyim, Sha'ar HaNekudot*

THIS ESSAY IS IN A CERTAIN SENSE A CONTINUATION of the previous essay,[1] and in any case it deals with the same topic: the relationship between an action and the intention that goes with it. In the previous essay, the emphasis was placed on the intention, which is the love and fear that a person feels and by virtue of which he performs the action. It was explained there that without the proper intention there is really no ascent of anything, not even words of Torah, which are themselves matters of holiness. This essay will mainly deal with the other side, the aspect of the action that ascends with the intention, why it is so important that there be a concrete action that ascends on high.

However, without reference to the previous essay, this essay has an independent theme and conceptual structure. Underlying the matter is the perception that reality in all its aspects, including the lower and the higher, the world and the Divine, wants to reach a union (*yiḥud*, unification, or *zivug*, fusion, in the terminology of the kabbalists). This unification is not only a nullification of what is found below within what is found above; in every fusion there is an aspect of reciprocity, of giving, and even of a certain nullification on the part of both sides. Why the lower beings want this is easily understood, for everything strives to connect to the source of its being and vitality, to receive more vitality; but

---

1. Indeed, in the first edition of *Kuntres Aḥaron* from the year 5574, this essay appears as a continuation of the first essay.

why would the upper beings want this? After all, the lower beings are ostensibly more external to and distant from the source. This short essay addresses this question and explains what is done and what should be done to inspire the upper beings to desire this union, to relate to the lower beings and bestow upon them.

This short discourse does not delve into long explanations of hasidic teachings, but merely resolves apparent contradictions with other sources in Kabbala. However, from the contexts that the author addresses, and the short sentences by way of which he illuminates his teachings, the inner, hasidic perception of the author the *Tanya* becomes manifest.

28 Ḥeshvan

27 Ḥeshvan
(leap year)

עַיֵּין עֵץ חַיִּים שַׁעַר הַנְּקוּדוֹת שַׁעַר ח׳ פֶּרֶק ו׳ שֶׁאֵין הַחְזָרַת פָּנִים בְּפָנִים כִּי אִם עַל יְדֵי מִצְוֹת מַעֲשִׂיּוֹת דַּוְקָא

See *Etz Ḥayyim, Sha'ar HaNekudot, Sha'ar 8,* **chapter 6,** where it explains that **the turning of face-to-face is** achieved **exclusively by means of mitzvot performed with a physical action.**

The passage in *Etz Ḥayyim* deals with the relationship between the faces of the Emanation – *Zeir Anpin* (the Small Countenance) and *Malkhut* (Kingdom), which in the language of the *Zohar* is the relationship between the Holy One, blessed be He, and His *Shekhina.* This relationship expresses the root of all the relationships between God and the worlds. *Zeir Anpin* expresses the face of God toward the world, the end point of the Divine from which He relates to the worlds. *Malkhut* expresses the Divine in the worlds, the *Shekhina,* the Divine Presence. The relationship between them is, therefore, the relationship between the Divine and the world as it is still in the Divine, in the world of Emanation. In this exceedingly important relationship, the ultimate end is that there be unification, a connection between them ("the unification of the Holy One, blessed be He, and His *Shekhina,*" mentioned everywhere), and furthermore, that this connection be "face-to-face," with desire and love on both sides, and not back-to-back, and with no back at all, for in that case the unification and the influence would not be complete.

It is explained in that passage, and it will be further explained in this essay, that the turning of face-to-face is brought about by the practical mitzvot that man performs below in the physical world. ☞

"Face" refers to the relationship from one side, whereas "face-to-face" refers to the relationship from the two sides. Usually there is a correspondence between the two sides, as the wisest of men said: "As water reflects a face to the face, so does the heart of a person to a person" (Prov. 27:19). But such a correspondence does not always exist. For example, if there is a relationship between two people, one may want the inner relationship, while the other regards the association as only an external necessity that he does not really desire. Such a relationship would be "face-to-back," and there can also be relationships that can be described as "back-to-face" or "back-to-back." Only when both parties have an internal interest and desire for the relationship will it be "face-to-face."

A relationship of "face-to-face" is a positive state of life and of a person, how he feels and lives and acts. This is a state of perfection that cannot be surpassed. It does not demand of the situation and of the person to be what he is not, but to continue what he is doing, to try harder, to ascend higher, because he feels that he can. This is not

FACE-TO-FACE

☞ Since we are dealing with spiritual worlds, which have no physical sides, we must explain what is meant here by "face" and "back." In the most basic sense, the distinction is between the main side, which is the goal, and is called "face," and the side that is called "back," which is the tool, the means, that is used for the sake of the inner side. The back is indeed necessary, though not because of its inherent importance, but only as a means to maintain the inner side, which is the goal. This distinction exists also in the physical world, where we find face and back in the same sense, such as in the distinction between the outside of a glass in contrast to its inside. The end and purpose is the inside of the glass that contains the drink, but it is impossible for a glass to have an inside without an outside. So too in spirituality and in matters of the soul there is something that we desire, but for that we "want" (need) many other things, which are the path, the means, and the foundation necessary for us to obtain what we desire. When we refer to something or someone as a "face," it means that we see that thing or person as an end in itself, and not as a way and a means to reach something else; and we will simultaneously turn our faces and eyes toward it on a physical level, and our innermost souls, our desires, and our life force on a spiritual level.

the perfection of repair like that in the time of the redemption, but it is the optimal initial state that can be realized at any time.

The truth is that this situation depends less on what a person does and more on his inner intention. When a person identifies the road leading to his inner intention in everything, his entire life is internal. When, however, something goes wrong, when the roads seem interminably long, when there is no end is visible in the dense thicket, life and one's attitude toward everything is casual and imposed upon him, and this is life facing the back side.

The assertion made in *Etz Ḥayyim* that "the turning of face-to-face is achieved exclusively by means of mitzvot performed with a physical action" requires explanation. What is the connection between performing the mitzvot and the emotional relationship of "face-to-face"?

וְטַעַם הַדָּבָר, כִּי עַל יְדֵי מַעֲשִׂים	**The reason is that through good deeds**
טוֹבִים גּוֹרֵם זִיוּוּג הָעֶלְיוֹן וכו'	**one causes the supernal fusion ....**

As is explained there in *Etz Ḥayyim*,[2] through the good deeds that a person performs, through the actions of the mitzvot and the repair of this world, he causes the "supernal fusion." "Supernal fusion" is the connection between the bestower and the recipient above in the world of Emanation. That is to say, it not only concerns the actual flow in the lower worlds, but higher up, as an influence upon the bestower within the *sefirot* themselves (from *Zeir Anpin* to *Malkhut*) which creates the direction and the manner of the flow upon our world.[3]

וּלְהָבִין אַמַּאי מַעֲשִׂיּוֹת דַּוְקָא   **In order to comprehend why** it is **specifically** mitzvot **performed with a physical action** –

It is understandable why the face-to-face relationship is achieved exclusively through the performance of the mitzvot, for, as is mentioned in many places, the term "mitzva" is derived from the word

---

2. See *Sha'ar HaHakdamot* for a more detailed discussion of the negation of the back side of the Father and Mother.

3. In the kabbalistic texts this is the union of Father and Mother, in contrast to the lower union, which is the union of *Zeir Anpin* and *Malkhut*.

tzavta, "togetherness,"[4] and it is specifically through a mitzva, which reflects the internal will of God above and is performed through the free and internal will and choice of man below, that this togetherness, the essential inner union between man and God, is created. However, this still does not explain why it is specifically mitzvot performed with a physical action that are necessary. Why is it so important that the supernal will reach all the way down? Why is it so important that the person fulfill the desire specifically with a physical act?

יוּבָן מִמַּה שֶׁכָּתוּב בְּשַׁעַר מ"ן וּמ"ד כִּי צָרִיךְ תְּחִלָּה לְהַעֲלוֹת מַיִּין נוּקְבִין דְּנוּקְבָא דִּזְעֵיר אַנְפִּין

this can be understood from that which is written in *Etz Ḥayyim, Sha'ar Mayim Nukvin UMayim Dukhrin,* that it is first necessary to raise the feminine waters of the feminine aspect [*Nukva*] of *Zeir Anpin,*

It is necessary,[5] as preparation for the fusion and the flow of the "masculine waters," to elevate the feminine waters of the feminine aspect of *Zeir Anpin. Zeir Anpin* (the Small Countenance) is, as it were, the face of God that relates to and influences the worlds, which are small in relation to Him, and the feminine aspect is *Malkhut,* which receives that flow on behalf of the worlds. For the sake of the fusion, which involves drawing the "masculine waters" from above, the feminine aspect, that is, the lower reality, must rise up from below its own "feminine waters," its desire and craving, to the male bestower.

The term "masculine waters" refers to the flow that comes down from above, from the bestower to the recipient. This is analogous to an idea that is channeled to the understanding and to its application in practice. The raising of "feminine waters" refers to the readiness of the lower side, both with respect to the desire and inner choice to receive from above, and with respect to the ability to receive, which includes the readiness of the utensil to receive the flow from above. This preparation involves not only the raising of information, but also

---

4. See also *Peri Etz Ḥayyim, Sha'ar HaLulav,* and *Torah Or* 6b; *Likkutei Torah,* Num. 55d, 57d, and many other places.
5. *Etz Ḥayyim,* 39. The reference may be to the beginning of Sermon 1.

the raising of the desire to receive, which awakens above the desire and craving to give.

וּמַיִם נוּקְבִין דְּנוּקְבָא הֵן בְּחִינַת עֲשִׂיָּה, כְּמוֹ שֶׁנִּתְבָּאֵר שָׁם (עץ חיים שער מ"ן ומ"ד) פֶּרֶק א' — and the feminine waters are the aspect of action (Asiya), **as explained there** (*Etz Ḥayyim, Sha'ar Mayim Nukvin UMayim Dukhrin*), **chapter 1.**

The feminine aspect of *Zeir Anpin* is, as stated, the *sefira* of *Malkhut*, which is the faculty of action with respect to the whole of spiritual reality, and what it raises is itself, that is, the quality of action. The ultimate action is, of course, the physical act.

וְהִנֵּה הַמַּעֲשִׂים טוֹבִים נִקְרָאִים כִּסּוּחַ וְקִיצוּץ הַקּוֹצִים הַנֶּאֱחָזִים בָּאֲחוֹרַיִים שֶׁהֵן בְּחִינַת עֲשִׂיָּה, כְּמוֹ שֶׁכָּתוּב בְּשַׁעַר מ"ז פֶּרֶק ה' — **Now, good deeds are termed "trimming and chopping the thorns" that are holding onto the "back side,"** which is the aspect of action (*Asiya*), **as written in** *Etz Ḥayyim, Sha'ar* 47, **chap.** 5.

"Good deeds," namely mitzvot performed with a physical action, in addition to their being the connection between man and God, also play a role in the world of action. In kabbalistic literature, this role is defined as trimming and chopping the thorns that are holding onto the back side.

The back side of all the spiritual worlds is the world of physical action; the outer side that is the furthest from the inner light and divine revelation.

In this back side, one does not see the inner intention and the source that gives it life and brings it into being. One sees only its outer outline, its action on the lowest plane of reality. The "thorns" hold onto such a view of action. Like the thorns in a vineyard, these thorns, which are the *kelippot* at their various different levels, are not the desired growth, and it was not for them that the vineyard was planted, but they too receive from the abundance of life, from the water and the light that is bestowed on the vineyard. This problem is exceedingly grave because not only do the thorns share the abundance of life with the vines, but when left undisturbed, they take over the vineyard, dry up its vines and become the main thing growing there. So too in the spiritual worlds, the "thorns" take hold of the world of action; not only do they conceal what is inside, which is the divine light, but, as it were, they work against it and against what reveals it. ☞

In this sense, "good deeds" resemble what gardeners do in a vineyard; they trim and chop the thorns that hold onto the back side, and thus they direct the bestower and the recipient to stand face-to-face, and turn the supernal flow to the good and the intentional, to the place and the manner that reveals the Divine even in this lower world.[6] The gardener, that is, the tzaddik (or anyone who performs "good deeds"),[7] does not turn the back side into interiority (because then it would no longer be part of the lower world), but only chops off the thorns, namely, the abnormal deviations of the back side, the evil drawing its nourishment from the back side. In this way the back side and the lower reality itself reveal the divine light.

TRIMMING AND CHOPPING THE THORNS

☞ As is explained there in *Etz Ḥayyim*, the state of "back-to-back" is the result of an unrepaired world, a world of chaos and disorder, a world in which there are "thorns," which directs the supernal influence flow to external matters, and not to internal and intentional ones. In this sense, "back-to-back" is like a safety valve that closes whenever there arises concern that the flow passing through will damage the lower worlds and reach places it should not reach. Therefore, when a person performs good deeds below, when he clarifies and repairs the lower reality and transforms it into a vessel that is ready and worthy to receive the supernal flow, he causes the turning of the face.

When we do not trust the person before us, when we are not pleased with the responses that he gives, we turn our backs to him and not our faces; that is to say, we do not reveal to him the inner aspects of our hearts and desires. The face-to-face relationship can only be restored when that person performs actions that will restore trust, when he creates from his place another reality that has a face, one toward which we would like to turn our faces.

---

6. And in greater force, for this is "dwelling in the lower worlds" in which He reveals Himself even more so than in the upper worlds.

7. For that which is stated about the tzaddikim relates in a certain sense to every member of Israel, as is explained in various places in connection with the verse "Your people shall be all righteous" (Isa. 60:21). See *Iggeret HaKodesh*, epistle 17; *Likkutei Torah*, Deut. 1a; and elsewhere.

וְהַיְינוּ עַל יְדֵי הַעֲלָאַת הַטּוֹב הַגָּנוּז
בָּהֶם הַמְלוּבָּשׁ בְּמִצְוֹת מַעֲשִׂיּוֹת
לִמְקוֹרוֹ לִקְדוּשַׁת הָאֲצִילוּת שֶׁכְּבָר
הוּבְרְרָה

This is achieved **through raising the good concealed within them – which is clothed in action-related commandments – to its source, to the sanctity of** *Atzilut* **that has already been distilled.**

Raising the good hidden within an action involves clarifying and raising the sparks of holiness from the *kelippot*. Good is hidden in everything, even in the back side and even in the *kelippot*; it is the spark of divine holiness that gives life and being to everything and every situation, for there is no existence and no life force without holiness. At times, however, the hidden good is not evident. This is the role of the person who performs good deeds, to reveal the good in that action and to raise it.

Not every spark can be raised, but what can be raised and it is a mitzva to raise it is that which is "clothed in action-related commandments." The togetherness of the commandment expresses itself also in its role in chopping the thorns and distilling the sparks. The act of the commandment is connected to the Divine, and from this emanates its power to reveal and distill and raise the sparks from within the *kelippa*.

This must be done through the performance of the commandment in actual practice, and it does not suffice to have the proper feeling or thought, since, as has been mentioned, the spark is trapped within the reality of action. It is true that there is also spiritual clarification, there are bad opinions and bad attributes in the soul, there are thoughts of madness and thoughts of impurity, but both the corruption and the repair of these things end up in action. And if the matter is not finished in action, it is not actually finished, and it does not reveal and raise up the feminine waters.

The ascent is to the "*Atzilut* that has already been distilled," that is, that was already distilled from the very outset – not through human action, but because this is how God made the world, that a part of it was already distilled and repaired. The knowledge and the fact that not everything is corrupted, neither in the worlds nor in the soul, is the foundation that enables the general repair upon which the entire service of distillation rests. The rule is that only one who is himself repaired can repair others, only a reality of a part that is fully repaired lead to the whole in its entirety being repaired. In man this is the divine soul within him, in the *sefirot* this is wisdom, and in the worlds, this is the world of *Atzilut*.

וּמַה שֶּׁכָּתוּב שָׁם שֶׁאָדָם הָרִאשׁוֹן תִּקֵּן גַּם כֵּן עַל יְדֵי תְּפִלָּה הַיְינוּ עַל יְדֵי אוֹתִיּוֹת הַדִּבּוּר, דַּעֲקִימַת שְׂפָתָיו הָוֵי מַעֲשֶׂה	That which is written there, that Adam the first man also rectified through prayer, that means using the letters of speech, as the moving of one's lips is considered an action,

Not only Adam,[8] but every person raises feminine waters with his prayers. Ostensibly, this contradicts what has been stated here, that the raising up of the feminine waters for the sake of fusion and the restoration of the face-to-face relationship is only through action.

A person speaks by way of moving his lips,[9] which is considered a physical action performed by his body, no less so than an action performed with his hand, or with an object of mitzva, like an etrog.[10]

כִּי הֵן מִנֶּפֶשׁ הַחִיּוּנִית שֶׁבַּגּוּף וְדָמוֹ אֲשֶׁר שָׁרְשָׁן מִנּוֹגַהּ	for they are from the vital, that is, animal, soul in the body and his blood, whose root is from *noga*.

Expression through the letters, like any other action that a person performs in the world, cannot be performed directly by the divine soul. The holy, divine soul does not directly animate the body, but only through the animal, vital soul.[11] Therefore, when the holy soul wishes to perform a mitzva, to relate a Torah teaching or to recite a prayer, it needs the animal soul that is clothed in the body.

The animal soul is also in a person's blood, in accordance with that which is known[12] that it is the blood that connects the spiritual, vital

---

8. *Etz Ḥayyim, Sha'ar Mayim Nukvin UMayim Dukhrin*, Sermon 1.

9. Based on *Sanhedrin* 65a; *Karetot* 3b; and elsewhere.

10. Though from other places it is evident that speech is not exactly the same thing as a physical action, and that speech is considered a "*ma'aseh zuta*," a minor action. See there in *Sanhedrin* and in *Karetot*.

11. See *Likkutei Amarim*, chap. 37.

12. See *Likkutei Amarim*, chap. 6; *Likkutei Torah*, Num. 11a, in the name of the *Kuzari*; and elsewhere.

soul to the physical body, as it is stated: "For the blood is the soul" (Deut. 12:23).

Man's vital soul and his body are from the *kelippa* of *noga*, like the material reality in which the action-related commandments are performed. As is explained in *Likkutei Amarim* (chaps. 6–7), *kelippat noga* is the *kelippa* that holds the sparks that we elevate as feminine waters. It turns out that through one's body and animal soul, through speech and action of holiness, man penetrates into the realm of *kelippat noga* and distills from there the holy spark that is hidden there.

> וְהִנֵּה הַבֵּירוּרִים דַּעֲשָׂיָּה עוֹלִין לִיצִירָה עַל יְדֵי שֵׁם ב״ן **Now, the distillations of *Asiya* ascend to *Yetzira* by means of the name of *Ban*,**

The name of *Ban* is one of the fillings or expansions of the Tetragrammaton, where the letters of the name of *Havaya* are themselves spelled out to express the inner value and meaning of the name. This expansion is seen as representing the *sefira* of *Malkhut*, the feminine aspect and the world of *Asiya* from among the four worlds; of course, not the world itself, but the light, the divine name, that descends into the world of *Asiya*, for in the end the name of *Ban* is also the name of God. And this name, which is the divine life force in the world of *Asiya*, is what distills the sparks of the world of *Asiya* and raises them to the world of *Yetzira*, as feminine waters, by way of the act of a mitzva performed by man. ☞

THE NAME OF BAN

☞ The name of *Ban* is one of the four fillings or expansions of the Tetragrammaton. This "full spelling" involves writing the letters of the name as words: the letter *yod* is written *yod-vav-dalet*, and the like. Since the letter *heh* can be expanded in several ways (*heh-alef, heh-heh, heh-yod*), and similarly the letter *vav* (*vav-vav, vav-alef-vav, vav-yod-vav*), there are several different fillings of the Tetragrammaton. The expansion, the numerical value of whose letters is *Ban* (52), is the expansion that in-

volves spelling the letters with a *heh* (*yod-vav-dalet, heh-heh, vav-vav, heh-heh*); the name *Mah* (45) is the expansion that involves spelling the letters with an *alef* (*yod-vav-dalet, heh-alef, vav-alef-vav, heh-alef*); the name *Ab* (72) is the expansion that involves spelling the letters with a *yod* (*yod-vav-dalet, heh-yod, vav-yod-vav, heh-yod*); and the name *Sag* (63) is the expansion that involves spelling the letter *heh* with a *yod* and the letter *vav* with an *alef* (*yod-vav-dalet, heh-yod, vav-alef-dalet, heh-yod*).

According to the Kabbala, the clarification that is achieved through the name *Ban* is the initial clarification, the distillation of the good from the absolute evil, from the dark *kelippa*, the main part of which is in the world of *Asiya*. This is the distillation referred to here, the distillation that involves elevating the feminine waters for the sake of fusion, etc. Afterward, by way of the supernal fusion in the repaired world of *Atzilut*, another clarification is performed, the second distillation, as will be explained below.

וּמִיְצִירָה לִבְרִיאָה וְלַאֲצִילוּת כְּמוֹ שֶׁכָּתוּב בְּשַׁעַר מַ"ן דְּרוּשׁ י"א סִימָן ז'

and from *Yetzira* to *Beria* and to *Atzilut*, as it is written in *Etz Ḥayyim*, *Sha'ar Mayim Nukvin UMayim Dukhrin*, Sermon 11:7.

The ascent to the repaired world of *Atzilut* is a gradual ascent, since the mixture of good and evil and the reality of the shattered vessels exists to a certain extent in all the created worlds: in *Asiya* it is all evil, in *Yetzira* half is evil, and in *Beria* it is mostly good. Therefore, after the clarification of the name *Ban* from the world of *Asiya*, the clarification ascends to the world of *Yetzira*, and continues to *Beria* and *Atzilut*, as is explained in *Etz Ḥayyim*, according to the Kabbala. The name *Ban* in the world of *Asiya* together with the soul of the tzaddik (a person who performs good deeds) bring out and raise the sparks of chaos that fell into *kelippat noga* in the world of *Asiya* to the world that is above them, the world of *Yetzira*, and from there to the world of *Beria*, and from there to the world of *Atzilut*. In any case, the clarifications are fundamentally clarifications of the world of *Asiya* that ascend from the world of *Asiya* by way of the actions of man.

וּבְזֶה יוּבַן דְּהִרְהוּר לָא עָבֵיד מִידֵי

Based on this, we can understand that contemplation does not perform anything,

Now we can understand what was said at the beginning in the name of the *Zohar* that only actions can bring about the supernal unification and the restoration of the face-to-face relationship, whereas contemplation cannot achieve anything. Contemplation alone does not do the one thing that really brings about a change in this world, namely, the raising of the feminine waters. Contemplation (intention) is of course important, because it raises the things that were done below to be noticeable and influential above, in the worlds of *Yetzira*, *Beria*, and *Atzilut*. But if there is no action, if there is no distillation and removal of the sparks from the *kelippa* in the world of *Asiya*, there is nothing that will ascend, and thus there is nothing.

כִּי בְּלִי הַעֲלָאַת מַיִּין נוּקְבִין מֵהַמְּלָכִים שֶׁבְּנוֹגַהּ אִי אֶפְשָׁר לְהַמְשִׁיךְ טִיפִּין מִלְמַעְלָה לְזִוּוּג זו"ן

since without raising the feminine waters from the "kings in *noga*" it is impossible to draw down drops from above for the fusion of *Zeir Anpin* and *Nukva*.

The "kings" mentioned here are the kings who died in the biblical metaphor for the shattering of the vessels (Gen. 36:31–39); they are the sparks of the lights of the chaos that fell into *kelippat noga*. Every king is a world, a vessel, and a kingdom, which in the reality of chaos cannot exist. The king dies, and the lights, the life and the culture, the intelligence and the beauty of the kingdom falls into what is *kelippat noga* in our reality. Without the raising of these great lights of the chaos from the *noga* it is impossible to draw down drops from above for the fusion of *Zeir Anpin* and *Nukva*. The idea is that the male, the bestower, must be aroused by the female, through her showing her desire and interest in him, so that he will turn to her and bestow upon her drops from above.

כִּי רוֹצֶה לִינַק מֵאִמּוֹ, וְלֹא לְהַשְׁפִּיעַ לְמַטָּה כְּמוֹ שֶׁכָּתוּב בְּשַׁעַר מ"ן דְּרוּשׁ ב'

For *Zeir Anpin* wants to suckle from his mother, not to bestow below, as it is written in *Etz Ḥayyim*, *Sha'ar Mayim Nukvin UMayim Dukhrin*, Sermon 2.

Because the bestower, the *Zeir Anpin*, wants to suckle from his mother, *Bina*, understanding, and not give to below, to the female, namely, to *Malkhut*, kingdom, as is written in *Etz Ḥayyim*. What is described here are the four faces of *Atzilut*: father, mother, *Zeir Anpin*, and *Malkhut*. The relationship between them is likened to the relationship between people who impact upon and receive from each other. *Malkhut* wants to seclude himself with *Zeir Anpin* and receive from him, but *Zeir Anpin* prefers that he himself should receive from his father and mother above him, and not give to *Malkhut* below him. This is the primary nature of things, that the recipient does not give and the bestower does not receive, and that as long as the recipient receives, he does not bestow. As it is written: "Therefore shall a man leave his father and his mother, and shall cleave to his wife" (Gen. 2:24). For he cannot cleave to his wife, and give to her, if he does not first leave and separate himself from those who give to him, his father and his mother.

In order for *Zeir Anpin* to face downward and give to *Malkhut*, something needs to happen, something that will make it do that. This is the role of the feminine waters. The feminine waters are, as stated, the refinements of the chaos, that is, the raising up of something that was indeed immersed below, at the bottom of the entire chain of emanations, captive and hidden within the *kelippa*, but at its root it is actually higher than anything above it. This chaos is a vast and powerful primal being, beyond what our world can contain, beyond everything we can achieve and appreciate with our own faculties. That is precisely why it is broken, why it does not exist in the limited dimensions and definitions of our world. However, through the service of man, his good deeds and the like, the sparks of chaos ascend and are repaired little by little. Every time something rises, it reveals an edge of the essence that is above it, something that even the *Zeir Anpin*, which is now above *Asiya* and above *Malkhut*, wants to be connected to and receive from. It will not receive from it as it had received from its mother, but it will awaken it to face downward, to give to what is below it, in order to awaken, reveal, and in the end receive its full greatness. This is similar to how every person discovers at some point in his life that his path no longer consists of receiving from his mother but rather he must give to another, to his wife and children, in order to receive from them what he lacks so that he can truly grow; not only as a child growing up with his mother, but to grow up like his mother and even more than her. ☞

TO SUCKLE OR TO GIVE

☞ This can also be explained based on the idea of *ratzo vashov*, "ascend and return," the state of longing to cleave to God, followed by a resolve to live within the context of material reality. The desire of the *Zeir Anpin* to receive from what is above and not to give to what is below is an expression of "ascending," but after the ascent there must be a "return." This is what the author is talking about here: how to make the transition from the "ascent" to the "return," from the ascent and

In continuation of what he cited from *Etz Ḥayyim*, that there is a
way of raising the feminine waters through prayer, by way of speech
which is considered an action, the author the *Tanya* presents a statement from the *Zohar* that is even more far-reaching:

וְעַיֵּין זֹהַר פָּרָשַׁת פְּקוּדֵי   See the *Zohar* in *Parashat Pekudei* (244b),
דַּף רמ"ד עַמּוּד ב': דְּאִית   that there is an order…to gaze upon….
סְדוּרָא כו' לְאִסְתַּכְּלָא כו'

The *Zohar* in *Parashat Pekudei* teaches that there is an order of prayer
that is fulfilled through words and there is an order of prayer that is
fulfilled through the desire and intention of the heart to know and to
gaze, namely, to gaze higher and higher to *Ein Sof*. That is to say, there
is a way to raise the feminine waters through prayer not only by way
of speech, which is considered an action, but also by way of the gazing,
contemplation, and intention of prayer.

Ostensibly, this contradicts everything that has been said up until
now, that the elevation of the feminine waters for the sake of unification
and the restoration of the face-to-face relationship can only be achieved
by way of an action.

The author of the *Tanya* explains:

וְהֵן כַּוָּונוֹת הַתְּפִלָּה וְיִחוּדִים   These are prayer intentions, and supernal
עֶלְיוֹנִים לַיּוֹדְעִים וּמַשִּׂיגִים   unifications, for those who know and
לְאִסְתַּכְּלָא כו'   comprehend how to gaze….

nullification to the acceptance of responsibility and fulfilling the supernal will below, despite the natural (and holy) desire
to ascend upward. The answer is, as with
humans, when a person extricates himself
from his personal "I," from what he feels,
from what he wants for himself, even in holiness, and moves on to the divine "I" beyond it. Great people make this transition
with full awareness in their general lives as
well, and every person should make these
transitions at all times, not with full awareness, but out of a sense that this line of

running is finished and he must move on to
the second line of returning. What drives
this and gives it force is the connection
to the action. The action below takes the
person out of himself, shows him that his
entire ascent upward is ultimately point-
less, because he will never be able to reach
there, and it takes him to what is beyond
him from above, to the divine essence that
he can never reach through the movement of "running," but he can perform His
will below, and thus reach Him through a
down-facing movement of "returning."

This is not a path that is equally suited for everybody, but for those who know and comprehend how to gaze upward there is in fact another path. There is prayer that relates to this world, to its difficulties, its illnesses, and also its beauty. In such prayer, holding onto this world, through speech which is considered an action, is essential, because the whole point of the prayer is that it elevates this world, in the sense of feminine waters, as has been explained above. But there is also prayer that is entirely "prayer intentions and supernal unions." In such prayer, the intention is the prayer itself, which the soul itself intends and adjusts itself to, in complete detachment (to the extent possible) from its connections to the affairs of this world. At that time, it is no longer concerned with raising the world, consecrating it, and uniting it with the Divine, but rather with the supernal unions in themselves. That is, with the unification of the different aspects of God Himself: right and left, the Holy One, blessed be He, and His Divine Presence; and further inward, with the holy names that are directed at His very essence. There are books of kabbalistic intentions which spell out these unifications in a detailed manner and lead the worshipper from letter to letter and from world to world. There are also ways that are less understood, that lead the worshipper in a more general way, in topics and paths of contemplation, and in different ways of bearing the soul on the words that are uttered with concentration and devotion and emerging out of the soul's liberation from everything else. This private journey is undertaken by the person alone, with his devotion to what is up above, according to his wisdom and his feeling at the time. In any event, such prayer and raising of the feminine waters belongs only to one who is truly found there up above; for whom at that time, at least, this is the actual reality of his life. When he engages in these supernal unions, that is the important thing, that is what touches his soul, that is his life, and that is what he raises up as feminine waters to arouse the supernal union and restore the illumination from above.

כִּי נר"ן שֶׁלָּהֶם עַצְמָן, הֵן מ"ן בִּמְסִירוּת נֶפֶשׁ עַל הַתּוֹרָה	For their own *nefesh, ruah,* and *neshama* are "feminine waters," by means of devotion to the Torah

One who prays in this way does not elevate anything from this world; in fact, he does not relate to this world at all. What then does he raise? For as has been repeatedly noted, the raising of the feminine waters involves raising something that had been down below. The answer to this question is that the parts of the worshipper's soul themselves – his *nefesh*, *ruaḥ*, and *neshama* – are what rise up from their place.

In the first type of prayer, the soul raises reality through its own levels, relating to it at an increasingly higher level within itself: from the relationship of an action to an inner feeling and to recognition in itself; from the aspect of *nefesh* to the aspect of *ruaḥ* to the aspect of *neshama*. The soul itself does not move from its place; only the things, the clarifications, the feminine waters rise up through it from level to level. But in the prayer of which we speak here, of supernal unions – those very parts of the soul, the *nefesh*, the *ruaḥ* and the *neshama* – are the feminine waters that rise upward.

In order for the soul itself to rise, it has to release itself. Just as when one hands something over to another person, he must stop holding it, and must remove it from his possession, the same is true about the delivering of one's soul. But who is the "I" who gives away the soul? As long as the "I" is found and identified in some corner together with the soul, it cannot give it away. Only when the soul's sense of "I" is completely eliminated, when the "I," to the extent that it exists, exists somewhere else – in the Divine Presence, in the Torah, in the Holy One, blessed be He – can there be a delivering of the soul. ☞

BY MEANS OF DEVOTION TO THE TORAH

☞ There are several aspects of "devotion to the Torah," of which the author the *Tanya* speaks. The Torah is God's Torah; not a feeling or a comprehension that a person achieves, but rather Torah that was given from above, from God. When a person adheres to the Torah, this is devotion and complete nullification that has no parallel in any other form of relationship between man and God. In the love of God and in the fear of God, at however high a level they may be, even at the level of the patriarchs, there is always a trace of the "I," who is the person who loves and fears. Only in the Torah is there complete nullification, because everything that the person feels and achieves on his own part does not matter: the speech is the speech of God who speaks in him, the thought is the thought of God who thinks in him (see *Torah Or* 56a, and elsewhere). Moreover, only the Torah is a vessel wide enough to receive and contain this devotion in its entirety. As explained, this devotion of the

וּבִנְפִילַת אַפַּיִם כַּנּוֹדָע and through **"falling on one's face"** in the *Taḥanun* prayer, **as is known.**

Falling on one's face[13] in the *Taḥanun* prayer is like a fall, a descent from the high point of prayer, from the place of emanation and complete union with God, back into this world. This fall is an act of devotion, for it is not a fall resulting from an accident, nor is it a fall of the person's personality, a collapse of the structure of his soul, but rather it is as if the person was going to a different place. He himself, as he is, descends from the place where he was revealed in his full stature to a different place, where none of this is revealed; but he descends because he needs to, because of and for the sake of something beyond him. This is a delivery of the soul, the soul itself, from here to there. ☞

ascent of the soul itself as feminine waters must take place with the entirety of the soul, which is only possible through the Torah, which is a vessel wide enough to receive the entire soul, in all its aspects and with all its connections in the world. When a person achieves such introspection in which the Torah becomes the true picture of the world, when his "I" is found in the Torah, adhering to and united with the divine will and wisdom in it, then he can transmit his soul, severing it from all its connections to the worlds and raise it as feminine waters to God. The world that we see is only its shadows and ramifications.

As an illustration of this point: I see reality, and I also hear what other people who cannot see it think about it. Similarly, for this person the Torah is the reality in which he is found, and the world that people see is what they imagine for themselves.

There is also another aspect to this. Devotion that is not towards the Torah can be devotion to chaos, to "ascending" from the vessels without "returning," where the person burns with an endless thirst and desire to nullify himself to *Ein Sof* forever. For the devotion to be not only in the running, but also in the returning, it must be directed towards the Torah.

FALLING ON ONE'S FACE IN THE *TAḤANUN* PRAYER IS A CLARIFICATION OF THE SPARKS

☞ Kabbalistic texts (*Peri Etz Ḥayyim*, ibid.) explain that falling on one's face in the *Taḥanun* prayer involves a descent for the purpose of clarification of the sparks. After reaching the world of *Atzilut*, and

being himself in a state of repair (as mentioned above, "*Atzilut* that has already been distilled"), a person can and should go down and repair "others" as well; the sparks of holiness that fell into the *kelip-*

---

13. See *Peri Etz Ḥayyim, Sha'ar Nefilat Apayim*. See also *Siddur im Daḥ* [*Divrei Elokim Ḥayyim*], *Sha'ar Nefilat Apayim* 91b.

This is a fall, a fall from the person's level, which is like death.[14] This is also devotion of the soul: first, his forsaking the level he had reached and his cleaving to God, all that he achieved through his prayer, and then his surrendering himself to God, "To You, O Lord, do I lift up my soul, and so forth."[15] ☞

This short essay, an "epilogue" to the chapters in *Likkutei Amarim* that speak of intention and action, dealt with the ways that lead to supernal fusion and the restoration of the face-to-face relationship. As an epilogue, it lacks an orderly conceptual structure, of the type found in the book of the *Tanya*, but presents the structuring of an idea through the referencing of citations (from *Etz Ḥayyim* and the *Zohar*) and through alluding, even if not explicitly, to the background as it appears there. The author first cited passages from *Etz Ḥayyim* which state that it is specifically actions that lead to supernal fusion, and he explained why this is so. What causes the supernal to face downward and to influence what is below is the

pot, to which he is connected, directly, indirectly, or in the most subtle of ways. This is the meaning of the confession, "We have sinned, we have betrayed, and so forth": to seek out and gather those sparks one by one; to search in "We have sinned," and if nothing is found, to search again and again in the most painstaking manner for the spark that is hidden there. And similarly, with "We have betrayed" and "We have stolen," and so forth.

THE DEVOTION IN THE FALLING ON ONE'S FACE IN THE TAḤANUN PRAYER AND THE DEVOTION TO THE TORAH

☞ What is common to these two expressions of devotion is that they both lead to action. Nothing is actually raised from the materiality of the world, as with an action or with speech that is considered an action, but there is a state of mind here that does not involve detachment from the world but just the opposite. In other words, this devotion is a devotion of "returning," and not of "running," of waiving personal love and cleaving, of seeing and delighting in God, and a reduction in role, in the study and observance of the Torah in this world, and a raising and repair of others, who are not repaired, through the falling on one's face in the Taḥanun prayer.

---

14. For anyone who has fallen from his level is considered as if he were "dead." See *Peri Etz Ḥayyim, Sha'ar Nefilat Apayim*, chap. 2.
15. Ps. 25, which is recited according to the rite following the usages of the Ari as part of *Nefilat Apayim*.

raising of the lower feminine waters, this lower water that is being raised being the sparks of holiness that fell with the kings in the chaos into the *kelippot*. This is what interests the supernal beings, this is what they lack, this is what they have been seeking ever since the world was created, and this is what stirs them to relate and give downward. And since these are found below, in action, they can only be raised through real action. In the continuation, once again by referencing statements from *Etz Ḥayyim*, he expands the matter to include not only action, but also the speech of prayer, for speech is in a certain way like an action. At the end of the essay, while explaining a statement in the *Zohar* that seems to contradict everything that had been said earlier, he expands the matter completely and includes not only the speaking in prayer but also the intention, as a way by which a person can not only raise the feminine waters from the world, but also raise his soul itself like feminine waters.

The meaning and importance of what has been stated here lies in seeing the whole picture. We are not dealing here with different ways, with "either this or that," but rather with a whole that works together. As the author explained at length in *Likkutei Amarim*, that intention and action are a single entity, two sides that complement each other – so too he says here in greater depth regarding the modes of intention. Everything is in the mind, and everything is in the action. Even when a person performs an action, it is not something external to him. Everything comprises part of his soul, all the sparks, all the parts of the Divine that are found in all places, they are essentially parts of himself. When he raises them, he should view that as raising his very own soul, with the same movement of devotion, because everything that he said about devotion and about uniquely gifted people is found in practice in anyone who engages in clarification and raises feminine waters to supernal unification. Similarly in the other direction, any spiritual undertaking, no matter how abstract it may be, should be treated as an action. That is to say, it is not in his imagination, it is not his private affair, but rather it operates in the real world, raising up or bringing down. What this means is that whether overtly or covertly, whether directly or indirectly, a person is responsible through his every mental movement for the whole of reality.

Essay 3
Understanding a Statement
in *Sha'ar HaYiḥudim*

THIS DISCOURSE, LIKE THE TWO PREVIOUS ONES, COR-responds to chapters 39–40 of *Likkutei Amarim,* and mostly addresses the same topic: intention versus action. It focuses especially on the intention of speech, which is considered the action, during Torah study and prayer. In contrast to the previous discourse, that emphasized the importance of action, this discourse highlights the power of intention: what effect the intention in the heart, which is love and fear, has on uttering words of Torah and prayer.

In chapter 39 of *Likkutei Amarim,* the author of the *Tanya* explains that when a person has intention while saying words of Torah and prayer, then his words ascend to the supernal worlds that correspond to his intention: If he has emotional intention, natural love and fear, then his words ascend to the world of *Yetzira.* If his intention is imbued with intellectual love and fear, then his words ascend to the world of *Beria.* Furthermore, not only do the words of Torah and prayer themselves ascend to the world that corresponds to one's intention, they even become subsumed into the ten *sefirot* of that world, which are the aspect of the Divine that corresponds to that world. This happens when a person's intentions are totally pure. However, what happens when a person does not have intention?

There are two types of a lack of intention. The first is when a person says the words out of habit. In this case, his words ascend to the world where his natural love and fear are,

273

meaning to the world of *Yetzira*. However, if he says the words and has selfish intentions, then the words of Torah do not ascend at all, but rather remain in the world of *Asiya*. These concepts comprise the basis of this essay in *Kuntres Aḥaron*, and lend depth and clarity to the corresponding chapters of *Likkutei Amarim* from various perspectives that were not fully addressed there, especially through the lens of additional references from the *Zohar* and the writings of the Arizal.

The author of the *Tanya* treated these topics in a general way in *Likkutei Amarim*, and did not distinguish between words of Torah and words of prayer. In this essay, he explores this distinction as well.

30 Ḥeshvan

29 Ḥeshvan
(leap year)

(In a twenty-
nine-day
month, study
also the
portion for 30
Ḥeshvan)

לְהָבִין מַה שֶּׁכָּתוּב בְּשַׁעַר הַיְּחוּדִים,
פֶּרֶק ב': דְּעַל יְדֵי תוֹרָה שֶׁלֹּא בְּכַוָּונָה
נִבְרָאִים מַלְאָכִים בְּעוֹלָם הַיְצִירָה

To understand what is written in *Sha'ar HaYiḥudim*, chapter 2, that through Torah studied **without intent, angels are created in the world of *Yetzira*.**

This source from the writings of the Arizal is also cited in *Likkutei Amarim* at the beginning of chapter 40 as support for the concepts he explains there.

The four worlds correspond to the four realms within every person. Therefore, when a person has conscious intent of love or fear, he is transported to the world that corresponds to his intention. Therefore, as explained in the *Tanya* there, a person who studies Torah without intention, without contemplating the greatness of God, does not generate this love and fear. One can conclude that it is the forces of natural love and fear that are hidden in the nature of his divine soul that impel him to study, as will be explained below. The fact that he is studying proves that he has love and fear of God. A person does not do something for no reason; he does something either out of love or out of fear. When a person does mitzvot and says holy words from within the nature of his soul, then he is like the holy *ḥayot* and *behemot*, the angels, as explained in *Likkutei Amarim*, chapter 39. Everything that these angels do to serve God is ingrained in their nature, in the world of *Yetzira* that they inhabit. When a person has this type of intention at the moment that he utters words and letters of prayer or Torah, he creates holy manifestations of his subconscious feelings of love and fear; these holy manifestations are what the author calls "angels in the world of *Yetzira*." ☞

וְשָׁם הֵבִיא מֵהַזֹּהַר פָּרָשַׁת שְׁלַח (חלק ג קסח,ב): דְּלֵית קָלָא דְּאִתְאֲבֵיד כו', בַּר קָלָא דְּאוֹרַיְיתָא וּצְלוֹתָא דְּסָלֵיק וּבָקַע כו'	He cites there from the *Zohar* in *Parashat Shelaḥ* (3:168b) that no sound is lost…, except for the voice of Torah and prayer, which ascends and breaks through…

No sound (or action) of any kind is ever lost; regardless of the form into which it transmigrates or the place to where it wanders, it never ceases to reverberate throughout the world. However, the sounds remain in the world, except for the sound of Torah and prayer that bursts through the firmament that surrounds the world and ascends into higher worlds. ☞

ANGELS ARE CREATED IN THE WORLD OF *YETZIRA*

☞ This is part of a larger-scale worldview wherein every mitzva that a person performs creates an angel (see *Avot* 4:11 and the commentaries there; *Ḥiddushei Aggadot* of the *Maharsha, Shabbat* 31b, and elsewhere). A good deed or a holy word, Torah or prayer, reverberates in the upper worlds and has meaning way beyond the world of *Asiya* in which it was done or said. What impact does it have on the higher worlds? How high does it go? This depends on the intention that the doer has. One's intention elevates the mitzva up to the world that corresponds to it. The inner meaning of an action or word becomes a spiritual being in the supernal world, and can have a real effect there. This is the "angel" created from a given action. The world of *Yetzira* is the lowest among the worlds that are above world of *Asiya*. A word of Torah automatically ascends to the world of *Yetzira*, even without special intention, as long as the person does not have in mind another antithetical thought, as will be explained below.

NO SOUND IS LOST

☞ This source from the *Zohar* explores worldly sounds of the world, the sounds of birth, death, and nature when various forces peak at the culmination of their inner processes. These are the sounds that erupt from the world at the moment the essence of life is extracted out of it. While these sounds are heard only at climactic moments, they always exist. Just as when a person is young, he is not aware that he is alive; he loves, yet does not feel the love. Only at the outer edges, the intersections of life, does he emit a sound expressing his love. Life reveals vitality and love, good

By presenting this source from the *Zohar,* the author of the *Tanya* is saying that the sounds of Torah and prayer are different than every other sound. The voice of a Jew who infuses his divine soul into these holy sounds and letters does not remain in this world but rather ascends above and beyond. The author of the *Tanya* also explained this in those chapters in *Likkutei Amarim.* Here, he goes into more detail and greater depth and introduces the difference between the sound of Torah and the sound of prayer.

וְהִנֵּה מִכַּוָּונַת הַתְּפִלָּה נִבְרְאוּ מַלְאָכִים בְּעוֹלָם הַבְּרִיאָה, כְּמוֹ מִכַּוָּונַת הַתּוֹרָה

Now, angels are created in the world of *Beria* from intent in prayer, as from the intent of Torah study,

When a person has pure intentions, then there is no difference whether he is uttering the words of the Torah as he studies or the words prayer; both ascend from the world of *Asiya* in which they were said to the world of *Beria* where the intention with which they were uttered belongs. This intention, which he calls "love and fear that are cultivated by the intellect," therefore belongs to the world of *Beria,* which is the world of the intellect. In the author of the *Tanya's* language, "Angels are created in the world of *Beria.*"

Until this point, there is no difference between prayer and Torah

and bad, and everything in between. When something is revealed, it makes a sound.

These sounds are never lost, because they are the expression of the world that they are in. They will always reverberate throughout the world; as other people hear the sound they resonate with it, and echo it back: "Me too." This is what the *Zohar* describes here: sounds that drift about from one end of the world to the other, from echo to echo. There is one exception: Torah and prayer. Not that their sounds are lost from reality, but rather, their truth and purpose do not relate to this world; they belong beyond world, and to a certain degree, beyond all the worlds, to the very

essence of God, as it were. The Torah is essentially the "sound" of God, His expression even before He created the world. As the Sages said: "The Torah preceded the world by two thousand years" (see, e.g., *Midrash Tehillim* 90:4, *Vayeshev* 4).

Prayer, on the other hand, in its deepest essence, is an expressing of a person relating himself to God Himself, not to God's attributes. Therefore, although the sounds of Torah and prayer can also leave echoes in the world, their essence ascends and bursts through the firmament, beyond the worldly dimension where they were uttered.

study. The difference arises when the words are uttered without intention.

וּבְלֹא כַּוָּנָה נִדְחֵית לְמַטָּה לְגַמְרֵי **but without intent**, the prayer **is rejected below entirely.**

Through Torah study without intention angels are created in the world of *Yetzira,* as explained above, while prayer without intention stays below, in the world of *Asiya,* and does not even ascend to the world of *Yetzira.*

כְּמוֹ שֶׁכָּתוּב בַּזֹּהַר פָּרָשַׁת פְּקוּדֵי דַּף **As it is written in the** *Zohar* **in**
רמ"ה עַמּוּד ב': גּוֹ רָקִיעַ תַּתָּאָה כו' *Parashat Pekudei* **(245b): Within**
דְּאִקְרֵין צְלוֹתִין פְּסִילָאן כו' **the lower firmament..., which are called invalid prayers...**

This section of the *Zohar* discusses prayers that are not fitting because they lack proper intention. Instead of ascending above the firmament, they remain down below. Furthermore, it states that these prayers are called "invalid prayers." They are still prayers; they are not like other mundane words; however, since they were not uttered with pure intentions, but rather with extraneous thoughts, they are invalid. Externally, they look and sound like prayers. However, they are not living prayers that bind the lower world to the higher sphere. The invalid prayers belong to an intermediate category: not prayers, yet not mundane speech. And they wait in this state "in the lower firmament" until the person who uttered them repents and recites another prayer with proper intention. Then all the invalid prayers ascend with it.

וְעַיֵּן שָׁם פָּרָשַׁת וַיַּקְהֵל דַּף ר"א עַמּוּד **See also there, in** *Parashat Vay-*
ב': אִי הִיא מִלָּה כִּדְקָא יָאוּת כו' *ak'hel* **(245b): If it is an appropriate word...**

The *Zohar* continues to state that if the word is spoken as it should be, with proper intent, then all the heavenly appointees kiss it and raise it up to the upper firmament, according to its intention. There it is heard. There it has power. When it is uttered without intent, however, it remains below in the physical world where it remains unknown and unheard.

The question is: Why is there a difference between Torah studied without proper intent and prayer spoken without intention?

אַךְ הַהֶפְרֵשׁ בֵּין תּוֹרָה לִתְפִלָּה
שֶׁלֹּא בְּכַוָּנָה מוּבָן מֵאֵלָיו, כִּי לִימּוּד
הַתּוֹרָה הוּא מֵבִין וְיוֹדֵעַ מַה שֶּׁלּוֹמֵד
דְּבִלָאו הָכֵי לָא מִיקְרֵי לִימּוּד כְּלָל

However, the difference between Torah and prayer without intent is obvious, for in the case of Torah study one understands and knows what he is studying, as otherwise it is not called "study" at all.

In contrast to prayer, it is impossible to study without some involvement of the intellectual faculty. Studying means understanding that which one reads on some level, because if a person does not understand at all, it is not called study. When a person studies Torah, he cannot be totally passive; he must pay attention, think, remember, compare, and conclude. He himself must change, from not understanding to understanding, from lacking knowledge to knowing. If he only looks at the words, and even says them out loud, without something shifting within him, it is not study. ☞

רַק שֶׁלּוֹמֵד סְתָם, בְּלֹא כַּוָּנָה לִשְׁמָהּ
מֵאַהֲבַת ה' שֶׁבְּלִבּוֹ בִּבְחִינַת גִּילּוּי,
רַק מֵאַהֲבָה הַמְסוּתֶּרֶת הַטִּבְעִית

It is simply that he studies for no purpose, without intent for its sake, out of the love of God that is manifest in his heart, only from the concealed, natural love.

Here, the author of the *Tanya* addresses a different type of love. Not the spiritually intellectual way of relating to that which a person studies, but rather the simple impulse within that drives him to study Torah, as

TORAH STUDY EQUALS UNDERSTANDING

☞ According to Halakha and hasidic teachings (see the *Shulḥan Arukh HaRav, Hilkhot Talmud Torah* 2:13), only when studying the Oral Torah is a person required to understand, and if not, it is not considered "study." However, this does not apply to the Written Torah, where by just saying the words, one fulfills the mitzva of Torah study, even if he does not understand.

opposed to something else. As explained elsewhere,[1] a person does not do anything unless he has love or fear in his soul that causes him to do it or to refrain from it. Love is the force behind everything a person does, creates, and grows; without love he would not do or change anything. It follows that the force in one's soul that brings him to study Torah is love of God. Without love, he would not study.[2] However, as explained in *Likkutei Amarim,* it could be that while this love impels him to do certain things, it is concealed; he therefore does not feel it in his heart. He may even be totally unaware of it. ☞

THE CONCEALED LOVE

☞ The author of the *Tanya* speaks about this love at length in *Likkutei Amarim* (mainly in chap. 18, and onward), and this is one of the pillars upon which the entire *Tanya* stands: that every Jewish person has a divine soul which loves God, not incidentally as another object of his desire, but rather as the love of his life, a love in contrast to which all his desires pale in comparison, upon which his whole life depends. This is not an acquired love, like other loves that a person adopts the more he grows spiritually and discovers that more refined things are worthy of his love. This is the most natural, primal love of the divine soul, by which he will be entirely consumed as long as it is not impeded. However, since the divine soul is generally occluded by the animal soul, then the love of the divine soul is hidden as well.

However, since it is natural, it acts upon the soul even when it is not revealed. If one does not obstruct it with other thoughts and intentions of the animal soul, it will be an active element of his being. As a distant example, some individuals are naturally people-lovers; they feel comfortable doing good for others, and if they are not impeded by negative influences or other constraints, they will do just that their whole lives. Similarly, every Jewish person naturally loves God; therefore, if others do not hamper or confuse him with foolishness, he will study Torah and do mitzvot, because it is good for him, even if he does not understand why. The author calls this type of Torah study "without intent...only from the concealed, natural love."

---

1. See the introduction to *Sha'ar HaYiḥud VeHa'emuna* ("Ḥinukh Katan").
2. See *Likkutei Amarim,* chap. 10, and the end of chap. 40 and elsewhere. This seems to echo the words of the *Shema*: "You shall love the Lord your God with all your heart, and with all your soul, and with all your might." And what should a person do with this force of love within him? That which is written later on, "These matters that I command you today.... You shall inculcate them in your children, and you shall speak of them and so forth": Torah study.

Since a person is not conscious of this hidden love in his mind, it does not elevate the Torah that he studies to its source in the world of intellect, the world of *Beria.* The Ba'al Shem Tov used to say[3] that a person is wherever his thoughts are; however, only if he thinks, meaning that he must articulate the particular concepts in his conscious thought. If the force of love is not within his conscious mind, and is only impelling him to study as a natural impulse of his soul, like angels and animals that act according to their inherent nature, then his Torah ascends to the world of *Yetzira,* which is the world of angels, whose love and fear are natural.[4]

אַךְ אֵינוֹ לוֹמֵד שֶׁלֹּא לִשְׁמָהּ **Yet he does not study literally not for**
מַמָּשׁ, לְהִתְגַּדֵּל כו' **the Torah's sake, for his self-aggrandize-**
ment…

The author of the *Tanya* comments here that this Torah study, performed without intent, that ascends to the world of *Yetzira,* refers to a lack of premeditated intent, but not to a person who has purposeful selfish intent, like the desire to earn respect from his community or to make money.

דְּהָא לָא סָלֵיק לְעֵילָא מִן **as in that case, the study does not ascend**
שִׁמְשָׁא כְּמוֹ שֶׁכָּתוּב בְּפָרָשַׁת **above the sun, as is written in the Zohar**
וַיְחִי דַּף רכ"ג עַמּוּד ב' **in Parashat Vayḥi (223b).**

The *Zohar* explains the verse "What advantage is there for man in all his toil that he toils under the sun?" (Eccles. 1:3) and adds that the Torah is different in that it transcends the sun. All the mundane activities that people engage in are "under the sun," meaning that they have no meaning beyond what occurs in this world. Torah study, on the other hand, has value beyond this world, "above the sun." Indeed, the *Zohar* qualifies this statement that even when it comes to Torah study,

3. See the *Toledot Yaakov Yosef, Ḥayyei Sarah:* "I heard explicitly from my teacher, that wherever a person thinks, his whole being is there." And see *Ba'al Shem Tov al HaTorah, Parashat Noaḥ, Amud HaTefilla,* 56.
4. *Likkutei Amarim,* chap. 39.

if one's motivation is to attain honor, then even his Torah study does not ascend and remains "under the sun."[5]

וְהַיְינוּ מִשׁוּם שֶׁמַּחֲשַׁבְתּוֹ וְכַוָּונָתוֹ הֵן מִתְלַבְּשׁוֹת בְּאוֹתִיּוֹת הַדִּבּוּר וְאֵינָן מַנִּיחוֹת אוֹתָן לְסַלְּקָא לְעֵילָא

The reason is that his thought and intent are enclothed in the letters of speech and prevent them from ascending upward.

The words that a person utters are so connected to him that they are almost incapable of leaving him. What a person thinks and feels, and the kind of person he is at the time the words are spoken, all of this is enclothed in the letters and words that he uses. His intentions at the time direct and change the meaning of the words he chooses. Therefore, when a person's intention is totally earthly, even if the words that he is saying are holy, they become bound below and cannot ascend above.

וְהָכָא נַמִי בִּתְפִלָּה שֶׁלֹּא בְּכַוָּונָה, שֶׁמְּחַשֵּׁב מַחֲשָׁבוֹת זָרוֹת

Here too, this applies **with regard to prayer without intent, when one thinks foreign thoughts**

When a person does not have love and fear of God in mind, but at least thinks about the simple meaning of the words that he is saying, then that is one level. But if instead of thinking about the simple meaning of the words, a person allows thoughts into his mind that are not connected at all to the words he is saying, "foreign" to his prayer, they prevent his prayer from ascending and leave that prayer right where it was uttered. The Lubavitcher Rebbe, Rabbi Menaḥem Mendel Schneerson, comments on the *Tanya*'s phrase "prayer without intent" that the kind of intent is "simply the meaning of the words. One

---

5. It is brought in "*Nitzotzei Zohar*" there: "The holy brilliant *Tanya* used a pure source from the Talmud *Pesaḥim* 3b: It is written, 'For Your mercy is great unto the heavens,' and 'For Your mercy is great above the heavens.' Here, where the verse says that God's mercy is above the heavens, it is referring to a case where one performs a mitzva for its own sake; and here, where the verse says that God's mercy reaches the heavens, it is referring to a case where one performs a mitzva not for its own sake. When a person performs a mitzva for its own sake, it ascends above the sun."

who does not have the simple meaning of the words in mind has not invalidated his prayer, since he has the general intention [to direct his prayers] to God. This is the continuation of the explanation: 'When one thinks foreign thoughts,' that is, not about the simple meaning of the words, because this foreign thought becomes enclothed in the speech and draws it down to its place below…" ☞

Prayer without intention is therefore different than Torah without intention. Torah, as explained, cannot possibly be without any thought or intention at all; it always entails the basic intentional thought that a person understands, to some degree, that which he is saying, because if that was not the case, it would not be called "Torah study." This thought and intention suffice to release the words of Torah from this material world.

A person cannot think two thoughts simultaneously, and one's intention to understand the content that he is studying means that there is no space for the totally external thought that has nothing to do with Torah, like thoughts of business or anything else of this world. This does not apply to prayer. Prayer can be said without any intention whatsoever; one's mouth could be moving, while his thoughts are swept up in things of this world, with no connection to what he is saying. These "foreign" thoughts become enclothed in the words of the prayer and do not allow them to ascend from this world at all. Therefore, unlike Torah studied without intention, prayer without intention does not ascend from this world at all, even to the world of *Yetzira*.

Below, the author of the *Tanya* makes a parenthetical comment, that prayer recited without any intention has an advantage over Torah

INTENTION DURING PRAYER

☞ Indeed, when hasidic teachings discuss intention during prayer, they mean much more than having in mind the simple meaning of the words. Thinking about the meaning of the words, on any level, is but the background for prayer, whose essence can be distilled to: the cleaving of the soul to the Divine with whom one speaks. This may happen through contemplating and feeling the content of one's prayer, or by cleaving to the letters alone, with love and fear and nullification before the presence of the Divine before whom he stands and speaks. The issue that the author of the *Tanya* is addressing here, however, relates to when even the bare minimum of intention, thinking the basic meaning of the words, is absent. Especially because, as explained in other places, this basic intention is a necessary component for the attainment of every higher level of intent in prayer.

study without intention. This comment is in parentheses because the author of the *Tanya* did not include it in his opening words of the discourse. This point nevertheless comprises an important element of the total picture.

(אֶלָּא מִפְּנֵי שֶׁכַּוָּנָתוֹ לַשָּׁמַיִם, לְכָךְ יֵשׁ לָהּ תִּיקּוּן בְּקַל לַחֲזוֹר וְלַעֲלוֹת כְּשֶׁמִּתְפַּלֵּל בְּכַוָּנָה	**(however, since his intent is to Heaven, it therefore has an easy rectification,** enabling the prayer **to ascend once again when he prays with intent,**

As explained above, a person who studies Torah can have totally impure, foreign intentions, such as to attain honor and so on. However, this is impossible with prayer. Prayer, unlike Torah, has no connection to this world; it does not enter the world, it leaves it. When it comes to Torah, a person can study, investing time and energy to understand well, all in order that people will honor him. Prayer, on the other hand, is essentially between the person and God; no one else can really know what is occurring in someone else's prayer. When a person prays, he turns to God, and even if other thoughts intrude while he is saying the words, they do not uproot the initial impulse to turn to God, which is what induces him to pray. This does not apply to Torah study, when the foreign, impure thoughts can drive his study and become enclothed in the Torah, and fundamentally invalidate it.

Therefore, even if a person has foreign thoughts during prayer, and therefore his prayer did not yet ascend at that time because it did not have proper intention attached to it, it is still not disqualified, but rather "frozen." The prayer remains a prayer, in the sense of a Jew turning to God, but it was simply not sent above, like a letter in a mailbox, waiting to be sent. "Therefore, it has an easy rectification" since it does not need to be transformed into something else; it just needs to be sent. How? All he needs to do is to recite one prayer with intention, and that sends the previous prayer as well.

אֲפִילוּ תְּפִלָּה אַחַת מְלוּקֶּטֶת מִתְּפִלּוֹת כָּל הַשָּׁנָה, כְּמוֹ שֶׁכָּתוּב בְּ׳מִקְדַּשׁ מֶלֶךְ׳ פָּרָשַׁת פְּקוּדֵי)	**even if** this is only **one prayer collected from the prayers of the whole year,** as is written in the commentary of "*Mikdash Melekh*" on the *Zohar, Parashat Pekudei*).

Even one prayer with intention can elevate the insincere prayers of
the whole year. This one heartfelt prayer gathers up all the prayers that
were stuck and unleashes them to the places that they were originally
directed. ☞

Below, the author of the *Tanya* will highlight a seeming contradiction between the two sources in the *Zohar* that he cited at the beginning.
Through the lens of Kabbala, he reconciles the contradiction and notes
additional layers of meaning about what he has explained until now
regarding Torah and prayer without intention.

וּמַה שֶּׁכָּתוּב בְּפָרָשַׁת פְּקוּדֵי
(רמה,ב) 'גּוּ רְקִיעַ תַּתָּאָה' בְּפָרָשַׁת
וַיַּקְהֵל (רא,ב) מַשְׁמַע דְּדַוְקָא אִי
אִיהִי מִלָּה כִּדְקָא יָאוּת סָלְקִין
עִמָּהּ עַד אֲוִירָא דִּרְקִיעַ דִּלְעֵילָא
כו'

As for what is written in the *Zohar*,
Parashat Pekudei (245b), "Into the
lower firmament," and yet it is indicated in *Parashat Vayak'hel* (201b)
that only if a word is appropriate
does it ascend with it to the atmosphere of the firmament above…,

The quotation from the *Zohar* in *Parashat Pekudei* says that prayer
without intention ascends to the lower firmament, while the *Zohar*

PRAYERS OF THE WHOLE YEAR

☞ For example, a person recites the prayer "Heal us" every day in the *Shemoneh Esrei* prayer. He generally says the words without thinking about their meaning, until one day, someone is sick at home, so he prays "Heal us" from the depth of his heart. At that moment, all the prayers that he said previously awaken and ascend with the intention and the intense need for healing that he feels when saying the prayer.

Every prayer, even one that did not ascend, is "written," but because it does not have an address, it has not yet been read. Who is it intended for? Who should be replying to it? Then, one prayer, marked clearly with an address, bursts forth and reveals the address for all the previous prayers; since all prayers really have the same address. Yes, the writers are seemingly different and their return addresses vary, but essentially they are one; they have a single pain, a single yearning. This is the yearning of the Divine Presence. Therefore, the deeper a person's intentions, on the one hand, and broader and more all-encompassing, on the other, not just relating to himself and his particular circumstance, but rather, as much as possible, to the whole of the Divine Presence, with its deficiencies and desires, the prayer said in that frame of mind elevates many more prayers. This is the power of the tzaddik, whose prayer can certainly elevate the prayers of the congregation and even those of people who are not present.

in *Parashat Vayak'hel* states that prayer without intention does not ascend at all.

לָא קַשְׁיָא מִידֵי: דְּרָקִיעַ תַּתָּאָה this is not difficult at all: For "the
מֵאִינּוּן רְקִיעִים דְּמַדְבְּרֵי גּוֹ עָלְמָא lowest firmament of those firma-
שֶׁבְּפָרָשַׁת פְּקוּדֵי, הֵן דְּמַלְכוּת ments that control the world,"
דַּעֲשִׂיָּה, וּדְפָרָשַׁת וַיַּקְהֵל הֵן דִּזְעֵיר which is the one referred to in
אַנְפִּין דַּעֲשִׂיָּה, כְּמוֹ שֶׁכָּתוּב בְּעֵץ *Parashat Pekudei,* is *Malkhut* of
חַיִּים שַׁעַר הַשֵּׁמוֹת פֶּרֶק ג' גַּבֵּי זְעֵיר *Asiya,* whereas that of *Parashat*
אַנְפִּין דַּעֲשִׂיָּה עַיֵּין שָׁם *Vayak'hel* is *Zeir Anpin* of *Asiya,*
as is written in *Etz Ḥayyim, Sha'ar HaShemot,* chapter 3, with regard to *Zeir Anpin* of *Asiya;* see there.

The sources refer to firmaments of different worlds; therefore, there is no contradiction between them. The *Zohar* in *Parashat Pekudei* refers to the firmament of *Malkhut* of the world of *Asiya.* Even the world of *Asiya* has higher spiritual levels and forces that affect its lower levels. *Malkhut* of *Asiya* is the lowest level of the world of *Asiya* and of all the levels in general; the *Asiya* of *Asiya.* Prayer without intention ascends to some degree, because it still is higher and holier than basic life, but only to the firmament of the lowest level: the "firmament" of the *Malkhut* of *Asiya.* On the other hand, when the *Zohar* in *Parashat Vayak'hel* states that prayers uttered without intention do not ascend to the firmament, it means the firmament of *Zeir Anpin* of *Asiya.* However, they do ascend to the firmament of *Malkhut* of *Asiya.* ☞

ZEIR ANPIN AND THE MALKHUT OF THE WORLD OF ASIYA

☞ The difference between *Zeir Anpin* and *Malkhut* even in the world of *Asiya* is the difference between reality as is (*Malkhut*) and one step higher than it, the next level (*Zeir Anpin*) that affects and changes *Malkhut.* When we say that prayer ascends, is heard, answered, and changes reality below, we mean that it ascends to the level of *Zeir Anpin* of *Asiya* (at least). On this level, reality is not fixed and determined as it is in *Malkhut.* Therefore, prayer that reaches that level can change something below. This is not the case with prayer that does not ascend to that level, but rather stays below on the level of *Malkhut* of *Asiya;* it cannot change anything, and is therefore a prayer that does not ascend and is not heard above, that is, for now.

וְהָא דְּמַשְׁמַע לִכְאוֹרָה בְּפָרָשַׁת
פְּקוּדֵי (שם), דְּגַם תְּפִלָּה פְּסוּלָה
עוֹלָה עַד הֵיכָל הָרִאשׁוֹן שֶׁמִּמֶּנּוּ
נִדְחֵית לְמַטָּה וְהוּא בִּזְעֵיר אַנְפִּין
דִּבְרִיאָה

As for the apparent implication in *Parashat Pekudei* (ibid.) that even invalid prayer ascends to the first chamber from where it is rejected to below, and that it is in *Zeir Anpin* of *Beria*,

The *Zohar* describes how all the prayers ascend until the entrance of the first palace where they are examined: If they are beautiful and fitting (in their intention) the gates open and they ascend through them. If they are not fitting, they are sent back down to the world of *Asiya* and stay there in the lowest firmament of *Asiya*, as explained above. We see from here that before they are rejected, they ascend higher than the world of *Asiya* to the first chamber. ☞

The question is: After showing that prayer without intention cannot really transcend the world of *Asiya* in which it was said, it is stated here that it seems to achieve a very high ascension, until the chamber that is in the heights of the world of *Beria*. How can this be reconciled?

לָא קַשְׁיָא מִידֵּי, שֶׁהֲרֵי אֲפִילוּ כָּל
הָעֲווֹנוֹת מַמָּשׁ, קַלּוֹת וַחֲמוּרוֹת,
עוֹלוֹת לְשָׁם, אֲפִילוּ עַד הֵיכָל הַד'
כְּמוֹ שֶׁכָּתוּב דַּף רנ"ב עַמּוּד א

that is not difficult at all: For even all the actual transgressions, light and severe ones alike, ascend there, even to the fourth chamber, as is written in the continuation of the *Zohar* there, *Parashat Pekudei*, page 252a.

THE FIRST CHAMBER

☞ The order of the chambers is a whole topic in and of itself that is beyond the scope of this work. The author of the *Tanya* refers to these matters since they are part of the *Zohar*'s discussion in the sections that he references. Still, in order to relate the ideas to what was addressed earlier, and to the conceptual frameworks about which he usually speaks, he comments that the chamber to which the prayers ascend is *Zeir Anpin* of the world of *Beria*.

As explained in kabbalistic writings (see *Zohar* II, 251–252, *Pardes Rimmonim*, *Sha'ar HaHeikhalot*, and in several places in hasidic works, such as *Ma'amarei Admor HaZaken* 5567, p. 99), the six palaces are the six steps of the throne (see the account of King Solomon's throne, I Kings 10:20). The throne is the world of *Beria*, meaning, the throne for divine *Malkhut* of *Atzilut*, as is known. God sits or descends, as it were, onto the throne to create continu-

The fourth chamber is even higher than the first in the world of *Beria* as well. The *Zohar* there speaks about the fourth chamber called the "chamber of merit."[6] This is the chamber of judgment, like the supernal Chamber of Hewn Stone where the Sanhedrin of the heavenly sphere sits. Everything a person does or says ascends there to be judged as a merit or demerit. It follows that even if sins embark on this ascension, then it must be a different type of ascension that is not reserved for the highest quality of meritorious actions, as the author of the *Tanya* goes on to explain.

אֶלָּא וַדַּאי שֶׁאֵין מַהוּת הָעֲלִיּוֹת שָׁווֹת וְאֵין עֵרוֹךְ וְדִמְיוֹן בֵּינֵיהֶם אֶלָּא בְּשִׁיתוּף הַשֵּׁם בִּלְבָד, וְדַי לַמֵּבִין

Rather, it is **certainly** the case **that the nature of the ascents is not the same, and there is no comparison between them whatsoever, apart from the shared name alone, and this is sufficient for one who understands** esoteric wisdom.

The ascension of the Torah and prayer spoken about earlier, and this ascension that even sins achieve, are two totally different phenomena; the only thing that they have in common is the shared name "ascension."

The ascension of prayer is an actual ascent; the words that a person says in prayer when he has intention, and infuses his mind, heart, and soul into the words, creates a spiritual force that transcends the space where it was uttered and reaches the realm that is related to the person's intention. The intent animates the words, and the words are like the body for the intent, as previously explained. This type of prayer is its own transcendent realm in which angels and souls sing and praise their creator. It becomes a living expression of the deepest true need, which is redemption, healing, livelihood, and it thereby ascends to its root and source.

ously the world that He is ruling over; that is the whole function of the world of *Beria*. The steps of the throne are the levels, or *sefirot*, of *Zeir Anpin* of *Beria*, which are the palaces themselves, meaning level upon level, room within room, until the level of the throne itself upon which the King sits (the *Malkhut* of *Atzilut*.)

---

6. See *Zohar* there, and the *Pardes Rimmonim, Sha'ar HaHeikhalot* 4.

The hasidic concept of prayer is not to stand below and cast a request heavenward. The author of the *Tanya* here explains that just through uttering the prayer, we reveal and create from within this world a refined, supernal, yet very real, essence that ascends, because now it belongs above. The prayer is therefore answered; it draws down divine abundance from above and transforms that which is below. The ascension of prayer is like the ascension of the worlds on Shabbat.[7] Worlds ascend because they transform into higher beings, without *kelippot,* without strict judgments and concealments, worlds that reflect palpable supernal divine delight. This is exactly what the ascension of prayer is, when the words, ideas, and the person who is praying actually ascend and become higher beings.

This does not apply to the second "ascension." Everything that a person does, including prayer without intention, and even sin, does not actually ascend, it does not automatically transform into its higher, more refined essence, but rather, it is mentioned above. Reality below is too complex and distorted; therefore, it is impossible to assess the true nature of a person's action or prayer in that environment. Insincere prayer uttered below ultimately stays below because that is where it belongs, like a body without a soul. However, since a person who has a holy soul and free choice did something and uttered a prayer, it has to be examined above.

Much is said in Hasidism about how we have no idea how to assess a Jew and the simple actions that he does. A person might be world famous for his wisdom and fear of heaven, and yet he may not ascend from the earth at all, and all his Torah and work might be going to the *kelippot,* because he is aware of his own greatness. On the other hand, there could be a Jew who does not even know how to read a siddur, but the sounds he makes ascend to the highest place, and his simple mitzva equals a whole world above. For this judgment of one's actions to be made, whether they are merits or sins, whether his prayers are fitting to ascend or not, they must be evaluated above and not below.

What ascends is therefore not prayer itself but rather information about it. For example, who appears before the king? Only one who he is worthy of it; a refined, extremely well-mannered and well-dressed

---

7. *Likkutei Torah, Vayikra* 41a, *Et Shabtotai Tishmeru,* and elsewhere.

person who can appreciate the loftiness of the king and his inner chamber; someone who will stand before him in fear and self-negation. In addition, and unrelated to these upstanding people who deserve to be brought before the king, the king gets a report that recounts the actions of all kinds of people in his kingdom so that he can judge them, and decide whom to absolve and whom to punish, whom to draw close and whom to distance.

וּבָזֶה יוּבַן גַּם כֵּן מַה שֶּׁכָּתוּב שָׁם דַּף רמ"ז, שֶׁבַּהֵיכָל הַב' (הַשֵּׁנִי) [אוּלַי צָרִיךְ לִהְיוֹת: 'אָזְדַּמַן הַמְמוּנֶּה' וְאוּלַי צָרִיךְ לִהְיוֹת: 'קַיְימִין הַלְּבוּשִׁים'] מְמוּנֶּה עַל הַלְּבוּשִׁים, שֶׁמַּלְבִּישִׁים הַנְּשָׁמָה מִמַּעֲשֵׂה הַמִּצְוֹת

Based on this, we can also understand that which is written there, in the *Zohar, Parashat Pekudei,* **page 247, that in the second chamber** is the one **appointed over the garments** [perhaps this **should** read: "**the one appointed** over the garments **is prepared**"; and perhaps it should read: "**the garments exist**"], **which enclothe the soul by the act of the mitzvot,**

The *Zohar* in *Parashat Pekudei* states: "One appointed over the garments is prepared," and the author of the *Tanya* comments on how the version of the *Zohar* should read, that perhaps it should be "the one appointed," instead of "one appointed," so that it reads: "The one appointed over the garments is prepared,"[8] or, alternatively, it should read: "The garments exist," instead of "one appointed over the garments." The meaning is as follows: What is the true value of a mitzva? What remains, beyond all its peripheral elements, a true and everlasting garment of one's soul? Which mitzva or aspect of it will constitute the eternal spiritual clothing of the doer that is deeply part of him, yet transcends his life in this world? These decisions are made in the second chamber of the world of *Beria.*

As stated, it is impossible to determine the value of spiritual merit in the lower worlds because they are deceptive and evaluate everything based on their own distorted frames of reference. Therefore, this judgment must ascend to the chambers of the world of *Beria,* which has no

---

8. According to a comment of the Lubavitcher Rebbe, Rabbi Menaḥem Mendel Schneerson, and similarly below.

independent identity, at least not one that obscures the truth. *Beria* is the world of pure intellect. Only in the light of the analysis of *Beria's* pure intellect, unfettered by the bias of the attributes of the worlds of *Yetzira* and *Asiya,* can the mitzva be properly assessed.

אַף שֶׁהֵן בְּגַן עֵדֶן הַתַּחְתּוֹן **even though they are in the lower Garden**
דַּעֲשִׂיָּה, כְּמוֹ שֶׁכָּתוּב שָׁם **of Eden of** *Asiya,* **as is written there,** in
דַּף ר״י **the** *Zohar* **there,** *Parashat Pekudei,* **page 210.**

The place where one acquires the garments is in this world, while the place where the soul wears those garments, feels them, and understands through them is in the lower Garden of Eden of the world of *Asiya.* ☞ ☞

GARMENTS OF EDEN

☞ As explained in many hasidic teachings, the soul is incapable of thinking, acting, and even feeling, without garments. The garments mediate between it and its surrounding environment. A person must don both physical and immaterial clothing appropriate for every place that he is in; immaterial garb includes thinking in the correct conceptual constructs and using the right words etc. Just as without these garments a person cannot enter a particular place, so too, the soul cannot be in the Garden of Eden without appropriate clothing. The term "Garden of Eden" refers to the revelation of the Divine on each particular level. However, the soul's garments in the physical world, its limbs of the body

and everything derived from them, prevent the soul from experiencing the Divine there.

Therefore, for it to enter and remain in the Garden of Eden, it must don other garments, and as explained above, these garments are the spiritual clothing created from thinking thoughts, speaking words, and carrying out actions of Torah and mitzvot in this world. When a person performs a mitzva, he is fulfilling the will of God, just as the hand fulfills the will of the soul. His action literally becomes a garment for the Divine when it makes the conscious choice to be an instrument for the fulfillment of that divine will.

LOWER GARDEN OF EDEN

☞ The Garden of Eden of *Asiya* is called "the lower Garden of Eden." There are higher levels of Eden in the worlds of *Yetzira* and *Beria*; however, a person can generally only reach them after he has been in the lower Garden of Eden. These high-

er levels of the supernal Garden of Eden in the worlds of *Yetzira* and *Beria* are levels that do not relate to the action a person does, but rather to the intention and spiritual infusion that the person had when he performed the action. A person can only

At any rate, what the author of the *Tanya* shows from the *Zohar* here is another angle of what he explained earlier, that there are different types of ascensions; one ascension occurs when something is done in a better way, is more refined and thus more sublime. In the other "ascension," which seems to reach even higher, the thing itself does not ascend, but it is only mentioned there; information about it ascends to be examined and judged.

וְהִנֵּה תְּפִלָּה פְּסוּלָה עֲדִיפָא מִתּוֹרָה שֶׁלֹּא לִשְׁמָהּ מִמַּשׁ שֶׁהִיא תַּחַת הַשֶּׁמֶשׁ וְהַתְּפִלָּה הִיא גּוֹ רָקִיעַ כוּ'

Now, invalid prayer is better than Torah studied entirely not for its own sake, which is under the sun, whereas prayer is within the firmament...

In conclusion, the author of the *Tanya* returns to the comparison between Torah and prayer from a different perspective.

The distinction between Torah and prayer outlined at the beginning of the essay was referring to devotional acts that, while lacking intention for its own sake, are also not filled with antithetical intentions. It was also explained that in this sense, there is a benefit to Torah, that at least ascends to the world of *Yetzira,* while insincere prayer remains in the world of *Asiya.*[9] Indeed, already there, the author of the *Tanya*

reach those levels from his place in lowly *Asiya,* by entering into the lower Garden of Eden through the action he does.

The lower Garden of Eden in *Asiya* reveals the Divine of that world. When a person performs a mitzva in the physical world of *Asiya,* he cannot experience its full power at that time; he often feels nothing at all. The Garden of Eden of *Asiya* is the super-spiritual realm where all the effects of one's mitzvot and Torah learning are revealed. It is where a person is able to experience the holiness, the good, and the supernal delight hidden in every holy action. It follows that only a person who performed good deeds and acts of holiness can reach this Garden of Eden. He is worthy to experience the Garden of Eden only because the positive effects of his actions actually belong to him. This is the significance of the spiritual clothing of the lower Garden of Eden.

---

9. According to the comments of the Lubavitcher Rebbe, Rabbi Menaḥem Mendel Schneerson, it seems that a distinction needs to be made between prayer that lacks intention (meaning that when it is being said, the person praying does not even have in mind the meaning of the words), but does entail a general intention

commented that if one studies Torah with intention that is truly tainted by insincere motives, for example, studying so that people will honor him, then that Torah study does not rise at all, and stays in this world "under the sun." Here he adds that in this case, there is a benefit to prayer, because prayer actually ascends in any case above the world of action, from the realm "under the sun" to "within the firmament" of *Asiya*. ☞

אֲבָל תּוֹרָה סְתָם, שֶׁאֵינָהּ שֶׁלֹּא לִשְׁמָהּ, רַק מֵאַהֲבָה מְסוּתֶּרֶת טִבְעִית

However, Torah studied **for no purpose, which is not "not for its own sake," but only out of the concealed, natural love,**

When a person studies Torah not for its own sake nor out of foreign personal interests, then what is impelling him to study? The author of the *Tanya* returns to the approach that he explained at the beginning of the essay, that it is the force of love for God, concealed in the soul of

PRAYER IS "WITHIN THE FIRMAMENT"

☞ The reason for this difference is that when it comes to prayer it is impossible for someone to have completely insincere intention. This is not true with Torah. To study Torah, a person must engage with worldly issues and delve into interpersonal and societal dynamics. A person could very easily have foreign intentions when involved in these matters. Prayer, on the other hand, is always conducted between a person and God, and is solely about connecting and cleaving to Him.

It is possible for a person to pray and not have the conscious intent toward Heaven, to connect with the Divine through the words that he is saying, which is "prayer for its own sake." However, he will not have any other intention either. At worst, he is distracted by thoughts about other things, and his mind wanders from the words of prayer. Therefore, prayer without intention, even if it does not ascend to another world, still remains neutral in relation to this world, separate from his concerns and machinations. It simply awaits another prayer filled with intent that will come and elevate it. This is the meaning of "within the firmament" as opposed to "under the sun." "Under the sun" refers to everything that a person does which becomes embroiled in this world, colored by one's calculations and interests, even his Torah study. It therefore could have no value or significance above. This is not true regarding prayer. Prayer is never "under the sun," but it is "within the firmament."

to pray to God, and between an invalid prayer that is recited even without this general intention. Further study is needed to establish what is considered "invalid prayer" that also ascends "within the firmament."

every Jew, that brings him to study Torah. The worldly thoughts and feelings of one's animal soul obscure only the higher levels of his love, and conceal the revelation of the palpable limitlessness and infinite power of it. However, every Jewish person is moved by this love to some degree; it impels him to do various things, such as study Torah. His Torah study becomes an expression of this love. This type of Torah, that is inspired by one's hidden, natural love, without any conscious intention of love or fear cultivated through his own conscious contemplation or other type of inner deliberation, is not considered to be invalidated by defective intention that is purposefully not for its own sake. Now, at the end of the essay, the author of the *Tanya* explores this essential simplicity and truth stemming from one's natural love of God that underlies this type of Torah study.

לָא גְרָעָא מֵהֶבֶל פִּיהֶן שֶׁל תִּינוֹקֹת שֶׁל בֵּית רַבָּן, דְּסָלֵיק לְעֵילָא מִפְּנֵי שֶׁהוּא הֶבֶל שֶׁאֵין בּוֹ חֵטְא	is no worse than the breath of the mouths of schoolchildren, which ascends upward because it is a breath without sin,

The Torah studied by schoolchildren is merely the "breath" of their mouths, because the children do not have intention and do not understand the words they are saying.

What distinguishes the words of Torah of small children is that they have no sin in them.[10] Just like the children themselves, their speech is untainted by sin. Sin distorts the soul and the reality of this world, preventing it from manifesting according to the supernal divine will. Speech tainted by sin is speech that is subject to this distortion because it emanates from a person whose internal misalignment prevents his own words from ascending. When Torah is uttered by children, they do not even understand the words that they are saying. It is therefore in the merit of what lies behind their words, the simplest, purest expression of Torah, the "breath without sin," that their Torah so naturally rises above this world and ascends heavenward.

This also applies to Torah study undertaken with hidden love. Particularly because it is hidden and not conscious, without any con-

---

10. According to *Shabbat* 119b, the *Zohar* in several places, and below.

sideration of this world, but a pure, natural force of the divine soul, it resembles the breath of the schoolchildren that has no sin. ☞

וְסָלֵיק לְעֵילָא אַף אִם הוּא שֶׁלֹּא and it ascends upward even if it is
לִשְׁמָהּ מַמָּשׁ, מִיִּרְאַת הָרְצוּעָה entirely "not for its own sake," for
שֶׁבְּיַד הַסּוֹפֵר example, **out of fear from the strap in the hand of the scribe.**

The breath of the mouths of schoolchildren ascends even in the case of what seems like intention that is actually not for its own sake. It is similar to a student who studies because he is afraid that the teacher will hit him, or because he'll get a candy if he studies well.

As explained, in the case of adults, intention that is truly impure does not allow the Torah to ascend; however, although children do not have intention to study for the sake of the mitzva of studying, they are still not tainted by sin; their simplicity stems from the fact that they never sinned; the consequence that they fear simply helps them to overcome their childishness. This type of impure intention does not affect or invalidate one's study; the connection between the intention and the action is purely superficial, while the studying itself,

CHILDREN WITHOUT SIN

☞ It's not that young children do not have an evil inclination, but rather, they do not have sin. This is a fundamental difference, similar to how the stages before sin and after sin are two totally different paradigms. Before the sin, even with an evil inclination, there is innocence, but after the sin, the innocence is no longer there. Before the sin, children are like angels; they have heard about the evil inclination and the reality of evil, but it is not part of their world; their bubble remains intact and unsullied. As long as a person is young (and perhaps, that is what keeps him young), he knows neither sin nor evil, neither from personal experience of sinning nor as internalized knowledge that sin and sinners are actually part of his world. As appears

from the continuation of the Talmud there (*Shabbat* 119b), this does not refer just to actual sin, but also to adults who, although they do not sin, have the awareness of the existence of sin and the complexity of this world that has evil and evildoers in it. In this sense, what small children uniquely have, as explained here, is their innocence; they have no conception or experience of sin. Schoolchildren without sin are, in a certain sense, like Adam before the sin (see *Torah Or* 5:3: "Behold, the man has become as one of us..."). He clearly had an evil inclination; yet as long as he did not sin, his world was entirely intact; he was living in the Garden of Eden. His thought and speech were whole. He lived below and reflected above.

the "breath of the mouths of schoolchildren," is still pure. The fear of the teacher does not stain the innocence with which the child relates to the Torah he utters; he understands according to his level that whatever he says is true: *Alef* is *alef* and *bet* is *bet*. This innocent way of relating to the words that he is saying directly elevates them way above all the calculations of this world.

וְעַיֵּין שָׁם דַּף רנ"ה עַמּוּד ב', שֶׁהַמַּלְאָכִים הֵם מַעֲלִים הַהֶבֶל שֶׁל תִּינוֹקֹת שֶׁל בֵּית רַבָּן עַד הָאֲצִילוּת

See there, in the *Zohar, Parashat Pekudei,* **page 255b,** where it states **that it is the angels who raise up the breath of the mouths of schoolchildren to *Atzilut*.**

When a person has intention to study Torah for its own sake with love and fear, the words of Torah that he utters ascend, as explained earlier. It can be said that love and fear create the angels, or they themselves constitute the spiritual forces, or angels, that elevate one's Torah. In the case of children who do not have intellectual love and fear, and are filled only with innocence and breath that has no sin, the angels themselves come, as it were, and elevate the words.

While breath without sin refers to physical speech, it is not caught up in the material world, like the speech of an adult, that is entangled in physical thoughts and emotions. Breath without sin is free, untethered pure speech, that just waits for an angel to pass by to elevate it; an angel that is just waiting for something to elevate. This angel is not the emotion or intention of the speaker; it is not created or activated by one's intention, but rather is like an abstract intention, or an abstract emotion, that exists beyond specific people with their specific life situations, beyond the bounds of all creation. In other words, as it belongs to the world of *Atzilut* beyond reality,[11] that is how high the angels elevate the breath of the schoolchildren.

The main focus of the author of the *Tanya* here is not this breath of schoolchildren, but rather the words of the Torah of any person, that

---

11. The actual quote from the *Zohar* reads: "The angels who elevate the breath of the mouths of schoolchildren to on high," which the author of the *Tanya* explains as "to *Atzilut*," because the world of *Atzilut* is beyond all created worlds and realities.

when spoken in innocence, without any ulterior motive, purely from the hidden love, ascends to the highest heights, like the breath of the mouths of the schoolchildren. This idea that comes as a summation of this essay, is, to a certain degree, the culmination of the first three essays in *Kuntres Aharon*. It is not a summary of the concepts outlined therein, but rather a concluding statement that can be presented only at the end of the whole process; for although it could have been mentioned at the beginning, it would not have made as great an impact as it does at the end.

The essay began with a clarification of the difference between Torah study and prayer without intention. Torah, even without intention, ascends to the world of *Yetzira,* while prayer without intention does not leave the world of *Asiya.* However, prayer has an advantage over Torah when a person is impelled to study Torah due to personal interest. Torah studied in this way stays tethered to this world and does not ascend at all; it sinks lower than prayer without intention. This does not apply to prayer, whose whole thrust is to connect a Jew to God, and which cannot be driven by ulterior motives. At worst, a person can suffer from distracting thoughts, yet still, at the foundation of his prayer lies his initial intention, which was pure: to pray to God. This prayer, even if it does not ascend to the highest heights, is also not chained to this world, and therefore, as soon as that same person utters a prayer with intention, it elevates all the prayers that were said without intention along with it.

The essay continues with the most foundational of clarifications: the nature of the ascension of Torah or prayer. The author of the *Tanya* explains that when a person undergoes an ascension, he, along with his speech and actions, becomes more refined and supernal. This differs from ascensions discussed elsewhere that do not entail immediate refinement and enlightenment of the person or practice. This is, rather, an ascension of information about the action which rises to be judged above.

The subject of the essay's conclusion is the one with which it began: the benefit of Torah studied simply, without conscious intention for its own sake, yet not with antithetical intentions, and powered by one's natural, concealed love. The benefit of this intention is that it is in some respect higher than any other intention, because it is not bound to the underlying shortcomings of intellectual intention, no matter how holy. There are no limitations to one's natural, concealed love, because it is intrinsically boundless, and can therefore ascend unendingly higher and higher. This is like the breath of the mouths of schoolchildren that has no intent and no apprehension, and therefore emanates from limitless innocence, which is irresistible to the angels who take it and elevate it higher than *Yetzira* and *Beria*, all the way to *Atzilut*.

Essay 4
Understanding a Statement
from *Pri Etz Ḥayyim*

THIS ESSAY, THE LONGEST AND MOST COMPLEX IN *Kuntres Aḥaron*, covers various topics that are addressed throughout the *Tanya*. These subjects are diverse, including prayer, the refinement of the soul and the elevation of the holy sparks, actions and the intention behind them, and the study of *halakha*. It would appear that this is not a systematic piece, with an introduction and a conclusion and a clear thread connecting them, but rather it is constructed in the form of a dissertation that meanders from one topic to another. Yet one must keep in mind that this is an essay from *Kuntres Aḥaron*, which means that it does not stand as an entirely independent essay, but contains topics that are discussed elsewhere in the *Tanya* and that complements the other sections therein. The connections to the themes found within the *Tanya* are the main focus of the essay, so the links between the parts of the essay itself are less evident. Nevertheless, since author of the *Tanya* did not write anything that lacks internal integrity, this essay also has a beginning and an end and a single thematic statement, even if it is less overt than in other instances.

In general, this essay addresses two main trajectories in the service of God: from below to above, which involves the ascension of man and the elevation of the holy sparks from the lower world, and from above to below, which constitutes the flow of the light of *Ein Sof* to the worlds. The first trajectory, from below to above, is expressed mainly, though not entirely, in prayer, while the other is embodied in mitzva performance and Torah study, particularly the study of *halakha*.

Many questions arise in this context: What is the relationship between these two trajectories in the service of God? Is one more important and central than the other? Moreover, how is prayer specifically related to elevating the sparks? Finally, what is so significant about the performance of mitzvot, which entail a seemingly petty preoccupation with this physical world, not only to us, but also to God Himself?

All these will be addressed in this essay.

2 Kislev
1 Kislev
(leap year)

לְהָבִין מַה שֶּׁכָּתוּב בִּפְרִי עֵץ חַיִּים דְּבַזְּמַן הַזֶּה, עִיקַּר הַבֵּירוּר עַל יְדֵי הַתְּפִלָּה דַּוְקָא

In this essay, we will come **to understand what is stated in** *Pri Etz Ḥayyim*, **that nowadays refinement is primarily achieved specifically through prayer,**

The author of the *Tanya* is referring to a statement that appears at the beginning of *Pri Etz Ḥayyim*.[1] It states there that nowadays, in this exile and particularly in recent generations, refinement is achieved mainly through prayer.

Pri Etz Ḥayyim, one of the central writings of the Arizal, is the foundational kabbalistic work on how to serve God, not in theory but in practice: what one should do, what intentions one should have when doing it, and how one should go about it. The text and order of prayer is, as a whole, the greatest and most systematic expression of the soul in its service of God. *Pri Etz Ḥayyim* thus starts with a kind of preface to the topic of prayer that focuses on the importance and necessity of serving God through prayer, because it is the primary way to achieve refinement.

What constitutes the work of refinement? As explained in the writings of the Arizal and hasidic teachings, our world is constructed on the fragments of a primeval world, one that was not physical but rather

---

1. *Sha'ar HaTefilla*, chap. 7.

was like a spiritual stage that preceded the reality of our world.[2] The shattering of that world was not the result of an external catastrophe but due to an internal breakage of vessels and entities that were unable to contain the light within them. That great light, which transcends all boundaries and vessels, is now scattered, its shards hidden throughout this world, within objects, deeds, and circumstances. Our task in life is to search for those shards and extract them from all those places. Sometimes one also senses a sanctified form of love, wisdom, or pleasure that is nothing other than a spark from that great light, whose discovery in its entirety is the entire purpose of our existence.

What, then, is this "nowadays" to which the author of the *Tanya* refers? The general assumption is that there are different phases in the service of God. Just as each person's life can be divided into different periods, in which he possesses various skills, life circumstances, and diverse roles, so too time in general is split into different periods, each of which has a different emphasis in the service of God. These periods are stages in the rectification of the world, in the revelation and development of the dimension of holiness within the world's materiality.

In our times, the primary service and refinement is through prayer. In general, "nowadays" refers to the time of exile, in contrast to the era when the Temple was standing. During the period of the Temple, the realm of holiness in the Land of Israel was more or less in order: It was clear exactly where the place of holiness was and what path one should follow to ascend to loftier levels of holiness. Everyone was well aware of what was holy and what was impure, what was prohibited and what was permitted.[3] The main work of refinement was achieved through the very existence of holiness. All that was required was to maintain a state of holiness and devotion through Torah study and the fulfillment of mitzvot, to be part of the edifice of holiness, so that it would shine even brighter, and the sparks scattered throughout the world would be collected automatically and become incorporated within the realm of holiness.

---

2. See *Torah Or* 51d, s.v. "*mi sam peh.*"

3. One of the reasons for this is that there were no halakhic disputes at the time, since every uncertainty was decided by the high court in Jerusalem. See Rambam, *Mishne Torah, Sefer Shofetim, Hilkhot Mamrim* 1:4.

During the exile, by contrast, when the side of holiness is not self-evident, one must descend to the place where the sparks are found in order to elevate them. This is achieved through the exile of the Jewish people among the nations,[4] and from the spiritual perspective, through the service of prayer. ☞

It is specifically through prayer that the divine light flows directly into this world in order to transform it and change man within it. It

REFINEMENT THEN AND NOW

☞ What is the implication of this term, "nowadays" in the author of the Tanya's prefatory statement, and what is its connection to prayer? In this regard, the Lubavitcher Rebbe comments:

"It would seem that what will be explained below [in Kuntres Aharon 8, which also discusses the importance of prayer in our generation] is not necessarily referring to these times. When [the author of the Tanya] states there, 'This was not the case for the early generations,' this means that then we were refined in an instant [that is, in the early generations, the souls were lofty and refinement through prayer occurred in an instant, which is not the case in our times, when much work is required], and then through reciting the Shema and Pesukei deZimra, not through Torah study and mitzvot.

"Perhaps here too, it has the same meaning [that nowadays one's prayers must be lengthy, and a moment's prayer is not sufficient]. The Pri Etz Hayyim states there 'that before the destruction of the Temple, Zeir and Nukva [the sefirot of Zeir

Anpin, which have a masculine energy, and the sefirot of Nukva, which has a feminine energy] were face-to-face...and they did not need our prayers...since the mohin [literally, 'brains' or 'intellect'\; the cognitive sefirot] never departed from them.' It can be inferred from this that when the departure [of the intellect] is greater, more prayer is required. [That is, nowadays, when people's intellect and awareness of the Divine are not as developed, they must pray more and at greater length]. See also Iggeret HaKodesh, at the end of epistles 5 and 9, regarding the relationship between charity and Torah. The same reasoning applies to the relationship between prayer and Torah.

"One might ask: Wasn't prayer [such as petitioning for the healing of the sick] also a positive mitzva from the Torah in the early generations as well? But there is no question here, since that is a separate matter that has no relevance to the discussion at hand, which is how the refinement of the sparks occurs and the purpose of the descent of the soul...."

---

4. This is reminiscent of the kabbalistic interpretation of the Rabbis' statement that the Jewish people were exiled among the nations "only so that converts would join them" (Pesahim 87b). This implies that these converts are sparks of holiness for which the Jewish people had to descend in order to elevate them, whereas during the Temple period they would come of their own accord. See Torah Or 10b.

is precisely prayer that elevates this world from below to above as a preparation and a petition for the divine light to flow forth into the worlds from above.

Furthermore, more effort is required nowadays for prayer than was the case in the past. Today, during the exile, when a person's thoughts throughout the day are remote from God, he has to work long and hard in order to achieve a state of closeness in prayer. This service, with its challenges, is the work of refinement.

אַף שֶׁתַּלְמוּד תּוֹרָה לְמַעְלָה מֵהַתְּפִלָּה — **even though Torah study is superior to prayer.**

Apart from the virtue of Torah study itself, that "Torah study is equal to them all" (*Pe'a* 1:1), that it is equal to all the other mitzvot together, there is also an apparent superiority to Torah study over prayer. The Torah provides the blueprint for the proper state of the world and man, as well as instructions on how to develop and maintain this order. When one studies the Torah, he achieves the necessary refinement through the very act of studying. ☞

If that is the case, how can we understand the author of the *Tanya*'s assertion that the primary way of achieving that refinement is specifically through prayer?

הָעִנְיָן הוּא שֶׁעַל יְדֵי תּוֹרָה וּמִצְוֹת מוֹסִיפִין אוֹר בַּאֲצִילוּת כו׳ — The explanation of **the matter is that** through Torah study **and mitzvot we increase light in** the world of *Atzilut* ...,

THE SUPERIORITY OF TORAH STUDY OVER PRAYER

☞ Torah study is superior to prayer because when a person studies Torah, the power he employs in performing this service fully originates from above. Unlike prayer, which is a service that comes from below, where a person praises God and makes requests of Him based on what he determines he needs, the Torah does not come from man's own understanding of how one should act. Rather, it is God's understanding of Himself, as it were, which He has given to man. One who says words of Torah is saying God's own words, and when he thinks about the Torah and apprehends the Torah, he is thinking and apprehending God's own thoughts, which is transcends anything that man himself can comprehend and think.

There are actually four worlds, or levels, in creation: *Atzilut, Beria, Yetzira,* and *Asiya.* The world of *Atzilut* is the loftiest of the four worlds, while ours is the lowest and is found in *Asiya. Atzilut* is not even a world at all, but it constitutes the Divine as it relates to the worlds. When a person studies Torah and performs mitzvot, he is not operating only in our world, in our reality, but primarily above, at the root of all worlds, the world of *Atzilut.* ☞

This Torah that he studies, which increases the divine light in the world of *Atzilut,* is the Torah of God, the innermost will and wisdom of the Almighty as they exist in their purest state before they manifest in the worlds below. By studying Torah and performing mitzvot down here, one draws forth a new light that had not previously existed even in the world of *Atzilut.*

This is why the author of the *Tanya* states that "we increase light in *Atzilut,*" because this illumination is an addition to what already exists in the worlds. It is like a new intervention on the part of God Himself in the construction and operation of the world. Although we say that God "continually renews the work of creation in His goodness" (in the *Yotzer Or* blessing), that renewal is entirely within the framework of the original creation, the same framework of what is, was, and will be, which is perpetually renewed and pulsates afresh at all times.

The increase of light through Torah study and mitzvot, by contrast, is always an addition. It is an increase also in the sense that it does not mix with the light of creation that belongs to the world, but rather it remains in its pure state, as the light of God. This light, even when

INCREASING THE DIVINE LIGHT IN *ATZILUT*

☞ Two hasidic Rebbes were engaged in conversation. One asked, "Why was man created?"

The other replied, "Man was created in order to rectify his soul."

The first Rebbe retorted, "Have you forgotten what we learned from our Rebbe? We learned that man was created to raise the heavens!"

This is what the author of the *Tanya* is saying here: that through Torah study and mitzvot, the heavens themselves are elevated as we increase the light in the world of *Atzilut.* In fact, in *Likkutei Amarim* (chap. 10), the author of the *Tanya* states that this is the service of the righteous, whom he calls "men of ascent" because not only do they elevate evil and darkness to a state of good and light, but their Torah study and mitzva performance ascends to the loftiest heights, elevating the good to an even higher place.

it descends to the worlds in the garb of Torah and mitzvot, is still of *Atzilut*. Like the world of *Atzilut*, which is purely divine, without any of the shattered vessels that could not contain the light, the existence of Torah and mitzvot, even in this world, is similarly divine, belonging to the reality of *Atzilut*. They are unadulterated divine wisdom and divine will, unchanged, as they exist on high.

פֵּירוּשׁ, אוֹר אֵין סוֹף בָּרוּךְ הוּא בְּכֵלִים דַּאֲצִילוּת	**meaning** that **the light of *Ein Sof*, blessed be He, is** drawn **into the vessels of *Atzilut*.**

The increase of light originates in the light of *Ein Sof*, but in order for it to be received, in order for it to have any substance, it must be contained in vessels. A light without a vessel has no meaning. For it to be an "increase," it must relate to that to which it is increasing, and this can be achieved only by its being received in vessels, in this case the vessels of *Atzilut*.[5]

עַל יְדֵי תַּלְמוּד תּוֹרָה בִּפְנִימִית, דְּהַיְינוּ הַמְשָׁכוֹת הַמּוֹחִין, וּבְקִיּוּם הַמִּצְוֹת בְּחִיצוֹנִית הַכֵּלִים שֶׁהֵם בְּחִינַת נֶצַח הוֹד יְסוֹד, שֶׁבְּי׳ סְפִירוֹת זְעֵיר אַנְפִּין שֶׁבַּאֲצִילוּת	**Through Torah study,** the light is drawn **into the inner dimension** of the vessels, or *sefirot*, of *Atzilut*, **which constitutes the flow of the intellect, and through the fulfillment of the mitzvot,** it is drawn **into the external dimension of the vessels** of *Atzilut*, **which are *Netzaḥ, Hod*,** and *Yesod* **among the ten** *sefirot* **of *Zeir Anpin* in *Atzilut*,**

There is a parallel between the human soul and its faculties and the structure of the sefirot in the world of *Atzilut*. Just as there is a difference between Torah study and the fulfillment of mitzvot for man,

---

5. As the author of the *Tanya* will explain, in this context, vessels refer to that which contains, and the light is the more spiritual substance that needs containment. A vessel will always be more external than the light, which is always internal. That said, what is considered a vessel in *Atzilut* might be considered a light in the other worlds, since it is more divine and internal than anything that exists in those worlds.

since Torah study is performed with the mind and the observance of mitzvot is done through action, the same applies to the flow of the light into the vessels, or *sefirot*, of *Atzilut* as a result of the Torah study and mitzva performance. The author of the *Tanya* thus makes a distinction between the effects of Torah study and mitzva performance on high: The former draws light into the cognitive *sefirot* of *Atzilut*, while the latter draws light into the *sefirot* of *Netzaḥ, Hod,* and *Yesod* of *Atzilut*, which are among the emotive *sefirot*.

Torah study employs the mind because the Torah is the divine wisdom. By studying the Torah below, the inner aspect of the divine light called *moḥin*, or intellect, flows from above into the internal dimension of the vessels or *sefirot* of *Atzilut*, which are the cognitive *sefirot*, Ḥokhma, Bina, and Da'at, or Wisdom, Understanding, and Knowledge. In man, this light, that of the intellect and cognitive awareness, is internal with respect to the emotions and practical application that are an expression of those emotions. The intellect constitutes a person's basic awareness of a thing, which is the way the soul relates to the thing internally. This is in contrast to the emotive attributes, where a person's relationship to the thing is expressed externally: how one feels about the thing, whether one loves or fears it, and so on. These feelings constitute a more external relationship. When a person performs a mitzva, utilizes these external faculties. Similarly, in *Atzilut*, the cognitive *sefirot*, or vessels, represent the internal intellect, the light, and the emotive sefirot are the external dimension of the vessels through which the intellect operates, just as awareness and thoughts fuel emotions and actions.

Thus, when a mitzva is performed below, the divine light is drawn into the external *sefirot* of *Atzilut*, which are the *sefirot* of *Netzaḥ, Hod,* and *Yesod*. These attributes turn outward from *Atzilut* to the created worlds in order to influence and operate within them. In the same vein, the created worlds are like an action with respect to the world of *Atzilut*, which is their soul.

All this occurs within the ten *sefirot* of the *partzuf*, or array of *sefirot*, known as *Zeir Anpin* of *Atzilut*. God relates to the worlds through this *partzuf, Zeir Anpin*, which literally means the "small countenance," since the worlds are in a state of smallness in relation to God. ☞

רַק שֶׁמִּתְלַבְּשִׁים בִּבְרִיאָה יְצִירָה **only** these flows of divine light **are**
עֲשִׂיָּה, בַּתּוֹרָה וּמִצְוֹת הַגַּשְׁמִיִּים **enclothed in** the worlds of ***Beria, Yet-***
שֶׁבָּעוֹלָם הַזֶּה ***zira,*** and ***Asiya,*** **in the physical Torah**
and mitzvot of this world.

The increase of the light of *Ein Sof* into the vessels of *Atzilut* flow forth into the other worlds. But it arrives in the worlds enclothed in the garments that are particular to these worlds, each world with its own distinctive garment. In this world, which is part of the realm of *Asiya*, it is enclothed in the garments of the physical Torah and mitzvot.

Granted, the light of *Ein Sof* is also enclothed in the garment of Torah that is within *Atzilut*. But in *Atzilut* this garment is one with the light itself, because "He and His attributes are one."[6] In the world of *Atzilut*, the garment of Torah does not conceal the light. It only reveals it and is completely unified with the essence of the light, which is revelation and bestowal. Likewise, the garments of the mitzvot in *Atzilut* are "the limbs of the King," God Himself. In essence, the garments in *Atzilut*, the vessels and the *sefirot* that contain the light, are one with the essence of the divine light. This is not the case in the other worlds, in which the revelation of the Torah and mitzvot is not a pure expression of the divine light, but rather there is always a gap between the Torah itself and the world.

In this world of ours, the Torah is not a part of the world, but is something additional, something that came later, totally different at

---

ZEIR ANPIN OF ATZILUT

☞ In kabbalistic terminology, a *partzuf* is a configuration of *sefirot* that comprises a complete structure of ten *sefirot*. The difference between a *partzuf* and a *sefira* is like the difference between a person's soul and a specific faculty or attribute that he has, between an individual who is a kind person at his essence and someone who merely experiences feelings of kindness and love. In this sense, the *partzuf* is an expression of the Divine, not merely a *sefira* or specific attribute. In view of this, the flow of the light of *Ein Sof* into the *partzuf* of *Zeir Anpin* through the performance of mitzvot does not involve one particular force or divine aspect, but a complete expression of God Himself.

---

6. *Tikkunei Zohar* 3b; see also *Iggeret HaKodesh*, epistle 20.

its essence. This world is a world in which broken vessels and sparks of light and holiness have scattered and hidden. The Torah and mitzvot, by contrast, constitute rectification at their essence, given to this world in order to refine and rectify it. When a person studies Torah with his physical intellect, a study that includes worldly concepts, and when he performs the mitzvot in practice with material objects, he draws the Torah and the light of *Ein Sof* that is enclothed in the Torah into this world.

In truth, the Torah and mitzvot could not exist in this world without this physical garb. Just as the soul cannot descend and operate in this world without a body, the light of *Ein Sof* cannot descend to this world without the physical garments of the Torah and mitzvot.

אֲבָל הַתְּפִלָּה הִיא הַמְשָׁכַת אוֹר אֵין סוֹף בָּרוּךְ הוּא לִבְרִיאָה יְצִירָה עֲשִׂיָּה דַּוְקָא	**By contrast, prayer is specifically the drawing forth of the light of** *Ein Sof*, **blessed be He,** directly **into the** worlds of *Beria*, *Yetzira*, and *Asiya*,

When one studies Torah or performs mitzvot, the intention is to draw forth light specifically into *Atzilut*, since the light is merely enclothed in the garments of this world but cannot be directly drawn into the world through Torah study or mitzvot. This is not the case with regard to prayer, in which the intention is to draw the light specifically into the affairs of this world.

לֹא בְּדֶרֶךְ הִתְלַבְּשׁוּת בִּלְבָד רַק הָאוֹר מַמָּשׁ, לְשַׁנּוֹת הַנִּבְרָאִים מִכְּמוֹת שֶׁהֵם, שֶׁיִּתְרַפֵּא הַחוֹלֶה וְיֵרֵד הַגֶּשֶׁם מִשָּׁמַיִם לָאָרֶץ וְיוֹלִידָהּ וְיַצְמִיחָהּ	**not by means of mere enclothing, but the actual light** descends to these worlds **to change created beings** from their current state, **so that the sick will be healed and rain will fall from the sky to the earth so that it may germinate and sprout.**

The light that is garbed in the Torah must reach the worlds enclothed in the Torah as it is manifest in those worlds. The light drawn forth by prayer is not enclothed at all. The light of *Ein Sof* itself descends directly to this world, without garments, to effect real changes to creation.

It should be noted that prayer here refers to the *Amida* prayer, in which one prays for the sick to be healed and for rain to fall so that the earth will produce fertile crops, among other things.

The purpose of prayer, simply put, is to change this world. When a person is sick, he prays to God that He change reality and the person will thereby be healed. This also applies on a deeper level: When we pray for the Divine Presence and the redemption of the Divine Presence, we do not have something theoretical in mind. We actually mean that there should be a revelation of the Divine Presence in everything, even on the physical level, in nature and in people, in the soul and in the body. This is prayer: that which connects what is most lofty to what is most lowly.

מַה שֶּׁאֵין כֵּן בַּתּוֹרָה וּמִצְוֹת, שֶׁאֵין שִׁינּוּי בִּקְלַף הַתְּפִילִּין עַל יְדֵי הַנָּחָתָן בָּרֹאשׁ וּבַזְּרוֹעַ

This is not the case with the Torah and mitzvot, where there is no change in the parchment of *tefillin* by their being placed on the head and the arm.

Although a mitzva is performed below, in this material, physical world, it does not effect any changes to this world. A person binds *tefillin* to his arm and head, but he does not thereby change the *tefillin* themselves. The *tefillin* remain the same after the performance of the mitzva as they were before.

Moreover, the person himself does not change through the fulfillment of the mitzva. It is true that when he dons *tefillin*, he does so with the intention of subjugating his mind and heart to God's service, of coming to love Him alone. But it is not the act itself that produces this change in his heart and mind but his focus and intent. It is the person who repents who transforms himself, the one who prays.

One who performs a mitzva effects and instigates changes above, in the world of *Atzilut*, while he himself merely carries out the action. The person, like the items used in the performance of the mitzva, is only an instrument, a tool, with which the service is executed. While the mitzva illuminates the person and the world in which it was performed, the illumination exists at the level of *Atzilut* in the soul, and it descends to the physical world, if at all, only indirectly and enclothed in garments.

וְגַם בְּמִצְוֹת שֶׁעֲשִׂיָּתָן הוּא גְמַר מִצְוָתָן **Even with regard to those mitzvot whose commandment is complete through their making** of the object with which it is performed,

When one performs the mitzva of donning *tefillin*, he uses a pair that has been fashioned beforehand. But there are cases where the mitzva act itself is in the creation of the object, such as the writing of a Torah scroll, circumcision, or the construction of a *sukka*.[7] Here it is perhaps possible to say that the act of the mitzva changes reality. Yet the author of the *Tanya* says that even then this is not the case.

הַשִּׁינוּי הוּא עַל יְדֵי אָדָם וְלֹא בִּידֵי שָׁמַיִם כְּבַתְּפִלָּה **the change is effected by man, not by Heaven, as with prayer,**

This change is part of the act of the mitzva that the person performs, an act that is itself part of the totality of the world. The reality of the world is not static; it is a reality that moves and changes within the framework of the boundaries and laws of nature. Just as the river flows into the sea, and man sows and reaps, he also performs deeds. But this is not the type of change that the author of the *Tanya* is referring to, the change that we request in prayer, which must come from God Himself, since it is a change that does not take into account the laws of nature and may even counter them.

שֶׁהִיא הַמְשָׁכַת הַחַיּוּת מֵאֵין סוֹף בָּרוּךְ הוּא, שֶׁהוּא לְבַדּוֹ כֹּל יָכוֹל **which is the drawing forth of the life force from *Ein Sof*, blessed be He, who alone is omnipotent.**

Prayer is directed to God Himself: "to Him and not to His attributes,"[8] to Him and not to the angels or His spiritual or physical forces. It is meant to change reality at its core, along with its own laws and parameters, as well as the forces and angels. Accordingly, the flow of light must come from high above, from *Ein Sof* Himself, who alone is able to effect such changes.

---

7. This is in accordance with the opinion that building a *sukka* is itself considered a mitzva. See *Shulḥan Arukh HaRav, Oraḥ Ḥayyim* 641.

8. See *Pardes Rimmonim* 32:2; *HaYom Yom*, 11 Tishrei.

וְהִלְכָּךְ כְּדֵי לְהַמְשִׁיךְ אוֹר אֵין   **Consequently, in order to draw forth**
סוֹף בָּרוּךְ הוּא לְמַטָּה, אִי אֶפְשָׁר   **the light of *Ein Sof*, blessed be He,**
בְּלִי הַעֲלָאַת מַיִין נוּקְבִין מִלְּמַטָּה   **below, it is impossible without the**
דַּוְקָא   **ascension of the feminine waters**
specifically from below.

There is a rule that there can be no flow from above, which is called the "masculine waters," unless there is an ascension of "feminine waters" from below. The ascension of the feminine waters is what is called by the *Zohar* an awakening from below, where the lower realm initiates an awakening in the upper sphere by drawing attention to itself and its need for a flow of light and life force from above.

It is natural that the greater the distance between giver and recipient, the more necessary and substantial the awakening on the part of the recipient. It is like a person trying to call attention to someone who is very far away: He must shout to be heard. This is never truer than with regard to prayer. Since one is praying to God Himself that He should draw forth the divine light directly into this world, this cannot simply happen automatically but must be achieved through awakening from below, from this place that is so lowly and far away, to which the flow of light must reach. ☞

מַה שֶּׁאֵין כֵּן לְתַלְמוּד תּוֹרָה   **This is not the case with regard to**
שֶׁבָּאֲצִילוּת, הַמְיוּחֶדֶת בְּלָאו הָכֵי   **Torah study, which has an effect in**
בַּמַאֲצִיל בָּרוּךְ הוּא   ***Atzilut*, which is in any case united**
with the Emanator, blessed be He.

"THE ASCENSION OF THE FEMININE WATERS

☞ The author of the *Tanya* stresses that it is impossible to draw down the light of *Ein Sof* directly into this world without the "ascension of the feminine waters" – without an awakening from below. When there is there is some sort of bond between giver and recipient, that very relationship and the mutual connection that exist between them, create the awakening. The recipient does not need to draw attention to himself, because he is already in the giver's sphere of influence. It does not matter wheth-er the giver is near or far. Provided that the distance is within a defined parameter, there will be a bond and the giver will be able to give and the recipient to receive. But when the distance is infinite, and when the possibilities are endless, the flow is impossible without the ascension of feminine waters from below. Only the ascension of the feminine waters, in the loftiest sense of the term, can breach the barrier of infinity and draw forth the divine light.

Although the Torah is studied below, its impact is felt above, as it draws and increases light in *Atzilut*, a realm that is "united with the Emanator, blessed be He." The world of *Atzilut* is not far from God Himself. It is one with Him in every aspect, and there is no need to elevate the feminine waters in order to draw forth this increase of light in *Atzilut*.

The whole significance and uniqueness of the giving of the Torah was that from that point onward everything one does below God likewise does above, as it were. But it is not like two actions, one evoking the other, but a single, simultaneous act.[9] When a person studies Torah, he is studying God's supernal wisdom. When he speaks words of Torah, they are the actual words of God speaking through his mouth, and when one performs mitzvot, the "limbs of the King," it is as though God Himself is carrying out the mitzva. In this sense, there is no negotiation between the lower and higher realms, no awakening from below or ascension of the feminine waters initiating an awakening above. There is only the revelation of the Divine in *Atzilut*, which flows through us, the realm of *Atzilut* penetrating all the way to this world itself. ☞

TORAH STUDY AND *ATZILUT*

☞ This concept can also be explained in a different manner, in accordance with the idea that the Torah constitutes an awakening above, which is loftier than an awakening from below (see *Or HaTorah*, Deut., vol. 1, p. 55). The source of the Torah is so lofty that no awakening from below can reach it. Therefore, the Torah does not flow as a consequence of an awakening from below, but rather in the form of an awakening of its own, a distinct expression of the Divine that is far higher than any possible relationship that could be awakened from below.

In view of this, the whole concept of elevating the feminine waters, of initiating an awakening from below, does not apply to Torah study, but to a different system, that of prayer. Prayer is the channel for the awakening from below. For each person, it begins from his lowly aim, from his *Malkhut*, the place where he is currently situated. It is from there that he prays, calling out to God, relating his woes, praising Him, beseeching. This is the ascension of the feminine waters that awakens and draws forth the flow of light from above.

---

9. See *Torah Or*, beginning of *Parashat Yitro*, where it states that the giving of the Torah was about "saying" (Ex. 20:1) – saying God's words together with Him.

וְהַעֲלָאַת מַיִין נוּקְבִין בְּמוֹחוֹ The ascension of the feminine waters
וְלִבּוֹ שֶׁל אָדָם in a person's mind and heart

All the holy sparks that a person collects in this world – the souls to which he connects, his deeds, words, and good thoughts – all ascend on high through the person's mind and heart. The mind and heart represent a person's consciousness and feelings, or, as it will be termed below, his cognitive love and fear. It is through his awareness and contemplation of God's greatness, and the love and fear that this evokes, that he binds his actions and his life to holiness. As the author of the Tanya says elsewhere,[10] these are the wings that elevate what a person says and does. This is the ascension of the feminine waters. ☞

THE ASCENSION OF THE FEMININE WATERS AND THE SOUL

☞ From a different perspective, it can be said that the ascension of the feminine waters in the soul of man is not like a passage through a channel, because what really ascends is first and foremost the person himself through the love and fear of God engendered and his contemplation of the Divine in his own mind and heart. Of course, outside factors affect a person, and he will react to events that occur and to people around him, but his actual service and elevation occur first and foremost when he changes within and elevates his soul. He raises upward everything that unfolds in his soul – the yearnings and challenges, the hesitations and the triumphs.

The ascension of the feminine waters must involve something precious and important, something that is missing there, as it were, and is only found down here below. Love, fear, wisdom – all of these are present, and in greater quantities, in the higher realm. Down below we have only the remnants of these qualities, and there-fore they do not have any real value on high. The only thing that exists below and not above is the uncertainty and struggle within the human soul, between the soul and the body, between the divine soul and animal soul, between the desire for one thing and its counterpart. In the personal, unique balance within each individual, this is the one thing that is not found above, nor in any other soul, and that is why it is so precious.

Of course, all of those developments in the soul are nothing but a reflection of what is happening in the world as a whole. The work is performed in the soul, but the soul is connected in all its strands to reality. When a person works on his soul, he has an effect on the world and on the soul of the world, which is the exiled Divine Presence and its holy sparks that are everywhere. When the soul elevates what it elevates from within itself, it also raises up those aspects of the Divine Presence, those divine sparks, that are in the world.

---

10. See, e.g., *Likkutei Amarim*, chap. 40.

The author of the *Tanya* refers here to "a person's mind and heart" because they incorporate all the faculties of a person's soul, both his intellect and emotive attributes.[11] Furthermore, the main work of the soul discussed in the *Tanya* involves the relationship between the mind and the heart, where the mind rules over the heart, rectifying and elevating the faculties of the heart and the animal soul. In a sense, the heart and the mind represent the animal soul and the divine soul in man,[12] which can be compared to the chaos and rectification in the worlds in general. Through the service of mind and heart, man gradually rectifies his soul and the world at large.

הִיא בְּחִינַת "רִשְׁפֵּי אֵשׁ" בְּלִי גְבוּל,   **is the embodiment of boundless sparks of fire,**

The ascension of the feminine waters is compared to sparks of fire.[13] Fire naturally reaches upward, leaping out of the vessel that tries to contain it. Similarly, the feminine waters are the holiness that we elevate from within this world by burning and consuming the vessels and garments in which it was hidden. It is like bringing an animal sacrifice upon the altar, which in the case of the soul is the elevation of the animal soul on the altar of the heart that burns with the love of God.[14]

וְנִקְרָא "מְאֹדֶךָ"   **and it is called *me'odekha*, literally, "your might,"**

Wherever it appears in the hasidic literature,[15] the term *me'od* always denotes that which is infinite, that which transcends boundaries, as in the requirement to love God *bekhol me'odekha*, "with all your might," as we are adjured to do in the *Shema*.[16] The implication is that we should love Him with unlimited love.

In the same sense, the ascension of the feminine waters is also called

---

11. *Likkutei Amarim*, chap. 3.

12. *Likkutei Amarim*, chap. 9.

13. Based on Song 8:6.

14. See *Likkutei Torah*, Deut. 35c.

15. See, e.g., *Likkutei Torah*, Num. 52c; *Torah Or* 53b.

16. From the famous verse in *Shema*: "You shall love the Lord your God with all your heart, with all your soul, and with all your might" (Deut. 6:5).

"your might." The author of the *Tanya* specifies *me'odekha*, "your might," and not simply *me'od*, "might," because unlimited might is not within the power of any man. "Your might," however, is attainable, and when someone breaks through his personal limits, that is his connection with *Ein Sof*. It also means that this point, the most significant in each person's service, is not something objective that can be equated or replicated from one person to another. Some might give a million dollars to charity, and that would still not be considered "with all your might," whereas others can give only ten dollars and that would be classified as "with all your might." The issue is not the specific sum that was donated, but what one has taken from himself. One who cannot afford it, and is also stingy by nature and is not in a particularly good mood today, must overcome these tendencies and go out of his way to give at least a small amount. This is "with all your might."

כְּדֵי לְעוֹרֵר בְּחִינַת אֵין סוֹף   **to awaken that which is infinite.**

How can man awaken the infinite, *Ein Sof*? Only when a person here below becomes in a certain sense infinite himself. Indeed, man is limited not only physically, but also in his mental and emotional faculties. His love is limited, and his reach is limited. After all, he is merely a created being, with boundaries and limits. Yet within the dynamic between the faculties within a person, in the contradictions, the struggles, and their integration, there is sense of infinity when a soul, or one of its faculties, succeeds in going beyond its previous limit.

A person possesses several infinite faculties that limit each other when they exist in a single place. But when he succeeds in changing the array of faculties, to break through the boundaries that define him, he attains infinitude. Divested of boundaries, he can touch the infinite.

וְהַיְינוּ עַל יְדֵי גְּבוּרוֹת דס״ג   **This is** achieved **through the *gevurot*,** the forces of restraint, **of** the divine name ***Sag*,**

The ascension of the feminine waters, the awakening below that initiates an awakening from above, drawing down the light of *Ein Sof*, occurs, in the terminology of Kabbala, through the forces of restraint of the divine name called *Sag*. This ascension can be seen as the elevation of the sparks of the divine light that fell upon the shattering of the vessels. These sparks belong both to the name *Sag* and to the side of *Gevura* and are therefore called "the forces of restraint of *Sag*." ☞

Every ascension from below to above employs the attribute of *Gevura*, as opposed to *Ḥesed*, which is poured forth in a movement from above to below and from the center outward. When *Gevura* is employed, it is through the opposite movement, from below upward and from the outside in, from the periphery to the core.

The same is true of the refinement of the sparks and their elevation: One who rises must do so through the strength of *Gevura*, in order to emerge and break away from the world and the *kelippot* in which the sparks are captive. Yet it seems that the *Gevura* that is required here in order to rise above the limits of the world to initiate an awakening of *Ein Sof* is beyond man's capacity. A person may rectify himself, change himself, but going beyond that to change reality with the power of *Ein Sof*, is not within his own abilities. This power is obtained only from

THE NAME SAG

☞ *Sag*, whose Hebrew letters, *samekh* and *gimmel*, have the numerical value of 63, is a holy name derived through a kabbalistic device known as *milui*, or expansion. This involves expanding the letters of the name of *Havaya* by spelling them out in their full form to reveal new letter combinations. Since certain letters can be spelled in different ways, there are several forms of expansion that can be derived from the name of *Havaya*. One of these is *Sag*, where the numerical value of the letters that comprise the name of *Havaya*, *yod*, *vav*, and *heh*, are totaled when the letter *heh* is spelled *heh-yod*, the *vav* is spelled *vav-alef-vav*, and the final *heh* is also spelled *heh-yod* for the final *heh*. These letters added together total sixty-three, or *Sag*.

When these letters of the name of *Havaya* are added together in other combinations, this results in other holy names.

These expansions of the name of *Havaya* represent the totality of existence (in the sense that each of these letters represent a different *sefira*, the forces through which God sustains and gives life the world). More than that, they represent the totality of all that has occurred in existence, shattering of the vessels and their refinement. Among these names and what they represent, the name *Sag* denotes the primeval existence that shattered due to an increase of light that was the capacity of the vessels to bear it. As a consequence, the lights fell down into the world below and the *kelippot*. Man's task in the world is to refine and elevate the lights of *Sag*, which are the shattered lights of *tohu*, the world of chaos, from among the *kelippot*. When they ascend, they are revealed in all their lofty essence, which is the name *Sag* that is above man.

within the process of refinement itself, from the power that is within the shattered sparks themselves.

The shattering occurred because the light was too great for the vessels of the world to contain, too intense for their parameters, so that it could not be contained. The light that emerged from the shattering, the sparks that fell, still carries with it a force that transcends limits.[17] This power of *Gevura* is called "the forces of restraint of *Sag*" in the language of Kabbala, and it refers to the unlimited forces of restraint of chaos, which can be found within the shattered sparks.

The massive power of these forces of restraint does not result from the ascension itself. At their essence, at their root, the sparks contain primal powers that are immensely greater than the forces of this world. These powers are released through their elevation, through the extraction of the sparks from the impure forces.

שֶׁהֵן הֵן הָרְפָּ״ח נִיצוֹצִין כו׳   **which constitute the 288 sparks...**

The name *Sag* is the source of the 288 sparks that fell from the world of chaos upon the shattering of the vessels. The number 288 represents the sum of the lights of the world of chaos that existed and was shattered before our world came into being.[18] The shards of these lights are the sparks that are concealed and held captive within the framework of

---

17. This can be compared to the difference between a righteous person and a penitent, a *ba'al teshuva*. A righteous individual is already rectified, so he cannot draw forth a new light and extract the sparks. In order to rise beyond his current status, he must become a *ba'al teshuva*. It is the penitent is going to extract the sparks from the *kelippot*. He is the one who is able to transcend limits. This is the meaning of the famous saying that in the place where *ba'alei teshuva* stand, even completely righteous individuals cannot stand (*Berakhot* 34b). This does not refer only to a *ba'al teshuva* who was formerly a sinner, since repentance is for the righteous as well.

18. See *Pri Etz Ḥayyim, Sha'ar Keriat Shema* 9; *Etz Ḥayyim, Sha'ar Rapach Nitzotzin*, chap. 1, which provide the calculations that explain how this number is reached. It is also explained that 288 was the number of holy sparks that descended within the world of *Atzilut*. When they fell into the worlds of *Beria* and *Asiya*, each spark split into many parts, until they numbered in the tens of thousands. See *Torah Or* 27d.

our world, and their elevation and rectification constitutes our divine service. ☞

וְלָכֵן נִקְרֵאת הַתְּפִלָּה 'חַיֵּי שָׁעָה',
הִיא מַלְכוּת הַיּוֹרֶדֶת בִּבְרִיאָה
יְצִירָה עֲשִׂיָּה, וְתוֹרָה 'חַיֵּי עוֹלָם',
הוּא זְעֵיר אַנְפִּין

Therefore, prayer is called "temporal life," which is *Malkhut* that descends into the dimensions of time and place in the worlds of *Beria, Yetzira,* and *Asiya,* and the Torah is called "eternal life," which is *Zeir Anpin,*

Prayer is called "temporal life" because its purpose is to draw the light of *Ein Sof* into this world, where the dimensions of time and place exist, in order to effect changes down below, such as healing the sick. Similarly, the *sefira* of *Malkhut* is "temporal life" since it constitutes the life force that descends into the dimension of time, into the fragments of time and the place of the worlds.[19] At its essence, time constitutes change, which is essential to prayer. When we pray, we are praying for a change. Even a prayer of praise is designed to draw down more of that praiseworthy quality and improve reality further.[20]

By contrast, the Torah is called "eternal life" because it draws, as stated, an increase of light into *Atzilut,* which is above time. Furthermore, it does not change anything in the worlds below. It does not

288 SPARKS

☞ The word *merahefet* in the verse "And the spirit of God hovered [*merahefet*] over the surface of the water" (Gen. 1:2) can be rearranged to form the words *rapah met,* "288 are dead" (see *Torah Or* 27d). This alludes that they fell from their lofty level, and they are the kings of Edom who are listed in the Torah (Gen. 36) as having reigned and died. The kabbalistic sources explain that this is the story of the seven *sefirot* or vessels (represented by the kings of Edom) of the world of *tohu,* the world of chaos, which were unable to remain intact because of the intensity of the light within them and they shattered. Those resulting sparks of light that fell at that juncture were scattered throughout the created worlds.

---

19. For this reason, we find that the Torah refers to the concept of time only with respect to *Malkhut,* Kingship, as in "The Lord reigns, the Lord reigned, the Lord will reign" (from the prayer service, based on Psalms 10:16, 93:1, and Ex. 15:18). See also *Sha'ar HaYihud VeHa'emuna,* chap. 7.
20. See *Torah Or* 30b; *Likkutei Torah,* Lev. 29c; *Derekh Mitzvotekha, Mitzvat Hallel.*

touch objects or enter them. On the contrary, the Torah raises the world to the dimension that is above time. ☞

כִּי רְמַ"ח פִּקוּדִין הֵן מִתְחַלְּקִין	for the 248 positive **commandments**
בי' כֵּלִים דְּעֶשֶׂר סְפִירוֹת דִּ"זְעֵיר	**are divided into the ten vessels of the**
אַנְפִּין" כוּ'	**ten** *sefirot* **of** *Zeir Anpin* ...

The connection between the Torah and *Zeir Anpin* is not merely a general equivalence, where *Zeir Anpin*, like the Torah, transcends the worlds and *Malkhut*. There is also a particular, structural relationship that pertains to their contents. The totality of the Torah can be viewed as the sum of the positive commandments, which number 248, a number that is related to the number of *sefirot* in *Zeir Anpin*.[21]

On a broader level, there is a link between the 248 positive commandments and the 248 limbs. On a basic level these mitzvot correspond to the 248 limbs of man. On a loftier level, they are the 248 limbs of the King, of God, which is *Zeir Anpin*, or more specifically, the revelation of God in the world as it is manifest through *Zeir Anpin*. Just as the 248 limbs of a person, metaphorically speaking, comprise the whole person, so too the 248 positive commandments comprise the entirety of God's revelation in *Zeir Anpin*.

TEMPORAL LIFE AND ETERNAL LIFE

☞ These terms are taken from a story recounted in the Talmud (*Shabbat* 10a): Rava saw Rav Hamnuna prolonging his prayer. He said about him, "They abandon eternal life and engage in temporal life." In other words, people such as yourself set aside Torah study, which is eternal life, since the study of Torah has eternal value for both this world and the World to Come, in favor of prayer, which is temporal life, since it constitutes a request for the needs of the hour alone, such as recovery from an illness or a livelihood.

---

21. As explained in several places (see, e.g., *Torah Or* 68c; *Likkutei Torah*, Num. 45d), when *Zeir Anpin* is regarded as having nine *sefirot* (without *Malkhut*, which is the feminine aspect of *Zeir Anpin*), each of which is comprised of nine *sefirot* themselves, this amounts to a total of 81. Since each of these contains three components – a head, middle, and end – that totals 243 (because anything that is not infinite has a beginning and an end, and perforce a middle). If we add to this the five aspects of Ḥesed, the forces of giving, this makes a grand total of 248.

Zeir Anpin represents God's countenance that He displays toward the worlds, so to speak – a revelation of God in the worlds. It is the manifestation of the Divine from the perspective of the worlds. When we in the world relate to God, to the Creator of the world, to His power, might, and wisdom, we are actually referring to the *partzuf*, or countenance, of *Zeir Anpin*. On an even broader scale, our perception of the Divine, which transcends *Atzilut* and the constriction of the divine light that emanates from it, passes through *Zeir Anpin*.[22]

The 248 mitzvot are thus the "limbs" of God. Just as the vitality of the soul is manifest within the limbs of the human body, within the faculty of thought in the brain, within the ability of the foot to move, within the sense of sight in the eyes, so too the mitzvot are the vessels and limbs through which God reveals His will, wisdom, and essence in the world.

At this point, the second section of the essay begins. As stated above, the essay compares the service of prayer, particularly when performed with love and fear, and the service of God through Torah study and the practical mitzvot. From here until the end of the essay, the emphasis shifts to its second theme: the fulfillment of action-related mitzvot and the study of *halakha*, which leads to that fulfillment, with an emphasis on the superiority of this service over service of the soul, of developing cognitive love and fear of God through contemplation of God's greatness.

However, since the author of the *Tanya* has mentioned that the mitzvot are rooted in *Zeir Anpin*, that they are the 248 limbs of the King, he presents a short discussion on the source of the mitzvot in general. Of course, God Himself commands us to observe the mitzvot, which represent His will. The purpose of this section is to clarify just how internal and lofty is the divine will behind the mitzvot.

3 Kislev

2 Kislev
(leap year)

וְהִנֵּה בְּמָקוֹם אֶחָד כָּתַב (עֵץ
חַיִּים שַׁעַר קִיצוּר אֲבִי"ע, פֶּרֶק ד)
שֶׁרְמַ"ח מִצְווֹת עֲשֵׂה הֵן בַּה'
חֲסָדִים, וְשַׁסַ"ה לֹא תַעֲשֶׂה
בַּה' גְּבוּרוֹת וכו'

In one place, it is written (*Etz Ḥayyim, Shaʾar Kitzur Abiya*, chap. 4) **that the 248 positive commandments are** rooted **in the five ḥasadim**, the spiritual forces of giving, **while the 365 prohibitions are** rooted **in the five gevurot**, the restraining forces…

---

22. See *Torah Or* 82b.

Generally, the mitzvot are categorized as either positive command-ments or prohibitions. This allocation has a deeper root within the *sefirot* of *Zeir Anpin*. The five *ḥasadim*, the forces of giving, and the five *gevurot*, or restraining forces, are the lights contained in the vessels, or *sefirot* of *Zeir Anpin*, and thus the root of the mitzvot above is the divine light that is contained in the *sefirot* of *Zeir Anpin*. The roots of the positive commandments is in the lights called five *ḥasadim*, while the roots of the prohibitions is in the lights called five *gevurot*. ☞

FIVE ḤASADIM AND FIVE *GEVUROT*

☞ These forces do not comprise the *sefirot* of *Ḥesed* and *Gevura* themselves. *Ḥesed* and *Gevura* are *sefirot* and attri-butes. While they are important attributes, the root of all the attributes in *Zeir Anpin* (since all *sefirot* that come after them are a mixture of the *sefirot* of *Ḥesed* and *Gevura*), each of them serves as a vessel for a specif-ic revelation of divine light. By contrast, the *ḥasadim* and *gevurot* refer to the light or vi-tality that is drawn into all the attributes.

We speak of five *ḥasadim* and five *ge-vurot* because they flow through the five attributes of *Ḥesed*, *Gevura*, *Tiferet*, *Net-zaḥ*, and *Hod*. As for the other five *sefirot*, the cognitive *sefirot* – *Ḥokhma*, *Bina*, and *Da'at* – are the source of these forces, of the *ḥasadim* and *gevurot*, while *Yesod* and *Malkhut* are the *sefirot* that receive and transmit them to the worlds.

The *ḥasadim*, the forces of giving, are the embodiment of the light of kindness, of giving and producing, each of the five *ḥa-sadim* comprising a different shade of this illumination. Similarly, the *gevurot* are the illumination of restraining forces, the pow-ers that preserve and overcome, the em-bodiment of might and restraint.

When the author of the *Tanya* says that the positive commandments are rooted in the five *ḥasadim*, this means that the vitality and strength to fulfill the positive commandments comes from those *ḥa-sadim*, which manifest in the attributes in the form of action and flowing forth. By contrast, the prohibitions are rooted in the five *gevurot*, meaning that the will and strength to refrain from doing something undesirable comes from the power of the *gevurot* that flow through the attributes. A person will perform a deed or refrain from committing an act in accordance with the attributes that manifest in his heart. On a deeper level, he will act or refrain from acting in accordance with the inner na-ture of those attributes, the forces of *ḥa-sadim* or *gevurot* as they are transmitted and expressed in each of the attributes that drive the deed.

The attribute of *Ḥesed*, for instance, is sweet; it is characterized by light and love. The question is, will a person want and de-sire it? Will he perform any action in order to actualize this desire? The answer de-pends on the way the attribute manifests. Something sweet can be sickening, and that which is bitter can become the spur for one's yearnings. It depends on the in-ternal dimension of the attribute being em-ployed, on the lights that are the *ḥasadim* and *gevurot* passing through the soul's fac-ulties, its cognitive awareness and emotions. The source of these forces are not only be-yond the faculties of the soul, but they ul-timately comprise all the faculties. What leads a person to perform or refrain from an action, then, is not only his attributes, but the *ḥasadim* and *gevurot* that fuel them.

וּבְמָקוֹם אַחֵר (זהר חלק ג קכט, א) but elsewhere (*Zohar* 3:129a) it is
כָּתַב שֶׁהֵן תַּרְיַ"ג אָרְחִין נִמְשָׁכִין written that they, the 613 mitzvot,
מֵחַד אָרְחָא כו', שֶׁהוּא לַבְנוּנִית וכו' are 613 paths that are drawn from a
single path…, which is the white-
ness…

Each of the 613 mitzvot, the 248 positive commandments and the
365 prohibitions, offer their own path through which the divine light
flows below, but they all have one source, a single path, which is
called "whiteness." White is the hue of kindness, or a specific aspect
of kindness that transcends all the faculties and that incorporates all
of them, just as one path can be the root of all paths. In contrast to the
root of the mitzvot in *Zeir Anpin*, where there is a difference between
the positive commandments and the prohibitions – where the positive
commandments are rooted in the *ḥasadim* and the prohibitions in
the *gevurot* – the whiteness referred to here is a far higher level that
incorporates all the mitzvot in a single path.

Moreover, it is explained in the teachings of Kabbala and Hasidism
that the color white is actually not a specific color, but rather it includes
all the colors.[23] This whiteness, then, is not among the *sefirot* in *Atzilut*
but rather is higher, on the level of *Atik Yomin*, the internal dimension
of the *sefira* of *Keter*. As the *Zohar* states (3:129a), "There is no left in
this *Atik*; it is all on the right." "Left" refers to the attribute of *Gevura*
in the level of *Atik*, which is the internal dimension of *Keter*. Rather, it
is all right, all *Ḥesed*.

It follows that there two different levels that are the source and root
of the mitzvot: It is either within the *sefirot* of *Zeir Anpin* in *Atzilut*,
which contain the five *ḥasadim* and the five *gevurot* or within the
whiteness of *Keter*. The author of the *Tanya* will go on to explain how
these seemingly contradictory concepts can be reconciled.

אַךְ הָעִנְיָן שֶׁכָּל הַמִּצְוֹת לְתַקֵּן רְמַ"ח The explanation of the matter is
אֵבְרֵי זְעֵיר אַנְפִּין that all the mitzvot serve to rectify
the 248 limbs of *Zeir Anpin*

---

23. See *Torah Or* 24b.

The impact of the mitzvot that we perform here, in this world, is activated in the world of *Atzilut*, as stated above. As the author of the *Tanya* puts it, they rectify the limbs of *Zeir Anpin* of *Atzilut*. This is the first level that is the root of the mitzvot: within the *sefirot* of *Zeir Anpin*. This is the place where they have an impact, where they bring about rectification. ☞

עַל יְדֵי הַמְשָׁכַת אוֹר אֵין סוֹף בָּרוּךְ הוּא בַּמוֹחִין הַכְּלוּלִין בה׳ חֲסָדִים וה׳ גְבוּרוֹת

by drawing the light of *Ein Sof*, blessed be He, into the *moḥin* that are incorporated in the five *ḥasadim* and the five *gevurot*.

The rectification of the attributes is achieved by drawing the light of *Ein Sof* into the *moḥin*, which constitutes the illumination of the intellect within the attributes. Here the author of the *Tanya* is calling the afore-mentioned lights, the five *ḥasadim* and the five *gevurot*, *moḥin*, since the source of these lights, which are channeled through the attributes, is in the *moḥin* of *Atzilut*. The cognitive *sefirot*, *Ḥokhma* and *Bina*, are like the father and mother that give birth to the other attributes. They generate

REPAIRING THE LIMBS OF *ZEIR ANPIN*

☞ *Zeir Anpin* is one of the *partzufim* of the world of *Atzilut*. In general, is a recti-fied world, yet the root of the shattering of the vessels in the worlds can be found in *Zeir Anpin* of *Atzilut*.

Zeir Anpin expresses the relationship of the Divine to the worlds, the counte-nance with which He turns to them. In a certain sense, anything that exists in the worlds in actuality exists in potential form in *Zeir Anpin*.

By way of analogy, the faculties of the human soul can be divided into the in-tellect and the emotive attributes. It is through the emotive attributes that man engages with the world around him. He becomes emotionally involved in it, iden-tifies with what is happening in it, and

reacts to it, with joy or anger, sadness or elation, depending on what is occurring in the world.

By contrast, when he employs his intel-lect, his state is static, because the intellect does not get involved with it, but remains objective, free of any personal bias, assum-ing that it is pure intellect rather than the rationale that results from a certain feel-ing or impulse.

Similarly, the limbs of *Zeir Anpin*, the attributes that are a revelation of God's will, penetrate, affect, and are influenced by creation. These limbs require rectifi-cation since the root of the shattering of the vessels can be found in these limbs of *Zeir Anpin*.

the awareness as a result of which the emotive attributes take shape. The light that reaches the attributes through the *mohin* has its origin in the supreme root of everything, which is the light of *Ein Sof*. ☞

The *mohin* flow into the attributes through the five *hasadim* and the five *gevurot*. The *hasadim* and *gevurot* are like the transmitters and translators of the *mohin* to the attributes. The *mohin*, or cognitive attributes that comprise the intellect, conclude either that there must be creation, expansion, and flow, which are the characteristics of the *hasadim*, or there must be caution, preservation, and internalization, characteristics of the *gevurot*.

It is the fulfillment of the positive commandments and the prohibitions down below that draw forth the *hasadim* and *gevurot*, directing and translating the conclusions of the intellect into the form of attributes. What is more, that which guides the intellect toward these conclusions is the fulfillment of the mitzvot.

The positive commandments draw forth the flow of the *hasadim*,

THE ILLUMINATION OF THE INTELLECT

☞ When the vessels of the world of *tohu*, of chaos, shattered, the light of *Ein Sof* entered a vessel that could not contain it, and so it broke. In the terminology that appears in the sources, there were too many lights in too few vessels. Consequently, rectification for this involves expanding the vessels by combining and joining the attributes to one another.

At its essence, each vessel is limited. Thus only way it can contain and manifest the light of *Ein Sof* is by joining with another vessel, through its emergence from itself, from being on its own, and attaching to another vessel, manner, and perspective. This expansion is achieved through the flow of the *mohin* into the attributes.

Returning to the analogy of the human soul, the attributes themselves cannot be combined with each other. One who becomes enraged is merely angry without limit; one who loves is simply a lover who accepts no criticism or boundaries. A connection between the two can be established only when a person comprehends why he is angry. At that juncture, the anger abates. In the language of lights and vessels, the lights are dimmed. Moreover, the person can feel love for the person with whom he is cross or have pity on him. This is an analogy for expanding and forming more vessels to contain the lights.

Furthermore, the *mohin* are always internal in relation to the attributes. The flow of the *mohin* reveals the internality of the attributes, and internally they are connected, just as in the physical world all things are connected at their root. Things that seem unrelated, even opposites, are fashioned from the same material internally. When viewed from the inside, they are the same entity (see also *Likkutei Amarim*, chap. 32, for a different perspective).

since these mitzvot reveal the supreme will of the Creator to bestow and produce, while the prohibitions draw forth the *gevurot*, since the restraint exercised by refraining from a prohibited action reveals the power of limitation and boundaries from above. On a deeper level, they reveal the supernal light that cannot be contained in any vessel, which manifests itself either as an absence or flow of light.

וּמְקוֹר הַמּוֹחִין הוּא לַבְּנוֹנִית כו', הוּא
הָעֹנֶג וְחֵפֶץ הָעֶלְיוֹן לְהַמְשִׁיךְ הָאוֹר
לְמַטָּה לִרְמַ"ח אֵבָרִין דִּזְעֵיר אַנְפִּין

The source of the intellect is the whiteness of *Keter*, **which is the supernal delight and desire to draw the light below into the 248 limbs of** *Zeir Anpin*.

These *moḥin* that flow through the attributes have a higher source than that of the attributes. In the human soul as well, the intellect is not the initial source for the soul's awareness and emotions, for the rationale behind why we think about a certain thing and why we understand something this way or that. It is not one specific faculty among the soul's faculties that we are speaking of here, but a general infrastructure that operates in the background, in the atmosphere where all the faculties of the soul exist.

In the terminology of the *Zohar*, this is called the "whiteness." Just as the color white is the source of all the colors, the whiteness constitutes the unlimited supernal kindness in which there is no mixture or limitation of any kind. In the terminology of Kabbala, it is "the internal dimension of *Keter*," while in hasidic teachings, it is described as the pleasure and desire that is the internal dimension of the will.

Similarly, the loftiest faculty in the soul, that which is the foundation of all the faculties, is the simple, primal will that has no specific definition or explanation. Yet it is what inclines the soul in one direction or another. Within that will, within that all-encompassing foundation, is pleasure. The flow of the light of the *moḥin* to the attributes does not begin with the intellect, where some course of action is prudent or wise, but even before that stage, there is the inexplicable pleasure it provides and the deep desire that it should be so.

The three levels that constitute the root of the mitzvot and appear in various sources can be reconciled into a single framework: The mitzvot we perform below rectify the vessels above, the limbs of *Zeir Anpin* in *Atzilut*. The rectification that is implemented through the performance of mitzvot below occurs when they draw the *moḥin* from above through the five *ḥasadim* and the five *gevurot*. The source of this flow is even higher, in *Keter*, in the supernal delight and desire that precedes even the intellect.

וּמִתְחַלֶּקֶת הַהַמְשָׁכָה לְתַרְיַ״ג **The flow** of supernal pleasure and desire
הַמְשָׁכוֹת פְּרָטִיּוֹת לְפִי בְּחִינַת **is divided into 613 individual channels**
עֵרֶךְ הַמִּצְוֹת **in accordance with the value of the mitzvot.**

The supernal desire within the whiteness of *Keter* is a single desire, a one-dimensional pleasure, which is drawn from above to below through the fulfillment of the mitzvot. Just as in this world there are 613 mitzvot that are known to us, in *Zeir Anpin* of *Atzilut* there are 613 individual channels, each corresponding to the value of the mitzva that draws it forth.

כְּגוֹן, בִּצְדָקָה וּגְמִילוּת חֲסָדִים **For example, through charity and acts**
נִמְשָׁךְ אוֹר אֵין סוֹף בָּרוּךְ **of kindness, the light of** *Ein Sof*, **blessed**
הוּא לְחִיצוֹנִית הַכְּלִי דְּחֶסֶד **be He, flows to the external aspect of**
דִּ״זְעֵיר אַנְפִּין״ וּבְקִיּוּם הַדִּינִין **the vessel of** *Hesed* **of** *Zeir Anpin*, **and**
בְּחִיצוֹנִית גְּבוּרָה וּבְרַחֲמִים כו׳ **through the execution of judgment it flows to the external aspect of** *Gevura*, **and through mercy, and so on.**

The author of the *Tanya* now goes into specifics: When someone fulfills a mitzva that involves an act of kindness, such as giving charity to the poor, he causes the light of *Ein Sof* to be drawn from the supernal delight and desire into the vessels of *Hesed* in the world of *Atzilut*.

Likewise, through the implementation of justice, whether it entails issuing a legal ruling or the execution of a sentence, either in an actual court of law, where the judge might dispense lashes and the death penalty, or within one's own soul, with respect to himself, one fulfills the mitzvot with the attribute of judgment. At that moment, he draws the light of *Ein Sof* from above into the external aspect of the vessels of *Zeir Anpin* and brings a flow of the *gevurot* into the world, which results in imposing justice on one's enemies, and on a larger, more general scale, dispensing life-giving sustenance to the world. The same applies to the fulfillment of the mitzvot that involve the attribute of mercy and *Tiferet*, and likewise to the other attributes. ☞

For the person performing a mitzva, this process can be described in the following terms: The light of the mitzva is the commandment of God. God commanded the mitzva, and its light comes from high above. Man as a whole is the vessel through which the mitzva is performed below, and he has an external aspect and an internal aspect. The internal aspect is his intentions, whether he fulfills the mitzva with love or fear, while the external aspect is the faculty of action, which overcomes any impediments to carrying out the action in practice. Likewise, in *Atzilut* above, the light comes from the whiteness in *Keter*, and the vessel is *Zeir Anpin* as a whole, through which the light is drawn and subsequently revealed in the worlds.

וְדֶרֶךְ וּמַעֲבַר הַהַמְשָׁכָה הוּא עַל יְדֵי פְּנִימִיּוּת הַכֵּלִים וּמוֹחוֹתֵיהֶן

The path and passage of the flow of the light of *Ein Sof* into the external dimension of the vessels **is through the internal aspect of the vessels and their intellects,**

THE EXTERNAL DIMENSION OF THE VESSELS

☞ The author of the *Tanya* is careful to state that the flow of light that results from a mitzva act goes to the external aspect of the vessels. Every vessel, on both the spiritual and physical planes, has internal and external dimensions, an outside and an inside. Contrary to what some think, a vessel is not an inert receptacle that only reveals the light as it is. The vessel also has its own essence, its own will, intellect, and character, so to speak, through which it expresses the light.

The vessel is like the body, which defines and directs the manifestations of the soul. It is like the letters, like words and language, that determine to a great extent how the meaning of what one is saying will be revealed and even what that meaning will actually be. Even the simplest devices have an influence on what is produced through them. Anyone who is involved in creative activity in any field is aware that the tools and materials they work with have a substantial effect on the nature of the final product and even its contents. This means that the vessel itself is like a distinct structure that has an intellect and attributes of its own (see *Or HaTorah*, Ex., vol. 3, p. 940). In general terms, the internal aspect of a vessel is the manner in which the vessel receives the light, while its external aspect is manner by which it activates and transmits the light.

Just as nothing flows directly from the innermost part of the soul to deed, but rather there is a complex path from will to action, so too the flow of the divine light to the exterior of the vessels in *Atzilut* is first channeled through the interior aspect of the vessels, which are the *moḥin*, the intellect or cognitive *sefirot*, within them. The *moḥin*, the intellect, is always the initial stage that brings about the activation of the emotive attributes, which then translates into external action. ☞

שֶׁהֵן דְּחִילוּ וּרְחִימוּ שִׂכְלִיִּים אוֹ טִבְעִיִּים   which are cognitive or innate fear and love of God,

The internal dimension of the vessels, and the internal dimension of the emotive attributes in the soul of man, through which one fulfills the mitzvot and has the proper intentions are "cognitive or innate fear and love [of God]." The internal faculty within a person that spurs him to fulfill the mitzvot is the love or fear of God.[24] Cognitive love and fear are related to a person's understanding and awareness: It is this understanding and awareness that evoke the love and fear. Innate love and fear, by contrast, are found latent in the soul and need only to be discovered. ☞

THE FULFILLMENT OF MITZVOT ABOVE AND BELOW

☞ The author of the *Tanya* appears to be describing two parallel systems in which the mitzvot operate, one below and the other above. Below, man fulfills the mitzvot, studies Torah, has the proper intention, and performs deeds. Meanwhile, above, in *Atzilut*, the mitzva rectifies and renders fit the vessels in *Atzilut* that correspond to the vessels with which the mitzva was performed below and draws into them an increase of the light of *Ein Sof* from high above in order to transmit it to the worlds below it.

If one takes a look, however, one will re-alize that there are not two separate systems here but a single system. When we fulfill the mitzvot in this physical world below, our minds and intentions should be that we are *Zeir Anpin*, that the soul correspondingly performs the mitzva in the spiritual world, effecting the vessels of *Zeir Anpin*. When a person has this in mind, when he identifies with the embodiment of *Zeir Anpin*, then whatever he does, he does together with *Zeir Anpin*: It is *Zeir Anpin* that is saying his words, *Zeir Anpin* that is performing his actions.

24. See *Likkutei Amarim*, chap. 4, and the introduction to *Sha'ar HaYiḥud VeHa'emuna*, where it is explained that love is the root of the positive commandments and fear is the root of the prohibitions.

שֶׁהֵן בְּחִינַת מוֹחִין דְּקַטְנוּת   and these are in a state of constricted
וְגַדְלוּת   or expanded consciousness in *Atzilut*
on high.

In the world of *Atzilut*, which is the realm closest to God and most defined by divinity, the internal aspect of the *sefirot*, of the attributes, by virtue of which the mitzvot operate in the world, constitute the *moḥin*, or intellect. The *moḥin* are the internal aspect of the attributes, since they activate the emotive attributes. Furthermore, corresponding to the cognitive and innate love and fear of God, there are two levels of *moḥin*: expanded or developed consciousness and constricted or undeveloped consciousness, or more literally the "small" intellect or "large" intellect. The difference between them is not in the depth or scope of the knowledge or awareness that they contain, but rather in the place that they occupy in the faculties of the soul.

For the sake of illustration, a child has a constricted consciousness, because his mind is dominated by his emotions and passions. It is constricted, or immature, because it is limited and serves the lowly faculties and facets of the soul.

An expanded consciousness is more evident in those who are mature in all respects, for whom the intellect is not influenced by the

TWO TYPES OF FEAR AND LOVE

☞   There are two fundamental levels of love and fear of God. One is love and fear that are engendered upon the contemplation and awareness of God's greatness, goodness, and kindness, in accordance with what can be observed in the worlds and in ourselves. The deeper and more intense this awareness, and the more convinced one becomes that this is the reality, the more he will feel love and fear for God. This is what the author of the *Tanya* terms cognitive fear and love.

The other is innate love and fear, which are not evoked through contemplation, but rather are intrinsic to the nature of every Jew, just as every person is born with a certain nature that he received, not through education, but is innate to him at the root of his soul and is inherited from his ancestors. Within the nature of every Jew's soul, there is an infinite love of God, and when it is uncovered, it conquers and consumes every other faculty in the soul. Granted, this love, like the divine soul itself, is concealed in this world, within the body and the animal soul, and man's task is to discover and direct it. But even when it is revealed, it is still innate love, which is not generated through the contemplation of the intellect, but already exists within the soul.

emotions. Such a person will think in a certain manner, not because he desires it, but rather he will desire something because that is how he thinks, because that is how he views reality with his intellect. An intellect of this kind is an expanded consciousness, a consciousness that is not limited or serves other purposes. When this intellect has an influence on the emotive attributes, it creates what is called "cognitive love and fear."

An expanded consciousness is thus consciousness itself, the *mohin* themselves, which engender cognitive love and fear. It consists of the cognitive attributes that are employed in the fulfillment of mitzvot. By contrast, a constricted consciousness are the *mohin*, the part of the intellect, that are brought to a state of awareness through the emotive attributes. This consciousness is contained within the attributes, since they require it in order to interpret the attributes and unveil them in the soul.

וְלָזֶה בִּיקֵשׁ מֹשֶׁה רַבֵּינוּ עָלָיו **It is for this** reason that **Moses, our**
הַשָּׁלוֹם מְאֹד לְקַיֵּים הַמִּצְוֹת **teacher, may he rest in peace, fer-**
מַעֲשִׂיּוֹת הַתְּלוּיוֹת בָּאָרֶץ **vently sought to fulfill the action-re-**
lated mitzvot that are dependent on
the Land of Israel,

God decreed that Moses would not be permitted to step foot in the Land of Israel, but he refused to give up and repeatedly implored God to allow him to enter the land. As emphasized here, he "fervently" pled with God to enter the land. The author of the *Tanya* employs the word *me'od* here, a word that connotes that which is limitless. When someone desires something "*me'od*," very much, he is prepared to pay any price, to give everything he has, to attain that which he seeks, because everything he possesses is worthless to him in comparison to the thing he desires.

For Moses, everything he had, his Torah knowledge, his intellectual attainments, his lofty level of prophecy, was nothing compared to entering the land. As the author of the *Tanya* explains here, the reason Moses wanted to enter the Land of Israel was in order to fulfill the commandments that could only be fulfilled there.[25]

---

25. See *Sota* 14a; see also *Torah Or* 46b, which states that the mitzvot that must

שֶׁהֵן תַּכְלִית הַהִשְׁתַּלְשְׁלוּת **since they are the purpose of the chain of progression**

The action-related mitzvot that are fulfilled in the Land of Israel are the purpose and goal of the chain of progression through which the divine light descends to the physical world. This is not self-evident. The question of where the purpose lies, whether above or below, on the spiritual or physical plane, is at the center of all theology. It was none other than Moses, whose spirit was loftier than anyone else, who determined that the purpose of the entire chain of progression is down here below.

Why is this so? What is the benefit provided by the practical service of God in the lower realm?

לְהַמְשִׁיךְ אוֹר אֵין סוֹף בָּרוּךְ הוּא לְבָרֵר הַכֵּלִים דִּזְעֵיר אַנְפִּין דִּבְרִיאָה יְצִירָה עֲשִׂיָּה, שֶׁבָּהֶן הֵן הָרְפָ"ח נִיצוֹצִין, עַל יְדֵי תּוֹרָה וּמִצְוֹת מַעֲשִׂיּוֹת שֶׁבִּבְרִיאָה יְצִירָה עֲשִׂיָּה דַּוְקָא

that draws forth the light of _Ein Sof_, blessed be He, to refine the vessels of _Zeir Anpin_ of _Beria, Yetzira_, and _Asiya_, in which there are the 288 sparks, through Torah study and action-related mitzvot, which are carried out specifically in _Beria, Yetzira_, and _Asiya_.

The advantage to fulfilling the Torah in the physical land is that the vessels of the worlds of _Beria, Yetzira_, and _Asiya_, in which the shattering of the vessels occurred, are thereby refined, and the 288 sparks of holiness that fell into them are elevated. ☞

THE PURPOSE OF THE CHAIN OF PROGRESSION

☞ Spiritual work on its own has an effect only in the higher worlds above. This entails contemplation of matters of wisdom and one's feelings, even about the significance of one's deeds, so that one senses the divine pleasure they might engender. One could understand why a person who is on such a lofty plane might not want to leave it. But someone on that level merely thinks about these matters, but he does not perform them himself and in fact does not really do anything at all. Everything stays where it is, the forces of the higher worlds remain in the higher worlds above and the inhabitants of the lower worlds remain below. There is no trajec-

be fulfilled in the land amount to almost four-fifths of all the mitzvot. See also _Likkutei Torah_, Num. 36c, 43d.

But the main significance of this descent is the rectification of the vessels and the elevation of the 288 sparks, as explained above. This rises above everything that exists, beyond all the worlds and even all the lights. The world of chaos was the initial attempt to reveal the light of *Ein Sof*, as it were, to bring the light of *Ein Sof* into the vessels. It would seem that this attempt was unsuccessful, because the vessels were shattered and the light of *Ein Sof*, instead of being revealed, was merely scattered and concealed in the broken vessels. By refining the sparks that fell from the world of chaos, which we achieve mainly through Torah study and the action-related mitzvot, it becomes clear that there is a rectification and a positive outcome to this process, a complete nullification of the vessel and its limitations, so that it can contain and reveal the actual light of *Ein Sof*. This is the purpose of the entire chain of progression that draws down the light, that brings about the revelation of the supernal delight itself in the actualization of the desire of the Divine to have an abode in the lower realm.

<table>
<tr><td>4 Kislev</td><td>וְהִנֵּה לְקִיּוּם מִצְוָה שֶׁאִי אֶפְשָׁר</td><td>**To fulfill a mitzva that cannot be per-**</td></tr>
<tr><td>3 Kislev
(leap year)</td><td>לַעֲשׂוֹת עַל יְדֵי אֲחֵרִים מְבַטְּלִין</td><td>**formed by others, we forgo Torah**</td></tr>
<tr><td></td><td>תַּלְמוּד תּוֹרָה</td><td>**study,**</td></tr>
</table>

This statement is the key to understanding the relationship between Torah study and the fulfillment of mitzvot.[26] It is a complex relationship.

tory of ascent or descent, not interaction between the spiritual realm above and the material world below.

It is only when a person actually does something, when he leaves the sphere of his thoughts and feelings and begins to interact with the reality that is outside and beyond him, to consider practical questions and engage in genuine action, that he brings about an awakening above, causing the flow of divine light to be drawn down

to the lower worlds whereupon something happens: The universe begins to stir, the inhabitants above descend while the inhabitants of the lower worlds rise.

This is why it was Moses of all people, with his ability to see further than anyone else, to perceive even what lay beyond his world, who could also discern the immense difference that the practical mitzvot could make and greatly desire it.

26. See *Mo'ed Katan* 9b; Jerusalem Talmud, *Pesaḥim* 3:7, *Ḥagiga* 1:7; *Shulḥan Arukh HaRav, Hilkhot Talmud Torah* 4:6.

On the one hand, it is based on the assumption that Torah study is equal to all mitzvot, a virtue attributed to Torah study that does not apply to the action-related mitzvot. On the other hand, if a person is presented with the opportunity to perform a mitzva and there is no one else available to perform it, the mitzva takes precedence even over Torah study. There is an assumption here that the mitzvot have greater value than everything else.

The conflict between these two extremes occurs when a mitzva cannot be done by others. It is impossible to both study Torah and fulfill the mitzva, and one must choose between the two. The ruling in that case is that the mitzva takes precedence. This indicates that the divine revelation from above that results from the fulfillment of a mitzva is always superior and more important, and any spiritual revelations that ascend from below must be negated in its favor. ☞

וַאֲפִילוּ מַעֲשֵׂה מֶרְכָּבָה וְכָל שֶׁכֵּן תְּפִלָּה שֶׁהִיא בְּחִינַת מוֹחִין וּדְחִילוּ וּרְחִימוּ שִׂכְלִיִּים וְהַטַּעַם כַּנִּזְכָּר לְעֵיל

even the study of **the workings of the** divine **chariot, and all the more so prayer, which is an expression of the intellect and cognitive fear and love** of God, **for the reason stated above.**

STUDY VERSUS ACTION

☞ Study and action are two extremes: There is, on the one hand, the ascension of man through Torah study, prayer, love, fear, and the knowledge of God. On the other hand, the performance of a mitzva, which brings about a revelation from above, is actually superior, more authentic and pure, the less the person's intellect is involved, the less one understands and feels, the less the faculties of his soul are engaged.

As opposed to Torah study, the mind does not necessarily have to be engaged during the performance of a mitzva. The act can be fulfilled even when one does not take into account one's understanding. That a certain mitzva can be performed by others means that there is no internal connection between this mitzva and the one who performs it. It has to be done, and it is not important who does it or with what attitude and intention. By contrast, when a certain mitzva cannot be performed by others, there is a profound, deep connection between this particular mitzva and the person who carries it out. This is a deeper bond than one of love or fear, a connection that touches on the essence of that individual.

It can therefore be said that the two extremes in the service of God, study and action, join together, in the most personal place, where they cannot be separated. Like Torah study, here is a mitzva act that

One forgoes even the study of the esoteric teachings of the Torah, such as the study of the workings of the divine chariot that appeared in the prophet Ezekiel's vision, the study of the Divine as it is divested from the materiality of our world and is manifest in the higher, spiritual realms.

Even more so one forgoes prayer. The main feature of prayer is the ascension of man, through contemplation of God's greatness and the development of cognitive love and fear of God. The prayers, accompanied by the love and fear of God, rise to the worlds of the spirit and the source of souls. They have nothing to do with the physical actions characterized by the performance of mitzvot, which is, as stated above, the entire purpose of the chain of progression through which the light of *Ein Sof* is drawn down to this world. Certainly, then, prayer, as well as Torah study, even when the study leads to practice, does not override a mitzva that cannot be fulfilled by others.

The author of the *Tanya* is not referring here to the quality of prayer in elevating the sparks through love and fear, but to the refinement itself, the extraction of the sparks from *kelippa* before they can be elevated, which is achieved specifically through action. ☞

וְעוֹד זֹאת, שֶׁבֶּאֱמֶת מְאֹד גְּדָלָה וְגָבְהָה מַעֲלַת הַמִּצְוֹת מַעֲשִׂיּוֹת וְכֵן לִימוּדָם, עַל מַעֲלַת הַמּוֹחִין שֶׁהֵן דְּחִילוּ וּרְחִימוּ שִׂכְלִיִּים

In addition, the virtue of the action-related mitzvot, as well as their study, is truly greater and loftier than the virtue of the intellect, which evokes cognitive fear and love of God,

requires this particular person, with his particular faculties and understanding .In this place. the deed and the intent of the one performing the mitzva prevails over every other aspect of divine service, and therefore it overrides Torah study, including even the study of the esoteric, mystical aspects of the Torah.

THE INTELLECT AND COGNITIVE LOVE AND FEAR

☞ The author of the *Tanya* states that prayer is an expression of the intellect and of cognitive love and fear of God, that which develops through the contemplation of God's greatness. It is not solely an expression of the intellect, because the intellect alone does not lead to an ascent. It may involve turning one's gaze upward, but the individual himself does not rise. It is only when the intellect engenders the emotive attributes, when it evokes love and fear of God, that the person himself ascends. That is when he is transformed, becoming more refined and lofty in his own right.

The study of action-related mitzvot entails the study of their *halakhot* in all their details: how one should fulfill the mitzvot in practice and how one should prepare himself for their performance. Such a mitzva takes precedence, not only because it is the purpose and will of God, but because the virtue of the action-related mitzvot transcends spiritual work, the contemplations of the intellect that leads to love and fear of God. This virtue is expressed in the connection with the Divine that a person attains through the mitzva act. It is not wonder that the word *mitzva* is derived from the term *tzavta*, which connotes a bond, a spiritual union. This is superior to any spiritual connection brought about through the intellectual understanding and sense of the Divine. ☞

כִּי הֲגַם דִּכְתִיב: "וּלְדָבְקָה בּוֹ" עַל יְדֵי מִדּוֹתָיו (דברים יא, כב) **for although it is written, "And to cleave to Him"** (Deut. 11:22), **by emulating His attributes,**

The Rabbis explain that this verse, "And to cleave to Him," means that we cleave to God by attaching ourselves to God's attributes and emulating them.[27] These divine attributes, the *sefirot* in *Atzilut*, are united with God through a wondrous unification that we cannot comprehend. As the *Tikkunei Zohar* states, "He and His attributes are one."[28] He, the light, and the vessels, or *sefirot*, are all one in the world of *Atzilut*. When a person conducts himself in accordance with those attributes, to the best of his ability, he cleaves to God Himself in a unique and

THE VIRTUE OF DEED VERSUS THE INTELLECT

☞ True virtue and what we perceive as a virtue are not the same thing. People in general, and in a sense every individual wherever he may be, have certain perspectives with regard to the higher worlds and this world below. Our unique composition of soul within body imparts to us the conception that body and materiality belong to the realm below, whereas all things related to the spirit belong to the realms above. We project this perception beyond our own selves into spheres of which we have no direct perception. A chasm is formed between what we feel, between what seems to be lofty, and what is actually lofty. The author of the *Tanya* will challenge these perceptions as he explains why a mitzva performed in this material world, with physical objects, is superior to the spiritual work of the intellect.

27. See, e.g., *Sota* 14a; *Shabbat* 133b.
28. *Tikkunei Zohar*, Introduction 3b; see also *Iggeret HaKodesh*, epistle 15.

more wonderful unification than can be imagined. Yet this unification would appear to occur only on the spiritual plane, on the level of God's attributes, and not in the realm of action. ☞

מִכָּל מָקוֹם אֵינֶנּוּ דָבֵק אֲפִילוּ בְּמִדּוֹת הָעֶלְיוֹנוֹת, אֶלָּא בִּמְצִיאוּתָן וְלֹא בְּמַהוּתָן even in the case of the supernal attributes one nevertheless cleaves only to the external manifestation of their existence and not their essence,

When a person cleaves to God's attributes by emulating them, he is certainly not cleaving to God Himself, and he is not even cleaving to His attributes. God's attributes are the most transcendent attributes of the world of *Atzilut*, with which God is unified. This means that His revelation within them is total, and nothing else is manifest within them but Him and Him alone. These attributes are as infinite as God Himself, and they differ in essence from anything we can fathom. Consequently, even when we conduct ourselves as much as we can to be like God, in our deeds and emotions, we are merely outwardly imitating these attributes.

In the words of the author of the *Tanya*, we are cleaving only to "[the external manifestation of] their existence and not to their essence." Existence, in contrast to essence, is an external parameter. It is a garment, a particular expression, color, or sound – something that says, "This is here." But we cannot touch the essence of the supernal

CLEAVING TO GOD'S ATTRIBUTES

☞ The explicit command to cleave to God would seem impossible. It is not only that this reality cannot apprehend God at all, but even if we succeeded somehow in getting closer to God and actually cleaving to Him, we would be consumed and any trace of our existence would be wiped out. God is infinite. He transcends all the parameters that define our existence. An unmediated encounter with Him, cleaving to Him, would break through those boundaries, and we would not be left with any existence or reality of our own.

Regarding this, the Sages cite the verse

"For the Lord your God is a consuming fire" (Deut. 4:24). In view of this, the only possible way to cleave to Him is through His attributes.

God's attributes are, by definition, measured and defined in light of the attributes of the world and our souls. We know a little about these attributes from the Torah: He is merciful and compassionate, He performs acts of kindness, He visits the sick, and more, and anyone can follow this path in accordance his own attributes and in his particular sphere.

attributes, what they actually are, no matter how much we work on ourselves and no matter how high we ascend in spiritual terms. The essence even of the supernal attributes is divine, which is completely distinct from the created essence of which we are a part.

וּכְמוֹ שֶׁכָּתוּב: "וְאָנֹכִי עָפָר וָאֵפֶר" (בראשית יח, כז) as it is written, "And I am dust and ashes" (Gen. 18:27).

This was the declaration of our forefather Abraham, who was a vehicle for the attribute of *Ḥesed* of *Atzilut*. Through his devotion and self-abnegation, he epitomized the divine attribute of *Ḥesed* in the most perfect form. His life in this world was nothing other than an expression of this attribute, yet he declared, "And I am dust and ashes."[29] I and my attribute of *Ḥesed* are like dust and ashes in relation to the supernal attribute of *Ḥesed*.

Ash is what remains of a tree after it has been burned. Just as only the element of earth remains from all the four elements of which it was composed (fire, earth, water, air), and just as the appearance and structure of the tree and its fruits has been reduced to mere ashes, which does not at all resemble the tree from which it came, so too only Abraham's attribute of *Ḥesed* remained from the supernal attribute of *Ḥesed* in *Atzilut*. Compared to that lofty divine attribute, his *Ḥesed* was mere ash and dust.

In the same sense, one's emulation of God's attributes is at best something external, similar to Abraham's emulation of divine *Ḥesed*. There is an awareness that the attribute exists, but otherwise it remains far removed from the essence of the attribute itself to an immeasurable degree.

וְכָל שֶׁכֵּן בְּאוֹר אֵין סוֹף בָּרוּךְ הוּא דְלֵית מַחֲשָׁבָה תְּפִיסָא בֵיהּ בְּאוֹרוֹ וְהִתְפַּשְׁטוּת הַחַיּוּת מִמֶּנּוּ יִתְבָּרֵךְ, כִּי אִם בִּמְצִיאוּתוֹ, שֶׁהוּא שֶׁמְּחַיֶּה אֶת כּוּלָם, וְלֹא בְּמַהוּתוֹ All the more so with regard to the light of *Ein Sof*, blessed be He, since no thought can apprehend His light or the emanation of the life force that is drawn forth from Him, but one can apprehend only His existence, that He gives life to all, and not His essence.

---

29. *Iggeret HaKodesh*, epistle 15.

If we are unable to cleave to His attributes, all the more so we cannot cleave to God Himself. We cannot even apprehend His light or the life force that He issues forth. It is not just that we cannot contemplate it in our thoughts, but our minds do not have the capacity to contain such thoughts. Our thoughts and capacity for apprehension relate to this world. It is possible that lofty individuals may have some perception of the spiritual worlds, but the human capacity to apprehend is still confined to the world that we understand, in which we are situated. Our minds cannot venture beyond it.

When discussing an understanding of the Divine, this refers only to the apprehension of the force and revelation of the Divine that gives life to the world or to the part of the world that we can apprehend, the present existence and the aspects of the world that we can grasp, but not its essence, which is beyond creation as we know it. ☞

אֲפִילוּ לָעֶלְיוֹנִים   This is the case **even for the supernal beings,**

The supernal angels that inhabit the higher worlds also have no concept of God's essence but apprehend only His existence within their world. The supernal beings differ from the lower ones only in their level of divine revelation. The Divine is completely concealed in our world, because this world reveals only itself and does not inform us of anything beyond it, while in the higher worlds the Divine is openly revealed. It is as though the higher world proclaims, "There is a God that brings me into existence, who sustains me, and acts through me." Yet even this revelation is no more than the discovery of the reality that there

THE MEANING OF ESSENCE

☞ Apprehending the essence of a thing means apprehending it on a deep, internal level. In other words, it is not how the thing is revealed, how and what it does and says, but what it is in truth.

That said, there are various degrees of interiority. Thought is internal compared to speech, because speech is what one hears when another person speaks whereas thought is contained within one's mind, confined to what one thinks. There is also an internal aspect of thought: what one feels and understands before it is wrapped in thought. Even deeper and more internal, there is what the thing is itself, its very essence.

is a Creator of the world, but it says nothing about the essence of the Creator Himself.

כְּמוֹ שֶׁכָּתוּב: "קָדוֹשׁ קָדוֹשׁ קָדוֹשׁ   as it is written, "Holy, holy, holy is
ה' צְבָאוֹת כו'" (ישעיה ו, ג)   the Lord of hosts..." (Isa. 6:3),

The supernal angels, who are the seraphim in the world of *Beria*, declare, "Holy, holy, holy is the Lord of hosts."[30] "Holy" connotes that which is separate. When an angel says "holy" it means that he apprehends that there is something separate from him. He sees the evidence and even senses a presence. But the essence of it is unfathomable. The greatness of this supernal angel is in his apprehension of what might be called "the existence of the essence," which is a deeper perception than understanding the reality of His existence alone. One who apprehends God's existence alone might think that with a little more effort and thought he can grasp His essence. But one who apprehends the existence of His essence knows with certainty that he will never be able to apprehend God's essence itself, and he therefore declares, "Holy."

The threefold proclamation of "holy" indicates that this lofty being understands that there is an essence that is separate and foreign to his understanding, and beyond that there is an essence that is separate and distinct from that essence, and beyond that, there is yet another essence that is separate from that separated essence. He recites "holy" three times but no more, because the angel relates only to the parameters of the worlds, and in general there are three levels of created worlds: *Beria, Yetzira,* and *Asiya.*[31]

לְבַד עֲלוּלִים הַנֶּאֱצָלִים, מַשִּׂיגִים   apart from the effects that emanate
כָּל אֶחָד בְּעִילָתוֹ   from the world of *Atzilut,* **each of which apprehend its cause,**

The *sefirot* and the *partzufim* of the world of *Atzilut* are "effects" that issue from one another and are clothed in one another in a chain of causes and effects. They do not apprehend the divine essence itself, but rather the essence of the *sefirot* in *Atzilut,* which are unified with the

---

30. See *Ḥullin* 91a.
31. See *Torah Or* 87a, 36b; *Likkutei Torah,* Num. 28d.

Divine, of which they are the effect. The essential connection between cause and effect means that the effect grasps the essence of its cause. This is the greatest extent of its apprehension. It cannot comprehend anything beyond that.[32]

כְּפִי הַסֵּדֶר שֶׁבְּעֵץ חַיִּים בְּהִתְלַבְּשׁוּת הַפַּרְצוּפִים   in accordance with the order as described in *Etz Ḥayyim* regarding the enclothing of the *partzufim*.

It is explained in *Etz Ḥayyim* that the *partzufim* of *Atzilut*, which are comprised of arrays of *sefirot*, are enclothed in one another. They do not merely converse with each other, so to speak, as we do through speech, but they are actually enclothed within each other, essence within essence. Speech constitutes an external relationship in which the listener does not apprehend the essence of the speaker himself, but only his speech. This is like the transition between *Atzilut* and *Beria*, where there is apprehension only of its existence but not its essence. By contrast, the enclothing of the *partzufim* of *Atzilut* within one another, where the exteriority of the higher *partzuf*, which stems from its very essence, is enclothed in the interiority of the lower one, where the lower *sefirot* of the upper *partzuf* are enclothed in the lower *partzuf*, entails an apprehension of essence, not just of existence. It is an enclothing of essence within essence.

This can be clarified with an analogy that relates to human relationships: If there is a deep bond between two people, where they both love the same thing, one does not need to explain anything to the other or issue commands to him, because they share a deep affinity. The second person grasps not only what the first one divulges to him, but even what the other feels. This is apprehension of the essence and interiority of one entity to another.

אֲבָל לֹא בַּנִּבְרָאִים אֲפִילוּ בִּנְשָׁמוֹת דַּאֲצִילוּת   But this is not the case for created beings, even for the souls of *Atzilut*,

---

32. See also *Iggeret HaKodesh*, epistle 20.

A direct cause-and-effect relationship exists among the levels within the world of *Atzilut* alone. This is not the case for the transition from the world of *Atzilut* to the created worlds below it. There is a gap, a partition, through which the essence of *Atzilut* does not pass. This barrier conceals the essence of *Atzilut* and conveys to the created beings a different light, one that which merely attests to the existence of the levels of *Atzilut* there.

"The souls of *Atzilut*" refers to the souls of the world of *Atzilut*, which cannot grasp the essence of the *partzufim* of *Atzilut* that are unified with the Divine. There is a difference between the *sefirot* of *Atzilut*, which are actual divinity, and the world in which they exist, reveal themselves, and operate.[33] The world of *Atzilut*, although purer and loftier than all the other worlds, is not part of the actual essence of the *sefirot*. The same is true of its inhabitants. In *Atzilut* there are also supernal angels and souls that emanated from the Divine. There is no distinct substance to them because they are nullified in the face of the Divine and serve as a vehicle for the Divine, yet even so they are not like the *sefirot* themselves, which are totally unified with the Divine. Rather, they belong to the boundary and scope of the world of *Atzilut*, which has no apprehension of the divine essence in the *sefirot* and the divine forces themselves. ☞

THE SOULS OF *ATZILUT*

☞ The souls of *Atzilut* do not exist only in the world of *Atzilut*. Even in our world there are souls of *Atzilut*. In fact, in a certain sense all souls (or at least the souls of Jews) are rooted in *Atzilut* before they descend and enclothe themselves in the body and the animal soul.

Moreover, there are a minority of souls who even in this world remember that they are souls of *Atzilut*. For most souls, their root in *Atzilut* is a general and vague status: There is a generality up high of which my reality below is a distant descendant. It is an important piece of knowledge, but it is not clearly evident. There is only a dim awareness of the soul's source. By contrast, those souls defined as "souls of *Atzilut*" are the exact same souls that they were in *Atzilut*. The same self, that specific soul itself, is now located below. This is not merely the general categorization of some distant source, but the actual existence of these souls in the physical body.

These people stand out for their sensi-

---

33. See *Iggeret HaKodesh*, epistle 20.

כְּמוֹ שֶׁכָּתוּב בְּמֹשֶׁה רַבֵּינוּ עָלָיו
הַשָּׁלוֹם, "וְרָאִיתָ אֶת אֲחוֹרָי כו'"
(שמות לג, כג)

as it is written regarding Moses, our teacher, may he rest in peace, "And you will see My back ..." (Ex. 33:23).

Moses's soul, for instance, was a soul of *Atzilut*, and he attained a greater degree of holiness than any other man. The verse that the author of the *Tanya* quotes here tells us how God told Moses, "And you will see My back, but My face will not be seen." Not even Moses, with his affinity for holiness, was able to apprehend the essence of God, the "face," but only His existence, the "back."

Moses's apprehension of the Divine was one of prophecy,[34] which entailed the divestment of materiality, and therefore his perception was not limited by the physical world and the body in which he was enclothed in this world. Yet still he could see only "My back." This restriction is a fundamental limitation of the divine revelation in the soul, even a soul of *Atzilut*, and all the more so the soul of some other person, who cannot in any way or degree grasp the essence of God, but only the back side, which constitutes only an awareness of divine existence.

In light of this, man's service through the faculties of his intellect and his cognitive love and fear, is limited. Although this is the loftiest service a man can perform, within the soul that transcends the body

tivity and affinity for holiness. Just as there are people in other fields who have a special talent – for music, for writing, for certain modes of thought – so that they do not have to work as hard as others in these fields, but rather they comprehend the relevant concepts and methods directly and immediately, these souls have an affinity and direct access to the realm of holiness.

An ordinary person may study matters of holiness from books or teachers, learning about the mitzvot, the Sabbath, proph-

ecy. He comes to understand what to do and what to say, but he cannot perceive the meaning and significance of Sabbath itself. It is related that as a child the Rebbe of Ruzhin once studied the *halakhot* of one who made a mistake in his calculations and did not know which day of the week it was. He said that he did not understand what the problem was: That person should simply look at the heavens and see whether it was the Sabbath (Rabbi Hayyim Mordekhai Perlow, *Likkutei Sippurim*, p. 370).

---

34. See *Iggeret HaKodesh*, epistle 19.

and the intellect, which comprise the loftiest and most abstract faculties of the soul, there is a limitation that cannot be traversed. The human soul, however lofty it may be, is a created and limited being, and no matter what it does, it is unable, on account of its own limitations, to achieve an essential connection with the Divine.

מַה שֶׁאֵין כֵּן מַעֲשֵׂה הַמִּצְוֹת, "מַעֲשֵׂה אֱלֹקִים הֵמָּה" הֵנָּה	**This is not the case** with regard to **the performance of the mitzvot, which are the work of God.**	5 Kislev 4 Kislev (leap year)

In contrast to cognitive love and fear, which are the work of man, the outcome of his intellect's contemplation and the application of his soul's faculties, the mitzvot are "the work of God."[35] What man cannot achieve from below, God can effect from above. In His infinitude, He bridges the infinite gap between the Divine and the worlds so that the divine essence is revealed there.

To illustrate: Everything that God created in His world is the work of God compared to what man achieves and creates. A person can analyze the nature of a flower, study botany and molecular biology and everything that people have written and could write about it, and yet all this will not constitute the flower itself. A single flower, like one drop in the ocean, incorporates the existence of the entire universe. Just as this flower encompasses all of nature and its laws infinitely more than anything that can be written about it, so a small mitzva act encompasses the divine essence, even if it is in a material and limited form, more than all the human conceptions and experiences can possibly encompass. ☞

THE WORK OF GOD

☞ While it is true that a person performs the mitzva, the mitzva he performs is not his work but the work of God and God's will. Here is the key difference: In contrast to all the lofty attainments that a person can achieve, the contemplation of the in- tellect and the fear and love for which a person toiled and which he developed in his soul, there are simple acts that man ex- ecutes below, not because he has investi- gated, understood, and desired them, but because it is God's will and the work of

---

35. Based on Ex. 32:16.

בְּדֶרֶךְ הִשְׁתַּלְשְׁלוּת מִכֵּלִים דַּאֲצִילוּת לִבְרִיאָה יְצִירָה עֲשִׂיָּה, מִמַּהוּתָן וְעַצְמוּתָן דְּחִיצוֹנִיּוּתָן

Within the chain of succession through which the mitzvot descend **from the vessels of** *Atzilut* **to** *Beria, Yetzira,* and *Asiya,* **from the essence and being of** those vessels' **external aspects,**

The descent of a mitzva from *Atzilut* to the worlds below it does not occur in the same manner as the creation of those worlds from nothingness. Rather, it comes about through a transmutation that passes along something of the essence of the thing itself, as explained above with regard to the *partzufim* of *Atzilut.* A mitzva in our world of *Asiya* is actually a transmutation of the vessels of *Atzilut,* a portion of *Atzilut* that has descended to this world and is now situated below, even if it is not perceived and felt. ☞

כְּמוֹ עַל דֶּרֶךְ מָשָׁל אֶתְרוֹג וּמִינָיו הִלְבִּישׁ בָּהֶן הַקָּדוֹשׁ בָּרוּךְ הוּא מִמַּהוּתָן וְעַצְמוּתָן דַּחֲסָדִים [פְּנִימִית] [פְּנִימִים] דִּזְעֵיר אַנְפִּין

such as, for example, an *etrog* **and its species, the Holy One, blessed be He, enclothed within them** something of **the [inner] nature and essence of the** *ḥasadim,* the spiritual forces of giving, **of** *Zeir Anpin,*

God. In view of this, it is God Himself, as it were, who is actually performing the mitzva that the person carries out.

But isn't it true that everything that occurs in the world are really the work of God? The difference is that in this world the works of God are concealed, and they are enclothed, one layer after another, through the chain of progression. At most

they reveal the existence of God who created the world. By contrast, a mitzva act is a direct act of God. It is precisely His will, wisdom, and work, where the Divine penetrates this world in the same sense as it does in *Atzilut,* with complete transparency between the world and the essence and being of God (see also *Likkutei Amarim,* chap. 53).

THE EXTERNAL ASPECTS OF THE VESSELS

☞ The descent of the mitzva from *Atzilut* involves only the external aspect of the essence of *Atzilut.* This exterior is the part and facet that projects outward. The

more external it is, the more it relates to the outside and is distant from its interior, the more hidden is its connection to the interior. And yet, although it is not

It is a mitzva to take the four species, the *etrog, lulav*, myrtle branch, and willow branch, on the festival of Sukkot and recite a blessing over them. The *etrog* and its species are physical produce that belong to this material world, and yet "the Holy One, blessed be He, enclothed within them [something] of the [inner] nature and essence of the *ḥasadim* of *Zeir Anpin*."

As explained above, the *ḥasadim* and *gevurot*, the forces of restraint, are the inner lights, or life force, that are passed down from high above within the *sefirot* and vessels of *Zeir Anpin* of *Atzilut*. Just as these lights, which were originally above even *Atzilut*, in the realm called the "whiteness" of *Keter*, were enclothed in the *sefirot* of *Atzilut*, they likewise enclothed themselves in this world through the materials and actions with which the mitzva is performed.

וְהַיְינוּ מִבְּחִינַת חִיצוֹנִיּוּתָן,   **meaning from the external aspects** of the
כַּנּוֹדַע בְּכָל מִצְוֹת מַעֲשִׂיּוֹת   *ḥasadim*, **as is known with regard to all action-related mitzvot.**

Only the external aspects of these lights can be transferred from one world to another. What is transmitted from the internal aspects of the *ḥasadim* high above to this world occurs through the external aspects of the external aspects, all the way down to the physical *etrog* and its species. The essence and being of these lights, then, are not stuck in the

apparent, even if it is the most external aspect of its exterior, it is still the essence of the thing.

To illustrate with an analogy from the realm of the mundane, one can refer to a book's inner content, which is its internal aspect, expressing the essence of the book as it would be viewed by the person who wrote it. One can also focus on the plot of the story, its structure, characters, and setting. This is a more external aspect, which can be perceived by those who are further removed from the deeper contents. Finally, one can relate to the book as a simple object, a printed and bound paperback that costs a particular sum of money

and weighs a certain amount. These features of the book can be discussed by people who are greatly removed from it, who might even be completely illiterate. Yet even those who pick up the book in order to consider it in this manner are still holding the book itself, its essence and being.

The same applies to a mitzva. That which descends to this world is the external aspect of its most external aspects, the aspect of it that can relate to the materiality of this world and its concepts. Yet one who performs the mitzva properly is holding its essence and being as it exists above in *Atzilut*, wholly transparent to the divine will.

world of *Atzilut*, but have descended to this very world, to be enclothed in the material objects of the action-related mitzvot, objects such as the *etrog* and the other species. ☞

מַה שֶּׁאֵין כֵּן הָאָדָם, אֲפִילוּ יֵשׁ **This is not so with regard to** the appre-
לוֹ נְשָׁמָה דַּאֲצִילוּת hension of **man, even if he possesses a
soul of** *Atzilut*.

Though the service of cognitive love and fear through the contemplation of his intellect is very lofty, his apprehension is still limited and he still cannot perceive the essence and being of the Divine as it is enclothed in a mitzva act. This is the case even if his is a soul of *Atzilut*. There are certain individuals whose soul is not only rooted in *Atzilut*, but the soul itself, even while within a body in the world of *Asiya*, belongs to *Atzilut*. It possesses the same affinity and sense of the Divine as that which is found in *Atzilut*, a sense of Divine without any blurring or clouding. Although such a soul is rare and precious, and only a few people in all of history have possessed such a soul, it is still limited, and this limitation has nothing to do with the soul's particular level.

ENCLOTHING THE ESSENCE OF THE ḤASADIM

☞ This descent and enclothing is not an isolated process. Something that descends from the higher realms through the chain of progression and numerous constrictions from one world to the next becomes part of the world to which it descends and its essence. Neither the vessel nor the light maintains the same identity below as they had above. But in the case of a mitzva, God enclothed within it "something of the [inner] nature and essence of the aspects of the *ḥasadim* of *Zeir Anpin*," implying that this essence remains unchanged throughout its descent.

This can be compared to a person who builds a house. He purchases the raw materials and hires a foreman who brings in laborers to do the job. It is quite likely that the workers have no idea who the owner is or what he wants. The foreman and the architect, of course, may know a few more details. The more practical the ideas and plans become, and as they reach the worker who will build the house with the actual materials, the less the owner of the house and his will are recognizable in them. Yet ultimately it will be the owner of the house himself who will live in it, and when he does so, he will enter the actual material house, not the architect's plans.

The owner's entry into the physical house is like a mitzva, which is a "limb of the King": It is enclothed in the external aspect of the external aspects, in the very materials of this world, but God Himself is still enclothed in it.

מֵאַחַר שֶׁמְּלוּבֶּשֶׁת בַּגּוּף, לֹא
יוּכַל לִמְצֹא בְּנַפְשׁוֹ, וּלְהַשִּׂיג
מַהוּתָן וְעַצְמוּתָן שֶׁל פְּנִימִית
הַחֲסָדִים דִּזְעֵיר אַנְפִּין דַּאֲצִילוּת

Since it is enclothed in a body, he will not be able to discover and apprehend through his soul the essence and being of the internal aspects of the ḥasadim of Zeir Anpin of Atzilut

The body conceals. Just as it obscures the Divine in the world, it conceals the lofty essence of the soul that it contains.[36] Even though the soul itself is from the world of Atzilut, it will not be able to apprehend the divine essence because it is enclothed in a body, the back side of the back side of existence, and therefore it is no longer able to uncover the internal aspects of the ḥasadim, the forces of giving, in Atzilut.

(כִּי הָאֲצִילוּת הִיא בְּחִינַת 'חַיָּה'
בִּכְלָלוּת הָעוֹלָמוֹת אֲצִילוּת
בְּרִיאָה יְצִירָה עֲשִׂיָּה, שֶׁהִיא
בְּחִינַת מַקִּיף מִלְמַעְלָה וְאֵינָהּ
מִתְלַבֶּשֶׁת בִּכְלִי כְּלָל)

(for generally Atzilut represents the level of ḥaya among the worlds of Atzilut, Beria, Yetzira, and Asiya, which constitutes an encompassing from above and is not enclothed in any vessel at all).

The structures of the soul and the worlds parallel each other. Since they were made as counterparts that are meant to complete one another, each of them has everything that is within the other, whether in a hidden or revealed state, whether in a state of perfection or in a damaged form that requires rectification. Despite their differences, and though there are elements that are attributed only to the worlds whereas others relate only to the soul, the kabbalistic works invariably discuss them interchangeably, so that what is known about one is true of the other.

This is exactly what the author of the Tanya is implying here. The soul is said to contain five levels: nefesh, ruaḥ, neshama, ḥaya, and yeḥida. But there are only four worlds: Atzilut, Beria, Yetzira, and Asiya. The fifth realm is that of Keter, which transcends all the worlds. If we view them as counterparts, that means that Keter corresponds to the soul

---

36. See Iggeret HaKodesh, epistle 15, which states that even in the case of Abraham, who was a vehicle for the attribute of Ḥesed of Atzilut itself, his soul was enclothed in a body, which meant that as much as he epitomized Ḥesed, it still did not resemble the attribute of Ḥesed in Atzilut.

level of *yeḥida*, *ḥaya* to *Atzilut*, *neshama* to *Beria*, and so on. When the author of the *Tanya* says that "*Atzilut* represents the level of *ḥaya*," he is merging the concepts, indicating that what is known with respect to the soul is the same with regard to the worlds.

Not all of the soul's levels are enclothed in the body. These levels are too lofty to be placed in a vessel. They remain forever in a state of encompassment, ever present, as if hovering in the atmosphere, but not actually contained within the body. This is the case, not because no individual has enough intelligence to apprehend that level of his soul, but because this level cannot be apprehended through the human intellect, no matter how lofty the person's level.[37] There is then a division in the soul between the levels of *nefesh*, *ruaḥ*, and *neshama*, which are enclothed in the body, and the levels of *ḥaya*, and *yeḥida* that are not enclothed and remain in state of encompassment. These two levels of the soul cannot be apprehended or reached through the faculties of the intellect or the emotive attributes. By stating that *Atzilut* corresponds to the level of *ḥaya*, the author of the *Tanya* connects the concepts: The essence of *Atzilut* cannot be apprehended by the aspects of the soul that are enclothed in the body. Just as the level of *ḥaya* is not enclothed or apprehended by the body, so too *Atzilut* is not apprehended within the other worlds.

כִּי אִם מְצִיאוּתָן עַל יְדֵי דְּחִילוּ   **Rather,** he can apprehend only **their**
וּרְחִימוּ שִׂכְלִיִּים   **existence through cognitive fear and love** of God.

This is love and fear that a person attains with his intellect. The intellect of man is a created entity, whose tools and concepts are taken from creation. Such an intellect cannot apprehend the essence of the divine light in *Atzilut*, but only the fact of its existence. ☞

וּמַה שֶּׁכָּתוּב: "וְרָאִיתָ אֶת אֲחֹרָי"   **As for the verse "And you will see**
(שמות לג, כג), הוּא בְּדֶרֶךְ נְבוּאָה   **My back"** (Ex. 33:23), **it** will occur
דַּוְקָא   **specifically through prophecy**

---

37. In *Sha'ar HaYiḥud VeHa'emuna*, chap. 9, the author of the *Tanya* offers a metaphor to illustrate this: If a person were to try to feel wisdom with his hands, everyone would laugh at him.

On Mount Sinai, at the moment of the revelation and illumination of the divine will, Moses submitted one more request to God: "Please show me Your glory" (Ex. 33:18). God responded, "You will not be able to see My face.... You will see My back, but My face will not be seen" (Ex. 33:20, 23). "My back" is also a revelation of the divine essence, beyond what man can apprehend of reality with his intellect. Seeing in general, and certainly spiritual perception, involves the perception of essence. One does not merely hear about a thing, but he actually sees it. Yet this does not involve cognitive fear and love that a person attains through the contemplation of his intellect, but rather a revelation through prophecy. In contrast to the apprehension and understanding of the intellect, prophecy is akin to sight,[38] in the sense that one sees the essence of the thing itself, even if it is only its back side. ☞

COGNITIVE LOVE AND FEAR

☞ The author of the *Tanya* here is referring specifically to cognitive love and fear, as opposed to innate love and fear (see *Likkutei Amarim*, chap. 43; *Torah Or* 73a), since he is referring here to a person's service through his intellect rather than a mitzva act. This is divine service that one performs through love and fear that is evoked through contemplation, awareness, and knowledge, which awakens feelings of love and fear toward the object of one's reflections.

This is not the case with innate love and fear, or with the discovery of higher degrees of love and fear, which relate to that which cannot be fathomed by the intellect. Innate love and fear is not the result of a person's efforts but already exist within him, and they are not necessarily awakened through the person's divine service. This love and fear exist in a state somewhere between that which is internal and that which encompasses. These feelings are internal, but they are not truly internal because they do not relate to a concept that can be comprehended in one's mind, but they may also relate to that which cannot be apprehended, that which mainly encompasses the soul, and yet the soul is still connected to it, and this is what evokes this innate love and fear.

THE THIRTEEN ATTRIBUTES OF MERCY

☞ From a different perspective, what was revealed to Moses on that occasion were the thirteen supernal attributes of mercy. These attributes come from above, from the level of *Keter* and the encompassing light that is not enclothed or limited by any law or intellect. Therefore, they are attributes of mercy and forgiveness that are transcend the intellect and the laws of the world. The author of the *Tanya* states here that the revelation of these attributes is not achieved through the intellect or through cognitive fear and love, but only through prophecy.

---

38. See *Iggeret HaKodesh*, epistle 19.

שֶׁהוּא הִתְפַּשְׁטוּת הַגַּשְׁמִיּוּת, כְּמוֹ) (which entails the divestment
שֶׁכָּתוּב בְּרַעְיָא מְהֵימְנָא פָּרָשַׁת of physicality, as it is written in
(מִשְׁפָּטִים *Raya Meheimna, Parashat Mish-
patim*).

According to the *Zohar*, in a prophetic vision, the person sees directly
with the soul, not through his body or even a faculty of the mind. ☞

In any case, in the context of this essay, the author of the *Tanya* is
not focusing on the attainment of prophecy, nor on the divestment of
materiality, but on the apprehension of the intellect and cognitive love
and fear. Through these faculties, a person can grasp only the existence
of the Divine, but not its essence.

וְהַיְינוּ הַטַּעַם לְפִי שֶׁאִי אֶפְשָׁר לַנִּבְרָא The reason for this is that it is
לְהַשִּׂיג כְּלוּם בְּמַהוּת הָאֱלֹקוּת שֶׁהוּא impossible for any created being
הַבּוֹרֵא to apprehend anything of the
essence of divinity, which is the
Creator,

The relationship between Creator and created being is that of existence
from nothingness, meaning that for the created being, who now exists,

THE DIVESTMENT OF MATERIALITY

☞ This concept is mentioned by the early authorities, as well as in the *Shulḥan Arukh* (Oraḥ Ḥayyim 98:1), in the laws of prayer, where it is applied in a broader manner: that there is a divestment of materiality that is not prophecy but is akin to prophecy. Here the divestment is a more attainable level that even someone who is not a prophet can achieve. According to the *Shulḥan Arukh*, a person can actually sense the soul itself, as if it were detached from the body, through meditation and introspection, where all thoughts are focused on the Divine, and through intense concentration during prayers.

To put it in simpler terms, the individual will still feel the body, but in the way

he feels about another body, as a distinct and separate entity from his soul. This is also a degree of divestment. When a person experiences such a feeling, his soul is not fully committed to his body, so he can at that moment apprehend and perceive things from a different perspective, one that is akin to a deep and essential apprehension of the Divine.

On another level, one that is less common, one can reach the point where his self, his awareness, is at the soul level of *ḥaya*, which transcends the body. At that moment, he will also achieve a more essential apprehension of the level of *ḥaya* in the worlds, which is the level of *Atzilut* that is above the other worlds.

the Creator is nothingness, invisible and entirely incomprehensible.[39] This is an essential feature of the relationship between Creator and created being: Were the creation to grasp the essence of the Creator, it would cease to be a creation, an entity with its own existential perception of reality. It is impossible to be on both sides at the same time. Either one is a created being, an independent entity, so to speak, and then one cannot attain this apprehension, or one attains it and then one is no longer a created being.

וּבְלִי הַשָּׂגָה אֵין זוֹ הַלְבָּשָׁה וּתְפִיסָא וּדְבֵיקוּת אֲמִיתִּית

and without apprehension of the divine essence **there is no true enclothing, grasping, or cleaving.**

If there is no apprehension of a thing, it is not truly enclothed and grasped within the person's being, in his understanding and emotions. Each entity exists on a separate plane, and there is no essential connection between them that could render them as one entity. ☞

מַה שֶּׁאֵין כֵּן הָאֶתְרוֹג, עַל דֶּרֶךְ מָשָׁל, חַיּוּתוֹ נִמְשְׁכָה וְנִשְׁתַּלְשְׁלָה מִמַּהוּת חִיצוֹנִית דְּכֵלִים דְּנוּקְבָא דִּזְעֵיר אַנְפִּין דַּאֲצִילוּת, שֶׁהוּא בְּחִינַת אֱלֹקוּת

This is not the case with regard to **the _etrog_, for example. Its life force is drawn forth and devolves from the essence of the external dimension of the vessels of the female aspect of _Zeir Anpin_ of _Atzilut_, which is an aspect of the Divine,**

"TRUE GRASPING AND CLEAVING"

☞   This phrase expresses a state of existence in which two become one. On the spiritual level, this can occur when a person thinks about an idea and understands it not only on a superficial, not only its external aspect, that it exists somewhere in reality, but he comprehends the idea at its essence. At that moment, the concept has been transferred to him so that it exists and lives in his thoughts as though he had actually formulated it, and it then continues to thrive and grow in his mind. This is "true grasping and cleaving," where the person and the idea he apprehends have become one essence, growing and changing together, so that they can no longer be separated.

39. See _Iggeret HaKodesh_, epistle 20.

The same applies to all physical items that are used for the fulfillment of the mitzvot. Their spiritual vitality, which gives them existence, stems from "the essence of the external dimension of the vessels of the female aspect of *Zeir Anpin*." *Zeir Anpin* is the level of *Atzilut* that bestows the divine light and life force upon the world, and it first bestows this light and life force to the vessels of its female aspect, or the *sefira* of *Malkhut* within this *partzuf* in *Atzilut*, One might say that it first bestows to itself what it received of the life force.

This can be compared to the way a person first gives from what he receives to what is inside him, in terms of his feeling and sensing it and understanding it. After that, it emerges through the external dimension of the vessels, which are analogous to speech, which is external to thought and is expressed to another.

At any rate, all the levels through which the life force devolves from *Atzilut* above to the worlds below, from feelings and thoughts to speech, all comprise the divine essence. Unlike a human being, where that which is below him truly becomes other, for God there is no other: Everything is contained within Him, analogous to the other entity when it is still in one's thoughts. The entire chain of progression through which the light and life force descends is the same, all the way down to the actual physical realm: Everything is contained within His essence, and every part of reality that devolves from Him and descends below is, in this sense, His very essence.

as it is written in *Etz Ḥayyim*, that all כְּמוֹ שֶׁכָּתוּב בְּעֵץ חַיִּים: שֶׁכָּל
fruits are in *Atzilut*. הַפֵּירוֹת הֵן בַּאֲצִילוּת

In contrast to man's grasp of that which is above from here below, which cannot touch on the divine essence, that which descends from above, from God Himself, is always divine essence. This can be observed even in the lowliest form of vegetation in the physical world, how it devolves

But the ability to absorb an idea in this way depends on a deep, internal apprehension. As long as the apprehension is external, as long as one merely grasps that such a thing exists and nothing more, the person and the thing remain separate. They might encounter each other at random, and even touch upon one another now and then, but there is no real connection between them.

and descends from the vessels of *Atzilut*, "essence in essence," as the author of the Tanya *states* below. ☞

כִּי לָמֶ"ד כֵּלִים דַּאֲצִילוּת יָרְדוּ   **For thirty vessels of *Atzilut* descended**

לִבְרִיאָה יְצִירָה עֲשִׂיָּה   **to *Beria, Yetzira,* and *Asiya***

The kabbalistic works describe the descent of *Atzilut* into the worlds: Each of the ten vessels, or ten *sefirot*, of *Atzilut* has an inner, middle and external aspect,[40] which means that together they total thirty vessels. The inner ten descend and become souls and life forces for the world

FRUITS AND *ATZILUT*

☞ Not only the *etrog* but all fruits sprout and grow and reproduce again and again, all through the vitality that descends from above. The difference is that in all other fruits the divine essence is in a state of concealment, whereas in the fruit used to fulfill a mitzva, the divine essence is revealed through the performance of the mitzva. This is described in several places in connection to the famous saying that "you find no blade of grass below that does not have a heavenly force that protects it and strikes it, telling it, 'Grow!'" (see *Likkutei Torah,* Num. 23a; *Bereshit Rabba* 10:6; *Zohar* 2:171b, 386a). This spiritual force itself has a spiritual source above it, and so on and so forth, each one higher than the other, all the way until their root in *Atzilut*.

An example of this is cited in the *Zohar*: The physical rose has thirteen leaves because that is the state of the spiritual rose, which stems from the illumination of the thirteen supernal attributes of mercy. When the author of the *Tanya* says, then, that all the fruits are in *Atzilut*, this does not mean they exist there as we see them here below. The higher spiritual levels are concealed from us, so that the physical fruit is here while its essence is in *Atzilut* above.

The reason the author of the *Tanya* specifies fruits, which are from the vegetable kingdom rather than the mineral kingdom, is that it is precisely those entities that emerge from the earth's vegetative power of growth that the power of *Ein Sof*, His power to create existence from nothingness, is revealed (see *Iggeret HaKodesh*, epistles 8, 20). The seed that was sown in the ground disintegrates entirely, while the new plant sprouts from what appears to be absolute nothingness. In actuality, the vitality that gives the plant life originates from *Atzilut*, and this is the meaning of "all fruits are in *Atzilut*."

40. Each *sefira* incorporates all ten *sefirot*, which are divided into inner *sefirot*, middle *sefirot*, and external *sefirot*. Thus, within each of the ten *sefirot*, Ḥokhma, Bina, and Da'at comprise the inner array, Ḥesed, Gevura, and Tiferet make up the middle, and Netzaḥ, Hod, and Yesod are the external dimension The inner *sefirot* are connected to the source, the middle *sefirot* represent the attributes themselves,

of *Beria*, the middle ten for the world of *Yetzira*, and the external ten for the world of *Asiya*.[41]

וְהֵן יו״ד מַאֲמָרוֹת שֶׁבָּהֶן נִבְרָא (and these are the ten utterances with
הָעוֹלָם) which the world was created)

The ten vessels that become the soul of the world of *Asiya* are manifest as the ten utterances that appear in the first chapter of the book of Genesis. These are the general life forces of creation that comprise and sustain everything in this world, as explained at length in *Sha'ar HaYihud VeHa'emuna*.

עַל יְדֵי הִתְלַבְּשׁוּת בְּנוּקְבָא by being enclothed in the feminine
דַּעֲשִׂיָה מַהוּת בְּמַהוּת aspect of *Asiya*, essence in essence.

The feminine aspect of *Atzilut* is *Malkhut* of *Atzilut*. The vessels, or *sefirot*, within *Malkhut* of *Atzilut* descend and are enclothed in the feminine aspect, or *Malkhut*, of *Asiya*, so that the essence of *Atzilut* is literally within the essence of *Asiya*. "Essence in essence" means that the essence itself is transmitted, not merely the awareness or knowledge of its existence. This means that there are no concealing transitions, as there are, for example, between the essence of something and one's thoughts about it, or one's thoughts about the thought.

That the essence of the vessels of the female aspect of *Zeir Anpin* are enclothed in the female aspect of *Asiya*, or *Malkhut* in *Malkhut*, means that it is enclothed not only in the head and body of *Asiya* – not only in the cognitive *sefirot* of *Hokhma*, *Bina*, and *Da'at* (the head), and not only in the emotive attributes, *Hesed*, *Gevura*, and so on (the body) – but also in the female aspect of *Asiya*, in *Malkhut*. This constitutes a bestowal of essence in essence, the essence of *Malkhut* within the essence of *Malkhut*.

This is analogous to a father teaching his son. When the father gives the son a rational explanation of what to do and how to act, this is not really "essence in essence," since the son has to convert the father's logic

---

while the external *sefirot* are those that bestow to the level below them that which they received from the level above.

41. See *Etz Hayyim, Sha'ar HaShemot*, chap. 1.

and rationale into deed. By contrast, when the father is not content with rational explanation but performs the action himself with his son, this is a communication of essence in essence.

כִּי הַכֵּלִים דַּאֲצִילוּת נַעֲשׂוּ נִשְׁמָה בַּעֲשִׂיָּה, שֶׁהִיא בְּחִינַת אֱלֹקוּת מַמָּשׁ

This is because the vessels of *Atzilut* became a soul in *Asiya*, which is literally an aspect of the Divine,

The vessels of *Atzilut* are, as explained above, the essence of the Divine itself. Their external aspects, the *sefirot* of the outer array, became a soul in *Asiya*. The soul of *Asiya*, of reality and physicality, is what sustains and brings everything there into existence and it is actual divinity. From the perspective of the Divine, there is no concealment, not of light or vessels, not in *Beria*, in *Yetzira*, nor in the physical world of *Asiya*, and therefore all of these vessels, all the way down to the world of *Asiya* itself, are divinity itself as it is manifest in *Atzilut*.

לְפִי שֶׁבַּאֲצִילוּת 'אִיהוּ וְגַרְמוֹהִי חַד', הַמַּאֲצִיל וְהַנֶּאֱצָל

since in *Atzilut* He and His attributes are one, the Emanator and the emanated.

God and the vessels or *sefirot* of the world of *Atzilut* are one, which constitutes the unification of the Emanator with the emanated. The Emanator is the light of *Ein Sof* itself, which transcends *Atzilut*, while the emanated is the world of *Atzilut* and the ten *sefirot*, which are the vessels of the world of *Atzilut*. Accordingly, the vessels of *Atzilut* on all levels, both their internal dimensions and their external aspects, are unified in the light of *Ein Sof*, and so they are divinity itself.

וְעַל יְדֵי הִתְלַבְּשׁוּת מַהוּת הַנְּשָׁמָה בְּמַהוּת הַכֵּלִים דְּנוּקְבָּא דַּעֲשִׂיָּה, נִתְהַוָּה הָאֶתְרוֹג

Through the enclothing of the essence of the soul, the life force that descends from the vessels of *Atzilut*, within the essence of the vessels of the female aspect of *Asiya*, or the ten utterances, the *etrog* came into existence.

The physical *etrog* came into existence through the enclothing of the life force that descends from the vessels of *Atzilut* within the essence of the vessels of *Asiya*. These are the ten *sefirot* of *Asiya* which are manifest, through *Malkhut* of *Asiya*, as the ten utterances of Creation. Thus, the life force that gives vitality to this physical *etrog* is thus the divine essence itself.

נִמְצָא כְּשֶׁתּוֹפֵס הָאֶתְרוֹג וּמְנַעְנְעוֹ כְּהִלְכָתוֹ, הֲרֵי זֶה תּוֹפֵס מַמָּשׁ חַיּוּתוֹ הַמְלוּבָּשׁ בּוֹ מִנּוּקְבָּא דַּאֲצִילוּת, הַמְיוּחֶדֶת בְּאוֹר אֵין סוֹף הַמַּאֲצִיל בָּרוּךְ הוּא

It follows that when one holds the *etrog* and shakes it, in accordance with the *halakha*, one is literally holding its vitality that is enclothed in it and that stems from the female aspect of *Atzilut*, which is united with the light of *Ein Sof*, the Emanator, blessed be He.

The author of the *Tanya* emphasizes that a person takes hold of the *etrog* "in accordance with the *halakha*," because otherwise the act is not a mitzva. When a person uses the *etrog* in fulfillment of the mitzva, he is holding the divine essence in his hand. In this way, he physically cleaves to the Divine, to the divine essence and being. ☞

THE ESSENCE OF AN *ETROG*

☞ Why does the author of the *Tanya* specifically highlight the *etrog* when it is being used to fulfill a mitzva? After all, the divine essence exists in all fruits, as the author himself stated above. What is lacking in the world that one has to perform a mitzva in order to seize hold of the life force of the physical world that is unified with the light of *Ein Sof*?

It is true that the divine essence is enclothed in all of physical reality. But this divine essence within the corporeal world is dormant, lacking substance or influence. It is present, but nothing more.

Furthermore, since this divine vitality is dormant, its external vessel and garb can take on a different meaning to divinity and holiness, even the converse of holiness. The great question of our world is

how to connect these two extremes: our apprehension of the Divine and our love and fear of God on one hand, which reveal divinity, though not the actual divine essence, and the life force that sustains and gives life to the reality of *Asiya* itself, which is the divine essence itself but is not revealed and has no substance. This dilemma has no evident solution, because even if we ponder and contemplate the divine essence that is contained in everything and try to uncover it, that would only constitute illumination and revelation from our perspective, but in no way is it the revelation of the thing itself.

The resolution to this paradox is the mitzvot. A mitzva is first and foremost a command from God, because a solution to such a dilemma can come only from Him,

מַה שֶׁאֵין כֵּן בְּכַוָּנָתוֹ אֵינוֹ מַשִּׂיג
וְתוֹפֵס, אַף הַיּוֹדֵעַ הַסּוֹד, אֶלָּא
מְצִיאוּתָהּ וְלֹא מַהוּתָהּ

This is not the case with regard to one's intention when fulfilling the mitzva. **Even one who knows the mystical wisdom** of Kabbala **apprehends and grasps only** the fact of **the existence** of the Divine, **not its essence.**

When a person fulfills a mitzva, his intent constitutes his focus on the spiritual meaning of the act in his heart and mind. Yet even one who has the loftiest intentions cannot apprehend or perceive the divine essence that is enclothed in the *etrog*. This is undoubtedly the case for one whose thoughts merely encompass that which he understands through logic he arrived at himself, but even someone who has studied the wisdom of the Kabbala, who is aware of ideas and concepts that cannot be known with one's intellect or logic, but rather he acquired them from his teachers who themselves acquired them in the same manner, or through prophetic intuition, can understand the fact of

from above, from *Ein Sof*. Through a mitzva, God enters physical reality but without interfering in it, without actually changing anything. He simply informs us about the significance of certain aspects and circumstances within reality, but there is no transformation of reality with which we can connect (through cognitive fear and love) in such a way that it would be experienced as divine intervention. Reality remains as it is; there is only an utterance here that chooses and refines objects within that reality. Through this choice, which is not based on any logical reasoning that human beings can discern, the essence gains access to our existence, so to speak.

In this way, when a person performs a mitzva, a connection between him and the divine essence is fashioned, not in his understanding and feelings, which can only perceive this reality, but in the grasp of the essence itself when he seizes hold of the object with which he performs the mitzva. This is not a connection through intellect or emotion, but it is a connection to the will and wisdom of God, which one does not understand but which one sets in motion.

Admittedly, even this connection forged by the fulfillment of a mitzva does not reveal an understanding or even an experience of the divine essence in this world, because that would be impossible. Yet one who is aware of this process can also perceive and feel something: that by performing the act in accordance with the *halakha*, in a precise manner, in accordance with those distinctions chosen by the supreme will, by distinguishing between one thing and another, between one way of performing an act and the other, what is correct and what is not, a wide path is created, a whole world that begins to utter the essence of the Divine.

the existence of the divine essence, but not the divine essence itself. It makes no difference that his capacity for apprehension is immense or that he learned these ideas from the loftiest of individuals. The human intellect is incapable of apprehending the divine essence. It can at best attain an awareness of its existence.

אַךְ בְּלִימוּד הִלְכוֹת אֶתְרוֹג, מַשִּׂיג **Yet with regard to the study of the**
וְתוֹפֵס הָאֶתְרוֹג מַמָּשׁ וּמִצְוָתוֹ **laws of the** *etrog,* **he apprehends and**
כַּהֲלָכָה, בִּבְחִינַת דִּבּוּר וּמַחֲשָׁבָה **grasps the actual** *etrog* **and its mitzva**
in accordance with the *halakha,*
through speech and thought,

Unlike spiritual thoughts and intentions regarding the meaning behind the mitzva, thoughts about the practical aspects of the fulfillment, such as the study of the *halakha,* constitute a perception of the divine essence within the mitzva act. There is no action without thought, without a spiritual element that fuels it. It is impossible to act without knowing what one is doing, and therefore the study and preparation that are related to the mitzva are an inseparable part of the act itself.

וְכָל שֶׁכֵּן הַלּוֹמֵד הַסּוֹד **and all the more so one who studies**
the mystical wisdom of the Kabbala.

Unlike the spiritual intention and meaning behind the mitzva that the author of the *Tanya* discussed above, this refers to the esoteric dimension of the actual *etrog* and the mitzva act performed with the *etrog.* It refers to the esoteric reasons behind the *halakhot* pertaining to the mitzva and their details. Furthermore, the study of the esoteric meaning is itself connected to the act, since many practical customs are based on esoteric teachings.

The author of the *Tanya* states "all the more so" because the study of the esoteric meaning of a mitzva entails understanding the mitzva act on a deep spiritual level: what an *etrog* is in the higher worlds, what happens there to the higher beings when we hold the *etrog* and *lulav* here below and wave them up and down, in accordance with the parameters of the *halakha,* and so on. In that case, the person's thoughts not only precede and prepare the body for the action, in the form of studying the *halakha,* for example, but it also executes the mitzva in the spiritual worlds itself together with the performance of the physical action.

אֲבָל דַּוְקָא סוֹדוֹת הַמִּצְוָה, דְּלָא גָרַע מִלִּימוּד הִלְכוֹתֶיהָ וְאַדְרַבָּה כוּ׳,

But this applies **specifically to the mystical meaning of the mitzva** itself, **which is not inferior to studying its laws, but on the contrary…**

5 Kislev (leap year)

The author of the *Tanya* stresses once again that in order for a person's study and intention to allow him to apprehend the essence within the mitzva, it must be related to the action, as is the case of the study of the *halakha* in practice.

But the author of the *Tanya* also implies that studying of the esoteric meaning of a mitzva is superior to the study of its *halakhot*. In this context, the virtue of studying the esoteric meaning lies in the discovery of the divine content within the act. The study of the *halakha* is also a spiritual activity, but it does not go beyond the realm of action, what to do and how to do it. It does not relate to the divine meaning behind the act. The study of the esoteric dimension of the Torah is generally on a different plane of reality, where the Divine is revealed to a greater extent. When one is focused on the physical *etrog* –what color a valid *etrog* should be, which marks are disqualifying, and other such factors – there is no divine revelation there, just as in the physical world itself one does not see the divine light within the fruit. But when one focuses on the spiritual essence of the *etrog*, such as the idea that *etrog* represents the *sefira* of *Malkhut* while the *lulav* represents *Yesod*, so that waving these species brings forth these forces into reality, then the Divine is openly revealed.

אַף שֶׁאֵינוֹ מַשִּׂיג הַמַּהוּת

even though he does not apprehend the essence of mitzva's spiritual meaning.

When a person studies Kabbala, even when he studies the esoteric mysteries that relates to a particular mitzva, one does not actually grasp the essence of the matter one is studying. The virtue of studying *halakha* is that we know what we are dealing with. We know this physical world, and not only the fact of its existence but also its very essence. We know exactly what an *etrog* fruit is, what the color yellow is, and so on, and therefore our understanding of the *halakhot* is an apprehension of the essence of the act itself.

By contrast, when we study kabbalistic concepts, this involves concepts that we do not actually understand, concepts such as angels, the *sefirot*, and spiritual lights. We can say the words, have a slight conception of what they might be so that we might know a little of how to connect one concept to the other, but we do not know what they actually are. In other words, we grasp the fact of their existence, but not their essence.

Nevertheless, as long as the study of these esoteric matters is related to the mitzva act, even if one does not actually apprehend the essence of the concepts one is studying, he is connected to the act in practice, which contains something of the divine essence itself.

This is akin to the particles that physicists work with. Though no one has any idea what they actually are, the physicists apply this knowledge and build devices that the entire world uses to maintain life in a very practical sense. The same applies to the relationship between the study of the esoteric meaning behind the act and the act itself: Even if one does not apprehend the essence of the concepts in question, the minimal knowledge of their existence and the relationships between them forms a connection between the person and the action and stimulates the deed.

6 Kislev | מַה שֶּׁאֵין כֵּן בְּסֵדֶר הַהִשְׁתַּלְשְׁלוּת | **This is not the case with regard to** the study of **the order of the chain of progression** by which the divine light descends to this world.

This refers to the study of the abstract concepts of Kabbala that are not directly related to mitzva acts, to what and how to think and do. It involves general knowledge of the structure of the worlds and how they transmute from one another. The chain of progression consists of the path and channel that extends from the Divine itself all the way down to this physical world, from the first constriction and the first level of lights and *sefirot* through the higher spiritual worlds down to our physical world and reality. The expression the "chain of the progression" thus encompasses the entire expanse of theoretical knowledge of the Divine and the worlds.

אַף אִם מַשִּׂיג הַמְּצִיאוּת לֹא עָדִיף מִצַּד עַצְמוֹ כְּלִימּוּד הַמִּצְוֹת, שֶׁמַּשִּׂיג וְתוֹפֵס הַמַּהוּת

Even if one does apprehend the fact of **the existence** of the chain of progression, **it is not as intrinsically worthy as the study of the mitzvot, where one does apprehend and grasp the essence** of the concepts he is studying,

Even if a person has studied Kabbala and knows how the worlds are structured and has learned of the existence of the divine forces and attributes and how they are positioned in relation to each other, this study is not as worthy as the study of the mitzvot. When one studies the subject for the sake of it and not in order to fulfill a mitzva or to evoke love and fear of God, such study does not have the special virtue of the study of mitzvot.

When a person studies the mitzvot, particularly *halakha*, one attains an apprehension of the essence of the concepts he is studying, since he is dealing with physical matters that are part of the world in which he lives. Even the study of the esoteric meaning of the mitzva, which also leads to action and practical application, is connected to the deed, and therefore also to the divine essence within the act itself.

וּמַעֲלֶה עָלָיו כְּאִילוּ קַיֵּים בְּפּוֹעַל מַמָּשׁ כְּמוֹ שֶׁכָּתוּב: "זֹאת הַתּוֹרָה כו'" (ויקרא ז, לז)

and God **ascribes him credit as though he actually fulfilled** them in practice, as it is written, "This **is the law** for the burnt offering, for the meal offering, and for the sin offering" (Lev. 7:37).

When one studies the *halakha*, both on the revealed level and in relation to the esoteric meaning of a mitzva, it is considered as though he fulfilled the mitzva in practice. The Rabbis expound from the verse cited here, "This is the Torah for the burnt offering, for the meal offering, and for the sin offering…," that one who studies the laws of the sacrifices is accredited as if he actually sacrificed the offerings.[42] The Torah itself ascribes the virtue of one who performs a mitzva to one who studies its laws. ☞

אֶלָּא שֶׁיְּדִיעַת הַמְּצִיאוּת מֵהַהִשְׁתַּלְשְׁלוּת הִיא גַם כֵּן מִצְוָה רָמָה וְנִשָּׂאָה But the knowledge of the existence of the chain of progression is also a lofty, exalted mitzva,

The author of the *Tanya* adds that even the abstract general knowledge of the chain of progression of the worlds, which is unrelated to a specific action-related mitzva or to the individual who knows it, is still a mitzva, even a "lofty, exalted" one. It is, in fact, the first mitzva discussed in the Rambam's *Mishneh Torah*: "To know that there is a Primary Being, and that He brought into being all existence. All the beings in heaven and earth, and whatever is between them, came into

STUDY EQUALS ACTION

☞ There is a general principle in Judaism that Torah study has intrinsic value, not only because it helps one to know what to do but as a goal in itself. Therefore, in many instances where a person is unable, for some reason, to perform a certain mitzva in practice, he is accredited with its performance by studying its *halakhot* and reasonings. Every mitzva can be fulfilled, not only in deed, but also in speech and thought on some level, or perhaps even in a different reality (*Likkutei Torah*, Num. 75a), and yet even these modes are considered actual fulfillment of the mitzva.

Generally, there are three levels in the performance of a mitzva: thought, speech, and deed. In the case of the sacrifices, for example, speech constitutes the study of the *halakhot*, thought refers to prayer, which has been substituted for the sacrifices, and deed, of course, is the actual

offering of the sacrifice. Admittedly, this is not exactly the same as performance of the mitzva on the physical plane, where a person is holding the thing itself, which is why it is merely "as though" one has fulfilled the mitzva. But this "as though" is the ascribing of credit by the Torah, the same Torah that commands one to perform the physical act and reveals the divine essence through it.

Ultimately, thought, speech, and deed require one another. The mitzva is constructed through each of these modes, and it is fulfilled only when all of them come together. It is true that they do not always join each other. Sometimes one has to wait for the next stage, perhaps even for several generations, but in the meantime none of what has been accomplished is entirely lost.

---

42. *Menaḥot* 110a.

existence only through the truth of His being" (*Sefer HaMadda, Hilkhot Yesodei HaTorah* 1:1). ☞

וְאַדְּרַבָּה עוֹלָה עַל כּוּלָּנָה, כְּמוֹ שֶׁכָּתוּב: "וְיָדַעְתָּ הַיּוֹם כו'" (דברים ד, לט)

and on the contrary, it surpasses all of them, as it is written, "You shall know this day and restore to your heart that the Lord, He is the God in the heavens above and upon the earth below; there is no other" (Deut. 4:39),

This is a general mitzva that in a certain sense encompasses all the mitzvot. It is a mitzva that empowers a person to fulfill all mitzvot, so from a certain perspective "it surpasses all of them."

The author of the *Tanya* emphasizes this point by quoting this verse from Deuteronomy. This verse adds a layer that is deeper than the knowledge one can gain from observing nature, as described by Rambam above. This deeper knowledge does not arise from contemplating the world merely through rational observation, but by virtue of this message from above that the Divine not only gives life to that which we see but that everything in existence is contained within the Divine and the Divine is contained within it. "The Lord, He is the God," or "*Havaya*," meaning everything in existence, "is God." That which brings into existence and that which exists are one and the same, as explained in *Sha'ar HaYiḥud VeHa'emuna*. There is nothing besides Him, not only with respect to the divinity that creates and give life, but there is no other within reality except for Him.

AN EXALTED MITZVA

☞ The world as we see it conceals the Divine and appears to exist independently. It seems as though everything is the outcome of a cause that has no apparent significance or source beyond reality itself. This mitzva offers a different awareness and perspective of the worlds, in which the Divine is no longer concealed, in which there is a cause and effect through the chain of progres-sion of the worlds, in which each detail and every occurrence is nothing other than a revelation of the Divine that brings it into existence and sustains them. This understanding does not come naturally or easily to most people: It requires work, the work of the intellect and the more internal work of changing one's perspective with regard to what one sees and thinks.

"דַּע אֶת אֱלֹקֵי אָבִיךָ כו'" (דברי and it is written, "**Know the God of**
הימים א כח, ט) **your father** and serve Him with a
whole heart and a willing mind…" (I
Chron. 28:9).

This verse is part of King David's final command to his son Solomon.
As in the verse from the Torah, here too there is a mitzva to know, to
investigate and reflect on God's greatness within the order of the chain
of progression and to take this knowledge to heart so that it is expressed
in one's service of God. But there is a personal addition here that does
not appear in the verse from the Torah: "Know the God of your father."
When one considers his own personal progression, his own origin in
the Divine – "the God of your father" – he will find his personal God.
He will become aware of the source of his life and his own personal
situation, which points to *Ein Sof* Himself.

וּמְבִיאָה לְ"לֵב שָׁלֵם" כו' שֶׁהוּא This knowledge **leads to a "whole
הָעִיקָר heart" …, which is the main thing.**

This is the "whole heart" that the verse from the Torah quoted above
mentions, implying that this level of knowledge of God's existence
leads to the rectification and perfection of one's attributes. A "whole
heart" means that one's soul will be whole, perfected, through that
which one understands, feels, and does. It is possible for someone to
understand a concept, and yet half of his heart is focused elsewhere. He
may also act in accordance with his understanding, while his feelings
about it contradict his actions. Only a foundation as deep and as wide
as possible of the knowledge of divine reality throughout the chain of
progression of the worlds, within all aspects of reality and in everything
that has occurred and will occur, can bring a person to the point where
his emotions, his love and awe, his yearnings and frustrations, accord
with his intellectual understanding and his actions and the practical
application of what he thinks and feels.

Developing a "whole heart" through the knowledge of the existence
of the Divine is not only a foundation and a source of strength for one's
divine service in practice. Rather, in a certain sense, it is the essence
and purpose of the service of God through the Torah and mitzvot. We

can infer this idea from yet another verse: "The Lord commanded us to perform all these statutes, to fear the Lord our God" (Deut. 6:24), which conveys that the purpose of the Torah and the mitzvot is the higher level of fear, the loftiest level of the human heart, and that is "a whole heart."[43] ☞

וְהַשָּׂגַת הַמְּצִיאוּת הוּא לְהַפְשִׁיט   **The apprehension of the existence**
מִגַּשְׁמִיּוּת כו׳   of the Divine **entails divesting from physicality…**

This brief comment has a far-reaching implications.[44] It expresses the approach of Hasidism in general, and that of the author of the *Tanya* in particular, with regard to the study of the esoteric teachings of the Torah. The study of these teachings in itself, which he defines here as "the knowledge of the existence of the chain of progression," is the knowledge of the existence of lofty spiritual essences throughout the immense chasm between us and God: what they are, how they are arranged, and how they relate to each other. Here he adds that this is not enough. Something more is required, another layer to this field of knowledge, without which none of this would constitute true knowledge of the Divine. It does not matter what we call the details, whether

---

A WHOLE HEART

☞   This level is attained when a person acquires the highest level of fear, where a person lives with the tangible feeling of the presence of God, that He is right there with Him. This fear is not merely apprehension of divine existence but a sense of the presence of the divine essence that transcends the intellect and any feeling that is familiar in our world. But a person can uncover God's essence only by serving God through Torah study and the action-re-lated mitzvot, as stated above. This is why the Torah is called the "gate to the courtyard" (see *Shabbat* 31b; *Yoma* 72b; *Likkutei Torah*, Lev. 5c). The fear, the sense of the presence of the divine essence, is the courtyard, while the Torah and the mitzvot are the gateway that leads to this level of fear. This is the whole heart that is "the main thing": It is the ultimate purpose of the Torah and mitzvot.

---

43. See *Likkutei Torah*, Lev. 5c.

44. For a different explanation of this concept, see the commentary to *Iggeret HaKodesh*, epistle 25.

they are the names of worlds or angels, or even if they are the names of God Himself, if all of it is nothing but knowledge of the names and the garments that enclothe the spiritual entities, if it is nothing but a physical garb that does not contain anything of the Divine.

Here physicality, in the broad meaning of the term, refers to the external *kelippa* that appears to be an independent entity, a thing in its own right, whether it is physical or spiritual. Not only is such study worthless, but it can even be dangerous.[45] This is why the author of the *Tanya* says that the apprehension of the existence of the Divine must be divested of physicality. ☞

DIVESTING FROM PHYSICALITY

☞   What does it mean to divest from physicality? In simple terms, this is precisely what the author of the *Tanya* does in his essays and discourses on Hasidism: He explains kabbalistic concepts and formulas in an understandable, accessible manner. When a person comprehends, as best as he can, the idea embedded within the words and concepts, he can, at least to some extent, separate the content from its physical garb. This is the divestment of physicality to which he refers.

This is true of any study that involves abstract concepts, but it is particularly the case with the study of Kabbala. When one studies the esoteric aspects of the Torah, which involves the mysteries of the chain of progression, the focus is not on this world but on the higher spiritual worlds, the *sefirot* and the divine *partzufim* that are even loftier than those spiritual words. One is engaged in matters of

which one basically has no concept, and he cannot call upon images or metaphors with which he is familiar. Therefore, all the names we give to these entities are taken from physical reality and are clearly inadequate. If one does not divest them of their materiality, to differentiate the wheels from the wheels, the feathers from the angels' wings, the Rachel and Leah we know of from the *partzufim* of *Atzilut* that are given these names, but continues to hold on to them with the same appellations that we give to things solely to enable us to relate to them as though they were the thing itself, such a person is in actual, mortal danger.

On a more profound level, this expectation, that one divest from physicality, applies to every individual. After all, it is a mitzva, and like every mitzva, it is not meant solely for righteous individuals. Yet the author of the *Tanya* himself states

---

45. See *Derekh Mitzvotekha, Shoresh Mitzvat HaTefilla,* 2, which states, "It is for this reason that the Ba'al Shem Tov instructed us not to study the works of Kabbala, since one who does not know how to divest the concepts from their physical garb will turn this study into something superficial, because he will develop an image of the Divine that fits the paucity of his mind. ..."

elsewhere (in *Iggeret HaKodesh*, epistle 25), "Nor should the listener suspect me of thinking that I have understood the words of the Arizal, how to divest them of their physical garb." This implies that the ability to divest from physicality belongs only to lofty tzaddikim, so much so that he does not even attribute such a skill to himself.

There is a way to divest from physicality so that a person can see that which is concealed behind it himself, just as a prophet might see, for example, an angel. Even the prophet sees something physical in a sense, but that does not matter, because for him it is divested of physicality. He sees an angel and nothing else, and it is only when he wishes to convey his vision to others that he clothes it in physical terms. This kind of divestment of the physical is indeed not within the capacity of all people, and this is especially the case with regard to the words of the Arizal, who attained such a lofty level of wisdom. It is with respect to the divestment of the physical on such levels, which even the Arizal attained only through wisdom, that the author of the *Tanya* states, "Do not suspect me of thinking that I understand them."

By contrast, it seems that here he does not have this divestment from physicality in mind. Rather, it is similar to what he himself does in epistle 25, and in a sense in all his writings, where he clarifies kabbalistic formulations through rational explanations, with images and metaphors that we can comprehend. Such explanations do not entirely divest the physical terminology from the abstract concepts. That is not possible with any logical explanation that a human being can comprehend, but they do constitute an attempt to replace the physical images with other descrip-tions and metaphors. The very replacement of one term for another comprises a degree of abstraction, a separation between the physical term that serves merely as a substitute and the deeper, actual content. Even if the concept is not completely divested of physicality, it can shine from within the physical garb, proclaiming its existence.

Granted, this still does not constitute an apprehension of the essence of these concepts, but it is at the least an apprehension of their existence, a recognition that these ideas exist and what they represent. Furthermore, since the metaphors that the author of the *Tanya* utilizes are taken from this world, with which we are very familiar and comprehend, at their essence and not just in the fact of their existence, we are able to divest them of their materiality to a certain extent. When we speak of *sefirot* and *partzufim*, we do not actually know what they are, but when we talk about the faculties and attributes of our soul, we have direct knowledge of what we are talking about. We understand the concept and essence of them behind the words, and that is what it means to divest them of their physicality. True, even then we remain in our own world, but by doing this, we can connect with the higher worlds and even have an effect on them. There is no other way to do this. What we apprehend and activate, each in his own soul and his own world, is what exists and happens all the way to the highest levels. This accords with a teaching of the Maggid of Mezeritch: "Know what is above you. That is, know that everything above, whatever happens and exists in the higher worlds, is all from you. it is the result of what happens to you below" (see *Or Torah* 480; *Sefer HaSiḥot* 5703, p. 12; *HaYom Yom*, 13 Iyar).

רַק שֶׁזּוֹ הִיא מִצְוָה אַחַת מִתַּרְיַ"ג
וְהָאָדָם צָרִיךְ לְקַיֵּים כָּל תַּרְיַ"ג

But this is only one of the 613 mitzvot, and a person must fulfill all 613 mitzvot,

Although the study and knowledge of the esoteric aspects of the Torah is a general mitzva that surpasses all the others, it is still only one of 613. It cannot replace the other mitzvot, but it is one of them, and one is obligated to fulfill it just as he is required to perform all the other mitzvot. ☞

לְפִי שֶׁהֵן הִשְׁתַּלְשְׁלוּת הַמַּהוּת
דְּחִיצוֹנִית דְּכֵלִים דַּאֲצִילוּת

for they descend from the essence of the external aspect of the vessels of *Atzilut*.

Each of the 613 mitzvot literally stems from the divine essence, and the essence it contains cannot be revealed through any other mitzva. If we were dealing with something external, where there is an obvious reason

---

A GENERAL MITZVA

☞　General mitzvot serve as the basis for other mitzvot and even all the mitzvot, such as belief and knowledge of God, Torah study, and *tzitzit*. There are also specific mitzvot. But there is one root for all the mitzvot that they share equally: Each mitzva is one of 613 manifestations of the supernal divine will, which transcends rationale and reason, higher than considerations of what is major and minor, more important and less important. Each and every mitzva is divine revelation itself.

To put it another way, every mitzva has two aspects. Each mitzva is drawn from the divine will in a particular manner, in which it differs from the other mitzvot. Thus, *tefillin* serves to draw forth the intellect and subjugate the heart to the mind, while *tzitzit* brings a person to accept the yoke of the kingdom of Heaven. On the other hand, all the mitzvot share something in common, which is the execution of the will

of God, not for the sake of something specific, nor to fulfill some desire, but for the sake of it, just to perform the will of God. From this perspective, every mitzva, even a lofty, exalted one such as the knowledge of God, is a single mitzva that is equal to each one of the 613.

Not only are the 613 mitzvot equal to one another, but they also need each other. In this regard, they can be compared to the limbs of a person. He has a head, and he has feet. The head includes the feet in the sense that it thinks about them and instructs them on when and how to walk, but the head cannot walk without the feet. Even if a person can function without a certain limb that may provide an external, relatively inessential function, this is not the case from an internal perspective. The essence of a person is manifest only when all of his faculties are complete.

and purpose for it to be that way, it might be possible for one mitzva to replace another or even several other mitzvot. But since every mitzva is drawn from the divine essence, which transcends all rationale and any purpose, no mitzva can substitute another.

לְכָךְ צָרִיךְ לְהַרְבּוֹת בְּלִימוּד כָּל הַתְּרְיַ״ג וְקִיּוּמָן בְּפוֹעַל מַמָּשׁ	**Therefore, one must increase the study of all 613** mitzvot **and their fulfillment in actual practice,**

While there are mitzvot that ostensibly incorporate other mitzvot, and a person may be more interested in certain mitzvot and more qualified to succeed in his fulfillment of them, he should still make an effort to fulfill all 613 mitzvot, both in study and practice. The study of the mitzvot itself is not merely a way of knowing what to do but represents a fulfillment of the mitzva itself on another plane, in another realm. But it is not actually part of the fulfillment of the mitzva at the level of action.

בְּמַחֲשָׁבָה דִּבּוּר וּמַעֲשֶׂה שֶׁהֵן בְּרִיאָה יְצִירָה עֲשִׂיָּה	**in thought, speech, and action, which** correspond to *Beria, Yetzira,* and *Asiya,*

Every mitzva should be fulfilled on three levels: thought, speech, and action.[46] Action means the actual physical act, speech is the study of the mitzva in the Torah, and thought includes the person's intentions, in terms of both the spirit and the purpose of that mitzva. In the case of the sacrifices, for example, the level of thought comprises prayer, which serves as a substitute for the sacrifices. With regard to the Sabbath, it entails refraining from thinking about secular matters on this day and sanctifying oneself and elevating oneself through the Sabbath prayers.

These three aspects of a mitzva correspond to the worlds of *Beria, Yetzira,* and *Asiya.* Everything contained within man exists in the worlds to their fullest extent. In relation to the world of *Atzilut,* which is also called "supernal man," the worlds of *Beria, Yetzira,* and *Asiya* are its thoughts, speech, and deeds. This means that when one fulfills a

---

46. See *Likkutei Torah*, Num. 75a.

mitzva at the level of action, one fulfills it in the world of *Asiya*. When one fulfills it through speech, one fulfills it in the world of *Yetzira*, and when one fulfills it on the level of thought, one fulfills it in the world of *Beria*.

לְבָרֵר בֵּירוּרִין אֲשֶׁר שָׁם **to refine that which must be refined there.**

A person must fulfill the mitzvot at all levels and worlds in order "to refine that which must be refined" in all the worlds, to extract the holy sparks from the impure *kelippot* and elevate them. Although the shattering of the vessels and the concealment of the Divine occurred primarily in the world of *Asiya*, the finer roots of these corruptions exist in the higher worlds, in *Yetzira* and *Beria*, and the service of refinement is therefore needed there too.

7 Kislev
6 Kislev
(leap year)

וְעוֹד זֹאת, שֶׁבֶּאֱמֶת הַבֵּירוּדִין
שֶׁבִּבְרִיאָה יְצִירָה עֲשִׂיָּה מְרֵפָּ"ח
עַל יְדֵי תּוֹרָה וּמִצְוֹת, בְּמַחֲשָׁבָה
דִּיבּוּר וּמַעֲשֶׂה, גְּבוֹהִין בְּשָׁרְשָׁן
מִנֶּפֶשׁ רוּחַ נְשָׁמָה שֶׁבָּאָדָם

Moreover, the truth is that the refinement that is effected **in *Beria*, *Yetzira*,** and *Asiya* by elevating the 288 sparks through Torah** study and mitzvot, in **thought, speech, and action, are loftier at their root than the *nefesh*, *ruaḥ*,** and *neshama* **in man,**

After the shattering of the vessels occurred, the lower three worlds became intermingled with a mixture of good and evil. The sparks of divine light fell among the *kelippot*. Now the worlds need to be refined and rectified through the extraction and elevation of these sparks. When the 288 sparks that fell to the worlds upon the shattering of the vessels are elevated by man through his service in this world, this results in the refinement and rectification of the worlds. When a person accomplishes this, he is loftier than the sparks, even though at their root, these holy sparks were originally loftier than man before they fell. This presents a paradox because only a higher entity can refine a lower one. But as the author of the *Tanya* goes on to explain, man originates from a loftier place than this world in which the sparks fell, and so he is able to refine and elevate them. ☞

The author of the *Tanya* stresses that man achieves this refinement through Torah study and mitzvot. Without Torah study and mitzvot,

LOFTIER THAN THE SOUL OF MAN

☞ The entity that refines is invariably loftier than the object of its refinement, the rectifier is higher than the rectified, and the doer transcends the deed. If it were otherwise, one would not be able to effect such changes. It is one's superiority in the situation that enables him to have any effect.

But after that initial stage of effecting change, it often becomes clear that the rectified has qualities that do not exist in the rectifier. The act of rectification and refinement does not bring anything from the outside. It does not create new realities, but simply evokes from within the entity that was rectified facets that were not conscious and active, that were hidden under layers of grime and distortion. Now that they are uncovered, it becomes apparent that there is something far greater and more powerful here than it first appeared, and it might even be loftier than the entity that refined and elevated it.

This is also true on the physical level. Many processes of energy production are based on this principle: One introduces a small amount of energy, changes the arrangement of the materials here and there, and the result is an exponential increase in energy.

Man's ability to refine the sparks and his ability to have dominion over them is not due to his higher status. Rather, it is because currently, in this reality, he is rectified, whereas the sparks are in an unrectified state. In other words, man is an orderly and purposeful being, while the reality is in a raw, undirected, and disorganized state so that it cannot employ its powers, and those powers may even work against it. Naturally, in this situation man, the one who is refining, whose faculties are organized and directed toward this purpose, is loftier that such reality and is able to effect the refinement.

To illustrate with a simple example, when a person, society, or army are organized, they can overpower and take control of a person or society that is bigger than them, that has more power, at least in potential, but is in a chaotic state.

This phenomenon, in which the refined turns out to be greater than the refiner, is not coincidental. There is a metaphor for this that appears in hasidic teachings (see, e.g., *Likkutei Torah*, Lev. 81b): When a stone wall falls, the stones at the top fall farther and break into more pieces. When we stand in front of the ruins and attempt to restore them, the more distant and broken stones must have been the higher stones. Similarly, everything that is now in a revealed state above, including the person who is refining that which must be refined and the faculties he employs, are at their roots lower than that which must be refined and elevated.

In view of this, that which has been refined and ascends from the 288 sparks that are scattered in the worlds of *Beria, Yetzira,* and *Asiya* are loftier than the soul levels of *nefesh, ruaḥ,* and *neshama* within man. Here too the wording is precise. It is loftier "than the *nefesh, ruaḥ,* [and] *neshama* in man" but not man himself.

There are soul levels that are higher than *nefesh, ruaḥ,* and *neshama.* There is also *ḥaya* and *yeḥida,* as well as the divine soul itself, which is an actual portion of the Divine on high. The levels of *nefesh, ruaḥ,* and *neshama* are enclothed in the body, in the life of this world, in the faculties of the intellect, emotions, and their consequent actions. It is with these faculties that a person operates in this world, and it is these faculties that he employs when he refines the sparks. It is in relation to these faculties that the author of the *Tanya* states that the sparks that man refines and elevates are loftier, but this statement does not apply to the essence of man himself.

a person could not do more than his status allows, and what he gives he will receive, no more. But when he fulfills the Torah and mitzvot, it is no longer his own private personal act. He serves as a vessel and garment for lofty wisdom and deed, which are far higher than the person himself. When a person operates below through the Torah and mitzvot, he will raise from there sparks and forces of holiness that transcend whatever he invested in this service.

כִּי הֵן מְס"ג שֶׁבִּפְנִימִית "אָדָם קַדְמוֹן", וְנֶפֶשׁ רוּחַ נְשָׁמָה שֶׁכְּבָר נִתַּקְנוּ עַל יְדֵי מ"ה, הוּא יוֹצֵא מֵהַמֵּצַח הָאָרָה בְּעָלְמָא

for they stem from the name *Sag* of the inner dimension of *Adam Kadmon*, whereas the *nefesh, ruaḥ*, and *neshama*, which were already rectified through the name *Mah*, emerge from the forehead of *Adam Kadmon* as mere illumination.

Here the author of the *Tanya* repeats what he just stated using kabbalistic terminology. *Adam Kadmon*, which is the loftiest and most internal spiritual world, constitutes the mapping out of all reality. The refinement that is effected is rooted in the divine name *Sag*, which itself stems from the internal dimension of *Adam Kadmon*, while the person who effected the rectification stems from the name *Mah*, which is only an external illumination that emerges from *Adam Kadmon*. This is another way of saying that the root of that which is refined is loftier than the person who effects the refinement.

When these concepts are analyzed in all their detail and depth, they paint a complex picture that is hard to understand without a kabbalistic background, which is why the author of the *Tanya* merely alludes to them here.

In summary, we might say that the refined sparks from the name *Sag* are rooted in the inner will of God itself, but because of their intensity and magnitude, the lights could not be contained and could not exist in reality. The person who effected the rectification stems from the name *Mah*, whose lights are more external and so not as intense, and it is precisely because it is merely an illumination, that it can exist in reality and that man can rectify the sparks. ☞

SAG AND MAH, CHAOS AND RECTIFICATION

☞ These two divine names are expansions of the name of *Havaya*. There are four principal expansions of the name: *Ab*, or *Ayin-Bet*; *Sag*, or *Samekh-Gimmel*; *Mah* or *Mem-Heh*; and *Ban*, or *Bet-Nun*. These names are derived by spelling out the four letters that comprise the name of *Havaya* and adding up their numerical value. The name *Sag* is derived from the expansion of the name where the letter *heh* is spelled with a *yod* and the letter *vav* with an *alef*, so that numerical values of the letters *yod-vav-dalet*, *heh-yod*, *vav-alef-vav*, and *heh-yod* are totaled and add up to 63, or *samekh-gimmel*. The name *Mah* is an expansion of the name where these letters are spelled with an *alef,* so that the numerical values of *yod-vav-dalet, heh-alef*, *vav-alef-vav*, and *heh-alef* are totaled and amount to 45, the numerical value of *Mah*.

The name of *Havaya* is the most inclusive name, which always refers to the revelation of God Himself as the divine light that is enclothed in the vessels or as the vessel that radiates with this light (*Torah Or* 10b). The expansions of the name of *Havaya* represent the various degrees and ways in which the divine light is revealed. In this particular context, the name *Sag* refers to the divine revelation in the so-called world of chaos, the primeval, unformed world whose power was greater than its ability to exist, which had multiple lights and too few vessels (see *Etz Ḥayyim, Sha'ar HaTikkun*, chap. 5). Since it could not contain the lights, it shattered, and the fragments of the vessels and the sparks of the lights formed the infrastructure of our reality.

The name *Mah* denotes rectification, illumination, and the balanced and measured divine revelation that rectifies the world of chaos to allow it to exist properly. The relationship between these names is thus clarifier and clarified, chaos and its rectification. But here, in referring to the names *Sag* and *Mah*, and to the level of *Adam Kadmon*, the author of the *Tanya* gives an additional facet to these relationships.

Adam Kadmon is the most comprehensive level of reality: It is the first *partzuf* that the supernal Emanator issued forth after the constriction of the divine light, the *Keter* or Crown of all reality, the will that incorporates the particular wills, from the light of *Ein Sof* before the constriction all the way down to the lowest point in this world. This entire space, the line, so to speak, that extends from the light of *Ein Sof* to that lowest point, is called *Adam Kadmon*. It is called *adam*, man, because it has the structure of a man formed from the ten *sefirot* so that one can speak of a head, feet, and forehead, as well as above and below, internal and external, in relation to it. It is called *kadmon*, primeval, because it precedes and incorporates all the *partzufim*. Accordingly, when the names *Sag* and *Mah* are related to the structure of *Adam Kadmon*, this is like defining the essence and position of something on the most comprehensive map of all time.

The name *Sag* stems from the inner dimension of *Adam Kadmon*, as the author of the *Tanya* points out. This refers to the essence of the supreme encompassing will. It is not a vehicle, a medium or intermediary through which the will is manifest, but rather it itself bears the will and revelation of *Ein Sof*, as it were. The sparks that man uncovers in the world stem from *Sag* and express the same infinite essence as divine revelation. By contrast, the individual who effected the refinement of the sparks, or more precisely, his *nefesh, ruaḥ*, and *ne-*

וְזֶה שֶׁכָּתוּב: "לִפְנֵי מְלוֹךְ מֶלֶךְ כו'"
(בראשית לו, לא)

This is the meaning of the verse "And these are the kings who reigned in the land of Edom, **before the reign of a king** for the children of Israel" (Gen. 36:31).

The name Israel is related to the divine name *Mah*, the rectifier, while the kings of Edom allude to the *sefirot*, which reigned in the world of chaos until the vessels shattered. Esau, who is Edom,[47] was the elder son, while Jacob, who was also called Israel, was the younger son. This verse thus hints that the kings of the world of chaos that stem from the name *Sag* preceded the kingdom of Israel, or the world of rectification.

וְהַיְינוּ טַעֲמָא שֶׁהָאָדָם חַי בִּמְזוֹנוֹת דּוֹמֵם צוֹמֵחַ חַי וּמְבָרְרָן במ"ה שֶׁבּוֹ וְחַי בָּהֶם, לְפִי שֶׁהֵם מס"ג

This is the reason that man lives on sustenance from the mineral, vegetable, and animal kingdoms, **which he refines through the** *Mah* **within him, and he lives through them, since they stem from** *Sag.*

It is an age-old question: Man lives on food from the mineral, vegetable, and animal kingdoms, but with his capacity for speech, he is above them. How, then, is it possible for him to receive his vitality from them? After all, the rule is that the higher entity bestows on the lower one, not the other way around. The answer is that man stems from the name *Mah*, whereas and the mineral, vegetable, and animal kingdoms come from the sparks of chaos that fell from the name *Sag*. When a person

shama, which carry out the actual refinement and rectification, belong to the name *Mah*, which emerges "from the forehead of *Adam Kadmon* as mere illumination." Without going into detail, the name *Mah* is a revelation of the Divine, but while it constitutes a full and balanced expression of all aspects of revelation, it is still only revelation and illumination. Consequently,

unlike *Sag*, which cannot be revealed and cannot exist in balance with any other aspect of revelation due to its immense light, the name *Mah* is only an illumination or reflection of the divine light. Although it is a diminished illumination, it is still divine revelation, but it is only a partial revelation of *Adam Kadmon*.

47. Gen. 36:1.

eats of one of these species with the proper intention, he extracts those sparks and elevates them to their root in the name *Sag*, which is higher than man and from which they give life to the person.[48]

This is not referring only to the life of the physical body. The question primarily concerns the spiritual existence of man and his lofty divine soul. In order for his soul to be vivified from the bread he ingests, he must, when eating, refine the food and extract the holy sparks it contains. In other words, it is not enough for him to physically eat. The mere physical act of eating, without intent and spiritual work, might sustain the body but not the soul. In fact, that kind of eating even makes a person more corporeal and weakens his spiritual faculties.

When a person eats, he must rectify the food, which means that he himself must have the status of a rectified being, at any rate with respect to this food and act of eating. He must position himself at least somewhat above the food, in a space where he can reveal the essence of the person he is as an embodiment of *Mah*. He will thereby awaken from the food the holy spark that is captured within it, which is the embodiment of *Sag*. The spark will then be elevated and refined, and the spiritual and divine portions of man will receive nourishment in turn.

וְעוֹד זֹאת, כְּמוֹ שֶׁכָּתוּב: "וּפָנַי לֹא יֵרָאוּ" (שמות לג, כג), שֶׁפְּנִימִית הָעֶלְיוֹן אֵינוֹ יָכוֹל לֵירֵד לְמַטָּה, רַק חִיצוֹנִיּוּתוֹ וּבְחִינַת אֲחוֹרַיִים

In addition, there is another reason that the fulfillment of the action-related mitzvot are superior to cognitive love and fear: **As it is written, "But My face will not be seen"** (Ex. 33:23), which means **that the supernal inner dimension cannot descend below, only its external aspect and back side,**

---

48. There is an alternative answer that is related to an explanation of the Arizal (in *Likkutei Torah, Parashat Ekev*) regarding the verse "Man does not live by bread alone; rather, it is by everything that emanates from the mouth of the Lord that man lives" (Deut. 8:3). It is not the physical bread that sustains man, but rather it is that which emanates from the mouth of God in the form of the ten utterances with which the world was created, which includes bread and other nourishment, that sustains the person who eats it (see *Keter Shem Tov* 194). And yet a question still remains: After all, wasn't man also created with those ten utterances? At this point, the author of the *Tanya*'s observation comes into play.

The author of the *Tanya* elaborates further on the advantages of the fulfillment of the action-related mitzvot over cognitive love and fear.

The inner dimension, the divine essence, by its very definition, cannot emerge outward, and that which does emerge is not the "face" but the "back." The author of the *Tanya* cited this verse at the beginning of the essay to impart the essential limitation of the divine revelation to the extent that even a soul of *Atzilut*, such as that of Moses, cannot see "My face," the divine essence. Here the author of the *Tanya* takes his analysis in another direction, pointing to what can descend and be apprehended by created beings. This relates to the previous words in the verse: "You will see My back, but My face will not be seen." This conveys that whatever descends to the worlds, which the people of the world can see, is the "back." To illustrate, when a person wants to teach someone, he cannot convey to him everything that he thinks and feels, but only the back side, his speech, which expresses the conclusions and ramifications of his ideas in terms that the other can understand.

שֶׁהוּא נוֹבְלוֹת חָכְמָה עִילָּאָה   **which are the withered fruit of supernal wisdom.**

The wisdom that descends from above is not wisdom itself as it exists on high, but only the "withered fruit of supernal wisdom." Wisdom is essence in every context, like the light in a vessel, like the world of *Atzilut* among the worlds, like the soul, and therefore it cannot descend in the same state as it is manifest above. What is transmitted and descends is like the withered fruit that falls from a tree, which has no taste or vitality, and seemingly no interior, but only an external form that recalls the fruit that once was on the tree. ☞

THE WITHERED FRUIT

☞ This expression is taken from a saying of the Rabbis: "Rabbi Ḥanina bar Yitzḥak said: There are three types of withered fruit: The withered fruit of death is sleep; the withered fruit of prophecy is a dream; the withered fruit of the World to Come is the Sabbath. Rabbi Avin adds another two: The withered fruit of the supernal light is the sphere of the sun; the withered fruit of supernal wisdom is the Torah." (*Bereshit Rabba* 17:5; 44:17)

This fruit, then, is not merely external *kelippa*. The Torah, for instance, is also something internal, but in the world below it is enclothed in the garments of this world. Likewise, the Sabbath is the withered fruit of the World to Come. There can be no World to Come within this world, but

וְעוֹד זֹאת, שֶׁהֲרֵי הַדִּבּוּר מִדְּבָרֵי
חָכְמָה עִילָאָה אֵינוֹ מוֹלִיד, וְהַטִּפָּה
שֶׁנִּמְשְׁכָה מֵהַכְּלִי דְּחָכְמָה עִילָאָה,
יֵשׁ בָּה כֹּחַ הַמּוֹלִיד וּמְהַוֶּוה יֵשׁ
מֵאַיִן.

Furthermore, speech from words of supernal wisdom does not produce offspring, while the drop that is drawn from the vessel of supernal wisdom has the power to produce offspring and bring about existence from nothingness.

The author of the Tanya offers another metaphor explaining the superiority of action-related mitzvot over the service of cognitive love and fear: Speech that emits from supernal wisdom transmits only the back side, the external dimension of existence, in contrast to the transfer of a drop of semen from male to female, which transmits that which is internal, actual essence. ☞ ☞

there is a Sabbath. The Sabbath is like a window, a template, of the World to Come, which can be enveloped within the reality and the materiality of this world. Whoever enters the Sabbath will have a sense, as if peering through a window, of the World to Come itself.

The same applies to the Torah: Even though it is enclothed in the materials of this world, such as the laws pertaining to an ox and a donkey plowing a field together or those of *tzitzit*, whoever enters its interior, even in this world, will see in it the supernal wisdom itself. One has to know how to read it, one must study and make the effort, but it is possible and necessary to perceive the supernal wisdom of the Torah even in this world.

SPEECH VERSUS THE DROP

☞ Throughout his writings, the author of the *Tanya* offers analogies for understanding the relationship between giver and recipient. One is the relationship between teacher and student. The teacher confers his wisdom to the student through speech. In this model, what is transmitted is merely external, a mere reflection of what the teacher knows and thinks. The other analogy is the transfer of a drop of semen from male to female, which in effect is a transference of his own essence (see *Iggeret HaKodesh*, epistle 15; *Torah Or* 8b).

When a person speaks words of wisdom, such as when one teaches his student, he conveys information that imparts what he thinks and feels. There is no transmission of the person's own essence here, but only an illumination and back side of what he contains within. An illumination of this kind, which is related to the higher faculties of the soul, the emotive attributes and the intellect, can be lofty and abstract and is capable of revealing an understanding of the Divine, at least as much as the human intellect is capable of comprehending it. By contrast, the drop that the male gives to the female, like a seed sown in the ground, seems to involve nothing but simple physicality, yet it transmits the very essence of the bestower. This drop will become an actual person, just like the

וְגַם הַמְשָׁכַת חָכְמָה עִילָאָה כְּלוּלָה
בָּהּ, וְהַטַּעַם, מִפְּנֵי שֶׁבָּהּ נִמְשָׁךְ
מַהוּתָהּ וְעַצְמוּתָהּ דְּחָכְמָה עִילָאָה

Also, the flow of supernal wisdom is incorporated within the drop of semen, **and the reason is because the essence and being of supernal wisdom flows into it,**

As was commonly supposed in the times of the author of the *Tanya*, the drop of semen is drawn from the brain in the form of the spiritual essence of the intellect and wisdom, which descends and materializes in the spinal cord until it becomes a physical drop of semen. It is not that the wisdom affects another part of the body, which then produces

giver himself is a person. It is not speech or even thought, but an essence like that of the father, who will think, understand, and feel on his own.

Consider, for the sake of illustration, the difference between a picture of a large, colorful tree with many fruits that impresses all who see it in its size and beauty. Meanwhile, next to it there is the seed of the tree, which is small, gray, and perhaps rotten. It does not resemble the tree in any way, yet nothing will be born from the picture, not even another picture, whereas from the small seed another tree will grow, bearing fruit that itself can reproduce.

EXISTENCE FROM NOTHINGNESS

☞ The author of the *Tanya* is discussing the birth of a new essence that did not previously exist, something from nothingness. It is only in the divine essence itself, and the point contained within the soul that constitutes that essence, that this special power exists, that can create something from nothingness. It is only at that point, where something was newly created, the something from the nothingness, that the essence of the bestower himself is present.

The supernal essence in all entities is enclothed in wisdom. The point of wisdom is the initial point of the apprehension and awareness of the soul, and just as it is the beginning of apprehension, it is also the beginning of the existence of the soul. Like the initial point of creation, it itself is nothingness, completely nullified, and therefore it is the only vessel that can contain infinity, as it were.

This flash of light that represents the point of wisdom, a light that does not constitute an actual vessel with dimensions of length and width, but consists only of the revelation of light itself, is a vessel that itself serves as the light contained in all other vessels, and it conveys the divine essence within it. Yet wisdom itself, although it conveys that which is infinite, is revealed only in the physical drop. The entire expanse of the soul and its faculties, like the divine *sefirot*, are nothing more than a transmitter of the essence itself, which is revealed only at the end of everything, at the emergence of the physical drop that gives birth to something from nothingness.

the drop, but rather the wisdom itself, its "essence and being," is drawn into the drop.

In the case at hand, since the physical drop contains all the information and potential needed to form a complete person, it is an embodiment of the point of wisdom, which is the initial point of the creation of the person that incorporates the entire spiritual essence of a human being.

מַה שֶּׁאֵין כֵּן בְּדִבּוּר וּמַחֲשָׁבָה, וַאֲפִילוּ בְּהַשְׂכָּלַת הַשֵּׂכֶל בְּאֵיזוֹ חָכְמָה	which is not the case for man's speech and thought, nor even the intellectual conception of some piece of wisdom.

This differs not only from the garments of the soul, speech and thought, but also from the intellect itself, even before it is enclothed in the letters of thought. This can be observed in the difference between speech and thought themselves, where not all thoughts are clothed in the letters of speech. We think of an idea, understand and sense it in a way that is clear to us, but the idea cannot be conveyed to another person comprehensively in words.

Likewise, there is a stage that precedes thought. It is impossible to fathom it, because it has not yet manifested itself in thought and it is imperceptible even to ourselves. Yet we know it exists, like the light that exists even before it is enclothed in vessels.

הֲרֵי חָכְמָה זוֹ רַק הֶאָרָה מִתְפַּשֶּׁטֶת מִמַּהוּת הַשֵּׂכֶל שֶׁבַּנֶּפֶשׁ וְעַצְמוּתוֹ	This intellectual conception of some piece of wisdom is merely an illumination emanating from the essence of the intellect that is in the soul and its being,

This intellectual conception, which has not even emerged into the intellect itself, is only a reflection of the intellect, which conceives of a certain topic. Though the intellect is employed in thinking of the concept, it does not constitute the intellect itself. It is a reflection or illumination of the intellect, stemming from the intellect but not the intellect itself.

וְהָאָרָה זוֹ הִיא רַק לְבוּשׁ לְמַהוּתוֹ
וְעַצְמוּתוֹ שֶׁל הַשֵּׂכֶל וְהַשֵּׂכֶל הוּא
הָאָרָה וּלְבוּשׁ לְמַהוּת הַנֶּפֶשׁ

and this illumination is merely a garment for the essence and being of the intellect, while the intellect is an illumination and a garment for the essence of the soul.

The intellect itself does not constitute a particular piece of knowledge or concept but is a faculty of the soul. It constitutes its ability to comprehend and conceive ideas, while the various conceptions that it conceives are the innumerable different illuminations and manifestations of the intellect. It is in these conceptions that the essence of the intellect is enclothed. Moreover, even the intellect itself is nothing more than a reflection and manifestation of the soul's essence.

This description of the intellect contained in the soul, from its most external manifestation as it is enclothed in speech to its more internal manifestation, which lies in thought, and the even more internal levels of awareness and the intellect itself, are nothing but a reflection and enclothing of the essence of the soul. As for the essence of the soul itself, as is the case with the divine essence, we have no apprehension of it at all.

מַה שֶּׁאֵין כֵּן הַטִּפָּה, נִמְשָׁךְ בָּהּ
גַּם מִמַּהוּת הַנֶּפֶשׁ וְעַצְמוּתָהּ
הַמְלוּבֶּשֶׁת בַּמּוֹחִין, וְלָכֵן מוֹלִידָהּ
בְּדוֹמֶה לָהּ מַמָּשׁ

This is not the case with the drop of semen. The essence and being of the soul, which is enclothed in the intellect, is also drawn into it, and therefore it produces that which is actually similar to itself.

In contrast to any other manner of giving, it is only through the drop of semen that the father imparts his soul's essence and being. It is evident that only the soul's essence, not any revelation or illumination that stems from it, can give birth to a being exactly like it. Only the essence of the soul bears within it the totality of everything, and only the essence of the soul carries with it the light of *Ein Sof*, the power that created it and that can also create a child who resembles his father.

The soul and the drop of semen are a metaphor for that which God Himself bestows on the world. He bestows an illumination that we have the capacity to receive, that of the faculties of the intellect, of love and fear. But there is nothing of His essence in any of these faculties, but merely a revelation of His existence. Yet God also provides, in the terms of the analogy, a "drop." It is through this drop, which is a mitzva that He gave us to perform, that God draws forth His essence and being into this world.

וְזֶהוּ הַהֶפְרֵשׁ בֵּין עֲבוֹדַת הַמַּלְאָכִים This is the difference between
הַיּוֹצְאִין מִ'נְשִׁיקִין' לְהַנְּשָׁמוֹת הַיּוֹצְאִין the service of the angels, which
מֵהַ'כֵּלִים' emerge through kisses, and that
of the souls, which issue forth
from the vessels.

The difference between the bestowal of the intellect and the bestowal of a drop, a mitzva, which contains God's essence, is like the difference between service performed with cognitive love and fear his service performed through the action-related mitzvot. This is also the difference between the service of the angels and the service of the human soul. This is only a general distinction, since like the angels, the souls also serve God with cognitive love and fear, but the human soul has another level of divine service, which no angel possesses, and that is service through the action-related mitzvot. ☞ ☞

ANGELS AND SOULS

☞ Just as angels and souls differ from each other in their manner of service, they differ at their essence. As the author of the *Tanya* points out, the angels are born of a coupling of spiritual kisses, whereas the human soul is born of a physical coupling. The former emerges from the lights, while the latter issues forth from the vessels. As in our world, every entity in the spiritual worlds is born from the mating of a male and a female. A male alone or a female alone cannot give birth to another living being. This can occur only through the union of them both, or coupling. The male is the giver, bestowing the light, while the female receives, collects, and contains the light within a particular space and time, allowing for the formation of offspring.

The kabbalistic teachings speak of two types of coupling: a coupling of kisses and a physical coupling. A coupling of kisses is a spiritual coupling, and just like a kiss in this world, it constitutes a spiritual closeness that reveals a deep emotion and intellect, but does not involve a physical drop. In the higher worlds, this resembles the coupling of *Ḥokhma* and *Bina*, which are also called Father and Mother. This coupling fertilizes *Bina*, which gives birth to the cognitive awareness and emotions expressed by the angels.

There is also a physical pairing, which produces not only intellects and feelings but an actual child. This is reminiscent of the coupling of *Zeir Anpin* and *Malkhut*, which produces actual offspring: the souls of Israel. These are not merely an expression of the holy *sefirot*, of the love and fear of God, but they are "children to the Lord" (Deut. 14:1). The child is the drop, or divine essence, which is more than the father's cognitive awareness

The author of the *Tanya* now goes on to explain how these ideas can be reconciled: how it is that the service of man is performed both with the vessels, or *sefirot*, of *Atzilut*, and the essence, or lights, of *Atzilut*, as well as the lights that spread from it throughout the worlds.

and feelings. It is in a sense an actual copy, a reproduction, of the father himself.

The difference between a person's intellect and that of his child is comparable to the difference between an angel and the soul, as well as the difference between the angel's service and the service of the soul. The service of the angel entails love or fear, which arise and are born from the intellect and awareness. The angel does not choose to serve God or not to do so, nor does it serve God sometimes in one manner and sometimes in another. Rather, the angel and his service are one and the same, just as all inanimate, vegetable, and living beings serve God and sing praise to Him through the very fact of their existence (as we find in *Perek Shirah*).

By contrast, the service of the soul is comparable to the service of the child in the author of the *Tanya*'s analogy. The child's service is not only an expression of the father's intellect, but it is an expression of the father himself. In this sense, the service of the soul is not like that of the angel, which serves God simply as it is, through its very identification as an angel. The soul's service entails an expression and revelation of the Father, of God, as it were. It strives to emulate God, to reflect His essence.

Yet a mortal person, however talented and superlative he is, cannot draw forth God's essence through his intellect, his wisdom or understanding, or through any degree of love and fear. The only that one can connect to the divine essence, to become a vessel for it, is through negation, the nullification of one's apprehension, love, fear, and all the faculties and manifestations of the soul (see *Likkutei Amarim*, chap. 35). Even this can be achieved only through the fulfillment of an action-related mitzva.

Furthermore, unlike the angel, man's service is a matter of choice, whether to perform the service or not, whether to act in this way or in some other manner. This constitutes loftiest manifestation of God Himself in the world, more than any faculty or intellect: the freedom of choice given to man. It is the preliminary condition for a person's service, and through it one can, as it were, bring God Himself into the world.

"FROM THE VESSELS"

☞ The author of the *Tanya* describes the physical coupling with the expression "from the vessels," because in contrast to the spiritual coupling of kisses, which is in essence a coupling of lights, such as Ḥokhma and Bina, which form the infrastructures for the intellect and emotions, the physical coupling also encompasses vessels, such as the lower sefirot like *Tiferet* and *Malkhut*. As is the case in this world, this coupling means that there will be giving and receiving within the parameters of the vessels, not only in terms of the relationship between male and female, but something of the essence is actually transmitted and received. In other words, it is not sufficient for the light within the vessels to move from one to the other, but rather the vessel itself must pass over. Only in this way is the essence itself transferred, as in the drop of semen that produces a child.

אַךְ הַכֵּלִים דַּאֲצִילוּת נַעֲשׂוּ נְשָׁמָה לִבְרִיאָה יְצִירָה עֲשִׂיָּה. וְהִלְכָּךְ דְּחִילוּ וּרְחִימוּ שֶׁכְּלִיִּים הֵן כְּמַלְאָכִים דִּנְשִׁיקִין, מֵהֶאָרַת חִיצוֹנִית דְּחָכְמָה בִּינָה דַּעַת בִּבְרִיאָה יְצִירָה עֲשִׂיָּה

Yet the vessels of *Atzilut* **become the soul of** the worlds of *Beria, Yetzira,* and *Asiya,* **and therefore** man's **cognitive fear and love** of God **are like** the service of the **angels,** which issue forth **from kisses,** but only **from the external illumination of Ḥokhma, Bina,** and *Da'at* **in** *Beria, Yetzira,* and *Asiya.*

There is no unambiguous, objective definition of lights and vessels. Something that is a vessel in the world of *Atzilut* becomes light and soul in the worlds below it when it descends there. Moreover, man's service through cognitive fear and love of God is like the service of the angels, which is a spiritual service, like the coupling of kisses, which is a spiritual union, rather than the physical service of drawing forth the divine essence, as occurs through the service of man. In other words, even man, in serving God with the faculties manifest in his soul, with his cognitive love and fear, is relating to the manifestations of the Divine in the worlds rather than the divine essence itself. These are not revelations of the essence of *Atzilut,* of the divine essence itself, but only "the external illumination of Ḥokhma, Bina, and Da'at." When the essence contained in the vessels itself descends to the worlds, it is not contained within the intellect or the attributes but rather manifests as a physical drop, or as an action-related mitzva. But when Ḥokhma, Bina, and Da'at descend into the worlds as Ḥokhma, Bina, and Da'at, this is a revelation of the Divine, merely an external illumination, not that of the divine essence.

וְהַטַּעַם מִשּׁוּם דִּפְנִימִית חָכְמָה בִּינָה דַּעַת, וּמַהוּתוֹ וְעַצְמוּתוֹ שֶׁל אוֹר פְּנִימִי, אֵינוֹ יָכוֹל לְהִתְגַּלּוֹת

The reason that the revelation is external **is that the internal dimension of Ḥokhma, Bina,** and *Da'at,* **and the essence and being of the inner light, cannot be revealed**

The worlds do not have the capacity to contain the internal dimension of Ḥokhma, Bina, and Da'at, which is the light that expresses the essence the *sefirot* of Ḥokhma, Bina, and Da'at in *Atzilut.* This is the light of intellect itself, the awareness and understanding of the essence of the Divine. Ḥokhma, Bina, and Da'at of Atzilut constitute a knowledge of the Divine at its essence, from the divine perspective of reality, where there is no barrier or concealment and there is no place for the worlds below to exist at all. Here, in the world of Atzilut, within the awareness engendered by these supernal sefirot, there is literally nothing else besides Him.

אֶלָּא עַל יְדֵי הָאָרַת הַכֵּלִים דַּוְקָא הַיּוֹרְדִים לְמַטָּה, כְּטִיפַּת הָאָדָם מִמּוֹחִין

except through the illumination of the vessels specifically, which descend below, like the drop of semen of man that issues from the brains,

The only way for this inner light to be revealed is through the "illumination of the vessels." The inner light, the essence, descend specifically through vessels.

The light is transparent and reflects what it is without concealment, but it has no ability to exist beyond the place and context in which it illuminates. By contrast, the vessel is opaque and conceals the light and that which it represents. It has its own existence, as it were, hiding the light within it. But it is for this very reason that it can bring down actual essence and transmit it to another reality, like the drop of semen that transfers the essence of the father to another reality within the child.

To illustrate with a more spiritual example: When one person speaks to another and thereby conveys ideas and feelings to him, what is actually transferred to the other person is only the words, or the vessels that contain those ideas. One cannot impart an idea without speaking. A person's idea or feeling may be strong and clear in his own mind, but without words they have no external existence.

Similarly, the light is specific and belongs only to the source of its illumination, whereas the vessel is universal. Thus, the words and letters can transmit the idea therein precisely because they do not illuminate on their own at all.

וּכְמוֹ שֶׁכָּתוּב: "וּפָנַי לֹא יֵרָאוּ"

as it is written, "But My face will not be seen."

It is with regard to this internal dimension, to the light and essence that are concealed, that God said to Moses, "But My face will not be seen." The word *panai*, "My face," is related to *penimiyut*, the internal dimension. This does not apply only to Moses, but to the entirety of the wisdom and Torah that he brought down for all generations. They are available solely in the form of "My face will not be seen" and "you will see My back."[49]

וּבַר מִן כָּל דֵּין   Apart from all this,

8 Kislev

7 Kislev
(leap year)

In addition to everything that has been said so far about the superiority of the action-related mitzvot over spiritual service, over developing love and fear of God, there is another, more weighty point to be made. This is not just about two different ways of serving God, since it is possible that one method without the other will not accord with the divine will in any case.

In general, there are two trajectories in the service of God. One involves ascension, when a person, by virtue of his service, elevates the lights from the vessels in this world to the divine source above.[50] The second is the flow from above to below, the drawing forth of the divine light into the vessels of this world. The work of elevation primarily involves the spiritual service of cognitive love and fear, where one

---

49. In this context, the Talmud states, "And I will remove My hand, and you will see My back' (Ex. 33:23) – Rav Ḥanna bar Bizna said in the name of Rabbi Shimon Ḥasida: This teaches that the Holy One, blessed be He, showed Moses the knot of *tefillin*" (*Berakhot* 7a). In terms of intellectual apprehension, Moses was indeed shown only the knot of God's *tefillin*, so to speak, which is behind the head, but with regard to the action-related mitzvot and Torah study, he was enclothed in the actual four passages of *tefillin* rather than merely the knot. See *Or HaTorah*, Num., vol. 1, p. 119.

50. Rabbi Menaḥem Mendel Schneerson, the Lubavitcher Rebbe, explains that there is another way of elevating, in which not only the lights ascend from the vessels, but the vessels themselves rise to a higher level, as in the ascension of the worlds on the Sabbath and Yom Kippur (see *Or HaTorah*, Lev., vol. 2, pp. 549ff). This ascent is entirely good, since the vessels are purified and become receptacles for loftier and more wondrous lights. That is not the case for the ascent and removal of the lights from the vessels, which is the main topic of discussion here.

apprehends the divine light itself and so desires and longs to emerge from the vessel below and cleave to the Divine.

The service of drawing down the divine light from above to below consists mainly of the performance of the action-related mitzvot. In the optimal circumstances, these two forms of service are intertwined: The upward trajectory awakens the desire to increase the flow downward, as described at the beginning of the essay. Accordingly, if the ascent from below to above does not lead to a flow from above to below, all we are left with is the lights leaving the vessels, of the soul and life force departing from the body. This is the opposite of the divine will, which always seeks to bestow and impart life to the vessels and the worlds. God wants to have an abode in the lower realm,[51] for the divine light and life force to be perpetually drawn down from above to this world.

אֲפִילוּ בִּנְשָׁמָה דַּאֲצִילוּת, אַף שֶׁהִיא מִכֵּלִים דַּאֲצִילוּת, וְכֵן בְּנֶפֶשׁ רוּחַ מִכֵּלִים דִּיצִירָה עֲשִׂיָּה

even in a soul of *Atzilut*, though it stems from the vessels of *Atzilut*, and likewise with regard to the *nefesh* and *ruah*, which stem from the vessels of *Yetzira* and *Asiya*,

A "soul of *Atzilut*" is a lofty soul, because not only is its root in *Atzilut* (as is the case for all souls), but its life experience, its service, belongs to *Atzilut* as well. This is the case even though "it stems from the vessels of *Atzilut*." The human soul, unlike the angels, emerge from the vessels, as explained earlier, and thus they are not merely a light of *Atzilut* but an essence of *Atzilut*. The same applies to the *nefesh* and *ruah*, which stem from the vessels of *Yetzira* and *Asiya*,[52] which refer to souls whose level of service is on a lower level, rooted in the worlds of *Beria*, *Yetzira*, and *Asiya*, since they too, on their level, stem from the vessels of those worlds and their essences.

---

51. See *Midrash Tanhuma, Behukotai* 3, *Naso* 16; *Bereshit Rabba* 3:9; *Bemidbar Rabba* 13:6; see also *Likkutei Amarim*, chap. 36.

52. According to the Lubavitcher Rebbe, Rabbi Menahem Mendel Schneerson,: "The manuscripts of *Kuntres Aharon* require scrutiny, since there is apparently something missing here, and it should read. 'And likewise with regard to the *nefesh, ruah*, and *neshama* and the vessels of *Beria, Yetzira*, and *Asiya* ... in the vessels of *Beria, Yetzira*, and *Asiya*, in the form of ...' But the text that appears in *Or HaTorah* is the same as the printed version."

הִנֵּה רְחִימוּ [אוּלַי צָרִיךְ לִהְיוֹת: their cognitive love of God [perhaps
דְּחִילוּ וּרְחִימוּ] שֶׁכְּלַיִם שֶׁלָּהֶם, this should read: fear and love] also
מְעוֹרְרִים גַּם כֵּן בְּכֵלִים דִּיצִירָה awaken in the vessels, or sefirot, of
עֲשִׂיָּה, בְּחִינַת הָעֶלְאָה מִמַּטָּה Yetzira and Asiya an ascent from
לְמַעְלָה, בְּאִתְעָרוּתָא דִּלְתַתָּא below to above through an awakening from below.

When the author of the *Tanya* says "their cognitive love," he is referring
to the divine service of the souls performed through cognitive fear
and love, which cause the lights in the vessels, or *sefirot*, of the worlds
of *Yetzira* and *Asiya*, to emerge from the vessels and ascend on high.
We see that such service elevates the lights also from the vessels in the
spiritual worlds above, not only in this world. ☞

וְזֶהוּ בְּחִינַת הִסְתַּלְּקוּת לְבָד חַס However, this is a form of departure
וְשָׁלוֹם alone, God forbid,

The ascent of the lights from the vessels, which does not incorporate
any thought or request for a flow of light from above to below, con-

AWAKENING AN ASCENT IN THE VESSELS

☞ The worlds, including the higher worlds, are dormant. The lights and vessels exist in an established order, and they remain in that state throughout the existence of the world. What changes, and thereby also causes a modification in the worlds, is man.

Man acts and changes and so effects alterations in his world, and in this way he brings about similar transformations in all the worlds above and beyond. A similar process can be observed in our mundane lives: People tend to become preoccupied with their daily routines and do not think or talk about certain issues, even when they are a matter of life and death. Then it might happen that someone, perhaps even a small child, will wake up and cry that he wants to go home, and his tears will cause others to open their eyes as well, and they will realize that they too want to go home. They would have gone on with their daily routines without ceasing if not for the change stimulated by the child's tears.

In the same vein, the soul of a man below is awakened through cognitive love and fear to restore his soul from among the dark vessels of the body and this world and bring it back to its source, to rejoin the divine light that it seeks to reach. This awakening in turn arouses in all the worlds the longing of the light to return home.

Everything that a person does below has significance above. But the more one is a "person," the more he behaves as the image of God that he is, holier and more connected to the higher worlds and the lofty lights and revelations, the greater and more meaningful will be his awakening.

stitutes a departure of the lights alone. With regard to this kind of ascension, when the light leaves the vessels without returning, the author of the *Tanya* exclaims, "God forbid." It is true that this is the most beautiful of ascents, when the soul pines with love for God to the point of expiration, but it is, at the end of the day, a death, and that is not what God desires. Life entails "running and returning":[53] In the stage of running, we follow through on the aspiration of our hearts, evoking love and devotion for God, yearning to escape all the materiality and darkness of the physical world and cleave to the holiness that we can perceive and sense, until the soul expires. Returning entails the soul's return to the vessel, to physical matter, to the life of this world. ☞

אֲבָל בְּחִינַת הַמְשָׁכָה מִלְמַעְלָה לְמַטָּה, הוּא עַל יְדֵי מִצְוֹת מַעֲשִׂיּוֹת דַּוְקָא, לְהַמְשִׁיךְ אוֹר בְּכֵלִים

whereas the flow from above to below is achieved specifically through action-related mitzvot, drawing light into vessels,

RUNNING AND RETURNING: A WAY OF LIFE

☞ "Running" involves a temptation – the temptation of the righteous, that which is holy, to reach for the Divine and proceed with this aim all the way to the end. But this is not God's way, nor is it a way of life, which involves the dynamic of both running and returning.

We do not always know where life will lead us, and we are even unaware of our destination, but this is the path that God wants us to take: to live, to continue on, to exist and allow God, so to speak, to fulfill His inner desire through us. The pining of the soul to the point of expiration entails our longing to apprehend and perceive the Divine to a greater degree. If one were to continue pursuing this aim, he would reach a limit beyond which his existence must end. But for God there is no limit, and the purpose that God has designated for us

and our world extends even beyond the infinity that we currently understand to exist. In this sense, the pining of the soul to the point of expiration would cut short, so to speak, the ultimate purpose for which God created the world and man, and it is regarding this possibility that the author of the *Tanya* declares "God forbid."

This does not refer solely to lofty and hidden matters. Even on a simple level, one can sometimes see such distortion mirrored in our own world. As soon as one views this kind of departure from a broader perspective, not only with regard to the soul that consumes itself but also with respect to the world it leaves behind, the beautiful picture is spoiled. Like the body from which the soul has departed, so too the whole world to which that person belonged is left for dead. This is the case not

53. Based on Ezek. 1:14.

The flow of light in the vessels can be drawn from above to below, and this flow is achieved mainly through the fulfillment of the action-related mitzvot. While the first type of service entails elevating the soul's faculties, the intellect, love and fear of God, to a more abstract level that is detached from the physical plane, here a person does the converse: He lowers the higher, abstract, and holy faculties of his soul to a lower realm and mode of expression, that which belongs to the physical world. He thereby effects the same trajectory in all the worlds, of the flow of the divine light from above to the vessels in the worlds below. ☞

particularly the external aspect of the vessels so that the external aspect of the higher level descends below, while the inner dimension of the lower level ascends upward,

וּבְחִיצוֹנִית הַכֵּלִים דַּוְקָא. שֶׁחִיצוֹנִיּוּת הָעֶלְיוֹן יוֹרֵד לְמַטָּה וּפְנִימִיּוּת הַתַּחְתּוֹן עוֹלֶה לְמַעְלָה

just in the physical realm, but the entire spiritual world that he built, encompassing his children, students, and friends, no longer exists. The vitality and power that he invested in working and building, bearing children and educating them, in studying and teaching, are like a body from which the spirit has departed.

DRAWING LIGHT INTO VESSELS

☞ When a person fulfills mitzvot with his body, he injects meaning and light into all the materials and vessels without which the mitzva cannot be performed. This meaning serves "to draw light into vessels." From now on, the body and all those parts of this world with which the mitzva was performed are no longer mere matter. They now have a higher function and purpose that illuminates and vitalizes them with a supernal light.

Furthermore, and this is the main point, the flow that occurs through the fulfillment of the physical mitzva is actually the drawing forth of the divine essence itself. The divine essence cannot be drawn through the intellect, or through love and fear, because these faculties do not apprehend the divine essence but only its existence. In other words, the divine essence cannot be grasped in the lofty spiritual worlds, which constitute the supernal intellect and emotive attributes, but only in this physical world. Even then, it is not apprehended in actual reality but through the mitzva that is performed within it. Accordingly, when a person performs a mitzva, a supernal light is drawn from above, not only in order to bestow, to do good for someone, but because the vessel that constitutes the mitzva is its particular vessel, through which the divine essence may be revealed.

Spiritual ascent and descent is not the same as in the physical realm, where the flow is invariably from a higher to a lower place. Instead, it resembles the soul, where that which is more lofty is the more internal, essential self, while that which is on a lower level is external, the aspect that relates to others. That which can descend is therefore not that which is internal, which is essence, the entity itself. Rather, what descends is the external aspect, and this is what is revealed below, through one's deeds.

Meanwhile, "the inner dimension of the lower level ascends upward." That which ascends is the more internal, abstract aspect of the entity. Therefore, every ascent entails that which is internal. The interiority of the soul is less tied to external forms, and consequently it can detach itself from them and connect to loftier forms. This is what constitutes an ascent, where a person comprehends something on a higher, more spiritual, and abstract level. ☞

וְזֶה שֶׁכָּתוּב בַּזֹּהַר פָּרָשַׁת פְּקוּדֵי (חלק ב רמד, ב) הַנִּזְכָּר לְעֵיל (סימן ב): דְּאִית סִדּוּרָא כו'

and this is the meaning of the aforementioned statement from the *Zohar, Parashat Pekudei* (2:244b), that there is an order...

The full quote reads, "There is an order that is established through words, and there is an order that is established through will and the

THE ASCENT OF THE EXTERNAL, THE DESCENT OF THE INTERNAL

☞ The emphasis here is on the systematic connection between the ascent and the descent. The soul in its entirety is a single entity with an interior and exterior, an above and below. Therefore, movement in one direction inevitably induces movement in the other. Like a wave rising and falling, the ascent rises higher and higher until it reaches the peak of the wave, at which point any further ascent is no longer of any significance. Even if the soul were to desire it, it would be futile. From there the trajectory will be downward, until it subsides, whereupon the wave, the movement

of life itself, the soul's entire being, will seek the ascent once again.

Any person who truly lives, who does not burn himself out or destroy himself, but seeks fulfillment, can sense this dynamic: the thread of life pulling him up after it has descended and leading him down when it has climbed sufficiently. It is the release of tension when one reaches the peak of the ascent, leaving things behind in the ensuing descent. As the tension rebuilds, and the light overflows from the vessels, the soul rallies its forces, ready for a fresh ascent.

intention of the heart."[54] There is an order and way of serving God through words and deeds, which is primarily the descent of the light into the vessels, which are the words and deeds. There is also the spiritual service of contemplating the Divine, of evoking love and fear of God, which mainly entails elevation of the light from the vessels.

וּשְׁתֵּיהֶן צוֹרֶךְ גָּבוֹהַ, הָעֲלָאָה וְהַמְשָׁכָה	**Both of them are needed by the Most High: the elevation and drawing down**

Taken together, all the methods of service for elevating and drawing down the flow of light are "needed by the Most High." In other words, they are a requirement of God. Contrary to what one might think, that only the elevation is for the sake of God, while the drawing down of the light is for the sake of man and the world, the author of the *Tanya* stresses here that both trajectories, the elevation and the descent, are "needed by the Most High."

עַל יְדֵי הַעֲלָאַת מַיִין נוּקְבִין מס"ג בִּבְחִינַת עוֹבְדָא וּמִלּוּלָא	**through the ascension of the feminine waters from** the divine name *Sag,* which is achieved **through action and speech.**

The elevation of the sparks through the performance of mitzvot is called the "ascension of the feminine waters from *Sag.*" These feminine waters that a person elevates are the holy sparks from the name of *Sag* that fell into the world upon the shattering of the vessels, as has been explained. Their ascent from of the world is achieved through man's divine service, starting from man's animal soul and body and radiating outward until it includes this entire physical world. When he rectifies these elements, both his physical self and the physical world, he releases the sparks of light that were concealed in them and elevates them to their root above, and this is the ascension of the feminine waters.

The essence of this elevation of feminine waters is that they awaken and draw forth the masculine waters, which is the flow of divine light and life force from above to below. Why do the feminine waters draw

---

54. See *Kuntres Aḥaron* 2.

forth the flow of the masculine waters? It is because they are from the divine name *Sag*. In other words, since the root of the feminine waters is from *Sag*, which is loftier than the person who elevated them. When they are extracted from this world and elevated, they in turn return and bestow light and life below to the person who elevated them and to the world from which they ascended as soon as they ascend and are refined. Moreover, the light that returns is greater and loftier light than it was before. This is the flow of masculine waters after the ascension of the feminine waters.

The author of the *Tanya* also notes that the ascension of the feminine waters occurs through the garments of action and speech. Since the soul itself belongs to the higher realms, it is only when it is enclothed in speech and deeds that it can have any effect in the lower physical world, and thereby elevate the feminine waters from there.

> וְזֶהוּ תַּכְלִית הַהִשְׁתַּלְשְׁלוּת, לְהִתְגַּלּוֹת אוֹר עֶלְיוֹן לְמַטָּה וְלֹא לַעֲלוֹת הַתַּחְתּוֹן לְמַעְלָה

This is the purpose of the chain of progression: to reveal the supernal light below, not to elevate the lower level above,

This is the purpose of the entire order of the descent of the light of *Ein Sof* from the loftiest plane down to this world, from level to level, in a chain of progression. Since it originates above, its purpose and aim is necessarily below because it can only follow the trajectory of above to below.[55] Yet after it has been explained that there is both an ascent and a descent of light in the order of progression, one might have thought that the ultimate aim is the ascent, that God brought down the lights, to people and to the world, for the purpose of their subsequent ascent. But once it has been made clear that both are "needed by the Most High," that they are not two opposing trajectories, independent of one another, but are actually a single trajectory, we see that the aim is the descent. If the ultimate purpose were the ascent, why would the service of drawing forth the flow downward be required? But if the purpose is achieved down below, the reason for the ascent is clear: It

---

55. See *Likkutei Amarim*, chap. 36.

is precisely that which rises from below that awakens the source above to issue forth to the vessel below. ☞

שֶׁזֶּה אֵינוֹ אֶלָּא לְפִי שָׁעָה. וְאַף גַּם זֹאת דַּוְקָא, עֲלִיּוֹת הַכֵּלִים לָאוֹרוֹת עֶלְיוֹנִים

for such an elevation **is only temporary, and even this** must be **specifically the elevation of the vessels to the supernal lights,**

The elevation is not an end in itself, but a temporary requirement in order to bring about the actual aim, which is the drawing forth of the light from above to the vessels below. Even this temporal ascent must be executed in a particular manner and method, which is "the elevation of the vessels to the supernal lights." Here the author of the *Tanya* adds another factor to the equation. He had previously spoken about an ascent and descent: the elevation of the lights from the vessels, and the flow of the divine light to the vessels below. Now he refers to the elevation of the vessels as well. The vessels can also ascend through the service of man. In fact, for the elevation to occur in the desired manner, it must involve the elevation of the vessels together with the ascent and purification of the lights.

הִיא מַעֲלַת הַשַּׁבָּת וְיוֹם הַכִּיפּוּרִים

which is a quality of the Sabbath and Yom Kippur,

THE ULTIMATE PURPOSE

☞   The idea that the ultimate purpose is to elevate the lights, the soul, the spiritual essence that is captive in this world, has occurred to many people throughout time, and they have attempted to fulfill it in practice. Yet this concept, which appears in several religions and worldviews, that the purpose of man is to disconnect and separate from his body and his world, leads people to nothing more than a state of delusion, and they become stuck on some lofty plane. Granted, there is a certain beauty in this effort, and it is admittedly impressive, but in Judaism it is considered akin to death.

Death is not necessarily bad according to those philosophies. In their view, it is the purpose of the soul, which is to leave the physical world. There are even those who took this idea to its logical conclusion and committed suicide. What is even worse, the claim that people should give up their lives for this purpose, and that it is for their own good, whether they desire it or not, has resulted in the slaughter of masses. For the Jewish people, on the other hand, who maintain the very opposite, that the ultimate purpose is to draw down life and vitality to this world below, death is evil itself, the most impure thing of all.

An example of this is the ascent of the worlds on the Sabbath and Yom Kippur.[56] On the Sabbath, and in a different manner on Yom Kippur, and in a sense on all the festivals, the worlds rise higher than on weekdays. "Higher" means that they are more divested from physicality, divisions, and boundaries, that they are more unified with the source of everything, and the Divine is a little less concealed.

On the Sabbath, for example, the world removes its weekday garments and becomes a more purified vessel to receive loftier lights. The worlds are vessels, which means that this is not an ascent of light alone, but an ascent of the world itself. Everything in the world – the food, the clothing, even the sky and the earth – is elevated on the Sabbath. ☞

All of this refers to the proper manner of ascent, whose ultimate purpose is the flow of light into the vessels and not the other way around. When the author of the *Tanya* speaks of the elevation of the feminine

THE ELEVATION OF THE VESSELS ON THE SABBATH

☞ The light rises from a vessel when a person does not, for example, eat the food that is in front of him, but first focuses his mind and spirit on loftier, spiritual matters. He thereby constructs another object for his desires, toward which he directs his love, fear, and life itself. The food remains below, and the body and animal soul also stay below with the food, while the light of the soul rises above.

There is also another way of attaining the same end: by eating in a state of holiness, in which one elevates from the world, not only his divine soul, but also his animal soul, and even his body and the food he eats. This is the elevation of the vessels.

In addition, there is a method of ascent in which nothing leaves the world because the world as a whole ascends, or at least part of the world. This happens when one does not have in mind to eat in a specifically holy manner, because the act of con-

sumption and the food itself are holy. This is the special quality of the Sabbath. While the Sabbath is indeed a gift from above, since it is a unique day that God has given us and we merely enter it, at the same time it is the perfect model for the service of elevating the vessels that we are meant to achieve on weekdays as well.

How can this type of service be achieved on the weekdays? One way is through prayer, which is said to be an aspect of the Sabbath. The ascent achieved during prayer echoes the ascent of the worlds that occurs on the Sabbath (*Likkutei Torah*, Num. 72b). During prayer, which mainly involves spiritual intent and focus, there is not only cognitive love and fear, but also words that must be uttered verbally. These words are the vessels of prayer that must be elevated. Prayer, then, when done properly, entails an ascent of both vessels and lights. Aside from the general intentions and awareness with which a

---

56. See *Pri Etz Ḥayyim*, introduction to *Sha'ar HaShabbat*, chaps. 1, 7; *Pri Etz Ḥayyim*, *Sha'ar Yom HaKippurim*, chap. 1.

waters, he notes that even though this is an ascent, it is "only temporary," in order to awaken and draw forth the light from above so that it will descend to the vessels below. Moreover, even this ascent itself is not an elevation of the light as it leaves the vessel, but an ascent that pulls the vessel along with it. When the initial purpose of the ascent is to bring the light down to the vessel, this means that the vessel is never abandoned even temporarily. The specific vessel in question rises, and the more comprehensive the intention and the more self-nullification involved, the more it encompasses the entirety of a whole world that mysteriously ascends to receive the light through revelation.

אֲבָל לֹא עֲלִיּוֹת וְהִסְתַּלְּקוּת **but not the elevations and departure of**
הָאוֹרוֹת חַס וְשָׁלוֹם **the lights** from the vessels, **God forbid,**

If the light were to merely ascend from the vessels, in such a manner that they depart and abandon them, regarding such an ascent the author of the *Tanya* declares, "God forbid." ☞

person enters the state of prayer, that he is standing before the King with love and fear, the first stage of prayer itself is the meaning and intent behind the words, which is what elevates the vessels, the words of prayer. When the words have been articulated while imbued with meaning, each person according to his ability, they exist in a higher and more purified state than their mundane reality, and at that moment wondrous lights shine from within them (*Or HaTorah*, Deut., vol. 4, p. 898), loftier than before the person prayed.

AN ASCENT WITHOUT A DESCENT

☞ Such service is contrary to everything that God desires from His world. It runs counter to the trajectory of the light and life force that God bestows on the worlds. The ultimate intention is to have an abode in the lower realm.

Yet the idea of a dwelling place for God down below is paradoxical, since it entails a link between the infinite God and the material, limited world. Even the concept of a connection between the spiritual and the physical, between the soul and the body, contains a built-in contradiction:

The soul does not feel good inside the body. It cries out that its experience there is bitter. Yet when a person tries to release the soul from the body, he in a sense returns the world to a state of chaos, because he contravenes God's will. On the one hand, he does resolve the paradox of the world and ostensibly makes things "normal," with that which is lofty positioned above and that which is lowly placed down below, but, on the other hand, he acts contrary to the will of God, who desires this very paradox.

כְּמוֹ שֶׁכָּתוּב בְּפְרִי עֵץ חַיִּים **as stated in *Pri Etz Ḥayyim* regarding the ascent of the worlds on the Sabbath.**

After discussing the lights and vessels in general terms, the ascent and departure of the lights and their ascent in the vessels, the author of the *Tanya* now applies these principles to man himself. ☞

וְנֶפֶשׁ רוּחַ נְשָׁמָה שֶׁל הָאָדָם **The *nefesh*, *ruaḥ*, and *neshama* of a** לְגַבֵּי גּוּפוֹ בָּעוֹלָם הַזֶּה חֲשִׁיבֵי **person in relation to his body in this** כְּאוֹרוֹת לְגַבֵּי כֵּלִים **world is like the lights in relation to the vessels,**

A person's soul is the light in relation to his body, which is the vessel. In view of this, what was stated about the elevation of the lights and their being drawn forth into the vessels applies equally to man himself. The ascent and departure of the lights is the elevation of the soul from the body, with all the beauty as well as the danger and dread that this entails. Likewise, the flow of the light to the vessel is the flow of the soul and life force to the body, in the form of the embodiment of the soul and its faculties. That the author of the *Tanya* specifies the *nefesh*, *ruaḥ*, and *neshama* indicates that it is specifically these soul levels that are comparable to the light that flows into the vessel that is the body. The remaining soul levels, *ḥaya* and *yeḥida*, are not actually enclothed in the body but encompass it.

וְכֵן דְּחִילוּ וּרְחִימוּ שֶׁכְּלַיִים לְגַבֵּי **and likewise cognitive fear and love** מִצְוֹת מַעֲשִׂיּוֹת דַּוְקָא **of God in relation to action-related mitzvot in particular.**

THE ASCENT OF THE LIGHTS AND VESSELS IN MAN

☞ Although the author of the *Tanya's* ensuing statements regarding the service of man and the elevation of the lights and vessels could be inferred from everything that has already been explained, it is important for him to spell it out explicitly, rather than for it to be derived by way of inference. The hasidic viewpoint is that one's primary and central focus must remain here, on man's service to God. Everything man does, on the physical and spiritual planes, starts from within himself. What he sees and changes internally, what he thinks and feels, affects all the worlds from the lowest to the loftiest.

The same applies to man's service of God. Cognitive fear and love of God resembles the light in relation to the performance of action-related mitzvot, which is like the vessels. The author of the *Tanya* already stated above that service through cognitive fear and love of God raises the lights from the vessels, while service through the mitzvot draws the lights to the vessels. Here he is adding that this relationship applies to the service itself, to these two types of service. Cognitive fear and love is the light, while the vessel is the service of fulfilling the mitzvot. Accordingly, there is nothing lacking in either of them. There is no deficiency in spiritual love and fear. But they simply should not have to operate alone, but rather should be drawn to the vessel, which is the service of fulfilling the mitzvot in practice.

וְלָכֵן הִתְפַּלֵּל מֹשֶׁה רַבֵּינוּ עָלָיו הַשָּׁלוֹם תְּפִלּוֹת כְּמִנְיַן 'וָאֶתְחַנַּן' עַל קִיּוּם מִצְוֹת מַעֲשִׂיּוֹת דַּוְקָא

Therefore, Moses, our teacher, may he rest in peace, offered prayers that amounted to the numerical value of the word *va'etḥanan*, specifically requesting that he might fulfill action-related mitzvot,

Moshe asked again and again for permission to enter the Land of Israel. There is a tradition that he prayed 515 times for this, which is the numerical value of the word *va'etḥanan*.[57] Why was he so persistent? What was there in the land that Moses needed to such an extent? The author of the *Tanya* explains that the Land of Israel has the action-related mitzvot.

The Land of Israel is the place where the mitzvot are meant to be fulfilled. Apart from the many mitzvot that can be fulfilled only in the land, such as those that depend on the cultivation of the land and the service of the Temple, the primary fulfillment of all mitzvot is actually in the land.[58]

It is for this reason that Moses yearned to enter the land. He in particular, who had achieved the ultimate spiritual perfection, was deficient in action-related mitzvot. These mitzvot are not just another facet, another layer, in the service of God, but an element without

57. See *Devarim Rabba* 11:10.
58. See Ramban, Lev. 18:25; *Torah Or* 46b; *Likkutei Torah*, Num. 36c.

which all spiritual work is worthless. As the author of the *Tanya* stated above, they are the vessel for spiritual work, and if the spiritual service is not drawn to the vessel, which is the action-related mitzvot, it might remain only as an elevation and departure of the light.

וְהוּא הַדִּין לְדִבּוּר גַּשְׁמִי שֶׁל הִלְכוֹתֵיהֶן **and the same applies to the physical utterance of their laws.**

The action-related mitzvot include the study of their *halakhot*, not only as a prerequisite and preparation for their fulfillment, but also as a value in its own right, as the fulfillment of the mitzvot on another level, on the level of speech rather than merely the level of action.[59] That is why the author of the *Tanya* emphasizes "the physical utterance of their laws." The light must be drawn to the vessels in some manner, the spiritual service in the mind and heart to physical vessels, whether they are the actions and objects of the action-related mitzvot or the letters of speech employed in the study of their laws.

On a deeper level, in the world of action, there are sparks of holiness whose root is on a very high plane, in the name *Sag*. When one performs a mitzva in the physical world, he extracts from it the spark of holiness that was held captive in this world, raising it to its lofty root, which is even loftier than the person who extracted it, since his soul stems from the name of *Mah*. The author of the *Tanya* proceeds to elaborate on these ideas, and he goes on to provide an analogy to explain them.

9 Kislev / 8 Kislev (leap year) — אַךְ לְהָבִין: אֵיךְ הָאֶתְרוֹג שֶׁהוּא מֵרְפָּ״ח שֶׁלֹּא נִבְרְרוּ עֲדַיִין **However,** it is necessary **to understand: How can the** *etrog*, **which stems from the 288 sparks that have not yet been refined,**

Before a mitzva has been performed with it, the *etrog* is like all other fruits. It is part of the framework of *kelippat noga*, the glowing husk that constitutes the mundane reality of this world. Any ordinary feature of this world is considered *kelippat noga*, because by itself it does not reveal the Divine but conceals it in its materiality natural order. The

---

59. See *Likkutei Torah*, Num. 75a.

holiness it contains, the part that is *noga*, constitutes the 288 sparks that fell to the *kelippa* from the world of chaos. It is true that these sparks are from a very lofty source of holiness, but as long as they have not been extracted from the *kelippot*, they remain covered and hidden. Not only are they not active or have any significant impact on the side of holiness, but they even nourish the *kelippa* in which they are concealed.

וְכֵן קְלַף הַתְּפִילִין יַמְשִׁיךְ אוֹר **and likewise the parchment of *tefil-***
בְּכֵלִים דִּזְעֵיר אַנְפִּין וְנוּקְבָא **lin, draw forth light into the vessels**
דַּאֲצִילוּת, שֶׁכְּבָר נִבְרְרוּ וְנִתַּקְּנוּ **of *Zeir Anpin* and *Nukva* of *Atzilut*,**
עַל יְדֵי שֵׁם מ״ה לִהְיוֹת בְּחִינַת **which have already been refined and**
אֱלֹקוּת? **rectified through the name *Mah* so**
that they are in a state of divinity?

Like the *etrog*, before the passages of *tefillin* are written on it, the parchment of *tefillin* is no different from any other animal hide, which like all items of this world is *kelippat noga*, a neutral *kelippa* that can be used for good or evil.

The question is, how do these lowly materials cause a flow of light in all the worlds, even in *Atzilut*, simply because a mitzva is performed with them? Surely the world of *Atzilut* is higher than this world, and indeed so are all the other worlds. Furthermore, the world of *Atzilut* is not only loftier than this world, but it is a refined and orderly world, in which the vessels fully contain the light within them, including all the divine lights in a single configuration. It is a world that is all holiness, one of total nullification and a perfect vessel for the divinity that is revealed in it. If so, how is it possible that a part of this physical world – a fruit or a physical piece of parchment – can draw light from so high above itself?

הִנֵּה הַמָּשָׁל לָזֶה הִיא הַזְּרִיעָה **The analogy for this is sowing and**
וְהַנְּטִיעָה **planting,**

The author of the *Tanya* uses an example from the physical world to explain how a physical object can draw a spiritual light: the analogy sowing or planting a seed in the ground.[60] This is a well-worn metaphor,

---

60. See also *Iggeret HaKodesh*, epistles 8, 20, and *Torah Or* 54b, 115c, where this analogy is also offered.

because what happens to the seed, which can readily be observed, has no obvious logical explanation. A small and completely unimpressive seed, a tiny grain of fibrous material that has completely disintegrated in the ground, sprouts into a large and magnificent tree, a living tree that likewise produces its own fruit and seeds, leading to more trees, ad infinitum.

What is going on here? How can a small and insignificant seed produce and give life to more trees and fruits?

The mitzvot work in a similar manner. The *etrog* or the piece of parchment draw forth, beyond any proportion to their physical existence, the actual light of *Ein Sof* into the world of *Atzilut*. ☞

שֶׁהַגַּרְעִין מְעוֹרֵר כֹּחַ הַצּוֹמֵחַ שֶׁבָּאָרֶץ, שֶׁהוּא דְּבַר ה': "תַּדְשֵׁא הָאָרֶץ כו' עֵץ פְּרִי כו'" (בראשית א, יא)	where the seed awakens the earth's **vegetative power, which is the word of God,** as it is written, **"Let the earth sprout** grasses, vegetation yielding seed, and **fruit trees** bearing fruit in its kind, in which there is its seed, upon the earth…" (Gen. 1:11),

It is not really the seed itself that grows. Nothing physical can sprout into something greater and more sophisticated than itself on its own. Rather, hidden within the earth is an immense power, an infinite power of growth, so that when the nucleus connects to this power and is subsumed in it, it produces any number of entities of the same species and form as the seed.

THE ANALOGY OF SOWING AND PLANTING

☞ There is another important point to be made regarding this analogy and the case to which it is applied. In both the physical and spiritual realms, it is natural for things to flow from above to below. Consequently, entropic processes occur on the axes of time and causality. In simpler terms, objects become lowlier and bulkier, less illuminated, less complex and orderly. In the material world, this means that the material of which living creatures and plants are made disintegrate into inanimate materials and soil, and a house becomes a pile of stones and dirt. But then there is also another converse and inexplicable trajectory: The nucleus of a seed, contrary to all the rules of entropy, consolidates earth matter into more complex forms instead of rotting and turning into yet another grain of soil. This tiny entity transforms into a large creation, and scattered, disorganized materials become a complex, organized entity incomparably more significant than the nucleus at its initial stages.

The author of the *Tanya* goes on to explain that the vegetative power in the earth is actually the word of God – one of the ten utterances with which the world was created: "Let the earth sprout...." These letters and words with which all vegetation was created, continue to be spoken in the earth throughout the existence of the world. They are the life force that perpetually causes all vegetation to sprout, with all their specific features, at all times. But the vegetative power itself, like the divine speech of the ten utterances, is a general, infinite power. In order for it to be revealed in individual plants, at a specific time and place, it is necessary for something to awaken it and circumscribe it precisely for this purpose, for this plant, at this time. This is stimulated by the seed that is sown in the ground.

עַל יְדֵי הַעֲלָאַת מַיִין נוּקְבִין **through the ascension of the feminine**
לְשָׁרְשׁוֹ **waters to** the seed's **root.**

The root of the seed is in this vegetative power that is in the earth. Here the author of the *Tanya* makes use of concepts from a different field, which belong more to the process he seeks to explain than the analogy itself. He states that this vegetative process is like the ascension of the feminine waters to the root. The root of the seed and all plants is in the vegetative power, which constitutes the life force that is inherent in the divine utterance "Let the earth sprout...." The seed that is sown carries the particular information pertaining to this plant to the root, in the form of the ascension of the feminine waters, to awaken the flow of the masculine waters above, which is the bestowal of the life force that causes growth. Accordingly, it is not the seed that brings about growth. The seed merely issues a request, an idea and a path, but the growth comes from the root, which assuredly has the power to bestow life and produce growth. ☞

THE FEMININE WATERS AND THE ANALOGY OF THE SEED

☞ In botanical terms, we might say that the seed contains the unique hereditary code for the tree, into which the vegetative power in the earth flows and begins to consolidate all the materials and energy around it in order to grow the tree. The seed itself is nothing. It is neither the substance nor the energy that produces the growth. It merely contains the information needed to specify the particular tree that should grow. This information is released as the seed decays and disintegrates.

כָּכָה מְעוֹרְרִים הַקְּלָף וְהָאֶתְרוֹג, **Thus,** when a mitzva is fulfilled with
עַד רוּם הַמַּעֲלוֹת them, **the parchment** of *tefillin* **and
the etrog are awakened at the loftiest
heights,**

The ascension of the feminine waters through a mitzva act rises higher
than all the worlds. The feminine waters ascend all the way to the Creator, above the creation. To emerge from the natural laws of the world,
where the power of creation is increasingly weakened, and where the
utterances of God gradually fade until they are virtually inaudible in
our physical world, it is necessary to elevate and reawaken the power of
the Creator. This is achieved through a new creation and illumination
that breaks out at the root from which the feminine waters originate.

This process resembles the growth of grass from earth, which to
us seems like a new creation. Likewise, the flow of light in the vessels
of *Atzilut* cannot be seen by mortal eyes but may be perceived by the
eye of the spirit.

This is the process that occurs when one performs a mitzva with
the *etrog* or with the parchment of *tefillin*. If no mitzva is fulfilled with
them, or even if the mitzva is performed but in an improper manner, it
will not awaken anything just as nothing will grow if one sows stones.
Only a combination of certain materials that have vegetative properties
can stimulate growth. Likewise, the *etrog* or parchment alone achieve
nothing. It is only when a mitzva is performed properly with them that
the combination of the object, the act, and the doer attains significance
above, in the divine will, which precedes all of creation. When the act is
performed in the appropriate manner, place, and time, as detailed in the
Written and Oral Torah, it becomes a vessel and a conduit for drawing
forth the divine light from the loftiest heights down to the creation.

שֶׁהוּא שֵׁם ס"ג שֶׁלִּפְנֵי הַשְּׁבִירָה **which is the name** *Sag* **from before
the shattering** of the vessels.

The awakening from below through a mitzva act reaches all the way
up to the level and essence called *Sag*. The names of *Sag*, *Mah*, and
Adam Kadmon were discussed above. Here the author of the *Tanya*
here refers to the ascension of the feminine waters from the mitzvot
to the name of *Sag* at the level it exists before the shattering. Each of

these names is a facet and a particular revelation of the bearer of the name. The name of *Sag* represents the divine revelation in the world of chaos before the shattering of the vessels. The world of chaos preceded our world, both chronologically and in order of magnitude. Since the light it contained was too great for the vessels, it could not survive as a world, and therefore it shattered. In this sense, when the author of the *Tanya* says "the name *Sag* from before the shattering [of the vessels]," this refers to the name, the light, and the divine revelation itself prior to its emergence from the divine essence to become a world and before it was shattered. This immense light could not exist as a world, as a durable entity of lights and vessels like the world of *Atzilut*, and yet deep within the divine essence it exists even now.

שֶׁהוּא מַהוּת וְעַצְמוּת אוֹרוֹת **This is the essence and being of the**
שֶׁבְּאָדָם קַדְמוֹן **lights in** *Adam Kadmon***,**

Adam Kadmon, literally, "Primeval Man," is the first structure and image that formed after the constriction of the divine light, incorporating all that existed at that stage.[61] *Adam Kadmon* is called "the crown of all crowns," meaning the highest, most abstract, most real entity that can relate to God himself from the totality of reality after the constriction. The name *Sag* refers to the light itself in *Adam Kadmon*.

As explained above, the lights that were revealed in the world of chaos were unlimited, without parameters. They were the essence of the lights of *Adam Kadmon*, which is why the vessels shattered. In that state before the revelation and placement of the lights in the vessels, represented by the name *Sag* before the vessels shattered, it was still a vast and infinite divine light. These lights are superior in that they are self-contained and unlimited, but they are also inferior in a different respect, since they cannot illuminate and become manifest in the form of a world because there are no vessels that can contain them without shattering.

---

61. In order for the world to be created, the divine light had to be constricted. Otherwise, the creation would be subsumed in the light. More, as the light descends from *Ein Sof*, it is constricted further, through numerous constrictions, layer upon layer, level after level, in order to allow it to be obscured and concealed in a physical world.

וְלֹא הֶאָרָה בְּעָלְמָא כְּמוֹ שֵׁם   not a mere illumination like the name
מ"ה שֶׁמִּמִּצְחוֹ   *Mah*, which stems from its forehead.

In contrast to the name *Sag*, which represents the infinite and uncontainable light of chaos, the name *Mah* represents the revelation and light of the rectification, which belongs to our world. The name *Mah* is illumination alone. It is an illumination that does not bear the infinity of the divine essence, but reveals only a facet of that essence, like the difference between an object itself and a glimpse of it.

As for the "forehead" mentioned here, that of *Adam Kadmon*, this is a kabbalistic expression used to contrast the illumination of the name *Mah* and the lights of the name *Sag*, which is the internal essence of *Adam Kadmon* that emerges through the eyes, as it were. Since the forehead is not an opening, what shines through it is not the inner light itself but only an illumination of it, an illumination of an illumination. This can be compared to a window through which some measure of light from inside passes through to the outside, as opposed to a veil, an opaque curtain, through which none of the light inside can escape, and yet a glimmer of the light is able to pass through. To use a different example, when one person instructs another to do something, his statement does not go beyond the world of speech, but when the listener does what he was told, the act has moved on into the world of action.[62] ☞

THE POWER OF THE NAME *MAH* TO RECTIFY THE LIGHTS OF THE WORLD OF CHAOS

☞ Although the light of *Mah* is relatively small and limited, it is for this reason that it can be manifest, enter vessels, and interact with various lights and vessels and other manifestations. It is true that the light is limited, but its very limitation makes room for the integration of all limited entities, and ultimately for the rectification and creation of a vessel that can achieve the supposedly impossible: the containment and revelation of the unlimited lights of the world of chaos, of the name *Sag* that stems from the internal dimension of *Adam Kadmon*.

This finds expression when a person performs a mitzva in accordance with the Torah's dictates, which is a revelation of the name *Mah*. In this way, he refines and rec-

---

62. See *Biurei HaZohar* by the Tzemah Tzedek, vol. 1, p. 282; see also *Derekh Mitzvotekha*, p. 68a, which provides another analogy: Light that passes through

וְכֵן בְּלִימוּד וְעִיּוּן הִלְכוֹתֵיהֶן מְעוֹרֵר בְּחִינַת חָכְמָה בִּינָה דַּעַת שֶׁבְּעֶשֶׂר סְפִירוֹת דְּכֵלִים דִּזְעֵיר אַנְפִּין וְנוּקְבָא,

Similarly, through the study and analysis of the laws of the action-related mitzvot, **one awakens Ḥokhma, Bina,** and *Da'at* **in the ten** *sefirot* of the vessels of *Zeir Anpin* and *Nukva* in the world of *Atzilut*

Studying the *halakhot* of a mitzva itself is in itself a fulfillment of the mitzva in a different, higher reality, like speech in relation to deed, as stated above. Since one studies with the intellect, by employing the attributes of *Ḥokhma, Bina*, and *Da'at*, the awakening above occurs in the same vessels: in *Ḥokhma, Bina*, and *Da'at* among the ten *sefirot* of *Atzilut*. Just as a kernel of wheat will sprout into wheat and the seed of an apple tree will grow into a tree that produces apples, the study of

---

tifies reality, its materiality and physicality, which constitutes the shattered vessels from the world of chaos. When a person refines and elevates that light to its root in *Sag*, which is in the internal dimension of *Adam Kadmon*, this is the ascension of the female waters that draws from above the light of the divine essence from *Sag*, which is now enclothed, through the refinement, in vessels of rectification.

Furthermore, the power in *Mah* to rectify even the lights of from the world of chaos, even though these lights are more internal and more intense, is because the root of the name *Mah*, which illuminates

only from the forehead, comes from the name *Ab*, which is within the internal dimension of *Ḥokhma* of *Adam Kadmon*. What the forehead conceals cannot be revealed in any other way than by illumination alone, which is the name *Mah*. The illumination, though it is small and external, is nevertheless an illumination of the greatest, loftiest entity. There, through an illumination of an illumination alone, a parable of a parable, the broadest expanse is ultimately revealed, which rectifies, organizes, and brings about the refinement of the worlds.

---

a hole, even if it is a tiny fissure, is like a sentence, or even one word, of what is stated inside. While a word is indeed only a single word, it encodes within it the essence of the inner light. Alternatively, what passes through the hole is merely an illumination of an illumination, which can be compared to an allegory. It is not the actual piece of wisdom that is contained within but another narrative, with its own world and concepts, and like a parable it can reveal that which is in to a completely different world. Furthermore, although it is not the essence of wisdom, it can disclose it more clearly and completely than any spark of inner light passing through.

a mitzva by employing the faculties of wisdom, understanding, and knowledge awakens and draws Ḥokhma, Bina, and Da'at from above.

וְעַד רוּם הַמַּעֲלוֹת, גַּם כֵּן בְּחִינַת	and up to the most elevated heights,
חָכְמָה בִּינָה דַּעַת שֶׁבְּסַ״ג דִּפְנִימִית	including Ḥokhma, Bina, and Da'at
אָדָם קַדְמוֹן	in Sag of the inner dimension of Adam Kadmon,

The ascension of the feminine waters through the study of halakha also ascends above Atzilut. It is not only a mitzva act performed in the material world that brings about such an elevation, but also the study of these topics raises sparks from the world of chaos to their source, which is in the name Sag in the interior dimension of the partzuf of Adam Kadmon, and even there they are raised to the level of the intellect, to Ḥokhma, Bina, and Da'at in Sag, where the root of that halakha lies. ☞

הַיּוֹצֵא דֶּרֶךְ הָעֵינַיִם כו'	which emerges through the eyes…

Unlike the name Mah, which is an illumination from the forehead of Adam Kadmon, the emergence of Sag is through the eyes of Adam Kadmon. The eyes are cavities, and the light that passes through them to the outside is the essence of the inner light, even if it is greatly constricted, like light passing through a small hole. Since it is the essence of the light itself, its power is greater than the light of Mah, which is merely an illumination of an illumination. Another analogy

ḤOKHMA, BINA, AND DA'AT IN SAG

☞ The sparks of the light that fell from the world of chaos exist not only in material objects, such as the etrog and parchment of tefillin, but they can be found throughout the existence of this world. This includes the spiritual faculties and the intellect, and in a certain sense also the spiritual levels that lead to this physical reality. Just as in the act of the mitzva the objects and materials are rectified, so too, when one is engaged in the study of halakha, he rectifies the intellect that he employs in the course of that study. What is more, the study of halakha on a broad scale is more than merely study for the purpose of performing the act. It is the study and analysis of these concepts in the mind and soul. When we know the place and value of everything in our thoughts, and we desire and sense the proper worth and purpose of everything, this itself constitutes a rectification of the world.

is given for this elsewhere:[63] The inner light is that which a person understands on his own and evokes within his soul, as opposed to an illumination of an illumination, which is like a person hearing from someone else what he has understood and is trying to awaken in him as well. Naturally, any conclusion that a person arrives at on his own will affect him more directly and meaningfully. But just as a person usually requires an external factor to awaken him within, so too the illumination of the name *Mah* must elevate the feminine waters from below in order to awaken *Sag* from within and above.

וְכָל הַנִּזְכָּר לְעֵיל הוּא בְּמִצְוֹת עֲשֵׂה, אֲבָל לֹא בְּלִימּוּד פְּרָטֵי הִלְכוֹת אִיסּוּרֵי לֹא תַעֲשֶׂה, לִכְאוֹרָה	Everything discussed above applies to the positive commandments, but not, it would appear, to the study of the details of the laws of the prohibitions,

All that the author of the *Tanya* has said about the study of *halakha*, that it is like fulfilling the mitzvot on a different level of reality, pertains to the positive commandments. What about the study of *halakhot* related to the prohibitions?

In truth, this question applies not only to study but also to fulfillment in practice. The difference between positive commandments and prohibitions is that in the case of a positive commandment one actually does something. One changes and adjusts something within reality, and this achieves the refinement and elevation of the sparks. This is not the case with prohibitions, since one does not do anything but merely refrains from taking action. Still, the question remains in reference to study, because the act of studying is itself considered fulfillment. One must then ask what value there is in study when its content is about what not to do, which apparently achieves nothing in terms of rectification and the ascension of the feminine waters.

וּבִפְרָט בִּדְלָא שְׁכִיחֵי כְּלָל, כְּמוֹ פְּרָטֵי הִלְכוֹת פִּיגּוּל וּכְהַאי גַּוְונָא	particularly those that are not at all common, such as the detailed laws of *pigul* and the like.

63. See *Derekh Mitzvotekha*, p. 282.

When the author of the *Tanya* asks whether the study of prohibitions is as effective as the study of the laws of the positive commandments, he does not refer merely to commandments that are rare, but to those that do not exist in our current reality, to a prohibition that is impossible for a person to come across in practice. He brings the example of *pigul*, a sacrifice regarding which the priest who offers it has in mind to offer up the animal or eat it after its allotted time. One does not have to do anything, even when the Temple is standing, to avoid violating this prohibition.

On the other hand, there are prohibitions regarding which the Rabbis stated, "If one sits and does not transgress, he receives a reward as one who performs a mitzva" (Mishna *Makkot* 3:15; *Kiddushin* 39b). He is considered like someone who has performed a mitzva because he must actively resist temptation to avoid violating the prohibition. But when the prohibition is uncommon, even this connection does not exist, and if so, what benefit is provided by their study, even on the spiritual plane?

To answer this question, the author of the *Tanya* takes the rest of this essay to analyze other aspects and qualities of the study of *halakha*, in addition to those he has mentioned to this point.

10 Kislev
9 Kislev
(leap year)

אַךְ עוֹד זֹאת, הַשָּׁוֶה בַּכֹּל כִּי כָּל דְּחִילוּ וּרְחִימוּ שִׂכְלִיִּים שֶׁל הַמַּלְאָכִים הֵן בְּחִינַת נִבְרָאִים מֵאַיִן לְיֵשׁ

There is yet one more characteristic that is shared by them all, for all cognitive fear and love of God of the angels are created as an existence from nothingness,

There is another characteristic of Torah study, and here there is no difference between positive commandments and prohibitions. In this case, the study of the mitzva is not regarded as a level of fulfillment, but as a distinct, separate act in itself, the drawing forth and revelation of supernal wisdom from above. From this perspective, it makes no difference whether the study focuses on a positive commandment or a prohibition.

Above, the author of the *Tanya* contrasted the service of God through cognitive love and fear with service through the performance of the action-related mitzvot. In the same vein, he presents the concept of cognitive love and fear versus the study of *halakha*.

The cognitive fear and love of the angels that the author of the *Tanya* mentions here does not refer only to the fear and love of the angels but even those of man, which is akin to the cognitive love and fear of the angels. Cognitive love and fear belong to the rank of created beings. They are apprehended and felt by those who are not nullified by the Divine, who are part of the worlds and the existence of created realities.

The angels are the beings that express the reality of the higher spiritual worlds, just as man, as a physical being, expresses the physical world through his emotions and intellect, in his ability to feel, touch, and see it. We know whether the world is frightening or beautiful through our feelings. It is through human intelligence and comprehension that we understand the world and know that it is subject to rational explanation. Similarly, through the angels' feelings and understanding of the spiritual worlds, we too can feel and understand those worlds. That is why the author of the *Tanya* mentions the cognitive fear and love of the angels, because they are reflected in the cognitive fear and love of man. ☞

וְהֵן בְּחִינַת נֶפֶשׁ רוּחַ דִּבְרִיאָה יְצִירָה עֲשִׂיָּה **and they are** the levels of *nefesh* and *ruaḥ* of *Beria, Yetzira* and *Asiya.*

The service of cognitive love and fear are related to the levels of *nefesh* and *ruaḥ*, as opposed to *neshama*, and to the worlds of *Beria, Yetzira,* and *Asiya* as opposed to *Atzilut*.

THE COGNITIVE FEAR AND LOVE OF THE ANGELS

☞ The author of the *Tanya* does not mention the cognitive fear and love of man, since in the case of man there is an internal quality to his love and fear that does not apply to the love and fear of the angels, and he is not speaking about that quality here. The uniqueness of man over the angels is the level of *neshama*, which is part of the world of *Atzilut* and the Divine in relation to the created beings. The expression of this level is man's love and fear of God, which are also the internal aspect of mitzva fulfillment: Love is the root of the fulfillment of the positive commandments, while fear is the root of the observance of the prohibitions.

The soul levels of *nefesh, ruaḥ,* and *neshama* are replicated in every world and soul. There is nothing that is truly dead and inanimate in reality. There is a certain measure of life in every object and every place, the divine light and life force within it. The Divine does not merely exist somewhere above all the worlds and creations, but an element of God is found in every world and level. This is the level of *neshama* in that world, while cognitive fear and love, which are the apprehension and feelings of the created being toward the Creator, are apprehended only on the level of *nefesh* and *ruaḥ* of the worlds of *Beria, Yetzira,* and *Asiya.*[64]

אֲבָל פְּרָטֵי הַהֲלָכוֹת הֵן הַמְשָׁכוֹת חָכְמָה עִילָּאָה דְּהַמַּאֲצִיל בָּרוּךְ הוּא

But the study of **the details of the** *halakhot* **are a drawing forth of the supernal wisdom of the Emanator, blessed be He,**

The supernal wisdom that exists in the *halakhot,* in the laws of the Torah, and is drawn forth all the way down to us in the world of *Asiya* no longer belongs to the realm of created beings, to the levels of *nefesh* and *ruaḥ* of the worlds. Rather, by virtue of the study of these *halakhot,* they belong to the level of wisdom, which is the *neshama* of the worlds, enclothing and expressing the divine essence within the worlds. ☞

HALAKHA AND THE SUPERNAL WISDOM OF THE CREATOR

☞ The *halakhot* of the Torah constitute the divine thought that passes into our lower world. Metaphorically speaking, they are like a person's unadulterated thoughts, not like the conclusion that is the outcome of all the stages of thought, of the planning and analysis down to every last detail, but like the initial thought, which starts the whole process within the person himself. This inner thought is like the supernal wisdom of the Emanator, which is the level of wisdom that resides within the soul's essence, that transcends any faculty or parameter in the soul. It is the spark in the soul that is ready to be absorbed in the faculties of the soul, in the intellect and the emotive attributes, and from there to be expressed through the soul's garments, its thoughts, speech, and actions. This spark of wisdom, beyond everything that God says and creates, beyond the cognitive love and fear of the angels and of man, is the essential expression of God Himself.

It is well known that *Hokhma* always parallels the world *Atzilut* in hasidic thought, and *Atzilut* is divinity itself. Accordingly, the revelation of the supernal wisdom achieved through studying the *halakhot* of the Torah constitutes the revelation and flow of the divine essence.

64. See also *Iggeret HaKodesh,* epistle 20.

הַמְלוּבֶּשֶׁת בְּגַשְׁמִיּוּת **which is enclothed in physicality.**

The supernal wisdom is drawn forth to this world directly through the details of the practical *halakhot*, of what one should do and how to do it. In this sense, it is clothed in physicality. Its essence is not enclothed in any spiritual layers, nor is it obstructed in its path by any spiritual levels or forms, but rather it is channeled directly into the physical realm. ☞

וְהַלְבָּשָׁה זוֹ אֵינָהּ כְּהַלְבָּשַׁת חָכְמָה עִילָאָה בִּדְחִילוּ וּרְחִימוּ שִׂכְלִיִּים **This enclothing is unlike the enclothing of supernal wisdom in cognitive fear and love** of God,

The supernal wisdom is also enclothed in cognitive love and fear. After all, supernal wisdom in *Atzilut* is the beginning of everything that exists, whether it is emanated, created, spiritual, or physical, and in this sense it is enclothed in all things, certainly in cognitive love and fear as it is employed in man's relationship with the Divine, as well as the wisdom that can be found within creation, or, more precisely, the part of creation that he has the capacity to apprehend. Consequently, the supernal wisdom is not enclothed solely in the study of *halakha* but also in cognitive love and fear. Yet, as the author of the *Tanya* points out, not all enclothing is equal.

דְּהָתָם הַלְבוּשׁ הוּא מֵעָלִים וּמַסְתִּיר לְגַמְרֵי כְּהֶסְתֵּר וְהֶעְלֵם הָאָרֶץ הַחוּמְרִיּית לְגַבֵּי חָכְמָה עִילָאָה הַמְלוּבֶּשֶׁת בָּהּ **for there the garment completely hides and conceals** the divine essence, **just like the hiddenness and concealment of the material earth with respect to the supernal wisdom enclothed within it,**

CLOTHED IN PHYSICALITY

☞ This does not mean that supernal wisdom reaches the physical realm only in the form of a conclusion arrived at through the wisdom, but rather as the wisdom itself, as a thought that relates to the material: what to do and what not to do, how, where, and when. It is not just in the *halakha* that one arrives at in the end of the thought process, but in all the details that one studies in order to get there. Moreover, it is part of the laws of the Oral Torah by virtue of the flexibility and freedom of the attribute of wisdom. The halakha is not always given to us explicitly. It must be arrived at through questions and answers, deliberation, and even disputes, methods that are employed through the faculty of wisdom.

Cognitive love and fear fully conceals the Divine until it cannot be seen at all. Although cognitive love and fear are essentially spiritual, and can even reach a very lofty level of spirituality, it is nevertheless the spirituality of a created being, and the garment of that being hides the essence of the Creator and the supernal wisdom in which His divinity is manifest.

This is a fine distinction, since we are speaking about the apprehension of the Divine. Yet because it is achieved through the man's intellect and emotive attributes, it is necessarily an apprehension only of the existence of God, not His essence. It is precisely because it is only an apprehension of His existence within reality that this apprehension cannot go beyond the limits of reality, and therefore it conceals the divine essence.

On account of the subtlety of the point he is making here, the author of the *Tanya* explains that the concealment inherent in cognitive love and fear is like the concealment of the material earth with respect to the supernal wisdom it enclothes. Just as in the physical world, one sees only matter, not that which is spiritual and certainly not the Divine, so too spiritual cognitive love and fear allows one to perceive only the existence of the Divine, essentially an external illumination, and not the essence of the Divine, that which is deep and internal.

כְּמוֹ שֶׁכָּתוּב: "כּוּלָם בְּחָכְמָה עָשִׂיתָ" (תהלים קד, כד) וְהַיְינוּ חִיצוֹנִיּוּת דְּחִיצוֹנִיּוּת דְּכֵלִים דְּמַלְכוּת דַּאֲצִילוּת שֶׁבַּעֲשִׂיָּה

as it is written, "In wisdom have You made them all" (Ps. 104:24), which refers to the external aspect of the external dimension of the vessels of *Malkhut* of *Atzilut* in *Asiya*,

Everything was created, fashioned, and formed with wisdom, with the supernal wisdom of God, of *Ḥokhma* in *Atzilut*. Accordingly, His wisdom is enclothed in everything, even if we cannot see it. How does the wisdom of *Atzilut* descend and become enclothed in the created entities of the world of *Asiya* to give them life?

That which descends from *Atzilut* is "the external aspect of the external dimension of the vessels of *Malkhut* of *Atzilut*" as they are manifest in *Asiya*. Once again, we can use the example of two people conversing with one another. Only the letters and the words – the vessels – pass between them, not the meaning behind the words that exist in the speaker's mind, which is like the light contained in the words he spoke. Similarly, the vessels of *Atzilut* are enclothed in *Beria*, while in *Yetzira* only the external aspect of the vessels exists, that which has been created from the vessels in the world of *Beria*. Finally, only the external aspect of their external aspect, that which was fashioned from the external aspects of the vessels from the world of *Yetzira*, is enclothed in the world of *Asiya*. It follows that the enclothing in *Asiya* is the external dimension of the external aspect of the vessels of *Malkhut* that is in *Atzilut*.

שֶׁהִיא מְסוּתֶּרֶת לְגַמְרֵי בְּרוּחַ נֶפֶשׁ דַּעֲשִׂיָּה   **which is entirely concealed in *ruaḥ* and *nefesh* of *Asiya*.**

The wisdom that stems from *Atzilut*, which has reached all the way to *Asiya*, is entirely hidden within the being and existence of the world of *Asiya*, in the levels of *ruaḥ* and *nefesh* of the world of *Asiya*.

This concealment "in *ruaḥ* and *nefesh* of *Asiya*" hides the internal aspect of supernal wisdom, the level of *neshama*. In the case of man, this means that on the levels of *nefesh* and *ruaḥ*, in the feelings of the soul through which it perceives physicality and grasps the existence of spirituality in *Asiya*, the apprehension of wisdom is concealed. This is the apprehension of the essence and interiority of the spiritual, the apprehension of the Divine in *Asiya*.

וְכֵן בִּבְרִיאָה, הִיא מְסוּתֶּרֶת לְגַמְרֵי בְּרוּחַ נֶפֶשׁ שֶׁהֶם בְּחִינַת נִבְרָאִים, בְּהֶסְתֵּר וְהַעֲלֵם הַבּוֹרֵא מֵהַנִּבְרָא   **Likewise, in *Beria* it is entirely concealed in *ruaḥ* and *nefesh* of *Beria*, which are created entities made distinct and separate through the hiddenness and concealment of the Creator from created beings.**

As in the world of *Asiya*, where the supernal wisdom is concealed in the levels of *ruaḥ* and *nefesh*, the same applies to the world of *Beria*. Although they are far more lofty and spiritual than in *Asiya*, the *ruaḥ* and *nefesh* of *Beria* are still created beings, which means that the Creator is concealed from them.

Supernal wisdom is not just another divine force like all the other *sefirot.* It carries the divine essence itself, *Ein Sof*, which is beyond all powers. The concealment of the divine essence exists not only in *Asiya*, which is lowly and corporeal, but even in the world of *Beria*, the loftiest of the worlds that contain created beings. Though it is the realm of the intellect and intellectual beings, the supernal wisdom is hidden there, just as it is concealed in the world of *Asiya*.

To clarify further, let us return to the metaphor of two people engaged in conversation. The listener can hear what the other person is saying, and he can even sense what the person is feeling and even grasp what he understands. Since it is all within the parameters of this world, others can theoretically also apprehend all these things. But we can never apprehend the essence and being of the other person, just as he himself cannot perceive it. The author calls of the *Tanya* refers to this as the concealment of the creator from that which was created.

A created being can apprehend the existence of the Creator when it is clothed in actions or speech, and even in thought (represented by *Beria*, *Yetzira*, and *Asiya*). He can perceive a divine act or thought, knowing that there is One who is acting or thinking. Yet he cannot apprehend God himself, the one who is acting or thinking.

<table>
<tr><td>10 Kislev
(leap year)</td><td>מַה שֶּׁאֵין כֵּן הַהֲלָכוֹת, הֲרֵי הָאָרַת
הַחָכְמָה מְאִירָה בָּהֶן בְּגִילּוּי</td><td>**This is not the case with the *halakhot*, in which the light of wisdom shines openly,**</td></tr>
</table>

The wisdom of *halakha* is not enclothed and concealed in the garments of the worlds through which it passes, unlike the life force that stems from Ḥokhma and gives life to the worlds. That wisdom is enclothed in every level and world and is manifest as wisdom characteristic of that world. This wisdom is enclothed in each world, in the logic, feelings, and the entire framework of the relationships between them that pertain to it, and therefore it is essentially manifest as the wisdom of that world and place. The wisdom imbued in *halakha*, by contrast, is unadulterated. It is manifest in our world in its essence without being affected by the intellect of our world, without any connection to its causal, internal logic.

Why does one take hold of an *etrog* on the festival of Sukkot? Why don *tefillin*? For that matter, why does the *tefillin* contain verses written specifically on parchment fashioned from the hide of a kosher animal?

Why are *tefillin* boxes square? And so on and so forth. It would seem that there is no logical reason for any of these *halakhot*, that they bear no relation to what is happening in this world. The actual reason, which we do not understand, is the supernal wisdom itself, and no wisdom belonging to the world, no wisdom in creation, can conceal it. ☞

However, since the *halakhot* are also enclothed in the garment of action, and we study these laws in order to implement them, how does its garment differ from all other garments?

וּלְבוּשׁ הָעֲשִׂיָּה הוּא דֶּרֶךְ מַעֲבָר לְבַד   **and the garment of *Asiya* is merely a passageway,**

This light only passes through this garment of *halakha*. It is not affected by it or influenced to become like it. ☞

THE LIGHT OF THE WISDOM OF *HALAKHA*

☞ When the author of the *Tanya* states that the supernal wisdom shines openly in the *halakhot*, this does not mean that it is open and revealed to us. We describe as "open" or "revealed" that which is enclothed in our own intellect, yet the supernal wisdom in the *halakhot* is not enclothed in the intellect of any created being. Rather, this means that it is not enclothed and concealed within any other wisdom or intelligence. True revelation is not necessarily that which I can comprehend and seems logical to me right now, but what is not actually concealed, but is revealed and openly manifest.

The question is, of course, what meaning there is to a revelation that is not open and accessible. We might suggest that it is true that we cannot grasp the supernal wisdom, in all its depth, with the tools of wisdom and intellect at our disposal. Yet

in the manner that the supernal wisdom is given to us, through the laws of the Torah, which gives us specific parameters for implementing the mitzvot in deed, we are able to contain it within our reality. When we study the *halakhot* using our limited intellect, we are able to comprehend this particular structure within which the supernal wisdom has enclothed itself.

Furthermore, when we study the laws in order to put them into practice, and then actually perform the acts, we penetrate beyond the layer of the clothing. What the mind cannot fathom, the entirety of a person, his entire being, can apprehend at his essence, through his emotions and deeds, that inner spark within, which transcends the faculties of his individual soul. Even if he fails to grasp it with his mind, even if he is unable to expressly feel it, he senses and grasp it at his essence.

A PASSAGEWAY VERSUS ENCLOTHEMENT

☞ Here the author of the *Tanya* touches on an essential distinction for understanding Hasidism (see *Torah Or, Parashat Teru-*

ma 81b; *Likkutei Torah*, Num. 89b). A light can descend from a higher world below in one of two ways: through enclothement or

With enclothement, the entity that is being transmitted has changed and has not retained its original essence. Yet what passes through has been wholly transmitted, in its entirety, including the intellect, emotions, and deeds, and the recipient can understand what has been transmitted since it has been translated into terms that can be understood in the lower plane to which it has been delivered. By contrast, in the case of a passageway, what is transmitted is exactly

what the author of the *Tanya* refers to as a passageway. When enclothed, as occurs when the divine light devolves through the chain of progression, from one level to the next, the entity from the higher world is enclothed in an entity in a lower plane, and the higher entity reveals itself and operates below through the lower entity. In that case, what is revealed is not the higher entity, but the lower one that enclothes it. That which has descended has undergone a fundamental change. It is not the same intellect, the same inner world, that it was above, but rather it has become a different intellect, a different conceptual world, translated through the intellect and concepts of the lower realm into which it has descended.

A passageway, by contrast, is when the lower entity is merely a conduit for the higher entity. A conduit does not interfere with the thing that is passing through it, nor does it affect its essence. It merely brings down that entity to a lower place and transfers it to another plane, but it does not change it in any way. What descends is the same as that which existed above.

To illustrate, an enclothement is similar to a person clarifying an idea to a group of people from a different conceptual and cultural world. He takes aside one of their members whom he knows and explains the idea to him, and that person subsequently explains the idea to the others.

The intermediary will explain the idea in the way that he understands it and in terms that the others can absorb it. The essence of the idea necessarily changes in the delivery. It is transmitted in the words, not of the first individual whose idea it was, but of the second.

A more common example of this provided in hasidic sources is an analogy or metaphor. The purpose of the metaphor is to transmit content from one area of thought and concepts to another, such as from technical terminology to popular science or from the conception of an adult to that of a child. The metaphor apparently deals with completely different ideas, such as physical rather than spiritual concepts, or those a child can relate to as opposed to those that resonate with an adult, yet it can be transferred from one conceptual plane to another. Moreover, what is transmitted is the metaphor itself, not the actual message, the higher concept it is trying to convey, that is contained and concealed within it.

By contrast, a passageway is compared to a person writing down his thoughts. The medium of hand and pen is merely a passageway, a conduit through which the thoughts pass from the person's mind to the paper. The hand does not understand anything of what it writes, does not change the content in any way, but only writes down exactly what the person is thinking.

what was above, but for precisely this reason it does not pass in its entirety. What passes through are only letters, deeds that cannot be understood and felt, and these are the *halakhot*. The *halakhot* are the supernal wisdom of *Atzilut* that is not enclothed in the garments of the lower world, and therefore it is impossible to understand, sense, and perceive meaning in them. The meaning merely passes through them, like the hand that writes down the thoughts of the mind until it is enclothed in the form of letters on paper, or in our case, in the practical *halakhot* of this world.[65]

כְּמוֹ בְּיוֹם טוֹב, שֶׁחֶסֶד דַּאֲצִילוּת הַמְלוּבָּשׁ לְגַמְרֵי בְּחֶסֶד דִּבְרִיאָה מְחַיֶּה עוֹלָם הַזֶּה הַגַּשְׁמִי עַל יְדֵי מַעֲבָר חֶסֶד דִּיצִירָה וַעֲשִׂיָּה	as on a festival, when the *Ḥesed* of *Atzilut*, which is completely enclothed in the *Ḥesed* of *Beria*, gives life to this physical world via the passageway of the *Ḥesed* of *Yetzira* and *Asiya*.

The author of the *Tanya* gives another example of a passageway: Unlike the weekdays, when the life force that reaches the lower worlds is enclothed in all the stages of the order of progression, such as *Ḥesed* of *Atzilut* devolving and being enclothed in *Ḥesed* of *Beria*, then *Yetzira*, then *Asiya*, on a festival the life force is enclothed only in *Beria*, from which it passes through *Yetzira* and *Asiya* in the form of a passageway. ☞

THE FESTIVAL AND THE PASSAGEWAY

☞ A festival is not an ordinary day. It is a day when the life force that descends to the lower worlds is superior to that of the weekdays. In general, all the worlds receive their life force through the chain of progression of the *sefirot* and the worlds, from

---

65. With that said, it must be that the enclothing of *Beria*, at least, is a garment and not just a passageway, since otherwise the supernal wisdom could not be absorbed in the worlds at all. It would be too intense, too undiluted and impossible to contain. Therefore, the descent from *Atzilut* to *Beria*, from the Divine to the created beings, must always involve an enclothing. But the descent from *Beria* to *Yetzira* and *Asiya*, where the difference between them and *Beria* is not so fundamental, since they are all created, separate entities to a certain degree, can be in the form of a passageway alone. See *Or HaTorah*. Lev., vol. 2, pp. 462, 470.

הַנִּקְרָא גַּם כֵּן הִתְלַבְּשׁוּת, שֶׁאִם
לֹא כֵּן לֹא הָיָה פּוֹעֵל בְּגַשְׁמִיּוּת
עוֹלָם הַזֶּה

This is also considered enclothing, because otherwise it would not have an effect on the materiality of this world.

The passageway from Ḥesed of Beria to Ḥesed of Yetzira and Asiya is, in a certain sense, also an enclothement. It is for this reason that the author of the Tanya refers to the "garment of Asiya" as a passageway. Although it is a passageway, it is still called a garment, because if there were no enclothing at all, the halakhot could not enter the world of Asiya at all. Returning to our analogy, while the hand that writes down words of wisdom is only a passageway, so to speak, and the written words are ascribed to the mind from which they came and not the hand, those words of wisdom could not have been formed as ink on paper without the hand.

Similarly, the Ḥesed of Atzilut that is enclothed in the Ḥesed of Beria could not enter and act on this world if it did not enclothe itself in the Ḥesed of Yetzira and Asiya and pass through them. Admittedly,

one level to other. In this chain of progression, the light of Atzilut is enclothed in Beria, the light of Beria is then enclothed in Yetzira, and the light of Yetzira in then enclothed in Asiya. This light is the life force that gives life to the worlds to sustain them. It is the natural life force that fashions and reveals the worlds, while concealing the infinite God who creates and controls them. Every enclothing necessarily conceals the higher reality, so that these layers of enclothement, from one level to the next, from the higher worlds down to this world, completely hides the divine light itself.

Yet from time to time flashes of the divine light penetrate certain places and certain times within the lower world, revealing the Divine beyond and elevating those times and places to another level of reality. This is how a weekday becomes a festival and a mundane act a mitzva. Such revelations stem from the same divine light and life force that descends to the world through the order of progression, but instead of being enclothed in all the levels of the progression, it skips over certain stages and passes through them only in the manner of a passageway.

This is the mystical meaning of all revelation: The question is only which light is being revealed, which steps it has skipped, and whether it has arrived in this world through enclothement or through a passageway.

This is also the case for the halakhot, which constitute the light of the supernal wisdom that is enclothed in Beria and transferred to the physical world of Asiya as through a passageway. The same is the case for the Torah in general, the words of the prophets, in accordance with the prophet's level, and the special days of the year: the Sabbath and festivals.

this is not the same enclothing as the manner of enclothement in which the divine light disappears completely because it is so heavily concealed. But it is an enclothement in the sense that the *Ḥesed* of *Beria* is enclothed in the clothing of *Yetzira* and subsequently in the clothing of *Asiya*, in order that it can enter the world of *Asiya*. Like the written word on paper, it is still ascribed to *Ḥesed* of *Beria*, but it is nevertheless "written": It exists in a physical form in the world of *Asiya* as well.

It is true that, like words on paper, it is merely recorded there; it does not itself reveal the true essence of its Creator, as in the world of *Beria*. But those who know how to read it can receive the same revelation that exists in *Beria* down here in the world of *Asiya*. It is thus possible to interpret the analogy in the following manner: One who fulfills the mitzvot of the festival in practice is like someone who reads the letters written on the paper. When he tries to understand what is written there, to connect the letters and formulate words that have meaning for him, it is as though he is actually reading what *Ḥesed* of *Atzilut* has written about that day in *Asiya*.

The same is the case for the *halakhot*, and in a certain sense, every divine revelation in our world. There is an enclothing of lofty levels, from *Atzilut* and *Beria*, within the physical world. This enclothing occurs in the manner of a passageway, a kind of enclothing that reveals those higher levels but they are still enclothed in a way that they can be revealed and exist in the physical reality.

וְאַף שֶׁגַּשְׁמִיּוּת עוֹלָם הַזֶּה וַדַּאי מַסְתִּיר לְגַמְרֵי אֲפִילוּ הַחֶסֶד דַּעֲשִׂיָּה **Although the physicality of this world definitely conceals** the divine light **completely** and **even** conceals **the Ḥesed of Asiya,**

The materiality of this world conceals the divine light, not only when it is enclothed in the lofty levels of *Atzilut* and *Beria*, but it even conceals *Ḥesed* of the world of *Asiya*. ☞

THE CONCEALMENT OF PHYSICALITY

☞ The physical world is completely sealed off from everything above it, from every being that is not physical. We can tangibly sense this. Even *Ḥesed* of *Asiya*, which is the spiritual aspect of this physical reality, the spirituality that is nearest to

מִכָּל מָקוֹם, הַהֲלָכָה עַצְמָהּ אֵינָהּ the *halakha* itself is nevertheless
גַּשְׁמִיּוּת מַמָּשׁ not actually physical.

Although the *halakha* is enclothed and expressed through physical reality, it in itself is not solely physical. True physicality is the reality whose spiritual, intellectual, and emotional components are also essentially physical. They are not comprised of matter that can be touched, but the reasonings and considerations related to them are corporeal: What can I get out of it? Perhaps it is food or money, and so on. By contrast, *halakha* is comprised of supernal wisdom, the Ḥokhma of *Atzilut*, which is merely manifest in a physical law but is not actually physical. One can see the physical tip of the iceberg, so to speak, the cow and the donkey, but one cannot see the other end, the intellect and the reasoning behind it, which are not physical and cannot be understood by a physical mind.[66] ☞

שֶׁהִיא בְּחִינַת רָצוֹן הַנִּמְשָׁךְ מֵחָכְמָה It is the divine will that is drawn
עִילָאָה from supernal Ḥokhma,

The physical realm is not a vehicle for revealing wisdom in general, but merely the divine will that is drawn from the wisdom, the conclusion of the wisdom that expresses the divine will, whether it should be like this or that.

it, is not revealed within it. The supernal wisdom of *Atzilut* is certainly not visible to the mortal eyes with which one perceives physical reality.

For example, there is a *halakha* that deals with someone who acquires a donkey by exchanging it for his cow. It turns out that the cow has calved, and both the erstwhile cow owner and the one who ac-

quired it lay claim to the calf (Mishna *Bava Metzia* 8:4); see also *Ba'al Shem Tov al Ha-Torah, Parashat Behar* 4). When one sees a physical cow being exchanged for a donkey, and each animal passes from the possession of one person to another, one does not perceive the wisdom of *Atzilut* or *Asiya* in this exchange. One simply sees a physical cow and donkey and nothing more.

---

66. As for what we call the reasons behind the mitzvot, whether explicit or esoteric, these exist only for us. For a certain person, the standard reason might be enough, while someone else might feel that a different justification is more convincing. But the truth of the matter is that from God's perspective there is in fact no reason for the mitzvot, certainly not one that we can fathom.

לְהָקֵל אוֹ לְהַחְמִיר   **for leniency or for stringency,**

A halakhic conclusion invariably takes one of two forms: a leniency or a stringency. It is true that the *halakha* also deals with other matters, including descriptions of objects and actions, but the ultimate purpose of all these details is to determine whether or not God wishes something to be this way or that way, whether He wishes one to be lenient or stringent.

רַק שֶׁיּוֹרֵד וּמֵאִיר בִּבְחִינַת גִּילוּי
בַּגַּשְׁמִיּוּת כַּמַּיִם הַיּוֹרְדִים מִמָּקוֹם
גָּבוֹהַּ כו'   **only it descends and illuminates in a revealed manner in the physical realm, just as water descends from a high place…**

This expression of the Divine, the question of whether one is to be lenient or stringent, descends and shines in every world, according to its level, all the way down to this physical reality. What is revealed and visible in each world is the garments of that world, its spiritual and material states. The one common denominator that reveals the divine wisdom itself in all worlds is this point of the *halakha*, whether to be lenient or to be stringent.

The analogy that the author of the *Tanya* offers here, of water cascading from a higher place to a lower one, has a further implication. In the case of a waterfall, the waters above and the waters below comprise the very same substance. Similarly, the divine wisdom that descends from *Atzilut* to the physical world of *Asiya*, despite all the garments and degrees of concealment through which it passes, is still the same essential wisdom, without change or distortion.

ACTUAL PHYSICALITY

☞ True physicality is a reality that has devolved through all the stages in the order of progression and is subsequently clothed in thicker layers of concealment. But the *halakha* does not fall into this category, because it is not enclothed as it passes through the stages in the progression, but merely passes through. It is indeed enclothed in the material world of *Asiya*, but in the form of a passageway alone, like that aforementioned hand that writes down one's thoughts on paper. Just as that writing is not the wisdom of the hand, but the wisdom of the intellect, so too the *halakha* is not physical wisdom, but the wisdom of the Divine.

וְהַדָּבָר הַגַּשְׁמִי עַצְמוֹ שֶׁבּוֹ
מְדַבֶּרֶת הַהֲלָכָה, בֶּאֱמֶת הוּא
מַסְתִּיר לְגַמְרֵי כְּמוֹ הַמַּחֲלִיף
פָּרָה בַּחֲמוֹר, וְכֵן בְּשַׂר הַפִּיגּוּל
אוֹ לֹא פִּיגּוּל וְכָשֵׁר

The physical object itself that the *halakha* discusses, such as one who exchanges a cow for a donkey, and likewise that which concerns **meat that is pigul** and is prohibited **or that is not pigul and is kosher, truly does conceal** the supernal wisdom **completely.**

This object is the physical garment through which the *halakha* is revealed. When one focuses on the physical garment, the situation and material object that the *halakha* discusses, the concealment is actual. The cow and donkey themselves in the case where one is exchanged for the other, and likewise the meat that is the subject of the debate as to whether or not it is *pigul*, both completely hide the supernal wisdom. ☞

רַק הַהֲלָכָה בְּעַצְמָהּ, עִם
הַטַּעַם הַנִּגְלֶה

However, the ruling itself, with the revealed reason,

This refers to the *halakha* itself, whether to be lenient or stringent or whether an item is invalid or kosher, as well as the reasoning and understanding behind the ruling of the *halakha*. ☞

הִיא מִבְּחִינַת מַלְכוּת דִּבְרִיאָה
וִיצִירָה דִּבְחִינַת נְשָׁמָה שֶׁהוּא
אֱלֹקוּת

stems from *Malkhut of Beria* **and** *Yetzira,* **whose source is the level of** *neshama,* **which constitutes divinity**

THE ACTUAL PHYSICAL OBJECT

☞ This distinction has an effect on how the *halakhot* are studied. The *halakhot* we study are always enclothed in the physical framework of this world. Holiness and divine wisdom are not revealed in the garment itself, but in the *halakha* that is sought through it, whether one should be lenient or stringent. If one focuses too much on the garment, on the physical objects and framework, he might lose the main point, which is the divine wisdom

contained within the Torah he is studying. Although the Torah is holy, and every word of the Torah is holy, it is nevertheless possible for a person to lose himself in all the materiality. Despite one's keen engagement with the details of the physical world in order to ascertain the correct *halakha*, one should not forget what he is seeking here: the divine wisdom and will, whether God wishes him to be lenient or stringent.

The place for the halakhic ruling along with its revealed reason in the worlds is *Malkhut* of *Beria* and *Yetzira*. On every level, *Malkhut* is the *sefira* that descends to the world below. It is the *sefira* and vessel enclothed in the reality of that world and to which they transfer the life force from above. This is like a person's speech, which passes from one person to another, transferring information from speaker to listener.

The *halakha* descends from *Atzilut* to *Beria* as it exists in the supernal wisdom in *Atzilut* through the nullification to the divine will. At that stage, there is no rational reason for the *halakha* that man could comprehend. But once it is in *Beria*, the revealed reason of the *halakha* is disclosed. Subsequently, *Malkhut* descends from *Beria* and *Yetzira*, which is the place of the ruling of the *halakha*. This accounts for the concept that "the Talmud is in *Beria*, and the Mishna is in *Yetzira*."[67] The talmudic analysis of the reasons for the *halakhot* belong to *Beria*, which

THE REVEALED REASON

☞ Every *halakha* has a logical, rational structure that relates to other *halakhot* and to this world in which it is practiced. On the basis of this structure, a sage will issue a ruling in the form of a leniency or a stringency. This is what the author of the *Tanya* terms the "revealed reason." It is not the divine reason behind the *halakha* known only to God. We have no access to that at all. Rather, it is the operative reason, based on which we debate the case and issue halakhic rulings.

Furthermore, the revealed reason is part of the essence of the *halakha* itself. It is a kind of spiritual space that surrounds every physical *halakha*, where the *halakhot* encounter each other and enter the life of the person who must fulfill them.

The revealed reason does not come from us, from what we comprehend. It comes from above, together with the *halakha* itself, and it is directed at the deep, hidden roots of the *halakha* that we cannot apprehend. Yet by studying and applying the revealed reason, so that we ourselves, through our intellect, knowledge, and feelings, can connect to it, we can arrive at the halakhic ruling, which is the revelation of the supernal wisdom in this world.

There are also hidden reasons for the *halakhot*, but those reasons deal mainly with the intentions that accompany the performance of the mitzva and its effect on the spiritual worlds, whereas the revealed reason applies to the way the mitzva should be executed in the physical world. The hidden reason is thus like the intention that accompanies the mitzva. It is not part of the act of the mitzva itself but an addition to it, certainly an important and even essential addition but an addition nonetheless (see *Likkutei Amarim*, chaps. 39–40).

---

67. See *Pri Etz Ḥayyim, Shaʿar Hanhagat HaLimud; Iggeret HaKodesh*, epistle 26.

is the world of the intellect, whereas the practical ruling of the *halakha*, which appears in the Mishna and the *Shulḥan Arukh*, is in *Yetzira*.

The source of the revelations of the *halakha* in *Beria* and *Yetzira* is "the *neshama*, which is the Divine." This *halakha* that descends from *Atzilut* to *Beria* and then *Yetzira*, and from there to *Asiya*, from the reason for the *halakha* to the practical ruling of the *halakha*, constitutes the divine life force on the level of *neshama*, which is the Divine. ☞

הַמְחַיָּה וּמְהַוֶּה נֶפֶשׁ רוּחַ   **that sustains and brings into existence**
דִּבְרִיאָה יְצִירָה עֲשִׂיָּה   *nefesh* **and** *ruaḥ* **of** *Yetzira* **and** *Asiya.*

The level of *neshama*, which constitutes the *halakhot*, gives life and existence to the levels of *nefesh* and *ruaḥ* of the worlds of *Yetzira* and *Asiya*. Just as on the broader scale God creates and sustains the world, so too the level of *neshama* is the crystallization of the Divine in the life force, and this is what sustains and brings into being that which gives life to the external frameworks of the world. In the same vein, the deeper, unfathomable reason behind the *halakhot* that is concealed

THE *NEFESH, RUAḤ,* AND *NESHAMA* OF THE WORLDS

☞ The life force that descends to the worlds, like the soul of man that descends and gives life to his body, is broadly comprised of three levels: *nefesh, ruaḥ,* and *neshama*. Two of these, *nefesh* and *ruaḥ*, are relatively external, and they constitute and give life to the worlds themselves, to the external frameworks that lend the worlds their existence. The level of *neshama*, on the other hand, is more internal and carries the divine light itself into the worlds (see *Iggeret HaKodesh,* epistle 20). Though the Divine itself transcends all levels and worlds, encompassing the world, the inner light within every world and level contains a facet in which the Divine reveals itself within that world. This is the *neshama* of that world.

In the human soul, by way of comparison, the levels of *nefesh* and *ruaḥ* are the

life force that give life to the body and manifest in his senses and attributes, the emotions by which he lives and interacts with the world. By contrast, *neshama* is the level of the intellect, man's recognition and awareness of himself and his world. At this level, the soul contains the soul's essence, the person's very self. Here the soul is not led by one's senses and feelings but actually directs them toward another end, to something higher, which the person himself understands to be necessary and good.

In the same way, God created and sustains His world with the life force that is called *nefesh* and *ruaḥ*. He also enters His world through His will and wisdom, via the *halakhot* and their reasons, and this is the level of the life force called *neshama*, which is a facet of the Divine itself.

sustains the revealed reasons and conclusions that we can see openly in the lower realm.

שֶׁהֵן דְּחִילוּ וּרְחִימוּ שֶׁל הַמַּלְאָכִים וְהַנְּשָׁמוֹת וְחָכְמָה בִּינָה דַּעַת שֶׁלָּהֶם, מֵאַיִן לְיֵשׁ

The levels of *nefesh* and *ruaḥ* constitute the fear and love of the angels and the souls and their *Ḥokhma, Bina,* and *Da'at,* which the *neshama* brings into existence from nothingness.

The life force of the worlds at the levels of *nefesh* and *ruaḥ* are the emotive attributes, such as love and fear, from which a person receives his vitality. This life force is expressed by the angels, whose entire being and service is this fear and love. The angel who loves God is an expression of the divine attribute of love, not as it actually exists in *Atzilut*, but as it is enclothed and defined in the worlds below it. The essence of the angel is the love that relates to a certain recognition of the Divine, a recognition that characterizes the parameters of the angel. This is why the author of the *Tanya* specifies "their *Ḥokhma, Bina,* and *Da'at.*" These are the cognitive attributes that constitute a being's awareness. This awareness and cognition of the angels is part of their being and service, which is cognitive love and fear, the emotions evoked as an outcome of their awareness of the Divine.

In general, the levels of *nefesh* and *ruaḥ* in the worlds is the realm of the angels, which is a created reality below the world of *Atzilut*, but also a spiritual and pure one. This means that the angels' task is easier, since their intellect is expansive and clear, without any interference, and their love and fear are absolute. For them, there is nothing else. It is their entire being and is threaded throughout their conceptions and feelings. The soul, by contrast, exists not only on the level of *nefesh* and *ruaḥ*, in the spiritual realms, but it is also clothed in a body. On the levels of *nefesh* and *ruaḥ*, in the world of the angels, the soul's cognitive fear and love is the same as the fear and love of the angels. There, the soul can sense and worship God like the angels. It is not that simple, and not always clear-cut, but it is the same cognitive love and fear as that of the angels.

The author of the *Tanya* tells us here that the level of *neshama* in the worlds, which is revealed by the *halakhot* of the Torah, gives life and existence to the levels of *nefesh* and *ruaḥ*, to the angels and souls in those realms.

וְלָכֵן הִיא מַרְוָה צִמְאוֹנָם **Therefore,** the *halakha* that descends from above and bears the supernal wisdom **quenches their thirst**

The *halakha* that descends from above quenches the thirst of the angels and souls that serve God with cognitive fear and love. ☞

קוֹדֶם שֶׁיָּרְדָה לָעוֹלָם הַזֶּה כַּמַּיִם **before it descends to this world, just**
הַיּוֹרְדִים כו' **as water descends…**

Before the *halakha* descended to be enclothed in this world, it was a spiritual essence in the spiritual realms of *Beria* and *Yetzira*. The angels cannot fulfill the mitzvot in practice, nor can they relate to the world of action, just as those in the world of action cannot relate to the angels. But the angels can receive something of the intellectual aspect of the *halakha*, its spiritual essence, in their own unique manner, as it exists before it descends to the world of *Asiya*. ☞

THE THIRST OF ANGELS AND SOULS

☞ This description of the *halakha* quenching the thirst of the angels, and essentially all created entities, is a portrayal of the entire creation, all of which studies Torah, so to speak. This is similar to the well-known Jewish concept that everyone should study Torah and that it is the duty of each Jew to study something each day, even if it is only one mishna or one chapter from the *Shema*, because he draws his inner vitality from there. On a broader scale, Torah study is important for all the worlds, since it quenches their thirst for life. The created beings, who are apparently separated from God, thirst for a Torah that is always connected, at every level, to the divine essence.

AS WATER DESCENDS

☞ The author of the *Tanya* returns to the analogy that compares the descent of the *halakha* from *Atzilut* to water descending from a high place to a low place. It does not illuminate below, or activate something else, or send something, but like water, the *halakha* itself flows down. Water remains in the same state below as it was above. The same applies to the *halakha* as it descends through all the levels: Despite the fact that it passes through each level and is enclothed in its own hue and matter, it is still the same divine will and the same supernal wisdom with which all yearn to quench their thirst.

וְגַם אַחַר שֶׁיָּרְדָה לַעֲשִׂיָּה, הִיא
לְמַעְלָה מַעְלָה מִבְּחִינַת חָכְמָה בִּינָה
דַּעַת דַּעֲשִׂיָּה, אֲפִילוּ דִּבְחִינַת נְשָׁמָה
שֶׁהִיא אֱלֹקוּת

Even after its descent to *Asiya*, it transcends *Ḥokhma, Bina,* and *Da'at* of *Asiya* and even the level of *neshama*, which constitutes divinity.

Although the *halakha* is enclothed in materiality, and the divine essence is not easily detected in it, it still transcends the highest levels of the world of *Asiya*, what is considered the intellect of *Asiya*, its spiritual realm. It even transcends the level of *neshama*, which is the divine essence in *Asiya*. This is the internal aspect of *Asiya* that represents the Divine that creates and sustains the world of *Asiya*, including its intellect, its *Ḥokhma, Bina,* and *Da'at*. The revelation of the *halakha* when it is enclothed in *Asiya* is still higher than all those levels, since it is an actual expression of the Divine in *Atzilut* – not the Divine in *Asiya* but the Divine in *Atzilut* – that resides and is revealed here below within the physical matter with which the *halakha* is involved.

וְהַטַּעַם מִשּׁוּם דְּחָכְמָה בִּינָה דַּעַת
דַּעֲשִׂיָּה דִּבְחִינַת נְשָׁמָה, הוּא מְקוֹר
הַחַיּוּת דְּחָכְמָה בִּינָה דַּעַת דְּנֶפֶשׁ
רוּחַ, וְתוֹלְדוֹתֵיהֶן וְהִתְהַוּוֹתָן מֵאַיִן
לְיֵשׁ עִם תּוֹלְדוֹתֵיהֶן עַד סוֹף הָעֲשִׂיָּה
הִיא הָאָרֶץ וְכָל צְבָאָהּ

The reason for the difference between divine light that descends through the chain of progression and the divine light within *halakha* **is that Ḥokhma, Bina,** and *Da'at* **of** *Asiya*, **on the level of** *neshama*, **is the source of the life force of Ḥokhma, Bina,** and *Da'at* of the levels of *nefesh* and *ruaḥ*, **and their offspring and their coming into existence from nothingness with their offspring until the ends of** *Asiya*, **which is the earth and all its hosts.**

11 Kislev

11 Kislev
(leap year)

Here the author of the *Tanya* seeks to explain the difference between the divine light that descends and progresses through the all the worlds, in which it is enclothed and concealed, and the divine light within the *halakhot*. The latter also descends into physical reality but is not hidden in it, but rather the divine essence remains, despite all the levels it passes through, essentially as it is above.

The reason for this difference is that *Ḥokhma, Bina,* and *Da'at* of *Asiya,* which essentially is the presence of the Divine in *Asiya,* the level of *neshama* of this world, is the source of the life force of *Ḥokhma, Bina,* and *Da'at* of the levels of *nefesh* and *ruaḥ,* which represents the head, or root, of the life force in *Asiya* itself. Their "offspring" is the physical world of *Asiya,* the levels of *nefesh* and *ruaḥ* within it, and "all its hosts," which includes everything that exists inside it, down to the smallest details of every inanimate, vegetable, and living creature. Thus, the *Hokhma, Bina,* and *Da'at* of *Asiya* are a source of life for the created beings.

אֲבָל חָכְמָה בִּינָה דַּעַת דַּהֲלָכוֹת בְּטַעֲמֵיהֶן שֶׁבְּמַלְכוּת דִּבְרִיאָה וִיצִירָה, עִנְיָן הַחָכְמָה הִיא בְּתִיקוּן פַּרְצוּפֵי הָאֲצִילוּת

But the *Ḥokhma, Bina,* and *Da'at* of *halakhot,* along with their reasons, are in *Malkhut* of *Beria* and *Yetzira.* The *Ḥokhma* within the *halakhot* effects the rectification of the *partzufim* of *Atzilut,*

By contrast, the *Ḥokhma* of the *halakhot* with which one engages in the study of those *halakhot* descends within *Malkhut* of *Beria* and *Yetzira,* as well as *Asiya.* Although the *halakhot* apparently involve physical objects and actions, it actually affects the *partzufim* of *Atzilut* above. We may do the action in *Asiya,* but what we activate is in *Atzilut* above. To return to the analogy we have used above, when we write, we fashion the letters by hand, but these written forms have almost no intrinsic meaning. Their meaning exists in the world of the spirit, in the ideas, beauty, and love that the words express. In view of this, rather than being a source of life force for *Asiya* and all that it contains, it is a force of rectification for the world of *Atzilut* above. ☞

THE RECTIFICATION OF THE *PARTZUFIM* OF ATZILUT

☞ This rectification is required, not because something is corrupt there, since the world of *Atzilut* is Divine and rectified by its own nature. But because the world of *Atzilut* constitutes the countenance of God and the way He relates to the created

שֶׁבָּהֶן תְּלוּיִן כָּל טַעֲמֵי הַמִּצְוֹת: מִצְוֹת עֲשֵׂה בה׳ חֲסָדִים, וּמִצְוֹת לֹא תַעֲשֶׂה בה׳ גְּבוּרוֹת

upon which all the reasons for the mitzvot depend: **The positive commandments** depend **on the five ḥasadim,** the spiritual forces of giving, **and the prohibitions on the five gevurot,** the restraining forces.

The five ḥasadim and the five gevurot are the lights that are drawn from above to below into the attributes of Atzilut, and their drawing forth into Atzilut and the worlds below Atzilut depends on the fulfillment of mitzvot. The illumination of the positive commandments are drawn forth through the ḥasadim, the forces of giving, while that of the prohibitions is drawn forth through the gevurot, the restraining forces.

וּמִשּׁוּם הָכֵי נַמִי כְּשֶׁיָרְדוּ לְהִתְלַבֵּשׁ בַּנִּבְרָאִים, הֵן בְּמַלְכוּת דִּבְרִיאָה וִיצִירָה דִּבְחִינַת נְשָׁמָה דַּוְקָא, שֶׁהוּא מִכֵּלִים דַּאֲצִילוּת וְלֹא בִּבְחִינַת נֶפֶשׁ רוּחַ

Therefore, even when the halakhot descended to be enclothed in created beings, they descended in Malkhut of Beria and Yetzira, specifically on the level of neshama, which stems from the vessels of Atzilut, and not the levels of nefesh and ruaḥ.

The halakhot descended in order "to be clothed in created beings," to be studied with the intellect of created beings and so that they should ultimately be fulfilled in practice. The levels of nefesh and ruaḥ are the spiritual realms of the worlds, while neshama contains the divine essence and life force that give the worlds their vitality. When the halakhot descend to the worlds, they are clothed solely in the vessels of Atzilut rather than the vessels of the worlds. Since they are clothed only in the

worlds, it is possible that from the perspective of the worlds different situations might arise within the interactions between the partzufim of the world of Atzilut, and the rectification of these interactions depends on our study and practice of the mitzvot.

This is because the mitzvot we perform here are like a direct connection between us and Atzilut. They are the way in which we can operate in Atzilut and open up the channels of the flow of goodness for us and all the worlds.

vessels of *Atzilut*, the divine wisdom in them is not concealed, since the vessels of *Atzilut* do not conceal the Divine. There is a constriction of the divine light and essence within the materials and circumstances in which the *halakha* must be carried out, but there is no constriction or concealment of the divine wisdom that is in *Atzilut*, which descends as it is until the *halakha* is fulfilled down below with material objects. ☞

THE DESCENT OF THE LIGHT AND THE *HALAKHOT* OF THE TORAH

☞ The fundamental distinction between the descent of the Divine to sustain the worlds through the chain of progression and the descent of the Divine in the *halakhot* is related to the aforementioned distinction between a passageway and an enclothing. There is a divine source that descends from above to below, to the worlds and to the angels' cognitive love and fear, and is literally enclothed in the affairs of the worlds below. This divine source, this light, descended for this very purpose, to be enclothed in the worlds and give them life. It is the enclothing itself that constitutes their vitality and sustains their existence. Of course, this light is not revealed below in the state that it exists above, as the unadulterated divine essence, but rather as the life force of the worlds below.

As explained above, this is the mode of enclothement, in which a higher entity reveals itself only through the intermediary of a lower entity, through its parameters and faculties. Yet this mode of revelation provides an understanding and feeling with which we can connect, a sense of spirituality and the forces of the Divine. This understanding and feeling are nothing other than the cognitive love and fear of the angels and souls.

By contrast, the divine light in the *halakhot* and their reasons was designed not for the created worlds but for *Atzilut*. This is the whole purpose and concern of the *halakhot*, to effect and rectify the *partzufim* of *Atzilut*. Therefore, their descent to the worlds is not a descent in the form of enclothing, but in the manner of a passageway. The content of the *halakhot* is not enclothed at all in the worlds but merely passes through them in order to be written down in the lower reality. For this reason, it is not manifest in the worlds, but it is also not hidden in them, in their existence and affairs. Instead, it remains a divine revelation as it is above and can be revealed to us only through their fulfillment below and through the study of their reasons in the Torah.

Moreover, the *halakhot* are internal because they relate to the supernal will itself, to the primary, internal purpose, which initiates everything, as opposed to the light that is enclothed in the worlds. This light is external, because it is designed to create the structures within which the internal will can operate. Consequently, this light is enclothed in the worlds, in the vitality that gives life to the worlds, and translates into cognitive love and fear, into the garments that relate to the lower worlds. This is not the case with the inner light of the *halakhot*: All of its garments are divine garments. They are always divine will and wisdom, and such garments never conceal

וְאַף דְּחָכְמָה בִּינָה דַּעַת דִּבְרִיאָה
יְצִירָה דִּבְחִינַת נְשָׁמָה, שֶׁגְּבֹהַּ
מְאֹד מַעֲלָתָן עַל בְּחִינַת מַלְכוּת
דִּבְרִיאָה יְצִירָה דִּנְשָׁמָה, וְאַף עַל
פִּי כֵן הֵן מָקוֹר לְחָכְמָה בִּינָה דַּעַת
דִּבְרִיאָה יְצִירָה שֶׁל בְּחִינַת נֶפֶשׁ
רוּחַ שֶׁהֵן הַמַּלְאָכִים

Although Ḥokhma, Bina, and Da'at of Beria and Yetzira on the level of neshama far transcends Malkhut of Beria and Yetzira of neshama, they are nevertheless the source of Ḥokhma, Bina, and Da'at of Beria and Yetzira on the levels of nefesh and ruaḥ, which are the angels.

Ḥokhma, Bina, and Da'at of Beria and Yetzira on the level of neshama are the source of the worlds and of cognitive love and fear since they contain the divine essence. They far transcend Malkhut of Beria and Yetzira of neshama, through which the halakhot pass. Even though these sefirot are all on the neshama level, that which contains the divine essence itself, Ḥokhma, Bina, and Da'at are much loftier than Malkhut, which is the lowest sefira. The revelation of the Divine in Ḥokhma, Bina, and Da'at is higher than the revelation of Malkhut, just as the intellect is higher, or precedes, action. Yet this lofty revelation of Ḥokhma, Bina, and Da'at of neshama is the source of Ḥokhma, Bina, and Da'at of the levels of nefesh and ruaḥ, which are the life force of the worlds and the service of the angels alone. In other words, it is not revealed below as divinity, but as Ḥokhma, Bina, and Da'at, or the intellect of the worlds, which are the angels. Yet the apparently lower revelation in Malkhut that appears in the worlds in the physical forms of the halakhot is actually a revelation of the divine wisdom itself in the world of Atzilut.

what is within. This inner will and wisdom merely passes through the worlds like a person going down the stairs. Though he is descending, he is still himself with each step he takes.

The inner garments do not conceal because they themselves are internal. Someone who is wearing his own clothes is not hidden. A soldier who wears his uniform displays to everyone who he is. Garments hide only when one is wearing someone else's clothes. Here too, when the interiority of the will is enclothed in the realization of that will, it is not hidden, but when it is enclothed in external desires, in the supplementary structures and intermediate stages that must constrict it, then it is concealed and may even be completely forgotten.

לָא קַשְׁיָא מִידֵי דְּבֶאֱמֶת
הַמַּלְאָכִים וְהַנְּשָׁמוֹת אֵינָן אֶלָּא
מִטִּפָּה הַנִּמְשֶׁכֶת מֵחָכְמָה בִּינָה
דַּעַת דִּנְשָׁמָה לִיסוֹד זְעֵיר אַנְפִּין
וְנִיתַּן לַנּוּקְבָא, וּמִשָּׁם יָצְאוּ
בִּבְחִינַת לֵידָה

This is not a question at all, because in truth the angels and the souls, which are created from Ḥokhma, Bina, and Da'at of Beria and Yetzira of neshama, come only from a drop that is drawn from Ḥokhma, Bina, and Da'at of neshama to Yesod of Zeir Anpin, and was given to the feminine aspect of the sefirot, which is Malkhut, from which they emerged in the form of a birth.

This apparent reversal, in which the lofty reveals that which is lowly (the worlds), while a lower entity reveals that which is lofty (Atzilut), is not actually a contradiction at all. The souls and angels that were created from Ḥokhma, Bina, and Da'at of Beria and Yetzira on the level of neshama were created in a simulation of a birth of a new being, as opposed to being the result of a direct flow from above to below from the divine essence.

Metaphorically speaking, this is like the difference between a person's own being, which extends from his intellect to the faculties and limbs of his soul, and the child he fathers. Despite the father's many sacrifices in the course of his upbringing and their close relationship, the child remains a different person. Likewise, in the realm of the Divine, this is the difference between the beings of the world of Atzilut, which are the "limbs of the King," and the worlds below it, as well as the souls and angels, which are separate beings, as it were, distinct from the Divine and the world of Atzilut.

כִּי אַף אִם תִּמְצָא לוֹמַר
שֶׁנִּבְרְאוּ מֵהֶאָרַת הַכֵּלִים
דְּנוּקְבָא דַּאֲצִילוּת, הֲרֵי הֵם
הַיּוֹרְדִים וְנַעֲשִׂים נְשָׁמָה

Even if you say that they were created from the illumination of the vessels of the feminine aspect of Atzilut, they themselves, these vessels, descend to the worlds of Beria, Yetzira, and Asiya and become the neshama of the worlds.

One might propose that the created souls and angels were created from the vessels that descend and become the neshama the worlds, the divine essence that descends and is found within every created being in all places.[68] But this descent and enclothing in the worlds is like the light of offspring, something apart from the divine essence, so to speak, and not the actual divine light that exists in *Atzilut*.

אֲבָל עַצְמוּת חָכְמָה בִּינָה דַּעַת דִּנְשָׁמָה, מִתְפַּשֵּׁט בּוֹ׳ קְצָווֹת דִּזְעֵיר אַנְפִּין וְנוּקְבָא, וְשָׁם הֵם שִׁיתָּא סִדְרֵי מִשְׁנָה וּגְמָרָא	But the essence of *Ḥokhma*, *Bina*, and *Da'at* of *neshama* extends to the six extremities of *Zeir Anpin* and *Nukva*, where they constitute the six orders of the Mishna and Talmud.

The six extremities refers to the six *sefirot* of *Zeir Anpin* that passes the divine light directly to *Malkhut*. They are called six extremities because this alludes to the six directions, north, east, west, south, up, and down. This progression is not like a birth, generating offspring that stem from *Ḥokhma*, *Bina*, and *Da'at*, but it is the actual light of *Zeir Anpin*.

The essence of these six extremities, or six *sefirot*, are the six sections of the Mishna and Talmud. This split into six sections of the Torah actually occurs in *Zeir Anpin*. The transition from abstract awareness to something that can interact with reality unfolds in *Zeir Anpin*, where the world and its six dimensions takes shape. As the essence of these six extremities, or six sections of the Torah, descends, it becomes even more particularized: They split into the Talmud in *Beria* and the Mishnah in *Yetzira*, then take the form of the Mishna and Talmud that we study in this world. We see that the supernal wisdom itself descends and extends from *Atzilut* all the way to this world: From the *Ḥokhma*, *Bina*, and *Da'at* of *Atzilut* – from the cognitive *sefirot* in that lofty world – to the study of the *halakhot* in this world, it is all the same supernal wisdom wherever it passes through.

וּמַה שֶּׁכָּתוּב בְּעֵץ חַיִּים (וְשַׁעַר הַיִּחוּדִים)	As for the statement in *Etz Ḥayyim* (and *Sha'ar HaYiḥudim*),	12 Kislev ⎯⎯⎯⎯ 12 Kislev (leap year)

---

68. The teachings of Kabbala say that thirty vessels of *Atzilut* descended to the worlds of *Beria*, *Yetzira*, and *Asiya* to serve as their *neshama*, the divine essence that gives life to the worlds. See *Etz Ḥayyim*, *Sha'ar HaShemot*.

In relation to this idea, the author of the *Tanya* cites an apparently different claim from *Etz Ḥayyim*.[69] After the sin of Adam, the garments of man's divine soul, his body and animal soul, his senses, his apprehension and awareness, and the way he lives and experiences reality, became garments of *kelippat noga*, with good and evil intermingled. Through Torah study and the fulfillment of mitzvot, man refines those garments and prepares holy garments for his soul. Specifically, it is clarified there that there is an order to the preparation of these garments. There is a special manner in which one should engage in Torah study and the performance of mitzvot from which the appropriate garments may be fashioned for each of the levels of the soul, for its *nefesh, ruaḥ,* and *neshama*.

These garments are associated with the three levels of the soul, thought with the level of the *neshama*, speech with *ruaḥ*, and deed with *nefesh*. With respect to the service of God, the thought is the intention behind the mitzva act, the speech is the study of Torah, and the deed is the mitzva act itself.

שֶׁעַל יְדֵי הַכַּוָּונָה נַעֲשֶׂה לְבוּשׁ
נְשָׁמָה וְעַל יְדֵי הַתּוֹרָה לְבוּשׁ רוּחַ
דְּרוּחַ, עַל יְדֵי מִשְׁנָה דִּיצִירָה,
וְרוּחַ דִּנְשָׁמָה דִּבְרִיאָה עַל יְדֵי
הַגְּמָרָא

that through intent when fulfilling the mitzvot and studying Torah **a garment is formed for** the soul level of *neshama*, **and through Torah** study itself, **through the study of Mishna, a garment** is formed **for *ruaḥ* of *ruaḥ* of *Yetzira*, and for *ruaḥ* of *neshama* of *Beria* through** the study of **the Talmud,**

One's intent when studying Torah and fulfilling mitzvot is loftier than the mitzva act and Torah study themselves, and therefore the garments for the soul level of *neshama*, which is more internal, are fashioned from them. Through Torah study itself, a garment is formed for the soul level of *ruaḥ*, since Torah study in general is in the realm of speech, and speech is in the world of *Yetzira* and the level of *ruaḥ*. More specifically, the garment for the soul level of *ruaḥ* of *ruaḥ* is formed through

---

69. *Sha'ar* 49, chap. 5. See also *Torah Or* 16a, 16c.

the study of Mishna of *Yetzira*,[70] since the Mishna, and the study of halakhic rulings in general, belong to the world of *Yetzira*, the world of the attributes where the correct relationship toward everything is determined, whether to be lenient or stringent.

Finally, the garment for the level of *ruaḥ* of *neshama* is formed through the study of the Talmud. The study of Talmud occurs in the world of the intellect, which is the world of *Beria*. Consequently, through this study, the garments of *ruaḥ* of the level of *neshama* are fashioned for the soul.

Etz Ḥayyim also states that the garment for the level of the *nefesh* is formed from the actual mitzva acts, but since the author of the *Tanya* here is focused on Torah study, he does not mention this. In any case, it can be inferred from the statement in *Etz Ḥayyim* that Torah study belongs to the level of *ruaḥ*, which is a level of created beings, not the level of *neshama*, which constitutes divine essence. ☞

it can be explained that this is specifically through the Torah study of man in this world, which ascends upward, יֵשׁ לוֹמַר דְּהַיְינוּ דַּוְקָא עַל יְדֵי תּוֹרַת הָאָדָם בָּעוֹלָם הַזֶּה הָעוֹלָה לְמַעְלָה

THE GARMENT OF THE TORAH

☞ It is explained elsewhere (see *Torah Or* 16a, 16c) that these garments of the Torah and mitzvot are designed specifically for the created soul. Since it is created, through a process of birth, it cannot grasp or communicate directly with the Divine. It is unable return to the experience of the Garden of Eden, neither after the life of this world nor through its service in this world itself, other than through the garment of the Torah. The Torah becomes a kind of medium, since on the one hand it belongs to a higher existence, but on the other hand it can connect to mortal man through his actions and thoughts in this world. In any case, the Torah that a person studies becomes a garment and vessel for the levels of *ruaḥ* in his soul so that he can understand and relate to that which he studies. It would seem that this idea put forth in *Etz Ḥayyim* is not the same as the statement cited earlier, which is that the Torah that descends to the worlds is not actually enclothed in the worlds and cannot in fact be grasped by the intellect of created beings.

---

70. Each of the five soul levels are further divided into levels. For example, the lower part of the level of *ruaḥ* is the *nefesh* of *ruaḥ*, while the higher level is *ruaḥ* of *ruaḥ*.

When *Etz Ḥayyim*, and other hasidic sources, speaks of the Torah becoming a garment for the created beings, it is referring to a person's Torah study in this world, not the Torah itself. When a person studies Torah, he uses his mind, emotions, and knowledge of this world. As described in *Likkutei Amarim*,[71] not only does the Torah enclothe the person who studies it, the individual himself also enclothes it with his intellect and understanding. The Torah he studied rises upward, unlike the Torah itself, which descends, just as water always descends from a higher place to a lower one. From the letters and words spoken or written in material form, from the understanding of the human mind and the physical human experience, it ascends to an increasingly deep apprehension. In the course of this ascent, the Torah enclothes the *nefesh* and *ruaḥ* of the person, so that he may be capable of receiving the divine light, which means that his soul becomes more spiritual and capable of apprehending a higher aspect of the Divine.

אֲבָל הַתַּלְמוּד עַצְמוֹ שֶׁנִּיתַּן בְּסִינַי הוּא בִּנְשָׁמָה   **whereas the Talmud itself, which was given at Sinai, is** in the level of *neshama,*

The entire Torah was given at Sinai, not only the Ten Commandments and not only the Written Torah, but also the Oral Torah, the Mishna and the Talmud, including all the teachings that future sages of Israel would innovate through the generations.[72] Of course, what was handed down at Sinai was not the precise words of Abaye and Rava, but rather the light and wisdom expressed by Abaye and Rava in their language and through their personalities, the supernal wisdom itself that was given at Sinai.

וְלָכֵן הוּא מְבָרֵר הָרוּחַ   **and therefore it refines the *ruaḥ*,**

The Talmud itself, which was given at Sinai, is always in *neshama* and is always divine, no matter the level at which it is enclothed, in which words, or through which form of intellect. Its content is always divine, and it simply passes through those words. Consequently, since it is a

71. Chap. 5.

72. See, e.g., *Megilla* 19b; Jerusalem Talmud, *Pe'a* 2:4; *Vayikra Rabba* 22:1; see also *Likkutei Torah*, Num. 76a; *Likkutei Siḥot* 19, p. 252.

divine entity, neither corrupted nor hidden, it refines, rectifies, and rearranges every created reality through which it passes. A created being knows that God is truth, and this is correct and proper, but he can actually apprehend the Divine only through the Torah. Therefore, the Torah that a person grasps, at every level, refines and regulates the level of *ruaḥ*, which is the life force of man and of creation.

> **וְכֵן בְּמִשְׁנָה דִּיצִירָה**   **and the same applies to the Mishna of *Yetzira*.**

Just as one's understanding of the reasons of the Torah through the Talmud refines the world of the intellect in general, and the mind of the individual who studies it in particular, so too the study of the Mishna refines the world of the emotive attributes, the world of *Yetzira*. These are the attributes employed to determine when leniencies or stringencies must be applied and what items must be rejected and what should be embraced, in the world and in the soul.

> **וְאַף אִם תִּמְצָא לוֹמַר שֶׁגַּם הַנִּיתָּן**   **Even if you say that what was given**
> **מִסִּינַי הוּא בְּרוּחַ דִּבְרִיאָה יְצִירָה**   **at Sinai is also enclothed in *ruaḥ* of**
> **Beria and *Yetzira*,**

If you say that the Torah itself, not the Torah a person has studied, is enclothed in *ruaḥ* of *Beria* and *Yetzira* upon its descent to the worlds, in the letters and affairs of this world below, how can it then be claimed that the Torah is in *neshama* alone, that it is not enclothed? In order to explain this, the author of the *Tanya* cites an example from a different area, from the existence of angels, who also transmit divine light from above to below in two ways.

> **הֲרֵי נוֹדָע שֶׁכָּל מַלְאָךְ שֶׁהוּא שָׁלִיחַ**   **it is known that every angel that is**
> **מִלְמַעְלָה אֲזַי נִקְרָא בְּשֵׁם ה' מַמָּשׁ**   **an emissary from above is literally**
> **הַשׁוֹכֵן בְּקִרְבּוֹ**   **called by the name of God, who resides within it.**

An angel is an emissary of God.[73] Just as "a person's agent is like himself" (*Kiddushin* 41a), so too an angel, for the duration of his mission, is in

---

73. See *Iggeret HaKodesh*, epistle 20; *Likkutei Torah*, Lev. 1c, Song. 20c; *Hemshekh Ayin-Bet*, vol. 2, p. 761.

a certain sense like God. This principle applies in the case of the angel even more than it does to human agency. Since an angel is a holy being, without a body or animal soul and without *kelippot* that conceal and confuse it, it executes its mission perfectly, with complete transparency to the Sender. The angel does not do anything else. It does not think and has nothing else in mind, nor even does it have an existence outside the mission. Therefore, throughout the period of its mission, it does not have a name of its own, and it is called by the name of God.[74]

מַה שֶּׁאֵין כֵּן כְּשֶׁאֵינוֹ שָׁלִיחַ, יֵשׁ לוֹ שֵׁם אַחֵר כְּפִי עֲבוֹדָתוֹ **This is not the case when it is not an emissary:** Then **it has another name in accordance with its service,**

An angel is a created being, an entity that exists in a spiritual world and was created as part of that world. An angel thus has a defined reality in the worlds in that it exists even when it is not performing God's mission. Once again our analogy of a person's hand can be instructive: When a person executes a task, such as cooking or writing, we do not say that the hand itself is cooking or writing but that the person is cooking writing. The writing is ascribed not to the hand but to the individual himself. This is not the case when it is not being employed for a particular task, when it hurts or looks beautiful or is dirty. Then we speak of it as a separate entity: "That hand hurts" or "This hand is dirty." ☞

THE OTHER NAME

☞ The other name of the angel that the author of the *Tanya* refers to here is its definition as a reality unto itself, separate, as it were, from the divine essence. While this definition constitutes a constriction and limitation of the Divine, that is not necessarily a negative thing, as is the case in this world. In this world, a limitation of this kind could end up in *kelippa*, concealing and even opposing God. But in the case

74. One can observe a similar paradigm in the case of the prophets, who are also called messengers or emissaries (see Num. 20:16, and Rashi ad loc.). The prophet who successfully divests himself of physicality so that he is a complete, transparent vessel for the word of God that is spoken through him no longer exists as a separate entity either. Thus, he can declare. "I am God" (Lev. 19:4), or "I will provide the rain of your land" (Deut. 11:14). See *Likkutei Torah*, Lev. 27c, 50a.

וַאֲזַי קוֹרֵא: "קָדוֹשׁ קָדוֹשׁ קָדוֹשׁ and then it proclaims, "Holy, holy,
ה' כו'" (ישעיה ו, ג), כְּלוֹמַר שֶׁשֵׁם holy is the Lord…." (Isa. 6:3), mean-
ה' מוּבְדָּל מִמֶּנּוּ ing that the name of God is separate
from it.

"Holy" means separate, and thus when an angel proclaims "holy is the
Lord," it means that God is distinct from it. The concept of "holy" in
relation to God is the fullest extent of that angel's grasp. Those who
are greater, who can go beyond this reality and apprehension of God,
will say "holy" one more time, and there are yet others who will say
"holy" three times.[75] These three declarations correspond to the three
general levels of constriction and the parameters of the inner light, and
with each declaration they rise another level. These levels are called
head, middle, end, of which the ten *sefirot* are comprised, the head
being *Ḥokhma*, *Bina*, and *Da'at*, the middle being *Ḥesed*, *Gevura*, and
Tiferet, and the end is *Netzaḥ*, *Hod*, *Yesod*, which parallel the worlds of
Beria, *Yetzira*, and *Asiya.* ☞

of an angel, this definition, that its name is "in accordance with his service," means that even when it is not performing a mission, he is executing his task just by his very existence. The angel's existence and service are one and the same. It is, in fact, the angel's very definition as a separate being that constitutes its service of God.[76] In its praise of God, its song, the angel draws God within the worlds, as it were, each angel in accordance with its rank, in the world to which it belongs and in the manner and perspective by which it reveals the Divine. By contrast, when an angel performs a specific mission for God, it merely serves as a conduit for the revelation of God's inner essence and being. But even when it is not carrying out a mission, it still reveals Him in a particular world to a specific creation.

WHEN AN ANGEL PROCLAIMS "HOLY"

☞ This is, of course, a declaration of praise. When a person feels that he is separate from God, that is a terrible thing, because it means he is distant from God and cannot sense His greatness. But when an angel realizes that God is separate, there is no higher perception than that, since it can be separate yet still apprehend God. It is not that the angels fail to grasp the truth, but rather its apprehension of the Divine is distinct from that of the worlds, a thing in itself that transcends anything

---

75. *Ḥullin* 91b; see *Likkutei Torah*, Num. 28dff; *Torah Or* 86a.

76. For example, the angel Gabriel is the left hand of God, so to speak, and is the embodiment of the attribute of judgment. Sometimes he is sent on a mission,

וְכֵן הוּא מַמָּשׁ, בִּבְחִינַת הִתְלַבְּשׁוּת
הַתַּלְמוּד בִּבְחִינַת רוּחַ דִּבְרִיאָה,
וְהַמִּשְׁנָה בְּרוּחַ דִּיצִירָה

The exact same thing applies to the enclothing of the Talmud in *ruaḥ* of *Beria* and of the Mishna in *ruaḥ* of *Yetzira*:

The Torah may be compared to an angel fulfilling its mission of bringing down the light of God. The enclothing of the supernal wisdom that is Torah within the structure and methodology of the Talmud occurs in the world of *Beria*, while the enclothing of the supernal wisdom in Mishna occurs in the world of *Yetzira*. This enclothement is like an angel serving in its role as emissary, when it is not called by its own name but by the name of God. The same applies to the Torah in the Talmud of the world of *Beria*: Although it is in the world of *Beria*, the Torah is not attributed to this world but to God Himself, to His will and wisdom. This applies to the Mishna in the world of *Yetzira*, and so too in our world when we study the Talmud and the Mishna.

הֵם שְׁלוּחֵי ה' They are emissaries of God,

The *halakhot* laid out in the Talmud and Mishna are the emissaries of God.[77] Just as an emissary is called by the name of the one who sent him, and everything he says and does is considered as though his sender himself is saying and doing it, so too the *halakhot* are God's emissaries, and no matter which garment they are enclothed in or which level they pass through, they are called by the name of God, and constitute both His will and His wisdom. They are not named after anything

we can see and apprehend. It is the ultimate apprehension of the Divine, since any apprehension that is defined by specific parameters is not true apprehension of the Divine. Only the realization that God is not one thing or the other is true apprehension of the Divine. To be more pre-cise, this is not just a negative definition, as it is with us, in which we say that such-and-such is not God. For an angel, there is nothing else. There is no other perception of reality than this, and so it is a positive apprehension – "this is the Divine; this is holy!" – rather than a negative one.

such as the destruction of Sodom. But even when he is not executing a mission, it is still the embodiment of the attribute of judgment, just by his very existence.
77. See *Midrash Tanḥuma, Vayigash* 6; *Likkutei Torah,* Lev. 2a.

else that they pass along the way. They do not take on the features and characteristics of the world or level they pass through.

דְּהַיְינוּ, כֵּלִים דְּנוּקְבָא דַאֲצִילוּת הַחִיצוֹנִים בַּתַּלְמוּד וְהָאֶמְצָעִים בַּמִּשְׁנָה, אֲשֶׁר הַמִּשְׁנָה וְהַתַּלְמוּד שֶׁבָּהֶם נִמְשָׁכִים מִיְסוֹד אַבָּא

which means that they are the vessels of the feminine aspect of *Atzilut*, which is *Malkhut*, which are external in the Talmud and intermediate in the Mishna, since the Mishna and Talmud contained within them issue forth from *Yesod* of *Abba*,

Nukva, or the feminine aspect, of *Atzilut* is *Malkhut* of *Atzilut*, which is also divine speech. The vessels of speech are the letters and words, which are like the emissaries of man when he is speaking to others. The words do not state their content; they have no mind or will of their own. They merely convey what that person is saying. Similarly, the words of the Torah, through the words and concepts of the Talmud and Mishna, are the emissaries of God and His supernal wisdom, and the worlds are no more than conduits of that supernal wisdom.

The Torah that is enclothed in the worlds of *Beria* and *Yetzira*, the Mishna and Talmud that we study, are drawn from the *Yesod* of *Abba*. *Abba* is the *Ḥokhma* of *Atzilut*, the attribute of Wisdom, and the *Yesod* of *Abba* is the drawing down of that wisdom as it passes through the worlds and receives its garment within each world, the garment of the Talmud in *Beria* and garment of the Mishna in *Yetzira*. ☞

THE *YESOD* OF *ABBA*

☞ The *Yesod* of *Abba* (literally, "Father") constitutes the direct flow of wisdom from *Atzilut* to *Malkhut*, and not through an enclothing in the intellect and the emotive attributes on the way. It is the *sefira* of Yesod that is the power of connection and flow of *Ḥokhma* from the higher realms to the lower realm. The *Yesod* of *Abba* is longer and extends lower than the *Yesod* of *Ima* (literally, "Mother"), which is *Bina*.

This is similar to the dynamic that unfolds in the soul: That which is defined through the attribute of *Bina*, of Understanding, can be passed on to one who understands on his own, to those who think in similar terms to the bestower of the information that was understood and share the same concepts with him. By contrast, wisdom itself can also be expressed in illogical ways, in a certain unaccountable sense in the soul that something is correct and true. Furthermore, wisdom can

הַמְקַבֵּל מֵחָכְמָה סְתִימָאָה דַּאֲרִיךְ אַנְפִּין, שֶׁבּוֹ מְלוּבָּשׁ אוֹר אֵין סוֹף בָּרוּךְ הוּא

which receives from the sealed Ḥokhma of Arikh Anpin, which is the Ḥokhma in Keter, the source of Ḥokhma in Atzilut, in which the light of Ein Sof, blessed be He, is enclothed.

In general, Ḥokhma is the garment and vessel for the light of Ein Sof, which means that the light of Ein Sof is enclothed in Ḥokhma. [78] Ḥokhma is characterized by an almost invisible point; it is almost undetectable because it is mostly light and has no existence and definition of its own. For this reason, it is the only sefira that can be a vessel for the light of Ein Sof. Therefore, it is Ḥokhma that acts as a channel for the flow of the divine light to the sealed or hidden Ḥokhma in Keter – the sefira of Ḥokhma contained in Keter but because it is so lofty it is concealed from creation – and from there to Ḥokhma in Atzilut, and subsequently to the Torah that descends like water to the created worlds, from one world to the next.

וְנִמְצָא שֶׁאוֹר אֵין סוֹף, הוּא שֵׁם ה׳ שׁוֹכֵן בָּרוּחַ דִּבְרִיאָה יְצִירָה עֲשִׂיָּה בְּמִקְרָא וּמִשְׁנָה וְתַלְמוּד

It follows that the light of Ein Sof, which is the name of God, resides in the level of ruaḥ of Beria, Yetzira, and Asiya, in the Tanakh, Mishna, and Talmud.

The light of Ein Sof, although it too is Ein Sof, is merely a revelation of Ein Sof Himself. In other words, it is the name that reveals and indicates to others the essence called by this name. In this sense, the name of God is the light and revelation of Ein Sof directed toward the worlds.

be expressed directly through the faculty of speech. The reason for this is that the Yesod of Ima is fundamentally a recipient, so that it actually transmits knowledge that it received and subsequently understood, and the act of receiving requires vessels. It cannot work without receptacles. The Yesod of Abba, on the other hand, is the ultimate giver, and so it essentially breaches boundaries: First it passes through, and only then does it search for vessels to receive it.

---

78. See *Likkutei Amarim*, chap. 35; see also *Iggeret HaKodesh*, epistle 15.

This name of God, this light, is the Torah, the supernal wisdom that descends below, which resides in the worlds and sustains them. This light resides in the *ruaḥ* level of the worlds, which is the life force that sustains the worlds, in contrast to *neshama*, which is the divine essence itself that resides in the worlds.

In other words, the Torah does not directly and visibly give life to the worlds, but rather it is something that sustains and gives meaning to life in the worlds. Deep within this life force lies the supernal wisdom, which is revealed in the worlds through the Torah. The light of God, the name of God, enters the worlds through the Torah, the section of the Torah that specifically belongs to it: the *Tanakh* in *Asiya*, the Mishna in *Yetzira*, and the Talmud in *Beria*. ☞

וּכְשֶׁהָאָדָם לוֹמֵד, מַמְשִׁיךְ אוֹר **When a person studies** these sections
אֵין סוֹף בָּרוּךְ הוּא בָּעוֹלָם הַזֶּה   of the Torah, **he draws the light of** *Ein Sof*, **blessed be He, into this world**

When a person who is living in this world studies Torah, employing his intellect and experiences of this world, he draws the light of *Ein Sof* that is in the Torah to this world, where he himself is situated. Just as an angel is emissary of God, so is man when he studies Torah. The Torah and God are one[79] in the sense that Torah that is spoken is said by God and Torah that is thought is thought by God. When a person

THE *TANAKH*, MISHNA, AND TALMUD

☞   The main study of the *Tanakh*, the Written Torah, is through its letters, by reading and writing them. The letters are like *Asiya* with respect to their content.

The Mishna is in *Yetzira*, because the Mishna constitutes the rulings of the *halakha* and the determination of one's proper relationship to each case, such as whether or not a food is kosher. Such determination is employed through the realm of the attributes: *Ḥesed* is characterized by revelation and drawing near, while *Gevura* limits. This is the realm of *Yetzira*.

Finally, the Talmud is in *Beria*, because the Talmud, which involves the analysis of the reasons for the laws, is an expression of the intellect, which is the concern of the world of *Beria*.

---

79. This is in accordance with the well-known saying that "the Torah and the Holy One, blessed be He, are entirely one," which appears in many hasidic works, even though its source is uncertain.

studies the Torah, he is like God's emissary in the most internal sense: God Himself speaks and thinks through him and is drawn into the world through him. ☞

לִהְיוֹת נִכְלָל וּבָטֵל בְּאוֹרוֹ יִתְבָּרֵךְ   **for it to be incorporated and nul-**
"כִּי זֶה כָּל הָאָדָם" (קהלת יב,יג)   **lified in His light, "for that is all of man"** (Eccles.12:13).

When the light of *Ein Sof* flows to the world, the world itself is nullified in the face of it. The world is no longer a separate entity from the Divine, but is incorporated in it. This is man's task and mission in this world: To draw forth the divine light through himself, thereby connecting and uniting himself with the Divine.

The author of the *Tanya* now proceeds to explain how the nullification of this world in the face of the Divine is achieved through the study of the *halakhot* of the Mishna and Talmud. Of course, all this has already been stated in this lengthy essay. Here he is merely tying up loose ends.

THE NULLIFICATION AND UNIQUENESS OF MAN IN THE STUDY OF TORAH

☞ Unlike an angel, whose essence is automatically negated in favor of its mission, since its entire essence is the mission itself, man has a choice and it takes an effort to negate his self. But this unique quality of man has great significance: One who negates his entire being to the Torah, who has no thoughts and feelings of his own apart from the Torah, will be able, as is related about great sages and righteous individuals, to do what he wishes in this world, and not even the angel of death has dominion over him (see *Likkutei Torah*, Lev. 22a).

But whether or not a person is able to nullify himself in this way makes no difference to the essential mission to bring down the light of *Ein Sof*. As long as the Torah is studied properly, it is drawn to this world together with the light of *Ein Sof*. Indeed, when a person is studying, despite his incomplete understanding, his headaches, and even his evil inclination, all these are facets of this world through which the Torah is drawn. When he succeeds in understanding something of what he is studying with his limited intellect, he draws the light of *Ein Sof* into that intellect. Moreover, when he studies despite the headache, he draws the light of *Ein Sof* into the unrectified and painful part of the world. The person himself, with his virtues and flaws, is both the emissary and the vessel through which the Torah and the light of *Ein Sof* are drawn to this world.

וְזֹאת הָיְתָה עֲבוֹדַת רַבִּי שִׁמְעוֹן
בַּר יוֹחַאי, וְכָל הַתַּנָּאִים וְאָמוֹרָאִים
בְּנִגְלֶה

This was the service of Rabbi Shimon bar Yoḥai and of all the *tannaʾim* and *amoraʾim* in the revealed portion of the Torah,

Rabbi Shimon bar Yoḥai is described as a person whose vocation was the study of Torah.[80] The revealed aspect of Torah referred to here is the Mishna and Talmud, which for us are the place where the Oral Torah encounters the Written Torah. It is where the entire Oral Torah that is known to us originates and emerges.

In a certain sense, the Written Torah constitutes the Torah exactly as it exists in the higher worlds, of which we have no true grasp, while the Oral Torah is the Torah that penetrates our world. It is the Oral Torah that we try to understand with our intellect and logic. It is the Oral Torah that tells us how the mitzvot written in the Torah apply in our world. Determining the basic conclusions of the concepts found therein and the appropriate mode of thought when studying it was the great work of the *tannaʾim* and *amoraʾim*. Any efforts made to study the Oral Torah beyond that is merely a continuation of the same effort.

The author of the *Tanya* is precise in specifying the revealed portion of the Torah. This is because when a person studies the revealed Torah, it is drawn into this physical world. The study of the esoteric Torah, on the other hand, the hidden portion of the Torah, remains above this world or concealed in the recesses of the soul, whereas the study of the revealed portion of the Torah is directly applied to this world,

---

80. See *Shabbat* 11a. The question is, why is Rabbi Shimon bar Yoḥai singled out here? It can be suggested that Rabbi Shimon bar Yoḥai had a unique status among the *tannaʾim*, to the extent that he was extravagantly praised (see, e.g., *Zohar* 2:38a, 3:144b). The hasidic sources explain that Rabbi Shimon bar Yoḥai had a soul of *Atzilut* (a lofty type of soul discussed at the beginning of this essay), and the flow of divine light and life force that was drawn forth by the *tannaʾim* from the supernal wisdom to the earth below, was drawn forth by virtue of Rabbi Shimon bar Yoḥai (see *Maʾamarei Admor HaZaken* 5574, p. 106). If so, Rabbi Shimon may be considered the root of the service of all the *tannaʾim* and *amoraʾim*, which explains the wording that the author of the *Tanya* uses here: "Rabbi Shimon bar Yoḥai and all the *tannaʾim* and *amoraʾim*."

with all its cracks and faults, with its conceptions and beliefs as well as its falsehoods.

לְהַמְשִׁיךְ אוֹרוֹ יִתְבָּרֵךְ וּלְבָרֵר
בֵּירוּרֵי נוֹגַהּ כָּל מֶשֶׁךְ זְמַן הַגָּלוּת

to draw forth the divine light and to effect the refinement of the kelippa of noga throughout the duration of the exile,

The light of Ein Sof is drawn down to this world in order to refine and raise the sparks of holiness that fell into kelippat noga. The time for this refinement is the duration of the exile, when Jews are scattered throughout the nations and the souls of Israel descend to the kelippot. Through their Torah study and performance of mitzvot among the nations, they elevate the sparks of holiness that can be found there.

דְּשָׁלְטָא אִילָנָא דְּטוֹב וָרַע

when the tree of the knowledge of good and evil has dominion,

The time of the exile is "when the tree of [the knowledge of] good and evil has dominion," referring to the tree of knowledge whose fruit Adam ate. From that moment, the perfection of the reality in which Adam was created was impaired. Man was expelled from the Garden of Eden, and the time of exile commenced. Exile, then, can be seen as the time when good and evil are intermingled, a state of affairs that has taken over reality, until it is no longer possible to distinguish between them.[81] The good provides the life force and existence that sustains the world, but evil conceals the divine light that provides this vitality and clothes the life force in various other identities.

כְּמוֹ שֶׁכָּתוּב: "עֵת אֲשֶׁר שָׁלַט
הָאָדָם בְּאָדָם כו'" (קהלת ח, ט)

as it is written, "Whenever man controlled man, it was to his detriment" (Eccles. 8:9).

On a deeper level, this verse can be read as saying that whenever the kelippa in man had dominion over the holiness in man, it was to the detriment of kelippa in man."[82] When kelippa prevails over holiness,

81. See Torah Or 5c.
82. See Avodat HaKodesh 3, chap. 7; Pardes Rimmonim, Sha'ar 16, chap. 7; see also Iggeret HaKodesh, epistle 25.

concealing the holiness and using it for its own purposes, it will ultimately turn out to be to the *kelippa*'s detriment. There will come a time when the holiness it swallowed, that is now inside it, will grow and awaken until the entire infrastructure of the *kelippa* collapses.

There is a certain relationship between *kelippa* and holiness that preserves the *kelippa*'s upper hand. It is a relationship of light and shadow that creates a reality of shadows, of imaginings and delusions. When this relationship falters, because the *kelippa* has swallowed more than it can contain and there is a greater illumination of the side of holiness, *kelippa* falls from its superior position and vanishes as though it never existed. *Kelippa*, after all, has no substance. It is merely concealment, confusion, and falsehood. It is only a veneer. Thus, when the truth is revealed, the *kelippa* dissipates like a bad dream.[83]

| כִּי זֶהוּ תַּכְלִית הַהִשְׁתַּלְשְׁלוּת, שֶׁיֵּרֵד הָעֶלְיוֹן לְמַטָּה וְיִהְיֶה לוֹ דִּירָה בַּתַּחְתּוֹנִים | **This is the purpose of the chain of progression, that the Most High should descend below and have an abode among the lower creations** |

The ultimate purpose of the creation of the world is God's desire for a dwelling place in the lower realm.[84] In order for Him to have an abode in the lower realm, two things are required: There must be a lower realm, and God must reveal Himself there. During the exile, one can see the lower realm, a reality that is apparently independent from all that is holy, which brings it into existence from nothingness. The presence of the Divine will only be revealed there at the time of redemption.

This does not mean that the Divine will be revealed and the lower realm will no longer be lowly, because that would not constitute "an abode in the lower realm." Rather, the lower realm will continue to be lowly, but instead of concealing the Divine, it will reveal it. Like the vessels of the world of *Atzilut*, which do not cease to be vessels just because of the revelation of the Divine that is so blatant in that realm, but rather they are the kind of vessels that do not conceal the Divine and instead reveal it through Ḥokhma, Ḥesed, and so on. In a similar manner, but to an even greater extent, the lower realm will discover

---

83. See *Torah Or* 28c.
84. *Likkutei Amarim*, chap. 36; *Bereshit Rabba* 3:9; *Bemidbar Rabba* 13:6.

those whose "beginning is affixed to their end" (*Sefer Yetzira* 1:7), the revelation of the divine essence itself, which is loftier even than the revelations of *Atzilut*.

כְּדֵי לְהַעֲלוֹתָן לְמֶהֱוֵי אֶחָד בְּאֶחָד   **in order to elevate them so that they may be united as one.**

When God descends to this world in order to have an abode in the lower realm, the inhabitants of the lower world are elevated and united with God. This is a unity that even the created beings of the higher worlds are not privileged to attain. When beings of the lower worlds are elevated in this manner, they are not only unified, but "united as one" with God.[85] The lower beings themselves become one down below and subsequently ascend and unite with the One above. They are then "united as one," literally, "one in one," because the singular being from below remains significant, even though it is now united with the One above.

This occurs every Sabbath eve in the internal dimension of the worlds, and the same will occur to existence in general upon the final redemption, when all refinements have been effected and the lower realms have been revealed as an abode for God.

This concludes the description of the great virtue of man's service through the study of the *halakhot* and their application. The author of the *Tanya* concludes by returning to the main point of the essay, which is the study of *halakhot* in contrast to service through cognitive love and fear.

מַה שֶּׁאֵין כֵּן עֲבוֹדַת הַמַּלְאָכִים, דְּחִילוּ וּרְחִימוּ שִׂכְלִיִּים, אֵינָהּ בִּבְחִינַת הַמְשָׁכָה כְּלָל וּכְלָל רַק הִסְתַּלְּקוּת כו'   **This is not the case with regard to the service of the angels,** which is **cognitive fear and love** of God. It is **not considered drawing forth at all, but only a departure** ...

Unlike a person's service through the fulfillment and study of *halakhot*, which draws forth of the light of *Ein Sof* from above to below, service

---

85. See *Zohar* 2:135a–b.

through cognitive fear and love, which is essentially the service of the angels, involves only an ascent and departure from the world. As has been explained in this essay, and numerous hasidic teachings, the ultimate purpose of the creation of the world and the entire order of progression is the drawing down of the divine light below, not merely a departure of the lights from below to above. Although one is impossible without the other, because there can be no drawing forth in the absence of any departure, no "returning" without "running" (in the kabbalistic parlance, referring to the descent of the divine light after the ascent of the sparks), one must know what the main aim is, what is internal and essential and what is external.

The fundamental difference here is that the service of the angels, and of anyone who is serving God with cognitive fear and love, is ultimately for themselves. It is lofty, holy, and wonderful, but the service is completed solely within the angel himself, as it ascends and is subsumed within the Divine. By contrast, man's service in fulfilling and studying the Torah is not only done on his own behalf, but such service is in a sense service for God. On a higher level, it is the service that God Himself performs, since He Himself passes from His completely abstract state as *Ein Sof* into this world through this service, so that He may have an abode in the lower realm.

וּבָזֶה יוּבָן מַה שֶּׁנִּבְרָאִים מַלְאָכִים
מֵאַיִן לְיֵשׁ עַל יְדֵי עֵסֶק הַתּוֹרָה

Now we can understand how angels are brought into existence from nothingness through the study of Torah,

As the Rabbis taught, with each and every word that God utters, an angel is created.[86] Furthermore, every word of Torah articulated by a person is in essence the speech of God Himself. Unlike the divine speech that created the world, His speech that constitutes the Torah descends in the manner of a passageway through all the worlds until it emerges from the mouth of the person who articulates it. In this way, the study of Torah generates the creation of angels, just like the speech of God.

---

86. Ḥagiga 14a.

An angel is essentially an emissary of God in this world, and consequently it is always internal in relation to the world to which it is sent and in which it is active. An angel is never merely an object or a physical or spiritual force. It is always a particular divine statement, of love or fear of the Divine, as it relates to the place in which it appears. The same applies to words of Torah: At every level in which they appear, they are a revelation of the divine wisdom that relates to that place. Just as in the soul the attribute of wisdom generates secondary faculties, that of the intelligence or emotions that arise from it, the words of the Torah create angels everywhere, who are like emissaries of the divine wisdom in that place. ☞ ☞

אֲפִילוּ שֶׁלֹּא בְּכַוָּונָה שֶׁהוּא בְּחִינַת רוּחַ
בִּלְבָד שֶׁאֵינָה אֱלֹקוּת כְּלָל

even without intent, which is merely the level of *ruaḥ* that does not constitute divinity at all.

ANGELS CREATED FROM NOTHINGNESS

☞ The ability to create something from nothingness is God's power alone. The author of the *Tanya* is thus emphasizing that the creation of angels through Torah study occurs through the power of God Himself as revealed in the Torah. Through the study of *halakhot* as well, in which the Torah is enclothed in the physicality of this world, angels are created from nothingness. It is true that one does not always see angels during the study of the *halakhot*, if one does at all – it is easier to perceive them in the study of the esoteric teachings of the Torah – but the creation of angels does not depend on what a person sees or feels.

WHEN A PERSON STUDIES TORAH

☞ To return to our analogy of the hand that writes words of wisdom, the hand does not understand what it writes, nor does it absorb their meaning in any way. Likewise, one who studies Torah is not supposed to see the angels that are created through it. Yet if we take this analogy a little further, particularly sensitive people may sometimes find that that their hand trembles when they transcribe serious ideas. Something of the content, of their meaning, penetrates the body as well, and the fingers actually shake.

This is so much the case that occasionally, when a person is aware of the magnitude and importance of what he is about to do, his body will not let him carry it out, whereas a coarser individual, who is not so aware, can write anything. Regardless, when a person studies Torah, his intent and sensitivity to the ideas do not affect the divine message it contains.

When a person studies Torah without the proper intent, when he does not have in mind that what he is saying is the speech of God and divine wisdom with all that this implies, it is "mere *ruaḥ*." The life force of all beings includes the levels of *nefesh, ruaḥ,* and *neshama,* as in the soul of man, as explained above. The level of *neshama* is the divinity within the life force, that essentially belongs to the Creator and is still a portion of the One who bestows the life force. The levels of *nefesh* and *ruaḥ* are the life force that belongs to the created being, the life force that is itself considered to be created. When a person studies Torah without the requisite intent for the sake of Heaven, his study belongs solely to the level of *ruaḥ,* not that of *neshama.*

אֶלָּא לְפִי שֶׁאַף עַל פִּי כֵן שֵׁם ה'
שׁוֹכֵן וכו'
Even so, nevertheless, the name of God resides in Torah that is studied even without intent,

The Torah is the internal aspect of divine wisdom, which is the name of God, wherever it descends, including within the person who articulates its ideas, even if he has something else in mind. This person, in his present state, is the locus through which the Torah speaks, and as in every other realm, here too divine speech and wisdom are the same as they are above. Angels are thus created from nothingness even from these words of Torah.

וְדַי לַמֵּבִין.
and this is sufficient explanation **for one who understands.**

Although the observations and concepts presented in this essay concern matters that cannot be fully understood, since they are rooted in the esoteric teachings of the Torah, each person's understanding of these concepts is sufficient for his Torah study to have an effect on himself and the world.

It is no coincidence that this long essay concluded with the idea that angels are created through Torah study. The essay as a whole contrasted the service of the angels with the service of fulfilling and studying the *halakhot* written in the Torah. It might be supposed that when a person serves God like an angel, with cognitive love and fear, there is nothing loftier, since he is employing all his mental and emotional faculties. By contrast, one who focuses on *halakhot* seems to delve into all the petty work of the technical details, which do not require the involvement of the spirit and do not provide any spiritual ascension or completion. Yet the essay takes precisely the opposite direction, showing how the study of the revealed Torah, through the Mishna and Talmud, is far loftier than the service of the angels, so much so that by means of one's Torah study, even without the proper intent, angels are created.

In truth, the two types of service are incomparable. The service of the angels is the personal service of a created being, an angel or a person who stretches his faculties to their fullest extent so that he can cleave to God. By contrast, the service of fulfilling and studying the *halakhot* of the Torah is not the work of created beings at all but God's work. It is a service that the person himself does not perform, nor is he the purpose of that service. Rather, it is the purpose of everything, of unity and divine revelation.

Yet the author of the *Tanya* by no means indicates that a person should put aside all other service and engage only in the study of *halakhot*. The other side, of serving God with cognitive love and fear like the angels, which is actualized through prayer, is not superfluous or "for beginners only." It is an essential, indispensable aspect of divine service. It is for this reason that the essay opens with the assertion that "nowadays refinement is primarily achieved specifically through prayer." In order for the divine light to be drawn from above to below, there must be an awakening and elevation from below, and the vessels must be prepared to receive that light.

All of this is achieved through the service of refinement below, through the extraction and elevation of the good and holy sparks from among the *kelippot* of this world. This is not only the need of a specific hour, in order to rectify a particular fault, but rather it is a requirement of the entire world, all of which consists of that "hour" and that "fault." The ultimate purpose of creating an abode for the Divine in the lower realm necessarily consists not only of drawing the light of *Ein Sof* from above to below, but also of the creation and perfection of the lower realm. This service has to originate from the lower realm itself, since otherwise it would not be a lower realm at all.

In general, this service is the service of prayer, the aspect of man's service that resembles that of the angels in that it is performed with cognitive love and fear. The difference is that man performs this spiritual service from within his lower physical being by transcending all levels and worlds and cleaving to God Himself. He thereby fulfills the ultimate purpose of the world, which is to be an abode for *Ein Sof*, for God Himself. It is what the author of the *Tanya* here calls a "departure," which may not be the ultimate goal but is in any case part of the system that creates the possibility for the drawing of the light of *Ein Sof* to the lower realm in turn.

Essay 5
Understanding the Details of
Halakhot That Are Not Common

THIS ESSAY, LIKE THE ONE BEFORE IT, FOCUSES ON ONE main point: the value and purpose of studying *halakhot* that are not actually performed. Seemingly, the reason for studying *halakha* is to know what to do. If that is the case, why study the laws of a practice that will never be performed?

The author of the *Tanya* laid the foundation for these matters in the previous essay. There he explained that the purpose of studying Jewish law is not just to know what to do; there is value to the very study itself. Since mitzvot are fulfilled on every level of reality – action, speech, and even thought – simply learning *halakha* has real worth. He then asked the question: What about prohibitions that do not entail an action, and are therefore not fulfilled even in speech or thought? Furthermore, what about mitzvot that are not realistic, practices that even avoiding doing them is neither realistic nor possible? The answer that he gave in the previous essay was connected to its context; however, the questions themselves were left unanswered. This essay completes the picture and delves into the significance of studying *halakha* that will be fulfilled neither practically nor in thought.

The reexamination of this subject highlights its importance beyond the details of those rare *halakhot*. The significance of studying those uncommon *halakhot* underlines the importance of the act of study itself, and uncovers a deeper layer of Jewish law and Torah study in general.

וּלְהָבִין פְּרָטֵי הַהֲלָכוֹת דְּלָא שְׁכִיחֵי
כְּלָל

And we wish **to understand the details of** *halakhot* **that are not common at all,**

There are mitzvot that are not only rare, but that will virtually never become applicable in practice.

וְאֶפְשָׁר שֶׁלֹּא הָיוּ מֵעוֹלָם בִּמְצִיאוּת
מִכָּל שֶׁכֵּן שֶׁלֹּא יִהְיוּ לֶעָתִיד לָבוֹא
כְּמוֹ פְּרָטֵי דִינֵי פִּיגוּל וּכְהַאי גַּוְונָא

and which possibly never came to exist in reality – all the more so, **they will not** actually occur **in the future** – **such as the details of the laws of** *piggul* **and the like.**

Some *halakhot* applied only in particular eras, and others only when specific conditions arose. Here the author of the *Tanya* speaks about the specifics of Jewish law that never were, and never will be, applicable.[1]

In the future times of the ultimate redemption, the world will be more rectified than it was during Temple times, since even during the First and Second Temple periods, the Torah was not fulfilled in its entirety. There were flaws in reality that did not allow for it; therefore, the Temples were ultimately destroyed. This will not be the case in messianic times, which will herald a perfected reality and ultimate fulfillment of the Torah. There will be no mishaps in the running of the world, nor in the fulfillment of mitzvot.

When a person offers a sacrifice and during one of the four stages (*sheḥita, kabbala, halakha, zerika*) has in mind that the sacrifice will be offered or eaten after the appointed time, it is called *piggul*. This type of sacrifice is invalid and anyone who eats it is deserving of excision. The details of the laws that set out under which circumstances a sacrifice is deemed *piggul* are extensive and complex. For example, not every thought renders the sacrifice *piggul*; only a thought regarding a deviation in time. Additionally, there must not be any other thought accompanying the first. Also, this prohibition does not apply to every sacrifice or to every Temple practice, only to that which was otherwise fit for sacrifice. The chance that a person will find himself in a situation that satisfies all the specific conditions to create a *piggul* issue is unlikely. It certainly will not happen in messianic times.

---

1. Such as *piggul, ir hanidaḥat, ben sorer umoreh* (see *Sanhedrin* 71a), and more.

הִנֵּה מוּדַעַת זֹאת שֶׁכָּל אִיסוּר שֶׁבָּעוֹלָם Now, it is known that every pro-
יֵשׁ לוֹ שֹׁרֶשׁ וּמְקוֹר חַיִּים בַּקְּלִיפּוֹת hibition in the world has a root
and source of life in the *kelippot*,

Every element of reality in the world has a source above in the spiritual dimension. The novelty of this idea is that even the forbidden, which is contrary to God's will, has a source in spiritual reality. Its source lies in the inner workings of the *kelippot*.

This is a difficult concept because, as explained earlier in the *Tanya*, there is no other source of existence besides God Himself. Therefore, how can there be a divine source for something that is contrary to God's will? This is the implication of "It is known." Those who are familiar with esoteric wisdom know about the "exile of the Divine Presence" (also discussed in the *Tanya, Iggeret HaTeshuva* 6). The Divine Presence can place its power and vitality in a foreign garment and will (*kelippa*); this is a prohibition.

שֶׁאִם לֹא כֵן, לֹא הָיָה יָכוֹל לִהְיוֹת for otherwise, it could not be in
בִּמְצִיאוּת בָּעוֹלָם בִּלְתִּי הַשְׁפָּעָה the reality of the world, without
עֶלְיוֹנָה the flow from above.

This means that the forbidden act and the person performing it would not be able to exist in the lower world without a flow from a higher spiritual reality. ☞

וַאֲפִילוּ הַמְסַלְסֵל בִּשְׂעָרוֹ וּכְהַאי Even one who twirls his hair, and
גַוְונָא מְקַבֵּל חַיּוּתוֹ בְּרֶגַע זוֹ מֵהֵיכָלוֹת the like, receives his vitality at
הַקְּלִיפּוֹת, כְּמוֹ שֶׁכָּתוּב בַּזֹּהַר that moment from the palaces
of the *kelippot*, as is written in
the *Zohar*.

WITHOUT THE FLOW FROM ABOVE

☞ These concepts reach even greater heights; prohibitions are not only rooted in spirituality but are actually rooted in holiness. Just as falsity cannot subsist without a kernel of truth, and every person, especially Jews, cannot live without at least a modicum of goodness and kindness, even if misdirected, the *kelippa* cannot exist without being rooted in goodness and truth. That drop of good can maintain (in a twisted manner) a whole world of *kelippa* and evil.

"One who twirls his hair"[2] is an expression that appears in midrashim and relates to a person who is not wicked per se, but rather feels overly good about himself and therefore looks at himself and prettifies his appearance to impress other people. This shows some arrogance on his part. This is not a serious prohibition; it is not even technically forbidden. Yet, when he does this, he shows that he has been distracted away from the *yiḥud*, from living with God, and instead, is self-absorbed. Even this person, who is not wicked and not transgressing a prohibition, receives his vitality from the chambers of *kelippa*, since at that moment he is not connected to holiness.[3]

To say that a person receives his vitality from this world from the palaces of *kelippa* does not mean that he actually has to violate a prohibition of the Torah. It is enough that he should envisage, or even feel in his heart, a sensation that is separate from holiness; at that moment, he is receiving his vitality from the palaces of *kelippa*.

From here we see that prohibitions receive their vitality from the *kelippot* in the spiritual world as well, before they emerge into actual physical reality. This spiritual source exists above as a spiritual fact, whether it becomes actualized in the physical world or not. ☞

The choice of from where to receive one's vitality lies in the hands of every person.[4] He can choose to receive it from the palaces of holiness by binding himself to the inner workings of those chambers, for example by connecting himself to his rabbis or to the Torah in general or his particular portion in the Torah, with righteousness, kindness, and humility. He thus becomes an extension of them. Or he

---

2. Like the Sages say about Joseph, see *Tanḥuma, Vayeshev* 8, and elsewhere (and in the context of a different topic in *Rosh HaShana* 26b and elsewhere). In several places, the author of the *Tanya* speaks about the twirling of the hair in supernal holiness, since just as the hair is drawn from the mind, Jewish laws are drawn from supernal *Ḥokhma*, and a person who twirls his hair is one who engages in *halakhot* in depth, and clarifies them, separating them one from another etc. (see *Torah Or* 31:4; *Likkutei Torah, Vayikra* 27a; there in *Bemidbar* 73a; and elsewhere).
3. Even a person who innocently "twirls his hair," and outwardly is still engaged in serving God in a general sense, and does not think any actual antithetical thoughts (as appears in several places, and see, for example, *Ba'al Shem Tov al HaTorah, Parashat Noaḥ, Amud HaTefilla* 52).
4. *Iggeret HaTeshuva* 6.

can choose to receive his vitality from the palaces of *kelippa*, because he finds an entire internal rationale there as well; networks that enliven and sustain him in his forbidden act, even in evil acts. There one finds an internal logic built upon "justice" and "kindness" as well, because without them, it would not be able to exist. However, these imagined rationalizations in the name of "justice" and "kindness" bring with them not construction, but destruction.

This vitality of the forbidden act, as an independent, enticing option, can be explained as drawing from what seems to be a lofty, spiritual chamber. It masquerades as life, yet truthfully it is only an external *kelippa* and sheer fantasy.

וְהִלְכָּךְ גַּם פְּרָטֵי הָאִיסּוּרִים שֶׁלֹּא בָּאוּ לִידֵי מַעֲשֶׂה מֵעוֹלָם בָּעוֹלָם הַזֶּה הַגַּשְׁמִי, מִכָּל מָקוֹם שָׁרְשֵׁי חִיּוּתָם הֵן בִּמְצִיאוּת בְּפוֹעַל מַמָּשׁ בְּהֵיכָלוֹת הַקְּלִיפוֹת

Therefore, even with regard to **the details of the prohibitions that have never been fulfilled in practice in this physical world, nevertheless, the roots of their vitality exist in actual reality in the palaces of the** *kelippot.*

Those details of Jewish law that are not applied in practice are applicable in the spiritual dimension. If the Torah describes a given reality, like the details of *piggul,* that is virtually impossible in this world, it

THE PALACES OF THE KELIPPOT

☞ The Divine Presence in our world manifests itself through spiritual structures called "palaces." These chambers are whole systems of inner reasoning in and of themselves, like an environment, like a whole world, through and according to which creations receive their vitality, like a social or business network that is structured with an internal order and logic that nourishes and sustains itself in general, and everything inside of it in particular. There are holy chambers that transmit the inner vitality as divine will and Godly influence, and there are also chambers of *kelippa* in which the divine vitality is in exile. These chambers transmit only the *kelippa,* that which conceals the divine source and displays a superficial vitality instead. They present shells of meaning as seemingly independent entities that sometimes seem to negate holiness entirely. This vitality, that is channeled through palaces of *kelippa,* can sustain something forbidden and even give life to a person at the very moment that he is doing something forbidden, while he is acting contrary to God's will.

must operate in the spiritual dimension, somewhere in the order of progression.

The material world is limited in terms of time and space and what can happen in it; not everything that a person thinks he does, and every possibility does not eventuate in reality. The *Tanya* is saying here that the thought and potential exist spiritually, even if they are not manifested physically. This applies to both the realm of holiness and that of *kelippa*.

וְגַם הַפְּרָטִים שֶׁיּוּכַל לִהְיוֹת שֶׁלֹּא הָיוּ וְלֹא יִהְיוּ לְעוֹלָם בִּמְצִיאוּת   This applies **also to the details that perhaps never were and never will be in reality,**

This applies not only to that which never happened in the past, because the right conditions never arose, but also to that which will never happen in the future, because the probability of it happening in the physical world is negligible.

כְּגוֹן טָעוּת וּשְׁגָגוֹת שֶׁטָּעָה וְקָרָא לַתְּשִׁיעִי עֲשִׂירִי כו' וּכְהַאי גּוֹונָא   **such as errors and unwitting acts,** for example, **when one erred and called the ninth "tenth"… and the like,**

In the laws of tithing cattle,[5] the following situations are described: To separate a tenth of one's cattle, a person puts his flock in a pen with a narrow opening and stands next to it. As the cows leave, he counts them one by one, and makes a color mark on every tenth cow. The tenth cow becomes the tithe. The questions that the Mishna and the Talmud address here at length are: What is the law if the counter makes a mistake in his counting, and calls the ninth or the eleventh, the tenth? Does his deeming that animal as the "tenth" sanctify it, or does it have to be sequentially the tenth?

דְּלֹא שַׁיָּיךְ בְּמֵזִיד לִהְיוֹת קְלִיפָּה שׁוֹרָה עַל זֶה וְיוּכַל לִהְיוֹת דְּכְהַאי גּוֹונָא אֵינוֹ בִּמְצִיאוּת בְּהֵיכָלוֹת הַקְּלִיפּוֹת   **for it is not applicable for a *kelippa* to rest on this through an intentional act, and perhaps in such cases it does not exist in the palaces of the *kelippot*.**

---

5. See *Bekhorot* 9:8.

These errors do not happen intentionally, but rather by accident. There is a distortion of the mitzva, but without any distortion of the intention.

Since this distortion does not have a root in the *kelippa* in one's soul, it could be that it does not have a root in the spiritual palaces of *kelippa*.

Here the author of the *Tanya* brings a gloss, in square brackets, from the *Tzemaḥ Tzedek*, the grandson of the author of the *Tanya*, the third Lubavitcher Rebbe.

[הַגָּהָ"ה מֵאַדְמוֹ"ר בַּעַל צֶמַח צֶדֶק ז"ל נִשְׁמָתוֹ עֵדֶן: נִרְאֶה לִי מַה שֶׁכּוֹתֵב "וְיוּכַל לִהְיוֹת" אַלְמָא דְּלָא בְּרִירָא לֵיהּ הַיְינוּ מִשּׁוּם שֶׁהַשְׁגָגוֹת בָּאוֹת מִנּוֹגַהּ, אִם כֵּן יֵשׁ לוֹמַר דְּיֵשׁ לָהֶם שֹׁרֶשׁ בְּהֵיכָלוֹת דְּנוֹגַהּ]

[A note by the Admor, the author of the *Tzemaḥ Tzedek*, of blessed memory, may he rest in peace: It seems to me that he writes "perhaps," implying that it is not clear to him, because unintentional acts come from *noga*, and therefore it can be said that they have a root in the palaces of *noga*.]

The wording of the author of the *Tanya* is strange. What does "perhaps" mean? Either there is a reality like this, or not. Therefore, he explains: unintentional sins do not have a source in the impure *kelippot*; however, they do have a source in the palaces of *noga*. In contrast to intentional transgressions, when a person intends to do evil, this action has a source in his soul and in the palaces of impure *kelippot*, and is contrasted with a person who is forced to sin, who does not have any source in the soul or in the palaces of *kelippa*.

The wording of the author of the *Tanya* thus can be understood: "perhaps," as the *Tzemaḥ Tzedek* explains, means that it is not clear. The *kelippat noga* is a *kelippa* that lies on the interface between holiness and *kelippa*. The very reality of *kelippat noga* is undetermined, unclear. It is unknown where the *kelippa* ends and the holiness begins. It depends on the person and what he does, if he elevates it to holiness, it will be holy and not *kelippa*, and if not, it will be *kelippa*. ☞

THE PALACES OF *NOGA*

☞ In Judaism, the definition of what is unintentional generally does not include coercion [*ones*]. "*Ones*" refers to an action for which a person is not responsible, and it is therefore considered purely a deed with no spiritual root in the soul.

For example, if a person did not know that something he was doing was forbidden, that is called *ones*. However, if he forgot that it was forbidden, that is deemed "unintentional." The person forgot because it was not important enough to him. Since in the depths of his heart he did not really want to internalize the matter, it stays external to him, and at the first opportunity, it is totally forgotten. This type of situation that is not accompanied by a bad intention, yet also does not have a holy intention attached to it, is the world of *kelippat noga*. In other words, it is the realm of the mundane: neither mitzva nor transgression, not holy, yet not impure. It is rather ordinary life with its permitted actions, conducted according to the whims of one's animal soul. *Noga* is at play in the everyday life of a Jew who is working to earn his livelihood. He eats his breakfast, and sets out to work. His world is not one of holiness, nor is it one of impurity, but rather, it is a world that is waiting to see what will done within it. If a person does not use it for holiness, nor for impurity, if he does not do anything, the end product is the "unintentional." "Unintentional" is the result of the palace, the spiritual reality, of *noga*.

מִכָּל מָקוֹם, עַל כָּל פָּנִים, יֶשְׁנוֹ בִּמְצִיאוּת, לְהַבְדִּיל, בְּחָכְמָה עִילָאָה, שֶׁנִּתְפַּשְׁטָה בִּפְרָט זֶה, לְמֹשֶׁה רַבֵּינוּ עָלָיו הַשָּׁלוֹם בְּסִינַי

Nevertheless, in any case, it does exist – not to equate the cases – in the supernal *Hokhma*, which expands in this detail, in the Torah that was given **to Moses, our teacher, may he rest in peace, at Sinai**

These rarely occurring, unintentional transgressions exist neither in the physical world nor do they have a source in the spiritual world. How, then, does studying them achieve the refinement the holy sparks from the *kelippot* and their elevation to God?

The author of the *Tanya* explains that these phenomena come from God's supernal wisdom [*Hokhma*], the soul of the Torah; that is, the

Ones can happen to anyone: a wise person, a fool, the righteous or the wicked. There is no connection between an action due to *ones* and what one planned or intended; therefore, he is not held responsible for this transgression. "Unintentional," on the other hand, refers to an action that although the person did not plan for it to happen, it happened through his negligence; he did not take the proper precautions to prevent it from happening.

root of forbidden and unintentional actions is in the *sefira* of Ḥokhma.[6]
Even if certain halakhic situations are highly unrealistic in life as we
know it, they exist in the Torah, in Jewish law. This applies not only to
cases stipulated in the Torah given to Moses at Sinai, but also in every
subsequent halakhic decision and discussion since then.

[כְּמַאֲמַר מַה] שֶׁכָּל תַּלְמִיד וָתִיק
עָתִיד לְחַדֵּשׁ כו׳

[as in the statement that] anything
that an experienced student will
introduce in the future ...,

The details of Jewish law progressively branch out from generation to
generation. Every new incident examined by *halakha*, every new piece
of reasoning and every new responsum that the rabbis of the generation
institute adds another sphere to the purview of Jewish law. This saying
of the Sages, that the author of the *Tanya* quotes,[7] asserts that all the
halakhic details, discussions, and explanations that ever were and would
be throughout history are proliferations of the supernal wisdom that was
given to Moses at Sinai. Each one bears the holiness of the Torah that
was given at Sinai. The author of the *Tanya* adds that it follows, given
the content of this essay, that these details are applicable in the spiritual
dimension, even if in the physical world there never was and nor ever
will be a halakhic situation that applies them.[8]

וְכָל פְּרָטֵי הָאִבַּעְיוֹת דְּרַבִּי יִרְמְיָה
(ע,א) ׳וּכְרַכְתּוּ כו׳ פֶּרֶק ד׳ דְּחוּלִּין

and all the details of the dilemmas
of Rabbi Yirmeya, such as "If one
wrapped it...," in the fourth chapter of *Ḥullin* (70a).

---

6. See *Iggeret HaKodesh* 26, where the author of the *Tanya* explains at great length
the difference between Torah itself, which is holy in every dimension and on
every level, and the topics that it discusses, that can be bad, even the *kelippa* of
absolute evil.

7. See *Megilla* 19b, Jerusalem Talmud, *Pe'a* 2:4, *Shemot Rabba* 47a, *Vayikra
Rabba* 22a, and many more places in the midrashim and the *Rishonim,* and in
works of Kabbala and Hasidism (and see in the name of the Lubavitcher Rebbe,
Rabbi Menaḥem Mendel Schneerson, in the *Tanya* with sources and collected
commentaries).

8. The text in the square brackets does not add anything important; it is simply
a phrase that appears in certain manuscripts but not in others.

Rabbi Yirmeya is famous in the Talmud for his borderline questions, that stretch the *halakha* to its outer limit, by suggesting absurd and even impossible cases.[9]

This source in the Talmud discusses the laws of firstborn animals. For the holiness to take effect on the firstborn, it needs to be "*peter reḥem*," the "opening of the womb." The question is: What is the definition of a first birth that has the effect of redeeming the womb, and how are borderline cases judged that are not necessarily realistic; for example if the newborn is wrapped in one's hands and taken out in a such a manner that it does not touch the opening of the womb (according to Rashi; Rabbeinu Tam explains this as referring to a case where two animals are born, one a female, and that animal wraps the male around its legs).

These instances discuss serious cases in Jewish law that relate to extremely rare and even impossible situation. Yet, they nevertheless exist in the Torah reality that addresses them.

כִּי הִתְפַּשְּׁטוּת חָכְמָה עִילָאָה הִיא בִּבְחִינַת אֵין סוֹף הַמְּלוּבָּשׁ בָּהּ בְּפוֹעֵל מַמָּשׁ **For the expansion of supernal *Hokhma* is an expression of *Ein Sof* that is enclothed within it in actual reality,**

The supernal *Ḥokhma* of the Torah is infinite, and its expansion in reality manifests in unending details and situations, far beyond what the physical world can design. That which we are capable of speaking and thinking about is limited, because we think in terms of concepts of a world that we already know. This does not apply when we think about Torah, and about life in the light of Torah, which is far vaster than what is realistically possible. This principle emerges out of the gulf that lies

9. For example, the discussion in *Bava Batra* 23b about young doves that are found: Who do they belong to? The Mishna says that young doves that are found within fifty cubits of the dovecot, they belong to the owner of the dovecot; and if they are found farther than fifty cubits from the dovecot, they belong to the finder. In the course of the discussion, Rav Yirmeya asked: What is the law if a young dove was found with one foot within less than fifty cubits and one foot at a distance of more than fifty cubits, to whom does it belong? The Talmud relates that he was removed from the *beit midrash*.

between mundane life and Torah Ḥokhma, in those "*halakhot* that are not common at all": the Torah and supernal Ḥokhma are infinite. ☞

וְכָל פְּרַט הֲלָכָה הוּא שַׁעַר,	and all the details of halakha are a gate,
נִמְשָׁךְ מֵחָכְמָה עִילָּאָה דְּיָסַד	which is **drawn from supernal Ḥokhma**
בְּרַתָּא׳	of "the father that **founded the daughter,**"

The *Zohar* says[10] that the father, which corresponds to Ḥokhma, founded, generates, and creates the "daughter," which is the *sefira* of *Malkhut*. Despite the distance between Ḥokhma and *Malkhut*, Ḥokhma being the first and *Malkhut* being the last, there is a direct relationship between them, which is the meaning of this statement, that "the father founded the daughter."[11]

It is particularly in *Malkhut* that quintessential Ḥokhma manifests in its original purity, in its power of creativity and even in its reve-

THE EXPANSION OF SUPERNAL WISDOM: INFINITE

☞ The author of the *Tanya* only touches upon the deep significance of this special expression, whose true meaning lies beyond the scope of this section. The infinite divine light manifests in everything; there is no molecule of life devoid of it. However, it does not manifest "literally actually" in the creation, even in the supernal attributes of *Atzilut*, but rather only through the limited parameters which characterize that creation. Truly infinite spiritual garb, "actually literally," albeit seemingly impossible, exists only in supernal Ḥokhma.

The author of the *Tanya* received an explanation of this point from his rebbe, the Maggid of Mezeritch, as mentioned in *Likkutei Amarim* (chap. 35, gloss). The light of *Ein Sof* is not unified, even in the world of *Atzilut*, except through the *sefira* of Ḥokhma. He explains there that since the blessed *Ein Sof* is the true Oneness alone, with no other, and this is the level of Ḥokhma....

Ein Sof, God Himself, is certainly not comprehended at all. However, human beings, who relate to Him from within the dimensions of the world, proclaim Him to be absolutely one, as we say in the *Shema*. In all the dimensions of the world, He is one, and there is no other. This is also the level of the utterly transcendent, supernal Ḥokhma; like the initial flash that lights up all reality: in one momentary spark, subsuming all of reality in it, every sensation, apprehension, emotion, and sense of being. This is supernal Ḥokhma that is clothed in the Torah, and in whoever engages in it, literally actually.

---

10. *Zohar* 3, 248b; ibid. 256b and more.
11. Similar to the wording of the verse "In (through) Ḥokhma the earth was founded" (Prov. 3:19).

lation of the infinite. The aspect of *Malkhut* in the Torah is the Oral Torah,[12] and it is particularly through the Oral Torah, through all the details of the *halakhot* that become clarified and decided in it, that supernal *Ḥokhma* in all its purity becomes manifested. *Ḥokhma* is meaningless unless it illuminates something, like physical light, that if passing through an empty space, without something to shine on, is meaningless; it is a light that does not shine. This is how supernal *Ḥokhma* operates; it only shines when it meets reality. Every place and situation that is illuminated with the light of *Ḥokhma* becomes another instrument, an additional angle, through which supernal *Ḥokhma* manifests in endless configurations. These infinite possibilities are every detail of the *halakhot* of the Oral Torah, which are like the gates through which *Ḥokhma* manifests and shines into our world.

וּמְלוּבָּשׁ בָּה, וּמִמֶּנָּה נִמְשָׁךְ וּמִתְלַבֵּשׁ בִּבְרִיאָה יְצִירָה עֲשִׂיָּה and is enclothed in it, and is drawn from it and enclothes itself in *Beria*, *Yetzira*, and *Asiya*.

The light of *Ein Sof* of *Ḥokhma* becomes enclothed in "the daughter," in the *Malkhut* of *Atzilut*, and from there in all the worlds. This kabbalistic description explains exactly what happens through the study of *halakha*. *Halakha* permeates all realms and is applicable to every life issue, every substance, every wisdom, every folly. Anything relating to the purview of *halakha*, even the most indecent of places, replete with *kelippa*, is illuminated by supernal *Ḥokhma* that pervades all.

After explaining the meaning of the *halakhot* and the way in which they draw down supernal *Ḥokhma* into every single physical and spiritual space, the author of the *Tanya* goes even further: he explains that when Jewish law and supernal *Ḥokhma* are drawn to that space, they clarify and rectify it. The permeation of supernal *Ḥokhma* through *halakha* is not like an illumination from afar, like, for example, a sage who sits in his room and tries to understand what is happening out on the street. The drawing down of *Ḥokhma* into *halakhot* in the worlds of *Beria, Yetzira,* and *Asiya,* entails an actual penetration that literally changes and rectifies the worlds; it teaches

---

12. *Likkutei Amarim*, chap. 53; *Torah Or* 53:3; ibid. 80a, and more.

what to do there according to supernal *Ḥokhma.* Here, the author explains how this happens.

וְנוֹדָע כִּי יְנִיקַת הַקְּלִיפּוֹת מֵאֲחוֹרַיִים דְּעֶשֶׂר סְפִירוֹת דִּקְדוּשָׁה	**It is known that the *kelippot* suckle from the "back side" of the ten *sefirot* of holiness,**

God is good, holy, and the source of everything that is in existence. Therefore, how can a reality of evil, *kelippa,* and idol worship, that seem to come from another source, exist? The answer is right here: the *kelippot* leech from the back side of the *sefirot*. The ten *sefirot* are the instruments through which God emanates vitality to the worlds; through intellect, love, fear…. For creative divine vitality to reach the worlds there must be vessels to receive it. Now, every vessel has a front and a back. When the leeching is from the back side and not from the front, it can reach the *kelippot* as well. ☞

וּבִפְרָט מִלְּבוּשִׁים דְּעֶשֶׂר סְפִירוֹת דִּבְרִיאָה יְצִירָה עֲשִׂיָּה	**specifically from the garments of the ten *sefirot* of *Beria, Yetzira,* and *Asiya,***

THE LEECHING OF THE *KELIPPOT* FROM THE BACK SIDE OF HOLINESS

☞ The ten *sefirot* are holy. However, they, like any receiving instrument have a front, which is the inside, and the intended purpose of its use, and the back side, which has no independent use. A vessel cannot possibly have an inside without an outside. Likewise, a spiritual vessel, no matter how ethereal, has an inside, a front, which is the intention of the vessel, and a whole outer structure whose purpose is to aid the front to fulfill its function.

For example, so that a person will truly have free will, he must have more than one option. The second, unwanted option, and the whole universe that enables it, is the "back side." The back side is not necessarily bad, because one does not have to choose it. However, the reality of *kelippa* leeches from it. The *kelippa*, as a negative reality of evil, is not, therefore, something that God created, but is rather a consequence of human beings focusing on the back side. When we relate to the "back side" as what is primary, as an independent entity, with no connection to the inside, then the reality of evil and idolatry is created. As long as a person connects the back to the front, then it is good and necessary for the sustaining of the good. However, when a person disconnects from the inside, the outside becomes a *kelippa* in every sense of the word: an opaque screen that hides the holiness beyond it. When people turn the back side into a source in and of itself, then automatically, anything that comes from it is false, evil, impure, and connected to death.

The leeching of the external forces is in a general sense from the back side of the ten holy *sefirot,* specifically from the garments of the ten *sefirot* of Beria, Yetzira, and Asiya, which are the created worlds, not from the ten *sefirot* of the world of *Asiya.*

The *sefirot* of *Atzilut* are unique in that they are unified in God Himself to the ultimate degree. In the language of the *Zohar,* "He and His life are one, He and His vessels are one."[13] This indicates that even their back side is not actually posterior; instead of concealing the divine light within them, they solely reveal it. Therefore, the ten *sefirot* of *Atzilut* do not allow for direct, actual leeching of the external forces; they are simply the source and influence for the ten *sefirot* of the created worlds. Only the ten *sefirot* of those lower created worlds, that possess a distinctive character which is separate from the Divine, as it were, have a back side that is not totally transparent to the divine reality. One can perceive in them something else as well, and particularly from there *kelippot* can begin to leech.

וּבִפְרָט דִּיצִירָה וַעֲשִׂיָּה הַמְעוֹרָבִים בַּקְּלִיפּוֹת כַּנּוֹדָע, שֶׁיְּנִיקָתָם מִבְּחִינַת הַלְּבוּשִׁים	specifically from *Yetzira* and *Asiya* that are intermingled in the *kelippot,* as it is known that their suckling is from the garments.

There is a hierarchy in the created worlds as well: the lower a world the more its garments conceal divine light.[14] Accordingly, within these worlds there is more leeching of *kelippot.* In the higher world of *Beria,* which is mostly good, there is a clear distinction between good and evil. There is also a reality of concealment and evil, because that is the nature of a created world; it is impossible for something created to not have the other side. In *Beria,* however, it is clear that the darkness is a necessary part of creation. No one gets confused there. Therefore,

---

13. According to the introduction to *Tikkunei Zohar* 3b. And see above, *Iggeret HaKodesh,* beginning of epistle 5, and in the explanations and comments there.
14. See *Likkutei Amarim,* chap. 7, *Likkutei Torah, Bemidbar* 3:4, and in many places in hasidic teachings. This is according to the known saying that the world of *Beria* is mostly good with a little bit of evil, the world of *Yetzira* is half and half, and the world of *Asiya* is mostly evil (See *Etz Ḥayyim* 43, and in the introduction, 47:4, 48:3, and more).

there is no real situation of leeching *kelippot*. This does not apply to the world of *Yetzira*, in which the *kelippa* is intermingled with holiness, and it becomes extremely complicated to distinguish between them. The world of *Asiya* is the lowest, the one with mostly evil, and that is where the *kelippa* masquerades as the most natural option.

וְעַל יְדֵי עֵסֶק הַהֲלָכוֹת, בְּדִבּוּר וּמַחֲשָׁבָה, מִתְפָּרְשִׁים וּמִתְפָּרְדִים מֵהַקְּדוּשָׁה, כְּמוֹ שֶׁכָּתוּב בַּתִּיקוּנִים וְרַעְיָא מְהֵימְנָא: לְאַפְרְשָׁא [כו']

By means of engagement in the *halakhot*, in speech and thought, the *kelippot* separate and become detached from the holiness, as is written in the *Tikkunim* and *Raya Meheimna*: To separate […].

This is the point that the author of the *Tanya* wanted to reach: the function of studying Jewish law in the spiritual worlds, in the worlds of *Yetzira* and *Asiya*, irrespective of the feasibility of the mitzva. He answers that when a person contemplates matters on the spiritual level of his soul, on the level of "*Asiya*" or "*Yetzira*," what is permitted and forbidden, how and in which situations, and so forth, he creates a distinction between good and bad, forbidden and permitted, and so forth, and in so doing separates the *kelippa* from the holiness. As explained, the problem in these worlds is the commingling of the *kelippa* with holiness. When there is no clear distinction between them, then the *kelippa* receives power along with holiness. However, from the moment that a person can separate between them in his mind, when he studies and analyzes the *halakhot* of the Torah, the *kelippa* loses its power and negative influence, and once again becomes the back side of holiness, a facilitator of good. ☞

BY MEANS OF ENGAGEMENT IN THE *HALAKHOT*, THE *KELIPPOT* SEPARATE AND BECOME DETACHED

☞ Something similar to this dynamic happens in a person's inner world. The phenomenon that something has the power to mislead or scare a person generally begins because a person does not know for sure if that thing is good or bad, true or false. However, the moment that it becomes entirely clear to him that it is totally false, it loses its power to affect him.

There is a story that appears in various versions (see, for example, Rabbi Shlomo

וְהַיְינוּ כַּנּוֹדָע מִמַּה שֶׁאָמְרוּ עַל שֶׁלֹּא בֵּרְכוּ בַּתּוֹרָה תְּחִלָּה כו׳

This is the same idea **as is known from** what the Rabbis **said: Because they did not recite a blessing on the Torah prior...,**

The Talmud asks,[15] "Due to what was the land lost?" (Jer. 9:11). And God answers, "Due to their abandonment of My Torah" (Jer. 9:12.) Rabbi Yehuda explains in the name of Rav, "They did not recite a blessing on the Torah prior." Torah study is a mitzva upon which a blessing is recited. The purpose of this blessing, like that of blessings on all other mitzvot, is to reveal the connection between the mitzva performance and God, who commanded that it be done. However, a person can study Torah like he studies any other subject: to improve intellectually, to use it for some other purpose, or even to know how to perform the mitzvot. If a person studies the Torah in these types of ways, purely as a means to an end, he disconnects it from God. This is why the land was destroyed. However, when a person first recites the blessing, "Blessed is God... who has sanctified us and commanded us to engage in words of Torah" and "who has chosen us... and given

Yosef Zevin, *Sippurei Ḥasidim, Torah* 552, beginning of *Parashat Ha'azinu*) about a hasid who was drawn to a place of terrifying external forces (demons). As his rebbe had instructed him previously, he said to them, "I am not afraid of you. You are nothing." Suddenly, a few disappeared. He then said, "You are just a figment of my imagination, you do not exist at all," and more disappeared. He continued to speak to them in this manner and to contemplate how they are nothing at all, until they all disappeared. These external forces, *kelippot*, leech from the back side that lost its connection to the inside. When a person says to them, "You do not have any independent existence, what you receive from the back side is total falsity," at that mo-ment the essence of that *kelippa* disappears entirely.

Indeed, the wisdom of the Torah is not like worldly wisdom that distinguishes between beneficial and not beneficial, between what is good for us and bad for us. While it clothes itself in worldly, human wisdom, the Torah's *Ḥokhma* is always supernal divine *Ḥokhma,* the wisdom of God Himself. Furthermore, as will be explained below, the light of *Ein Sof* is enclothed in supernal *Ḥokhma* (*Likkutei Amarim,* chap. 35, in the name of the Maggid of Mezeritch) that transcends all *Ḥokhma,* and therefore, during the study of the *Ḥokhma* of the Torah, the very Divine enters the world, and the reality of God is the power that distinguishes and clarifies it.

---

15. *Bava Metzia* 85b and in *Nedarim* 81b. And see *Likkutei Siḥot* 15:3.

us His Torah," he declares that he studies because God commanded him to study, and that the Torah is God's Torah: divine wisdom, and divine will. Through this, one binds the Torah below to God Himself above.

שֶׁהוּא עַל יְדֵי הַמְשָׁכַת אוֹר אֵין סוֹף בְּחָכְמָה עִילָאָה הַמְלוּבֶּשֶׁת בָּהֶן, וּבְחָכְמָה אִתְבְּרִירוּ׳ בְּאוֹר אֵין סוֹף שֶׁבָּה	which is by drawing the light of *Ein Sof* in the supernal Ḥokhma that is enclothed in them, and "with wisdom [*Ḥokhma*] they are refined" in the light of *Ein Sof* within it.

Hasidic teachings explain that the deeper meaning of the word "blessing" [*berakha*] is "drawing down" (like "grafting [*hamavrikh*] a vine,"[16] which means to pull down a branch and bury it in the ground). Therefore, when one blesses on the Torah, he draws down God's supernal Ḥokhma, and the very light of *Ein Sof* that is clothed within it, through the intricacies of the practical *halakhot* of the mitzva that he is performing. For more on this concept, see *Zohar, Heikhalot, Pekudei* 254:2, and in many other hasidic sources. See also *Iggeret HaKodesh*, epistle 28.

In a more general sense, the blessings of the Torah establish an overall intention for one's Torah study: that it should be for the sake of Heaven, Torah for its own sake. The blessing and the intention connect the Torah to the Giver of the Torah (as signified by the wording of the blessing), and as they say in hasidic circles, draws down the light of *Ein Sof* into the Torah. The Torah that we have is an intricate arrangement of words and wisdom that bear significance on several levels simultaneously – *peshat, remez, derush,* and *sod* – and in the various worlds (as there is Torah that is studies in the Garden of Eden). A person who studies Torah may only understand it in terms of its outward expression that relates to the particular realm in which it is being studied. Torah study for its own sake, study that draws down the light of the *Ein Sof* into the Torah, transcends all its particular manifestations, and permeates Torah as it was at Sinai. The blessing transforms one's Torah study into an intimate union with the *Ein Sof*

---

16. *Kilayim* 7:1. And see *Likkutei Torah, Vayikra* 40b, and ibid., *Devarim* 29a.

who gives it. A person's blessing turns him not only into a recipient of Torah, but into a giver of the Torah as well, because he is the one who sparks the infusion of the light of the *Ein Sof* into it.

As explained, Torah study generates the refinement of the worlds, and separates the *kelippa* from holiness. Through this, the *kelippa* is altogether eliminated. Here the author of the *Tanya* adds that this clarification does not just happen through halakhic decisions that definitively render some things permitted and others prohibited, but rather, the very penetration of the supernal *Hokhma* and light of *Ein Sof* into the worlds causes the good to be filtered out from the bad. Sparks of holiness ascend from within the shards of broken vessels and *kelippot,* and the world becomes rectified.

The concept that "with *Hokhma* they are refined" means that on the level of *Hokhma* things get clarified. An abysmal situation of confusion between holiness and *kelippa* is resolved as it ascends to the level of *Hokhma*. The level of *Hokhma,* in one's soul and in the world, is a rectified level in and of itself. (In the overarching four-world scheme, *Hokhma* corresponds to the world of *Atzilut,* and in particular it corresponds to the *Atzilut* of every world.) There can be no concealment or obscurity on this level, nor the presence of *kelippa*. A person who is on this level, to whatever extent this can be achieved in reality, experiences total subsummation of his being. He is not consciously aware of his state of being, nor does it cause him to feel or think something in particular at that moment. Therefore, "with *Hokhma* they are refined" means that there is no comprehension of the *kelippa* there, and it falls away and dissipates on its own. Still, in actuality, this concept is connected mostly to Torah study, because Torah, and he who studies it, reveals the supernal *Hokhma* and light of *Ein Sof* within it.

וְהַמְשָׁכָה זוֹ נַעֲשָׂה עַל יְדֵי דְיוֹקַן הָעֶלְיוֹן שֶׁל הָאָדָם הָעוֹסֵק גַּם כֵּן בַּהֲלָכוֹת אֵלּוּ לְמַעְלָה בְּשָׁרְשׁוֹ

This drawing forth is performed by means of the supernal image of the person who is also engaged in these *halakhot* above, in his root,

A person is not just comprised of a soul that clothes itself in a body. He is not the sum total of what he feels and thinks through his bodily senses's faculties. The entire spiritual stature of a person[17] ascends way up, into the highest worlds and realms. As he studies Torah in this world, his supernal root engages with Torah in the supernal worlds as well. This lofty experience does not necessarily become actualized in the physical world.

בְּנוּקְבָא דִּזְעֵיר אַנְפִּין דִּבְרִיאָה   in *Nukva* of *Zeir Anpin* of *Beria*, *Yet-*
יְצִירָה עֲשִׂיָּה   *zira*, and *Asiya*.

The feminine aspect of *Zeir Anpin* corresponds to *Malkhut,* the Divine Presence, and the light that fills all the worlds that receives from *Zeir Anpin.* If *Zeir Anpin* corresponds to the divine attributes as they are above and beyond man (the aspect of the holy) the *Nukva,* or the feminine aspect is that which receives from *Zeir Anpin* according to its capacity. It cannot receive the totality of *Zeir Anpin,* just as a person cannot receive from another person the very essence of his soul, but rather just a particular revelation of it. However, since the *Nukva* is the feminine tailored to *Zeir Anpin,* it is the abstract recipient, without particular limitations of a particular world, person, or situation below. Therefore, the author of the *Tanya* identifies this level as the source and supernal image of man, as he is in his root and his very essence. Spiritual influence continues from there to descend through particularized channels that every person creates through his way of being and life in this world.

While in the world of *Atzilut,* the *sefirot* and *Zeir Anpin* and *Nukva* are the general ones, the spiritual structure of every world includes ten *sefirot* and *partzufim* of *Zeir Anpin* and *Nukva,* that manifest in particular ways in order to impact the unique character of each world, as previously explained. The author of the *Tanya* also explained that while every person experiences life through his body in this world, the root of his soul belongs to a very high spiritual world. Some souls (albeit only a few) find their root in *Atzilut,* others in *Beria,* some in *Yetzira,* and others in *Asiya.* This supernal root above is the "image" of that person who is studying the supernal Torah corresponding to the Torah study he does below in his physical body.

---

17. See further the explanation of this concept above in the first essay of *Kuntres Aḥaron.*

וּבָזֶה יוּבָן חִיּוּב כָּל נֶפֶשׁ רוּחַ נְשָׁמָה
לְהַשְׁלִים כָּל הַתַּרְיַ"ג בְּמַחֲשָׁבָה
דִּיבּוּר וּמַעֲשֶׂה, שֶׁהֵן פְּרָטֵי הַהֲלָכוֹת

Now we can understand the obligation of every *nefesh, ruaḥ,* and *neshama* to complete all the 613 mitzvot **in thought, speech, and action, which are the details of the** *halakhot.*

In light of the above, the significance of the existence of the *halakhot* and their study is not restricted to what a person does in this world; both one's soul and the mitzvot are rooted far above this world, and they can have many roots, as befitting the worlds. This therefore explains the teaching brought in hasidic works,[18] that every person is obligated to fulfill all 613 mitzvot.

And if a person cannot perform them practically, then he should fulfill them in speech, when he studies them, or thinks about them, that is, attuning the soul to those mitzvot to the best of his ability. For example,[19] sacrificial offerings were practical actions performed in the Temple with animals that were offered on the altar. There are sacrificial offerings in speech, when a person studies the laws of sacrifices in the Torah, and then there is the devotion in thought, which is the fulfillment of the mitzva of prayer that is "a substitute for sacrificial offerings," with love, when the heart ascends and is burned on the altar due to its love of God. It follows that every person can perform every mitzva in one of these ways, and is therefore obligated to fulfill all the mitzvot.

This is especially the case since, as explained in this essay, it is through the spiritual fulfillment of the mitzva, by studying every detail of its laws, practical or otherwise, that the good is distilled from the bad in its root. A rectification is made in the source of reality, in the root of evil and *kelippa,* regardless of whether a person sees the effects of that rectification in this world or not. It was explained that studying

---

18. In *Sefer HaGilgulim 4, Sha'ar HaGilgulim,* introduction 11:16, and the introduction to *Sha'ar HaMitzvot* (and in *Etz Ḥayyim* 49:5), it is abridged, and therefore not difficult there. See also Shelah, *Torah SheBikhetav BiTeḥilato* (the comments of the Lubavitcher Rebbe, Rabbi Menaḥem Mendel Shneerson, epistle 29). And see *Torah Or* 16:4, and ibid. 32:4; *Likkutei Torah, Bemidbar* 38:4, and in many other places.

19. See *Likkutei Torah, Bemidbar* 75a, and onward.

halakhot impacts the soul on every one of its levels, from the source of the image of supernal man until its life in a body below, on all levels of reality, to refine and rectify them. The obligation of every person undertaking this task stems from the uniqueness of each person. No person is identical to another, and this is not arbitrary, because every person, according to the structure of his soul in all of the myriads of details that are unique to his particular life, engages, through the minutiae of the *halakhot,* in another angle and another detail of life that no one else can rectify.

וּצְרִיכוֹת לָבֹא בְּגִלְגּוּל לְהַשְׁלִים הַתּוֹרָה בְּפַרְדֵּ"ס

And every soul **must be reincarnated to complete the Torah in** *Pardes*,

Pardes refers to the four layers of the Torah: *peshat, remez, derush,* and *sod.* This is virtually impossible to do in one lifecycle. Whatever a person does not accomplish in one incarnation must be fulfilled throughout the course of additional incarnations.

כְּדֵי לְבָרֵר כָּל הַבֵּירוּרִין הַנּוֹגְעוֹת לָהֶם מִכָּל הָרַפָּ"ח שֶׁהִיא קוֹמַת אָדָם שְׁלֵמָה, תַּרְיַ"ג בְּחִינוֹת כְּלָלִיּוֹת וּפְרָטִיּוֹת

in order to perform all of the refinements that apply to them from all of the 288 sparks, **which is the full height of man, 613 aspects, generalities and particulars.**

Two hundred and eighty-eight is the number of the roots of all the sparks in all time and worlds that all the souls must refine. From these, every soul has specific sparks that are relevant to it, sparks that it, and only it, can refine. Since this can be achieved by him alone, and by no one else, this very soul must return in an additional incarnation.

This spiritual undertaking reflects the spiritual makeup of man's soul. Just as the overall spiritual stature of a person is a complete analogue of the mitzvot, having 248 limbs and 365 sinews (physically and spiritually), so too the ultimate purpose of the soul is the function that corresponds to it, which is the complete analogue of the Torah, comprised of a total of 613: 248 positive commandments and 365 prohibitions. There are the general 613 mitzvot of the Torah and the myriad particulars, with 613 detailed *halakhot* for every individual soul. There is an all-encompassing mitzva, like "Remember the Sabbath day," that is relevant to all people, and then there are almost endless details of specific *melakhot* that relate to individual circumstances: how a given person must fulfill a particular mitzva in the specific circumstance in which he finds himself, be it in action or in study. These halakhic details are integrally bound up with the relevant individual soul, bringing refinement to the essence of the person's soul, through every particular life circumstance that he experiences.

The author of the *Tanya* has been explaining the topic of the work of refinement until now, which is the function of this world. Refinement entails "positive" and "negative" undertakings; the positive gives life to and elevates the good, while the negative separates the bad and undermines its vitality. Torah study, like action, does this through the clarification of Jewish law: what to do and what not to do, what is permitted and what is prohibited. However, in the times to come, when there will no longer be a reality of evil in the world, then how will this work and Torah study look?

אֲבָל לֶעָתִיד לָבוֹא כְּשֶׁיִּשְׁלַם הַבֵּירוּר יִהְיֶה עֵסֶק הַתּוֹרָה בִּבְחִינַת ׳עֲשֵׂה טוֹב׳ לְבַד. לְהַעֲלוֹת הַנֶּפֶשׁ רוּחַ נְשָׁמָה מַעְלָה מַעְלָה עַד אֵין סוֹף

In the World to Come, however, when the refinement will be complete, the engagement in the Torah will be solely an expression of "do good" alone, to elevate the *nefesh, ruaḥ,* and *neshama* above and beyond, until *Ein Sof.*

The "World to Come" refers to the time that follows the completion of the work of refinement. Good and light are infinite, but darkness and evil are limited. Darkness and evil are the concealment of the Divine, that hides and limits; therefore it is intrinsically limited. Light and goodness are divine revelation that knows no end. Therefore, the work of refinement, transforming darkness into light, bitter into sweet, is intrinsically work that has an end. When the work will be finished, the world will be a transformed, unrecognizable place. That world will be characterized by its own purpose and work, however; instead of the work of refinement of good from the bad, it will entail only doing good.[20]

---

20. See also *Iggeret HaKodesh*, epistle 26.

After the good has been distilled from the bad, what is left is to make the good even better, to elevate it infinitely higher and higher.

Man's divine soul is unified in its source, a literal part of God above. However, when it descends to the worlds, it is divided, so to speak, into *nefesh, ruaḥ,* and *neshama. Nefesh* interacts with physical matters of the world of *Asiya, ruaḥ* with emotional matters of the world of *Yetzira,* and the *neshama* with intellectual matters of the world of *Beria.* Therefore, the author of the *Tanya* specifies the division of the divine soul here, "to elevate the *nefesh, ruaḥ* and *neshama,*" because since it is submerged in the worlds – thankfully, not in evil, but in physicality and limitation of this world – it can ascend from the state of separation to infinite oneness and purity.

Like the work of refinement in this world, the ascension in the future will be according to the Torah. Through the clarification of the details of Jewish law, through the clear distinguishing between permitted and prohibited, all the holiness was distilled from the *kelippa.* In the future, through the study of the reasons for the *halakhot,* they will ascend to their source in the highest heights, every detail of them, with the person who studied and performed them.

וְגַם בְּשְׁסָ"ה לֹא תַעֲשֶׂה, בְּשָׁרְשָׁן לְמַעְלָה שֶׁהֵן גְּבוּרוֹת קְדוֹשׁוֹת | This **also** applies **to the 365 negative** commandments, **in their root above, which are the holy aspects of *Gevurot*,**

We will not only engage with positive commandments in the future, but with negative commandments as well. Although it seems that now prohibitions deal with blemish and evil, phenomena that have no place in the future, the root of the prohibitions is bound to the essence of *Gevurot,* which, in its supernal source, is eternally holy.

While in our world, one of the functions of negative command-ments is to protect a person from evil, in their roots above, they are holy, no less so than positive commandments. Since positive command-ments are drawn from aspects of lovingkindness, the infinite light that is the aspect of *Ḥesed,* so too the prohibitions express and draw down holy, supernal *Gevurot.* The image of the Divine that interacts with the world is necessarily comprised of aspects of both *Ḥesed* and *Gevura* together. It is impossible to draw a picture with just one color, or play music with one note; so too, above, it is impossible for the Divine to reveal itself with just *Ḥesed*. Every limitation and delineation of *Ḥesed*, every picture with other colors, comes from the side of *Gevura*. In its source, *Gevura* is not concealment (and certainly not evil). *Gevura* is the revelation of that which we do not see, which is, in a certain sense, the more immense revelation.[21] This is the revelation of everything that cannot be revealed or expressed except through a negative statement. It is that which the eye cannot see, and the mind cannot understand. It is the root of the 265 negative commandments.

וּלְהַמְתִּיקָן בַּחֲסָדִים בִּרְמָ"ח מִצְוֹת עֲשֵׂה וּלְכָלְלָן יַחַד

and to mitigate them through the aspects of *Ḥesed* of the 248 positive commandments, and to incorporate them together.

The endeavor relating to negative commandments of the future can be seen as being mitigated in aspects of *Ḥesed*. One does not engage in studying them through wariness of and protection against evil, but rather as part of the performance of good, since in this world, in order that true good will materialize, limits must be set that do not stem from the will not to give, but rather from the will to give, so that goodness will be received. This limitation, that serves the giving and the *Ḥesed*, is called "the mitigation of *Gevurot* in aspects of *ḥasadim*."

The mitigation of *Gevurot* in the aspects of *ḥasadim*, of negative commandments in positive commandments, is an inclusion of both together, a unification of the overall divine influence, making it better, more refined, and more suitable, not just in general, but in terms of every aspect of reality. This is the significance of engaging in the study of both common and rare *halakhot*, now and in future times.

וְעַל כֵּן הַתּוֹרָה כּוּלָּהּ, נִצְחִית, בִּכְלָלָהּ וּבִפְרָטָהּ

Consequently, the whole Torah is eternal, in its generality and particulars,

---

21. See *Torah Or* 9:3 about this, and in great detail about the high level of negative commandments in *Likkutei Torah*, Pekudei 6:3.

When the author of the *Tanya* says, "The whole Torah," he means the positive and negative commandments alike.

The eternality of the Torah is both now and in the future, both in the exile and in redemption. The holiness and the truth of the Torah is eternal, in its overall, general aspect, and every single mitzva and *halakha* in particular, that will or never will happen. ☞

שֶׁגַּם פְּרָטֵי הַהֲלָכוֹת דְּשַׁסָּ"ה לֹא תַעֲשֶׂה, הֵן הֵן עֲנָפִים מֵהַכְּלָלוֹת	as even the details of the *halakhot* of the 365 negative commandments are the very branches of the generalities,

"Generalities" mean the eternality of the Torah as expressed in its overall kindness [*Hesed*] and bestowal. "The details of the *halakhot*" are, as explained, the offshoots of the general principle, like branches of a tree that particularly, because they are separate branches, comprise the entire tree: many that are one.

וְיֵשׁ לְכוּלָּם שֹׁרֶשׁ לְמַעְלָה בה' גְּבוּרוֹת דִּקְדוּשָׁה כְּמוֹ הַשַּׁסָּ"ה לֹא תַעֲשֶׂה עַצְמָן, שֶׁהֵן לְמַעְלָה בְּחִינַת הַדָּם הַמְחַיֶּה הָאֵבָרִים וְכֵלִים דִּזְעֵיר אַנְפִּין.	and they all have a root above, in the five holy aspects of *Gevurot*, like the 365 negative commandments themselves, which are above, in the manner of blood that sustains the limbs of the vessels of *Zeir Anpin*.

Every detail of *halakha* of the negative commandments finds its root in the five aspects of *Gevura*. The five aspects of *Gevura* and the five aspects of *Hesed* are the holy lights from above, which correspond to the light of the *Ein Sof* that pours forth its effect to the worlds through the *sefirot* of *Zeir Anpin*.

Like man below, the supernal divine has 248 limbs and 365 sinews,

"ETERNAL"

☞ As explained in other places (see *Likkutei Torah*, Deut. 67:4), eternality is not synonymous with infinity, because the eternal is a factor of time; eternality encompasses all time. The Torah's eternality does not mean that it transcends time, but rather that it belongs to all time.

which are the blood vessels that circulate blood to all the limbs to give them life. The 248 positive commandments correspond to the limbs of *Zeir Anpin,* "the limbs of the King," and the 265 prohibitions are like the blood that lends vitality to the limbs.

It follows that negative commandments, that are like the blood that enlivens the limbs, are even higher than positive commandments. And as explained elsewhere, the level of prohibition is actually higher than the positive commandments, more abstract and all-encompassing, and supplies the parameters and vitality to the positive commandments. They are the five aspects of *Ḥesed* and the five aspects of *Gevura* above, which encompass all divine abundance; the five aspects of *Ḥesed* are the observable divine influence, the "limbs," while the five aspects of *Gevura* are the substratum, the background from which the aspects of *Ḥesed* burgeon forth. The aspects of *Ḥesed* are the revelations that are visible, while the more powerful revelation that is invisible, *Gevura,* completes the revelation of the *Ein Sof* in the world. The Divine is divine and the *Ein Sof* is *Ein Sof* anywhere; however, just the tip is revealed and the rest is concealed. The revealed are the aspects of *Ḥesed,* the limbs of *Zeir Anpin,* and the greater hidden part comprises the aspects of *Gevura* and corresponds to the blood that provides vitality to the limbs.

This short essay addressed one question: Why engage in the study of *halakhot* that are rarely practiced because they depend on the occurrence of highly unrealistic situations? Why is it important to know if someone in that situation would be liable or exempt, if something would be permitted or prohibited? The author of the *Tanya* began by explaining that whatever is forbidden below is rooted in *kelippot* above, whether it is practical or not. There is a world of *kelippot* only a fraction of which actually comes into existence. The rectification and clarification of that world in general is man's work and the purpose of his coming to the world. Since the source of this world and, therefore, its essence is not a physical world, its rectification is not only practical, but also activated through study, through the thought and the speech of the person who is studying the *halakhot.*

Every detail of *halakha* is like a gate through which the supernal

Ḥokhma penetrates the worlds; every *halakha* of a prohibition relates to particular ways and situations in which the *kelippa* clothes itself and mingles into holiness. When a person engages in study of Jewish Law, and thinks about *halakha*, relating it to it in his soul, a soul submerged in the world and its *kelippot* to a certain degree, he literally shines the light of Ḥokhma into all those places.

This description of a person's spiritual work is our task in the exile; a person must work tirelessly to rectify the brokenness of this world and distill the good from the bad. Therefore, the end of the essay touches upon the future times of redemption, when these refinements and rectifications will not need to be done. Torah study will also be different then; it will not be the study of refinement of evil, as explained earlier, but rather a study that elevates the good and improves it more and more. It is important to say this because particularly through this the deeper facet of Torah emerges, not only as an instrument that fixes what is broken, but rather as a goal in and of itself of elevation and cleaving to God Himself, who is one with the Torah.

Essay 6
"David, You Call Them Songs?"

THIS ESSAY FROM *KUNTRES AḤARON* IS ONE OF THE MOST fundamental and famous of all hasidic discourses. It deals with the essence of the Torah on its innermost level, where it does not relate to humankind or to the world, but only to the Holy One blessed be He Himself.

This essay is also unique in the broader context of the totality of hasidic works. Generally, the purpose of hasidic writings is to bring the higher intellects down below, to the mind and service of man in the world, and yet this essay, in a certain sense, is aimed in the opposite direction. The author of the *Tanya* gathers what we know about the Torah, and all the ways in which we can relate to it, and elevates them: What you currently understand and are doing is good, but there is something higher and deeper. Even if you are unable to achieve it in your service of God, you should be aware of the existence of this layer of the Torah, which extends all the way to its innermost core.

This essay has a number of parallels and is mentioned in numerous hasidic discourses,[1] while in many other places it is cited as "*Iggeret HaKodesh* at its end," "*Iggeret*

---

1. The most important parallels, which elaborate on the topic at hand, can be found in *Ma'amarei Admor HaZaken* ("*Et'halekh Lyozna*"); *Likkutei Torah*, Num. 18 and onward, and in *Derekh Mitzvotekha* (by the *Tzemaḥ Tzedek*), *Mitzvat Masa HaAron BaKatef*. See also *Hemshekh Ayin Bet* 5672 (1912), vol. 1, p. 170 and onward.

HaKodesh," "Iggeret HaKodesh, section 36," "According to the saying of the Rabbis, 'David, you call them songs?'" and various other titles.

In terms of its content, this essay is related to the previous one. Like the previous essay, which deals with the significance of Torah study in the spiritual worlds and in future times, this essay also discusses the inner spiritual meaning of Torah study. Even more than in the previous essay, the focus here is on the distinct divine meaning of the Torah, which is higher than even all spiritual levels. As will be explained, this particular meaning has no relevance to the soul and the world, but only to the Divine.

'דָּוִד זְמִירוֹת קָרֵית לְהוּ כו'?'

"David, you call them songs…?"

14 Kislev
_____
14 Kislev
(leap year)

This opening phrase directs our attention to a rabbinic saying which forms the basis of the entire essay.[2] The Bible[3] recounts how David returned the Holy Ark (which had earlier been in the possession of the Philistines) to Jerusalem. He had his men place the Ark on a new wagon and they traveled on. However, when Uzza, who was accompanying the wagon, thought that the Ark was about to fall off, he reached out his hand to support it, at which point God struck him and he died. Greatly shocked by the incident, David realized that something was wrong and that he was the one at fault. The Talmud clarifies what went awry and explains David's surprising lapse through an exposition of Rava: For what reason was David punished? Because he called words of Torah "songs," as it is stated: "Your statutes were songs to me in the house of my sojourning" (Ps. 119:54). The Holy One blessed be He said to him: It is written about words of Torah: "If you cast your eyes on it, it is gone" (Prov. 23:5), [and yet] you call them songs?! I will cause you to stumble in a matter that even schoolchildren know, as it is written with regard to the wagons brought to the Tabernacle: "But he did not give [wagons for carrying] to the sons of Kehat, because the sacred

---

2. The phrase is from *Sota* 35a, where it appears as "And you call them songs?" The source for the precise version as written here, and which also appears in other hasidic works, is unclear.

3. II Sam. 6:7. See also I Chron. 13:9.

service [is upon them; they shall bear on the shoulder]" (Num. 7:9). And he [David,] brought it in a wagon.

הִנֵּה בַּזֹּהַר (חלק ג ח,ב): שְׁבָחָא Now, it is said **in the Zohar** (3, 8b):
דְּאוֹרַיְיתָא וּרְנָנָה כו' "**The praise of the Torah and its chant…**"

In order to understand this rabbinic saying, the author of the *Tanya* first explains the purpose of the joy of Torah study. In this source, the *Zohar* is referring to one's joy in the service of God, in accordance with the verse "Serve the Lord with joy" (Ps. 100:2). It states that when the Temple was standing, this joy was attained through the sacrifices, which would atone for a person's sins and draw him closer to God, and he would accordingly praise the Lord and rejoice. Nowadays, however, when there are no sacrifices, the joy is derived through the study of Torah.

וּלְהָבִין, מַהוּ הַשֶּׁבַח להקב"ה, We need **to understand: What is**
כְּשֶׁזֶּה אָסוּר אוֹ מוּתָּר? **the praise of the Holy One, blessed be He – when this is prohibited or permitted?**

It is not difficult to understand the praise of God when we grasp His exalted status and the abundant goodness that He bestows upon us. However, it is more challenging to comprehend the praise and great joy in the Torah, a large part of which consists simply of determinations of what is permitted and prohibited.[4]

הִנֵּה הוּא עַל דֶּרֶךְ "מַה גָּדְלוּ מַעֲשֶׂיךָ **This is in the manner of: "How**
ה' מְאֹד עָמְקוּ מַחְשְׁבוֹתֶיךָ" (תהלים **great are Your works, Lord; how**
צב,ו) **profound Your thoughts"** (Ps. 92:6).

---

4. The Lubavitcher Rebbe, Rabbi Menaḥem Mendel Schneerson, notes that when one delves into the specifics, the *Tanya* in several places actually refers to six categories: permitted, kosher, and pure, and their opposites. It seems that the author of the *Tanya* chose only "prohibited or permitted" here because these include a basic level of meaning that applies to all of those categories. As stated in *Likkutei Amarim* (chap. 7; see also chap. 8), the term *assur* ["prohibited"] is derived from the way it is bound [*assur*] and tied up by the *sitra aḥara* (the "other side," that which is not holy), whereas the permitted is no longer bound up, and therefore it can ascend to the holy.

This verse, which praises God, refers to His deeds and thoughts. His deeds are great, and when one reflects upon them – the oceans, mountains, sky, and the countless stars – one is motivated to marvel and to extol the One who created them all, His power and kindness that are revealed through His actions and wisdom. Yet there is also a more internal thought, which is the wisdom revealed in the Torah, upon which the externality of His wisdom in creation ("Your works") depends.

As will be stated below, is not easy to perceive the praise of the Torah. Yet when one reflects on "How great are Your works," and that this is connected to "How profound Your thoughts," one can comprehend the praise of the Torah. This is not merely a general connection, but a specific, particular connection of every individual entity in the great wide world to Jewish law and the minutiae of each particular *halakha*, as the author of the *Tanya* proceeds to explain:

> כִּי הִנֵּה נוֹדַע שֶׁכָּל הָעוֹלָמוֹת עֶלְיוֹנִים וְתַחְתּוֹנִים תְּלוּיִם בְּדִקְדּוּק מִצְוָה אַחַת
>
> **For it is known that all the upper and lower worlds depend on the precise** performance **of one mitzva.**

The wisdom of the Torah involves the definition of the mitzvot: What is a mitzva, under what exact conditions must it be fulfilled, and the like. The precise features of a mitzva are the same as its minute details, why in such circumstances is it considered a mitzva, but not otherwise. These boundaries are called "the precise features of a mitzva" because they deal with its minute and exact definitions, which sometimes make no sense to us. And yet it is these very definitions and minutiae that structure the character of the mitzva, so that it will have a real image and existence in the world, precisely in this manner and not otherwise. If a single aspect is not followed properly, then the mitzva is no longer worthy of the name. The great wonder for which the entire vast world was created, that at a certain point it will have a mitzva and a bond with God, will remain unfulfilled.

> דֶּרֶךְ מָשָׁל: אִם הַקָּרְבָּן כָּשֵׁר, נַעֲשָׂה יִחוּד עֶלְיוֹן וְעוֹלִים כָּל הָעוֹלָמוֹת לְקַבֵּל חַיּוּתָם וְשִׁפְעָם
>
> **For example, if an offering is fit, a supernal union is achieved and all the worlds ascend to receive their vitality and flow.**

On the inner level, a sacrifice ascends from the world to the Holy One, blessed be He. It is detached from the world through the acts of slaughter and burning, and so on, and it is drawn closer to God when it is offered and placed upon the altar. Each specific sacrifice is merely a representative of all the worlds,[5] both the upper and the lower ones, which ascend and are drawn closer together with it, and are thereby incorporated into their Creator. All animals would ascend together with the animal that was brought as a sacrifice, and all plants by means of the one-tenth of an ephah of fine flour. Thus, the entire ascent and drawing close of the worlds depend on the performance of this rite in exactly the proper manner according to the precise definitions and rules of the Torah.

וְאִם שִׁינָה שֶׁקִּיבֵּל הַדָּם בִּשְׂמֹאלוֹ דֶּרֶךְ מָשָׁל, אוֹ שֶׁלֹּא בִּכְלִי שָׁרֵת כָּשֵׁר, אוֹ שֶׁהָיְתָה חֲצִיצָה אֲזַי נִתְבַּטְלָה עֲלִיּוֹת הָעוֹלָמוֹת וְחַיּוּתָם וְשִׁפְעָם מֵחַיֵּי הַחַיִּים אֵין סוֹף בָּרוּךְ הוּא

But if one deviated, as he, for example, received the blood in his left hand, or not in a kosher service vessel, or there was an interposition, the ascents of the worlds, and their vitality and flow from the infinite source of life, *Ein Sof*, blessed be He, are negated.

One who receives the blood after the slaughter must do so in his right hand, and he must use a specific vessel designated for the Temple service, which has been anointed with the anointing oil or which has served a holy purpose. If he used just any regular vessel, the sacrifice has been invalidated. Another example is an interposition[6] between the priest and the service vessel, or between the priest and the floor of the Temple, or between the priest and his garments.[7] All of these are

---

5. See *Likkutei Amarim*, chap. 34.

6. For all of the laws mentioned here, see *Zevaḥim* 2:1, 3:2, and also Rambam, Mishne Torah *Sefer Avoda, Hilkhot Pesulei HaMukdashim*, chap. 1 and elsewhere. The Lubavitcher Rebbe notes that "received the blood in his left hand" is an example of an invalidation involving the person; "not in a kosher service vessel" is an invalidation involving the vessel; while "or there was an interpolation" is an invalidation in which there is nothing wrong with either of those two elements.

7. As stated in a note of the Lubavitcher Rebbe.

examples of precise requirements of the mitzva of the sacrifice. Any deficiency in their fulfillment culminates in the negation of the "vitality and flow" of the worlds, which they receive "from the infinite source of life, *Ein Sof*, blessed be He." All the worlds ascend by virtue of the sacrifices, as stated. This ascent is not a minor issue, but rather it is the essence of the existence of the worlds. On the one hand, when they ascend, they fulfill the purpose of their creation, as they rise upward and return to God all that He has granted them. On the other hand, in their ascent they receive new life from the life and source of all life, which is *Ein Sof*, for the continued existence of the worlds and another cycle of ascents. ☞

The service of the sacrifices is, of course, only an example, for the same is true for all the mitzvot. Every mitzva embodies a bond with the Divine, and everything that is part of the mitzva ascends and connects to God, including the person himself, his body, and the objects of the world with which he performed the mitzva. Whether the act itself is an explicit mitzva or whether it is related in some way to a mitzva (in Hasidism this possibility is unlimited), in its ascent it draws with it part

"THE ASCENT OF THE OFFERINGS IN THE TEMPLE"

☞ The offerings are part of the mystery of the bond between the worlds and the Divine. The entire system of the Temple and the sacrificial service serves as a medium for connecting the higher and the lower. There, in the reality of the Temple – which is a site that is not a place, which does not belong to any tribe, which differs in its holiness from any other location in the world, which does not really belong either to the lower realm or the upper realm – we find the meeting place. This encounter and connection is complex, since tying together all the details, so that the worlds will truly become linked, in order that the influence from above to below will indeed flow through all the right channels, requires a complete theory. Even in the material world, when it is necessary to join together two complex systems, there are a huge number of details that must be executed so that they are implemented in exactly the correct manner: the red wire must go here and the yellow wire there; this valve has to be attached there, and so on and so forth. If you change any element, in one case it simply won't work, while in other situations it can even destroy the entire world. With the alteration of a small, apparently insignificant detail, everything changes. When compounding a medicine, the variation of a single molecule can make the difference between a cure and a poison. The same applies, to an even greater extent, to the sacrifices. The Torah provides the "technical specifications" on how a sacrifice must be brought up to God, and if there is a deviation in even one detail from what is written in the instructions, none of it will work.

of an entire world, from both the lower and the upper ones. However, when the precise details of the mitzva are not performed properly, all of this is nullified and they do not ascend.

וְכֵן בִּתְפִילִין כְּשֵׁרוֹת מִתְגַּלִּים מוֹחִין עֶלְיוֹנִים דזו"נ שֶׁהֵם מְקוֹר הַחַיִּים לְכָל הָעוֹלָמוֹת וּבִדְקָדּוּק אֶחָד נִפְסָלִין וּמִסְתַּלְּקִין הַמּוֹחִין

Likewise, in the case of kosher *tefillin*, the supernal *moḥin*, brains, of *Zeir Anpin* and *nukva* are revealed, which are the source of life for all the worlds, but through one particular detail they are invalidated and the *moḥin* depart.

Every mitzva belongs to part of the soul (and body) and part of the world on the one hand, and all of the mitzvot are "limbs of the King," the Holy One blessed be He on the other hand. The "King" from the perspective of the created beings, is the countenance of *Zeir Anpin* (the "small countenance"), the aspect of the countenance of *Ein Sof* above, which is directed toward the worlds, as explained in the kabbalistic sources, while the *nukva* of *Zeir Anpin* is the feminine, receptive side of the Divine that belongs to *Zeir Anpin*, through which the *shefa*, the divine abundance, flows to the worlds.[8] The *tefillin* of above are the *tefillin* that are donned by God, so to speak (see *Berakhot* 6a). A manifestation of *Zeir Anpin*, their function is to direct the flow of the supernal *moḥin* from the cluster of *sefirot* known as Ḥokhma, Bina, and Da'at, and from even higher than that. Just as the limbs of a person draw the vitality of the soul into those limbs – the power of intellect to the brain, or the power of vision to the eye – so too the mitzvot draw forth and connect the divine life force from below to above and from above to below.

The *tefillin* of above and the *tefillin* of below, those which we don, are linked to one another. The same applies to every mitzva: what we do below is performed likewise above. On the deepest level of the mitzva, the *tefillin* below and the *tefillin* above are the very same *tefillin*, but in order for the unification between them to be revealed, for the vitality

---

8. These terms are explained in the writings of the Arizal, in *Pri Etz Ḥayyim, Sha'ar HaTefillin*. See also, e.g., *Derekh Mitzvotekha, Mitzvat Tefillin; Likkutei Torah*, Song. 45a and onward; *Siddur im Divrei Elokim Ḥayyim, Sha'ar HaTefillin*.

to flow in unity, we must, in the only place in all of creation where there may be any opening, close the circuits by fulfilling the mitzva in all of its specific requirements. At that hour, the unity between above and below, between the encompassing and the internal, between the Divine and everything else, is drawn out and revealed.

The phrase "which are the source of life for all the worlds" refers back to the *mohin* that are drawn forth by means of the mitzva of *tefillin*. ☞

The author of the *Tanya* adds that "through one particular detail" of the *halakhot* of *tefillin*, e.g., if a single letter is missing or written incorrectly, or if the boxes of the *tefillin* are not square or the straps are not black, as required, the *tefillin* are invalidated, and in essence they are no longer *tefillin*. At that point the vessel, which drew the *mohin* to the person and all the worlds, has ceased to function. ☞

וּכְהַאי גַּוְונָא בְּדִקְדּוּקֵי מִצְוֹת The same applies to the precise details
'לֹא תַעֲשֶׂה of negative commandments.

"THE SOURCE OF LIFE"

☞ The drawing forth of the *mohin* is man's life. This is both because the light and vitality from beyond (the light of *Ein Sof* enclothed in *Ḥokhma*) are drawn via the *mohin*, and because a person's *mohin* – his consciousness, awareness, capacity to examine situations and make decisions, ability to direct all of his forces of mind and body in accordance with his understanding (so that the mind rules over the heart) – are what make him human. These quali- ties sever him from the mineral, vegetable, and animal entities, in which he exists only in his current state and does not live a true, independent life corresponding to the divine life force. The same applies to human society, which cannot continue to exist if new *mohin* are not constantly drawn to it in order to understand changing situations, to set goals, and arrange all the various details into a single entity and action.

"THEY ARE INVALIDATED AND THE *MOHIN* DEPART"

☞ This consequence is not immediately evident. Although the *tefillin* are invalidated, everything appears to go on as before. The same is true of all the mitzvot, as the flaw is in the interiority of the life force, not in its external aspect. Accordingly, the exterior life ("everything as usual") contin- ues for the time being, but this is not the case for the inner aspect of the life force. For those who are sensitive to this – and there are such individuals – the world has been destroyed, and it is impossible for the situation to continue, since the rectification must be implemented immediately.

In the case of negative commandments, there is no action or element whose omission can render the mitzva unfulfilled. Instead, there is a no less complicated system of actions that are forbidden to perform. Just as positive commandments connect a person's deeds below to all the worlds, so too negative commandments define precisely those actions that if performed in a particular manner will detach the person and that part of the world from the Divine, and sully the world with corruption from one end to the other. ☞

וְהִלְכָּךְ, הַמִּתְבּוֹנֵן מַה גָּדְלוּ מַעֲשֵׂי ה', שֶׁבְּרִיבּוּי הָעוֹלָמוֹת וְכָל צְבָאָם

Therefore, one can reflect on "how great are Your works, Lord," in the proliferation of the worlds and all of their hosts,

The reflection begins, as stated, in the first part of the verse: "How great are Your works." We reflect on what we can observe, on God's actions and the worlds He has created, in their immeasurable size and number.

For them, if the *tefillin* are invalid, a sealed wall has materialized, there is no passage of light and *moḥin*, as is known from the many tales about holy individuals who recognized such things in people who visited them. However, this is true for every person as well; even if he doesn't feel it immediately, if he fails to correct the defect over time, the world will keep changing. This is perceived even by less sensitive people, if only they have eyes that see and a mind which can understand.

"THE PRECISE DETAILS OF NEGATIVE COMMANDMENTS"

☞ On a deeper level, the significance of the negative commandments is not merely whether someone performed them "in accordance with their *halakha*." Rather, in their very existence in the world as actions that may not be done, they draw forth a flow that is even higher than that of a positive commandment. Whereas positive commandments draw forth that which can be perceived in the worlds, both physical and spiritual influences, negative commandments bring down what cannot be perceived in the worlds, which lies beyond conceptions, definitions, and feelings, and which cannot be related to as an entity but at most as that which is beyond entities. Negative commandments thus draw forth the infrastructure for everything that exists, and all the precise details of negative commandments, when they are not performed, sustain the hidden infrastructure upon which man and the world survive. (This idea was partly developed toward the end of the previous essay, and it appears in many other places in the hasidic literature that deal with the negative commandments, such as *Likkutei Torah, Parashat Pekudei*, s.v. "*eleh pekudei HaMishkan*").

This appreciation is not self-evident: a person can live in the world without recognizing these facts. People become habituated, they take things for granted and then the wonders cease to be significant. That is why it is necessary to articulate and meditate on "how great are Your works," as though it has all just been created, and one is seeing it for the first time and marveling.

וְאֵיךְ כּוּלָם בְּטֵלִים בִּמְצִיאוּת לְגַבֵּי דִּקְדּוּק אֶחָד מִדִּקְדּוּקֵי תּוֹרָה, שֶׁהוּא עוֹמֶק מַחֲשָׁבָה הָעֶלְיוֹנָה וְחָכְמָתוֹ יִתְבָּרֵךְ, אֲשֶׁר בְּדִקְדּוּק קַל עוֹלִים כָּל הָעוֹלָמוֹת וּמְקַבְּלִים חַיּוּתָם וְשִׁפְעָם אוֹ לְהֵיפֶךְ חַס וְשָׁלוֹם

and how they are all negated in reality in relation to a single detail of the details of the Torah, which is the depth of the supernal thought and His wisdom, as through a slight detail all the worlds ascend and receive their vitality and flow, or the opposite, God forbid.

The second stage of the reflection is "how profound Your thoughts." We neither see nor understand the thoughts, the supernal wisdom, and therefore, in order to establish the connection, our wonder for the depth of His thoughts, we must observe and marvel at the magnitude of His works. When one reflects that all this immensity and multiplicity is sustained and exists on the basis of "a single detail of the details of the Torah," he will begin to relate to the precise details of the Torah, and, indeed, the Torah as a whole, in a very different manner. When we consider the fact that the Torah in our possession, which we study and fulfill, is the supernal wisdom itself, the wisdom of the Holy One blessed be He who created the worlds, it becomes clear that all of the worlds, in their current state, depend on the precise details of that thought. If the thought were otherwise, all the works would change accordingly.

When one reflects in this manner, the whole perception of the world changes. One's initial view of reality is that there is a large world which maintains a stable existence, and irrespective of that fact, there is also a Torah that certain people follow. However, when one looks at it in the above fashion, that perception is reversed: there is a Torah, which is the deep wisdom of the Creator and leader of the world, and events unfold in accordance with the Torah and this wisdom. This is comparable to a desire one has that is subsequently fulfilled, or a wise perspective with which one sees and comprehends things and then they come into being according to that understanding. The great world is not at all stable in its existence; it changes and is created anew every moment from absolute nothingness, in accordance with the Torah and all of its particulars, as we study and fulfill it.

וּמִזֶּה נִתְבּוֹנֵן גְּדוּלַת עוֹמֶק מַחֲשַׁבְתּוֹ יִתְבָּרֵךְ, שֶׁהוּא בִּבְחִינַת בְּלִי גְבוּל וְתַכְלִית וּמַעֲלָתָה לְאֵין קֵץ וְתַכְלִית עַל מַעֲלוֹת חַיּוּת כָּל הָעוֹלָמוֹת, שֶׁכָּל חַיּוּתָם שׁוֹפֵעַ מִדִּקְדּוּק אֶחָד מִמֶּנָּה

From this we can reflect on the greatness of the depth of His thought, which is unlimited and infinite, and whose quality is endlessly and infinitely superior to the quality of the vitality of all the worlds, as all their vitality flows from one particular detail of it.

The depth of the thought of the Holy One blessed be He according to which the world was created, is greater than the world. If the world God created occupies all limits and measures (because limits and measures are themselves part of the creation), the wisdom with which the world was created extends beyond that limit and purpose of the world.

The "vitality of all the worlds" is a spiritual life force, so that "all their vitality," of the worlds, "flows from one particular detail of" the Torah. The connection between the Torah and the physical world cannot be seen with physical eyes, and therefore one must use his conceptual powers in order to perceive it with the eye of the mind. Every physical entity has a spiritual vitality that constitutes and animates it. When one relates to those spiritual life forces and dimensions, it is easier to proceed to the divine dimension and vitality. If a divine mitzva is performed precisely in accordance with the divine will and wisdom, it will release a stream of will and wisdom, which are the vitality of all the worlds. ☞

"THE DETAILS OF THE TORAH"

☞ What is the meaning of this concept of "the details of the Torah," which the author of the *Tanya* reiterates repeatedly? First, it is necessary to disabuse the reader of the notion that all the lofty ideas he expresses about the Torah apply only to the Torah in general, but not to the details, and especially the seemingly "bothersome" halakhic minutiae. Instead, he emphasizes that all the life of the worlds "flows from one detail..." In addition, there is an inner statement here that has important relevance for the rest of the essay (an "inner statement" is not necessarily a

שֶׁהוּא נִמְשָׁךְ מִמְּקוֹרוֹ, הוּא עוֹמֶק
מַחֲשַׁבְתּוֹ יִתְבָּרֵךְ כְּמוֹ שְׂעַר הָאָדָם
הַנִּמְשָׁךְ מִמּוֹחוֹ עַל דֶּרֶךְ מָשָׁל,
וְכַנּוֹדָע מֵהַתִּיקוּנִים וְהָאִידְּרָא רַבָּא

For it draws from its source, which is the depth of His thought, like the hair of a person that is drawn from his brain, metaphorically speaking, and as is known from the *Tikkunim* and *Idra Rabba*.

Every particular detail of the Torah, even of it seems like something ordinary that does not display any profound wisdom, actually flows from the depth of the divine wisdom, as explained above.

The *Tikkunim* (*Tikkunei Zohar*) and *Idra Rabba* (a section of the *Zohar*, from *Parashat Naso*) explain that the revelations of the Torah, of the Divine in the world, are like hairs drawn from the brain. A hair contains vitality from the brain, but it is so limited that it cannot be seen, and certainly one is unable to perceive its source. However, for this very reason the hair can transfer the vitality of the intellect to places that are so distant that they are no longer intellect at all, and yet the hair reaches there as well. ☞

Up to this point, the essay has discussed the superiority of the Torah in relation to the worlds. Although it is above the worlds, it is related to and refers to them; it is higher than the worlds, but it constitutes them and all of their greatness. Now, in the second part of the essay, the author of the *Tanya* will talk about the true virtue of the Torah,

more abstract formulation, but rather a statement that explains the thing itself, in terms of its own purpose, not as a means for something else). A particular detail involves a double message, both a positive and a negative one. It is not merely a positive statement alone, that one should "do such-and-such," but also a qualification: "Act in this manner, and not otherwise." These restrictions of "Do this," although they appear to be limitations, are indicative of the weighty nature of the statement. To take a mundane example, when a doctor says, "Do this and don't do that," his instruction is clearly serious, as opposed to when he simply says, "Do this," which is a casual general statement that doesn't amount to anything real. Beyond that, a statement that includes both a "yes" and a "no" bears within it something of the object itself, not just a certain manifestation of it. For, as explained earlier, the "yes" discloses what can be revealed to its audience in accordance with their intelligence and status, while the "no" reveals what cannot be exposed to them, because it lies beyond their understanding. In this sense, it is the particulars themselves, which contain both a "yes" and a "no," that convey something real (even if not in an explicit manner) about the entity that cannot be grasped with our understanding and intellect.

which does not refer at all to the worlds created by God, but only to the Holy One blessed be He Himself.

וְזֹאת הָיְתָה שִׂמְחַת דָּוִד הַמֶּלֶךְ עָלָיו הַשָּׁלוֹם, שֶׁהָיָה מְזַמֵּר וּמְרַנֵּן לְשַׂמֵּחַ לִבּוֹ בְּעֵסֶק הַתּוֹרָה בְּעֵת צָרָתוֹ

This was the joy of King David, may he rest in peace, as he would sing and chant to gladden his heart in the engagement of the Torah at his time of trouble.

15 Kislev

15 Kislev (leap year)

That is, this superior quality of the Torah, which is such that all the worlds are nullified in favor of a single of its particulars, "was the joy of King David." When King David was troubled by the affairs of this world, when he was persecuted by his enemies and he did not have "this world" in which to rejoice, he would gladden himself by engaging in the Torah. When he reflected and sensed that all the worlds are negated by the Torah in which he was occupied, as explained above, he could rejoice in this fact, even though externally he was still involved in a time of trouble.

אַךְ מַה שֶׁהָיָה מִשְׁתַּבֵּחַ בִּתְהִלַּת הַתּוֹרָה בְּמַעֲלָתָהּ זוֹ, וְאָמַר "זְמִרוֹת הָיוּ לִי כוּ'" (תהלים קיט,נד) נֶעֱנַשׁ עַל זֶה

However, when he glorified himself in the praise of the Torah for this quality, declaring, "Your statutes were songs to me..." (Ps. 119:54), he was punished for that,

---

HAIRS

☞ It is explained in many hasidic sources (see, e.g., *Likkutei Torah*, Num. 30c and onward, *Torah Or* 82b) that the analogy of hairs drawn from the brain serves to explain the apparently impossible flow from the encompassing to the encompassed, from *Ein Sof* to the limited boundary. A hair is not like all the other limbs of the body. In fact, it is not a limb at all, as one can cut it off without the person feeling anything. And yet it emerges from the brain itself and contains a certain vitality, since it grows and changes. Similarly in the case at hand, the "hair" carries with it a certain content, but it itself is not connected in any visible way to the source, and therefore it can extend beyond its domain. A more abstract metaphor has also been suggested in this regard (see *Torah Or*, ibid.): The hair is like the letters of speech, which convey an idea from one person to another. The letters are not the speaker's idea itself, because that idea could theoretically be explained with other letters as well, and yet the influence of the idea passes by means of and through those letters.

As long as he rejoiced in his study of the Torah, this was not a problem. On the contrary, a person should be happy and rejoice as much as he can, and if he is able to do this while engaging in the Torah, this is all to the good. The trouble begins when one turns his joy in the Torah into a praise of the Torah itself, that this is his relationship to the Torah, in its quality as "songs to me in the house of my sojourning."

וְאָמַר לוֹ הקב״ה: זְמִירוֹת קָרֵית   and the Holy One blessed be He said
לְהוּ   to him: You call them songs?

You dare to call this Torah, which is the deep wisdom of the Holy One blessed be He Himself, mere songs? That is, not the wisdom we receive and not what all the higher worlds and angels can attain, but God's own, inner wisdom, in relation to which all the worlds are considered external – is that what you, David, call songs? Do you rejoice in that, by making it an externality for something else? ☞

The divine will is His self-expression, like the highest desire in the soul that expresses what lies beyond the wisdom of the soul and beyond

"YOU CALL THEM SONGS?"

☞ This point is further developed elsewhere (*Derekh Mitzvotekha, Mitzvat Masa HaAron BaKatef*), and some of those ideas will be cited later in this essay as well. David declared, "Your statutes have been my songs." Statutes are those mitzvot for which we can perceive no discernible reason, and therefore we observe them only because they are the will of God. In truth, every mitzva has certain features of a statute, since beyond any reason that can be given for it, a mitzva is the will of God and that is why we perform it. From this perspective, there is actually no difference between the mitzvot. While each mitzva represents a different will, in relation to the novelty and wonder in the very fact that we are fulfilling the will of God there is no difference between one will and another. However, this wonder is that of a person looking from the outside at what he is doing, and in this sense, it is external with

respect to the act itself. When David says, "Your statutes have been my songs," he is expressing, notwithstanding all the beauty and holiness in his statement, the same "external" reference point, that these statutes are like songs for him. One sings a tune repeatedly, each time enjoying the same musical phrases, which is not the case for phrases of speech. It makes no sense to repeat the same sentence over and over again. After we have understood what was said, there is no point in reiterating it. It is only when looking at the external wrapper, namely that all the mitzvot are God's will, without referring to the specific content of each mitzva, that the Torah is like a song. This is not a trivial point; it is a true and exalted reference to the Torah and its commandments. However, God expects more than that from King David, "David My servant."

what it loves: the soul itself, when it desires not for an external reason but due to its very nature. Nevertheless, the will invariably refers to the external; it is expressed in the soul's desire and relation toward something that is external to it. However, the soul itself also has an inner expression, which is the power of pleasure. Like will, pleasure is also an expression of the soul itself, but this pleasure relates inward, for it is the pleasure of the soul in its essence. This is what the Holy One blessed be He said to David: Are you calling them songs? Are you treating them as a will without a reason? I would expect you to relate to the lofty, inner side, to the divine pleasure of a mitzva, a pleasure that distinguishes between the particulars of every mitzva, each of which has a different reason. It is true that David cannot comprehend the reasons for the statutes, but this is not about David's powers of reasoning or those of anybody else, but rather the reason that God Himself receives from the mitzvot, as it were, such that a person who attains the nullification of his entire reality can, by means of this negation, also relate to this level of the reason and pleasure within the Divine.

מִשּׁוּם שֶׁבֶּאֱמֶת מַעֲלָתָהּ זוֹ, שֶׁכָּל הָעוֹלָמוֹת בְּטֵלִים לְגַבֵּי דִּקְדּוּק אֶחָד מִמֶּנָּה, הִיא מִבְּחִינַת אֲחוֹרַיִים שֶׁל עוֹמֶק הַמַּחֲשָׁבָה

Because truly that virtue, in relation to a single **one of whose details all the worlds are negated, is considered the "back side" of the depth of the thought,**

The virtue of the Torah in comparison to all the worlds is not an internal merit of the Torah itself, but only its external reference to the worlds. We marvel at the fact that all the worlds are subsumed in the Torah because we can see the worlds and appreciate their greatness, and through this admiration we also appreciate the Torah. However, this is of course not an evaluation of the Torah, nor even of its relation to the worlds, but rather of the worlds' relationship toward the Torah. ☞

"ALL THE WORLDS ARE NEGATED"

☞ This can be compared to a small child who has no idea of how great his rabbi is; he does not have the words, concepts, or feelings to apprehend his essence. And yet when he sees his father and the whole congregation standing in holy fear before the rabbi, he too will sense something, only his feeling will be related not to the rabbi himself but to what the others are feeling, and this is called the "back side."

כְּמוֹ שֶׁמְבוֹאָר בְּמָקוֹם אַחֵר בְּשֵׁם
הָאֲרִיזַ״ל עַל מַאֲמַר רַבּוֹתֵינוּ ז״ל:
נוֹבְלוֹת חָכְמָה שֶׁלְּמַעְלָה תּוֹרָה

as explained elsewhere in the name
of the Arizal, on our Rabbis' statement: Torah is the withering fruit
of wisdom that emerges **from above.**

"Withering fruit"[9] refers to those fruits that have fallen and are no longer
attached to the tree. The analogy, as discussed elsewhere,[10] in the name
of the Arizal,[11] is that the source of the Torah in our possession is the
supernal wisdom, but like the fruit that has fallen from the tree, the Torah
we comprehend and refer to is likewise not the supernal wisdom as it is
internally, connected and united at its root, but as it relates to the worlds.

אֲבָל פְּנִימִית שֶׁבְּעוֹמֶק, שֶׁהוּא
פְּנִימִית הַתּוֹרָה, הִיא מְיוּחֶדֶת
לְגַמְרֵי בְּאוֹר אֵין סוֹף בָּרוּךְ הוּא
הַמְלוּבָּשׁ בָּהּ בְּתַכְלִית הַיִּחוּד

However, the internal aspect of the
depth, which is the internal aspect
of Torah, is completely united in the
light of *Ein Sof*, blessed be He, which
is enclothed within it in ultimate
union.

The Torah is the interiority of God's thought, so to speak, what He thinks
in His own mind, and therefore it is completely unified within Himself.
Just as for a man, his thought is a garment and a vessel for the soul, so
too in the realm above, a thought is a garment and a vessel for the light
of *Ein Sof*. The more internal the clothing, the more it is connected and
identified with what it covers. Just as thought is more internal than speech,
and is more connected and identified with the mind than speech, the
same relationship exists between an internal and a more external thought.
The Torah, which is the interiority of the interiority of the supernal
thought, and not merely "withering fruit" as we perceive it below, is the
innermost garment, united by the light of *Ein Sof* that it enclothes.

וּלְגַבֵּי אֵין סוֹף בָּרוּךְ הוּא כָּל
הָעוֹלָמוֹת כְּלֹא מַמָּשׁ וְאַיִן וָאָפֶס

And in relation to *Ein Sof*, blessed be
He, all the worlds are insubstantial

9. *Bereshit Rabba* 17:5, 44:17.
10. Note of the Lubavitcher Rebbe: "See *Iggeret HaKodesh*, epistle 19."
11. In *Iggeret HaKodesh*, epistle 19, the author of the *Tanya* references the Arizal's *Likkutei Torah, Parashat Ki Tisa* and *Sha'ar HaNevua*. Explicit reference to this section is found elsewhere in the writings of the Arizal, such as *Pri Etz Ḥayyim, Sha'ar Keriat HaTorah*, chap. 1; *Likkutei Torah, Parashat Zot HaBerakha*; and others.

מַמָּשׁ, כִּי "אַתָּה הוּא עַד שֶׁלֹּא נִבְרָא הָעוֹלָם וכו'" and literally nothingness, for "You are He, before the world was created…"

This phrase appears in the prayer book: "You are He, before the world was created; You are He, after the world was created."[12] If the worlds are not considered to be anything in relation to God, but "are insubstantial and literally nothingness," then the creation of the world did not change anything with respect to God Himself: as He was before the world was created, so He remains after it was created, without any change at all. The negation of the worlds is absolute; they are not just smaller than Him and of lesser value; they are completely non-existent in reference to the light of *Ein Sof* itself.

וְהִלְכָּךְ גַּם לִפְנִימִיּוּת הַתּוֹרָה, אֵין לְשַׁבְּחָהּ כְּלָל בִּתְהִלַּת חַיּוּת כָּל הָעוֹלָמוֹת, מֵאַחַר דְּלָא מַמָּשׁ חֲשִׁיבֵי Therefore, the internal aspect of the Torah should also not be praised at all with the praises of the source of vitality of all worlds, for they are considered insubstantial,

Since the Torah in its interiority is truly united in *Ein Sof*, and all the worlds are literally nothingness in relation to *Ein Sof*, they are not considered to be anything, and their existence and life have no meaning in relation to the interiority of the Torah. Therefore, there is also no cause to praise the Torah for its relationship with the worlds. True words of praise must be appropriate for the one who is being praised, as otherwise it is not real, internal praise, but only an external commendation that does not relate to him on his inner level. ☞

THE PRAISES OF THE VITALITY OF ALL WORLDS, WHICH ARE CONSIDERED INSUBSTANTIAL

☞ Not only is praise of this kind not true praise, it can actually be considered a slight to the object of the praise. The Talmud (*Berakhot* 33b) relates that a man stepped forward to serve as prayer leader in the presence of Rabbi Ḥanina, and began by declaring: "God, the great, mighty, awesome, powerful, mighty, awe-inspiring, strong, fearless, steadfast, and honored." Rabbi Ḥanina waited for him to finish and then rebuked him: "Have you concluded all of the praises of your Master? We have

---

12. Based on *Tanna deVei Eliyahu Rabba* 24; start of *Yalkut Shimoni* 836, and several other sources.

וּבִבְחִינַת פְּנִימִיּוּתָהּ, אֵינָהּ שִׂמְחַת
לְבַב אֱנוֹשׁ וְשַׁעֲשׁוּעָיו, אֶלָּא כִּבְיָכוֹל
שִׂמְחַת לֵב וְשַׁעֲשׁוּעַ הַמֶּלֶךְ הקב״ה
שֶׁמִּשְׁתַּעֲשֵׁעַ בָּהּ

and with respect to its interior aspect, it is not the joy of man's heart and his delight, but rather, as it were, the heart's joy and the delight of the King, the Holy One blessed be He who delights in it.

David took delight in the externality of the Torah, but in its inner level the Torah is not the joy of the human heart, but the joy of the heart of God alone. A person can be happy, frolic, and take delight in the Torah when it relates in some way to the structure of his soul, when he understands and senses something, if not in the Torah itself then at least in the wonder of what he can grasp, the world and everything it contains. However, he cannot rejoice or delight in the internalities of the Torah, which cannot be compared at all to anything with which he is familiar. The internality of the Torah is the inner thought of God in His own mind, as stated, on a more interior level than His relationship toward everything else, and therefore it is the joy of God's heart and the delight of God[13] alone.

כִּי אֱלֹקִים הֵבִין דַּרְכָּהּ וְיָדַע מְקוֹמָהּ
וּמַעֲלָתָהּ בִּידִיעַת עַצְמוֹ כִּבְיָכוֹל

For God understands its way and He knows its place and its quality, through His knowledge of Himself, as it were,

The garment of the Torah is so internal that understanding and knowing it is like knowing God Himself, so to speak, which He alone knows. Therefore, only God understands the way of the Torah (where it goes), its place[14] (from where it comes), and its individual quality, through His knowledge of Himself.

only three ('great, mighty, and awesome'), and had Moses our teacher not said them in the Torah and had the members of the Great Assembly not incorporated them into the prayer, we would not be allowed to recite them either." He proceeded to compare this to a king who possessed many thousands of golden dinars, and yet he was praised for having silver coins. Wouldn't that be regarded as an insult?

13. This expression is derived from the verse cited below, and from a statement of the Rabbis in *Shabbat* 89a and elsewhere: "You have a hidden treasure in which You delight every day."

14. Based on Job 28:23. The expression that immediately follows, "It is concealed

אֲבָל נֶעְלְמָה מֵעֵינֵי כָל חַי, כְּמוֹ שֶׁכָּתוּב: "וּפָנַי לֹא יֵרָאוּ" (שמות לג,כג), דְּהַיְינוּ בְּחִינַת פְּנִימִיּוּתָה, כְּמוֹ שֶׁכָּתוּב שָׁם (אגרת הקדש סימן יט) בְּשֵׁם הָאֲרִ"י ז"ל

but it is concealed from the eyes of all living beings, as it is written: "But My face will not be seen" (Ex. 33:23), meaning its internal aspect, as is written there (*Iggeret HaKodesh*, epistle 19) in the name of the Arizal.

This essential concealment of the Torah, like that of God Himself, is of the "internal aspect." The internality of the Torah, the Torah as it is with God, as it is itself, is not within the comprehension of even our teacher Moses.

וְזֶה שֶׁאוֹמֵר הַכָּתוּב: "וָאֶהְיֶה אֶצְלוֹ כו' שַׁעֲשׁוּעִים" (משלי ח,ל) 'אֶצְלוֹ' דַּוְקָא, "מְשַׂחֶקֶת לְפָנָיו" (שם) - 'לְפָנָיו' דַּוְקָא, דְּהַיְינוּ בִּבְחִינַת פְּנִימִיּוּתָה

This is the meaning of the verse" "I was with Him … a delight" (Prov. 8:30) – "with Him" is meant specifically; "playing before Him" – "before Him" is meant specifically, that is, its internal aspect.

The full verse reads: "I was with Him, as a protégé; I was a delight." The author of the *Tanya* infers that "with Him" is meant specifically, that is, the Torah is a delight only for God, not humans.

וְעַל זֶה אָמַר: "וָאֶהְיֶה אֶצְלוֹ אָמוֹן" - אַל תִּקְרֵי אָמוֹן אֶלָּא אוֹמֵן כו'

And with regard to this it says: "I was with Him, as a protégé [*amon*]" (Prov. 8:30); do not read *amon* but rather *omen* …

This is referring to the interiority of the Torah, that it was like an artisan [*omen*] with God.[15] It is further stated at the beginning of *Bereshit Rabba*: "*Amon* means pedagogue … *amon* means hidden." On this level, the Torah is like the Holy One blessed be He Himself, when

---

from the eyes of all living beings," is from verse 21.

15. *Tanḥuma, Bereshit* 1, and in several places in the *Zohar* (e.g., 1:134b, 2:161a). This saying also appears in a slightly different form in *Bereshit Rabba* 1:1.

He acts solely as a giver[16] and sustainer, not as one who receives or is comprehended in any manner. ☞

וְעַל בְּחִינַת אֲחוֹרַיִים אָמַר:
"מְשַׂחֶקֶת בְּתֵבֵל אַרְצוֹ וְשַׁעֲשׁוּעַי
אֶת בְּנֵי אָדָם" (משלי ח,לא)

And with regard to the "back side" it says: "Playing in the world of His earth, and my delights are with the sons of man" (Prov. 8:31).

In contrast to the interior aspect which is not grasped and which does not refer to the worlds, the "back side" does relate to the worlds, as the author of the *Tanya* earlier mentioned that all the worlds are negated in relation to any particular halakhic detail. This is the meaning of the phrase "playing in the world of His earth," that this reflection provides joy and delight for a person, when he maintains his focus on the Torah even when he is troubled by the affairs of the world.

כִּי הַתּוֹרָה נִתְּנָה בִּבְחִינַת פָּנִים
וְאָחוֹר, כְּדִכְתִיב בִּמְגִילָה עָפָה
דִּזְכַרְיָה: "וְהִיא כְּתוּבָה פָּנִים
וְאָחוֹר"

For the Torah was given in the form of "front and back," as is written with regard to Zechariah's flying scroll: "And it was written front and back."

Our Rabbis explained that this scroll, which was "written front and back,"[17] is the Torah that was given at Sinai, as it has both a front and a back: its front, interiority, is in God's inner thought, in His

AMON – HIS ARTISAN TOOLS

☞ Another meaning of *amon*, which is also mentioned in the midrash there, is God's artisan tools [*kli umanuto*]. God creates and makes all the worlds, and His artisan tool, the instrument with which

He performs the work, is the Torah. The meaning is the same: the Torah and God are alone on one side, the internal side, while all of the worlds are on the other side.

---

16. As explained in several places in the hasidic sources (see *Torat Menaḥem* 8, p. 14), "*Amon* means pedagogue" in relation to the revealed Torah, which provides its influence openly, while "*Amon* means hidden" in reference to the interiority and esoteric teachings of the Torah.

17. Ezek. 2:9. See Zech. 5:1 and Rashi there, who explains, based on *Eiruvin* 21a,

understanding and the joy of His heart alone; and its back, exteriority, is its relationship with our worlds and ourselves, our understanding and the way in which we fulfill it.

The most significant part of this statement is that the Torah was given to us in the form of "front" as well. In interpersonal relationships, when one teaches his friend wisdom, he delivers only the exterior. Whatever the listener manages to understand, what relates to him and his world, that is what he receives, whereas the interiority of the wisdom necessarily remains with the giver, since he cannot convey the depth and subtleties of his understanding and feeling as they are within himself. It might have been thought that if this is the case between human beings, all the more so between man and God, whose interiority is immeasurably higher than man's, and He gave us the Torah only in the form of "back," not "front." ☞

"THE TORAH WAS GIVEN IN THE FORM OF FRONT AND BACK"

☞ This statement has different meanings from two different perspectives. First, from God's perspective: a giving of interiority also means an inner giving, that is, not only the giving of a thing (an object or intelligence) for a specific need, but like a person giving to one whom he truly loves, such that he would actually desire nothing more than to give his very self, and everything that he gives in practice is nothing more than a means and a clothing for the inner gift, which is himself. One act of giving is for the needs of the recipient, and that will always be a giving of externality, whereas another act of giving emerges from the needs of the giver, especially when the desire and need are internal, in which case it will be the most internal giving of all. Accordingly, the statement that the Torah was given "front and back" means that the To-

rah is an internal giving by God, that He gives us Himself, as it were. This is in the vein of the well-known interpretation of the Ba'al Shem Tov (see *Degel Mahaneh Efrayim, Parashat Yitro*, s.v. "*veyesh bazeh*"; *Parashat Ki Tisa*, s.v., "*vehamikhtav*") on the rabbinic saying (*Shabbat* 105a) that the word *anokhi* ["I am," the first word of the Ten Commandments] is an acronym for *ana nafshi ketivat yehavit* ["I, Myself, wrote, gave"]. The plain meaning of this phrase (as Rashi states there) is "I Myself wrote and gave the Torah," whereas the Ba'al Shem Tov explains: "I wrote and gave Myself" (see a similar idea in the name of Rabbi Shneur Zalman in *Likkutei Torah*, Num. 44d, and in many places in the writings of the author of the *Tanya*). God gives by means of these words, with this wisdom and these mitzvot, through which we attain a unity that is unparalleled in

___
that the scroll Zechariah saw is the very same scroll of Ezekiel, and that it was the Torah.

וּלְפִי שֶׁתָּפַס דָּוִד בִּבְחִינַת אֲחוֹרַיִים,
לְכָךְ נֶעֱנַשׁ בִּשְׁכְחָה הַבָּאָה מִן
בְּחִינַת אֲחוֹרַיִים וְנֶעֱלַם מִמֶּנּוּ לְפִי
שָׁעָה מַה שֶּׁכָּתוּב: "עֲבוֹדַת הַקֹּדֶשׁ
עֲלֵיהֶם בַּכָּתֵף יִשָּׂאוּ" (במדבר ז,ט)

Because David grasped hold of the "back side" aspect, he was therefore punished with the forgetfulness that comes from the "back side" aspect, and he temporarily overlooked the verse: "The sacred service is upon them; they shall bear on the shoulder" (Num. 7:9)

our world (as explained in *Likkutei Amarim*, chap. 5), a unity with God Himself.

The other perspective is that of man. If God also gave us the interiority of the Torah, as it is with Him alone, this means that we have a share in it, that there is something we can and should do with it within our souls and in our world. What is this addition that we can do, beyond our best efforts (each in accordance with his ability) to study the Torah, perform the mitzvot, and in the service of God, more than cleaving to Him in every act, speech, and thought, with our utmost strength? In several places in the hasidic sources (see *Likkutei Amarim*, chap. 10, and elsewhere; and in *Hemshekh Ayin Bet* 5672 [1912], vol. 1, p. 346 and onward, where this issue is discussed in the context of our essay), it is said in different ways that beyond all of those factors there is a higher dimension in the service of God, in which the great change is the shift of the center of gravity from man to God. When a person no longer refers to his own work and the purification of his soul, his love and fear, ascent and devotion, but solely to the Holy One blessed be He a transition has occurred onto another rung of the ladder, to another plane of life where everything looks different. It can be said that his "self" has transferred from him (in all levels, up to the highest and most abstract) to the Almighty Himself. At that stage, he does not "make

his heart rejoice," not with love and fear, nor even with the study of the Torah and mitzvot. Rather, he no longer has a heart of his own at all but exists, even if not he cannot sense this, in the joy of God's heart, in God's delight in the interiority of the Torah, as explained above.

It is true that such a share in the interiority of the Torah is a distinctive quality that only unique individuals (or an ordinary person at a special time for him) can attain, and only a few "men of ascent" (see *Likkutei Amarim*, ibid.) can live their lives in this manner. Nevertheless, since the Torah was given "front and back," and the Torah is one (not two, with one Torah being the "front" and the other the "back"), this means that no matter how a person holds the Torah, he is also holding its interior. Since we know that the Torah has an interior, and since we know that it too was given to us, the ideas are interpreted in such a manner that reflects their interiority. Whatever I saw and sensed, whatever I did without feeling, perhaps from one perspective and interpretation they can be instructive of nothing, of flights of the imagination or dead ends, and yet from a different perspective they inform us that this is the interiority of the Torah, which we know is present there. For example, when a person fulfills the mitzvot (including Torah study) by simply accepting the yoke of Heaven, not in order to ascend

This occurred when David rejoiced in the quality of the Torah, in the endless vitality of the worlds that flows from a single particular of it, which he called "songs." It is known[18] that forgetfulness comes from the "back side," as we see that a person can forget what is not important to him, what is only secondary and "back side," whereas he will not forget anything that is deemed vital to him and essential to his existence, upon which his life depends.[19] The cited verse from Numbers teaches that the Holy Ark must be carried on the shoulders, not on a wagon, as David did.[20] ☞

לְחַבֵּר וּלְיַחֵד אֶת הַכְּתֵפַיִם, שֶׁהֵן בְּחִינַת אֲחוֹרַיִים, אֶל 'עֲבוֹדַת הַקֹּדֶשׁ' הִיא חָכְמָה עִילָאָה בִּבְחִינַת פְּנִים, שֶׁמִּשָּׁם נִמְשְׁכוּ הַלּוּחוֹת שֶׁבָּאָרוֹן

to join and unify the shoulders, which are the "back side" aspect, to "the sacred service," the supernal *Ḥokhma*, in a form of internality. For the tablets in the ark were drawn from there,

and become this type of person and attain any particular achievement, but because God commanded it, because it is His will, this can be interpreted in all kinds of ways, but once we know that the Torah was given to us "front and back," we understand that this is its internality.

"PUNISHED WITH THE FORGETFULNESS"

☞ The ensuing event, the death of Uzza, resulted from the punishment, but the punishment itself was the forgetfulness, and not just any loss of memory, but a failure to remember a matter that was precisely related to David's "lapse." This is an internal perception of punishment, that it is not something separate from the sin but merely an expression, from another angle, of the sin itself. Even Gehenna is nothing more than a person's perception and sense of the sin he has committed, with the evil he committed tormenting him (as it is stated in Jeremiah 2:19: "Your own evildoing will chastise you, and your deviations shall reprove you"). This is especially true here, where the sin is particularly subtle. The punishment is likewise, but of such a nature that one can see the sin within it. Such a punishment, when a person receives it properly, knowingly, and with the appropriate feeling, is already the beginning of his rectification, as is indeed described in the continuation of the biblical account.

---

18. See *Notes on Lamentations*, p. 33 (by the *Tzemaḥ Tzedek*, later printed in *Or HaTorah* on the Prophets and Writings, vol. 2, p. 1085 – from a note of the Lubavitcher Rebbe that appears elsewhere).

19. See *Iggeret HaKodesh*, epistle 4.

20. See the discussion in *Sota* 35a.

Here the author of the *Tanya* explains why the Ark must be carried on the shoulders. The internal reason for this mitzva of bearing the Ark on one's shoulders is the unification of the "front" and "back." The shoulders are the bodily expression of the "back side"[21] with which the "sacred service" is performed. This is a service that is separate from us, which belongs not to us but to the interiority of God's Torah that belongs to Him alone, and that is the bearing of the Ark and the Tablets that are inside it.

The Ark, and the Torah inside the Ark, inscribed on the Tablets of the Covenant, are the expression in this world of that inner Torah. The Ark was placed in the Holy of Holies in the Temple, in the innermost place of all the worlds, in the interiority of the Land of Israel, the interiority of Jerusalem and the Temple, in the Holy of Holies and within the Ark itself. No man enters that inner place, the place of the Divine Presence alone, where the Tablets, the inner parts of the Torah, are located, as will be explained.

כְּמוֹ שֶׁכָּתוּב: "כְּתוּבִים מִשְּׁנֵי   as it is written: "Inscribed on both
עֶבְרֵיהֶם כו'" (שמות לב,טו)   their sides…" (Ex. 32:15),

Various interpretations have been offered for this verse. Based on Rashi's commentary, it seems that the letters were miraculously engraved from one side of the Tablets to the other, such that they could be read from both sides.[22]

וּכְמוֹ שֶׁכָּתוּב בִּירוּשַׁלְמִי דִּשְׁקָלִים   and as is written in the Jerusalem
(פרק ו הלכה א) שֶׁלֹּא הָיְתָה בָּהֶן   Talmud, *Shekalim* (6:1), that they
בְּחִינַת פָּנִים וְאָחוֹר, עַיֵּין שָׁם   did not have a front and back; see
there.

The interpretation of the Jerusalem Talmud is even more far-reaching. It states: "'From this side and from that side they were inscribed' (Ex. 32:15) – *tatroga*." In Greek, *tatroga* means a square, or a cube (*Korban*

---

21. This is always the case in the hasidic sources; see, e.g., *Torah Or*, 102a, s.v. "*va'ani natati Lekha shekhem eḥad.*"

22. See also the Responsa of the Radbaz, vol. 3, 549.

HaEda there). In other words, the text could be read not only from two sides, but actually from all four sides.

Our world was created in such a manner that it and everything within it has a "front" and "back." There is no reality in the world of a "front" without a "back." Since the Tablets are read from all sides, that is, all its sides were "front," meaning that the letters could be read from each side, the Tablets were thus not a separate "creation," unlike anything in this world. This absolute interiority, the "physical state" of the Tablets, reflects the interiority of the Torah (which was written on the Tablets), as discussed in this essay. It was not an interiority in relation to a specific externality, that is, a more internal explanation of something that is explicitly understood, but an internality that is entirely separate from any external observation, from any reference to the world, the intellect, and worldly concepts. This interiority belongs to God Himself; it is between Him and Himself, as stated.

According to the punishment, we can understand the nature of the "sin." The sin was not that David failed to recognize the existence of such an internality of the Torah, but that he did not connect it to the "back side." After all, we cannot do anything with respect to the interiority of the Torah itself. We cannot refer to it at all, since it is by definition "unavailable" to us. What we can do is to connect the "back side," which is the focus of our engagement, to the interiority, and this is "the sacred service is upon them; they shall bear on the shoulder." The service as regards the sacred, the distinct interiority of the Torah, is to connect to it and to unify with it the "back side," that is, the way in which we relate to the Torah and fulfill it in our world.

In this essay, the author of the *Tanya* delved into the stage of the practical fulfillment of God's will, how we achieve the connection of "they shall bear on the shoulder" in our lives, through our Torah and mitzvot. The *Tzemaḥ Tzedek* mentions this issue in his discourse *Masa HaAron BaKatef* (at the end of that discourse, in *Derekh Mitzvotekha*, p. 44b), where he states that an analogous kind of connection exists in the life of each person himself. This is the connection between the power of pleasure and the power of simple will in one's soul, since he should direct the power of pleasure solely to the Torah and its mitzvot, whereas the power of simple will, which he should perform without reason at all, he should direct toward the affairs of the world as a whole. One who lives in this manner thereby absorbs into his life, into this "back side," which is his activity in the world, the interiority that is beyond his personal powers, namely the interiority of the Torah as only God Himself, as it were, senses and takes delight in.

This essay, however, does not analyze that stage, since its entire purpose is to sing the praises of the Torah itself, as stated. This is a praise that goes beyond all praises: Know that there is an inner self to the Torah that you cannot attain and you are unable to sense, and everything you achieve and feel will always be the "back side." You should further know, with respect to everything you do, study, and attain, that there is an internality to this Torah you study and comprehend, which reaches down to the very essence and self of God. And this is what Rabbi Shneur Zalman would always request, as he could be heard chanting in his devotion: "I do not desire Your Garden of Eden; I do not desire Your World to Come; I desire only You" (as cited in the *Tzemah Tzedek's Derekh Mitzvotekha, Shoresh Mitzvat HaTefilla*, chap. 40 [138a], and also transcribed in *HaYom Yom*, 18 Kislev; see also *Sefer HaMa'amarim Melukat*, vol. 3, p. 144, and onward).

Essay 7
"And Charity Like a Constant River"

THIS ESSAY, AND ALL OF THE SUBSEQUENT ESSAYS OF *Kuntres Aḥaron*, are not essays but epistles, much like those found in *Iggeret HaKodesh*. Like many of the epistles in *Iggeret HaKodesh*, this one is concerned with galvanizing the hasidim to give charity.

Like the epistles of *Iggeret HaKodesh*, here too, only the general, theoretical sections of the original epistle were printed in the *Tanya*, while the passages relating to the particular time and place in which it was written were omitted. To complete the picture, we have included, in an appendix at the end of this chapter, the epistle's unpublished ending. This concluding section contains an entreaty to the hasidim, and a record of the particular needs and difficulties that prompted the author of the *Tanya* to write this epistle.

Nonetheless, the section of the epistle that is printed in the *Tanya* is, for all intents and purposes, a hasidic discourse. In fact, it even parallels certain other hasidic discourses.[1] Its subject, which links it to the previous essay of *Kuntres Aḥaron*, is the flow of God's inner essence to the inner aspect

---

1. See *Likkutei Torah*, Deut. 18a and onward; *Ma'amar Amar Rabbi Yehoshua ben Levi BeKhol Yom*, 5688, of the sixth Lubavitcher Rebbe, Rabbi Yosef Yitzḥak Schneerson (cited by the Lubavitcher Rebbe, Rabbi Menaḥem Mendel Schneerson, in *Lessons in Tanya*). See also *Or HaTorah*, Deut., vol. 2, pp. 635, 662; *Sefer HaMa'amarim* 5633, vol. 2, p. 448.

of the heart, which is the innermost point in the human being. The essay begins by discussing the nature of this flow and the way in which it illuminates the inner aspect of the heart. However, the main body of the essay, which addresses its practical purpose, delineates what each of us, in our own unique circumstances, can do to awaken and reveal this flow of inner essence.

As he does in a number of his other discourses, the author of the *Tanya* opens this essay with a verse that will serve as its motto.

16 Kislev

16 Kislev
(leap year)

"וּצְדָקָה כְּנַחַל אֵיתָן" (בְּעָמוֹס   **"And charity like a constant** [*eitan*]
סוֹף סִימָן ה' פָּסוּק כד)   **river" (in Amos, end of chapter 5,** verse
    24).

This verse juxtaposes charity with a "constant river." At first glance, these terms seem completely unrelated to each other. This essay of *Kuntres Aḥaron* is concerned with understanding the connection between them.

פֵּירוּשׁ: כְּמוֹ שֶׁנַּחַל אֵיתָן הוּא   This means: Like an *eitan* river, which
הַמְשָׁכָה הַנִּמְשֶׁכֶת מִבְּחִינַת   is a flow that flows from the aspect of
אֵיתָן'   *eitan* ["constant; firm"],

First, the author of the *Tanya* discusses the concept of an "*eitan* river," in the spiritual sense rather than the physical. A river is a drawing forth. In the physical world, for example, water emerges and flows as a river. The river that is "*eitan*" is one whose flow possesses the aspect of *eitan*, meaning that it is strong, stable, and unchanging.[2] This is a reference to the source of the flow, which is the essence and origin of all revelations and flows. This essence itself is immutable.

In kabbalistic terms, the "*eitan* river" is the manifestation and illumination of *Ḥokhma* (Wisdom) in *Bina* (Understanding): *Eitan* is *Ḥokhma* and the river is *Bina*. Similarly, wisdom is the source of every

---

2. See *Sefer HaMa'amarim* 5703, pp. 71 and onward, which enumerates, based on verses from *Tanakh*, three different aspects of the term *eitan*: power, rigidity, and age.

manifestation and flow in the human soul. This is because wisdom receives the flow of the soul's essence, which is on a higher level than all of the soul's various manifestations. Furthermore, the lights of wisdom are revealed within the soul by means of the attribute of understanding. Through understanding, these lights expand and flow into all of the soul's faculties, attributes, and garments.

שֶׁהִיא בְּחִינַת 'נְקוּדָה בְּהֵיכְלָא',	which is an expression of "a point in
וּ'תְרֵין רֵיעִין וכו'"	the sanctum," and "two spouses…"

The "eitan river" is equated with two expressions used in the Zohar to refer to the union of Hokhma and Bina. Just like wisdom in the human soul, Hokhma is a "point," a flash of light that is lacking any dimension, having no length or width. It has reality and meaning only in the "sanctum" of Bina, which absorbs, develops, and reveals the light within its own, defined dimensions. This is the meaning of the expression "a point in the sanctum."[3] Elsewhere, Hokhma and Bina are compared to "two friends who are not separated."[4] They are the two cognitive faculties that have no substance or meaning when separate from each other. Consequently, they always occur together in reality. ☞

NOT SEPARATED

☞ The union of Hokhma and Bina is the source of the worlds' existence. Like the union between male and female, which is the origin of new life in the physical world, the joining of Hokhma and Bina in the world of Atzilut is absolutely essential, since it produces the flow of the worlds' life force and reality. If this union were to be disrupted even for one moment, the worlds would cease to exist. While other unions may be severed, this one is described in Kabbala as the continuous union that ensures the worlds' existence. Consequently, at least from our perspective, the union of Hokhma and Bina is continuous and has remained unbroken since the beginning of the world, because without it there could be no existence. In the formulation of the kabbalistic sources, it is "a continuous union for the existence of the worlds, for there are other unions that are discontinuous, and so forth." The second Lubavitcher Rebbe, Rabbi Dovber Schneuri, interprets the verse "In the beginning, God created" (Gen. 1:1) in this light: "'In the beginning' refers to Hokhma, and 'God' refers to Bina" (Peirush HaMilot 93c).

---

3. See, for example, Zohar 1:20a.
4. See, for example, Zohar 3:4a.

וְאוֹתִיּוֹת 'אֵיתָן' מְשַׁמְּשׁוֹת לֶעָתִיד   Each of **the letters of** *eitan* **are used to** indicate **the future tense,**

Every future-tense verb in the Hebrew language begins with one of the four letters of the word *eitan*: *alef, yod, tav,* or *nun*. Accordingly, the word *eitan* contains an allusion to the World to Come.

פֵּירוּשׁ 'אֲנָא עָתִיד לְאִתְגַּלְיָא' כְּמוֹ   meaning "I will reveal myself in the
שֶׁכָּתוּב: "הִנֵּה יַשְׂכִּיל עַבְדִּי וְגו'"   future," as it is written: "Behold, My
(ישעיה נב,יג)   servant will succeed ..." (Isa. 52:13).

The most significant difference between this world and the World to Come is that in this world, we act but do not see the results of our actions, whereas in the World to Come, we will see them clearly. In other words, the World to Come will be an era of revelation, namely the revelation that ensues from our labor. Therefore, it belongs only to the World to Come, the stage that comes after we have toiled, when everything that was previously concealed will be revealed.[5]

The verse cited here depicts the Messiah, who will reign in the World to Come.[6] It illustrates the fact that the level of revelation in that era will surpass all previous revelations.[7]

וְהַיְינוּ שֶׁיִּתְגַּלֶּה אָז אוֹר אֵין סוֹף   **That is, the light of** *Ein Sof,* **blessed**
בָּרוּךְ הוּא וְיִחוּדוֹ יִתְבָּרַךְ תּוֹךְ   **be He, and His unity, will then be**
פְּנִימִית נְקוּדַּת הַלֵּב   **revealed within the internality of the point of the heart,**

---

5. The concept of "I will reveal myself in the future" is found in the *Zohar* (3:11a, 3:65b).

6. See *Targum* ad loc.; *Yalkut Shimoni*, Isa. 476.

7. The word *me'od*, "very," in this verse signifies limitlessness. It is also an anagram of "Adam [*alef-dalet-mem*]" (see Rashi ad loc.; *Zohar* 3:246b; *Bereshit Rabba* 8:5). Consequently, it may be inferred from the verse that the Messiah will be on a higher level than that of Adam before the sin, and likewise, revelation in the Messiah's time will be on a higher level than revelation prior to the sin. Elsewhere, *me'od* is interpreted as an acronym for "Moses, Adam, David" (see *Torah Or* 46d). Accordingly, the verse indicates that the revelation received by the Messiah will be higher than the revelations that were received by these three illustrious figures.

The tremendous revelation that is to take place in the World to Come consists of three key stages: The first stage is the revelation of the light of *Ein Sof* in this world. At this stage, we will not yet comprehend the nature, meaning, or impact of the light of *Ein Sof*, but simply the fact that it exists. In other words, the physical realm will no longer be closed off to it. The second stage is the revelation of the fact that the light of *Ein Sof* is "one": It is not made up of a number of lights from various sources. There is only one light, and it encompasses the whole of reality, both the upper and lower realms. The third stage is the revelation of these things within the innermost point of the heart. Since the revelation of the World to Come is a revelation granted to human beings, it has both an external aspect and an inner aspect: Intellectual revelation, the knowledge of reality, is external, while emotional revelation, which is manifested in the heart, is internal. It is a revelation that affects us; it moves us and can even change us. The revelation to the innermost point of the heart is very deep, to the core of the soul, which is truly the manifestation of the very essence of soul. ☞

עַל יְדֵי הַמְשָׁכַת נַחַל אֵיתָן, הוּא הָאָרַת חָכְמָה עִילָאָה שֶׁיָּאִיר בִּפְנִימִיּוּת הַלֵּב	by means of the flow of the *eitan* river, which is an illumination of the supernal *Ḥokhma* that will illuminate the internality of the heart,

THE INNERMOST POINT OF THE HEART.

☞ The deeper levels of the heart experience a wider scope of inner emotion, and are more able to directly perceive its own essence and the essence of the matter. Accordingly, the innermost point of the heart perceives the essence of the soul, if this is possible. A revelation in the innermost point of the heart is not an everyday occurrence. Similarly, we are able to perceive the meaning of life only occasionally, when we question it. In *Iggeret HaKodesh*, epistle 4, it states, "There is sometimes an extremely important matter on which a person's entire life depends, and it affects a person to the core, up to and including the innermost point of the heart." The emotion described here is comparable, both in substance and significance, to the revelation of the light of *Ein Sof* in the innermost point of the heart. However, the perception that results from that revelation will not relate only to the individual's own life, but to the essence of all life and existence. It will relate to the light of *Ein Sof*, which is beyond all worlds, revelations, and definitions. Furthermore, it will take place in the innermost point of the heart, which is beyond comprehension and emotion.

The revelation in the World to Come is, as explained, the illumination of the "point" of *Ḥokhma* in *Bina* and in the attributes and the internality of the attributes (the point of the heart). The inner dimension of the emotive attributes, which is the inner dimension of the heart, is where the illumination is extremely impactful, affecting the essence of the soul itself.

The illumination of supernal *Ḥokhma* in the inner dimension of the heart is the actual revelation of supernal *Ḥokhma*, and of the light of *Ein Sof* and the divine essence enclothed within it. This is the one and only level at which the soul's aspect of *eitan* is revealed. This illumination is the flow of the fine point of its very essence, to the extent that this can be described in words. It cannot be revealed in a person's intellect, nor even in his emotions, but only in the innermost point of his heart.[8] By analogy, human beings are also "revealed" in different ways: With respect to his child, a person is revealed as a "parent." At his place of work, he may be regarded as an "employee" or a "manager," and so forth. But where is a person's essence revealed? One is most likely to reveal his true self to a person who truly cares about him, who does not wish to take anything from him, who is entirely concerned with his wellbeing, and who nullifies himself and his own needs for the sake of the person he cares about. Thus, the innermost point of the heart is more than just the revelation's end point: it is the place where the revelation actually takes place.

לִיבָּטֵל בְּיִחוּדוֹ יִתְבָּרֵךְ בְּתַכְלִית מֵעוּמְקָא דְּלִבָּא אַחֲרֵי הֲסָרַת הָעָרְלָה מִתַּאֲוֹות הַגַּשְׁמִיּוֹת וכו' — to be absolutely negated in God's unity, from the depths of the heart, after the removal of the foreskin, from physical lusts...

When nullification occurs in the depths of a person's heart, he has the sensation, and even the status of being completely subsumed in the unity of the light of *Ein Sof*.

However, this occurrence is subject to a certain condition. Although

---

8. As stated in numerous hasidic works, "No thought can grasp it, but it is grasped in the desire of the heart" (based on the introduction to *Tikkunei Zohar*, 17a). Likewise, it states in the *Zohar*, "It cannot be known and it cannot be understood... except in the desire of the heart" (*Zohar* 3:289b, *Idra Zuta*).

it is associated with the World to Come, this does not mean that it is purely time dependent. Time is a key element, but certain events must occur, and specific things must change, at the right time. If they do not, the era is largely insignificant, or it is significant in a different way.

The condition is that the "foreskin of the heart" must be removed. When a person is consumed with physical desire, his heart becomes enclosed in an additional "covering," which prevents it from feeling anything other than physical desire. Consequently, it is capable of experiencing only those feelings that can be expressed in physical terms. In their lower form, these include physical desires for food, material possessions, and so on. In their higher form, they include more personal desires such as fulfillment and growth. In any case, such a person is unable to perceive what is good and true at all, and he is certainly incapable of sensing the spiritual reality, namely the existence and essence of God. ☞

THE FORESKIN OF THE HEART

☞ This "covering" is essentially an emotional barrier. It does not necessarily diminish the person's intellectual capabilities, but it negates his perception of the reality of spiritual concepts. It is with his heart that a person determines what is real and what is mere speculation. Consequently, this covering primarily affects, and distorts, one's personal ideas and beliefs. Eventually, he stops thinking about spiritual matters altogether, since he perceives them as devoid of substance.

The basic layer of the "foreskin of the heart" is simply the reality of the physical world. This reality determines a person's initial feelings and perceptions, since one begins to connect to the physical world around him by means of physical concepts and his physical senses. The nature of physicality is that it conceals not only the Divine, but the entire spiritual realm. The physical world creates the impression that it embodies the whole of existence, that there is nothing else but physical matter and energy. This belief is so deeply ingrained in us that a person can never rid himself of it completely, even if he manages to develop an understanding of the fact that there is a spiritual reality. The erroneous belief that there is nothing but physicality sustains a world in which emotions relate only to the physical reality, producing the basis for what the author of the Tanya refers to as "physical lusts." There is, however, an additional layer to the foreskin of the heart, and it is to this layer that the author of the Tanya is referring here when he mentions the removal of the foreskin "from physical lusts." The additional layer is formed when the individual does not simply reside in the physical realm, but immerses himself in it, choosing to receive his vitality from it rather than from the Divine. When a person does this, he loses the ability to perceive the spiritual realm and the Divine,

וְהִנֵּה עַתָּה, בַּגָּלוּת הַחֵל הַזֶּה, יֵשׁ
גַּם כֵּן עֵצָה וְעוּצָה לְהָאִיר קְצָת
אוֹר ה' מִבְּחִינַת אֵיתָן לְתוֹךְ נְקוּדַת
פְּנִימִיּוּת הַלֵּב, כְּעֵין לֶעָתִיד

Now, in this exile that has begun, there is also a devised plan to shine a little of the light of God from the aspect of *eitan* into the internal point of the heart, in the manner of the future.

The phrase "this exile that has begun" (see Obad. 1:20) is a reference to the current exile.[9] This is the final exile, which will come to an end only with the full redemption, in the World to Come. In that forthcoming, complete redemption, there will be no more evil. This exile, however, also refers to the different flaws of this world: not only was the Second Temple burned down and the Jewish people were driven out of their land, but even more significantly, the entire world is in a state of divine concealment and sorrow. This has been defined as the state in which the divine sparks are trapped in the husks, and we are obligated to

and furthermore, he can no longer receive "real" vitality from God.

Elsewhere, it is explained that there is a "thick foreskin" and a "thin foreskin" (see *Iggeret HaKodesh*, epistle 4; *Likkutei Torah*, Deut. 18c, section 3; *Etz Ḥayyim, Sha'ar Ha-Ona'a*, chap. 3; *Ta'amei HaMitzvot, Lekh Lekha*). In the physical act of circumcision, the thick foreskin is removed by means of cutting, *mila*, and the thin membrane is removed by means of uncovering, or *peria*. Spiritually, the thick foreskin signifies our base desires. These desires are forbidden, wrong, and repulsive, yet this "barrier" is the easier one to remove. The thin foreskin, on the other hand, signifies more "refined" desires: what the individual craves is not expressly forbidden, but it does not constitute attachment to God. Such desires are more difficult to eliminate. As explained, the thin foreskin represents our physical reality. Not only is it permitted

and necessary to engage with this reality, but in a certain sense, it is even a mitzva to do so. However, a person's connection with the physical world can easily turn into physical desire, and when this happens, he must sever this connection. Accordingly, the verse states, "Remove the foreskin of your heart" (Deut. 10:16). It is clear from this verse that it is the individual's responsibility. Of course, a human being is not able to completely remove this "foreskin," because it is his own physical reality. Therefore, another verse states, "The Lord your God will remove the foreskin from your heart" (30:6). Certain matters are in the hands of God alone: the removal of the barrier between the human heart and the Divine, and likewise, the removal of this world itself, which will lead to the arrival of the World to Come. This entire reality is in the hands of God, like the reality of the World to Come.

---

9. See Ibn Ezra ad loc.; *Or HaḤayyim*, Gen. 28:5.

extract them through the mitzvot. This exile of such a great scope will be rectified only when there is a fundamental shift in the center of gravity of the world. The entire belief system of the physical world must change: what is important and what is not, what is real and what is not, and so on. As mentioned, this shift is ultimately in the hands of God, and will be implemented in the World to Come. However, it states here that within the microcosm of the individual human being, there is a way to receive the aforementioned illumination, or something akin to this illumination, or perhaps "just a glimmer of it," in the here and now. The author of the *Tanya* explains this idea below.

In theory, there is no question that this illumination, the light from the aspect of *eitan*, is capable of penetrating the innermost point of the heart even in the present day. However, the physical world, which is situated between them, prevents it from happening. The various possible paths that the light may take are false and lead elsewhere. Nonetheless, the world is not completely impermeable: occasionally, something that has the capacity to get through it succeeds in doing so. This is not possible everywhere, and moreover, it can change after a day, an hour, or even a minute, because the physical world, which is dynamic and ever-changing, will certainly proceed to conceal whichever paths are uncovered. Nonetheless, in the right time and place, and with the right person, God's light is able to shine from the aspect of *eitan* into the innermost point of the heart, as it will in the World to Come.

The author of the *Tanya* observes that we are provided with a strategy for bringing on this momentous revelation: ☞

A DEVISED PLAN TO SHINE A LITTLE

☞ This embodies the approach of the author of the *Tanya*, and conveys the very essence of the *beinoni*. That which a tzaddik is able to do constantly, a *beinoni* can do only on occasion. Nonetheless, because the *beinoni* is able to do it time and time again, he too is considered, in his own particular way, to be in a state of perfection. Specifically, the tzaddik is capable of going beyond the removal of the foreskin from his physical desires, and reaching a state where physicality itself is stripped away. In other words, the physical world continues to exist, but it is not his reality. He is able to understand the fact that others live in the physical reality, and why the existence of that reality is essential. However, his own consciousness resides with the higher soul, rather than with his body in the physical world. In this sense, the tzaddik is already in the World to Come.

וְהַיְינוּ, עַל יְדֵי שֶׁמְּעוֹרֵר עַל נִיצוֹץ
אֱלֹקוּת שֶׁבְּנַפְשׁוֹ בְּחִינַת 'רַחֲמִים
רַבִּים' הָעֶלְיוֹנִים

That is, by arousing the aspect of supernal "great mercies" upon the divine spark in his soul.

The ability to draw the light of *Ein Sof* into the innermost point of the heart is not within a person's ability, with his intellect or will, and so forth, but relates to something else entirely: the arousal of the supernal great compassion. Compassion is unique in that one can feel it for someone he does not know, or something that is totally outside his scale of values, even a drenched bird, a dying tree, and so on. Consequently, in order to arouse God's mercy, even though we are entirely worthless in comparison to it, if we are only aware that we are far from God, this ability is always within our grasp. For example, compassion is a force that emanates from the soul's essence and flows through the middle "array" of the *sefirot*, which rises to the *sefira* of *Keter*, Crown. This is especially true with regard to the supernal great compassion mentioned here, God's attribute of compassion, which is on a higher level than the intellectual faculties. More than any other spiritual faculty, the attribute of compassion embodies God's deep, essential connection to the world. Thus, we are capable of arousing the supernal great compassion, and moreover, this compassion flows from the highest level, the light of *Ein Sof*. ☞

THE DIVINE SPARK

☞ The author of the *Tanya* explains that the compassion that one arouses is "upon the divine spark in his soul." He emphasizes this point because it is not immediately apparent who or what the object of this compassion is supposed to be. This is especially the case since, as will be explained below, supernal compassion is aroused by means of an awakening from below. In other words, the individual awakens within himself that which he seeks to evoke in the upper realm, namely compassion. If so, compassion for oneself does not impact the lower realm in any way, so it certainly does not impact the upper realm either.

Accordingly, the awakening from below must involve compassion for someone or something else.

For if compassion is directed toward oneself, it is nearly the exact opposite of the supernal compassion we wish to evoke. Supernal compassion must start from the supernal essence of a person and descend to the lowest realms. On the other hand, compassion for oneself comprises a withdrawal into the self: the individual sees only his own experience and is oblivious to everything else. This certainly does not evoke supernal compassion, and moreover, it may evoke the supernal attribute

כִּי בֶּאֱמֶת כָּל זְמַן שֶׁאֵין הָאָדָם
זוֹכֶה שֶׁיִּתְגַּלֶּה אוֹר ה' מִבְּחִינַת
אֵיתָן בִּנְקוּדַת פְּנִימִית לְבָבוֹ,
לִיבָּטֵל בְּיִחוּדוֹ יִתְבָּרַךְ מֵעוֹמְקָא
דְּלִבָּא עַד כְּלוֹת הַנֶּפֶשׁ מַמָּשׁ,
אֲזַי בֶּאֱמֶת יֵשׁ רַחֲמָנוּת גְּדוֹלָה
עַל הַנִּיצוֹץ שֶׁבְּנַפְשׁוֹ

For in truth, as long as a person does not merit that the light of God will be revealed from the aspect of *eitan* in the point of his internal heart, to be negated in His unity from the depths of the heart, until the actual expiration of the soul, then there is truly a great pity for the spark in his soul.

The author of the *Tanya* teaches us the fundamental truth about the current exile. When the world, and the individual, are in exile, the divine spark within the soul deserves compassion. This does not pertain only to specific individuals who are worthy of compassion because they are either wretched or, whether intentionally or not, wicked. Rather, it is true for everyone, including complete tzaddikim. When the divine light illuminates the innermost point of a person's heart as it will in the World to Come, the person's self-conception is completely nullified. This means that the person himself, as we know him, is completely nullified.

כִּי הַנִּיצוֹץ נִמְשָׁךְ מִבְּחִינַת
חָכְמָה עִילָאָה מַמָּשׁ, וּכְשֶׁאֵינוֹ
יָכוֹל לְהָאִיר מִבְּחִינָתוֹ לְתוֹךְ
פְּנִימִיּוּת הַלֵּב שֶׁשָּׁם מְקוֹם גִּילוּי
הָאָרָה זוֹ, הֲרֵי זֶה בִּבְחִינַת גָּלוּת
מַמָּשׁ

For the spark is drawn from the actual supernal Ḥokhma, and when it cannot illuminate from its own aspect into the internality of the heart, which is the place for the revelation of this illumination, then it is in an actual state of exile.

of judgment and create even more distance and separation between us and God. This is why the author of the *Tanya* emphasizes the fact that the compassion that is aroused is compassion for "the divine spark in his soul." While it is true that the divine spark within a person is, in a sense, the person himself, but it is also the point at which he is no longer separate from God. That part of his "self," with needs and wants, is no longer separate from God but is subsumed in the Divine and becomes one with Him. Accordingly, there is reason to feel compassion for the divine spark, because as long as that spark is enclothed within a person, together with his earthly thoughts and feelings, it is very distant from God. However, this compassion is not directed toward the self, but toward the Divine, since it pertains to the point where the individual "self" is thrust something that is beyond his self.

The divine spark in the soul is drawn from the supernal *Ḥokhma* of God Himself, which is in the world of *Atzilut*. In other words, it comes from the source of all reality: the inner dimension of *Ḥokhma*, which enclothes the light of *Ein Sof*. In addition to being a part of the Divine, this spark is the supernal source of the human soul.

As explained, the supernal illumination of the divine spark can be revealed only in the innermost point of the heart. This is analogous to a king who shows himself only in his royal chamber. Everywhere else, the king himself is concealed, though when necessary, he reveals himself partially in order to address different local needs. Likewise, the divine spark within a person is truly revealed only in the innermost point of the heart.

Exile is the state in which a person's unique essence is not revealed or actualized. Instead, it is used for the benefit of other people and the surrounding environment. Likewise, when the soul's unique essence, the divine spark within it, is not revealed for its own sake, but is only something that gives strength and vitality to other parts of the human being, this is considered "true exile."

וְעַל יְדֵי ׳רַחֲמִים רַבִּים׳ הָעֶלְיוֹנִים יוֹצֵא מֵהַגָּלוּת וְהַשִּׁבְיָה	**But through the supernal "great mercies" it emerges from exile and captivity,**

The spark can be brought out of exile by means of the great compassion. As mentioned, compassion refers to the capacity of the highest level to connect to that which is farthest away from it. Thus, it is the connection formed by the Divine, or the aspect of supernal *Keter*, to the human being who, with his thoughts and actions, is on an extremely low level. Likewise, it is the connection of the soul's essence, the aspect of *eitan*, to the farthest of all the places where the soul is concealed. When the connection described here is formed, and the feeling of compassion is experienced, the divine spark comes out of exile.

Moreover, exile and spiritual captivity, and in a certain sense, physical captivity, too, depend more than anything else on the person's level of awareness. When one does not know that he is a captive, that he is serving others, he is in the deepest exile.[10] However, once compassion

---

10. The Ba'al Shem Tov comments on the verse "And I, I will conceal [*haster astir*]"

has been aroused, he begins to understand that he is not who he thought he was, that he does not belong there, and that his current situation is dire. He realizes that he is deserving of compassion, and at that very moment, he begins to emerge from the exile. Thereafter, though his physical reality may be different, he knows that this reality is external and temporary. ☞

וּמֵאִיר לְתוֹךְ נְקוּדָּה פְּנִימִיּוּת הַלֵּב בְּחִינַת אַהֲבָה רַבָּה זוֹ — **and illuminates into the internal point of the heart, in this form of great love,**

The connection formed by compassion reveals the fact that a connection has always existed, though it may have been concealed. This refers to the concealed love between all Jewish souls, wherever they may be found, and the supernal divine essence. The *Tanya* discusses this love extensively.[11] It is present in every Jew, even those who are furthest away, for it expresses the fact that the Jewish soul is truly part of God. Furthermore, when this bond of love is revealed within an individual, it is expressed as "great love."

Ordinary, "minor" love relates primarily to divine revelation and action in the world. These are matters that we are able to comprehend. In contrast, great love is the love for God Himself, who is above all the worlds and beyond all comprehension. Consequently, the only "place" where great love can shine its light in a revealed manner is in the

GREAT COMPASSION

☞ This compassion is beyond the intellect and man's stature. In contrast, compassion that is "below" the intellect is part of the framework of the soul. The compassion that is found in our emotive attributes, below the intellect, is not capable of being directed toward the spark of the Divine within the soul. The divine spark is not part of the person's intellect, nor his unique, finite self. Rather, it is an actual part of the Divine, and it connects to the person, not as an individual being but as a part of God. Compassion for this spark can be aroused only through the "great compassion" within a person. It awakens the corresponding great compassion in the upper realm, and this causes the light to shine from the aspect of *eitan* into the innermost point of the heart.

(Deut. 31:18), that the hardest form of exile is the one in which the concealment itself is concealed (see *Ba'al Shem Tov al HaTorah, Parashat Vayelekh* 4).

11. *Likkutei Amarim*, chaps. 15, 18, and onward.

innermost point of the heart. This is where one's very being, and the divine soul itself, shines its light. Furthermore, God Himself, who is beyond all revelation, intellectual and emotional, also connects to this "place."

כַּנּוֹדָע מִמַּה שֶׁכָּתוּב: "לְיַעֲקֹב אֲשֶׁר פָּדָה אֶת אַבְרָהָם" וּכְמוֹ שֶׁנִּתְבָּאֵר בְּלִקּוּטֵי אֲמָרִים פֶּרֶק מ"ה — as is known from the verse: "To Jacob, who redeemed Abraham," and as explained in *Likkutei Amarim*, chapter 45.

The Sages explain that this quote, which is based on Isaiah 29:22,[12] means that Abraham was saved from the fiery furnace because of the merit of Jacob, his unborn descendant.[13] In *Likkutei Amarim*, chapter 45, this verse is explained in terms of the spiritual attributes embodied by our forefathers. Each of the forefathers was the vehicle for one of the supernal attributes of *Atzilut*. Each embodied his particular attribute perfectly in his life, to the point where he and the attribute became one, over the course of his lifetime at least. Abraham was the attribute of kindness [*Ḥesed*] and love, Isaac the attribute of restraint [*Gevura*] and fear, and Jacob the attribute of beauty [*Tiferet*] and compassion. Accordingly, the phrase "Jacob, who redeemed Abraham," indicates that the attribute of compassion redeems the attribute of love. Moreover, the attribute of compassion can even awaken within us the attribute of supernal love, the love of God that is concealed in our souls. The fact that Abraham is redeemed does not mean that the attribute of love was previously nonexistent, but that it was concealed or in captivity, and the attribute of compassion redeemed it.

The next part of this essay is more practically oriented. Above, we were advised to arouse the supernal compassion. However, we do not yet know how to do this. How can a person in the lower world awaken an attribute of God? In the broader context, this is a fundamental

12. The Lubavitcher Rebbe, Rabbi Menaḥem Mendel Schneerson, notes, "The verse states, 'the house of Jacob.' However, *Sanhedrin* (19b) and *Bereshit Rabba* (63:2) explain plainly that it is 'Jacob, who redeemed Abraham.' The phrase is likewise cited in many other sources. Indeed, this too is the meaning in the continuation of this very verse (quoted in *Sanhedrin* 19b and elsewhere), 'Not now will Jacob be ashamed.'"

13. See *Tanḥuma, Toledot* 4; *Bereshit Rabba* 63:2.

question. In fact, it may be the most important question that can be asked about divine service: Do our efforts in the lower realm have the power to influence the operations of the upper realm? And if so, how does this work?

וּמוּדַעַת זֹאת כִּי אִתְעָרוּתָא דִּלְעֵילָא בְּאִתְעָרוּתָא דִּלְתַתָּא דַּוְקָא תַּלְיָא מִלְּתָא

It is known that the matter of the awakening from above depends specifically on the awakening from below,

We learn two things from this statement. The first is the simple fact that what it describes is actually possible. God established a connection in this world, between the flow from above and the events that occur below. Consequently, we are able to influence the divine conduct in the higher realm through our actions, speech, and thoughts in the lower realm, and likewise, God's actions in the higher realm influence our personal attributes and deeds in the lower realm. In truth, human beings have no significance whatsoever with respect to God, and accordingly, we are powerless to affect His actions. Nonetheless, when He created this world and determined its essential nature, He decreed that the awakening from above is contingent on the awakening from below. This means that an awakening from below is necessary in order to arouse the divine attribute of compassion and induce the divine flow.

The second thing we learn is that this is actually the preferred order of things. Occasionally, when it is absolutely necessary, the awakening from above happens first and evokes the awakening from below.[14] However, the ideal is that the awakening from below comes first. ☞

AWAKENING FROM ABOVE THROUGH AWAKENING FROM BELOW

☞ Our world is structured in accordance with this model, and even our interpersonal relationships function this way. A person who desires an answer must start by asking a question. Thereafter, provided that his question is good enough, the answer will become clear. However, if the answer emerges before the question is asked,

---

14. See *Likkutei Torah*, Lev. 2b, s.v. "*adam ki yakriv*." See also *Torah Or* 1b, s.v. "*ki ka'asher hashamayim haḥadashim*," and the commentary, which states that the order will change only in the World to Come.

דְּהַיְינוּ עַל יְדֵי הִתְעוֹרְדוּת רַחֲמִים
רַבִּים בְּלֵב רַחֲמָנִים וְגוֹמְלֵי חֲסָדִים
לְהַשְׁפִּיעַ לְמַטָּה הַשְׁפָּעָה גַּשְׁמִיּוּת
– זָהָב וָכֶסֶף וכו'

that is, through the awakening of
great mercies in the hearts of merciful ones and those who perform
acts of kindness, to bestow a material flow below – gold and silver…

To awaken the attribute of supernal compassion, we must first awaken
the great compassion within the individual in the lower world. Compassion and kindness are defining characteristics of the Jewish people.[15]
These attributes are part of our nature, even in the reality of the physical
world, where they are found in our animal soul and the body. Human
beings are capable of feeling a certain level of compassion and acting on
it to help someone in need. When a person has "human" compassion
for another, he carves out an opening and creates within himself a
vessel for receiving supernal compassion. ☞

the person is unable to receive it properly, since he does not have a suitable vessel for it.

It is important to understand that the
relationship between the awakening from
below and the awakening from above is
not simply one of "action" and "reaction."
Rather, intrinsically, they are the same, a
single essence that moves from one realm
to the other. The awakening from above,
which comes from God Himself, "depends"
on the awakening from below, which stems

from the individual, because in essence,
the human soul is part of the Divine. The
soul's actions in the lower realm are related to the fundamental purpose of all existence, which embodies the essence and
will of God. Therefore, God's actions and
flow are enclothed in the individual's actions in the lower world, provided that the
individual in question does not have any
kind of intention that breaks or damages
their connection.

IN THE HEARTS OF THE MERCIFUL ONES
WHO PERFORM ACTS OF KINDNESS

☞ As stated earlier, the essence of the
awakening from below is not simply the cry,
or prayer, that is sent to the upper realm
from within a person's heart. Rather, it is

primarily the act that the person performs
in the lower world. Put another way, it is not
simply "in the hearts of the merciful ones,"
but is chiefly the domain of those "who

---

15. It states in *Yevamot* (79a), "There are three distinguishing marks of this nation,
[the Jewish people. They are] merciful, [they are] shamefaced, and they perform
acts of kindness." This quote also appears in Rambam, *Sefer Kedusha, Hilkhot
Issurei Bia* 19:17. See also *Iggeret HaKodesh*, epistle 10.

Just as we desire that the awakening from above should not remain in the upper realm, the compassion that is awakened in a person must not remain a mere "feeling" in his soul. Instead, it must produce a tangible result, a concrete action in the physical world. This is the act of giving charity to the needy. ☞

וְלָכֵן פְּעוּלַת הַצְּדָקָה הִיא פְּעוּלַת   Therefore, the act of charity is the
נַחַל אֵיתָן מַמָּשׁ   actual act of the *eitan* river,

As explained above, the *eitan* river is the flow from the aspect of *eitan* in the soul. It emanates from the soul's essence, which is enclothed in Ḥokhma, and travels to the soul's faculties: the intellect and emotions. Although the awakening from below begins in the lower realm, with the preparation of the vessels, and so forth, its function is to convey the flow of Ḥokhma from above. In this way, it resembles a real, physical "constant river."

In particular, when a person gives charity, he feels what the other person is feeling, and provides for his needs. Even if the giver does not consider the fact that he is creating an awakening from below, he is nonetheless affected. Anyone who gives in the physical world feels an internal illumination: he senses that something is filling his soul from above. In some cases, the individual has a higher level of awareness, and

perform acts of kindness." The awakening from below does not, in essence, resemble a prayer. Its deeper meaning lies in the act that is performed in the upper realm at the very moment when the individual acts in the lower realm.

TO BESTOW BELOW

☞ When an individual effects an awakening from below, he is no longer just a "receiver." He has awakened the upper realm, and consequently, he must now view himself like the higher realm, as a giver. He must feel compassion and contemplate how to give, and moreover, he must take action and give in reality. In kabbalistic terms, he assumes the role of *Zeir Anpin* rather than *Malkhut*, Kingship. He should regard himself in precisely these terms: His kindness is "*Ḥesed* of *Zeir Anpin*," his "left" is "*Gevura* (Restraint) of *Zeir Anpin*," and so too, his compassion, dominance, splendor, and foundation correspond to the remaining *sefirot* of *Zeir Anpin*. He is not the receiver of compassion, but the giver. He is the mercy that flows through *Zeir Anpin* itself. Thus, he must consider how to have compassion and how to bestow, and more than that, how to actually bestow to the feminine aspect of *Zeir Anpin*.

he also reflects on the awakening from above, the flow of the *eitan* river, and the revelation of the Divine in the innermost point of the heart. At such times, the illumination acquires a higher and more clearly defined form: the flow of the *eitan* river itself.

The author of the *Tanya* concludes this section of the essay with an idea that he discusses in a number of places: when charity is necessary for the sake of the giver's soul, the halakhic restrictions, such as not giving more than one-fifth of one's property, do not apply.[16] These restrictions apply when a person gives away his money purely in order to help others. They are imposed to prevent the giver himself from becoming impoverished. However, in the case described here, the person's donation constitutes an investment in himself.

וְהִנֵּה מוּדַעַת זֹאת מַה שֶּׁכָּתוּב
(איוב ב,ד) כִּי "עוֹר בְּעַד עוֹר וְכֹל
אֲשֶׁר לָאִישׁ יִתֵּן בְּעַד נַפְשׁוֹ"
הָאֱלֹקִית לְהָאִירָהּ בְּאוֹר הַחַיִּים
אֵין סוֹף בָּרוּךְ הוּא.

and the verse is known, that "skin for skin, everything that a man has he will give for his soul" (Job 2:4) – his divine soul, to illuminate it with the light of life, *Ein Sof*, blessed be He.

A person's soul may require that charity be given so that it can receive atonement (see *Iggeret HaTeshuva*, chap. 3) or supernal great compassion. For, as explained here, supernal great compassion is drawn into the soul by means of an "awakening from below," namely the act of charity. When charity is necessitated by the soul, for either purpose, the individual is permitted to give everything he owns.[17]

The author of the *Tanya* explains the verse by attaching the word "divine" to it: one should be willing to give everything he has for the

16. Regarding these restrictions, see *Ketubot* 50a; Rambam, *Sefer Hafla'a, Hilkhot Arakhin VaHaramim* 8:13; *Shulḥan Arukh, Yoreh De'a* 249:1, in the gloss.
17. The Lubavitcher Rebbe, Rabbi Menaḥem Mendel Schneerson, comments on the verse quoted here by the author of the *Tanya*, "In *Iggeret HaKodesh*, at the end of epistle 16, the phrase 'skin for skin' is included as well. This is not the case at the end of epistle 10, and so too, in many other places [which quote only the conclusion of this verse: 'Everything that a man has he will give for his soul']. Perhaps, since the [verse's opening] phrase 'skin for skin' signifies a limited degree of charity according to the plain meaning of the verse, it is quoted [here and elsewhere] only when this scope of charity is also being discussed."

sake of his divine soul. On the other hand, he is not required to give everything he has for the sake of his life in the physical world, or for the sake of his animal soul, because these things change over time. They are not essential to the soul. Rather, they are vital only at a certain point in time, in a particular situation. Consequently, they are inherently limited.

Through the actual, physical wealth that a person gives away for the sake of his divine soul, he is able to illuminate that soul with the light of *Ein Sof*. ☞

Like many other discourses that deal with the topic of charity, this short essay addresses the spiritual benefit that a person receives from the charity he gives. But what is unique about this essay is its account of the path to the soul's highest level of worship, namely the drawing down of the essential light of *Ein Sof* into the innermost point of the

THE ESSAY'S CONCLUSION

☞ The final paragraph of this essay was not printed in *Kuntres Aḥaron*, but it is included in *Iggerot Kodesh Admor HaZaken*, epistle 57:

This is the basis for my case. For I do not wish to become a burden on all my loved ones and friends, whom I inundate each year with my pronouncements, entreating them to be extremely generous, and to contribute even more than they can afford in these difficult times, may God have mercy on us, toward the costs of the *gor kikh* [shelter for the poor]. These costs have been substantial in recent years, since new hasidim arrive every day, penniless vagrants and virtuous paupers, and it is necessary to give them provisions for their journeys in addition to feeding and sustaining them while they remain within our gates. Today, there is a new expense, which never existed before: the *biletin* [fee for documents authorizing travel between Russian cities]. This is an enormous sum,

which the faithful envoy who bears this letter must set aside each year, may God have mercy. Therefore, may my plea come before you, and may my life be granted to me with my wish. My request is reiterated and unfolded before the entire community, my loved ones and friends, both new and old. I entreat them not to diminish from the holy, God forbid. Certainly, giving less than one's [officially determined] "value" must not even be mentioned. I have compiled a list of these amounts, which is in the possession of the faithful, honest, veteran emissary who carries this letter, Rabbi Shmuel, may his light shine forth. To anyone who gives more, may God in Heaven give additional blessings and life.

Like his own soul and the soul of a beloved, I love them, and I desire your peace and prosperity with all my heart and soul. [Signed,] Shneur Zalman, son of Barukh, my rabbi and teacher, may his memory be a blessing in the World to Come.

heart. This is also called the *eitan* river. As explained, this lofty goal pertains to the full revelation of the light of *Ein Sof* in this world, which is possible only in the innermost point of the heart. However, as a result this revelation cannot occur in the world's current reality. Rather, the full revelation of the light of *Ein Sof* can take place only after our world has undergone complete rectification, and its essence has been transformed. In other words, it can take place only in the World to Come. The great tzaddikim are the one exception to this. They are already fully rectified, and in essence, they already inhabit the perfect reality of the world of *Atzilut* and the World to Come. However, there is also a way to bring something akin to this revelation into the current reality of every *beinoni*, and this is the main focus of this section of *Kuntres Aharon*. The *beinoni* cannot transform the world's basic structure to make it similar to that of the World to Come, but he is able to create a connection between all the extremities. This connection is formed when an individual in this world is aware that *Ein Sof* is present in his soul, yet is concealed and exiled, and as a result, the individual feels compassion for *Ein Sof*, and likewise he feels compassion for himself, since he is unable to perceive *Ein Sof*. This connection may consist of compassion alone, but sometimes it also includes love, and occasionally even "great love." However, at other times, it consists of nothing but latent potential. Thus it is sometimes "full" and sometimes absent, just like content, light, and emotions, which come and go. It is possible to actualize the connection by bringing compassion all the way down to the lowest realm and into a physical action, namely the act of giving charity to one who truly needs it. This is the meaning of the verse "Charity like an *eitan* river." In particular, when one does not limit his contributions, this keeps the connection open to unlimited compassion and great love.

Essay 8
"The Report That I Hear Is Not Good"

THIS ESSAY IS IN THE FORM OF AN EPISTLE, LIKE THE previous one. It addresses one topic: the purpose and importance of prolonged public prayer, especially in contemporary times.

This essay differs from most of the other essays in that it opens with the concrete-practical part and concludes with the analytical. It begins by addressing an appeal to a particular hasidic community following a rumor that the author of the *Tanya* heard, and concludes with general hasidic teachings, directed at every person for the depth of one's soul, about the loftiness of prayer and how to pray. This reversal of the order of subjects, while it is evident also in other essays, seems to emanate from the author of the *Tanya*'s desire to respond to the troublesome rumor, and the necessity to prevent people from sin. Only afterward does he turn to words of peace and hasidic thought, to explain the inner dimension of the *halakha.*

The novelty of this essay lies first and foremost in the fact that the author of the *Tanya* addresses an actual specific situation, which always concretizes the concepts and brings them to life, although they were already discussed conceptually. Nevertheless, in the second and essential part of the essay, short as it is, there are points that are not found in previous epistles or essays, like the importance of the work of prayer, which is considered literally as the obligation of Torah study and a foundation for the fulfillment of the entire

Torah. Another aspect, already discussed in *Kuntres Aharon*, in the fourth essay, though it was not covered exhaustively there, is the connection between prayer and the refinement of sparks.

17 Kislev

17 Kislev
(leap year)

הִנֵּה לֹא טוֹבָה הַשְּׁמוּעָה שָׁמַעְתִּי
וַתִּרְגַּז בִּטְנִי (חבקוק ג,טז)

Now, the report that I hear **is not good; I heard and my stomach trembled** (Hab. 3:16) –

This essay, directed at a particular community in regard to a disturbing report, opens with the report that the author of the *Tanya* heard. The expression "the report that I hear is not good" is from I Samuel 2:24. The Lubavitcher Rebbe, Rabbi Menaḥem Mendel Schneerson, comments: "It should be noted that there (in I Samuel) it is referring to the sacrifices (*Shabbat* 55b) and the delayed union of *Ze'ir* and *Nukva* – prayer, the unification of the Divine Presence, and the Holy One, blessed be He" (*Lessons in Tanya*). He is suggesting that this is referring to the same issue, only the topic here is prayer, which is also the unification of the Holy One, blessed be He, and the Divine Presence. ☞

A REPORT THAT IS NOT GOOD

☞ From its inception, Chabad Hasidism was a highly organized group; there were rules and regulations, even in writing, such as the "Regulations of Lyozna" (see above, *Iggeret HaKodesh*, epistle 24) that Chabad hasidim were obligated to follow. Whoever disobeyed the regulations of the Rebbe, had certain sanctions imposed upon them. This stemmed not only from the orderly nature of the Chabad Rebbes, but from the demands of the time. The author of the *Tanya* had many more followers than other hasidic groups at the time, and this alone dictated a different, more established character of leadership. Furthermore, the students of the author of the *Tanya* were not observing from afar, coming every so often to get the Rebbe's blessing; they themselves were active partners with the Rebbe in the fulfillment and life of Hasidism.

A hasid of Chabad is a *"beinoni,"* or at least, is striving to be a *beinoni*, as described at length in the *Tanya*. He is a person who serves God himself and endeavors to perfect his soul. He does not receive from the Rebbe free gifts of kindness from above, but rather, a system of instructions, guidance, and supervision, with mechanisms of encouragement and consequences (see, for example, *Iggeret HaKodesh*, epistle 1). In this sense, the opening of the essay, "The report is not good..." is not something out of the ordinary, but rather a common expression of the special relationship that the author of the *Tanya* had with his hasidim.

אֲשֶׁר עַם ה׳ מַעֲבִירִים מִלִּפְנֵי הַתֵּיבָה that the people of God are removing the prayer leader **from before
the Ark,**

Turning toward the leaders of the congregation, using gentle language,
he attributes the report to "the nation of God," who are guilty of
removing the prayer leader "from before the Ark" (since the prayer
leader is positioned before the *Aron Kodesh*) to appoint another person
in his stead. ☞

Therefore, when the prayer leader would not pray well, or would not
arouse the congregation to pray with fervor, there would be grounds
to replace him. However, in this instance, the negative report that the
author of the *Tanya* heard is that they were replacing the person who
was actually praying appropriately, and was prolonging the prayers
with intention, because they wanted to finish the prayer quickly. In this
essay, the author of the *Tanya* mentions this other reason for replacing
the prayer leader.

הָאִישׁ הֶחָפֵץ בַּחַיִּים וַאֲרִיכוּת יָמִים a man who desires the life and
שֶׁל כָּל אַנְשֵׁי שְׁלוֹמֵנוּ, שֶׁבַּמִּקְדָּשׁ length of days of all of our col-
מְעַט הַזֶּה שֶׁל אַנְשֵׁי שְׁלוֹמֵנוּ. leagues who are in this "minor
sanctuary" of our colleagues, in
כְּמַאֲמַר רַבּוֹתֵינוּ ז״ל (ברכות נד,ב): accordance with our Rabbis'
שְׁלֹשָׁה דְּבָרִים מַאֲרִיכִים יָמָיו שֶׁל statement (*Berakhot* 54b): **Three**
אָדָם, וְאֶחָד מֵהֶם הַמַּאֲרִיךְ בִּתְפִלָּתוֹ **matters extend a person's days,
one of which is "one who pro-
longs his prayer."**

The "man who desires life..." refers to the fitting prayer leader, who
desires the length of days not only for himself but for all the hasidim of

REMOVING THE PRAYER LEADER FROM HIS POSITION IN HASIDISM

☞ The prayer leader plays an extremely important role, especially in hasidic circles. More than just a person who would
recite aloud the words from the siddur, he
would be the true messenger of the congregation, guiding the spirit of the community with his intention and fervor. He
enlivens the prayer and determines to a
large extent the character and value of
the prayer. Many of the great hasidic Rebbes in the early generations, including the
Ba'al Shem Tov, his students, and the author of the *Tanya* himself, would famously lead the public prayer.

the community that has appointed him as their emissary. The "minor sanctuary" refers to the synagogue.[1]

The challenge of the author of the *Tanya* is that, if this prayer leader who is prolonging the prayers is good for the community and lengthening their lives, why are they replacing him?

Furthermore, one could argue that he who prolongs his prayer does so in his own personal prayer, which is characteristic of Chabad hasidim who would spend a long time in prayer and contemplation. However, a lengthy personal prayer is not part of his duties as the communal prayer leader. As can be seen in the situation at hand, when the community is not with him, but to the contrary, the extended length of the prayer is actually a burden to them, therefore it seems that in this situation they are justified in replacing him. In response to this argument, the author of the *Tanya* emphasizes that the intention of the prayer leader when lengthening his prayer is for the well-being of the congregation. He is not implying that the prayer leader has lofty, esoteric intentions, of which, perhaps, the congregation is unaware, but rather, he is referring to the simple goal of granting them the merit of a long physical life, as the Sages stated in the Talmud. ☞ ☞ ☞

SOMEONE WHO PROLONGS HIS PRAYER

☞ The connection between length of life and length of prayer finds its source in the Talmud. "There are three matters which, when one who prolongs their duration, they extend a person's days and years. They are: one who prolongs his prayer, one who prolongs his mealtime at the table, and one who prolongs his time in the bathroom." These activities should be done with patience, while rushing them can even cause opposite results, namely shortened days, Heaven forfend. When a person rushes his prayer, he generally fails to connect the words that he is saying to what he thinks and feels which then leads to bitter disappointment, and frustration. To really think about the words and the matters that a person is uttering whilst he is praying, to allow them to truly enter into his psyche so that he can live them, takes time.

During prayer, the soul ascends from daily life and attempts to connect to higher, more complete, and more revealed levels; to the oneness of the Divine. To get used to this, to disconnect from and let go of one's world below, to become immersed in the world above, demands, first and foremost, time (although there are differing opinions in hasidic thought regarding the

---

1. See *Megilla* 29a.

prolonging of prayer, the author of the *Tanya* and Chabad hasidim would greatly extend their prayers). In return for the time that a person invests in prayer, he receives time from above, length of days. He is not guaranteed a quantitatively long life, but rather is granted a fullness of days while he is alive (for more on this topic of length of days, see *Likkutei Torah*, Deut. 12b; see also *Ma'amarim Melukatim* 5738 [1978], s.v. "*veAvraham zaken*," 1:300 and onward). When a person truly lives every moment of his day, deeply feeling each and elevating it, this is considered a truly long day. This is length of days. This is exactly what prayer gives a person; respite from the daily race, from running from one day to the next

without being present in any. It inspires one's presence of mind and connection to the present moment. This is a long life.

On a deeper level, even more than Torah and mitzvot, prayer is not a part of life in this world. When a person studies Torah, he at least knows something that he did not know before; when he does a mitzva, he has done something in the world; but when he prays: nothing. Seemingly, it is time lost, but it is specifically because of this that prayer grants time. It is particularly the time that seems lost, that seems meaningless, that is actually eternal time, the time that expands the limited days of our lives in particular and the limitations of time in general.

A LONG TIME PRAYING

☞ There is a famous story (for example, *Reshimot Devarim* by Rabbi Chitrik 1:150) about Kotzker hasidim who asked the fourth Lubavitcher Rebbe, Rabbi Shmuel Schneerson, also known as the Rebbe Maharash, why Chabad hasidim spend so much time in prayer. They challenged them: "Is it not true that when people are traveling in a wagon through a village, and foul people throw stones at them, then

the best thing to do is to go faster?!" The Rebbe Maharash answered them: "This is the right advice if those villains are on the ground and the travelers are in the wagon. However, when the attackers are already in the wagon and striking their heads with stones, then this is not the right thing to do. Instead, stop the wagon and throw the attackers off."

PROLONGED PUBLIC PRAYER

☞ The author of the *Tanya* does not mean to say that a person should spend endless time in prayer. While there were always hasidim called "*ovdim*," who would sometimes pray for many hours in the course of one day, as previously mentioned, this was not during public prayer. Public prayer should also be long, but with a limit. Elsewhere, the author of the *Tanya* does give a specified time for public prayer: an hour to an hour and a half, which seems

to be the length of time that it took for them to concentrate on the words they were saying. See *Iggeret HaKodesh*, epistle 1: "To spend a long time in the morning prayers, at least an hour to an hour and a half, every day of the week." See also *Iggerot Kodesh*, vol. 81: "From *Hodu* until after *Shemoneh Esrei* should take an hour, and no less." This length of prayer is what he is talking about here as well.

וְאַף גַּם מִי שֶׁהַשָּׁעָה דְּחוּקָה לוֹ בְּיוֹתֵר, וְאִי אֶפְשָׁר לוֹ בְּשׁוּם אוֹפֶן לְהַמְתִּין עַד אַחַר עֲנִיַּת קְדוּשָׁה שֶׁל חֲזָרַת הַשְּׁלִיחַ צִיבּוּר הַזֶּה

And even someone who is extremely pressed for time, and for whom it is absolutely impossible to wait until after the refrain of *Kedusha* in the repetition of this prayer leader,

There are parts of the prayer service, like *Kedusha, Barekhu,* and *Kaddish,* that are recited only in the presence of a quorum. Often people are rushing to recite these prayers in order to fulfill their obligations, even though this leads to lack of the proper intention. Human nature causes a person faced with accomplishing a time-bound action to give up on that which is less prescribed and not limited in time. Here, the author of the *Tanya* says that when it comes to prayer, this should not be the case: one's heartfelt intention takes precedence.

הֲלֹא טוֹב טוֹב לוֹ שֶׁלֹּא לִשְׁמוֹעַ קְדוּשָׁה וּבָרְכוּ מִלֵּירֵד לְחַיֵּיהֶם שֶׁל הַחֲפֵצִים בַּחַיִּים

it is far better for him not to hear *Kedusha* and *Barekhu* than to harass those who desire life.

The author of the *Tanya* gives a halakhic ruling here, like in *Iggeret HaKodesh,* epistle 1, that a lengthy and mindful public prayer is more important than ensuring that those individuals who cannot wait will be able to hear the *Kedusha.* Therefore, although they will not hear *Kedusha,* they must not hurry the congregation's prayer for that purpose. And here he adds another reason: since a long prayer extends the life of the congregants, then the prayer leader is harming the whole community that desires life. ☞

WHO DESIRE LIFE

☞ One can posit that there is a second layer of meaning here. Those who "desire life" also refers to the people who strive to elicit the life and vitality that is packed into every word of prayer, which in this context refers to the words that comprise the *Kedusha* and *Barekhu* prayers. It is impossible to derive this vitality through merely reciting the words automatically. One must break through the externality of the words. To do so, he must cultivate heartfelt concentration and contemplation that is only possible through allotting plenty of time to one's prayers.

וְאוֹנֶס רַחֲמָנָא פַּטְרֵיהּ. וְהַשְׁלִיחַ צִיבּוּר מוֹצִיאוֹ יְדֵי חוֹבָתוֹ אַף שֶׁלֹּא שָׁמַע כְּאִילוּ שָׁמַע, שֶׁהוּא כְּעוֹנֶה מַמָּשׁ

The Merciful One exempts a victim of coercion, and the prayer leader fulfills his duty on his behalf, such that **even though he did not hear, it is as though he heard, and he is like one who literally responds.**

A person who has an urgent reason to leave and cannot hear *Kedusha* or *Barekhu* because the congregation is prolonging their prayer is considered coerced [*anuss*]. This halakhic principle is applied in various situations in many parts of the Torah, and stipulates that a person who is a victim of circumstances beyond his control is freed of his obligation. The novel point here is that the author of the *Tanya* calls a person who prolongs his prayer "coerced". This set of circumstances beyond one's control looks very different from other examples of this principle; for example, when a person has some sort of life-threatening situation, or other combination of various pertinent factors that leave him with no option but to not fulfill a particular mitzva. The author of the *Tanya* explains that God frees even a person who is "coerced" because he is praying for a long time from his obligation to join the group prayers.

In other situations beyond one's control that render a person exempt from a particular mitzva he nevertheless misses out on the mitzva. In this situation, however, the person does not miss out on the mitzva, but rather the *halakha* is that the prayer leader fulfills his obligation.

A person who is a victim of circumstances beyond his control and therefore cannot respond to *Kedusha* or *Barekhu*, or for example, is up to a part of prayer that he is unable to make a response, and he listens, then he is considered what the halakhic principle calls "he who hears is as if he answers."[2]

וְכִדְאִיתָא בַּגְּמָרָא (רֹאשׁ הַשָּׁנָה לה,א) גַּבֵּי עַם שֶׁבַּשָּׂדוֹת דְּאַנִּיסֵי, וְיוֹצְאִים יְדֵי חוֹבַת תְּפִלַּת שְׁמוֹנֶה עֶשְׂרֵה עַצְמָהּ בַּחֲזָרַת הַשְּׁלִיחַ

This is **as taught in the Gemara** (*Rosh HaShana* 30a) **with regard to the people in the fields who are constrained by circumstances beyond their control, and they fulfill their duty of the**

---

2. *Shulḥan Arukh, Oraḥ Ḥayyim* 109:3.

צִיבּוּר כְּאִלּוּ שָׁמְעוּ מַמָּשׁ, וְגַם קְדוּשָׁה וּבָרְכוּ בְּכְלָל

Shemoneh Esrei prayer itself by means of the repetition of the prayer leader, as though they actually heard it, and *Kedusha* and *Barekhu* are also included in this *halakha*.

The Talmud here discusses people who, for example, work in the fields and are unable to recite the *Shemoneh Esrei* prayer, even on their own; it is as if they heard even when they did not hear. The practice of the prayer leader repeating the *Shemoneh Esrei* was established to fulfill the obligation of other people who do not know how to pray or are unable to pray themselves. When they would hear the prayer leader and have intention that he serve as their mouthpiece, this would suffice to fulfill their obligation. This is the prooftext for the principle that, as explained above, whoever finds himself in circumstances beyond his control and cannot hear, fulfills his obligation through the prayer leader.

He who prays alone does not fulfill his obligation of hearing the *Kedusha* and *Barekhu*. Yet if he finds himself in circumstances beyond his control, even if he was not in the synagogue at all, he fulfills his obligation through the prayer leader.

This ends the first part of the essay. In review, the author of the *Tanya* opened with the troublesome report that he heard, and makes an urgent call to the hasidim that they should cease taking the proposed action immediately. He explains the simple reason why it is such a serious issue, and how to act in the future. He continues in a more placating manner in this second half of the essay, and in continuation of the concepts that he mentioned, presents a general yet profound explanation about the power of the prayer of the individual, especially in these generations, and why it is so important to invest time and concentration into it.

וְהִנֵּה זֹאת חֲקַרְנוּהָ כֵן הוּא אַף גַּם בַּדּוֹרוֹת הָרִאשׁוֹנִים שֶׁל חַכְמֵי הַמִּשְׁנָה וְהַגְּמָרָא, שֶׁהָיְתָה תּוֹרָתָם קֶבַע וְעִיקַר עֲבוֹדָתָם וְלֹא תְּפִלָּתָם

Now, we have investigated this and it is so – even in the early generations of the Sages of the Mishna and Talmud whose Torah was fixed and was their main occupation, rather than their prayer,

"We have investigated this,[3] it is so" refers to the halakhic principle that stipulates that although prolonged prayer is not a defined halakhic obligation, it still takes precedence over more definitive halakhic obligations, like reciting *Kedusha* and *Barekhu*.

The proofs that the *Tanya* brings about the supreme importance of prayer come from the Sages of the Mishna and the Talmud, whose "Torah was fixed rather than prayer," which means that they engaged primarily in Torah study as the core of their service of God rather than in prayer. ☞

וּמִכָּל שֶׁכֵּן עַתָּה הַפַּעַם בְּעִקְבוֹת מְשִׁיחָא, שֶׁאֵין תּוֹרָתֵינוּ קֶבַע מִצּוֹק הָעִתִּים	all the more so now, in the times of the approach of the Messiah, when our Torah is not fixed, due to the distressful times.

The full picture of the Messiah is like an analogue of history. The beginning of history is like the head, then there are years that correspond to the hands and body, and then there are the generations that parallel the legs and heels, which is the time that immediately precedes the coming of the Messiah, the end or culmination of time. Just as in the heel there is no intellect or sensation, so too, this time of the "heels of Messiah" are intellectually and emotionally benumbed, relative to the

THEIR TORAH WAS FIXED

☞ Throughout the course of a person's life, different times call for different emphases in serving God, as explained in essay 4. This can be seen over the course of history as well. One time may call for a greater emphasis on Torah, which would then occupy the main focus in one's service of God, while another time, it is prayer. This does not mean that people in that time were exempt from engaging in the other avenues of divine service, but there are changing priorities in the spiritual connection to the total service of God; which is the means and which is the goal. The Torah can be seen as a means to keeping the mitzvot correctly and praying well, or prayer can be viewed as the preparation for Torah study for its own sake. Therefore, at the time of the *amora'im* and the *tanna'im*, Torah study was fixed; it was their main occupation, and the only means by which they reached prayer and charity. Nevertheless, even then prolonged prayer was not deferred for Torah study or other halakhic obligations.

---

3. This wording comes from Job 5:27.

rest of the "body." These times of suffering and concealment lack the power of Torah understanding as well.

וְעִיקַר הָעֲבוֹדָה בְּעִקְבוֹת מְשִׁיחָא הִיא הַתְּפִלָּה, כְּמוֹ שֶׁכָּתַב הָרַב חַיִּים וִיטַאל ז״ל בְּעֵץ חַיִּים וּפְרִי עֵץ חַיִּים

The main service in the approach of the Messiah is prayer, as Rabbi Ḥayyim Vital, of blessed memory, wrote in *Etz Ḥayyim* and *Peri Etz Ḥayyim*.

Rabbi Ḥayyim Vital writes about the difference between these times and Temple times. In kabbalistic terms, during Temple times when *zun* (*Zeir Anpin* and *Nukva*) were face to face, they were in a constant state of expanded consciousness, and the *moḥin* did not depart from them. In simpler terms, people had a clear awareness of the Divine and were cognizant of constant divine revelation. That which lies almost entirely beyond our grasp today, and can only be glimpsed through extraordinary effort or divine beneficence, as an illumination from above that shines into our lives for a moment, was for them a basic everyday perception. Therefore, they did not need to struggle to attain divine understanding or cleaving to the Divine, but rather, as soon as they would think about it, they would experience it. This is not the case in this day and age, when immense effort and time is required to arrive at this type of level. This is the work of prayer, which is therefore the main devotional work of this time. ☞

PRAYER: THE MAIN WORK IN THE TIMES BEFORE THE MESSIAH

☞ How does this work? In the times before Messiah, there is no obvious divine revelation in the world. Therefore, a person whose spirit searches for the Divine yet does not find it, neither intellectually nor in expanded consciousness, finds it in prayer. Prayer is from below, and is therefore always present for every person in the place where he is, even when he does not have expanded consciousness, intellectu-al awareness, or emotion in his soul. This place he can transform into prayer. As King David said, "I am prayer" (Ps. 109:4; see, for example, *Torah Or* 93:3, *Likkutei Torah*, Song 2:3). The essence of prayer is what a person does with his "I," from the unique, ever-evolving spiritual and material place that he finds himself, with his joy and his sadness, his despair and his hope; with whatever he has in him: this is prayer.

מִכָּל שֶׁכֵּן וְקַל חוֹמֶר שֶׁרָאוּי
וְנָכוֹן לִיתֵּן נַפְשֵׁינוּ מַמָּשׁ עָלֶיהָ,
וְהִיא חוֹבָה שֶׁל תּוֹרָה מַמָּשׁ

Surely, all the more so that it is proper
and correct to give our lives literally
for it, and it is an actual obligation of
the Torah

Since in these days we have nothing else, prayer is the path and connection to the Divine. Therefore, certainly, one should give everything
for it, not only a little bit of time and a little bit of soulful energy, but
"with all of your soul." As explained in the context of a similar concept:
"Everything that a man has he will give for his life" (Job 2:4).[4]

Irrespective of the question of whether the obligation of prayer is
from the Torah or rabbinically mandated,[5] when a person engages in
the service of prayer, he fulfills several mitzvot that are undoubtedly
of Torah origin, like loving God, fearing God, declaring the unity of
God, and more, which lay one's spiritual foundation for the fulfillment
of the entire Torah. ☞

TORAH OBLIGATION

☞ As the author of the *Tanya* says himself, "Although the form of prayer and the
three prayer services a day are rabbinically mandated, the essential act and essence of prayer comprise the foundation
of the entire Torah: to know God, to recognize His greatness and splendor with
absolute and settled awareness and with
understanding of the heart, and so forth"

(*Iggerot Kodesh*, vol. 10; a similar conclusion is implied by his comments here and
elsewhere). And as he concludes there:
"However, in these times, anyone who is
close to God and has ever savored the
taste of prayer one time will understand
and discern that without it a person will
not lift a hand or a foot to truly serve God,
and will learn by rote."

---

4. This verse is cited in many places in *Iggerot HaKodesh* (see *Iggeret HaKodesh*,
epistles 10 and 16, and in the previous essay) in reference to charity, which serves
to atone for one's soul and to heal it.

5. The Rambam in his *Sefer HaMitzvot,* positive commandment 5, wrote that daily
prayer is a Torah obligation, and the Ramban disagreed. The author of the *Tanya*
in his *Shulḥan Arukh HaRav* 106:2 cites both opinions and concludes that the
Ramban's opinion takes precedence. He also writes in *Likkutei Torah, Bemidbar*
70:3, that the obligation is rabbinic. And see more in the *Iggerot Kodesh* of the
author of the *Tanya,* vol. 10.

לְמְבִינֵי מַדָּע, תּוֹעֶלֶת הַהִתְבּוֹנְנוּת וְעוֹמֶק הַדַּעַת קְצָת כָּל חַד לְפוּם שִׁיעוּרָא דִּילֵיהּ

for those who understand and have knowledge of the advantage of the contemplation of prayer, and a little depth of this knowledge, each according to his own capacity [shiura].

The author of the *Tanya* says, "for those who understand…," because this experience is difficult to explain to one who has never tasted it.

The work of prayer entails contemplation of God; His greatness, His kindness, and so forth, and the deepening of one's knowledge of Him, even a little bit. When a person does not just understand, but rather strives to forge this connection, this closeness, this personal contact with every fiber of his being, this is the deepening of his "knowledge," which is an unending pursuit. While there were hasidim, "*ovdim*," who lived and dedicated their entire lives to this, for the average person, even a lesser degree is beneficial. Anyone who does this will reap the benefits of his contemplation in many areas in his life, in ways that are beyond one's intellectual comprehension. When a person accustoms himself to deepen his knowledge for a period of time, even "a little," he will awaken his emotions as well: his love and fear of God, his wonder at the splendor and harmony of life, and so forth. The appearance of these emotions is not automatic. It is not a necessary outcome of contemplation, but rather is like a surprising effect that results from it, that arises at unexpected moments, since these two dimensions are not directly connected.

This language, which comes from the *Zohar*,[6] means according to the one's capacity [*sha'ar*], measure [*shiur*], and unique way. The extent of the contemplation and depth of one's knowledge necessary to awaken his emotions varies from one person to the next, and from one concept to the next. One person may have a refined intellect and a soul that is sensitive to holiness, so that through only a modicum of contemplation, he can attain the excitement of love and fear, while

<hr/>

6. The language of the *Zohar*, see *Zohar* I, 103a, as an extrapolation of the verse: "Her husband is renowned at the gates" (Prov. 31:23). This is also referenced in the introduction to the *Tanya* and in many hasidic teachings.

another person must contemplate longer and invest more effort to reach a bit of emotion. ☞

בְּסִדּוּר שִׁבְחוֹ שֶׁל מָקוֹם בָּרוּךְ הוּא, בִּפְסוּקֵי דְזִמְרָה וּשְׁתֵּי בְרָכוֹת שֶׁלִּפְנֵי קְרִיאַת שְׁמַע, יוֹצֵר וְאַהֲבָה

The contemplation of prayer is **in the arrangement of the praise of the Holy One, blessed be He, in** *Pesukei DeZimra* **and the two blessings before the recitation of the** *Shema*: *Yotzer* **and** *Ahava.*

As the author of the *Tanya* describes in other essays, the Sages established *Pesukei DeZimra* on one level, and the blessings before *Shema* on the next level, as preparation for the recitation of the *Shema* itself, for the unification of God and His love. (The *Shemoneh Esrei* is even higher, and brings with it total nullification of one who stands before God, the King.) The preparation entails contemplation and deepening of one's knowledge of the words that one recites there, which are entirely praises of God.

To connect with God, who is holy and separate from this worldly life, who cannot be fathomed or felt in a normal way, one must enter into a process of speech and thought about Him. Indeed, since we are incapable of thinking about God Himself, who is utterly abstract and separate, these thoughts and words must traverse this familiar world that praises God who created it and sustains it. This is "the arrangement of the praise of the Holy One." Praise of God is that which relates to what one sees and understands in the created worlds:

EACH ACCORDING TO HIS OWN CAPACITY

☞ This can be read as a guiding statement: "When does the intellect reach emotion? When one's contemplation is according to his own personal measure." Every person has a particular intellectual and emotional capacity. What type of intellect does a person have? How broad, how deep, how subtle? How much information, conceptualization, experience, and ability can he access? What type of emotion? Some people have a sensitivity and openness to love; others easily cultivate reverence; and then others naturally possess other attributes, in one way or another. Only when a person contemplates according to his personal intellectual and emotional capacity will he succeed in deepening his knowledge and awakening his emotions.

physical mountains, oceans, animals, and people, and spiritual forces, angels that love and fear God. They all are praising, with words and emotions, the One who created them. This is the essence of their existence. Words and thoughts about these ideas, formulated by each person according to his capacity, raises a person little by little, higher and higher, into an elevated spiritual plane in which God is present in a more tangible way. ☞

לְעוֹרֵר בָּהֶן הָאַהֲבָה הַמְסוּתֶּרֶת
בְּלֵב כָּל יִשְׂרָאֵל לָבֹא לִבְחִינַת
גִּילוּי

The aim is **to awaken through them the hidden love in the heart of all Israel, so that it is revealed**

ARRANGEMENT OF PRAISE OF THE HOLY ONE

☞   This is a concise formulation that means the contemplation of the praises of the Holy One in *Pesukei DeZimra* and the blessings of the recitation of *Shema*. As mentioned elsewhere, just as the Sages established the voicing of songs and blessings before *Shema*, since they needed this extra preparation, in this day and age we must add to this preparation. This is what the author of the *Tanya* and hasidim who engaged in the service of prayer throughout all time did: they added to the very saying of the words of the siddur, layers of learning and contemplation of those concepts. See *Hayom Yom*, 20 Tammuz: "There are three types of contemplation. The first is analytical contemplation: after a person understands a concept clearly, he contemplates the depth of that concept, until he understands it fully. The second, before one's prayer, when one feels that concept that he studied, not the intellectual emotion of analytical contemplation. And the third, during prayer, the feeling of the Divine in that which he studied. These three are rungs in the ladder of cultivating emotion, and only with the beneficence of God who is with us do we sometimes feel

the Divine without any work at all, which is due to the divine essence that is in one's soul. However, from the perspective of the actual power of the service, all of the above three are needed." So that the saying of the words, and even the thoughts about them, will affect one's soul, there must be a spiritual foundation that makes a deep connection between the words and their depth of meaning: there is a whole world that lies behind each word, behind a sentence and paragraph of prayer.

The most basic layer is simply studying a hasidic teaching to become familiar with the world of concepts that allow for the contemplation of spirituality and the Divine, to understand and to know the frameworks in general, and in particular, that are described in these passages. A practice that is closer to prayer is to study and contemplate before prayer. Chabad hasidim have the custom, even today, to study a hasidic discourse before their morning prayers, so that each person will understand according to his capacity. The study of a particular discourse becomes the lens through which the devotee can focus on the prayer he is saying

Prolonged contemplation during *Pesukei DeZimra* and the blessings of the *Shema,* even on the simplest level of contemplation, is enough to unearth the hidden love in the heart of all Israel. This love is discussed at length in *Likkutei Amarim* (mostly in chap. 18 and onward). It is the love of the divine soul that inhabits every Jewish person, because it is an expression of the soul being a literal part of God above. Yet, since the divine soul is clothed in this world, in the vital soul and in the body, this love become concealed in the loves of the animal soul, that express themselves as desires for the material things of this world.

Nevertheless, as explained there, that which within aa person can be, wants to be, and ultimately will be revealed. A person must simply ensure that he does not actively suppress it, on the one hand, and on the other hand, he must strive to reveal it, if not through emotion, then in speech and action. The work of prayer, as the author speaks about it here, is to articulate words that express one's love and fear,

with added spiritual intensity. He thus cultivates a more personal connection with the words and can literally enter into the prayer.

The early hasidim used to ask each other, "With what did you pray today?" The meaning of the question is with which understanding, what point of relating that one took from one word to the next, that strings the words together and brings them under a fluid roof of meaning. This would be gleaned from the study of the hasidic discourse that was undertaken before prayer. The closest layer is the hasidic contemplation at the time of prayer itself, that could be more general relative to the hasidic teaching, yet more specific when in contact with the words of prayer and in the heart of the person himself who is praying.

The author of the *Tanya* does not elaborate here because, among other reasons, he speaks here about public prayer, and these additional layers are intended mostly for one's individual prayer; even when he is praying with the congregation in the synagogue, he answers what he is supposed to answer, and so forth. His prayer service is necessarily deeply personal, and its time cannot be fixed like public prayer. This does not imply that communal prayer should not be deep, or that it should not be long or contemplative.

After all, this is what this whole essay is intended to address: the minimal measure of prayer in the congregation that must be at least a recitation of the words while thinking about their actual meaning. Since if this does not happen, then the prayer has no value, neither in light of the Torah obligation nor the rabbinical mandate. As mentioned earlier, prayer is literally enjoined by the Torah, and the obligation that the author speaks about is not just the obligation to pray, however that will look, but rather, the prayer as the foundation of the mitzvot, an aspect of prayer which is certainly from the Torah. This type of prayer comprises the bedrock of one's soul for his fulfilling the entire Torah.

words that are recited before the *Shema* as praise for the Holy One, and if he only has intention for these matters, and restrains himself from thinking extraneous thoughts, then he automatically reveals the hidden love. This too demands a certain amount of time, and this is the topic of this essay.

בְּהִתְגַּלּוּת הַלֵּב בִּשְׁעַת קְרִיאַת שְׁמַע עַצְמָהּ, שֶׁזֹּאת הִיא מִצְוַת הָאַהֲבָה שֶׁבַּפָּסוּק "וְאָהַבְתָּ גו' בְּכָל לְבָבְךָ גו'"

through the openness of the heart at the time of the recitation of the *Shema* itself, which is the mitzva of love that is commanded in the verse "And you shall love ... with all of your heart ..."

The preparation before reading the *Shema* is designed to ensure "the openness of the heart at the time of the recitation of the *Shema* itself." This mitzva of "You shall love the Lord your God with all your heart, and with all your soul" is written in the *Shema*. While the deeper dimensions that lie behind these words are manifold, on a simple level it speaks of the heartfelt feeling of love, an extremely strong emotion that transforms a person and his behavior. And the question is: How can a person fulfill a mitzva that calls for a particular emotion? Are a person's emotions within his control? Can he choose how to feel?

The Rambam's approach to this, and the author of the *Tanya* explains it in the same way as well,[7] is that a person fulfills this mitzva by contemplating that which causes love, because this is within his control. This is what it says here, that through contemplation and deepening one's knowledge through the praise of the Holy One during *Pesukei DeZimra* and the blessings before *Shema*, a person fulfills the mitzva of "You shall love" when he recites the *Shema*. Because, whether the

---

7. In the comments of the Lubavitcher Rebbe, Rabbi Menaḥem Mendel Schneerson, on *Derekh Mitzvotekha*, p. 420, and in several other places, it is cited in the name of Rabbi Epstein Halevi from Homel (in his book *Shenei HeMeorot* 2:2): "I heard face to face from the Rebbe (the author of the *Tanya*) in this wording: 'This is what I received from the Rav the Maggid of Mezeritch, and this is what he received as well from the Ba'al Shem Tov, that the mitzva of 'You shall love' entails pegging one's thoughts and mind in concepts that arouse love. And whatever results from that is not the main mitzva.'"

love is revealed in a person's heart or not, he nevertheless does his part and therefore fulfills the mitzva when he says, "You shall love." It goes without saying that if he spends enough time in serious contemplation so that the words he says will percolate, then they will certainly reach the heart and open it. A person needs to know that even when he feels some emotion, it takes time and perspective to give it a name and define it as "love of God." Therefore, a person could have love of God and not know it when his particular social circle and intellectual associates do not discuss or openly work toward this lofty goal.

| הַנִּמְנֵית רִאשׁוֹנָה בְּתַרְיַ"ג מִצְוֹת, כְּמוֹ שֶׁכָּתַב הָרַמְבַּ"ם ז"ל שֶׁהִיא מִיסוֹדֵי הַתּוֹרָה וְשָׁרְשָׁה, וּמָקוֹר לְכָל רְמַ"ח מִצְוֹת עֲשֵׂה | This is listed first amongst the 613 mitzvot, as the Rambam, of blessed memory, wrote, that it is one of the foundations of the Torah and its root, and a source for all of the 248 positive commandments. |

Love of God is the first mitzva of a Jew (Rambam, *Sefer HaMadda, Hilkhot Yesodei HaTorah* 2:1);[8] first, he loves, and afterward, from the force of his love, he performs other mitzvot. A person does not do anything unless he is driven by a force in his soul. As it the case between people, the motivating force to act on behalf of another is love. When a person does something out of fear or for any other reason, he does so because of the other reason. Love is the only motivation that causes someone to do something truly for the other person. How much more so when it comes to performing God's mitzvot. Love of God is the source in one's soul for every mitzva he does.

This is not the case only in one's soul. Since it is the power of a

---

8. The Lubavitcher Rebbe, Rabbi Menaḥem Mendel Schneerson, commented as follows (printed in *Lessons in Tanya*): "This demands some further study (in the Rambam's *Sefer HaMitzvot*, love of God is the third mitzva. In the *Zohar* I, 11b: 1. fear; 2. love; 3. knowledge of God; and so forth). The Sages state (*Avoda Zara* 73a) that a substance is "nullified little by little." In this context, the first is nullified relative to the mitzva of love that comes next. Also note in the introduction to the *Tanya, Ḥinukh Katan* (introduction to *Sha'ar HaYiḥud VeHa'emuna*), that love is the root of all the positive commandments (including the positive commandment of fear [which is the root of the negative prohibitions] and therefore), the root of all the mitzvot."

person's love of God that propels him to perform mitzvot, the manifestations of love are essentially the fulfillment of the mitzvot; all the mitzvot are essentially a revelation of that love. In this sense, love is the foundation and root of the Torah, since all the mitzvot are only revelations of that foundational existing love between the Jewish people and God.

כִּי עַל אַהֲבָה הַמְסוּתֶּרֶת בְּלֵב כָּל
יִשְׂרָאֵל בְּתוֹלַדְתָם וְטִבְעָם לֹא שַׁיָּיךְ
צִיוּוּי כְּלָל

For no command applies at all to love that is hidden in the heart of all Israel, in their pedigree and nature.

As long as the love is only in one's heart, as long as it does not manifest in other things like spoken words or actions, the love is hidden. As explained, the hidden love, the essential connection of one's soul to God, exists in the spiritual configuration of one's soul. It is not something acquired; it exists. Therefore, it is not comprised in a commandment. The mitzva "You shall love your God" is the mitzva to reveal it.

The uncovering of the love begins with contemplation and deepening one's knowledge in prayer, awakening and manifesting the love as an operative force in the heart. If possible, it appears in the form of the emotion of love, and if not, as the force in the soul that causes a person to behave and act like someone who loves, like someone who feels love, for his Beloved, to do His will. This is the ultimate goal of the revelation of the love.

וְדַעַת לְנָבוֹן נָקָל, כִּי כְּשֶׁהָאַהֲבָה הִיא
מְסוּתֶּרֶת הִיא עוֹדֶינָה בְּנֶפֶשׁ הָאֱלֹקִית
לְבַדָּה, וּכְשֶׁבָּאָה לִבְחִינַת גִּילּוּי לַנֶּפֶשׁ
הַחִיּוּנִית, אֲזַי הִיא בְּהִתְגַּלּוּת הַלֵּב
בֶּחָלָל שְׂמָאלִי, מְקוֹם מִשְׁכַּן נֶפֶשׁ
הַחִיּוּנִית

And knowledge of this **is easy for the discerning** – for when the love is hidden it is still in the divine soul alone, but when it comes to a state of revelation in the vital soul, it is revealed in the heart, in the left chamber, the place of the vital soul.

Knowledge of this matter is simple for someone who contemplates it, as is stated below. As explained, the hidden love is the love of the divine soul, and because it is in the divine soul it is defined as hidden, just as the divine soul is hidden in the material world. The vital animal soul of man manifests and acts in this world, and the divine soul manifests only through its enclothement in it. Similarly, the hidden love manifests only through the vital soul, and further, through and behind the vital soul's loves and desires in the physical body, which is in the left chamber of the heart, as explained in *Likkutei Amarim* (chap. 9 and elsewhere). ☞

וְזֶהוּ עִנְיַן 'בֵּירוּר נִיצוֹצוֹת' הַמּוּזְכָּר שָׁם בְּעֵץ חַיִּים וּפְרִי עֵץ חַיִּים גַּבֵּי תְּפִלָּה

This is the meaning of the "refinement of the sparks" that is mentioned there in *Etz Ḥayyim* and *Peri Etz Ḥayyim*, in connection to prayer.

This revelation of the divine love of God through another love of the animal soul is the way a person accomplishes "refinement of the sparks" in the most personally significant way. Therefore, the work of prayer is the main service of refinement of sparks (and as mentioned

MANIFESTATION OF THE HIDDEN LOVE IN THE LEFT CHAMBER

☞ *Likkutei Amarim* states that the vital soul resides in the left chamber of the heart, and the divine soul resides in the right chamber. The difference between the right and left chambers is like the difference between Ḥesed and Gevura, between the place that reveals and the place that conceals, meaning that reveals through that which conceals. The sanctuary of the divine soul is in the right chamber of the heart in the sense that it is revealed through the attribute of Ḥesed and love; love manifesting as is, as unadulterated love of God, deep love for its own sake, and nothing else.

In contrast, the vital, animal soul dwells in the left chamber in the sense that the love there is always enclothed and hidden and necessarily reveals itself through other mediums. In its root, it too is a holy soul that loves God. However, since it is

bound and clothed in the body and in all worldly things, it manifests itself through those other things, through worldly yearnings, loves, and fears. Therefore, it too has a rectification and revelation, yet through and from behind those masks and garments. For example, when a person elevates and binds his worldly love to holiness, connecting his desire for something down below to his desire for God, it is not a direct revelation, but rather a revelation that happens through other mediums, through precisely those things that conceal the revelation. Yet, when a person succeeds in revealing the hidden, there is a release of the concealed unlimited power that manifests particularly through the attribute of Gevura, which is a revelation of the hidden love in the vital soul as well, and in the left chamber of the heart.

and explained above in *Kuntres Aḥaron* at the beginning of the fourth essay.) ☞ ☞

שֶׁלָּכֵן הִיא עִיקַר הָעֲבוֹדָה בְּעִקְּבוֹת מְשִׁיחָא, לְבָרֵר נִיצוֹצוֹת כו' שֶׁהוּא בְּחִינַת אִתְהַפְּכָא אוֹ אִתְכַּפְיָא שֶׁל נֶפֶשׁ הַחִיּוּנִית לַנֶּפֶשׁ הָאֱלֹקִית כַּנּוֹדַע

For this reason, prayer **is the main service in the approach of the Messiah, to refine the sparks…** This service **is the transformation or subjugation of the vital soul to the divine soul, as is known.**

Unlike the revelation of love in the divine soul, which is like the self-expression and self-actualization of the divine soul and entails an

THE MAIN SERVICE

☞   The refinement of the sparks is spiritual work that has needed to be done since the beginning of creation. This work will reach its culmination with the coming of the Messiah. Some times are particularly remarkable, like when the Temple stood, and when there were supremely eminent Torah minds, through which the work of refinement of sparks was performed automatically. Then, it was natural for people to work toward the ultimate spiritual good, engaging constantly in light and holiness, without having to pay attention to the fact that they were refining sparks; they did not have to wage war with the evil and concealment because the sparks were distilled and refined automatically.

And then there are times, especially at the termination of exile, the heels of the Messiah, which are times when Godly awareness and sensation are intensely hidden, times when we do not feel or see the holiness, only the *kelippa* that is hiding it. In this case, the only way is to work hard, to work with the difficulty, to break the *kelippot* in these low places, to fight the last battle against the darkness, evil, and concealment, within the darkness and concealment, even when you do not see or feel. This is the work of the heels of the Messiah.

REFINEMENT OF THE SPARKS

☞   The revelation of the hidden love of the divine soul is the revelation of man's divine spark, and when it manifests in the vital soul, in what it wants and what it fears and all the places that it is scattered in the world, it collects and elevates all the sparks that were scattered there. All are like his sparks that belong to him, that are hiding in the desires, fears, beauty, splendor, triumphs, and bindings of his soul. Those holy sparks are the enlivening essence of all those phenomena; they are the soul and hidden light that is in everything, even in the *kelippot*. During prayer, when the hidden love is aroused and becomes revealed in the vital soul and its scattered aspects of self in the world, then these sparks are distilled out from the realm of earthly existence and ascend and unify with their shining and conscious source; all then rise into supernal holiness. This is the "refinement of the sparks."

unsurpassed delight, to which every other delight pales in comparison. For the vital soul to feel or even activate love without feeling it, it needs to change, to transform from its original nature; it needs to be like the divine soul. Changing anything is not easy, as everyone knows; it does not happen on its own. For change to happen, one must work and sometimes even fight.

Hasidic teachings address two levels of change in the vital soul: "transformation" and "subjugation." Transformation is when the vital soul changes to be something else. It does not transform into a divine soul; however, it transforms into a garment that is nullified to the divine soul that wears it. It then receives the desires and the loves, and so forth, of the divine soul, acquiring them as its own. This is considered a high level in divine service, the level of great tzaddikim, whose souls are rectified to become a microcosm of the supernal world of *Atzilut,* a perfectly integrated unity of light, vessels, and *sefirot,* in each other. Subjugation, on the other hand, is when the vital soul is unable to attain this internal nullification and transformation, and the person must subjugate it against its will, as it were, to do the will and love of the divine soul. This is considered a lower level, and in a general sense, is the level of the service of the *beinonim,* and of times of small-mindedness and concealment: the paradigm of the created worlds.[9] ☞

The refinement of sparks in prayers is not just a refinement of the

SUBJUGATION AND TRANSFORMATION IN PRAYER

☞ This work is primarily undertaken during prayer, because prayer effects changes in the soul. A person can study Torah and perform the mitzvot, yet not change. This is not the case regarding prayer; prayer forces a person to change. If a person prays seriously, with contemplation and deepening of the mind, he already transfers himself to a different place. During Torah study, a person works on Torah and during mitzva performance, he works on the world. However, during prayer, he first and foremost works on himself. When he prays, he plows and harvests in his soul (see *Likkutei Torah,* Lev. 40:3, and onward, for the spiritual parallel of all the steps for making bread in one's soul). Therefore, he leaves prayer a different person to the one who entered. As explained earlier (start of essay 4), it is prayer that effects changes in the world, such as rainfall and healing, and certainly changes to one's soul.

---

9. It is also explained in some hasidic works that in another, perhaps deeper, sense, the work of subjugation is the higher path, even higher than transformation (see *Torah Or* 89:3 and elsewhere.)

vital animal soul itself, that ascends and approaches the Divine in prayer, but it also refines aspects of the actual world that are bound to the soul that is being refined.

כִּי הַדָּם הוּא הַנָּפֶשׁ כו' (דברים יב,כג), וְהַדָּם מִתְחַדֵּשׁ בְּכָל יוֹם מֵאוֹכָלִין וּמַשְׁקִין

For the blood is the soul... (Deut. 12:23), **and the blood is renewed every day through food and drink,**

The spiritual soul is bound to the physical body in the blood. When a person eats every day, his food comes from all corners of the earth, with sunlight, water, and earth involved in its growth, and all combine together to ascend with the body and the vital soul in love of God which is manifested in it in the moment of prayer.

וְגַם מִתְפַּעֵל וְנִתְקָן מִמַּלְבּוּשִׁים וְדִירָה כו'

and it is also affected and amended by one's **clothing and place of residence...**

While garments are not ingested and do not enter the bloodstream, they still affect the soul. When a person wears a new garment, he feels new, he feels different. When he lives in dwelling place, the environment surrounding him affects his soul and mood. When he translates all these factors into serving God, when he utilizes the forces and possibilities that he has received from his garments and domicile, he elevates and refines the holy sparks that are in those garments and home. ☞

GARMENT AND DOMICILE

☞ It is explained elsewhere (see *Likkutei Torah*, Deut. 10:4, 99:1) that "garment" and "home" are levels of surrounding light. Garment is a closer surrounding light while home is farther: the surrounding light of the surrounding light, the distant surrounding light. Therefore, the author of the *Tanya* specifies and adds "garment" and "home" to indicate that even the influences of surrounding lights, even the distant surrounding, more encompassing light, that does not immediately nor directly affect a person's mood, but rather has a more long-term influence that makes a mark sometimes only after many years, even those connect and ascend with the vital soul when it transforms itself, all the influences that it gets from this world, to love of God.

All these gather together and are refined with a person's soul in the work of prolonged and contemplative prayer that the author of the *Tanya* addresses here.

מַה שֶּׁאֵין כֵּן בַּדּוֹרוֹת הָרִאשׁוֹנִים, שֶׁהָיוּ נִשְׁמוֹת הָאֱלֹקִית גְּדוֹלֵי הָעֵרֶךְ, הָיָה הַבֵּירוּר נַעֲשֶׂה כְּרֶגַע, בִּקְרִיאַת שְׁמַע לְבַד, וּבְרָכוֹת שֶׁלְּפָנֶיהָ וּפְסוּקֵי דְזִמְרָה בִּקְצָרָה וְכוּ' וְדַי לַמֵּבִין

This was not the case for the early generations, when the divine souls were of great quality – the refinement occurred instantaneously, through the recitation of the *Shema* alone, and the blessings before it and *Pesukei DeZimra* in brief form..., and this is sufficient explanation for one who understands esoteric wisdom.

Therefore, back then, there was no need to especially prolong prayer. This does not apply to these days, preceding the coming of the Messiah, in which in order to refine one's soul and reveal the hidden love through prayer, one must prolong his prayer to a greater extent in preparation for the recitation of the *Shema* and the *Shemoneh Esrei.* ☞

"DIVINE SOULS OF GREAT QUALITY"

☞ When speaking about a great soul, one means a soul that has a unique capacity for holiness. Like in every dimension, a person who has a special talent for music, mathematics, or anything else can achieve significantly more in much less time than anyone else. This also applies to holiness. A person with a Godly, lofty soul, a person who has an almost intuitive sense about every spiritual matter, does not need extensive work to prepare for prayer. The moment he says the words "Hear O Israel, God our Lord is one" he feels immediately, almost viscerally, the reality and unity of the Divine and love of God "with all of his heart and soul." In contrast, an ordinary person must work hard, sometimes hours, every day anew, to reach the level of feeling something spiritual when he utters those words.

Ostensibly, what is the benefit of a Godly, lofty soul? After all, there will always be an animalistic soul that is equally strong. Opposing the loftiness of his intellect and spiritual sensitivity there will necessarily be intellectual and emotional sensitivity that parallels it in the earthly realm. As the Sages have said (*Sukka* 52a): "He who is greater than his friend has a greater evil inclination." Nevertheless, because of the greatness, the whole struggle happens on a very lofty plane, and the victory of the divine soul will be immediate, since the vital soul will understand the matter automatically, and the adjustment from one love to the other will be easy and quick. This

While this essay begins with a local issue, with the negative behavior that the author of the *Tanya* heard attributed to a specific community, yet what he writes is not just applicable to that particular situation, but rather to the entire Jewish world, especially to those generations living at the end of exile. Because, particularly in this time of the heels of the Messiah, of concealment of the Divine in the world, the work of prolonged and intentional prayer is imperative, because it is the only way to reveal the hidden love of the Divine that lies latent in the heart of every Jew. As he highlighted in this essay, this is not a peripheral matter in one's service of God; this work is literally a Torah obligation, because in so doing the person fulfills the first commandment of the Torah of actually loving God, and since this is the work that refines and prepares one's soul and his whole world for service of God in this day and age in the heels of the Messiah.

does not happen with low souls, where on every angle the person is dealing with small details, and low, coarse places, where translating them to love of God, even to an elementary degree, demands work and time. This is what the author of the *Tanya* addresses here: in this time of the heels and end of history, the time when all the small details are reaching conclusion, the souls are well suited for that work. So that the vital soul that deals with worldly details can relate to the Divine at all and bind its loves and desires to God, it needs to recite the *Pesukei DeZimra* and the blessings before the *Shema* for a long time.

Essay 9
"You Shall Surely Rebuke Your Fellow"

THIS FINAL ESSAY, WHICH CONCLUDES *KUNTRES AḤARON* and the book of the *Tanya* as a whole, broadly focuses on practical matters. In the style of a summary and a conclusion, it reviews some of the main topics that have been discussed previously, and presents them in the form of practical conclusions. The essay can be divided into three parts, each of which centers on a different topic. The first continues from where the previous essay left off, by addressing prayer, specifically public prayer with intention and patience, and the important role of the prayer leader. The second part deals with the study of the Talmud in public, as mentioned in the first epistle in *Iggeret HaKodesh*, while the third part concerns the Sabbath. Although the author of the *Tanya* discusses the Sabbath only briefly throughout the *Tanya*, this is the topic with which he chooses to end the book.

"הוֹכֵחַ תּוֹכִיחַ אֶת עֲמִיתֶךָ" (ויקרא יט,יז), אֲפִילוּ מֵאָה פְּעָמִים (בבא מציעא לא,א) "You shall surely rebuke your fellow" (Lev. 19:17), **even one hundred times** (*Bava Metzia* 31a).

There is a mitzva from the Torah to rebuke one's colleague if he is observed acting in an unseemly manner. As is the case for several other mitzvot (such as sending away the mother bird from the nest and returning lost property), the Gemara asks how many times one is required to repeat this mitzva, and the answer given is that one must do it "even one hundred times," i.e., there is no upper limit. Since the mitzva is for a person to perform an action, not that the task itself must be done, it follows that it has no limit. Even if it seems to him that he is repeating the same act over and again without reason, it does not matter if it is the first or the hundredth time. This is especially true in the case of the mitzva of rebuke, since here the significance of one's persistence goes beyond the fact that he is not relinquishing or limiting the mitzva; he is thereby demonstrating his refusal to give up on the other person.

וְלָזֹאת לֹא אוּכַל לְהִתְאַפֵּק וּלְהַחֲרִישׁ מִלִּזְעוֹק עוֹד בְּקוֹל עֲנוֹת חֲלוּשָׁה

Accordingly, I cannot hold back and remain silent from shouting out more, in a "sound of a cry of weakness":

The phrase a "sound of a cry of weakness" was uttered by Moses upon his descent from Mount Sinai, in reference to the noise he could hear from the sin of the Golden Calf (Ex. 32:18). As explained by Rashi, it means the sound of a people fleeing in war; that is, a sound of distress, a cry of despair. The author of the *Tanya* uses this harsh language to express the sense of crisis he feels, after he has already spoken and reproved his audience many times to no avail, so that he does not know what else to say. His message is that even so, because the idea is so important and serious, he cannot refrain from articulating it yet again.

בְּמָטוּתָא מִינַּיְיכוּ בְּרַחֲמִין נְפִישִׁין חוּסוּ נָא עַל נַפְשׁוֹתֵיכֶם, וְהִשָּׁמְרוּ וְהִזָּהֲרוּ מְאֹד מְאֹד עַל הַתּוֹרָה וְעַל הָעֲבוֹדָה שֶׁבַּלֵּב זוֹ תְּפִלָּה בְּכַוּוֹנָה

I implore you, with great mercies, please have compassion upon your souls, and be watchful and exceedingly careful with regard to the Torah and the "service of the heart," which is prayer with intent –

This is an exceptionally severe warning, that one must be extremely careful with respect to both Torah study and the service of the heart, which is prayer with intent. As will become clear below, this grim warning refers specifically to the public services of communal Torah study and congregational prayer. The author of the *Tanya* pleads[1] with his hasidim to "have compassion upon your souls," as their very lives will be endangered if they fail to listen to him. The importance and power of public service is immeasurably greater than that of any single individual. At the same time, an individual who is part of the collective is usually unaware of the power he shares, as part of the community. It is true that each individual is only a small portion of any collective, but he is an indispensable part, and if he does not function properly he might interfere with and disrupt the service of the entire congregation. Furthermore, the service of the community, the *minyan*, is not merely the sum of its parts, for the collective together discovers the encompassment that lies beyond the dimensions and vessels of all the particulars.[2] Therefore, it is precisely with regard to public service that warnings and precautions are most necessary. ☞

The author will start by speaking about prayer, and later he will also address the issue of communal Torah study. While it is necessary to be "watchful and careful" with regard to all the mitzvot, it has been accepted from the earliest generations that special caution is necessary when it comes to all requirements of public prayer, such as praying

ME'OD ME'OD

☞ It is explained in several places in the hasidic sources that *me'od* means without limit, i.e., the level of encompassment that is higher than any definition and limitation, while the double expression *me'od me'od* expresses a level of encompassment in relation to the encompassment. Accordingly, when it comes to public service, which is considered an encompassment with respect to the service of an individual, and also an encompassment of an encompassment with respect to the personal encompassment of each person, one must be *me'od me'od* "watchful and careful" (see *Iggeret HaTeshuva*, chap. 7; *Likkutei Torah*, Num. 37a–b).

---

1. The expression "I implore you" comes from the Talmud (e.g., *Berakhot* 35b), while the phrase "with great mercies" is from the *Seliḥot* liturgical poem "*Maḥei UMasei*."

2. This can be metaphorically compared to a word that reveals an additional meaning which goes beyond the mere combination of its letters, as explained elsewhere with regard to the Rabbis' statement that "the Divine Presence dwells in any place where there are ten [Jews]" (*Sanhedrin* 39a). See *Iggeret HaKodesh*, epistle 23, and the commentary there.

together, refraining from talking, and not disturbing the communal prayer. Any lapse here can lead to a tangible and immediate danger.[3] These requirements of communal prayer are the minimum. The author is not addressing especially holy individuals to encourage them to do more, but all Jews, exhorting them not to diminish what they can and are obligated to do.

לְהַתְחִיל כּוּלָם יַחַד כְּאֶחָד, מִלָּה בְּמִלָּה וְלֹא זֶה בְּכֹה וְזֶה בְּכֹה, וְזֶה דּוּמֵם, וְזֶה מֵשִׂיחַ שִׂיחָה בְּטֵילָה, ה' יִשְׁמְרֵנוּ

that everybody should start together as one, word by word, not this one here and that one there, this one silent and that one engaging in idle conversation, may God preserve us.

Everyone should begin the prayer together, and also continue in this manner, as much as possible, throughout the entire prayer, reciting it word by word along with the prayer leader. The phrase "this one here and that one there," which is derived from I Kings 22:20, means that each person is in a different place in his prayer. The final comment, "may God preserve us," applies specifically to someone "engaging in idle conversation," since he is disturbing those who are trying to pray.

When a communal prayer is recited together, it pierces through all the heavens and there is nothing greater than this. However, when not everyone prays together, and some do not even pray at all but actively disturb others, "may God preserve us" from such danger. The loftier the sanctity, the more severe the impurity when it is negated; the steeper the ascent, the harder and more dangerous the fall. ☞

PUBLIC PRAYER

☞   The basic idea of public prayer is that the prayer of the many should become one: they should think and say one thing, like one person. When that happens, it becomes the kind of communal prayer that is always accepted and never returned

---

3. A special prayer (which blesses all those who are careful not to talk during prayer time) was instituted by Rabbi Yom Tov Lipmann Heller, the author of the *Tosefot Yom Tov*, at the time of the Cossack riots. This was due to the assumption, expressed by several leaders of Israel, that the persecutions and the devastation they wreaked were connected to this sin of engaging in idle conversation during communal prayer.

וְעִיקַּר הַסִּיבָה וּגְרָמָא בְּנִזְקִין הוּא
מֵהַיּוֹרְדִים לִפְנֵי הַתֵּיבָה, שֶׁהוּא
הֶפְקֵר לְכָל הָרוֹצֶה לִפְשׁוֹט רַגְלָיו
הַחוֹטֵף אֶפְרָתִי אוֹ מֵחֲמַת שֶׁאֵין גַּם
אֶחָד רוֹצֶה וכו׳

The main reason for and cause of this **harm is due to those who pass before the Ark** as prayer leaders, a position **that is free to whoever wishes to stretch forth his legs to snatch** it, someone who considers himself **an Ephrathite,** that is, a member of a distinguished family, **or because there is not even one** other person **who wants** to do it.

The clause translated as "to stretch forth his legs[4] to snatch [it, someone who considers himself] a member of a distinguished family" is literally

empty. For why should a prayer not be accepted in any situation? Because it was not whole; some word, thought, or a part of the soul was lacking. However, when everything is actually one, uniting all the powers of the soul from within the words of the prayer, then the prayer will be answered. For such a prayer, a word, is already operating and fulfilling the request. Similarly, in a public prayer, the combination of ten people together is like the combination of a single person's ten spiritual, divine powers together, which nothing can withstand. This is related to the well-known comment of the Mitteler Rebbe, Rabbi Dovber of Lubavitch, that when two Jews discuss matters pertaining to service of God, there are two divine souls against one animal soul (see *Sefer HaSiḥot*, 5697, p. 71, and *HaYom Yom*, 20 Tevet). The advantage of public prayer is that it is feasible, since no individual is required to exhaust all his powers in such a way that nothing is held back. For an individual this is a difficult requirement, which only virtuous individuals are capable of meeting, and not even these people at all times. But as part of a congregation, the very connection between different people neutralizes much of the *kelippa*, the separate being and coarseness of each individual person. Even if the heart and thought of the individual fails to achieve the same perfection, an entire structure of holiness is created from the community that operates independently, without taking into account all kinds of remnants of private thoughts and feelings that its members must inevitably have had. Since these remained private, did not come into effect, and did not join the public prayer, they do not impair it, as might occur in the prayer of an individual. Nevertheless, this clearly depends on the recitation of the public prayer together, word for word, and all the other conditions. Even if it is not perfect in terms of thought or intent, at the very least the words must be said together.

---

4. This expression is used by the early commentaries in precisely this context, that someone unworthy is not permitted "to stretch forth his legs" and pray (see,

rendered as "to stretch forth his legs, HaḤotef the Ephrathite."[5] This is a poetic turn of phrase, referring to a specific *tanna*, because whoever snatches [*hotef*] the position of prayer leader considers himself a person of distinguished lineage, an "Ephrathite."[6] The author adds that if no worthy individual agrees to serve as prayer leader, the role will be taken up by someone who is unsuitable.

The author of the *Tanya* thus lays the blame for this state of public prayer, where people are not praying together and there are other problems, on the prayer leader. He considers this a kind of an "administrative defect," which means that correcting the situation depends on the proper organization and leadership of the praying congregants, under the supervision of the prayer leader. This is, after all, the function of the prayer leader: to serve as the public leader and guide during the course of the prayer.

וְאִי לָזֹאת, זֹאת הָעֵצָה הַיְעוּצָה וְתַקָּנָה קְבוּעָה, חֹק וְלֹא יַעֲבוֹר עוֹד חַס וְשָׁלוֹם, דְּהַיְינוּ לִבְחוֹר אֲנָשִׁים קְבוּעִים הָרְאוּיִים לָזֶה עַל פִּי הַגּוֹרָל אוֹ בְּרִיצּוּי רוֹב הַמִּנְיָן:

As such, this is the devised plan and the permanent enactment, a statute that shall no longer be violated, God forbid, namely to select people in a fixed capacity, who are worthy of this, by lottery or through majority consent.

The beginning of the solution is to choose the right people, and that they will be the only ones to serve regularly as prayer leaders. ☞

The author adds that the "permanent enactment," i.e., the order

---

e.g., Responsa of the Rashba, vol. 1, 450, 791; Responsa of the Maharitz 104; also cited by the *Beit Yosef* and *Shulḥan Arukh HaRav, Oraḥ Ḥayyim* 53). In general, it is a way of displaying arrogant behavior, attributed here to one who forces himself on the public. The Lubavitcher Rebbe commented likewise in a note.

5. Rabbi Yosei, son of HaḤotef the Ephrathite, mentioned in Tractate *Kilayim* (3:7).

6. Note of the Lubavitcher Rebbe (according to *Likkutei Biurim*): For "snatch [*haḥotef*]," see *Ḥullin* 133a ["a priest who seizes [*hateif*] gifts"]; *Yalkut Shimoni* (as cited by Rashi), *Parashat Balak*, 769: "They quickly read [*hotfin*] the Shema." "Ephrathite" is perhaps a reference to the two explanations of this term mentioned by the Radak (I Samuel 1:1): A person of noble lineage; or someone distinguished by holiness.

of when each of them will lead the prayers, should be determined by lottery. The advantage of a lottery is that it eliminates the possibility of arguments, since it is independent of any specific person's opinion or wishes, and thus it is equally binding upon everybody. Another option, which is preferable, is that the majority of the congregation should express their preference for a particular individual.

דְּהַיְינוּ שֶׁמִּתְפַּלְּלִים מִלָּה בְּמִלָּה, בְּדֶרֶךְ הַמִּיצוּעַ, בְּקוֹל רָם, וְלֹא מַאֲרִיכִים יוֹתֵר מִדַּאי, וְלֹא מְקַצְּרִים וְחוֹטְפִים חַס וְשָׁלוֹם	**Specifically,** it should be **those who pray word by word, in a moderate manner, out loud, who do not overly prolong** the prayers, **nor do they shorten** them **and swallow** the words, **God forbid.**

That is, a prayer leader must know how to articulate each word separately, and he should neither hurriedly swallow his words nor stretch them out too much. His voice must be loud enough that the congregation can hear him and join in with him. Overall, he should not take longer than the majority of the congregation can bear and still maintain their concentration, and conversely he must take care that each word is enunciated properly and audibly.

"THE DEVISED PLAN"

☞ Even when he is speaking about serious matters, which must be expressed in a "permanent enactment, a statute that shall no longer be violated," the author calls this "the devised plan." The approach of the author of the *Tanya* (and of the Chabad Rebbes in general) is not to issue unequivocal instructions, in the manner of directives, but at most to offer advice, and even then usually only by way of an allusion. Apart from the fact that this is a wise approach to leadership in general, because those who wish to obey will do so anyway, while those who have no desire to comply will not be swayed even by an explicit command, there is a specific essential point here that characterizes the leadership of the author of the *Tanya*. His approach to leading his hasidim was that each hasid must do the work for himself. The Rebbe is not supposed to do anything on the hasid's behalf, and this includes not giving explicit and unambiguous instructions, since that would mean that the Rebbe was undertaking the responsibility, and in effect performing the act himself. The Rebbe merely advises, and even then only in such a manner that the choice and responsibility will be that of the hasid, to the greatest extent possible.

וַעֲלֵיהֶם מוּטָל חוֹבָה לֵירֵד לִפְנֵי
הַתֵּיבָה, כָּל אֶחָד וְאֶחָד בְּיוֹמוֹ
אֲשֶׁר יַגִּיעַ לוֹ, וְלֶאֱסוֹף אֵלָיו סָבִיב
סָמוּךְ כָּל הַמִּתְפַּלְלִים, בְּקוֹל קְצָת
עַל כָּל פָּנִים וְלֹא בְּלַחַשׁ וְלֹא
חוֹטְפִים חַס וְשָׁלוֹם

They have the obligation to descend before the Ark as prayer leaders, **each one on his designated day, and to gather around him, next to him, all those praying, with at least some voice, and** who are **not whispering or swallowing** the words, **God forbid.**

As stated, the main task of the prayer leader is to ensure that the congregation will recite the prayer together.

וְכַמְבוֹאָר בְּתַקָּנוֹת יְשָׁנוֹת בְּכַמָּה
עֲיָירוֹת. וְעַתָּה בָּאתִי לְחַדְּשָׁן
וּלְחַזְּקָן וּלְאַמְּצָן בַּל יִמּוֹטוּ עוֹד
לְעוֹלָם חַס וְשָׁלוֹם

This is as explained in **the old enactments of some towns, and I have now come to renew them, and to strengthen them and adopt them so that they should never fail again, God forbid**

As already implied at the beginning of the essay, the author of the *Tanya* is not saying anything new here; rather, he has repeatedly issued such demands in different places and on various occasions. In some towns these requests have even been accepted as written, binding enactments. In this essay, he is not seeking to add any new requirements, but simply to reinforce those existing decrees.

(בִּכְתַב יָד: גְּוֶואלְד גְּוֶואלְד)   (in the manuscript: *Gevald, gevald!*).

In this essay, which the author composed in his own handwriting, the author of the *Tanya* adds a colloquial Yiddish expression that comes straight from the heart: "*Gevald, gevald!*"[7] This phrase, for which there is no adequate translation and which does not appear elsewhere in the

---

7. See the Lubavitcher Rebbe, Rabbi Menaḥem Mendel Schneerson, *Iggerot Kodesh*, vol. 4, epistle 829: "My teacher and father-in-law, the Rebbe [Rabbi Yosef Yitzḥak Schneerson], may I be an atonement for his resting soul, said in one of his sermons that when speaking about something vital and heartfelt, [members of previous generations] would sometimes switch to Yiddish. As an example of this, he cited the comment of the author of the *Tanya* in *Iggeret HaKodesh*, 'You shall surely rebuke your fellow': '*Gevald, gevald!*'"

Tanya, shows how deeply he was affected by this issue of public prayer and prayer in general.

עַד מָתַי יִהְיֶה זֶה לָנוּ לְמוֹקֵשׁ (שמות י,ז)   "**Until when will this be a snare for us?**" (Ex. 10:7).

The "snare" is the fact that the public prayer is not as it should be, with everyone joining together in their recitation and intention, without any talking or interruptions, Heaven forfend. This quote is based on what Pharaoh's servants said to Pharaoh when he refused to learn the lesson from all the calamities that were befalling Egypt, and insisted on acting as though there was no connection between the plagues and Moses's demands. The same applies here: After all the retributions from which have been inflicted upon them, can they still fail to understand that these are due to improper prayer?

וְלֹא דַּי לָנוּ בְּכָל הַתּוֹכֵחוֹת וְהַצָּרוֹת שֶׁעָבְרוּ עָלֵינוּ ה' יִשְׁמְרֵנוּ וִינַחֲמֵנוּ בְּכִפְלַיִם לְתוּשִׁיָּה, וִיטַהֵר לִבֵּנוּ לְעָבְדוֹ בֶּאֱמֶת   **Are all the punishments and troubles that have befallen us not sufficient for us, may God protect us and comfort us with a double measure of wisdom, and purify our hearts to serve Him in truth.**

As stated, it was an accepted view that all the material troubles that had befallen the Jews, which were such terrible events that he does not wish to specify them but merely states "may God protect us," were to a large extent the result of this corruption of public prayer.

After his harsh comments, the author concludes this section with words of comfort and encouragement: May God "comfort us with a double measure of wisdom,"[8] i.e., they should rise up through the strength of their repentance and rectifications, and then they will receive a double portion of goodness than what they had before. The salvation will come through the very thing that was corrupted, for

---

8. The phrase "comfort us with a double measure" is from, e.g., *Eikha Rabba*, end of chap. 1, while "double measure of wisdom" comes from Job 11:6. For an interpretation of this expression, see the commentary on epistle 37.

God will "purify our hearts to serve Him" in the service of the heart, which is prayer. In order that our prayer will be "in truth," assistance is needed from Heaven. On our part, we can only serve God as best we can, but in order for our speech to be true, appropriate, and connected to the higher will, as an embodiment of "O Lord, open my lips so my mouth may declare Your praise" (Ps. 51:17), we require purification from above. This is the truest response of the Holy One, blessed be He, to our prayers.

חִזְקוּ וְיַאֲמֵץ לְבַבְכֶם כָּל הַמְיַחֲלִים   **Be strong and have your hearts**
לה'   **take courage, all of you who hope
in the Lord.**

This phrase is derived from Psalms 31:25. In order to attain this prayer, it is first of all necessary to work hard, because prayer always starts from below, from where we are situated. In this regard, the author states: "Be strong and have your hearts take courage." We must await God's response and hope for His salvation, for no matter what we do, say, and strive for, it will never match up to that for which we yearn, which is achieved only through the beneficence of God.

This concludes the first part of the essay, which focused on prayer. The second section deals with the study of Torah. Here too, the author addresses the congregation rather than individuals, as his request is specifically for a communal form of service.

גַּם לִגְמוֹר כָּל הַשַּׁ״ס בְּכָל שָׁנָה וְשָׁנָה   **Also,** it is important **to complete**
וּבְכָל עִיר וָעִיר   **the Six Orders** of the Talmud **each
year in every city,**

This is also a reproof, albeit not as severe a criticism as the previous one. As is the case for prayer, so too there is extra value and worth to Torah study performed in public. However, unlike public prayer, there is no fixed framework to public Torah study (mandated by *halakha* or custom) that must be observed carefully. Nevertheless, it is necessary to create and maintain such structures. The author of the *Tanya*'s idea is to create a framework that unifies time, place, and people in a shared study of Torah. Indeed, ideas of this kind are applied nowadays almost everywhere, on various topics, including the study of the Talmud, Bible,

Rambam, *Zohar*, and more. The aim here is "to complete the Six Orders [of the Talmud] each year in every city." ☞

לְחַלֵּק הַמַּסֶּכְתּוֹת עַל פִּי הַגּוֹרָל and I would suggest **dividing up the**
אוֹ בְּרָצוֹן **tractates by lottery or by consent.**

The author of the *Tanya's* suggestion is to divide up the tractates in a similar manner to the arrangement he proposed earlier with regard to prayer leaders. In order for the service of the public to succeed in general, all the details must be organized in a fixed order, which does not depend on people's constantly changing will or possible lack of will. He therefore suggests that the order be determined by lottery, since this removes any considerations of preferences or personal motives. In a lottery everyone is treated equally, which is why it is a suitable framework for the service of the collective. He adds "or by consent," since there is certainly no reason to prevent someone who has a personal preference to study a particular treatise from doing so. If a person's will and heart draws him to a specific topic, he will be more engaged there, and his study will accordingly be more successful.

וְעִיר שֶׁיֵּשׁ בָּהּ מִנְיָנִים הַרְבֵּה If a city has many congregations, each
יִגְמְרוּ בְּכָל מִנְיָן וּמִנְיָן one of them should complete it,

It is not only the collective that is important, that the community should study the entire Talmud in the same place, but each individual is also of significance. Every person should study at least one tractate a year. Therefore, where there is a large community, they should not allow a portion of the public to fulfill the duty on behalf of everyone,

COMPLETING THE SIX ORDERS OF THE TALMUD

☞ This custom, which the author of the *Tanya* instituted among his hasidim, was already mentioned in the first epistle of *Iggeret HaKodesh* and is practiced to this day among Chabad hasidim, for every congregation and *minyan* undertakes to study the entire Six Orders of the Talmud. At the cel- ebrations of the nineteenth of Kislev (the "New Year's Day for Hasidism") the hasidim divide the Six Orders among themselves: each takes it upon himself to study one tractate, and thus between them all, in the same year and place, the entire Six Orders will be studied.

but rather they should divide the Talmud many times over, so that everyone will be allotted a tractate.

וְאִם אֵיזֶה מִנְיָן קָטָן מֵהָכִיל, and if one congregation is too small
יִצָּרְפוּ אֲלֵיהֶם אֲנָשִׁים מֵאֵיזֶה to manage it, they should be joined
מִנְיָן גָּדוֹל, בְּבַל יְשׁוּנֶּה חֹק וְלֹא by men from some other, larger con-
יַעֲבוֹר gregation, without deviating from the requirement, a statute that shall not be violated.

The main thing is that each person should study some part of the Talmud, as part of the study of the entire Six Orders.

The author of the *Tanya* presents another requirement to those who study the Talmud:

וְכָל אֶחָד וְאֶחָד מֵהַלּוֹמְדִים And each and every one of those stu-
הנ"ל יִגְמוֹר לְעַצְמוֹ בְּכָל שָׁבוּעַ dents shall complete by himself, every
הַתְּמָנְיָא אַפֵּי שֶׁבַּתְּהִלִּים קי"ט week, the eightfold verses of Psalms 119.

Psalm 119, which is the longest in the book of Psalms (and, indeed, the longest chapter in the entire Bible), is structured alphabetically, eight times over.[9] In other words, it comprises eight verses, all of which start with the letter *alef*, followed by eight that begin with a *bet*, and so on for the whole alphabet. This lengthy psalm consists entirely of praises of the Torah, which is blessed with every possible laudatory name, such as "Your statutes," "Your precepts," "Your mitzvot," "Your saying," "Your laws," "Your edicts," and others. All this in one psalm of eightfold eight verses, for each letter of the alphabet.

The author of the *Tanya* addresses this request specifically to those studying the Talmud, that they recite this chapter every week. This is to ensure that the Torah does not become like other professional activities and fields of knowledge, since it will help them remember and reflect at all times that it is the Torah of the Holy One, blessed be He, Himself. Since the Torah has been brought down to us, and it deals mainly with the affairs of this world, its connection to its higher source is not evident in most cases, and thus we have to establish a

9. See *Berakhot* 4b.

framework in order to remember that we are dealing with not only oxen and donkeys, agriculture and tort law, but the wisdom and will of God Himself, which He revealed to us and desires from us. Furthermore, when we contemplate the Torah we are united in God's wisdom and will, and with Him Himself, in a unity that has no equal anywhere in any world.[10] When one reflects upon this, while reciting the eightfold verses of praise of the Torah that is within each letter, he will not only remember but actually feel like one who can see before him the Giver of the Torah Himself, as he keeps his focus on the Torah.

The author of the *Tanya* expects that each person should complete the eightfold verses himself, because this connection of the Torah to its Giver should be fully experienced by everyone, not only as a part of a community but for himself, in his personal being, his "measure," so that it touches him and enters the interiority of his heart. No person can share this engagement with anyone else; one cannot receive or give it. It is here, in his innermost self, that he must complete the entire eightfold chapter. ☞

It can be said that in this request to recite Psalm 119, the author of the *Tanya* links the study of the Talmud to the prayer he discussed in the earlier part of the essay. Accordingly, these are not two unrelated topics that he just happened to address in the same essay, but part of the same idea and message that he wishes to convey to his hasidim. This idea continues, it can be suggested, into the third part of the essay as well.

"WHY HAS THE LAND BEEN LOST?"

☞ The response to the prophet's question, "Why has the land been lost?" which is: "Because they have forsaken My Torah" (Jer. 9:11–12), is understood by the Sages to mean that they did not recite a blessing before studying the Torah. In other words, although they did study the Torah, they did not deem it necessary to recite a blessing over it, and thus they failed to mention and connect it to the Giver of the Torah, and this is why the land was lost. As stated, this is the topic of the whole essay: Why has the land been lost? Why are Jewish congregations and communities perishing? It is because they do not serve God with the power of the collective; they are not careful that public prayer is performed in the proper manner, and that the Torah is studied in every congregation and in the appropriate way, which is to recite a blessing before studying the Torah.

---

10. See *Likkutei Amarim*, chap. 5.

וְלִהְיוֹת מֵחֲמַת חֲלִישׁוּת **Since, due to the weakness of the gen-**
הַדּוֹר אֵין כֹּחַ בְּכָל אֶחָד וְאֶחָד **eration, not everyone has the strength**
לְהִתְעַנּוֹת כָּרָאוּי לוֹ **to fast as he should,**

This sentence appears to be a continuation of some comments that are missing. Whether there is an omission here or not, we ourselves should be able to fill in any possible gap. It appears that in this essay, which comes at the end of the book of the *Tanya*, the assumption is made that we have already studied the previous sections. Indeed, the background to this sentence can be found in *Iggeret HaTeshuva* (chap. 3), from which one can at the very least gauge what the author is referring to here. The subject of that chapter in *Iggeret HaTeshuva* is the atonement for one's sins by means of fasts, and the weakness of recent generations, who are unable to complete the number of fasts required by the *Tikkunei HaTeshuva* of the Arizal. It is stated there that as a result, one must nowadays give more to charity, a mitzva that corresponds to the fasts. Here he takes the same idea in a different direction.

The "weakness of the generation" is more a spiritual than a physical weakness. The issue of fasting does not only raise the question of what it does to the body, but mainly relates to a person's spiritual attitude toward the fast. It is clear that nowadays it is more difficult to fast; people are used to eating more, several times a day and between meals, and thus one's psychological dependence on food is greater. A person who has not eaten for several hours can hardly think of anything else apart from food. If a person fasts and fails to do anything useful on that day, the harm this causes outweighs any potential benefit of fasting. Furthermore, if one successfully completes the fast, he will feel so proud of himself that it would have been preferable for him not to have fasted at all.

לְזֹאת עֵצָה הַיְעוּצָה כְּמַאֲמַר **accordingly, the devised plan follows**
רַבּוֹתֵינוּ ז"ל (שבת קיח,ב): כֹּל **our Rabbis' statement (Shabbat 118b):**
הַשּׁוֹמֵר שַׁבָּת כְּהִלְכָתוֹ מוֹחֲלִין **Whoever observes the Sabbath in**
לוֹ עַל כָּל עֲווֹנוֹתָיו כְּהִלְכָתוֹ **accordance with its halakhot, God forgives him all of his transgressions –**
דַּוְקָא **"in accordance with its halakhot" is meant specifically.**

What is the connection between the Sabbath and repentance [*teshuva*]? There is indeed a conceptual link between them, apart from the similarity of the letters of which the two words are comprised. Repentance involves the return to one's roots, the homecoming of someone who has wandered off, back to his place of origin. The Sabbath is also, in its inner meaning, the ascent of all things back to their roots, as they were before they were created, and their return to the One who created them. Therefore, one who observes the Sabbath in accordance with its *halakhot*, like one who repents, will reach the root of his existence, which is above the array of laws and definitions that constitute this world. In that place, he can also obtain forgiveness for his sins. Although any action he has performed cannot be undone, when he is above the restraints of the causality of the world in which he performed the act, he may no longer be bound by its results.

However, in order to be with God alone, without any interference from anything else, one must be within the Sabbath in all its perfection, which means observing the Sabbath in accordance with its *halakhot*. If one fails to keep the Sabbath in accordance with any single *halakha*, it is as though a limb, hand, leg, or ear has not entered the Sabbath to be there with God, but has remained outside, separated.

לָכֵן מוּטָל עַל כָּל אֶחָד וְאֶחָד לִהְיוֹת בָּקִי בְּהִלְכְתָא רַבָּתִי לְשַׁבְּתָא	**Therefore, each and every person must be expert in the great *halakhot* of the Sabbath.**

The "great *halakhot*"[11] of the Sabbath are very severe: One who willfully desecrates the Sabbath, in the presence of witnesses, is liable to death by stoning. And yet they are among the most common *halakhot*, since once every seven days there is a whole day of the Sabbath. Whatever a person does on the Sabbath, such as eating, walking, or talking, he must know if it is permitted or not. It is related[12] that Rabbi Bunim of Peshischa once said: "When I was a boy and I first understood matters, I was afraid to stand up after having sat down on the Sabbath, and after I arose I was afraid to sit down again, for I was worried that I might be

---

11. The expression comes from *Shabbat* 12a.
12. See *Siaḥ Sarfei Kodesh*, vol. 1, *Shabbat Kodesh* 23.

desecrating the Sabbath. Therefore, for my own preservation I had to study the laws of the Sabbath."

וְגַם יִזָּהֵר מְאֹד שֶׁלֹּא לָשׂוּחַ שׁוּם   He must also be very careful not to
שִׂיחָה בְּטֵילָה חַס וְשָׁלוֹם   engage in any idle conversation, God
   forbid,

The prophets taught that certain forms of speech are forbidden on the Sabbath; see for example the verse "[You call the Sabbath a delight and the Lord's sacred, honored, and you honor it by refraining from doing your business,] from seeking your needs and from speaking of matters" (Isa. 58:13). We learn here that one may not speak on the Sabbath about issues that are "your needs," which do not concern the Sabbath or God. The author is stating that in order for the Sabbath to be an atonement for one's sin, he must observe the holy day in accordance with its *halakhot*, not only in deed but also in speech, and as much as possible in thought as well, in order to be connected with God in all the garments of one's soul.

The sanctification of one's speech and thought on the Sabbath, even with respect to what is permitted according to *halakha*, has a far-reaching inner meaning:

בִּהְיוֹת מוּדַעַת זֹאת לְיוֹדְעֵי חֵן,   as it is known to those initiated in the
כִּי בְּכָל הַמִּצְוֹת יֵשׁ פְּנִימִיּוּת   esoteric wisdom of the Kabbala that all
וְחִיצוֹנִיּוּת   the mitzvot have internal and external
   aspects.

The esoteric wisdom is also called "the internality of the Torah," because the most basic concept it reveals is that there an internality to the Torah and the mitzvot. In the internality of the Torah we are taught that even on the Sabbath there is both a visible layer, of one's deeds in the physical external reality, and also more internal layers of speech and thought, through which one observes the Sabbath as well. ☞

"ALL THE MITZVOT HAVE INTERNAL AND EXTERNAL ASPECTS"

☞   When we speak of "internality" with respect to the Torah and mitzvot, we are   not referring to their basic status as the internality of God's will and wisdom, since all

וְחִיצוֹנִית מֵהַשַּׁבָּת הוּא שְׁבִיתָה
מֵעֲשִׂיָּה גַּשְׁמִיִּית, כְּמוֹ שֶׁשָּׁבַת
ה' מֵעֲשׂוֹת שָׁמַיִם וָאָרֶץ גַּשְׁמִיִּים
וּפְנִימִית הַשַּׁבָּת הִיא הַכַּוָּונָה
בִּתְפִלַּת הַשַּׁבָּת וּבְתַלְמוּד תּוֹרָה –
לִדְבְקָה בַּה' אֶחָד

The external aspect of the Sabbath is the rest from physical activity, just as God rested from making the physical heavens and earth, while the internal aspect of the Sabbath is one's **intent in the Sabbath prayers and in Torah study, to cleave to the one God.**

The general rule is that we must strive to be like God. The Sabbath of God consisted of a rest from the creation of the physical heavens and earth, as described in the second chapter of Genesis. The same applies to our Sabbath, on which we rest from similar activities. Just as God rested from the creation of the world, which is separate from Him, as it were, so too for us the rest is from all our actions in the world. We leave them behind and return to the soul itself. We do not carry out tasks, nor do we speak of or think about them, but rather we transcend

aspects of the Torah and mitzvot are internal, at every level and in every place. This is in fact the meaning of the Torah in contrast to the entire reality of this world, for the Torah has no externality and is entirely internal. It is the worlds that reveal the externality of the will, what God does in order to have what He desires, internally, whereas the Torah invariably reveals precisely His true wishes, on the internal level. However, the inner nature of the Torah, which is revealed by the esoteric wisdom, is that there is a reality and revelation to the Torah even in the inner, hidden worlds. It is explained in the revealed Torah, both the Written and Oral Torah, that a mitzva is revealed in the external worlds, in the world of physical activity where the mitzva is actually performed. Meanwhile, the esoteric wisdom reveals that the mitzva is also "performed" in the inner spiritual levels of reality, one level above the other, where there is no further action but only

speech, and even at a level where there is not even speech but merely thought.

Here we can cite an example, to which we have frequently had recourse: There is a mitzva to sacrifice a burnt offering, and this is a practical obligation that must be performed in the Temple, along with many other conditions. Yet even when one merely studies the *halakhot* of a burnt offering, in speech alone, and not through action, this has the same significance and value as the fulfillment of the mitzva, to a certain degree. On an even more inner level, simply thinking about drawing closer to God, i.e., prayer, which is the "service of the heart" that corresponds to the offerings, is equivalent to fulfilling the mitzva of bringing an offering with all its specific requirements, in an inner, spiritual dimension, as explained in various ways in the works of esoteric wisdom (see, e.g., *Menaḥot* 110a; see also *Likkutei Torah*, Lev. 24d and onward, Num. 13a and onward).

them in order to relate to the Divine Himself, as He is in His rest from the labor of the world.

How can one observe "the internal aspect of the Sabbath," in one's speech and thought, in the higher reality that is above this world of physical actions? As on the external level, so on the internal level, there is a division between positive and negative commands, between what must be done and what has to be avoided on the Sabbath. This is a division that the Sages attribute to two verses that appear in the Ten Commandments: "Remember the Sabbath day" (Ex. 20:8) and "Observe the Sabbath day" (Deut. 5:12).

The "positive commandment" of the inner Sabbath is to have "intent in the Sabbath prayers and in Torah study, to cleave to the one God." On the external level, in practice, the mitzvot of the Sabbath are mainly negative commandments, since the mitzva is to rest as God did, and rest involves refraining from activity. What did God do on the day of the Sabbath; what did He create? Nothing. We too do nothing on the Sabbath, as much as this is possible. This applies on the external level, but when it comes to the internal aspect of the Sabbath the situation is different. For just as God Himself did not create heaven and earth but was Himself, so we do not take action on the Sabbath, but we exist, to a greater extent than on other days, as ourselves: in our thoughts, we focus on the intention to cleave to the one God.

Cleaving to the one God, as He is incomparably Himself, is our Sabbath. It is thus like the Sabbath of God: We become ourselves by resting from all activities that operate in and are connected to another world. Then, when we are ourselves, at our roots, beyond all actions, thoughts, feelings, and cognitions, we are truly one with Him.

The author here emphasizes one's intent, not necessarily the recitation of prayer or the words of the Torah, but one's intention at the time. Of course, as long as we live in this world we cannot literally do nothing, not think or not feel anything. However, we can reach the stage where our action or speech will not be important for itself, but merely the framework for the pure intention, which is one's cleaving to the one God. We pray on the Sabbath, with words, from a siddur, in the synagogue, and so on, but this is nothing more than the vessel for our intention to cleave to God. An expression of this idea is that on the Sabbath we do not pray for the affairs of this world, for healing or a livelihood, and the like. Instead, the eighteen blessings of the standard *Amida* prayer are shortened to a mere seven, and these focus on praising and thanking God and describing the nature of the Sabbath day. Likewise, Torah study on the Sabbath is not like the study of the Torah on weekdays, but is mainly geared toward helping one cleave to God alone. Accordingly, this is the way to observe the Sabbath on the internal level: to meditate on and intend to cleave to the one God.

> כְּמוֹ שֶׁכָּתוּב: "שַׁבָּת לַה׳ אֱלֹקֶיךָ" (שמות
> כ,י) וְזוֹ הִיא בְּחִינַת "זָכוֹר" (שמות כ,ח)

As it is written: "A Sabbath for the Lord your God" (Ex. 20:10), **and this is an aspect of "Remember"** (Ex. 20:8),

A person's Sabbath day, his actions, words and thoughts, indeed his whole being and existence on the day of the Sabbath, transcend the world "for the Lord your God."[13] This is of course a consequence of one's intention, since a person's actions on the Sabbath are basically the same as those of the weekdays, with regard to eating, drinking, and his other deeds. The difference on the Sabbath lies in one's intent behind those actions and words, that they should be "for the Lord your God."

Whereas for the external conduct of the Sabbath one must "remember" the limited halakhic requirement of sanctification, with respect to the internality of the Sabbath this "remember" has a much broader meaning, that one's intent in all his actions and speech must be "for the Lord your God."

> וּבְחִינַת "שָׁמוֹר" (דברים ה,יא) בִּפְנִימִיּוּת,
> הִיא הַשְּׁבִיתָה מִדִּיבּוּרִים גַּשְׁמִיִּים, כְּמוֹ
> שֶׁשָּׁבַת ה׳ מֵעֲשָׂרָה מַאֲמָרוֹת שֶׁנִּבְרְאוּ
> בָּהֶם שָׁמַיִם וָאָרֶץ גַּשְׁמִיִּים

while an aspect of "Observe" (Deut. 5:12), **in the internal aspect, is resting from physical speech, just as God rested from the ten utterances with which the physical heavens and earth were created.**

---

13. A similar expression appears in the sources with respect to festivals as well (see *Pesaḥim* 68b): "A solemn assembly for the Lord your God" (Deut. 16:8), in contrast to: "A solemn assembly for you" (Num. 29:35). See also *Likkutei Torah*, Lev. 14d and onward.

On the external level the rest is from activity, while on the internal level it is from speech: to refrain from discussing the affairs and building of the world, just as God rested from the speech of the ten utterances with which the world was created. ☞

כִּי "זֶה לְעוּמַת זֶה" (קהלת ז,יד).   **For** "God made **this corresponding to that**" (Eccles. 7:14).

With respect to both the Sabbath and the internal aspect of speech there is "this speech corresponding to that speech." There is a speech of the Sabbath, of ascending and cleaving to God, while corresponding to it there is a mundane, material speech, which desecrates the Sabbath on the internal level. Thus, the choice to observe the Sabbath applies on all levels, from the physical level of an actual violation of the *halakhot* of the Sabbath, through the kind of speech that opposes holiness, diverting one's thoughts away from the Sabbath to secular concerns, to a thought that desecrates the Sabbath in the soul. ☞

"REST" IN THE EXTERNAL AND INTERNAL ASPECTS

☞ The difference between interiority and exteriority is, metaphorically speaking, comparable to the difference between what others, from the outside, see in a person, and how he views himself. The same applies to God's creation of the world. We from the outside see events, the formation of heaven and earth, whereas He, from His perspective, as it were, sees speech:

"And the Lord said, and so forth." With respect to human conduct as well, an action expresses the external, what exists in actuality, whereas speech expresses the internal, what we desire and intend to bring into existence. This is what is stated here, that on the external level one rests from action, whereas on the internal level one rests from speech.

FOR "[GOD MADE] THIS CORRESPONDING TO THAT"

☞ The esoteric sources interpret this verse as referring to the existence of evil as opposed to good. God made both of them, as it were, as two sides, two options, of seeing the existence of our world. The world is one of choices, in which holiness in

not easy to perceive. Contrasting with every aspect of holiness is an opposing force of impurity that conceals it, or at least ensures that the expression of sanctity will not be unambiguous. For if that were the case, man would not have free choice.

This essay dealt with three topics: public prayer, communal Torah study, and the Sabbath. Each of these has two aspects, the external level and also the internal level, which is revealed from the external.

The essay starts with prayer. Ostensibly, it deals with the external framework of public prayer: everyone must begin together, recite the prayer word for word, avoid talking during the prayer, find a way to select a prayer leader, and so forth. However, there is also an interior aspect to prayer, which the author of the *Tanya* imparts through an unusual exclamation in reference to this issue, that is so important to him. No similar expression can be found throughout the book of the *Tanya*, and it is "uncharacteristic" of the author of the *Tanya* not to have a measured response to the situation but simply to shout out the informal cry: "*Gevald, gevald!*" For within this apparently simple framework of public prayer, which is often taken for granted, there lies the most inner content of the loftiest connection between Israel and the Holy One, blessed be He, which is higher than wisdom and words. For this reason, he cries out and begs his audience to act for their own sakes, since their very lives depend on this matter.

The author then proceeds to talk about Torah study; not the study of the Torah by exceptional individuals, but the seemingly external framework of the study of all Six Orders of the Talmud by the entire congregation. Yet here too, his demand penetrates into the interiority of the study, that the Torah must be studied for its own sake, in order to draw the light of the *Ein Sof* into the wisdom of the Torah. As was the case for public prayer, he derives this feature precisely from the externality, from the Torah studied by the public. For more than any single individual, the collective can express the inner essence of Israel and the internality of our relationship to the Divine Himself, which continuously bestows His influence through the Torah itself.

Finally, he discusses the Sabbath, stating that whoever observes the Sabbath in accordance with its *halakhot* will be forgiven for all of his transgressions. Here too, he is referring to the external framework of the Sabbath observance in accordance with its *halakhot*, for it is only when performed in this manner that one's sins are forgiven. He adds that it is not enough to observe the Sabbath on the external level; one must keep the Sabbath on the internal level as well, in one's speech and thought, and thereby rest from all the affairs of the world and cleave to the Divine.

This short essay, which concludes the book of the *Tanya*, focused mainly on externalities, like a seal that is impressed on the outside. Nevertheless, a seal is not merely a lock; it guards the content not because it cannot be smashed but because people are wary of breaking it, because the seal represents the one who put it there. Indeed, this is the point of this essay: it deals with externalities and yet testifies to the innermost levels that lie within.

The *Tanya* is considered the Written Torah of Hasidism, and therefore this internality, if we can attempt to distinguish it, is an inner point for the hasidic approach in general. As stated, the internal line that runs through all parts of this essay is the deep connection between Israel and God. In Hasidism in general, what emerges from all the teachings, stories, and anecdotes about leadership is that the most important thing for God is the Jew himself. A Jew can be the greatest of the great or the simplest of the simple; his entire Torah and mitzvot are only the background and the clothing that surround and define him. The uniqueness of each member of Israel for the Holy One, blessed be He – and this is the attitude we should all have – is precious beyond all definition.

Summary of Chapters – *Iggeret HaKodesh*

The following is a summary of the thirty-two epistles which comprise *Iggeret HaKodesh*.

Epistle 1: Starting with a benediction

The main topic of this epistle, which begins with a blessing to the hasidim for completing the Talmud, is faith: Strengthening one's faith by studying *halakhot*, and the power of faith to establish and reinforce one's love and fear of God.

Epistle 2: "I am unworthy of all the kindnesses"

An epistle from the author to his hasidim after his acquittal and release from prison on 19 Kislev, 1798. In the wake of the kindness that God has bestowed upon them, his hasidim must humble themselves and act with meekness and modesty.

Epistle 3: "He donned charity like armor"

An epistle on the virtue of charity. All of the mitzvot are drawn from the light that encompasses all worlds to the light that fills them, but charity extends this flow to our material existence as well. Furthermore, charity protects us by preventing the external forces of impurity above from also drawing sustenance.

Epistle 4: The Jewish people are redeemed only through charity

An epistle on the virtue of the mitzva of charity. There is an external dimension and an inner dimension to the feelings of the heart. The external dimension is attained through contemplation, while the inner dimension is an expression of the internality of the heart that transcends contemplation. Not all people merit this dimension, but during prayer a person can merit internality as well, and this awakening from below is achieved through charity.

Epistle 5: "David made a name"

An epistle on the virtue of charity. Charity draws the light of *Ein Sof* from supernal Ḥokhma to this world, which is like the drawing down of Ḥokhma to the letters. From here the epistle moves on to a lengthy discussion of the nature of the letters in general, and the ramifications of these ideas for man's service of God through the Torah and the mitzva of charity.

Epistle 6: "The sower of charity has a true reward"

An epistle on the virtue of charity. The reward for charity is the attribute of truth. The epistle clarifies the nature of the attribute of truth in the service of God, and how it can be attained through the attribute of compassion by giving charity, especially to the residents of the Holy Land.

Epistle 7: "We are fortunate. How good is our portion"

In its inner meaning, this epistle focuses on the connection between the mitzvot and soul. Every Jew has a unique portion, a special mitzva and service that belongs to the root of his soul and which purifies it as necessary.

Epistle 8: "He sows charity and brings forth salvation"

An act of charity performed by Israel below awakens the drawing down of the kindness of God from above to shine upon man, especially at the time of prayer. This is particularly true of charity given to the Land of Israel, since one thereby awakens the supernal Land of Israel.

Epistle 9: My beloved ones, my brethren and friends

The main service of God in this period of "the heels of the Messiah" is charity. The Jewish people are redeemed only through charity, and one who slaughters his evil inclination through the mitzva, by opening his hand and heart, will "merit seeing with actual eyes the return of God to Zion."

Epistle 10: After greetings of peace and life

The importance of giving charity. Since "we are not perfect and complete," we require God's infinite kindness. We must therefore give unlimited charity, even more than the standard one-fifth, because charity heals the soul.

Epistle 11: To enlighten you with understanding

In order for the light of God to dwell within a person he must dedicate himself absolutely to the divine, without reserving any inner desire for this world. The way to attain this level is through a true faith that everything is from God and that no evil descends from above.

Epistle 12: "The act of charity will be peace"

There are two levels of giving charity: The "act of charity" and the "service of charity." The "act of charity" is what the soul is naturally drawn to do, while the "service of charity" is what the soul performs that goes beyond its nature. Corresponding to the charity that a person gives below, he merits charity and a divine revelation from above, on those two levels: A revelation in accordance with his measure, and an immense revelation that is without measure.

Epistle 13: "How great is the goodness You have"

In general terms, those who serve God can be divided into two types: The right side and the left side. The left side is the attribute of constriction and the fulfillment of mitzvot in a limited manner, which one is obligated to do according to the Torah, and by "walking humbly." The right side is kindness, expansiveness, and the fulfillment of mitzvot in an unlimited manner. Every Jew incorporates both sides; the only difference is which side is revealed.

Epistle 14: To awaken the old love

The virtue of giving charity to the Holy Land. Such charity is positioned directly opposite the supernal land, which receives the light of *Ein Sof* from supernal Ḥokhma. The epistle explains at length that the light is drawn down every year afresh, and giving charity to the Holy Land awakens this drawing forth with even greater strength.

Epistle 15: "To understand proverbs and aphorisms"

A basic epistle that deals with the ten *sefrot*, clarifying them according to Hasidic teachings, as paralleling the faculties of the soul of man.

Epistle 16: My beloved ones, my brethren and friends

A call to give charity in the usual manner, even when the giver is himself destitute and has to give his own basic necessities. For one's dedication in giving charity will be his salvation at a time of need.

Epistle 17: It is known that an awakening from below

This epistle deals with the reward for giving charity, whose "fruit is eaten in this world while the principal remains for the World to Come." The emphasis is on the reward for the mitzva in the World to Come, both the recompense in the Garden of Eden and the reward at the time of the resurrection of the dead. The epistle clarifies the nature of the reward in the World to Come, and how this relates specifically to the mitzva of charity.

Epistle 18: "How fair you are and how pleasant you are"

A Hasidic essay on the topic of the love for God, which explains the difference between two types of love: The "love of delights" and the love of desire and yearning for God's closeness.

Epistle 19: "Enveloping with light as if with a cloak"

A Hasidic essay on the Torah, specifically on the relationship between the Torah in supernal Ḥokhma, and the Torah in our possession. Notwithstanding all of the garments in which the Torah is enclothed until it reaches our world, it is the very same Torah and wisdom as it is above. The epistle also discusses the nature of the attainment of the Torah, and the difference between the comprehension of a Sage and that of a prophet.

Addendum to Epistle 19: The letters revealed to us

A short essay on the Hebrew letters. In addition to the content that they transmit, the letters themselves constitute a profound essence that cannot be grasped, which is always the meaning of speech.

Epistle 20: He and His life forces

A complex essay, written mostly in the language of the Kabbala, on the unity of the *sefirot* in the light of *Ein Sof*, and on the power of *Ein Sof*, which is revealed whenever there is a creation "existence from nothingness," how it descends and unfolds from one world to the next, in the form of "their beginning is affixed to their end." The practical message is the virtue of the mitzvot that are fulfilled through action, whose beginning is likewise "affixed to their end."

Epistle 21: After inquiring into the welfare

On the charity given to the Holy Land, which must be increased on a weekly basis, for it is a great virtue to give on many occasions, For when a mitzva is performed many times over it draws down an abundance from above.

Epistle 22: My beloved ones, my brethren and friends

This epistle is an attempt to regulate the relationship between the hasidim and the Rebbe. It calls on the Hasidim not to come to ask the Rebbe about material problems, but only to inquire into their service of God, while for the affairs of this world they must place their trust in God.

Addendum to Epistle 22: My beloved ones, my brethren and friends, on account of my great preoccupation

A rousing call to the hasidim to pray with pure intent, and to strengthen the bond of love between the hasidim themselves.

Epistle 23: "By the decree of the angels"

The sanctity of a *minyan*. "Ten who are sitting and are engaging with the Torah, the Divine Presence rests amongst them," and this is all the more true when they are praying. Accordingly, one should not sit idly in the synagogue, but rather there should be communal Torah study between the afternoon prayer and the evening prayer, and on the holy Shabbat they should study the laws of Shabbat.

Epistle 24: My beloved ones, my brethren

The sanctity of the synagogue. A synagogue is a "miniature sanctuary" in which the King, the Holy One blessed be He, reveals Himself to each person through the letters of the prayer, in accordance with his intellect and the root of his soul. One who is preoccupied with his own needs at the time disparages the King, and therefore a person should not engage in idle conversation from when the Prayer Leader begins until the end of the prayer.

Epistle 25: *Tzava'at Rivash*

An interpretation of a teaching in the book *Tzava'at Rivash* on the enclothing of the Divine Presence in the *kelippot*, which aroused the objection of the *mitnagdim*. The author of the *Tanya* wrote this interpretation as a model for all the apparently puzzling teachings of the early hasidic masters, which have profound meanings when they are explained in accordance with hasidic thought.

Epistle 26: "The wise"

This epistle is basically an interpretation of a seemingly puzzling teaching of the *Zohar*. It presents the hasidic approach to the study of the inner dimension of the Torah and the revealed Torah in these times and the messianic era.

Epistle 27: A letter of condolence for the passing of Rabbi Menaḥem Mendel of Vitebsk

This epistle explains that the life of a tzaddik in this world is not "a life of flesh." Thus, even after his death the tzaddik continues to have an influence on those who are connected to him. This applies both on the internal level and in the form of an encompassing, hidden influence that reaches every Jew.

Epistle 28: A letter of condolence for the passing of Rabbi Levi Yitzḥak of Berditchev

A Kabbalistic and hasidic interpretation of the Sages' teaching that just as the red heifer grants atonement, so does the passing away of the righteous.

Epistle 29: "A woman of valor"

On the study of the *halakhot* of the Oral Torah. These *halakhot* reveal the supernal will, which is the garment and externality of the supernal delight. Accordingly, the fulfillment and study of *halakhot* is the garment of the soul through which it receives the supernal divine delight of the Garden of Eden.

Epistle 30: "Whoever is accustomed to coming to the synagogue"

This epistle is addressed to those hasidim who had stopped giving charity in their accustomed manner. It discusses the virtue of charity when it is performed on numerous occasions and at fixed times.

Epistle 31: "Known in the gates"

On the importance of the bond between the hasidim, and that there should be peace between them. The souls of Israel are called the "limbs of the Divine Presence," while the Divine Presence itself is the heart. Just as the health of the body depends on the proper connection between the organs and the flow of blood between them, so too the vitality of the worlds and the redemption of the Divine Presence depend on the cleaving of the souls together and their attachment to one another.

Epistle 32: "Bless, O Lord, their might"

This epistle starts with an expression of thanksgiving and a blessing to the hasidim for a great act of charity in their community. It continues with an explanation of the inner nature of charity, which is revealed through its future reward, before concluding with a call of awakening to the love of God through prayer, which is the spiritual stage that precedes and precipitates the act of charity.

Summary of Chapters
Kuntres Aḥaron

Below is an outline of the essays of *Kuntres Aḥaron* and a brief summary of their content:

Essay 1: "**To understand how one who reads all the narrative stories in the Torah is connected to the supernal wisdom.**"

This section addresses a topic discussed in *Likkutei Amarim* (chap. 40) and elsewhere: the essential connection in a person's divine service between his intention and his speech or action. Here, the author of the *Tanya* relates to this matter from a different perspective, primarily addressing what happens to an intention that is not accompanied by an action or utterance. Toward the end of the section, he also discusses what happens to speech that lacks intention.

Essay 2: "**See *Etz Ḥayyim, Sha'ar HaNekudot*... where it explains that the turning of face to face is achieved exclusively by means of performative mitzvot.**"

This section deals with the same topic as the previous section: intention and action. Here, this matter is addressed through the most fundamental question regarding divine service: How do we awaken the supernal union and flow from the lower world? In order to make this possible, how do we return the upper and lower realms to a state of being "face to face"? What part does action play in this, and what part does intention play?

Essay 3: "To understand what is written in *Sha'ar HaYiḥudim*."

This section relates to the same chapters of the *Tanya* and addresses the matter of intention and speech, where speech is equated to action. Specifically, it considers the outcomes of intention and speech with regard to Torah study and prayer. It shows that there is a difference between Torah study and prayer in this regard, and explains why this is so.

Essay 4: "We wish to understand what is written in *Peri Etz Ḥayyim*."

This, the longest and most complex section of *Kuntres Aḥaron*, is concerned with divine service. It begins with a discussion of prayer, through which the individual, and the sparks of holiness in the world, ascend to higher realms. Later, it addresses Torah study and the practical mitzvot: God Himself is "drawn" to the person who performs these acts in the physical world.

Essay 5: "We wish to understand the details of *halakhot* that do not apply."

This section addresses the study of *halakha* in general, and in particular, the study of those *halakhot* that do not apply in any real-life situations, whether in the past, present, or future. Thus it emphasizes the value of studying *halakha* for its own sake rather than simply to learn how to behave.

Essay 6: "David, you call them songs?"

This is one of the most fundamental essays of hasidic thought. It is concerned with the praise of Torah, or more precisely, with the intrinsic glory of the Torah, which is beyond all praise. Any praise used to describe the Torah detracts from its inner essence, which is the delight of God alone.

Essay 7: "And charity like a constant stream."

This section is an epistle addressed to the hasidim of the author of the *Tanya*. Accordingly, in addition to its highly abstract subject, the flow of the inner dimension of the Divine to the inner dimension of the human heart, it discusses the practical way to achieve this flow: by giving charity.

Essay 8: "Now, the report that I hear is not good."

This too is an epistle, which addresses the subject of communal prayer. It begins with a condemnation of improper procedures in hasidic prayer services, and ends with deep hasidic insights concerning the greatness of prayer and how to pray.

Essay 9: "You shall rebuke your neighbor."

This is the final chapter of the *Tanya*. It is an epistle that deals with three topics: communal prayer, communal Talmud study, and halakhic and spiritual Sabbath observance, which atones for our transgressions.

Glossary

alef First letter of the Hebrew alphabet

aliya Immigration to the Land of Israel

Amida Silent prayer recited three times daily

amora'im Sages of the Talmud who lived from approximately 200 to 500 CE

Arizal Rabbi Yitzḥak Luria of Tzefat (1534–1572), the most influential kabbalist of modern times

Ashkenazic A Jew who originated from northern and eastern Europe, primarily Germany and its environs

Asiya The world of Action, the fourth and lowest of the spiritual worlds

Atzilut The world of Emanation, the highest of the four spiritual worlds and closest to the source of creation

ayin Nothingness; the sixteenth letter of the Hebrew alphabet

Ba'al Shem Tov Rabbi Yisrael ben Eliezer (1698–1760), founder of the hasidic movement

beinonim Literally, "intermediates"; those who are on a level where he is neither wicked nor righteous

Beit Hillel Literally, "House of Hillel"; a school of thought named after the mishnaic Sage Hillel, who founded it

Beit Shammai Literally, "House of Shammai"; a school of thought named after the mishnaic Sage Shammai, who founded it

Beria The world of Creation, the second of the four spiritual worlds

bet The second letter of the Hebrew alphabet

Bina Understanding, one of the ten divine attributes known as *sefirot*

Chabad An acronym of the three cognitive attributes, *Ḥokhma, Bina*, and *Da'at*; the name attributed to Lubavitch Hasidism, founded by Rabbi Shneur Zalman of Liadi

Da'at Knowledge, one of the ten divine attributes known as *sefirot*

dalet The fourth letter of the Hebrew alphabet

Ein Sof God's infinite being

etrog Citron, one of the four species waved on the festival of Sukkot

gaon An outstanding Torah scholar

Gevura Restraint, one of the ten divine attributes known as *sefirot*

gimmel The third letter of the Hebrew alphabet

Haggada Book that tells the story of the Exodus to be related at the Seder on the first night of Passover

halakha (pl. halakhot) Jewish law

hasid (pl. hasidim) Literally, "pious individual"; a follower of Hasidism, the movement initiated by the Ba'al Shem Tov

Havaya A reference to the four-letter name of God known as the Tetragrammaton

ḥaya The second highest of the five soul levels

ḥayot Angelic creatures that appear in Ezekiel's mystical vision

heh The fifth letter of the Hebrew alphabet

Ḥesed Kindness, one of the ten divine attributes known as *sefirot*

ḥet The eighth letter of the Hebrew alphabet

Hod Splendor, one of the ten divine attributes known as *sefirot*

Ḥokhma Wisdom, one of the ten divine attributes known as *sefirot*

Ḥumash The five books of the Torah

Ibn Ezra Abraham ben Meir ibn Ezra (c. 1092–1167), a Spanish poet, grammarian, and biblical commentator

Kabbala The mystical teachings of the Torah

kaf (or khaf) The eleventh letter of the Hebrew alphabet

kelippa (pl. kelippot) Literally, "husk"; the aspect of the universe that is unholy and conceals the Divine

kelippat noga Literally, "glowing husk"; a form of *kelippa* that contains an element of goodness that can be elevated

Keter Crown, one of the ten divine attributes known as *sefirot*

Kislev The third month in the Jewish calendar, which falls out during winter

kof The nineteenth letter of the Hebrew alphabet

lamed The twelfth letter of the Hebrew alphabet

lulav Palm frond, one of the four species waved on the festival of Sukkot

Maggid of Mezeritch Rabbi Dovber (d. 1772), a disciple of the Ba'al Shem Tov and the teacher of Rabbi Shneur Zalman of Liadi, author of the *Tanya*, who strengthened the Hasidism of his master, anchoring it firmly in Jewish thought and practice

Maharal An acronym for Rabbi Yehudah Loew of Prague (1525–1609), one of the outstanding scholars and Jewish leaders of the sixteenth century

Malkhut Kingship, one of the ten divine attributes known as *sefirot*

mem The thirteenth letter of the Hebrew alphabet

menora Candelabrum with eight lights traditionally lit during the festival of Hanukkah, also known as a *hanukkiya*

mezuza A parchment scroll on which four portions from the Torah are inscribed and affixed to the doorpost of a Jewish home

Midrash Collection of homiletic interpretations of the Scriptures by the Sages of the Talmud

mikveh Bath used for ritual immersion

Mishna A concise summary of the teachings of the Sages on all topics of Torah, which was redacted in the beginning of the third century CE by Rabbi Yehuda HaNasi

mitzva (pl. mitzvot) A Torah commandment

mohin Literally "brains"; the *sefirot* corresponding to the cognitive faculties

nefesh The soul; specifically, the lowest of the five levels of the soul

neshama The soul; specifically, the third of the five soul levels

Netzah Dominance, one of the ten divine attributes known as *sefirot*

nun The fourteenth letter of the Hebrew alphabet

parasha (pl. parashiyot) Torah portion

partzuf (pl. partzufim) Literally, "divine countenance"; a particular arrangement of the ten *sefirot*

peh The seventeenth letter of the Hebrew alphabet

peruta Coin of a small denomination

Rabba Rabba bar Nahmani (died c. 320 CE), a prominent third-generation talmudic Sage from Babylon

Rabbeinu Bahya A rabbi and scholar (1255–1340), best known for his commentary on the Torah

Rambam Maimonides; Rabbi Moses ben Maimon (1138–1204), a leading halakhic authority and philosopher

Ramban Nachmanides; Rabbi Moses ben Naḥman (1194–1270), renowned for his commentary on the Torah and Talmud

Rashi Rabbi Shlomo Yitzḥaki (1040–1105), one of the foremost commentators of the Torah and Talmud

resh The twentieth letter of the Hebrew alphabet

Rosh HaShana Jewish New Year

ruaḥ Second of the five soul levels

samekh The fifteenth letter of the Hebrew alphabet

Sanhedrin A tribunal of sages consisting of seventy-one members

se'a A unit of volume measurement used in talmudic times

sefira (pl. sefirot) One of the ten divine attributes with which God creates, sustains, and directs the worlds

shamash Attendant

Shema Prayer recited three times daily in which one declares one's faith in the oneness of God

shin The twenty-first letter of the Hebrew alphabet

shofar Ram's horn sounded on the festival of Rosh HaShana

siddur Prayer book

sitra aḥara Literally, "the other side"; a general term for evil, including all aspects of the universe that counter the Divine

sukka Hut or shelter with a roof of branches and leaves used as a temporary residence during the festival of Sukkot

Sukkot The harvest festival celebrated in the fall during which Jews leave their houses to live in temporary shelters

tallit Prayer shawl

Tanakh An acronym for *Torah, Nevi'im, Ketuvim* (Torah, Prophets, Writings), comprising the twenty-four books of the Scriptures

tanna'im Sages who lived in the period spanning 332 BCE to 220 CE whose views were recorded in the Mishna

tav Twenty-second letter of the Hebrew alphabet

tefillin Leather boxes worn on the arm and forehead containing certain biblical passages that declare the unity of God and the miracles of the exodus from Egypt

tet Ninth letter of the Hebrew alphabet

Tiferet Beauty, one of the ten divine attributes known as *sefirot*

Tosafot Medieval commentators of the Talmud

tzaddik (pl. tzaddikim) Righteous individual; a person born with the extraordinary ability and brilliance to perceive God

Tzemaḥ Tzedek The third Lubavitcher Rebbe, Rabbi Menaḥem Mendel Schneerson (1789–1866), grandson of the author of the *Tanya*, Rabbi Shneur Zalman of Liadi

tzadi Eighteenth letter of the Hebrew alphabet

tzitzit Strings that are affixed to four-cornered garments

vav The sixth letter of the Hebrew alphabet

Vilna Gaon Rabbi Eliyahu of Vilna (1720–1797), a commentator and kabbalist who was known as a leader of the opponents of Hasidism

yeḥida The highest of the five soul levels

yesh Existence, substance, entity

yeshiva (pl. yeshivot) An academy dedicated to the study of Torah

Yesod Foundation, one of the ten divine attributes known as *sefirot*

Yetzira The world of Formation, the second of the four spiritual worlds

yod The tenth letter of the Hebrew alphabet

Yom Kippur The Day of Atonement, when the Jewish people engage in fasting, prayer, and repentance

zayin The seventh letter of the Hebrew alphabet

Works Cited in This Volume

Avodat HaKodesh A kabbalistic work by Rabbi Meir ibn Gabbai, a kabbalist born in Spain in 1480

Avot deRabbi Natan A commentary and exposition of the teachings of the *Pirkei Avot*, compiled during the geonic period (c. 700–900 CE)

Ba'al Shem Tov al HaTorah A compendium of teachings on the Torah and the festivals by the founder of the hasidic movement, anthologized by Shimon Menaḥem Mendel Vodnik

Beit Rebbe A biography of the author of the *Tanya*, Rabbi Shneur Zalman of Liadi (1745–1812), and his successors by Chaim Meir Heilman

Beit Yosef Written by Rabbi Yosef Karo (1488–1575), a commentary on the halakhic work *Arba'a Turim* by Rabbi Yaakov ben Asher

Bemidbar Rabba Midrash comprising a collection of homiletical interpretations of the book of Numbers

Bereshit Rabba Midrash comprising a collection of homiletical interpretations of the book of Genesis

Degel Maḥaneh Efrayim A work of hasidic teachings on the Torah by Rabbi Moshe Ḥayyim Efrayim of Sudilkov (c. 1748–1800)

Derekh Ḥayyim A work by the second Lubavitcher Rebbe, Rabbi Dovber Schneuri (1773–1827), on the subject of repentance

Derekh Mitzvotekha Hasidic discourses on the esoteric meaning of the mitzvot by the third Lubavitcher Rebbe, Rabbi Menaḥem Mendel Schneerson (1789–1866), also known as the Tzemaḥ Tzedek

Devarim Rabba Midrash comprising a collection of homiletical interpretations of the book of Deuteronomy

Eikha Rabba Midrash comprising a collection of homiletical interpretations of the book of Lamentations

Etz Ḥayyim   The fundamental work of the Arizal's Kabbala, compiled by his disciple, Rabbi Ḥayyim Vital

Gevurot Hashem   Commentary on the exodus from Egypt and the Passover Haggada by Rabbi Judah Loew, the Maharal of Prague (c. 1520–1609)

HaMa'asar HaRishon   An account of the incarceration of the author of the *Tanya* by Rabbi Yehoshua Mondshein

HaYom Yom   An anthology of hasidic aphorisms and customs arranged according to the days of the year, compiled by Rabbi Menaḥem Mendel Schneerson, the Lubavitcher Rebbe (1902–1994)

Hemshekh Samekh Vav   Compilation of hasidic discourses by the fifth Lubavitcher Rebbe, Rabbi Shalom Dovber Schneerson, all of which were taught between 1905 and 1908

Hemshekh Ayin Bet   Compilation of the hasidic treatises of the fifth Lubavitcher Rebbe, Rabbi Sholom Dovber Schneerson (1860–1920), from the Hebrew year 5672 to 5676 (1911–1916)

Ḥiddushei HaRim   Work of hasidic teachings by Rabbi Yitzḥak Meir Rothenberg Alter (1799–1866), the first Rebbe of Gur

Hilkhot Talmud Torah   Literally, "Laws of Torah Study," published anonymously by the author of the *Tanya* in 1794

Idra Rabba   A section of the *Zohar* on *Parashat Naso*, in which kabbalistic mysteries that Rabbi Shimon bar Yoḥai revealed to nine of his students are transcribed

Iggeret HaTeshuva   The third section of the *Tanya*

Iggerot Kodesh   A comprehensive collection of correspondence written by the Rebbes of Chabad, including those of the fifth Lubavitcher Rebbe, Rabbi Shalom Dovber Schneerson (1860–1920), and seventh Lubavitcher Rebbe, Rabbi Menaḥem Mendel Schneerson (1902–1994)

Jerusalem Talmud   Written in the Land of Israel, an extensive work built upon the foundation of the Mishna like its better-known counterpart, the Babylonian Talmud

Kad HaKemaḥ   An encyclopedic work of ethical instruction and self-improvement written by Rabbeinu Baḥya ben Asher, the topics organized alphabetically according to the letters of the *alef-bet*

Kehillat Yaakov   Kabbalistic dictionary by Rabbi Yaakov Tzvi Yalish of Dinov (1778–1825)

Kerem Chabad A journal founded and edited by Rabbi Yehoshua Mondshine, comprising articles on Chabad hasidic teachings and history, published between the years 1987 and 1992

Keter Shem Tov Collection of teachings of the Ba'al Shem Tov (c. 1698–1760), compiled from the works of his disciples, by Rabbi Aharon HaKohen

Kol Mevaser A collection of essays compiled from the works of the students of Rabbi Simḥa Bunim of Peshisḥa and published by Rabbi Yehuda Menaḥem Baum in 1991

Kol Sippurei HaBa'al Shem Tov A collection of stories and chronicles on the life of the Ba'al Shem Tov compiled and arranged according to topic by Rabbi Yisrael Yaakov Klapholtz

Kuntres Aḥaron The fifth and final section of the *Tanya*

Likkutei Amarim The first section of the *Tanya*

Likkutei Amarim Also known as *Maggid Devarav LeYaakov*, a collection of teachings of Rabbi Dov Ber, the Maggid of Mezeritch (c. 1700–1770), compiled by his disciple, Rabbi Shlomo of Lutzk)

Likkutei Biurim LaSefer HaTanya Explanations on the *Tanya* culled from other works of Chabad Hasidism, including the discourses of the seventh Lubavitcher Rebbe, Rabbi Menaḥem Mendel Schneerson (1902–1994), compiled by Rabbi Yehoshua Korf

Likkutei Dibburim A series of books containing the teachings of the sixth Lubavitcher Rebbe, Rabbi Yosef Yitzḥak Schneerson (1880–1950)

Likkutei HaShas A collection of the Arizal's writings on the Talmud

Likkutei Levi Yitzḥak A collection of marginalia from the *Tanya* of the kabbalist Rabbi Levi Yitzḥak Schneerson, the father of the Lubavitcher Rebbe, Rabbi Menaḥem Mendel Schneerson

Likkutei Siḥot The collected discourses of the seventh Lubavitcher Rebbe, Rabbi Menaḥem Mendel Schneerson (1902–1994) on the Torah and festivals

Likkutei Torah Hasidic discourses by the author of the *Tanya*, Rabbi Shneur Zalman of Liadi (1745–1812) on the last three books of the Torah and the festivals

Likkutei Torah Collection of mystical teachings of the Arizal (1534–1572) on the Torah (not to be confused with the work written by the author of the *Tanya* of the same name)

Ma'amar Bati LeGani The title of the last hasidic discourse of the sixth Lubavitcher Rebbe, Rabbi Yosef Yitzḥak Schneerson (1880–1950), and the first, as well as subsequent, discourses of his successor Rabbi Menaḥem Mendel Schneerson

Ma'or Einayim Hasidic teachings on the Torah by Rabbi Menaḥem Naḥum Twersky of Chernobyl (1730–1798)

Me'orei Or Kabbalistic reference book by Rabbi Meir Paprish (1624–1662)

Metzudat Zion A commentary on Prophets and Writings by Rabb David Altshuler that focuses on explaining difficult or unfamiliar words in the verses

Metzudot Referring to the commentaries of Metzudat Tzion and Metzudat David on Prophets and Writings by Rabbi David Altshuler, Metzudat Tzion focusing on unfamiliar and difficult words in the verses and Metzudat David delving into the meaning of the verses

Mevo She'arim An introduction to the wisdom of Kabbala from the writings of Rabbi Ḥayyim Vital

Midrash Shoḥer Tov Midrash comprising a collection of homiletic teachings expounding the Psalms; another name for *Midrash Tehillim*

Midrash Tanḥuma Midrash comprising a collection of homiletic teachings expounding the Torah

Midrash Tehillim Midrash comprising a collection of homiletic teachings expounding the Psalms

Mishneh Torah Code of Jewish law composed by Rambam (1138–1204), containing fourteen books, including *Sefer HaMadda* (the Book of Knowledge), which addresses fundamentals of Judaism

Olat Tamid A work on meditations in prayers by Rabbi Ḥayyim Vital based on the teachings of the Arizal

Or HaTorah Compilation of hasidic discourses on the *Tanakh* and festivals by the third Lubavitcher Rebbe, Rabbi Menaḥem Mendel Schneerson (1789–1866), also known as the Tzemaḥ Tzedek

Otzar HaMidrashim Collection of two hundred minor midrashim, compiled by Yehuda David Eisenstein

Pardes Rimmonim The primary exposition of the kabbalistic system of Rabbi Moshe Kordevero, famously known as the Ramak (1522–1570)

Pirkei Avot Literally, "Chapters of the Fathers"; a tractate of the Mishna dealing with ethics and piety

Pirkei deRabbi Eliezer Homiletic work on the Torah containing exegesis and retellings of biblical stories

Pri Etz Ḥayyim Mystical teachings of the Arizal on rituals and holidays as recorded by his disciple Rabbi Hayyim Vital

Raya Meheimna Subsection of the *Zohar* presenting a kabbalistic exposition of the commandments and prohibitions of the Torah

Sefer HaArakhim An encyclopedic work of hasidic concepts compiled by Rabbi Yoel Kahn and Rabbi Shalom Dovber Lipsker

Sefer HaBahir A kabbalistic work attributed to first-century talmudic Sage Rabbi Neḥunya ben HaKanah

Sefer HaIkkarim A fifteenth-century work on principles of Judaism by Rabbi Yosef Albo (1380–1444)

Sefer HaKen An anthology of articles on the life and work of the author of the *Tanya*, Rabbi Shneur Zalman of Liadi, compiled and edited by Rabbi Adin Even-Israel Steinsaltz at the behest of the Lubavitcher Rebbe, Rabbi Menaḥem Mendel Schneerson

Sefer HaMa'amarim A series of works containing the collected hasidic discourses of the Lubavitcher Rebbes, arranged by year

Sefer HaMa'amarim Melukat Selected discourses by the Lubavitcher Rebbe, Rabbi Menaḥem Mendel Schneerson, arranged according to the festivals

Sefer HaSihot A compilation of discourses delivered by the sixth Lubavitcher Rebbe, Rabbi Yosef Yitzchak Schneerson

Sefer Mitzvot Katan A halakhic work by Rabbi Yitzḥak of Corbeil (d. 1280) that is a summary of *Sefer Mitzvot Gadol* by thirteenth-century scholar Rabbi Moshe of Coucy, containing an enumeration of the 613 commandments

Sefer Yetzira Ancient mystical work attributed to the biblical Abraham

Sha'ar HaGemul Treatise on divine justice by Nachmanides

Sha'ar HaGilgulim A kabbalistic work based on the teachings of the Arizal on the topic of reincarnation and the nature of the soul

Sha'ar HaKavanot A kabbalistic work based on the teachings of the Arizal on the mystical underpinnings of daily rituals and the daily prayers

Sha'ar HaYiḥud VeHa'emuna The second section of the *Tanya*

Sha'ar Ruaḥ HaKodesh A kabbalistic work based on the teachings of the Arizal containing hundreds of meditations geared toward purifying the soul and attaining higher levels of consciousness

Sha'arei Kedushah Mystical work on piety by Rabbi Ḥayyim Vital (1542–1620)

She'eilat Ya'avetz Halakhic responsa by Rabbi Yaakov Emden (1697–1776)

Shemot Rabba Midrash comprising a collection of homiletic interpretations of the book of Exodus

Shir HaShirim Rabba Midrash comprising a collection of homiletical interpretations of the book of Song of Songs

Shivḥei HaBa'al Shem Tov Biographical stories of the Ba'al Shem Tov and his disciples

Shulḥan Arukh The most important and influential codification of Jewish law, compiled by Rabbi Yosef Karo of Tzefat (1488–1575)

Siddur Admor HaZaken Prayer book edited in accordance with the teachings of the author of the *Tanya*, Rabbi Shneur Zalman of Liadi (1745–1812)

Sifra Midrash containing halakhic exegesis on the book of Leviticus

Sifrei Midrash containing halakhic exegesis on the books of Numbers and Deuteronomy

Tanna deVei Eliyahu A compilation of midrashic teachings ascribed to the prophet Elijah

Targum Yerushalmi An Aramaic translation and commentary on the Torah

Targum Yonatan Aramaic translation and commentary on Prophets composed by Rabbi Yonatan ben Uziel

Tikkunei Zohar Also known as the *Tikkunim*, an appendix to the *Zohar* consisting of seventy commentaries on the opening word of the Torah, *bereshit*

Torah Or Hasidic discourses by the author of the *Tanya*, Rabbi Shneur Zalman of Liadi (1745–1812), on the books of Genesis and Exodus, as well as on Hanukkah and the book of Esther

Torat Ḥayyim The collected discourses of the second Lubavitcher Rebbe, Rabbi Dovber Schneuri (1773–1827), on the books of Genesis and Exodus

Torat Kohanim   The halakhic Midrash to the book of Leviticus

Torat Menaḥem   The comprehensive collection of discourses and speeches of the seventh Lubavitcher Rebbe, Rabbi Menaḥem Mendel Schneerson (1902–1994)

Torat Shmuel   A collection of discourses by the fourth Lubavitcher Rebbe, Rabbi Shmuel Schneerson (1834–1882)

Vayikra Rabba   Midrash comprising a collection of homiletical interpretations of the book of Leviticus

Ya'arot Devash   Collection of the sermons of Rabbi Yehonatan Eibeshitz

Yalkut Shimoni   Collection of homiletic teachings on the books of *Tanakh*, compiled between the eleventh and fourteenth centuries

Zohar   One of the fundamental texts of Kabbala (Jewish mysticism) that consists of the teachings of Rabbi Shimon bar Yoḥai (second century CE), as recorded by his close disciples

אגרת הקודש

אגרות כז-לב

קונטרס אחרון

לכ"ק אדמו"ר הזקן

הרב רבי שניאור זלמן מליאדי

בעל התניא והשו"ע

אגרת כז

יב בחשון פשוטה
יא בחשון מעוברת

מה שכתב ליושבי אה"ק תובב"א לנחמם בכפליים לתושיה על פטירת הרב הגאון המפורסם איש אלקים קדוש נ"י ע"ה פ"ה מהור"ר מנחם מענדל נ"ע.

אהובי   אחיי ורעיי אשר כנפשי כו' עליהם יהיו חיים עד העולם ויצאציהם אתם זרע אמת ברוכי ה' המה מעתה ועד עולם.

אחד"ש כמשפט לאוהבי שמו באתי לדבר על לב נדכאים הנאנחים והנאנקים ולנחמם בכפליים לתושיה אשר שמעה אזני ותבן לה על מארז"ל דשבק חיים לכל חי כי צדיק באמונתו יחיה ובירֵאת ה' לחיים וברשפי אש שלהבת אהבתם מחיים לכל בהן חיי רוחו [נ"א ונשמתו] כל ימי חלדו ויהי בהעלות ה' רוחו ונשמתו אליו יאסוף ויעלה בעילוי אחר עילוי עד רום המעלות שבק חיי רוחו פעולתו אשר עבד בה לפנים בישראל פעולת צדיק לחיים לכל חי היא נפש כל חי הקשורה בנפשו בחבלי עבותות אהבה רבה ואהבת עולם בל תמוט לנצח אשר מי האיש החפץ חיים לדבקה בה' חיים בעבודתו תדבק נפשו והיתה צרורה בצרור החיים את ה' בחיי רוח אפינו אשר אמרנו בצלו נחיה בגוים אשר שבק לנו בכל אחד ואחד כפי בחי' התקשרותו באמת ואהבתו אהבת אמת הטהורה מקרב איש ולב עמוק כי כמים הפנים וכו' ורוח אייתי רוח ואמשיך רוח ורוחו עומדת בקרבינו ממש כי בראותו ילדיו מעשה ידיו בקרבו יקדישו שמו יתברך אשר יתגדל ויתקדש כאשר נלך בדרך ישרה אשר הורנו מדרכיו ונלכה באורחותיו נס"ו. וז"ש בזוה"ק דצדיקא דאתפטר אשתכח בכלהו עלמין יתיר מבחיוהי דהיינו שגם בזה העולם המעשה היום לעשותם אשתכח יתיר כי המעשה (גדל) [גדל] והולך גידולי גידולין מן אור זרוע לצדיק בשדה אשר ברכו ה' המאיר לארץ ולדרים וגם אנחנו אלה פה היום כולנו חיים בדרכיו דרך הקדש יקרא לה. זאת בעבודת ה' במילי דשמיא. ובמילי דעלמא בפירוש אתמר בזוה"ק דצדיקייא מגינין על עלמא ובמיתתהון יתיר מבחייהון ואלמלא צלותא דצדיקייא בההוא עלמא לא אתקיים עלמא רגעא חדא וכל הקרוב קרוב אל משכן ה' בחייו קודם לברכה:

יג בחשון פשוטה
יב בחשון מעוברת

ביאור על הנ"ל:

יד בחשון פשוטה
יג בחשון מעוברת

איתא   בזוה"ק דצדיקא דאתפטר אשתכח בכלהו עלמין יתיר מבחיוהי כו'. וצריך להבין בעולמות עליונים אשתכח יתיר בעלותו שמה אבל בעוה"ז איך אשתכח יתיר. וי"ל ע"ד מה שקבלתי על מאמר חז"ל דשבק חיים לכל חי כנודע שחיי הצדיק אינם חיים בשרים כ"א חיים

רוחניים שהם אמונה ויראה ואהבה כי באמונה כתיב וצדיק באמונתו יחיה
ובירא'ה כתיב ויראת ה' לחיים ובאהבה כתיב רודף צדקה וחסד ימצא חיים
וחסד הוא אהבה ושלשה מדות אלו הם בכל עולם ועולם עד רום המעלות
הכל לפי ערך בחי' מעלות העולמות זע"ז בדרך עילה ועלול כנודע. והנה
בהיות הצדיק חי על פני האדמה היו שלשה מדות אלו בתוך כלי ולבוש
שלהם בבחי' מקום גשמי שהיא בחי' נפש הקשורה בגופו וכל תלמידיו
אינם מקבלים רק הארת מדות אלו וזיוון המאיר חוץ לכלי ע"י זה ע"י דבוריו
ומחשבותיו הקדושים. ולכן ארז"ל שאין אדם עומד על דעת רבו וכו' אבל
לאחר פטירתו לפי שמתפרדים בחי' הנפש שנשארה בקבר מבחי' הרוח
שבג"ע שהן שלש מדות הללו לפיכך יכול כל הקרוב אליו לקבל חלק
מבחי' רוחו שבג"ע הואיל ואינה בתוך כלי ולא בבחי' מקום גשמי כנודע
מארז"ל על יעקב אבינו ע"ה שנכנס עמו ג"ע וכ"כ בספר עשרה מאמרות
שאויר ג"ע מתפשט סביב כל אדם ונרשמים באויר זה כל מחשבותיו ודבוריו
הטובים בתורה ועבודת ה' (וכן להיפך ח"ו נרשמים באויר המתפשט מגיהנם
סביב כל אדם) הלכך נקל מאד לתלמידיו לקבל חלקם מבחי' רוח רבם
העצמיית שהם אמונתו ויראתו ואהבתו אשר עבד בהם את ה' ולא זיוום
בלבד המאיר חוץ לכלי לפי שבחי' רוחו העצמית מתעלה בעילוי אחר
עילוי להכלל בבחי' נשמתו שבג"ע העליון שבעולמות העליונים ונודע שכל
דבר שבקדושה אינו נעקר לגמרי מכל וכל ממקומו ומדרגתו הראשונה גם
לאחר שנתעלה למעלה למעלה ובחי' זו הראשונה שנשארה למטה בגן עדן
התחתון במקומו ומדרגתו הראשונה היא המתפשטת בתלמידיו כל אחד
כפי בחי' התקשרותו וקרבתו אליו בחייו ובמותו באהבה רבה כי המשכת
כל רוחניות אינה אלא ע"י אהבה רבה כמ"ש בזוה"ק דרוח דרעותא דלבא
אמשיך רוח מלעילא רק אם יכון לקראת אלהיו בהכנה רבה ויגיעה עצומה
לקבל שלש מדות הללו כדרך שהורהו רבו וכמארז"ל יגעת ומצאת תאמן.

והנה יש עוד בחי' הארה לתלמידיו רק שאינה מתלבשת בתוך מוחם ממש
כראשונה רק הארה מאירה עליהם מלמעלה והיא מעליית רוחו ונשמתו למקור
חוצבו דהיינו לחקל תפוחין קדישין וע"י נעשה שם יחוד ע"י העלאת מ"ן
מכל מעשיו ותורתו ועבודתו אשר עבד כל ימי חייו ונזרעו בחקל תפוחין
קדישין אורות עליונים מאד לעומת תחתונים אשר הם תורתו ועבודתו
והארת אורות עליונים אלו מאירה על כל תלמידיו עובדי ה' על ידי
תורתו ועבודתו והארה זו שעליהם מלמעלה מכנסת בלבם ההרהורי תשובה
ומעשים טובים וכל המעשים טובים הנולדים מהארה זו שמאירה מאורות
הזרועים בשדה הנ"ל נקרא גידולי גידולין והארה זו היא בהעלם והסתר
גדול כמו שמש המאיר לכוכבים מתחת לארץ כדאיתא בתיקונים על משה

רבינו ע"ה שאחר פטירתו מתפשטת הארתו בכל דרא ודרא לששים רבוא
נשמות כמו שמש המאיר מתחת לארץ לששים רבוא כוכבים:

אגרת כח

מה שכתב למחותנו הרב הגאון המפורסם איש אלקים קדוש ה' נ"י ע"ה פ"ה
מו"ה לוי יצחק נ"ע אב"ד דק"ק בארדיטשוב לנחמו על פטירת בנו הרב
החסיד מו"ה מאיר נ"ע:

למה נסמכה פ' מרים לפ' פרה לומר לך מה פרה מכפרת וכו'. וצריך
להבין למה נסמכה דוקא לפרה אדומה הנעשה לשלש מחנות
אלא דחטאת קריי' רחמנא [בכת"י הנוסחא הנעשה בחוץ. ומן תיבת לשלש
עד תיבת רחמנא ליתא בכת"י] ולא נסמכה לפ' חטאת הנעשה בפנים על גבי
המזבח כפרה ממש. אמנם נודע מזוה"ק והאריז"ל סוד הקרבנות שעל גבי
המזבח הן בחי' העלאת מ"ן מנפש הבהמית שבנוגה אל שרשן ומקורן הן
בחי' ד' חיות שבמרכבה הנושאות את הכסא פני שור ופני נשר וכו'. ועי"ז
נמשכים ויורדים מ"ד מבחי' אדם שעל הכסא הנקרא בשם מלכא וז"א.
אכן בשריפת הפרה אדומה הנה ע"י השלכת עץ ארז ואזוב וכו' ונתינת
מים חיים אל האפר נקרא בשם קידוש מי חטאת במשנה והיא בחי' קדש
העליון הנקרא בשם טלא דבדולחא כמ"ש בזוה"ק שהיא בחי' חכמה
עילאה ומוחא סתימאה דא"א ועלה איתמר בדוכתי טובא בזוה"ק בחכמה
אתברירו ואתהפכא חשוכא לנהורא דהיינו עולם התיקון שנתברר ונתתקן
ע"י מוחא סתימאה דא"א מעולם התהו ושבירת הכלים שנפלו בבי"ע וכו'
כנודע. ולזאת מטהרת טומאת המת אף שהוא אבי אבות וכו' ולמטה מטה
מנוגה:

והנה מודעת זאת דאבא יונק ממזל השמיני הוא תיקון נוצר חסד נוצר
אותיות רצון והיא עת רצון המתגלה ומאיר בבחי' גילוי מלמעלה
למטה בעת פטירת צדיקי עליון עובדי ה' באהבה במסירת נפשם לה'
בחייהם ערבית ושחרית בק"ש שעי"ז היו מעלים מ"נ לאו"א בק"ש כידוע
(וכן בת"ת דמחכמה נפקא) ועי"ז היו נמשכים ויורדים בחי' מ"ד מתיקון
ונוצר חסד והם הם המאירים בבחי' גילוי בפטירתם כנודע שכל עמל האדם
שעמלה נפשו בחייו למעלה בבחי' העלם והסתר מתגלה ומאיר בבחי'
גילוי מלמעלה למטה בעת פטירתו והנה ע"י גילוי הארת תיקון ונוצר חסד
בפטירתן מאיר חסד ה' מעולם עד עולם על יראיו ופועל ישועות בקרב הארץ
לכפר על עון הדור אף גם על הזדונות שהן מג' קליפות הטמאות שלמטה
מנוגה לפי שמזל דנוצר דא"א מקור הבירורים ואתהפכא חשוכא

דשבירת הכלים לנהורא דעולם התיקון. משא"כ בקרבנות שע"ג המזבח
שאינן מכפרים אלא על השגגות שהן מהתגברות נפש הבהמית שמנוגה
כמ"ש בלקוטי תורה פ' ויקרא ולכן נסמכה לפ' פרה דוקא מה פרה וכו'
ובילקוט פ' שמיני הג' מי חטאת וכו':

אגרת כט

אשת חיל עטרת בעלה כו'. איתא בגמ' פ"ד דמגילה ודאשתמש בתגא
חלף כו' זה המשתמש במי ששונה הלכות כתרה של תורה כו'
תנא דבי אליהו כל השונה הלכות מובטח לו כו'. וצריך להבין למה נקראו
ההלכות בשם תגא וכתרה של תורה וגם למה השונה הלכות דוקא מובטח
לו כו' ולא שאר ד"ת. וכן להבין מארז"ל בפי"א דמנחות אפי' לא שנה
אדם אלא פרק אחד שחרית כו' יצא י"ח ולמה אינו יוצא י"ח בשאר ד"ת:

אך מודעת זאת מ"ש האריז"ל שכל אדם מישראל צריך לבא בגלגולים
רבים עד שיקיים כל תרי"ג מצות התורה במחשבה דיבור ומעשה
להשלים לבושי נפשו ולתקנם שלא יהא לבושא דחסרא כו' לבד מצות
התלויות במלך שהוא מוציא כל ישראל כי הוא כללות כולם כו' והטעם
הוא כדי להלביש כל תרי"ג בחי' וכחות שבנפשו אחת מהנה לא נעדרה
כו'. וביאור ענין הכרח וצורך לבושים אלו מבואר בזהר ומובן לכל משכיל
כי להיות שנפש רוח ונשמה שבאדם הן בחי' נבראים וא"א לשום נברא
להשיג שום השגה בבורא ויוצר הכל א"ס ב"ה וגם אחרי אשר האיר ה'
מאורו ית' והאציל בבחי' השתלשלות מדרגות רבות מדרגה אחר מדרגה
בבחי' צמצומים עצומים ולבושים רבים ועצומים הידועים לי"ח ונקראים
באד"ר בשם שערות וכדכתיב בדניאל ושער רישיה כעמר נקא כו' אעפ"כ
לא יכלה הנפש או הרוח ונשמה למסבל האור כי טוב ומתוק האור וכו'
כמ"ש לחזות בנועם ה' לשון נעימות ועריבות ומתיקות ותענוג עצום לאין
קץ כמ"ש אז תתענג על ה' והשביע בצחצחות כו' לשון צחה צמא כמ"ש
בזהר ואין בכחה לקבל הנעימות ועריבות הצחצחות שלא תצא מנרתקה
ותבטל ממציאותה כנר באבוקה אם לא שמסבחי' אור זה עצמו תשתלשל
ותמשך ממנו איזו הארה מועטת בדרך השתלשלות מדריגה אחר מדרגה
בצמצומים רבים עד שיברא ממנה לבוש אחד נברא מעין מהות אור זה
להלביש הנפש רוח ונשמה ודרך לבוש זה שהוא מעין אור זה תוכל ליהנות
מזיו אור זה ולהשיגו ולא תבטל ממציאותה וכמשל הרואה בשמש דרך
עשיית זכה ומאירה וכו' וכמ"ש ויבא משה בתוך הענן ויעל כו' שנתלבש
בענן ועלה וראה דרך הענן וכו' כמ"ש בזה"ב דר"י ורכ"ט. והנה אור זה
הגנוז לצדיקים לע"ל הנק' בשם נועם ה' וצחצחות להתענג על ה' וד'

מאות עלמין דכסופין דמתענגי בהון צדיקייא כו' כמ"ש ארבע מאות שקל כסף כו' הנה יש בו מעלות ומדרגות רבות מאד גבוה מעל גבוה אך הארה מועטת היורדת מדרגה אחר מדרגה לברוא לבוש זה היא מבחי' מדרגה האחרונה שבאור זה ונקראת בשם מדרגה החיצונה ואחוריים דרך משל כמ"ש בזהר דר"ח ע"ב (עיין בס' מק"מ) ור"י ע"ב ומה דאשתאר כו' והנה כמו שבנשמת האדם יש בה כח התענוג שמתענגת ממה שיש לה ענג ממנו כמו מהשכלת שכל חדש וכה"ג ובחי' חיצוניות ואחוריים של כח ובחי' התענוג שבה היא בחי' כח הרצון שבה שהוא שהוא רוצה מה שהוא רוצה דהיינו דבר שאינו צער שהצער היפך התענוג. וככה עד"מ באור א"ס ב"ה ג"כ כביכול הרצון העליון ב"ה היא בחי' חיצוניות ואחוריים לבחי' ענג העליון ונועם ה' וצחצחות ועלמין דכסופין הנ"ל הגם שהם מיוחדים בתכלית היחוד שהוא ית' ורצונו אחד ולא כרצון האדם ח"ו לא מיניה ולא מקצתיה ואין דמיון ביניהם כלל אעפ"כ דברה תורה כלשון בנ"א לשכך האזן מה שיכולה לשמוע במשל ומליצה מנשמת האדם הכלולה מכח התענוג והרצון והחכמה והבינה וכו'. וכנראה בחוש שכשאדם משכיל איזה שכל חדש נפלא אזי באותה רגע עכ"פ נולד לו תענוג נפלא בשכלו מכלל שהתענוג הוא למעלה מעלה מבחי' השכל והחכמה רק שמלובש בבחי' שכל וחכמה וכשהאדם מרגיש השכל וחכמה דהיינו שמשיגה ומבינה היטב אזי מרגיש ג"כ בחי' התענוג המלובש בחכמה ולכן נקראת בחי' בינה בשם עוה"ב כי בזוה"ק שהיא בחי' התגלות החכמה עם התענוג המלובש בה שמשיגים הצדיקים בג"ע ומשכילים בפנימיות התורה דאורייתא מחכמה נפקא ואורייתא וקב"ה כולא חד:

והנה רצון העליון ב"ה מכונה ונקרא בפי חכמי האמת בשם כתר עליון ובו תר"ך עמודי אור וכו'. פי' דרך משל כמו שיש עומדים בבית חומה גדול נצבים בארץ וראשם מחובר בתקרה. ככה ממש עד"מ כתר עליון ב"ה הוא למעלה מבחי' מדרגת החכמה והוא מלשון כותרת שהוא מכתיר ומקיף על המוחין שבראש שהם בחי' חב"ד וזה נתלבש בתרי"ג מצות התורה וז' מצות דרבנן שרובם ככולם הן מצות מעשיות וגם התלויות בדבור הא קי"ל דעקימת שפתיו הוי מעשה וגם התלויות במחשבה או בלב הרי המצוה ניתנה לאדם הגשמי שבעוה"ז דוקא שהוא בעל בחירה להטות לבבו לטוב וכו'. משא"כ הנשמה בלא גוף א"צ לצותה ע"ז. ונמצא שהמצות הן עד"מ כמו העמודים נצבים מרום המעלות רצון העליון ב"ה עד הארץ הלזו החומרית והן עד"מ כמו העמודים חלולין שמקיפין ומלבישין נשמת האדם או רוחו או נפשו כשמקיים המצות ודרך עמודים אלו עולין הנר"ן שלו עד רום המעלות לצרור בצרור החיים את ה'. פי'

כא בחשון פשוטה
כ בחשון מעוברת

להיות צרורות ומלובשות באור הכתר הוא רצון העליון ב"ה וע"י לבוש
זה יוכלו לחזות בנועם ה' וצחצחות שלמעלה ממעלת הכתר והן פנימיותו
עד"מ (והגם שנתבאר במ"א שהמצות הן פנימיות רצון העליון ב"ה הנה
מודעת זאת לי"ח ריבוי בחי' ומדרגות שיש בכל בחי' ומדרגה ממדרגות
הקדושה כמה בחי' פנים לפנים וכמה בחי' אחוריים לאחוריים לאין קץ
וכו'). והנה ז' מצות דרבנן אינן נחשבות מצות בפני עצמן שהרי כבר נאמר
לא תוסף אלא הן יוצאות ונמשכות ממצות התורה וכלולות בהן במספר
תרי"ג להלביש תרי"ג בחי' וכחות שבגבר"ן האדם. וז"ש בזוה"ק פ' פקודי

כב בחשון פשוטה
כא בחשון מעוברת

(דרכ"ט ע"ב) דאינון עובדין טבין דעביד בר נש משכי מנהורא דזיווא
עילאה לבושא כו' וחמי כו' בנועם ה' וכו'. והגם דהתם מיירי בג"ע התחתון
שהלבושים שם הם ממצות מעשיות ממש אבל בג"ע העליון הלבושים הם
מרעותא וכוונה דלבא באורייתא וצלותא כמ"ש בזהר שם (דר"י) הרי
הכוונה היא כוונת עסקו בתורה לשמה מאהבת ה' ומצות ת"ת ג"כ
מכלל מצות מעשיות דעקימת שפתיו הוי מעשה והרהור לאו כדבור דמי
ואינו יוצא י"ח בהרהור לבדו וכן בתפלה ומה גם כי מעלת הכוונה על
הדבור ומעשה אינה מצד עצמה כו' אלא מצד הארת רצון העליון כו' כמ"ש
בלק"א ח"א פל"ה באריכות ע"ש. והנה מודעת זאת כי הנה רצון העליון

כג בחשון פשוטה
כב בחשון מעוברת

ב"ה המלובש בתרי"ג מצות שבתורה שבכתב הוא מופלא ומכוסה טמיר
ונעלם ואינו מתגלה אלא בתורה שבע"פ כמו מצות תפילין עד"מ שנאמר
בתושב"כ וקשרתם לאות על ידך והיו לטוטפות בין עיניך והוא מאמר
סתום ונעלם שלא פירש הכתוב איך ומה לקשור ומהו טוטפות והיכן הוא
בין עיניך ועל ידך עד שפירשה תורה שבע"פ שצריך לקשור בית אחד
על היד וד' בתים על הראש ובתוכם ד' פרשיות והבתים יהיו מעור מעובד
ומרובעים דוקא ומקושרים ברצועות של עור שחורות דוקא וכל שאר
פרטי הלכות עשיית התפילין שנאמרו בע"פ ועל ידך היא הזרוע דוקא
ולא כף היד ובין עיניך זה קדקוד ולא המצח. וכן כל מצות שבתורה בין
מ"ע בין מצות ל"ת אינן גלויות וידועות ומפורשות אלא ע"י תורה שבע"פ
כמצות ל"ת שנאמר בשבת לא תעשה מלאכה ולא פי' מה היא מלאכה
ובתורה שבע"פ נתפרש שהן ל"ט מלאכות הידועות ולא טלטול אבנים
וקורות כבידות. וכיוצא בהן הן כל המצות בין מ"ע בין מל"ת הן סתומות
ולא מפורשות וגלויות וידועות אלא ע"י תורה שבע"פ ומשום הכי כתיב
על תושבע"פ אל תטוש תורת אמך כמ"ש בזהר שעד"מ כמו שכל
אברי הולד כלולים בטיפת האב בהעלם גדול והאם מוציאתו לידי גילוי
בלידתה ולד שלם ברמ"ח אברים ושס"ה גידים ככה ממש כל רמ"ח מ"ע
ושס"ה מל"ת באים מהההעלם אל הגילוי בתושבע"פ ורישי' דקרא שמע בני
מוסר אביך קאי אתורה שבכתב דנפקא מחכמה עילאה הנק' בשם אב.

וז"ש אשת חיל עטרת בעלה כי התורה שבע"פ הנק' אשת החיל המולידה ומעמדת חיילות הרבה כמ"ש ועלמות אין מספר אל תקרי עלמות אלא עולמות אלו הלכות דלית לון חושבנא כמ"ש בתיקונים וכולן הן בחי' גילוי רצון העליון ב"ה הנעלם בתושב"כ ורצון העליון ב"ה הוא למעלה מעלה ממעלת חכמה עילאה וכמו כתר ועטרה שעל המוחין שבראש לכן נקראו ההלכות בשם תגא וכתרה של תורה והשונה הלכות מובטח לו שהוא בן עוה"ב ע"י התלבשות נר"נ שלו ברצון העליון ב"ה כנ"ל:

אגרת ל

כד בחשון פשוטה
כג בחשון מעוברת

מודעת זאת משארז"ל כל הרגיל לבא לבהכ"נ ויום א' לא בא הקב"ה שואל עליו שנאמר מי בכם ירא ה' וכו' וכן בכל המצות ובפרט מצות הצדקה ששקולה כנגד כל המצות הגם שהיא בלי נדר ח"ו אעפ"כ כל החיל אשר נגע יראת ה' בלבם לא יאתה לנפשם האלוקית לתת מגרעות בקדש מאשר כבר הורגלו מדי שנה להפריש ממאודם להחיות רוח שפלים ונדכאים דלית להון מגרמיהון היא בחי' סוכת דוד הנופלת וכו' לקומם ולרומם וכו' למהוי אחד באחד וכו'? והכל לפי רוב המעשה וכו' ולפי החשבון כמארז"ל כל פרוטה ופרוטה מצטרפת לחשבון גדול וכו' על דרך מארז"ל אימתי גדול הוי' כשהוא בעיר אלהינו וכו' היא בחי' ומקום החשבון כמ"ש עיניך ברכות בחשבון והמכוון כנודע כי באתערותא דלתתא המשכת חיים חן וחסד במעשה הצדקה ברצון הטוב וסבר פנים יפות אתערותא דלעילא יאר הוי' פניו הוא הארת והמשכת חן וחסד ורצון עליון מחיי החיים א"ס ב"ה אשר לגדולתו אין חקר והשגה כלל אל בחי' מלכותך מלכות כל עולמים דאתגליא עלמא דאתגליא המחיה כל הברואים שבכל ההיכלות עליונים ותחתונים שהן בבחי' מספר וחשבון כמ"ש אלף אלפים ישמשוניה וזהו חשבון גדול שע"י רוב מעשה הצדקה שלום. כי פי' שלום הוא דבר המחבר ומתווך ב' קצוות הפכיים שהן קצה השמים לעילא בחי' ולגדולתו אין חקר וקצה השמים לתתא המתלבש בבי"ע גבול ומספר וד"ל:

אגרת לא

כה בחשון פשוטה
כד בחשון מעוברת

נודע בשערים מ"ש בתיקונים דשכינתא איהי מרעא בגלותא כבי'. פי' עד"מ כמו חולי הגוף המבדיל בין קדש וכו' שסיבת החולי והבריאות היא התפשטות והילוך החיות מהלב אל כל האברים המלובשת בדם הנפש היוצא מהלב אל כל האברים וסובב סובב הולך הרוח חיים והדם תוך תוך כל האברים והגידים המובלעי' בהם וחוזר אל הלב ואם

סיבוב והילוך הרוח חיים הלז הוא כהלכתו תמידי כסדרו המסודר לו
מחיי החיים ב"ה אזי האדם בריא בתכלית כי כל האברים מקושרים יחד
ומקבלים חיותם הראוי להם מהלב ע"י סיבוב הלז אך אם יש איזה קלקול
באיזהו מקומן המונע ומעכב או ממעט סיבוב והילוך הדם עם הרוח חיים
המלובש בו אזי נפסק או מתמעט הקשר הלז המקשר כל האברים אל
הלב ע"י סיבוב הלז ואזי נופל האדם למשכב וחולי ה"י. וככה ממש עד"מ
הנה כל נשמות ישראל נקראים בחי' אברי דשכינתא הנקראת בשם לב
כמ"ש וצור לבבי וכמ"ש ושכנתי בתוכם פי' כי לשון שכינה הוא שאור
הוי' שוכן בעולמות בי"ע להחיותם והמשכת חיות זה היא ע"י התלבשות
תחלה בנשמות ישראל לפי שכל הנבראים אין ערוך להם אל הבורא ית'
דכולא קמי' כלא ממש חשיבין וא"א להם לקבל חיות מאורו ושפעו ית'
להיות נבראים מאין ליש וחיים וקיימים כ"א ע"י הנשמות שעלו במחשבה
וקדמו לבריאת עולמות שע"י בחי' הדבור כמארז"ל במי נמלך הקב"ה וכו'
כנודע במ"א. ונודע בשערים כי כל המשכת החיות וההשפעה מעליונים
לתחתונים מהם הן כמ"ש בס"י נעוץ תחלתן בסופן וסופן בתחלתן ובכתבי
האריז"ל מכונה בשם אור ישר ואור חוזר וכמ"ש והחיות רצוא ושוב אשר
ע"פ ע"פ הדברים האלה אשר א"א לבאר היטב במכתב נקראת
השכינה בשם לב והנשמות בשם אברים להורות לנו כי כאשר כל הנשמות
דבוקות ומקושרות יחד אזי סיבוב והילוך החיות וההשפעה סובב סובב
ונעוץ סופן בתחלתן לקשר ולחבר כולן להוי' אחד ולדבקה בו ית' וכמ"ש
אתם נצבים היום כולכם לפני הוי' אלוקיכם כולכם דייקא ולפני דייקא
ראשיכם כו' מחוטב עציך כו'. ובזה יובן מארז"ל כי חורבן בית שני ונפילת
ישראל בגלות והסתלקות השכינה וירידתה לאדום בבחי' גלות כבי' הכל
הי' בעון שנאת חנם ופירוד לבבות ר"ל ולכן נקראת חולה עד"מ כמ"ש
סומך נופלים ורופא חולים לשון רבים הם כל האברים וכו':

אגרת לב

ברך ה' חילם ופועל ידם ירצה לרצון להם לפני ה' תמיד כה יתן וכה
יוסיף ה' לאמץ לבם בגבורים ונדיב על נדיבות יקום להיות גדול
המעשה בכל עיר ומנין ותחשב לו לצדקה ועל העושה נאמר צדקתו עומדת
לעד עומדת לשון נקבה שמקבל התעוררות לבו הטהור מגדול המעשה
אעפי"כ עומדת לעד. פי' שכל הצדקה והחסד שישראל עושין בעוה"ז
מנדבת לבם הטהור הן הנה חיות וקיימות בעוה"ז הגשמי עד זמן התחיי'
שאז הוא זמן גילוי אלקות ואור א"ס ב"ה מבחי' סובב כל עלמין בעוה"ז
וכמ"ש באריכות במכתב דאשתקד וצריך להיות כלי ומכון להתלבש בו

אור א"ס ב"ה כמו הגוף לנשמה עד"מ כמ"ש הלא כה דברי כאש מה אש
אינה מאירה בעוה"ז אלא כשנאחזת ומתלבשת בפתילה כו' כמ"ש במ"א.
והגוף והכלי לאורו ית' היא מדת החסד ונדיבת הלב ולהשפיע חיות
למאן דלית ליה כו' כמ"ש בתיקונים וכמה גופין תקינת לון ואתקריאו
בתיקונא דא חסד דרועא ימינא וכל הגוף נכלל בימין וכך אמר הפייט
לבושו צדקה. וזהו שארז"ל אין הצדקה משתלמת אלא לפי חסד שבה
שנאמר זרעו לכם לצדקה קצרו לפי חסד שהקציר הוא גילוי הזריעה
הטמונה בארץ וכך הוא הצדקה והחסד שישראל עושין בזמן הגלות היא
טמונה ונסתרת עד זמן התחיה שיתלבש ויאיר אור א"ס ב"ה בעוה"ז
הגשמי ואיהו וגרמוהי חד הם בחי' הכלים דע"ס דאצי' וכ"ש וק"ו אור
א"ס ב"ה הסובב כל עלמין מלמעלה מעלה מבחי' אצי' ולפיכך נקראת
צדקה לשון נקבה צדקתו עומדת לעד שמקבלת הארה מאור א"ס הסובב
כל עלמין המתלבש בתוכה בעוה"ז הגשמי בזמן התחיה. אבל צדק לפניו
יהלך הוא לשון זכר היא מדת החסד המתעוררת בלב האדם מעצמו ע"י
התעוררות אהבת ה' בקריאת שמע ולדבקה בו ולמסור נפשו באחד ובכל
מאדך כפשוטו וכו' ובאתערותא דלתתא וכמים הפנים לפנים כן לב אדם
העליון כו' אתערותא דלעילא הוא המשכת אור א"ס ב"ה הסוכ"ע למטה
מטה בעוה"ז הגשמי בבחי' גילוי בזמן התחיה כמבואר במכתב דאשתקד
באריכות. וזהו לפניו יהלך שמוליך וממשיך פנים העליונים מלמעלה
מהאצי' עד עולם העשי' וכעת עת לקצר וכל טוב מהם לא יבצר הטיבה
ה' לטובים ולישרים בלבותם כנפש תדרשנו:

קונטרס אחרון

סימן א

עיין בלק"א ח"א פ"מ

כז בחשון פשוטה
כו בחשון מעוברת

להבין איך הקורא בסיפורי מעשיות שבתורה הוא מקושר בח"ע ע"פ מ"ש בכוונות דט"ז ע"ב כמו שהאדם עוסק למטה כך דיוקן האדם העליון למעלה כו' וכן י"ל בהרהור באותיות הכתובות. אבל הדבור י"ל דבוקע וסליק לאצי' ממש או לבריאה בדו"ר שכליים או ליצי' בדו"ר טבעיים ובמקרא סליק מעוה"ז לי"ס דעשי' משום דבקע אוירין וכו'. משא"כ בהרהור אלא הדיוקן שהוא שרש נשמתו וכו'. ומ"ש בזהר ח"ג דק"ה דהרהור לא עביד מידי כו' והיינו אפי' לטב ע"ש ובדל"א ע"ב י"ל דהיינו לאתערא לעילא שיומשך משם לתתא רק מחשבתו נשארה שם ומוסיפה שם אור גדול בתוספת וריבוי האור באצי' ע"י מקרא ומצות מעשיות שבעשי' שעיקר היחוד הוא למעלה רק הפירות בעוה"ז ע"י המשכת אור מזעיר למטה ע"י הדבור ומעשה משא"כ בהרהור לא נמשך כלום ולכן לא יצא ידי חובתו מה שירדה נשמתו לעוה"ז רק להמשיך אורות עליונים למטה כמ"ש בע"ח שכ"ו להמשיך אור וכו' אבל להעלות ממטה למעלה הוא דוקא ע"י מחשבה טובה דבלא דו"ר לא פרחא לעילא וכמ"ש בשער הנבואה פ"ב והמחשבה טובה כו' ומ"ש דבקע רקיעין וכו' והיינו אפילו בלא דו"ר במכש"כ מדברים בטלים [ז"א דגם שם יש איזו תאוה. בנ"א ליתא תיבות אלו] דמדה טובה מרובה היינו רקיעין דוקא שהן ההיכלות והבתים ולא בגוף האדם העליון וכש"כ בנר"ן אפי' באדם דעשיה שהן י"ס אורות וכלים וז"ש בתקונים דבלא דו"ר לא יכלא לסלקא ולמיקם קדם ה' דוקא:

סימן ב

כח בחשון פשוטה
כז בחשון מעוברת

עיין ע"ח שער הנקודות ש"ח פ"ו שאין החזרת פב"פ כו' א ע"י מצות מעשיות דוקא. וטעם הדבר כי ע"י מע"ט גורם זיווג העליון וכו'. ולהבין אמאי מעשיות דוקא ממ"ש ממ"ש בשער מ"ן ומ"ד כי צריך תחלה להעלות מ"ן דנוק' דז"א ומ"ן דנוק' הן בחי' עשיה כמש"ש פ"א. והנה המע"ט נק' כסוח וקיצוץ הקוצים הנאחזים באחוריים שהן בחי' עשיה כמ"ש בשער מ"ז פ"ה והיינו ע"י העלאת הטוב הגנוז בהם המלובש במצות מעשיות למקורו לקדושת האצי' שכבר הוברר. ומ"ש שם שאד"ר תיקן ג"כ ע"י תפלה היינו ע"י אותיות הדבור דעקימת שפתיו הוי מעשה כי הן מנפש החיונית שבגוף ודמו אשר שרשן מנוגה. והנה הבירורים דעשי' עולין ליצי' ע"י שם ב"ן ומיצי' לבריאה ולאצי' כמ"ש בשער מ"ן דרוש י"א סי' ז'. ובזה יובן דהרהור לא עביד מידי כי בלי העלאת מ"ן מהמלכים שבנוגה

א"א להמשיך טיפי' מלמעלה לזווג זו"ן כי רוצה לינק מאמו ולא להשפיע
למטה כמ"ש בשער מ"ן דרוש ב' ועיין זהר פ' פקודי דרמ"ד ע"ד דאית
סדורא כו' לאסתכלא כו' והן כוונות התפלה ויחודים עליונים ליודעים
ומשיגים לאסתכלא כו' כי נר"ן שלהם עצמן הן מ"ן במס"נ על התורה
ובנפילת אפים כנודע:

סימן ג

כט בחשון פשוטה

להבין מ"ש בשער היחודים פ"ב דע"י תורה שלא בכוונה נבראים
מלאכים בעולם היצירה ושם הביא מהזהר פ' שלח דלית קלא
דאתאביד כו' בר קלא דאורייתא וצלותא דסליק ובקע כו' והנה מכוונת
התפלה נבראו מלאכים בעולם הבריאה כמו מכוונת התורה ובלא כוונה
נדחית למטה לגמרי כמ"ש בזהר פ' פקודי דרמ"ה ע"ב ויקהל דר"א ע"ב
דאקרין צלותין פסילאן כו' וע"ש פ' ויקהל דר"א ע"ב אי היא מלה כדקא
יאות כו'. אך ההפרש בין תורה לתפלה שלא בכוונה מובן מאליו כי לימוד
התורה הוא מבין ויודע מה שלומד דבלא"ה לא מיקרי לימוד כלל רק
שלומד סתם בלא כוונה לשמה מאהבת ה' שבלבו בבחי' גילוי רק מאהבה
המסותרת הטבעית אך אינו לומד שלא לשמה ממש להתגדל כו' דהא לא
סליק לעילא מן שמשא כמ"ש בפ' ויחי דרכ"ג ע"ב והיינו משום שמחשבתו
וכוונתו הן מתלבשות באותיות הדבור ואין מניחות אותן לסלקא לעילא
וה"נ בתפלה שלא בכוונה שמחשב מ"ז (אלא מפני שכוונתו לשמים לכך
יש לה תיקון בקל לחזור ולעלות כשמתפלל בכוונה אפי' תפלה אחת
מלוקטת מתפלות כל השנה כמ"ש במק"מ פ' פקודי) ומ"ש בפ' פקודי גו
רקיע תתאה ובפ' ויקהל משמע דדוקא אי איהי מלה כדקא יאות סלקין עמה
עד אוירא דרקיע דלעילא כו'. לק"מ דרקיע תתאה מאינון רקיעי' דמדברי
גו עלמא שבפ' פקודי הן דמלכות דעשי' ורפ' ויקהל הן דז"א דעשי' כמ"ש
בע"ח שער השמות פ"ג גבי ז"א דעשייה ע"ש. והא דמשמע לכאורה בפ'
פקודי דגם תפלה פסולה עולה עד היכל הראשון שממנו נדחית למטה והוא
בז"א דבריאה. לק"מ שהרי אפי' כל העוונות ממש קלות וחמורות עולות
לשם אפי' עד היכל הד' כמ"ש דרנ"ב ע"א אלא ודאי שאין מהות העליות
שוות ואין ערוך ודמיון ביניהם אלא בשיתוף השם בלבד וד"ל. ובזה יובן
ג"כ מש"ש דרמ"ז שבהיכל הב' [אולי צ"ל אזדמן הממונה. ואולי צ"ל קיימין
הלבושים] ממונה על הלבושים שמלבישים הנשמה ממעשה המצות אף שהן
בג"ע התחתון דעשי' כמ"ש ש"ד דר"י. והנה תפלה פסולה עדיפא מתורה שלא
לשמה ממש שהיא תחת השמש והתפלה היא גו רקיע כו'. אבל תורה סתם
שאינה שלא לשמה רק לשמה מאהבה מסותרת טבעי' לא גרעא מהבל פיהן של

כח בחשון מעוברת.
בחודש חשון של
כט יום לומדים
ביום כט גם
השיעור של יום ל.

ל בחשון פשוטה

א בכסלו פשוטה

כט בחשון מעוברת.
בחודש חשון של
כט יום לומדים
ביום כט גם
השיעור של יום ל.

ל בחשון מעוברת

תינוקת של בית רבן דסליק לעילא מפני שהוא הבל שאין בו חטא וסליק
לעילא אף אם הוא שלא לשמה ממש מיראת הרצועה שביד הסופר וע"ש
דרנ"ז ע"ב שהמלאכים הם מעלים ההבל של תינוקת שב"ר עד האצי':

סימן ד

להבין מ"ש בפע"ח דבזמן הזה עיקר הבירור ע"י התפלה דוקא אף
שתלמוד תורה למעלה מהתפלה. הענין הוא שע"י תו"מ מוסיפין
אור באצי' כו'. פי' אור א"ס ב"ה בכלים דאצי' ע"י ת"ת בפנימית דהיינו
המשכות המוחין ובקיום המצות בחיצוניות הכלים שהם בחי' נה"י שבי"ס
ז"א שבאצי' רק שמתלבשים בבי"ע בתורה ומצות ומצות הגשמיים שבעוה"ז.
אבל התפלה היא המשכת אור א"ס ב"ה לבי"ע דוקא לא בדרך התלבשות
בלבד רק האור ממש לשנות הנבראים מכמות שהם שיתרפא החולה וירד
הגשם משמים לארץ ויולידה ויצמיחה. משא"כ בתו"מ שאין שינוי בקלף
התפילין ע"י הנחתן בראש ובזרוע וגם במצות שעשייתן הוא גמר מצותן
השינוי הוא ע"י אדם ולא בידי שמים כבתפלה שהיא המשכת החיות מא"ס
ב"ה שהוא לבדו כל יכול והולך כדי להמשיך אור א"ס ב"ה למטה א"א
בלי העלאת מ"ן מלמטה דוקא. משא"כ לת"ת שבאצי' המיוחדת בלא"ה
מאציל ב"ה והעלאת מ"ן של אדם בו במוחו ולבו בחי' רשפי אש בלי
גבול ונק' מאדך כדי לעורר בחי' א"ס והיינו ע"י גבורות דס"ג שהן הן
הרפ"ח ניצוצין כו' ולכן נק' התפלה חיי שעה היא בחי' מלכות היורדת בבי"ע
ותורה חיי עולם הוא ז"א כי רמ"ח פקודין הן מתחלקין בי' כלים דע"א
דז"א כו'. והנה במ"א כתב שרמ"ח מ"ע הן בה' חסדים ושס"ה ל"ת בה"ג
וכו' ובמ"א כתב שהן תרי"ג ארחין נמשכין מחד ארחא כו' שהוא לבנונית
וכו'. אך הענין שכל המצות לתקן רמ"ח אברי ז"א ע"י המשכת אור א"ס
ב"ה במוחין הכלולין בה"ח וה"ג ומקור המוחין הוא לבנונית כו' הוא הענג
וחפץ העליון להמשיך האור למטה לרמ"ח אברין דז"א ומתחלקת ההמשכה
לתרי"ג המשכות פרטיות לפי בחי' ערך המצות כגון בצדקה וגמ"ח נמשך
אור א"ס ב"ה לחיצוני' הכלי דהסד דז"א ובקיום הדינין בחיצוניות גבורה
ברחמים כו'. ודרך ומעבר ההמשכה הוא ע"י פנימי' הכלים ומוחותיהן שהן
דו"ר שכליים או טבעיים שהן בחי' מוחין דקטנות וגדלות ולזה ביקש משה
רבינו ע"ה מאד לקיים המצות מעשיות התלויות בארץ שהן תכלית
ההשתלשלות להמשיך אור א"ס ב"ה לברר הכלים דז"א דבי"ע שבהן הן
הרפ"ח ניצוצין ע"י תו"מ מעשיות שבבי"ע דוקא. והנה לקיום מצוה שא"א
לעשות ע"י אחרים מבטלין ת"ת ואפי' מעשה מרכבה וכש"כ תפלה שהיא
בחי' מוחין ודו"ר שכליים והטעם כנ"ל. ועוד זאת שבאמת מאד גדלה וגבהה

מעלת המצות מעשיות וכן לימודם על מעלת המוחין שהן דו"ר שכלים כי
הגם דכתיב ולדבקה בו ע"י מדותיו מ"מ איננו דבק אפי' במדות העליונות
אלא במציאותן ולא במהותן וכמ"ש ואנכי עפר ואפר וכש"כ באור א"ס
ב"ה דלית מחשבה תפיסא בי' באורו והתפשטות החיות ממנו ית' כ"א
במציאותו שהוא שמחיה את כולם ולא במהותו אפי' לעליונים כמ"ש קדוש
ק' ק' ה' צבאות כו' לבד עלולים הנאצלים משיגים כ"א בעילתו כפי הסדר
שבע"ח בהתלבשות הפרצופים אבל לא בנבראים אפי' בנשמות דאצי'
כמ"ש במשה רבינו ע"ה וראית את אחורי כו'. משא"כ מעשה המצות
מעשה אלקים המה הנה בדרך השתלשלות מכלים דאצי' לבי"ע ממהותן
ועצמותן דהחיצוניות כמו עד"מ אתרוג ומיניו הלביש בהן הקב"ה ממהותן
ועצמותן דהחסדים [פנימית] [פנימים] דז"א והיינו מבחי' חיצוניותן כנודע
בכל מצות מעשיות משא"כ האדם אפי' יש לו נשמה דאצי' מאחר שמלובשת
בגוף לא יוכל למצוא בנפשו ולהשיג מהותן ועצמותן של פנימית החסדים
דז"א דאצי' (כי האצי' היא בחי' הבי"ע שהיא בחי'
מקיף מלמעלה ואינה מתלבשת בכלי כלל) כ"א מציאותן ע"י דחילו ורחימו
שכליים. ומ"ש וראית את אחורי הוא בדרך נבואה דוקא. (שהוא התפשטות
הגשמיות כמ"ש בר"מ פ' משפטים). והיינו הטעם לפי שא"א לנברא להשיג
כלום במהות האלקות שהוא הבורא ובלי השגה אין זו הלבשה ותפיסא
ודבקות אמיתית. משא"כ האתרוג עד"מ חיותו נמשכה ונשתלשלה ממהות
חיצוניות דכלים דנוק' דז"א דאצי' שהוא בחי' אלקות כמ"ש כ"ה שכל
הפירות הן באצי' כי למ"ד כלים דאצי' ירדו לבי"ע (והן יו"ד מאמרות
שבהן נברא העולם) ע"י התלבשות בנוק' דעשי' מהות במהות כי הכלים
דאצי' נעשו נשמה בעשי' שהוא בחי' אלקות ממש לפי שבאצי' איהו וגרמוהי
חד המאציל והנאצל ועי' התלבשות מהות הנשמה במהות הכלים דנוק'
דעשיה נתהוה האתרוג נמצא כשתופס האתרוג. ומנענע כהלכתו ה"ז תופס
ממש חיותו המלובש בו מנוק' דאצי' המיוחדת באור א"ס המאציל ב"ה.
משא"כ בכוונתו אינו משיג ותופס אף היודע הסוד. אלא מציאותה ולא
מהותה אך בלימוד הלכות אתרוג משיג ותופס האתרוג ממש ומצותו
כהלכה בבחי' דבור ומחשבה אף שאינו משיג המהות. משא"כ
דלא גרע מלימוד הלכותיה ואדרבה כו' אף שאינו משיג המהות. משא"כ
בסדר ההשתלשלות אף אם משיג המציאות לא עדיף מצד עצמו כלימוד
המצות שמשיג ותופס המהות ומעלה עליו כאילו קיים בפועל ממש כמ"ש
זאת התורה כו' אלא שידיעת המציאות מההשתלשלות היא ג"כ מצוה
רמה ונשאה ואדרבה עולה על כולנה כמ"ש וידעת היום כו' דע את אלקי
אביך כו' ומביאה ללב שלם כו' שהוא העיקר והשגת המציאות הוא

ה בכסלו פשוטה
ד בכסלו מעוברת

ה בכסלו מעוברת
ו בכסלו פשוטה

להפשיט מגשמיות כו' רק שזו היא מצוה אחת מתרי"ג והאדם צריך לקיים כל תרי"ג לפי שהן השתלשלות המהות דהחיצוניות דכלים דאצי' לכך צריך להרבות בלימוד כל התרי"ג וקיומן בפועל ממש במחדו"מ שהן בי"ע לברר בירורין אשר שם. ועוד זאת שבאמת הבירורין שבבי"ע מרפ"ח ע"י תורה ומצות במחשבה דבור ומעשה גבוהין בשרשן מנר"ן שבאדם כי הן מס"ג שבפנימית א"ק ונר"ן שכבר נתקנו ע"י מ"ה הוא יוצא מהמצח הארה בעלמא. וז"ש לפני מלוך מלך כו' וה"ט שהאדם חי במזונות דצ"ח ומברן במ"ה שבו וחי בהם לפי שהם מס"ג. ועוד זאת כמ"ש ופני לא יראו שפנימית העליון אינו יכול לירד למטה רק חיצוניותו ובחי' אחוריים שהוא נובלות חכמה עילאה ועוד זאת שהרי הדבור מדברי חכמה עילאה אינו מוליד והטפה שנמשכה מהכלי דח"ע יש בה כח המוליד ומהווה ומאין יש מאין וגם המשכת ח"ע כלולה בה והטעם מפני שבה נמשך מהותה ועצמותה דח"ע. משא"כ בדבור ומחשבה ואפי' בהשכלת השכל באיזו חכמה הרי חכמה זו רק הארה מתפשטת ממהות השכל שבנפש ועצמותו והארה זו היא רק לבוש למהותו ועצמותו של השכל והשכל הוא הארה ולבוש למהות הנפש. משא"כ הטפה נמשך בה גם ממהות הנפש ועצמותה המלובשת במוחין ולכן מולידה בדומה לה ממש. וזהו ההפרש בין עבודת המלאכים היוצאין מנשיקין להנשמות היוצאין מהכלים אך הכלים דאצי' נעשו נשמה לבי"ע והלכך דחילו ורחימו שכליים הן כמלאכים דנשיקין מהארת חיצונית דחב"ד בבי"ע והטעם משום דפנימית חב"ד ומהותו ועצמותו של אור פנימי אינו יכול להתגלות אלא ע"י הארת הכלים דוקא היורדים למטה כטיפת האדם ממוחין וכמ"ש ופני לא יראו. ובר מן כל דין אפי' בנשמה דאצי' אף שהיא מכלים דאצי' וכן בנפש רוח מכלים דיצי' עשי' הנה רחימו [אולי צ"ל דו"ר] שכליי' שלהם מעוררים ג"כ בכלים דיצי' עשי' בחי' העלאה ממטה למעלה באתערותא דלתתא וזהו בחי' הסתלקות לבד ח"ו. אבל בחי' המשכה מלמעלה למטה הוא ע"י מצות מעשיות דוקא להמשיך אור בכלים ובחיצונית הכלים דוקא שחיצוניות העליון יורד למטה ופנימיות התחתון עולה למעלה וז"ש בזהר פ' פקודי הנ"ל דאית סדורא כו' ושתיהן צורך גבוה העלאה והמשכה ע"י העלאת מ"ן מס"ג בבחי' עובדא ומלולא וזהו תכלית ההשתלשלו' להתגלות אור עליון למטה ולא לעלות התחתון למעלה שזה אינו אלא לפי שעה ואף כי גם זאת דוקא עליות הכלים לאורות עליונים היא מעלת השבת ויוה"כ. אבל לא עליות והסתלקות האורות ח"ו כמ"ש בפע"ח ונר"ן של האדם לגבי גופו בעוה"ז חשיבי כאורות לגבי כלים וכן דו"ר שכליים לגבי מצות מעשיות דוקא ולכן התפלל משרע"ה תפלות כמנין ואתחנן על קיום מצות מעשיות דוקא וה"ה לדבור גשמי של הלכותיהן.

אך להבין איך האתרוג שהוא מרפ"ח שלא נבררו עדיין וכן קלף התפילין
ימשיך אור בכלים דזו"ן דאצי' שכבר נבררו ונתקנו ע"י שם מ"ה להיות
בחי' אלקות. הנה המשל לזה הוא הזריעה והנטיעה שהגרעין מעורר כח
הצומח שבארץ שהוא דבר ה' תדשא הארץ כו' עץ פרי כו' ע"י העלאת
מ"ן לשרשו כמה מעוררי' הקלף והאתרוג עד רום המעלות שהוא ס"ג
שלפני השבירה שהוא מהות ועצמות אורות שבא"ק ולא הארה בעלמא
כמו שם מ"ה שממצחא וכן בלימוד ועיון הלכותיהן מעורר בחי' חב"ד שבע"ם
דכלים דזו"ן ועד רום המעלות ג"כ בחי' חב"ד שבס"ג דפנימית א"ק היוצא
דרך העינים כו' וכל הנ"ל הוא במ"ע אבל לא בלימוד פרטי הלכות איסורי
ל"ת לכאורה ובפרט בדלא שכיחי כלל כמו פרטי הלכות פיגול וכה"ג. אך
עוד זאת השוה בכל כי כל דחילו ורחימו שכליים של המלאכים הן בחי'
נבראים מאין ליש וכן בחי' נפש רוח דבי"ע. אבל פרטי ההלכות הן המשכות
ח"ע דהמאציל ב"ה המלובשת בגשמיות והלבשה זו אינה כהלבשת ח"ע
בדו"ר שכליים דהתם הלבוש הוא מעלים ומסתיר כהסתר והעלם
הארץ החומריית לגבי ח"ע המלובשת בה כמ"ש כולם בחכמה עשית והיינו
חיצוניות דחיצוניות דכלים דמל' דאצי' שבעשיה שהיא מסותרת לגמרי
ברוח נפש דעשיה וכן בבריאה היא מסותרת לגמרי ברוח נפש שהם בחי'
נבראים בהסתר והעלם והעלם הבורא מהנברא. משא"כ ההלכות הרי הארת
החכמה מאירה בהן בגילוי ולבוש העשיי' הוא דרך מעבר לבד כמו ביום
טוב שהחסד דאצי' המלובש לגמרי בחסד דבריאה מחיה עוה"ז הגשמי ע"י
מעבר חסד דיצי' ועשי' הנק' ג"כ התלבשות שאל"כ לא הי' פועל בגשמיות
עוה"ז ואף שגשמיות עוה"ז ודאי מסתיר לגמרי אפילו החסד דעשיה מ"מ
ההלכה עצמה אינה גשמיות ממש שהיא בחי' רצון הנמשך מח"ע להקל
או להחמיר רק שיורד ומאיר בבחי' גילוי בגשמיות כמים היורדים ממקום
גבוה כו' והדבר הגשמי עצמו שבו מדברת ההלכה באמת הוא מסתיר
לגמרי כמו המחליף פרה בחמור וכן בשר הפיגול או לא פיגול וכשר רק
ההלכה בעצמה עם הטעם הנגלה היא מבחי' מלכות דבריאה ויצי' דבחי'
נשמה שהוא אלקות המחיה ומהוה נפש רוח דבי"ע שהן דחילו ורחימו של
המלאכים והנשמות וחב"ד שלהם מאין ליש שהם מרוה צמאונם קודם
שירדה לעוה"ז כמים היורדים כו' וגם אחר שירדה לעשי' היא למעלה מעלה
מבחי' חב"ד דעשי' אפי' דבחי' נשמה שהיא אלקות והטעם משום דחב"ד
דעשי' דבחי' נשמה הוא מקור החיות דחב"ד דנפש רוח ותולדותיהן
והתהוותן מאין ליש עם תולדותיהן עד סוף העשיה היא הארץ וכל צבאה.
אבל חב"ד דהלכות בטעמיהן שבמל' דבריאה ויצי' ענין החכמה היא בתיקון
פרצופי האצי' שבהן תלוין כל טעמי המצות מ"ע בה' חסדים ומל"ת בה"ג
ומשו"ה נמי כשירדו להתלבש בנבראים הן במל' דבריאה ויצי' דבחי' נשמה

דוקא שהוא מכלים דאצי' ולא בבחי' נפש רוח. ואף דהב"ד דבריאה יצירה
דבחי' נשמה שגבהה מאד מעלתן על בחי' מלכות דבריאה יצירה דנשמה
ואעפ"כ הן מקור לחב"ד דבריאה יצירה של בחי' נפש רוח שהן המלאכים.
לק"מ דבאמת המלאכים והנשמות אינן אלא מטפה הנמשכת מחב"ד
דנשמה ליסוד ז"א וניתן לנוק' ומשם יצאו בבחי' לידה כי אף את"ל שנבראו
מהארת הכלים דנוק' דאצי' הרי הם היורדים ונעשים נשמה. אבל עצמות
חב"ד דנשמה מתפשט בו"ק דזו"ן ושם הם שיתא סדרי משנה וגמרא ומ"ש
בע"ח (ושער היחודים) שע"י הכוונה נעשה לבוש נשמה וע"י התורה לבוש
רוח דרוח ע"י משנה דיצי' ורוח דנשמה דבריאה ע"י הגמ' י"ל דהיינו דוקא
ע"י תורת האדם בעוה"ז העולה למעלה. אבל התלמוד עצמו שניתן בסיני
הוא בנשמה ולכן הוא מברר הרוח וכן במשנה דיצי' ואף את"ל שגם הניתן
מסיני הוא ברוח דבריאה יצירה הרי נודע שכל מלאך שהוא שליח מלמעלה
אזי נק' בשם ה' ממש השוכן בקרבו משא"כ כשאינו שליח יש לו שם אחר
כפי עבודתו ואזי קורא קדוש ק' ק' ה' כו' כלומר ששם ה' מובדל ממנו וכן
הוא ממש בבחי' התלבשות התלמוד בבחי' רוח דבריאה והמשנה ברוח
דיצי' הם שלוחי ה' דהיינו כלים דנוק' דאצי' החיצונים בתלמוד והאמצעי'
במשנה אשר המשנה והתלמוד שבהם נמשכים מיסוד אבא המקבל מח"ס
דא"א שבו מלובש אור א"ס ב"ה ונמצא שאור א"ס הוא שם ה' שוכן ברוח
דבי"ע במקרא ומשנה ותלמוד וכשהאדם לומד ממשיך אור א"ס ב"ה
בעוה"ז להיות נכלל ובטל באורו ית' כי זה כל האדם וזאת היתה עבודת
רשב"י וכל התנאים ואמוראים בנגלה להמשיך אורו ית' ולברר בירורי נוגה
כל משך זמן הגלות דשלטא אילנא דטו"ר כמ"ש עת אשר שלט האדם
באדם כו' כי זהו תכלית ההשתלשלות שירד העליון למטה ויהיה לו דירה
בתחתונים כדי להעלותן למהוי אחד באחד. משא"כ עבודת המלאכים דו"ר
שכליים אינה בבחי' המשכה כלל וכלל רק הסתלקות כו'. ובזה יובן מה
שנבראים מלאכים מאין ליש ע"י עסק התורה אפי' שלא בכוונה שהוא
בחי' רוח בלבד שאינה אלקות כלל אלא לפי שאעפ"כ שם ה' שוכן וכו'
ודו"ל:

סימן ה

ולהבין פרטי ההלכות דלא שכיחי כלל ואפשר שלא היו מעולם
במציאות מכש"כ שלא יהיו לע"ל כמו פרטי דיני פיגול
וכה"ג. הנה מודעת זאת שכל איסור שבעולם יש לו שרש ומקור חיים
בקליפות שאל"כ לא הי' יכול להיות במציאות בעולם בלתי השפעה
עליונה. ואפי' המסלסל בשערו וכה"ג מקבל חיותו ברגע זו מהיכלות

יב בכסלו פשוטה
יב בכסלו מעוברת

יג בכסלו פשוטה
יג בכסלו מעוברת

הקליפות כמ"ש בזוהר. והלכך גם פרטי האיסורים שלא באו לידי מעשה
מעולם בעוה"ז הגשמי מ"מ שרשי חיותם הן במציאות בפו"מ בהיכלות
הקליפות. וגם הפרטים שיוכל להיות שלא היו ולא יהיו לעולם במציאות
כגון טעות ושגגות שטעה וקרא לתשיעי עשירי כו' וכה"ג דלא שייך במזיד
להיות קליפה שורה ע"ז. וויכל להיות דכה"ג אינו במציאות בהיכלות
הקליפות [הגה"ה מאדמו"ר בעל צ"צ ז"ל נ"ע. נ"ל מ"ש וויכל להיות אלמא
דלא בריר לי' היינו משום שהשגגות באות מנוגה א"כ י"ל דיש להם
שרש בהיכלות דנוגה]. מ"מ עכ"פ ישנו במציאות להבדיל בחכ"ע
שנתפשטה בפרט זה למשרע"ה בסיני [כמאמר מה] שכל תלמיד ותיק
עתיד לחדש כו' וכל פרטי האבעיות דר' ירמי' וכרכתו כו' פ"ד דחולין.
כי התפשטות חכ"ע היא בבחי' א"ס המלובש בה בפועל ממש. וכל פרט
הלכה הוא שער נמשך מחכ"ע דיסד ברתא ומלובש בה וממנה נמשך
ומתלבש בבי"ע. ונודע כי יניקת הקליפות מאחוריים די"ס דקדושה ובפרט
מלבושים די"ס דבי"ע ובפרט דיצי' ועשיה המעורבים בקליפות כנודע
שיניקתם מבחי' הלבושים. וע"י עסק ההלכות בדבור ומחשבה מתפרשים
ומתפרדים מהקדושה. כמ"ש בתיקונים ור"מ לאפרשא [כו'] והיינו כנודע
ממה שאמרו על שלא ברכו בתורה תחלה כו' שהוא ע"י המשכת אוא"ס
בח"ע המלובשת בהן. ובחכמה אתברירו באוא"ס שבה. והמשכה זו נעשה
ע"י דיוקן העליון של האדם העוסק ג"כ בהלכות אלו למעלה בשרשו
בנוק' דז"א דבי"ע. ובזה יובן חיוב כל נר"ן להשלים כל התרי"ג במחדו"מ
שהן פרטי ההלכות וצריכות לבא בגלגול להשלים התורה בפרד"ס כדי
לברר כל הבירורין הנוגעות להם מכל הרפ"ח שהיא קומת אדם שלמה.
תרי"ג בחינות כלליות ופרטיות. אבל לע"ל כשיושלם הבירור יהי' עסק
התורה בבחי' עשה טוב לבד. להעלות הנר"ן מעלה מעלה עד א"ס וגם
בשם"ה ל"ת בשרשן למעלה שהן גבורות קדושות ולהמתיקן בחסדים
ברמ"ח מ"ע ולכללן יחד. וע"כ התורה כולה נצחית בכללה ובפרטה.
שגם פרטי ההלכות דשם"ה ל"ת הן הן ענפים מהכללות ויש לכולם שרש
למעלה בה"ג דקדושה כמו השם"ה ל"ת עצמן שהן למעלה בחי' הדם
המחיה האברים דכלים דז"א:

סימן ו

יד בכסלו פשוטה
יד בכסלו מעוברת

דוד זמירות קרית להו כו'. הנה בזהר שבחא דאורייתא ורננה כו' ולהבין
מהו השבח להקב"ה כשזה אסור או מותר הנה הוא ע"ד מה
גדלו מעשיך ה' מאד עמקו מחשבותיך. כי הנה נודע שכל העולמות
עליונים ותחתונים תלוים בדקדוק מצוה א' ד"מ אם הקרבן כשר נעשה

יחוד עליון ועולים כל העולמות לקבל חיותם ושפעם. ואם שינה שקיבל
הדם בשמאלו ד"מ או שלא בכלי שרת כשר או שהיתה חציצה אזי
נתבטלה עליות העולמות וחיותם ושפעם מחי' החיים א"ס ב"ה וכן
בתפילין כשרות מתגלים מוחין עליונים דזו"נ שהם מקור החיים לכל
העולמות ובדקדוק אחד נפסלין ומסתלקין המוחין וכה"ג בדקדוקי מצות
ל"ת והלכך המתבונן מה גדלו מעשי ה' שבריבוי העולמות וכל צבאם
ואיך כולם בטלים במציאות לגבי דקדוק א' מדקדוקי תורה שהוא עומק
מחשבה העליונה וחכמתו ית' אשר בדקדוק קל עולים כל העולמות
ומקבלים חיותם ושפעם או להיפך ח"ו ומזה נתבונן גדולת עומק מחשבתו
ית' שהוא בבחי' בלי גבול ותכלית ומעלתה לאין קץ ותכלית על מעלות
חיות כל העולמות שכל חיותם שופע מדקדוק אחד ממנה שהוא נמשך
ממקורו הוא עומק מחשבתו ית' כמו שער האדם הנמשך ממוחו עד"מ
וכנודע מהתיקונים והאד"ר. וזאת היתה שמחת דהע"ה שהיה מזמר ומרן
לשמח לבו בעסק התורה בעת צרתו אך מה שהיה משתבח בתהלת
התורה במעלתה זו ואמר זמירות היו לי כו' נענש ע"ז וא"ל הקב"ה
זמירות קרית להו משום שבאמת מעלתה זו שכל העולמות בטלים לגבי
דקדוק אחד ממנה היא מבחי' אחוריים של עומק המחשבה כמ"א בשם
ה019 הארי"ז"ל על מארז"ל נובלות חכמה שלמעלה תורה. אבל פנימית
שבעומק שהוא פנימית התורה היא מיוחדת לגמרי באור א"ס ב"ה
המלובש בה בתכלית היחוד ולגבי א"ס ב"ה כל העולמות כלא ממש ואין
ואפס ממש כי אתה הוא עד שלא נברא העולם וכו' והלכך גם לפנימיות
התורה אין לשבחה כלל בתהלת חיות כל העולמות מאחר דלא ממש
חשיבי ובבחי' פנימיותה אינה שמחת לבב אנוש ושעשועיו אלא כביכול
שמחת לב ושעשוע המלך הקב"ה שמשתעשע בה כי אלקים הבין דרכה
וידע מקומה ומעלתה בידיעת עצמו כביכול אבל נעלמה מעיני כל חי
כמ"ש ופני לא יראו דהיינו בחי' פנימיותה כמ"ש בשם הארי"ז"ל. וזש"ה
ואהי' אצלו כו' שעשועים אצלו דוקא. משחקת לפניו לפניו דוקא דהיינו
בבחי' פנימיותה וע"ז אמר ואהיה אצלו אמון אל תקרי אמון אלא אומן
כו' ועל בחי' אחוריים אמר משחקת בתבל ארצו ושעשועי את בני אדם
כי התורה ניתנה בבחי' פנים ואחור כדכתיב במגילה עפה דזכרי' והיא
כתובה פנים ואחור ולפי שתפס דוד בבחי' אחוריים לכך נענש בשכחה
הבאה מן בחי' אחוריים ונעלם ממנו לפי שעה מ"ש עבודת הקדש עליהם
בכתף ישאו לחבר וליחד את הכתפיים שהן בחי' אחוריים אל עבודת
הקדש היא ח"ע בבחי' פנים שמשם נמשכו הלוחות שבארון כמ"ש כתובים
משני עבריהם כו' וכמ"ש בירושלמי דשקלים שלא היתה בהן בחי' פנים
ואחור ע"ש:

טו בכסלו פשוטה
טו בכסלו מעוברת

סימן ז

טז בכסלו פשוטה
טז בכסלו מעוברת

וצדקה כנחל איתן (בעמוס ססי' ה'). פי' כמו שנחל איתן הוא המשכה
הנמשכת מבחי' איתן שהיא בחי' נקודה בהיכלא ותרין ריעין
וכו' ואותיות איתן משמשות לעתיד פי' אנא עתיד לאתגליא כמ"ש הנה
ישכיל עבדי וגו' והיינו שיתגלה אז אור א"ס ב"ה ויחודו ית' תוך פנימית
נקודת הלב ע"י המשכת נחל איתן הוא הארת חכמה עילאה שיאיר
בפנימיות הלב ליבטל ביחודו ית' בתכלית מעומקא דלבא אחרי הסרת
הערלה מתאוות הגשמיות וכו'. והנה עתה בגלות החל הזה יש ג"כ עצה
יעוצה להאיר קצת אור ה' מבחי' איתן לתוך נקודת פנימיות הלב כעין
לעתיד והיינו ע"י שמעורר על ניצוץ אלקות שבנפשו בחי' רחמים רבים
העליונים כי באמת כל זמן שאין האדם זוכה שיתגלה אור ה' מבחי' איתן
בנקודת פנימית לבבו ליבטל ביחודו ית' מעומקא דלבא עד כלות הנפש
ממש אזי באמת יש רחמנות גדולה על הניצוץ שבנפשו כי הניצוץ נמשך
מבחי' חכמה עילאה ממש וכשאינו יכול להאיר מבחינתו לתוך פנימיות
הלב ששם מקום גילוי הארה זו ה"ז בבחי' גלות ממש וע"י רחמים רבים
העליונים יוצא מהגלות והשביה ומאיר לתוך נקודה פנימיות הלב בחי'
אהבה רבה זו כנודע ממ"ש ליעקב אשר פדה את אברהם וכמ"ש בלק"א
פמ"ה. ומודעת זאת כי אתערותא דלעילא באתעדל"ת דוקא תליא מלתא
דהיינו ע"י התעוררות רחמים רבים בלב רחמנים וג"ח להשפיע למטה
השפעה גשמיית זהב וכסף וכו' ולכן פעולת הצדקה היא פעולת נחל איתן
ממש. והנה מודעת זאת מ"ש כי עור בעד עור וכל אשר לאיש יתן בעד
נפשו האלקית להאירה באור החיים א"ס ב"ה:

סימן ח

יז בכסלו פשוטה
יז בכסלו מעוברת

הנה לא טובה השמועה שמעתי ותרגז בטני אשר עם ה' מעבירים מלפני
התיבה האיש החפץ בחיים ואריכות ימים של כל אנ"ש שבמקדש
מעט הזה של אנ"ש כמארז"ל שלשה דברים מאריכים ימיו של אדם ואחד
מהם המאריך בתפלתו. ואף גם מי שהשעה דחוקה לו ביותר וא"א לו בשום
אופן להמתין עד אחר עניית קדושה של חזרת הש"ץ הלא טוב טוב לו
שלא לשמוע קדושה וברכו. מלירד לחייהם של החפצים בחיים ואונס רחמנא
פטריה. והש"ץ מוציאו ידי חובתו אף שלא שמע כאילו שמע שהוא כעונה
ממש וכדאיתא בגמרא גבי עם שבשדות דאניסי וויוצאים ידי חובת תפלת
שמו"ע עצמה בחזרת הש"ץ כאלו שמעו ממש וגם קדושה וברכו בכלל.
והנה זאת חקרנוה כן הוא אף גם בדורות הראשונים של חכמי המשנה

והגמרא שהיתה תורתם קבע ועיקר עבודתם ולא תפלתם. ומכש"כ עתה
הפעם בעקבות משיחא שאין תורתינו קבע מצוק העתים. ועיקר העבודה
בעקבות משיחא היא התפלה כמ"ש הרח"ו ז"ל בע"ח ופע"ח. מכש"כ וק"ו
שראוי ונכון ליתן נפשינו ממש עליה והיא חובה של תורה ממש למביני מדע
תועלת ההתבוננות ועומק הדעת קצת כל חד לפום שיעורא דיליה בסדור
שבחו של מקום ב"ה בפסוקי דזמרה ושתי ברכות שלפני ק"ש יוצר ואהבה
לעורר בהן האהבה המסותרת בלב כל ישראל לבא לבחי' גילוי בהתגלות
הלב בשעת ק"ש עצמה שזאת היא מצות האהבה שבפסוק ואהבת גו' בכל
לבבך גו' הנמנית ראשונה בתרי"ג מצות כמ"ש הרמב"ם ז"ל שהיא מיסודי
התורה ושרשה ומקור לכל רמ"ח מ"ע כי על אהבה המסותרת בלב כל
ישראל בתולדתם וטבעם לא שייך ציווי כלל ודעת לנבון נקל כי כשהאהבה
היא מסותרת היא עודינה בנפש האלקית לבדה וכשבאה לבחי' גילוי לנפש
החיונית אזי היא בהתגלות הלב בחלל שמאלי מקום משכן נפש החיונית
וזהו ענין בירור ניצוצות המוזכר שם בע"ח ופע"ח גבי תפלה שלכן היא
עיקר העבודה בעקבות משיחא לברר ניצוצות כו' שהוא בחי' אתהפכא
או אתכפי' של נפש החיונית לנפש האלקית כנודע כי הדם הוא הנפש
כו' והדם מתחדש בכל יום מאוכלין ומשקין וגם מתפעל ונתקן ממלבושים
ודירה כו'. משא"כ בדורות הראשונים שהיו נשמות האלקית גדולי הערך
היה הבירור נעשה כרגע בק"ש לבד וברכות שלפניה ופסד"ז בקצרה וכו'
וד"ל:

סימן ט

יח בכסלו פשוטה
יח בכסלו מעוברת

הוכח תוכיח את עמיתך אפילו מאה פעמים. ולזאת לא אוכל להתאפק
ולהחריש מלזעוק עוד בקול ענות חלושה במטותא מינייכו ברחמין
נפישין חוסו נא על נפשותיכם. והשמרו והזהרו מאד מאד על התורה ועל
העבודה שבלב זו תפלה בכוונה להתחיל כולם יחד כאחד מלה במלה
ולא זה בכה וזה בכה וזה דומם וזה משיח שיחה שתהיה בטילה ה' ישמרנו ועיקר
הסיבה וגרמא בנזקין הוא מהיורדים לפני התיבה שהוא הפקר לכל הרוצה
לפשוט רגליו החוטף אפרתי או מחמת שאין גם אחד רוצה וכו'. ואי לזאת
זאת העצה היעוצה ותקנה קבועה חוק ולא יעבור עוד ח"ו דהיינו לבחור
אנשים קבועים הראוים לזה עפ"י הגורל או בריצוי רוב המנין. דהיינו
שמתפללים מלה במלה בדרך המיצוע בקול רם ולא מאריכים יותר מדאי
ולא מקצרים וחוטפים ח"ו. ועליהם מוטל חובה לירד לפני התיבה כל אחד
ואחד ביומו אשר יגיע לו ולאסוף אליו סביב סמוך כל המתפללים בקול
קצת עכ"פ ולא בלחש ולא חוטפים ח"ו וכמבואר בתקנות ישנות בכמה

עיירות. ועתה באתי לחדשן ולחזקן ולאמצן בל ימוטו עוד לעולם ח"ו (בכ"י גוואלד גוואלד) עד מתי יהיה זה לנו למוקש ולא די לנו בכל התוכחות והצרות שעברו עלינו ה' ישמרנו וינחמנו בכפלים לתושיה ויטהר לבנו לעבדו באמת. חזקו ואמצו לבבכם כל המייחלים לה'. גם לגמור כל הש"ס בכל שנה ושנה ובכל עיר ועיר לחלק המסכתות עפ"י הגורל או ברצון. ועיר שיש בה מנינים הרבה יגמרו בכל מנין ומנין. ואם איזה מנין קטן מהכיל יצרפו אליהם אנשים מאיזה מנין גדול בבל ישונה חק ולא יעבור. וכאו"א מהלומדים הנ"ל יגמור לעצמו בכל שבוע התמניא אפי שבתהלים קי"ט. ולהיות מחמת חלישות הדור אין כח בכל אחד ואחד להתענות כראוי לו. לזאת עצה היעוצה כמארז"ל כל השומר שבת כהלכתו מוחלין לו על כל עוונותיו. כהלכתו דייקא. לכן מוטל על כל אחד ואחד להיות בקי בהלכתא רבתי לשבתא. וגם יזהר מאד שלא לשוח שום שיחה בטילה ח"ו. בהיות מודעת זאת לי"ח כי בכל המצות יש פנימיות וחיצוניות וחיצונית מהשבת הוא שביתה מעשיה גשמית כמו ששבת ה' מעשות שמים וארץ גשמיים. ופנימית השבת היא הכוונה בתפלת השבת ובת"ת לדבקה בה' אחד כמ"ש שבת לה' אלקיך וזו היא בחי' זכור. ובחי' שמור בפנימיות היא השביתה מדיבורים גשמיים כמו ששבת ה' מיו"ד מאמרות שנבראו בהם שמים וארץ גשמיים כי זה לעומת זה כו':

A WRITER WRITES

A WRITER WRITES

*A Memoir by Stephen Birmingham, America's Leading
Social Historian and Best-Selling Author of* "Our Crowd"

STEPHEN BIRMINGHAM

Edited and Annotated by Carey G. Birmingham

Guilford, Connecticut

An imprint of Globe Pequot, the trade division of
The Rowman & Littlefield Publishing Group, Inc.
4501 Forbes Blvd., Ste. 200
Lanham, MD 20706
www.rowman.com

Distributed by NATIONAL BOOK NETWORK

British Library Cataloguing in Publication Information available

Library of Congress Cataloging-in-Publication Data
Names: Birmingham, Stephen, author. | Birmingham, Carey G., 1955- editor.
Title: A writer writes : a memoir by Stephen Birmingham, America's leading
social historian and best-selling author of "Our Crowd" / Stephen
Birmingham ; edited and annotated by Carey G. Birmingham.
Description: First Lyons Press edition. | Guilford, Connecticut : Lyons
Press, 2022. | Includes bibliographical references and index. | Summary:
"A memoir by the late, bestselling writer Stephen Birmingham, whose work
focused on the upper class in America. Birmingham was the author of "Our
Crowd" and more than thirty other books"— Provided by publisher.
Identifiers: LCCN 2021053848 | ISBN 9781493061907 (cloth ; alk. paper)
Subjects: LCSH: Birmingham, Stephen. | Authors, American—20th
century—Biography. | Social historians—United States—Biography. |
LCGFT: Autobiographies.
Classification: LCC PS3552.I7555 Z46 2022 | DDC 813/.54
[B]—dc23/eng/20211221
LC record available at https://lccn.loc.gov/2021053848

♾️™ The paper used in this publication meets the minimum requirements of American National
Standard for Information Sciences—Permanence of Paper for Printed Library Materials, ANSI/
NISO Z39.48-1992.

For Caitlin

Contents

CONTENTS

INTRODUCTION

My father, Stephen Gardner Birmingham, died in November 2015 at the age of eighty-six. At his side, in their apartment on Gramercy Park in New York City, was his partner of over thirty-eight years, Dr. Carroll Edward Lahniers, PhD (I call him "Ed," and he has become a close friend and confidant, and, although my dad and Ed never "married," I refer to him as my stepfather).

Although eminently unqualified as a writer, I was privileged to prepare and disseminate his obituary, which was widely distributed and printed in the *New York Times, L.A. Times, Washington Post*, and *Cincinnati Enquirer*, among others.

My father was gay. Or to be more accurate in today's complicated miasma of gender and sexuality, my father would be described as bisexual. He had to be, at least for a time, having been married to my mother and begetting three children.

Although we often had young men visiting our home during my father's rising notoriety in the early sixties, the first indication that something was different was when my father showed up at my sister's junior high school party at our house on Hidden Spring Lane, Rye, New York. The party, attended by several prepubescent boys and girls, was a gala affair and, since I was the younger brother (I am the youngest of the three), I was ignored and only allowed to observe. Midway into the festivities, my father appeared in a skintight T-shirt (he was very fit), red bandana tied provocatively around his neck, pink socks with Gucci loafers, and yellow (yes, yellow) vinyl hot pants. It was a scene, man. Perhaps he was making an announcement or wanted desperately to "come out," but the message I received in my prepubescent brain was confusion.

Prior to my father's display, I had sheltered sexual experiences, which is to say none. My earliest recollection of "sexuality" per se was my fascination along with my best friend Kevin O'Keefe with our fourth-grade teacher, Miss Jones (her real name). Miss Jones was probably twenty-five years old and attractive. We, however, were not so concerned with her outward beauty but one specific part of her anatomy: her *breastal region*. For reasons we could not understand at the time, we became infatuated with Miss Jones and her, uh, attributes, which were in fact quite spectacular (if memory serves fifty years later). We became so enamored, some might say obsessed, that we decided to give Miss Jones a not-so-thoroughly-thought-through, but appropriate, secret name: "Secret." As in "Here comes Secret," which we would whisper to each other when Miss Jones entered the playground at recess. This was about as close to sexual harassment, as its defined today, as two fourth-grade boys could get. This was not a particularly fortuitous beginning to exposure to the fairer sex.

When my father died, he had amassed an impressive portfolio of not less than twenty-eight books, both novels and "social histories," the latter of which required exhaustive research and interviews. He will be best known, perhaps, by his seminal work, *"Our Crowd": The Great Jewish Families of New York*, published in 1968. He also published innumerable articles on a wide range of topics for *Holiday* magazine and the *Saturday Evening Post*. His books alone resulted in over eight thousand pages and sold an estimated fifteen million copies worldwide since his first book, a novel called *Young Mr. Keefe*, was published in 1958. Assuming 150,000 words per book, he produced well over four million words, all typed with two fingers on a Royal Model HH manual typewriter at approximately one hundred words per minute.

Let us put this into perspective, both in the context of the times and my father's productivity.

First, during my father's writing career over a thirty-year period, my father wrote twelve novels (not including one unpublished novel written in 2003) and sixteen researched histories; each history called for at least twelve months of research. Comparing numbers only, some contemporaries of my father produced far less; Hemingway wrote twenty-four books, Kurt Vonnegut, twelve, J. D. Salinger, seven, and Mario

Puzo, eleven. I don't mean to compare my father with these icons, but he certainly deserves recognition for volume if not for producing the "great American novel."

Second, one must remember the times. Granted, we are not talking the era of Dickens or Poe, but writing in the late fifties into the eighties was done prior to the advent of the Wang Word Processor or Microsoft Word. Pages were inserted into the Royal with carbon paper between, and the writer, well, wrote—without the benefit (as I fortunately have) of advanced word-processing capabilities. The pages were written and edited with pencil or pen and then, laboriously by today's standards, retyped, again and again until the writer got it right. This is the process we witnessed growing up with my father.

Amid all his work, my father had to deal additionally with the creative sides of his progeny: my brother, Mark, my sister, Harriet, and me. While we tried to behave as good children should, the creative sides of our personalities, in particular with my brother and me, came forth and manifested themselves as what one would call *stressors* today. I don't know how much effect such stressors had on my father's decision to leave the family in 1974 (and perhaps make the final move toward becoming exclusively gay), but I can't imagine it helped. I've provided some anecdotes elsewhere in this memoir which, in their totality, could have driven anyone to drink (not to mention question whether having such children was a good idea in the first place) and finally conclude "I've had it," and give a call to Ed.

For example:

STRESSOR 1.0—THE FURNITURE INCIDENT

Our earliest rendition of a stressor provided to our parents occurred when I was young, perhaps four, so my memories are vague. Both parents, however, independently verified this story as true.

Shortly after my father's book *Young Mr. Keefe* was released, my parents' social star was on the rise and they were constantly entertaining, with my mother always the consummate hostess. Our job, as The Children, was to fill the cigarette holders prior to a party, make pleasant (and short) introductions and be relegated to the upstairs bedroom, and make no noise; children were to be seen and not heard.

This plan apparently did not sit well with us, The Children.

Our house on Hidden Spring Lane had three stories, with Mark's and my bedroom on the second floor. It was a corner room, directly over the main dining room on the first floor, with one of our windows directly above the dining room window, facing west.

Once, during our parents' holiday gathering of adults, a guest happened to glance out the dining room window. "Nan," he mentioned to my mother, "I think I just saw something fall outside the window." My mother, incredulous, watched for a moment and, sure enough, another object whizzed by, landing with a dull thud on the driveway. As discreetly as possible, my mother approached my father and asked him to go upstairs to The Children's room and see what is going on.

Upon entering the room, my father witnessed me sitting on the base-end of our *101 Dalmatians*–themed coatrack with my brother guiding the business end of it out the aforementioned second-floor window (this window was to play a significant part in our lives in the future), presumably with the intention of sending it to the tarmac below.

Already gone from the room were a myriad of smaller items, like clothes, hampers, stools, and toys. We had been going at it for a while, evidenced by the resultant pile outside.

STRESSOR 2.0—A CHRISTMAS STORY

In the earliest years of our family, we always had Christmas at Grandmother's house in Andover, Connecticut. In 1960, however, my father decided we would have Christmas at home in Rye, and he devised a plan for a Christmas Day to beat the band. Unfortunately, he failed to consult the band—that is, The Children, and without the band's consent, things can go dangerously wrong.

At 9 p.m. on Christmas Eve, Mark, Harriet, and I were awake and downstairs. There was no evidence of Christmas in our house, not even a tree, and certainly no presents. We, The Children, were confused. Didn't we always have stockings hung with care at Grandmother's? Where's the tree, whose bounteous boughs had brought forth gifts galore? In short, where's Christmas, this Christmas Eve? Finally, in resigned despair that Santa had indeed skipped us over (probably because of something like the Furniture Incident), we three went to bed; and our parents got to work.

Unbeknownst to us, our parents had planned The Great Surprise, no doubt a creation of my father's furtive mind, and had hidden all the presents and Christmas accoutrements in our garage determining only to begin assembly and placement after we were snoozing. They worked until 5 a.m. The patently unachievable goal of The Great Surprise was to greet The Children at the top of the stairs and, with wild anticipation in their young, properly behaved eyes, we as a family would gracefully go down the stairs only to open the doors of the dining room to find . . . the unimaginable! Santa had not forgotten us! All would be forgiven, and the family, as a loving cohesive unit, would celebrate the birth of Christ! My father had even purchased a handmade gingerbread house, almost identical to our own home! That was the Plan.

They should have cleared this Plan with us.

At 6 a.m. Christmas Day, while our parents were asleep after their all-night toil (and probably cocktails), my brother, the oldest, woke Harriet and me up and we three made our way ever-so-quietly downstairs to the dining room. The entry doors were, perplexingly, closed. Not to worry. Opening the doors, a crack, our eyes were visited upon by nothing short of a miracle. Whereas the night before there had been nothing, now there was a cornucopia of wrapped presents, a tree, lights sparkling, stuffed stocking and even a gingerbread house! Santa had indeed arrived! (In the after-action report delivered later during debriefing, our mother contended, "It was all too much for them. It overstimulated their senses.")

Overstimulated or not, we got to work. Barely being able to read at the time, I can't really be blamed for what happened next. We rushed into the dining room with abandon, like a horde of hungry locusts during an African drought. With little coordination, my brother would hand me a wrapped present and instruct me to open it, notwithstanding that I couldn't (or wouldn't) read the tag identifying its intended recipient. Once I realized the opened present was not for me, or us, it was summarily cast aside; a punch bowl for my grandmother here, a set of wine glasses for our aunt there; it made no difference. There were so many presents! We had a lot to do.

After a few hours of culling, we finally opened *all* the gifts, eliminated anything extraneous that was not within our purview, and settled down to play or rest, as the case may be. The room was a shamble, with wrapping paper and useless (read: not-for-us) gifts strewn about.

Then our parents awoke, maybe a little hungover, around 8 a.m., and upon descending the stairs found us amid a disaster. If it had occurred to my father at the time, he would have called the Rye Police, but instead he went on a rampage. Peacefully asleep under a mountain of gift wrap, I was aroused by my father who, enraged, kicked the gingerbread house across the room and to smithereens. Our parents' perfect plan crumbled under the weight of three creative children out, seemingly, to destroy the family.

STRESSOR 3.0—A BRILLIANT GAG

A few years after The Christmas Incident (TCI) and The Furniture Incident (TFI), on a wintry night, I invented a Brilliant Gag to play upon my unsuspecting parents. On such an evening, with a light snow covering the ground and Mom and Dad downstairs sharing a cocktail and the days' news, I decided to climb out my second-story bedroom window (yes, that window) on a rope.

The idea was to tie the rope from my bedstead out the window to the driveway below, climb down, and come nonchalantly through the front door past my parents lounging on the couch, and go back up to my room. The gag was obvious: my parents would see me come into the house from outdoors, but they did not see me leave. How could this be? After two or three times, my parents would stop me and ask, "What's going on?" They'd quickly see how innovative and funny I was (not to mention brave, climbing out a second-story window) and we'd all have a good laugh. That was the plan, and the Gag.

The first attempt went off without a hitch (I don't think my parents even noticed, but that too was part of the plan and process; *initial complacency*). However, as I began to make my second descent, as if right on cue, my sister, Harriet, popped into my room (we all had our own rooms by this time, the better to prevent conspiracies, my father thought) and began asking unfortunate questions like, "What are you doing?" Anyone with a sister knows that they are nothing but trouble and under these circumstances should just go away. "Go away," I said. She did not go away, but persisted with the added threat, "If you don't tell me, I'm telling [Dad]." I explained the Brilliant Gag and swore her to secrecy. "Only if I can do it, too" she said, adding, for no good purpose, "or I'm telling [Dad]." Everyone knew then, and should know now, that sisters should not be allowed to do certain things, and climbing out of a second-story window based on instructions from an eight-year-old is one of those things.

Leaving me no choice, I explained carefully how this Gag worked, saying to Harriet, "Lower yourself slowly out the window, grab the rope and climb down. Whatever you do, don't panic." Simple enough a monkey could do it, but not my sister. As soon as she grabbed the windowsill, she hung by the full length of her arms—and panicked. While she was screaming her head off, I bent out the window begging in a whisper, "Don't panic! Just grab the rope and climb down!" My entreaties fell on deaf ears. There was nothing but more screaming.

Eventually, Harriet's clamoring made its way down to the living room and my parents came running. Upon entering my room, they could hear screaming but couldn't see anything, my sister's fingers clinging to the sill being the only exposed part of her body. Finally, noticing the open window (a clear giveaway), my father stuck his head out to see what the ruckus was, and Harriet immediately released from the sill—and grabbed my father around his neck. My father was fit. But even he could not gain leverage, and gravity was slowly pulling him out the window along with Harriet. My mom rushed in, grabbed my father from behind and around his chest and *she* started pulling, the three looking like some strange, bent-over conga line.

Meanwhile, seeing my Brilliant Gag deteriorate before my eyes, I realized the end result would not be "a laugh was heard 'round!" but rather "this belt'll make a sound." Exit stage right.

Unbeknownst to me, all three of the conga line eventually pulled back through the window, my sister no worse for wear, but crying (as she was wont to do) uncontrollably. By that time, I had already been hiding under a bush across the street, in the snow, with my life ebbing away. "They will miss me," I thought, as I planned to slowly succumb to the snow and cold. Fate would not have me that night, however, as my father, knowing I had "run away" (fifty feet and under a bush constitutes running away in the Book of Kids), called from the front porch to inform me that I was not, in fact, in trouble and could come home. All was forgiven and in the coming years we would all have a good laugh about the Brilliant Gag Incident.

STRESSOR 4.0—DANCING SCHOOL

At twelve, that last thing I was interested in was girls (excepting my adoration of Miss Jones), and the only thing worse than girls was Dancing School.

My sister, Harriet, however, desperately wanted to attend dancing school, as I can only assume so many young girls want to. Conveniently, Management at the Apawamis Country Club Dancing School was experiencing a dearth of young boys to pair with the young girls, and a void in the Birmingham Dancing School Agenda was thereupon created, a void I was destined to fill against my wishes. In my mom's rationalization, I was sacrificed to the fourth graders' season of dancing school so my sister could attend the sixth graders'. A sacrifice it would be, but who would be placed on the altar of Apawamis Club? Not I, if I had anything to say about it.

A lot of planning had to go into my first night of DS, including obtaining a dark suit, which I didn't own and for which I refused to get fitted. The answer: Mom would get my brother's old blue suit, hem the pants and sleeves and, Bob's your uncle, we're good to go.

Finally, the big night arrived, and I was to attend my first session of dancing school, learn proper etiquette, and understand how to treat young women properly and with respect.

My mother came up to my room with less than thirty minutes until "school" started (Apawamis was conveniently five minutes away) and I was in my shorts and T-shirt.

"Why aren't you dressed?" she asked

My response, "I can't find my suit."

Not buying it, my mother called out, "Steve! We've got a Code Red!" (my mother's message was clear: we have breach and attempted escape of an inmate. Close all the exits and secure the perimeter.) My father appeared—in a homemade bikini comprised of three bandanas tied together, barely, and a paint-dabbled and torn T-shirt.

They two were going to make sure I got to that school, and the first step was to find the suit. To do so, they had to toss my cell, quickly discovering the contrabanded blue suit, now hopelessly wrinkled, under my mattress fortunately sans a shiv or soap-gun. Ten minutes to go, and both mom and dad tried to corral me like BLM wranglers meeting a mustang in Wyoming. I wasn't going down without a fight. Holding me down, they both managed, after twenty minutes, to get me in the suit, outfit me with a cockeyed tie, and throw me in the car. All the way to Apawamis Club I was festooning them with expletives as if I'd become possessed by the devil himself.

By the time we got to the Apawamis Club, one of the most exclusive and Brahmin-esque clubs in Westchester County (and one of the oldest, founded in 1890), I was thirty minutes late. My father, still in his "bikini," yanked me from the back seat and pushed me forward toward the grand entrance, thinking naively that my better manners would prevail once I was in public. The obligatory retired Rye Police officer who provided security looked askance, not only at this wrinkled kid coming in a half hour late, but also at the strangely dressed man who dropped him off.

Once inside, I was greeted by the hostess, an elderly, bejeweled woman with a substantial bosom and obvious patrician heritage. She smiled.

"What a sweet young man! Welcome. Although you're a little late, I'm sure you'll enjoy our Dancing School!"

I looked around her rather large frame to witness dozens of boys my age dancing with girls who wore white gloves. The boys looked like the undead, moving rhythmically to "right step, one, two; left step, one, two." I looked up at the hostess (I was short at the time). I looked around at the dancing. I looked back up at the hostess, who, despite my clear reticence to enter the premises, continued to smile politely. Staring up, I said, "Fuck you!" I then turned on my heels and ran.

As the matron gasped and clutched her chest ("Why, I never!"), the security guard started laughing hysterically, giving me time to make my break. I hadn't counted on my father waiting at the bottom of the steps like some crazily dressed goalkeeper. As I leapt, he caught me and dragged me, struggling, back into the club, while the hostess sat in a chair provided by the security guard and fanned herself.

Realizing I had no choice, I entered the dance hall proper and sat sullenly in a chair by myself, conquered, at least for the time being. I determined that I would not dance, no matter what. Finally, I succumbed to the social pressure of forty or so of my fellow doomed boys, who encouraged me to buck up and make it through, if for no other reason than to survive. The downside of my stubbornness was that, when I finally did hit the floor, the only dance partner left was the homely girl with the limp.

I never reconciled with Dancing School and managed, despite my father's best efforts, to avoid better than 70 percent of the sessions, using guile, obfuscation, and disinformation (I transposed School Dates with no School Dates on the family calendar). The Apawamis Club probably never recovered from that awful, awful Birmingham boy.

Stressors Nos. 5 and 6: It's All Fun and Games Until Somebody Gets Hurt

I was eight when I almost died the first time.

The backyard of our house was a children's paradise, with a small play yard containing a slide, sandbox, and a playhouse of about one hundred square feet. The playhouse had functioning windows and a front door with six glass panes, which when closed gave the little residence a weatherproof place for us to hide when needed. We had a large yard and a swimming pool about one hundred feet down from the playhouse/yard.

On this occasion, my parents were sitting by the pool on a sunny summer afternoon where my father, taking a break from his constant writing, was once again lounging in his signature bandana bikini.

Harriet and her best friend, Laura, were in the playhouse and would not let me join them. I was frustrated. Amid my yelling and the girls' mocking, I was determined to enter the playhouse by any means, even if it meant knocking down the door (unlikely, given my small stature at the time). With that in mind, I ran toward the closing front door with my right arm stretched out in front of me like a running back plunging into the line, aiming for the perimeter of the door. I missed.

My hand and arm crashed through one of the glass panes of the door and sliced a huge swath of muscle and tissue on my upper right bicep. Looking down at this severe wound, I think I immediately went into shock, while my sister and Laura started screaming. I recall that there was, surprisingly, not a lot of blood.

Running from the pool, my mother wrapped my injured arm with a towel while my father drove us to United Hospital Emergency, which was only minutes away. My father had managed to put on a T-shirt, but otherwise was barefoot and in his bikini as he carried me into the hospital.

I was rushed into surgery, and twenty-two stitches later, the doctors were able to save my arm. (I remember having a dream under the anesthesia in which I woke up and saw my arm in a jar of formaldehyde!) The surgeon explained how close I'd come to severing the main artery in my arm and "bleeding out." Nevertheless, the surgery was a success, and other than a conversation scar, I have complete use of my arm to this day.

My father accused my sister of trying to kill me.

Two years later, having fully recovered, my brother had his turn.

Our parents had gone into New York City for a dinner party and left Mark and me alone; never a good idea.

While outside, on a sunny spring evening, Mark constructed a crude bow and arrow from a sapling bough and some string (you can see where this is going—"you'll shoot your eye out!"), aimed at me and gave me "the count of ten to run." To this day, I don't know what prompted him to threaten me like that or, for that matter, not to wait until ten. At the count of three, he fired from about ten feet away. He shot my eye out. Well, not completely. The "arrow" struck the outside of my left eye, broke the retina, and caused other damage to the eye. I fell to the ground, now blind in that eye, but again with little blood loss.

In an age before cell phones, there was no way for us to contact our parents, so my brother helpfully walked me across to the Simmonses, our neighbors, whereupon Mrs. Simmons drove me to, where else, United Hospital. Good to see you again, Carey!

While I was in the emergency room waiting for surgery (again), somehow, someone was able to contact my parents and they arrived at the hospital, this time with my father properly attired and my mother in a fur coat. With their signature on the consent, I then spent three hours in surgery and the next five years in and out of New York Eye and Ear (East Fourteenth Street) having several complications and attendant surgeries. In the end, the doctors saved my eye, but my vision is 20/500 and it can never be completely corrected.

My father accused my brother of trying to kill me.

I've never blamed my brother nor held animosity toward him for his moment of directed violence, despite never knowing his motivation. On the contrary, I am extremely close to Mark even today, and, as you'll see, we had many misadventures scheduled for our future together after he let loose that arrow.[1]

I imagine that all these stressors, in addition to the others I've added to this memoir, helped my father call Ed in Cincinnati in 1974 and say, "I've had enough! I'm on my way!"

⸎

When my father died, he left a sizable estate, a result of his hard work, a creative mind, and generational parsimony. A large part of his assets, including a co-op in Gramercy Park and the house in Cincinnati (described later in this memoir) were bequeathed to Ed, and I can't imagine a more worthy beneficiary. An additional large amount of his estate was willed to a trust, the beneficiaries of which were scholarship funds set up at Williams College in Massachusetts and Hotchkiss School in Connecticut, both schools that my father attended in his youth.

The copyrights to all his written works were also part of the assets included in the trust, including any royalties and any theatrical rights that might accrue. I discussed this with the Trust's administrator and ended up purchasing all the copyrights to all my father's works in 2017. Shortly thereafter, Ed delivered this memoir, an unpublished but typewritten piece, along with another complete novel and half of an unfinished third work of anecdotal history (this history, *Unguarded Moments*, is included in the appendix), all apparently written between 2000 and 2013.

My siblings and I received nothing from my father's estate. His will, which we had to acknowledge with respective signatures, stated, "I, Stephen Gardner Birmingham, specifically make no provision in this Will for my children, Mark, Harriet and Carey." While some might consider this ignominious, or even cruel, I did not; I had expected it, since my father's and my reconciliation in the early 1980s. My brother and sister were not so understanding and remain bitter today. This is particularly true in the case of my sister, who has been, and remains, on public assistance after years of alcohol and drug abuse and periods of homelessness; she expected a payday. I like to think my father was, in a sense, getting even with us for all the stressors we put him through, which, as you'll see, often included the police.

Whatever my father's reasons for leaving the family so precipitously in 1974, the result was a long period of disruption, pain, and anger in Rye, New York, where we grew up. My mother, who adored my father, notwithstanding his "proclivities," never remarried nor, for that matter, had any serious relationships. She would never, however, forgive my father, even up until she died on my birthday in 2007. Although I was always close to my mom, I was the only one of us who really reconciled with my father after he left, recognizing him both as the man and talent he'd become. He, on the other hand, never exuded much warmth, and I always had the feeling he was holding back, perhaps to avoid any true intimacy with his children.

Harriet would call our father on occasion (most times inebriated), lugubrious and often seeking money. My brother did not contact our father for over forty years, and on that occasion only to ask for money to help in Mark's cancer treatment; my father gave him $10,000.

Throughout my reconciliation, I also managed to find a place in my heart for the man who took care of my father for thirty-eight years and who was at his side when dad died: Ed Lahniers.

It's interesting to note that, despite our reconciliation, my father never mentions me or my sister in this book but devotes an entire (if not altogether flattering) chapter to my brother, Mark. Perhaps, as you'll see, this was because my brother was the instigator of so many of our "hijinks" and, being the first child, the cause of so much of my father's angst.

While I've taken the liberty of peppering this memoir with my own personal recollections and anecdotes, this work is, in the end, my father's memoir, not mine. Nonetheless, I hope readers will enjoy my father's stories and my own and will gain some context into an author's life.

Carey Gardner Birmingham
San Antonio, TX
January 2020

PART I
THE EARLY DAYS

CHAPTER ONE

Buffy

STEVE:

HER NAME WAS JENNIFER BOYINGTON, AND HOW SHE ACQUIRED THE nickname I've no idea, but everyone called her Buffy. She was the prettiest girl I'd ever seen, and at the age of nine I was madly in love with her. Her image, as they say, filled my waking thoughts.

Buffy was an orphan, some sort of foundling, and as a child I imagine she had been raised in a series of Depression-era foster homes. But since she never talked about her past, and it never occurred to me to ask, I have no idea whether she knew who her parents were. I had heard my own parents say that Buffy was "illegitimate," which I gathered was not a desirable thing to be, though I'm not sure I even understood the meaning of the term. All I knew was that I loved her unbearably. She was seventeen years old.

She had dark, naturally curly hair, fair skin, wide-spaced dark eyes, and a band of pale freckles across the bridge of her small, perfectly formed nose. She had three dimples—one on each cheek, and one in the center of her chin. She had lived with friends of my parents in the little town of Andover, Connecticut, while their own children were growing up, and these friends had grown fond of Buffy. With their children grown and off to school and college, these friends felt that Buffy, who was fond of small children, needed a more stimulating home life. During 1941, it was decided that Buffy should come to live with us. She adapted beautifully to the change of address. My sister, Susan, was two and a half years younger than I. My mother explained that Buffy was to be what she called our "nursemaid."

As such, her duties were somewhat loosely defined. She helped my mother in the kitchen, fixing dinner, and with the cleanup afterward, but she ate her meals with us. She was expected to keep her bedroom tidy and to do a little light housework, but she was always given time to do her high school homework, and she was never required to pick up after us children, although she sometimes did. Today, I suppose she would be called an au pair girl, and for this, in addition to room and board, my mother paid her a small allowance, enough for Saturday-afternoon movies, the Mounds bars she liked to nibble on, the Lucky Strikes she smoked, her cosmetics, and other incidentals. Mainly, she was to be a surrogate for my mother, while she was off and about, busily running the little town.

It is important to remember that my mother was an alumna of Wellesley College, as was my grandmother before her. The Wellesley Woman, I was given to understand, was a special breed indeed. Once, on an alumnae questionnaire that my mother was filling out, I saw this question asked: "What was the most important thing you gained from the Wellesley experience?" My mother had answered this in three words: "Poise, I suppose." At Wellesley (at least in Mother's day, and I don't imagine it has changed that much), a young woman was required to master not just academic skills but social ones as well. If your posture was poor, Wellesley would correct it. If your speech was less than cultivated, Wellesley would fix that, too, with emphasis on proper vowel sounds. (One exercise was to repeat the phrase: *Papa, potatoes, poultry, prunes, and prisms.*) In order to receive her diploma a Wellesley woman had to be able to swim at least two lengths of the college pool.

Not that scholarship was overlooked at Wellesley. "At Wellesley," my mother once offhandedly remarked, "they teach you just about everything there is to know about everything." I remember one morning, when we were children, hearing that an atomic bomb had been exploded over Hiroshima, and my mother explaining to us how an atomic bomb worked, based on something called nuclear fission. In fact, she said, if she had the money to purchase the necessary parts and ingredients, she could have built an atomic bomb based on what she had learned in chemistry class at Wellesley. In my mother's mind, there was no doubt that my sister would also go to Wellesley, as indeed she did. And I know that it was a deep disappointment to her that her only granddaughter—my daughter—did not pass Wellesley's rigid muster and become the fourth generation in her family at the college.

Wellesley women were expected then—and this of course has changed—to marry, and have, on the average 2.5 children and then to throw themselves vigorously into community service. My mother took all this very seriously. She founded the local chapter—and naturally became chairperson of—the Parent-Teachers Association (PTA), and later served on the Connecticut State Board of Education. She headed the Andover Mother's Club, which was sort of an adjunct to the PTA. She was also on the Area Board of Education and was its chairperson for several terms. As an ardent New Deal Democrat in an overwhelmingly Republican village, she ran for and was elected to—Andover's Board of Selectmen, where one of her duties was seeing to it, on snowy nights that the town's one snowplow was called into service so that roads would be cleared by morning. She played the piano well and, though she had never played the organ, when the First Congregational Church (the only Episcopal house of worship in town) needed an organist, she volunteered for that, and was the church's choir director as well. She wrote a regular column of Andover news, also without pay, for the *Hartford Courant*. And there was a great deal more. As a result of all this activity, she was out virtually every evening of the week at some committee meeting or another. My sister and I might have resented this—in fact, we did, until Buffy came.

At some political gathering a former governor of Connecticut, Wilbur Cross, had referred to Editha Birmingham as "the smartest woman in the state." My mother took this seriously, too; it confirmed and made official what she had already suspected. But, naturally, a woman with that high an opinion of herself, and who undertook the running of such a little town—correcting its shortcomings and pointing it in what she knew to be the right direction—made her share of enemies. It used to embarrass us, as children, to hear our friends' parents inveigh against our mother as "that Birmingham woman." We knew that, at the regular Town

5

Meetings, there were other townsfolk who engaged her in angry shouting matches and called her ugly names. In the three-room schoolhouse we attended (yes, it was painted red), we knew that we received special attention. After all, our mother was chair of the School Board. But being teachers' pets did not endear us to our peers.

In fact, we both grew up supposing that Mother was one of the most disliked women in town, though it was obvious Mother didn't care. When she died in 1976, Susan and I decided, rather than a funeral, to have a memorial service for her at the church where she'd played for so many years. As we were leaving the house, Sue looked at me with panic in her eyes, and said, "My God—what if nobody comes to this?" The church was filled to capacity, with standees in the back.[2]

Meanwhile, it was more or less made clear to us that Buffy wasn't very bright; "simple" was the term my mother sometimes used for her, but "a good soul." It was not that she was feebleminded. Her IQ was probably in the low-average range. But at the regional high school she attended, she was not considered "college material," and the courses she took were in something called Home Economics. She also took courses in typing and shorthand, and I can see her at the small desk in her bedroom, practicing her typing, with a chart of the keyboard propped up in front of her portable typewriter and the letters on the keys themselves covered with adhesive tape. Later, I would watch her endlessly copying the hieroglyphics from Gregg's Shorthand Book into a spiral notebook. The school's theory, I suppose, was that if Buffy did not marry and have children, she could always find employment as a secretary or clerk-typist. She was conscientious about her homework, though her grades, I understood, were generally poor.

My father, who was a practicing lawyer in Hartford, had his jolly side. On Sunday mornings my sister and I would cuddle in bed with him while he read us the funnies from the *Courant*. Or he would tell us stories that he made up as he went along—usually about a pair of twins: "Ike and Mike, they look alike." He composed limericks: "There once was a schoolmarm named Little, who had no control o'er her spittle. She'd drip and she'd drool, while teaching her school, but she cared not a jot nor a tittle." But he could also be a stern and harsh disciplinarian. I had certain chores that I was required to do. Our house had been originally built in the middle of an apple orchard (the Great Hurricane of 1938 blew down all the trees), and one of my tasks was to pick up apples on the lawn as they began to fall, so they would not jam the blades of Father's lawn mower. I didn't mind picking up apples. I was paid ten cents a bushel for the job. What I didn't like doing was getting the eggs.

Our eggs were bought from a farm across the road, where the farmer's wife, Mrs. Gilchrist, kept chickens. To this day, I have no idea why I hated going to Mrs. Gilchrist's once or twice a week to buy a dozen eggs. It had nothing to do with Mrs. Gilchrist herself, who was always kind to me, and the walk from our front door to hers was no more than three hundred yards. But I considered my egg chore an enormous imposition on my time—eggs always seemed to be needed at inconvenient moments—and I finally hit upon a strategy that would rid me of this onerous duty forever. The next time my father told me to get eggs, I would simply say no. I remember my father stepping into my room with coins jingling in his hand. "Time to run over and get a dozen eggs," he said.

"No." I said, looking him bravely in the eye.

I was thereupon paddled so severely that I never dared to say no to him again.

My mother, meanwhile, was all Wellesley seriousness. She loved explaining things. If you asked her what made the wind blow, she would tell you in terms of temperature fluctuations, atmospheric pressure and shifting currents in the stratosphere, and this might lead to an explanation of different cloud formations—cirrus, cumulus, and so on. She also had a quick temper, and a habit of bursting into hysterical tears when things seemed not to go exactly as she thought they should. And so, it seemed a wondrous thing to have someone like Buffy living with us, whose mood was always sunny. She never moped, never sulked, never seemed to feel angry or misused or disappointed. My life, at the time, seemed nothing but a series of disappointments and frustrations. It was as though disappointments were contagious, like measles or whooping cough, and I had caught them all. I was disappointed that I couldn't seem to run as fast as other boys my age, that I couldn't seem to catch or throw a ball, that I was secretly afraid of water, and couldn't seem to learn to swim.

The thing that impressed me most about Buffy was her perpetual cheerfulness. She could not have had a happy childhood—I knew that—and yet she was always happy, always smiling; Buffy seemed immune to disappointment. She seemed to skip through life, untouched, uncaught. I longed to be *just like her*. I wanted to inhabit her body, her mind, her soul, and to learn the secret of her merry spirit. Because everybody, it seemed, loved Buffy. And nobody, it seemed, loved me—except Buffy, whose love was huge and unquestioning and enfolding, and took in all the world.

At right about the time Buffy came to live with us, I had begun developing a peculiar fascination—a fetish, even—involving female breasts. I know exactly how it started. It started with Miss Litwin, my third-grade teacher. Miss Litwin was a pretty young woman who fancied loose-knit dresses and skirt-and-sweater sets, which showed off her shapely bosoms to good advantage. I took to making secret pencil 1 drawings of women, always in profile, with enormous breasts, sometimes long and pendulous, sometimes pert and upturned, but always with little round nipples, like Miss Litwin's in her knits.[3] Somehow, Buffy seemed to have sensed that I had this secret vice. At seventeen, she had a fully developed figure, with traces of baby fat still lingering beneath her chin, around her armpits, and just below her buttocks, and she clearly enjoyed dancing and prancing around her room in her bra and panties (never anything less), and letting me watch her get dressed. And of course, I loved watching her. If there was a zipper to be run up the back of a skirt or blouse, she let me do this for her. This was one of our secrets kept from my mother.

I also loved watching her apply her makeup. In retrospect, I suppose she used much too much makeup for a high school freshman, but, as it was, preparing her face before she caught her bus to school took at least half an hour. She sat at her dressing table, facing a three-way mirror, and I would stand behind her as she worked with her brushes, sponges, pencils, and puffs and with little tubes of creams and blushes, erasing those irksome little freckles across the bridge of her nose, adding eye shadow here, re-sculpting the shape of her mouth with bright red lipstick. The only times I ever saw her frown were when she was dissatisfied with the arch of an eyebrow, or a bow of her lips. A small brown mole on her chin

8

regularly sprouted a hair, and I would watch, in fascination, as she artfully
tweezed this out.

When I was alone, I often sneaked into her bedroom to study the
array of cosmetics that covered her dressing table, sniffing the scents of
her lipsticks and powders and nail polishes, the brushes she used to apply
mascara and the dangerous-looking little clamp she used to curl her eyelashes. This dressing table also contained a drawer, and in this drawer, she
kept her diary, which I knew she wrote in every day. The diary was always
locked, but one day, in my snooping, I discovered where she hid the key.
Naturally, I unlocked the diary, expecting that all sorts of wonderful and
exciting secrets about Buffy and her magic formula for gaiety would
soon be revealed to me. But unfortunately, all the entries were written in
Gregg's shorthand, impossible to decipher.

Andover was so small (its prewar population was only about seven
hundred) that it did not have a downtown. Instead, it had what we called
"downstreet." Downstreet was the intersection of Long Hill Road, where
we lived, and US Route 6, which ran eastward from Hartford all the way
to the tip of Cape Cod. At this intersection was the town's only streetlight, which was regularly knocked out of commission by stone-throwing
teenage boys. Downstreet consisted, in addition to the three-room
schoolhouse (about ninety students), of the Congregational Church, the
little public library on the opposite corner, a railroad station (now gone,
the tracks torn up), a gas station, the post office, the building that housed
the Andover Volunteer Fire Department's one shiny red fire engine, and
Mr. Standish's General Store.

Trains did not stop at the Andover station unless there happened to
be a passenger on board wanting to get off there or waiting to get on.
Otherwise, which was most of the time, outgoing mail was placed, in a
sack, on a hook by the track, and was snatched off by a trainman as the
train sped through. In another sack, incoming mail was simultaneously
tossed on the platform. The Volunteer Fire Department was called out so
infrequently that the volunteers regularly set brush fires to keep themselves in practice, and their truck exercised and lubricated. There was no
local law enforcement person. In case of serious trouble, the Connecticut
State Police were called. A sign at the outskirts of town used to announce

"ANDOVER—THICKLY SETTLED." But it went down after the same teenage boys in charge of the streetlight kept painting out the "T" in THICKLY. This is what my parents, both city folk, had wanted when they built their house "in the country."

Mr. Standish's store, on the other hand, was quite a lively place. In addition to flour, sugar, salt, milk, butter, and other staples, Mr. Standish sold a few fresh vegetables—mostly onions—along with canned goods, galoshes, twine, fishing tackle, aspirin and toothpaste, laundry soaps, kerosene, cooking oil, brooms, mops, and candy—and of course a great deal else. School was just a short run from Mr. Standish's and so, at recess time, we would all flock into his store and fan out in all directions. When one of us was able to get Mr. Standish's attention with the possibility of an actual sale, the rest of us would stuff our pockets with candy. I always tried to get a Mounds bar for Buffy and, if I was lucky, a pack of Lucky Strikes as well. She rewarded me by letting me light her cigarettes for her and letting me take the first drag, another secret from my mother.

A couple of doors down from Mrs. Standish's was the town Post Office, where Mrs. Gatchell, the postmistress, ran a side business as a candy store. We did not like Mrs. Gatchell, nor patronize her. She was a mean and suspicious soul who kept her supplies of candy in a locked glass case. She did not produce her key—it hung from a string tied to her belt—until the proper amount of cash had been placed in her plump little hand.

"Don't tell your mother." These words had become something of a mantra in our family, and we took it completely for granted. These secrets—and sometimes they were downright lies—were a matter of course, and it was easy to see why. They made life easier; they helped avoid storms and ruckuses and unpleasant confrontations, which spilling the beans or telling the truth would certainly have created. My parents' marriage, for instance, had been considered a great *mésalliance*. Both my mother's and father's parents thoroughly disapproved of the union, and some members of both families refused to acknowledge it. As a result, I had aunts, uncles, and cousins on both sides of my family whom I never knew.

My mother was a Gardner from Massachusetts, a WASP family of some renown. Isabella Stewart Gardner, of the Boston museum fame, was a cousin by marriage. We were the "old" Gardners, I was assured. We were also called the "blind" Gardners, since our name had no "I" in it. The "one-eyed" Gardiners of New York, after whom Gardiner's Island is named, were considered to be the "new" Gardiners. As my grandfather Gardner used to put it, "We are the *original* Gardners. We are descended from Adam and Eve!" As a result of the Gardner connection, I have relatives with such distinguished New England names as Peabody and Parkman—the writer Francis Parkman is a several-times-removed cousin—and, through the Gardners, my mother's family can be traced directly back to one of the twenty-three original male *Mayflower* passengers, Richard Warren.

My father, by contrast, was the grandson of an Irish Catholic immigrant who made his way, penniless, to New England at the time of the Great Hunger. My grandfather Birmingham is listed in Hartford records as an "engineer," but this does not mean he had any sort of a degree. He had started out as a laborer, laying tracks for the New Haven Railroad, and had worked his way up to the front of the train, where he rang the bell and pulled the whistle. My father grew up in a poor—largely immigrant, largely Catholic—section of southwest Hartford with the unlovely name of Frog Hollow. He was one of six children—two boys, four girls—and the only one to put himself through college, and then on through Yale Law School.

When he married my mother, outside the Catholic Church, he officially gave up Catholicism, and appeared to give up religion altogether—though my mother was, even then, a church organist and choir mistress in the local Episcopal Church. As such, religion never played much of a role in my family's life that I could notice. On Sunday mornings, my father would go off to play golf. "There's no sweeter sound," he used to say," than the sound of church bells ringing across a golf course on a Sunday morning." At around the time Buffy joined the family, he began asking me to go with him. I could carry his clubs, be his caddy. We would toss his golf bag into the trunk of the car, and off we would go. But we didn't play golf. Instead, the unfathomable would occur. We went to morning Mass at the Catholic church in Columbia, the next town. I didn't understand the ritual at all—my father indicated when we should kneel and when we should rise—but I found the Latin incantations, the swinging of the censer, the music, the candles, the priests' and the alter boys' robes all quite mysterious and beautiful. If religious faith, I have often thought, is supposed to be something ineffable and, at bottom, beyond human grasp and comprehension, Catholicism must be the most religious religion of all. He never explained why, but his instructions were clear: "Don't tell your mother," he would remind me. Of course, I never did.

My father commuted by car between his law practice in Hartford and Andover five days a week, and he often went to the office on Saturday mornings as well. Saturday afternoons what with my mother's many meetings during the week—were usually the only times my parents spent in the house together. But they didn't really do "togetherly" things. My mother would putter in the rock garden she had created, or sit at her desk, writing her Andover news column for the *Courant*, or play Klondike, her favorite solitary game, or work on her nails. She was not much of a woman for cosmetics, but she was almost obsessive about her fingernails.[4] She would often apply, and remove, her nail polishes several times a day, changing the shade each time, while smoking many Pall Malls. Her desk was always a clutter of little pyramid-shaped bottles of all colors, along with emery boards, cuticle scissors, orange sticks, cotton balls and Kleenex.

Outside, my father might be mowing the lawn. He was obsessive about his lawn as my mother was about her nails, and it was a large lawn—at least a two-hour job to get it properly edged and manicured and this, more than golf, was his principal exercise. Then, when that was done, he'd go into the house and into the kitchen, and open his first bottle of beer.

I suppose he drank quite a lot. He was, after all, an Irishman, and drinking is supposed to be the Irish curse. Often, his speech would become slurred, and he would appear unsteady on his feet. My mother pretended not to notice when this happened. She was not a drinker. In fact, she could not really handle alcohol at all. Sometimes, when they entertained, she would have a martini. But a second one was too much for her. About halfway through her second cocktail, she would simply lie down on the sofa and fall asleep.

Saturday afternoons, meanwhile, were the best times for my sister and Buffy and me, particularly during the summer months, when school was out. "I'm taking the children downstreet for a walk," Buffy would say. "That's nice, dear," my mother would reply, not looking up from her card game or nail buffer.

Then we'd be off, on our way to glorious adventure, down Long Hill Road to where it met US Route 6, a distance of less than a mile. Buffy in shorts and halter (I'd zipped and tied her into these), her midriff bare, her breasts bouncing, a smile on her ruby-lipsticked lips.

In front of the library, facing the highway, there was a low stone wall. The wall was the end of our walk, and there we would sit, watching the cars go by on their way to and from Hartford, Providence, and the Cape. After a while, a car would slow down and stop, and Buffy would hop off the wall and have a conversation with the driver. Sometimes these conversations seemed to end in a disagreement, and the car would drive off, but usually they would end with Buffy motioning us to join her. She would get in front with the driver, and my sister and I would climb in the back. This man was her friend, Buffy would explain, introducing us.

Sometimes there was more than one friend in the front seat with Buffy. I remember at least one occasion when Buffy managed to squeeze herself into the front seat with three young men, all of them in the highest of spirits.

Then off we would drive, heading we knew not where, but usually soon turning off the main road onto one of the many country roads in the area that were mostly one-lane, unpaved, and rutted. Well into one of these sleepy, wooded lanes, the driver would stop his car, and turn off the ignition.

Susan and I knew what we were to do then. We were to lie down on our faces on the floor of the back seat of the car and wait until Buffy told us we could take our seats again. We always obeyed her unquestioningly. After all, hadn't our mother told us that, when Mother was not around, Buffy was in complete charge?

We had no idea what they were doing in the front seat, but it was clear that they were enjoying themselves immensely. There were whispers, giggles, little squeals, a lot of heavy breathing, more squeals. Then, when they had finished whatever they were doing, we were told we could sit up.

Buffy's friend or friends would then drive us all back down the dirt road to the main highway, and deposit us back at the library wall, where we'd wait for another joyride.

At the end of such an afternoon, we'd all three walk back home. "Don't tell your mother."

We didn't, ever.

Looking back from a distance of years, I'm quite sure that my sister and I both knew that Buffy was involving us in something that was quite wrong, even extremely dangerous—to ourselves, as well as to her—but if we were getting a lesson in sex education, we didn't realize it. And if we didn't tell Mother, it was not because Mother had told us that Buffy was boss. It was because we both loved Buffy so.

Of course, in the years since, I've often wondered whether Buffy charged money for her favors. Somehow, I just don't think she did. But if money were freely offered to her, I imagine she would have taken it.

During her senior year in high school, Buffy began dating a young man named William. William was a good-looking young fellow, a couple of years older than Buffy, tall, with a shock of blond hair, who would probably have been truly handsome if his face had not been badly pocked with acne scars. His family were considered lower class, though nobody ever came right out and said so. In that democratic, Republican little New England town—with its town meetings, where every citizen could have his say—there were no official class lines drawn, and every Andoverite was a peer. But his family lived in a shanty in the wrong part of town, with a privy in the back.

Buffy announced that she was going to marry William as soon as she got her high school diploma.

At that point, my sister and I were both too old to need a nursemaid, and soon I would be going off to boarding school. Also, I had fallen madly in love again—with Betty Lou Van Deusen, who was my age but a good six inches taller. I'd mastered at least one athletic ability—the bicycle. Betty Lou and I rode back and forth between our respective houses on our bikes.

Suddenly, early that spring, plans changed. Buffy would marry William without waiting to graduate. I remember a number of whispered conferences between Buffy and my mother. Buffy and Bill were married in February. Their first baby was born in June. I remember some of the townspeople commenting: "Well, after all, what can you *expect*?"

And my mother's dry observation: "First babies are often premature."

After that, we all lost track of Buffy. I never saw her again. Years passed, gathering their random harvest of memories and regrets.

Suddenly—everything happens *suddenly* in memory—it was 1985, and I had recently had a new book published, and was doing the usual promotional tour of talk shows and author luncheons for my publisher. I had appeared, if memory serves, as a guest on the *Merv Griffin Show*, and a few days afterward I received a letter, forwarded by the show. It was written on lined yellow paper, and it read:

> *My name is William [surname left out], and back in 1943 I married a girl named Jennifer Boyington who used to work for your Mom and Dad. In 1950, she disappeared with our three kids, and I have been trying to locate her ever since. By the way, she was always called "Buffy." Any help you can give me in helping locate both she and my kids would really be appreciated. Thanks.*

He gave a Florida address, but of course I couldn't help him. But I did think, yes, Florida—that's where she would have headed first, into the sunshine and a world of silvery mobile homes. Look for her first there, Bill, I thought, in some sunny place. Wherever she is, I'm sure she's managing to get by, even if just barely, with that sunny disposition and that sunny, dimpled smile.

Chapter Two

Grandfather's Castle

STEVE:

MY PROTESTANT GRANDPARENTS LIVED IN A CASTLE. THAT SOUNDS like a very grand assertion, but, to me, growing up, it seemed a grand situation to be in. A castle! How many other children could make such a lavish claim?

To be sure, it was not a large castle—not large enough to qualify as a mansion. But it was a castle nonetheless, with tiled, crenellated roofs that rose to pointed gables, with two stout square towers surmounted with battlements, with a fountain in the courtyard, and even a flying buttress supporting one tower wall. And its surrounding grounds were almost sizeable enough to be considered manorial—forty-five acres—and from the top of the castle's towers one had an unobstructed view of rolling pastures, virgin woodland, a rushing river, a waterfall, and not a single neighbor's house. The castle was (and still is) located in the rural farm country of southern New England, in the town of South Coventry, Connecticut, another town that adjoined Andover, where I grew up. From my house to my grandparents was a pleasant, woodsy three-mile walk, mostly along unpaved roads and wooden bridges.

The castle was built by my grandfather, my mother's father, whose name was Elam LeRoy Gardner. On his letterhead, which was stamped "E. LeRoy Gardner, Skungamaug Towers, So. Coventry, Conn.," he appeared to eschew his Old Testament first name, as though embarrassed by its oddness, and yet I never heard my grandmother address him as anything other than Elam. He had been brought up in Troy, New York, by parents who, I was told, though not particularly rich, took great pride in their aristocratic Gardner heritage. Also, an English earl, I understood, lurked somewhere distantly in the family tree. For this reason, my grandfather was not permitted to be educated with the ordinary schoolchildren at the public schools of Troy. He was taught by private tutors, and it was not until he reached college age that he was sent a short distance from home to Rensselaer Polytechnic Institute, where he received a degree in electrical engineering. My grandfather, I was always assured, was a genius.

My grandmother's background was similarly genteel and intellectual. She had been born Clara Maria Keefe[5] in eastern Massachusetts, and her distinction, of which she was inordinately proud throughout her life, was that she had graduated from Wellesley with the class of 1887, the ninth graduating class of that institution, in an era when higher education for women was quite rare. Even more unusual was the fact that Grandmother had been a member of the Wellesley College Crew, and her rowing oar, painted with the year of her college class, was always displayed prominently against her drawing-room wall. How my grandparents met I no longer have any way of finding out, nor was this a question I ever thought to ask, but I do know that for several years after graduating from Wellesley she worked at one of the few occupations open to an educated woman in those days, as a schoolteacher. I also know that when my grandparents married, in the 1890s, my grandfather had acquired—again, it would be interesting to know exactly how—the ownership of the Electric Light and Power Company of the little town of Chester, Massachusetts. Chester was one of the first towns in the state, outside Boston, to have electricity, and it was my grandfather who brought it to, and sold it to, the town. Ruth Gordon, the actress, who was a childhood friend of Mother's, often recalled how she and my mother used to swim in the various canals and mill races that were the basis of Grandfather's water-powered system, and how, either to alarm or tease the children, he would open and close valves that would turn a gently flowing stream into a rushing torrent, and back again. As the owner of the power company, Grandfather exerted considerable power of his own. For example, to summon his two daughters—my mother and my aunt— home for supper, he simply flipped the main switch of the plant off and on again three times, and all the lights of Chester, including, of course, the streetlamps, blinked off and on accordingly.

In Chester, my grandparents lived in a perfectly ordinary, solid ten-room house. I have seen photographs of that—the wide, street-facing veranda with four stone columns and the two-story, large-windowed residence itself. In the photographs, the house appears to have little architectural distinction, but what was uncommon about it was the fact that Grandfather had designed and built the house himself, absolutely singlehandedly, because he was also an accomplished stonemason and carpenter. All went reasonably well in Chester throughout the early 1900s. But shortly after World War I there was trouble, and that trouble was the beginning of the story of the castle in Connecticut.

I know all this because Grandfather wrote a novel about his later, unhappy experiences in Chester. At least he called it a novel. It was a curious, long-winded affair—over fifteen hundred author-typed pages (his huge old Oliver typewriter was set up in a corner of his dining room)—which was part straightforward, documentary journalism (complete with contemporary newspaper accounts, letters written and received by Grandfather, and legal documents, all about as exciting reading as lawyers' briefs), and part romantic storytelling. From hard-fact, first-person-singular reporting, my grandfather's narrative would suddenly vault into the third person, and into breast-beating passages which began with such phrases as, "And now, dear reader, let us watch as our handsome young hero leaves his humble home to brave the winds of inclement destiny, etc." The title of the work was *Just Compensation*, and this was intended to be ironic; the compensation which my grandfather received for all his efforts was, in his opinion, most unjust. Several attempts were made to find a publisher for this manuscript, but none was successful, which perhaps was just as well. And now, alas, after perhaps languishing in various family attics for many years, the manuscript has disappeared.

There were several villains in Grandfather's story—corrupt legislators, crafty attorneys, ungrateful townspeople—but chief among them was the Massachusetts Light & Power Company, which had begun stretching its tentacles westward from Boston and northward from Springfield, gathering up small local companies as it went and incorporating them into its network. By 1919, one of its targets was Chester. The power that my grandfather sold to the town was direct current (DC). The power that Massachusetts Light proposed to offer was the more "modern" alternating current (AC); it also proposed to offer this at a considerably lower cost per kilowatt hour. When Massachusetts Light made an offer to buy my grandfather's plant, which he refused, the larger company took its case to the town. There was a referendum on the subject, and the townspeople voted overwhelmingly, as might have been expected, in favor of the cheaper form of current. Now all that remained to be decided was how much Grandfather would be paid for his plant and equipment, and this was left to the courts. Unfortunately, after a long legal battle, the amount of "just compensation" which the court decreed was significantly less than the figure which Massachusetts Light had offered Grandfather in the first place.

Of course, I have always suspected that my grandfather's somewhat austere and autocratic personality may have been a factor in these decisions against him. Knowing him as I did, I am certain that he had made more enemies in Chester than he had made friends. Nonetheless, feeling bitter and betrayed by his neighbors and former customers, he decided to turn his back forever on both Chester and the state of Massachusetts. He began systematically to dismantle the house he had built himself in Chester and, on a series of railroad flatcars, the house was shipped, room by room and brick by brick, out from the hostile territory and across the border into Connecticut. He would never set foot in the state of Massachusetts again. Indeed, the site he chose to rebuild his house was, and is still, quite startlingly beautiful—a high, rocky cliff jutting out, rather in the shape of the prow of a ship, over a steep, narrow gorge carved out by the Skungamaug River. The place was called Wright's Mill. I have no idea who Wright was, but the property, when my grandfather acquired it, contained a sprawling and fairly dilapidated mill house at the river's edge, and there was a ruined stone foundation just below it, where an earlier mill house must have stood. These had obviously both been gristmills once, for a number of discarded grindstones, green with moss and lichens, could be found throughout the surrounding woods, half buried in the ground. Some of these circular stone slabs were fairly small and could be lifted and wheeled about by a pair of healthy children; others were enormous and appeared to weigh several tons apiece. Before my grandfather built his high dam across the river, creating his own waterfall, I suppose that the earlier mills had been powered by a natural waterfall, where the sleepy river left several miles of pastureland and suddenly plunged into that deep, dramatic gorge.

When—again, singlehandedly—my grandfather began rebuilding the Chester house on the Skungamaug riverbank, it quickly turned into an altogether different sort of house. It became a castle. The reason that he gave was that, when the structure was halfway finished, he discovered that he had run out of building space on his chosen promontory. He had two whole rooms left over, and so he decided to place them on the top of the house as a pair of towers. Then, as appropriate bits of exterior decoration, he added the other Arthurian fairy-tale details—the gables, turrets, battlements, and the flying buttress. This, at least, was the explanation he always gave. I never quite believed it. He was far too thorough and farsighted to have miscalculated his building space. Also, it was quite clear that there was plenty of extra square footage on the clifftop to accommodate two more rooms. I suspect that his castle was, in fact, an act of personal defiance. He felt he had been badly treated, and therefore decided to build a towering medieval fantasy to show the countryside at large that he no longer intended to live according to its conventions.

The castle was built of fieldstone and French burrstone, and into the mortar was mixed a green pigment to give it an instant mossy, weathered look. Otherwise, there were a few architectural peculiarities and anachronisms. The large "picture" windows that had graced the Chester house did not exactly lend themselves to the medieval style, but Grandfather used them anyway. Then there was the problem of the two front doors, which stood side by side barely ten feet apart. Each door was surmounted by a portico, one rather small and the other rather large. The smaller portico was intended to indicate that this was the service entrance, while the larger portico covered the main entrance. The trouble was that, since the smaller entrance was the one nearest to the drive, visitors always managed to miss the point and invariably came first to the service door.

The service entrance led into the laundry room, but, even so, this door became the customary means of access to the house and, in time, the main entrance was permanently locked and bolted. From the laundry room, a pair of doors led into the large, square kitchen. From the kitchen, of course, access to the dining room was possible through a swinging door, and the visitor was at last in the formal part of the house. Off the dining room was the long drawing room, and off the drawing room, behind heavy curtains, was the library. Coming into the castle, therefore, one had the sense of doing it all backward.

The three principal rooms on the ground floor all had walls and ceilings handsomely paneled in cherry, oak, and chestnut. The drawing room ceiling was particularly impressive; in the center of each of the dozens of panels was a naked electric light bulb. These were part of a system, operated by a panel of rheostats and switches, designed to create lighting effects that could be varied from a Broadway blaze to the faintest twinkle of starlight. Each of these three rooms also contained a stone fireplace, also electric. Above the library fireplace, Grandfather had placed one of the smaller grindstones he had found on the property, and its central axle-hole he had also electrified; a small lamp in this aperture illuminated, from behind, a tinted photograph—out of deference to my grandmother—of Lake Waban on the Wellesley campus.

From the drawing room, a paneled L-shaped staircase ran up to the second floor and an upstairs sitting room nearly as large as the drawing room below, and off the sitting room were two large bedrooms. Then, at each end of the sitting room, matching staircases ascended to the pair of bedrooms contained in the two towers. From these tower rooms, it was possible, with a ladder and by way of trapdoors, to climb to the top of the castle and to survey the valley, the river in its deep ravine, and all the hills beyond. The view from the south tower was the more satisfying, since the drop from the roof to the ground below was well over fifty feet. On this roof, Susan and I would imagine pushing our enemies head over heels across the merlons and seeing them crash to their deaths on the drive below or, if the enemies were already below, pouring boiling oil on their heads through the crenels. In the basement, furthermore, in addition to two garages and various storage and utility rooms, there was even a dungeon of sorts, suitable for keeping prisoners: the sunken root cellar.

The house had other peculiarities, based on my grandfather's idiosyncrasies. He believed, for example, that food was better digested when washed down with water, but he did not believe in water being served in glasses at the table; these simply created extra work for the person setting and clearing the table and washing the dishes. So, he installed a very businesslike drinking fountain against one of the dining room walls. One was expected, during a meal, periodically to leave the table and refresh oneself from the "bubbler," as he called it. He also considered bathrooms unnecessary luxuries. The castle had only one on the second floor. It was, however, nearly as large as the dining room below it, containing a huge old-fashioned tub on claw-and-ball feet and a correspondingly oversized washstand; adjoining, in a separate room, was the toilet. As a concession to my grandmother, he had built a single-stall shower off one of the second-floor bedrooms. Downstairs, in a space the size of a closet, was another toilet, which was just that. In other ways, however, the house contained certain extravagances. All the kitchen countertops, for example, were solid Carrara marble. And, since my grandfather was electrically minded, there were appliances which, though commonplace today, were almost unknown in the early 1930s—such as an electric dishwasher, which he had fashioned out of an old clothes-washing machine.

When, after a mild heart attack, my grandmother was advised not to take stairs, Grandfather devised what he called an "elevator" to lift her to the second floor. It was not so much an elevator as a vertical breeches buoy, manually operated with weights and pulleys, by which she could be jerkily hoisted up the stairwell to the landing above. I have often wondered why her vertiginous trips aboard this contraption did not cause her ailing heart to fail altogether. At the bottom of the stairs, Grandfather would strap Grandmother into her swing. As my sister and I watched in awe, Grandfather would then take the controls, and my terrified grandmother would begin to scream, "Elam! Don't let go the rope! Don't let go the rope!" Up he would haul her, sobbing all the way, until she reached the top. Then, after securing the rope with a half-hitch around the newel post, he would mount the stairs to help her out of her swaying perch at the end of her journey.

In retrospect, I suppose, my grandfather's castle, with its peculiar oversize windows, was really rather ugly, and it certainly was not very convenient. There were, for instance, no closets at all, since Grandfather was of an era when clothes and linens were all stored in tall armoires. But, as children, what we loved most about the place was the drama of the countryside around it. Along the front of the castle, facing the river, was a wide paved terrace. From this a short flight of stone steps led down to a larger, circular terrace, surrounded by a low stone wall and with a fountain at the center. At the outer edge of the round terrace, there was an opening in the wall, and another short flight of steps. At this point, the going became really dangerous, because one was now on the edge of the cliff, and the river boiled angrily some forty feet below. A steep, slippery path over wet, moss-covered rocks led down the face of the cliff to the water's edge, but this path was not for the unwary or untutored. One had to know exactly into which rock crevice to insert one's toe, and which limb of an outcropping tree to seize for support. Otherwise, one could have a quite nasty and probably fatal fall. And yet, though children and adults often clambered up and down this hair-raising path, there was never an accident.

Down by the river, it was usually possible to surprise a black water snake basking on the rocks, and watch it slither silently into the dark water. In the quieter pools and eddies, there were strange water bugs that could march across the surface of the water, occasionally disappearing into the jaws of one of the speckled trout, with which the Skungamaug teemed. On the wooded banks above the ravine, other wild creatures could be spotted: deer and rabbits. At dusk, the raccoons, porcupines, and possums would emerge for a drink from the river. Down by the river, too, were the rocky ruins of the original gristmill which, from early maps of the area, had been built at least 150 years earlier. As children, clambering in and out of the "rooms" of this damp ruin, and wondering what these spaces might once have been used for, was something we never tired of doing. In some childhood story I had read there had been a reference to a sunken rose garden. I used to imagine that, if the castle were ever mine, I would turn the ruined mill into something like that.

Not far from the ruin was a place where, by jumping across a series of boulders, one could reach the opposite shore of the river, where the gorge was faced with another imposing series of cliffs. These, too, could be scaled by the initiated and, at the top, there was a forest of hemlock and pine, its thick and spongy floor slithery with brown needles. Under the pines there was a lower cover of mountain laurel and, in thick patches, a ground cover of wild myrtle and princess pine. All this was our garden. In spring, all manner of wildflowers appeared: Star-faced wild anemones, jack-in-the-pulpit, lady's slipper, purple and yellow wild violets. In the center of one clump of violets reposed, on its side, one of the largest of the cast-off grindstones. How it got there, across the river and easily half a mile from the mill, was a mystery akin to that of the Easter Island moai heads; it must have taken two dozen strong men to carry it. Naturally, it suggested a fairy ring.

At one point, the cliff dipped down and then spread itself out into a wide, flat platform of rock. This platform directly faced the cliff opposite, where the castle stood. This natural outcropping resembled nothing more than a raised stage and would easily have accommodated a symphony orchestra; above it, the next stratum of projecting rock provided a proscenium. If it were my castle, I used to think, I would hire performers or musicians to put on plays and concerts from this stage, while the audience arrayed itself on the terraces of the castle, just across the river.

When my grandfather built his high dam of reinforced concrete across the river, creating a new millpond above it and a plunging waterfall, his object, of course, was to generate electric power. When his power station was completed, and the generator and dynamo installed, he had a facility ample to the task of lighting and heating half of Tolland County, and this was exactly what he had planned to do. Unfortunately, he again found himself thwarted by a giant utility concern. The Connecticut Light & Power Company, it seemed, had succeeded in getting a law passed through the State Legislature which made it illegal to string private power lines across state-maintained roads. Since Grandfather's property was surrounded by state roads on all sides, there was no one to whom he could sell his power but himself. If it was any comfort to him that never, as long as he lived, did he have to pay a single utility bill to heat and light his home, he never showed it. The 1929 stock market crash had wiped out whatever proceeds he had made from the sale of the Chester plant—or what was left of them, after what must have been the considerable cost of moving his house nearly a hundred miles by flatcar. Thoroughly embittered now, and growing older, he turned to farming.

Well before the conservationist views of today, my grandfather remained a staunch believer in the principle of deriving power energy from natural resources, such as rivers and streams, rather than from fossil fuels underground, which logic should tell us would not last forever. The world's tides, he often pointed out, could be harnessed by a process as simple as throwing a dam across a river. By use of a movable water barrier, or lock, an incoming tide could be caught in a tidal basin; then, as the tide receded, the lock could be gradually lowered and the basin water would be released, in a waterfall not unlike his own, and power could be generated. The process, furthermore, could be repeated endlessly, throughout time, or as long as our earth's moon could manage to stay hanging in the sky.

Since my parents lived not far from my grandfather's castle, every Sunday of our lives we were required to join my grandparents at noon for Sunday dinner. These were command appearances, and only very contagious diseases, such as mumps or measles, were accepted as excuses for failure to attend. Even family trips and vacations had to be planned around the ordeal of breaking the news to Grandfather that a Sunday dinner would be missed. The castle's cook was my grandmother. Though her repertory of dishes was somewhat limited, she did what she did quite well. She was particularly good at pies, mincemeat, squash, pumpkin, and apple, and she baked excellent biscuits and butter cookies. One dish we particularly looked forward to was a macaroni casserole in a cream sauce with stewed tomatoes. Also, because my grandfather raised chickens (and sold the eggs), chicken was a frequent item on her menu. At an early age I learned the meaning of the expression "running around like a chicken with its head cut off." Each time a chicken went under Grandfather's hatchet for a Sunday meal, we would watch, confounded with wonder, as the headless and obviously thoroughly exasperated bird ran about the yard, flapping its wings, sometimes becoming airborne, for what seemed like an incredible length of time while its head lay, unblinking, on the chopping block some distance away.

Otherwise, the Sunday dinners were not precisely festive affairs. For Susan and me, who were seated below the salt, there were two principal rules: Children should be seen and not heard, and, never speak until spoken to. Actually, we rather appreciated the second rule. My grandfather's questions, when addressed to us, tended to be boring and predictable; "What did you learn in school this week?" "Do you like your teacher?" We preferred to be left alone. After dinner, as part of the unbending routine, we were led into the drawing room, where my grandfather read to us the Sunday funnies. Even that was boring. My parents were the ones who got the Sunday paper and, after reading it, delivered it to him. So, we had already read the funnies. After that, however, we were free to go outside and explore the rocks and woods along the river.

In summer, when we were small, we swam in the millpond above the dam. There, a projecting ledge of rock just below the surface of the water provided a logical sitting-place, jumping-off place, and, for me, hanging-on place. To everybody's annoyance, including my own, my younger sister had learned to swim before I did. She paddled bravely around the pond and had even, or so she bragged, submerged herself so deeply in the pond that she had touched toes on the rocky bottom. As for me, I just clung to the rock ledge and kicked my feet. My grandfather had assured us that a water monster lived in a cave beneath that ledge, and so I was careful not to let my feet dip within the monster's reach.

I remember once when my grandfather, operating on an ancient, homegrown theory that holds that a child tossed into water will teach him- or herself to swim, suddenly reached down to where I was kicking from the ledge, lifted me by the armpits, and tossed me out into the deep water. I remember myself slowly sinking, and thinking to myself: well, so this is what it is like to drown; I am drowning now, and this is what it is like. As the water darkened around me, I made no effort to save myself, and simply let myself sink like a stone. Today, trying to explain this, I think that I had grown so accustomed to obeying my grandfather, and doing what he wanted, that I must have also thought: Very well, my grandfather wants me to drown, and so I must do as I am told. I was actually quite surprised when I felt someone's arms around me, pulling me to the surface, and realized that he had jumped into the pond to save me.

Needless to say, everyone was careful about swimming too close to the edge of the dam, where the smooth water of the pond suddenly picked up speed before cascading over and crashing down on the rocks below with a sound of continuous, distant thunder. Everyone was cautious, that is, except my grandfather. He routinely walked across the top of the dam, the white water curling in huge cuffs against his ankles, even though the dam's lip was slimy with algae, and to have fallen would have meant certain death. Further upstream, there was a bridge, but the dam provided the shortest means of access to his powerhouse on the other side. And so, surefooted as an aerialist, he walked across the dam.

Later on, when we were older, we discovered a swimming place even better than the millpond. This was in the rocky pools *below* the dam, which could be reached by the cliffside path. Here, hundreds of years of falling water had carved large submarine potholes in the rocks, which provided the exciting experience of stepping from water that was no more than knee deep into a sudden, seemingly bottomless pit. There were also some rocks, close to the base of the dam, where one could actually sit or stand *behind* the waterfall. By August, the summer sun had heated the water of the millpond to the point where it was really quite warm. Susan and I would station ourselves on these special rocks, screened from the world outside, invisible to it, by this glassy, tepid, opaque sheet of falling water. No sounds, no parents' (or grandparents') calls that it was time to go home, penetrated the thundering veil of water that enclosed us and provided us with a kind of private room. We would stay there, or so it seemed, for hours.

It often seemed my grandfather loved animals more than he loved people, to be sure. Despite this, he occasionally killed a pullet for his dinner table, but otherwise was proud and protective of his large brood of laying hens and his spreading incubators full of fertile eggs and baby chicks. In a series of large ledgers, he kept careful track of his egg production. He also kept a small herd of goats, animals he considered far more intelligent and interesting than cows.[6] Aside from the mill house and the powerhouse, the only other outbuilding on his property was the goat house. It was here that I learned that goats do not dine on garbage and tin cans, not Grandfather's goats, at any rate. His goats were fed a special diet of corn mash and sweet hay, of which the goat house smelled pleasantly, and each evening before milking the goats were carefully bathed and brushed. Then their teats were washed with an antiseptic solution, and Grandfather milked the goats wearing sterile surgical gloves.

Goats' milk was always served at his table. It had a not unpleasant, but faintly sourish taste, which we children didn't much care for. Also, compared with cows' milk, it seemed somewhat thin and chalky in texture, perhaps because goats' milk is naturally homogenized; that is, it has much the same butterfat content as cows' milk, but no cream separates and rises to the top. We preferred the goats' milk cheese that my grandmother made. Then, too, there were times, when the goats were let out to summer pasture, that the animals would happen upon some particular delicacy of green apples, wild mustard, dandelions, onion grass or juniper berries and make a feast of this. When this happened, the flavor of the milk that day was decidedly off. When we complained, Grandfather always had an explanation but never an apology. We learned to appreciate goats' milk, however, during the war, when ordinary milk was scarce. Every week, after Sunday dinner, my parents brought home goats' milk from the castle in a five-gallon can, enough for a week's supply.

The goats were named for the stars in the Pleiades—after the seven daughters of Atlas and Pleione: Alcyone, Asterope, Electra, Celaeno, Maia, Merope, and Taygete, and Grandfather attempted to match their names with their particular personalities. If, for example, a particular nanny goat seemed especially shy or withdrawn, she would be sad Electra, mourning for Troy. If another seemed cross or defensive, she was Merope, ashamed for having married a mortal, Sisyphus. Perhaps because the Pleiades were situated in the constellation Taurus, Grandfather drew a Bovidae connection. For reproductive purposes, there was always also a billy goat. His name was always, simply, Billy. During the war, too, when beef and lamb were all but unobtainable, we occasionally dined on kid or chevon—but always with a pang, knowing that the meat on our plates, which tasted quite like veal, was not veal, but was one of a succession of Meropes or Maias whom the lecherous Orion had pursued through the forest for years until Zeus translated the lot of them, including Orion and his dog, into the sky. Whenever Grandfather felt it necessary to slaughter one of the sisters, as he called them, there were tears in his eyes as he headed for the goat house with his pistol in his hand. In the castle, we would wait for the sound of the single shot.

He was also an apiarist, and the honey from his hives he boxed and sold under his private label. His honeys, all carefully marked as to their floral sources, varied according to the season and what flowers happened to be blooming at the time. Some of his honeys were conventionally flavored—clover honey, apple-blossom honey, and peach-blossom honey, for example. Others were more exotic, such as wild-primrose honey and mountain laurel honey and yellow sumac honey. When the asparagus in his garden came into flower, there was asparagus honey and, late in summer goldenrod honey. As children, we gave the boxlike hives of the honeybees a wide berth. We had watched Grandfather in his beekeeping clothes protective trousers, gloves, a hat with a long veil of netting to protect his face and shoulders, and his bellows-like smoker (smoke calmed the bees). But we knew that despite all this he was often stung. We were impressed, however, by the statistic that a single hive could produce as much as fifty pounds of honey in a summer season. Considering the small amount of nectar in the average flower, this was an impressive testimony to the industriousness of the bees.

One afternoon in early summer, after a swim in the millpond, my mother was sitting on the terrace of the castle, drying her long dark hair in the sun. A bee appeared, and then another, and suddenly a great many more. The bees, it seemed, had decided to swarm in her hair, and they festooned themselves there, buzzing loudly. My mother, knowing that bees in a swarm will almost never sting unless severely agitated, kept her composure, and sat quietly with the swarm hanging in her hair. My grandfather, meanwhile, quickly prepared a new hive to accommodate the swarm (swarming is an indication of overcrowding, and that the hive is making room for a new queen). After about forty-five minutes, the swarm departed as suddenly as it had come. Later, my mother would say that having the bees swarm in her hair that afternoon was the closest she had ever come to having a religious experience.

My grandfather's enemies were not animal. They were human, and he was always armed for them. Two pistols, a .44-caliber Colt revolver and a Smith & Wesson .22-caliber semiautomatic, fully loaded, always reposed under the pillow of his bed, ready to put the finish to an intruder who never appeared. As children, we would sometimes sneak into his bedroom, lift up the coverlet and pillow, and stare at the guns. Fortunately, we were never tempted to play with them or even touch them, because I don't recall anyone ever telling us that they were dangerous. We didn't touch them for a simple reason: no one dared touch any of Grandfather's things.

There were, however, frequent intruders of a sort. During the building of the castle, there had been a certain amount of local publicity about it. Sightseers, either assuming that Grandfather's castle was some sort of public attraction—a kind of early-day Disneyland—or drawn by simple curiosity by the sight, from the road, of two medieval towers looming above the trees in a rural valley of Connecticut, often appeared. They either wandered down the long drive, or approached, through the woods, to gawk at the castle from the cliff at the opposite side of the river. Sometimes they carried cameras and, occasionally, sketch pads. Grandfather was always on the lookout for these interlopers and we, as children, were trained to be also. Whenever a small band of curious innocents was spotted on the drive or in the trees, someone would cry out, "More Nosey Parkers!" Grandfather would march to his bedroom, seize his two pistols, jam them conspicuously in his belt and head out to confront the uninvited strangers, who always left very quickly and politely, with no bloodshed. It never seemed to occur to anyone that the castle, in itself, had become a local curiosity and celebrity, a tourist sight, and that it would have been simpler in the long run—though much less exciting—to let the visitors snap their pictures and sketch their sketches, and then depart in peace.

Despite the sounds emanating periodically from the goat house, I only saw him fire a pistol once. In warm weather, our Sunday lunches with my grandparents sometimes took the form of outdoor picnics. For these, a white tablecloth was laid out on a flat rock in a shady corner of the goat pasture, and the meal was spread on that, while we sat around the rock on folding canvas chairs set up on the grass. At one of these, I remember my grandmother suddenly leaping to her feet and screaming, "Elam! There's a spider! *A spider!* Elam!" Sure enough, there was a spider in the grass. It was not a particularly large or dangerous-looking spider—certainly no black widow or tarantula—but it was definitely making its way in my grandmother's direction, and she was screaming hysterically. Calmly, my grandfather reached for the Colt revolver in his belt and took careful aim. There was a sharp report, and the spider disappeared in a shower of dirt, summarily dispatched.

Much like the famous Winchester House in San Jose (sans ghosts), the castle was never really finished. Grandfather was always working on it, and there was always more to do. When he first started construction on it, my grandparents lived in the mill house, along with Grandfather's old Stanley Steamer. When the kitchen, dining room, and one upstairs bedroom (along with the bathroom), were finished off, they moved into the house. The mill house became the chicken house, and the Stanley Steamer's engine was dismantled and converted into the castle's basement water pump. Grandfather's workshop—where he kept his lathe, his planes and levels and hammers and other tools—moved accordingly. While he finished the drawing room, the workshop was set up there. Then it moved to the library, while that room was being done, and from there the workshop moved upstairs to the upper sitting room, and so it went, from room to room. The house always smelled of sawdust, drying plaster, and the great curls of wood shavings that littered the floor of whatever room Grandfather was working on, and in, at the time.

The castle was begun in 1929 (the year I was born), and by 1938, when I was still quite little, it was perhaps half finished; the sitting room was done, and the workshop had moved into the unfinished bedroom next door. The latter year was to provide one of the castle's great tests of strength, for that was the year of the Great New England Hurricane. I remember how hot and still and overpoweringly close that September day became. By early afternoon, the sky had taken on an ominous slate-gray color and, as if by instinct and some terrible event in nature was about to take place, we children came quietly into the house from play. Still no wind blew, and not a leaf stirred, and the sky grew darker, a strange mustard-colored darkness, for the sun was still up.

Then it began. In my parents' house, we watched as a whole orchard full of apple trees toppled, their trunks snapped off or their stumps uprooted. Three enormous old oak trees fell, one by one, across our driveway. The lights went out throughout the house and, as we could see, throughout the town. A great crash of masonry on the roof told us that part of our chimney was gone, and we could see the shingles from our roof flying through the air. Soon it was impossible to see anything from our windows at all; leaves torn from trees had cemented themselves solidly against every windowpane.

The next morning, when the sun came up brightly and cheerfully as though nothing in the world had happened, neighbors gathered in their yards to survey their respective and collective damage. Telephone and electric light poles, and their tangled wires, lay about the streets. "Live wires!" people cautioned—quite unnecessarily, since all the wires were snapped and perfectly dead. The landscape seemed leveled of trees. The First Congregational Church had lost its steeple.

Naturally, my parents' first concern was how my grandparents, with their private power station and their castle on the river's edge, had fared in the storm. The telephones were out and so, as soon as the roads were at least partway cleared, we all got in the car for the short drive to South Coventry.

I have never seen anything quite like it. The water in the millpond was so high that it covered the bridge, but the bridge had held. Over my grandfather's dam, which had also held, a sheet of white water was shooting out almost horizontally, carrying huge boulders and the trunks of uprooted trees with it. Suddenly someone's shed appeared at the edge of the dam and disintegrated in midair before crashing into the river below. Grandfather's electric dynamo, below the dam, was buried by the thundering waterfall, and the river beneath the castle had risen so high that my outdoor stage and amphitheater had disappeared completely. But the river had not reached the level of the castle. And the water-powered turbine which, in turn, powered the seventeen-kilowatt generator that lighted and heated the house, was still faithfully delivering its prescribed amount of current.

In our part of Connecticut, some houses were without heat and electricity for anywhere from thirty to forty-five days as a result of the Great Hurricane of 1938. My grandfather's house was never without these amenities for a single moment, nor, as he said at the time, had he expected that it would be.

When my grandmother died, my grandfather refused to go to her funeral. Understandably, this caused eyebrows to be raised in certain quarters. But Grandfather did not believe in funerals. He considered them a barbaric custom, had never attended a funeral, and did not wish to have one of his own. While the rest of us went to the church, he stayed home. He had always stuck to his principles. Once, when he needed a new suit, he went out to buy one but came home empty-handed, outraged at the prices being asked in the stores. Instead, he bought some fabric. Then, though he had never used a sewing machine in his life, he sat down at Grandmother's Singer and made a new suit for himself, using one of his old suits, which he had taken apart, for a pattern.

After my grandmother's death, he became increasingly taciturn and reclusive. She, it seemed, had been his only real friend and, aside from the family and an occasional Nosey Parker, there were no visitors to the castle. He was a man of many talents, but housekeeping was not one of them. Dirty dishes collected in the sink and, as the months went by, a thick layer of dust settled through the rooms. My mother worried, and tried to help, but he resented her interference. His habits became more eccentric. For convenience, he moved his bed down into the library, but he objected to having his bed linen changed. My mother had to do this surreptitiously, while he was out of the house, always careful to make sure that his guns were replaced in their customary positions under his pillow. For a while, a red-headed housekeeper, Mrs. Parrish, was tried, but he soon proved too irascible and despotic for her.

His manner of dress became odd. Now, in fair weather and foul, he wore only a pair of baggy brown khaki shorts, nothing more, and we would watch him, with our breath held, as he walked, bare-chested and barefooted, a man well into his seventies, across the top of his waterfall, the swift water cuffing around his ankles. He worried us in other ways. His stance toward the Nosey Parkers had become much more threatening and belligerent. Now he waved his guns at them as he approached. Also, though he didn't have that much money, he decided that he no longer trusted banks, and kept what seemed like an unwisely large amount of cash in his top dresser drawer. Still, he resisted all advice and suggestions, and of course no one dared to touch his money. He died in his sleep in 1946, while I was away at boarding school. But, since there was to be no funeral, I had no excuse to come home.

There were no ghosts in the castle, though my grandfather used to claim that the shade of old Chief Skungamaug patrolled the battlements at night. If it did, or even if there ever was such an Indian chief, I never saw or heard him. Sleep in the castle, in fact, was particularly easy and peaceful, lulled by the ceaseless rumble of the waterfall.

The castle was sold soon after Grandfather's death, and the property has changed hands once or twice since then. But whenever I am in the vicinity I go back and look at it, either venturing down the drive or approaching it through the woods, which I still know like the back of my hand, across the river, now one of the Nosey Parkers myself. The later owners of the place, however, have been much more tolerant of these incursions and have even, when I explained my former connection with the house, invited me in. The innards of Grandfather's old Stanley Steamer still pump the water in the house, and Grandfather's generator still spins out the seventeen kilowatts' worth of old-fashioned DC that he assigned to it. One subsequent owner, apprehensive about relying on a homemade electrical system that was approaching fifty years of age, had an auxiliary AC system run into the house in case of emergencies. To this day, it has never been needed.

The goats and the bees are gone, and the mill house has become, of all things, a dentist's office. Earlier owners converted Grandfather's goat barn into a charming guest cottage. But the dam and the millpond are still there, and children still swim under the waterfall. The fountain in the center of the round terrace is dry, but only because none of the subsequent owners has been able to figure out how Grandfather turned it on; he took that secret with him. No one, I think, has heard a concert

35

or a play performed from the stage of my rocky amphitheater, but black water snakes still curl on the rocks and slip into the water at the sound of a footfall, and in the spring the river still swells with trout.

Memory expresses itself in peculiar and tricky ways. Often, when I am taking a morning shower, I adjust the hot- and cold-water taps to get the right temperature, not too hot and not too cold, just lukewarm. Then, when I have the setting of the faucets exactly right, I stand and let the tepid water pour over my head and shoulders. I am there again, and I think with satisfaction: Ah, Grandfather's waterfall.

It has always seemed to me that I remained a sexual naïf for much longer than most people, and that this was my mother's fault. Perhaps "fault" is too strong a word, but it was certainly her doing. Partly, it was because, as chairwoman of the local School Board, she could pull certain strings, and one of these had been to have me enrolled in the first grade at the Andover Public School when I was barely five years old. Also, through some local demographic quirk, it would turn out that for most of the eight years I spent at that red, three-room schoolhouse, I was the only boy in my class. This meant that all the other boys in school were at least a full two years older than I was, and even the girls were taller.

(My only male contemporary in the town had been my friend Teddy Lockwood, who had drowned the previous summer at Andover Lake. I was there when it happened. We were all playing on the beach, and suddenly we noticed that Teddy was no longer with us. His body was pulled out three days later. There was a funeral, with an open casket, and several of us children were asked to be honorary pallbearers. I remember Teddy's pale, bloated face, looking not at all like the boy we'd known. I think it was the trauma of that experience that led to my irrational fear of water. For a long time, I couldn't even bring myself to wade in Andover Lake, thinking of Teddy's body lying there so long beneath its surface.)

Being the class baby, and the only boy, offered no advantages at all that I could see. When sides were divided up for sports, I was always the last one chosen, to the obvious displeasure of my teammates; having me on their side almost guaranteed that their team would lose. I was teased unmercifully about my size and age, though most of the abuse was verbal, and not physical. One of my chief tormentors was an older boy named

Troy Jenkins. One day I had come to school with a new lunch box, of which I was particularly proud. I remember it vividly. It was green, with Disney characters painted on it; the Seven Dwarfs danced across its lid. That afternoon, after school, while we all waited for the bus that would take us home, Troy Jenkins came after me again. I don't remember what he said, but I had had enough. I raised my lunch box and brought it down hard on Troy's head.

Troy—his head spurting blood—ran back into the schoolhouse for first aid. I looked at my lunch box, which now had a large dent in it and would not shut properly, and I began to cry. At that point, a little old lady was walking down the street, and she stopped and asked me, "What's the matter, little boy?" "Look at my new lunch box," I sobbed. "My mother's going to *kill* me!" She patted me on the head, and then reached into her purse and handed me a dollar bill.

Sometimes, as Blanche DuBois would say, there's God—so quickly!

One should thank the Deity, too, I suppose, for other small blessings. My mother, it turned out later, had originally wanted to enter me in *second* grade at age five, where I would have been even smaller, lonelier, and more miserable, skipping first grade altogether. Fortunately, the school authorities drew the line at this. But, to my mother, I was some kind of prodigy, or genius like my grandfather, or even Mother herself, this went without saying. And so, all through my years in elementary and secondary schools, my fate was to be the littlest—and the most belittled—in my class. It was not until I got to Williams College that I began to see that my youth might actually convey some special sort of status. There, my classmate and fraternity brother, Stephen Sondheim, and I found ourselves the only sixteen-year-old freshmen (Our birthdays are only weeks apart). A large number of our classmates, furthermore, were men who had returned from the war, and were completing their education under the G.I. Bill. These men had come back with tales of military and sexual exploits in such faraway places as Kwajalein Island, Guadalcanal, and Anzio. They were four, five, or even six years older than we were, and some were married and had started families of their own. They were also men who had been robbed of a certain segment of their boyhoods. To them, Steve Sondheim and I were objects of a certain amount of awe. We were treated as wunderkind.

The reason, meanwhile, why my mother had marked me as a gifted child was that, before the age of five, I had taught myself to read, and had even begun to tap out—using the two-finger system that I still use, with only my two index fingers and my thumb on the space bar—short sentences on the typewriter. But this feat was to a large extent my mother's doing, too. Starting when we were both quite small, my mother read aloud to my sister and me every night, as we sat on either side of her on her big bed. No matter how busy she might be, she always found time for this. Also, she didn't read to us from so-called "juvenile literature," or books with lots of illustrations. Those bored her. Instead, she read to us the novels of Dickens, Mark Twain, James Fennimore Cooper, and the Brontës. And, of course, she read to us only if we had been reasonably well-behaved that day, and these nightly reading sessions soon became so important to us both that the most severe punishment from her was, "No reading tonight!" It was the punishment reserved for the direst of offenses.

Her rule was simple: one chapter per night of whatever novel it happened to be. Of course, many of the chapters of the novels she read have cliffhanger endings, and we would beg her to read just one more chapter to relieve the suspense. But she was always firm. At a chapter's end, she would close the book, kiss us goodnight, and be off to one of her inevitable civic meetings. Left alone, my sister and I would study the pages of the next chapter, trying to figure out what was going to happen next. Sometimes we'd try to guess the outcome of the particular plot situation. Sometimes we'd guess right.

I remember how I started learning to read. "What do those little wiggly marks mean?" I asked my mother. They looked to me like tiny polliwogs.

"Those are called quotation marks," she said. "They indicate the characters are talking to each other, having a conversation."

From then on, she began tracing the lines of her text with the lacquered tip of her index finger, pointing out new or interesting or unfamiliar words as they occurred. Suddenly, it seemed, the small, inky symbols on the page began to turn into letters, the letters into sounds and syllables, and then into whole words and English sentences. I'm sure it didn't happen as quickly as all that, but, before long—after Mother had departed for the night—I was able to pick up the book again and, word by word, decipher the next episode of the story. Soon I was putting words on paper myself. My mother was turning me into a writer.

On the matter of sex education, however, I was for a long time mostly in the dark. Dickens, Twain, Cooper, and the Brontës often wrote about love, but they left sex to the imagination of the reader. It was not that my mother neglected to tell me the so-called Facts of Life, but when she did it was in a scientific, Wellesley-esque, chemistry-class way, explaining these facts the way she explained the weather, in terms of sperm and egg cells, one cell fertilizing the other, a matter of gametes and ova, tubes and seminal vesicles and microorganisms. It all sounded very dull and complicated and mechanical to me, and I couldn't understand why grown-ups considered sex so important. Why did people do sex? "They do it when they want to have children," my mother said. "A wife does it when she wants to become a mother, and when her husband wants to become a father." If that was the case, I gathered that my parents had had sex exactly twice.

In that assumption, I may not have been far off the mark. I often suspect that my mother, having produced two children—one boy, one girl, neatly spaced chronologically—may have felt that she had completed her wifely duties to my father. With that out of the way, she took up the task of toiling for her community. Years later, from certain of my parents' friends, hints were dropped to the effect that my father had other girlfriends on the side. Considering my mother's feelings on the subject, I'm sure he did.

"How long does it take?" I remember asking her.

"Not long. It's over very quickly."

"What does have sex *feel* like?"

She thought a moment. It was clear that she was uncomfortable with this line of questioning. "It's like a little sneeze," she said, finally.

A *sneeze*? Why all the fuss, all the seriousness, over a little sneeze? One day, in the schoolyard, one of the older boys—and, naturally, they were *all* older boys—whispered to me, out of a clear blue sky, "Do you know what *fucking* is?" I didn't—the word was new to me—and so he told me in terse, graphic, and somewhat violent terms. Still, this was closer to what I wanted to know about. Sometime later, at the family dinner table, the subject of the Facts of Life came up again—more about ova and gametes, X and Y chromosomes, and cells that kept dividing until they turned into a baby." Oh," I said, brightly and helpfully, "you're talking about fucking."

A ghastly silence descended on the table. "Leave this table at once," my father ordered. "No dinner for you!"

"No reading tonight!" my mother added.

I decided to ask my parents no more questions about sex, at least for a while.

Next, my mother presented me with a couple of pamphlets from the United States Printing Office that I presume she'd sent away for, and that dealt with sex education for young people, in this case boys. "Read these," she told me. "They'll answer all your questions."

I read them avidly, but these booklets left me with more questions than before. There was a section, I recall, headed "Nocturnal Emissions and Masturbation." The text was not at all clear on what, exactly, nocturnal emissions were, except that they were normal. As for masturbation, I read that this, too, was normal, even pleasant, and relaxing, quite harmless, and that all boys did it. But what I couldn't figure out was *how* one did it. The government pamphlet didn't say. If it was pleasant and normal, harmless, and all boys did it, I wanted to know *how*. The dictionary was no help, either, with terms like "self-abnegation," "auto-eroticism," and "Onanism."

At around that time, the newspapers were filled with lurid stories about the actor Errol Flynn, who had been accused of something called "statutory rape." I'd seen Errol Flynn in the movie *Robin Hood*, and loved it, and I knew, in a vague sort of way, what rape was. It was forcible fucking. But what was *statutory* rape? Once more, I turned to the dictionary. Statutory, I read, meant "pertaining to statutes," so I looked up *statute*. There I learned that statute derived from the Latin *stature*, meaning, "to stand up." I therefore concluded that statutory rape meant forcible fucking in a standing position.

Not long after answering that question for myself, I overheard my mother talking with a couple of her woman friends. They seemed to be talking about cooking, and I wasn't paying much attention. Then I heard one woman say, "I always make mine with broccoli rape."

"I *love* broccoli rape," a second woman said.

Broccoli rape? What was this? Rape performed with a bunch of broccolis, my least favorite green vegetable.

Across the street, some neighbors were building a new house, and the builder let me explore the structure as it was being framed up. He pointed out the locations of the various rooms in the finished house. "This will be the kitchen," he said, "and over here, in this corner, will be the berfusnook." He led me up a flight of carpenter's stairs to the second floor. "Here's going to be the master bedroom," he said.

He was using terms that were unfamiliar to me, and that night, at dinner, I told my parents about my tour of the unfinished house, and asked them, "What's a berfusnook?"

They both looked puzzled, and my mother asked, "Where is it located?"

"In a little corner, off the kitchen."

My mother laughed. "I'm sure he said *breakfast* nook," she said. "Honestly—the way these country people talk!"

"He said one of the bedrooms was a master bedroom," I went on. "What's a master bedroom?" Then I added, "Does it have something to do with masturbation?"

All smiles faded around the table, and another of those ghastly silences fell. "Leave the table," my father said sternly. "Go to your room."

"No reading tonight!" my mother echoed.

I went up to my room, bewildered. I knew by then that *fucking* was a vulgar word, inappropriate for use at a family dinner table, with lady's present. Was *masturbation* a dirty word as well? But how could it be, when our very own United States government had devoted an entire chapter to the subject in an official pamphlet my mother had given me to read? It made no sense to me at all.

How old was I when these events took place? Memory and the calendar do not always see eye to eye, but I see that the Errol Flynn trial took place in 1940, so I must have been ten or eleven.

The Andover Public School had no gymnasium, no pool, no locker rooms where boys undressed together and engaged in locker-room sort of talk. Our only playground was an open field. In spring, this became a baseball diamond, and in fall it was a football field. Aside from such sissy games as shooting marbles, playing hopscotch, or skipping rope, these were the only two athletic choices offered, and I had long ago decided that I just "couldn't do" either of those sports. Partly, it was because it was made clear to me that those huge, hulking brutes—as I perceived those sixth-, seventh-, and eighth-grade boys to be—didn't want a skinny little runt like me playing on their teams. But mostly it was because nobody had taught me how to play either game. I didn't know any of the rules. I didn't understand the various positions of the players, or what each position was entitled—or supposed—to do. Profound in my ignorance of both baseball and football, I was too timid and shy—or perhaps too proud—to ask for guidance and information. For a while, I supposed I might be able to pick up the rules of these games by some sort of osmosis, but, from the outset, it was clear that this was not going to work.

My first "away" game for the Andover school was an example. We were there on the field. It was late in the game, and the score was heavily in our favor, when the kindly coach decided it was safe to put the little kid into the game. He sent me out to right field, but with no instructions as to what I was to do when there. A fellow from the opposing team came up to bat, and I noticed that he was a left-hander. I was clever enough to realize that, if he hit the ball, it would probably head in my direction, but beyond that I knew nothing.

Then, with a resounding smack, he hit the ball on the first pitch, and the ball came flying toward me and landed at my feet, where it lay. Then I picked it up. "Throw it to first!" my teammates screamed. Then, "Throw it to second! Throw it to third!" I did not know which base was which, so I just stood there, holding the ball. The result, of course, was a home run for the other side.

"Why didn't you *catch* the ball? Why didn't you *throw* the ball?" they screamed to me in fury, even though we'd won the game by a big margin. All the way home on the bus, no one would speak to me.

Thus disgraced, thus vilified, and scorned, I decided to give up on the game forever. That first game was my very last.

Summers were better times. When school was out, the delineations of age, and class, and caste became blurred. School kept us sorted and segregated according to grade, and room. "The Little Room" was for first and second graders. "The Middle Room" was for grades three, four, and five, and "The Big Room was for the sixth, seventh, and eighth grades. But in summer all those walls came down, the school-year barricades tumbled, and we all—big kids and little—swam together from the beach at Andover Lake, or fished in the streams that ran in and out of it. Yes, I eventually learned to swim.

Then there was the summer that Frank Corelli [not his real name] came to town. Frank was a dark-haired, sweet-faced kid who'd come to spend the summer with his aunt and uncle and teenage cousins who had a house on the lake, not far from the beach. Frank was bright and affable and funny. He played the guitar and sang. But the most interesting thing about Frank, to most of us, was that he was from East Hartford. That meant he was a city kid, wise to the ways of the city streets. To us country yokels, he seemed wonderfully savvy and sophisticated. Frank took a shine to me and included me in all his larky antics and songfests. Best of all, he seemed to forgive the fact that I was a few years younger than he was. I was twelve then, and still small for my age, and Frank was fifteen, but that didn't seem to matter, and it soon began to seem to me that I had found what I had lost years before when Teddy Lockwood drowned: A true best friend.

I knew I'd miss Frank when summer ended and he went back to East Hartford. But he assured me we'd keep in touch. East Hartford—light-years distant in lifestyle and tone—was, after all, only fifteen miles away. "It's not like going to the moon," Frank said. "Next year, I'll have my driver's license. I'll come to see you."

I not only had a best friend. I would have a best friend *with a car.* The days sped by. Through the years of being the youngest in my class, I'd developed a little shell around me, a kind of chrysalis impervious to hurt or prying. Frank seemed to draw me out of that private, protective shell.

Then, one afternoon, after a day at the beach, Frank and I went back to his aunt's house to change from our swimming trunks into our regular clothes. This was not our usual routine, but I thought nothing of it. Undressing, in Frank's room, I noticed that he had a crop of dark curly hair at his groin, but this neither surprised nor particularly interested me. I'd seen Frank's hairy armpits at the beach and knew that Frank had passed into a phase of young manhood that I longed to enter but had not yet. Suddenly Frank said to me, "Have you got a hard-on?"

In actual fact, as I recall, I did not, but the truth was that I did not have the slightest idea, at that point, what this expression meant. And so, since it was the answer Frank seemed to want, I said, "Yes?"

Then he began to fondle me. The sensation was rather pleasant, and so I figured I ought to reciprocate. Perhaps, I recall thinking, this was what good friends did to one other in such worldly-wise big cities as East Hartford. Then Frank said, "There's another way to do it."

He instructed me to lie down, naked, on my stomach on his bed, and told me to spread my legs. Then he climbed on top of me.

I had no idea what was supposed to happen next, nor, as it would turn out, was I going to find out that afternoon. Because, just then, there was a noisy banging on the door. It was Frank's aunt, calling, "What's going *on* in there?"

We both quickly hopped off the bed and into our clothes.

I rode home on my bicycle, my head swarming with unanswered questions. Though nothing had really happened, I knew that something rather important had.

The next day I saw Frank on the beach. He was sitting tailor-fashion in the sand, playing his guitar, a group of other kids around him. I approached them, but when he saw me coming, he turned his head away. "What's the matter, Frank?" I asked him, and he turned to me and snarled, "Get away from me, you creep!"

I turned and walked away quickly, trying to blink back the tears.

Of course, I realized what had happened. Frank's aunt had seen nothing, but she had intuited something, and her intuition had been, unfortunately, correct. That evening, she, and probably Frank's uncle, too, had delivered a so-stern little lecture to him, and Frank had simply turned the tables on me, claiming that I, and not he, had initiated the little exercise at which Frank had obviously had some practice, and gained a certain amount of expertise. I could understand why he lied. If he had confessed the truth, his summer hosts might have sent him packing back to East Hartford, where he would have spent the rest of his vacation on the steamy city streets, far from a lazy, lakeside beach. He had obviously repeated the lie to others as well, by way of explaining why he and I were no longer friends. Soon other older boys were greeting me with little smirks and leers and giggles, little hissing noises, and whispery suggestions. I supposed it wouldn't be long before the whole town had heard Frank's version of that afternoon's events in Frank's room. Frank was making sure he covered his bets, saved his backside, so to speak, and continued to be the life of the party.

I did not go back to the beach for the rest of that summer, and spent it retreating back into my shell, weaving another layer of my cocoon, adding another convolution to my private chrysalis.

And yet—sometimes, there's God—so quickly!

Not long after that summer of treachery and betrayal, I enrolled at the Hotchkiss School, a private boys' school (now coed) in northwestern Connecticut. There I discovered a new sport.

I had already decided that football was a senseless, brutal sport. I had seen too many boys being carried off the field with injuries; a boy I knew had broken his leg playing football. To me, a broken arm was one thing. I wouldn't have minded breaking an arm. A person with his arm in a sling was somehow *interesting*. The sling suggested that this person had a *history*, a story to tell, and I even devised a sling out of kitchen towels, to see how I would look in one. But the idea of hobbling around for six weeks on crutches struck me as no fun at all.

And baseball, it seemed to be, was an awfully *slow* sport. A baseball game seemed to go on and on, and watching one was mostly watching players walk back and forth, not doing much of anything, between arguments with the umpires over what seemed to me over insignificant calls and decisions. To this day, I could not tell you what constitutes an inning, or what it means, in football, to run around your own end.

My sport was basketball. Basketball was fast-moving, and it was fun. The size of the teams was small, and the positions of the players were graspable, and the rules were easy to follow. The object of the game was simple: toss the ball through the basket, and you made a score. And the scores mounted rapidly, which added to the excitement. The game was also player friendly, and relatively injury free. I don't mean to imply that I became a great basketball star at Hotchkiss. Far from it. I was not a particularly good player, and the fact that I had to wear glasses—this was in the days before contact lenses became commonplace—made things awkward. But I did love the game.

I forget which other school team we were playing that afternoon, but there were only a few seconds of play left, and the score was tied. Suddenly the ball was thrown to me. The basket was behind me, out of sight, but I raised the ball and threw it blindly backward, over my head. Then I turned and watched the ball rising in a perfect arc and dropping into the hoop without even brushing the rim. I had scored the winning points.

Not many of us, I suspect, experience those perfect moments when we are truly happy—when everything seems to come together in one implosive flash, when sheer joy blinds the mind to everything else, even consciousness, the heartache of awareness, the rough exigencies of life, the demands and agonies of love, the certainty of mortality itself. Those moments come, of course—a marriage, the birth of a child—but they don't come very often, and certainly not often enough. As my teammates crowded around me, hugging me, thumping me on the back, even lifting me lightly on their shoulders to carry me off the court, this was one of those moments. Tears were appropriate. Suddenly, though not technically, I was an adult, and had learned all the facts of life I would ever need to know.

And as for you, Frank Corelli, my lying, duplicitous and treacherous false and fair-weather friend, I send just one wish to you: Wherever you are, I hope that camels are shitting on you and your mother's grave.

CHAPTER THREE

A Hat

STEVE:

AND WHERE, THE READER MIGHT ASK, WAS MY FATHER THROUGH ALL of this? He was there, of course, but he worked hard. He had a forty-five-minute commute, each way, between our house and his Hartford law office, and he usually left for the office before we children left for school and was seldom home before dinnertime. He was active in the community, too, though not to the extent that my mother was. For a number of years, he served as chairman of the Andover Democratic Town Committee. Also, once a week, he had his poker evening with a group of male friends, a gathering that moved from house to house. As a result, with the exception of those occasional secret trips to Sunday Mass, there weren't many things that my father and I did together as I was growing up.

To me, my father was always somewhat distant and aloof, a stern—and even frightening—authority figure. Perhaps it had something to do with the whipping I received when I tried saying "no" to getting the eggs. I'm sure he loved me, in an abstract sort of way, but I never got the feeling that he really liked me or enjoyed my company. My younger sister, in the meantime, was his clear favorite. It was he who taught her how to swim at such a young age. When she was barely two, she was swimming fearlessly out to the raft that was anchored in the lake. The raft had two diving platforms, a low one, and another that was easily twelve feet high. She'd clamber up the ladder to the high board and, holding her nose, leap off into the deep water. She'd repeat this again and again, and I remember spectators on the beach exclaiming, "Just look at that little girl! Look at

47

that *little girl.*" Yes, she was definitely Daddy's Girl, and I, by default if not by choice, became Mamma's Boy.

I sometimes think that, if I had had a chance to get to know my father as an adult, we might have become close, even friends. But, after boarding school, I went off to college. Soon after graduating, I got married, and not long after that I was drafted into the Army. And while I was in the Army my father died—much too young, he was only forty-six—of cancer. During the school and college years, he and I had only become more distant, more embattled. And most of our battles, I'm sorry to say, involved money.

There were certain ironies here. In grammar school, my kid sister, Susan, and I were known as "the rich kids." This was because our father was "the lawyer"—the only man in that profession in Andover at the time—and, in Andover's mind, being a lawyer was synonymous with wealth. At home, on the other hand, poverty was the persistent theme. "I can't afford that" was my father's inevitable response to anything that involved an outlay of cash.

Looking back, I'm sure that this had a lot to do with the times in which we were living then. My father graduated from Trinity College in 1924, and, after completing three years of law school at Yale, he and my mother were married in 1928. They then took off for a grand and extended tour of Europe and Scandinavia, and when they returned my mother was pregnant with me. I was known as "the Bavarian baby," and some friends of my parents presented me with a pair of knee-length lederhosen, with a bib top, and a green Bavarian cap with a feather in it, which I vaguely remember. Later I learned that this was because my parents believed I had been conceived in the German resort town of Garmisch-Partenkirchen, in the Bavarian Alps.

Back home, they purchased the property in Andover—four acres on a hilltop, at the foot of which ran a pretty brook—and started to build their house. It was not a grand house by any means—designed in a traditional Colonial style, part stone, part shingle. But, by Andover's modest farmhouse standards at the time with five bedrooms and three baths—it was bigger than most. All this, of course, was in the Roaring Twenties, when President Hoover had assured the nation that America had achieved "a permanent plateau of prosperity," and it must have seemed to my parents at that particular moment that they could look forward to lives of ease and comfort, if not a certain amount of luxury.

Then came the Stock Market Crash of 1929, followed by the long, grinding years of the Great Depression, when all dreams and hopes were shattered, and the grim realities of hard times everywhere slowly settled in. I sometimes think that the Depression, coming so early in my father's career, permanently shaped his thinking, and his attitude toward money. Even when times eventually got better, my father's mind remained rooted in those Depression years. My father's life seemed to fall into two halves: Coolidge's Prosperity, and Hoover's Depression. He remained in the Depression until the day he died, almost into the Eisenhower years.

My earliest memories seem to involve endless, small economies. My mother did all her own washing and ironing, mended our underwear, and darned our socks. (I still have her white china darning egg, now missing its handle.) New shoes, when we outgrew or outwore our old ones, were a cause for a family council of war. My father would insist that the purchase could be postponed at least a month, or two months, or six: "Do you think I'm made of money?" In the end, he might say he had a "friend" or a "client" who had a shoe store, who would either sell us cheap shoes at a discount or let us have them free in lieu of a legal fee.

I remember an argument about trays. My mother wanted to buy a tray, to help her bring on and remove the dinner dishes. "A *tray*?" I remember my father wailing. "Why would you need a *tray*? Why would anyone with two good hands need a *tray*?" These scenes left me baffled. I had friends whose parents I knew were much worse off than we were. Their mothers had a tray, sometimes two or three trays.

I knew that times were hard. Tramps, as we called them, would come to our door for handouts. I've heard it said that the tramps would leave little symbols, in chalk, at the foot of driveways or at the gates of households where they were well received. If that was true, one of those chalk marks must have been inscribed at the foot of our drive, because the tramps seemed to come by our house in a steady stream. My mother would give these homeless men something to eat, and even let them spend the night on an old Army cot in the garage, but they were expected to perform some service for us in return: washing windows, waxing the car, painting the kitchen ceiling.

Sometimes, in those days, it seemed to me that my father's law practice was conducted in a similar fashion, on a kind of barter system. A good deal of it probably was. For years, for example, my father drove a Fleetwood Cadillac. This was an impressive machine, a rich man's car. The only thing was that it was secondhand, a used-car dealer's payment to my father for some legal service. My mother had a little fisher fur jacket that I thought looked very snappy on her. But it, too, had had a previous owner. One client paid my father with a Hoover electric floor-polisher, and my father presented it to my mother for her birthday. Not the most romantic gift, it was always referred to by my mother as "the birthday present" not without some sarcasm, I'm sure, since it was well-used by the time it came to her. Still another client's fee came in the form of three large Oriental rugs. These turned out to be old and fine, and are still in the family, I'm happy to say.[7]

In the meantime, my father—during the Depression—became a much-loved figure in Andover. This was because, in addition to his city practice, he also served as a kind of country lawyer for the local populace, and for this he charged little, or nothing at all. Or a farmer might pay him with a freshly plucked and dressed chicken, or a quart of tomatoes or a bushel of corn from his garden. The "cases" that he handled here almost never came to court, and for the most part involved disputes where some sort of impartial mediator, or referee, was needed to smooth things out, or simmer down hot tempers. Mrs. Gifford, a widow down the road, claimed that Mr. Chambliss, another neighbor, had made an "improper proposal" to her while they were both on volunteer Air Raid Warden duty together. (The war had started by then.) Mrs. Gifford wanted Mr. Chambliss exposed for what he was, a masher, and she went to my father with her injustice. This was a ticklish situation since the Chamblisses were our next-door neighbors.

My father paid a call on Mr. Chambliss, who explained that all he had said to the woman was something to the effect that widowhood must be a lonely life. Mrs. Gifford had interpreted this to mean that Mr. Chambliss was offering to relieve her loneliness. Meetings were held, back and forth, but Mrs. Gifford would not be mollified. In the end, the situation grew to such proportions that the Chamblisses packed up and moved to another town.

A neighbor's dog got loose, and went into a farmer's henhouse, where it killed two chickens. Under normal circumstances, the farmer would simply have shot his neighbor's dog. There would have been hard feelings all around, to be sure, but this would have been considered country justice, and it would have effectively put an end to the matter. But the aggrieved farmer came up with a more insidious form of revenge. The dog owner, it seemed, worked for Pratt & Whitney Aircraft in East Hartford, and was being considered for a promotion (again, this was after America had entered the war) to a position that required top secret security clearance. In making its routine background check on this man, the FBI visited various of his neighbors, and the farmer told the FBI that he knew, for a fact, that the Pratt & Whitney man was a card-carrying member of the Communist Party.

This was a serious charge, and it took several weeks of delicate arbitration before my father was able to persuade the warring parties to shake hands and get out of the ring. The Pratt & Whitney man paid the farmer for his chickens, plus enough to compensate him for the loss of egg production. The farmer formally withdrew his treasonous allegations.

The Pratt & Whitney man paid my father with a horse. She was an even-natured mare who had been his children's saddle horse. But the Pratt man had a new job and was moving to the city where there would be no place to keep her. We named the horse Merry. We stabled her and pastured her on a farm across the road, and I learned to ride on Merry. I helped cut bridle paths for Merry through our woods. My father decided to have her bred, and Merry produced a filly foal. I watched her being born, legs first and kicking as she came, and named her Merrylegs. Merrylegs was a wild, skittish colt, and no one could get near her. It was my mother—of all people—who finally succeeded in roping her, throwing a saddle on her, and breaking her. In time, my father sold Merrylegs and, at last, some actual money changed hands.

The woman who ran the local gas station was Mrs. Hendricks. She was a powerhouse. She wielded the nozzle of a gas-pump hose as though wrestling an anaconda. Her husband was sickly and suffered from a number of undiagnosed ailments, which his wife treated with a series of enemas. "I cleaned him out real good last night, and he's feeling a little better," I'd hear her say. I don't know what Mrs. Hendricks's legal problems were, but there seemed to be many. Apparently, she could make no business arrangement without saying, importantly, "I'll have to consult with my attorney"—pronouncing the second syllable of "attorney" to rhyme with "horn." Every time my father stopped to fill up—and Mrs. Hendricks had a monopoly along that stretch of Route 6—she would summon him inside her station for a lengthy conference on whatever the current matter was, while we waited patiently in the car. In her station, Mrs. Hendricks also sold newspapers. Her payment to my father for his services was a free copy of the Sunday *Courant*. "No charge!" she would say grandly, as she presented us with the paper on Sunday mornings. It apparently never occurred to her to give him a free tank of gas.

At home, my father was very much the Old World, head-of-the-household sort. His home was his castle, and he ruled it accordingly. His theory was that, as the family's breadwinner, he and he alone would decide how, and to whom, the bread was to be distributed. We all grew accustomed to begging him for anything we wanted or felt we needed, and when he refused us—"No, I can't afford it"—that was final, and any further argument was to no avail.

None of us had any idea of how much money my father earned, and it would have been fruitless to try to find out. When he prepared my parents' joint income tax returns, he held his hand over the figures while my mother affixed her signature. She was permitted to have no checking or other bank accounts, nor was she allowed any charge accounts. He had an almost paranoid fear of being in debt. It was credit, he often said—no doubt correctly—that had brought on the Great Crash. Whatever bills came in, he paid from the office, where he kept his checkbook—its balance always a secret, though once I did see a check sitting on his desk, payable to him, for $5,000. It seemed an astonishing sum; so, we couldn't be *that* poor. During the war, he was appointed assistant United States district attorney for the State of Connecticut. This gave him a second office, and a second secretary, in the Federal Building in Hartford. It also paid him a government salary, in addition to what he earned from his law practice, but we had no idea what that salary might be.

There were hints, nonetheless, that the family's financial situation had improved somewhat. In his Justice Department post, he was required to make frequent trips to Washington, and sometimes—during the summer months, when we were home from school—he would take us with him. We would put up, rather grandly, at the Mayflower Hotel on Connecticut Avenue, and take the Pullman sleeper train back and forth. This was outright luxury, but mostly I remember the draining, sweltering heat of summers in Washington in those pre-air-conditioning days. Wartime Washington worked year-round. There were no summer recesses for Congress or anyone else, and I used to imagine President Roosevelt sweating, in drenched shirtsleeves, in his White House office. Still, in terms of family spending, my father remained flintily frugal. When I was about fourteen, I had become quite girl conscious, and also more than a little clothes conscious. In the window of Stackpole, Moore & Tryon, which was then—and still is—one of Hartford's finest, and priciest, men's clothing stores,[8] I had seen a handsome pair of red-and-yellow argyle socks, which I coveted. Using money saved from my allowance I decided to buy them. They cost $1.50 which was, I imagine, about the equivalent of a $20 pair of socks today. My shopping done, I went back to my father's office, where he immediately spotted the Stackpole bag.

"What's in there?" he wanted to know. I showed him my new argyles.

"How much did you pay for those?" he demanded. "A dollar-fifty," was my reply.

"A dollar and a *half*? For *socks*? Jim!" he roared, calling to his law partner, Jim Kennedy, across the hall. "Jim! Come here and look at what this son of mine has done! Look at this—he's paid a dollar and a *half*—for socks—from *Stackpole's*, no less!"

Both men stood there, shaking their heads in disbelief at what this feckless, foolish, spendthrift adolescent youth had done.

Still, there were moments in those days when my father seemed to relax about money, and to slip back, however briefly, into a pre-Depression modality. I remember, not long after the socks episode, seeing him leave a $2 tip for the waitress in the dining room of the Mayflower, where we'd just had dinner. I blinked at the size of the tip but did not comment that he was simply giving away—*giving away*—more money than I had paid for a perfectly serviceable, not to mention elegant, pair of socks.

At the Hotchkiss School, which was then—and still is—one of the costliest New England boarding schools, I found myself rubbing shoulders with boys whose names were Ford, Mellon, Pillsbury, Pullman, and du Pont. These were *seriously* rich kids. I had been accepted at Hotchkiss on a scholarship, which my parents assured me was a great honor. But I soon discovered that there were certain drawbacks to this. Scholarship boys were required to perform certain "scholarship duties" every day—sweeping the corridors, waiting on tables in the dining room, cleaning blackboards in the classrooms. The scholarship duties limited one's extracurricular activities somewhat, and clearly marked the scholarship boy as economically disadvantaged, one of the deserving poor.

I was at the age, the early teens, when kids often worry incessantly and needlessly that their parents may not quite measure up, in looks or in manners, against the parents of other kids. I had observed the parents of other Hotchkiss boys when they came to visit their sons at school. The fathers were usually tweedy, with golfing tans, and the mothers, usually blondes, were uniformly turned out by Bonwit Teller, De Pinna, or Lord & Taylor. I knew I could never get my father into tweeds, but in one of his dark business suits, and driving his Fleetwood Cadillac, he'd do. And my mother, in her chic yellow fisherman's jacket, would probably pass muster. There was only one thing. All the other Hotchkiss mothers, it seemed to me, wore hats when they visited the school. My mother did not have a hat. On my first weekend home from school, I mentioned this situation to her. Before she visited me at school, I wanted her to buy a hat.

"I'll mention it to your father," she said.

For the next two days, the only topic in the house seemed to be hats.

"How much does a hat cost?" my father wanted to know.

She had no idea. She'd never bought a hat. She was proud of her full head of naturally curly dark brown hair—now lightly mixed with gray—and felt no need for a hat, and thought that a hat would "flatten" her hair. But now she was asking for a hat.

"I'll run over to Fox's tomorrow and find out," my father promised her. At the time, G. Fox & Co. was another of Hartford's leading department stores, although it closed in 1993.

It is amusing to picture my tall and stockily built father scouting the millinery department of G. Fox & Co., pricing women's hats. But that apparently was what he did because he came home the next night to announce, in awestruck tones, "Do you realize, Edda, that some of those hats cost as much as *fifty dollars?*"

But Mother stuck to her guns. I think she had actually begun to like the idea of buying a hat. Wisely, she didn't tell my father that it was I who was behind the idea of a hat and was pushing it. If she had, that would have killed the project altogether because my father had already written me off as a hopeless profligate when it came to money. And, in the end, he relented. He took out his wallet and handed her $45. "See what you can find for that," he said, with a little sigh.

I thought the hat she chose was very pretty. It was light blue, palettes of colored glass around the brim, and a small half-veil.

"How much was it?" my father asked her when she modeled it for us the evening of her purchase.

"Why, forty-five dollars, of course," she said. "That's what you gave me." But as she said this, she tossed me a little wink, and I was certain that she had paid more than that and had scraped together the extra cash from some secret source of her own.

As far as I can remember that pale blue hat with the colored spangles at the brim and the half-veil was the only hat she ever owned.

CAREY:

I am reminded of a joke my father told me long ago, demonstrating his unique sense of humor and perhaps recollecting the shopping episode by my grandmother:

After a long pregnancy, a woman gave birth and the resulting male child was, sadly, only a head but otherwise healthy.

The delivering doctor tried to assuage the woman's shock and grief by explaining, "Mrs. Johnson, please don't fret. Someday, a person will give birth to only a body, and the technology will allow us to join your son and his problems will be solved."

Somewhat mollified, the woman raised her son, the Head, into his teens when, coincidently on her son the Head's fifteenth birthday, the birth doctor called with excitement to explain, "Mrs. Johnson, I have good news! Fifteen years ago, another woman gave birth to only a body. We have worked diligently to keep the body healthy and we are now happy to report we have the technology and can join your son, the Head, onto this healthy teenaged body!"

The mother, ecstatic, raced into her son the Head's room and exclaimed, "Son, I have the most wonderful birthday present for you!"

Her son, the Head, sardonically responded, "Not another hat."

STEVE:

In 1952, I was in the Army, stationed in California, when I received word, from the Red Cross, that my father was gravely ill. My mother had told me nothing, possibly because she herself was unwilling to accept the seriousness of the situation. I applied for, and was quickly granted, an emergency leave, and flew home to Connecticut.

It was a shock to see him—my once robust and hefty father—lying there, pale, and shrunken and hollow-cheeked, on the hospital bed, his hand lying, palm-upward, above the bedclothes. My mother and I sat beside his bed, while a private-duty nurse sat nearby, knitting, and reading a magazine at the same time. His doctor had told us that a final piece of exploratory surgery had been just that. His body had been riddled with cancer, and so the incision had been closed again, but the trauma of the surgery had left him in an even more weakened state.

Mostly, he just slept—a fitful, drug-induced sleep from the painkillers that dripped into his wrist through a clear plastic tube. But there were occasional moments of lucidity. At one point, he opened his eyes and turned his head to me where I sat in my Army uniform; I had recently attained the lofty rank of sergeant and wore three stripes on my sleeve. "Why don't you run out and buy yourself a new suit?" he said. I wondered if he was remembering all the times, I had asked him for money to buy clothes, and he had refused.

"I'll do that," I said. Those were his last words to me.

From time to time a Catholic priest appeared, and paused at the doorway of his room, but my mother, the always stalwart Episcopalian, waved him away. Finally, she said to him, "We don't need your services, Father, and we don't want your services. Please go away."

It was not that my mother was anti-Catholic, exactly. But chemistry major that she was, she associated Catholicism and its Church with supernaturalism—with visions, miraculous cures at Lourdes, and weeping statues of the Virgin, whom my mother often referred to as Our Lady of Perpetual Recrimination.

Presently, my mother had to go to the bathroom, and as soon as she had left, I went quickly out to the nurse's station and found the priest. I knelt at the foot of my father's bed, while the priest stood over him and blessed him. He began to speak in Latin, and from my Hotchkiss Latin classes I recognized the words, "*Ego te absolvo in nomine Patris . . .*" and I watched as the priest made the sign of the cross. Then the priest removed a small silver box from his pocket. It contained the consecrated oil, and he gently dabbed the chrism on my father's forehead, speaking again in Latin. Then he put the box away and uttered a final blessing. It was over, my father had received the Last Rites, and the priest had departed before my mother returned from the ladies' room.

I never told my mother what I'd done, of course. It was my father's and my last secret from her. After all, I saw nothing wrong with the notion that my father should join his Irish ancestors in heaven.

Soon it was time for us to leave him for the night. The private-duty nurse—who had not looked up from her *McCall's* or her needlework during the priest's visit—gestured to the nightstand beside my father's bed. "Better remove all his personal stuff from that drawer," she said. "He's not going to make it through the night."

I glared angrily at her, but did as she suggested, and we emptied the drawer. It contained his billfold, his reading glasses, and some other odds and ends.

Early the next morning, the telephone rang, and I knew it was the hospital calling, and that he was dead.

After his funeral—to which, it seemed, the whole town of Andover turned out—my mother and I discovered some surprising things. In a pocket in his billfold, we found a key, and the key turned out to belong to a safe-deposit box that we'd never known he had. In the box were a number of savings bank passbooks, dating from more than twenty years back, showing regular deposits and very few withdrawals. We found government, municipal, and corporate bonds, some in quite large amounts, their coupons never clipped. We found stock certificates—many of them purchased in the darkest years of the Great Depression—mostly in Hartford's old-line, gilt-edged insurance companies: Aetna, Travelers, Hartford Life, and Connecticut General. He'd been squirrelling away money for years, without telling a soul.

He was by no means a millionaire, but his estate turned out to be worth several hundred thousand dollars. We also found his will, which left everything to my mother.

Wellesley may have taught her the principles of building an atomic bomb, but it had not taught her how to manage and balance a checkbook. Many months later, I went back to Andover again and saw, on her desk, a pile of unopened bank statements. I offered to bring her checkbook up to date, and quickly discovered that she had overdrawn her account by almost $500. Some recent checks had already been returned to her, stamped "UNPAID INSUFFICIENT FUNDS." She had a quick solution for this: she would simply write a check, on the same account at the same bank, for $500 and send the check to the bank. It took some explaining before I was able to make her see that this tactic would simply have the effect of doubling the size of her overdraft.

In recent years, I've become reasonably active in alumni affairs for the Hotchkiss School. It used to be called "Fundraising." Then it was renamed "Development." And now, in our age of the ever-expanding euphemisms, it is becoming known as "Institutional Enhancement." On one of many visits back to the school, one of the school officials asked me if I'd enjoy looking at my old school records from the days when I was a student there. I said sure, and he produced a thick file folder. But when I opened it, I quickly wished I hadn't, and I suddenly began to feel a little ill.

The first document I saw was a questionnaire my father had filled out, called "Application for Financial Aid," and it asked him to list his financial assets and liabilities: "Please list any savings accounts you maintain, along with current balances."

My father had written "None."

"Please list, by company and share amount, any stocks, bonds, or other equities you own."

Again, "None."

"Is there a mortgage on your home? Please state current unpaid balance." My father had answered, that, yes, there was $100,000 on the mortgage. But there had been no mortgage.

My father had lied about his financial situation to avoid paying my tuition at the school. I closed the folder and handed it back.

In the years since making that unhappy discovery, I've often tried to puzzle out my father. What went wrong? Something—I'm convinced of it—surely had. Sometimes he appears to me, a bit contentiously and defensively, in dreams, and I try to ask him questions. But of course, I get no answers. Did it have something to do with my mother marrying a Protestant, out of the Church, and then trying to live a double life, both in and out of it? Somehow, I keep coming back to the Depression.

I see him—I'm just guessing now—back in the Roaring Twenties, young, handsome, full of wonderful ambition. The ambition must have been there, to get out of Frog Hollow, because he was the only member of his large Irish-Catholic family to go beyond high school. I see him dreaming of a career in politics. (In New England, politics and the Irish have long gone hand in hand.) In Hartford, he had a lot of politician friends. U.S. Senator Thomas Dodd (father of Congressman Christopher) was one, and so was Tom Spellacy, for many years Hartford's mayor, and Hartford's answer to Boston's "Honey Fitz." I see my father planning to run for Congress, then the Senate. Or he may have had a loftier ambition. He once told me that the highest goal a lawyer could achieve was to be appointed a justice of the United States Supreme Court.

"Being a Supreme Court justice is even better than being president," he said. "A justice doesn't have to run for office every four years. He's got the job for life."

But then the Depression came, killing all those dreams. When I was ten or eleven, I thought I might like to be a lawyer, and follow in his footsteps. "Don't," he told me. "Why not?" I asked him. I remember his gnomish reply: "Because you might have a son who'll want to be a lawyer."

My father was a contemporary of Scott Fitzgerald, another Irishman. In fact, he had met Fitzgerald once, when the latter was in Princeton, and was unimpressed with him. "Kind of a pasty-faced guy, with lips like a girl's," was the way he described the chronicler of that era. In his closet, my father kept a very natty-looking pair of gray-and-white plaid golfing knickers, in the style that golfers wore back then with knee socks and shoes with ghillie flaps. I never saw him wear those knickers, yet he never threw them out, keeping them in his closet for years after they had gone out of fashion. Nostalgia?

Contrary to its intent, Prohibition seemed to encourage Americans to drink more, not less, and it was during this period, I'm sure, that my father, like Fitzgerald, acquired his taste for alcohol. "Goodness, but we all drank a lot in those days," an old friend of his, Ruth Guy, said to me not long ago. "The best parties were always at your parents' house, and your father always knew how to find a bootlegger. Your father drank with the best of them, but he was always a jolly drunk, never a mean or maudlin drunk."

But none of this explains why, at some point, he chose to wear a mask of failure—to his family, as well as to strangers—when he really wasn't one. Like me, my sister went to boarding school and college on a series of scholarships, and so I have to assume that he made similar misstatements about his worth on other questionnaires.

By the time I got to college, I was no longer in awe of him. If anything, I was ashamed of him, embarrassed by him, with an embarrassment that no purchase of a new hat could disguise. He was becoming a slob; there's no other word for it. He never used to—but now he did— bring a quart of beer with him to the dinner table and pull on it as he ate. Halfway through the meal, he'd go to the kitchen for another quart. In the evenings he was hardly ever sober. My mother used to worry about him driving from his late-night poker games, when often he would have to be helped upstairs and into bed. Because of her worry, no, let's call it what it was, her nagging, he now often didn't come home at all, but slept off the evening on a friend's sofa. To me, there was something almost perverse about this—something deliberate, and hostile. Once I brought a friend home with me from college for the weekend. We returned, in black ties, from a coming-out party at the Hartford Golf Club to find my father, wearing only his undershorts, sitting in a dining room chair, passed out, face forward, across the table. Several empty beer bottles lay about the floor.

My father, the Bowery bum.

I could have gladly killed him at that point. But I didn't kill him— just turned off the dining room lights and closed the door.

I sometimes wonder: Was he trying to punish me with this sort of thing, when the old punishments, bending me over his knee, no longer worked? It was true that it upset him when I was asked to parties at the Hartford Golf Club. This was because, when he was my age, no Irish were permitted to enter the club, except as groundskeepers. My father had worked there one summer when he was in high school, as a groundskeeper.

Let's leave my father there, but I'll add one more element to the riddle. In his safe-deposit box, my mother and I also found about a thousand dollars' worth of unused American Express travelers' checks. Had he, at some point, been planning a grand escape from all of us? Back to Paris . . . Munich . . . Oslo . . . Copenhagen, where they'd gone when they were young and happy? The travelers' checks were naturally undated, and so it was impossible to tell how long he'd had them there.

A couple of years ago, I was able to establish a trust fund for the Hotchkiss School, and to create my own scholarship fund. I'm not trying to pat my own back here, though I'm proud to have done it. I did it partly because I do believe that an elite education—such as that which schools like Hotchkiss provide—should be within the reach of as many students as are willing and able to do the work. The work is hard. These schools demand a lot from their students and make short shrift of the indolent or sloppy. But I also made this gift out of a sense of guilt and shame, hoping to atone—at least in part—for the lies my father told them years ago.

CAREY:

The irony of my father describing his father as a drunk and a Bowery bum is not lost on me in 2019. My father, throughout the years I knew him, was what could euphemistically be called a "functioning alcoholic." Unlike my grandfather, whom I never knew, my father's drink of choice was not beer but a vodka or Bombay Gin martini, yet no one would ever find him passed out in his underwear. When he did pass out (which to be truthful, I don't recall happening very often), he was usually resplendent in finery, having just come from a celebrity party of some sort. He was voted one of *Gentlemen's Quarterly*'s 10 Best-Dressed Men in America in 1970.

In those days, the mid-1960s, it was common for grown-ups to have a cocktail hour. Such was the case in our house. It was an everyday occurrence that after my father had completed his day's work writing, he and my mother would enjoy several martinis while we, The Children, were sent upstairs. I remember many nights when I was young crawling into my parents' bed and smelling alcohol on my father's breath. To this day, the smell of vodka or gin brings back those difficult memories.

My father was not a mean drunk, except on a few occasions. When he drank alone (after my mother stopped joining him at cocktail hour around 1971), he appeared morose and introspective. I remember vividly his drinking martinis alone and listening to Don McLean's recording of "Starry, Starry Night" over and over again on the phonograph in our sunroom, perhaps interpreting the lyrics and how they reflected his life.

I do, however, recall unfortunate instances when his drinking got out of control.

One evening when I was nine years old, our family attended a dinner party with some friends nearby in Rye. While my brother, sister and I were sent upstairs to play with the hosts' children, my father got, well, plotzed. When it was time to leave, an argument ensued in the hosts' driveway as my mother insisted on taking car keys and driving. My father, well into his cups, was having none of it. The ride home was terrifying, as my father weaved across lanes and kept taking his hands off the wheel.

In such circumstances, each member of the family had a role. My mother sat stoically (if afraid), buckled into the front passenger seat. My sister, prone to throw gasoline on any fire, belittled my father and mocked him from the back seat, making matters worse. My brother zoned out of the entire mess, closed his eyes, crossed his arms on his chest and mind-traveled who-knows-where. Me? Although I was the youngest, my job was the negotiator and, as such, perched between the two bucket seats, also in the rear of the Thunderbird, I did my best to "talk my father down." We made it home that night, but it was harrowing

On another occasion, my father was arrested in our hometown of Rye for "drunken driving," as it was known then, before DUIs, DWIs, and "impaired driving" took its place. The incident occurred when I was in elementary school, and, since my father was a local celebrity of sorts, was reported in the local press. The *Rye Chronical*, and probably the *Daily Item* crowed "Local Celebrity Arrested for Drunken Driving." (There weren't many celebrities in Rye at the time.) I vividly recall this, my first introduction into spin control, as my mother briefed each of us how to handle the questions from classmates that would inevitably arise. Only one or two comments were made when I got to school and, as instructed, I responded with "I don't know anything about it," the next best thing to "no comment." In those days, there were probably many of my elementary school peers who had experienced similar circumstances of parents' drinking and thought better than to cast stones.

At a different time, in the waning days of my parents' marriage, they both had driven into New York City for a party to celebrate the publication of *Real Lace*, one of my father's more successful books after *"Our Crowd."*

While our parents were partying in town, my gasoline-on-the-fire sister, Harriet, thought this would a good time to have a party at our house on Hidden Spring Lane, and word got out to the local lowlifes in Rye. My brother signed on, to a degree. Sure enough, as was designed into this particular business model, the lowlifes began to accrete literally out of the woods (our house backed up to a stretch of trees between our yard and the street), and the party was on. At the time, I was thirteen, but saw what was racing toward a debacle.

My brother, seventeen, and his invitees (numbering three or four) thought this party would be as good a time as any to drop LSD, and shortly thereafter one friend began experiencing the textbook "bad trip." In the meantime, various losers numbering perhaps twenty to thirty were in our backyard pool getting drunk, stoned, and basically tearing up the place, a classic teenage party. All the while, my parents were finishing up late-night partying themselves and driving home from New York. A storm was brewing on the horizon. Looking back, I can't imagine what my siblings were thinking. Did it really not occur to them that our parents would return? Did they think twenty to thirty drunk teenagers would be welcome in our house upon our parents' return?

As this tragedy began to unfold, my brother, who was tripping, did his best to control his out-of-control, bad-tripping friend, even going so far as to consider another boy's suggestion that they hold bad-tripper down and punch him in the head until he was out cold (fortunately, the idea was discarded).

My parents returned about midnight, just as my sister's party was in full swing. When the Thunderbird's headlights wafted past our front yard, the various losers scattered like cockroaches in a New York apartment, and my brother's friends quickly abandoned him to solve "bad-tripper's" problem on his own. Mark's solution: take the LSD-addled kid away, and fast. It was with some relief that we realized my father was completely passed out in the back seat of the car, and my mother, who despite having been drinking herself, quickly regained composure and went into rush damage control, knowing that when my father awoke the tumult would begin in earnest.

Meanwhile, the main problem became apparent. In fleeing, party attendees had abandoned their cars in our driveway, three cars to be precise, and the owners (with their keys) were in the wind, nowhere to be found. Indeed, one car belonged to LSD-kid, and he, in a fit of acid-fueled reason, had hurled his own car keys into the nighttime woods, thank you very much, saying he was traveling to another dimension.

The storm awoke.

Mind you, during the entirety of these events I was a benign observer—OK, I admit I thought it would be cool if they actually beat LSD-kid into unconsciousness as was suggested, just to see what would happen, but I would not take part. In retrospect, I was the only completely sober person there, and I chronicled all for posterity.

Amid my father's rage, there was, of course, screaming by all parties (except me) and plenty of belt to be aimed at participants (including me). When all else fails, my father always thought the best approach was to call the local police and demand "they remove those cars from my driveway!" When the police did promptly arrive (our address was well known to the Rye PD at this point, but that's a later story), they advised my father that they were not, in fact, a towing service and now, at 1 a.m., they had better things to do, including a major accident on nearby I-95. This response was unacceptable to my still half-drunk father, and he repeatedly hurled the "*Do you know who I am?*" question at them. The police left. The cars remained. During this, my mother cried, my sister laughed and ridiculed my father (she being drunk herself, which only exacerbated matters), and I observed, keeping a low profile having already being whipped with a wide 1960s belt in the early stages of the storm.

The next morning a towing service hauled the cars away to who knows where. The aftermath witnessed a stolen TV, smashed tables, countless beer and wine bottles strewn about, and plenty of bruises and welts from the belt. Drunken rages run deep.

Mark wandered the streets of Rye deep into the early morning, finally disposing of LSD-kid, leaving him passed out on a bench with as much compassion as Mark could muster and made his way home, having come down from his own LSD trip. Our dysfunctional family life resumed.

Sad to say, these tales were not isolated incidents, and other less memorable rages, fights, and symptoms of dysfunctionality occurred before and well after, including, I'm sorry to say, after my father left. None, however, were as violent and drink fueled as that night in 1968, a year in which the nation had its own violent and historic events to deal with.

At one point, in 1995, my father was invited to speak at Baylor University in Waco, Texas, during a symposium on John Marquand, my father having written the definitive biography, *The Late John Marquand*. The event was held in the alumni dining room with dinner. My wife at the time and I drove up from San Antonio, where I live, to attend the lavish affair, which was well attended.

Born in Connecticut and not having had long experience in Texas, my father can perhaps be forgiven for not understanding the venue. Baylor is Southern Baptist and alcohol is not tolerated. Nevertheless, when a waiter came by the table to take orders for drinks, my father ordered a Bombay martini with an olive. An awkward moment passed and the waiter, discreetly, reminded my father alcohol was not served. Nonplussed, my father held a beat (perhaps incredulous that dinner should not be served without a cocktail prior) and ordered iced tea. The awkward moment passed, my father rose to the occasion and gave a thorough, if not rousing, talk about Marquand. Departing afterward, we immediately hit a bar in his hotel nearby.

Throughout this entire period, my father, the functioning alcoholic, managed to create and produce numerous books and magazine articles, with much success and many bestsellers.

Chapter Four

Tall Tales

STEVE:

A tissue of lies is an apt metaphor, it seems to me. A lie is such an airy, diaphanous creation, as fragile as a spiderweb, as flimsy and easy to penetrate as Kleenex. Most lies eventually become unwoven, and fly apart of their own, insubstantial weightlessness into the nothingness from which they came. Like a gift box from Saks or Gucci they conceal the truth, but are quickly ripped open, and discarded, revealing the surprise or lack thereof within. I've told plenty of lies of my own, of course, and I've also known a number of truly world-class liars.

A writer, I suppose, is a liar by trade. As novelists, we fabricate our characters, invent motivations for them, twist and distort their reactions. In our stories, we mislead our readers. We plant false clues to seduce our readers into supposing that the outcomes of our tales will be quite different from the ones we've planned. We like to spring on our readers from behind their backs, to get them to gasp in astonishment. We prevaricate, we equivocate, we break promises—all in the interest of keeping readers turning our pages. I've always been puzzled by critics who use the phrase "a real page-turner" as a term of disparagement. If a reader didn't want to turn the pages, what would be the point of reading a book?

As novelists, we also take people we know in real life, invent new names for them, give them new hairdos and other disguises, falsify the facts of their lives to suit our fictional whims, and then make up words for them to speak. Many of these real people have not led happy or successful lives, but, because half the world loves a happy, or at least satisfying ending with the good guys triumphing and the bad guys getting their comeuppance, we manipulate facts and circumstances, and avoid the truth in order to end the story the way it *should* have ended. In fact, most true stories do not end the way they ought to. We all know that.

Even the most respected journalists—winners of Pulitzer Prizes—bend the facts to suit their needs. To add drama, color, poignancy, intimacy—or to get their stories printed on the front pages of their newspapers—they also lie. Whenever, in a newspaper account, you see the phrase, "A White House spokesman who asked not to be identified" or "A source close to the Royal Family, who spoke on condition of anonymity," you can be fairly sure that the anonymous quote came from the reporter himself. He or she needed a quote to liven up the story at that point. Unable to get one, he or she made one up, rationalizing that this was something somebody might have said, or ought to have said. Or else it reflected a thought the reporter had himself and wanted to see in print.

When I first started out, writing articles for magazines, a newspaper-man who was one of journalism's elder statesmen said to me, "Young man, I'll give you two pieces of advice. One, never check out an interesting fact. And, two, always make up the quotes—they're bound to be better."

He was only partly joking. Failure to check out an interesting fact can be dangerous, as I learned, early on, the hard way, when a fact I'd heard from a source I thought was reliable turned out not to be a fact. The result was an expensive lawsuit. But the advice about the quotes was pretty sound. Most people, when they talk, do not speak in complete English sentences. They speak with gestures. They mutter and mumble and ramble inconclusively, leaving thoughts unfinished. They utter half-sentences, change their minds in midsentence, contradict themselves and repeat themselves. Most people, if writers quoted them verbatim, would sound very much like Kato Kaelin testifying in the O. J. Simpson case. There was a difference there, of course. Kato Kaelin really *was* dumb, so he came by his inarticulateness honestly. This is why transcriptions of tape-recorded conversations so often sound incomprehensible. When the black box is retrieved from the wreckage—well, what, exactly, *were* the pilot and the copilot discussing just before the plane went down? Ditto the famous tapes of Richard Nixon in the White House. Well, he *should* have destroyed them because, only here and there in the thousands of hours of spinning reels is it clear what any of those people were talking about.

I've often found myself interviewing a subject while he cast about, incoherently, trying to phrase some sort of answer to a question. I've found myself saying, "I think what you're trying to say is . . ." With that, the interviewee snaps his fingers and says, "Yes! That's it!" And so, I've done it. I've made up the quote. In journalism, of course, there's a euphemism for this. It's known as "cleaning up the quotes."

Still, I've had people complain that they've been misquoted, which usually translates as, "I wish I hadn't said that." Or that they've been quoted "out of context." I've never been sure what that means, since most humans, when they speak, do not speak in any context whatsoever. A writer, on the other hand, does have—or ought to have—a context, and it is quite easy to lift a writer' s words from their surrounding apparatus, and make them mean something quite different from what the writer meant to say. For this reason, I've always been leery of newspaper interviews. If you make a fool of yourself on television, that's it. It's done, you've done it, and you've no one to blame but yourself. A reporter from the print media, on the other hand, if he doesn't like the lift of your eyebrow or the curl of your lip, can make you sound foolish right at his keyboard.

And as for sources who speak "on condition of anonymity," I've never met anyone who really wanted to be anonymous, aside from the writers of crank letters. In Philadelphia, I once telephoned a Main Line dowager whom I wanted to interview. She quickly agreed but added a warning. "In Philadelphia," she said, "we are *not* like New York. We do *not* like publicity. We do *not* like to see our names in print. I'll talk to you, but you must promise not to use my name." I promised—her name was not one that would have meant much to my readers, anyway—and when I got to her house, she spent over two hours telling me the most scandalous things about her friends and neighbors, defamatory gossip that even the *National Enquirer* would have qualified at printing. I left her, thinking that the whole afternoon had been a waste of time. But the next morning, she telephoned me to say, "I've been thinking about our conversation yesterday, and I've decided, on second thought, that you *may* use my name!"

I couldn't bring myself to tell her that I intended to use neither her name nor the scurrilous information she'd provided. It would have disappointed her too much.

Lillian Hellman, by contrast, was a writer who always spoke with great precision and great care. In conversations with her, you could almost see—on that craggy, furrowed, handsome face of hers—as she meticulously composed, and edited, her thoughts in her mind before uttering them. Lillian, to be sure, was sometimes accused of being untruthful in her work—most notably by Mary McCarthy who asserted, on national television, that every word Lillian wrote was a lie, including "the" and "and." The result was a lengthy lawsuit between Lillian and Mary that dragged on until both litigants were dead. It has been said that Lillian's account of her relationship with the great love of her life, Dashiell Hammett, was grossly exaggerated, and that Hammett had no more than a brief and passing interest in her. And a little research has shown that Lillian's story, "Julia," in her memoir, *Pentimento*, was almost certainly a total fiction, though she presented it as historical fact. Nonetheless, no one can deny that "Julia" made a hell of a good story.

When I was writing my biography of the novelist John Marquand, Lillian was one of many people I interviewed. She produced painstakingly articulate, perfectly phrased quotes. I was pleased, after the book was published, when Lillian telephoned me to say, "I don't think I have ever been so accurately quoted!"

It was a nice compliment but, if it was so, it was thanks to her, not me. As to whether the things she told me about Marquand were true or not, Marquand himself was by then dead, and so I have no idea.

Louis Auchincloss told me a lovely story about John Marquand. Gretchen Finletter, a popular New York hostess, had had a dinner party at her house, and the guests had included Auchincloss, Marquand, and Mrs. August Belmont, the Metropolitan Opera patroness. The conversation had turned to the terrible lack of taste and reticence in young people, which all the guests deplored. Marquand then changed the subject to some abdominal surgery he had recently undergone, after which some sessions of abdominal massage were prescribed. Marquand, according to Louis, then told the table of how a nurse, massaging him, had said,

"It's so wonderful, Mr. Marquand, to be able to rub the lower abdominal muscles of a man like you!" After a brief silence, Eleanor Belmont turned to him and said, somewhat icily, "And where, Mr. Marquand, is the taste and reticence in that anecdote?"

But there are a couple of things wrong with this story. Dana Atchley, Marquand's lifelong physician, told me that Marquand had never had any surgery, abdominal or otherwise. He had had a heart attack, but abdominal massage is never prescribed, and was certainly not prescribed by Dr. Atchley, for this ailment. And Mrs. Finletter, who did recall such a dinner gathering at her house, had no recollection of such an interchange. Furthermore, though she hadn't kept any record of it, she was sure that there had been no more than eight at her dinner table that night. Eight was her favorite number, and sixteen was the absolute capacity of her dining room. I, in the meantime, had come up with twenty-nine different people who, in slightly varying versions, told the same story, all of whom swore they had been at Gretchen Finletter's house that night.

"Never check out an interesting fact." Well, there are times when it is essential to do so. As I said earlier, I learned this the hard way. My source for this one was a highly respected small-town newspaper editor, and I was young enough—and foolish enough—to suppose that a highly respected small-town newspaper editor would not lie. He told me a story about a fellow in his town who was rabid on the subject of Roman Catholics. This man hated Catholics to the point of obsession. He was so obsessed on the subject that he offered to convert, free of charge, any Catholic to any other religion—Judaism, Protestantism, Buddhism, Shintoism. This man had had certain brushes with the law— arrested for passing out anti-Catholic literature on the playgrounds of parochial schools, for example. He and a lady friend often dressed up in costumes—he as a priest, and she as a nun—and put on performances for audiences of interested bigots, demonstrating the wicked lives led by the Catholic clergy in convents, monasteries, and seminaries. In these stage shows, the performers danced, held hands, embraced, and so on. But what my editor told me was that this same couple, in their liturgical garb, had driven out to a suburban shopping mall in an open convertible, where they had parked and, with the top down, in broad daylight, indulged in a heated necking session. Scandalized passersby murmured, "Look at that *priest* . . . with that *nun!*"

It was such a wonderful story I saw no need to check it out. "But I ought to warn you," the editor said, "this guy likes to sue people."

I paid no attention, wrote up the story, and it was published in a national magazine. I had not used the man's name, thinking that that would protect me, forgetting that the man in question was so notorious locally that everyone in the town knew who I was talking about. The man promptly sued me for $1 million on a charge of criminal libel. He went even further than that. He sued the publisher of the magazine, my literary agent, and even the printing press where the magazine was printed. Suddenly I found myself in a considerable mess.

The case dragged on for months, while my lawyers searched for evidence to back up my story. We found photographs of the "priest" and the "nun" dancing. We found photographs of them holding hands, and hugging. But I had said "necking," and we could find no photographic evidence of that. Furthermore, we could find no witnesses to the alleged event. My unimpeachable source, the newspaper editor, turned out not to be so unimpeachable. Yes, he said, he had heard the story, or something like it, but he had heard it from someone else—he couldn't remember who. Clearly, he didn't want to become entangled in the lawsuit. It began to seem as though the event I had reported had never actually happened.

Then we suddenly got lucky. Investigators my lawyers had hired discovered that the event I described had indeed happened, though it hadn't involved the people I said it had. Not directly, anyway. Instead, the performing couple had hired two teenagers to dress up in their costumes and go out and neck in the parking lot. Of course, I was still wrong, but these new embarrassing and sordid facts—plus the possibility of the illegality of hiring minors to put on such a performance—caused the plaintiff to lower his demands considerably. The case was settled for a small sum, though I was presented with a hefty legal bill. No, I would *not* encourage a young writer not to check the facts of an interesting story very carefully.

Still, it's hard to understand why a writer would accuse another writer of being a liar. We all lie, in ways large and small, but we call it by its euphemism, "creativity." Lying is one of the tools of our craft, part of the delicate tissue of trying to entertain, to amuse, to shock, to scare. It's what we wrap our surprises in—in what we hope will be our little gifts to our readers. None of us are expected to write what we write under oath. Mary McCarthy, I'm sure, was guilty of telling the occasional whopper in her time. I've known several of her Vassar classmates who recognized themselves in her novel, *The Group*, and who felt that she misrepresented their stories, falsified details of their lives, and in general treated them unfairly.

All writers are in the lying game, which may explain why writers distrust each other so. We're wise to our own unreliability. I'm often asked why, since 1975, I've made my home in the quiet, gentle, red brick riverbend city of Cincinnati, where the skyline still includes church steeples. There are three in the view from my hilltop windows right now. Don't I miss the excitement of New York, and the company of other writers? The answer is, not at all. One of the nicest things about Cincinnati is that there are very few writers here. Even nicer, we've never met each other. To me, there's nothing more discouraging than a roomful of writers, except possibly a roomful of actors who are usually "between engagements," which means out of work. When writers get together, they lie more enthusiastically than ever, and—worse—most of the time they lie about money.

Here is a typical exchange between two writers we might imagine meeting at the bar of such a writerly watering-place as Elaine's, on Manhattan's Upper East Side:

Writer number one: I see you've got a piece in this month's *Vanity Fair*.

Writer number two: (feigning modesty): Yeah.

Writer number one: How much did they pay you for it?

Writer number two: (pulls a wildly exaggerated figure out of his head.)

Writer number one: Hmmm. Gee, they pay me a lot more than that.

There are some writers who only lie occasionally. There are some writers who lie a lot. Then there was Truman Capote.

To me, Truman was a writer who became so addicted to telling lies that he couldn't stop. His lies became a narcotic to him, a monkey on his back, a habit he couldn't shake. And, like any other addict, his daily craving for new material to lie about escalated steadily until, at the end, he spun completely out of control. It was as though, when he couldn't lick it, his habit killed him: Death by falsehood. Even in death, he left more lies behind him.

This is not to say that when Capote wrote—which, as it turned out, was not all that often—he didn't write like an angel. He did; he was a brilliant writer, the envy of us all. But I always thought it was fortunate for him that in his masterpiece, *In Cold Blood*, all the principal characters were dead, so there was no one left to dispute him, or to claim that things hadn't happened quite the way he said they had. Publication of that book had to wait until Dick and Perry, the killer-heroes of the story, were finally hanged, and this was delayed by various appeals and stays of execution. I can remember Truman fuming, "Why can't the state of Kansas just *kill* those boys, so I can write my *ending*?"

Later, he wrote a beautiful short piece for the *New Yorker* called "Music for Chameleons," about a West Indian woman whose piano playing had the effect of drawing dozens of small lizards into her house to listen. The trouble was, when others tried to track down this woman in order to observe the phenomenon, she could not be found.

The stories he told in person were even more fanciful and farfetched than that—though not always as delicious. Whether it was a black-tie dinner at Gloria Vanderbilt's town house or swathed in a towel in the locker room of the Continental Baths, all it took was a lull in the conversation to send Truman off and running on one of his outlandish flights, speaking in his breathy, italicized style: "I was standing in the men's room at the *Ritz*, doing what one does *naturally*, and who should walk in but Indira Gandhi. She walked into a *booth*, and without even closing the *door*, she lifted up the skirts of her sari, sat down, and *farted*."

"I was having dinner at the Vatican with the pope and some of the younger, more *attractive* cardinals, and the cardinals were passing around, under the *table*, some really *dirty* pictures. His Holiness noticed this and asked to look at one of them. One of the cardinals handed him one, and John Paul looked at it, and then said to the cardinal, 'Your sister, I presume?'"

"I was having dinner at the White House, and Jackie asked me to come up to her bedroom. 'Look what I found in Jack's dresser drawer,' she said, and it was dozens and *dozens* of *condoms*."

On and on it went like that. There was no stopping him. It was all wonderfully entertaining stuff, of course, and it was easy to see why, for a while, he was much in demand as a guest at fashionable New York parties until he turned the tables on his hosts and hostesses and began telling vicious and scandalous stories about *them*. There were many dinner-at-the-White-House stories, and one of these, involving the writer Gore Vidal, so enraged Vidal that he sued Truman for libel, and won. It hadn't taken Vidal much research to find out that Capote had never been a guest at the White House. Many of the tallest of these tales made their way into Truman's official biography, by Gerald Clarke, who seems never to have questioned their veracity. And so now they stand immortalized, enshrined in the Library of Congress.

The last time I saw Capote, not many months before he died, was at his New York apartment at United Nations Plaza. For the better part of twenty years, he had been talking, in television talk show interviews—which had become his principal form of artistic expression—about the Proustian magnum opus he was writing, a novel with the beautiful title of *Answered Prayers*. Over the years, short bits, and snippets of this had appeared in various magazines, and his fans were salivating to see the completed whole. "It's *finished!*" he crowed that night in his apartment. "It's finished—my *arbeit*. All I'm doing now is some final polishing of the jewel!" To prove it, he lifted a great stack of paper from a drawer and brandished it in front of us. "Here it *is*," he squealed. "Here it is—all of it!" He replaced the stack of paper, and stood there, swaying slightly, a drink sloshing in his hand.

He was wearing a T-shirt and blue jeans. He had started out as a wispy, winsome lad with a gardenia-like complexion, but by now too many rich dinners and far too much wine had transformed him, almost literally, into a balding Mr. Five-by-Five. As he stood there—talking, swaying, drinking—the waistband of his jeans crept inexorably downward across the bulge of his great belly. Soon it had fallen below the line of his pubic hair, but he seemed unaware of this. Finally, a friend stepped over to him and gently hitched up his trousers for him before they cascaded to his ankles. He seemed oblivious of this kind gesture and did not acknowledge it.

"My novel will be the first novel in history that will have an *index!*" he exulted.

"Vladimir Nabokov's novel, *Pale Fire*, had an index," I pointed out to him.

He gave me a narrow look. He did not like me much, certainly not just then.

"But my novel will have a *real* index," he said at last. "The index to *Pale Fire* wasn't a real index."

And yet, when he died, real index or not, no manuscript of *Answered Prayers* could be found among his effects. Then what did that stack of pages consist of when he pulled them out that night? Just blank sheets of typewriter paper, I suppose. Whenever someone asks me what I'm working on, I usually try to dodge the question, and give some vague, evasive answer. I'm a little superstitious in that regard. If a writer talks too much about a book he's writing, it doesn't get written. Perhaps that's what happened to Truman, as a result of all those talk show interviews. The most talked-about book of the period turned out to be the book he wasn't writing. Or perhaps he'd talked about his novel so much that he actually believed he was writing it.

Perhaps he'd fallen into that final, fatal trap of the most prodigious liars. They begin to believe their own lies.

Someone—I can't remember who it was—once said, "Beginning writers are influenced. Mature writers steal." And it's true that we writers do commit larcenies, both grand and petty. I'm not talking about plagiarism. I'm talking about the way we pick up little pieces of other peoples' lives as we pass through them, and pocket them, the way one might pocket an ashtray from a swank hotel. We are always pinching material that wasn't really ours to take. This is why I often think writers are dangerous people to have as friends.

I'll give you a personal example. I was talking, several years ago, to one of the daughters of the late Julius Rosenwald, the founder of Sears, Roebuck & Co. She said, "You knew we children had two different sets of parents, didn't you?"

I asked her what she meant, and it was this. When the senior Rosenwalds were first married, they had three children in quite rapid succession. These children knew a mother who scrubbed the kitchen floor on her hands and knees and packed their father's lunch in a paper bag. At night, their parents tucked them into bed, and sang them lullabies. There followed a hiatus of eight years, and then two more children were born. In those eight years, Julius Rosenwald had become rich. These younger children were raised in a mansion on Chicago's North Shore, with a guard in a sentry box by the gate. They were brought up by governesses and nannies, while their parents toured the country in their private railroad car or set off for Europe in their yacht. When their mother was home, these children were allowed a fifteen-minute visit with her at teatime. They hardly saw their father at all.

The younger two children resented the older set because it seemed to them, they had received so much more of their parents' love. The older three children resented the younger ones because they had so much more money.

I quickly snatched this situation from its rightful owners and made it the basis of the plot for my novel *The Auerbach Will*.

After my first nonfiction book, *"Our Crowd,"* was published, and became a surprise best seller, there was a certain amount of huffing and puffing and sword-rattling among New York's *haut Juif* set. One of its most offended members, it seemed, was Gerald Warburg, one of Felix Warburg's sons. He kept calling me up and screaming at me about how I was "airing the family's dirty linen in public." At first, I had no idea what Gerald Warburg was talking about, and he was too angry to articulate it, but I finally discovered what it was.

I had written about Felix Warburg's many philanthropies, particularly in the musical arts. He had set up many musical scholarships and had made many promising musical students his personal protégés. A number of the latter, I added, had remained his lifelong friends, and I mentioned a few names—among them Hulda Lashanska, a German singer who sang the lieder. Well, it seemed—though I didn't know it when I was writing the book—that Mme. Lashanska had been much more than a lifelong friend. She had been Felix Warburg's mistress for more than thirty years. She lived with the family in the great house at 1109 Fifth Avenue, which is now the Jewish Museum. Her bedroom was next door to Mr. Warburg's and Mrs. Warburg slept down the hall. This design-for-living arrangement was further complicated by the fact that, as far as anyone could tell, Mrs. Warburg and Mme. Lashanska were the dearest of friends. They lunched together often at the Plaza, went to the theater and opera together, and even traveled to Europe together as a twosome.

Still, it must have been a confusing—even painful—situation for the Warburg children when they were growing up, as witness Gerald's rage at the mere mention of Lashanska's name, even though the three principal players in the drama were by then long dead.

Anyway, I liked the story well enough to pinch it, change the names and venue, and use it in a novel.

In another of our *"Our Crowd"* families, the Lewisohns, there was a mystery. Adolph Lewisohn, the founder of the family fortune, had a younger brother whose name, I think, was Julius. Even his name was part of the mystery because he disappeared from all the records and memorabilia at about the age of twenty. His name was excised from the family tree. His picture was not just turned against the wall, it was destroyed. In group photographs, his face was cut from the prints with a razor blade. He became a nonperson. What had this young man done to deserve this treatment? Was he gay? Did he go to jail? Had he been insane, and been institutionalized? Or was he guilty of an even greater sin, marrying the wrong sort of girl—a Christian or, what would have been far more unforgivable in the family's eyes in those days, an "Oriental" Jewess from Russia or Poland? There were a number of living relatives of this young man at the time who must have known the answer. But, if they did, they were not telling me. In the meantime, the situation intrigued me enough to use it as a plot element in my novel, *The Auerbach Will*, where I would invent a solution to the riddle.

Years later, one of Adolph Lewisohn's granddaughters confided the dark family secret to me. "He was a homosexual," she whispered. As it turned out, I had guessed right.

To most writers the urge to purloin a good tale is irresistible. A number of years ago, a fellow writer-friend recounted the following story:

My friend had been rushing to meet a deadline that day and had skipped lunch. Much of his hurry was due to the fact that he'd promised a hostess in Connecticut that he'd catch the 4:23 train out of Grand Central to Westport, Connecticut, where he was to be met and driven to a cocktail party hosted by a couple he'd never met, but where he was to be the celebrity guest of honor. He'd made it to the train, and to the party, but that was virtually the last thing he remembered of the evening, except that, on his empty stomach, he had probably had a few more drinks than was his custom.

The next thing he knew was when he awoke in an unfamiliar bed, in his undershorts, in a strange, dark bedroom. He groped about in the darkness for a light. Touching a bedside table, he tried to find a lamp, and, in this process, his hand brushed against an object and knocked it to the floor. Reaching down to discover what it was, his hand touched something wet on the carpet. It appeared he'd knocked over a glass of water. He felt about for broken glass, but apparently there was none, and so he got out of bed and began feeling along the walls for a light switch. He finally found one and turned on the lights.

He discovered that what had knocked off the table was an inkwell, and his inky fingerprints were arrayed across the walls of the room against what looked like fresh, and rather expensive wallpaper. In a panic, he raced into the bathroom, found a washcloth, and began trying to wash the inky stains off the walls and white carpet. But soapy water only made the ink stains bigger and more pronounced. Miserably, he decided the only thing to do was to go back to bed and wait for morning.

In the morning, he awoke, dressed himself, and made his way downstairs where he found his hostess of the night before at the breakfast table.

"I'm terribly sorry . . ." he began.

"Oh, you were perfectly fine," his hostess said. "You just had a bit too much to drink, but our guests loved meeting you. Fortunately, there were two strong men who carried you upstairs to the guest room."

"You mean I . . . passed out. and had to be carried."

"You were perfectly fine," she said. "Don't think a thing about it. Fortunately, my decorator had just finished redoing the guest room."

"There was an inkwell beside my bed," my friend said. "I'm afraid I accidentally tipped it over."

Her fingers went to her throat. "The white V'Soske carpet?" she said.

"Yes, and I'm afraid—the wallpaper."

"The wallpaper? Well, don't think a thing about it. I'm sure the carpet can be cleaned. And the wallpaper—well, I was never that crazy about it. Sit down and have some breakfast."

"I'm terribly sorry."

"Please don't think a thing about it. Please sit down."

With that, he pulled out a chair and sat down. There was a horrible screech, but it was too late. He had sat on the family cat and killed it.

"Please don't think a thing about it," his hostess kept repeating. "Don't think a thing about it."

Of course, this story is almost too good to be true. It has the requisite three parts—the beginning, the middle, and the end—that a writer looks for: the passing-out, the ink, the cat. And did it ever happen—to anyone? I have no idea, but I'm almost certain it didn't happen to the fellow who told the story to me. Over the years, I've heard the story from several other people. It happened in Beverly Hills. It happened in Palm Beach. It happened in Seattle. The details are nearly always the same. An inkwell is nearly always pivotal. But sometimes the cat is a small dog. It always ends the same.

But the discerning reader might ask a few questions. Why would an inkwell be placed on a bedside table in a guest room? And who, in this day and age, uses inkwells?

Still, the story is so delicious that I've sometimes been tempted to steal it, and claim it happened to me. In fact, if it weren't for the incongruity of that inkwell . . . .

I've often wondered how these maybe-true-but-probably-not stories get started, and I think I have a clue or two.

For one thing, they all contain certain elements in common.

They frequently hinge upon the unlikely placement of an object, such as an inkwell on a nightstand. I'm thinking of the Bloomingdale's ladies' room story, for example, which has circulated around New York for years, attributed to various people, usually a "close friend" of the tale's narrator. In this account, a Manhattan matron has stepped into the ladies' room at Bloomingdale's to refresh herself. Once inside her cubicle, she slung her handbag by its strap over the hook on the inside of the door. Settled there, and temporarily incapacitated, she was aghast to see a woman's hand extend over the top of the door and sweep away her bag. As soon as she was able to pull herself together, she reported the caper to the store's security office. It was not so much the cash in her purse, she explained— no more than $30—but the loss of other personal objects in her bag that distressed her: house keys, credit and library cards, her driver's license, and baby pictures of her children that could never be replaced.

The security people were sympathetic but explained that there was really little they could do at that point. They did, however, take down her name, address, and telephone number, and promised to get in touch with her if anything turned up. The distraught woman returned home, many blocks uptown.

Later that afternoon, her telephone rang, and the caller identified herself as a member of Bloomingdale's security staff. The stolen bag had been found in the store; she was told. The cash purse was empty, but everything else—keys, credit cards, and the precious baby pictures— appeared to be intact. If the shopper would return to the store right away, with some form of identification, the bag and its contents would be returned to her. She departed at once for the store.

But when she got there, no one knew what she was talking about. No bag had been recovered. No one in the security office had made that tele-phone call. Again, the store was sympathetic; there must have been some sort of mix-up. The poor woman went home again, more distraught than ever, only to find that her apartment had been thoroughly burglarized.

Once again, the story divides itself neatly into three parts: setting the stage, the theft of the bag, and the surprising denouement. Once again, the tale involves the inappropriate placement of an object—the bag on the hook. Over the years, I've asked various women friends what they do with their handbags when visiting a public ladies' room. Their answers are nearly always the same. They might hang a coat or jacket on a hook, but never a bag with valuables in it. Nor would they set it on the floor, where it could be temptingly within reach of the occupant of the adjacent booth. On the lap seems to be the preferred positioning of such an important accessory to a woman's wardrobe.

And not long ago, on a short shuttle flight from Washington, I found myself in conversation with my seatmate who turned out, of all things, to work for Bloomingdale's security department. I asked him if he had ever heard this story, or one like it. He smiled faintly. Yes, he had, and he had heard it more than once, with slightly varying details. But to his knowledge nothing of the sort had ever happened at the store. "Why is it always Bloomingdale's?" he wondered aloud. "Why doesn't it ever happen at Saks or Lord & Taylor?" I suggested that it was probably because Bloomingdale's is New York's most celebrated store, the only one that Queen Elizabeth wanted to visit on her first trip to the city.

Quite often these dubious tales involve the death of a pet—a dog, if not a cat. There's the one about a New York hostess who, having been presented with a box of rare wild mushrooms, decided to try a few of them out on her dog a few hours before having her cook prepare them for dinner guests that evening. The dog gobbled up the mushrooms without any apparent ill effect, and so the delicacies were served at the table that night. But in the middle of dinner her cook appeared from the kitchen and whispered in the hostess's ear, "The dog is dead!"

Immediately the hostess rose to the occasion, announced that the mushrooms they had all just eaten were apparently poisonous, and that she was summoning an ambulance to rush the entire party to a nearby emergency room to have their stomachs pumped out. That ordeal over, the hostess returned home and found her cook in the kitchen. "Where's the dog?" she wanted to know. "Why, he's still out in the street where the car hit him," was her cook's reply.

And sometimes the victim is a human, not an animal. A Manhattan couple were on a motoring trip in Canada with their children, accompanied by an elderly grandmother. One morning, a knock on the door of Granny's motel room failed to rouse her. The couple entered the room to find that Granny had died in her sleep. In a quandary as to what to do next, the couple telephoned their lawyer in New York. The problem, a lawyer explained to them, was that Granny had expired in a foreign country. A great deal of bureaucratic red tape, not to mention expense, would be involved in shipping a corpse across national borders. "If you can bring yourselves to do this," the lawyer advised the couple, "I'd put Granny in the trunk of the car and drive back into New York State as quickly as possible. Once you're across the border, everything will be simple."

But what about going through Customs? The couple wanted to know. "Just pray that they don't ask you to open the trunk," was the lawyer's reply.

Well, it seems the couple did as the lawyer suggested, and the family made it across the border without incident. But, once safely back in the United States, everyone was in such an anxious state that the first thing everyone had to do was go to the bathroom. They pulled into the nearest service station, and each member of the party dispersed himself and herself in the appropriate directions.

But when they returned, the car was gone. In their haste, the keys had been left in the ignition, and the car had been stolen. To this day, neither the car nor Granny's corpse has ever been seen or heard from again. Interestingly, this is another story of a theft involving a public toilet.

I began collecting these no doubt apocryphal tales several years ago when, with a little frisson of recognition, I discovered that I had become the originator of just such a myth myself. Of course, to confess to having created a myth is the same as admitting that I once told a lie. It was not a major lie, perhaps, but it was certainly a conscious distortion of the truth, a misrepresentation of fact, a quite deliberate failure to attribute a story to its correct source. I confess this now only to help explain how myths get into circulation. And also to make the point that all of us lie a <u>little</u> now and then, and that, when we hear a temptingly lively anecdote, it is hard for some of us to resist the temptation to take a small moral sidestep and, with that out of the way, to appropriate that story either as our own or as the property of someone we know well.

I can't remember the exact date when I took one of these little side-steps, but it would have been sometime in the late 1950s and I recall the circumstances well. I was having lunch at the University Club in New York with my friend and literary agent, Carol Brandt, who, with her husband Carl, ran the venerable New York agency of Brandt & Brandt, now Brandy & Hochman Literary Agents, Inc. Until 2013, the agency was headed by her son, another Carl, who died in 2013. Carol Brandt was telling me a story about one of her favorite clients from the past, a writer named Frederick Faust, whom everybody called Heinie.

I never knew Heinie Faust, but there are many lovely stories about him. He was apparently a big teddy bear of a man, with many friends and a wide acquaintanceship. He was also a writer who dreamed of one day writing the Great American Novel. That dream forever eluded him, but, instead, he wrote a great deal of what he wrote very well: pulp fiction.

It was said that he was saving his real name to attach to the master-work that was never written. In the meantime, he wrote under a variety of pseudonyms, the most famous of which was probably Max Brand, the name under which he produced a long series of novels and short stories about a character called Dr. Kildare. Readers of the pulps snapped up his Dr. Kildare stories, and so did Hollywood. In the decade between 1937 and 1947, the Dr. Kildare series of films became one of the most popular and successful series ever produced by Metro-Goldwyn Mayer. In all, there were sixteen Dr. Kildare movies. In the year 1940 alone, three Dr. Kildare films were released. Three more followed in 1942. In most of these, Lew Ayres appeared in the title role, and his kindly, curmudgeonly medical cohort, Dr. Gillespie, was played by Lionel Barrymore in a wheelchair. Any number of actors and actresses who later became major stars got their start appearing in Dr. Kildare pictures, including Lana Turner, Ava Gardner, Robert Young, Laraine Day, Van Johnson, and Red Skelton. The film series became a radio series and, in due course, a series for television. It could truly be said that every television drama or soap opera with a hospital setting owes a debt to Dr. Kildare.

Dr. Kildare earned Heine Faust millions of dollars, but no amount of money, it seemed, could quite match the Fausts' capacity for spending it, which was prodigious. Faust and his wife Dorothy lived in a lavish villa on the Italian Riviera, where they entertained like mad and where Faust demonstrated an equally prodigious capacity for alcohol. Like a Depression-era version of Zelda and Scott Fitzgerald, life for the Faust's became a continuous house party. Faust was like Fitzgerald in other ways. Though he had become one of the highest-paid writers in America, he was nearly always broke.

At one point—and this was the point of Carol Brandt's story to me at lunchtime—the Fausts' financial straits became so desperate that the couple set sail for New York to seek help from Brandt & Brandt. Naturally, they traveled First Class.

Scott Fitzgerald—sometimes sending Zelda on the begging mission—was occasionally able to borrow money from his agent, Harold Ober. But Carl Brandt was firm in his resolve never to get involved in that sort of thing with Heinie. His solution was to let the Fausts stay at the Brandts' Manhattan apartment, where Heinie was given a room, as far removed from the liquor closet as possible, with a typewriter and plenty of paper, where he could pound out more Dr. Kildare stories for the pulps and for the films. Carol Brandt's assignment was to take Dorothy Faust aside and give her a few lessons in thrift: the importance of setting up a household budget and sticking to it strictly; of shopping at the A&P rather than Maison Glass; of looking for sales and bargains, and collecting in-store coupons.

Dorothy Faust had listened politely to these tips on domestic economies for a while. Then she looked at her watch, and said, "Excuse me, but I must telephone Italy. I forgot to remind my butler that there are a dozen breakfast trays that need to be sent to Milano to be re-lacquered."

"When she said that," Carol said to me, "I knew I was never going to get anywhere with Dorothy."

Now I must digress briefly with a few words about the late Carol Brandt. She was a tall, handsome, and elegantly dressed woman, who was often swathed in furs and was usually gloved and hatted. As a younger woman, she was often mistaken for the film actress Mary Astor. She lived in a grand apartment with a dramatic view of Central Park and the reservoir, furnished with splendid American antiques and an imposing collection of Steuben glass. There was a certain imperiousness about Carol, a certain theatricality. Some people found her intimidating. Like her friend the publisher Blanche Knopf, she was fond of large, important pieces of jewelry, and these appeared on her person in the forms of chunky rings, bracelets, necklaces, earrings, and glittering pins and brooches. Someone once said of her, "Literary agents are supposed to be little brown wrens who scuttle about with rolled umbrellas. Carol Brandt makes *writers* feel like little brown wrens with rolled umbrellas." In her prime, when I first knew her, she was known as the Queen Bee of New York agents, and I'm sure she enjoyed that title to the hilt. Flamboyant might be too strong an adjective to describe her but suffice it to say that she was a woman who never entered a room unnoticed. I adored her.

Not long after that lunch with Carol, I was again lunching in New York with another friend. I don't remember who this was, but I do know that it was a man in no way connected with the worlds of writing and publishing. He couldn't have been, or he wouldn't have asked me the question that he did. During lunch, he asked me, "What's this Mrs. Brandt like?" I thought a moment, trying to find some words that would properly sum her up. Finally, I said, "Well, she's the kind of woman who once interrupted a business meeting to phone her butler, reminding him to send a dozen breakfast trays to Milan for re-lacquering."

Of course, it wasn't true and more accurately attributable to Dorothy Faust, but it somehow seemed to capture Carol's persona. It sounded like her. It was something I could almost imagine her doing. And she did have a butler.

Now, years pass. Envision, if you will, the calendar pages fluttering across the screen, the way they used to in old movies. It is now the early 1970s, some fifteen years later, and I am living in Rye, New York. Down the pike, in Larchmont, live friends Jean and Walter Kerr, he the distinguished drama critic and she the wonderfully comic author and playwright, who is just as amusing in person as she is on the printed page. The Kerrs have come to my house for dinner.

I'd been aware that Jean and Walter Kerr had both been clients of Brandt & Brandt, and so, during the course of the evening, I was a little surprised to learn that they no longer used the Brandts and had gone to another agency.

"What happened?" I asked Walter Kerr.

"Oh, Carol Brandt is just too la-di-da for us," he said.

I asked him what he meant.

"In the middle of a business meeting, she suddenly telephoned her butler to ask him to send a dozen breakfast trays to Milan to be re-lacquered," he said.

I was too astonished to reply. My own falsehood had come back to me intact, almost verbatim. It had come full circle, after what sort of a long, roundabout route I couldn't imagine, through all those torn-off calendar pages blowing in the wind.

At the time, Jean Kerr had a hit play, *Mary, Mary*, on Broadway. Walter Kerr was sort of an emeritus drama critic for the *New York Times* and would soon have an important midtown Manhattan theater named after him at 219 West 48th Street. So, I somehow couldn't bring myself to say to him, "Walter, that's not true!" Like so many other maybe-true-but-probably-not stories, this one involved a theft: my stolen anecdote. In the other stories, there is usually a victim, and in this case, there were two: Walter and me. All I could do was blush at what could have been our mutual embarrassment. But I often wonder what would have been his reaction if I'd said, "Walter, that was my lie. I stole it first."

CHAPTER FIVE

Two Steves

STEVE:

AT THE BEGINNING OF OUR FRESHMAN YEAR AT WILLIAMS COLLEGE IN 1946, all freshmen were asked to arrive a week before the start of classes in order to participate in a general orientation of the campus, as well as to take part in "rush week," during which the dozen or so Greek letter fraternities (Williams was an all-male institution in those days) sized up the incoming underclassmen and decided which were deemed worthy to be invited to join their clubs.

The fraternity situation at Williams was, I knew, a little lopsided at the time. Nearly eighty percent of the students belonged to fraternities. The others, the fraternity rejects—or those who simply had no interest in joining a fraternity—were relegated to something called the Garfield Club. The Garfield Club was more of a social club and clubhouse and occupied a building on the other side of the campus, far from Fraternity Row. Garfield Club members had no power on campus, political or otherwise. They were not even pariahs. They were simply ignored. They were nonpersons, and nobody knew their names. The Garfield Club was dissolved in 1952. If the Club had weekend parties, as the fraternities did, nobody heard about them. Clearly, if one was going to be a full-fledged Williams man, one was supposed to join a fraternity. This was all made clear to us during rush week.

As a scholarship student, I had no idea whether my father would allow me to join a fraternity. Fraternity membership meant monthly dues, plus an initiation fee, and it would not have surprised me if he had come back with his usual reaction, that he couldn't afford this additional expense. On the other hand, he had been a member of Phi Gamma Delta at Trinity College, and often spoke warmly of the good times there, and so it struck me that I might have a chance. I decided to participate in rush week and was rather pleased to receive second bids from eleven of the twelve houses, who invited me back for a second look-over. After that, I was supposed to narrow down my personal choices to three houses and, if all three still wanted me, I was to take my pick and become a pledge to that house.

One balmy evening of that first week at college, I was walking down the street on my way from the Freshman Quad to my third interview at the Beta Theta Pi house when a slightly built young fellow fell into step with me, and said, "Hi. My name is Steve, the same as yours. "I asked him where he was headed. "Beta Theta Pi," he said. "Same as you. "I was surprised that he seemed to know so much about me, including my name, since I couldn't recall having laid eyes on him before. He told me that his full name was Stephen Sondheim, and that he had pretty much decided to make Beta Theta Pi his final choice. We walked together to the Beta house. It was a calm beginning to a long and intensely complicated relationship.

I'd pretty much decided on Beta Theta Pi myself, and for reasons that—as it turned out—were based on some horrible in-house error. At the other houses I'd visited for my second round of interviews, I'd been chatted to by a steady stream of members. The interviewing teams worked in relays. One member would greet me at the door, talk with me for a few minutes, and then another member would appear to relieve the first. By the end of the hour-long visit, I would have talked to as many as twenty different members—all pleasant, but rather forced small talk, of course, and by the time the interview period was over, all the names and faces of the men I'd talked to were blurred and indistinguishable.

But Beta Theta Pi seemed to operate on a different system. The whole time I was there I was interviewed by only one member. After the first five minutes of our talk, this fellow began to appear decidedly ill at ease. He was visibly perspiring. Of course, there was a reason for his distress. He was wondering what had become of his replacement, who was overdue but who, through some behind-the-scenes mix-up, never did appear. He had run out of questions to ask me. He was like a stage actor who, having delivered his cue line for the next performer's entrance, finds himself alone on an empty stage. He repeats the entrance cue more loudly, but still nothing happens.

Hoping to make him feel more comfortable, I began asking this young man questions about himself. It turned out he had an interesting history. He was a member, he told me, of the Oxford Group, a Buchmanite. He explained how this movement had been founded, back in the 1920s, by a German American, Frank Buchman, who claimed to have had a vision of the Cross in the English Lake District. Buchman had worked as an evangelist-missionary for the YMCA in Asia. He claimed to be able to "change lives" through something called the First Century Christian Fellowship and had organized groups all over the world under the general rubric of Moral Rearmament. All this stuff was new to me, and fascinating. My interviewer, I decided, was a bit of an oddball, but an interesting oddball, and a nice oddball. And I thought: How nice. Instead of giving me a parade of interviewers whom I never got to know at all, they gave me just one guy whom I really got to know quite well.

Steve Sondheim, it turned out, had quite a different reason for wanting to join Beta Theta Pi. Upon joining, he would become that fraternity's first Jewish member. Back at the fraternity's national headquarters, in Oxford, Ohio, there had already been a good deal of huffing and puffing about this. But the Williams chapter, in a spirit of postwar enlightenment, had determined to break the old gentlemen's agreement. And Steve had all the qualifications for membership. He was good-looking and well-dressed. His father was, in the parlance of the times, well off. And at the George School in Pennsylvania, where he had gone before Williams, he had been a brilliant, straight-A student. Steve himself had no objection to being Beta Theta Pi's token Jew; in fact, he relished the idea. After all, most of the Jews on campus ended up in the Garfield Club. Even as a sixteen-year-old freshman, Stephen Sondheim was a star. Attention was to be paid.

(There was only one Black member of my class of 1950 at Williams. He, of course, was in the Garfield Club. I can't recall any Asiatic or

Hispanic classmates at all. Later, as upperclassmen, we wanted to take a Black freshman into Beta Theta Pi. Steve Sondheim joined me in this effort. But such was the outcry from Oxford, Ohio—with threats to cut us off from funds—that we caved in. Not many years after we all graduated, fraternities at Williams were abolished altogether.)

After being pledged to Beta Theta Pi, there followed several weeks of performing "pledge duties." These involved memorizing certain sacred Beta songs and chants, addressing all upperclassmen as "sir," running little errands for them, and doing chores such as dusting, running the vacuum cleaner, and waiting on tables in the dining room. Then, just before the ritual of initiation, came what was known as Hell Week.

We'd all heard lurid stories about what went on during Hell Week. Pledges were forced to eat human feces. (At least they were told it was human feces; it was in fact just peanut butter). A pledge would be driven miles from Williamstown, stripped of his clothes, and left by the side of the road in the winter night to fend for himself. We Beta pledges braced ourselves for the worst. As it turned out, I handled my own Hell Week experience rather cleverly.

Late one night, asleep in my bed in the dorm, I felt the bedclothes being yanked off of me and knew something was up. Two strong young men—I never did get a good look at their faces—lifted me by the ankles and armpits and carried me into the shower, where they dropped me on the floor and turned-on cold water. I decided to play dead, and just lay there, trying not to breathe, while the cold water poured over me. Soon I heard their whispers. "My God, did we—" "Is he all right?" "Did he hit his head on something?" "Do you think it's a concussion?" "Let's get him out of here!" The water was quickly turned off, and the two lifted me again. I made myself a limp, dead weight, my eyes still closed. They carried me back to my room, stripped off my sopping pajamas, found a dry pair for me, and pulled me into those. Then they lifted me back onto my bed, pulled the covers up around me, and tucked me in. At one point, I let my eyelids flutter open and murmured groggily, "Wha—wha happened?" "Don't worry," they whispered, "you'll be all right." Then they tiptoed away, and that was the end of Hell Week for me.

Steve's father, Herbert Sondheim, was an extremely successful dress manufacturer on Seventh Avenue. The elder Sondheim's dresses were sold at such high-end retail outlets as Bendel's, Bergdorf's, Saks, and Neiman-Marcus. Steve's mother, Frances Sondheim, whom everyone called Foxy, had been her husband's chief designer. But there had been a bitter divorce, Herbert Sondheim had remarried, and most of Steve's growing-up years had been spent with Foxy.

From early on, it seemed, Foxy Sondheim had decided that her son was a musical genius. At the age of twelve or thereabout he had written a full-length musical comedy. To help further her son's career in musical theater, Foxy had bought a house in New Hope, Pennsylvania, near where her friends Dorothy and Oscar Hammerstein II had a home. The Hammersteins had a son roughly Steve's age, and Foxy's hope had been that the famous lyricist would take her son under his wing and make him a sort of protégé—which Oscar Hammerstein had generously done. Steve always referred to the older man fondly as "Ockie."

But, despite his mother's doting gesture, it puzzled me to discover, from our earliest acquaintanceship, that Steve appeared at the time to have some contempt for his mother. I used to ask him why he appeared to have such ambivalent feelings toward her to such a degree. Well, for one thing, he alleged, she seemed to only want to associate with rich and famous people. That didn't strike me as so awful. After all, as a top designer, she needed well-known names and faces to buy and display her clothes, didn't she? She was also an uncompromising hostess, he claimed. "Everything has to be cooked in wine," he said. "The lobster was cooked in wine. She'll have a dinner party, and announce, the string beans were cooked in wine." All in all, that did not seem so bad.

The irony of all this was brought home to me a couple of years later, when I met Foxy Sondheim at a cocktail party in New York. When she learned that her son and I were classmates at Williams, she said, "You know my Stevie is a true genius, don't you?" A small, animated woman, her voice rose with enthusiasm as she extolled her son's talents. "He was always a gifted child, a true prodigy. He'll be incredibly famous one day, wait and see. He's going to be the next George Gershwin—or even greater than that! My son is going to be to twentieth-century music what

Mozart was to the eighteenth! Do you realize that?" she repeated, jabbing her finger at my chest for emphasis. "Do you realize how great his talent is?" Perhaps her sin was loving her son too much.

Meanwhile, at Williams, Steve Sondheim and I had become known as "the two Steves." (There was actually a third Steve in our class, but he was one of those returning-war-veteran types, and he spelled his name Stefan, and was not in our league.) We were conspicuous not only because we were the two youngest members of the class, but—so it appeared, when the grades from the first marking period were posted— we were also the two smartest. There were not many jocks in the Beta house. The jocks tended to be Phi Delts, while the Dekes were the real Animal House. The Betas prided themselves on their scholastic standing. Now, thanks to Steve and myself, the Betas had become the top-ranking fraternity, scholastically, on the Williams campus. And we'd both started shaving only a couple of years before.

From all of this, our classmates assumed that Steve and I must be the best of buddies. This was not the case.

There was no question but that Stephen Sondheim was very, very bright. For their final examination in the Music Major course, the students were given a one-sentence assignment: Compose a sonata. They were given three hours to do this. Steve Sondheim completed his composition in less than half an hour, turned in his paper, and walked out of the examination room whistling. Needless to say, he got an A-plus.

But long before that moment, I had begun to see a change come over him. The modest, almost shy boy who had caught up with me on the sidewalk during rush week ("Hi, my name's Steve, the same as yours") had begun developing a new persona, now that he suddenly found himself, early in freshman year, a big man on campus.

My own braininess always seemed to express itself best on paper. In a classroom, I tended to listen, and not to express strongly or harshly worded opinions. Steve was just the opposite. He had a brilliant and witty tongue, and his opinions were nearly always expressed caustically. I soon found that I could not be in conversation with him for awfully long without experiencing a kind of dull ache somewhere behind my eyes. Verbally, he was always getting the better of me. He invited unflattering nicknames for some of our classmates. Dominick Dunne, for instance, was "Dominick Dung." Because he announced that he found me "hopelessly naive," he called me "Na-Steve." He was a master of the verbal put-down.

In the late 1940s, a new young writer came bursting on the literary scene. His name was J. D. Salinger, and the first Salinger story to catch our collective attention, published in the *New Yorker*, was called "A Perfect Day for Bananafish." We were bowled over by this story, with its dark suggestions of pedophilia and the strong phallic implications of its title. We who dreamed of one day becoming writers were dazzled by such technical effects as Salinger's use of italics ("Oh, what's the *difference*, Mother?") Whereas most young writers tend to overpower their fiction with too much detail, Salinger's power seemed to come from how much he'd left out—leaving the reader to imagine a whole landscape of meanings and emotions. With a single, quick detail—a girl "putting her weight on her right leg"—he could say more about the girl's character, background, and even physical appearance than most of us would have spent a paragraph trying to do. On top of everything else, there was the mystery surrounding Salinger himself—who he was, where he'd come from—a mystery that continues to surround the reclusive author to this day. For days after it appeared, all anyone could talk about were the wonders of "Bananafish."

That is, until we learned what Steve Sondheim thought of the story. "It's a very careless, very amateurish piece of work," he announced. "The author hasn't thought the situation through at all. Take the character of the little girl, Sybil. He writes that Sybil won't need the bra top of her swimsuit for another 'nine or ten years.' What age do girls start wearing bras? Twelve or thirteen? That makes Sybil about three years old. Yet her mother wanders off to leave this kid, who's not much more than a toddler, and who can't swim, alone and untended on a Florida beach while Mom has a cocktail with a friend—and while the kid could be picked up by any sort of pervert, and almost is. Would any mother, no matter how awful, do a thing like that? But that's a relatively minor point. The main flaw in the story is: Why would Seymour Glass, who's supposed to be this sweet, sensitive, poetic, *bruised* guy, ever have been attracted to a vain, shallow, dumb clotheshorse like Muriel—much less have *married* her? That's what's totally unbelievable. And as for the ending—Seymour puts a bullet through his head. That's nothing but pure, cheap shock melodrama."

Of course, the trouble with Steve's analysis of the story was that, once you thought about it, he was absolutely right. Much as we'd all admired the story, now that Steve had demolished it for us so thoroughly, we had to admit that "Bananafish" didn't make a hell of a lot of sense. We were left wondering why no one else had thought of these points before

Sacred cows were among Steve's favorite targets, and the greater the icon, the greater was his relish in removing it from its pedestal. My generation—as well as that of my parents and grandparents—had always been taught that the greatest writer in the English language, and of all time, had been—who else?—William Shakespeare. That was before the oracle spoke. "Shakespeare wrote a whole lot of very bad plays," he said. "Most of them are never performed, and there's a reason. They're unperformable. *Hamlet* is one of the worst. Shakespeare should never even have attempted to write it. He was out of his depth from start to finish. He should have known you can't make a tragic hero out of a weakling. *King Lear* is even worse, and *Macbeth* is worse than that. And as for the comedies—has anyone ever got a laugh out of any of them? He did write one play that's at least *partially* successful—*Julius Caesar*." The audacity of the man! He dared to pillory *Shakespeare*! We were dumbfounded by his gall. (And yet I have never since been able to sit through a Shakespeare play without recalling that Sondheim appraisal.)

For an English class, we were asked to write a book report on Henry James's novel *The Spoils of Poynton*. Literary critics will, I think, agree that this is not one of the master's most important works, and Steve's report was audaciously brief:

This is an exceptionally long, very boring book about a lot of furniture.

Of course, he got an A+.

It wasn't long before we gave more weight to Steve's pronouncements than to anything our college professors had to say. Other passions of our day included the songs of Cole Porter and Rodgers and Hart. (Porter was a Williamstown neighbor.) Though Lorenz Hart had been superseded by

Richard Rodger's new writing partner, Oscar Hammerstein, I once dared to opine that I preferred the perky lyrics of Lorenz Hart. Steve gave me one of his withering looks. "That shows how little you know about music," he said. "Actually, Larry Hart's lyrics were incredibly sloppy. Take just one song—'Blue Room.' He writes, 'We will thrive on, keep alive on, just nothing but kisses, with Mr. and Mrs. on little blue chairs.' Come *on*. Did you ever hear of a couple with 'Mr. and Mrs.' written on their *chairs*, like 'His and Hers' on towels? He just needed a rhyme for 'upstairs,' and *chairs* was the best he could come up with." I had to admit that he had a point. He always did.

On Broadway, the sensation of the day was Tennessee Williams's new play *A Streetcar Named Desire*. All of us—faculty and students alike—who could afford to had gone down to New York to see *Streetcar* performed at the Barrymore Theatre at least once, if not several times, and those of us who hadn't seen it had read it. It seemed to us simply the greatest American play ever written. But, needless to say, Steve Sondheim did not agree. He found the play "seriously flawed." The flaw was the rape scene, where Stanley Kowalski rapes Blanche near the end. "It's <u>completely</u> out of character for Stanley to rape Blanche," he said, "especially while his wife is off at the hospital having their first baby. Stanley feels nothing but disgust for Blanche. He sees how she's destroying his marriage, and all he wants is to get her out of the house. He's even bought her a bus ticket back to Laurel. There's been no indication that he's ever thought of fucking her. Of course, Blanche may have secretly wanted Stanley to rape her—but if that's the case, the last thing he'd have done would be to accommodate her. He'd have chosen a subtler way to humiliate her. But the rape turns Stanley into a complete animal, which leaves Stella looking like a stupid twit for marrying him."

Of course, the rape scene is the play's climax, the story's great dramatic peak. Without it, *Streetcar* would lose all its resonance and power. Still, thanks to Steve's analysis, another idol bit the dust.

Though I was always uncomfortable in conversations with him—which kept me warily waiting to be one-upped by him—it wouldn't be true to say that I actually disliked the other Steve. I was fascinated by him, always a little scared of him. I think we all felt that way. There was a certain seductiveness about his sort of confidence, and we all fell under his spell. Though waiting for the next barb that might fall from his bitter tongue was a little like watching a cobra preparing to strike, we all tried to amuse him, to please him, to find favor with him. One of our fraternity brothers once said to me, "You know, I think that maybe I'm witty. Steve Sondheim actually laughed at one of my jokes." This was indeed unusual. His usual response to any attempt at wit was simply a shrug. He had one of the most effective sneers I've ever known, a marvelous curl of the lip that left its recipient red-faced and apologetic, with his toe curled in the rug.

I envied him his seductiveness and the authority it gave him over other people. I longed to be able to play the game the way he played it—play it and win. Looking back, I think he provided me with a rare gift, something I'd always lacked and needed: the sense that I had a competitor. Though he and I have always worked in quite different and noncompeting fields, I find myself to this very day—when I've completed a piece of work—asking myself: What would <u>he</u> think of this? Would he give it a nod of approval?

When he happened to agree with something you said, he would respond with, "<u>Exactly</u>!" But his tone implied that his was a conclusion he had reached long ago, and that he was surprised that it had taken you so long to reach it. My envy of him grows fiercer as I remember that "Exactly."

Several years later, I was having lunch in Switzerland with Noel Coward and his two longtime companions, Cole Lesley and Graham Payn, in their pink chalet high in the mountains above Montreux. It was one of the most delightful afternoons I have ever spent. I knew some lyrics to some Coward songs, and we sang on and off throughout the luncheon, while the silhouette of Mont Blanc glistened outside the dining room windows. Noel Coward, it turned out, was a fan of mine, and this naturally added to my enjoyment of the occasion. I had recently published a book called *The Right People*, and Coward had assumed—mistakenly, though I did not disillusion him—that I had taken the title from one of his songs. ("Why, oh, why, do the wrong people travel, when the right people stay back home?") Actually, my original title for the book had been *The Best People*, but my publisher decided that "Right" had a better ring to it than "Best."

By then, Steve Sondheim's name had become well-known on Broadway; he had won a brace of Tony Awards and was widely regarded as a rising star. During the lunch with Sir Noel, Steve's name came up. Coward looked thoughtful. "Interesting talent," he said. "But why doesn't he write one or two really *pretty* songs? I'm sure he could if he wanted to. But he doesn't even seem to want to try. To me, he hasn't written a single song that I'd call pretty."

"I think he doesn't want to be labeled a sentimental, like Hammerstein," I said.

Coward shook his head. "No," he said, "I think he's terrified of sentiment."

I ran into Steve not long afterward in New York and, because I considered Noel Coward one of the giants of modern theater, I thought I'd pass that comment along to Steve. The familiar curl of the lip immediately appeared. "Noel Coward," he said. "Well, considering the source, I consider that remark a distinct compliment." And so, another of my heroes lay shattered at my feet.

But I'm getting ahead of my story. At Williams, Steve and I did not get involved in too many of the same activities. Steve spent most of his spare time working with the college theater group. I worked with this group for a while and acted in two or three productions. But I soon grew tired of the politics and ego battles that theater work seemed to involve. Steve wrote, produced, and directed a full-length musical comedy based on college life. It was enthusiastically received, and Steve's own ego swelled proportionately. He claimed, for instance, that he could solve any of the crossword puzzles in the New York *Times* without looking at the clues. As an avid puzzler myself, I knew how hard some *Times* puzzles could be, so I suspected some hyperbole in his boast. But the interesting thing was that none of us dared to challenge Steve's claim or ask him to prove up his ability.

My ambitions were more literary and journalistic, and one of the organizations that both Steve and I worked for was the college humor magazine, the *Purple Cow*. By the end of our junior year, he and I were named coeditors of the magazine. So, there we were again, the two Steves, our names linked at the top of the masthead.

Like other college humor magazines of the era, the *Purple Cow* was an almost abject attempt to imitate the *New Yorker*, in format and in content. Steve and I were both smart enough to know that we could never equal the *New Yorker*'s level of excellence, so we set our sights a little lower. We thought we could at least turn out a magazine on a par with the *Harvard Lampoon*, which was almost always a pretty funny publication. But it was soon clear that Williams simply lacked the huge talent pool of that much larger university—a young writer named John Updike was already appearing regularly in the *Lampoon*—and so we never even got close to rivaling our paradigm, try as we might. In the end, we would be writing most of the material that went into the *Purple Cow* ourselves, using pseudonyms and cryptic initials as signatures. (A couple of my pieces were actually selected for publication in anthologies of college humor, though since I'd disguised myself, I got no author credit.)

Longing as I did—as all of us did—for that rare thing, a word of praise from the other Steve, I tried a new tactic as the two of us put our little magazine together: flattery. "That's a very clever piece, Steve," I'd say to him, after reading one of his efforts. "It's really terribly, terribly funny." It didn't work, of course. My flattery was never reciprocated. The best I could hope for, after he'd gone over a piece of mine, was a shrug, and, "I guess it's okay," or "It'll do," as he tossed it into the "Accepted" pile of manuscripts.

We graduated, both of us with high honors, both Phi Beta Kappas, and I got married not long afterward to a California girl named Nan Tillson, whom I'd been courting for about two years. Nan and I moved into a small apartment in, of all places, Kew Gardens. I never knew where Kew Gardens was, exactly. If it lay outside the Borough of Queens, it did so just barely. But it didn't matter, because we knew we would not be living in Kew Gardens long. My Draft Board in Connecticut, it seemed, had other plans for me, which I'll get to shortly. There seemed no point in buying much in the way of furniture, and so, by artfully draping various gaily printed sheets and tablecloths we'd received as wedding presents over trunks and crates and packing boxes, we created tables and chairs and other pieces, with results, we decided at the time, that were cozy and charming and inviting, if a bit primitive. We called the atmosphere of our first home "Bohemian." That's how young we were.

Nan was an excellent cook. She had attended classes at the Cordon Bleu in Paris, and it wasn't long before we decided we were ready to give our first dinner party as newlyweds.

I was working as a copywriter in New York, and we decided to invite Bill Sisson, a fellow copywriter, and Mary Meade, a bright and amusing girl he sometimes dated. We asked another couple, whose names I forget. And we'd recently met a very pretty young English girl named Gemma Something—blonde, sweet-faced, with a peach-and-cream English complexion, she was barely twenty. Gemma had been in America only a few months, but she'd found herself a job she considered quite exciting. It actually wasn't much of a job, and consisted mostly of filing correspondence, but her employer was the Metropolitan Museum of Art. We invited Gemma and, because we wanted to do a dinner for eight and wanted to even out the sexes, I suggested that we ask Steve Sondheim.

Steve didn't appear to be doing much in New York at the time. Still ahead of him were the Broadway credits that would begin to make him well-known—the lyrics for Leonard Bernstein's *West Side Story*, and, even more brilliantly, the lyrics for *Gypsy*. I'd told Nan a little bit about him but, as far as she was concerned, he was just a college fraternity brother of mine. We invited him, and he accepted.

Nan toiled for several days in our tiny kitchen on her dinner menu, which was quite elaborate and designed to impress her new bridegroom's friends. On the night of our party, the guests arrived, cocktails were served, and by the time we all sat down at the table things seemed to have gotten off to a splendid start. Then somehow the talk turned to theater, and Gemma spoke up. "I saw the most wonderful musical show on Broadway the other night," she said.

Immediately, Steve's head cocked in her direction. "Really?" he said. "What show was that?"

"I don't remember the name of it," she said, "but it was awfully clever. And the girl who was the star of it—she was tall, with lots of blond hair, great big eyes, and a funny, squeaky voice. Oh, she was terribly good."

"Really?" said Steve, feigning the most intense interest. "Who could she have been, I wonder?"

"Oh, I wish I could remember," Gemma said. "It seems to me it was Carol—Carol Something."

"Carole Lombard?" said Steve, mentioning an actress who had been dead for quite a few years.

"No, I don't think it was Lombard—"

From our opposite ends of the table, Nan and I realized what was going on. Steve was launching into a classic send-up, and he had found the perfect innocent victim. Nan gave me an anxious look, and we both tried to change the subject. But it was too late, things were moving too fast and were spinning out of our control.

"Tell me more," said Steve. "Tell me more about this show. I'm really interested!"

"Well, there was one song in it that was really darling," Gemma said. "Something about diamonds. Something about diamonds being a girl's best friend."

Steve looked at her evenly for a moment. "By any chance," he said, "is there a possibility that the show your describing is called *Gentlemen Prefer Blondes*, starring Carol Channing, with music by Jule Styne, lyrics by Leo Robin, based on the 1925 novel by Anita Loos, which has been playing since a year ago last December at the Ziegfeld Theatre, 256 West 47th Street, directed by . . ."

There was no doubt that he would have gone on reciting the names from the show's program, right through the casting director, wardrobe mistress, stage manager and house physician, but Gemma, covering her mouth with her hand, uttered a little cry, jumped up from the table and ran sobbing from the room.

Nan followed her into our bedroom where she lay weeping into the toss pillows. "I won't go back into that room," she sobbed. "I won't! I *won't!*" Nan tried to comfort her, and to persuade her to rejoin us at the table, but Gemma was adamant. Eventually, Nan led her out through the kitchen door and back to dinner, where we all tried elaborately to pretend that nothing had happened, as the conversation, though strained, turned to other matters.

After dinner, he announced that, among his other talents, he could rattle off the casts of old movies. Name any old movie, he said, and he could give you the names of the two principal stars, at least two of the supporting actors, and names of the director and producer. To my surprise, my usually shy friend Bill Sisson announced that he could do the same thing. And so suddenly a contest was on between the two men. Taking turns, each man named an old movie title, while the other shot back with the credits. The rules were simple. The first man to stump the other would be the winner. Back and forth they went, with titles of old movies the rest of us had never heard of. It became rather exciting and, after the disturbance Steve had created earlier, it was understandable that the rest of us were rooting solidly for Bill. Finally, after dozens of titles had passed through this mental sparring match, Bill came up with a title that, after a little hesitation, Steve admitted he didn't know. Bill then recited the credits, and, with a little nod, Steve acknowledged defeat. A round of cheers went up for Bill Sisson.

(A few years later, Bill Sisson had begun drinking heavily. Drinking and smoking in his bed, the coroner's inquest concluded—a glass of vodka had spilled in his bed, his cigarette had ignited the alcohol, and he died, horribly, in a fire that destroyed his apartment. I miss him to this day.)

That evening, after our last guests had said their thank-yous and goodbyes, with Steve Sondheim appearing somewhat sulky and contrite, Nan leaned against the closed front door. There was, as they say, fire in her eye. Not known for her tolerance of the various celebrities we entertained, she said, "Never again will I allow that young man to set foot in my house."

"But he's brilliant," I said. Foreshadowing Steven Sondheim's illustrious future career, I added, "He's going to be famous someday—wait and see."

"I don't care," she said. "As God is my witness, that young man will never set foot in my house again!"

And, unfortunately, he never did.

Our story now jumps forward by some forty years. Steve and I had run into each other from time to time over the intervening years, usually at other peoples' houses, and these meetings, though brief, had always been cautiously cordial. But in the early 1990s Williams College embarked on its Third Century Fund-Raising Campaign, through which it hoped to raise some $50,000,000 through alumni giving. Since I'd gone through Williams on a scholarship, I thought it would be appropriate to pay the college back by contributing enough funds to create the Stephen Birmingham Scholarship Fund.

This gift naturally endeared me to the college's development office, and so I was not surprised one day to have a telephone call from the director of development, asking for my help. "We're having a little problem with your classmate, Stephen Sondheim," he said. "We have him tagged as capable of making a six-figure gift, and we've tried various ways of approaching him. We've invited him to Williamstown for weekends, to luncheons and dinners in both New York and Los Angeles, but he always declines. Does he have something *against* Williams, do you think?"

The college's attitude toward Steve, it seemed, had become one of bemusement. After graduating, the college had awarded him with a special two-year grant for further study in music. Several years later, the college had given him an honorary doctorate degree in music, the first such Doctorate in the college's two-hundred-year history. Over the years, Steve had responded to the Annual Alumni Fund drives by sending a check, but these checks had often been for modest amounts. While the college perhaps felt, understandably, that they had done almost everything they possibly could for him, they also felt that Steve had done little commensurate in return for Williams.

"Do you think you could help us out?" the development director asked me. "Do you think you could persuade him to dig into his pockets a little deeper for Williams? Be a little more generous? It occurred to us that if you explained to him what you've done for the college, it might make him decide that he ought to do the same thing. After all, you were the two Steves—you're two of the stars from your class."

And so there we were again, our names inextricably linked, like conjoined twins joined at the hip. Furthermore, we were being squared off again as competitors.

"You mean maybe I could *shame* him into making a matching gift?" I said.

"Well, yes, that's more or less what we had in mind," he said.

"That won't be easy," I said. "Shame isn't exactly in Steve's repertory of emotions."

"It might make him feel that he'd like to do you one better," he said.

"That notion might appeal to him more," I said. "Well, what the hell? I'll give it the old college try. But I can't promise you much."

I could tell Steve was puzzled when I telephoned him and told him I wanted to see him. "What's this about?" he asked me. "Do you have some sort of idea for a collaboration?"

"Well, sort of," I said, "but not in any sort of artistic sense. I'd rather explain what's on my mind when I see you." And so, we set a date.

For some reason, I was terribly nervous about this meeting. For one thing, I've never been particularly good at fundraising. I dislike asking other people for money. But there was much more to it than that. More than anything I feared that harsh, erudite tongue of his. I was still somehow in his thrall. Surely, you've outgrown all that, I told myself. But I hadn't.

I fretted endlessly over what to wear when I went to see him. Dress for success, I decided. I wore my bespoke blue blazer from Mortises, a Turnbull & Asser shirt, a Hermès tie, Burberry grey flannel slacks and Ferragamo loafers. I had my hair cut by Jerry at Bergdorf's. In my nervousness, I arrived at his house fifteen minutes ahead of schedule. I killed the time by walking around the block a few times, puffing furiously on a cigarette.

Steve's house is in Turtle Bay Gardens, a famous double row of handsome 19th-century brownstones placed back-to-back on two parallel streets in the East Forties. Each house has its own small garden in the rear which opens onto a lovely private garden, invisible from the street, which runs the length of the block, and is maintained by the residents, with fountains and statuary. Steve's house is on the Forty-ninth Street side of Turtle Bay, and I remembered that Nan and I had once looked at a house on the Forty-eighth Street side that was being sold by a writer Dorothy Thompson. I remembered that she was asking $90,000 for the house at the time. It would have been a good investment. Today, Turtle Bay houses sell for millions.

I thought how odd it would have been if the two Steves had ended up being neighbors, running back and forth through our backyards to borrow a cup of sugar.

Steve's doorbell was answered by a young male secretary. "He'll be down shortly," he said. He fixed me a rather watery drink, and I sat down in a living room sofa. That is an important part of celebrityhood, of course: the little wait. Celebrities never answer their own doorbells. There is always that mandatory little wait. They're never quite ready to receive callers.

Presently Steve appeared, and immediately put me at my unease. "Please don't sit in that sofa," he said. "I have a bad back, and I need to stretch out." I quickly moved to another seat. "Goodness, you're all dressed up," he said. He was wearing corduroy pants and a sweatshirt. "I have to go on to a dinner party from here," I said, which was a lie. We chatted for a few minutes, and then I decided the time had come to make my pitch. "Look," I said, "at Williams, you and I were known as the two Steves. It seems we still are. We were the two youngest in our class, the two smartest, we were in the same fraternity, and we coedited the magazine. We both work in the arts, though not in competing fields. We've both had our share of failures, which is par for the course, but on the whole we've both had more successes than failures."

"Not in my case," he said. "I've had lots more failures than I've had successes."

"I disagree," I said. "But the point is we're both considered successes by those who know us. To those who know us, the two Steves have been successful."

"Possibly." His look was wary.

"I think we both owe a lot to the kind of education we got at Williams College," I said. "This year, the college is celebrating its two hundredth anniversary, and there's a special fund drive which I'm sure you've heard about. I was able to make a six-figure gift to this fund, and I thought—and the college thought—that it would be nice, that it would be fitting, and that it would also be great fun for you to consider making a similar gift."

"I don't have that kind of money," he said flatly.

I let this pass and went on to point out the various way's funds could be turned over to the college—in the form of a trust, or an annuity, or even in such a manner that, while the college received principal sum the donor could keep the lifetime income from it. "So, you can give money away, and get to keep it too," I said. I went on to mention the considerable tax advantages and savings that would result from such a gift.

But he kept shaking his head.

"The college would do everything possible to publicize your gift," I said. "And it would be the best possible publicity. In show business, I'm sure you appreciate the value of good publicity."

"Have you taken up doing this sort of thing?" he asked me. "Fundraising?"

"No," I said. "You're my only victim. The college asked me to approach you because, frankly, they've tried all sorts of other ways. It's because we're the two Steves. We're the only two of our classmates who are listed in *Who's Who in America*, the *Celebrity Register*, and *Who's Who in Arts & Entertainment*. Whether we like it or not, we're thought of as a matched set, a pair, a duo, like a pair of bookends."

"I don't think of us as that at all," he said.

"Neither do I," I said, "but you can see why some other people do."

"Well," he said. "It's not that I have anything *against* Williams. It's just that I can't afford to give anything more to Williams than I've given already."

He then launched into a brief litany of his impoverished state. At least, I thought, I seem to have triumphed in perhaps one aspect of our long competition; I seemed to be richer. But that was cold and dreary comfort. And I wasn't sure how much of all this I really believed. After all, he owned a five-story Manhattan town house at a smart address. Katherine Hepburn was his next-door neighbor. He also owned a weekend and summer place in Connecticut. He'd never married and had no children or other visible dependents. (In New York theater circles, he was widely assumed to be gay, but I'd had no evidence of that; he lived alone.) He'd recently come out with a new album of his songs, with Barbra Streisand, and she, at least, was a person who didn't work cheap.

"Well, think about it, anyway," I said at last. "I didn't expect you to make any commitment today. But maybe I've planted a seed. In my business—and in yours, too, I'm sure you never know when somebody is going to walk through the door and offer you a bagful of money. If you get one of those sudden windfalls, think of Williams."

Changing the subject abruptly, he said, "You live in Cincinnati."

"Yes," I said.

"Why?"

"I like it there," I said. "It's a great place to work. I get a lot more work done there than when I lived in New York. I love New York, but life in Manhattan is just too—too *jagged* for my taste."

He rose to escort me to the door. Celebrities always escort you out of their houses, but never into them.

At the door, he said, "You know, once a month Howie Erskine and Chuck Hollerith and I have lunch at the Four Seasons." Howard Erskine—tall, blond, and handsome—was one of our campus glamour pusses. Hollerith, bubbly and with apparently lots of money, was one of our party boys. Both men are now theatrical producers in New York. "At these lunches of ours," Steve said, "we just dish everybody. Howie Erskine will get such a kick out of it when I tell him you live in *Cincinnati!*"

I thought to myself: There you go again. I may be leaving your house emptyhanded, but I'm not going to leave with you implying that I live in some inappropriate, even ridiculous, place.

I looked at him. "I don't think Howie Erskine is going to get much of a kick out of learning that," I said. "In the twenty-odd years I've lived there, Howie's visited my house in Cincinnati several times—at least twice for dinner."

It wasn't much of a retort, I admit. As a feat of one-upmanship, it was hardly up to the Sondheim standard. But from his surprised look I could tell it had had its effect. And so, we shook hands and parted, two intimate strangers, two hostile friends, two unfraternal brothers, two Steves, begrudging admirers of each other's talents.

CAREY

Postscript:

Several weeks prior to final editing of this book, I contacted Stephen Sondheim asking if he'd like to review the chapter on him and my father's history and possibly add a quote for the back jacket. I heard back within a few days via email that Mr. Sondheim (whom I've never met) would appreciate a read of this chapter, but declined to offer any endorsement or quote.

On November 17, 2021, I sent Sondheim this chapter and had hopes of interviewing him about his and my father's history and convince him to perhaps provide a quote. Unfortunately, he died just ten days later, and I missed an opportunity to talk with him and gain his insight.

In the end, the competition and rivalry between these two creative men resulted in a decisive Sondheim win, as news of his passing traveled around the globe. My father's ego chased fame equal to Sondheim, but never quite reached its sought-after apogee. While my father was revered for his talent and his written works, it appears that the competition of those Williams days remained with him throughout his life.

Chapter Six

US 51011172

STEVE:

I WAS DRAFTED INTO THE UNITED STATES ARMY IN 1951, ON MY WED-ding day. Though I'd been expecting this notification to come, it was not the most welcome of wedding presents. The Korean War—or "Conflict," as it was more politely called—was in full swing. American soldiers were fighting there and being killed.

My new bride, Nan, and I spent the next few weeks preparing for my departure closing the apartment we'd rented in New York, packing, and arranging for a two-year leave of absence from my job. To a twenty-one-year-old, I probably don't need to add, two years seemed like an eternity, a prison sentence. I tried not to think that it could end in death. A few days before I was scheduled to report for duty, we said goodbye to our New York friends and loaded up the car to drive to my parents' home in Connecticut. A friend, in a borrowed pickup truck, was to follow us with the rest of our possessions. We headed north on the Merritt Parkway.

The Merritt Parkway, we soon discovered, barred trucks of any sort. Our friend was soon stopped by the police and ordered to reroute to local streets, which meant US Route 1, the old Boston Post Road, with its many traffic lights, which ran roughly parallel to the Parkway. Our friend kept trying to sneak back onto the Parkway wherever possible, but vigilant troopers kept ushering him off again. In the end, we arrived in Andover first, and our frustrated friend turned up an hour or so later. That night, my mother gave a little farewell dinner party for me. There were toasts, and a few tears. I was to report at the induction center in Hartford at 6 a.m. the following morning.

Something about the date on my orders had always struck me as a little odd. I was instructed to report on February 24, 1951, a Saturday. I knew enough about how the US government operated—my father, after all, was with the Justice Department—to know that, even in times of war, federal employees seldom worked on weekends. One reason why the Japanese surprise attack on Pearl Harbor was so devastating was that the Japanese had sprung it on a Sunday, when most of the military personnel at Hickam Field were out playing baseball, or dozing in their bunks, or otherwise far from their battle stations. Still, that was the date clearly typed on my very official-looking orders. There was no disputing it. The orders also contained threats of the direst consequences for failure to report as ordered.

My father had volunteered to drive me to the induction center. And so, early that morning, I kissed by sleeping wife goodbye, and we set off for Hartford before dawn's first rays had hit the sky.

We arrived at the induction center promptly at six o'clock. All the doors were closed and locked. Repeated knocks produced no response. We decided to go around the corner for a cup of coffee. We returned at 6:30 to find the place still locked. We returned to the coffee shop, ordered a full breakfast, and studied the orders. There was the date: February 24. It corresponded with the date of the morning newspaper, and so there was no mistake. But when we returned at 7:45, the induction center was still very much closed. Clearly, though I was ready to join the Army, the Army was not ready for me. "Let's go home," my father said. "We can phone them later in the day and find out what's happened."

So, we went home, to be greeted by a surprised—even disappointed— wife and family. After all, all the goodbyes had been said the night before, and yet here I was, back again, like a bad penny. We all spent a confused and rather aimless weekend, wondering what was up. Periodically, I telephoned the induction center, but there was never any answer.

On Monday morning I telephoned again. This time, a perky-voiced woman said, "Oh, but Mr. Birmingham, didn't you receive our notice? You've been given a thirty-day postponement. You're not to report until

March twenty-eighth." My father, it turned out, had requested this, hoping to use his government connections. But he hadn't told me about it and, when he heard nothing, assumed that his request had been denied.

Now my wife and I looked at each other. I'd quit my job. We had no place to live, except in my parents' house, which was not an exactly exciting prospect. An idle span of more than four weeks yawned ahead of us, with no plans. Suddenly, the solution seemed clear. We'd had no real honeymoon. Here we were in wintry New England. The solution was obviously a Caribbean cruise. I immediately phoned a travel agent, and the next day we boarded ship in Brooklyn and set off for the sunny isles.

March 28 was a Wednesday, and there was no doubt that the Army would be in business. But the night before I'd come to a decision, a decision, as it would turn out, that would affect my entire career in the military. "Getting into the army has caused me enough irritation and expense," I announced. "I'm going to get my revenge. I'm going into the army, but I'm going into it in *style*. I'm going to pack a full wardrobe, including my dinner jacket. After all, who knows where I'll be stationed, or what I might need when I get there? I'm going to take my tennis racket, and my portable typewriter, plus plenty of books to read."

"You are a damned fool," my father told me flatly. "All that stuff will be stolen from you in ten minutes."

But I disagreed. Something—a sense of personal theater, perhaps—told me that If I was going to be inducted into the Army and asked to fight for a cause in which I didn't particularly believe, this was the only sensible way to do it. And so, when I arrived at the induction center early that Wednesday morning, I was dressed in Brooks Brothers flannel trousers, button-down Oxford shirt, jacket, and tie. My father opened the trunk of the Cadillac, and I unloaded two large suitcases, my portable typewriter in its case, my tennis racket in its press, and an over-the-shoulder garment bag.

It was quite clear from the scene on the street that the Army was very much open for business that morning. Several hundred other young men crowded the sidewalk outside the building, waiting for the doors to open. The sight of me and my luggage immediately drew jeers and catcalls, but I'd expected that. "Where the fuck do you think you're going—to some country club?" one fellow yelled at me. I merely smiled and shrugged and cleared a space for my luggage on the sidewalk. I could tell at a glance that most of my fellow inductees were at least three years younger than I was—eighteen-year-old kids. I'd been given a deferment to let me finish college. Most of these young men were barely out of high school. I began to feel that I had a slight edge on them.

Promptly at 6 a.m., the doors to the building opened, and we began to file inside. I found a place to park my luggage in a corner of the building's lobby, wondering, briefly, if I would ever see it again. Next, we were ushered into a large room fitted with desks and chairs, where a brief intelligence, or scholastic aptitude test, was administered. There followed a fifteen-minute interview with an Army psychiatrist, whose main interest seemed to be to find out whether any of us had ever had a homosexual experience, which we all stoutly denied. (If one was going to be rejected by the US Army, it wasn't going to be for that.)

Then we were told to strip naked, and to line up for final immunization shots. Naked, my Caribbean tan also drew comment and questions, and when I explained how it had come about, I realized that most of my soon-to-be-fellow Army men had never heard of the Caribbean Sea. As we moved along in single file, medics on both sides of us punched at our arms with needles.

It was at that point in the process that a voice came over the loudspeaker: "Is Mr. Birmingham in the group? Please report to the desk sergeant at the back of the room." I dutifully stepped out of line and made my way to the man in question. "The commanding officer would like to see you in his office," he told me. I indicated my unclad state. "Yes, you can put on your clothes before going in to see him," he said. The commanding officer turned out to be a smooth-faced young captain who offered me a seat in front of his desk. "Is that your luggage out there?" he asked me.

I said it was.

"I see you've done a bit of traveling," he said. I should add here that, for the hell of it, my wife and I had plastered our suitcases with stickers advertising the various hotels we'd stopped in, and the ports of call we'd made. I explained the mix-up on the induction dates, and how we'd spent the past few weeks.

"Ever been to Mexico?" he asked me.

At that point, I hadn't, and he then proceeded to provide a colorful travelogue on a recent holiday he and his wife had spent in that country. "You really ought to spend some time in Mexico," he said, "It's a fascinating country." I had no idea where all this might be leading.

Then he said, "Are you by any chance a writer?" He'd obviously spotted my typewriter case in the lobby.

"Well, I hope to be," I said.

"You know," he said, tipping back in his chair, "I do some work for the Public Information Office in Washington. Most of these kids being drafted into the army are scared to death. They're scared shitless. They're scared they're going to be fed lousy food. They're scared they're going to be made to sleep on beds without sheets or pillowcases. They're scared of basic training, which every G.I. has to have. They're scared they're going to be bullied and mistreated by senior NCOs. And of course, they're scared they're going to be killed. I've been thinking of having someone write a weekly column for the Army *Times*—just five, six hundred words—a column written by a typical draftee, writing about what life for the typical draftee is really like. I mean, we're *proud* of our Army meals. We *do* provide sheets and pillowcases, and clean linen once a week. We try to make Army life as civilized as we can make it. I'm looking for a typical draftee to write a column, telling it like it really is. Would you be interested in doing something like that?"

I told him that I would indeed.

He scribbled the name and address of the person to whom I should send my copy in Washington. "Just once a week," he said. "Don't skimp on the tough parts, but mention the good parts, too. A little humor would be good, too. Just an honest weekly story of what life in the Army is like for the typical GI draftee—that's what we're looking for."

I told him that I thought it would be a most interesting assignment. "Human interest stories," I said. "Personal stories. Anecdotes."

"Exactly," he said. Then he said, "Of course the Army can't pay you for this. But is there anything I can do for you in return?"

I hesitated, and then I explained that, in fact, there might be. My new wife's father, who lived inland from San Francisco, had recently undergone major surgery for colon cancer. Now it had been discovered that the cancer had spread. Her father was not expected to live much longer and, even as we spoke, my wife was preparing to board a flight to California to be with her parents. "If there's any way I could be stationed in Northern California during these next few months, that would be wonderful," I said.

He spread his hands. "Well, I'm afraid there's nothing I can do about that," he said. "I'm sorry, but that's entirely out of my hands. But I wish you good luck in the Army." He stood up. We shook hands. The interview was over. I left with the directions for where to send my stories but realized I had not even made a note of the young captain's name. I returned to the inoculation room, stripped again, and received the balance of my shots.

From there, we were lined up, dressed once more, raised our hands, uttered the pledge, and made the symbolic one step forward. We were now officially members of the United States Army. I was now US 51011172, a number I was instructed to commit to memory.

From Hartford, we boarded buses for the recruitment center in Fort Devens, Massachusetts. As we stepped aboard the bus, Red Cross volunteers handed each of us a doughnut and coffee in a paper cup. The Salvation Army had a more interesting gift, one that was actually useful. Each of us was presented with a small packet containing a razor, extra blades, a toothbrush, toothpaste, a sewing kit, and a Bible. The Bible, it was noted, had magical properties. In combat situations, if the Bible was placed in the left-hand breast pocket, it would deflect an otherwise fatal bullet. Incidences of these occurrences were well documented. This gift left me with a permanently warm spot in my heart for the operations of the Salvation Army. And it marked the beginning of my disillusionment with the humanitarian efforts of the American Red Cross, of which I'll have more to say shortly.

Fort Devens, at the time, was a vast reception center for thousands of draftees and new recruits from throughout the New York and New England area. It was from here that we would be assigned to various

Army posts across the country to begin our mandatory basic training. My four days at Fort Devens were neither particularly harsh nor particularly pleasant. The late-winter weather in Eastern Massachusetts was cold and rainy. The streets of Fort Devens were uniformly muddy, and we were not permitted to leave the base. At Fort Devens, we were given our boots and uniforms; mine was particularly ill fitting. We each received the usual three-minute GI haircut. We were housed in a series of huge, glum barracks, each one filled with double-decker bunks. I was lucky enough to grab a lower bunk, which turned out to be a mixed blessing, since my bed had to be used as a step for the man who slept above me. At least my lower bunk gave me space in which to store my luggage under my bed. The thing I remember most vividly about Fort Devens was the smell of the barracks, which was nothing more than the smell of mass male humanity. At night, a neighboring bunk became the center of a certain amount of homosexual activity, which the rest of us tried to sleep through.

There was good deal of this sort of thing in the Army, by the way. It was always ignored. To me, this made President Bill Clinton's "historic" stand on homosexuality in the military, and the resulting fuss that was made over it, seem a little silly and beside the point. But, after all, Clinton himself had managed to avoid the draft. So, what would he know?

During the days at Fort Devens, there was a regular schedule of lectures and training films. But, since no attendance was taken, it didn't seem to matter whether one partook of these events or not. Periodically, a loudspeaker in the barracks would order us all to "fall out" for something or other. But, if I chose to stay in my bunk, where I was rereading Scott Fitzgerald's *Tender Is the Night*, nobody seemed to care. I found my Army boots bulky and uncomfortable, and so I switched to a pair of penny loafers that I'd brought along. No one noticed the change of footwear. I noted all this for my weekly column.

Then, on the fifth day, all of us at Fort Devens received our reassignment orders. These were posted on a huge blackboard in the mess hall: 1,678 enlisted men were being assigned to Camp Atterbury, Indiana; 2,840 enlisted men were being shipped to Camp Polk, Louisiana. One enlisted man was being sent to the 504th Signal Base Maintenance Company at the Sacramento Signal Depot in California.

There was a certain amount of hemming and hawing about how I was going to make this trip. One man did not seem sufficient to require an entire Army bus, and there was no troop train headed in that direction, as there would be to the two other destinations. In the end, I was given a first-class rail ticket for a private roomette across the country. This seemed to me a slow way to get there, and so, in Boston, I cashed in the ticket for a plane ticket to San Francisco, and even got to pocket a little change. I arrived in California four days ahead of time and was met at the airport by Nan.

I often think of the 504th Signal Base Maintenance Company as the Army unit the Pentagon forgot. Though, as it would turn out, I would spend my entire two-year Army career with this little outfit, it was never clear to me what its mission was. The Sacramento Signal Depot was—still is—a large civilian installation, run by the Army Signal Corps, located in the south suburbs of the state capital—a series of squat, squared-off buildings sitting in a sprawl of tract housing. Security was tight there. The Depot was surrounded by high, barbed-wire, electric fences. An identification card had to be shown to the armed guard at the gate when entering or leaving the place. Unscheduled or unexpected visitors were challenged. More than two thousand men and women worked there, but what sort of work they did behind those windowless walls I never had a clue. I was merely told that it was all Very Important, and that it had to do with "communications." Did they manufacture communications systems there, or did they simply repair them? I never knew, though large eighteen-wheeler semis were always rolling importantly in and out, loaded to the Peirsol line with important-looking equipment.

The 504th Signal Base Maintenance Company was located about a mile behind the Depot proper. It consisted of about ten buildings: six barracks, the mess hall, an auditorium, the company headquarters building, two buildings containing showers and latrines, and a largish garage-like building called "the shop." When I arrived at the 504th, its military population consisted of about eighty men. There were never more than 120, because that was its housing capacity. Officially, these soldiers were stationed there to provide military "backup" to the Signal Depot's operations. But what this meant in fact was a mystery, since the Depot never called on the Maintenance Company to do anything, though I learned that the soldiers were often able to earn extra money babysitting for civilian families on the base.

My initial appearance at this tiny military outpost was greeted with a certain amount of puzzlement. The First Sergeant of the company, MSG Pakula, to whom I reported and handed my orders and slim packet of military records, studied these documents for several minutes, scratching his head.

"This is a Signal Corps outfit," he said at last. I replied that I'd gathered as much.

"You work with radios? Radar?"

"No," I said, adding that my experience with radios was limited to turning one on and off.

"Why'd they put you in the Signal Corps?" he asked me.

I answered that I didn't know that I was in the Signal Corps.

"Well, you are," he said. He reached in a desk drawer and pulled out a Signal Corps insignia to be pinned on the shoulder of my uniform. "Wear this with pride, Soldier," he said solemnly. It seemed to me that I was being given some sort of medal, and so, not knowing what my response was expected to be, I saluted him.

"Don't salute *me*," he said gruffly. "I'm not an officer."

I apologized, and then explained my special assignment—to write a weekly column for the *Armed Forces Times* on the daily life of a typical draftee. He looked at me as though I was speaking Chinese. Then he looked back at my records. "You haven't been through basic training yet," he said.

I answered that I was aware of that.

"Well, we have no facilities to give you that here," he said. "We'll have to send you somewhere else for that." Then his eyes fell on my portable typewriter in its case. "Can you type?" he asked me. I answered that I could. "Well, maybe we could use you here in the orderly room," he said. "We got a guy now whose M.O.S. is clerk-typist, but he can't type worth shit." With that, he handed me back my records. "Anyway," he said, "I got nothing for you to do right now. Take a couple of weeks off. Get to know the city. Find yourself a place to live."

I was dumbstruck. A place to *live*? I had always assumed that, in the Army, one lived with—well, with the Army.

"We got no space for you in the barracks now," he said. "Don't worry, we'll give you an off-post living allowance. I'll put that through right away. That'll be a hundred and ten a month. You should be able to find a decent place for that."

My starting pay, as a lowly private, was, if memory serves, about $120 a month. An additional $110 a month sounded like a fortune. My wife had dropped me off at the Signal Depot earlier that afternoon, and we'd assumed we were facing another lengthy farewell. "I know this sounds a little surreal," I said when I telephoned her to explain what had happened.

"Are you sure they really want you in the Army?" she asked me.

We spent that night in a Sacramento motel. The next day, armed with the classified section of the Sacramento *Bee*, we found ourselves a pleasant one-bedroom furnished apartment near the center of town, a block from the State Capitol building and the pretty park it faced. The rent: $110 a month. That did not give us much left over for luxuries, but of course we had some savings.

My duties in the orderly room of the 504th Signal Base Maintenance Company, when I finally took them up, turned out to be fairly routine: typing up and filing reports, and handling official correspondence for the company commander, Major McCandless, a pleasant, soft-spoken man who was spending his time, it turned out, waiting for his fiftieth birthday, when he could retire from the Army, on a comfortable pension, and return to San Luis Obispo where he planned to grow peaches on some land he'd purchased there. He was an undemanding boss. At first, he dictated his letters to me. But soon he'd simply call me into his office, tell me roughly what he wanted to say, and let me compose the letters for him.

But then, all at once, something really exciting happened. Major McCandless called me in one morning, and said, "Colonel Wilson wants to see you. Colonel Wilson is the commanding officer of the entire Signal Depot!"

I promptly reported to the colonel's big corner office. It was my first time inside the depot proper, and I gave the colonel my snappiest salute.

"Armed Forces Day is coming up, Private!" he barked in his thoroughly commanding voice. "There'll be a big parade through downtown Sacramento. Every military installation in the area will be represented by a float in that parade. I want the Sacramento Signal Depot's float to be the biggest and the best! I'm giving you the assignment of designing that float!"

I mumbled something about having no idea how to design a float for a parade.

"What?" he said, glaring at me. "It says right in your personnel file that you have a bachelor of arts degree! Draw up a design for me!"

So, I agreed to design the float.

"We'll provide you with a flatbed truck," he said. "We'll give you all the materials and supply the personnel you need to build it for you—to be your designees. But you're the designer! Now get cracking on it, Private!" He shook his fist at me for emphasis.

Once I got to know Colonel Wilson, I came to be quite fond of him. Despite his blustery, whip-cracking manner, he turned out to be a tender-hearted soul. And he had a terrible secret. Colonel Wilson was illiterate. He could neither read nor write beyond signing his name in big, scrawl letters. He had received his commission "in the field," meaning that he had been made an officer as the result of some act of bravery—what it was, I never knew—and had never attended Officer Candidates School, or any other military place of learning. He had been a kid from West Texas who lied about his age and joined the Army at sixteen. He had been pulled out of third grade by his father to help on the family farm. His first name was actually Hoot—"Because I hooted and hollered so when I was a baby!"—but, as a colonel, he decided that name was undignified, and so he signed himself Harold J. Wilson. The "J" didn't stand for anything. He cried easily—particularly later on, when I told him my wife was pregnant. He and his wife, he told me, had never been able to have children, and adoption is difficult for military couples.

Still later, he told me the reason for the Wilsons' barren state. A childhood bout with mumps, he said, had left him impotent as well as sterile. It was another terrible secret, and he wept openly confessing it. "You're the first confessee I've confessed this to," he said.

As time went by—and on Major McCandless's recommendation—I began writing letters for Colonel Wilson as well. He had a peculiar speech habit, I discovered. He liked adding "ee" to verbs and nouns. His sentences were filled with words like "confessee." He spoke of enlistees, draftees, absentees, presentees, appointees, licensees, loanees, vouchees, confirmees, trainees, escapees, surrenderees, transferees, remitees, payees, and so on. I suppose he thought this made him sound both erudite and official. He would often telephone me to perform some errand for him. Once one of our sergeants was performing a series of tests on a group of new arrivals. "Go ask Sergeant Amick how his testees are doing," Colonel Wilson told me. I decided to have some fun with this one. I reported back, "Amick says they're doing very well, considering his age and physical condition." He scowled. He didn't get the joke.

But I'm getting way ahead of my story. First, I had to design the float for the Armed Forces Day parade.

That night, armed with colored pencils and drawing paper, I drew up my design. It was not, I must admit, terribly original. At one end of the flatbed, I sketched and igloo with a polar bear standing nearby, and at the other end was a clump of palm trees. At either end was a radio transmitting tower, and between the two towers were stretched a banner reading: SACRAMENTO SIGNAL DEPOT: COMMUNICATIONS AROUND THE WORLD! I sketched in some other figures on the float. At the "North Pole" end, we would place some of us better-looking soldiers, dressed in cold-weather gear. At the "tropical" end, we would borrow some pretty young women from the Depot typing pool to loll around in bathing suits.

"What does it say on that banner?" Colonel Wilson said when I showed my sketch to him in the morning. "I can't read it without my glasses." I read it to him. "Brilliant!" he said. "You've carried out this assignment brilliantly. You're an excellent assignee, Private." He began pressing buttons. Carpenters from the Depot maintenance staff were assigned to construct the igloo, the palm trees, and the pair of radio towers. I was placed in charge of the construction. We were even able to locate a polar bear rug at a local taxidermy shop. Draped over a pair of sawhorses, he looked quite fiercely realistic.

Armed Forces Day arrived, and our float was completed. The pretty girls in swimsuits, and the soldiers in their winter wear took their places on the flatbed, and we were ready to set off for the starting point of the big downtown parade. But we hadn't moved much more than a hundred feet when we discovered we had a major problem. Our palm trees were so tall that they would not clear the telephone lines that ran across the street. There was only one solution. A couple of extra servicemen were assigned to tilt the palm trees on their sides whenever we approached an intersection and set them right again when our float had passed. Fortunately, no one saw the irony in this—that a giant communications outfit could have built a float without considering overhead phone and power lines.

Meanwhile, life in the orderly room continued in its routine. Three of us worked there. I was the typist, another man was in charge of the files, and a third man handled the military payroll. Supervising us was the first sergeant, MSG John Pakula. In an Army unit, I soon discovered, the first sergeant is a very important person, if not the most important person. He might be outranked by the commissioned officers above him, but I noticed that none of the officers at the base were able to get much out of our little company without first seeking the first sergeant's advice and approval.

Periodically, Sergeant Pakula would pull out my file, scowl at it, and say, "We've got to get you sent somewhere for basic training." But weeks, and then months, went by, and nothing happened, and I did not press the issue.

Of course, the three of us in the orderly room had our little games with Sergeant Pakula. He, for example, was in charge of the air-conditioning in our offices. As spring drew on into a hot, humid Central Valley summer, it was he who decided whether it was hot enough to turn on the air conditioner or not. If it was, he would stride officiously across the room and flip the switch. No one else had this privilege. The air conditioner itself was a primitive affair. It consisted of a fan mounted in an outside wall. Outside the building, on a platform, could be placed a large block of ice, and when the fan was turned on slightly cooler air blew into the room. One morning, when the temperature in Sacramento had already topped 100, one of us—I'll never say who it was—had the notion of covering the blades of the fan with shaving cream from an aerosol can. While the three of us did our best to look busy at our desks, Sergeant Pakula marched into the room, flipped on the switch, and was immediately sprayed with foam.

We three in the orderly room had another responsibility. We were to prepare the weekly duty roster—the list of men who were assigned that week to work as kitchen police or to perform guard duty. Needless to say, we ourselves were exempt from such duties. No one minded KP duty—it principally involved wiping down tables and sweeping the mess hall after each meal. (The Army had machines to peel potatoes.) But guard duty, quite simply, was a bore. It required that a man sit up all night, with a loaded rifle on his lap, guarding the premises. But guarding them from what? There were never any intruders. Nothing ever happened at the base at night. When the guard on duty filed his report the next morning, it was always "Incidents: None."

We tried to be fair in parceling out these jobs, rotating the names in alphabetical order. But we were continually besieged by men whose names were up for guard duty, and who offered various excuses for getting out of it. We listened, we haggled, we worked out compromises and substitutions, trying to keep everybody happy. What it all meant, really, was that it behooved the other soldiers in the company to be particularly nice to us.

And, besides that, what did the other men stationed at the 504th Signal Base Maintenance Company actually do? The answer, I'm afraid, is practically nothing at all that could be said to contribute to the Korean War Effort. In the building known as the Shop there were a number of work benches and stools, along with a supply of tools and parts. At these benches, the enlisted men spent their days tinkering with their personal radio transmitters and receivers, with their television sets, record players, and even with the innards of their cars. No specific work was ever assigned to the Shop, nor did anyone ever come by to check on what these men were doing. Sometimes they just played cards. Once again, I wondered whether the Pentagon was aware that this strange little Army unit existed.

In the meantime, I found myself faced with an increasing moral dilemma. It was a kind of catch-22 situation. I had obviously been granted my request to be stationed in Northern California, and, in return, I'd agreed to write a weekly firsthand report about Army life as experienced by the typical draftee. But it was increasingly clear that I was not leading the life of a typical draftee. I'd been sending out my stories regularly, but I'd begun relying on interviews with other soldiers, and relating their tales, and I'd begun to feel that my copy lacked a certain feel of authenticity, that I was making up stories, saying I'd experienced things I really hadn't. I felt I was not holding up my end of the bargain.

Adding to my frustration was the fact that, as far as I could tell, my stories were not being printed. My dispatches to the address in Washington were never acknowledged. From time to time, a copy of the *Armed Forces Times* would drift into the orderly room. I looked in vain for my byline. I began to feel I was sending off my words into some huge bureaucratic vacuum.

I mentioned my problem to Betty Sknolnik, the attractive young civilian woman who bore the title of public information officer for the base, and she had a quick solution. Instead of writing my weekly column, or non-column, she suggested, why didn't I write up news of servicemen's doings for their hometown newspapers? It would keep the name of the Signal Depot, and the Maintenance Company, in the press. And so, I became sort of the society-page reporter for the 504th. Whenever a man received a promotion, or became engaged, or got married, or had a baby, I would call the base photographer, have his picture taken, and ship the story off to his hometown paper. The papers, particularly in smaller towns and cities, snapped these stories up and, indeed, these seemed to have an immediate, positive effect on the morale of the servicemen involved. A Letter of Commendation was always good for a story. These were given out, with some regularity, by the Company Commander to anyone who behaved himself reasonably well. LOCAL GI RECEIVES COMMENDATION was the way the headlines usually read.

It was in this capacity that I began to receive promotions myself. First, I was elevated from ordinary private to private first class. Then I became a corporal, and then a sergeant, with three gold stripes on my sleeve. I don't know whether or not these promotions were actually illegal, but they certainly ran against military orthodoxy, which clearly stated that no enlisted man could be promoted without completing basic training. But the promotions, ordered by Colonel Wilson, and endorsed by Sixth Army Headquarters at the Presidio in San Francisco, went through without a hitch. I began to entertain a fantasy. What if I prepared an order for Colonel Wilson's signature granting me an honorable discharge from the United States Army, along with a handsome lifetime pension? He would certainly have signed it, as he signed every other document, I prepared for him. But I decided not to push my luck that far. It was enough that, without having undergone basic training, without ever having handled a weapon, I could not legally be shipped overseas, where the war in Korea was still going on. I was grateful for that.

And it was not long before I became the assignee of another very important assignment from Colonel Wilson. I was asked to be the armed forces public information coordinator for the annual California State Fair. This meant that I would be working not only with the commanding officer of the Sacramento Signal Depot, but also with the commanders of McLellan and Mather Air Force bases nearby, as well as officers from a small Navy and WAVE detachment in Sacramento. We'd work together to design a space at the fairgrounds where we'd display, as best we could, what we were all up to. For this job, I was supplied with a vehicle, an olive-drab Army station wagon. I'd gained a few pounds on starchy mess hall food, but my Army-issue uniform still didn't fit me very well, and so I argued that, since I'd be dealing with high-ranking officers, I'd do better in this job in civilian clothes. Colonel Wilson looked at me in my baggy sergeant's outfit and agreed. I didn't add that civilian clothes would also spare me the chore of saluting to all the brass, since saluting was something I still didn't do very well.

I won't say that our display of military might was the most popular attraction at the California State Fair that year. The farm folk of the Central Valley were more interested in ogling a prize Duroc hog, or a

1,200-pound watermelon, or a Guernsey cow whose milk had the highest butterfat count ever recorded. But I did score one coup. I'd read that Jack Benny was coming to Sacramento for a couple of performances. I telephoned the Benny office in Los Angeles and asked whether he could spare the time for an appearance at the Armed Forces display at the Fairgrounds. He was immediately enthusiastic. "Something for the boys!" he said. "Sure, I'll do it!" (I learned later that Benny's nose was bent considerably out of joint by the fact that Bob Hope had claimed for himself the role of principal comedy entertainer of troops overseas.)[9]

I picked up Benny at his hotel, and drove him out to the fairgrounds, where we'd built a stage and set up a microphone for him. He proceeded to perform one of his funny, thirty-minute standup routines. I think Benny was disappointed that his audience consisted mostly of civilians, rather than "the boys," but that didn't matter. He was clearly a hit. Both Sacramento papers, the *Bee* and the *Union*, had sent photographers to cover the event, and, afterward, when Benny was posing with various servicemen and -women, I noticed Colonel Wilson standing in the sidelines, looking unhappy. I knew at once what had to be done. I tapped the *Bee* photographer on the shoulder, and said, "Look—this is really important. You've got to get a picture of Jack Benny shaking hands with Colonel Wilson."

The next morning, there it was, on the front page of the newspaper, with the headline: SIGNAL DEPOT COMMANDER WELCOMES JACK BENNY TO STATE FAIR. I think the colonel was even happier when we sent the picture to his hometown paper in Texas, where it was also front-page news.

Meanwhile, with my wife's pregnancy advancing, and her father's physical condition worsening in Modesto, it was decided that she should return to her family and have the baby there, where her family doctor was. Of course, she would have been entitled to have the baby in an Army hospital, the way other Army wives did, but there was a possibility that the baby would have to be delivered by C-section, and we didn't entirely trust the military with that. My first son, Mark, was born in the Modesto hospital in March 1952. I'd been in the Army for not quite a full year. As predicted, Mark was a cesarean baby, as would be my other two children.

Cesarean babies, though hard on the mother, are nearly always beautifully formed. Ours certainly was.

Nan's father had died a few months before and did not live to see this grandson.

While all this was going on, I gave up the apartment in downtown Sacramento to move to the base, but it wasn't exactly barracks living that I was about to experience. One of the barracks buildings had been converted into a pair of apartments for noncommissioned officers and their wives. One of these was vacant, and I was offered this. Its furnishings were Spartan, but it contained a small sitting room, a bedroom, and its own private bath. There was even a telephone. I wondered whether it handled long distance and, to find out, called my parents in Connecticut. It worked. Soon I was calling friends all over the country, and even some friends in England. I never received a phone bill.

I remembered an old song from, I think, World War II: "This is the Army, Mr. Jones . . . No private rooms or telephones . . ."

My next-door neighbors were two sergeants who were the head cooks in the mess hall. Next to the first sergeant, the most important people in any Army unit are the cooks, the theory being, I suppose, that if an Army cook is not happy, he will find quick ways to seek revenge. These men were great neighbors and, because they controlled the key to the larder, there was never any shortage of after-hours snacks. Every payday we would lay in our liquor supply for the month to come.

Periodically, of course, First Sergeant Pakula would pull out my personnel file, make clicking noises with his tongue, and say, "'We've got to get you sent away somewhere for basic training." But, since my two-year stint as a draftee was now more than half over, I began to seriously doubt that this would ever happen. Pakula used it as a threat, I'm sure, to make sure I stayed in line.

But, with nothing as exciting as the California State Fair on my work agenda, I began casting around for things to do. I bought a little blue Renault to get around in. It was so lightweight that four or five strong men could easily carry it, and they often did. My fellow soldiers were always making me play hide-and-seek with my car. One time I found it inside one of the barracks. Another time they'd carried it into the latrine.

I still had time on my hands. I wrote some freelance advertising copy for Weinstock, Lubin, and Co., a Sacramento department store. I'd done some acting in college, and had worked in summer stock, so I tried out for a part with a local amateur theater group and was cast as Henry in Thornton Wilder's *The Skin of Our Teeth*. I joined the Sutter Lawn Tennis Club, where Sacramento "society" hung out. I saw a newspaper ad that said, "Earn up to $2,000 a week in your spare time—car needed," and answered it. We all met in a suite at the Senator Hotel downtown, where I learned what this lucrative job entailed. We were to read birth announcements in the newspapers, and then follow these up by ringing the doorbells of the new parent s to try to sell them a crash-proof baby's car seat. Prospective salesmen were asked to shell out $75 for the sample. I turned that offer down.

And, in my spare time—at my desk in the orderly room or in my little barracks apartment, on my portable—I wrote short stories, as I'd done at college. I typed them up neatly and sent them off to magazine editors along with self-addressed stamped envelopes for their return. And returned was what most of them were. But then, wonder of wonders, I opened an envelope one morning and out tumbled a check. I had actually sold a story—and for the princely sum of $100!

The editors who bought it were the husband-and-wife team of Whit and Hallie Burnett. For several years, the Burnetts had edited *Story* Magazine. Recently, they had begun publishing collections of short fiction in hardcover, concentrating on young, hitherto unknown authors. My story, the Burnetts informed me, would be included in the fourth volume of this series, to be called *Story Number 4: The Magazine of the Short Story in Book Form.*

The next miraculous thing to happen was that, when the book was published, it was actually reviewed in the Sunday *New York Times Book Review*. The reviewer, William Peden, wrote: "The Burnetts have introduced the work of several promising young authors, at least two of whom possess talent which deserves to be called striking." The first of the two singled out was John Knowles, who went on to write a memorable boarding school novel, *A Separate Peace*. Mr. Peden went on to say:

*Another newcomer of palpable ability is 24-yearold Stephen Birming-
ham whose depiction of a rather traditional middle-aged governess in
"Reappearance" becomes a warm and moving experience rather than
the glib clinical study a young writer of less talent might produce.*

I was floating on cloud nine that Sunday morning. The word "talent"
had been used twice in the same paragraph to describe me and my work.
But I was enough of a realist to know that one published short story and
a few words of praise in the *New York Times* were not enough to guaran-
tee me a brilliant future as a writer, much less make me suppose I could
ever earn a living at it.

In the meantime, life in the Army was not all routine, and even had
its interesting moments. Though I appeared to have become a permanent
fixture at the 504th, its population was always changing. Solders arrived
from, and departed for, Korea, and some of the arrivals had acquired
exotic habits in Asia. I remember one enlisted man who had let his fingernails grow long and kept them polished with bright red lacquer. He
had also taken to using crimson lipstick. This was dismissed as a symptom
of stress, or battle fatigue, and perhaps that was all it was.

The attitude toward homosexuality in the military was also eye-
opening. There was definitely a double standard here. For a soldier to
allow a man to perform fellatio on him—that was tossed off as normal
fun. It was even regarded as rather macho. But the man who performed
the act—he was a *queer*. A list of places Off Limits to Military Personnel
was consistently posted on the company bulletin board. Most of these
turned out to be gay bars in nearby San Francisco. I gathered that these
off-limits spots were not policed in any way, because the list proved to be
a handy guide for servicemen who were looking for a bit of offbeat adventure on their weekend passes to the city. They returned with no end of
lurid tales of their homoerotic encounters. One man boasted that a dozen
men had lined up to give him blow jobs in the men's room of one bar.

Then we had the problem of Junior. Junior was his given name, and
he hailed from somewhere in the Ozarks. I found Junior to be a sweet
kid, though he was obviously simple-minded. His IQ scores placed him
in the low-average range. Physically, on the other hand, he was a giant.

At six-feet-eleven, he should probably not have been drafted into the Army in the first place. His feet stuck out over the end of his Army cot, and the standard Army sheets and blankets were too short to cover him. It was difficult to find uniforms that would fit him, and boots for his size-sixteen feet had to be specially made. But the most troublesome thing about Junior was that he was a bed-wetter. Every morning, without fail, he would be found in a sopping-wet mattress.

Draconian measures were applied to try to correct this. At night, the guards on duty were instructed to wake Junior on the hour and escort him to the latrine. This didn't help matters in the slightest. Finally, a meeting was held in the orderly room by the senior officers on the base to try to solve the Junior problem, and it was decided that Junior should be given a Section Eight discharge. Section Eight was reserved for men who were "mentally unfit" for the service. It could also be interpreted to mean "insane."

It was hardly my place to interrupt a meeting between officers, but when I heard this decision, I spoke up. "Sirs," I said, "I know you haven't asked for my opinion, but I think a Section Eight is wrong. That sort of thing could follow him for the rest of his life. Every time he tries to get a job, and they look at his military record, they'll see the Army thought he was crazy. I have another suggestion."

"What's that?" they wanted to know.

"Promote him," I said. "Make him a corporal. Give him a little authority. It might not work, but it wouldn't hurt to try."

At first, there was consternation at this notion. But finally, in a spirit of nothing ventured nothing gained, it was agreed to give my suggestion a try. As a corporal, Junior all at once fairly bristled with authority. He strode around the company grounds barking orders to lower ranking enlisted men. He volunteered for jobs no one else wanted—including guard duty. The bed-wetting stopped. As a corporal, Junior was transformed into the perfect, robotic soldier. Soon he was asking to be sent to Korea. He wanted, he said, to see some "action." He wanted to see some "real fighting." His request was granted. I have no idea what finally became of him, but I'm sure that for the rest of his Army career he conducted himself bravely, and with honor.

One of my last special assignments in the US Army was to head up the annual fund drive for the American Red Cross. I must say it was one of the most unpleasant jobs I've ever tackled. I'd had no idea in how much contempt—hatred, really—the Red Cross was held by the average soldier, particularly those who had served in combat. Thousands of people, myself included, have donated blood to the Red Cross, and I'd always assumed that this blood was administered for free to wounded servicemen in the field. This turned out not to be the case at all. The wounded received blood, but they had to pay for it, and at the time the price was $15 a pint. Furthermore, in order to receive it, they were required to sign a Class A Allotment to the Red Cross, allowing the cost of blood to be deducted from their pay. "Class A" meant that a soldier's indebtedness to the Red Cross took precedence over anything else. Often, a soldier who had required large amounts of blood in the battlefield recovered to find that there was nothing left in his pay envelope at all. It was all going to repay the American Red Cross.

At the same time, orders had come down from above—perhaps from the Pentagon itself—that every serviceman was expected to contribute to the annual fund drive. Nothing less than 100 percent participation in the drive would be tolerated by Headquarters, and it was implied that the man who failed to contribute faced a court-martial, or the brig, or even worse. The minimum acceptable contribution was $1. To a soldier who earns only $4–$5 a day, a dollar is a significant sum—a quarter of his daily wage. As I went from man to man, soliciting their dollars—and few gave more than that—abuse was heaped upon my head, and upon the American Red Cross. One man tossed a hundred pennies on the floor beside my feet and told me that if I wanted his contribution to the Red Cross I would have to get down on my hands and knees and pick up every penny. "Fuck the Red Cross!" he said and raised his middle finger in a significant gesture.

If there was a crisis at home, the Red Cross would arrange for a soldier to take an emergency leave and would handle his transportation arrangements. But, again, if a soldier needed an airplane ticket home, the Red Cross would not give it to him. He was required to sign another Class A Allotment for the sum, and it would be deducted from his pay.

It struck me as odd that the Red Cross seemed to be in the position of ordering the United States Army what to do. But this civilian, supposedly humanitarian organization, seemed to have a stranglehold on the military. I began to wonder if this was quite what Clara Barton had had in mind.

One disadvantage I had as a member of the 504th Signal Base Maintenance Company was that I—with my car, my tennis racket, and my preppy wardrobe—was known as "the rich guy." About a week before payday, every soldier in the unit seemed to be broke, and I was an obvious target for requests for loans. These were usually for small sums and were always repaid when payday rolled around. But then one day a pleasant young sergeant named Bill approached me and asked me if I could lend him $500. This, in enlisted men's terms, was a lot of money. But his need seemed pressing enough. His girlfriend needed an abortion, and he felt it was his duty, as a soldier and a gentleman, to pay for it. I let him have the money. Several months—and paydays—went by, and though Bill always greeted me cheerfully when we met, there was never any mention of repaying the loan. Then, from my sensitive post in the orderly room, I saw Bill's orders come through; he was being sent to Korea. I decided it was inhumane to confront a man who was about to go off to risk his life for his country, and so I decided to write the whole matter off.

On the day that Bill and a couple of dozen other men were to ship out, they all lined up to board a bus to San Francisco. The rest of us in the company stepped outside to wave the men goodbye. Seeing me in the crowd, Bill suddenly broke out of the line, ran over to me, and said, "I've been looking for you." He pressed five $100 bills in my hand. Later, I heard that he had been killed by a sniper's bullet near Panmunjom.

And, despite my father's dire warnings, none of the things I'd brought into the Army with me—the luggage which, after all, had got me where I was—was ever stolen. There was a strict code of honor among servicemen. A man's money, and his possessions, were sacred. They were more sacrosanct than his wife or girlfriend. This is not to say that other forms of larceny, both grand and petty, were not condoned—even encouraged— by the military. A popular practice, for example, when a man learned he was about to be shipped overseas, was for the man to hurry downtown and purchase a large diamond ring for the girlfriend or the wife. Small retail jewelers were happy to part with such an item for as little as $100 down, and a signed contract promising to pay off the balance at $10 a month for years to come. Needless to say, once the man was safely in some remote part of the world, all monthly payments stopped. In the orderly room, we were always getting calls from irate jewelers seeking the whereabouts of their vanished creditors, but we were never furnished with soldiers' forwarding addresses and could offer no help at all. Sometimes the jewelers took their grievances to Washington, where the Pentagon piously informed them that it would constitute a severe breach of National Security to reveal the location of any of the Army's troops. This sort of scam would not have worked with the purchase of, say, an automobile, which would be fairly easy to trace and repossess. But the diamonds were gone forever.

With the end of my two-year tour of duty just months away, and the possibility of my being shipped anywhere else growing remoter by the day, my wife and I decided to rent a house for ourselves and our new baby. We chose one from the sprawl of tract houses near the Signal Depot. It didn't matter to us that the floor plan of our house was identical to those of all the other houses on the street, which were differentiated only by the cutouts on their window shutters (some were cut out in the shape of pineapples, some in quarter-moons, some in the shape of pine trees.) Thirty-six-thirty-eight MacMillan Drive was our first real house, with a lawn to mow and water, and a hedge to trim. Nothing says domesticity like a diaper service.

When we moved into this house, my friends the Army cooks insisted on giving us a housewarming party. This, they explained, was an Army "tradition." From the Mess Hall larder, they presented us with huge, Number-10 jars of mustard, mayonnaise, catsup, and pickles. They gave us several twenty-pound tins of tuna, a fifty-pound carton of powdered milk, and a fifty-pound vat of butter. We said no to an offer of a whole side of beef, since we couldn't think of a place to refrigerate or store it, and so the cooks substituted a few dozen sirloin steaks. There was a good deal else—huge bags of flour, a gross of eggs, bags of salt, a hundred pounds of frozen frankfurters. It went on and on. My little car was so weighted down with stolen government property that its rear end scraped the pavement when we reached the guard at the gate of the Signal Depot and were waved through.

The night before I was due to receive my discharge from the Army, my wife and I decided to have a party for all our friends at the base. We invited the two cooks, of course, and First Sergeant Pakula, Major McCandless and his wife, and Colonel and Mrs. Wilson. There was a certain amount of huffing and puffing about this. It was against Army etiquette for officers and their wives to socialize—"fraternize" was the word used—with mere enlisted men. I suggested that we might all wear civilian clothes to reduce any differences created by rank. But I was told, it wasn't just rank; it was a matter of *status*. Still, in the end, they all accepted our invitation—out of curiosity, perhaps, more than anything else.

The evening got off to a rather stiff and edgy start, particularly among the wives, who were more status-conscious than their husbands. But, after a few drinks, everyone began to feel more comfortable. Nothing breaks down the most rigid of class barriers better than whiskey.

Colonel Wilson spent the evening begging me not to accept my discharge, but to reenlist, apply for Officer Candidate School, and make the Army my life's career. He spoke of the generous retirement benefits, the free health care, the liberal leave policy. "You'd make an excellent officer," he assured me. "You'd be an excellent officer candidate. I'll even give you a Letter of Commendation." I demurred as politely as possible.

After a drink or two, I turned to First Sergeant Pakula. "Pakula" I said, "admit it, you never had any intention of sending me somewhere else for basic training, did you? The minute you saw that typewriter of mine, and found out I could use it, you decided to keep me here."

At first, he scowled. I was accusing him, after all, of ignoring Army regulations, if not actually flouting them. He went to the bar, poured himself another drink, and then turned to me and gave me a slow wink.

I have a soft spot in my heart for M/Sgt Pakula to this day.

Chapter Seven

Marquand

Steve:
There used to be an unwritten rule in my profession that writers always tried to help other writers, the theory being, I suppose, that most writers are in some sort of trouble most of the time. It was a nice rule, but I'm not sure that it's honored much anymore. When I first started publishing, in the mid-1950s, publishing and bookselling were still something of a cottage industry. The local independent bookstore was still a viable part of any neighborhood. The bookseller pretty much knew who his customers were, and knew their tastes, and would recommend titles and authors accordingly. If a particular customer's Aunt Grace went to the hospital, the bookseller usually had a list of books that Aunt Grace would enjoy reading during her stay. The independent bookstore owner saw his role as something akin to that of the grandmotherly village librarian. He was performing a community service, and earning a small, but comfortable, living by doing so.

Today, the independent bookstore is all but nonexistent, having been driven out of business by the mighty chains. At vast emporia such as Barnes & Noble and Joseph-Beth, it is hard enough to find a salesperson to wait on you, much less one who has actually read any of the books in the store; service personnel amount to the people at the end of the cash-register line with their electronic scanners.

The chains—and these increasingly include chains of supermarkets where books are sold—have profoundly changed the nature of book publishing. What used to be called "an occupation for gentlemen" is now big business, an occupation for entrepreneurs. The chains, with their huge centralized and computerized buying power, are now effectively able to dictate what sort of books get into print. The chains want big, blockbuster best sellers—they discount these, further boosting sales—and publishers are under pressure to deliver them. As publishing has become big business, once-small publishing houses have been snapped up by conglomerates, in some cases international ones, to whom the slightest indication of red ink is a signal that heads must roll. The same thing is happening in Hollywood, of course. The pressure to turn big profits is on. It used to be that publishers were willing to fly by the seat of their pants—publishing books that sometimes made money, but sometimes didn't, while the publisher stayed afloat with the occasional boost of a surprise best seller. But no more. Today, the average shelf life of a non-best-selling title is not much more than that of a quart of milk. If a title doesn't sell, off it goes to be remaindered and, soon afterward, shredded to become recycled paper.

At the bottom end of this feeding frenzy is the author, who is under the most pressure of all. The fact is that today the author of a slender, sensitive, elegantly crafted first novel has an extremely difficult time finding a publisher in this fierce climate. I suspect that many writers sensing the current situation, simply give up, and turn to some other line of work. Those who persevere are now too busy covering their own hindquarters, while keeping a wary eye over their shoulders at what the competition is doing, to give much thought to helping other writers. Nowadays, it's every man for himself, and to hell with the others. As to what this portends for the future of writing in America, I have no crystal ball. But I try not to be too pessimistic.

As for myself, I was lucky enough—and writing is a career, I should remind the reader, where one must be willing to be lucky—to find not one, but two established writers who were able, out of nothing but sheer generosity, to give me a much-needed boost. I'll always be grateful to those two men, who came into my life out of the blue.

I'd been working as a copywriter for a New York advertising agency called Doherty, Clifford, Steers & Shenfield. (It later became Needham, Harper & Steers, and is now, after a series of mergers, known as D.B.B. Needham, Worldwide, Inc.) I found writing advertising copy to be almost embarrassingly easy. Fortunately, I had not been hired to write copy about laxatives, deodorants, and mouthwashes, though the Bristol-Myers drug company was one of our biggest clients and had products in all those categories. My job was writing advertising promotion for *Ladies' Home Journal*. "Advertising promotion" meant that the ads I wrote were designed to persuade advertisers to buy space in the magazine—advertisers from the automotive industry, in particular. We'd learned that, in the all-male bastions of such places as the Detroit Athletic Club, the idea of placing car ads in women's magazines was considered sissy stuff. My job was to try to change that attitude.

The slogan I offered was "Never Underestimate the Power of a Woman." The idea behind it was that the man in the family might be the one who wrote out the check for the new car, but it was more often his wife and the mother of his children who had the final say about the car's make, model, color, and styling. It seems a simplistic notion today, in the wake of the feminist movement, but at the time it was considered quite startling and original—equating women with *power*, of all things. And I note that *Ladies' Home Journal* still carries my slogan on the spine of the magazine, though I doubt that anyone there today knows where it came from.

We ran about one full-page ad a month in the *New York Times* and other big-city newspapers (including Detroit's), and an occasional ad in the *New Yorker*, considered a strong medium for automobile advertising. As I said, I found this to be not a terribly taxing production schedule. I soon began to feel as though I could write these ads in my sleep. The irony was that I was apparently very good at writing them, and was rewarded with what seemed to me an absurdly high salary, and one that was supplemented with regular, generous raises and bonuses, all of which were naturally welcome in a household where, in addition to a wife, there were already two, and soon would be three, small children.

To write one ad a month took me, at most, an hour. Of course, in the agency business one doesn't just submit one ad to the client for approval. It's far better to offer the client a choice of three or four—one that you know is good, and a few more that you know are less good. This gives the client the important psychological power of *standing in judgment* over your work, the power of *rejection* of some of it. Never underestimate the feelings of power enjoyed by those who can exercise the power of the veto—in my case, the husband-and-wife team of Bruce and Beatrice Gould, who were then coeditors of the *Journal*.

At the same time, submitting several choices of ad copy for the client's approval gave the client the impression that you had been working and thinking tirelessly about the ways of promoting his product, at the expense of all else, since your last meeting. But even if I turned out half a dozen proposals for *Journal* ads a month, that effort—to me, at least—did not consume much more time than a single working day. I hope this doesn't sound like boasting. It was just that this sort of writing came to me so easily. And I should add that I was fortunate in having a client that was not particularly demanding. Things were going well for the *Journal* in those days. Circulation was climbing, soon to top five million. Ad pages and revenue were going up, too—whether thanks to my efforts or not I have no way of knowing. Nor, in the ad game, does anyone else.

There are many wonderful people in the advertising business, and I made a number of friends at the agency, particularly in the so-called "Creative" departments, Copy and Art. At the same time, advertising struck me as—there's no other word for it—a shitty business. One of our important clients was Seagram, and we handled the advertising for several important brands of Seagram liquors. Seagram was then headed by the despotic and mercurial "Mr. Sam" Bronfman. We thought Mr. Sam was happy with us, but then something happened. Mr. Sam was an inveterate gin rummy player, and he played for high stakes. Another agency may have won his business in a gin rummy game; who knew? But one morning we were informed that he was taking his business to another shop, and that was that. That same day, forty employees of our agency were out on the street, looking for jobs. That sort of thing went on all the time, and it was not pretty to watch.

At about that time, Bill Steers, who was president of the company as well as president of the American Association of Advertising Agencies, began telling me that he had me in mind to succeed him as president. (Bill, a dear man, and a good businessman, was also, alas, a man who had trouble expressing himself verbally, and I'd been writing his speeches for him. In his obituary, a number of years later, his theories about the advertising business were extensively quoted, and I was touched to recognize some of the words I'd put into his mouth for addresses at Four-A's meetings and conventions.) But when he began hinting that the presidency of the company could be mine when he stepped down, I tried to be properly appreciative, though the truth was I didn't want to be president of an advertising agency. I wanted to be a writer.

CAREY:
The Mad Men *Connection*

Many will recall the highly entertaining TV series, *Mad Men*, which ran on AMC from 2007 until 2015. My wife, Lisa, and I watched, enthralled, as I recounted to her some of my father's experiences at Needham, Harper & Steers in the 1950s and '60s, the period in which both the series and my father's advertising career overlapped. As we binge-watched the series, it brought back many memories of my father coming home from New York, much as Don Draper did.

Once enveloped, I noticed several parallels between the series and the Birmingham experiences in advertising:

- In more than one episode, the firm name, Needham, is mentioned. This alone would not necessarily be coincidental since Needham Harper was an established firm during the time frame. However, during one episode, as Lisa and watched transfixed, one character says to another, "Did you hear Birmingham left Needham?"

- Elsewhere, Glen Bishop, the young boy who is attracted to Betty Draper, attends Hotchkiss School, my father's high school alma mater.

- The Drapers end up moving out of New York City to the burbs, and select Rye, New York, as their new home. Rye is where I grew up, and my parents purchased our house in 1954.

- In one episode, a partygoer at Ted and Betty Chaough's house comments to the effect, "there was already trouble on Peck Avenue." Our house was among five others in a small cul-de-sac with the only exit onto Peck Avenue. It's curious that the party guest should mention Peck Avenue, because it's a nondescript street that connects Midland Avenue and Post Road in Rye, with its only claim to fame that it had an entrance to Avon Products headquarters (Avon's address was, in fact, on Midland Avenue.) I can't imagine what "troubles" might have occurred on this short, three-quarter-mile street in the *Mad Men*'s writer's mind.

- Ted Chaough, a partner at Cutler, Gleason, is married to "Nan" in the series. While not necessarily a unique name, "Nan" was my mother's name, derived from Janet.

- Robert Morse plays Bertram Cooper in the TV series, the patriarch of the advertising firm Sterling, Cooper & Partners. Robert was a close friend of our family in the 1960s. Indeed, when I was in seventh grade at Rye Junior High School, I got the part of Barnaby Tucker in our middle school's production of *The Matchmaker*. (Robert Morse immortalized that role on Broadway.) I will never forget on opening night at our junior high school when I received a telegram from Robert wishing me luck and, in classic Broadway style, hoping I'd "break a leg!"

All coincidences?

As I write this, I have reached out to both Matthew Weiner and Robert Morse via their agents to see what, if any, connection the show had to my father's time in advertising, either directly or tangentially. I got no responses.

STEVE:

Among the other copywriters in our department, there were several young men and women who harbored ambitions to become "serious" writers. Their excuses for not having made the giant step were the same: after a hectic day in the rat race of the advertising business they had no energy left to work on the plays and novels and television scripts they someday wanted to write. But as for me, since I found the pace of my job so un-hectic, I needed something to do to fill my hours at the office. So, I wrote short stories, as I'd been doing through most of my years at college, as an English Major, and through two years in the United States Army.

It's important to remember that the early 1950s were still part of a kind of Golden Era for the short story. There were magazines about, such as the *Saturday Evening Post* and *Collier's*, that published three or four short stories a week. So did the *New Yorker*, which, though it paid little for short fiction, was where every young writer dreamed of being published. Then there were the monthlies—*Harper's*, the *Atlantic*, *Redbook*, *Cosmopolitan*, *McCall's*, *Ladies' Home Journal*, *Mademoiselle*, *Good Housekeeping*, *Esquire*—all of whom offered markets for the short-story writer. I submitted my output to all of these. Sitting at my desk in my office, hunched over my typewriter, with a plentiful supply of paper in the agency supply room—I'm sure I gave the impression to passersby of great industry. No one guessed that I was actually working for myself. At the end of the day, I carried my works-in-progress home, where I worked on them some more, in a very businesslike looking attaché case.

And I collected the printed rejection slips. Despite my first sale, there were soon dozens of these, then over two hundred. I kept a careful chart which showed which story had been submitted to, and rejected by, which publication. From time to time, I would receive a rejection slip with the word "Sorry!" handwritten across the face of it. That was always a thrilling moment. It meant that some anonymous editor had actually felt sorry that he'd rejected my work! That indicated progress! But of course, it really didn't. It simply meant that my work was still unacceptable. And, as my desk drawer began to overflow with unpublished, and seemingly unpublishable, short stories, I began to get discouraged. Perhaps, I decided, it was time to face some hard facts. Perhaps I should give up on this. That was the point at which, quite by accident, Jerry Weidman came into my life.

Jerome Weidman was a prolific and versatile writer. He'd written many short stories and books, perhaps the best known of which were *I Can Get It for You Wholesale*, *What's in It for Me*, and *The Horse That Could Whistle "Dixie."* He'd also written for Broadway, and had collaborated, with George Abbott, on the hit musical "*Fiorello!*" about New York's colorful ex-mayor LaGuardia. I'd never read any of his work, but there he was, with his pretty wife Peggy, at a cocktail party at the home of mutual friends in Westport, Connecticut, where the Weidmans then lived.

Later that evening, as my wife and I were leaving, he suddenly turned to me and said, "Do you do any other writing besides the advertising?" I muttered that I'd written a few short stories. "I'd like to read them," he said. "Will you send them over to me?" He gave me his address and phone number. That night, I pulled all my short stories out of their drawer and shipped them off to Jerome Weidman.

What happened next seems, in retrospect, to have happened fast. A few days later, Weidman called me and said, "I like some of your stories very much—some more than others, of course. But if you don't mind, I'd like to show them to my agent, Carl Brandt. He's a terrific guy." I hastily assured him that I wouldn't mind at all. I'd be hugely grateful, in fact.

Then, a few days after that, I had a call from Carl Brandt. He'd like to see me at his office to discuss my work.

Carl Brandt was a courtly, soft-spoken gentleman from the Old South whose dignified demeanor belied the fact that he had the reputation of being a tough agent and a driver of hard bargains on behalf of his stable of writers, many of whom were well known. At the time, Brandt & Brandt was known as the "Tiffany of literary agencies," in part because it had been around longer than almost any other. In the past, it had represented such writers as Joseph Conrad, Thornton Wilder, Booth Tarkington, and John Dos Passes. When I arrived at his office, Carl Brandt had divided my manuscripts into two neat piles—those he thought he could sell, and those he didn't. He handed the latter pile back to me.

Within two weeks, he had sold three of my stories to national magazines, one of them to a magazine that had previously sent it back with a rejection slip. A week later, he sold two more—one of them, I was rather tickled to note, to *McCall's*, which was then "my" *Ladies' Home Journal's* chief rival in the women's magazine field.

Perhaps understandably, I was unable to keep the news of my "overnight" success from my fellow workers at the office, and that was when I had an experience that would sour me even further on the advertising business. One of my fellow senior copywriters, whom I'll call Fred Jones, came to me with a proposition. Fred was a bright young man, a graduate of Harvard where he's been a member of the Hasty Pudding Club. I liked Fred, and I was still young and naive enough to think that a man with an Ivy League education had to be morally above reproach. Fred had also been writing short stories, with no success, and here was his proposal. "Look," he said, "why don't you take some of my short stories, put your name on them, send them over to Carl Brandt, and let him sell them? You and I can split the money fifty-fifty."

I was so flabbergasted by this suggestion that I was barely able to speak civilly to Fred again.

I never really got to know Jerome Weidman very well, though I used to run into him from time to time. In those days that was not hard to do, since he was very much the man on the go in New York and Hollywood. But I've always been grateful to him for introducing me to the Brandt office, which has represented me ever since.

Thanks to Carl Brandt, I began turning out, and selling, more short stories, and soon I was being assigned nonfiction pieces for various magazines, including *Life, Sports Illustrated, Vogue, Harper's Bazaar, Travel & Leisure, and Town & Country*.[10] For some reason, I was never able to sell anything to *Ladies' Home Journal*, for whom I was still writing ad copy. Perhaps it was because the editors there saw me as a person wearing one hat, that of their copywriter, and had trouble envisioning me wearing any other. In fact, the *Journal* is one of the very few national magazines that has never published anything of mine.

One day Carl Brandt called me into his office. "Look," I remember him saying, "You can go on writing for magazines for as long as you like. The editors like your stuff, and you always make your deadlines. But a lot of magazines are in trouble right now. *Esquire* is in trouble, and so are the Curtis magazines. Hearst is retrenching, and I think both *Life* and *Collier's* are about to fold. And the market for short stories is shrinking. The short story form seems to be going out of style." (He was remarkably foresighted; today, forty years later, the market for short stories is virtually nil.) Then he added words I'll never forget, "A writer's literary estate lies between hard covers." I went home that night and started writing a novel. For the next eight months, I worked on virtually nothing else.

Carl had told me that he liked to spend his weekends reading manuscripts, undisturbed, at home. So, when my manuscript was in what I considered a good first draft form, I dropped it off on a Friday morning with the doorman at the Brandts' Fifth Avenue building. This was in the late spring of 1957. The next afternoon, I had a telephone call from Carl's wife, Carol. "I've had an unpaid reader reading your manuscript," she told me, "and he'd like to talk to you about it. Can you come by the apartment for drinks at six o'clock? His name is John P. Marquand."

From the mid-1930s through the 1950s, the novels of John P. Marquand had appeared, almost without exception, on best seller lists across the country. They were nearly always bought for serialization by magazines, and more often than not eventually became motion pictures. His first "serious" novel, *The Late George Apley*, published in 1936, won the Pulitzer Prize for Fiction that year. Prior to that, Marquand had made a more-than-comfortable living writing detective novels whose hero was a seemingly timid but cunning and intelligent Japanese sleuth named Mr. Moto. Mr. Moto's characteristic response to the uncovering of an important clue was, "Ah, so!" The Mr. Moto tales had also been snapped up by the movies, and between 1937 and 1965 there were nine Mr. Moto movies, and they established the acting career of Peter Lorre, who played the title role in most of them.

The Late George Apley was considered a radical departure for Marquand, and someone at his publisher—Little, Brown—actually suggested that it might best be published under a pseudonym, so closely was Marquand's name associated with Moto. But *Apley* was clearly the right departure for Marquand. After that book, his many novels—*Wickford Point, H. M. Pulham, Esquire*, and others—enjoyed not only popular success but critical acclaim. By 1957, he also had the distinction of being one of the five judges at the Book of the Month Club. He was very much an Important Figure in American Letters, and a rich man. Unlike Heinrich Faust, however, who was a Californian, Marquand was a thrifty New Englander who managed his finances shrewdly and, proper Bostonian that he was, lived "on the income from his income."

Given the size of John Marquand's reputation at the time, it strikes me as both curious and sad that, if you asked the average college English major today who John Marquand was, he would probably look at you blankly and scratch his head. It is not that his books have not withstood the passage of time or seem old-fashioned. Though they deal with an earlier generation, they also portray a segment of New England society— particularly Boston society—that has hardly changed at all over the years and is serenely proud of that fact. The novels of John Marquand are surely no more dated than those of Jane Austen, Henry James, or Edith Wharton, novels of manners that have lately been enjoying an enthusiastic renaissance, both in bookstores and on the screen. Why have John Marquand's books been allowed to sink without a trace? Some mysterious law of public relations must be at work here.

Ironically, the works of John Marquand that have survived the longest are the ones of which he was least proud, the Mr. Moto stories. And these have maintained a life of their own in a curious milieu: the world of crossword-puzzle creators and solvers. Whenever a puzzler encounters the clue "Fictional sleuth," the four-letter answer is almost certain to be "Moto."

But perhaps the major books have not sunk entirely without a trace. Whenever I am in a public library, I check the Marquand section on the fiction shelves. From the cards in their little envelopes, I can see that his novels still circulate. Some people are still reading him. But no one seems to want to talk about him except in a few, somewhat arcane circles. At Baylor University in Texas, for instance, a group of English professors recently offered a series of Marquand symposiums. But, after all, Baylor University is not Yale, Princeton, Brown, or Marquand's own beloved Harvard, which, in his novels, he was able to anatomize so deftly.

Meanwhile, I knew that Carl and Carol Brandt's relationship with Marquand was a complicated one, to say the least. For several years before I met either of them, the Brandts had had what I guess is best called an "open marriage." The Brandts were clearly devoted to one another, both as husband and wife and as business partners. And yet, as far as their sex lives were concerned, both had come to an amicable agreement that each partner in the union was at liberty to go his and her own way. This always struck me as a very sophisticated, and yet sensible, notion. It provided a certain glue that held the marriage together. It was like the European custom known as *cinq-à-sept*. In a *cinq-à-sept* arrangement, the husband is allowed to leave the hours between five o'clock, when he leaves his office, and seven, unaccounted for. How he spends these two hours is no one's business but his own, and he may spend them at his club, or with any sexual partner of his choice. The only stipulation—and this rule is strictly adhered to—is that he be home by seven o'clock, for dinner with his family. His wife, if she so chooses, is offered the same privilege. The *cinq-à-sept* tradition is said to help account for the fact that divorce rates are much lower in Europe than in Puritan-minded America.

In the Brandts' case, there was a slight difference. John Marquand was probably Carl Brandt's closest friend, and certainly one of his most profitable clients. Carl Brandt thought highly of Marquand's work, and Marquand valued Brandt's opinion of it—more so, in fact, than he did that of his editors at Little, Brown. At the same time, when Carol Brandt told me that Marquand had read my manuscript and invited me to meet him for drinks at her apartment, I knew that Carol and Marquand had been lovers for the better part of fourteen years. It was an arrangement that suited everybody—or, rather, everybody except Mrs. Marquand and Marquand's five children, none of whom had been able to quite grasp the elegance of this design for living.

There are a great many wonderful Carol Brandt stories, but, in terms of her love life, I have a few favorites. She once said to me, "Englishmen make the best lovers. It's those all-male public schools that do it. By the time they're sixteen, they've learned how to do absolutely *every*thing. I adore being taken over a man's knee and being spanked, for instance. *Nobody* gives a better spanking than an Englishman!" On another occasion she remarked, "The only trouble with being a woman agent and taking lovers is that sooner or later the lovers come back with a manuscript for me to read." My old friend Margaret Thalken, who worked as an editor for various fashion magazines—*Glamour* and *Vogue*—was between jobs at one point and, since no one knew the magazine world better than Carol, I suggested that Margaret and Carol should have lunch. During the course of this, Carol asked Margaret, "My dear, can you write?" Margaret replied that she could, though her experience consisted mostly of writing captions for fashion photos. "Why don't you write a novel about the fashion magazine business?" Carol suggested. Margaret said, "Well, Mrs. Brandt, if I were to tell the truth I'd have to point out that most of the top women editors are married to homosexuals." "Oh, but they make marvelous lovers, dear," Carol said. "I disagree, Mrs. Brandt," Margaret said. "Most of the men I know are very cruel to their wives." Carol gave Margaret a long look through her jeweled lorgnette. "My dear, I didn't say *husbands!*" she said.

All this was part of Carol's pose, of course, her outrageous persona. I grew to see another side of her, as a woman of great honesty, integrity, intelligence, and courage. Her life had not been without its vicissitudes. She had suffered through Carl Brandt's alcoholism (though by the time I met him he had been sober for many years.) By the time she died, she had been widowed three times. Her only daughter, Vicky, was killed in a plane crash with her young husband. One of her young grandchildren died in another tragic accident. Through all of these exigencies, her upper lip remained extraordinarily stiff, the facade in place.

Not long before Vicky's death, Carol had asked me to serve as Vicky's legal guardian, since I was close to Vicky's age. "If anything happens to me," Carol said, "I just want you to see to it that Vicky's money doesn't go to a lot of Hollywood divorce lawyers." And so, Vicky was my official ward. When I read of the plane crash, and phoned Carol to express my shock and sympathy, her first words to me were, "Well, darling, you're off the hook!"

John Marquand had used Carol Brandt as the model for the character of Marvin Myles in *H. M. Pulham, Esquire*, Harry Pulham's first and only great love—a bright, free-spirited young New York career woman, somewhat incongruously played by Hedy Lamarr in the film version.[11] Marquand was always sparing in his physical descriptions of his fictional characters, preferring to let their words and actions create pictures of them in the minds of his readers. His description of Marvin Myles is typically lean and terse, and he says of her only that "Her eyes and mouth were both straight and defiant." That is an apt summation of Carol Brandt.

As it happened, on the afternoon that Carol invited me to have drinks with her and John Marquand to discuss my manuscript, I had read none of Marquand's novels. The only work of his I'd read was a very clever short story called *The End Game*, based on a game of chess. Obviously, caught short by this invitation, I had no chance to catch up on my reading of Marquand, and knew I was going to have to wing it when I met him later in the day.

When he stepped into the library of the Brandts' apartment that evening, the first thing that struck me about him was that he didn't look like a writer. I don't know what I expected a famous novelist to look like, but Marquand looked more like a bank vice president or a Wall Street lawyer. He was a handsome, compactly built man in his early sixties with carefully combed silver hair and a small, neatly trimmed moustache. He was dressed in a dark, three-piece suit, white shirt, and conservative necktie. His manner, as Carol introduced us and we shook hands, struck me at first as reserved and almost courtly. I'd rehearsed what I was going to say to him, and so, as we sat down, I said, lying, "Of course I've read and enjoyed many of your novels, Mr. Marquand. But I must say that one of my favorite pieces of yours is a short story called 'The End Game.'"

All at once he was positively beaming. "Well!" he said, slapping his knee. "Is that so? You know, I've always been rather proud of that short story. If I do say so, I think it's one of the best things I've ever written!" Once again, I'd managed to be lucky. From that moment on, John Marquand and I were friends. Nathan, Carol Brandt's elegant Black butler, took our orders for drinks.

What had happened that weekend, I learned later, and the reason why Marquand had read my manuscript, was this: Marquand had been staying with the Brandt's, as he usually did when he was in New York, and on Saturday morning Carl Brandt had suddenly felt ill and had been rushed to a hospital with what was feared to be a heart attack. (It turned out not to be.) As Carol Brandt and Marquand sat alone in the apartment, waiting for word from the doctors and the hospital, Carol said, "Look, there's no point in the two of us just sitting here worrying about Carl. Let's get to work. Here's a manuscript that's just come in—a first novel by a young writer named Stephen Birmingham. Let's read it and see what we think." They sat there in the Brandt's' library, passing the pages of my manuscript back and forth between them.

After reading about thirty pages, I was later told, Marquand put down the script and said, "I'm sorry, but I'm afraid this really isn't very good." "Give it a few more pages," Carol said.

Marquand sighed, and read on. A few minutes later, he said, "Actually, it's beginning to get better." And he read on, to the end, at which point he said, "It's really rather good. I'd like to meet the young man."

And now he was saying to me, "I enjoyed your novel very much, though it gets off to a slow start. I'd do some heavy cutting in the first thirty or so pages if I were you. You've got to grab the reader right at the beginning of a book preferably on the first page, even better in the first sentence of the very first paragraph. If you haven't grabbed the reader by the third or fourth page, he's going to put your book down and never pick it up again. Also, your writing is overly adverbial. Remember—nouns and verbs are the workhorses of the language. A string of heavy adjectives won't help a weak noun, and adverbs are the weakest words of all. If I were you, I'd go through this script and delete every word ending in 'ly.' And you don't need to tell the reader how a particular line of dialogue is spoken, you don't need to say, 'he implored,' or 'she demanded.' If your dialogue is good enough the tone of voice is implicit. Just write, 'he said,' or 'she said,' and only when the reader could be confused as to who's saying what."

He then sprang to his feet and, his glass of whiskey swinging in circles in his hand as he spoke, began to give us a demonstration of what he meant, improvising a scene from an imaginary novel:

"'Have you fed the baby?' she demanded mincingly.

'Not yet,' he riposted cagily.

'Why not?' she inquired coyly.

'I thought you were going to do it,' he countered uncomprehendingly.

'But it's your turn,' she expostulated wearily.

'Are you sure, dearest?' he threw back at her fiercely. 'Of course, I'm sure' she retaliated winsomely.

'You're wrong,' he ejaculated triumphantly."

It went on for some minutes, and when he sat down at the conclusion of this little act, I decided that if John Marquand had not chosen to be a writer, he could have earned a tidy living as a stand-up comic in Las

Vegas. He was an extremely funny man—even funnier, somehow, in his bespoke, pinstriped three-piece suit.

He also had some ideas about titles. I'd titled my manuscript *The Year of the Avocado*, a title I found (and still do find, a little) poetic and evocative, since the hero of the tale, Jimmy Keefe, is a young man whose wife has left him, who is drifting into alcoholism as well as into an affair with his best friend's wife, while haplessly and fruitlessly (my penchant for adverbs still pops up from time to time) trying to grow an avocado tree from a seed pierced with toothpicks over a glass of water in his lonely kitchen.

"Don't call it that," Marquand said. "You'd be amazed at the number of people who don't know what an avocado is, much less how to pronounce the word. In bookstores, people get shy and reluctant to ask for a book if they're not sure how to pronounce a word in the title. People like to read books that are about people, so I try to put peoples' names in my titles—*The Late George Apley*; *H. M. Pulham, Esquire*; *Sincerely, Willis Wayde*; *Melville Goodwin, U.S.A.*; *B.F.'s Daughter*. I still wish I'd given Apley a different name. Nobody knew how to pronounce it. People kept coming into stores and asking for *The Late George Appleby*. I'd have sold a lot more copies of that book if I'd given Apley a different name."

He then returned to the subject of my title. "Don't get fancy with titles," he said. "Keep them simple. Your novel is about a young man named Keefe. Why not call it *Young Mr. Keefe*?"

"I will," I said.

At the time, John Marquand was considered the master of the flashback technique. Many of his novels begin in the present, and then take leisurely detours backward in time, then move forward, and wind up in the present again at the end. Marquand found my flashbacks a little bumpy and awkward. "Take more time with your flashbacks," he said. "Just add a few more sentences, with a bit more detail, to help your reader realize that you're moving from one point in time to another. You have to *ease* the reader into the flashback. Don't make the shift too abrupt, or the reader will be confused about where he is in the story, and what's going on."

Marquand and I got on famously that first meeting—so famously, in fact, that I wasn't keeping any track of time. Marquand liked the fact that I was working in advertising. His first job after Harvard, it turned out, had been as a copywriter for Young & Rubicam, and we swapped advertising horror stories. (He'd used his experiences, I discovered later, to hilarious effect in *Pulham*.) Now we were joined in the room by Carol's butler, who announced, "Dinner is served, ma'am." I jumped to my feet to go.

"Please stay for dinner, darling," Carol said.

I started to demur, but Carol insisted. "You're both having so much fun," she said. "All we need to do is set another place at table."

"Add some water to the soup!" Marquand said.

And so, I stayed. It was nearly midnight when I finally took my leave. "I'd like you to do me a favor," Marquand said as I was leaving. "I'd like you to let me take your book to my publisher, Little, Brown."

A favor! I was overjoyed.

"Oh," said Carol, pretending disappointment, "and I had my heart set on Scribner for Steve."

"It's not that there are any brilliant editors there," he said. "In fact, the term 'brilliant editor' is an oxymoron. Most editors are idiots who don't have any idea what they're looking for. But Little, Brown needs some new young talent. They've got this one young man, J. D. Salinger. He's good, but he's also crazy as a loon. Very undependable. But the thing I like about Little, Brown is that they're better than anyone I know of at the job of *selling books*." I saw one reason why John Marquand looked like a banker. He treated the craft of writing as a business. ("I'd write jingles for greeting cards if they paid me enough money," he once said to me with a wink.)

The next day, I attacked my manuscript, discarding the first thirty pages entirely, crossing out every adverb I could lay my hands on, making my flashbacks less abrupt, and giving the book its new title. Then I shipped the novel off to Marquand at his home in Newburyport.

I didn't realize it at the time, but Marquand wielded great power at Little, Brown. He was their best-selling author, and they would do anything to please him. If he said he liked a manuscript, that was it; Little,

Brown published it, without a single editorial query or suggestion. They didn't even correct my occasional grammatical lapses or misspellings. The minute I opened the finished book, I spotted one. I had meant to write "The wind blew." Instead, I had written "the wind blue." If Marquand had passed on the book's content, the publisher must have felt, that was the way the sentence was supposed to read.

I don't know who may have suggested that Marquand might provide a blurb for the book's dust jacket. It may have been Carol Brandt. But whoever did must have approached the subject very gingerly because I knew that Marquand disapproved of this sort of literary logrolling and, to my knowledge, he'd never done this for another writer before. But he did one for me. It was, I must admit, a very guarded endorsement. It was:

"One of the best first novels I have read in several years."—John P. Marquand.

There are quite a few qualifiers in that statement. He did not say, "The best novel I have ever read." But it was, I now see, a carefully thought out—and thoroughly honest—appraisal, and as good a one as the book deserved. And it looked very impressive splashed, in large type, across the book's cover. And it was that endorsement, I'm quite sure, that caused *Young Mr. Keefe* to appear, albeit briefly, toward the bottom of the *New York Times* best seller list. And it also caused reviewers—including Orville Prescott of the *Times*, to compare and liken my novel to those of Marquand, even though, when it was written, I had read only that one short story of his.

I saw John Marquand often after that first meeting. When he came to New York for Book of the Month Club meetings, we usually had lunch, and usually with Carol Brandt. I began to feel he regarded me as a sort of surrogate son, and he often confided to me his varying degrees of disappointment with his own children. One son spent most of his time in and out of mental hospitals. His oldest son, and namesake, was a particular source of frustration to him. Johnny Jr. was a couple of years older than I was and had been dating a pretty brunette named Jacqueline Bouvier—much to Jackie's mother's displeasure. ("Writers don't make any real money," Janet Auchincloss had cautioned her daughter.)

In 1953, Johnny Jr. had published what still seems to me a very creditable novel called *The Second Happiest Day*. Not wishing to appear to be hanging on to his famous father's coattails, Johnny had published this under the name John Phillips (he was John Phillips Marquand, Jr.) But book reviewers had penetrated this disguise and had reviewed his book comparing him—often unfavorably—with his father. Bitter about this, Johnny had written nothing of substance since, and this state of affairs annoyed Marquand Sr. "Damn it," Marquand said, "why *shouldn't* his writing sound a lot like mine? I'm his *father*, aren't I? Why shouldn't I be his major literary influence? Why can't he get on with it until he finds his own voice? Why has he just—*stopped?*"

Marquand had even less use for book reviewers than he had for editors. "They're all horses' asses," he said. "Most of them are frustrated novelists who couldn't write a decent piece of fiction if they tried. Why does Johnny pay any attention to what those horse's asses have to say? No book reviewer has ever helped a writer write a better book."

Marquand was also in the process of divorcing his second wife. She was the former Adelaide Hooker, an heiress to two considerable fortunes. On her father's side was the Hooker Chemical Company, the major polluter who gave us, in the 1970s, what became known as the Love Canal Disaster. Adelaide's mother was a Ferry, of the Ferry Seed Company, though Marquand liked to say that the Ferrys made their money "in shovels and manure." Adelaide' s sister, Blanchette, had married John D. Rockefeller II.

Marquand's first wife, Christina, had been a beauty if a bit of a scatterbrain. She often walked her dog in the Boston Common holding only the leash, having forgotten to attach the dog. Adelaide, by contrast, was not at all pretty. She was a large woman, and, in the course of bearing Marquand three more children, she had grown ever larger—some might say even fat. None of Marquand's friends had ever been able to fathom what it was he saw in Adelaide unless—and this was my guess it was because she was so much richer than his first wife' s family, the Sedgwick's.

For complicated tax reasons, during the Adelaide marriage several of Marquand's novels had been copyrighted in both their names. It infuriated Marquand to discover that Adelaide was going around using the copyright line to claim that she and John had written the books in collaboration. At our lunches, John would often do hilarious—and quite cruel—imitations of Adelaide, mimicking her stilted, high-pitched speech, describing her fondness for dirndl skirts and peasant blouses and other costume getups, giving his impression—exaggerated, of course—of her portly waddle. He would usually end these Adelaide parodies by slamming the heel of his palm against his forehead, and saying, "But, by God, my brother-in-law is John D. Rockefeller!"

I began to see John Marquand as a character he had invented for himself the way he created the characters in his fiction. He was a poor boy from a fine old New England family who, thanks to a ne'er-do-well father, had been cheated out of the wealth and status he should rightfully have enjoyed as a young man. He had been forced to attend Harvard on a scholarship. He hadn't had the money to join one of Harvard's elite clubs, such as the Porcellian, which should have been part of his birthright. In his personal flashbacks, his tale was as bittersweet as Henry Pulham's or George Apley's.

But he had gone to work and worked hard. And now he was rich and famous. He had joined all the right clubs—the exclusive Somerset Club in Boston, and the Myopia Hunt. He had homes in Newburyport, in Aspen, in Hobe Sound, and in horsey-golfy Pinehurst, North Carolina, where his neighbor was General George C. Marshall. He was in the *Social Register.* His brother-in-law was John D. Rockefeller. He had been appointed to Harvard's prestigious Board of Overseers. He had marched in a Harvard alumni parade alongside John F. Kennedy. But it was all dust in the mouth to him.

He had not found love. Not the right love, anyway.

"Now I'm meeting and mingling with the sort of people I used to dream of meeting and mingling with," he said to me. "And they're all a bunch of goddamned bores and horses' asses!"

I suspect he enjoyed the fiction he had made of his life as much as he'd enjoyed any of the fictional characters he invented.

The last time I saw him was in the spring of 1960, and we lunched at the old Voisin restaurant, off Park Avenue. As usual, Carol joined us. By then, John and Adelaide were divorced, and Carol, now widowed, had taken over the presidency of Brandt & Brandt. John was in a jolly mood, and was feeling like having several drinks, and Carol and I cheerfully kept up with him. He had just come back from a safari in Africa and had mastered a hilarious imitation of a hippopotamus snuffling and wallowing in the mud. Even Voisin's staid and proper waiters were laughing.

As we all ordered a third martini, he suddenly turned to Carol, and said, "Well, you and I won't have any trouble on *that* score, will we?" John enjoyed his drinks, but drinking had become a problem for Adelaide.

Then all at once the conversation became serious, and I began to feel I'd become part of a scene in which I didn't really belong. He was asking Carol to marry him.

"No, no," she said firmly.

"*Please!*" he begged.

"No, no . . ."

"Then at least come back with me to Boston on the train tonight. We'll have dinner together and spend a few days in Newburyport."

"John, I have a business to run. I have to be back at the office this afternoon, and I have appointments all day tomorrow."

"Please."

"No, no."

When the three of us said goodbye after lunch, he seemed visibly shaken. We stood on the sidewalk outside the restaurant, and John stood on his tiptoes to kiss her; I hadn't realized that Carol, in heels at least, was a couple of inches taller than he was. At the sight of that kiss, I felt a definite tug at my heart. Like Marvin Myles in *Pulham*, Carol was John's one true love.

I offered to drop Carol off at her office, and on our way downtown in the taxi asked her, "Why don't you marry him?"

"Never," she said. "I run a business in New York—a business I happen to love. I'm very fond of John, but I don't want to be dragged off to Newburyport and become Mrs. John P. Marquand, his wife and hostess. As lovers, it was quite different. He can be very demanding. I remember once in Versailles, I was still in bed and he phoned me from downstairs in the hotel lobby, complaining about not being able to find the right kind of stamp for a letter he wanted to mail. He was screaming and shouting. I just dropped the receiver and let it hang by the bed, while he went on yelling. If I was his wife, I couldn't have done that. I'd have had to climb out of bed, get dressed, and go downstairs to help him find his goddamned stamp."

A few months later, in 1960, John Marquand died in his sleep at his house in Newburyport. Carol telephoned me with this news so I wouldn't read it in the next day's paper. He was sixty-seven. "He should not have done this without consulting us," Carol said.

Marquand had served as my informal editor for my second novel, to which I had dutifully given the Marquandian title *Barbara Greer*. Once again, the book had gone from Marquand's hands to the printer without a single comment or suggestion from anyone at Little, Brown. He was waiting to do the same thing for my third book as soon as it was ready.

But with Marquand's death I suddenly discovered that there were such things as professional editors up there in Boston. The manuscript for my third novel, *The Towers of Love*, came back to me with dozens—scores—of little picky queries and comments. In that novel, I'd written an idyllic little scene, of which I was quite fond, in which a group of little children splash about merrily, naked, in a woodland brook on a summer afternoon. In the margin of that scene, the editor had written "But wouldn't the children be bitten up by mosquitoes?"

With a heavy heart, but at the editor's insistence, I slathered all the children with citronella. The scene now positively reeks of citronella. To my mind, the stench of citronella robbed my pretty scene of any charm or piquancy it might have had.

And somewhere, I'm sure, John Marquand was laughing.

Chapter Eight

Ava

CAREY:

AVA GARDNER WAS A FIXTURE ON OUR HOUSEHOLD WHILE I WAS GROW-ing up. Whether she was there in person (which I am sure she was), or not, she was always a presence in our lives, at least in the early 1960s.

At the time, during a visit to our home, Ava took a shine to my sister, Harriet, with whom she had a connection much like mother-daughter. My sister was perhaps eleven, and Ava never had any children. Ava doted on Harriet during that period, as well as subsequent visits.

When Harriet turned eighteen, Ava Gardner, fabulous film star, invited Harriet to visit her luxurious flat located in the Knightsbridge neighborhood of London. Upon arrival, Ava looked upon not the little eleven-year-old girl she remembered, but a stunning, full-grown young lady who would turn heads around the town. Seeing Harriet, Ava, in her own waning years of beauty and fame, had a moment of serious jealousy and quickly relegated my sister to the basement to live with the staff. Gone were Ava's promises of touring around London with a famous film legend; my sister ate and visited with the cook and butler, and, at least for a week, was rarely outside.

The visit to Ava Gardner was supposed to be for two weeks. However, after one week, having had virtually no contact with her, Ava promptly gave Harriet the boot, saying Harriet had to leave. (As I wrote this, I interviewed my sister about the event. I said, "inviting you to stay for two weeks and kicking you to the curb after one? That seems kind of rude." My sister, a forgiving person, gave Ava the benefit of the doubt, saying "She probably had things to do and I didn't think it was rude." I think it's the definition of rude.)

Not having anywhere to go, my sister called my mother, who, fortunately, had another friend from the film business, Angela Allen, a film continuity director, who lived in London and took Harriet in until she could get her flight back to the states.

We never heard from Ava Gardner again.

STEVE:

I've always loved the theater, and, in school and college, I performed in various amateur productions. I also spent a summer with a stock company at Lake George, New York, and, in those days, I used to think I'd like to become a professional actor. But I had one problem—my voice. In a small auditorium, I was fine, but in a larger hall I had trouble getting my lines heard by the audience in the back rows. I have what one director called a New England voice; it possesses what is known as a glottal stop. That is, its projects from somewhere just behind my tongue, and not, as a stage actor should, from the diaphragm. My voice hasn't enough resonance for stage work. To be heard in the last row, I had to shout, and shouting is not what a good actor is supposed to do.

Stage acting is all about voices and gestures vocal and body language. It doesn't matter that much how an actor or actress looks. In films and television, on the other hand, it's all about faces. An actor can speak in whispers, and his eyes can convey everything he needs to say. Whenever I've met a film star in the flesh, I've often been astonished by how unprepossessing he or she is in physical appearance. Watching the early films of Katherine Hepburn, I'd always assumed she was a tall, willowy figure. When I met her, I discovered that she is actually a tiny creature. Would Hepburn have become a great star without those cheekbones? Would Bette Davis—another small woman—have made it without those extraordinary eyes? I once saw Bette Davis in a stage play. Because of her size, she had no stage presence at all and, to make herself heard, she had to shout. Tom Cruise has a great face—those dimples!—but, in person, he's just a little guy, who was probably considered shrimpy in high school, and had trouble getting a date for the senior prom. One actor I've met who looked the way he was supposed to was Gary Cooper. He really *was* tall, lean, and lanky.

I suppose, with the proper exercise and training, I could have got rid of the damned glottal stop, which made me sound as though I was speaking through my nose instead of from my chest. But, by then, I'd decided that a career in the theater was not for me. Mostly, it was because I didn't much like other actors.

If a roomful of writers is pretty bad, a roomful of actors is much worse. Actors, as a rule, are interested only in talking about themselves. Turn the conversation to anything else, and the actor grows silent and glum. Any subject besides himself bores him. I once took a date to a party in New York where I knew there would be a lot of actors. When I told her this, she didn't want to go. She found actors depressing, she said, mainly because they are usually out of work. But I gave her a bit of advice. "When you meet an actor, I said, "start off by saying 'You are *wonderful!* You have the most marvelous eyes hair—nose—body'—whatever comes into your head." She followed my advice and was the most popular girl at the party.

Sometimes I think that actors aren't real people—they're just human shells waiting to be handed scripts with lines for them to read, gestures for them to make, and emotions for them to pretend to feel. Without scripts and parts to play they sit around like zombies. There are exceptions to this, of course.

Elizabeth Taylor, whom I first met in 1963, is a warm and generous woman with a sly, almost elfin, sense of humor, even when it comes to poking fun at herself. I remember sitting with Elizabeth while she sat in front of her makeup mirror. She was then thirty-one. She stuck out her tongue at her reflection, and then composed that beautiful face again. "Well," she said to the mirror, "I guess we can give it about five more years." As it turned out, the face would last quite a few more years than that.

Again, she didn't look quite the way I'd expected her to look. In all that's been written about Elizabeth Taylor, I've never seen any mention of the large brown birthmark that covers much of her lower jaw and upper throat. This can be covered easily enough with makeup, but it's still a major beauty flaw, and, when she appears without her warpaint, I've heard people whisper, "Who is that?" And on the subject of beauty flaws, I should mention her figure. When she's in trim fighting shape, she has a great figure—in profile. But when she's viewed straight-on, she's straight up and down, with no hips, like a boy.

I first met her in Puerto Vallarta, where Richard Burton was filming *The Night of the Iguana*. Elizabeth and Richard were not married—for the first of their two times—yet, and she was in the process of divorcing Eddie Fisher, while Burton was in the process of disentangling himself from his first wife, Sybil. Elizabeth and Richard had rented a lovely house, called Casa Kimberly in what was known as Vallarta's Gringo Gulch, overlooking the Pacific. Here, periodically, flotillas of lawyers in suits and carrying fat briefcases arrived from New York and California to help sort out the couple's respective marital situations.

Also present at Casa Kimberly, and on the *Iguana* set, were dozens of reporters and journalists—including myself—who had been sent by newspapers and magazines from all over the world to cover the adulterous Burton-Taylor romance that had begun, notoriously, on the set of "*Cleopatra*" a year or so earlier. Everywhere the couple went, paparazzi snapped photos of them.

Richard Burton, I found to be a good-natured bore. After a day's shooting, everyone would gather at the bar that had been set up hard by the film's principal location, and here, over drinks, Burton would hold forth. In his rich baritone, he would start reciting poetry. He would recite all of Hamlet's soliloquies, and then move on to *Macbeth*, *Othello*, and *Lear*." He would then recite the works of Dylan Thomas, including an entire short story about a child's Christmas in Wales. This was entertaining for a while, but Burton didn't seem to know when to stop or, as they say in the theater, "get off." After a certain number of drinks, he would start repeating himself, and we'd be treated to Hamlet's soliloquies all over again. Night after night this went on, and there seemed to be no way of cutting off these endless verbal concertos, and through it all Elizabeth would gaze at him with an expression of utter rapture—real or feigned, it was hard to tell.

After many evenings of this, where the rest of us were his captive, often glassy-eyed, audience, there came a moment when Burton seemed briefly to run out of breath. He turned to Elizabeth and said, "It's so wonderful to have poetry in your heart, in your soul, in your gut! There must be some poetry that you know by heart, luv!"

"Oh, but I really don't, Richard," she said in her little-girl voice.

"Oh, come on, luv," he said.

"I honestly don't," she said.

"You must know some poetry. What about that thing you did for the British telly on Shakespeare's London?"

"But all I did was read from the teleprompter," she said. "I didn't *memorize* anything!"

"I can't believe that a nice Jewish girl like you wouldn't know a single line of poetry—not a single poem!"

She giggled. "Well, I guess I do know one poem," she said. "But it's just a silly little poem my father taught me when I was a little girl."

"Ah, luv," he said. "How wonderful! Let's hear it. Out with it!"

She lowered her eyes modestly, and an expectant hush fell around the bar. "Well," she said, "it goes like this." And suddenly her voice became harsh, almost strident. The actress was at work:

> *"What'll you have?" the waiter said,*
> *as he stood there picking his nose.*
> *"Hardboiled eggs, you son of a bitch,*
> *You can't put your fingers in those!"*

Everyone in the room roared with laughter, though Richard looked unhappy. Elizabeth Taylor had just upstaged the great Shakespearean actor.

Often, with Elizabeth, it was hard to tell whether she was being slyly humorous or deadly serious. Once she announced, quite out of the blue, "Richard and I spent the most wonderful night last night!"

Once again, the room fell silent, and then someone asked, "Well, what did you do?"

"Richard sat up with me and read Shakespeare to me until five o'clock in the morning!" she said.

She also had an odd way of dealing with Richard's drinking. One evening they came into the bar together, and Richard astonished the assembled customers by ordering a glass of ginger ale instead of his usual double vodka. "Oh, Richard!" she exclaimed. "Aren't you going to have a drink?"

"Nope," he said firmly. "I'm doing close-ups in the morning. Can't have bloodshot eyes."

"Oh, Richard! Have a drink. Have a vodka. You'll feel so much better!"

"Nope!"

"Oh, please! Have some vodka. Have some rum, or some tequila. Have a whiskey!"

"Nope! Not tonight."

"Oh, please." She continued with this wheedling for a while, with Richard standing firm.

"Just one drink wouldn't give you bloodshot eyes, Richard!"

And finally, he caved in. "All right," he said. "Give me a double vodka."

Then, about fourteen double vodkas later—and after more poetic orations—it was time for Richard Burton to be carried to his car by a couple of members of the camera crew. Looking back at the rest of us, Elizabeth was apologetic. "I'm afraid Richard had a little too *much* to drink," she said.

From incidents like that, some of us wondered: Did sex play any role at all in what the tabloids were calling the Romance of the Century?

We had our answer a few nights later at a small party I gave for some fellow journalists and members of the *Iguana* cast. At one point, a young journalist who had been hitting the tequila bottle with particular enthusiasm, called to Elizabeth from across the room in a loud voice, "Hey, Liz!"

Now the silence was one of deep shock because we all knew that, though the tabloids had been using that name for years, she hated being called Liz. But she looked across at the young man inquiring, "Yes?"

"Is it true that you're a lousy lay?"

Now the shock was even more profound. This, after all, was no ordinary mortal he was addressing. This was the great film star, Elizabeth Taylor, and I could see my little party headed for disaster.

But Elizabeth chose to address the question seriously. "Well, you see," she began, "when I was a young girl, I played a part in a film called *National Velvet*. I was only twelve years old, and it was my first really important picture. It was a story about a girl who wants to have her horse entered in the Grand National Steeplechase, and I played the girl."

Once again, I wondered: Was she pulling our collective leg? She was describing details of her early professional life that everyone in the room if not most of the civilized world already knew.

"I had to do a lot of scenes on horseback in that film," she went on. "Liz Whitney—she was Mrs. Jock Whitney, and a famous horsewoman at the time—gave me special riding lessons. But one day on location I had a really bad fall from my horse, and I really hurt my back. I've had problems with my back ever since. Sometimes the act of sex can be terribly painful for me. Sometimes I can't do it at all unless I'm loaded with painkillers. Does that answer your question?"

It certainly did, and the conversation quickly turned to other matters.

Elizabeth had brought to Mexico with her, her young daughter, Liza Todd, whose father had been the impresario Mike Todd, Elizabeth's third husband. Liza Todd was then eight or nine, and she had inherited her mother's gorgeous eyes, as well as her father's punishing jawline. Also, in the *Iguana* cast was the New York actress Grayson Hall, and she had come to Mexico with her husband, the television writer Sam Hall, and their young son Matthew, who was about Liza Todd's age. Since Sam wasn't working on the film, and since I had time on my hands, and since Elizabeth liked to sleep late—seldom arriving on the set until well after lunchtime—Sam Hall and I were often selected to accompany the two children to the beach.

The most popular beach in Puerto Vallarta was—still is—the public beach called Los Muertos. Los Muertos Beach is lined with hotels, shops, restaurants, and open-air bars that are jammed with tourist's night and day. As we watched Liza and Matthew at play in the sand and kept an eye on them when they were in the water, Sam and I became aware of a couple of things. For one thing, it was soon apparent that Liza Todd's education had been somewhat sketchy. It surprised us, for instance, that a little girl that age did not know her alphabet did not know, in fact, that such a thing existed. We tried teaching it to her, using the familiar singing rhyme that goes up and down the scale. It also seemed to us that Elizabeth paid little attention to her daughter. In fact, the only words of advice I ever heard Elizabeth offer Liza was once, when the two were seated at a restaurant table and, as usual, cameras were snapping furiously in their direction. I heard Elizabeth murmur to Liza, "Never look directly into the cameras, dear."

Elizabeth had also brought with her to Casa Kimberly an English couple, who served as her butler and cook-housekeeper. We would often see the English couple sitting at the beachside bar chatting with tourists who were obviously buying them coco-locos, rum drinks served in a coconut shell. Periodically, one or the other of the English pair would come down to the beach where the children were playing, take Liza by the hand, and say, "Come along, dear. There are some nice people at the bar who want to meet you." Liza would then be trotted back to the bar, out would come the tourists' cameras, and Liza would be required to pose for photos with the tourists.

It struck both Sam and me as wrong that the little girl should be exploited in this fashion, that the English couple were selling photographs of Liza in return for drinks. We decided that Elizabeth should know about this, but, rather than report the situation directly to Elizabeth, which might upset her, we decided to tell one of Elizabeth's secretaries, who might be able to handle the problem discreetly, without involving Liza's mother.

There were two of these secretaries, both winsome, pretty young men who looked so much alike that they could have been taken for twins. Each day, they performed a kind of striptease on the beach. They would arrive wearing normal swimming trunks, which they would then remove to reveal bikinis. Then the bikinis would come off, leaving them wearing what amounted to codpieces. What secretarial duties this pair performed for Elizabeth was never clear to me. Mostly, it seemed, they went shopping for her, and this proved to be something of a hardship for the rest of us. I'd had the idea of buying something in a bright Mexican print to take home to my wife. But whenever I saw anything in a shop that struck me as the least bit pretty, I was told that the item had been earmarked to be sent up to Casa Kimberly for Elizabeth's approval. Would I be able to tell my wife that the only articles of clothing available in Puerto Vallarta were Elizabeth Taylor rejects?

In any case, Sam Hall and I approached the twin secretaries as they sunbathed on the beach and told them about the problem with the English couple. They listened solemnly. "Of course, we won't breathe a word about this to Elizabeth," they promised. "Don't worry. We'll handle it."

But of course, as we should have known, the first thing they did was to tell their boss. Her reaction was a curious one. "Liza can never swim at that beach again!" she decreed. And so, thereafter, Sam and I were instructed to take the children to a remote beach at the far north end of Banderas Bay, a beach that was neither popular nor populated because of the rocky shoreline and the treacherous undertow. It struck us that the wrong people were punished. I ran into Liza Todd not long ago. She is now a shy, pretty woman and talented sculptor.

The unit publicist on the *Night of the Iguana* set was a pleasant young man named Greg Morrison. Because of the Taylor-Burton affair, the film was getting far more publicity than it needed or probably deserved, but Greg Morrison welcomed all of it. "You can talk to anybody you want to," he'd said to me when I first arrived on the location. "You can talk to Burton, you can talk to Taylor, you can talk to John Huston, the director, and to Deborah Kerr. The only exception is Ava Gardner. I must ask that you leave her strictly alone. She doesn't like the press. She distrusts journalists and hates all writers. There was a writer once whom she befriended, and who later betrayed her in print." (Later, I would learn there had been several, notably including the film critic Rex Reed.) She wanted a closed set for this picture, meaning no journalists or outside photographers. She didn't get her way on that one, and I think she's a little ticked off that so many people from the press are here."

And so, I did as Greg had asked me, and gave Miss Gardner a wide berth. I watched her from the sidelines on the set, of course, and, though her fortieth birthday was only weeks away, I was struck by her extraordinary beauty. She was one of the last stars to come out of the old studio system and had come to Hollywood as a teenager to become an MGM contract player. Her studio had begun calling her "the world's most beautiful animal." She was certainly that.

The set for *The Night of the Iguana* had been built just outside the tiny Indian village of Mismaloya, about fifteen miles across the water from Puerto Vallarta. Today, a modern highway connects the two towns, and the old movie set, in a somewhat crumbling state, has become something of a tourist attraction. But in 1963 the only way to reach Mismaloya from Vallarta, except by muleback, was by boat. The lowlier members of the film company more or less camped out in Mismaloya, while the film's stars were given houses in Vallarta, and were given speedboats—and native boat boys—with which to make the daily commute back and forth. Richard Burton had his own boat, and so did Elizabeth Taylor, who wasn't even in the film. Ava had her own boat, but Deborah Kerr, who played a major character, had for some reason not merited a boat of her own, though Sue Lyon, who played a very small part, somehow got a boat named, appropriately, the *Lolita*, for her personal use. At the time, Miss Lyon was considered a rising star. Later, after *Iguana*, it was decided that she was not.

Late one afternoon, after a day's shooting, a group of us had gathered at the bar. Burton was doing his usual thing, and suddenly Ava appeared with her personal maid and male secretary in tow. She ordered, and downed, a quick martini, and then someone from across the room called to her, "Ava—we're going back to town now. Do you need a ride?"

"No thanks," she said. "I'm going to water-ski back. Anybody want to join me?" She looked around the room, but there were no immediate takers.

I raised my hand. "I will," I said.

She looked me coolly up and down. "Okay," she said. "C'mon—let's go.

I followed her down to the boat dock. Ava walked with small, quick steps, and I almost had to run to keep up with her. At the dock, her two Mexican boat boys were waiting for her, and we all climbed aboard the boat and started off at high speed. Left behind, on shore, were several fellow journalists who had followed us down, wondering, no doubt, how I had earned this special privilege. Among them I spotted Herb Caen from the San Francisco *Chronicle*, Gary Wills, Barnaby Conrad, and a very drunk Budd Schulberg—all of whom were "doing a piece" on the film. I rationalized that I hadn't really broken my promise to Greg Morrison. I hadn't approached her. She, in a sense, had approached me.

When we were a little distance out in the bay, I said to her, "Well, who's going to ski first?"

"You are," she said, and so I pulled on a pair of skis, grabbed the tow rope, and jumped into the water. The Mexican boys fed out the rope to me.

When I got to my feet on the skis, I could see her, in the boat ahead of me, whispering instructions to the Mexican youth behind the wheel. Suddenly the boat slowed down, almost to a stop, which meant that I sank down to my chin in the water. Then the boat would quickly accelerate, jerking me to me feet again. Then it would slow again, then speed up again. This happened several times. Then the boat began zigzagging, at top speed, across the water, meaning that I was forced to jump back and forth across the wake. From her wicked grin, I could tell what she was trying to do. She was trying to throw me off the skis. But I am a fairly good water-skier, and I was determined not to let her succeed. Partly, on such short acquaintance, I was not at all certain whether or not, if she did succeed, she would tear off in her boat and leave me floating in the Pacific Ocean where, earlier that week, several sightings of sharks had been made. I waved cheerfully to her from my skis to indicate that I was having a hell of a good time with her little game, which of course I wasn't.

Finally, she grew tired of it and waved to me, signaling that she wanted a turn on the skis. The boat slowed down, I dropped the rope, and the boat circled back to pick me up. She then skied the rest of the way back to Puerto Vallarta. She was, one of the Mexican boys explained to me, *una novata*—a newcomer to the sport—and it pleased me to see that she was much less confident on the skis than I was. "*Tu es mas mejor esquiar que ella*," he confided to me. But what she may have lacked in experience, she more than made up for in stamina, as I was soon to learn.

"Come back to my house for a drink," she said as she toweled herself.
I said I'd enjoy that, and so the two of us hopped into the back seat of
her Jeep, with one of the young Mexicans at the wheel.

I sat beside her while, at her dressing table, she removed her movie
makeup, using many tissues, smoking many Winston's, sipping a drink.
"I really hate this work," she said. "I only do it for the loot—only for the
loot." I decided that she looked even more beautiful without her warpaint—she had pale, clear, luminous skin—and I told her so. "Yes, I guess
I'm pretty. That's all I've got. No talent." I told her I disagreed, and that
some of the scenes I'd watched her do in this film seemed strong indeed. I
told her I'd loved her in *The Barefoot Contessa*, particularly in the haunting
little scene toward the end when she performed a little barefoot Gypsy
dance. "I hated that film," she said. "The only picture they let me do some
acting in was *On the Beach*, where I played a drunk. One critic wrote that
I'd never acted better or looked worse." I said that someone had suggested
that she might get an Oscar nomination for *Iguana*. "Puh-*lease!*" she said.
"What would I do with one of those stupid statues? And please—don't
suggest something vulgar!"

She pulled her dark curly hair back and fastened it in a ponytail with
a rubber band. With her hair away from her face, she looked like a Spanish girl; she had three dimples, one in each cheek, and one on her chin.
She excused herself then and came back in a pair of jeans cut off at mid-
calf and a baggy sweatshirt—one of her favorite outfits, I was to learn.
She still looked beautiful. There seemed to be no way she could help it.

We had more drinks, and we talked. She talked about her girlhood
in Grabtown, North Carolina—"How does that grab ya?"—her many
brothers and sisters, and her mother who had worked for many years
as a cook in a boardinghouse for spinster teachers, and her father who
was not, as MGM publicity releases often stated, a "sharecropper," but a
tenant tobacco farmer, which was something quite different. The family's
fortunes went up and down depending on the price of tobacco at the
annual auctions. It amused her to find out that my middle name was
Gardner. "We're cousins!" she cried.

She put some flamenco music on the stereo and danced to that. She
showed me how she could stand on her head and walk on her hands.

Then she played some Frank Sinatra records, and the two of us danced to these. The evening grew quite late. The Mexican boat boys wandered off into the night to join their novias on the waterfront promenade. The male secretary excused himself and went back to his hotel. The Spanish maid went off to bed in another part of the house, and Ava and I were alone with the night sounds of crickets chirping and palm leaves rattling in the breeze. Suddenly she turned to me and kissed me on the lips. "I'm so goddamned lonely!" she said. We became lovers that night.

It was the first time I'd strayed from strict marital fidelity. But it wouldn't be true to say I hadn't wanted it to happen. I had, just as much as she had. And it wouldn't be true, either, to say that I was filled with guilt or remorse over the deed. I knew I'd betrayed my wife, of course, and yet I felt oddly exhilarated, released, as though some great inhibiting burden had been lifted from my shoulders. Corny as it sounds, I felt born again. The next morning, I went to the window, opened it, and took great happy gulps of sweet sea air. I felt like a new person and, having made this giant step, I knew I would never be quite the same again, or think about myself in the same way again. It was like first sex, though I was thirty-two, and the father of three young children. Having made this giant step, I knew that all the baby steps that followed would simply have to follow, one after another, leading me who knew where.

Movie people often joke," You can't take a film on location without at least *one* good love affair developing." Well, I thought, that was what this was going to be, a nice love affair to remember. But, as it turned out, it was to be a bit more than that.

"I want to marry you," Ava said.

I reminded her that I already had a wife to whom, at the time, at least, I was happily married.

"Oh, we can fix that easily enough," she said airily.

That frightened me. All the ugly words floated across my mind. Divorce. Lawyers. Child custody battles. Money fights. Our names in the papers. Adultery. Mental cruelty. . . . Who gets the house?

I'm afraid I weaseled at that point. "Let's think about all this very carefully," I said.

At this point, I have to ask myself: Was I really in love with her? I was enchanted by her, yes, infatuated with her, loved being with her, both in and out of bed. And it was impossible not to be stunned by the sheer look of her. But the trouble was that the more I got to know her the more I felt sorry for her, and love and pity are not two emotions that mix well.

It was not just that she insisted she hated her film work that she did "only for the loot." She might hate her work, but she was always very professional about it always on time, ready when the cameras were ready for her, sure of her lines. She did not throw temper tantrums, bully the crew, or threaten to walk off the set. It had more to do with the way the motion picture business treated its female performers. They were treated more as decorative objects than human beings. It takes a certain toughness, it seems to me, for a woman to survive in the movie business. Elizabeth Taylor had developed that toughness, that *nil admirari* attitude. After all, she had started out at a much younger age than Ava had and had grown insensitive to the battering the industry is capable of inflicting on its women. Ava, when I first met her, had been badly bruised by the industry, and the emotional scars still showed in her bitterness toward the profession. I watched the many ways the movie business had of humiliating and demeaning her, and these were not pretty sights.

The producer of *Iguana*, for instance, was Ray Stark. I found him to be a nasty little man. Later, he would go on to be called "the most powerful man in Hollywood," who would then become eclipsed by Mike Ovitz, who, in turn, would be eclipsed by someone else. At the time, Ray Stark was principally famous for being married to Fanny Brice's daughter, and for having produced *Funny Girl*, based on the latter's career—"A labor of purest love," as he described it, for his late mother-in-law. I was not impressed with Stark's brassy wife, Fran, either. Once, at a dinner party over which Ray Stark presided, he spent some time describing an article he had read about female orgasms. There were two kinds, he said, vaginal and clitoral. He then turned to each of the women guests and demanded to know which type of orgasm they had. When he got to Ava, she said, "It just depends on who I'm fucking," which shut him up.

Ray Stark came down to the *Iguana* set from California from time to time, always unannounced. Ava disliked him as much as I did but, as her producer, she had to be nice to him. He always came loaded with gifts for her—armfuls of the latest hit records for her stereo, among other things. The fashion rage at the moment were the bright print outfits of Emilio Pucci. Stark also brought dozens of Pucci dresses and blouses for Ava. As it happened, Ava hated Pucci's designs, but she always thanked him prettily before giving them to her maids. At the same time, despite the lavish gifts, he could also be totally insensitive to her feelings, if not downright insulting. "I've got a great part for you, honey," I heard him say to her." It's a great story, and you'd play Natalie Wood's mother." Ava was deeply hurt by this. She might have been a few years older than Natalie Wood, but she was certainly not old enough to be Natalie Wood's mother.

Age is a ticklish subject for any performer, but it is a particular problem for a female film star. A biological fact is at work here, and that is that men and women age in different ways. Male actors—a Clark Cable, Cary Grant, Gary Cooper, Clint Eastwood, or Paul Newman can stay looking great, and get great roles, well into their sixties or even their seventies. But, in Hollywood's eyes, an actress over forty is over the hill. And Ava knew she was approaching that watershed year. In fact, though Ava made quite a few more films after *Iguana*, that was her last major role.

Women stars of Ava's magnitude are given one concession not granted to men—one that rankles with men. Women are allowed to take up to five days off from work every month if they need to. Elizabeth Taylor used to giggle that she got the five-free-days clause written into her contracts, even though she'd had a hysterectomy years before, and had no need for those days. One morning in Vallarta, Ava was not feeling up to snuff—actually, she was suffering from a massive hangover—and she decided to phone in and ask for one of her "bonus" days. Ray Stark replied that she could have the day off, but he added a degrading stipulation. First, he would send a doctor over to her house to examine her and verify her condition. Needless to say, she made it to the set.

John Huston had directed Ava in several other films before this one, and, as I watched him work with this company, I often wondered what it was that made him revered as such a great director. He was certainly easygoing, almost to the point of sloppiness. In charge of continuity on this film was a young Englishwoman named Angela Allen. Continuity is an important, painstaking job. A single short scene may take days to film, and so it is essential that everything on the set match from one day to the next. If, for example, the clock on the mantel says ten past seven at the beginning of the scene, it would not say half past twelve a few seconds later. Angela was always catching Huston in mistakes like this. His attitude was that the audience wouldn't notice. Firmly, Angela would insist that the scene be shot over with the hands set right.

Huston hardly ever offered his actors any suggestions as to how they might interpret their roles. A year or so later, I watched him direct Marlon Brando in *Reflections in a Golden Eye*. Huston had nothing at all to say to Brando about how he delivered his lines. Perhaps Brando is the kind of actor who doesn't need direction, but Ava was not. One day she asked him, "What's my character—Maxine—really feeling in this scene? Is she in love with Shannon—or what?" Shannon was the character played by Burton. Huston simply laughed at her. "Don't worry your pretty head about it," he said. "All you have to do is stand there and look beautiful."

He had a certain sadistic streak. The cast of *Night of the Iguana* included, needless to say, an iguana, and several of these large lizards had been captured for this purpose. In one scene, an iguana is supposed to leap ferociously as though to attack an enemy. But despite prodding with sticks, the iguanas all remained sluggish, refusing even to bare their teeth. "Rub some turpentine on its ass," said John Huston. Some time was spent by the iguanas' handler locating that part of its anatomy but, when it was finally found, and the turpentine was applied, the animal leaped into the air again and again, screeching and writhing with pain, and Huston got his shot.

"You can do the same thing with horses," Huston confided to me. "If you want a horse to really buck and rear, just rub some turpentine on its ass." This humane suggestion was from the man who, at home in Ireland, was Master of the West Galway Hounds.

Some years earlier, when directing *Treasure of the Sierra Madre*, Huston had taken a shine to a young Mexican boy named Pablo. Without consulting his wife, and with the permission of the boy's parents, Huston had legally adopted Pablo and brought him home with him to California. This unexpected new addition to their family was said to have caused the breakup of that particular Huston marriage. Now Pablo Huston had matured into a seriously disturbed young man of twenty-something. He'd been given some menial gofer's job with the film unit, and he was a pedophile. He spent his off-work hours in Vallarta's central plaza, trying to lure young local schoolgirls up to his room. His adoptive father found this activity terribly amusing.

But Huston was capable of acts of kindness. Ava had a scene in which she was preparing a fresh fish for dinner. She was supposed to deliver the line, "I really loved old Fred," and then come down, *whack*, with her cleaver and behead the fish. For some reason, she kept blowing the line, and it kept coming out, "I really loved old Frank." So, what the camera caught was:

"I really loved old Frank"—whack—"Oh, shit!"

Each time this happened, of course, she had to be provided with a new fish. But the others on the set all interpreted her fluffs as Freudian slips, indicating that the man still most on her mind was Frank Sinatra. That night, when he showed the daily rushes, Huston thoughtfully cut the sound on that scene so that Ava would not have to hear herself blow that simple line.

After she finished *Iguana*, Ava went back to Madrid, where she then lived, and I went back to New York. We kept in touch by phone. But Ava Gardner's work for *Night of the Iguana* was not really done. Ray Stark planned to open the film with a gala World Premiere at New York's Lincoln Center, which was then quite new. It would be a black-tie affair, with all sorts of stars and dignitaries flown in at Stark's expense. All the principals in the film would be there: Burton and Taylor, who were by then married, Ava, Deborah Kerr, and Grayson Hall. Sue Lyon was not to be invited. After seeing the finished film, Stark had loudly announced, "That girl's career is over!" And, cruelly enough, it was. Other stars were invited: Tony Curtis, Lauren Bacall, Edie Adams, Lena Horne, and on and on. After a screening of the film in the New York State Theater, there would be an elaborate dinner, followed by dancing. Ava was being flown in from Madrid—first class—along with her Spanish maid (economy class) and was being put up in a large suite at the Regency Hotel on Park Avenue. Sydney Guilaroff was flown in from MGM just to do Ava's hair.

Ava had wanted me to accompany her to the premiere, but Ray Stark had other ideas. He thought Ava would make a more dramatic entrance if she arrived at the theater solo in her limousine, and not with a man who would require identification by the photographers and television cameras on the sidewalk. He arranged for me to follow Ava's car in a limo of my own. We'd meet in the lobby and be seated together in the theater. This arrangement was all right with me. And Ava did make a particularly lovely personal appearance; we watched it later on the evening news—and she looked radiant and happy. In the theater, Tennessee Williams had been seated directly in front of us, and he'd considerately brought along a flask of vodka. We passed this back and forth as we watched the movie.

The dinner afterward was held in the theater's lavishly decorated open courtyard. I don't remember what we ate, but there were many elaborate toasts and speeches as various members of the film community rose to congratulate each other, and themselves, on this magnificent motion picture achievement. The evening was beginning to sound like an Academy Awards night, and I could tell that Ava was beginning to be a little bored and restless. Finally, she whispered to me, "Let's go up to Birdland and hear some good jazz." So, we got up and made our way out of the room as inconspicuously as possible. Outside, her limousine was waiting, and we were driven uptown to Birdland.

It was nearly two in the morning when we'd both finally had enough, and I called for the check. But when we got outside on the street there was no sign of her car. Upper Broadway was empty. I stepped back inside the club and phoned Buckingham Livery, the outfit that had supplied all the cars for the event. "Miss Gardner's limousine service ended at midnight," I was told. "Those were Mr. Stark's instructions."

"The driver might have told us that," I said.

"Sorry!"

I went back out and explained the situation to Ava. There we were in the small hours of the morning, on an empty street on the fringes of Harlem, Ava in a long Galanos gown, me in a dinner jacket. Eventually, I spotted a cab at a distant intersection. I ran for it and was able to flag it down.

When she arrived in New York a few days earlier, Ray Stark had filled her suite at the Regency with dozens and dozens of yellow roses, her favorite flower. Some theater people believe that yellow roses bring bad luck, but Ava believed the opposite.

As we sat in the suite the morning after the premiere, eating a room-service breakfast, the roses were looking a little weary. We passed the reviews of the film back and forth between each other. Mostly, they were very praising of Ava's performance, though most of the critics agreed that the movie had been based on a second-rate Williams play. At around eleven o'clock, there was a knock on the door. I went to open it, and it was none other than the producer Ray Stark himself. For a moment I wondered how he'd managed to get up to the suite unannounced, but then I realized that, since he was paying for it, he'd have had no trouble.

He was all business and bustle. "I've only got a minute, Ava, honey," he said," but there's a few last-minute things we've got to clear up. First of all, here's your plane ticket back to Madrid." He handed it to her.

She looked at it. "Economy class?"

"That was the deal, honey. First class over, economy home. Of course, you can always upgrade to first if you want to—at your own expense, of course."

"What about Graciella?" Graciella was her Spanish maid.

"I guess you didn't look at the deal very closely when you signed it, honey. I only agreed to pay one-way on her. If she wants to fly back with you, she'll have to buy her own ticket. Or you can buy one for her, of course."

"Of course."

"Now check-out time here at the hotel is one p.m. You can keep the suite longer if you want to, of course, but that'll be at your own expense. Now there's just one more thing." He reached into his jacket pocket. "Just a few expenses you ran up on the set. Here's the bill." And he handed her a bill for $87.12. I'll never forget that figure: $87.12.

Most of the items on the bill were for drinks she had charged at the bar in Mismaloya. But I remember one other item:

Sun hat for maid: *75 cents.*

I never saw Ava cry, but when she walked to her desk, took out her checkbook, and wrote out the check her eyes were opened very wide.

She handed him the check without looking at him, and without a word.

"Thanks, honey. Well, gotta run. Call me the next time you're on the Coast, honey. Bye-eee!" And he was gone.

At that point, I think I hated the movie business even more than she did. She stood in the center of the room in her robe and slippers and heaved a great sigh. "Let's get rid of these fuckin' roses," she said.

She still periodically spoke of marriage, and how simple it would be, but it didn't seem quite that simple to me. And the fact was that, much as I loved her, and much as I felt sorry for what she saw as her lonely, unappreciated existence, I really didn't want to marry Ava Gardner, and for a number of reasons.

Elizabeth Taylor, for instance, had developed a technique for avoiding intrusions on her privacy when she was in public places. In Puerto Vallarta, in order for her to get from her car to her boat, she had to walk down across a public beach. She was always escorted, of course, and sometimes I was the escort. As we crossed the beach, she stayed close beside me, her face turned up to mine, talking animatedly—about the weather, what she had had for breakfast, whatever came into her head, an uninterrupted stream of chatter. Though camera shutters clicked, no one approached her. Once aboard the boat, and safely out of the public's reach, the chatter stopped altogether.

Ava was just the opposite. We'd be sitting in a restaurant, and someone across the room would recognize her, and catch her eye. She'd immediately smile warmly at that person and, the next thing we knew, that person would be standing beside our table, and Ava would invite him to join us for a drink. Her friend the poet Robert Graves once wrote a poem that he told her she might want to take personally. It included the lines, "She speaks always in her own voice, even to strangers." And, "She is forever wild and beautiful, pledged to love through all disaster." It was a good description of her. Some of the strangers she picked up in public places turned out to be perfectly nice people, but others could be tedious bores, particularly when they decided to spend the evening with the two of us. Then it would be up to me to try to get rid of these admirers. There was a low rattlesnake sound that she would make in her throat. It was a signal, and it meant, "Dump this guy!"

Frank Sinatra, I gathered, had the same problem, and it was one of the main causes of the breakup of their marriage. Women would approach Frank at a table to ask for his autograph or to shake his hand, and Frank would ask them to join him, which made Ava wildly jealous. Or a man would approach Ava, and the same thing would happen, and Frank would fly into a jealous rage.

Meanwhile Sinatra, or "Albert Francis" as she always referred to him, was still an important factor in Ava's life, though I was never sure how important. He telephoned her often, from wherever he happened to be, and Ava' s personal phone book was filled with Frank's various unpublished numbers, which changed with some frequency. Whenever Frank called, I always stepped out of the room and closed the door, so I have no idea what these conversations were about, though they were often quite lengthy. Though I once spent a delightful evening with Ava and Artie Shaw, another of her ex-husbands with whom she'd remained friendly, I only met Sinatra once. Ava was staying in an apartment he kept at the Waldorf Towers, and Sinatra dropped by for a drink. He seemed to me a pleasant, soft-spoken man, quite unlike the raffish, brawling George Raft type I'd expected. At one point, he was looking up a number in the Manhattan phone book, but he hadn't brought his glasses. "Try mine," Ava suggested, and she handed him a pair of Ben Franklin-style half glasses that she wore for reading. He slipped them on. "Hey," he said, "these work for me! That's another reason why the two of us should get back together!"

Later, I asked her, "Why don't the two of you get back together?"

"We'd be at each other's throats in two days," she said.

If I'd married her, I'd have had to deal with a number of other complicated personal relationships of hers. There was her former brother-in-law Larry Tarr, for instance, who'd been married to Ava' s ten-years-older sister, Bea. Larry Tarr had once been an important New York photographer, and it was his photograph of the teenage Ava that he'd sent to an MGM talent scout that got Ava started on her film career. She always felt that she owed something to him. But, by the time I met her, Larry Tarr had turned into a noisy drunk who was always in some sort of trouble. He was always turning up, always unannounced, begging Ava to help him out of some mess or other.

One night we were having dinner at Trader Vic's in New York, and there were sounds of a noisy scuffle at the headwaiter's station. It was Larry Tarr, though how he'd found out we were there I have no idea. When he spotted us, he began calling, "Ava! Ava! They won't let me in, but I've got to talk to you!"

The captain stepped over to our table. "Mr. Tarr was here last night," he said, "and I'm afraid he created a bad scene. Trader Vic's has asked that he never come back."

Ava said nothing.

"Do you want Mr. Tarr to join your party, Miss Gardner?" the captain asked. Ava looked at me. I shrugged. By then I was familiar with Larry Tarr's antics. But then Ava very slowly and deliberately shook her head back and forth. With that, two waiters grabbed Larry—he was a slightly built man—one by the belt, and one by the collar, and carried him bodily to the front door and threw him out into the street. Ava continued to sip her mai tai, but I could tell the episode had upset her.

Then there was the complex relationship between Ava and her sister Bea, whom she called Bappie or Bee-At. When Ava had first come to Hollywood, Bappie had come with her as her chaperon, and Bappie was still very much a part of Ava's life. At times, the sisters would act like the closest of friends but, at other times, they fought bitterly, and one never knew, from one day to the next, what their feelings were going to be toward each other. Their fights always ended up over the same thing: Aunt Ava's pearls. Their aunt Ava, after whom Ava had been named, had died years before, and Ava had wanted Aunt Ava's pearls to be buried with her. But Bappie—so Ava said—had removed the pearls from the corpse before the casket was closed and had kept them. Bappie denied this. "Thief!" "Liar!" "Grave robber!" "Liar!" they would end up screaming at one another. Bappie's second husband was a Hollywood property man named Art Cole, who openly hated Ava. "That sexy walk of hers," he'd say. "Do you know how they taught her to do that? They had her walk with a fifty-cent piece up her ass, squeezed between her cheeks!" Did I want to marry into that disputatious, dysfunctional family?

Ava had a number of remarkable friends who were genuinely loyal to her, people like Robert Graves, Adlai Stevenson, Salvador Dalí, Patricia Neal, Princess Grace, and the bandleader Peter Duchin. But there were others who struck me as questionable, even dangerous—the writer James Baldwin, for example.

Having grown up in the segregated South, Ava had the naive belief that all Black people deserved to be treated with kindness and generosity, that all could be trusted to be her friends. I'd always considered James Baldwin a dishonest writer. He passed himself off as a man who'd grown up in the mean streets of Harlem, who'd fought his way singlehandedly out of the ghetto of poverty and discrimination and, against all odds, had achieved fame and success. In fact, Baldwin had had a particularly privileged childhood. His gifts as a writer had been recognized early by his teachers, and he'd been awarded special scholarships to special schools, where much more attention and financial assistance had been lavished upon him than the average Black youth would have expected. To Blacks who really knew Harlem, Baldwin was considered a fraud and a poseur. He had no experience in common with ghetto Blacks at all.

One night in the winter of 1965, when Ava had come to New York from Spain on one of her periodic visits, she was staying at the St. Regis, where she often stayed, and she announced that she felt like hell. I put my hand on her forehead, which felt feverish, and I suggested we call the hotel doctor, who presently arrived. It turned out she was running a temperature of 102, and the doctor suspected she might be coming down with the flu. We'd been planning to go out to dinner that night, but the doctor recommended against this. Outside, the February night was cold and windy, with rain mixed with snow, and the streets were awash with slush. The doctor gave her a shot of antibiotics and told her to get lots of rest. After he left, Ava began supplementing the antibiotics with medicine of her own: Vodkas on the rocks. It was at this point that the phone rang to announce that Ava had a visitor. Jimmy Baldwin was downstairs. "Send him up!" she croaked.

Jimmy arrived, bustling with news and excitement. Arthur Miller's new play, *After the Fall*, had recently opened in the Village, and the whole so-called "artistic community" of New York was up in arms about it. The play was said to be cruelly exploitive of Miller's former wife, the late Marilyn Monroe, and Baldwin was organizing a band of writers, artists, and performers to picket that night's performance outside the theater. It was essential that Ava join the picket line. "With a star of your magnitude, we'll get network TV coverage!" he said.

"Darling, I'm really not feeling so hot," she said. "The doctor thinks it might be the flu."

"But you've *got* to come!" he insisted. "With you, we can get all three networks. We can get the *News* and the *Mirror* and the *Post*, and maybe even the *Times*."

Ava looked out at the stormy night. "Can I carry an umbrella?" she asked him. I could see she was beginning to weaken.

"Absolutely not! The cameras won't recognize you under an umbrella! But we've got a sign for you to carry—'Down with *The Fall*! Save Marilyn's memory!'"

"But what about my hair?" she asked him.

"If your hair looks a little disheveled in the rain, that'll be all the better! It'll show how deeply and passionately committed you are to the memory of Marilyn."

"Well, all right. I'll do it for you, Jimmy," she said.

"Now hurry!" he said. "Get your face on! Get into your most glamorous gown! We've got to get down to the theater before curtain time!"

She went into the bedroom to change her clothes.

"Isn't this wonderful!" he squealed. "I've got Ava Gardner! We might even make the eleven o'clock news, don't you think?" He started for the phone to notify the media of his coup.

"I'll tell you what I think," I said, in what are usually called measured tones. "I think you're a little shit, Jimmy."

He put down the phone and stared at me, his oddly exophthalmic eyes seeming to grow more bugged. "What do you mean?" he said.

"The girl is sick," I said. "She told you so. She's running a temperature of a hundred and two. She's also a little drunk. The doctor just gave her a shot and told her to get to bed. And you're going to make her walk up and down the street for two hours in the freezing rain. She doesn't give a damn about the Miller play. She never even met Marilyn Monroe."

"What should I do?" he asked.

"Just leave," I said.

"Without saying goodbye to her?"

"Without. Just leave." I pointed to the door. "Get out of here." He was out the door with surprising alacrity.

Presently Ava reemerged from the bedroom, looking, I must say, gorgeous. She had put on a long white Balenciaga gown, and was carrying the full-length mink coat she'd been given as one of her perks for *Seven Days in May*, which she'd just finished. Her cheeks were flushed, and her eyes were bright, if not from makeup, from fever. "Where is he?" she wanted to know.

"He had to leave," I said. "I guess it took you too long to change."

She sank into the sofa with a deep sigh. "Thank God," she said. "I really feel like hell." She lay down on the sofa and closed her eyes. I arranged some sofa cushions around her head and covered her with the big mink coat. I pressed my palm to her forehead again. It was still warm, but the fever did seem to be receding. I sat there with her for a while, thinking troubled thoughts. Would this beautiful creature always be pursued by people who used her for their own gain, as well as by her own demons?

After a while, seeing that she was in a deep sleep, I drew the shades and closed the curtains tightly—she could only sleep in a completely darkened bedroom, and often pinned heavy blankets across her windows for blackout shades—and turned out the lights. Then I also left.

The more I got to know her, the more I realized that her personal life was disorganized to the point of chaos. She always had a secretary, usually male, and, like Elizabeth's, they were mostly willowy young men who were willing to trade much in the way of salary in return for the supposedly glamorous life with a nomadic, international film star. Ava had a long series of these, and none of them lasted more than a few months. One of the most faithful of these was a nice young man named Ed Schaeffer, who genuinely loved her, but whose employment was only in spurts. She'd beg him to come back to her, and he'd consent, but it was only a matter of time before she'd blow up at him over something, and he'd fly home to rejoin his longtime lover, a prominent hairdresser in Los Angeles.

She was forever losing things. She had a pair of emerald earrings that she particularly liked, but, at a bar or a restaurant where we had dinner, she'd often slip these off and leave them at the table, perhaps rolled up in a napkin. Then, when she got home and missed them, it would be up to Ed or me, or sometimes both of us, to retrace the itinerary of the evening, either by taxi or by telephone, in search of the emeralds, while restaurant staffs searched through piles of soiled table linen. Miraculously, the earrings always turned up. She also had a gold cigarette case and matching Dunhill lighter that Frank had given her and, wherever we went, these were always getting left behind. I soon learned, whenever we left a party or a restaurant, to be sure she still had her full inventory of belongings: "Have you got your earrings? Have you got Frank's case and lighter?"

Once, when she and Ed were flying back to Spain, she'd asked me to accompany them to Kennedy Airport. But, when, at the last minute, it was time to remove her jewelry case from the hotel's safe-deposit box, neither of them could find the key. We searched for this high and low. In the end, we waited in the limousine while the hotel blew up the box with blasting caps. We could hear the muffled explosions from the street. Later, Ed Shaeffer told me that, after boarding the plane, he'd found the missing key in his jacket pocket.

She had a lovely duplex apartment in Madrid at number 11, Avenida Dr. Arce, in a new building just off the Paseo de la Castellana. It had a large terrace, and the terrace had been filled with potted trees and tropical plants. But, when she left for Mexico for four months to do *Iguana*, she forgot to arrange for anyone to water her plants, and when she got home, they had all died. She never got around to replacing them.

One of Ava's neighbors in the building was Juan Perón, the exiled Argentinean dictator, along with—for a while at least—the mummified remains of his late wife, Eva. Ava's terrace overlooked Peron's, and occasionally we would see him standing there, facing the street in a military posture, much as he must have stood on the balcony of the Casa Rosa in Buenos Aires addressing the Argentine masses. Ava would sometimes yell down to him, *Mala leche!*"—the Spanish equivalent of "Bastard!" Without acknowledging her, he would turn stiffly and disappear inside his apartment. Ava enjoyed doing anything that would irritate Sr. Perón. She often invited Gypsy dancers up to her place from a local nightclub, and joined them in noisy, foot-stomping flamenco performances that went on late into the night. Once, when Perón had had enough of this, he called the police. But, when the Guardia Civil arrived, the soldiers were so delighted to find themselves in such glamorous company that they simply poured themselves drinks and joined the rowdy party.

Meanwhile, Ava had no sense at all about money. That she had any financial security at all was thanks entirely to her big sister Bappie. Early in Ava's film career, Bappie had shrewdly placed all of Ava's financial affairs in the hands of the Los Angeles management firm of Morgan Maree & Company, who managed money for a number of important stars. From them streamlined offices on Wilshire Boulevard, Morgan Maree negotiated the details of Ava's contracts, collected her money for her, invested for her, saw to it that she carried sufficient insurance, and paid all her bills, including her taxes. She was kept on a strict cash allowance of $500 a week. Even so, she was always running short. When she first started borrowing money from me, I frankly wondered whether I'd ever see it again but, to her credit, she was incredibly good about repaying these small loans. Otherwise, she was a reckless spender. Her closets were filled with dresses, furs, and shoes that she'd never worn. Once, at a Balenciaga show, she got so excited that she ordered the designer's entire fall collection. When the people at Morgan Maree heard about this, they made her send most of the outfits back.

But her greatest financial crisis occurred in 1970, when she received a notification from the Spanish government claiming that she owed $1,000,000 in Spanish income taxes. Immediately the people at Morgan Maree were galvanized into action. Jess Morgan of that firm flew to Spain, armed with briefcases full of receipts and newspaper clippings. He planned to launch a double-barreled defense. On the one hand, he intended to demonstrate that Ava had poured a great deal of money into the Spanish economy. He also would argue that, what with her well-publicized flings with bullfighters and such, Ava had actually become a

Spanish tourist attraction as, in a real sense, she had. A meeting was set up with a Spanish cabinet minister named Manuel Fraga Iribarne.

Sr. Fraga was Spain's minister of tourism, and the police. This always struck me as a quaint combination of cabinet posts but, with these twin responsibilities, Fraga was an important figure in Generalissimo Franco's government. A couple of years earlier, I'd had some personal dealings with Fraga, in which I'd actually extracted an apology from the great man, and so it was suggested that I might be helpful at the meeting.

My earlier meeting with Fraga had come about this way. I'd been assigned to go to Spain to do an article for a major travel magazine that was planning to devote an entire issue to Spain. The Franco government, at that point, was very sensitive to anti-Franco sentiments in the United States, and so Sr. Franco's office had decreed that if the American magazine was to get any cooperation from his government on the project, the magazine must submit a full list of the writers and photographers involved, for the government's approval.

The list was submitted, and, a few weeks later, a dossier arrived from Madrid by way of United Nations Headquarters in New York. Most of the men and women involved passed Spain's official muster, but I was astonished to learn, I had not. When I was shown my section of the dossier, I read, "Stephen Birmingham is a well-known British writer of little note." I didn't mind being mistaken as British, nor did I mind being called well known. But to be told in the same sentence that I was "of little note" rather hurt my feelings. The report went on to say that I was known to be "a hater of Spain," that I was a card-carrying member of the Communist Party, and that, in 1932, I had written a series of articles denouncing Generalissimo Franco in the *Daily Worker*.

At that point, I'd never been to Spain, and so couldn't see how I could have developed a hatred of the country. I'd never had any sympathy with Communism. And, in 1932, I was barely a toddler, so to have written articles for the *Daily Worker* would have been quite a feat. The minute I got to Spain I made an appointment to see Sr. Fraga-Iribarne, to try to clear my name. If I didn't, I was sure I'd be harassed by his police at every turn.

With some embarrassment, Fraga explained that his staff had done their researches on us under much pressure and in some haste. An error had indeed been made. There actually had been another writer, an Englishman, with the same name as mine. My prior namesake had indeed been anti-Franco and had written for the *Daily Worker*. But further research had turned up the fact that this fellow had been dead for thirty years. Sr. Fraga was most apologetic. He hoped that his office's earlier report on me would cause me no embarrassment or inconvenience. If there was anything his office could do to assist me in my researches, I should not hesitate to call on him personally. Now, though I doubted he'd remember our previous meeting, I was to meet with him again, in Ava's tow this time.

Ava refused to take this meeting very seriously. She knew, she insisted, how to deal with Spanish bureaucrats like Manuel Fraga Iribarne. She kept jokingly referring to him as "Señor Bragas," the Spanish word for underpants. I said I wasn't sure that this was such a laughing matter. The workings of Franco's government were often devious and mysterious. After all, El Caudillo had granted political asylum to Juan Perón in Spain when the latter was expelled from Argentina. It might just be that Perón had grown tired of hearing insults and obscenities shouted at him from his film star neighbor and had gone directly to the top. I counseled extreme tact and caution.

We chose Ava's wardrobe for the meeting very carefully, and I suggested that we select something from a Spanish couturier, even though Fraga might not recognize this patriotic gesture. We settled on a moss green wool suit from Balenciaga, with a low stand-up collar, long sleeves, and a slim skirt. We accessorized this with a silk scarf and ostrich handbag from Loewe, the Spanish equivalent to Hermès in Paris, and the scarf would be tied in such a way that the signature showed.

I also reminded Ava of the way Spaniards prefer to conduct business meetings. Spaniards find Americans' brusque, down-to-brass-tacks approach to negotiations extremely rude. Instead, Spanish etiquette demands that the first five or ten minutes of any meeting be spent exchanging personal pleasantries. "How is your lovely wife?" "Is your son doing well at his university?" "I heard your mother-in-law was ailing." "I hope she's feeling better." Et cetera.

On the afternoon of the meeting, we were ushered into Sr. Fraga's office at the Ministerio, the size of which even King Farouk might have envied. We all shook hands, and I reminded Fraga that he and I had met a year or so before. "Ah, yes," he said. "You are not the dead English Communist!" He then turned his attention to Jess Morgan. "Did you have a pleasant flight from Los Angeles?"

"I did indeed. In my opinion, Iberia is the finest airline in the world."

"And your hotel accommodations here in Madrid? Are they comfortable?"

"Comfortable? They're superb! There's no hotel anywhere to equal the Ritz."

And so on. I thought things were getting off to a nice start. But Ava had lighted one of her Winstons and was puffing on it furiously. She had crossed her legs in her chair, and her right foot had begun swinging in small circles, a sign that she was growing impatient with all this polite backing and filling. I tried to catch her eye but couldn't.

Finally, Fraga turned to some papers on his desk, and said, "Ah, Senorita Gardner, I see we are here to discuss your indebtedness to the Spanish government of ten thousand dollars."

Ava stamped out her cigarette. "What the fuck?" she cried. "I thought it was a million!"

Sr. Fraga—who spoke and understood English perfectly—frowned and looked down at the papers in front of him.

"Well, which is it?" Ava said. "Make up your cotton-pickin' mind!"

Sr. Fraga continued to frown, while passing his fingers across the documents. Then he looked up at her and said, "Ah, Senorita Gardner, I see you are quite right. The figure *is* a million dollars."

The meeting was over. Ava had been offered an out—a mere 1 percent of the original bill—but she had managed to blow it. She was given ninety days in which either to pay the million dollars, or to wind up her affairs in Spain and leave the country—permanently. She chose the latter course, and that was when she decided to move to London, even though it meant leaving her two beloved corgis, Rags and Cara, for weeks in

British quarantine. She could never go back to Spain, not even as a tourist. If she had tried, she would have been met at the Customs desk by the Spanish tax collector.

If Juan Perón had been involved in the whole caper, he had won.

No, the more time I spent with her the more certain I became that I did not want to marry her. Sometimes I wondered whether, more than a husband, she simply wanted a permanent male companion, someone with whom to share her lonely evening hours. Even the series of male secretaries she employed could not fulfill that function. I'd known a couple of men who married film stars—Peter Viertel, who married Deborah Kerr, Roald Dahl, who married Patricia Neal—and had seen how much of their lives was spent shepherding their wives' luggage through airport departure lounges and hotel lobbies. I knew that marriage to Ava would be the end of my career as a writer. Taking care of her would be a full-time job.

There was also the matter of her drinking. I won't say that she was an alcoholic, but she did like to drink, and she drank a lot. ("Liquid courage," she called it.) But she didn't like to drink alone, and most of the male secretaries she hired were also supposed to serve as her bartenders and drinking companions. I remember one November when I happened to be in Madrid over Thanksgiving and Ava invited half a dozen of us for a traditional American Thanksgiving dinner at her apartment on Dr. Arce. She was an excellent cook, and it was almost like watching a child as she enthusiastically prepared this feast—the huge turkey with apple and hazelnut stuffing, candied yams, corn pudding, cranberry relish, and three pies for dessert: apple, mincemeat, and a three-berry recipe that had been her mother's. She'd scoured the local markets for just the right ingredients—many of which were not exactly staples of the Spanish diet—and did all the cooking herself. But, on Thanksgiving Day, as she toiled in the kitchen, she called out to me, "Fix me a vodka on the rocks, darling!" And, by the time, her dinner was ready to be served, she had reached capacity and had slipped away upstairs to her bedroom and passed out. We sat down to her Thanksgiving dinner without our hostess, all of us elaborately pretending that nothing out of the ordinary had happened.

At other times, when drinking, she would become suspicious and obsessed with the notion that even her closest friends were spying on her, or secretly plotting to exploit her for their own personal gain. I suppose she had been exploited for so long by Hollywood that she no longer really trusted anyone and could convince herself that everyone with whom she came in contact had some sort of sinister private agenda designed to take advantage of her. Her frequent blow-ups with her private secretaries were usually over matters like this. There was a tabloid magazine at the time called *Confidential*, which specialized in printing scurrilous stories about film stars. She would suddenly turn to the secretary of the moment and say, "You're planning to sell a story about me to *Confidential*, aren't you?" No amount of denying would convince her otherwise. The secretary would then depart, often in tears.

The drinking made her a difficult friend, and a demanding lover. It would have made her an impossible wife.

There was a Movado wristwatch I wore at the time of which I was quite fond. It was an unusual-looking piece because there were two dials on its face. Designed for travel, one dial could be set for the time at home, while the other could be set for local time. One night she suddenly turned to me and said, "That watch is a tape recorder, isn't it? You're recording everything I say!" "Honestly, it isn't, honey," I said, and I tried to show her how the watch worked. But she would have none of it. "I won't let you make love to me with that watch on," she said, and so I removed it and left it in another room.

I decided to deflect the talk of marriage by using a technique that still seems rather cowardly. I decided to make her a friend of the family. I invited her to my house in Rye to meet my wife and children and, when she was in New York, she was our frequent dinner and party guest. I should probably now address the question of whether my ex-wife knew of Ava's and my affair. I'm quite sure Nan did know. I think wives always know, though Nan and I never discussed it. Ava was not the cause of our eventual divorce. That was brought about by less tangible matters, which I'll get to. And, though I'm sure that my former wife would deny this hotly, I'm also sure that she thoroughly enjoyed having this beautiful and famous woman as our guest and friend. Ava was an exciting change from our somewhat stuffy suburban neighbors, bankers and lawyers and insurance executives, members of the West Chester Country Club crowd, whom I used to refer to as the Lilly Pulitzer set, since both the women and their husbands at the time favored the splashily colored cotton prints by that designer. Against this backdrop, Ava—who usually dressed simply, usually in skirt-and-sweater ensembles, or in jeans and a boy's Brooks Brothers shirt—was still unmistakably the glamorous Ava Gardner. I've seen her put up her dark, naturally curly hair with toothpicks from her martinis. She still looked gorgeous. "The only thing I've ever learned about this business is how to find the key light," she used to say. On every movie set, there's a key light. Once you find it, you have to let it touch the tip of your nose." She could find the key light in my living room, and her beauty would be breathtaking.

She was a great box office draw for our parties. Nan liked that.

As Ava's and my affair began to cool as I'd hoped it would—and as Nan helped me maintain the charade, and it was already a charade, that she and I were a perfectly happy suburban couple, with a pretty house and garden and a pool, the cooling was helped by the fact that Ava had found a new love. He was the actor George C. Scott, with whom Ava costarred in *The Bible*, another film directed by John Huston.

"The only thing I know about him," Ava said before flying off to Rome to do the picture, "is that he's an ex-drinker. Well, I'm just going to have to change *that*!"

She did, in fact rather quickly change that, with disastrous results for all concerned.

When sober—I never saw him drink, fortunately—George Scott was a mild-mannered, soft-spoken man with an almost shy demeanor. When drunk, he apparently turned into a raging, fist-swinging bully. He was a big, powerfully built man, but his wife at the time, the actress Colleen Dewhurst, was also a large, muscular woman who apparently was able to slug him back with as much force as he slugged her. Their marital fisticuffs had become the stuff of movie legend. He towered over Ava, and, once she got him drinking again, she quickly began to pay the price. At first, they had only food fights. But these soon escalated into really rough stuff. On the set of *The Bible*, it got so bad that even the normally laissez-faire John Huston found it necessary to speak to Scott about it. Huston could simply not afford to have his film delayed while his leading lady recovered from the batterings she was receiving from the leading man.

One time during all this I met Ava at Heathrow Airport, and her arm was in a sling. Scott had broken her collarbone, torn out a large hunk of hair, and blackened her left eye, in which she still had double vision. Suddenly I was disgusted with her. "How can you have anything to do with this creep?" I asked her.

"I can't help it," she said. "I've fallen for him."

I tried to rationalize this new relationship. Perhaps, I thought, as a little Tarheel farm girl from North Carolina, she had grown up in a world where domestic violence was not uncommon, even considered acceptable. I began to think of my relationship with Ava in terms of a rather nasty little game Truman Capote had invented, called Linkages. In this he "linked" various well-known personalities through their various sexual encounters. Through Ava, via Frank Sinatra and with a bit of chronological leapfrogging, I could claim a link to Mia Farrow and, through Woody Allen, to Farrow's adopted daughter Soon-Yi Previn. Through Ava's affair with Howard Hughes, I could link myself to Katherine Hepburn, and, through Artie Shaw, I had a link to Lana Turner and Evelyn Keyes, and on and on. It was a grimly amusing game to play.

One night Ava invited me for drinks at her London town house in Alexandra Square. When I arrived, George Scott was sitting on the living room sofa, his face covered with scabs and oozing sores. Ava pulled me into the kitchen, where she was fixing drinks. "Did you see George's face?" she whispered. I said it was hard to miss. "What happened?" I asked her. "Last night he got drunk," she said, "and he suddenly threw himself face-first into the fireplace and the open fire. My maid and I had to drag him out by the feet." In the next breath she added, "George and I are going to get married!"

After that encounter, it was nearly a year before I saw her again, though we talked occasionally on the phone between New York and London. But our affair was not quite over.

One afternoon I was coming from a haircut at a shop I used to go to on Madison Avenue in Manhattan, and, as I walked down the street, I saw a bellhop wearing a St. Regis uniform walking two corgis. I immediately recognized them as Ava's Rags and Cara. I stepped into the hotel lobby and called her on the house phone. "Darling, come up here at once," she said. "A terrible thing has happened, and I need you desperately!"

I then telephoned Nan. "Ava's in town," I said. "She's in some sort of trouble. I'm going to see what I can do to help her."

"Of course," my wife said.

The trouble, it turned out, was not quite as desperate as Ava had made it sound. What had happened was that Ava had come to New York to interview candidates for a new secretary-companion. She had found a young man she liked and had planned to fly back with him to London the following night. She had given him a $500 advance on his salary. But, at the last minute, it turned out that the young man did not have a valid US passport, and he had also disappeared with the money and was nowhere to be found.

We had a few drinks, and Ava's spirits improved considerably. I suggested dinner at Trader Vic's, where we'd often gone before. Ava excused herself to change from her jeans and sweatshirt.

At Trader Vic's we ordered mai tais and steaks—she was a great steak eater—and she told me how the affair with George C. Scott had ended. In the end, he had gone back to Colleen Dewhurst, and to the fistfights they both seemed to relish so. In fact, he had already divorced Colleen once before meeting Ava, and had then married her again. Once more, Ava was alone in the world. "I just want someone to cuddle," she said. "Just someone to cuddle." Though she still looked great, the movie roles were not being offered to her the way they once were. John Huston had offered her a cameo role, playing Lillie Langtry in *The Life and Times of Judge Roy Bean*. There was a small part in a B disaster film called *Earthquake*, in which she would end up being sucked down into a storm sewer. There were a couple of things for television, which she didn't want to do. "Television is for children," she said bitterly.

From Trader Vic's, we went on to a bar on West 46th Street, which was one of Frank's favorite hangouts, and where much fuss was made over

Ava, which she enjoyed. In high spirits again, she announced that she was still hungry, and we went on to a Third Avenue steak house called Christa's, where she devoured a second sirloin. Here, the owner, who had heard she was in town and hoped she might drop by, had set aside a special bottle of *añejo* tequila for her, in anticipation of a visit. Did she want him to open it for us? No, she said, she wanted to keep this beautiful bottle intact forever, as a permanent reminder of their friendship.

The hour was now growing late, approaching 3 a.m. The restaurant had closed its doors to further customers, but of course the proprietor let us stay on, undisturbed, and we each had a couple of more martinis. Finally, it was time for us to go, and we left Christa's and went out into the quiet street where we were able to flag down a late cruising taxi.

Now, at this point, the retelling of what happened next during that long night becomes a little tricky. Ava had an American friend named Betty Sicre, who had married a Spanish businessman and was living in Madrid. The Sicres had a son, named Ricardo, who was a freshman at Princeton, and, before leaving for New York, Ava had promised Betty Sicre that she would try to look in on Ricardo to see how he was faring at his American university. Ava had lamented that, on this trip, she just wasn't going to have time to go down to Princeton to visit young Ricardo. She wished she could do it, but she couldn't.

In the taxi, exuberant and expansive from martinis, I said, "Why don't we ask this cab to drive us down to Princeton and see Ricardo?" She was immediately enthusiastic, and so the cab turned toward the Lincoln Tunnel and the New Jersey Turnpike and headed for Princeton, a good two-hour drive from Manhattan. In the taxi, we both dozed a bit to regain our stamina, and the morning sun came up somewhere over New Brunswick.

When we reached the Princeton campus, the then all-male students were heading for their first classes of the morning. I asked Ava if she knew where Ricardo lived, which dorm he was in, but of course she had no idea. "We'll ask," she said, and we began stopping little knots of students on the street and asking them if they knew where we could find Ricardo Sicre. Nobody had ever heard of him.

We then began stopping in front of every building that looked as though it might be a college dormitory. Ava would then hop out of the cab, still clutching her precious bottle of tequila, and run into the entry-way calling, "Ricardo! Ricardo!" to no avail.

It wasn't long before she was recognized, and word soon spread across the Princeton campus that Ava Gardner, in a New York taxicab with some unknown gentleman, was wandering about the campus streets looking for someone called Ricardo. Soon a small band of students was running behind our taxi, slapping its fenders, and yelling, "Hey, Ava! Ava!"

"This is ridiculous," she said at last. "There's only one way to get any-thing done. We've got to go directly to the top. Who's the president of this damn university, anyway?"

I happened to know the answer to that one. "His name is Robert F. Goheen," I said. I'd seen him mentioned in the *Times* a few days earlier.

"Let's find his house," she said. "Anybody ought to know where the president's house is!"

We asked for, and received, directions, and presently we pulled up in front of the president's residence, a huge red-brick Georgian mansion, as I recall. Ava started to get out of the cab, but I put my hand on her shoulder.

"Now wait a minute," I said. "Let's think about this. Let's think about this whole thing very carefully. You are, after all, Ava Gardner, and you have a reputation for being—well, a little wild. You know, with bullfight-ers and all that. We both had a lot to drink last night, and we haven't had much sleep. Neither of us is looking our absolute best right now. I under-stand why you won't let go of that bottle of tequila, but—think about it. The president of Princeton, if he's home, is probably still in his robe and slippers, having breakfast with his wife. If you go charging in there now, asking for Ricardo—well, it's possible you could have the poor kid kicked out of college by this afternoon!"

She sighed and sank back in her seat. "You're right," she said. "Let's go the hell back home."

And so, we headed back for New York City. We stopped for some breakfast at a Howard Johnson's on the turnpike. After that, she dozed some more in the cab. Then suddenly she sat bolt upright. "Jesus Christ," she said. "It's *Yale*!"

It makes a lovely anecdote, doesn't it? It even made its way into her autobiography. But the trouble is—I warned you that this gets a little tricky—that most of it isn't true. We never went to Princeton. This was all a lie that Ava and I composed together in order to explain to my wife why I had been gone from home, without a word, for more than twenty-four hours.

What actually happened was this:

After leaving Christa's we got in a cab and headed back to the St. Regis. Ava sat back in her seat staring blankly into space, her face a mask, and suddenly I was filled with an almost unbearable sorrow for her. Here she was, still looking more beautiful than any forty-six-year-old woman had any right to look, but where was she? She was one of the last products of the old studio star system, a system that had been invented by her old boss, Louis B. Mayer, whom she despised. The studio had taught her how to walk with a fifty-cent piece clenched between her cheeks. The MGM speech school had taken all the North Carolina out of her accent, and given her that rich, throaty speaking voice. The one thing she had resisted was letting them pluck her eyebrows because, when that happened, they often never grew back. They had taught her to find the key light, and to let it perch on the tip of her nose. In scores of films, for the better part of thirty years, she had been assured that she had no acting talent, and that all she had to do was stand there, in the key light, and look beautiful. She insisted she hated every film she made, and had done them "only for the loot, only for the loot." ("Of course," I used to kid her, "I guess you could have opted for being a housewife in the Bronx. Would that have been better?")

Sitting in the taxi with her, I realized that I was witnessing the twilight of a great star. The important scripts were no longer being offered to her, and soon, indeed, she might be playing Natalie Wood's mother. All of us, of course, must come to the moment when it is time for us to step out of the parade, but the moment seemed to have come too suddenly for Ava, and had caught her unawares. And now what was left for her? Well, there was a slimy young man who applied for a job as her secretary, but who had left her in the lurch and run off with her money. There was the bartender at Frank's favorite West Side gin mill who had fussed over her and flattered her. There was the owner of the East Side Steak joint who had given her a bottle of aged tequila, worth perhaps $12. What else?

She sat there in the taxi, cradling the bottle of tequila as she might have cradled the baby she always wanted, but never had. She'd aborted two pregnancies with Frank that he'd never known about. If he'd known about the abortions, he'd have been furious with her, but she'd had them done because the pregnancies would have interfered with her film schedule. Sinatra's career was in a slump at that point, and they needed the money. I reached out for her in the taxi and took her in my arms.

"Shall we go to our place?" she whispered at last. I nodded.

"Our place" was the Hotel Elysée on East 54th Street. We'd gone there often before. In New York, she usually stayed at the St. Regis because she enjoyed the luxury and the service. But she distrusted the hotel's staff and suspected them of spying on her. She was certain that the St. Regis telephone operators were eavesdropping on her telephone calls, gathering information to try to sell to tabloids like *Confidential*, and, in fact, when using the phones there I'd heard little clicks on the line that suggested someone might be listening in. But they knew her at the Elysée, and she trusted the smaller hotel to keep her comings and goings secret. She had nicknamed it the "Hotel Easy-lay," and who knew with how many other men it had become "our place." It didn't matter. As we stepped into the lobby, the night manager spotted us instantly and hurried us into an elevator. We signed the hotel register in the elevator, on our way up to the suite. This was part of the service. The Easy-lay always kept the mechanisms for an assignation well-oiled.

We made love, and then opened the bottle of tequila. Then we made love again. We slept until past noon the next day, and by then the empty tequila bottle was in the wastebasket. I somehow knew that this would be our last time together, but she kept begging, "Just stay with me a little longer."

But soon it was time for us to start concocting the lie that we would both tell my wife. She actually *had* mentioned Ricardo Sicre, who actually *was* at Princeton (instead of visiting him, she'd called him on the phone), and so a trip to Princeton seemed to be a good starting point for the deception; it would account for all those missing hours. "If you're going to lie, it's important to lie *big*," I reminded her, "and it's important to throw in lots of little details." One by one, we added these—the students banging on the fenders of the cab, the visit to President Goheen's house, the breakfast at Howard Johnson's, and so on—until Ava giggled and said we sounded just like an old MGM story conference, at which, Scheherazade-like, writers would sit around a table and talk until a screen story had been developed out of thin air.

When we both had our story down pat, Ava clapped her hands and said, "I love it!" Then she added, a little sadly, "It sounds exactly like something I'd do."

We both told our story to my wife, who accepted it, or pretended to, and the story was retold so many times that I almost began to believe it was true. Our fictitious junket to the Princeton campus always got a good laugh. It was such a good story, in fact, that I rather hate to surrender it, as I do herewith.

After that New York visit, it was nearly twenty years before I saw Ava again, though I usually tried to telephone her on her birthday, a date about which she was particularly sentimental. It was an easy date to remember—December 24th, the day before Christmas. As a little girl, she'd felt cheated by this birthday. Her older brother and sisters got to get gifts twice a year. But she, the youngest, always received combination birthday and Christmas presents, which she found unfair.

In November of 1989 I was in London and decided I must see her. It was as though our affair had just petered out, and needed some form of closure, some final scene. But when I phoned her, she didn't seem particularly eager to see me, and kept waffling about the date. "Let me take you out to dinner at some swell place," I said. Her reply was, "After a stroke and double pneumonia, I don't go out to swell places anymore." But eventually a date was arranged; my friend Ed Lahniers and I were to come to her place for a drink on a Thursday, at five o'clock—a week away. I began to suspect that she didn't want me to see the way she looked, and even when I rang her doorbell, I wasn't at all sure she'd let us in. But she did.

She was then living in an elegant floor-through flat at 34 Ennismore Gardens, in Kensington, and she greeted us in a baggy pair of sweatpants and shirt, barefoot, her Ben Franklin half-glasses perched on her nose.

The legendary beauty had indeed been smudged by age, but she was still pretty. A stranger, seeing her on the street, might not have recognized Ava Gardner, but would surely have thought, "What a pretty woman!" The stroke had left her with a slight limp, and only partial use of her right arm. Arrayed on her living room sofa were dozens of pairs of high-heeled shoes, which she could no longer wear. She was in the process of giving the shoes away. She had been medicated for the pneumonia with cortisone, and the drug had caused her to gain weight. She was not fat, but neither was she as reed slender as she had been when I first met her. She lived alone with a Peruvian cook-housekeeper, and now only one corgi, named Morgan, after Jess Morgan, her business manager. She would turn sixty-seven the following month, but she seemed in good spirits, and no one could have foretold that just two months later—in January 1990— she would contract pneumonia again and die.

She no longer drank, she explained—"My maid gets so angry with me when I drink." But she still puffed enthusiastically on the Winstons she loved so much, and she had a smoker's cough. She had been finishing her memoirs, and her publisher, Doubleday, had been concerned about her health, worried, perhaps, that she might not be well enough to tour to promote the book when it came out. They'd sent a doctor to see her and, through some mix-up, the doctor's large bill had been sent to Ava, instead of Doubleday. "Don't send me any more doctors!" she had written angrily to the publisher.

She'd sold all her jewelry which she no longer wore, including the emerald earrings for which we'd undergone so many late-night searches. I asked her what she did for exercise. "Nothing anymore." She'd always been so athletic. She'd been a good golfer, and an excellent tennis player. Once, she and I had played a rather drunken set of mixed doubles at the Beverly Hills Hotel—in our bare feet, since we hadn't brought the proper shoes. I kept apologizing to my male opponent for the rotten shots I was giving him and complimenting him on his fine returns. "You're really a very good tennis player!" I remember telling this man. Only when the set was over and we shook hands at the net did I discover that I'd been playing against Alex Olmedo, the 1959 Wimbledon champion, who had become the hotel's tennis pro.

"What about swimming?" I suggested. She'd always been a strong swimmer. Surely there must be a swimming club in London with an indoor pool where she could work out. "No, no," she said, and I suspected that she no longer liked the way she looked in a swimsuit. I told her that London's damp and foggy winter weather couldn't be the best thing for her damaged lungs. Why didn't she go back to Southern California? After all, she owned the house on Rinconia Drive where her sister Bea and her husband lived. "No, no." She never wanted to go to Hollywood again.

Scattered about the apartment were photographs of Ava in her glory days, including an astonishing full-length portrait by Man Ray, in which she was dressed as a Gypsy queen. "Yes, I really was pretty, wasn't I?" she said, looking at it. And the sad fact seemed to be that this girl who had always been reassured that her only talent was her beauty had given up on life.

We talked about her memoirs, which were designed, she said, to put an end to "all the lies" that had been written about her, including a *Confidential* story claiming that she and Lana Turner had been caught in bed together, suggesting a lesbian affair. The two had, in fact, once spent the night together, but only because they were trying to hide from Frank who was on one of his marauding rampages.

She wanted to call her book *In Her Own Voice*, from the Robert Graves poem that he'd told her she could take personally: "She speaks always in her own voice, even to strangers." (Wisely, I think, her publisher dissuaded her from that title, and the book, published after her death, was called, simply, *Ava*.)

In her London living room that afternoon, I quoted the next line of the poem: "She is forever wild and beautiful, pledged to love through all disaster." She looked at me, astonished. she asked me. "How did you ever remember that?"

"I was very much in love with you once—remember?" I said.

PART II
LIFE IN RYE AND BEYOND

Chapter Nine

"Our Crowd"

CAREY:

THE PUBLICATION OF *"OUR CROWD,"* MY FATHER'S SEMINAL WORK AND his most successful, was a turning point in our family, and we considered the two-to-three-year period onto which he embarked on the project as B.O.C. and A.O.C., Before *"Our Crowd"* and After *"Our Crowd."* Before *"Our Crowd,"* we had a relatively calm and ordinary life, notwithstanding our unscheduled get-togethers with the law. After *"Our Crowd,"* things began to fall apart in the family on Hidden Spring Lane.

The City of Rye and the Rye Police Department

The City of Rye, New York, not to be confused with the Town of Rye, New York, was formed by English settlers in 1660 when three families purchased land from the Siwanoy natives of the Algonkian Nation paying eight coats, seven shirts and fifteen "fathom" of wampum.[12] Once the transaction properly closed, the previous inhabitants promptly moved on, and the City of Rye expanded dramatically, becoming what today is a wealthy enclave of hedge fund managers, investment bankers, and their ilk commuting by rail to the canyons of power in Manhattan.

According to the 2010 census, Rye had an overall population of 15,720 and per capita income of $94,959 (2012 dollars), making it one of the wealthiest small cities in America on the basis of median household income. In 1960, at the beginning of our family's "creative period," the City had 14,225 making the total population increase 10 percent in fifty years. The City had 2019 operating budgeted tax revenues of approximately $41 million, not including school taxes.[13]

In 2014, the Rye Police Department reported a total of ten full-time and five part-time peace officers.[14] In 1960, there were probably five full-time officers, including the detectives Mark and I were to encounter on several occasions. The first encounter was around that time.[15]

Mark and I Introduce Ourselves to the Rye Police Department

When my older brother and I had run-ins with the detectives in Rye, it was not our fault. Necessarily. While Mark and I were on a virtual first-name basis with the Rye Police by the mid-1970s, it was always for strange and non-prosecutable infractions. On the other hand, our father had, in fact, been the only Birmingham convicted of a crime after his DUI arrest in 1964. Nonetheless, the Rye Police kept a sharp eye out for the Birmingham progeny.

The first run-in occurred when I was young, perhaps five years old. My brother, who was nine, and I were dropped off at the local Rye Recreation ("Rye Rec") Park. While we spent time on swings and generally running around, three "big kids," who were probably twelve or thirteen, grabbed us and told us we all are going into an abandoned mansion located adjacent to Rye Rec, on Milton Road. We didn't know these boys, and I have no idea why they picked us, since there were plenty of other children (but few adults) in the Park that day. Although it sounds like a horror story about to unfold, the actual events were kind of boring. Until the police got involved, that is.

The boys forced Mark and me through a chain-link fence surrounding the vacant property and promptly broke a window to get in. After dragging us inside, they made us sit in a hallway while they ransacked closets and various rooms, presumably looking for things to steal. The house was virtually empty, yet I remember vividly Mark and I looking at each other with confusion as the boys hit found tennis balls down the hall with purloined rackets.

Before we knew it, the boys had gone. My brother and I sat for several minutes until we realized we were alone. With that we left and continued with our playtime in Rye Rec. After a time, Mom picked us up, and we told her of the incident. She seemed unconcerned, since we showed no outward injury, and that was that. Or was it. Enter the Rye Police.

A few days later, the incident, and specifically the break-in, found its way into the Burglary/Robbery Division (comprised of one detective) of the Rye Police Department, with no doubt a Code Red designation. Officers had corralled the principal suspects and those suspects, in turn, had cracked like a cheap watch, named names, and somehow implicated Mark and me.

We were brought downtown. Without benefit of counsel, the chief (and only occupant) of the Burglary/Robbery Division, using police best practices, separated us, and tried to sweat out confessions (putting us under the lights!). Although only five years old, I'd been taught to tell the truth and did so. The persistent badgering, however, finally made me break down and confess that we had been *forced* into the abandoned house by some "big kids." I started crying, professing my innocence, and explaining in detail the events. The detective would have none of it and kept on detecting, assuming I was obviously a cog in a much larger burglary ring he would expose.

Our parents, who were outside the interview room, must have finally realized that there was something perhaps unconstitutional, or at least wrong, about the cop's procedures, and called an end to the interview. I like to think I invoked my Fifth Amendment rights, but I don't recall. With all the bluster he could muster, the detective agreed to release us, without bail and on our own recognizance. That was the end of it.

In calmer moments, I try to believe that the detective was trying to scare us straight. At other moments, however, I think he was just being mean. Whatever his motives, we were more victims than criminals, and this must have frustrated him since it was after all *his collar*.

After this event, my father seemed predisposed to call the Rye Police at the drop of a hat, and did so on numerous occasions, so much that the Birmingham name became well known in the corridors of the Rye Police Department.

∽∞∾

My father's work on *"Our Crowd"* consumed him, and although he shrugs it off in this chapter, the work involved was momentous and straining to him, our mother, and the family. He spent countless hours on research and traveled far and often to interviews. Many were the nights I could hear the thump-tick-tick-tick-thump of his Royal typewriter, as he worked late into the night.

Despite all the anxiety we delivered onto our father, he dedicated *"Our Crowd"* to us, "The Children, Mark, Harriet and Carey." In addition, a random photograph I took of my father at his desk managed to find its way onto the back cover of *"Our Crowd"* as the author's photo, and I was given credit. Although photographically amateur, I still think my *"Our Crowd"* jacket photo is the best photo of my father, showing him as a writer and not some model.

STEVE:

In the mid 1960s I was working on a book I didn't really want to write. There was a young editor at Harper & Row (later to become Harper-Collins) named Roger Klein, who was widely considered to be brilliant. Roger's parents, I understood, were well-to-do New Yorkers of Belgian-Jewish background, and his father was an international diamond merchant; the family moved on the social fringes of New York's Jewish haute bourgeoisie. Roger had a book idea that he had been pestering me about since 1962.

Well, perhaps *pestering* is the wrong word. Every few weeks, he'd call and invite me to lunch at one or another of New York's snappiest restaurants, and at every lunch the topic would be the same: his book ideas, and his belief that I was the ideal person to write it for him.

In 1962, Frederic Morton had published *The Rothschilds: A Family Portrait*. Morton's book was essentially a collection, in hardcover, of a series of articles he had written for *Holiday* magazine, and, though collections of magazine pieces traditionally do not sell well—one theory being that everyone interested in the topic has already read them—*The Rothschilds* had become a surprise best seller. It was making millions for its publisher, Athenaeum, with a tidy percentage of those earnings going to the author himself. Roger Klein's idea was that a similar book could be written about New York' s German-Jewish banking families. Though these families were not all conveniently named Rothschild, as had been the case in Fred Morton's book, they were all, as Roger pointed out, intricately interrelated to one another through marriage. Dynasty had interlocked with dynasty to the point where these families could be treated as a single *mishpocheh*. "And you," Roger kept reminding me," have made yourself a recognized authority on rich people."

This, I suppose, was true, and this had come about in a roundabout, almost accidental way. I, too, frequently wrote for *Holiday*, and this was in the heyday of the Curtis Publishing Company, its corporate parent. *Ladies' Home Journal*, as I've mentioned, was a leader in the field of women's service magazines. *Holiday*—big, glossy, full of color and unafraid of controversy—was displayed prominently on tables in doctors' waiting rooms across the country, and in the reading rooms of every important country club. Curtis's entry into the tots' field, *Jack & Jill*, was taught in every self-respecting kindergarten and nursery school. *Holiday* was particularly financially successful because it alone among Curtis titles would accept liquor advertising, an important source of revenue.

Flushed with success, Curtis threw money around with delightful abandon. Curtis maintained luxurious suites of offices in both New York and Philadelphia, certainly not an arrangement designed for thrift, and its editors traveled back and forth between the two cities sipping martinis in Pullman chairs. *Holiday* paid its writers and photographers top fees and offered them what amounted to unlimited expense accounts— first-class air tickets, five-star hotels, and even chauffeur-driven limos when needed. Indeed, all this extravagant spending may have contributed to the magazine's eventual demise, but at the time those of us who worked for *Holiday* lived it up.

My editor at *Holiday* (he was Fred Morton's too) was the irrepressible Harry Sions, a man whose capacity for enthusiasm knew no bounds. My assignments from Harry had been mostly straightforward travel pieces, or what he liked to call "city portraits"—E. B. White's *New York* and John Marquand's *Boston* had been popular *Holiday* features in this genre. *Holiday*'s resident authority on the rich and high society had for several years been Cleveland Amory (*The Proper Bostonians, The Last Resorts, Who Killed Society?*).

But one night at dinner in New York, where Harry and I had met to discuss some other writing job, he began complaining about Amory. Harry wanted Amory to write a major story on the American debutante scene, but Amory was dragging his heels. Amory, Harry told me, had said it would take him at least six months to research such a story. It would entail travel to at least a dozen US cities, and an extensive stay in each of them. It was beginning to sound as though all this would put a strain on even *Holiday*'s bounteous budget. (As it turned out, Amory was beginning to lose interest in the doings of the moneyed and was turning his attention to wildlife and the plight of baby seals being slaughtered for the fur industry.) After a while, I said, "Look, if Clip Amory really doesn't want the job—if he's willing to give up the assignment—I can write you a piece about debutantes without leaving my desk." After all, I'd been on the debutante circuit myself not that many years before and bringing myself up to date on the situation seemed to involve little more than a few phone calls. And so that was how I came to fill Amory's slot at *Holiday* and become an "authority on rich people." For a while, I even heard myself described as "the poor man's Cleveland Amory."

But as for Roger Klein's idea for a book on New York's wealthy Jewish families, I kept demurring, and for several reasons. For one thing, I had published five books, all of them novels. I felt comfortable with fiction. Though I'd written lots of nonfiction pieces for *Holiday* and other magazines, and felt I'd mastered the trick of that, I wasn't at all sure I wanted to write, or was up to writing, a full-length nonfiction book. For another, I knew some of the Jewish families involved. At Hotchkiss, a schoolmate of mine had been John L. Loeb Jr., whose father headed C. M. Loeb Rhoades & Company on Wall Street. Johnny Loeb and I had been on the swimming team together. (I was the team manager.) At Williams, one of my best friends became Bob Bernhard, who was Johnny Loeb's first cousin. Their mothers were sisters whose maiden name was Lehman, of the Lehman Brothers banking family. An uncle had been Herbert H. Lehman, who was both a United States senator and governor of New York State. Herbert Lehman had given Williams College one of its most elegant dormitories, Lehman Hall. It had become even more complicated when my Williams classmate, Edgar Bronfman, married Johnny Loeb's sister Ann.

At Williams, Bob Bernhard seemed to have gotten the idea that I was Jewish—or at least that was my impression when he came into my room one night with a shocking story. Bob had joined the Phi Gamma Delta fraternity, to which Herbert Lehman had also belonged, and Bob's younger brother Billy was at that point shopping for colleges. Quite naturally Billy had visited Williams, with which the family by then had strong ties, and had dinner at the fraternity house with Bob. After dinner, the president of Phi Gamma Delta had taken Bob Bernhard aside. "Look," he'd said to Bob, "we don't care where your brother decides to go to college. But we want to make it clear that, if he chooses Williams, he'll not be taken into this fraternity. We took your uncle in, and we took you in, but there's got to be a limit. Otherwise, Phi Gamma Delta will be overrun with you people."

"What would you do?" Bob Bernhard asked me.

I was stunned by the question. And why was he asking me what I would do?

"I'll tell you what *I* would do," I said quickly. "I'd resign from that fraternity tonight. I'd toss that fraternity pin right in your president's face. I'd tell him to take that pin and stick it in some other part of his anatomy!"

But of course, he didn't do that. He stayed with Phi Gamma Delta, and brother Billy chose some other college.

"I know some of those New York families," I said to Roger Klein. "They're perfectly nice people, but they're also a little dull. They're not a bit glamorous, like the Rothschilds. The Rothschilds got their start in the eighteenth century. They financed European wars and dealt with kings and queens. They became lords and barons, and even Hitler was afraid to mess around with them. The New York families came here around 1850, started out as peddlers, and didn't begin to make any money until around the time of the Civil War. What's so exciting about a bunch of Wall Street investment bankers?"

But Roger kept insisting it was a brilliant book idea.

Meanwhile, friends to whom I mentioned the idea were less than enthusiastic. "Rothschild is an internationally known name," they said. "But the Loebs? The Lehmans? The Schiffs and Warburgs? Who's heard of them outside a small corner of Manhattan?" My Jewish friends were also uneasy with the notion. Oscar and Marian Distel were friends and neighbors of ours in Rye. The Distels were Jewish, and Oscar Distel was the head of a major paperback publishing house. "It's a terrible idea," he told me flatly. "In publishing, it's what we call a Hollywood idea. You have a hit with a book like *The Rothschilds*, and so you try to follow that with something sort of like it." My old friend the novelist Beverley Gasner was even more outspokenly against the project. Her parents were second-generation Russian Jews who had started out on the Lower East Side and prospered in the garment industry. To people like them, the "Uptown" German Jews were the enemy. Though the Germans had established the settlement houses in the beginning, little more than delousing stations—to "assist our less fortunate brethren" who were arriving at Ellis Island by the millions at the turn of the century, the Germans' true purpose was seen as something else by the Eastern Europeans: It was to get the Poles and Russians to shave off their beards and side curls, stop using Yiddish, and start behaving like "real Americans." To the assimilated Germans, the Jews of the Lower East Side tenements were simply an embarrassment. "They're perfectly dreadful people!" Beverly said. "Who'd want to read a book about them? Not I, or anyone I know!"

I was getting a taste of Jewish anti-Semitism.

And members of the families themselves, when I mentioned the idea to them, were hardly supportive. "We've always tried to stay out of the limelight," said Frances Lehman Loeb, Johnny Loeb's mother. "We do what we have to do, but we try to do it quietly, without publicity. We don't push ourselves forward or try to see our names in print. I think you should talk to our lawyer before going ahead with this."

The lawyer in question was Joseph Proskauer, who had represented many of the families in legal matters for many years. When I went to see him, he addressed me as though I was a naughty schoolboy. "This is not only a very bad idea," he said "It is a dangerous one. Any association of Jews with great wealth will be inflammatory. It will simply stir and fan the flames of anti-Semitism. I strongly urge you not to pursue this project, Mr. Birmingham. And if you persist, I shall instruct my clients not to cooperate with you. Goodbye."

I reported all these negative reactions to Roger Klein. But he was not to be dissuaded from his mission, and our lunches on the subject continued.

At the same time, I was also beginning to have something of a problem with Roger Klein himself. He may have been a brilliant editor, but he was also striking me as a little weird. He had become, I discovered, an enthusiastic advocate of LSD, and he kept trying to push the hallucinogen on me. "Take some," he kept urging. "You'll go on the most amazing trips! You and your wife should take it together. You'll love what it does for you! Why, you'll go on acid trips that will last a whole weekend!" I kept trying to explain to him that, with three small children, my wife and I simply didn't have the time to go on weekend-long acid trips.

"I've got something new for you," he said one day, trying to press some controlled substance into my palm. "You'll love this! *Mescaline!*"

But I remained as resistant to his drug recommendations as I was to his book idea.

Then one day, quite out of the blue, I had a telephone call from my friend Bob Bernhard' s mother, Dorothy Lehman Bernhard. Would I come for tea? I replied that I would be delighted.

The Bernhards lived in a nineteenth-century New York brownstone in East 70th Street, one of the loveliest streets in Manhattan. From the outside, it was no different from the other houses on the block—tall and narrow, with the kitchen in the basement and the "parlor floor" one flight up from the street entrance. In the same block, between Madison and Park Avenues, I later learned lived seven other members of the Lehman family in similar houses. Also, on that block lived General David W. Sarnoff, the founder of RCA. The Sarnoffs, I knew, were not considered the social equals of families like the Lehmans, since the Sarnoffs were Russian Jews and David Sarnoff had been born and raised in a tenement on the Lower East Side. To the Lehman's and their like, General Sarnoff was "that Russian radio man," though his status had improved somewhat when his son Robert married one of the banker Paul Warburg's twin daughters.

Inside the Bernhards' house, the effect was homey and comfortable, but hardly grand or pretentious. It had what was called a lived-in look, with a touch of shabby-genteel. I had the impression that nothing much had been changed in this house, in terms of decor, in more than fifty years. The house had a private elevator, to be sure, and little maids in frilly white caps and aprons scuttled about with feather dusters. But the window curtains showed signs of strain and sun-rot, the upholstery was faded, the sofas a little butt-sprung, and the carpeting was threadbare in many places. I noticed that Mrs. Bernhard's teaspoons were heavy antique German silver, with the milky glow that good silver acquires when it is polished every day, and from a peek at the underside of my saucer I saw that her china was fine old Meissen, though my teacup had a chip in it. Still, it was all a far cry from the palaces and chateaux that Frederic Morton had described in his book about the European Rothschilds.

Until one looked at the walls, that is. On one wall I spotted a van Gogh, on another a couple of Cézannes. Over there was a Renoir, and just beyond that a Degas ballerina, then a Manet, then a Rousseau, then one of Monet's waterlilies. This was all, my hostess explained, just a part of the collection assembled by her grandfather, Adolph Lewisohn, that had been divided among his grandchildren.

"I've been thinking about your idea for a book," Dorothy Bernhard said to me as her maid passed little cucumber sandwiches on the thinnest possible slices of crustless white bread. "I don't think it's such a dreadful idea as some members of my family seem to think. After all, it seems to me we've accomplished quite a bit in just three generations' time. I think we've got quite a bit to be proud of. Of course, if one of us were to write such a book, it would seem like—boasting. As though we were trying to pat ourselves on the back. But you, coming from a different— background—well, it casts a different light on things, I think."

I should put in here that Dorothy Bernhard was a Wellesley graduate. In fact, she and my mother had known each other slightly at college, though they hadn't been in the same class. I like to suppose that Wellesley had given Mrs. Bernhard that Wellesley sense of superior enlightenment.

"I'd like to show you something," she said, and she went to a desk drawer and withdrew a yellowed and slightly dog-eared manuscript. "This is something my grandfather dictated quite late in his life," she said. "It's sort of a memoir, of how he got started in America. It's never been published. Take it home and read it. I think you might find it interesting."

I hadn't known very much about Adolph Lewisohn. I knew that he'd made a great deal of money in banking and in copper mining. I knew that he had a large mansion on Fifth Avenue, and that he'd assembled a major collection of Impressionist art, as well as a collection of Shakespeare first folios and illuminated Bibles, most of which now reposes in New York's Metropolitan Museum of Art. I knew that he'd donated Lewisohn Stadium to New York's City College.

But when I got his manuscript home, I learned a great deal more. I learned, for one thing, why his story had never been published. Born in southern Germany, he had never learned to master the English language very gracefully. But there was more in his manuscript than that. In it, I learned that when he was growing up, in the 1850s, Germany was going through a reactionary period. When he was nine or ten, his mother began to worry that her oldest son might be conscripted into the Kaiser's army. When that happened to a Jewish boy, his family usually never saw or heard from him again; conscription, for a Jewish youth, was for life. And so, his mother decided that it was time for young Adolph to set off for the *goldeneh medina*, America, where she had heard the streets were paved with gold.

In the best tradition of Jewish motherhood, his mother had managed to save, in a cookie jar, the equivalent of about $80, which seemed like a fortune to the young boy. She sewed the money into the lining of his trousers. It would take about $15, she figured, to get him to the port city of Hamburg. Another $10 would get him across the Channel to England. For about $30, he could buy steerage passage to New York. With luck, when he arrived, he would have a little money left over, and this was to be used to buy wares to peddle, on foot, in the New World. This, his mother had heard, was the way everyone got started. And so, he set off, alone, this ten-year-old, across the face of Europe and the Atlantic Ocean. And from this start had come the Fifth Avenue mansions, the Cézannes, the first folios, and a college athletic field. Only in America!

On the steerage voyage, which lasted about six weeks, young Adolph's diet consisted of unvarying rations of water, beans, and salt pork. So, he quickly discovered that what, in his parents' kosher household, had been considered *trayf* did not poison him, and, as a result of that, by the time he reached Ellis Island he was well on his way to becoming an Americanized Jew. Also, before leaving home, his mother had reminded him that he owned only one pair of shoes. As a foot peddler, he would need those shoes. And so, he wrote in his manuscript, all across the ocean he had gone barefoot, with his precious pair of shoes slung over his shoulders, tied together with the laces.

I wondered: If there were stories as touching as this one in just one family's history, what others might turn up in terms of the other New York families? And that was when I decided, if I agreed to write a book, what the focus of the book would be. It would not be a book about the quotidian doings of a group of Wall Street bankers. It would be about how they got to where they were—how they had managed to emerge, in such a short period of time, from the cocoon of immigrant poverty and had come to occupy positions of affluence and influence in the New World. A nineteenth-century Cinderella story.

It began to seem to me like a I also realized that, with someone like Dorothy Bernhard in my corner, I could approach the project with a distinct advantage. Mrs. Bernhard was very much a grande dame among New York's Jewish matrons and, with her endorsement, I felt certain that others would fall into line willingly, even eagerly. After all, it seemed unlikely that the other matrons would simply sit back and let Dorothy Bernhard dominate the book's progress. Others would want to have their stories told as well. If need be, I decided, I could always resort to a bit of journalistic blackmail. If, for instance, Mrs. Warburg declared her unwillingness to talk to me, I could always respond with, "Well, then I'll just have to believe what Dorothy Bernhard has to say about you." And so, I decided to ignore Judge Proskauer's dire threats and warnings. I agreed to write the book, a contract with Harper & Row was drawn up, and a small advance was paid.

But my problems with this project were far from over. At the time, Harper was headed by the legendary Cass Canfield. I'm not sure why I use the word *legendary* to describe him, except that this was the descriptive term most often applied to him at the time. What had made him a legend in the publishing world? Well, his adopted son, Michael, had once been married to Jackie Kennedy's sister Lee, and Michael himself was often rumored to have been the illegitimate son of the Duke of Kent. This rumor Cass Canfield refused either to confirm or deny, which kept the tongues wagging. Cass Canfield had risen to eminence in the publishing world through the most surefire of possible ways: he had bought his way in. He was a scion of an old-line WASP family from the Hudson River Valley—the Canfield Casino in Saratoga Springs was operated by an ancestor—and, after graduating from Harvard, he found himself with a tidy inheritance. He decided to invest this in a publishing company. As an important stockholder in Harper & Row, his rise in that company was predictably rapid.

He was, I hasten to add, a charming man—tall, courtly, elegantly tailored, and gently mannered. It was simply that, in Cass, I never detected any hint of editorial acuity or even of business brilliance. He struck me as decidedly old-fashioned and Old World (for years, there was no ladies' room on the executive floor of Harper's offices.) There was also something of the absent-minded professor about him. Once, landing at LaGuardia Airport after a short shuttle flight from Washington together, he reached in his wallet and handed me a dollar bill when the plane's wheels touched the ground. "You won your bet," he said to me. What bet? "You bet that the sun would have set before we landed in New York," he said. "It was a good bet." I'd made no such bet, but I accepted the dollar.

On another occasion he handed me a chapter of a memoir he was writing and asked me to read and comment on it. It was a chapter dealing with his days at Harvard, where he'd been a member of the Porcellian Club, whose membership selection process was very much based on family wealth and pedigree. "I've often heard the Porcellian called snobbish and elitist," he wrote. "But all I can say is that when I was there it was the gayest place on campus." I suggested that Cass might consider another superlative, since the word "gay" now had other connections. He had no idea what I was talking about, and when I explained it to him, he looked dumbfounded, shocked. "What other word would you use, then?" he asked me. "Merriest?" I suggested.

After we'd signed the contract for a book on New York's Jewish banking families, he took me aside. "We're proud to be publishing your book, of course," he said to me. "But I just don't want you to expect too much from us. It is, after all, a regional book, and there'll be no market for it outside the five boroughs of New York City, if even that much. We can't afford to budget any advertising for the book. And we can't afford to send you on any sort of publicity tour or put you on television talk shows and things like that. I just hope you understand." I did understand, but with a heavy heart since no advertising and no publicity usually means no reviews.

At the same time, as I began my researches, Cass Canfield began to treat me as an expert on all things Jewish. One day he telephoned me to ask me, "What's a bagel?" I tried to explain bagels to him as best I could, and added, "There's nothing better on a Sunday morning than lying in bed eating a fresh buttered bagel and reading the *New York Times*. Try it." Later, I asked him if he'd tried my suggestion. "I had my housekeeper order some bagels," he said. "It's a kind of Jewish doughnut that tastes like cement. I think I'd rather lie in bed and eat the *New York Times and* read the bagel."

Of such stuff are publishing legends made.

Meanwhile, my researches into such families as the Lehmans, Loebs, Lewisohns, Seligmans, Schiffs, and Warburgs were revealing some curious facts. It was quite clear that these families considered themselves a kind of Jewish elite, certainly in New York City, if not the entire country. In this respect, they were very Jewish. Their names decorated the boards of all the leading Jewish philanthropies—United Jewish Appeal, Bonds for Israel, the World Jewish Congress. They held directorships of Mount Sinai and Montefiore Hospitals, and were officers of the most fashionable Jewish house of worship, Temple Emanu-El. They belonged to the best Jewish clubs, the Harmonie in Manhattan, and the Century Country Club in Westchester County. And yet, in other respects, they didn't seem Jewish at all.

A great deal of emphasis was placed on celebrating Christmas, for instance—with Christmas tree–trimming parties, Christmas family dinners, and fathers dressed up as Santa Claus passing out presents to the children. The same was true of Easter, with Easter baskets, lilies, and egg-hunts. How curious, I thought, that so much attention was paid to what I'd always considered the principal Christian holidays while, in many cases, Yom Kippur and Passover were hardly observed at all or, if so, in only a perfunctory way. While weddings and funerals were usually celebrated at temple, there were no bar mitzvahs or bat mitzvahs, and the idea of keeping a kosher household was considered barbaric. It was all a part, I decided, of becoming assimilated, or secular Jews, but it seemed to me that many of these families wanted to be Jewish and Christian at the same time. The result often seemed a bit schizophrenic. For instance, those who toiled hardest and invested most heavily in Bonds for Israel expressed no desire at all to visit that beleaguered little country or to become involved in its politics.

Meanwhile, there was plenty of snobbery. The German Jews, I was told, were the best, but it went further than that. "Actually, the best Jews are from Frankfurt," a member of the Schiff family assured me, and of course Frankfurt was where the Schiffs—along with the European Rothschilds—had started out. Jews from Hamburg and Munich were placed somewhere below the salt. The Guggenheims were a problem. They had immigrated from German-speaking Switzerland, but they had also become extremely rich. At one point the Guggenheim fortune was nearly on a par with that of the Rockefellers, but the Guggenheims had made their money mostly due to a fluke, rather than hard work. (The first American Guggenheim had accepted some shares in an abandoned mine in settlement of a debt. Visiting his new mine, he had found it contained one of the richest veins of copper ore in the world.) The Guggenheims were variously dismissed as "the smelters" or, more disparagingly, as "the Googs."

Jews from Eastern Europe—who far outnumber Germans in America—were regarded as brash and uncouth upstarts, and the fact that many of these later-arrived immigrants had slowly become successful was acknowledged somewhat sniffily. In a sense, it was old money versus new, but it went even deeper than that. I'd had a sense of how deep it went back in 1953, when my friend Johnny Loeb's sister, Ann, announced her engagement to my Williams classmate, Edgar Bronfman.

As college freshmen, the name Bronfman meant nothing to us. All we knew was that he was from Montreal and that, by maintaining his Canadian citizenship, he was going to be able to avoid the US draft. We had no idea his family was rich. In fact, Edgar usually seemed short of pocket money. We often bought him beers and paid for his way into the movies. He took a part-time job as a caddy on the Williamstown golf course, where he worked for tips. The first hint of wealth as when his parents arrived for a visit in a huge custom-built Rolls-Royce with both a chauffeur and a footman, and mink lap robes in the back seat. It was then that we discovered that his father, "Mr. Sam" Bronfman, the head of Seagram's, was at the time conservatively estimated to be worth $800 million.

Despite this, when his engagement to Ann Loeb was announced, there was consternation among the German-Jewish families whom I knew. "But they're *Russians!*" someone explained, and someone else said, "But those Bronfmans have just come down from the trees!" Various others referred to Sam Bronfman as "that bootlegger."

At the advertising agency where I worked, Sam Bronfman was a client, and we handled several Seagram brands, so I'd had some personal dealings with Mr. Sam. One thing I knew was that he did not like being called a bootlegger. He often pointed out that, during the 1920s, the manufacture and sale of liquor was perfectly legal in the Province of Quebec since there was no Prohibition there. But he did admit that he had a good business relationship with men such as Meyer Lansky, who was a bootlegger, on the southern shore of Lake Erie. "I never counted the empties on the other side of the lake," Mr. Sam used to say.

At the time of the engagement, the senior Bronfmans had come down from Canada to New York, where they ensconced themselves in several suites at the Sherry-Netherland Hotel and sent out invitations to a huge celebratory party. Everyone of any importance, Jewish and Christian, in the Tri-State area was invited, including the mayor of New York, the top city commissioners, and celebrities of the stage and screen. For several weeks before the party, rumors circulated about the upcoming

Bronfman bash. Five hundred people had been invited to a seated dinner, where there would be a footman behind every other chair. Five hundred more had been invited for dancing afterward, where Meyer Davis and his orchestra would play. There would be magicians and acrobats and fortune-tellers and *tableaux vivants*. Ethel Merman would belt out some songs, and Danny Kaye was being flown in from Hollywood to perform a stand-up routine. Cases of Iranian caviar had been purchased, a planeload of orchids was coming from Hawaii, special wines were being shipped from France, and on and on. Of course, how much of this was true no one knew for sure, but still the rumors flew.

Of course, none of the invited guests was going to miss this spectacular affair. But among my German-Jewish friends, the reaction was, "Oh, dear. How vulgar. How ostentatious. Do you suppose we really have to go? Well, I suppose we must, since it's a party for poor, dear Ann, who's marrying into this peculiar family." John Loeb Sr., the father of the bride-to-be, was overheard to comment drily, "Now I know what it's going to feel like to be a poor relative."

The party was scheduled, interestingly enough, for Christmas Eve, 1953. Early in the morning of December 24th, it began to snow. By nightfall, some twenty-five inches of snow had descended on New York City. Surface traffic had come to a standstill. The subways stopped running. The airports closed. Pedestrians used skis and snowshoes to make their way across the mounds of buried automobiles. Small children dug tunnels and caves in the drifts across Fifth Avenue.

As a result of this, the Bronfman party was rather sparsely attended; only those in the immediate neighborhood could make their way to the Sherry-Netherland. The mayor was too busy marshalling snow-removal equipment to handle the emergency to make an appearance at the Bronfman's, and Danny Kaye, if he was indeed being flown in from California, would have had no place to land.

The next day, Christmas, when things were more or less returned to normal, I happened to be at the house of Mrs. Arthur Lehman, the maternal grandmother of the bride-to-be, for a small gathering. Mrs. Lehman, who, like so many others, had been housebound by the storm, was practically rubbing her hands with glee at the disastrous outcome of the Bronfman party. "That," she said triumphantly, "will show those parvenu Bronfmans that they can't just *buy* their way into our society!" It was as though she believed an Old Testament Deity had dumped twenty-five inches of snow on Manhattan just to mete out biblical justice on the Bronfmans for their sin of pride, or chutzpah.

Some years after the Loeb-Bronfman nuptials, Louis Auchincloss found himself seated at a dinner party next to Mrs. John L. Loeb Sr., Ann Bronfman's mother. Mrs. Loeb was bubbling on about her wonderful son-in-law, how happy her daughter was, and the beautiful and well-behaved Bronfman grandchildren the union had produced for her. Louis, who admits he may have had a bit too much to drink, blurted out, "But those Bronfmans are terrible people! During Prohibition, they had people *killed*!"

He immediately suspected he might have made an inexcusable social gaffe. But the next morning Mrs. Loeb telephoned him to say, "I so enjoyed talking to you last night! I want you and your wife to come to dinner. I want to hear more about the Bronfmans." And so, the old aversions still lingered on.

Other aspects of my research were more rewarding. Philip Lehman, a third-generation descendant of the family that founded Lehman Brothers, had begun collecting art earlier in the century. His son, Robert Lehman, who was then the head of the investment banking firm, had inherited his father's collection, and had greatly added to it. When I first met Bobby Lehman, his had become one of the most important private art collections in the world. When Bobby Lehman died several years later, the entire collection went to the Metropolitan Museum of Art, and an entire new wing of the museum had to be built to display it. On the other hand, I was able to view most of the Lehman Collection when it still hung on the walls of his house in 55th Street.

And so, in due course, I completed a first draft of the book, and shipped it off to Roger Klein at Harper. That was the last I was to see of it for a long time. Weeks passed, then months, and I heard nothing from Roger Klein. I learned that he had been transferred to Harper's London office, and, presumably, had taken my manuscript with him. I really didn't know what might have become of it. Later, I heard that an important reason for his move to England had been to pursue a romance with a young Englishman, and this news caused me to have certain qualms. I had further qualms when I heard, through the publishing grapevine, that this affair had turned out unhappily, and that Roger had asked to be returned to New York. I began to resent what seemed to be the fact that Roger Klein's personal sex life was interfering in the progress of my book from manuscript to print.

But, when I finally heard from him, I forgave him everything, and saw why he was considered a brilliant editor. The trouble with my first draft, I see now, was that I had approached the various New York families with a sense of Boy Scout fairness, believing that each family deserved time and space equal to all the others. But the fact was that some families had quite interesting stories to tell, while others simply did not. The material was all there, but it needed organization, and it needed cutting. In just a few pages of notes, Roger explained how this could be done, rearranging paragraphs, even whole chapters, indicating where cuts should be made and where bits of connective tissue should be added. All at once, in a series of deft strokes, he had transformed all those pages of my writing into something that had a real narrative pull. He'd turned a manuscript into a book. Roger Klein had been called a "creative" editor, and at last I saw why.

But my problems with the book were not yet over, despite Roger's valuable input. In publishing, one of the last things to be decided is a book's title. Carol Brandt used to say, "A good title is the title of a good book," and I have always tended to agree with her, but most publishers do not. A good title, the feeling seems to be, should somehow suggest something of the book's content to the purchaser or reader. But then how does one explain the success of a novel titled *Peyton Place?* Who would guess, from that title, that this was a novel about sexual shenanigans in a small New England town? As a New Englander, I've never heard of a town with the word "Place" in it. Instead, *Peyton Place* to me suggests a fashionable Manhattan address, such as Sutton Place or Beekman Place.

But, in publishing, everyone gets into the act when it comes to a title not just the editors, but the art directors and, of course, the salesmen, whose responsibility it is to present the book to booksellers. The author's choice of a title is given little weight, and rarely has a book of mine—or magazine story, for that matter—been published with the title I originally chose for it. Usually, I ended up surrendering my book title ideas in favor of those proposed by publishing experts who, supposedly, Knew Best.

The title Harper had chosen for this book was *The Jewish Grand Dukes*. I thought this was a terrible title and said so. To me, it had a condescending, snotty, even mocking ring to it. Furthermore, it did not seem at all descriptive of these New York families. There was nothing particularly grand about them, and nothing at all ducal. They did not live ostentatiously, but quietly, self-effacingly, and even a bit self-consciously. They did not comport themselves like dukes and duchesses and, in the scheme of things in New York society, they did not have the status of nobility, but only of a particular segment of the *haute bourgeoisie*, solid city burghers who went about their business with a sense of probity and duty. The next title proposed was *The Golden Ghetto*, which I liked a little better, but I felt that any title with the word "ghetto" in it would be off-putting to readers. Harper then offered a third title, *Many Mansions*. "But it's from the wrong Testament!" I squealed.

The title I wanted was *"Our Crowd,"* with the words in quotation marks, and with the subtitle, *The Great Jewish Families of New York*. I'd first run across the phrase in a novel called *Red Damask*, by Emanie Sachs, who was married to Walter E. Sachs of the Goldman, Sachs investment banking family. Mrs. Sachs's novel dealt with the world I was writing about in the 1920s and 1930s, and the title referred to what seemed to be the fabric of choice for upholstery, for window treatments, among proper New York Jewish families of the period. In her book, Mrs. Sachs deplored what she saw as the rigidly conformist and ritualized lives these upper-crust Jewish families led. A character named Abby declares:

> *Our crowd here. They cover their walls with the same silks. Why, there isn't a house we go to, including Sherry's, that hasn't a damask wall! They go to the same dentist and the same grocer and the same concerts. They think alike and act alike and they're scared to death not to talk alike. The men go to jobs their fathers or grandfathers created, and all*

they do is to sit at desks and let the organizations work. They haven't enough physical courage to go in for sports like the rich gentiles, and a little too much brains. So, they go in for art collections with an expert to help. They wouldn't risk a penny on their own tastes. They wouldn't risk anything!

Red Damask was published in 1927, but, forty years later, I'd observed much the same thing, except that by then the damask was a little faded and water spotted. Conformity continued to reign. Sons were sent to predominantly Christian boarding schools such as Hotchkiss, Taft, and Deerfield, but not to Groton or St. Paul's, which were considered "too Christian," since they were headed by clergymen. They went on to Harvard, or perhaps Yale, but rarely to Princeton, which was considered anti-Semitic, and never to Columbia, which was "too Jewish." Girls went to schools like Shipley or Madeira, then on to one of the Seven Sisters colleges. The families lived on the East Side of Manhattan because the West Side was "too Jewish," and children attended Miss Viola Wolff's dancing classes, because the Christian de Rham classes did not take Jewish children. The families had created their own exclusive German-Jewish country club, the Century, and men's club, the Harmonie, just across the street from the non-Jewish Metropolitan Club. They all belonged to Temple Emanu-El, but rarely attended services. In other words, they walked a careful tightrope between being just a little bit Jewish and not appearing to obtrude too much into the Christian world around them.

For years, Jewish high society adhered to a social schedule as inflexible as that of the Christians, but with certain differences. The New York social season began right after Labor Day, and continued through New Year's, and then it was off to Florida. But the Uptown Jews considered Miami "too Jewish," and preferred Palm Beach. As a result, Palm Beach began to take on a particular Jewish character all its own; its Jews were bankers and stockbrokers, while those in Miami were dismissed as "Seventh Avenue types." Christian families in Palm Beach who didn't care for this trend moved either northward to Hobe Sound, or across the peninsula to such West Coast resorts as Naples. The Florida season ended on March 31, and then it was back to New York for the so-called "little season" of April, May, and June, with the latter month reserved for weddings, graduations, and coming-out parties.

For the summer months, the Christian Establishment had already thoroughly staked out Newport and the Hamptons, on Long Island's South Shore. Some Jewish families built summer homes on the North Shore, in Sands Point and Oyster Bay, but most preferred to establish beachheads on the New Jersey shore, in the towns of Elberon and Deal. The month of July was for the seashore, but August was for the mountains, and many Jewish families built elaborately rustic "camps" in the Adirondacks where, in the mornings, the gentlemen fished and, at lunch, joined the ladies for rather formal picnics where the women wore long dresses and ropes of pearls. Once again, the Catskill Range, to the south, was considered "too Jewish" for the German Jewish crowd.

These families were involved then—and still were, forty years later—in a cautious process called assimilation or Americanization. But, as Mrs. Sachs had seen and noted, it was also a process based on fear—a fear of taking too many risks, of making too many waves, of overturning a delicately balanced applecart. By being a little bit of this, and a little bit of that, the German-Jewish families were determined not to come across as too much of either. It was no wonder that, by the third American generation, so many members of these families spent several hours a week on psychoanalysts' couches.

There is a story, possibly apocryphal, that the publisher Bennett Cerf once took a Southern lady author to lunch at the Century Country Club. After lunch, the woman commented, "That was a lovely lunch, Mr. Cerf, and it's a beautiful club. But I wonder—well, some of the members looked Jewish."

Still, they were an entity, a "crowd," a particular principality of wealth and power, intricately related to one another through marriages or business partnerships or, in many cases, both. During my research, I'd often heard the phrase "our crowd." At the time of the Bronfman engagement party, for instance, several people had remarked, "People in our crowd just don't *give* parties like that." It was a party that was, simply, far too Jewish. And so, after much wheedling and coaxing, Harper & Row finally relented and let me have my title.

The next thing I had to deal with was the jacket design, an area in which an author is almost never allowed to have any vote at all. Words may be an author's domain, but design is firmly in the art director's bailiwick. But the artwork produced by Milton Glaser—who was himself Jewish—for the initial design struck me as truly offensive. It depicted a group of men in tall silk hats and swallowtail coats, sitting around what appeared to be a boardroom table. All the men were overweight, with cartoonish big noses, and all were puffing fat cigars. Talk about Jewish stereotypes! I'd tried to write about these families with understanding, with sympathy and even love, but this drawing seemed downright hateful. Once more, I protested loudly. "What about a montage of family photographs," I suggested, "like something you might find in an old family photo album, or scrapbook that turned up in Grandmother's attic?" Miraculously, I got my way on that one too, and the final design, by Seymour Chwast, captured the exact feeling I wanted, and Chwast had the inspiration to arrange the family photos against a lacy filigree background, suggesting a doily or an embroidered antimacassar, or an old-fashioned Valentine.

And so *"Our Crowd"* was finally published without—as I'd been warned—any advertising, publicity, or any other sort of fanfare. The daily *New York Times*, at the time, sometimes published "postscript" reviews. That is, it would publish one major review on the book page, and then, as a kind of afterthought, add a short review of a second title, leaving the implication that this book was of less importance than the book that was featured. *Crowd* got one of these, and it was so short and inconspicuous that I missed it myself in the newspaper, and I'm sure most other readers did too.

Then, in the Sunday *Times Book Review*, there was a longer review. It was neither hostile nor particularly praising, but it was, Roger Klein and I agreed, "respectful." Though it was not the sort of review that would send customers rushing to bookstores on Monday morning, it was certainly better than no review at all. I suspected that the Sulzberger family, who own the *Times*, felt they could not overlook the book altogether, since they were related to several of the families I'd written about.

After that, I didn't hear much or see much in the press about the book, and several weeks went by. Then, one day, a friend in California called me to say," Did you know that your book is on the best seller list in the *L.A. Times*?" I did not know, and neither did my publisher. Next, I learned that *"Our Crowd"* had appeared on the best seller list of the *Salt Lake City Tribune*, where, it seemed, even the Mormons were interested in reading about people they called "Gentiles." And presently the book appeared on the only bestseller list that really counts in publishing, that of the weekly *New York Times Book Review*. And so, the great Cass Canfield had been wrong. Instead of finding an audience "only in the five boroughs of New York," the book's popularity seemed to have started on the West Coast and surged eastward. Canfield himself was flabbergasted. As the sales figures climbed, he declared, "Why, there aren't that many Jews in the country!" The answer seemed clear. The book had struck a responsive chord among Jewish and non-Jewish readers alike.

As the book climbed steadily up the *Times* list, I found myself faced with a dilemma often encountered by authors: friends began calling to say they couldn't find the book in stores. "I've tried every bookstore on Fifth Avenue," said one, "and nobody has it. They can't even say when they'll have it back in stock." Nothing is more frustrating to authors than this sort of thing, since books are often purchased on impulse and, if a prospective buyer can't find the title he wants, he either buys something else or forgets all about it. This, and the fact that books often seem to be shipped to stores by Pony Express, are the cause of great woe and lamentation among those of us who earn our living putting words on paper.

I felt I'd already nagged and complained to Harper enough about this project, but when it appeared that what was now the number one best-selling title in the entire country was unavailable for sale in any retail outlet, I decided to lodge one more gripe. I called Harper's director of sales. "Yes," he said, "we're aware of the problem. We've ordered another large printing of the book, and the printing is ready. The books are in our warehouse in Scranton, Pennsylvania, ready for shipping. But the fellow who's in charge of the warehouse is on vacation. He's on a fishing trip somewhere in the Maine woods, and he seems to have taken the only key to the warehouse with him. Nobody can get in there until he gets back." I replied that I'd be happy to travel to Scranton with a locksmith or, for that matter, a stick of dynamite, if that was what it would take to open the warehouse door.

With *"Our Crowd"* in the number one spot on the *Times* list, Harper & Row was galvanized into action. An elaborate national advertising campaign was launched, along with a city-by-city publicity tour. I was quickly booked on every local radio and television morning talk show, as well as the big national shows—Johnny Carson, Merv Griffin, Dick Cavett, Mike Douglas, and the rest. Book and author luncheons were arranged, and it seemed as though every Hadassah chapter in America wanted me as a speaker. A great part of the excitement was that it was all so unexpected.

Why, I began to wonder, would a book about a relatively small number of New York Jewish families, whose names were really not nationally famous, have gained such widespread popularity? I really don't have the answer to that question, unless it was because of the Horatio Alger quality of the stories about the founders of these family fortunes who had gone, literally, from rags to riches in less than a generation's span. But these were no fictional Ragged Dicks or Tattered Toms; they were real people, even though their rise might seem like a nineteenth-century fairy tale. They had succeeded against enormous odds, not the least of which was that none of the founders arrived on these shores speaking a word of English. They had succeeded, furthermore, through a combination of hard work and probity, with a willingness to gamble and the courage to be lucky. That they arrived in America at a lucky time—just before the Civil War—was merely a coincidence. Their instinct for fairness and honesty was perhaps Talmudic. Their Christian contemporaries were justifiably labeled the Robber Barons. It was William H. Vanderbilt who, when asked how one of his high-handed deals might affect the public, replied, "The public be damned." It was E. H. Harriman who, when workers on one of his railroads threatened to strike, hired goons with machine guns to keep his crews in line. The success of the German Jewish entrepreneurs involved little dirty work at the crossroads. Most of all, perhaps, the reason why their stories struck such a popular chord with the public was that these were young men who had come to America believing in the American Dream. Their successes proved that if you believe in a dream thoroughly enough, and pursue it doggedly enough, it will often enough come true.

Postscript

The commercial success of *"Our Crowd"* in the literary marketplace did its share to increase the value of Roger Klein's stock in the publishing business. From Harper & Row's standpoint, he had stubbornly persisted with a book idea that no one in the industry thought had much merit or sales potential, and the result had turned out to be a hit. The millions that his employers were making from his notion were proof that he was an editorial genius, and, still in his thirties, he was on his way to becoming a publishing legend. In publishing, the ability to pick a winner is all that is needed to become a hot property.

From my standpoint, his genius lay in his ability to take the mishmash of my research and turn it into a coherent whole, shaping and rearranging my material so that it had narrative shape and dramatic pull. This skill of his was as artistic as it was impressive, and for that I remain awed and grateful. At the time, I thought Roger must have been a happy, or at least professionally satisfied, man.

I really didn't know him very well. That is, I liked him and admired him, but didn't really consider him a close friend. In fact, he rather alarmed me with his enthusiasm for mind-altering chemicals. Why, I've often wondered, would anyone with a good mind seek to alter it? The only personal dissatisfaction that I knew Roger had about himself was that he was unhappy with his physical appearance. He was not tall. He was not dark but had a kind of prison pallor and was prematurely losing his hair. He was pleasant looking, but certainly not handsome and, in glasses, had a somewhat owlish look. In school, he once told me, he had been considered an oddball, a geek. But it seemed to me that lack of good looks, which is something nobody can do much about, should not have ruled out a fulfilling life. Not all of us grow up to be an Adonis; in fact, most of us do not.

Still, it was a shock when, one morning in 1968, I received a telephone call saying that, the night before, Roger had gone berserk in his parents' apartment, smashing furniture, and destroying art objects, and then had taken his own life.

In the Jewish custom, his funeral took place quickly, and the main chapel of Frank Campbell's Funeral Home was filled to capacity with mourners, including most of the important figures in the New York publishing world. The rabbi spoke eloquently of life's mysteries and enigmas, of promises both fulfilled and unfulfilled in a life cut off too short, and of how, even amid apparent triumph there can lurk secret failures.

I returned home from Roger's funeral to find a letter from him in my mailbox. It had been written the day he died, but it contained no hint of anything that might be wrong. In fact, it was a perfectly ordinary letter; its purpose was simply to congratulate me on the fact that my book had been on the best seller list for a solid year. I've never known the exact circumstances of his suicide, though I suspect that drugs must have had something to do with it. I have no idea what manner of private demons and furies may have been pursuing him, and in fact I don't really want to know. Some questions are better unanswered. In some ways each human life will always remain a riddle.

CAREY:

It was during the period that my father was working on "Our Crowd" when my brother and I had our second run-in with Rye Police.

Mark and I Reintroduce Ourselves to the Rye Police

On one of his many travels to promote the upcoming "Our Crowd," my father visited Kentucky to give a short speech on the book. While there, probably around 1967, he was introduced to a new technology, the Solex motorized bicycle. Originally made in France, a small Kentucky company had begun importing them to the United States and my father promptly purchased one and had it shipped to our home in Rye.

It didn't take long for Mark and me (along with our sister, Harriet) to take advantage of this new mode of transportation. The Solex was basically a bicycle but had a small 1.5 hp motor hanging over the front tire which, in turn, had a small wheel which made contact with the front tire and voilà! you had motorized transport. In the alternative, one could simply pull back on a lever and the motorized aspect of the device was suspended, leaving only a pedal-powered bike as a result—your choice.

On occasion, Mark and I would take the Solex for short trips to downtown Rye, with me riding on the back package-carrier (ordinally for bread and wine baskets, I suppose) and Mark engaging the throttle on the handlebars for thrust—downhill with a tail wind, the Solex could only manage 15–20 mph. Enter the Rye Police.

On one such journey, we parried with cars on Purdy Street on our way to the soda shop and no sooner began to pick up speed on the down-hill when we passed one of Rye's patrolmen (there were only six).

As we passed, we could see the officer's head turn as on a swivel, carefully watching and analyzing this strange conveyance and its obviously underage operator. We imagine his thought bubble: "There must be a law against that!"

Before we knew it, he gave chase, calling, "Hey, you kids! Stop! Police!" Quick-thinking Mark, having had experience with law enforcement, recognized a potential threat and immediately pulled back the lever, disengaging the small engine, and started to pedal as, well, a bike, just as the Solex was designed.

We pulled over and the breathless cop started yelling that we were operating a motor vehicle obviously underaged and without a license. Mark countered that, "No, we are just riding our bike," the motor having ceased its sputtering by this point.

This perplexed the officer to no end. He continued to accuse my brother of operating a motor vehicle without a license. When the inexorable logic of Mark's argument slowly leaked into the officer's mind, he nonetheless had concluded that there *was* a law against what we are doing! He said, "Come on, I'm taking you in," as in downtown, although the police station was only a block from where we were "arrested."

Our parents were called, and my father lamented, "not again." His wishes, like most wishes, were premature.

The officers at the station house, no doubt with the help of prosecutors, finally determined the charge, dusting off a law from the 1800s, "Riding Double on a Bicycle." My brother and I were released, for a second time, with no bail required and on our own recognizance. My parents paid the fine of $5.

This, however, was not the end of our troubles with the Solex or, for that matter, the Rye Police. Shortly after this incident, the entire Rye bureaucratic machine began assembling to answer one question: what, if anything, was the City of Rye going to do with this consarn, new-fangled gizmo those Birmingham boys are riding around like will-o-the-wisps!? Mopeds had not yet made the scene.

As with most bureaucracies, the City took the most bureaucratic approach and notified my father by registered mail of their decision. He was told the Solex (1) had to be registered as a motor vehicle *and* a bicycle, and (2) it had to be insured, and (3) the "driver" had to be eighteen or over and have a valid motorcycle license, and (4) the "driver" (and any passenger—although you could not ride double—I don't know how that was supposed to work) had to wear approved motorcycle helmet protection.

My father took our beloved Solex to the dump the next day.

Like any good story, however, ours with the Rye Police was not yet over.

Not a year had gone by after the "Solex Affair" when, as an energetic eleven-year-old, I purchased my first handgun, and it really wasn't that difficult. Somehow, I wrangled up enough money to walk to the local Korvette's department store and purchase it, a .17 caliber air-powered pellet gun. Today, a twelve-year-old could no sooner purchase a pellet gun than fly to the moon, yet that's exactly what I did. What made this tale even more interesting is that the gun was a spitting image of the classic .45 ACP 1911—standard sidearm for officers in World War I and World War II. It was black steel and shot one pellet at a time; I loved it.

One sunny fall afternoon, when my sister and mother were out of the house, my father informed my brother and me he was going to walk downtown to buy a paper and "not to get into any trouble" while he was gone. We consented, saying, in unison, "Yes, Dad." He should have known better.

No sooner had he disappeared from Hidden Spring Lane on foot that Mark and I, bored, broke out my pellet gun. From our bedroom window on the second story of our house (yes, that window) we began taking potshots at a tree here, a squirrel there, a rock. We were seeking more meaningful targets when we saw a van stopping at our neighbors to deliver dry cleaning. It was a mere twenty yards away as the driver stepped out to make his delivery. Being creative, I made the connection: van/pellet gun. Pellet gun/van. It seemed all very logical.

With Mark watching over my shoulder, I aimed my gun at the side of the van and POP, BANG! The pellet hit the van and rang out like Notre Dame at Christmas. The driver came running from the neighbor's house, scanning the horizon for the source of the shot. As he did so, we peeked over the windowsill and saw him. Like a grainy figure in the Zapruder film, he stood pointing at our open window. It was the Book Depository all over again.

The driver ran over to our house and began knocking on our front door and ringing the bell. We did what any self-respecting kid would do, having fired upon an unsuspecting civilian—or at least his van: we hid under our beds. Eventually, the driver gave up and drove away. As we extricated ourselves from the box springs, we had a good laugh. Scared the heck outta that guy! Too soon, our revelry was to come to an end. Within minutes, we heard the sounds of sirens; the Rye Police were on us again.

Looking out from our sniper's window, we saw them, three police cars, coming down our little, quiet Hidden Spring Lane on this lovely fall day, lights-a-flashin', followed by the dry-cleaning van, who no doubt could identify the window if not the actual culprits. As they all pulled into our driveway, Mark and I did the only honorable thing: we hid under our beds again and waited for them to go away. This time, however, they did not go away.

This event must have energized the Rye Police like no other previous event, since they now produced their bullhorns, no doubt dusty from tenure in a closet. "Come on out!" they called through the horns, "We know you're in there!" We discussed our options, and decided we'd get less time in the slammer if we gave up.

Mark opened a window in front of the house, also on the second floor, and shouted "Okay! We're comin' out! Don't shoot!" To be fair, the officers had not brandished their firearms, if indeed the Rye Police carried them. We walked out the front door with our hands held high, and the senior officer asked to see "the weapon," which I promptly, and carefully, produced. Nonplussed, the officer said, "why, this is just a toy . . ." We agreed. Whereupon he proceeded to lecture us sternly about firearm safety, even in the case of a pellet gun and confiscated my gun, adding, "Say, aren't you the Birmingham boys?"

At just about the time we were receiving our lecture, just twenty minutes after he left, our father comes traipsing down idyllic Hidden Spring Lane (I think he was even whistling—not for long), newspaper in hand, without a concern in the world until: three cop cars in his driveway, two sons in virtual handcuffs and a sergeant holding what appears to be a .45, obviously taken from those same sons. His jaw was agape.

So much for his instructions. I can't remember what the punishment was, but it fit the crime. At least we didn't have to go downtown. Again.

(Ironically, when I was seventeen, I again had a run-in with Rye Police and it too involved a gun, or in this case a "rifle." A friend and I were in my backyard when some young school children crept into the woods behind my house and began catcalling. Racing up to my bedroom closet, I grabbed my old popgun, complete with string and cork, and ran back to the yard and, like a curmudgeon, yelled at the kids—get off my property, whippersnappers!—ostentatiously brandishing the popgun.

As the kids ran off, I looked up to Peck Avenue to see a Rye Police cruiser drive slowly by, the officer staring at me with saucer eyes—"Man with gun!" The jig was up. I slowly walked into my front yard just as the cruiser pulled in and held up the popgun above my head, making sure the officer could see I was no threat. As he examined the "rifle" with which I "attacked" the children he said, "Why, this is just a toy . . ." followed by, "Say, aren't you one of those Birmingham boys?" Our name had gotten around. Weapon confiscated. Long lecture. No charges.

I imagine somewhere in the archives of the Rye Police Department's Crime Division there exists a board with weapons of violence confiscated by police in their line of duty and, glued to that board, much like the boards showing soap guns and shanks made by federal prison inmates, my pellet gun and popgun are proudly displayed.)

Later that year, in the midst of a very cold winter, after the Book Depository Incident, my brother and I had the urge to ride our Flexible Flyers down Hidden Spring Lane. While not a particularly steep grade, the Lane had a pronounced slope and length, plenty good enough to achieve, and maintain, a modicum of speed. However, the lane had been plowed to the tarmac on this particular day, and we were distraught. That is until we came up with a plan; we would take buckets and watering pails and ice down almost the entire street, leaving a swath of perhaps ten feet of raw asphalt at the end to decelerate (as it turns out, abruptly) upon reentry. Below this deceleration point lay a swamp in which we had no intention of ending up should our speed and control run awry.

We began after dark when the temperature was well below freezing and our parents, as well as the neighbors, were quietly enjoying their evening cocktails. After only an hour or two we achieved success, leaving only a thin strip along the side to access the top without slipping. In fact, we were so successful on the initial test run that we had to extend the deceleration patch (negative G-forces and plenty of sparks from the runners) and don hockey shin pads, helmets, and gloves to avoid (further) injury.

We had a great time. Until morning.

Needless to say, Mark and I slept well after numerous runs and crashes on our self-made bobsled run, despite scratches and bruises, some from reentry. We woke up, however, to the ominous sound of bias-ply tires wildly spinning—vvvvvvzzzzssss! vvvvvzzzzzsssss!—out in front of our house. Apparently, in our search for the perfect combination of a 0-friction coefficient and speed, we neglected to consider that inhabitants of our "laboratory" had to go up our street to get out in the morning to go to work and, well, our ice fields provided an impediment to same. Hmm . . . we'd have to work on that.

My father put two and two together and concluded that the cacophony on quiet Hidden Spring was the result of Mark's and my outside antics. Our neighbors skidded into our pachysandra and yelled out "those Birmingham boys!" My father called the Rye Police.

Although they provided a multitude of services to the community, maintaining plowed streets was not within the Rye Police's purview and, after they too skidded into ground cover, they angrily pointed this out to my father. He did not take it well, and we were promptly Sent to Our Room! (After spending hours spreading salt on the street and undoing our masterpiece of icy speed.)

CHAPTER TEN

Home Life

STEVE:

BEING THE AUTHOR OF THE NUMBER ONE BEST-SELLING BOOK IN THE United States changed my life in many ways, some of which were pleasant and some of which were less so. For one thing, if Cass Canfield's estimate of the sales potential of *"Our Crowd"* was somewhat wide of the mark, so—happily—were Judge Joseph Proskauer's dire predictions that the book would "fan the flames of anti-Semitism" in America. If anything, the book seemed to do just the opposite.

From the fan mail that flooded in at the time—and it still trickles in, thirty years later, since the book has never been out of print—it was clear that the book was being read by Christians and Jews alike. Sometimes the ethnicity of the letter writers was given away by their names, but most of the time the writers told me whether they were Jewish or not. I had to hire a part-time secretary to help me handle the mail, and she and I soon discovered that most of the letters fell into one of three categories and could be handled with one of three almost formulaic responses.

To begin with, there were the letters—often exceedingly long—from Jewish readers who said, in so many words, "My family was just as good as the ones you wrote about. Why wasn't my family included?" These readers would then enclose lengthy pieces of documentation to show that their ancestors were worthy of note, or even worthier of note, than the ones I'd chosen. I replied that my choices had, of necessity, been somewhat arbitrary, and that I'd had to stop somewhere. Then there were many letters, again from Jewish readers, from young people—teenagers—who asked me genealogical questions. The name Loeb, for example, is a fairly common Jewish name (in Spanish it occurs as Lobo, and in German as Wolf or Wulff) and a number of high school students, exploring their ethnic roots, wrote to ask if great-grandmother, whose maiden name was Loeb, was any relation to the two unrelated Loeb banking families of New York, or even to the also-unrelated thrill-killing Loeb of Chicago.

Usually, I was unable to answer their questions, but I tried to direct them to family members who might be able to help them.

Then there was a third category of letters, the largest of all, that seemed unconfined to any religious or national boundaries. This I called the nostalgia category. A typical letter would say in effect that the reader's grandmother had been born in Italy—or France, or Spain, or Ireland, or on an American Indian reservation in the Southwest—and that, as a little girl, Granny had tried to regale her with tales of the Old Country, and what it was like, and how the family had made its way to, and made its mark in, the New World. But, at the time, the children had all been too busy, too eager to get outside and play with their friends, to pay any attention to Granny's stories—to record them, or even remember them. And now Granny was gone, and her stories with her. My book, these readers said, made them wish they had paid more attention to Granny while she was still around. This sort of letter was particularly touching to receive.

Meanwhile, as a result of *"Our Crowd,"* many people who had tended to keep such matters under wraps before stepped forward to boast of Jewish ancestors. My old friend Charles Van Rensselaer, of the old-line Hudson River Dutch patroon family, came out of the closet with the fact that there were several Jews in the Van Rensselaer family tree. Louis Auchincloss often considered the archetype WASP, whose prolific Scotch Presbyterian family has more listings in the *Social Register* than any other, told me that one of his Auchincloss relatives had married a Smedberg—"Obviously an old New York family," he said with a wink. And the writer-cum-bullfighter Barnaby Conrad, whose genealogical claim to fame was always that he was a collateral descendant of Martha Washington, revealed that he also had forebears named Levy. "I'm the only Jew in the Burlingame Country Club," he wrote me gleefully from California.

During the course of my publicity tours for the book—and, instead of none, as I'd been promised, there were eventually more than a dozen—I appeared on countless local radio and television talk shows of the sort that take telephone call-ins from listeners and viewers. It is to these shows, I'm convinced, that America's craziest people stay tuned, by their telephones, wanting to talk to the guest with their questions and comments and opinions. In many cases, the craziest calls are screened out, but often they're welcomed, and I must say that I never encountered a caller who voiced anything that could be remotely considered anti-Semitic. And so, though there are certainly anti-Semites about, their flames were not being fanned by my book or, if they were, I didn't hear from those people.

But wait. That's not entirely true. I did get one letter that contained every anti-Semitic epithet in the book. It was a strange and violent letter, obviously self-typed and written in such a fit of fury that the sentences ran wildly off the edge of the paper so that its content was all but unintelligible. It was postmarked from Tucson, Arizona, and it was signed by a man I thought was long dead. At first, I thought the letter was some sort of lunatic hoax. But I telephoned the Public Library, and was told that, indeed, Mr. Westbrook Pegler was still alive and well and spewing hate in Arizona. He has since, thankfully, been gathered to his Maker.

Pegler had started his newspaper career as a much-admired sportswriter for Hearst, but at some point, in the late 1930s to early 1940s he had veered off on a virulent anti-Communist, anti–New Deal, and anti-Semitic kick. He regularly vented his spleen on all the Roosevelts—the president (whom he sometimes called "President Rosenfeld"), his children, his dog, and, most particularly, his wife. When asked how she could withstand so much verbal venom from Pegler's pen, Mrs. Roosevelt replied, "I understand he's very good to his wife." (Pegler's wife, interestingly, was Jewish.) His defamatory output continued to accelerate until 1949 when, after a notably below-the-belt attack on the newsman Quentin Reynolds, Reynolds sued Pegler for libel. On the witness stand, Pegler seemed to have become mentally unhinged. At one point in the trial, Reynolds's lawyer, Louis Nizer, read Pegler a newspaper story and asked him what he thought of it. "Communist propaganda," said Pegler.

Then Nizer revealed that the author of the story was Pegler himself. During the trial, it was noted that not a single executive of the Hearst Corporation would come forward in Pegler's defense, an indication that his bosses no longer held his services in much esteem. Reynolds won the case and was awarded $175,000 in punitive damages. Pegler then retired to Arizona to lick his wounds. Drink had always been a problem for him, and, in Arizona, he continued to deteriorate.

What had roused Westbrook Pegler's anti-Semitic bile again, in terms of my book—as far as I could make out from his incoherent letter—turned out to be an episode in the family of the banker Jacob Schiff that had occurred many years earlier, before the turn of the century. A man who had worked for the Schiffs as a butler or majordomo had made a homosexual pass at Schiff's young son, Marti. Schiff had the man arrested. He was tried, convicted, and sent to prison. Pegler felt that this was cruel and unusual punishment, and typical of the Jews' lust for blood revenge. On the other hand, Jacob Schiff was very much a product of the Victorian era. The Oscar Wilde–Lord Alfred Douglas scandals were on everyone's lips. And what the butler did was not really nice; at best, it was unprofessional. Would a parent in the 1990s behave much differently?

Though it was unpleasant to receive a letter as hateful, and obscene, as Pegler's, at least it was comforting to know that the writer of this missive was probably certifiably insane.

"Our Crowd" also elicited a thoughtful letter from Rabbi David de Sola Pool, who for many years headed New York's Congregation Shearith Israel, the oldest Jewish house of worship in the United States. In my book, I'd devoted a short paragraph to the old Sephardic Jewish families in America who, originally from Spain and Portugal, had first made their way to these shores two hundred years before the Germans, in 1654. In his letter, Rabbi de Sola Pool chided me lightly for being what I guess could be called anti-semantic. I had referred to Shearith Israel as a "temple," but, he pointed out, it was like plums and prunes. All temples are synagogues, but not all synagogues are temples. His congregation, being Orthodox, preferred the designation "synagogue."

In the course of his letter, Dr. de Sola Pool invited me and my wife to have dinner with him and his wife, Tamar, at their home, and to tell us more about the old Sephardic families. We accepted, of course, and at the Pools' dinner party they included members of New York's Hendricks, Nathan, Gomez, and Mendes families, old-line Sephardim all. It was at this dinner party that I first tasted such delicacies as Sephardic eggs— eggs that have been hard-cooked for months and months, and which acquire, in the process, a brownish color and a not unpleasant oily texture. It was this dinner party, also, that gave me the idea for a second book of Jewish social history, *The Grandees*, in which I traced the history of the Sephardim from the time of Ferdinand and Isabella's Expulsion Edict of 1492, when all Jews were ordered either to convert to Catholicism or leave the Iberian Peninsula, down to their present descendants who have addresses on Park Avenue.

And this book led, in turn, to the third book of my Jewish trilogy, *The Rest of Us*, about the Eastern European Jews in America, who were forced out of Russia and Poland by Czarist pogroms between 1880 and 1914. These books also became best sellers, and so I owe a debt of gratitude to David de Sola Pool for pointing out my error in terminology.

With the success of *"Our Crowd,"* friends began asking me why I stayed at the advertising agency, and in a business for which I had always professed dislike. Well, for one thing, it was difficult to contemplate giving up a regular—and almost embarrassingly generous—twice-monthly salary check for the uncertainties, and inevitable ups and downs of a writer's income. On the other hand, I did try to quit my agency job. I went to the agency's president, my friend Bill Steers, and told him of my intention to resign.

By then, I had been permitted to buy stock in the company, but this I assumed would present no problem. The stock's per share price was based on the book value of the company, and I knew that, when I left, I would simply sell my shares back to the company without losing any money in the transaction. I also knew that the company had a profit-sharing plan for its employees, but I'd never paid much attention to that. When I went to Bill Steers that day, he said he'd be sorry to see me go. Then he said, "But you know, Steve, you have quite a bit of money in your profit-sharing account," and he mentioned a quite astonishing sum. "And if you resign, you're only entitled to 10 percent of that. If you stay with us a full ten years you get the whole sum, which ought to amount to a good deal more by then. Of course, if you're fired you get the full amount. So why don't you let us fire you? It's just a matter of bookkeeping, after all." I told him I'd like to think about that offer and get back to him the next day.

Of course, I thought about it that evening, and talked it over with my wife, Nan. To both of us, the offer seemed a kind of double-edged sword. On the one hand, Bill was simply trying to be helpful. On the other, neither of us liked the idea of my getting fired. I'd never been fired from a job before. Was this the note on which I wanted to start my career as a full-time writer? I decided it was not. I went to Bill the next morning and told him I'd decided to stay. Then he said, "What if you were to give us just three days a week? That would give you four days a week to work at home."

And so that was our arrangement. Soon, however, that dropped to one day a week at the office, and the rest of the time at home. And that one day a week mostly involved writing speeches for Bill Steers.

Meanwhile, the success of *"Our Crowd"* was presenting another problem. When the royalties for the book started to come in, I knew I was going to be catapulted into a much higher income tax bracket. There was plenty of time to prepare for this. One of the continuing peculiarities of the publishing business is that, even in today's high-speed age of the computer, it still takes publishers more than a year to pay an author the royalties he's earned on a book. That is, the moneys earned by an author up until the end of June in one year are not paid out to him till at least April of the following year. No one knows why an accounting procedure needs to take so long, but it always has, and it always does. And of course, no one knows what publishers do with these funds over the intervening months, but it may explain why a few hardy writers have tried to buck the system by going into self-publishing.

At the same time, the Internal Revenue Service is not particularly fair to the self-employed. Though a writer never has any idea how much money he will make in any given year, the IRS fixes each year's tax bill on the basis of his performance the year before. If a writer has a good year followed by a lean year, the lean year's taxes are based on the good year's earnings—and, of course, he can apply for a credit or a refund at tax-filing time. If it's the other way around—a lean year followed by a good year he will find himself with a hefty tax bill, along with interest and even penalties. And of course, the IRS has never been known to pay interest on overpaid taxes. They get you, as they say, coming and going.

But I knew the dangers that lurked for the unprepared taxpayer. Bel Kaufman, a delightful former teacher in the New York public school system, had also written a book, *Up the Down Staircase*, that had become a surprise best seller. When she suddenly received a giant royalty check, she went on a happy buying spree, purchasing for herself all sorts of things she'd never been able to afford on a schoolteacher's salary. She had a lovely time with her windfall money until tax time, when she discovered she'd spent it all. She told me with chagrin that she'd practically had to declare bankruptcy to satisfy the pitiless demands of the tax collectors.

I began talking to various friends, lawyers, and accountants about ways in which I might possibly lessen my upcoming tax burden. Louis Auchincloss, who was a friend and also my lawyer at the time, told me of an arrangement he had made with his publisher, Houghton Mifflin, some years before. He had drawn up an agreement with Houghton Mifflin whereby the publisher paid him a fixed annual amount of a few thousand dollars a year, rather like a salary. That way, he insured himself against unpleasant surprises from the IRS. But he warned me, such agreements are shatterproof, and cannot be broken at any future date. Since signing this, Louis had published a number of successful books. Now he was faced with the knowledge that Houghton Mifflin was sitting in Boston with several hundred thousand dollars of what was technically his money, paying him no interest, and using it for God only knew what—even paying it out as advances to other authors, no doubt—while he continued to receive his modest annual check. So, Louis did not necessarily recommend this tactic.

One of the people I mentioned this to was my old friend Bob Bernhard who, not surprisingly since he was a member of the family, was by then a partner at Lehman Brothers. "Come down to the office for lunch," said Bob. "We'll meet with some of the partners and talk about it."

At the time, Lehman Brothers was the only New York investment banking firm with its own building, a skyscraper at One South William

Street, just off Wall Street.[16] The day before our lunch date, I had a call from Lehman Brothers. A car would call for me at my house in Rye, and I would be driven to Manhattan for our meeting.

The car, a gleaming black Bentley with a uniformed chauffeur, arrived at my front door, and as the driver hopped out and helped me inside and we drove off I could only hope that some of my suburban neighbors were watching from their windows across the street. The car had a telephone in the back seat. I'd never used a car phone and, as we sped down the turnpike, I decided to call my wife. But Nan had stepped out, and I got Daisy, our Black cleaning woman. "I'm calling from a car," I said. "Well, that's real nice," said Daisy.

As we pulled up in front of One South William Street, a uniformed doorman immediately stepped out and opened the car door. "Welcome to Lehman Brothers, Mr. Birmingham," he said, tipping his cap.

Inside, an elevator was waiting. "Welcome to Lehman Brothers, Mr. Birmingham," said the elevator operator with a little bow. I was whisked up to the top floor where a secretary was waiting at the elevator door, with the same greeting. "And now your first reward," she said. "Mr. Lehman's office," and she ushered me into Robert Lehman's office. "Mr. Bernhard and the others will join you shortly."

Robert Lehman, I knew, who was the firm's most senior partner, prided himself on the fact that his was the smallest office in the building. It was indeed small, but from its walls gleamed a few specimens from his collection—a couple of van Goghs, an Utrillo, and several pieces from the Sienese School. How appropriate, I thought, that an international banker should have concentrated heavily on paintings executed in gold leaf. On a small table were displayed signed and warmly personalized photographs of every United States President from Herbert Hoover through Lyndon Johnson. Robert Lehman himself, I learned, was out of the country, but clearly to be allowed to use his office as a waiting room was a great honor. Presently Bob Bernhard and a couple of the other partners joined me.

Our next move was into the Partners' Room, richly paneled in dark walnut, where portraits of the three founding Lehman brothers—Henry, Mayer, and Emanuel—gazed down sternly at us from above the mantel. These were the three young men who, having started out as foot peddlers in the rural South, had moved on to a horse and wagon, then to a small store and, by the outbreak of the Civil War, had established themselves as cotton brokers in Montgomery, Alabama. In the Partners' Room, sherry was passed by a butler wearing white gloves. "Are we lunching in the small dining room or the big dining room today?" someone asked. "The Shah of Iran is in the small dining room, so we'll use the big one," said someone else. I could only wonder what Henry Lehman, the oldest of the three brothers who had been struck down by yellow fever at the age of thirty-three, would have made of all this.

We next made our way to the big dining room, with its spectacular view of New York Harbor, where perhaps a dozen more partners joined us. I was led to the head of the big oval table, where I noticed several bottles of pills had been laid out next to the place setting. Thinking that this was where I was to be seated, I started to sit down, but someone touched my elbow. "No, no," this man murmured. "This is where Mr. Lehman sits. We just thought you'd like to see it. No one sits there but Mr. Lehman." I was then shown to a chair further down the table.

The menu was on a printed card at my place. Today there was a choice, for starters, of cold vichyssoise or a bisque of Maryland terrapin. For the main course, there was filet mignon, Rock Cornish game hen, or broiled live Maine lobster out of the shell. I opted for the lobster, noting the irony that, in kosher Jewish households, all shellfish is *trayf.* The Lehman Brothers chef, I was told, had come to them from Chambord, one of the great French restaurants in New York. The chef had decided he only wanted to do lunches, not dinners, and that was how Lehman Brothers got him. The lunch was served by waiters in dark jackets with white gloves. There were three wines.

At lunch, the conversation was general. This was an unwritten rule at Lehman Brothers: No business talk at lunch. I wondered what the group lunching with the Shah were talking about. But each man at the table had read (been instructed to read?) *"Our Crowd,"* or enough of it to be able to ask me intelligent, well-thought-out questions about the book, and the questions went around the table. It was all very civilized and cordial, and I was having an exceptionally good time.

Throughout the meal, the place at the head of the table—fully set with china and silverware—remained empty. It was like the custom, at a Passover Seder, of leaving an empty place at the table, and a goblet of wine, to welcome the Prophet Elijah, whose appearance will herald the coming of the Messiah.

After lunch, Bob Bernhard, a couple of the other partners, and I repaired again to Robert Lehman's office, and the door was closed. "Now," said Bob, "we're here to discuss what Steve can do to avoid excessive taxes on his earnings from the book." One of the partners spoke first. Tenting his fingers thoughtfully, he said, "Two solutions to the problem come immediately to mind. For one thing, he can ask to have his royalties paid to him in the form of Harper & Row stock. That way, the money would be taxed as capital gains, not ordinary income, which would result in considerable tax savings. For another, he could sell his financial interest in the book to a charitable or religious organization—the Catholic Archdiocese of New York, for example. He wouldn't realize as much money from such a sale as he would from royalties, but, again, it would be taxed as capital gains."

I was awestruck. None of the attorneys, tax specialists or accountants I'd talked to had proposed such elegant tax-saving techniques. How fortunate I was, I thought, to have a friend such as Bob Bernhard—so highly placed in a great banking house—to come to my assistance. "If you're interested," said Bob, "we'll ask Mr. Bernstein from the Accounting Department to come upstairs and work out the details." I nodded eagerly, and Bob began pushing buttons.

Presently, there was a tap on the door and Mr. Bernstein was admitted. He was a slight, fidgety man in shirtsleeves with ink-stained hands, wearing elastic sleeve garters and a green eyeshade. I could picture him working with his ledger books in a windowless cell somewhere in the basement. He looked like a Jewish accountant out of central casting, and, from his nervous demeanor, I suspected that he had never been in Robert Lehman's office before. As the partner who had offered the twin proposals outlined them to him, Mr. Bernstein' s eyes kept darting anxiously about the room, clearly uncomfortable in the presence of these banking giants in their expensively tailored dark suits.

But, as my new tax adviser began moving from Plan A to Plan B, I noticed that Mr. Bernstein had begun slowly shaking his head. "What's the matter?" the partner asked him. "Both those things are against the law," said Mr. Bernstein. The Lehman partner looked briefly flustered. "Well!" he said. Then he stood up and extended his hand to me. "Well, it was certainly a pleasure meeting you," he said. "Your car and driver are downstairs, whenever you're ready."

Then we all stood. I thanked them for the pleasant lunch, and we shook hands all around.

Then I left. I did not use the phone on the drive home.

In the meantime, working at home as I was now doing was causing some unexpected difficulties. "A woman marries a man for better or for worse, but not for lunch" is the old cliché, and, in fact, it was lunch that presented us with our first problems. At the office, when not entertaining a client, I'd always had lunch around the corner at a neighborhood burger joint. Or, if I happened to be busy, I'd phone the same establishment and have a carryout sandwich sent over to eat at my desk: pastrami on rye with extra mustard.

At home, I worked in a quiet study on the second floor where I could turn off the phone and close the door to avoid distractions. During the first few weeks of this, Nan would occasionally tap on my door. "I didn't hear your typewriter," she'd say. "Just wondered if you were all right." I tried to explain that a writer's day is not entirely spent pounding at the keyboard. In fact, a good part of a writer's day is spent postponing the act of writing, while attending to such other important matters as sharpening pencils, sorting the big paper clips from the little paper clips, and solving the *Times* crossword puzzle.

Then there was the matter of lunch. Nan had long had—deservedly— a certain reputation as a cook. When we entertained, she often spent days beforehand in the kitchen preparing glorious meals, and she took the matter of our having lunch together very seriously. Every day, and shortly after twelve, she would tap on my door with our lunch on a tray— watercress soup with a dollop of sour cream floating in the center, an herb-crusted chicken breast on a bed of angel-hair pasta, an avocado salad, and a fresh-baked dinner roll. So much time and care had obviously gone into preparing such splendid repasts that it seemed churlish not to be appreciative of these lunches, or to tell her that, when hungry, I'd just as soon go down to the kitchen and peel a banana or open a container of yogurt.

It wasn't long before I began resenting, even dreading, these elaborate lunches of hers, assembled with such thoughtfulness and gustatory imagination. They came, regardless of whether I was in the middle of untangling a sentence or undangling a participle. Often the lunches were so rich and filling that I had to lie down and rest after one of them. I was sure she didn't eat like this when she was alone in the house. We were both gaining weight. But it was too late. A pattern had been established.

I mentioned this problem to a few writer friends. They knew what I was talking about. John Updike told me that he'd rented a room over a local bank in Ipswich, Massachusetts, where he lived. Barbara Tuchman showed me the separate studio she'd built for herself on a hill behind her house in Connecticut. But my local bank had no rooms for rent, and there was no room on my Rye property to build a studio.

At the same time, I'm sure my children suffered from my working-at-home arrangement. They were always being told to turn down the volume of their stereos "because Daddy's working," and nothing goes so much against the adolescent grain as soft music, as every parent surely knows. Sometimes they'd ask to have friends over after school, but the answer was usually, "No, because Daddy's trying to finish a chapter." With everyone in the house being so considerate of me, or trying to be, why was I the one who was feeling resentful? It was because I was the one who appeared selfish and demanding, a new domestic chore for my wife and an ogre to my children.

In terms of our social life, there were also some unexpected problems. New York is a city that worships success, no matter how sudden or brief—in fact, the more sudden the better. It is a city that simply ignores failures and, in its Delman pumps, blithely steps over the drunks and derelicts that lie sprawled across its fashionable East Side sidewalks. As the author of the number one best-selling book, I was suddenly the new celebrity on the block, the number one catch for the party-tossing set. All at once, Nan and I found ourselves being invited to dinner parties by the top hosts and hostesses of the day—Diana Vreeland, Pauline Trigère, Marjorie Reed, William and Pat Buckley, Gloria Vanderbilt, the art collectors Robert and Ethel Scull, Jack and Marion Javits, John and Susan Weitz, Sonny and Marylou Whitney. At the latter's Fifth Avenue apartment, dining off gold service, I found myself seated next to a pleasant but rather boring woman whose place card identified her only as "Doris." Only after the party was over did I learn that my dinner partner had been Doris Duke.

At first, we found this to be all great fun. In fact, we often accepted invitations from people we didn't even know. We'd look at an invitation, and ask ourselves "Who are these people?" Our rule was simple: if the party was being held at a good address, we'd go. I knew all this was ephemeral and transitory, not to be taken too seriously, the frosting on the cake. But the trouble was that Nan seemed to begin mistaking our popularity on the Manhattan scene for the cake itself. She began saving clippings from the society gossip columns in which our names appeared, copying them, and sending them home to her mother in Modesto, California, who was herself a frustrated socialite, never able to understand why the elite of San Francisco refused to embrace a rancher's wife from the Central Valley, even though she bought all her clothes at I. Magnin.

I was still doing quite a lot of traveling, promoting the book, and I remember one afternoon when Nan had a phone call from a then-prominent New York hostess named Joanne Winship. Could Nan and I come to a small dinner at her house next Thursday? (A small dinner in New York meant no more than forty people.) Nan replied, "Well, Steve is going to be out of town next week, but I'd love to come!" There was a short silence on the other end of the line. Then Mrs. Winship said, "Oh, but I'm afraid that would upset my table seating. We'll do it again when Steve can make it." If that alone wasn't enough of a blow to Nan's self-esteem—being told that she herself had no value as a guest other than as the celebrity's wife, and not even a trophy wife at that—we read about the Winship party later in one of the columns, Liz Smith's or Suzy Knickerbocker's, and learned that the dinner was a buffet. I never mentioned this to Nan, but I know she was deeply hurt. It was incidents like this that began to make hobnobbing with New York's upper set seem less like fun.

I'd been getting a lot of requests to make speeches and deliver lectures before various groups around the country, and I finally decided to engage the lecture bureau of W. Colston Leigh to represent me. Though lecture agents such as Leigh charge a hefty fee—35 percent—they can make life a lot easier. They handle all travel and hotel arrangements and try to extract the highest honorariums for their speakers that they feel the traffic can bear. There is one unalterable rule of the lecture circuit, however, that the speaker should always bear in mind. That is, that no matter how witty or brilliant or stimulating a speaker may be, he or she will never be invited back to speak before the same organization again. The reason for this is simple. Every women's club or campus group or book-and-author series elects a new program chairperson every year. The last thing the new chairperson wants to do is repeat anything from last year's program; it must be all new. So, there is no repeat business. In this respect, it is a little like the undertaking profession. There are always new clients waiting in the wings, but nobody ever comes back to have it done again.

Sensing Nan's growing frustration and dissatisfaction with her role as the author's wife, I had an idea. She'd always had a winning and sparkly personality and was good on her feet with funny anecdotes. What if she, too, were to go out on the lecture circuit? Everyone likes applause and earning some herself might be good for her spirits. She liked the idea, and so we outlined a few lecture topics that she might offer—her culinary secrets, of course, being one of these. Then we set up a meeting with Bill and Ardis Leigh, and some of their regional sales representatives, where Nan would make her pitch for some lecture dates of her own.

The meeting was a huge success. At her bright and animated best, Nan charmed the Leigh people, and it wasn't long before the bureau came back to her with a heavy schedule of appearances across the country.

The lecture season begins soon after Labor Day, takes a break in mid-November through the holidays, and then picks up again in mid-March and continues through early May, at which point people get too involved in working in their gardens, playing golf, seeing their kids graduate, and making summer plans to want to attend lectures. And so, the busy lecturer takes to the podium for about five months a year.

And Nan's first lecture season was certainly busy. The Leigh Bureau had her booked to appear before audiences such as the Women's Club of Rock Island, Illinois, and the Officers' Wives' Club of an Air Force base in Texas, with stops anywhere they could book her in between. She'd arrive back home on weekends tired, but still on an adrenaline high, full of stories of her misadventures—the nearly missed commuter planes, the breakdowns of airport limousines, the rooms in motels that charged hourly rates for the rooms above the bar, and the sometimes-idiotic questions that audiences threw at her in the Q and A period after the talk. The "comment sheets" that the sponsors were asked to fill out and send in to the agency after the talks were uniformly enthusiastic, but her tales of what went on behind the scenes were often hilarious—to the point where our old friend Joan Rivers, who often filled in for Johnny Carson on the *Tonight* show, invited her on the show to do a segment.

Those five months, I often think, comprised some of the happiest times of her life. She was a hit, she was a star of the chicken-salad circuit, she was applauded for something she was doing on her own. And, for the first time since our marriage, she was working and making money at it. It was a wonderful antidote to her bruised self-esteem.

"They loved me in Wichita!" she would exclaim when I'd collect her at LaGuardia Airport after a week of touring. "Quite a few people told me that they wanted to get me back again next year." "Well, don't count on it," I warned her. "It's nice of them to say that, but they're really only saying it to be nice. Next year there'll be a new program chairman and remember the old saying about the new broom."

(Actually, I have been invited back to speak before the same sponsoring group—exactly once. The group was the Wellesley Club of Dallas, and their re-invitation came about fifteen years later when, I'm convinced, everybody in the audience had forgotten that I'd ever spoken before them in the first place. When I mentioned that this was a repeat appearance in my opening remarks, I saw Madame Chairman of the luncheon begin fanning herself with her program. Would she catch hell from her membership, I wondered, for her oversight?)

One August afternoon, when Nan had finished with her tour, we were sitting with friends around the pool in Rye. Suddenly Nan said, "I can't understand why I haven't received my fall and spring lecture schedule from my agent. I really can't plan anything for the next few months until I find out where they've got me going." Her tone was a bit self-important, but that was understandable. Hadn't some self-importance been what I'd wanted to give her? She reached for the phone, a pencil, and a pad of paper. "In fact, I'm going to call them right now," she said. "They can at least give me the schedule for the first two months." She dialed the number of the Leigh Bureau.

The rest of us sat there, not wanting to listen in, but unable not to. When she got Ardis Leigh, we heard Nan say, "Nothing? You've got nothing for me? . . . Nothing for the fall? . . . Nothing for the spring? . . . Nothing ?"

When she hung up the phone her expression was horrible to behold. None of us said anything. I couldn't bring myself to say, "I told you so." But I often wonder why it is that many people listen only to the things they want to hear. She had simply saturated the market. Our friends tried to change the subject, but Nan merely sat there looking dazed, stunned, defeated.

After that, Nan fell into a prolonged and deep depression. Worse, it was a depression laced with bitterness and anger—anger at me. It was as though she blamed me for having sent her on this happy joyride which had ended, as all joyrides do, with a thump on the brake pedal. I tried to cheer her up by suggesting that she take some of the money she had earned on the lecture circuit and buy herself something utterly useless, beautiful, and extravagant. Nothing worked. We began using separate bedrooms.

One morning not long after that I stepped into her bedroom and found her in bed with a male friend who'd been our weekend houseguest. Her eyelids fluttered open, and I'm sure she saw me, though I quickly closed the door and walked away.

Our friend was a young black makeup artist who worked in films and television. Working with foam rubber, polyurethane, silicone, and gels, his makeup specialty was creating space aliens and monsters. At the time, he was living with a pretty young actress. I never said anything to Nan about finding her in bed with him. How could I? After all, my own record of marital fidelity was far from unblemished, and so it hardly behooved me to make a scene, or to play the role of the outraged, cuckolded husband. And we'd all had quite a lot to drink the night before.

But the episode left me feeling incomparably sad—just sad. Sad that our marriage of more than twenty years, a marriage that had started out with so much fun and hope and promise—so many giggles!—was all but over.

It was, as Scott Fitzgerald once wrote, like turning the calendar at June to find December on the next leaf.

When our houseguest left to drive back to New York that afternoon I said goodbye to him warmly. Then I watched from my upstairs window as Nan followed him out to his car. She got in on the passenger side, and I watched as they sat parked in the driveway and had a long and serious conversation. I have no idea what they talked about. I told myself I really didn't care.

But that was a lie, of course. I did care. I cared a lot.

CHAPTER ELEVEN

Druggie

STEVE:

A NUMBER OF YEARS AGO I WAS IN SALT LAKE CITY AND HAD BEEN asked to lunch by one of the town's leading businessmen. He was not, as might have been expected, a banker or the president of an insurance company, but a funeral director. But I'd been told, this was not just *any* funeral director. He was Salt Lake's most prominent funeral director, and all the most important burials in the city were handled by his establishment. He was the second generation of his family in the business, and a much-admired member of the Mormon community. He'd asked me to meet him in his office.

I haven't been inside too many funeral parlors, but I know they're generally not intended to be cheery places. Their mood is expected to be solemn, even somber. But this one, housed in a huge stone Victorian mansion not far from the center of town—with its famous statue of Brigham Young, pointing westward from a mountaintop and declaring, "This is the place"—was truly grandiose in its lugubriousness. Inside, its tall windows were swagged with heavy draperies of purple velvet, drawn closed to shut out any valley sunshine. Chandeliers with cut crystal prisms glowed dimly from the high ceilings, walls were paneled with dark mahogany, and more purple plush and velvet covered oversize chairs and sofas that were trimmed with heavy black fringe. Marble statues in mournful poses filled niches in the walls, and soft, sad music played from hidden speakers.

A flight of heavy carpeted marble steps led downward from the entrance to the main reception room, and as I started down the steps a pretty young woman was heading upward toward me. In one hand she was carrying what looked like a blanket from a child's crib. The blanket was pink, its piped edges somewhat frayed, and as we met on the steps, she stopped in front of me. She was not weeping, but the expression on her face was beyond grief. She looked utterly betrayed and lost, and she held up the small blanket to me. "I don't understand," she said. "I don't see why not. Why can't she take this with her? I just don't understand." Then she hurried past me, up the steps, and out the door.

Of course, I had no idea what she was talking about, but I mentally composed a scenario for her. Her child had died, and she wanted the blanket from the child's crib placed in the coffin with her. But someone, or something—a rule of the Mormon Church, perhaps?—had vetoed this idea. Or perhaps it was just too late to change the arrangements in that one small way. I never did know what the true story was, or what the exact circumstances were, but the stricken look on that woman's face has stayed with me for more than twenty years. It was a look of infinite sadness.

That's how sad we were at home.

I've often argued, quite seriously, that parents should be required to have licenses before being permitted to have children. It is incomparably more difficult to learn to raise a child than to learn to drive a car. There are so many more maneuvers that can lead to errors and misjudgments and accidents. A child can be totaled in so many different ways. The rules of the parental highway are enormously more complicated, and the rules keep changing, and all the roads are filled with chuckholes. Licenses to be parents should not be issued to the untutored or the unready.

My friend and partner, Ed Lahniers is a clinical psychologist in private practice in Cincinnati and he and I often discuss the various new rubrics that keep appearing in the mental health community to describe unwelcome personality traits. In the public school system, for example, some students are now being described as suffering from H.A.S., or homework aversion syndrome. These are kids who don't like to do homework, and I can recall many of this breed when I was in school. Similarly,

I suppose, a person who doesn't like to hold down a job could be called a victim of occupation aversion syndrome. A person who used to be considered scatterbrained is now diagnosed as having attention deficit disorder, while the stupid—or simply mulish—child can be categorized as learning disabled. Not to be outdone, Ed Lahniers has come up with a diagnostic classification of his own for certain patients that he sees on a regular basis: exemptive personality disorder. I am convinced that this is what has long afflicted Nan's and my oldest son, Mark.

A person with E.P.D. is perfectly aware that there are certain rules and conventions in a civilized society that are designed to promote calm and civic order. But, for one reason or another, the person with E.P.D. believes he or she is exempt from these rules. An anarchic type like this, needless to say, often finds himself in trouble with his peers, not to mention the police. Mark designs and crafts his own line of furniture in Colorado, and his designs have won a couple of national awards an indication that he has talent. On the other hand, he has not been particularly successful because he simply refuses to adhere to what might be considered standard business practices. He works when he feels like it, not when he doesn't. If a customer orders a piece of furniture, and wants it by Christmas, the piece may not turn up until the following June.

Mark's feeling is that she's lucky to get it at all. Not long ago, a shipment of lumber, clearly marked for another purchaser, was delivered by mistake to his address. Mark saw no reason why he shouldn't keep it. After all, it was the shipping company's error, not his. More recently, he was having so much fun hiking in the nearby mountains that he decided to ignore an appointment he'd made with a potential customer two hundred miles away. He finally showed up for the appointment, three hours late, and was summarily thrown out of the office. His response was a shrug. If a customer wanted to do business with Mark, he'd have to do it on Mark's terms. If the customer found this behavior unprofessional, or just downright rude, well, that was the customer's problem.

We'd had trouble with Mark's E.P.D. from the time he was a child when we labeled it stubbornness or pure cussedness. None of the rules we tried to lay down as a family seemed to apply to him. In school, he was a poor student—not because there was anything the matter with his brain (tests showed that), but simply because he refused to do the work. He was required to repeat third grade, with no visible results. From public school, we moved him to Rye Country Day School, where classes were smaller and life was supposedly more structured, but nothing much changed.

When he was about twelve, we took all three children to Mexico for the Christmas–New Year's holidays. Citizens were required to purchase tourist cards to enter Mexico; one half of the card was surrendered to Customs upon entry, and the other half was to be turned over upon departure. With the misguided idea that this would teach Mark some responsibility, I put him in charge of his and the younger children's tourist cards while we were on vacation, explaining that these were valuable documents needed to get home. But when we were leaving Mexico, and were asked to produce the tourist cards, Mark explained that he had simply thrown the three tourist cards away. He didn't see why he should be required to produce a piece of paper just to go home. Fortunately, our friend Sloan Simpson, who worked for Braniff International Airways, was at the Acapulco airport and was able to get us through Mexican Customs without what could have been a lengthy bureaucratic delay, not to mention expense.

One the plane, Mark rather proudly explained that he had not exactly lost the tourist cards. Instead, he had sold, or rather bartered them on the streets for ten ounces of Acapulco Gold. He showed us the packet of drugs in his pocket. Terrified of what could happen to us if we were caught smuggling marijuana into the United States, I immediately snatched the packet away from him, and flushed the contents down the airplane's toilet, causing what sort of trouble I could hardly imagine with the plumbing of the aircraft. There followed a long, preadolescent sulk, during which I tried to explain not only the dangers of smuggling controlled substances from one country to another, but also the dangers— mostly the legal ones—of drugs themselves. He saw nothing wrong with marijuana. A lot of the kids in his school used it. He'd promised to bring home some Acapulco Gold to share with his friends.

I've often wondered what might have become of the illegal immigrants who entered the United States using tourist cards issued in the names of my three children. But, most important, I discovered that Mark and his friends were already into drugs—and not just marijuana, but also hashish, LSD, various forms of speed, and, later, cocaine in several guises that drifted in and out of fashion on the drug scene. This, of course, was in the 1960s, when everyone was blaming everything on the war in Vietnam.

We tried the usual things: long, heart-to-heart parental talks with our son. I'd smoked marijuana myself a few times, I told him, but found it did nothing to heighten the fun of the party, or to heighten my consciousness or expand the powers of my imagination. I much preferred the "hit" from an extra-dry martini. But the point was, I tried to explain, that martinis were legal, whereas marijuana was not. I've long argued that all drugs should be legalized for no other reason than to take them out of the hands of criminals. After all, it was the dismal experiment of Prohibition that had created the Mafia in the first place. If legalized, and taxed, the government could exercise some sort of control over drugs that reached the marketplace in terms of their quality.[17] If Americans were permitted to kill themselves with tobacco and alcohol, as they are now, why not with other narcotics? I realize that this is not a popular stance, and that thousands of government employees now futilely engaged in fighting the War on Drugs would be thrown out of work if my plan were ever put into effect. And what would we do with those people?

"Then you agree that the laws are wrong," my son said.

"There are probably a lot of laws that are wrong," I said. "But until you can get them changed, isn't it best—safest—to try to obey them?" I was talking to a stone wall.

I told him about my one experience with hashish, which had been quite unpleasant. It had occurred in, of all places, Kansas City, at the home of a wealthy Kansas Citian whose family had made its fortune in, of all things, farming and farming machines. The Kansan's other claim to fame at the time was that he had recently had Maria Callas as his houseguest, while she was wandering across the globe bemoaning her loss of Aristotle Onassis to Jackie Kennedy. Callas, it seemed, had been a demanding guest. She had insisted that her host create the illusion that time was passing rapidly for her. "Today is the first of December," he would say to her. "Tomorrow will be Christmas, Friday will be Valentine's

Day, and on Sunday it will be Easter." This technique had done much to assuage her grief, he told me.

After a dinner party at his house, which had included a number of Kansas City's bright young socialites, the host produced what looked like a cake of brown soap. There were oohs and ahs among the guests at the sight of this. It was a cake of pure hashish and must have cost him at least $5,000, one guest whispered to me. Using a penknife, our intrepid and accommodating host chipped off flakes from the cake and placed them in the bowl of a pipe. The pipe was lighted and passed around the room. The volume of the music was turned up, and the lights were dimmed. Then everyone began to take off their clothes. What followed was I guess supposed to be an orgy. It was more like a high-class group grope.

My hotel was in Kansas City's famed Country Club Plaza, just a couple of blocks from the hashish house—an easy walk. But when the party was over, I was having trouble walking, having partaken perhaps too much. Ahead of me I could see the lighted sign of my hotel. If I can just keep that sign to my left, I can make it, I told myself. But then I'd look up, and the sign would be on my right. I was walking in circles. It was a terrifying experience, and it kept recurring—the sign on my left, then on my right again. It seemed to take an eon to reach the lighted entrance of the hotel and, once inside, it took another eon to cross the lobby to the elevators. Inside the elevator, I pressed the button for my floor—the third. Years passed before the elevator reached the second floor, and then more years passed before the elevator finally delivered me to three. I fell into bed fully dressed.

The next morning, I discovered that I was wearing an unmatched pair of socks, neither of which had ever belonged to me. I was also wearing a woman's pair of panties. I felt utterly stupid. I also felt nothing like a familiar hangover. Instead, I felt what I can only describe as a sense of total lethargy, of listlessness, of loss of energy or ambition. The feeling hung over me like a dark cloud all day. It was an effort just to put one foot in front of the other. Mixed with all this, of course, were feelings of guilt over the silly business—or what I could remember of it—that had gone on the night before. This, I decided, was no fun at all. It was certainly nothing that I craved to repeat.

"You just didn't know how to use hash, Dad," Mark told me helpfully.

One night Nan and I invited some friends in for a drink after a neighborhood party. As we walked into the living room, I saw a large and unfamiliar shopping bag sitting on the sofa. I looked inside and saw that it was filled to the brim with marijuana. There were at least ten pounds of the stuff in the bag, far more than any individual would require for personal consumption. To me, this meant only one thing: Mark was dealing, though he himself was nowhere in sight. My first impulse was to take the bag to the basement, toss it into the furnace, and then raise the thermostat a notch or two until it kicked on. But Nan objected. The fumes emanating from our chimney from so much burning pot, she insisted, would have everybody in our neighborhood woozily hallucinating. I didn't think this would actually happen, but I acceded to her wishes and hid the bag instead in a little-used basement refrigerator, planning to have words with Mark about this later.

Presently Mark, accompanied by an older friend, appeared at the front door, clearly surprised to see us home from our party so early. The two boys looked nervously about the room. "Did anybody see a shopping bag we left here?" Mark asked. We all elaborately pretended not to know what he was talking about. With that, the two began tearing through the house, running upstairs and down, through room after room, searching for their stash. There was a terrible desperation about their search, convincing me that the contents of the bag were worth quite a lot of money. Then I heard them dash down the basement stairs, then up again, and then I heard the back-door slam, and they were off into the night. They had found the bag where I had hidden it. It had taken them less than five minutes to do so.

Things got worse. There were reports of truancy from his school. One day the police called, and Mark and the same friend had been arrested for shoplifting from a local clothing store. Mark was now fourteen, and one evening I opened the garage door and found my car was gone. So was Mark, and I knew that his friend had been giving him driving lessons. I called the police, and presently the underage and unlicensed driver, along with the car, were returned. In tears, Nan begged that no charges be pressed, and none were. But now I had to be careful where I kept the car keys.

His bedroom reeked of marijuana now most of the time. In a search of his room, I found cigarette papers, hash pipes, glassine envelopes containing a white powder, and other drug paraphernalia casually strewn about in one of his dresser drawers. I also found half a dozen copies of my car's ignition key that he'd obviously had made. I confiscated these but had no idea what to do with the rest of the stuff, since he'd made no secret of his habit.

None of this was exactly conducive to a serene home life, nor did it do much to stabilize Nan's and my already shaky marriage, and at the heart of the problem lay the fact that she and I could not seem to agree on what should be done about the situation. Nan, having been born and raised in California, felt that the matter should be turned over to outside experts. A series of psychiatrists, psychologists and other counselors were consulted. Some prescribed medication, which required supervision to be sure that Mark took it. At least one prescribed drug seemed to drive him berserk, and after one dosage he ran out of the house in his underpants and began throwing rocks through the big plate glass windows of our sunroom. In desperation, the doctor who prescribed the drug was called. He announced that Mark should be hospitalized, and an ambulance was called, and I had the painful experience of watching my son being subdued by paramedics, strapped to a hospital gurney, and carried off to the Disturbed Ward of St. Vincent's Hospital in Harrison, New York.

We were told not to visit him for at least a week. When we finally did, I was shocked to learn that the doctor who had committed him to that institution had not once come by to see how his patient was doing. We decided to bring him home, and to try another doctor.

Perhaps it's a strain of Yankee individualism in my genes, but I distrusted all the behavioral scientists and mental health professionals who were being dragged into the case, and at no small expense to me. What I felt was needed was tough, hands-on action from Mark's parents. For one thing, I felt that he should be given absolutely no money to spend. "But you can't do that!" Nan protested. "All his friends have spending allowances!" Still, I was determined to try. I'd already noticed cash missing from my wallet, and now I decided that my wallet would be on my person at all times, and for a while I even slept with it tucked inside my pillowcase. But, as anyone who has ever tried it knows, there is no safe place to hide anything from a determined thief. Once, having left my billfold for a few minutes in the hip pocket of my trousers while they lay across a chair, I returned to find it emptied of both cash and credit cards. When I confronted Mark with this, his reply was flippant: "Never trust a junkie, Dad!"

Nan also objected to my periodic searches of Mark's room, and to my eavesdropping on his telephone conversations. "The boy's got to be given some privacy! "she insisted.

Boarding schools were tried. At one of these, in northern Massachusetts, I was invited by the headmaster to speak to his students about careers in writing. My talk was in the school auditorium, and all the students were required to attend. One of my themes was that writing, and reading, can deliver a "high" or a "rush" that is just as satisfactory, and a lot healthier than any high produced by drugs. After my talk, the headmaster invited me into his office, and I assumed he was going to thank me for driving all that distance to talk to the kids. Not at all. During my lecture, the school had taken the opportunity to search Mark's room for contraband. In Mark's laundry bag, the school authorities had turned up a large stash of marijuana. I was told to have Mark pack his things and be off the campus that night.[18] The ironies of that situation didn't escape me. Soon a new breed of expert had entered our lives: The professional school-placement consultant.

After Mark's expulsion, as we were leaving the school, he asked me to stop the car near a wooded area just off the campus. It seemed he wanted to collect some young marijuana plants he'd been growing there. When I objected vehemently, Nan said, "But they're his plants!" One of the most valuable talents of the exemptive personality is the ability to divide and conquer the authorities.

Of course, I must accept some share of the blame for what was becoming a seemingly insoluble mess. A writer is not an easy person to live with, probably under any circumstances. A writer's mind, particularly when he is writing a book, is often far away from the situation at hand.

I suppose it is a little like an engineer in the midst of designing a bridge across a canyon. While his personal life is demanding his attention, his mind is somewhere else, computing angles of stress, the placement of struts, cables, bolts, and rivets. In terms of myself, it is a little different. I tend to see my mind as a kind of darkened screening room, and the events I witness as parts of an unfolding drama. I often find myself less interested in what the characters are doing and saying, or even feeling, than in how the whole story will play to an audience. Will the audience believe this, or do certain elements of the story need to be heightened, beefed up, and others edited out? I tend to block out my personal feelings in favor of what the crowd will buy. I'm not at all sure that, while the events I've just described were taking place, I wasn't mentally planning how they might translate as words on paper, as I'm doing now.

I'm certainly not describing the ideal parent, or even husband. If I'd been required to have a license to be a parent, I wouldn't even have passed the first battery of tests, the written part. I certainly would have flunked the road tests.

And so, Nan and I roared on toward the inevitable denouement, a divorce. As always, I tried to let it all roll over me, to keep it all at arm's length, to let the final reel spin out. Then we would shake hands and get out of the ring.

Louis Auchincloss is a man with a wonderful subtle mind. One of the charms of knowing him is never being sure whether some of the things he says are said in a kind of campy jest or in total seriousness. One day at lunch we were discussing the *Social Register*, and whether it was really an accurate or meaningful list of who was who in American society. "Well," Louis said at last, "the *Social Register* has gotten so enormous that it looks rather peculiar if one's *not* in it." Another time we were talking about the abortion issue. "My stand on abortion is quite simple," he said. "The people who ought to be getting abortions aren't." At one point I'd written a profile of Jacqueline Kennedy's mother, Janet Auchincloss, who was married to a cousin of Louis's. Janet and Hughdie Auchincloss had invited me to spend a weekend at Hammersmith Farm, their lovely estate in Newport overlooking Narragansett Bay, where, among other things, Jack and Jackie Kennedy had been married.

For some reason—I still don't know what it was—my story had displeased Janet Auchincloss. This was not long after Jackie Kennedy had had her highly publicized dust-up with the writer William Manchester, whose book *The Death of a President* she had originally supported, but then changed her mind about, and tried to suppress altogether. Again, no one quite knew what Jackie was upset about, but it seemed to have something to do with the news that Manchester stood to make quite a lot of money on his book, and that *Look* magazine had paid him $600,000 for the serialization. Jackie, it appeared, preferred to think of writers as starving in garrets. There was a lawsuit and Jackie, in tears, lost her case.

After my story on Janet was published, Janet called Louis to complain about it, inveighing against me and ruing the day she had ever allowed me into her presence. Louis said to me, "And so I was able to make a *mot*. It was quite a nice *mot* if I do say so. I said to her, 'My dear Janet, you—*and* your daughter—will simply have to learn not to talk to authors with the names of British industrial cities.'"

When I came to Louis, as my lawyer, to tell him that Nan had engaged a lawyer to represent her in the divorce, he sighed. "I don't do that sort of thing," he said. "I *used* to do divorces when I was much younger. But it's such unpleasant work. It's like being an undertaker, you know. *Somebody* has to do it. But even though I can't help you, I can certainly fix you up with someone who can. But first I'll see if I can find out something about this shyster lawyer your wife has hired. He's obviously a total shyster. I'll find out whatever I can about this shyster, and let you know."

A little later he called me back. "I'm sorry," he said, "but apparently your wife's lawyer is *not* a shyster, after all. I looked him up in *Who's Who in American Jurisprudence,* and he's a graduate of Yale!"

I'm sure there's no such thing as an amicable divorce. The phrase is an oxymoron, and the Latin derivation of the word, meaning to go different ways, is freighted with unfriendliness. But with Nan represented by her obviously gentlemanly Yale man in her side of the dispute, I found I had support from an unexpected quarter.

I was sitting in the Cafe Pierre in New York one afternoon, having a drink with my old friend Mary Meade from Dallas, when two men approached our table. Both wore dark pinstriped suits. One was tall and heavy set, and must have weighed close to three hundred pounds, and the other was a small and squirrelly, wearing dark glasses and a diamond pinky ring. "You're Stephen Birmingham, aren't you?" the heavy man said. I said I was.

"We're friends of your father's," the heavy man said. Then he nodded in Mary's direction. "Maybe your lady friend can go powder her nose or something," he said. "We'd like to talk to you for a minute." Mary glanced at me, I shrugged, and Mary excused herself.

The two men sat down at the table. The heavy one did all the talking, and the smaller man in the dark glasses kept looking anxiously around the room as though expecting someone.

"He was a wonderful man, your father," the heavy man said. "A wonderful man. A prince."

My father had been dead for more than fifteen years, but I nodded in agreement.

"He was a big help to us once," he said. "A big help. And more than once. Quite a few times, in fact. We've never forgotten that."

I began to get the drift of what he was talking about. As a kid, I'd often waited in the car outside the Wethersfield State Penitentiary while my father went to visit a client of his who was on the inside. These clients were obviously from cases he had lost, but there were undoubtedly other cases that he'd won.

"We'd like to do something to pay him back for all that help," the heavy man said.

"What exactly did you have in mind?" I asked him.

"We hear your wife is giving you a lot of trouble," he said. In fact, there had been an item in one of the gossip columns about our split-up. "We'd like to help you," he said.

"Well, thank you," I said. "But how?"

He drummed his fingers on the tabletop. "There's ways," he said. "She could have an accident. She could fall out a window."

Suddenly, though the room was cool, I could feel perspiration dripping down my back, and gathering across my scalp. My vision blurred, and my throat constricted so I could hardly talk. "Well," I said, finally, "it's true we're having our difficulties, but I really—I mean I don't really want her *killed*."

The man nodded. "Okay," he said. "Just thought we'd offer."

Then they both stood up, and the heavy man extended his hand. "Nice to meet you," he said. "You look a lot like your dad."

We shook hands, and then they were gone. I realized they'd never given me their names.

"Well!" said Mary when she returned to the table. "What was *that* all about?" She looked at me. "You're white as a sheet!"

I decided not to violate omertà or break the code of silence. "Just some friends of my father's," I said.

"Your father must have had some peculiar friends," she said."

"Yes, I guess he did," I said.

But I've often wondered how Nan might have reacted if she'd known that, with a simple nod of my head, I could have had her, as they say, bumped off.

CAREY:

When my parents divorced, it seemed so sudden. I mean, my father just *left*. One moment I was in dorm room at Franklin Pierce College in New Hampshire routinely calling home and the next minute, so it seemed, my mother was telling me that my father had moved out. I never spoke to him before he left, and it would be three years until I spoke to or saw him again. Strangely, in his last visit to the house on Hidden Spring Lane, he claimed ownership of, and departed with, the dining room chairs (not the table) and two high barstools we used around the kitchen table, without which you had to stand to eat meals; My mother never replaced the bar stools, and we often ate standing up until she sold the house in the 1980s. My wife often remarks even to this day how I still stand to eat my meals while in the kitchen.

My father's departure occurred in December 1973. I came home from New Hampshire in January 1974 amid the Arab embargo. At that time, schools and colleges in the Northeast were closing for short periods to conserve heating oil, which was in short supply. My college was no different and elected to close for the month of February. At the same time, my mother was completely immersed in a depression caused by my father's leaving and thought the best thing to do with this unanticipated February houseguest was to ship me off to Outward Bound School for 21 days. When she suggested this plan to me, I thought, well, I guess so. . . . Where is this school? Moosehead Lake, Maine. In February. Not far from the arctic circle. Sure! Sound like great fun!

We had to work fast, since the school started in seven days and my mother and I scrambled to get winter (arctic?) gear for me to take with me. Fortunately, I had lots of experience camping and rock climbing with my brother, so I had lots of stuff, but not extreme winter clothes suitable for below-zero temperatures.

As it turned out, the hurt and emotions I held about my father's leaving were, in the parlance of psychology, submerged, and only (apparently) subzero temperatures, sleeping in an unheated chicken coop with twelve others, and ice-cold showers managed to bring my emotions to the fore. After seven days at OB, I wanted out.

The director of the Moosehead Lake Outward Bound School was a young man who had a younger female assistant, both of whom, however, were older than me and my fellow OB candidates. They lived in heated trailers and enjoyed warm food and showers. Upon my telling them of my decision, they told me I could not leave without my parents' permission, so I got my mother on the phone (yes, they had one) and had a tempestuous, expletive-filled and tearful talk, with her finally telling me "No! You can't come home! [Crying] You need to stick it out!" "No," I said, "I'm coming home," and hung up.

Turning to the director and his assistant I expected them to demand that I remain since I *clearly* had not obtained my parents' permission to leave. In a moment of what can only be called clarity, the director simply said, "Okay. Walk two miles down the plowed path until you see a paved road. Take Route 6 south to Route 15, which will take you to Bangor and I-95. If you need a place to sleep, check with local churches." He shook my hand. "Good luck." His intuition was spot-on: I did not need a lecture, consoling, or encouragement. Although I had only recently turned eighteen, all I needed was to be by myself and go home. The director must have sensed that, and I've been grateful to him since, a man whose name I can't remember but whose simple understanding made such an incredible impact on my life.

It took me four days to hitchhike from Outward Bound—Moosehead Lake, back to Rye, spending the first night in Bangor at a flophouse right out of *Catcher in the Rye*, which I was reading at the time. "Checking in," at the flophouse I was told $5 per night or $7 if you wanted a shower. After eight days in a chicken coop, I paid the extra $2. I don't know how I had money, but I managed to pay for the room (and subsequently two others elsewhere during my journey) and even went down to a dive bar after my shower to have some beers with the locals. The entire trip was a catharsis.

After I arrived home, it took my mother and me a month to reconcile, and by then I was already on my way back to college. I would stay at Franklin Pierce for one more year, only to leave in spring 1975, whereupon I embarked on other adventures, which would define my life. I never forgot, however, that winter day when I left Outward Bound and became an adult, able to stand on my feet.

The next time I saw my father was 1975, almost three years after he left. The occasion was an ill-conceived plan by my mother to attend several "family therapy" sessions with a local husband-and-wife team of therapists. The ostensible goal was for "closure," but it quickly became clear that my sister's drinking (and drugs) was to be the main topic of conversation. To this end, my father was invited to attend one of the sessions. It did not go well. After no communication for three years, none of us really had much to say, the therapists were no help, and my sister kept denying she had a drinking problem, evidence notwithstanding. At the session's expiry, as I shook my father's hand, he invited me to join him and Harriet for drinks at a local bar. Drinks? Were we just at the same therapy session?

Nonetheless, I went to the local bar and met my sister and father, both of whom were well on their way to inebriation. In a fit of pique, I then laid into my father, saying horrible and hurtful things about his tenure as our dad. Much of what I said was true, but my presentation was poorly timed. Years later, when I was going through my own divorce,

I called my father and gave a heartfelt apology for my hurtful words in 1975. He didn't remember any of them.

It was again almost five years later until I saw him again, this time in New York City. I was attending New York University in 1979, and I read that my father was giving a talk at the University Club in New York, and the public was welcome. I rustled up a threadbare business suit and took the train into New York to attend the event. After the talk, I mingled among my father's admirers and managed to get close enough to shake his hand. "Do I know you?" he asked (maybe it was my mustache). Stumbling, I replied with the only thing I could come up with, "I'm your son." Momentarily confused, he said only, "Oh! So good to see you!" With that the throng closed in and I melted into the background, eventually just going home. Like other instances, my father said he'd forgotten about that moment. But I didn't believe him. He had an incredible memory for people and events. It would be another few years until we began our reconciliation.

STEVE:

"There are no second acts in American lives," Scott Fitzgerald once wrote. Like many such pronouncements, that one has the ring of profundity. But, frankly, I've never been entirely sure what Fitzgerald was talking about. Why are there no second acts in American lives? Why are our lives cut off after the first-act curtain? And why are American lives any different from, say, European lives? Don't our lives even merit an entr'acte? I used to know Fitzgerald's beautiful daughter, Scottie Lanahan (later Smith), and I asked her once about that line. She confessed that she didn't know what her father meant, either.

I know my life has had an interesting second act, and I'm not convinced it won't have a third. Having been sternly told—in no uncertain terms—in a letter by Nan's Yale lawyer to move out of the house in Rye by a specific date, I did so. ("Vacate the marital premises" was the term he used.) Later, during the court proceedings, I was surprised to hear that I had "abandoned" her. But, in any case, I have never been one to stick around for a fight. At the first sign of unpleasantness I try to make myself scarce. I don't even like to take part in, or even witness, verbal sparring. Perhaps that is part of my own exemptive personality. When I sense a storm brewing, I quickly exempt myself from its path, with a hasty sidestep, to get as far away from the storm as possible, preferably to another hemisphere.

At first, I moved to the Williams Club in Manhattan. Then I began considering ways to leave New York altogether, at least until the skies cleared.

My psychologist friend Ed Lahniers offered to let me share his apartment in Cincinnati, located not far from the campus of the University of Cincinnati. By coincidence, a fellow member of the Coffee House, a men's luncheon club I belonged to in New York, was Warren Bennis, then the president of U.C. When he heard that I might be moving there, Warren suggested that I might be interested in conducting a writing workshop at the university, as a sort of writer-in-residence. I'd conducted such workshops before—notably at Indiana University in Bloomington, and at Barnaby Conrad' s workshop in Santa Barbara—but these had been for adults. The idea of working with young people intrigued me. The second act of my life was about to begin.

One night in Cincinnati, our friends Dan and Ceil Waldrip came by Ed's apartment for a drink. At the time, Don was Cincinnati's superintendent of schools, and Ceil was a former beauty queen from a small Texas town. Ceil had been Larry McMurtry's inspiration for a leading character in his novel *The Last Picture Show* and later for the film McMurtry cowrote with Peter Bogdanovich. The Waldrips lived in one of those huge stone monstrosities that Midwesterners were so fond of putting up in the years after the Civil War to advertise their new prosperity. The third floor of their house was given over to a ballroom in which a hundred couples could have easily danced. But now their children were grown and heading off to schools and colleges, and the Waldrips were shopping for a house with less acreage for floorspace.

"We looked at a beautiful house today," Ceil said. "It's really one of the most beautiful houses I've ever seen—fourteen-foot ceilings, a marble entrance hall. But it's an absolutely impossible house. I mean nobody could actually *live* there. It has only eight rooms, and they're absolutely beautiful, but the way they're laid out is crazy—simply impossible." She went on and on about this beautiful-impossible house, so gorgeous but so impractical, and my curiosity was piqued. The next day I called the real estate agent she'd mentioned and asked if I could look at this oddity.

The house was in an old section of the inner city called Mount Adams. On this hilltop, with its commanding views of the Downtown skyline and oxbow bends of the Ohio River, Nicholas Longworth, father-in-law of Alice Roosevelt and a member of an Old Cincinnati family, had established a vineyard in the last century. Longworth's vines had produced grapes for America's first champagnes. But then his vines had been stricken with grape phylloxera, and had been plowed under, and Longworth had turned his property into real estate, building many modest row and townhouses, which had been snapped up mostly by German and Irish immigrants. Two Roman Catholic churches were erected, since the Germans and the Irish could not be expected to worship under the same roof. By the 1930s and 1940s, the area had become an urban slum, and in the 1960s it became a favored hangout for hippies and druggies who patronized its many sleazy bars and head shops.

But then, in the early 1970s, the neighborhood had begun slowly to turn around. Young professional couples without too much money but with plenty of taste and imagination had taken a look at Mr. Longworth's nineteenth-century row houses—some of geranium brick and some of clapboard, and most with as many as four working fireplaces—and begun snapping them up, at bargain prices, and renovating and remodeling them. The proximity of Mount Adams to downtown Cincinnati was an important drawing card. So was the fact that the neighborhood skirted the city's premier park, that the Cincinnati Art Museum was within a short walking distance, along with Cincinnati's famous Playhouse in the Park. And then, of course, there were the spectacular hilltop views, which no one seemed to have noticed before. The sleazy bars had been upgraded with ferns and hanging plants and outdoor sidewalk café tables, and the head shops had become boutiques and antique shops and art galleries. From a New Yorker's point of view, Mount Adams was being given the Columbus Avenue or the SoHo treatment. The neighborhood was almost fashionable.

By 1976, the "gentrification" process was far from complete. A splendidly restored house stood next door to one that wasn't much more than a shack. But this created a village atmosphere that was pleasantly mixed. Some homeowners drove home in a Mercedes or BMW, while others came home in panel trucks. White and black families lived in comfortable proximity to one another.

The house Ceil Waldrip had been talking about was one where the owners—a young stockbroker and his wife—had begun a quite ambitious renovation. The roof of what had once been the attic had been raised to create two more rooms on the top floor. Two of the four working fireplaces had been closed off to make room for extra bathrooms. The former basement, with its original fieldstone walls, had been opened up with a floor-to-ceiling wall of glass to face the descending hillside below. And so, what had originally been a two-story house was now four stories, with a long spiral staircase winding from top to bottom through the center of the house.

The house had already been featured in *House Beautiful*. But then, for some reason—the so-called Nixon Recession may have had something to do with it—all work on the place stopped, the owner and his wife moved to an outlying town, and there was still much work to be done. The house was for sale.

What Ceil called the "impossible" aspects of the house were quite apparent. For one thing, though it wasn't clear why, the kitchen and dining room had been placed on the top floor, and the bedrooms on the bottom. It seemed, at first glance, all upside down, and this arrangement definitely meant that bags of groceries would have to be lugged up many flights of stairs. But what perhaps Ceil hadn't noticed was that the owner had also created mini-kitchens on two other levels, each with a refrigerator and icemaker, which alleviated the situation somewhat. It was still a dauntingly tall and narrow house, sixteen feet wide, forty-five feet tall, with two rooms to a floor.

At the time, Ed Lahniers was director of psychology at the Rollman Psychiatric Institute in Cincinnati. But he was also seeing a few private patients on the side, was renting office space for this purpose near the university, and was hoping to make the transition into full-time self-employment, with his growing private practice. When we looked at the house, Ed and I were both quick to see how it would fulfill our individual needs. The lower level—originally the basement—would make a perfect studio for me, along with a bed-sitting room, bath, and mini-kitchen. The next level, with its entrance from the street, would provide Ed with an office, its own bathroom, and a separate waiting room for patients. The top two floors would become shared space. In 1976, this seemed an ideal arrangement.

We even envisioned how, on a ten-foot-wide strip of property between the house and the house next door, a narrow lap pool could be built. It's now there.

But meanwhile, as we dickered with the owner over the selling price, the seller kept pointing to all the luxurious frills he had employed in his still incomplete renovation. Wall-to-wall carpeting was by V'Soske, "the most expensive, and the best." Bathroom fixtures were from Sherle Wagner in New York. All the kitchen and laundry appliances were top-of-the-line. One elaborate overhead lighting fixture, involving many direct and indirect bulbs, had been custom made and designed by the Yale School of Architecture. The concealed control panel for this fixture alone consisted of more than a dozen dimmers and switches. "Why, that panel itself cost me twenty-five thousand dollars!" the owner exclaimed. "Very nice," we replied. "But what else are you going to do with it?"

It still works, though I still have to consult the diagram to find which switch does what.[19]

As for Mark, we keep in touch, though I don't see him often. When one of his furniture designs wins an award, he is always careful to send me the news clipping about it, and I dutifully write back with my congratulations. Several years ago, he came to me desperately asking to borrow money. I don't suppose I really expected to have the loan repaid, and of course it wasn't. The exemptive personality feels exempt from such mundane obligations. But this, and unhappy memories from the past, have resulted in a certain coolness in our relationship.

He insists he no longer uses drugs to the extent he used to, "except for a little recreational marijuana." Fortunately, he has a good and sensible wife, who teaches school and who helps keep his household on an even keel.

He has announced that he never wants to have children. "I've done so many drugs in my day that I'm sure my genes are thoroughly fucked up," he says. And so, he's exempted himself from that responsibility, too, and perhaps wisely.

Still, it's a statement that makes me a little sad. I know I shouldn't care whether he has kids or not, and yet I do. And I can't help wondering whether, in the random genetic lottery where luck counts as much as in Russian roulette, some of those exemptive genes might have come from me.

Chapter Twelve

In the Groves of Academe

STEVE:

LOOKING BACK, IT SEEMS A BIT IRONIC THAT, JUST AS ED LAHNIERS WAS weaning himself from the thrall of a state-run bureaucracy, I was hurling myself into one—albeit part-time. Teaching a writing course at the University of Cincinnati was not to be the piece of cake it had first seemed to be.

To begin with, there were certain preliminary protocols to be undergone. First there was a business lunch with Warren Bennis, the university's president. There followed a dinner party at the Bennises' house, an imposing, turreted Victorian mansion. It was there that I first met Neil Armstrong, who had also joined the university's faculty, teaching a course in astrophysics. Armstrong turned out to be a rather diffident fellow, quite in contrast to his ebullient wife, Jan, who seemed more interested in talking about the cattle on his farm in Lebanon, Ohio, than his historic walk on the moon. He was already growing pudgier than the youthful figure we all saw being beamed back to earth on television. Talking with him, I found myself repeatedly looking down at his feet, which were surprisingly small, in their lace-up oxfords, and remembering that those were the same feet that had made such giant imprints on the sands of the lunar surface and that, presumably, are still there.

"Tell me," I asked him, "when you first stepped out of the capsule and onto the moon, were you—even just for a few seconds—just a little bit scared?" "Well, no," he said carefully. "Because we'd all had a certain amount of training for it. And, besides, we were all wearing pressurized protective suits." Oh. Later, I asked him," Tell me something else. At night, are you ever tempted to step outside your house and look up at the moon, and say to yourself, 'Gee, I was *there!*'" He thought about this a minute. Then he said, "But the moon isn't visible every night, you know." Oh, again. Later we talked about the butterfat content in the milk from his Guernsey cows.

With these social formalities out of the way, there was more serious academic business to attend to. The first and seemingly most important matter involved obtaining a sticker for my car's windshield that would allow me to park on campus. These stickers, it turned out, were not handed out to just anyone. I had to fill out a lengthy questionnaire that wanted to know which felonies and misdemeanors I had been convicted of. Had I ever had my driver's license suspended for any reason? Was I an abuser of alcohol or any other controlled substance? Had I ever been cited for moving traffic violations? Finally, I was issued a temporary sticker, "pending review," of my application for a permanent sticker.

Then there were meetings with various members of the English department faculty, including the department head. And then the most delicate matter of all was raised: the question of my salary.

At the time, I was in the middle of my research for my biography of the Duchess of Windsor, and I was spending a certain amount of time traveling, to New York and Palm Beach, and also to London, interviewing friends and acquaintances of the Duchess, as well as to Paris, where I was dealing with the Duchess's formidable lawyer, Suzanne Blum. It was Maître Blum as she liked to be called, who by then had taken over complete control of the Duchess's life, as she would do for more than a dozen years. Though the poor Duchess was bedridden and incontinent, and suffering from senile dementia, Maître Blum had reduced the Duchess's household staff to just two people and had refused to allow her to have any visitors. "When people come to see her, her blood pressure goes up," Maître Blum told me. But couldn't a rise in blood pressure also indicate pleasure? Of course, it could, but there was no prevailing on Suzanne Blum. And so, the Duchess spent her final years in total isolation in her house in the Bois de Boulogne while, in Paris, rumors flew to the effect that Maître Blum was systematically pirating the Windsor fortune, selling off the Duchess's jewels and household goods. (When the Duchess finally died, these rumors proved to be quite untrue; the estate was in perfect order.)

In any case, because of this, I didn't want to be tied down to a strict classroom schedule. I wanted my schedule to be as loose and flexible as possible, allowing me to come and go as my needs arose. I explained this to the English department chairman. I was also certain that any salary he offered me would be quite small, and so I told him that I would prefer to offer my teaching services on a pro bono basis, as a service to the college and the community. The chairman looked quite relieved, even delighted, at this suggestion, and he thanked me profusely. But, as it would turn out, this was a major political and public-relations error on my part. I'll get to that shortly.

Meanwhile, my Prose Writing Workshop, as it was announced in the university's catalog of courses, sounded pretty simple. My class would meet one afternoon a week for two hours; it must have struck students as an easy way to pick up an academic credit, and I was told that "quite a number" of students had signed up for the course. The classroom I'd been given was large enough and contained a long conference table at which perhaps two dozen people could be seated. But when I walked in for my first class that fall semester, I was appalled to see some eighty-five students waiting for me. There were nowhere near enough chairs for everyone, and students were perched on radiators and windowsills and even seated on the floor. I wondered how I'd even be able to remember names to attach to each student in the sea of faces, much less how I'd be able to read the literary output from so many would-be writers.

I'd planned our first meeting to be a sort of get-acquainted session, and I started by outlining what I saw to be the objectives of the course. The emphasis, I pointed out, would be on professionalism—that is, writing with an eye to publication. We would only deal with prose, no poetry or drama. All manuscripts submitted to the class should be neatly typewritten, double-spaced, with no interlinear insertions, and typed on standard white 8½" × 11" typewriter paper, as they would be if they were being submitted to an editor. Do not use corrasable paper, I told them, because editors as a rule don't like it. (If an editor spills a cup of coffee on the page, the words disappear, and the pages stick together.) Regular Xerox paper, I suggested, was the cheapest and the best.

Type should be pica size, no fancy fonts, or serifs, because that is the type most editors are accustomed to reading. If you can't type, I said, find a friend or significant other to do your typing for you. Manuscripts written in longhand would not be acceptable. I explained a few more basics of manuscript form, such as margins and page-numbering, but as I went through these rules, I noticed that many of my students were responding with glassy-eyed stares.

I pointed out that since different students would obviously be working on different things some might be writing novels, some short stories, some working on nonfiction books or articles—it didn't seem fair to apply a strict grading system to a student's output in terms of A's, B's, and C's. Instead, the course would be graded on a simple pass-fail system. And all that would be needed to pass the course would be to turn out two thousand words of writing a month.

With that, a collective groan ran around the room.

Don't worry, I said. I'm not going to spend my time laboriously counting the number of words each of you has written. I know what two thousand words looks like. On my typewriter, it's six or seven pages. Many professional writers, I pointed out, can easily turn out two thousand words a day, but I realized that these students had other courses with work to prepare for, and I felt that two thousand words was not too much to ask for over a four-week period. Of course, if a student wanted to do more than that he could obviously do so.

Our first session broke up, and a few students left me with manuscripts they'd already been working on. When I took these homes and read them, it seemed to me that one or two might possess real ability and promise. This was encouraging. But, the following week, I was even more encouraged when exactly eight people showed up for my second class. The others, it seemed, had all dropped out. It had just sounded like too much work. But now I had a class of a workable size. And, even more important, I had a class of young men and women who really wanted to write, and who really wanted to be writers.

As a rule, I read the students' works out loud, and then the others in the class and I would offer comments, suggestions, and criticism. The students, I discovered, could be surprisingly harsh to one another—harsher than I could ever bring myself to be—and these discussion periods often erupted into heated arguments and even angry tears. But if we decided that a piece of work might be publishable, I would suggest editors to whom it might be sent. I also supplied a list of reputable literary agents who might be queried.

And it wasn't long before we began to have a few successes. One young woman sold a short humorous piece to *The Atlantic Monthly*. She has since gone on to publish two books—one a novel, and the other a biography, and now writes and directs television documentaries. Another young man sold two poems to the *New Yorker*, though I can't take any credit for that, since poetry didn't fall within our class's purview. Still another young woman began writing a regular column for the *Cincinnati Post* on local personalities, and now earns a tidy income writing author-for-hire books, specializing in corporate histories. One of the happiest moments of that first semester was when a young woman who had never been in print before sold an article to the *Sunday Magazine* section of the *Cincinnati Enquirer*—for $50. She brought a magnum of champagne and plastic cups to class to celebrate the sale.

Of course, we had our share of failures, too. The class was not limited to university undergraduates and was also open—for a fee—to members of the community. One of these was a highly placed member of the Cincinnati City Council. Being a politician, he was affable and charming and articulate, and his criticism of the work of others was usually well-received. He never missed a class, but the trouble was that he never submitted any work of his own. Periodically, I'd remind him of this, and, like a politician, he'd always promise to get something to me right away, but he never did. At the semester's end, when I was expected to give out grades, I didn't know what to do about this worthy. On the one hand, since he'd done no work at all, I didn't feel I could mark him down as having passed the course. On the other hand, in view of his position, I didn't feel comfortable about giving him a failing grade. So, I waffled, and gave him a grade of "Incomplete," which really counts as failing, though it sounds a little better.

Grades were posted publicly on a central bulletin board, and a local gossip columnist from one of the papers got wind of the story. It appeared under the headline: Councilman Flunks Writing Course. The councilman was not very happy.

In fact, he was furious. From his position at City Hall—and since the university was funded, at least in part, by the city—he kicked up a terrible fuss, demanding that his grade be changed, that a retraction be printed at the paper, that I be censured, and making all sorts of dire threats of reprisals if his demands were not met. President Bennis, the English department chairman, and I had a late-night conference call over what to do about the situation. In the end, it was decided that the grade was fair, and it was allowed to stand. I occasionally see the ex-councilman—he was defeated in the next election—at social functions. We are careful to stand at opposite sides of the room.

Meanwhile, the reactions of other members of the English department to me, as an unpaid member of their faculty, were strange but, perhaps, predictable. They looked on me as someone from out of town who was doing, for nothing, what any one of them could be doing for a little more money. The stakes here seemed pitifully small, but I realized I'd made a big mistake not asking for some sort of compensation, even if it was just a token sum. And I also realized how fortunate I was not to have chosen a career in the groves of academe and in this world of infighting and petty jealousies. If teaching the kids had been a lot of fun, my glimpse of faculty politics was dispiriting.

The English Faculty Wives asked me if I would be their speaker at a dinner meeting at the Faculty Club. I accepted and, when I arrived, I discovered that there was a cash bar. I hadn't brought my wallet, but no one offered to buy me a drink. When it was time for the ladies to go into the dining room, I found that no place had been set for me. The ladies had all paid for their chicken dinners in advance, it seemed, and I had only been invited to be their speaker, not their dinner guest. I sat outside in the hall while the ladies ate and waited until the chairwoman of the event came out to call me to the microphone.

In the English department office at the university, each faculty member was assigned a pigeonhole for mail. The "mail" consisted entirely of interoffice and intradepartmental memos, which were of no interest to me, but when I checked my mailbox once a week, I found my memos had been torn to shreds. One day I found an anonymous note in my box. It read, "Why should you get any mail, you son of a bitch? You're not getting paid!"

I wondered if this note was from the professor whose office was next door to my classroom. I never knew this gentlemen's name, but he had his own peculiar form of revenge. The building was not air-conditioned, and, in warm weather, we usually opened all the windows in the classroom and, to generate a breeze, often left the door open as well. As classrooms go, ours was not particularly noisy. But this man developed the habit, whenever entering or leaving his office, of slamming his door closed with a ferocious bang, and then, for good measure, slamming our door closed as well. In the class, we made a joke of it. Whenever we'd hear his heavy footsteps pounding down the corridor, one of us would whisper, "Oops! Here he comes!" Then we'd plug our fingers in our ears and wait for the double whammy: SLAM! SLAM!

It was men like this who were entrusted to instill a love of learning among American' s young.

I'm not really sure how good I was as a teacher. And I'm not sure that writing is a craft that can be taught at all, though even the best writing can nearly always be improved. I used to ask my students, "When you dream, do you dream in pictures or in words?" If they answered that they dreamed in words, I suggested that they'd probably make good writers, though I'm not sure whether this test has any real validity.

Some members of my class followed my teacherly advice, and some did not.

There was, for instance, the case of the young man I'll call Joe. Joe was nineteen or twenty, and his family was from Appalachia mountain folk who had come down from the hills of West Virginia in hopes of finding better times in the big city. Joe's family lived in the dirt-poor little town of Dayton, Kentucky, just across the Ohio River. Dayton is a town so poor that it has never been able to afford the dikes and levees that protect other river towns from flooding and, usually once a year after the spring thaws, Joe's parents' house would at least partially disappear beneath the flood waters of the river, and the family would evacuate itself to a church basement on higher ground.

Joe would have been a good-looking kid, except for the fact that most of his front teeth were missing. His live-in girlfriend, who was helping to pay his tuition, worked as a topless go-go dancer in one of the bars along "the strip" in Newport, Kentucky. When Joe spoke, his accent was pure Dogpatch, but he had bright, merry eyes and a witty, winning personality, and he wrote . . . and wrote . . . and wrote. Every week he arrived with a new stack of neatly typed (by the girlfriend) pages of the novel he was writing.

At least he called it a novel. I'm not sure how to describe it. It was neither science fiction nor fantasy but was a little bit of both. The setting was, at times, outer space, and at other times it was deep within the earth's core. At still other times, it was set in some Oz-like city of the imagination. There were wizards and dragons and elves and archangels in the story. There were strange, humanoid clown characters with crazy names like *Oofla* and *Mpfrls*. There were space aliens and talking animals and dancing microbes. I remember a tightrope-walking pair of knitting needles that somehow featured in Joe's narrative, and then there were characters who were described as blobs of jelly on one page, then flew to the moon on the next or simply exploded into thin air. I could make no sense of Joe's tale. It sounded as though it had been put together in a marijuana haze, and it probably had. I could see no commercial possibilities for the darned thing and yet, despite its nuttiness, the class always looked forward to Joe's next installment. Reading his chapters as they poured out became one of the highlights of our weekly meetings.

Despite my misgivings, he began sending chunks of his manuscript to editors at publishing houses in New York, Philadelphia, and Boston. These were always returned to him without comment. But this did not discourage our Joe, who was forever the cockeyed optimist. One day when he announced that he was about to type "The End" on the last page of his novel, he told me that he had found a printer in Cincinnati who had agreed to print a thousand copies of the book including his own weird drawings that accompanied the text—for $5,000.

I strongly urged him not to do this. I was certain that he could ill afford the money and, I said, it would be like throwing $5,000 out the window, that he'd never see a penny of it again. But Joe was not to be dissuaded. With small loans from parents, relatives, and friends, he raised the necessary capital, the book was printed in soft cover, and he presented me with a first copy. It was full of typos and misspellings but, considering the wackiness of the whole project, that didn't seem to me to matter much. With a heavy heart, I wished him luck.

As it turned out, he didn't need it. With their familiarity with the local bar scene, Joe and his girlfriend set out with stacks of copies under their arms to peddle the books directly to bar customers—at $10 a copy, plus another dollar for the author's autograph or $2.50 for a personal inscription. Soon, it seemed, bar patrons were talking about the book; they loved it. And, within weeks, Joe had sold every copy, more than doubling his original investment. With this success, he ordered a second printing, and this sold out as well. The book had generated a cult following, albeit a local one. And I've often wondered whether a New York publisher may have missed the boat by not snapping up what might have become a surprise best seller, another *Jonathan Livingston Seagull*.

Then there was the case of a fellow I'll call Bill. Bill was a university senior, and I can only describe him as a geeky-looking guy. Tall and stooped and skinny, he wore thick glasses and was prematurely losing his hair. His face was savagely pocked with acne scars. Unlike Joe, who was as bubbly as a glass of champagne, Bill took himself with great seriousness. He was writing his autobiography. It was essentially the story of his own sexual awakening, and it was as somber as Joe's was loony. Instead of giggles, Bill's life story often evoked sobs among his readers and listeners.

Bill, it turned out, was president of the student Gay Alliance on campus. In his story, he told he told how he had come out of the closet as a young teenager, to the horror and disgust of his Southern Baptist family. His father, an uncle, and an older brother had all given him severe beatings, thinking this would straighten him out and, when it hadn't, he'd been told never to darken his family's door again. It had been close to eight years since he'd had contact with any of his family, who called him a "queer" and a "faggot," and said that he would burn in hell for the sins of his flesh.

In his manuscript, he also revealed that he was a cross-dresser as well, and that he earned extra money on weekends performing, in drag, on the stage of a local gay night spot. Bill's classroom demeanor was owlish and melancholy. With me, he was terribly formal. Though the other students all called me by my first name, Bill always insisted on addressing me as "Professor Birmingham," though I had no academic claim to the title. It was hard to imagine Bill prancing about the stage in wigs and false eyelashes, in jewels and ball gowns and stiletto heels, and some of the other outfits he described. He invited us all to come to one of his performances, but as far as I know none of us ever did.

In about chapter 6 of his autobiography he announced his intention to have a sex-change operation, and he described in full and often quite gruesome detail the various surgical procedures that would be involved in the transformation. In addition to the most obvious one, and the hormone injections, he explained how the bones of his rib cage would be broken and reset in order to form a womanly pair of breasts. Having once cracked a rib, I could only shudder at the thought of the pain he was planning to endure. The entire changeover was going to cost him, he estimated, about $45,000, and he admitted he had no idea where he was going to come up with that kind of money. And so, instead of having the whole thing done at once, he was planning to have it done little by little, one step at a time. The full process might take years, he said, but he was determined to go through with it because only by inhabiting a woman's body would his life achieve any meaning or purpose.

At the end of the school year, Bill was about to graduate with high honors, and I invited the members of my class to a kind of wrap-up party at my house. I served beer and cheese and wine, and I may have tossed back a little too much of the latter because I found myself seated on a sofa next to Bill and heard myself saying to him, "Bill, I really wish you'd give up on this sex change thing. For one thing, it's going to be terribly expensive, and you don't have any money. Even if you did, would it be worth it? Wouldn't it be better to spend your time and effort, and use that good mind of yours, trying to make the most out of the life and body you've already got?"

Bill looked thoughtful but said nothing.

"Then there's the matter of pure aesthetics," I went on. "You're a nice guy, and a bright guy, but you're not by any stretch of the imagination a handsome guy. You're not even a particularly good-looking guy. Just looking at you, it seems to me you'd make a really ugly-looking woman."

"You think so?" he said.

"I really do," I said. "Look at your height. Look at the size of your hands, and the size of your feet. As a woman, you'd look grotesque!"

He blinked once or twice, and, thinking I'd already said more than I should have said, I changed the subject.

The next afternoon my telephone rang. "Professor Birmingham!" he cried, "I just wanted to tell you that I took your advice!"

It was a moment or two before I recalled what advice I'd given him. "I've gone completely straight!" he said. "I'm not gay anymore! I've even got a new girlfriend, and last night we had sex! And I've got a new job for the summer—as a salesman at Brooks Brothers! And the best thing about it is that I can buy clothes there—good, *straight* clothes—at a big discount. I just bought two new suits!"

I was so stunned I didn't know what to say, and I don't really remember what I said. But I think I said, "Congratulations."

"By the way," he said, "you know that girl Priscilla in our class? Have you got her phone number?"

I said I did, and I looked it up and gave it to him.

"Thanks," he said. "She loaned me some jewelry and a couple of cocktail dresses. I've got to get that stuff back to her, since I won't need it now."

"Sure," I said.

"Thanks," he said again. "Thanks for *everything*, Professor Birmingham!"

All that was a long time ago. I never heard from Bill again, and I'm sorry to say that I've lost track of him. But wherever he is and whoever he is now, I wish him well and hope he's happy, even in that new life, if he really chose it, that I apparently helped him choose. Even for a little while.

I'm not very sanguine about that, of course. But at least one can be hopeful.

CHAPTER THIRTEEN

A Country Ham

STEVE:

MARK TWAIN SUPPOSEDLY COMMENTED THAT, WHEN THE END OF THE world came, he wanted to be in Cincinnati. This was because everything that happened in Cincinnati happened twenty years after it had happened everywhere else. This observation is still largely true today. Cincinnati is a city with its own particular urban style, but with absolutely no sense of, or interest in, fashion. Several years ago, a truck came through town loaded with women's midthigh-length jackets in many sizes and colors, all copies of a design made popular by Chanel in the late 1970s. Cincinnati women rushed out to buy these knockoffs. They are still the Cincinnati woman's favorite mode of Downtown attire; the jackets have held up that well.

When I first moved here, people used to say, "You can fly anywhere you want from Cincinnati—as long as it's Chicago." Now that's considerably changed. Delta Air Lines has made Cincinnati its most important Midwest hub, and today we have daily international flights to London, Paris, Zurich, Frankfurt, and Munich, with nonstop service to Rome and Madrid soon to be added to their European schedule. Still, though thousands of travelers fly in and out of Cincinnati every day, they do not come to visit and most of them see no more of the city than the airport. Cincinnati has not become a "destination city" like New York, Los Angeles, or San Francisco, or even like Boston, New Orleans, or Dallas. People route themselves through here on their way to someplace else, which is exactly the way Cincinnati likes it.

When I announced to my New York friends my intention to make Cincinnati my new home, they asked but one question: *Why?* My new Cincinnati neighbors tend to phrase the question a little more politely. Once they've gotten to know me, they inevitably ask, "What, exactly, made you decide to settle here?" They seem to acknowledge that, while many large corporations ship executives here for tours of duty, no one seems to settle here voluntarily. It's just not that sort of place.

My Easterner friends may not think of Southwestern Ohio as a territory populated by cowboys and Indians. But they do tend to think of it as a flat and endless prairie filled with amber waves of grain and long green rows of corn. Then there is always the problem of how to spell the city's name, how to organize all those hard consonants. Perhaps this is because, though there are at least two New Yorks in the country, three Hartfords, four Andovers, and though virtually every state in the Union has a Springfield or a Columbus or a Columbia, there is only one town in the entire world called Cincinnati. It is unclear why, in 1790, the City Fathers chose to change its original, prettier name of Losantiville, in order to rename it after the Roman general Cincinnatus, whose alleged feats of daring and conquest are open to serious historical doubt. Perhaps it was because, like Rome, Cincinnati is said to array itself across seven hills, though no one has ever been able to attach seven names to those hills.

So—why do I choose to live here? Let me offer a few answers by way of explanation.

As I write this, it is late August and, from the window-wall of my studio, after a rainy spell, all I can see are the lush green leaves of trees. A pair of cardinals has just alighted on my window ledge, and I could easily be in the deep woods of Vermont. Only the low hum of downtown traffic, and from an interstate that snakes through the city, reminds me that I am actually in an urban setting, just a few minutes' walk from the center of the city. When the leaves begin to fall, the silhouette of the downtown skyline will loom back into view with its centerpiece skyscraper, the Carew Tower, the tallest building in the world to have been built entirely of brick. With my telescope, I will be able to check out the activity in the rooms of the Omni Netherland Hotel.

Downtown Cincinnati, a matter of some twelve square blocks, is for the most part glistening and new, shiny towers of steel, granite, and glass. But the rest of the city is nearly all from the nineteenth century or earlier, when this was a bustling river port, one of the biggest cities in America, connected to the Eastern marketplace by the Erie Canal System. It is still a red brick city, with gaslit streets in some neighborhoods, brick sidewalks, and some streets (such as one around the corner from me) still paved with brick, and a few where the rails of the old trolley cars still peek through.

Change does come to Cincinnati, but it seems to come more slowly here. Those old enough to remember them still mourn the loss of the old trolleys, or "streetcars" as they were called, which were clean, safe, quiet, and efficient, and transported the citizenry wherever it wanted to go for a nickel. The streetcars were a far cry from the huge, lumbering, exhaust-belching buses we have now which, with the awkward wide turns they must make to navigate the city's steep, winding, and often narrow streets, succeed in stopping traffic in all directions. Also gone is the Mount Adams Incline, a cable railway that carried passengers up and down the hill between Downtown and the city's premier park. The disappearance of the streetcars and the Incline is viewed with the same sort of nostalgia that Boston reserves for the cast-iron mud-scrapers on the front steps of houses on Beacon Hill, a reminder of an older, more naive, muddier but not forgotten time.

Like other American cities, Cincinnati has experienced a loss of downtown businesses and shops, and a sprawl to outlying suburban malls. But here the problem seems less dramatic, with downtown still a vibrant place, with theaters, museums, many excellent restaurants, and stores like Brooks Brothers and Saks Fifth Avenue and, even after dark, with many pedestrians for human reassurance. For the last dozen or so years, I have not owned an automobile. Before that I drove one of the last luxury-model Thunderbirds, a big, gleaming monster of a machine with all the options. But, whenever I took it out, something seemed to go wrong with it. It seemed to be forever in the shop. Finally, I asked my mechanic, "What's wrong with this damn thing? Have I got a lemon?"

He looked at the odometer and said, "Look, you've owned this car for four years, but you've driven it less than a thousand miles. A car is like a horse. It needs to be *exercised*. You need to drive it more. Take it out on the freeway and drive it a hundred miles every weekend. Put some miles on it."

I realized that what he said was true. I owned my fancy car, but I wasn't using it. I didn't need to. Within two blocks of my house were both a deli and a grocery store. So were half a dozen restaurants and bars. The liquor store delivered, and so did the drugstore and the flower shop. The only times I drove my car were to and from the airport and, with the problem of parking out there, it was easier and quicker, and often cheaper, to take a taxi. And I realized, and this came as a terrible psychological jolt, since I'd owned a car since my college days—*that I simply didn't need a car.*

I was in for an even worse jolt. This was during the Arab oil crisis, with long lines at the pumps, and my Luxurious Thunderbird was nothing if not a prototypical gas-guzzler. Still, having accepted the fact that the car was a superfluous part of my life, I decided to sell it, and I took it down to the dealership where I'd bought it, to their used-car department. There, I pointed out the car's excellent condition, the many extras that it had, its low mileage, and it's like-new tires. "It sure is in good shape," the dealer said. Encouraged, I said, "Well, what'll you give me for it?" "Nothing," he said. "Nothing?" "Nope," he said. "I couldn't sell a car like this in this market. It would just cost me money, taking up space on my lot." And so, my beautiful car was worthless.

"But I don't want it anymore," I said. "What am I going to do with it?"

He gave me a narrow look. "Is something the matter with it?" he asked me.

"No, but I just don't want it anymore."

"Well, if you want to take it over to the showroom, they'll probably give you something on it as a trade-in for a new model," he said.

"But you don't understand," I said. "I don't want *any* car."

Now he was looking at me as though I were speaking Chinese. Finally, he shrugged. "Well, I guess you could run an ad in Classified," he said.

I drove home, discouraged. When I mentioned putting an ad in the classified section, friends strongly urged me not to do this. "You'll get some guy who'll pay you $50 down and promise to pay you $10 a month for the next ten years, and that's the last you'll see of him," one friend said. And so, it seemed that, having made up my mind that I no longer needed an automobile, I was now stuck with one anyway.

Nevertheless, I decided to place an ad in the paper. That evening, my telephone rang, and it was a caller responding to my ad. As we talked, and he quizzed me about my Thunderbird's features, something about the man's voice sounded familiar. He hadn't given me his name, and I hadn't given him mine, but he sounded like Bob Braun, who had a locally popular television talk show at the time, and I'd been a guest on his show many times. Finally, I said, "Is this Bob Braun?" It was him all right, and I told him who I was, and invited him by for a drink and to look at the car.

Bob Braun collected classic cars. He had a couple of Rollses, a Bentley, an old Packard, a Stutz Bearcat, a Cord—a whole barnful of cars at his place in the country. He'd always wanted a Thunderbird, and mine, being the last luxury model, had become a collector's item. He was at my house in half an hour. He looked over the car, and I handed him the keys so he could drive it around the block a few times. He returned, wrote out a check for the price we'd agreed upon, and drove off with the car. I've been contentedly without wheels ever since.

I mention this episode only because it is quite typical of Cincinnati that the first person to respond to my anonymous ad in the newspaper should have turned out to be a friend. It is a small enough city so that it is almost impossible to walk down the street without bumping into someone you know, or to dine out in a restaurant without seeing one of your neighbors sitting across the room. It is not like New York, where one can disappear, unrecognized, for days at a time, and for those who prize the queer gift of privacy, Cincinnati is not the best place to live. I've heard the complaint that it's impossible to conduct a discreet love affair here because, wherever you choose as a trysting place you'll be spotted and identified and, by tomorrow morning, the news will have traveled all over town. When lovers meet, they must choose a place far from this city, preferably in another state. This fact may explain why adultery, so popular in larger cities, is less common here, and the divorce rate is lower. Adultery is only for the foolhardy, and the very rich.

And Cincinnatians seem to be particularly faithful in other ways as well—to the city itself, and to its institutions. Many Cincinnati families are very rich today because, way back in 1837, they invested money with a young man named William Cooper Procter and his brother-in-law, James Gamble, by buying stock in their fledgling Procter & Gamble Company. Through the generations, and through countless splits, these old families held on to their P&G stock, reinvesting their dividends, to the point where, today, many are as well off as some Mellons and Rockefellers.

Still, a certain polite reserve and tastefulness prevents rich Cincinnatians from flaunting their wealth. You will see the occasional Rolls-Royce on the street, and private jet at the airport, but you can be sure that these represent "new money." Cincinnati women may own important jewels, but they hardly ever leave the vault. Until recently, Cincinnati had more Savings and Loan associations per capita than any other city in America. Clearly, this is a city of savers, rather than spenders.

Cincinnatians' affection for, and protectiveness of, their money—coming, as it does, from a local source—is reflected in their feelings toward each other. They are most comfortable in each other's company. This does not mean that they are unwelcoming to, or distrustful of, strangers and visitors from other places. After all, Cincinnati—except by conventioneers—is not a place that is visited much, and so new faces are always a welcome sight. But that has nothing to do with the serene self-satisfaction that Cincinnatians feel toward themselves. As Mr. Willing, the fictional biographer of Marquand's *The Late George Apley*, says of Apley's fellow Bostonians, "When the individuals of one group find a complete peace and happiness and fulfillment in the association with one another, why should they look farther?"

When Cincinnatians travel, they travel in little groups of other Cincinnatians. In New York, Cincinnati has its own favorite hotel, the comfortable but modest Windsor, and it has taken some adjustment here to the fact that several years ago the Windsor was taken over by Leona Helmsley, who is about as un-Cincinnatian as a woman could be. In London, Cincinnati stays at Brown's. Back in the nineteenth century, to escape the steamy Ohio River Valley summers, Cincinnatians established a summer colony in northern Michigan in and around the lakeshore town of Charlevoix. Today, of course, since everyone has air-conditioning and nearly everybody has a pool, there's no real reason for Charlevoix. The lake is too cold for swimming, and the summer colony is bound by annoying regulations (no outdoor barbecues). Still, it's a tradition, and so everyone flocks there for at least part of the summer, and there they see and entertain the same people they've seen and entertained the rest of the year. It is as though Cincinnatians possess the ability to transport their own soft-spoken culture to every place they visit.

Few cities I've known—except, perhaps, Boston—exert such a powerful sense of *home*. I know at least one Cincinnati family who have lived in the same house for five generations, with a sixth generation waiting in the wings and fully expecting to do the same thing. Among my neighbors here I suspect I am considered rather worldly, since I've managed to live, more or less successfully and for extended periods of time, in a couple of other places. Not long ago, a social worker friend of mine phoned to say that she had a young man in her caseload who wanted to become a fashion photographer. Would I look at some of his photographs and tell her whether I thought he had any talent? I told her I knew next to nothing about photography—my own pictures usually turn out out-of-focus or with my thumb over the lens—but I said I'd be happy to talk to the man, and see if I could help him.

He arrived at my house—he was twenty-three or twenty-four—with a briefcase full of his work. I looked at his photographs and, to my untrained eye, they looked quite good. I told him so, and suggested that if he could get himself to New York, I had at least two friends—Richard Avedon and Francesco Scavullo—who were successful fashion photographers and who could offer him better career advice than I could give him. He looked horrified. "Oh, I could never go to New York!" he said. Well, what about Los Angeles, I asked him. He positively shivered with revulsion. "I could never go there," he said. Then I suggested Chicago which, after all, is less than an hour by plane from here. But Chicago was also out of the question. It turned out that the only place where he wanted to be a fashion photographer was in Cincinnati and, though the opportunities in such a field seemed quite limited here, he would never dream of leaving home.

And when Cincinnatians do leave home, they nearly always turn around and come back before long. No other place will quite do. A case in point is Bob Braun, who bought my Thunderbird. For years, he had an enormously popular morning television talk and entertainment show, which was syndicated in several nearby cities. The *Bob Braun Show* was considered especially important for books and authors, and a booking on Bob Braun was the pivotal reason why publishers included Cincinnati authors' book tours. I could see why. After being interviewed on Braun, the entire studio audience—mostly women—would follow me out of the building and down the street for two blocks to Shillito's department store where, in the book department, I'd sit at a table while they bought and had me autograph their books.

But the only trouble with the *Bob Braun Show*, it seemed, was that his audience—in the studio and at home—was aging with him. Every time I did the show there seemed to be more gray heads out there. His audience, the demographics showed, was getting beyond the ages of twenty-five to forty-five that advertisers consider their prime market, people who shop for baby powder and Pampers. His show, despite high ratings, was abruptly canceled.

The Brauns then took themselves to Los Angeles and, for a time, it was rather sad to recognize the face of the man who had been such a major star in Cincinnati when it turned up in bit parts and walk-ons in films. The Brauns, needless to say, hated California and, before long, they were back. Today, Bob Braun is reading radio commercials.

Another popular television personality was Nick Clooney, brother of Rosemary and father of George. Nick Clooney is an older version of his movie star son and, as a news anchor, had become something of a local heartthrob. As a result of his popularity, he was offered—at a considerable hike in salary—a news job at a Southern California station. But, like the Brauns, Clooney and his wife just didn't feel at home on the West Coast. They then tried Arizona and were just as unhappy there. And so, it wasn't long before Nick Clooney was back in Cincinnati, writing a column for one of the local newspapers, where, as though to remind readers of his former high profile and visibility, he makes frequent references to "my sister, Rosemary," and "my son, George."

A third, much-loved television celebrity was roly-poly Ira Joe Fisher. Ira Joe read the weather reports, and his special talent was his ability to stand behind a glass weather map and write, backward, across the face of it. This striking accomplishment brought him to the attention of a New York station, which also made him a lucrative offer to come to Manhattan. But that familiar Cincinnati malaise, homesickness, soon afflicted him. He came back, of course, and tried to establish his own television talk show. This, however, was a failure, and as of this writing he is giving New York a second try, still mirror-writing the weather forecasts. The jury is still out as to whether he'll remain there this time, but most people feel that, sooner or later, Ira Joe will be back in some guise or other.

They always seem to come back—later, if not sooner. One woman I know married and moved east with her husband some forty years ago. Then, not long ago, after her husband's death, she decided to return to the hometown of family and childhood friends. "And do you know," she said wonderingly to me, "when I came back, nobody asked me where I'd been."

They've been called the Serene Cincinnatians, a label they don't mind at all. And serene they remain, serene and sedate and self-satisfied, and not a little smug. After all, Cincinnatians have always had quite a bit to feel smug about. For years, they were smug about having Pete Rose, a native son, as a national sports hero playing for the hometown team, the Cincinnati Reds, the oldest ball club in the country. My own encounter with Rose was brief. As I've mentioned, I rarely turn to the sports pages and, not long after moving here, I found myself on a short flight home from Atlanta. After we were served drinks, my seatmate and I fell into conversation. "What do you do?" he asked me. I told him I was a writer, and he asked me my name. I told him, and he said, "Well, I can't say I've ever heard of you. But then, I'm not much of a reader." I asked him his name. "Pete Rose," he said. "And what do you do?" I asked him. "I'm a ballplayer," he said. "Oh? Do you play baseball or football?" I asked him. "Baseball," he said. We went on to chat about other matters.

That evening, at a cocktail party, I asked, "Has anyone here ever heard of a baseball player named Pete Rose?" There were shrieks of disbelief from around the room.

Later, after Rose was suspended from the sport for gambling and other alleged ethical infractions, many Cincinnatians came forth to say that they'd never really liked him, that they'd always found him a bit vain and arrogant, and somewhat thick between the ears. There was talk that the street that had been recently renamed in his honor, Pete Rose Way, should revert to its previous, more prosaic designation as Second Street. But, in the end, it was decided that, for all his faults and misdeeds, Pete Rose was a rather good ballplayer, and that the new street name should be allowed to remain. Once again, charity and good taste prevail in Serene Cincinnati.

Disgraced, Pete Rose left town under a cloud, vowing never to return. But, some day, when the storm has subsided and the scandal has been forgotten, it is more than likely that Rose will head back to the city where he was born. All will be forgiven and, politely, no one will ask him where he's been.

One doesn't have to live here long before one begins to share the sentimental and nostalgic feelings of attachment that Cincinnati has for its institutions and traditions. During the Great Depression, Cincinnatians like to point out, the hard times were hardly felt here. No banks closed, and Procter & Gamble went right on turning out soap that Americans, for richer or poorer, still had to buy. No Cincinnati stockbrokers leaped from window ledges. There were no breadlines or apple vendors here. As a result, Cincinnati likes to think of itself as "recession proof."

Cincinnati is equally proud of its race-relations history. Though the city has a large Black population, Blacks and whites have always had a comfortable, even cordial, relationship with one another. In the 1960s, when other cities exploded into racial violence, arson, and looting—as in Detroit, Cleveland, New York, and Washington, D.C.—Cincinnati remained calm. This is largely because Cincinnati has no distinct and self-contained Black ghetto as such, like New York's Harlem or Chicago's South Side. Instead, Cincinnati's Black poor live in a series of mini ghettoes scattered throughout the town. Scattered here and there are also pockets of Black affluence, where home-owning Black businessmen and professionals and their families live. At the same time, there are also neighborhoods (such as my own) where Black and white families live within close proximity to one another. And there are some pleasant middle-class sections of town where Black families have taken up residence on one side of the street, while white families live on the other.

Cincinnati takes equal pride in its excellent public library system—in its gleaming new Central Library downtown, and its many satellite branches. In terms of the sheer number of volumes in its collection, the city boasts the third-largest public library in the country, topped only by New York and Boston. It also claims to have the highest return rate of any library system in the nation; though it loans out close to ten million books a year, borrowers who fail to return their books number in the hundreds. And this is despite a very liberal system of fines on overdue books. The Public Library has always refused to impose a fine higher than the original cost of the book itself. The Cincinnati Library also offers a service that was long ago abandoned by the New York Public Library—its Telephone Information Service. By picking up the phone and calling the appropriate department, one can verify a date, check a quotation or the spelling of a name, or obtain other information on the subject at hand. Though the library admits that this service is often used to settle wagers, it still cheerfully provides it. The library will even look up foreign telephone numbers and zip codes from its extensive collection of city directories.

Cincinnati also has its own private library, originally called the Young Men's Mercantile Library. (The "Young Men's" part of the name was later dropped for sounding sexist.) For a small annual membership fee, subscribers can order books or tapes by phone, and these will be mailed out to them, along with return mailers. In its elegantly paneled Victorian reading room, downtown businesspeople are encouraged to bring their lunches and read while eating. The Mercantile Library—unheard-of in this day and age—even provides ashtrays for smokers, adding to the club-like nineteenth-century ambience.

The Mercantile Library owes its privileged status to the generosity of the founder of the Fleischmann (yeast and distilling) family fortune, one of the more redoubtable hereabouts. When he was putting up an office building downtown years ago, the elder Fleischman made a magnificent gesture. He offered the Mercantile Library a lease on the top two floors of his building, with a splendid view of the Ohio River, for a thousand years at the rate of $1 a year. Needless to say, the Mercantile snapped up that lease.

But that lease has, in years since, become the cause for much squabbling. The elder Fleischmann's grandson, Charles Fleischmann III, who inherited the building from his namesake, began to see those top two floors as potentially lucrative office space that was earning him not even a pittance in rent. He tried various legal tactics in an attempt to break the lease, but without success. In retaliation—out of spite, his critics say—the younger Fleischmann then built a new, taller building on the lot next door, completely cutting off the library's river view. The library's reading room had originally contained two magnificent stained-glass windows. Though the new building would block the windows from any sunlight, the library had made plans to light them electrically from behind.

But, during the new building's construction, Fleischmann' s contractor recommended that the windows be removed "for their protection." This was done but, when the building was completed, the precious windows were nowhere to be found. Upon investigation, it turned out that Fleischmann had donated the windows to the Cincinnati Art Museum! The library's board protested. Those windows, the library rightfully claimed, had not been Fleischmann's to give away. And so, in some embarrassment, the Art Museum returned the windows to their donor, claiming that this was all their legal position permitted them to do. All this was quite a few years ago before I moved to Cincinnati, in fact—but the Battle of the Windows still goes on. No one knows for sure where the windows are today, but they are suspected to be locked somewhere in the basement of Charles Fleischmann's house. In any other city, this fight might be considered too petty to worry about. But, in Cincinnati, the matter is about as serious as any conflict between Culture and Capitalism can get.

Cincinnati has its sacred monuments, its urban treasures that no one would dream of tinkering with. One is the Suspension Bridge, the first bridge to cross the Ohio River from Cincinnati to Kentucky. The Suspension Bridge was designed by the great John Augustus Roebling, who went on to design the Great East River Bridge in New York, more popularly known as the Brooklyn Bridge. Indeed, Cincinnati's Suspension Bridge was the prototype for the Brooklyn Bridge, with the same steel web truss across its span to keep it from swaying in the wind. In appearance, the Suspension Bridge is almost identical to, if somewhat shorter than, the Brooklyn. Roebling did not live to see the completion of the Brooklyn in 1883, but he was here in person during every phase of his Cincinnati project.

To some observers, the Suspension Bridge seems to cross the river at an odd angle and can be approached at either end only by making a series of peculiar zigzag turns and backtracks. This, it turns out, was done to accommodate the state of Kentucky, which feared that if the bridge connected directly with main thoroughfares on either shore it would facilitate the escape of slaves into Abolitionist Ohio. A few years ago, the suspending cables of the bridge were festooned with lights, but not without much handwringing from local traditionalists who argued that electric lighting had not been a part of Mr. Roebling's original design, even though the Brooklyn Bridge, which is newer, had had its cables decorated with strings of lights at least twenty years before.

The resistance to any sudden or dramatic change has helped give Cincinnati its sense of permanence and continuity—serenity, if you will. This might make Cincinnati seem a little boring, but Cincinnatians don't feel that way. Nor do I. On the contrary, life here has often offered more excitement than I would personally have wished for, and enough oddball characters have entered my existence here to thoroughly overpopulate a Tennessee Williams play.

My first landlady, for example, was a woman named Verna, who had obviously been a great beauty in her youth. In her sixties, she still tinted her hair by dusting it with pink face powder. Her husband was a doctor who, she explained, had cured her of tuberculosis using a novel method: he had prescribed circus bareback riding. And she had gone further than that. She had learned not only to ride bareback, but to ride standing, barefoot, while straddling a pair of prancing white circus horses. Her best friends became the Flying Wallendas! She had photos of herself from her performing days to prove it, and her robust appearance gave no hint that she had ever been consumptive.

Her German-born husband, whom she always referred to as "Doctor," also had an interesting history. He had been the personal physician of Kaiser Wilhelm II after the latter's abdication and exile to the Netherlands. Though an ardent German Royalist, Doctor was hardly a Nazi. Still, his German origin, and accent, put him under a cloud, professionally, during the War and he was placed in an American internment camp. He may have married an American woman to try to ease this situation. It was certainly an unusual marriage. Though he lived in another part of town, Doctor always appeared on Verna's doorstep every night for dinner.

If I'd expected Cincinnatians to be a bit reserved and reticent, I was in for a surprise. After buying our hilltop house, a young woman we'd barely met stopped by one summer evening for a drink. Soon she was having such a good time that she leaped, fully clothed, into the pool. Then, encumbered by sopping wet garments, she shed every stitch, and splashed around some more in the altogether. We sent her home, later on in the evening, wrapped in an old raccoon coat of mine from college days, and carrying her clothes in a plastic bag. Her last question to me was, "How am I going to explain this to my husband?" Since I wasn't aware that she had a husband, I had no good suggestions.

At a cocktail party, I found myself in conversation with a tiny silver-haired woman named Crystal who said to me, "You know, I'm going to be ninety next month, and I have just one wish. I'd like to go back to Paris just once before I die. But I'm a widow, and I don't want to go alone." In a moment of whiskey-induced exuberance, I said, "I'll go with you!" The situation rapidly escalated. It seemed that Crystal had a friend named Hermina, another widow of the same vintage, who also wanted one last trip to Paris. And so, Ed Lahniers was recruited as the second escort, and the four of us set off together for the City of Light.

We established ourselves in a suite of rooms, with a common sitting room, in a small hotel just off the Avenue Foch. We'd agreed that, during the days, we'd each do whatever we wanted, and then meet in the sitting room for cocktails before continuing on to dinner. The two diminutive nonagenarians proved to be astonishingly energetic; they nearly wore us out. Every morning after breakfast the two would charge off, travelers' checks in hand, in the direction of Avenue Victor Hugo or the rue Saint-Honoré to shop. They visited every couturier and *parfumerie* in Paris, and every cocktail hour was spent with the ladies displaying their purchases. They shopped competitively, it seemed. If Hermina bought six Hermès silk scarves, Crystal would buy a dozen. If Crystal bought a Chanel suit, Hermina would feel compelled to buy two. If Hermina came home with four scented Rigaud candles, Crystal would buy twice as many. The people at Baccarat must have rubbed their hands with glee when the two appeared, together, at the famous store in the Rue du Paradis and began ordering crystal stemware, each one trying to outdo the other with orders for cocktail, wine, and highball glasses. It all seemed to be getting somewhat out of hand when Hermina admitted that she already owned several crates full of Baccarat from an earlier trip that she'd never unpacked.

One evening Hermina came home with, among other things, an over-the-shoulder handbag from Louis Vuitton. I saw Crystal's eyes narrow as she planned to buy an even fancier bag the next day. "But Hermina," I pointed out, "that bag is exactly like the one you brought with you to Paris!" "No, this one is a little different," she said. "This one has a little pocket on the inside, with a little mirror in it." "That's silly," I said. "I'm sure you have lots of compacts with mirrors in them. I'm going to insist that you take this one back to the store." Which, reluctantly, she agreed to do. I saw Crystal's face relax. That took her off the hook as far as a visit to Vuitton was concerned.

The night before we were to head home, and as we surveyed the mounds of packages that represented the ladies' costly purchases, I said, "You know there's a limit to how much you can take in duty-free. I'm sure you're both way over that limit. I hope you both have cash enough left to pay the duty on all this stuff when you go through customs." This thought had not occurred to either of them. "Will customs take credit cards?" One of them asked. I said I doubted it, and both women began looking worried.

But I had a suggestion. I'd heard that people in wheelchairs were often whisked through customs at airports without questions or having to open their luggage, and so I said, "Look, you're both getting on in years. Why don't I call the airline and tell them we need wheelchairs to meet you both at Kennedy?" I did this, and it worked—though their respective sons, who had come to meet their mothers at the airport, were briefly horrified to see their previously spry little mothers wheeled out onto the sidewalk by airport personnel. Both men looked at Ed and me as though we had been responsible for disabling their parents when, in fact, it had been very nearly the other way around.

Within a year after that trip, both women died—but peacefully and happily, I'm sure, and went to their rest wearing some of their Paris finery.

And who would have thought that in sedate, decorous Cincinnati I would encounter my first serious stalker, and that this disturbed character would end up stalking me for the better part of seventeen years?

Since she's still around, and may resurface at any moment, I'll change her name. I'll call her Ingeborg. Ingeborg is a large woman in her fifties, of Latvian extraction, with broad shoulders, big peasant paws, thunder thighs, a mop of unwashed hair, and a case of halitosis that would probably warrant an article in the journal of the American Dental Association. It all started with Ed, and so I'll have to backtrack a little.

In the late 1970s, Ed was working a couple of afternoons a week running group therapy sessions at an inpatient treatment center for alcoholics. Ingeborg had checked herself into this facility for a two weeks' stay, and this was where Ed first encountered her and marked her as a troublemaker, since she was frequently cursing, threatening, and fighting with the other patients. After her discharge from the center, Ingeborg expressed her wish to continue to see Ed on a private basis. He agreed to see her, and, once she discovered where we lived, the nightmare started. My theory is that she fell in love with him, but that's just a guess.

I've never been entirely sure what Ed does when he sees his stream of patients on the floor directly above my own. An intercom system that used to permit people to chat from room to room throughout the house has been disconnected, so I've never been able to tune in to eavesdrop. At times, I've heard an angry cry, or the stomping of feet on the ceiling overhead. Once there was a loud crash, as a desk clock was hurled across Ed's office by a woman who had clearly been told something she didn't want to hear. But, for the most part, I hear the sounds of people sobbing when they go into his office and laughing when they emerge fifty minutes later.

Ed saw Ingeborg in therapy exactly twice. Ostensibly, she stopped seeing him because she could not afford his fees; his bill to her was never paid. But then her campaign of harassment began. She harassed in person, and she harassed by telephone, but the telephone was her favorite medium. And when she learned of my existence her efforts redoubled.

Her preferred time for telephoning was after midnight when the household was asleep. The answering machine would cut her off after about a minute, and so she would simply press her "redial" button and call again. The phone would ring throughout the night. Often, she would run through an entire tape on the machine before finally running out of gas. A great deal of the time her drunken ramblings were unintelligible. Sometimes she sang, and sometimes she read from the Bible. Sometimes she repeated, "I love you. . . . I love you both. . . . God loves you. . . . Let Jesus into your lives." But at other times her messages were more menacing: "I'm going to cut your balls off! I'm going to see that you're both dead meat! I'm coming out there with a gun and kill you both!" We knew that she did indeed have a gun because she'd once shot her husband in the leg, not fatally, and her Kentucky neighbors had complained that she often brandished a shotgun in their direction. Because Ed and I shared a house, she assumed we were homosexual lovers, and often her message was, "I hope you both get AIDS, and rot away with cancer, and die." And there were the usual epithets: faggots, queers, pansies, cocksuckers.

In the front of the telephone directory, the following warning is printed:

"It is a crime under state and federal law for anyone to make obscene or harassing telephone calls. In Ohio, the law imposes penalties of up to five (5) years' imprisonment and/or $500 fine. If harassing calls continue, contact your local police or Cincinnati Bell Telephone's Annoyance Call Bureau at 397-7366 for what options are available to you."

We followed that advice. We called the police first. But, it seemed, the Cincinnati police had no jurisdiction over anyone calling from

Kentucky. And, naturally, the Kentucky police explained that they could not handle complaints coming from the state of Ohio. We next tried the Annoyance Call Bureau where we learned that the options available to us were very few. Cincinnati Bell appeared to be quite reluctant to take any steps that might cost the company a subscriber. "Why don't you just leave the phone off the hook?" was their best suggestion. But we reminded them, as a psychologist Ed occasionally received late-night calls that were actual emergencies. And, by now, Ingeborg's calls were coming throughout the daytime hours as well, and what was the point of having telephone service at all if the phone was always off the hook? "For a small extra monthly charge, we can give you a new unpublished number," they offered. But a doctor's office with an unpublished number didn't make much sense, either.

We tried moving higher up in the hierarchy of the telephone company, and finally contacted a supervisor who seemed actually willing to help. She could, she suggested, set up tracing equipment on our line which would automatically record the calling number of each harassing call. For our part, all we had to do was record the exact time of each call. The hitch was that the tracing equipment could be put in place for one week only.

The equipment was set up, and we and the telephone company synchronized our watches. But, uncannily, Ingeborg seemed somehow to sense that her calls were being tracked, and for the next week there was no sound from her at all. And, no sooner had the tracing equipment been removed than her calls started up again with a vengeance. We were getting nowhere.

I decided to try a more human tactic. I tried telephoning Ingeborg myself—calling her during the morning hours when, I hoped, I'd catch her in a moment of sobriety. I tried asking her why she was doing this to us, and what she hoped to accomplish through her relentless campaign. Though sober, her explanations were vague and rambling. She did it, she said, because she lived close to a cemetery and, at night, dead souls often spoke to her urging her to do what she did. Also, airplanes passing over her house she lived near the airport sometimes radioed signals to her with coded instructions. She had, she said, talked to the CIA in Virginia about

Ed and me, and the Agency had given her official permission to call us as often as she liked, at whatever hour of the day and night she chose. Was she working for the CIA? I asked her. "Yes, unofficially," she said.

It occurred to me that talking to a relative might help. I knew I wouldn't get very far with her husband, since he often joined Ingeborg in her telephone tirades, but I did get the name of her mother-in-law and called her. "I want nothing to do with that drunken bitch," her mother-in-law said before hanging up on me.

The calls continued. The tracing equipment was set up again and, this time, Ingeborg was more obliging. I sat up all night one night, faithfully noting the times of some ninety different calls between two and six o'clock in the morning. I reported these to the telephone company and, reluctantly it seemed to me, they agreed to disconnect Ingeborg's line, from which all the calls originated. I asked about the jail sentence and the fine that the warning in the phone book had promised, but disconnecting her service seemed to be as far as the company was willing to go.

We then looked forward to a period of peace, but our hopes were soon dashed. Deprived of a telephone, Ingeborg began appearing at our house in person. One evening the doorbell rang and, when Ed answered it, Ingeborg forced herself inside. Ed is a skinny six-footer, weighing about 150 pounds, but Ingeborg outweighed him by at least that much again. She threw him to the floor and began ripping off his shirt. On another occasion, when Ed's grandmother and great-aunt were visiting us, Ingeborg easily snapped through the chain lock, ran into the two ladies' bedroom and jumped into bed with them both. Then she charged upstairs to where I was watching television and leaped—all three hundred pounds of her—onto my lap screaming, "Fuck me! Fuck me!"

Needless to say, the police were called, and it usually took at least two brawny Cincinnati cops to subdue and handcuff her. But all the police could do with her, it seemed, was to escort her back across the Ohio River to Kentucky where she belonged. The morning after one of these forays, her husband telephoned us, but not to apologize for his wife's intrusions. "When the police were wrestling with Ingeborg in your driveway last night, trying to get the handcuffs on," he said, "they apparently knocked the diamond out of her engagement ring. Do you mind if I come over and look around your driveway for the diamond?"

Phoneless, she devised ever more demonic forms of torture. At four o'clock one morning our doorbell rang, and it was a Cincinnati policeman. "Your friend Ingeborg called," he said, "and told us she'd seen no activity around your house for some time. She's worried that the occupants of this house are all dead. We're required to make a routine check of the premises." One morning an agent from the United States Secret Service telephoned. "We had a tip from a woman named Ingeborg that someone at this number is plotting to assassinate President Clinton," he said.

We succeeded in having a restraining order issued, forbidding her to come within half a mile of our house. Of course, she ignored this, and the neighbors became used to seeing flashing lights from police cars outside our front door. Then the phone calls began all over again. The telephone company had restored her service.

Someone suggested that we might sue the telephone company, but that sounded as though it might be counterproductive and could end up disrupting our own phone service. Someone else proposed that, since the warning in the telephone directory mentioned "federal law," and that much of the problem seemed to be that it crossed state lines, we might report our plight to the FBI. We did this. A very polite FBI agent paid a visit, listened to our tapes of some of Ingeborg's more violent ravings, and jotted down a few notes in a little black notebook. He promised to "start a file" on Ingeborg. I suppose he did this, but that was the last we heard from the FBI.

Finally, we did what perhaps we should have done from the beginning. We hired a lawyer. A lawsuit was instituted against our tormentor and, court calendars being what they are, this all dragged on—with depositions, and all the rest for a good two years. In the meantime, Ingeborg's husband divorced her, remarried and, the day after his remarriage, suddenly died—of natural causes, we were assured. But this complicated things further since our lawsuit had been against both Ingeborg *and* her husband. But at least our lawyer was getting a taste of what we were going through. He began getting telephone calls from Ingeborg in which she threatened not only his life but those of his wife and children. And of course, her calls to us kept right on coming.

Finally, the court awarded us a judgment of $1 million in damages for our long ordeal. This decision was appealed to the Ohio State Supreme Court and was upheld. Victory! But it was not quite that, because Ingeborg had nothing even close to $1 million.

She lived in a tarpaper shack with a yard strewn with derelict automobiles and an old refrigerator standing on the sagging front stoop. It was a typical Appalachian farmhouse, surrounded by a few ramshackle outbuildings. (Appalachians, it seems, seldom discard their cars after they have ceased to function. They pile them around their yards and scavenge them for spare parts as needed.)

But what she did have was a spread of some twenty-six acres of wooded land behind the house. It was very pretty property covering several rolling hills, and a splashing stream ran through it. This property, we were told, would now have to be sold at a sheriff's auction to satisfy our legal claim against her.

It was not a merry prospect. Though we bore no love of Ingeborg, we had not set out on this course intending to create a homeless person. But the wheels of the law were in motion now, and there was nothing we could do to stop it. A date for the auction was set. An announcement appeared in the newspapers. For some legal reason, we were required to be present at the sale. Also, it would be necessary for us to make an initial bid on the property for a figure based on a percentage of the land's assessed value. This figure turned out to be $45,000. No money would actually change hands but, if there were no higher bidders, title to the twenty-six acres would automatically pass to us, the plaintiffs.

It was pointed out to us that this land lay close to a new industrial park and shopping center that was being developed and could turn out to be worth a lot more than $45,000. But we didn't want the land. We didn't want to become real estate developers. We especially didn't want the unpleasant—even scary—task of having to evict Ingeborg from her property. Suppose she started shooting again? All we'd ever really wanted was for her to stop telephoning us in the middle of the night.

We were fairly sure that Ingeborg herself would appear at the auction. And, because of Ingeborg's reputation for violence, our lawyer suggested that we hire an off-duty police officer to accompany us to the event—a SWAT team member, to be exact—and so we did this. And when we arrived at the country courthouse steps where the auction would be held, there she was, looking mad as hell. There were no metal detectors at the courthouse, and so our police bodyguard had Ingeborg body searched by a matron. Then the sheriff banged his gavel, and the auction was on.

Besides ourselves, our two suited lawyers, our bodyguard—who carried a can of Mace, but no weapon—and the lady herself, there weren't many people in the audience. This was not a good sign. An auction can't build up a head of steam without quite a few bidders. Our principal attorney stepped forward and made our bid. "I have $45,000 bid on the property," the sheriff said. He repeated the figure. There was silence, and our hearts began to sink. "Going for $45,000," the sheriff said. "Going . . . going . . ." He raised his gavel once more.

But just then a young man who looked barely in his teens, who looked as though he hadn't a nickel to his name or a friend in the world, raised his hand. "Fifty thousand," he said. Of course, he could have outbid us by raising our bid by as little as a penny, but he had no way of knowing that. "I have fifty thousand," the auctioneer said. "Do I have any more bids? Going for fifty thousand. Going . . . going . . . *gone!*" And down came the gavel. It was over.

The young man took out $5,000 in hundred-dollar bills from the pocket of his tattered dungarees and handed this to the sheriff. "I'll get the rest of the money from my grandmother," he said. "You'll have to have it here, in cash, within an hour," the sheriff warned him. "I will," he said. And apparently, he did because, that very afternoon, a cashier's check was hand-delivered to us. It covered our legal expenses, and a little more.

It would be nice to say that that was the end of our telephone torture from Ingeborg, but it wasn't. She started calling that very evening, angrier and more abusive than ever. But, by one of those strange coincidences with which life is filled, that same week the telephone company announced a new service called Call Blocking. It took only a phone call to put this service in place. And now, from wherever she calls, all I have to do is press a three-digit number, and she can never call from that number again. Ah, the wonders of modern technology! If only Call Blocking had been available those many years ago, we'd have been spared the whole miserable ordeal. But then I'd have been robbed of a good story.

And it turns out that we did not actually create a homeless woman. It seems that Ingeborg once worked as, of all things, a schoolteacher, and has a comfortable pension to live on. Still, whenever my doorbell rings when I am not expecting a visitor, I experience a frisson of fright. Usually, though, it is just Jehovah's Witnesses, and not that massive figure with the matted hair and fetid breath.

No, Cincinnati has not turned out to be a boring place to live. And its quirks and oddities and special charms have, for me, far outweighed any tribulations I have encountered here. It is a great party town, for one thing, and I've always been more than a little party—and invitation—prone and, now that I'm single again, I've rediscovered an odd but interesting fact: An extra single man is nearly always welcome at a party whereas, often, an extra single woman is not. Cincinnati loves to give parties, and everyone tries to outdo everyone else when it comes to entertaining. There's a saying I've heard here: "In New York, they ask you how much money you make. In Boston, they ask you where you went to boarding school. In Philadelphia, they ask you what your grandmother's maiden name was. Here, they ask you, 'What'll you have to drink?'"

Cincinnati's priciest—and most party-giving—suburb is Indian Hill, to the east of town. As in many cities, the East side of town is more fashionable than the West. This, supposedly, is so that businessmen who commute to and from downtown every day will be able to drive both ways with the sun at their backs, and not in their eyes. But it wouldn't be accurate to describe Indian Hill as a suburb. It calls itself an "incorporated village," and was conceived, early in the century, as a place with wooded hills and open fields where wealthy sportsman such as Julius Fleischmann, John Emery, and Oliver de Gray Vanderbilt (no kin to those other Vanderbilts) could stable their horses and ride to the hounds. The oldest estates in Indian Hill were originally laid out as farms.

Indian Hill has its own police force and its own fire department, but it has no hospital. It has its own Zip Code, but no post office. It has its own country club and its own school, but no shops or business establishments. It has many horse trails and bridle paths, but no sidewalks or streetlights. There is but one traffic light, a cautionary yellow blinker. There is one church (Episcopal). A number of years ago, at a gathering of Indian Hill village folk, it was suggested that, hard by the church, Indian Hill ought to have its own cemetery so that the villagers, who had spent so much of their lives together, could all repose together at the end. There was an immediate angry outcry at this suggestion. "Why should we want another cemetery," someone shouted, "when we have Spring Grove?"

Spring Grove Cemetery is one of Cincinnati's most sacred institutions. it was laid out in the nineteenth century by the celebrated landscape architect Frederick Law Olmsted, who also designed New York's Central Park and Prospect Park in Brooklyn. Olmsted created hills and glens, sweeping vistas, dotted with groves of trees and topiary and banks of wildflowers. There are lakes and ponds and gentle streams, hushed waterfalls, and quietly splashing fountains. Colonies of swans and geese and ducks were established there, and nightingales were imported from England to fill the trees with song. (Only the waterfowl survived.) Here, entombed beneath monuments of granite and marble, and in mausoleums of extravagant design, lie members of Cincinnati's oldest and most prestigious families—Tafts, Hollisters, Bardeses, Stettiniuses, Procters, Gambles, and Fleischmanns. Needless to say, the First Families staked out the best locations, on hilltops with the finest views. But lesser folk have also been given space in this serene, parklike setting where every prospect is a pleasant one.

As in most cemeteries, sections have been set aside for various religious denominations, for Catholics, Protestants, and Jews. But Spring Grove is unusual in that one hillside has been designated as a resting place for a tribe of Gypsies. According to the legend, an itinerant Gypsy princess was passing through Cincinnati many years ago, where she was taken ill and died. But she was given such excellent and considerate medical care and treatment before her death that her family decided to have her buried here. Since then, dozens of members of the princess's extended family, from all over the country, have elected to join her in Spring Grove.

Each year, on Memorial Day, the hillside of Gypsy grave sites is decorated with elaborate floral displays—huge blankets and baskets and sprays, nearly all of them constructed with fresh white, pink, and purple orchids, orchids by the thousands. Hundreds of thousands of dollars must be spent annually on these floral tributes and, oddly, all of them are created by one small and obscure florist's shop in Northern Kentucky. No one knows why the Swan Floral & Gift Shop is always given the assignment of building these orchid extravaganzas, and if the Swan people know why they annually get the Gypsies' business, they will not say. "It is obviously our reputation for quality and service," replies Swan's proprietor a little stiffly. Is there some sort of connection between Swan's and the Gypsy tribe? "Not that I am aware of," he says. Naturally, he will not tell me what the Gypsies' annual bill for orchids runs to. He will only reveal that Swan's has been in charge of decorating the Gypsy graves "since the early nineteen-fifties."

If you arrive at Spring Grove early enough in the morning of Memorial Day, you will find two or three limousines filled with swarthy-faced men and women, paying tribute to their departed kinfolk.

Cincinnati is full of surprises like Spring Grove. But to me the most astonishing thing about living here is that Ed Lahniers and I have decided—independently of each other, and without ever discussing it—to spend the rest of our lives in this not particularly important city. (To me, there are only five important cities in the world: New York, London, Paris, Rome, and maybe Madrid.) After more than twenty years of living under the same roof, we both feel utterly satisfied with this arrangement, and can really envision no other. It was not planned that way as far as I can recall. There was no commitment to each other's comfort and convenience if, by commitment, one means some sort of promise. On the contrary, when I first moved into Ed's apartment (with the ex–circus performer landlady), I viewed it as a temporary solution, a sensible port in the storm of an unhappy divorce. Then, as the months and years passed by, it began to seem very nicely permanent. What started out as a sort of jolly palship has weathered into a deep and meaningful friendship, requiring no explanations or apologies, and with very few complaints.

We're in some ways, I suppose, the Odd Couple. We're like the bright and dark sides of the moon. Don Fernando, my Spanish language teacher, describes my personality as *"laconico,"* somewhat uncommunicative and given to long silences. (Nan used to accuse me of being "a cold New Englander"; she, by contrast I guess, was the sunny Californian.) Ed is the opposite of me: bubbly, enthusiastic, voluble, and funny, the life of the party. I tend to be a listener while he's a great talker. I find him wise in many ways that I am not, and yet I find that he respects my mind as well. Fortunately, we both have plenty of money, and together enjoy the things we are able to spend it on. So, there's no arena for quarreling there, and I've always felt that money fights were the worst fights of all—far worse than battles involving sex.

We argue and disagree, of course. But mostly we argue about the proper height to hang a picture, or what temperature to keep the pool. (When he's not looking, I raise the thermostat a notch or two; when I'm not looking, he lowers it.) The layout of our house is such that each of us has blessed privacy throughout most of the day. But at the end of the day, when we sit down together for a drink before dinner (a meal we more or less take turns at preparing), we can't wait to rehash the news of the day, the stories in the morning paper, what new tricks our dog has learned—I've taught him to tell time by a digital clock. These shared times are blessed, too. After so much time together, we can often read each other's thoughts and finish each other's sentences.

Is this what love is? It certainly is what respect is—what trust and forgiveness and patience are, most of all. I don't think I have ever been in love. I've said "I love you" to many people—too many, I suppose, lying again, in the heat of passion, which is love's opposite. I was not really in love with Ava, I see that now. It was pity, which is love's killer. I've tried in my fiction, which is truth's opposite, to describe love in its various manifestations. And, in the process, I've found myself in love with make-believe people. When Essie Auerbach died at the end of my novel, I found myself weeping so uncontrollably that I couldn't read the words I'd typed on the page. But I do believe in need. We all need some other person. Just one. So perhaps that's what love is. Dependency. I do believe in that.

Love surrounds most people, in one form or another. I guess love is what God is—unattainable, doubtful, suspicious, comforting, all-encompassing, all-justifying. Love is a total suspension of disbelief, a refusal to accept reality. Are these enough stabs in the dark? Even Sigmund Freud was unable to come up with a meaningful definition of love.

Ed Lahniers is, among other things, a talented musician, and we've written several songs together—The lyrics mine, music his—and one of those is called "Long Live Love." The lyric goes in part:

> Love is grief, love's a thief, it's a brief refrain,
> A crazy combination of delight and pain,
> A bolt of lightning from above,
> Love is sweet, love's a cheat, it will wax and wane,
> as fickle as the sunshine or an April rain,
> the kind of love I'm thinking of . . . .
> Love, like happiness, is the bird in the hand. So—long live love.

We're invited out a lot. Two single men often seem more in demand than one, and many of our married friends seem actually to envy us our partnership. We probably don't entertain as often as we could or should, and sometimes we both feel a little guilty and selfish about that—that we don't share our pretty house to the extent that we might. Do we just enjoy each other's company too much? But when we do entertain, we like to do it right, with a certain amount of flair and pizzazz. And it was in the course of preparing a dinner party that I discovered country ham.

Another beloved Cincinnati tradition revolves around the reverence for Kentucky country ham. Indeed, there is almost a mystique surrounding the preparation of an authentic Kentucky country ham, and one approaches a full ham presented on a silver platter, garnished with spiced crabapples and cilantro, with a mouthwatering sense of awe. "Oooh, a *country ham!*" people squeal with delight and anticipation when the great roast appears.

A woman friend of mine, who had been entertained by friends in the East recently, sent her host and hostess a Kentucky ham as a thank-you gift. She was considerably put off, even insulted, when a note came back saying, in part, "Thank you so much for the meat." "Imagine!" my friend said. "Can you imagine anybody calling a country ham *meat*? Can you even *imagine*? That wasn't meat—it was a genuine *country ham!*"

You will find, on the shelves of the meat department in many local supermarkets, as well as on the bills of fare of any number of diners and truck stops and cafes, many items that call themselves "country ham." These are not the real thing. When eaten, these imposters are dry, almost unbearably salty, and so tough that they are virtually unchewable. As everyone knows, there is only one place to buy the real item, and that is at the Burlington Hardware Store in Burlington, Kentucky.

Burlington, Kentucky is about a twenty-five-mile drive from here, but once you are in Burlington you will have no trouble finding the Burlington Hardware Store. It stands on one of the four corners that comprise the little town. No one knows how or why the hardware store got into the ham business, but there they hang, on ropes, along with the hammers and saws and wrench sets and trays of screws and barrels of nails. The hams hang there, looking not a bit out of place, and they look as if they have been hanging there, gathering dust, for years. Ask the proprietor to cut one down for you. Never mind the price. More important than whether you can afford a country ham is the question of whether you have the time to devote to preparing it properly.

There is only one way to ready a country ham for the table. Anything else is considered sacrilege, and there are no shortcuts. First off, you must wash it thoroughly, to remove the years of grime it has accumulated while hanging in the Burlington Hardware Store. For this, a stiff wire scrub brush is recommended, along with a mild detergent. Most country hams are too big to fit in a conventional oven, and so the next thing to do is to cut off as much of the lower leg bone as necessary, and for this you'll need a sharp and sturdy hacksaw. The bone can be reserved for use in a stock or soup.

Next the ham must be soaked in water to cover it, and a deep sink or laundry set tub is a good place to do this. The ham should soak for at least twenty-four hours, but most cooks recommend up to seventy-two hours, changing the water several times a day. Now the ham is ready to begin the cooking process. Place it in a large kettle, cover it with water, bring the water to a boil. Lower the heat, cover the kettle, and let the ham simmer for three to four hours. Remove from the heat and let cool. Now, with your ham on a good working space, using a sharp knife, remove the rind and all but a thin layer of fat beneath the rind. Discard all this trimmed-off stuff. Now the top surface of the ham can be scored, dotted with whole cloves, and glazed, though this last step is optional. Place the ham in a deep roasting pan, and preheat your oven to moderate (300°F). Bake for three to four hours, or until the ham is golden brown and has begun to smell good. Your Kentucky country ham is now done.

A while back, I invited some friends for dinner, and I decided to offer this classic regional entree as the pièce de résistance of my dinner party. Starting a week beforehand, I'd gone through all the above steps and, the night before, I'd finished everything. My ham looked gorgeous. I hadn't quite decided whether to serve the ham warm or at room temperature—there are two schools of thought about this—but I'd just about settled on the latter. Still, I covered the ham with aluminum foil and placed it in the refrigerator for overnight. An entire shelf had to be cleared out to accommodate it.

Late that night—or, rather, early the next morning, around three a.m.—my little dog began to bark. Groggily, I wondered what he might be barking at. He barked for about ten minutes, and then stopped. I rolled over and went back to sleep.

The next morning, Ed Lahniers called down to me from the floor above. He'd found a strange flashlight on a bench just inside the front door. I went upstairs to look at the flashlight. It was certainly no flashlight either of us had ever owned. I remembered the dog barking. Apparently, we'd had an intruder during the night.

How he or they—gained entry was no mystery. We hadn't locked the front door. Ours is a quiet, well-lighted residential street where everyone knows everyone else and where the only pedestrian traffic at night consists of neighbors walking their dogs, and we'd seldom bothered locking our doors. And so, our burglar had just opened the door and walked in.

We began going through the house looking for missing objects. In a dresser drawer Ed kept a few rolls of coins—quarters, dimes, nickels, and pennies—waiting until he had enough rolls to make a trip to the bank worthwhile. The rolls of quarters and dimes were gone, but the pennies and nickels had been left behind. Upstairs, in the living room, we'd had a small portable black-and -white television set. When I'd bought it (from a catalog), it had been advertised as a "Tummy TV." About half the size of a cereal box, it operated on batteries and was designed so that the viewer could rest it on his stomach while lying in bed and catch the eleven o'clock news. It had cost, if memory serves, about $49, and was more a novelty item than anything else. That, too, was missing. We looked at the flashlight again. For some reason, its handle was greasy.

And when we got to the kitchen on the top floor, we discovered the answer—and what had been the main focus of our burglary. My country ham had been removed from the refrigerator, placed on a kitchen countertop, and stripped of its foil wrapping. A carving knife had been removed from a drawer. A jar of mayonnaise had also been taken out, along with a loaf of bread. A large, ugly gash had been cut from the meat. Our burglars—and, from the size of the gash, I'm sure there were at least two—had fixed themselves ham sandwiches, heavy on the mayo.

There were quite a few other valuable objects in the house that they could have made off with. We have a small but respectable collection of contemporary paintings including an Andy Warhol and a Jack Youngerman. But most of these are quite large and would have made an awkward burden to carry down a spiral staircase. From mothers and grandmothers, we also have an unnecessarily large collection of sterling flatware—enough, in fact, to lay out for a buffet of fifty to sixty people. Much of this is in a discontinued Reed & Barton pattern, and some of it is antique coin silver. We even have such arcane and never-used utensils as silver iced-tea spoons and ice cream forks, sometimes called sporks. All this stuff was in the kitchen drawer next to the one where the burglars had found the carving knife, but none of this was taken.

Also, on display was a nice collection of sterling silver mint julep cups, along with silver sipping straws from Tiffany. (When Sotheby's had its garage sale of Jacqueline Onassis's household goods, a set of seven of these straws was illustrated in the catalog and sold for thousands upon thousands of dollars. Mine are identical, and I have more of them than she had.) My burglars had no interest in any of this.

In fact, when, in my writerly way, I began envisioning the crime scene, I decided that the tiny TV set and the dimes and quarters had been stolen as afterthoughts. On their way out, after making their sandwiches, one of the thieves must have said to the other, "Look, now that we've entered this house illegally, and fixed ourselves something to eat, we really should take a few other odds and ends, shouldn't we? After all, sandwiches aren't a *real* burglary." Then, with their hands full of sandwiches, rolls of coins, and a pint-sized TV set, they had simply left their flashlight behind.

We telephoned the local police precinct, and, in a jiffy, two uniformed officers and a plainclothes detective were at our doorstep. The plain-clothesman dusted the flashlight and the mayonnaise jar for fingerprints. One of the police officers nodded his head knowingly, and said, "We have a pretty good idea who did this." I'm sure he was lying. Certainly, the police never came up with any suspects. Was there actually a felon at loose in Cincinnati whose MO was to enter peoples' houses while the owners slept, and after the bars had closed, and have a late-night snack? I doubted it.

But more on my mind at the time was what to do with my debauched and deflowered Kentucky country ham. I had no backup main course to offer my guests that evening. The only alternative I could think of was pizza or takeout Chinese. And I'd been so proud of the way my ham *looked*, so succulent and juicy, tender, and delicious. Now it looked like hell.

Normally, a good burglary provides the burgled party with conversational fodder to dine out on for weeks thereafter. By a *good* burglary, I mean a burglary in which no one was hurt, where everything stolen is replaceable and is fully covered by insurance. My situation was a little different. Though at least 90 percent of my ham remained intact, I felt I couldn't carve it and tell my guests that what they were being served had been pawed by who knew how many pairs of grubby hands of strangers the night before. Yet, in view of the time I'd spent preparing it, I couldn't throw the whole thing out. I had to serve it.

Finally, I hit upon a solution: parsley. I bought a bunch of fresh parsley at the grocery store, and draped it artfully and gracefully over the ham to cover the gash that had gone into the burglars' stomachs.[20] A chorus of ooohs and ahs ran around the table that night when I presented my ham on its silver platter. "Oooh, a real Kentucky *country ham!*"

It was pronounced mouthwateringly delicious, and I accepted my congratulations for its perfect preparation with seemly modesty. I don't remember now who exactly was on my guest list that night—after all, I was, as the country folk out here say, "pretty fairly nervous"—but there were no reports of deleterious aftereffects from that meal. My thank-you notes were uniformly praising. And I have kept a secret of our odd burglary until now when, after so much time, perhaps I will be forgiven for serving my friends a tainted delicacy.

Pull your bed rolls closer to the campfire, children. I have a tale to tell. Hurry, it's growing late. Look. there are still a few more marshmallows in the bag. Skewer them on that sharp stick and let's toast them in the fire before the embers die and it's time to sleep. Listen, there are two stories I can tell you. One is about a very, very bad little boy. The other is about a very, very good little boy. Which one do you want to hear? Don't bother answering that. I can read the answer in your eyes . . . .

I often think of my country-ham burglars as a metaphor for the city where I live. They were tasteful. They were reticent. They were discreet and conservative. They had a solid set of values. They knew that a country ham was more to be treasured and enjoyed than jewels or precious metals. Money is only money, but a good country ham is a dream. A country ham, in all its finished, tempting glory embodies a tradition and has a history, a story that was begun years before in a rural Kentucky smokehouse, and was brought into being by loving hands.

But isn't there also, in this episode, a metaphor for a writer's craft? I think so. It's in those dainty sprigs of parsley. We create a deception. We dissemble. We deal in artifice and decoration, in camouflage and disguise. We embroider and falsify and fantasize, but throughout we Write.

A writer writes; yet we weave crisp and leafy, delicate, and frangible tissues of lies.

Epilogue

CAREY:

MY RECONCILIATION WITH MY FATHER BEGAN IN EARNEST IN 1982, shortly after I graduated from New York University and started work at an architectural firm doing public relations and marketing. We agreed to meet at the Four Seasons and there I would have an opportunity to finally meet Ed. We had a great evening.

Since that evening dinner, I've visited Ed and my Dad numerous times in their Cincinnati home and New York apartment on Gramercy Park. Both have visited me and my wife, Lisa, in San Antonio, and we've enjoyed trips elsewhere together. I am pleased that I remain close to Ed and consider him a part of my family. And I will forever be grateful to him for taking care of my father for thirty-eight years and for being at my father's side at his passing.

After my father left in 1974, my life took twists and turns. I attended college in New Hampshire for two years studying, of all things, early childhood education—the third graders I student-taught thought I was great, but I was a terrible teacher. Leaving college, I worked at an elevator factory, a sporting goods store, an industrial film company in Los Angeles, a lumber company in Modesto, and an iron works until I decided to attend NYU and graduate with a journalism degree in 1980. After I landed a job with the architectural firm, I began studying real estate law, appraisal, and finance at NYU's Real Estate Institute, graduating with an advanced degree (now the equivalent of an MBA) in 1983. After that I worked for two years in commercial real estate at New York Life in

Manhattan, eventually going on to another real estate company, which transferred me to San Antonio, Texas, where I married my first wife and had my daughter, Caitlin in 1989.

Today, I refer to myself as a serial entrepreneur. Like my father, I've always had difficulty conscripting myself to the corporate world and continue to endeavor to make it on my own. I've started several companies with as many successes as failures. My father and Ed even invested in one of my companies, an automated test equipment business, and unfortunately lost their investment. My father never let me forget it, thinking, I believe, that his investment somehow enriched me personally rather than enhancing the business's capital. Despite my explaining to him that I had lost five times as much as he lost, my explanations fell on deaf ears. He took every opportunity to remind me of his loss in the ensuing years.

I was fortunate that Ed contacted me just two weeks before my father died in 2015, and I visited both in Cincinnati. My father was confused as to the reason I was there, thinking perhaps I was there for a handout. I spent two or three days with Ed and my Dad, after which Ed took him to Gramercy Park, where he stayed by my father's side until November 15.

In April 2019 I met Ed in New York and sprinkled a small amount of my father's cremated remains in the Gramercy Park garden, under the dark of night. In July Ed installed a commemorative bench with my father's name in Gramercy Park in memory of my father, a man of acerbic wit, vast intelligence, and a dedication to his craft. A writer writes.

Appendix 1

Unguarded Moments:
Some Memories of Some Noted People

By Stephen Birmingham

PREFACE

WHEN I LIVED IN NEW YORK'S WESTCHESTER COUNTY, ONE OF MY favorite neighbors was the poet and essayist Phyllis McGinley. On Sundays, Phyllis and I used to help each other out with the *New York Times* crossword puzzle. Actually, it was usually I who phoned Phyllis for an answer, rather than the other way around. She was a somewhat more adept puzzler than I.

We also, as telephone buddies, had little games that we would play. One was to compose lists. One was a list of Overrated Famous People. On that list went such literary luminaries as Brendan Gill, Gloria Steinem, and Susan Sontag. We considered adding Rosa Parks to the list. ("After all, all she ever did was sit there.") I wanted to add Shakespeare to the list. Shakespeare wrote only one good play, I argued—*Julius Caesar*. *Hamlet*, as a piece of theater, is a total mess.

Macbeth—as anyone who has ever tried it will attest—is almost impossible to stage. As for some of the Bard's other works—*Titus Andronicus*, *Coriolanus*, *Cymbeline*, *Pericles*—there's a reason why these gems are rarely produced.

But I was voted down. Phyllis argued that we should stick to people who were roughly our contemporaries.

We also made a list of Worthwhile Famous People whom we had met. "Remember," Phyllis used to say, "there are only about thirty people in the world, at any given time, who are worth knowing. And, before you're through, you will probably meet them all." One summer afternoon, a number of years ago, I thought I had come up with a good candidate. My telephone rang, and a man's voice said, "Mr. Birmingham? This is Charles Lindbergh." I almost said, "Sure, and I'm the King of Siam." Then I realized that this was indeed Colonel Lindbergh. It was because, some months earlier, as part of my research for my biography of the novelist John P. Marquand, I had sent out more or less form letters to people who had known Marquand. Marquand's second wife, Adelaide, and Lindbergh had both been active in a pre–World War II organization that called itself the America First Committee. The America Firsters argued that the United States should stay out of the war, that we should let Hitler have Europe, if that was what he wanted, on the condition that he leave America alone. Of course, after Pearl Harbor, the America Firsters no longer had any platform, and the organization collapsed of its own weight.

Some people had responded to my letters. Some had not. I hadn't really expected Lindbergh to respond, but now he was responding. "My wife and I are hoping that you could have dinner with us tomorrow night at the Colony Club," he said. Of course, I said yes.

"Can Lindbergh go on my list of Worthwhile Famous People?" I asked Phyllis the next time we talked.

"No," she said flatly. "He goes on the overrated list."

"But Phyllis," I said, "back in the 1920s, Charles Lindbergh was easily the most famous man in the world. He was a great American hero."

"All heroes," said Phyllis, "are horses' asses."

I was thinking the other day about Phyllis's comment about the thirty famous people I would encounter before I was through. I have, I realized, crossed paths with a number of newsworthy people. I started counting, and I made a list. I didn't make it to thirty names, but I did come up with more than twenty-five, which seems close enough.

Some of these people—the Queen of England, for example—I met by sheerest accident, or luck, by happening to be in the same place that a famous person was, and at the same time. Others I met through my work, as a writer. Starting out—with a wife, a house with a mortgage, and three small children—I did a lot of magazine work. Some magazine assignments excited me, but others really didn't, and I accepted them anyway because magazines paid good money in those days. Quite often, these assignments involved interviewing celebrities (would I do a piece on Raquel Welch? I would!). As always, the writer's trick with a celebrity was to try to catch that person in an unguarded moment, which will reveal something about that person that readers have not read about dozens of times in dozens of other publications before.

Sometimes I succeeded in capturing unguarded moments, and other times I did not. And so here, instead of providing a compendium of Big Names, I have tried to provide a few more intimate revelations, glimpses I have stumbled upon or perhaps even induced when getting to meet some of the rich and famous.

And, out of deference to my old friend Phyllis, I have had nothing to say about my bland and unrevealing dinner with Charles and Anne Lindbergh, other than that we all had the salmon croquettes.

Oh, and one other small observation. When we entered the dining room of the Colony—a toney women's club in Manhattan—Anne Lindbergh said to the captain, "A reservation for Lindbergh."

The captain said, "How do you spell that?"

Sic transit gloria.

S.B.

May 2013

HER MAJESTY THE QUEEN

In 1949, in the summer of my junior year at Williams College, I'd applied for enrollment in an exchange-student program sponsored by the Institute of International Education, a project funded by the Rockefeller Foundation. I'd been accepted in the program and set off to England aboard the original *Queen Elizabeth*, recently demobilized from service as a military transport vessel. In England, I was scheduled to take courses in English literature at University College, Oxford. There were about a dozen of us, from different American colleges, in my group.

For us, in 1949, World War II had become little more than a distant memory. We were all too young to have been touched by it directly. But in England, the terrible reminders of war were everywhere. In London, though the rubble had been cleaned up, whole sections of the city were bombed-out shells. The great dome of St. Paul's Cathedral still bore a gaping hole. Rationing, far more draconian than anything we had had to endure in the United States, was still in effect, and strictly enforced.

Oxford, on the other hand, had suffered relatively little war damage. And University College, a time-blackened eminence on the city's main street, the High, appeared to have changed little since the reign of Edgar the Peaceful. Situated in a quadrangle of eleventh-century stone buildings, surrounding a grassy courtyard, our rooms were large but unheated. Heat could be obtained from a fireplace that required cannel coal, which was expensive if you could find it, or from a gas ring on the window ledge that took a sixpence coin to provide fifteen minutes of flame for warming up a teakettle.

The communal toilet (we were all males at University) was an evil-smelling stone structure located about a quarter of a mile from the main quadrangle. (At night, this distance was, naturally, unlighted.) Our rooms were supplied with chamber pots but, for most occasions, an open window was usually the most convenient convenience.

Each entry on the quad—there was one at each of the four corners—had its own basement bathroom, and the bathroom, as the word implied, was for bathing only. In each of these damp and cavernous spaces stood three or four enormous bathtubs. If you wanted to take a bath, you put on your robe, took your skinny sliver of soap (all that was supplied), descended a dark flight of cellar stairs, and notified your "scout" of your plans. Each entry had a scout—sort of a male scullery maid—and the scout would appear with main pails of scalding water (heated elsewhere on the premises) that it took to fill each giant tub. Since scouts expected tips for such services, we learned to bathe only when absolutely necessary.

England, in 1949, provided a lesson in how to do without. Chocolate, for instance, was almost impossible to find—a particular hardship for most Englishmen, who could easily devour a pound of Cadbury's opera creams in the course of a matinee. Households were restricted to something like one egg per week.

Meals in the University College dining hall—a vaulted, medieval chamber dimly lit by tiny light bulbs from chandeliers high above—were something of a gustatory challenge to us spoiled American kids. It had been a good year for the British cabbage crop, we decided, since boiled cabbage was most often the featured entree of the dinner menu. The sea had also offered up a good haul of a flatfish called plaice. Plaice were related to flounder, I decided, because when one first appeared at dinner, I saw both its eyes were on the same side of its head, as it gazed, balefully and accusingly, up at me from my plate.

But we learned little tricks. In a tearoom, a pot of hot water, poured into a teacup with some bottled catsup from the table, made a very presentable cup of tomato soup.

And, in spite of the exigencies of English college life, all of us managed to have a wonderful time at Oxford. None of us had any money to speak of. My spending allowance, as I recall, was $10 per week. We did some studying. We went to lectures from time to time. My roommate's name was Parker Handy, a jolly ex-Marine and then an undergraduate at Brown. Parker and I spent many a bibulous evening at one or another of the local pubs. We became skillful at scaling the College's daunting stone walls after the College locked up for the night at eleven p.m.

We took dates out for punting on the Isis (actually the Thames, though whimsically renamed when it passes through Oxfordshire). We saw everything, went everywhere. Like much else, petrol was rationed, but we didn't care since we didn't have a car. Instead, we had bikes. These we "borrowed" from the bike racks behind the college. The only rule was that you had to return the bike to its proper owner's slot at the end of the day (most of the bike owners were off for their summer holidays). We also took frequent trips, by train, down to London to enjoy the pleasures there.

That particular Saturday afternoon, Parker and I had gone to London to meet a couple of Smith girls we knew who were coming into Victoria Station on the boat train from Paris. The Smith girls, all about to enter their senior year, were doing what all properly bred young ladies were expected to do in those days—making the Grand Tour of Europe. Since college girls were expected to become engaged immediately after graduation, if not a few weeks before, the Grand Tour was intended to supply these young women with enough culture and conversation from visiting castles, cathedrals museums and historic sites—to amuse and entertain, if they were lucky, the young men who would soon become their husbands.

The Smith group's highly organized itinerary was called The Marsh Tour. Our little joke: "How's the Marsh Tour coming along? It's gotten bogged down" was the answer.

That afternoon, our train delivered us to London a little early. The train from Paris was not due in Victoria for another two hours, giving us time to kill. The National Gallery had mounted a much-talked-about exhibit of Viennese tapestries, so we decided to take that in.

A word about how we were dressed. We both had a two-day growth of beard. That was part of the fashion of the times. I was wearing a T-shirt that had Beta Theta Pi emblazoned across the front of it. Jeans were not yet de rigueur, but we both wore un-ironed khaki pants, which were. And we were both wearing what men's college chic demanded, white buck shoes with heavy red rubber soles. But those white bucks were supposed to be—as ours were—thoroughly scuffed and soiled.

In other words, Parker Handy and I were walking examples of perfect 1940s American college frat house couture. Only a prude would have suggested that we were inappropriately clad for a visit to London's stately National Gallery of Art.

As we made our way along one particularly narrow corridor of the exhibit, admiring the elaborate stitcheries of Imperial Vienna, I became aware of a small party of a man and two women who were heading toward us from the opposite direction. It was clear that one woman was leading this expedition, since she was moving slightly ahead of the other two. She was short and plump, and all in beige. Her shoes were beige, and her dress was beige, sparkly with what I believe are called bugle beads. Her outfit was topped with a somewhat rakish, off-the-face beige hat decorated with just a whiff of beige veiling. Something about the lady looked familiar to me, and I suddenly realized who she was.

"My God," I whispered to Parker. "It's the Queen!"

This was Her Royal Majesty, Queen Elizabeth of England, mother of the present Queen.

"What should we do?" I said to Parker.

"Absolutely nothing," he hissed. "Stand very still and pretend to be looking awfully hard at the tapestry. Don't show any sign of recognition and let them pass behind us."

I did as I was told, as the Queen approached us on a collision course.

I stood rigidly staring at the wall until Her Majesty was just behind us, and I heard her say, "Are you Americans?"

We both turned now, and, mutely, nodded. "Are you having a pleasant stay in England?" Once again, we both nodded yes.

She held out one beige-gloved hand.

I had read somewhere that no one is supposed to touch Royalty, but when Royalty offers you its hand, surely it would be the height of rudeness to refuse it. I took the beige-gloved fingertips in my own. There was the slightest squeeze.

Suddenly, for some reason, when she lifted her hand, I became aware of her scent. At that moment, I thought it was gardenia, but I have never been good at identifying fragrances. It could have been lilac, or vetiver or roses or lavender or lotus or cinnamon or apple blossom, or some concoction of all these created just for the Royal Patent by some New Bond Street perfumer. But I remember thinking, how strange that no one has ever written about how wonderfully the Queen of England smells!

"I'm afraid we're still not looking our best here in London," she said. "Still a bit tattered from the war. But we're getting back to our old self. I hope you'll continue to have a pleasant stay in our country." She tilted her head and gave me a twinkly smile.

"Thank you very much, your . . ." And I couldn't think what I was to call her. Your Majesty? Your Highness? Your Excellency?

"Thank you very much your Queen," I said.

(When I told a waggish friend this story, he said, "She might have answered, 'Not at all—your trump!'")

My mother, when I wrote her of my gaffe, was indignant. "I though you knew better," she wrote back. "You're not a British subject, so you don't call her 'your' anything. The proper term of address for you is 'Ma'am.'"

Our encounter with the Queen that summer afternoon solved a problem that had been nagging at Parker Handy and me for several weeks. We'd both received invitations to the Royal Garden Party, which was to take place in about ten days.

The invitations came about due to what turned out to be my friend's important family connections. His father, Truman P. Handy, was at the time head of the European Economic Commission in Paris. Parker's mother, when she came to visit us, brought us bottles of Scotch whisky and cartons of American cigarettes in the diplomatic pouch. Mrs. Truman Handy herself was an important interior decorator in New York. Though not as well known as the likes of Syrie Maugham or Lady Mendl, or even Sister Parish, she had many socially prominent clients.

She was a Douglas—Parker's full name was Parker Douglas Handy—and one cousin was Lewis Douglas, formerly US Ambassador to the Court of St. James, the father of Sharman Douglas, Princess Margaret's best friend.

To us, the invitations had come as a complete surprise. But they were not to be taken lightly. Gentlemen were expected to wear tall, gray silk top hats, striped trousers, tailcoats, gray silk ascots, and other formal odds and ends. We'd already made inquiries of a London tailor, who had agreed to rent us the necessary accoutrements for the occasion—at enormous expense.

We'd known all along that we couldn't afford to attend the Royal Garden Party, and meeting the Queen clinched it. We sent our regrets. Because what if we'd gone and had been invited into the Royal Enclosure—a remote possibility, of course, but still a possibility—to be presented to Their Majesties—and what if the Queen had cried out: "I remember you! You're the two galoots from the National Gallery who called me 'Your Queen!'"

It probably wouldn't have happened, but it might have. Who knew? Why takes a chance? And it gave us an excuse to decline the invitation.

And it left me with a haunting memory of Her Royal Majesty's perfume.

DAVID SMITH

In the spring of 1969, one of the major cultural events in New York City was the retrospective one-man showing of the works of sculptor David Smith, at the Guggenheim Museum. Crowds lined Fifth Avenue to buy tickets for the show, and continued down side streets for the show's March-to-May run. David Smith's national reputation had been growing over the previous several years. He worked almost exclusively with metals, and his success had enabled him to create massive objects, some of them with rare or precious metals, including sterling silver. His fame had then been spiked by his sudden death, in his forties, in an automobile crash in upstate New York, near his home in Bolton Landing. As always happens when an artist dies, the prices for his work—since there will be no more of it—shot sharply upward.

It was more than twenty years before the much-publicized Guggenheim opening—another summer while I was still a student at Williams—when I met David Smith. A classmate, Ford Wright, had invited me to spend the month of August at his family's cottage on Lake George. With the invitation came a bright red Ford convertible, and a gleaming mahogany sixteen-foot Chris-Craft cruiser. Who could turn down an invitation like that?[21]

But being a guest for a month is a long time, and so is being a host. Ford and I had lots of fun. There was swimming in the lake, and water skiing and aquaplaning from the Chris-Craft. There were parties and dances and tennis at the Lake George Club. But life among the idle rich had begun to be a little boring by the end of the first week, and we were both casting about for something a little different to do. In a barn in the nearby village, a troupe of young New York actors was barely making ends meet with a summer stock company that called itself the Bolton Landing Players. We dropped by their barn to see if we could do something to help them out—paint scenery, perhaps.

To our astonishment, we were both immediately cast in a play they were currently rehearsing. It was the George Kaufman classic *George Washington Slept Here*. I was even given a line. I came on briefly in the second act to say something like, "Tennis, anyone?" except that I remember I had to carry a pair of ice skates for my entrance.

We'd only been at our new career for a day or so when an invitation drifted in for the entire company. A young sculptor named David Smith and his wife would like us all for dinner Sunday night, when our theater was dark. I suppose the Smiths though the Bolton Landing Players were starving artists like themselves and would appreciate an evening out. It would be very casual, and BYOB.

One of the young women in the cast would, several years later, turn out to be the woman I married—but that's another story.

Nobody'd ever heard of a sculptor name David Smith, and it seemed like a very forgettable name.

The Smiths lived in a tiny shack on a hill high above the lake. It was indeed a shack, just one room, and the Smiths' bed was in one corner. There was no electricity, and lighting was by candles and kerosene lamps. There was no running water, David Smith cheerfully informed us, so if we needed the facilities, we should just wander off into the woods and find a tree. (What the Smiths did for more serious bathroom matters, I could only imagine.)

David Smith was a big-boned, hearty young man with a great bushy beard. His wife, also an artist, was a tiny woman full of quick, merry outbursts and bright enthusiasms. The dinner she had prepared was her own special recipe for a tossed chicken salad, and she served it in a large wheelbarrow. It was the same wheelbarrow, she explained, in which she and her husband took their baths.

After a certain amount of wine had been drunk by everybody, the Smiths revealed that they were Communists. In those days, to us, being a Communist was just an odd, interesting fact. This was long before the rantings of Senator Joe McCarthy and the Un-American Activities Committee. No one talked of a Red Menace or an Evil Empire. The news that one was a Communist elicited the same reaction that might come if friend had announced that he had become a Vedantist or a Jehovah's Witness.

And I got the impression that the Smiths' commitment to Marxism was not all that strong, as we all joined in lustily to such songs as "Meadowlands" and "The Peat Bog Soldiers."

As the evening progressed, David Smith invited me to visit his forge. This was housed in another shanty, a few hundred yards down the hill. In it were the trappings of an old-fashioned blacksmith's shop, an anvil, sledges, wedges, hammers, tongs, a blowtorch, and an acetylene flame helmet. Outside, in a good-sized pile, were what Smith told me were his "rejects"—pieces that were unfinished and abandoned, or that had not worked out to his satisfaction. "Take any of this stuff you want," he said. "I'm done with it. It's yours."

The pieces in the reject pile were interesting representations of shapes and bodies, but most were large and, when I tried to lift one, very heavy. It would take two strong men to carry one of these abstractions away. I couldn't imagine how one would fit in the back seat of the red convertible, or in my dormitory room at college, much less in my own small bedroom in my parents' small house in rural Connecticut.

I said, "Thanks a lot, David. But, really, no thanks."

Of course, I realize today that even a David Smith reject would have brought enough to send a son through Yale.

Years pass. The calendar pages fly off in the wind, as the seasons change from the snows of winter to the blossoms of spring, the way they used to do in old movies. It is years later, at least ten—make it 1959. I am working in New York City, and living in the suburbs, with a wife, three small children, and a house with a mortgage. Owning art is not our first priority.

A friend of ours at the time was going through an unpleasant divorce, if that is not a tautology. Her husband was being mean about money, and his lawyers were being even meaner. She had decided to pull up stakes, sell everything she owned, and move to Paris, where she planned to start life anew. One of the things she wanted to sell was a David Smith bronze head. She wanted $500 for it.

Over the years, David Smith and his works had become better known, though he was still not nationally famous. His work had been acquired by several important collections, and a few museums, including New York's Museum of Modern Art.

Our friend offered to let us borrow the head for a few days, to see how we liked it. It sat on our living room coffee table for about a week.

It was roughly the size of a human head, and full of angles and shadows, depths, and mysteries. We liked it a lot, and it had a certain resonance for us both, recalling that evening at the artist's shanty and forge at Bolton Landing. But, in 1959, $500 seemed like a lot of money. It certainly did for us. Yes, we could have afforded it, but the price would have put a serious dent in our budget, which, we decided, should really be allotted for other, more essential items. Reluctantly, we sent the head back. And we soon lost track of our friend.

Move forward again in time—another ten years. It is the spring of 1969, the opening of the David Smith retrospective exhibit at the Guggenheim. The show had something of an air of a memorial service, since Smith had died at a tragically young age not long before. I moved down the whirligig ramp that circles the Guggenheim's interior. Larger pieces—some of them monumental size—filled the main floor, and the museum's principal exhibit space. Smaller pieces were displayed in niches along the descending ramp. About halfway down, there—sure enough!— was "my" head, on loan, its label read, from an anonymous collector. It was all I could do to keep myself from reaching into the niche, grabbing the bronze head, and crying, "This is *mine!*"

Instead, I gazed at it for a long time, filled with that bittersweet feeling, a mixture of rue and wonder that accompanies the acknowledgment of lost chances.

JACKIE BOUVIER

One more Williams College memory.

We called it "mono," short for mononucleosis, the so-called "kissing disease" that seemed to infect every college student in those days, at one time or another.

I don't know whether mono is still the campus scourge it once was.

Medical science has doubtless come up with some preventative or cure, but in those days, it was practically endemic in the Ivy League. And when it struck, its attack was vicious. Its symptoms were fever, violent headache, nausea, ague, and a whole catalog of related unpleasantness, and its victims usually had to be hospitalized. The only plus side to this ailment was that it rarely lasted more than forty-eight hours, and once it had made its way through the collegiate bodily system, it hardly ever recurred.

At Williams, meanwhile, the principal social event of the college year was the winter house party weekend. A fraternity brother of mine, whom I'll call Art, had been planning to attend this event, and had invited a date from nearby Vassar named Jackie Bouvier. Then, at virtually the last minute, Art had been laid low by mono. From his college infirmary bed Art asked me if I would pinch-hit for him with Jackie, at least for the first day of the weekend until, presumably, he would be back on his feet. I agreed and took off to meet Jackie at the Greyhound from Poughkeepsie.

I had no trouble recognizing her. She was, after all, already sort of famous. Her photograph had been in *Life* magazine, and the society gossipist Igor Cassini, who wrote under the name Cholly Knickerbocker, had named her Queen Deb of the Year.

At eighteen or so, Jackie was not by any means what I would call beautiful, as in later life she almost became. She still carried a bit of baby fat, and her arms and hands were a little chubby, with that small, bunched business around the chin that young girls often have. Her eyes were a little too far apart, her nose was almost nonexistent, and her hair was short and tightly curly. (Later, I suspect, she used a straightener.)

Since this was a girl who would become an icon of American high fashion, I often wish I could remember what she was wearing when we met, but I cannot. I do remember that every eastern college girl at the time had to own a shorty sheared-beaver jacket, and penny loafers were the required footwear. So, let's assume that was what she was wearing.

I also remember that Jackie did not seem at all pleased to see me. She had clearly not perfected her radiant, almost feral smile that almost always appeared when there were photographers, later on. In fact, the expression on her face when we were together was closer to a pout.

These arrangements, after all, had been very last minute, and this was obviously not a girl who was accustomed to blind dates. This one, in fact, may have been a first for her, and if I was going to be the stand-in for her regular escort, she was patently unhappy with the substitution.

So, what do you do with a girl on an early Friday afternoon when you're stuck with her for God only knows how long? You take her to the movies. Or at least that's what I did.

Once we were comfortably in our seats, Jackie immediately lighted a cigarette. In those days, movie theaters had smoking sections, either in the back few rows or in an upstairs balcony. The little Williamstown theater had no such provision for smokers, but there were only a handful of others in the audience, and no attendant to admonish us, so I decided to let the situation ride. And now, with bags of butter-pop on our respective laps, and the credits for the show rolling, I placed my arm very casually across her shoulders.

The adverb "casually" is important here. In my day, way back when, the arm across the shoulders was an entirely casual thing. It was a gesture of companionship, of palship. It was not to be considered an invitation to romance. Brothers and sisters watched films this way, for crying out loud, as did children and their parents. All it meant was, "Hey, good buddy, let's enjoy this movie together."

Put another way, if I had been trying to put the make on a fraternity brother's girlfriend, that would have been considered a cardinal sin. I would have been disciplined, probably forever ostracized by my fraternity brothers, if not kicked out of the house for good and all. If I had put my hand on Jackie's knee, of course, that would have been quite another matter.

In any event, what happened was that Jackie quietly reached back, removed my hand from her shoulder, and placed it on the armrest of my seat. I don't remember what happened in the movie after that.

That evening there were cocktail parties at various fraternity houses, and we had been invited to several of these. At each of these, Jackie seemed most interested in who else was there. "Is the president of your class here? Is the captain of the football team here?" In my class—as in everyone's class, I imagine—there was one man who stood out wherever he went. Tall, blond, and blue-eyed, he was movie-star handsome. He had the physique of a young Greek god and was a star in every athletic endeavor he undertook, the classic golden youth. When he entered a room, men and women alike drew in their breath, and stared. That night, this young Adonis suddenly appeared at one of the crowded cocktail parties we attended. "Is that man a friend of yours?" Jackie wanted to know.

Alas, he was not. I'm sure he didn't even know my name, and so there was no way I could introduce her to him. She was obviously disappointed. I introduced her to the manager of WMS, the college radio station. She was unimpressed.

(After college, Adonis's career was what you might expect. He went, under full sail, to Wall Street to join one of the prominent white-shoe firms, where he became an alcoholic and a suicide at thirty-four.)

The next day, Saturday, was the Big Day of the college weekend. There was a football game in the afternoon, and a big, black-tie ball in the evening in the college gym. Fortunately for me, my friend Art was discharged from the infirmary that morning and could take over the task of entertaining Jackie Bouvier. My responsibilities were over. I wish I could say that Jackie flung herself into Art's arms when he appeared, but, if anything, she seemed pouty with him as well.

Perhaps she was cross at him for having been palmed off on me. In any case, I saw little of her for the rest of the weekend.

And I'm afraid that whole weekend was a total loss for all of us involved. When a girl has been nominated Deb Queen of the Year, I'm sure she has a very heavy social schedule and can hardly keep her dates straight or remember where she has been from night to night or when she had been there or with whom. In any event, when asked about it years later, Jacqueline Bouvier Kennedy Onassis said, "I don't recall ever going to any parties at Williams College."

I remember reading somewhere that, when asked to reveal her life's ambition, she wrote in her boarding-school yearbook at Miss Porter's School, "To be queen of the circus, and marry the man on the flying trapeze."

She certainly fulfilled that prophecy and married the man on the flying trapeze not only once, but twice.

JEAN KERR

My first job after graduating from college was as a copywriter for a mid-size advertising agency in New York, where the account I was to work on was called *Ladies' Home Journal* Advertising Promotion. "Advertising Promotion" meant just that—we were trying to promote advertising in that venerable women's magazine that had been going strong since before your grandma's day, and only recently has finally faded from existence. We were after specific categories of advertising. For instance, at the time the *New Yorker* was considered an excellent medium for automotive advertisers. We argued that, while the man of the house might choose the make of the car, it was usually the woman who decided on the model, color, and accessories of the family automobile. In the macho confines of the Detroit Athletic Club, any auto exec who suggested buying an ad in a woman's magazine was suspected of having dubious sexual tendencies. Our advertising for the *Journal* was out to try to change all that. Our slogan was "Never Underestimate the Power of a Woman."

One of my campaigns to sell ad space in the *Journal* involved getting testimonials from prominent American women—in business, government, and the arts—who would speak glowingly of how the *Journal* had affected their lives and, of course, by implication, their spending habits. These testimonials then appeared in full-page ads in the *New York Times* and other publications across the country. Naturally, these women were paid for their testimonials. In 1958, one of the women we chose was Jean Kerr.

Prior to that year, Jean Kerr, had been known primarily as the wife of Walter Kerr, the chief drama critic for the *New York Times*. (I will have more to say about Walter Kerr later on.) But she had also published a number of short humor pieces for magazines like *Vogue* and *Saturday Evening Post*, most of which had been about the comic rigors of being married to a famous theater critic. These pieces had then been collected in a slender volume called *Please Don't Eat the Daisies*, which—to the astonishment of everyone in the publishing world—had become a huge best seller. *Please Don't Eat the Daisies* now topped every nonfiction best seller list in America. Hollywood had bought the title for an outrageous sum, and in New York a television series was in the making. Jean Kerr was rich, famous, and an ideal celebrity for one of my ads.

My wife and I knew the Kerrs in a casual sort of way. They'd been to dinner at our house, and we'd had dinner at theirs, just down the road in Larchmont, where they lived in a big, weird Charles Addams-ish house on Long Island Sound. The house had a clock tower that contained an electric carillon that played the duet from *Carmen* every day at noon—among its other oddities.

Like other friends of theirs, we'd speculated about what the Kerrs' marriage must be like now that Jean had leapt to stardom. As top drama critic for the *Times*—which made him unquestionably the top critic in the country—Walter certainly made good money. But now that his wife's earnings easily eclipsed his own, how was Walter taking it? Well, the answer seemed to be: Just fine. The Kerrs, who'd been college sweethearts, seemed to be a genuinely happy married couple, with many attractive and well-mannered children to prove it, despite all the fuss over *Daisies*.

Jean Kerr, meanwhile, was a rather odd-looking woman, in the fact that her face didn't go with the rest of her. She had a very pretty youthful face—the face of a young Irish colleen, I always thought. But from the neck down—well, she was a large woman, not fat, exactly, but with a build that might be described as Junoesque. Her face was sweet and innocent looking, but her body was almost intimidating. I'd heard that Mrs. Kerr had a temper, and though I'd never seen examples of it, I could believe it.

She and I worked on her testimonial copy over a couple of afternoons at her house, and it was a thoroughly happy experience. Almost all of the words were her own, though there were a few copy points I needed to insert. (After all, an ad is simply an attempt to sell something.) When it was done, everyone was pleased with the result, including—most important—the client, based in Philadelphia where the *Journal* was published.

All that remained was the sometimes-sticky matter of Mrs. Kerr's compensation.

Jean telephoned me to say that her accountant had advised her not to receive any more money in that calendar year. To do so would push her into an even higher tax bracket than the one she was in already, meaning that anything we paid her would go to the IRS. He suggested that she take some other form of payment. She said, "How about a mink coat?" We said fine, and that seemed to make everything clear sailing.

But when the client started pricing mink coats, it turned out that a decent full-length mink would cost at least $10,000, and that was more than the *Journal's* budget would take. Would Mrs. Kerr consider a mink jacket? She said fine. In the end, the most mink that the budget could handle was called a capelet—a sleeveless, over-the-shoulder fur piece that fastened at the throat and extended to about elbow length. Jean said she would be happy with that.

It was decided that I should make the presentation of the piece. And Dick Ziesing, the *Journal's* executive publisher, who wanted to meet the famous authoress, was to come with me. We drove to Larchmont together.

When she opened the box, and unfolded the layer of tissue paper, she squealed with delight and buried her face in the lustrous, black skins. "It's beautiful," she cried. She jumped to her feet and tossed the capelet over her shoulders. She began dancing around the room, nuzzling the fur as she went. "I love it, I love it, I love it!" she sang. "And I not only love it to pieces, I really *like* it. Oh, thank you so much, oh it's so beautiful. It's the most beautiful thing I've ever seen! Where did you find it?"

"Some little kike furrier on Seventh Avenue," said Dick Ziesing.

All at once there was, as we say, fire in Jean Kerr's eye. She snatched the fur from her shoulders, flung it at Dick Ziesing, catching him with it in his face.

"Take it back!" she almost shouted. "Take it back and get out of my house! Get out! Get out! *Now.*"

We hurried toward the door, Dick clutching the capelet. As I said, Jean Kerr was a large woman, and this was a large, terribly angry woman. We opened the front door as quickly as we could, and just as quickly she reached out and snatched the capelet. "I'll take that," she said, and slammed the door in our faces.

We drove back to Manhattan, red-faced and in silence. Never underestimate the power of a woman.

ANDY WARHOL

Andy Warhol had a singular ability. He could *materialize*.

I mean, you could be standing in a room with other people standing all around, and suddenly—out of nowhere—there was Andy Warhol, standing silently beside you. He had come in through no doorway, stepped off no elevator. He was just *there*. He was able to de-materialize just as magically. One minute, you were in his presence, and the next minute you weren't. He had disappeared, vanished just as quickly and mysteriously as Banquo's Ghost.

To be sure, Warhol's physical appearance helped create the impression that this was a specter, not a living, breathing human being. If he had not been born exactly handsome, it always seemed to me that he did his best to be almost defiantly ugly as a grown man. His acne-scarred face had a kind of prison pallor, and his clothes hung on his skinny frame as though he found them in a dumpster. He favored snow-white fright wigs combed in shaggy styles that would have defied the most creative hairdresser. In other words, since he had learned how to come and go like a phantom, he had evidently decided to look like one as well.

I'd been assigned by a magazine to do a story on the Warhol phenomenon, and I was spending afternoons at what he called his "Factory," then on Union Square in Lower Manhattan. It was a factory, however, that produced no goods, as far as I could tell. A number of people could usually be found lounging about this drafty, loft-like space. Now and then they spoke with one another, but mostly they seemed to loll. Some of these people were what Andy called his "superstars," but others seemed just on-hangers who hung out there, awaiting the appearance of the Master, and to do his bidding, whatever that might be. Mothlike they fluttered around his flame, as he faded in and faded out.

These folks consisted of an odd mixture of slumming *Social Register* types, East Village hippies, and Eurotrash. Some had actually starred in Warhol films.

Though rarely there all at the same time, some of the Warhol camp-followers I spoke with were Joe Dallesandro, Monique van Vooren, Francine LeFrak, Candy Darling, Baby Jane Holzer, Loulou de la Falaise, Edie Sedgwick, and Honeychile Hohenlohe—all of whom seemed to have committed their lives to Warhol's genius. Andy seemed to have been drawn to them by their exotic names.

Somehow, I had expected Andy Warhol's factory to be awash with drugs and sex. If drugs were being used there—and I can only assume they were—they were not used while I was around. The factory's personnel seemed too self-absorbed to be interested in any outside stimuli from controlled substances. As for sex, the factory's atmosphere was almost monastic, and it all seemed to emanate from the Grand Lama himself. I'd heard that he was gay, but he projected such an aura of asexuality that it was hard to imagine Andy Warhol cuddling with anything.

To me, Andy's genius seemed as elusive as his presence, which was now-you-see-me-now-you-don't. On most days, he carried with him a small Polaroid camera, and, when he materialized in a room, he glided about randomly taking pictures of this and that. When I tried to ask him a question, he would impishly turn and point the camera at me, snap my picture and then hand me the developing print. Needless to say, interviewing Andy Warhol was no walk in the park.

An important member of the Warhol coterie, I discovered, was a young man named Bob Colacello. Colacello, it seemed, played a major role in the writing and publication of *Interview*, a magazine that was periodically turned out by Warhol's factory, and that was gaining a certain respect in the New York literary underground.

"I know Andy doesn't like to talk much," Colacello said to me one afternoon.

Yes, I said. I noticed that.

"And I know you need some quotes from him for your article," he said. Yes, I admitted. That would be nice.

"Well," he said. "Just ask me any questions you have for Andy, and anything I say you can say came from Andy. It'll be that simple. We do that with journalists all the time."

"In other words," I said, "stuff I've heard that Andy said is really stuff that *you* said?"

"It's just that we think alike, and sometimes I can phrase things better than he can."

"What about that famous Warhol quote?" I asked. "Something about everybody being famous for fifteen minutes. Did he say that, or did you?"

He smiled. "I honestly don't remember," he said.

I didn't say that Bob Colacello seemed to have made himself into a sort of ventriloquist's dummy. Or that the kind of journalistic sleight of hand that he was recommending could be considered journalistic laziness, if not downright journalistic dishonesty.

After all, readers of my story might be expected to want to know what the great artist had to say, not what somebody named Bob Colacello had to say while pretending to be Andy Warhol. But in the end, I decided to compromise a bit. Most of the quotes I gathered were from the various Warhol groupies, with a few Colacello/Warhol comments thrown in for balance. The result I cannot claim to have been my best writing effort, to say the least. In fact, I can't remember the name of the magazine that published it. But through it all, I couldn't help asking myself the question: Was the whole Andy Warhol phenomenon some sort of elaborate hoax, a well-planned, extremely profitable but essentially harmless put-on?

Certainly, it was part theater, part circus, with Andy as the ringmaster, silently waving the magic wand. Certainly, the Campbell's tomato soup cans and the Brillo boxes were fun, but they were also totally original images; no artist had ever done such things before and dared to call them art. But those images also made a wry comment on the commercialization of modern art in America. Legend has it that the soup cans were not even Warhol's original idea but came from a friend. Nevertheless, it was Warhol who saw the brilliance of the idea, took it, and ran with it until, today, who can look at a tomato soup can and not think: Andy Warhol? Through some vision that was all his own, his name is now secure in the pantheon of great American artists of the twentieth century.

(After my story was published, I ran into Andy Warhol a couple of times. Once, at a large gathering, I was chatting with the sculptor Louise Nevelson and spotted Andy across the room. "There's Andy Warhol," I said. "Would you like to meet him?" "Oh, yes," she said. "Bring him over!" I crossed the room to Andy. "Would you like to meet Louise Nevelson?" I asked him. "Sure—bring her over," he said. They never did meet.)

Several months later, my wife and I were at a dinner party at Gloria Vanderbilt's house on the Upper East Side. Suddenly, without appearing to have entered through any normal doorway, there was Andy. My dinner partner on my right was old Mrs. William Woodward, mother-in-law of the infamous Ann Woodward, a former showgirl turned socialite, who had shot and killed her husband, shooting him many times, claiming she thought he was a burglar. What startled New York society at the time was the Woodwards stood stonily behind Ann's very fishy claim, and the scandal was quickly brushed under a North Shore Long Island rug.

At the Vanderbilt dinner party, meanwhile, I saw that Elsie Woodward had been given, as her right-hand dinner partner, Andy. So, he sat two places down from me and I was able to observe the two of them in animated conversation. Except it wasn't a conversation. It was more like a monologue, with Elsie Woodward doing all the talking.

This is something society ladies seem to have been taught to do from their mothers' knees: bright chitchat. I often wonder whether the famous "Misses" schools—Miss Chapin's, Miss Spence's, Miss Hewitt's, Miss Porter's, and Miss Madeira's—offered courses in Small Talk 101, because, by the time they graduate, these schools' alumnae are experts at it. It is talk that is gay and charming and intimate, about everything in general and nothing in particular, carefully well-mannered and usually flattering to the male sex, members of which society ladies will expect to be seated between at dinner parties such as the one I am describing, for the rest of their lives.

Out of the corner of my eye, I watched as Andy reacted to Elsie Woodward's bravura performance that evening as a bona fide New York society grande dame. At times, he smiled slightly; at other times he blinked. Sometimes, his pale eyes closed altogether, and he appeared to be asleep.

As the soup course was being removed, we noticed that our hostess had turned the conversation. Now Elsie Woodward turned to me. "Isn't Andy Warhol absolutely the most fascinating man?" she gushed. "So deep!"

Of course, as far as I could tell he had said or done absolutely nothing. But this, I thought, is part of the Warhol phenomenon, part of the

Warhol mystique, the Warhol genius, if you will. Not only could he conjure himself into being, and then simply evaporate when the show was over. He could also charm and fascinate an audience without lifting a finger or opening his mouth or moving his lips. He could do this with or without someone like Bob Colacello serving as his mouthpiece. It was an art. He had it.

ELIZABETH TAYLOR

I think no one will disagree that Elizabeth Taylor was one of the century's most beautiful women. But the thing that always struck me most about her beauty was that it was nontransferable. By "transferable" I mean that it didn't seem to transfer well from the motion picture screen to everyday life, where the great beauty became just another pretty face. I've been at a number of gatherings where Elizabeth was present, and someone has whispered, "Who's that girl?" Told who it was, people act surprised: "I never would have recognized her!"

Of course, this is really not surprising. Elizabeth had spent almost her entire life—from the time she was a little girl—working in front of cameras. She had learned how to use a camera, how to make it her friend and handmaiden, so that whenever she appeared in front of one, it would make her look her loveliest. She had learned, as a film star, the importance of lighting in film work. "In every scene in a movie," she once explained to me, "there's always a key light. If it's outdoors, using natural light, the key light is the sun. A performer has to know how to find that key light. I know I've found it when it just hits the tip of my nose."

If lighting and camera work helped create Elizabeth's beauty, Mother Nature had given her little help at all. She had a large, brown, flat birthmark that extended from her right chin to her upper throat. This never appeared in photographs and was easily covered with makeup, but to most women it would be considered a major beauty flaw. Then there was her figure. Though she always battled with weight, her silhouette, viewed from the side, was usually exemplary. But viewed straight on, she had no hips, or rather the silhouette of a boy, straight up and down. Also, since I first met Elizabeth in tropical Mexico where we were often in swimsuits, I couldn't help noticing that she had rather chunky legs. The cameras were never allowed to focus on any of these traits, needless to say.

It was in the winter of 1966. I was in Puerto Vallarta, doing a magazine piece, and she was there with Richard Burton, who was making a movie. The Burtons had not yet married (for what would be the first of two times) but were in the process of divorcing their respective spouses. Periodically, batteries of Hollywood lawyers, in suits with briefcases bulging with important legal documents, would appear at Elizabeth's and

Richard's rented villa high on a hillside overlooking the river, the village, and the sea. All this activity was considered very newsworthy, and Puerto Vallarta also teemed with reporters from the world press. (Burton and Taylor had just survived a steamy and well-publicized extramarital love affair on the set of *Cleopatra*, when it was being filmed in Rome.)

With Elizabeth was her daughter Liza Todd, who was then nine or ten, from an earlier marriage to producer Mike Todd. Somehow it had been decided that my friend Sam Hall and I should be the ones assigned to take the little Liza to the beach every day. (Sam's wife, the actress Grayson Hall, had a supporting part in the film. Sam Hall and I, both being writers, probably looked as though we had nothing better to do than beach-sit Liza.)

Actually, we enjoyed it. Sam and Grayson had a son, Matthew, who was about Liza's age, and we watched the children doing things children do at the beach, building sandcastles and swimming in the gentle surf of Banderas Bay. Liza Todd was a bright and pretty little girl, who had inherited her mother's spectacular eyes, as well as—unfortunately—her father's punishing jawline. We were surprised that, at her age, she had never learned the alphabet, and so we spent some time teaching her that with the familiar singsong rhyme.

We also became aware of something that was more disturbing. The principal beach at Vallarta was called *Los Muertos* ("The Dead," for some reason). And, at the time, it was one of the busiest social centers in the town, with a lively beachside bar, strolling vendors and mariachi bands, and white sands strewn with bronzed and baking bodies of tourists and townsfolk smelling of sunscreen and coco-locos. Elizabeth had brought with her an English couple who served her as butler and housekeeper, and who, by noon, could usually be found at the bar by the beach. There, they seemed to make quick friends among the tourists, who would buy them rum punches. A pattern emerged. After a few drinks, one or the other of the English couple would come over to where we were sitting, take little Liza by the hand, and say, "Come along, darling, there are some nice people over here that I want you to meet."

The tourist couple who had been buying the drinks would then pose for photos with Liza. (Once they were back home in Wilkes-Barre, they could put their color slides on the carousel and say, "And here we are on the beach with Elizabeth Taylor's daughter.")

Sam and I asked ourselves, Would Elizabeth really want her domestic staff selling pictures of her little girl for piña coladas? We realized that, with two nasty divorces brewing at home, Elizabeth already had a lot on her plate. So, we decided to bring the matter up with her secretary. Actually, Elizabeth's secretary had his own secretary, and so did Richard Burton's. These willowy young men, in spandex shirts and toreador pants, were virtually indistinguishable from one another, but we located one of them and described the situation to him. "No need to bother Elizabeth with this," we said. "Just so you know what's going on." He assured us he wouldn't tell his boss and would take care of the matter.

Of course, he immediately told Elizabeth, and her response was quick and decisive. "Liza can never swim at that beach again," she announced.

I could see her point, sort of. Good servants were hard to find, particularly in Mexico, particularly a couple, particularly an elegant butler with a plummy British accent who wore white gloves when he served drinks. Firing an English couple in a foreign country presented a number of travel- and visa-related problems. Elizabeth's solution was the quickest and easiest.

The only other beach in the area was a distant stretch of shoreline on the then-undeveloped north side of Banderas Bay. The beach was rocky and unswept, strewn with seaweed, plastic bottles, driftwood, and other pieces of flotsam that the tides had carried in. A tricky undertow and jellyfish made for unpleasant swimming, and naturally nobody went there. I don't think the children minded it much, but Sam Hall and I certainly did, as we tried to find comfortable places to spread a towel amid windrows of drying kelp. We soon were making excuses as to why we could no longer beach-sit Liza Todd.

Meanwhile, in the little winter colony of Puerto Vallarta, there was a great deal of speculation about how the about-to-be-newlyweds, Richard and Elizabeth, were getting along. Outwardly, at least, all seemed happy-happy, and there was a good deal of public romantic demonstrativeness—kissing, hugging, handholding and so forth. There were no hints of quarrels or even disagreements, and yet there were signs that this was not exactly going to be a marriage made in heaven.

Richard Burton was a very heavy drinker. When speaking of someone of Burton's celebrity and professional status, one does not use the word *alcoholic*. You might say that person "has a little drinking problem." In Richard's case, on nights when he had passed out at the bar and had to be carried to his car by waiters, the polite phrase was, "Richard has reached capacity." He reached capacity often.

One day at lunch, Elizabeth chirped brightly, "Richard and I had the most wonderful night last night!"

Our ears pricked up, thinking that we were about to learn about some new erotic diversion that the pair had come upon.

"Richard read to me from Shakespeare until four o'clock this morning!"

That was the other thing about Richard Burton. When he was drinking, he became verbose. He told wonderful tales about his growing-up years in Wales, and about characters he had encountered in his upward climb to stardom of the stage and screen—Sir Ralph Richardson, Alec Guinness, Laurence Olivier, and many more. He could also quote from memory many poets. He could recite all of Shakespeare's soliloquies, and many of the sonnets, and he could quote from Dylan Thomas, William Butler Yeats, Eliot, and Auden.

All this was very entertaining, up to a point. The trouble was that the more he drank the more he talked, or maybe it was the other way around. Once he had launched into one of his great verbal concertos, he became impossible to stop.

After all, he was Richard Burton, with that gorgeously mellow stage-trained voice that could have carried, I'm sure, into the back rows of Yankee Stadium without a microphone. One couldn't just get up and leave the room during one of these performances. Once he had started, one felt trapped until the great artist finally ran out of steam and, of course, as such evenings wore on, he tended to start repeating himself. The yawns became harder and harder to suppress.

This happened one evening after a small party for the film cast in Puerto Vallarta. Richard paused briefly to catch his breath between recitals, and suddenly he said, "It's a wonderful thing to have some poetry in your heart—in your soul! Everyone should have some poetry in his heart." Turning to Elizabeth, he said, "You must have some poetry in your heart, luv."

"No, Richard, I really don't," she said.

"What about that Shakespeare show you did for the British telly, luv?"

"But all I did was read the lines from the teleprompter," she said. "I didn't *memorize* any of those lines."

"Oh, c'mon, luv," he said. "There must be some little bit of poetry you know by heart. There's *got* to be!"

She considered this. "Well, there is one little poem that my father taught me when I was a little girl," she said.

"Ah, you see, luv?" he cried. "There is something. Something your father taught you. Wonderful! Out with it, luv!"

"Well," she said with a giggle, "it's just a silly little poem but it goes like this: 'What'll you have?' the waiter said, as he stood there picking his nose? 'Hard boiled eggs, you son of a bitch, you can't put your fingers in those.'"

There was silence in the room, then polite laughter, and a smattering of applause. It was getting late. It was time to go home. Everyone had to work tomorrow. Someone had finally gotten Richard to shut up.

NEIL ARMSTRONG AND BUZZ ALDRIN

In 1973, I moved to Ohio where, among other things, I conducted a Prose Writing Workshop at the University of Cincinnati. One of my first invitations, to cocktails, came from Warren Bennis, who was then the university's president. "Neil and Jan Armstrong will be coming," President Bennis added.

I knew that Armstrong, who lived just outside the city, had been given a post at the university, teaching a course in something like Aeronautical Engineering. But I was still awed to meet him.

After all, can anyone in the world who was alive at the time ever forget that thrilling moment on July 20, 1969, when the first human footsteps appeared in the dust of the moon, when John Kennedy's miraculous inaugural prediction actually became a miracle come true? A man on the moon! Remembering that first image on television still sends shivers up my spine. It couldn't be happening, and yet it was.

My first remarks to Neil Armstrong were not terribly original, I'm afraid. I said, "I met Charles Lindbergh not long ago, but all he did was fly to Paris. You've flown to the moon—and back!" Armstrong smiled. I wondered if he knew who Lindbergh was. The latter's accomplishment had occurred before Armstrong was born. I couldn't resist looking down at Armstrong's feet. Those footprints that first appeared in the moon's sand—and are presumably still there—had seemed enormous. Neil Armstrong had fairly small feet. In fact, he was not a large man, and he still had the bright, boyish good looks that had grinned at us from TV screens all over the world when he alighted at the end of the mission. He still looked like the boy next door. He looked about eighteen. A miracle. (The grin stayed with him into his eighties, as the face and frame grew chubby.)

On our first meeting there in Cincinnati, I longed to ask him questions that would provoke revealing answers. I said, "Tell me, do you ever step outside your house at night, and look up at the moon, and ask yourself, 'Was I really there, or was it all a dream?'"

"Well, the moon isn't visible every night," he said.

Oh.

I tried a different tack. "Tell me, when you first stepped out of the capsule onto the surface of the moon, were you even just a little bit—scared?"

"Well, you see, we were wearing these protective suits," he said.

Oh, again. "But weren't you just a little bit worried that you might never get home again?" I said.

"The amount of fuel that it would take for the return trip had been very carefully calculated," he said.

Oh, and it was a good thing someone had thought of that.

I guess I shouldn't have been disappointed. I shouldn't have expected Neil Armstrong to be a poet or a philosopher. He was, after all, an engineer, more at home with slide rules, quotients, and equivalents. I found his wife to be just as practical-minded. Later, talking to Jan Armstrong, she mentioned the farm they had bought outside of Lebanon, Ohio, where they planned to raise Black Angus cattle.

"That should be fun," I said.

"Fun? Well, maybe," she said. "But we hope to make a little money too!"

I had naively supposed that the wife of a great adventurer who had sailed beyond the earth's boundaries into the unknown wilds of space would be above such worldly matters. But I was clearly wrong.

Time passed. I continued to live in Cincinnati, though no longer connected to the university. I'd found, and bought, an 1870s house in an old neighborhood in the center of the city that had become a slum and was in the process of being—I hate the word—"gentrified." Neil Armstrong continued to live nearby. We never became friends, though we ran into each other from time to time, usually at some sort of civic function—nodding acquaintances, at best.

In 2001, I was invited to be a guest lecturer aboard the *Queen Elizabeth II* then in service between New York and Southampton, England. My compensation? Two deluxe first-class round-trip tickets, and all I had to do for this was deliver three forty-five-minute lectures to the ship's passengers. Who could say no to that? Once aboard, I discovered that my fellow guest lecturer was Buzz Aldrin.

On first meeting Aldrin, I mentioned that I lived in Cincinnati, and that I occasionally ran into Neil Armstrong there. His reaction left me dumbfounded.

"Wow," he whistled. "Neil *Armstrong!* That's a name I haven't thought about for years."

You'd have thought that those two men, having been sent off into the sky together on the century's most glorious mission and adventure, having had only each other for companionship in a tiny space capsule, not knowing whether they would even succeed in the mission, much less return from it together—that those two would have been bonded for life. Wouldn't you think that they would telephone each other every now and then, just to see how the other guy was doing? Wouldn't there be an annual—at least—get-together, over beers, where the two could reminisce and swap tales and catch up? Wouldn't they at least exchange Christmas cards? Apparently not. It seems they had not spoken to each other in over thirty years.

Some months later, I happened to meet a scientist who had worked for NASA and knew both men. "Those two never liked each other, from long before the moon mission," he told me. "The dislike was more on Aldrin's part than Armstrong's. Neil was a pretty easygoing guy, but nobody could get along with Buzz Aldrin. There was a lot of professional jealousy there. And by the time of the launching of the moon mission, I think the two actually hated each other."

Would the psychologists at NASA, I wondered, actually, deliberately choose two men who hated each other to be sent into space together? Did some sort of chemistry occur between enemies that made them work together better than two pals? It didn't seem very sensible to me. But there it was.

A great deal hung, my friend pointed out to me, on who was going to be the first man to plant his feet on lunar soil. Most of it could be measured in terms of dollars. There would be speakers' fees. There would eventually be a book deal.

There would probably be a movie deal, or a TV miniseries deal, or both. And then there were the lucrative possibilities of commercial endorsements. The first man to take those steps was certainly going to be able, if he wished, to cash in. The second man would be little more than an also-ran. All this added to the tension and animosity between the two astronauts.

But somebody had to be number one. The pair could not step off the spacecraft hand in hand. Various solutions were proposed—a drawing of straws, a cutting of cards, a coin toss. Nothing satisfied the two participants.

"Finally, it was the *Life* magazine thing that settled it," my friend said. It seemed that long before the lunar landing had left the drawing boards, *Life* had—for a certain sum—acquired the first refusal rights for all print photographs of the venture. "*Life* felt that Armstrong was by far the better-looking and the most photogenic of the two," my friend told me. "*Life* strongly urged that the first man out would be Armstrong. That more or less settled it."

I don't imagine Aldrin was pleased to learn he was not handsome enough to be on the cover of *Life*.

In the little town in eastern Connecticut where I grew up, there were open fields on all sides of our house, and there were no city lights to compete with the full glory of a starry night. As a kid, I used to lie on my back in the grass on clear nights and look up at the whole starlit universe. Clear nights with a full moon were best when you could really read by moonlight. The moon seemed near and personal to me, and full of mystery. It only showed one face to the earth; its other face was always hidden. And yet the moon controlled the earth's tides, and even, in some obscure way, the menstrual cycle of women. A turn in the tides could change the earth's weather, and the moon seemed somehow in charge of time itself, since all the world's calendars were based on phases of the moon and had been for as long as anyone knew. The very rhythm of life itself seemed to be in the moon's hands.

But since meeting the two moonwalkers, I've never felt quite the same about the moon as when it was my moon. Now I kind of resent its sands having been disturbed by alien human feet. Knowing that those feet belonged to two guys who can't stand each other doesn't help. Nor does realizing that, instead of a Great Adventure, the moon walk was more of a media spectacular, a public relations stunt with photo ops. And nothing but envy and hard feelings afterward.

No, the moon and I will never again feel quite the same about each other.

And watching Buzz Aldrin flogging his book to *QE2* passengers didn't help, either.

LORETTA YOUNG

I should state right off: I never knew Loretta Young. But her second husband, Tom Lewis, was a good friend, and her daughter, Judy Lewis, lived up the road from us in Greenwich, Connecticut. At the time, I learned the following family facts from Judy and her stepfather: Judy was no longer on speaking terms with her mother, who was threatening to sue her, nor with her real father, who had never spoken to her. Tom Lewis was no longer speaking to his wife. Judy's daughter no longer spoke to her grandmother. And very soon, it would turn out, Judy and her husband, Joe Tinney, would stop speaking to each other and would be headed for a rancorous divorce. The baleful eminence for whom all this domestic discord and dysfunction was blamed was Loretta Young.

The more I learned about the situation, or situations, the more I began to sympathize with Loretta, who was being given, I decided, something of a bum rap. Having been dealt a bad hand, she had played her cards masterfully. Or tried hard to.

When Tom Lewis spoke of his stepdaughter, it was usually as "poor Judy." When Joe Tinney spoke of his about-to-be-ex-wife, it was "poor Judy" again.

Trying to give both men's stories some perspective, I tended to side with Poor Loretta.

The deal was this: In 1934, Loretta had made a movie with Clark Gable. It was a fairly forgettable film called *Call of the Wild*, and was filmed in the wilds of the Yukon Territory. At the time, Gable was just beginning to emerge as a major male star—this was his fifth picture—and Loretta Young, just twenty-one, was also considered to have great promise. Clark Gable was married at the time to an older woman named Ria Langham, with three small children. Loretta had been married as a teenager and divorced. Before the filming was completed, Loretta had become pregnant by her costar. "I don't think it was any grand passion, or great romance," Tom Lewis told me. "It was probably some chilly night up in the North Woods, when they both had a bit too much to drink—though Loretta always denied this." In any case, the two participants in the coupling—Loretta, in particular—faced a sizable problem.

Everyone in show business knew what the fallout from a Hollywood sex scandal could be. A few years earlier, the popular star Fatty Arbuckle had been banned from films for life over some drug-related hanky-panky in a San Francisco hotel room. Draconian censorship rules had evolved from this: even a husband and wife could not be pictured sitting fully clothed on a double bed. A few years later, Ingrid Bergman, a major actress and box-office draw, had been permanently blackballed by the industry for having revealed that she was pregnant by her director, Roberto Rossellini, and was going to bear his child.

If Loretta's pregnancy by Gable had become public knowledge, Gable, perhaps, could have survived it. This, in the double standard of the day, was because he was a male, and all men were supposed to be like that. Men strayed from their wives; it was their nature. But Loretta—she was the Other Woman, the homewrecker, the adulteress, the wearer of the Scarlet Letter. Her budding career in movies would be forever over.

This mattered not only to her. She had become the principal breadwinner for her mother and three sisters, in this fatherless family. Something had to be done. Loretta was a devout Roman Catholic, which put abortion out of the question. She had already committed one mortal sin, adultery, in the eyes of the Church, and could not bring herself to commit another.

"I'm sure she considered putting the baby up for adoption," Tom Lewis said, "although she always denied that there was ever such a question. I'm sure she and her mother and sisters put their heads together, and decided: she should keep the baby, and the ladies worked out the details of the secret conspiracy."

It worked like this. Loretta, claiming "exhaustion," would take a couple of months off from film work (though she worked into the sixth month of her pregnancy, her secret undetected) at which point she would quietly check into a Catholic home for unwed mothers, where her daughter was born. After a few weeks, she would fill out formal adoption papers, and bring her "adopted" baby home.

In this cover-up scheme, Loretta was enormously aided by Louella Parsons, the powerful Hollywood gossip columnist for Hearst newspapers. "Louella would often do favors for her pet stars, and write what they asked her to say," Tom Lewis said. "Especially if the stars had been generous with her at Christmastime." Louella wrote breathlessly of how Loretta Young had opened her heart to the orphan baby she had named Judy and was offering her a privileged childhood and a loving home and mother, whereas the infant might have otherwise faced a life of deprivation and neglect.

And where did Clark Gable stand in all of this? Very much at arm's length, it would seem, which would seem to be what he, his wife, and two stepchildren, and Loretta all wanted. As far Judy herself knew, her biological father had come to see his child just once. At the time, Gable had handed Loretta four $100 bills, with instructions, "Buy something for the baby." Otherwise, he would certainly be given no awards for gallantry in the matter. Asked about how his paternity had come about, he said merely, "Well, she'd been married. I thought she knew what she was doing."

Once the secret, and the cover-up, had been set in place, Loretta refused to change her story—on the theory, perhaps, that once another person knows the secret, it is a secret no longer. As Judy Lewis—she had taken Tom Lewis's name—matured into young womanhood, the resemblance to Clark Gable became ever more striking. She had Gable's wide-spaced eyes, his high cheekbones, slightly hooked nose, his dimples, and—most noticeably—his flyaway ears.

Surgery to "fix" little Judy's ears was performed, and this helped. So did her mother's insistence that Judy's curly hair should always be combed forward, to cover the ears, and this helped some more. But the ears remained a giveaway. At school, one of her nicknames was "Dumbo."

People who knew Loretta were able to do the arithmetic with the dates between Loretta's work on *Call of the Wild* and Judy's birth. The secret, in the Hollywood community, became increasingly ill-kept. Still, Loretta stuck to her guns. Judy was told that she was adopted, and when she asked who her birth parents were, she was told they were both dead. Even Tom Lewis did not learn the truth about Judy's birth until several years after marrying Loretta. At the time of their marriage, Judy was listed as Loretta Young's "ward." When Judy accused her mother of lying, Loretta insisted, "I adopted you."

"The sad thing was," Tom Lewis told me, "that Loretta went overboard trying to be a perfect mother to Judy. She showered her with gifts for every occasion. There were always nurses and governesses for the little girl, and the best private schools and colleges. But Judy, always aware that something was "wrong" about her birth, and that she was being lied to, never seemed to appreciate any of her mother's efforts.

"How would you feel being told that you were a mortal sin?" Judy once asked me.

"I'm sure Loretta never told her that," Tom Lewis told me. "Loretta didn't have much education, but she wasn't stupid. Loretta had committed a mortal sin in the eyes of the church, and she knew it. But Judy didn't commit any sins, and Loretta knew that too."

Still, when Judy finally knew for sure that Gable was her true father, she could not forgive him for not coming forward. She could not forgive Tom Lewis for not being her true father. She could never forgive her mother for her lies. In the end, when it all blew up over Loretta's failure to attend Judy's daughter's wedding, with screaming accusations from all concerned, threats of lawsuits, and everyone in the family vowing never to speak to anyone else again, one can't help but wonder: Would it have ended more happily if Loretta simply given up the baby for adoption?

Perhaps the moral to this sad tale is: There are some secrets that can be kept for too long.

Tom Lewis told me that he believed Loretta had spent the rest of her life trying to atone for the mortal sin that had resulted in her daughter. She had finally confessed her long-maintained lie to him, it was in such an oblique way that, at first, he had had no idea what she was talking about. In the end, he felt it was the long lie that resulted in the collapse of her marriage, though they never divorced. Though always devout, she became an almost obsessive Catholic. Wherever she was, she tried to attend Mass every day. She was one of the three female film starts famous for their devotion to Los Angeles's Church of the Good Shepherd, often called "Our Lady of the Cadillac" for the affluence of its congregants—the other two women being Irene Dunne and Rosalind Russell.

At one point, the Lewises rented one of the cottages on the Doheny Ranch in Beverly Hills. The "cottage" contained more than thirty rooms, and the ranch covered a Beverly Hilltop. The ranch had been created by the late California oil tycoon, Edward Doheny, a prominent figure in the Teapot Dome oil scandals of the 1920s and, at the time, probably California's richest man.

His widow, Estelle, liked to style herself as "the Countess Estelle Doheny," since she was given the papal title of countess, in thanks for her generosity to the Mother Church. One afternoon, the countess decided to pay a call on her new tenant and fellow faithful, Loretta Young.

But Miss Loretta Young was always first, and foremost, a great film star. She was not accustomed to receiving unexpected and uninvited guests, no matter how important they might well be. When the countess's presence downstairs was announced, it took Miss Young a little time to prepare her face and wardrobe for her visitor, and when she finally made her entrance into her drawing room, with her usual flair, the room was empty.

The Countess Estelle Doheny had gone home. Poor Loretta.

WALTER KERR

Big lies tend to backfire, and the bigger the lie, the louder the noise.

Smaller lies merely ricochet. When the former NBC news anchor Brian Williams, offered his first public acknowledgment of "exaggerations" or "misstatements" in his televised news reports, it was noticed that he did not go so far as to use the "L" word. I can understand why. He did not see these departures from hard fact as actual lies. I had a favorite author whose favorite word was "vividify." She would hold up a piece of copy of mine and cry, "Vividify! Vividify! Vividify!" Brian Williams was simply vividifying.

Erik Preminger, Gypsy Rose Lee's son, once told me that when his aunt, June Havoc, was reading the galleys of her sister's memoir, *Gypsy.* which became the basis of the musical, Miss Havoc put down the proofs and said, "But Gypsy, some of this just isn't true!" "Who cares if it's true?" Miss Lee replied. "It makes a hell of a good story, doesn't it?"

Miss Lee was an entertainer. She was in show business. So, in a real sense, is a TV news anchor. Brian Williams wasn't hired for his newsgathering acumen. He was hired for his good looks, his shy smile, his twinkle, and his poise. The actual TV news is gathered, and mostly composed, by others. The anchor simply reads it.

But on the infrequent occasions when a TV news anchor leaves his desk in New York to go "on location" to a place where major news is actually happening, it must be a temptation for the newsman to make himself part of the action—to become one of the bold War Correspondents of yore. This, I suspect, was the cause of Mr. Williams's misstep and eventual downfall. He needed an Ernie Pyle moment, and so invented himself one.

A drama critic, of course, is a quite different sort of writer—closer to Gypsy Rose Lee, an entertainer, in show business himself. His job is to analyze, interpret, imagine, and even invent for his audience, to perform and do tricks for the edification and entertainment of his readers. And so, when I caught my late friend Walter Kerr in a misstatement of fact, I couldn't say he was a liar. He was just a vividifier.

But the special thing about this particular vivification was that it had been one of my own manufacture. A fiblet I had told years before came back to me, like a boomerang, to hit me in my somewhat reddened face about ten years later.

It came about like this:

For many years, my literary agent was Carol Brandt, whom many considered to be the Queen Bee of New York agents. It seemed that two young women appeared on the Manhattan literary scene in the 1930s, more or less simultaneously and more or less out of nowhere. One was tall and dark and beautiful—that was Carol. The other was tiny and blonde and beautiful. That was Clare Boothe. The two knew each other but were not exactly friends. They worked in parallel fields. Both were drawn to powerful men. Both became forces.

Being tall, Carol Brandt always wore—and could get away with—large, chunky jewels. Carol had a black standard poodle named Beau, and Beau was so beautifully behaved that a number of top New York restaurants allowed him into their dining rooms where he would sit in a chair, paws politely folded, until lunch was over. It was said that literary agents should be little brown wrens scurrying about in raincoats with rolled umbrellas. Carol was the opposite of this stereotype, and made authors feel like little brown wrens. I, on the other hand, always enjoyed and admired her style.

One day at lunch, she told me an amusing story. It involved a one-time client named Frederick Faust, who wrote under the name Max Brand. Max Brand wrote mainly for what in those days were called the "pulps," and his most famous creation was Dr. Kildare. Dr. Kildare stories appeared not only in the pulp magazines, but also in radio soap opera series and literally dozens of motion pictures. Max Brand can be said to have invented a genre—the hospital soap, a TV staple today—and Dr. Kildare's creator made lots and lots of money.

The trouble was that Frederick Faust and his wife always managed to outspend their income. They lived in great style in a villa on the Italian Riviera and were perpetually broke. At one point, the Fausts' financial situation became so dire that they sailed to New York and arrived on the doorstep of Carol Brandt and her partner-husband, Carl Brandt, crying for help. Creditors on both sides of the Atlantic were after them, this time seriously.

Carl Brandt's solution was to offer Faust a room in the Brandts' apartment, hide the liquor, give him a typewriter, and keep him in there until he churned out more Dr, Kildare stories. Carol Brandt's job was to take Dorothy Faust aside and give her a few lessons on homemaking thriftiness. She told her about the importance of keeping a household budget, of looking for sales and special offers at stores and supermarkets, about layaway plans and Christmas clubs and discounts and how to save in-store coupons. In the middle of all this, Dorothy Faust suddenly looked at her watch and exclaimed, "Oh! It's getting late in Italy. Excuse me but I must phone my butler and tell him that there are twelve guest breakfast trays that he needs to send to Milan to be re-lacquered."

"At that point," Carol told me, "I gave up trying to talk to Dorothy Faust about household economies."

Some time went by—I forget how much. I was talking with a friend. I don't even remember who it was, but he asked me, "What's Carol Brandt really like?" She had, by then, become something of a legend in the relatively small world of New York publishing. I remember describing how Carol lived—in a large, rather splendid Fifth Avenue apartment overlooking Central Park. The apartment even contained a wine cellar, and even the servants' rooms in the back had views of the East River. Here Carol held forth with the aid of a Black couple, her cook, and her butler, who were always dressed in formal attire.

And I suddenly blurted out, "She's the kind of woman who'll interrupt a business conversation to say, 'Oh, I must remind my butler to send out twelve guest breakfast trays to Milan to be re-lacquered.'"

I have no idea what made me reapply that anecdote to Carol Brandt. It wasn't really like her at all, and I actually cannot imagine her saying anything of the sort. I guess I thought the story, though untrue, added to what I always thought was her glamour, her sense of personal theater, the extravagance of her presence, her vivacity. Anyway, there it was, I'd said it, and it was too late to take it back.

More time went by—years, in fact. As I mentioned earlier, Jean and Walter Kerr had become neighbors of ours in Westchester County. Despite an earlier kerfuffle involving a mink tippet for Jean, we'd remained good friends. Walter Kerr, the drama critic for the *New York Times*—making him the most influential voice in the American theater— had even had a Broadway theater named after him, probably the highest accolade a critic can receive. The Kerrs had come to dinner at our house.

I knew that for a number of years both Jean and Walter Kerr had been represented by Brandt & Brandt, and I'd heard that they'd recently changed literary agencies. Over dinner, I asked Walter why. "Carol Brandt was just a little too la-di-da for us," he said. "In the middle of a business conversation, she suddenly said, 'Excuse me, but I must call my butler and remind him that there are a dozen guest breakfast trays that need to be sent to Milan to be re-lacquered.'"

I was speechless. My little fabrication had come back to me, after all these years, almost word for word, virtually intact, the perfect boomerang. How many ears had heard, and how many mouths had spoken those words before they reached Walter Kerr, and finally zoomed back home to me I could only imagine?

My feelings were decidedly mixed. On the one hand, I was embarrassed that my falsehood had hung around New York for as long as it had, crediting my friend Carol with something that she never could have said, and allegedly costing her a client. On the other hand, it was kind of nice to know that my pilfered anecdote had been good enough for someone as distinguished as Walter Kerr to feel that it was worth re-pilfering.

MARILYN MONROE

It began to look as though I was never going to have my interview with Marilyn Monroe. For five successive days her publicity man, John Springer, and I had shown up at her address, in the East 50s and Sutton Place, for 5 p.m. appointments. Each time, we were told Miss Monroe was not at home. She might return soon, or she might not, no one knew. One day it was, "She went to Connecticut with Paula Strasberg. They should be back soon." Other days it was vaguer. Usually it was, "Come back in half an hour." Every time it was, "She's sorry, because she *really* wants to do this interview."

Naturally, with Miss Monroe not home, we were not allowed to wait for her upstairs in her apartment. And her doormen would not allow us to wait for her in the lobby of her building. Too many fans had tried that, just in hopes of catching a glimpse of the star. And we'd noticed small gatherings of folk, mostly teenagers with autograph books, waiting on the sidewalk outside the building for the same reason.

John Springer and I had discovered a small coffee shop around the corner, where we waited for Marilyn. Usually, after an hour or so, we gave up. "Come back tomorrow," we were told. "She really *wants* to do this interview."

That was the ironic part of it. I hadn't asked for the interview. *She* had. My magazine assignment was for an article to be called "Richard Avedon, Photographer of Beauty." Avedon had recently taken a series of photographs of Miss Monroe in the nude, dancing with nothing but a pair of pink ostrich-feather fans. She and Avedon had apparently hit it off, and, hearing of my article, she had asked to be part of it, which, of course, was fine with me.

And naturally I had heard of Marilyn's problems with lateness, or, as it was called politely, "time-management issues." Her perennial lateness and failures to show up for work had annoyed—even infuriated—her fellow performers and directors and had recently gotten her fired halfway through her most recent film, *Something's Got to Give.*

Now I was getting a sampling of Marilyn Monroe's famous tendency, and I was becoming more than a little annoyed with her, prepared to dislike her a lot, after wasting one afternoon after another in that coffee shop. John Springer was more philosophical. He was used to it. "She'll either show up today, or she won't," he'd say with a shrug.

Then, on the sixth day of our postponed meetings, there was suddenly different news from upstairs. "Miss Monroe is expecting you," the doorman said. We were whisked into an elevator, and up to the apartment, and ushered into a small anteroom where a secretary sat at a desk with two "In" mailboxes—one labeled "Marilyn Monroe," and the other "Arthur Miller." The couple was by then separated but apparently still shared a secretary. "Miss Monroe will be with you shortly," the secretary said. "Please have a seat." We sat.

After about fifteen minutes, a small man in a dark business suit emerged from the apartment proper. Obviously a doctor, a stethoscope hung around his neck, and he carried the signature little black bag. To the secretary we heard him say, "I've just given her a shot. She'll sleep now."

The secretary nodded, and John Springer and I exchanged apprehensive looks. Obviously, a woman who has just been given a knockout shot was not going to be in the best shape to grant an interview. The secretary continued typing, and we continued to wait.

Then, all at once, a tiny creature with a whiff of blonde hair appeared in the doorway. "Hi, I'm Marilyn Monroe," she said.

She was wearing black toreador pants, black slip-ons, and a kind of see-throughy white cotton blouse, and, as far as I could tell, no makeup, and yet she glowed. There must be some kind of makeup that a woman can wear that, though invisible, makes them glow, or maybe hers was some sort of inner radiance that just shines naturally through the skin. I thought immediately: Tinkerbell.

I once saw a production of *Peter Pan,* in which Tinkerbell was portrayed by an incandescent electric light bulb that danced and flitted across the stage.

This was Marilyn Monroe. A sex symbol? How can a bit of fairy ectoplasm be sexy?

She served us tea. I have never been particularly good with crockery, teacups in particular, and usually end up with most of my tea sloshing in my saucer. But Marilyn Monroe could manage to balance a teapot in one hand, a teacup in the other, and move effortlessly around the room, pouring tea with more poise and grace than a finishing-school headmistress.

Where could that have come from? I had heard that her upbringing had been desperately fraught—an absent father, a mentally unstable mother, an orphanage, dreary foster homes with abusive foster parents—just about as many disadvantages as a childhood could chalk up. Did classes at Lee Strasberg's Actor's Studio teach such polish? It was a naturalness that seemed more inborn than acquired.

We talked about Richard Avedon. Some critics had claimed that Avedon's photographs displayed a cruel streak. A recent series of photos of the Duke and Duchess of Windsor, for instance, seemed harsh on the poor couple, showing every wrinkle and ravage of age—the Duchess's gnarled and liver-spotted hands fiercely straightening the Duke's necktie. "Oh, no, not cruel!" Marilyn cried." He's not cruel! I can sense a cruel person from a mile away. Dick is just—*articulate*. Is articulate an articulate word?"

Yes, John Springer assured her, articulate was an articulate word.

The smallest of possible miniature white poodles came bouncing into the room, jumped into its mistress's lap as she sat cross-legged on the sofa, and began licking her face. "His name is Maf," she said. "Short for Mafia. Frank Sinatra gave him to me."

She gave me a tour of the apartment. It was all done in shades of white, including a white grand piano. She showed me the closet where she stored her bicycle, and she showed me the black wig and the oversize dark glasses she wore when she rode her bike in Central Park.

Did the disguise fool the gathering of fans I'd noticed on the sidewalk outside her building, I asked her?

"Oh, no," she laughed. "They're on to that."

But wasn't it kind of a nuisance, I asked her, having to make her way through a gamut of admirers every time she came and left her home?

"Oh, no!" she said. "They're all nice kids. They're my friends! I know most of their names. There's Chewy, and Chewy's brother, and Nick and Bobby—they just want to chat and visit with me for a few minutes."

She took me into her all-white bedroom. There I was, alone in her bedroom with Marilyn Monroe in an almost-transparent blouse, alone with an international sex symbol. Why weren't my thoughts even in the slightest way libidinous? If anything, I would describe my feelings toward her at that moment as *protective*.

This woman seemed so small—much tinier in real life than she appeared to be on the screen—so dainty and fragile and easily woundable—that she seemed misplaced in the roughneck male world of the movie business. I felt like saying, "If you ever need help, will you call on me?"

Back in the living room, I looked at my watch. It was nearly nine o'clock. I had spent almost four hours with Marilyn Monroe for an interview that I had not expected to last more than forty-five minutes. In the anteroom outside, the secretary had gone for the night. The *nil admirari* John Springer was suppressing a yawn.

Clearly the soporific that the doctor had administered had affected our hostess not at all, and when we rose to say goodnight, she actually seemed sorry to see us go, and I felt a little guilty myself to be leaving her all alone in that big, all-white apartment.

At the front door, she stood on tiptoe and lightly kissed my cheek. "Take care," she said.

Though not a native, I had spent most of my working life in and around New York City, and felt that I knew Manhattan like the back of my hand. It was a warm summer night, and I decided it would be an easy walk from East 55th Street, south to Grand Central Station, where I could catch a train home to Westchester.

I had walked for a while when I suddenly looked up and discovered that I was in a neighborhood I'd never been in before. Nothing looked familiar, not a street sign, not a house. I was totally lost in my familiar city.

I'd walked twenty blocks in the wrong direction.

ARTHUR RUBINSTEIN

The pianist Arthur Rubinstein was publishing the first volume of his memoirs, *My Young Years*, and his publisher, Alfred Knopf, was throwing a publication cocktail party for the maestro. Appropriately, Knopf had decided to hold the party on the stage at Carnegie Hall, on an afternoon when there was to be no performance. I'd been lucky enough to receive an invitation.

As the guests mingled and moved about the stage, I found myself standing with the guest of honor himself.

"I can't believe," I said to him, "that I'm standing in the center of the Great Stage at Carnegie Hall, speaking to the great Artur Rubinstein."

"And look what they've given us," he said, gesturing into the vast auditorium. "An empty house!"

JANET AUCHINCLOSS

I can almost visualize it—the monthly editorial meeting where the editors of the popular women's magazine gathered to plan their next issue.

"There must be something new we can do about Jackie Kennedy," someone must have said. "But what?"

Silence. Then, "What about her mother?"

"Her mother! Of course! Nobody knows anything about her mother!"

"Her mother's married to some rich guy . . ."

". . . named Auchincloss."

"That's it. I've got the title—'How Her Mother and the Fabulous Auchincloss Clan Shaped Jackie Kennedy's Style.'"

"Beautiful! Let's get Birmingham to do it."

Something like that, I'm sure, is how that magazine assignment came about.

"That idea is perfectly ridiculous," said my friend Louis Auchincloss, a cousin of Jackie's stepfather, Hugh D. Auchincloss. Louis also happened to be my lawyer at the time. "Jackie and her sister were not close to their mother at all, and they make jokes about poor Hughdie. The girls have never forgiven Janet for divorcing their father when he lost all his money, and then marrying Hughdie simply for *his* money. Hughdie Auchincloss is probably the most boring man you'll ever meet. There is no 'Fabulous Auchincloss clan.' We were thread merchants. Hughdie's mother bought him a seat on the stock exchange because nobody could figure out what to do with him. You can't say that either Hughdie or Janet had anything to do with Jackie's style."

"But that," I replied, "is exactly what I'm going to have to do."

When you take on a magazine assignment, you cut the cloth to suit the customer.

They'd invited me to Hammersmith Farm, that big, rambling single-style estate on a hilltop in Newport, overlooking Narragansett Bay, for the weekend. It was here that John and Jacqueline Kennedy had been married in the summer of 1953, in a so-called "Wedding of the Century."

In the Auchincloss family, it was often said, "There are no rich Auchinclosses—except Hughdie." This is more or less true, though the Auchincloss family in America, of doughty, thrifty Scotch Presbyterian stock, have been prolific and for the most part "respectably prosperous." They have also had the good fortune to marry into other respectably prosperous American families, and at one point the *New York Social Register* contained the listings of more Auchinclosses than any other family.

Hughdie Auchincloss, meanwhile, became richer than all his relatives more or less by accident. His mother, who married an Auchincloss, was a daughter of Oliver H. P. Jennings, a partner of John D. Rockefeller in Standard Oil. With his seat on the New York Stock Exchange, Hughdie was able to have his own stockbrokerage firm.

Gore Vidal, whose mother was married to Hughdie Auchincloss before he married Janet Bouvier, once described Hughdie to me as "sublimely dull." I saw what he meant when the patriarch took me on a tour, in his Jeep, of Hammersmith Farm and its features. We passed a large herd of black cattle. "Black Angus?" I asked him. "I'm not really sure," he said. "I just rent them for the summer." Why? I asked him. "I've always liked to look out the window at cows grazing," he said.

I could see I was going to have a hard time showing how the fabulous Auchincloss clan had influenced Jacqueline Kennedy's style.

His wife was another matter. A small, sharp-faced woman with a brisk and breezy manner, she was clearly the one who ran the Auchincloss *ménage*. She was complaining that afternoon, that her monogram, "J.L.A." had been hand-painted on the doors of her new Jaguar using much too large lettering. The lettering would all have to be done over. (I had read somewhere that Jackie Kennedy carried a Chanel over-the-shoulder bag, but with the Chanel double-C logo removed. Aha! Here was something.)

I expressed an interest in seeing the original Auchincloss summer home in Newport, and Janet offered to drive me there in her car. It was in what was by then a rather run-down section of the city, she warned me, and hadn't been that much of a house to begin with. But if I wanted to see it, she'd take me, and so off we went.

The house, a Victorian affair, was indeed in shabby repair on an even shabbier street and had become a retreat house for an order of Stella Maris nuns. We parked in the street outside. "Seen enough?" Janet asked.

"Do you suppose," I said, "that if I rang the bell, they'd let me have a look inside?"

"Do you really *want* to?"

"It might give me an idea of what it was like."

"Oh, well—go ahead."

I got out of the car, went to the front door, and rang the bell, leaving Janet in the big Jaguar.

The door was answered by a little nun in full habit, and I explained my interest in the house.

She hesitated, looking at Janet's car. "Is that," she whispered, "Mrs. Auchincloss?"

I said it was.

"Our . . . Jackie's . . . *mother?*"

"Yes."

"Oh, do you suppose she'd possibly come in to see us? Our Mother Superior would be just thrilled to meet her."

"Well, I'll ask her."

Back at the car, I explained the situation to Janet. "How did they know it was me?"

"I guess it was your car," I said. I didn't mention the oversized monograms.

"Oh, all right." She climbed, rather crossly, out of the driver's seat. Back at the house, we were met by the first nun, another sister, and the Mother Superior of the house, who greeted us profusely and with blessings. "We want to give you a tour of our home," they said.

Inside, the Stella Maris retreat house was even drearier than it appeared from the street. The sisters showed us the refectory, where they and their retreatants took their meals, a stark, cavernous room with heavy curtains and peeling walls. "Beautiful . . . absolutely beautiful," Janet Auchincloss kept murmuring, as we passed through the dismal rooms. They showed us the tiny cells where the retreatants stayed. Each cell, which had a narrow window high in the wall, was furnished with a steel cot, a crucifix, a water bowl and pitcher, and a chamber pot. "Such a wonderful sense of *peace* here," said Janet. "Do you suppose someone like myself, a civilian, could come here for a retreat?"

"Absolutely, Mrs. Auchincloss," said the Mother Superior.

"*Could* I? I would love to come for a few weeks."

"We'd be thrilled to have you stay with us, Mrs. Auchincloss," said Mother Superior.

We entered the chapel, and, seizing the handrail of a pew, Janet Auchincloss flung herself to her knees, silently mouthing some sort of sacred incantation. We all stood there, awaiting her moment of rapture to pass.

"Well, thank God that's over," Janet said when we were back in our car. "And look—it's going to make us late for lunch!"

"At least you made a few little nuns awfully happy," I said. "I'm afraid I got you into that."

"It's made us late for lunch," she said again, applying the gas pedal. "And the first course is a soufflé. It will have fallen, of course. Damn!"

A few months later, my article appeared. I did not include the Stella Maris episode, but I heard from others that Janet was not pleased with it. "Full of inaccuracies," she complained to Louis Auchincloss. "I wasted a whole weekend with that friend of yours!"

After listening to Janet fulminate against me for some time, Louis told me, "I was able to make a *mot*." All this, of course, was not long after Jacqueline Kennedy made a very public display—and had instituted, and lost, a lawsuit—against the writer William Manchester, trying to stop the publication of his book *The Death of a President*.

"I made a *mot*," said Louis. "I said, 'My dear Janet, you, *and* your daughter, will have to learn not to become involved with writers with the names of British industrial cities.'"

NORA EPHRON

The town of Des Plaines, Illinois (pop. 58,720), is a prosperous, unpretentious middle-class suburb of Chicago. It does not possess the toniness of some of the towns to the north, along the lakeshore, but it is doing fine, thank you very much, and does not go to the trouble of trying to Frenchify the pronunciation of its name. It is plain old DEZ PLAYNZ, and that's all there is to it. But there's plenty of culture in Des Plaines, don't worry about that.

The city of Des Plaines was having its first-ever book-and-author dinner, sponsored by the Friends of the Des Plaines Public Library.

The event had been at least two years in the planning. Events like this require the toiling of many volunteers, mostly women, of many different committees, over many months. One committee must work with New York publishers over the availability of certain authors on certain dates. And of course, everyone wants authors who are currently "hot" or in the news, and the trouble with that is so does every other community in the country having a book-and-author dinner.

One committee must handle the pre-event publicity, wooing local newspaper editors and radio and television producers. Another committee must handle ticket pricing and sales. Still another must handle the dinner menu, another is in charge of author transportation and hotel accommodations, and yet another must arrange to have the authors met at airports on their flights. And so it goes.

Over the entire hierarchy of committee-dom reigns supreme one woman, usually Madame Program Chairman, who among other things will have the honor of introducing the speaker or speakers at the beginning of the program, and upon whose shoulders the success or failure of the evening will ultimately fall.

Now all was in readiness for the evening's program. Over two hundred tickets had been sold. The weather had obliged—it was a lovely spring evening. There had been one or two glitches leading up the event, but they had been resolved without too much difficulty, and everyone agreed that Madame Program Chairman had done a superb job organizing everything. There were to be three guest speakers: Nora Ephron, Mary Higgins Clark, and me.

Of the three, Miss Ephron was clearly the star, and the chief drawing card of the evening. She had recently published a sort-of memoir, in which she had dealt with the flagrant infidelity of her former husband, Carl Bernstein—of the famous Woodward-Bernstein Watergate reporting team—and how she had managed the discovery that her husband, by whom she happened to be pregnant, had also been sleeping with one of her best friends.

The audience that evening was looking forward to some spicy anecdotes.

There was only one problem. Waiters had started serving the dinner's first course—a fruit cup, naturally. But Miss Ephron was nowhere to be found.

There had been a series of frantic telephone calls between Madame Program Chairman and her minions at O'Hare Airport. The meeting committee had been at the gate in plenty of time. She had not gotten off the plane. The flight's manifest, furthermore, did not show her as a passenger on that flight.

Madame Chairman suggested that her committee members stay for the next flight from New York, in case Miss Ephron had missed the first one. Calls to her publisher in New York were unavailing. Their offices (on Eastern time) had closed for the day.

Madame Program Chairman, needless to say, had not touched her dinner. There were visible tears in her eyes. Meanwhile something had to be done. An announcement had to be made. The audience had begun to notice the empty chair at the speakers' table. There were stirrings of unrest.

Finally, there was word from New York. Someone had contacted Nora Ephron. She had felt a cold coming on that afternoon and decided not to come to Chicago.

Who should quickly step forward to try to save the day but Mary Higgins Clark, a former airline stewardess trained to handle crowds in emergencies? "I'll take over the keynote spot," she said. "I had a lousy marriage too. I'll tell them all about that."

Which, when the time came, she proceeded to do, with great aplomb and charm and good humor. She may not have been Nora Ephron, but her talk was certainly entertaining. She certainly managed to dispel much of the audience's initial disappointment.

Best of all, as far as the harried program chairman was concerned, there were no requests for their money back from members of the disappointed audience. Nora Ephron, you made money for the Des Plaines libraries in spite of yourself.

I'd met Nora Ephron a couple of times, had lunch with her in New York at least once, and always enjoyed her sharp, funny essays in magazines. When I ran into her a few weeks later, I mentioned that we missed her in Des Plaines.

At first, I don't think she knew what I was talking about.

"Oh, that," she said at last. "What was that? Some prairie town in Iowa? I couldn't care less about that."

"Well," I said, "that prairie town happened to have bought quite a few copies of your book to autograph and sell."

"Oh?" she said, and I thought I saw her wince. No, I didn't think I saw her wince. I wanted her to wince. "How many copies?" she asked.

"Oh, a couple of hundred," I said. It was a lie. I had no idea how many copies the Public Library had bought. Maybe ten. But I wanted to turn the screw a little more, to make her really wince. "But, of course, I assured them that all the books could be returned for credit," I added.

I think I got my wince.

All hail Des Plaines, Illinois! All hail Mary Higgins Clark!

Appendix 2

List of Works by Stephen Gardner Birmingham

	Nonfiction		
	Title	**Est. Print and Digital Copies Sold**	**Pages**
1	"Our Crowd"	1,750,000	450
2	The Grandees: America's Sephardic Elite	1,500,000	300
3	The Right People: A Portrait of the American Social Establishment	1,650,000	310
4	America's Secret Aristocracy	880,000	400
5	The Jews in America Trilogy	100,000	300
6	The Rest of Us: The Rise of America's Eastern European Jews	590,000	410
7	The Grandes Dames	450,000	300
8	Duchess: The Story of Wallis Warfield Windsor	400,000	300
9	California Rich	400,000	318
10	Life at the Dakota: New York's Most Unusual Address	980,000	235
11	The Golden Dream: Suburbia in the Seventies	350,000	300
12	Jacqueline Bouvier Kennedy Onassis	400,000	300
13	Certain People: America's Black Elite	400,000	229
14	The Right Places	680,000	300
15	Real Lace: America's Irish Rich	1,250,000	300
16	The Late John Marquand: A Biography	275,000	300
		12,055,000	3,292

Fiction

	Title	Est. Print and Digital Copies Sold	Pages
1	*Heart Troubles*	175,000	210
2	*The Wrong Kind of Money*	275,000	400
3	*Carriage Trade*	225,000	450
4	*The Rothman Scandal*	325,000	450
5	*Shades of Fortune*	425,000	450
6	*The LeBaron Secret*	500,000	450
7	*The Auerbach Will*	650,000	425
8	*Fast Start, Fast Finish*	200,000	350
9	*Those Harper Women*	220,000	375
10	*Barbara Greer*	280,000	360
11	*The Towers of Love*	158,000	300
12	*Young Mr. Keefe*	100,000	350
		3,533,000	4,570

Unpublished

	Title
1	*A Writer Writes: A Memoir*
2	*The Headmaster's Wife*
3	*Unguarded Moments*

Acknowledgments

This book would not have been possible without the help and cooperation of Dr. C. Edward Lahniers, my father's partner in Cincinnati of more than forty years.

Upon my father's death in 2015, my siblings and I received letters from his estate informing us that our father had left many of his assets to a trust for the benefit of scholarships in his name at the Hotchkiss School and Williams College. Among those assets were the copyrights to all of his twenty-eight books and innumerable other articles and publications, and I immediately knew that neither of these institutions would do anything to promote the titles conveyed or my father's legacy. I, therefore, approached Dr. Lahniers ("Ed") for a solution, since he was trustee of the aforementioned trust.

Over the years since I reconnected with my father, I had also become close with Ed and even now consider him my stepfather. Shortly after my father's death, I confided with Ed about my strong feelings that the authored works of Stephen Birmingham should remain with his children and grandchildren, to be passed onto future Birminghams. Ed thoughtfully agreed and worked diligently with the estate attorney to find an equitable solution which balanced the needs of the estate, his fiduciary duty to same, as well as my wishes to further my father's literary legacy. Ed, in his graciousness, came upon a fair price acceptable to the trust and myself.

So, I became the copyright holder to all my father's works in 2016 and continue to make attempts to promote the sale of his books, including exploring film and television opportunities as they arise and simply "working the asset" to maximize its value.

Upon completion of the copyright purchase, Ed delivered to me three of my father's typewritten but unpublished manuscripts, including this one. My father, until the end, produced all his letters and works on an old Royal typewriter and never got the hang of computers and particularly word-processing software. He would produce typewritten words on vellum and deliver the pages to an assistant who would, presumably, scan and convert them into a word-processed document, returning computer generated paper pages to my father for editing with handwritten notes in the margin. Eventually my father's handwritten changes would be returned to the assistant for subsequent and final drafts. It was in this form that I received this book, along with two other manuscripts. One of the manuscripts was an unfinished compendium of short anecdotes of celebrity interviews and stories which I've incorporated here as an Appendix, *Unguarded Moments*. The amalgam of stories I received included several of my father's handwritten notes and ideas for additional stories which, sadly, he never finished.

Despite our best efforts, neither Ed nor I could determine who, if anybody, held the digital copies of the unpublished works. As a result, I took it upon myself to have the paper version scanned into a pdf document and then embarked on converting that document into an Microsoft Word document for editing for format, spelling, grammar, and eventual content which may have been confused in the process of translation from four hundred pages of written manuscript to a digital, and editable, work. The result is *A Writer Writes*.

As we say in Texas, that may be a long way 'round the barn to explain how this book came about, but it could not have even begun to be created without the help of Ed.

My additional thanks goes to my publisher, Lyons Press, and Gene Brissie for taking a risk on an unpublished work, as well as my untested editing skills.

Thanks always to my wife, Lisa, and my daughter, Caitlin, for all their patience, support, and love for the past six years while I undertook this project.

San Antonio, Texas
2022

Notes

1. Among other things, I was with Mark when (1) I became hypothermic and almost froze on the side of a New Hampshire cliff three hundred feet off the ground in 1973, (2) fell five stories to the ground off a cliff in the Adirondacks in 1976, and (3) almost drowned when I got caught underneath a rock while navigating a Class 4 rapid on the Colorado River in 1979.

2. CAREY: I was living in Los Angeles at the time of my grandmother's death, and my father flew me back on a red-eye through LaGuardia Airport and somehow to Andover. As a result of the long flight and jet lag, the entire episode is a blur. I crashed early, and the family (such as were there) had the reading of my grandmother's will. I was to receive a German beer stein, but since I was asleep, I was never apprised of this and, to this day, have never had the chance to have a cold one from my grandmother's largesse.

3. CAREY: Like my father, I also had a fascination with my elementary school teacher's breasts, in my case Miss Jones. Unlike my father, presumably, my fascination with that part of a woman's anatomy continues to this day, along with all the other requisite parts.

4. CAREY: My earliest recollections of my grandmother include her almost obsessive concern for my siblings' and my cuticles, offering us numerous nail treatments during our visits.

5. CAREY: My father's first novel, which many think is highly autobiographical, was titled *Young Mr. Keefe*.

6. CAREY: Apple far from the tree? Many years later, my brother, Mark, perhaps channeling our grandfather, started collecting goats; pygmy circus goats, to be more precise. I say collecting, because in Mark's case he did not end up eating them but regarded them (and still regards them) as pets with free roaming rights of his house in Colorado.

7. CAREY: I don't know where these rugs are in 2019, but I could probably use them.

8. Named Morneault's Stackpole in 2008

9. CAREY: My roommate during my freshman year at Millbrook School in Millbrook, New York was Mike Rudolph, the first grandson of Jack Benny. Rudy, as we know him, was one of only sixteen freshmen—including me—who survived four years at Millbrook, and he remains a friend today. Rudy was valedictorian of our Class of 1973. Me? Not so much. Rudy went on to medical school and has been an emergency room MD in Los Angeles since the '80s, where he often consults for television shows involving medicine. My father never mentioned this segment of his Army story to me, despite knowing that Rudy was my roommate.

10. CAREY: Not long after my father's departure, my mother began a long career as a travel writer for *Travel + Leisure* and as contributing editor for *Town & Country*, producing numerous city profiles and traveling around the globe.

11. CAREY: A few years after my parents' divorce, Hedy Lamarr, star of over thirty-five films from 1930 to 1989, including *Samson and Delilah*, became close friends with my mother and lived in our house in Rye for several months.

12. https://www.ryehistory.org/brief-history

13. https://www.ryeny.gov/government/city-comptroller-finance-department/budget Approved Fiscal Year Budget, City of Rye, New York, for year-ending December 31, 2019.

14. http://www.ryepolice.us/personnel.

15. CAREY: When I turned eighteen, I drove my mom's car down to a local Rye pub and had beers with some friends. Later that evening, recognizing I should not be driving, I chose to walk home, knowing I would retrieve the car the next day. Upon returning to the car the following day, I had received a parking ticket, which required I either (1) Pay a $15 fine or (2) Appear before Judge so-and-so at 8:30 a.m. on such-and-such date. Looking around my environs (it was a Sunday morning, and the parking area was empty save for my mom's Mazda RX-3) and so no indication that parking was not allowed, anywhere! I determined to fight this wanton use of the law. When such-and-such date arrived, I went to the Rye Police Department and entered the small courtroom off the main entrance. It was completely empty, although I was there promptly at 8:30 a.m. A detective approached me and asked me harshly, "What do YOU want?" I told him, "I am here to contest this parking ticket I received." He responded, "You can't do that. You just have to pay the fine; besides the judge is busy. Say, aren't you one of those Birminghams?" I said I was but that wasn't the point. "There are no No Parking signs anywhere, yet I got this ticket. How could this be?" "The No Parking signs are on the outskirts of the city to be read as you enter the City of Rye," he said, "They state that there is No Parking on any City of Rye street between midnight and 6 AM." "So, let me get this straight," I asked, "I have to drive out of town and then back into town to determine where to park?" His face was flushing red by this time and he began to raise his voice, apparently forgetting some constitutional basics like due process, and said, "You just have to pay the fine!" "I want to see the judge!" I said, equally loud. We were getting nowhere, and the argument was devolving quickly. Finally, as other officers surrounded the increasingly angry detective (I gathered they weren't there to protect ME from HIM), I tore up the ticket and stormed out, perhaps gesticulating with a finger while leaving, with the detective screaming at me, "That's government property you just destroyed, and you just have to pay the fine! The judge is busy!"

16. CAREY: Lehman Brothers was one of the first casualties of the financial crisis of 2008 and closed that same year after declaring Chapter 11 bankruptcy.

17. CAREY: At this writing, thirty-nine states have legalized or decriminalized marijuana for either recreational or medical use, or in some cases both, by individuals.

18. CAREY: I remember this night clearly, as our whole family was there to see my brother and attend my father's talk. The school's dean delivered his verdict of expulsion upon my father's completion of the speech, and just after my father graciously turned down the small honorarium the school had offered. I recall that, in a flash, we had

Mark's belongings, along with my mom, my sister, and me, stuffed into our Thunderbird to make the three-hour-plus trip home to Rye. Not a word was spoken the entire trip, as Mark sat sullen in the back seat. Upon his return, Mark had to make arrangements to enter Rye High School mid-semester. I was in seventh grade and would visit Mark in the auditorium often while he was in study hall. I remember a broken soul, lonely, with no friends, and uncertain prospects for the future. Later that year, he was welcomed into Avon Old Farms preparatory school in Avon, Connecticut, from which he graduated, but not without controversy.

19. CAREY: My father bequeathed the Cincinnati house to Ed Lahniers, who ended up selling it in 2018 and moving nearby.

20. CAREY: This story involving parsley echoes a similar tale from my parents' early entertainment days. It was a holiday turkey and my grandmother, Editha, was visiting. In an effort to "help," Editha chose to stuff the turkey and, much to mother's chagrin, stuffed and stuffed and stuffed, until the poor turkey was bulging at its sides. Despite my mother's protestations, my grandmother knew best and insisted that the volatile, close-packed bread crumb mixture was just what the turkey needed. Midway through its cycle in a 350° oven, the turkey had enough, and its side exploded, just as my mother had predicted. With time running short, and guests arriving any minute, my mother hit upon the idea, "Breach the wound with parsley!" When dinner was served, everyone was impressed, and my mother broached a wise saying: "Never explain and never apologize" when serving a meal.

21. Ford Wright was one of my wealthier college classmates. At Williams, he was known as something of a playboy.

INDEX

Arab oil crisis, 292
Arbuckle, Fatty, 359
argument, about trays, 49
Armed Forces Day parade float, 121, 122–23
Armed Forces Times, 115, 119, 125
Armstrong, Neil, 277–78, 353–57
Army, 48, 56, 127, 132–33; basic training, 117, 128; discharge from, 135; draft, 111–12; homosexuality in, 117, 130–31; number for, 116; stationed in California, 118–25; style in, 113–14; writing for, 115–16, 124
Army cooks, 128
arrests, 261
art, 334, 345
Attention Deficit Disorder, 257
Auchincloss, Hughdie, 372–73
Auchincloss, Janet, 264–65, 372–75
Auchincloss, Louis, 70–71, 220, 238, 372
auction, of Ingeborg property, 309–10
The Auerbach Will (Birmingham, S.), 77, 78–79
authors, 138
autobiographies, 285
Ava (Gardner, A.), 200
Avedon, Richard, 295, 367, 369
Avon Old Farms preparatory school, 385n18

backyard, xviii
bagels, 216
Baldwin, James, 181–82
Balenciaga, 185
"Bananafish" (Salinger), 95–96
Banderas Bay, 167, 350
banking, 58
"Bappie." *See* Bea "Bappie" (Gardner, A., sister)
Barbara Greer (Birmingham, S.), 158
bareback riding, 301–2
The Barefoot Contessa (film), 170
barstools, 267
baseball, 42–43, 45–46
basic training, 117, 128
basketball, 46
"Bavarian baby," 48
Baylor University, 65–66
Bea "Bappie" (Gardner, A., sister), 180
beach, 43–45, 349–50; death at, 36; Los Muertos, 165–67, 349; in Puerto Vallarta, 165–67, 178
Beacon Hill, 291
beauty: of Monroe, 368; transferable, 348
beekeeping, 30–31
beer stein, 383n2
Bennis, Warren, 271, 277, 353
Benny, Jack, 127
Bergman, Ingrid, 359
Bernhard, Billy, 209